THIRD EDITION

UNDERSTANDING HUMAN BEHAVIOR
AND THE
SOCIAL ENVIRONMENT

Nelson-Hall Series in Social Work

Consulting Editor: Charles Zastrow
University of Wisconsin—Whitewater

THIRD EDITION

UNDERSTANDING HUMAN BEHAVIOR
AND THE
SOCIAL ENVIRONMENT

Charles Zastrow
University of Wisconsin–Whitewater

Karen K. Kirst–Ashman
University of Wisconsin–Whitewater

NELSON-HALL PUBLISHERS ■ CHICAGO

Project Editor: Dorothy Anderson
Production/Design: Tamra Phelps
Illustration and Photo Research: Nicholas Communications
Compositor: E. T. Lowe
Manufacturer: Courier Corporation
Cover: Joe LaMantia
Cartoonist: Don Baumgart

Library of Congress Cataloging-in-Publication Data

Zastrow, Charles.
  Understanding human behavior and the social environment /
Charles Zastrow, Karen K. Kirst–Ashman. — 3rd ed.
    p.   cm.
  Includes bibliographical references and indexes.
  ISBN 0-8304-1377-4
  1. Social psychology.   2. Behavioral assessment.
3. Developmental psychology.   4. Social work education.
5. Life change events.   I. Kirst–Ashman, Karen Kay.   II. Title.
III. Series.
HM251.Z37   1993
302—dc20   93-4904
                                                   CIP

Manufactured in the United States of America

10 9 8 7 6 5 4 3

TM The paper used in this book meets the
minimum requirements of American
National Standard for Information
Sciences—Permanence of Paper for
Printed Library Materials, ANSI
Z39.48-1984.

Sections of Chapters 2, 5, 8, 12, 15 and 16 were adapted
from *Introduction to Social Welfare Institutions*, 2d ed., 1982 by
Charles Zastrow. Adapted by permission of The Dorsey Press,
Homewood, Ill.

Sections of Chapters 2, 5, 8, 9, 10, 11, 12, 15 and 16 were
adapted from *Social Problems: Issues and Solutions*, 1984 by
Charles Zastrow and Lee Bowker. Adapted by permission of
Nelson-Hall, Inc., Chicago.

The material on Freud in Chapter 4 and the material on
parent effectiveness training in Chapter 8 were adapted from *The
Practice of Social Work*, 2d ed., 1985 by Charles Zastrow. Adapted
by permission of The Dorsey Press, Homewood, Ill.

Sections of the material on identity formation in Chapter 7
were adapted from "Who Am I: Quest for Identity" by Charles
Zastrow. In *The Personal Problem Solver*, Charles Zastrow and
Dae Chang eds, 1977, pp. 365–370. Adapted by permission of
Prentice-Hall, Inc., Englewood Cliffs, NJ.

TO SMOKEY, RUTH, AND CHRISTOPHER

Contents

Part Two
Adolescence and Young Adulthood

CHAPTER 6
Biological Systems and Their Impacts on
Adolescence and Young Adulthood   239

A PERSPECTIVE   240
Adolescence   241

Part Three
Middle Adulthood

CHAPTER 10
Biological Systems and Their Impacts on Middle Adulthood   389

CHAPTER 11
Psychological Systems and Their Impacts on Middle Adulthood   427

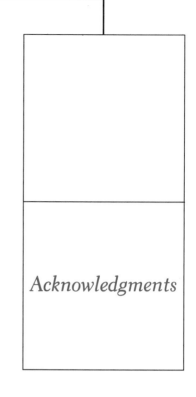

Acknowledgments

We wish to express our heartfelt appreciation to the following people and organizations. Many thanks to illustrator Donald Baumgart. A sincere thank you to Nick Ashman, David Cohen, Andrea Drollinger, Susan Drollinger, Rachel Kolberg, Tim Larson, Phil McCullough, Kathy Moretz, Steve Noll, David Runyon, and Kristine Zastrow for helping to conceptualize various chapters and for assisting in a number of ways with the writing. We want to express our indebtedness to Steve Ferrara who encouraged us to undertake this project, and who was an invaluable consultant in helping us to write this text.

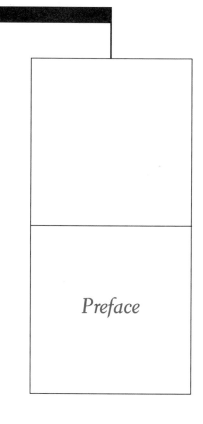

Preface

An eighteen-year-old man, who sees no reason to live anymore, threatens to kill himself. A couple suddenly separates after twenty-three years of marriage. A young family plagued by unemployment is evicted from their apartment and moves into a tent. A demonstration is staged because a local factory refuses to hire African American workers. Why do people do what they do? The main focus of this text is on *assessment*; that is, material is presented to help readers understand the underlying reasons why people act the way they do and to evaluate the strengths and deficits in the development of people. A variety of theories and research about human growth and development are presented. The theories cover both the internal and external variables that influence human behavior.

This text is especially written for undergraduate and graduate courses in human behavior and the social environment (HBSE). The Council on Social Work Education (CSWE), the national accrediting body, provides the following guidelines for HBSE content in its Curriculum Policy Statement:

Programs of social work education must provide content about theories and knowledge of human bio-psycho-social development, including theories and knowledge about the range of social systems in which individuals live (families, groups, organizations, institutions, and communities). The human behavior and the social environment curriculum must provide an understanding of the interactions between and among human biological, social, psychological, and cultural systems as they affect and are affected by human behavior. The impact of social and economic forces on individuals and social systems must be presented. Content must be provided about the ways in which systems promote or deter people in the maintenance or attainment of optimal health and well-being. Content about values and ethical issues related to bio-psycho-social theories must be included. Students must be taught to evaluate theory and apply theory to client situations.*

---

*Council on Social Work Education, "Curriculum Policy Statement," revised, (Alexandria, VA: Council on Social Work Education, July 1992).

This Curriculum Policy Statement also requires that content on the following be incorporated throughout the curriculum: social work values and ethics, diversity, promotion of social and economic justice, and populations at risk.

For a number of years social work programs have struggled to develop a HBSE curriculum that covers the extensive content mandated in the Curriculum Policy Statement for HBSE. This text is designed to facilitate such content. The text has the following thrusts:

- It uses a systems model, entitled The Systems Impact Model (described in chapter 1), which incorporates some ecological concepts. This model allows the authors to present a vast array of theories and research to explain and describe human development and behavior. The model also allows the authors to describe the following terms: families, groups, organizations, communities, institutions, social systems, cultural systems, and the social environment.
- It presents substantial information on human diversity and populations at risk, including material on racial and ethnic groups, gender, and sexual orientation.
- It uses a life span approach that allows for a description of human growth and development from conception through adulthood.
- It identifies biological, psychological, and sociological systems that influence development for each age group.[1] Interactions among these systems are discussed in some depth. For many of the bio-psycho-social theories described, content about values and ethical issues is included.
- It presents material on strategies to promote social and economic justice.
- It describes normal developmental tasks and milestones for each age group.
- It describes the impact of social and economic forces on individuals and social systems.
- It presents material on the attainment and maintenance of optimal mental and physical health and well-being. It also describes the ways in which systems promote or deter health and well-being.
- It presents material using a four-faceted approach to evaluate theory, and describes how diverse theories can be applied to client situations.

---

1. In some cases the biological, psychological, and sociological variables overlap. For example, a midlife crisis often involves a combination of biological, psychological, and sociological variables. Therefore, the authors may, rather arbitrarily, include some material under one heading (for example, covering biological aspects) when a reader can make a strong case that it should be covered under some other heading (that is, psychological aspects or sociological aspects).

A major thrust of this text is to present the material in an educational and readable fashion. Numerous case examples, photographs, and line illustrations are used in presenting provocative and controversial issues about human behavior. As much as possible, jargon-free language is used so that the reader can readily grasp theory.

It should be noted that the accompanying Student Manual has been designed to enhance students' ability to comprehend and assimilate course content. All chapters are outlined to assist in note-taking during lectures and while reading the text. Additionally, a variety of classroom exercises, role plays, and issues for discussion are included for each chapter. The authors have found that student involvement through the use of such experiential exercises and classroom discussion greatly improves both students' understanding of content and their ability to relate content to social work practice. Use of this Student Manual also minimizes the need for supplementary handouts.

In those instances where the text is used for a one semester course, the authors have found that it is useful to divide the text into four components for the purpose of administering examinations. Each component focuses on one of the four specified phases of the lifespan. These phases are infancy and childhood (Chapters 2 through 4), adolescence and young adulthood (Chapters 6 through 8), middle adulthood (Chapters 10 through 12), and later adulthood (Chapters 14 through 16). The text is composed of sixteen chapters. A fourth chapter chosen from the remaining chapters may be added to each component. The remaining four chapters are: Chapter 1, Introduction; Chapter 5, Ethnocentrism and Racism; Chapter 9, Gender Roles and Sexism; and Chapter 13, Sexual Orientation.

In those programs which use the text for more than one semester (for example, those programs which spend one semester on each half of the lifespan), the four lifespan phases can be broken down even further in a fashion similar to that mentioned above. The authors have been asked how so much material can be covered in such relatively little time. When told the topic of the text, a friend (who happens to be an accountant) asked, "Human behavior? Well, isn't that everything?" Our response must be that, yes, it involves everything about people that social workers need to know. We have found that we must make choices regarding what content is most important to cover. Those programs which allow more time for HBSE can address the significant issues and topics examined in the text much more thoroughly. We ourselves have found that requiring prerequisite courses in biology, psychology, and sociology has allowed us to spend more time focusing on issues critical to social workers in practice.

Our overall intent is to provide a dynamic, inter-esting, and relevant social work perspective on human behavior and the social environment. We strive to enhance students' understanding of social work values, develop their ability to empathize with people in situations different than their own, and help them focus on the need for changes in the impinging environment and sometimes in the client. We hope students will be able to relate these values and this knowledge to how social workers make assessments in real practice situations. We endeavor to portray social work as the fascinating, useful field it is.

The Systems Impact Model

. . . and away we go!

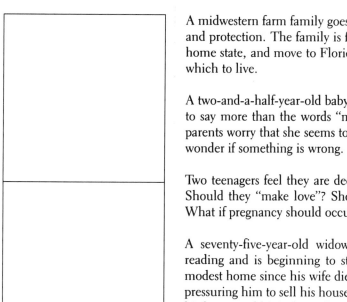

A midwestern farm family goes bankrupt after losing federal financial support and protection. The family is forced to pack up all of its belongings, leave its home state, and move to Florida, where they can afford only a canvas tent in which to live.

A two-and-a-half-year-old baby girl has not yet begun to take her first steps or to say more than the words "mama" and "dada." She is an only child. Her parents worry that she seems to be lagging behind other children her age and wonder if something is wrong.

Two teenagers feel they are deeply in love. They struggle with many issues. Should they "make love"? Should they use some method of birth control? What if pregnancy should occur? Should they get married?

A seventy-five-year-old widower finds his health failing. He has trouble reading and is beginning to stumble frequently. He has lived alone in his modest home since his wife died twelve years ago. His two adult children are pressuring him to sell his house and move into a nursing home. He likes both his home and his independence. What should he do?

Each of these vignettes reflects a real-life situation involving individual persons, each with unique qualities. Additionally, all of them are addressing issues which are related to their current period of life. In each situation people are raising questions, facing crises, or making decisions. Human behavior is often complicated and confusing. Why do people behave the way they do? The basic task of social work is to "help people meet their needs and carry out their responsibilities" throughout their life spans (Siporin, 1975, p. 3). In other words, social workers help people enhance their own functioning. Yet, in order to help people do this, social workers must first understand the process themselves. Only then can they apply techniques and skills in order to help clients make decisions and solve problems.

A PERSPECTIVE

The goals of this text are to explore the dynamics of human behavior and prepare a foundation of knowledge upon which to build practice skills. Social workers assist people in making decisions and in solving their problems. One of the primary steps in the helping process is assessment. Assessment involves evaluation of some human condition or situation. It also involves making decisions about what aspects of the behavior or situation need to be changed.

Social work is unique in that it emphasizes a focus that stretches far beyond that of the individual. Assessment in social work addresses all aspects of clients' situations. Social workers need to concentrate on understanding the many aspects of any particular client problem. A social worker assesses not only the individual client's behavior but also aspects of all the social systems in which the client is involved. These systems include families, work groups and environments, social agencies, organizations, neighborhoods, communities, and even local, state, and national government.

In many cases it is not the client's "fault" that problems exist. Rather, something outside of the client may be causing the problem. The client's whole family may not be functioning well. There may be difficulties beyond the client's control in his or her workplace. Existing social service organizations may not be providing what clients need. Resources may be too difficult to obtain, inadequate, or even nonexistent. Organizational policies or laws affecting the client may be unfair. Thus, assessment in social work targets clients' relationships with individuals, groups, organizations, and communities. Deciding what to do about any specific problem may directly involve any of these systems.

This chapter will:

- Discuss the importance of foundation knowledge within the purpose and process of social work.
- Explain the significance of foundation knowledge for assessment.
- Describe general systems theory and its relevance for social work.
- Formulate a model for viewing, assessing, and understanding human behavior that concentrates on the interactions of micro, mezzo, and macro systems.
- Define organizations as macro systems and explain their involvement with clients.
- Discuss communities as macro systems and examine their impacts on human behavior.
- Describe some of the major roles assumed by social workers as they practice within the context of micro, mezzo, and macro systems.

Foundation Knowledge and the Purpose of Social Work

In order to recognize the significance of foundation knowledge, the purpose and process of social work need to be understood. Social work may be viewed as having three major thrusts (Baer and Federico, 1978, p. 68). First, social workers can help people solve their problems more effectively and cope with their situations. Second, social workers can work with systems, such as public and private agencies and organizations, so that people can have better access to the resources and services they need. Third, social workers can "link people with systems" (Baer and Federico, 1978, p. 68), so that clients have access to resources and opportunities. Much of social work, then, involves people's social functioning.

People interact with other people and with organizations such as government and social service agencies and also with small groups such as families and colleagues in the workplace. Social work targets not only how individual persons behave but also how these other systems and people affect each other.

An example is a family of five in which both parents work at low-paying jobs in order to make a marginal living. The father works at a small, non-unionized leather processing plant. The mother works as a waitress at a short-order diner. Suddenly, through no fault of his own, the father is laid off. For a short time the family survives on unemployment compensation. When that runs out, they face a serious financial crisis. Despite great effort, the father is unable to find another job. In desperation, the family applies for public assistance. Due to some unidentified error in the lengthy application process, which involves much "red tape," the payments are delayed for two months.

Meanwhile, the family is forced to eat poorly and is unable to pay rent and utility bills. As a result, the phone is disconnected, the electricity is turned off, and the landlord threatens to evict them. Reacting to the externally imposed stress, the parents begin to fight verbally and physically. The children complain because they are hungry. This intensifies the parents' sense of defeat and disillusionment. Out of stress and frustration, the parents hit the children to keep them quiet.

Although this example has not been presented in detail, it nonetheless illustrates how people are integrally involved with other systems in their environment. A social worker reviewing this case might assess how the family and other systems in the environment have had an impact on each other. First, the father's life is seriously affected by his place of employment, the leather factory, when he is laid off. He then seeks unemployment compensation, which affects that system by dipping into its funds. When those benefits cease, the family goes to the public assistance system for financial help. The family then affects this system by drawing on its funds. The public assistance system, in turn, impacts the family by delaying their payments. The resulting frustration affects all family members, as the parents are unable to cope with their stress. The entire situation can be viewed as a series of dynamic interactions between people and their environment.

Social workers today are generalists. A generalist practitioner is one "whose knowledge and skills encompass a broad spectrum and who assesses problems and their solutions comprehensively" (Barker, 1991, p. 91). Social workers must be able to view a problem situation from multiple perspectives in the context of the entire social environment. This sets the stage for numerous intervention approaches.

Foundation Knowledge and the Process of Social Work: The Importance of Assessment

Social work practice usually involves several basic steps. First, the problem or situation is scrutinized and understood. In other words, an *assessment* of the problematic situation is made. Second, a specific *plan* of action is developed in which goals are carefully selected and clearly specified. Third, the actual *intervention* occurs; this is the "doing" part of the process. It may involve providing counseling to an individual, or it may entail working with a large organization to change its policies so that the organization better accommodates its clients' needs. Fourth, progress toward solving the problem is subject to *evaluation*. To what extent have the goals established with the client been met? Fifth, the social work process calls for a *termination* of the intervention. This includes talking about ending the process and summarizing what has been accomplished (Shulman, 1981, pp. 17–28).

The problem of a missing person is individual, familial, and societal. The social worker involved with the parents of a missing adolescent needs to keep these dimensions of the problem in perspective.

Accurate assessment of the person, problem, and situation is well documented as a critically important step in the social work process (Baer, 1979; Loewenberg, 1977; Richmond, 1917). Information about the problem or situation needs to be gathered, analyzed, and interpreted. Such situations may involve parents who have difficulty controlling the behavior of their children or families not receiving the public assistance they desperately need for survival. Regardless of the type of situation, careful thought is necessary in order to make effective decisions about how to proceed.

According to Siporin (1975, p. 119), assessment is "a process and a product of understanding on which action is based." This process involves basic knowledge and assumptions about human behavior. Knowledge about how people normally function provides the structure into which bits of information can fit. Social workers need to have a foundation of information and understanding about human behavior so that they can help clients identify and select alternatives.

For example, a social worker who is trying to help a potentially suicidal adolescent needs certain types of information. The worker needs to know some of the reasons why people commit suicide so that he or she knows what questions to ask, how to react to and treat the person, and what alternatives and supports to pursue. Working with clients whose racial and ethnic backgrounds differ from the worker's own provides another example of the importance of foundation knowledge. The worker needs to have at least general information about clients' cultural values and the potentially differential treatment they have experienced (for example, racial discrimination). Only then can the worker empathize with a particular client's situation and help the client identify realistic alternatives.

Additionally, the worker must be able to identify what resources are readily available to suicidal adolescents. How can the crises be addressed immediately, simply to keep them alive? What supportive resources are available to keep them from suicidal thoughts in the future? Where can a social worker refer them to get help?

Bartlett (1970) calls for a common base of social work practice. This base involves common values such as the belief that each individual has the right to make decisions about what to do in his or her own life. This base also involves common skills. For example, social workers need to know how to conduct an interview and how to help people identify and evaluate their various alternatives. Finally, social workers need a common base of knowledge. They must have access to certain types of information in order to plan effective interventions. They must be educated in the basic knowledge of human behavior before any skills can be applied.

This book focuses on how people act within the context of their environments. People are dramatically affected by the other people, groups, and organizations around them. A young child may be devastated by a sharp scolding from a parent. The presence or absence of friends and social supports within office work environments may determine whether employees love or hate their jobs. Which candidates are elected to Congress may affect the taxes an individual is required to pay, the types of freedom a person can enjoy, and the absolute quality of life itself.

This text aims to clarify some of the reasons why people behave the way they do. It will present basic concepts in human development and examine normal developmental life events. It will do so within the context of the communities and environments in which people live. It will also concentrate on the impacts that organizations, policies, and communities have on individuals.

Impacts of Systems in the Environment

Because the environment is so important in the analysis and understanding of human behavior, the conceptual perspective must be clearly defined. Social work focuses on the interactions between individuals and various systems in the environment. Such a conceptual perspective provides social workers with a symbolic representation or picture of how to view the world.

Systems theories make up a broad category of such symbolic representations. They involve concepts that emphasize interactions among various systems. They stress "the relationships among individuals, groups, organizations, or communities," and "they focus on the interrelationships of elements in nature, encompassing physics, chemistry, biology, and social relationships" (Barker, 1991, p. 233). Systems theories provide a broad approach to understanding the world and can be applied to a multitude of settings.

General systems theory, on the other hand, is a subset of the larger body of systems theories. General systems theory more specifically aims at analyzing "the behavior of people and societies by identifying the interacting components of the system and the controls that keep these components . . . stable"; it then emphasizes living things, "from microorganisms to societies" (Barker, 1991, p. 92). This contrasts with the larger category of systems theories that can be applied to virtually anything.

This text assumes a general systems theory approach. It also incorporates some basic concepts from the ecological perspective (which will be discussed in the next section). Such a perspective provides a way for social workers to interpret and examine their clients' situations. People are thought of as being involved in constant interaction with various systems in the environment. These include family, friends, work, social service, political, employment, religious, goods and services, and educational systems. Systems theory portrays people as being dynamically involved with each system. Social work practice is directed at improving the interactions between clients and systems.

Case Example: Child Abuse

The Presenting Problem

As she was baking Christmas cookies, Mrs. Green overheard Mr. Horney in the next apartment screaming at his son, Jimmy. Mrs. Green became very disturbed. Jimmy, who was only six, was crying. Next, Mrs. Green heard sharp cracks that sounded like a whip or a belt. This was not the first time; however, she hated to interfere in her neighbor's business. She recalled that last summer she had noticed strange looking bruises on Jimmy's arms and legs, as well as on those of his four-year-old sister, Sherry. She just couldn't stand it any more. She finally picked up the phone and reported what she knew to the public Social Services Department. She asked that the Horneys not be told who had called to report the situation. She was assured that the report would remain confidential. State law protects persons who report suspected child abuse or neglect by ensuring their anonymity if they wish.

The Investigation

Ms. Samantha Chin was the Protective Services Worker assigned to the case. She visited the Horney home the day after Mrs. Green made the report. Both Mr. and Mrs. Horney were home. Ms. Chin explained to them that she had come to investigate potential child abuse.

Harry Horney was thirty-eight years old. He was a tall, slightly overweight, balding man dressed in an old blue shirt and coveralls. He spoke in a gruff voice, but expressed a strong desire to cooperate. He also had a faint odor of beer on his breath.

Marion Horney was a pale, thin, soft-spoken woman of thirty-two. Mrs. Horney looked directly at the worker, shook her head in a determined manner, and stated that she was eager to cooperate. However, she often deferred to Mr. Horney when spoken to or asked a question.

Ms. Chin asked to examine the children. She found slash-like bruises on their arms and legs. When Mr. Horney was asked how the children got these bruises, he replied that they continually made noise when he was trying to watch the football game on television or sleep. He stated they had to learn discipline in order to survive in life. He just strapped them a little now and then to teach them a lesson. It was no different from his treatment at the hands of his own father. He also stated that his neighbors could just keep their noses out of his business and the way he wanted to raise his kids.

Ms. Chin replied that the state's intent was to protect children from abuse or neglect. She continued that citizens were encouraged to make a report even if the abuse or neglect was only suspected. Ms. Chin added that the anonymity of people who made reports was protected by state law.

When asked how she felt about discipline, Mrs. Horney said she agreed with her husband regarding how he chose to punish the children. Mr. Horney was the main disciplinarian, and Mrs. Horney felt all he was doing was teaching the children a lesson or two in order to maintain control and respect.

The Children

Jimmy was an exceptionally nonresponsive child of relatively small stature for his age. When he was asked a question, he tended to avoid eye contact and mumbled only one-word answers. When his father asked him to enter or leave the room, he did so immediately and quietly. His mother mentioned that he was having some problems with reading in school.

Sherry, on the other hand, was an extremely eager and aggressive child. When asked to do something, she initially ignored the request and continued her own activities. She refused to comply until her parent raised his or her voice. At that point she would look up and very slowly do what she was told, often requiring several proddings. At other times, Sherry would aggressively pull at her parents' clothing, trying to get their attention. She would also scream at them loudly and ask for things such as food, even though this interrupted their ongoing conversation.

Parental History and Current Status

In order to do an accurate assessment, Ms. Chin asked the Horneys various questions about themselves, their histories, and their relationship with each other. Mr. Horney came from a family of ten. His father drank a lot and frequently used a belt to discipline his children. He remembered being very poor and having to work most of his life. At age sixteen he dropped out of high school because he was able to get a job in a steel mill.

Mrs. Horney came from a broken family; her father had left when she was three. She had two older brothers who, she felt, often teased and tormented her. She described her mother as being a quiet, disinterested woman who rarely stated her own opinions and liked to keep to herself. The family had always been on welfare. Mrs. Horney also dropped out of high school to marry Mr. Horney when she was seventeen. At that time Mr. Horney was twenty-three and had already held six different jobs since he had started working at the steel mill seven years before.

The Horneys' marriage had not been an easy one. It was marked by poverty, frequent unemployment on Mr. Horney's part, and frequent moves. Mr. Horney had been laid off nineteen months ago from his last assembly-line job at a local tractor factory. He stated that he was "very disgusted" that the family had to rely on welfare. Despite his frequent job changes, he had always been able to make it on his own without any assistance. Yet this time he had just about given up getting another job. He stated that he didn't like to talk to Mrs. Horney very much about his problems because it made him feel weak and incompetent. He didn't really have any "buddies" he liked to talk to or do things with either. All he seemed to be doing lately was watching television, sleeping, and drinking beer. He was even starting to watch the daytime soap operas.

Mrs. Horney was resigned to her fate. She did pretty much what her husband told her to do. She told Ms. Chin that she never did have much confidence in herself. She mentioned that she and Mr. Horney were never really able to talk much.

The Horneys had been living in their current apartment for the past six months. However, as usual, they were finding it hard to keep up with the rent and thought they'd have to move soon. Moving so often made it hard to get involved and make friends in any neighborhood. Mrs. Horney said she'd always been a lonely person.

The Assessment of Human Behavior

Factors which must be considered in the assessment of a child-abuse case include physical and behavioral indicators, and certain aspects of social functioning which tend to characterize abusive families. Before Ms. Chin could plan an appropriate and effective intervention, she needed to understand the dynamics of the behavior involved in this family situation. Additionally, she needed to know what resources were available to help the family.

Physical Indicators of Abuse

According to the U.S. Department of Health, Education and Welfare (1979a), physical indicators of abuse include bruises and welts, burns, lacerations and abrasions, skeletal injuries, head injuries, and internal injuries. Often it is difficult to determine whether a child's injury is the result of abuse or a simple accident. For instance, a black eye may indeed have been caused by being hit by a baseball instead of a parent's fist. However, certain factors suggest child abuse. These include an inconsistent medical history, injuries that do not seem to coincide with developmental ability (for example, it is not logical that an eighteen-month-old girl broke her leg when running and falling when she is not yet old enough to walk well), and odd patterns of injuries (for example, a series of small circular burns from a cigarette or a series of bruises healed to various degrees).

In Jimmy's and Sherry's case, slash-like bruises were apparent on their arms and legs. Upon further investigation, the worker established that these did result from disciplinary beatings by the children's family. Cases of discipline often involve a discretionary decision on the part of the worker. The issue concerns parental rights to discipline versus children's rights and well-being. The worker must assess the situation and determine whether abuse is involved.

Behavioral Indicators of Abuse

Ms. Chin needed to know not only what types of physical indicators are involved in child abuse but also the behavioral indicators of abused children. These types of behaviors differ from "normal" behavior. She needed to know the parameters of normal behavior in order to distinguish it from the abnormal behavior typically displayed by abused children.

Abused children are often overly compliant and passive. If a child acts overly eager to obey and/or is exceptionally quiet and still, this may be a reaction to abuse. Such children may be seeking to avoid further abuse by maintaining a low profile and avoiding notice by the abuser. Jimmy manifested some of these behaviors. He was afraid of being disciplined and so maintained as low and innocuous a profile as possible. This was a logical approach for him to take in order to avoid being hurt.

(continued next page)

A number of terms are important to an understanding of general systems theory and its relationship to social work practice. They include *system, boundaries, subsystem, homeostasis, role, relationship, input, output, feedback, interface, differentiation, entropy, negative entropy,* and *equifinality.*

A *system* is a set of elements that are orderly and interrelated to make a functional whole. A large nation, a public social services department, and a newly married couple are all examples of systems. For our purposes, we will refer primarily to social systems, that is, those systems that are composed of people and affect people.

Boundaries are the repeatedly occurring patterns of behavior that characterize the relationships within a system and give that system a particular identity. A boundary may exist, for instance, between parents and their children. Parents maintain family leadership and provide support and nurturance to their children. A boundary may also exist between the protective service workers in a large county social service agency and those who work in financial assistance. These are orderly and interrelated groups set apart by specified boundaries in terms of their designated job responsibilities and the clients they serve. Yet, each group is part of the larger social services agency.

A *subsystem* is a secondary or subordinate system. It may be thought of as a smaller system within a large

Case Example: Child Abuse (continued)

Sherry, on the other hand, assumed an aggressive, attention-getting approach. She frequently refused to comply with her parents' instructions until they raised their voices, and often demanded additional prodding. She also tried to get their attention by pulling at them and screaming requests at them. This approach is also typical of certain abused children. Since Sherry was not getting the attention she needed through other means, she was acting aggressively to get it, even though such behavior was inappropriate. Ms. Chin needed to be knowledgeable about the normal attention needs of a four-year-old in order to understand the dynamics of this behavior.

One other symptom typical of abused children is a lag in development. Jimmy was small for his age and was having difficulty in school. Ms. Chin needed to be aware of the normal parameters of development for a six-year-old in order to be alert to developmental lags. She also needed to know that such lags were potential indicators of abuse.

Family Social Functioning

Not only the children but also the parents must be assessed. A worker must understand the influence of both personal and environmental factors on the behavior of the parents. Only then can these factors be targeted for intervention and the abusive behaviors be changed.

Personal parental factors that are related to abuse include unfulfilled needs for nurturance and dependence, isolation, and lack of nurturing child-rearing practices. Ms. Chin had discovered in her interview that in this case both parents were isolated and alone. They had no one to turn to for emotional support. There was no place where they could appropriately and harmlessly vent their frustrations. Nor had either parent learned appropriate child-rearing practices in their respective families of origin. Mr. Horney had learned excessive discipline. He had learned to be strict and punitive. Mrs. Horney had learned compliance and passivity. She had learned to be helpless and to believe she could have no effect on others no matter what she did.

Environmental factors are equally important in the assessment of this case. Specific factors related to abuse often include lack of support systems, marital problems, and life crises.

Neither parent had been able to develop an adequate support system. Due to frequent moves, they had not been able to develop relationships with neighbors or others in a community. Nor could they turn to each other for emotional support. They had never learned how to communicate effectively within a marital relationship. Finally, they were plagued by the serious life crises of poverty and unemployment.

All of these things contributed to the abusive situation. Ms. Chin, as the initiator of intervention, needed to have substantial knowledge about normal physical and emotional development, social and emotional needs, and the impacts of the surrounding physical and social environment on all family members at various life states. Only then could she understand the dynamics of the behavior involved in the situation and begin to plan interventions.

system. Obvious examples of subsystems are the parental and sibling subsystems within a family. On the one hand, parents form a subsystem. On the other, children form a subsystem by virtue of their dependent status. The group of protective services workers in the large social services agency forms one subsystem and the financial assistance workers another. These subsystems are set apart by designated boundaries, yet still are part of the larger, total agency system.

Homeostasis is the tendency for a system to maintain a relatively stable constant state of balance. If something disturbs the homeostatic system, that system will work "to adapt" and "restore the stability previously achieved" (Barker, 1991, p. 103). A ho-meostatic family system is one that is functioning in such a way that it can continue to function and stay together. A homeostatic social services agency is one that works to maintain its ongoing existence. However, neither the family nor the agency is necessarily functioning as well or effectively as possible. Homeostasis merely means maintaining the status quo. Sometimes that status quo can be ineffective, inefficient, or seriously problematic.

A *role* is "a culturally determined pattern of behavior that is prescribed for an individual who occupies a specific status" (Barker, 1991, p. 203). Each individual involved in a system assumes a role within that system. For instance, a person in the role of profes-

Making Connections with Available Resources

Ms. Chin considered several treatment directions. Of course, in order for an option to be considered, it must exist. This illustrates the critical importance of resource availability in the client's community. If resources had not been available, Ms. Chin may have faced quite a dilemma. Should she work to help get appropriate resources developed? If so, what kind? How should she proceed? This would involve focusing on aspects of the larger social systems in which her clients lived.

However, the Horneys' community had a number of resource possibilities. A Parents Anonymous group and various social groups were available to decrease the Horneys' social isolation (Parents Anonymous is a self-help organization similar to Alcoholics Anonymous for parents who have abused or neglected their children). Individual and marital counseling were available to improve the Horneys' personal self-images and to enhance marital communication. A visiting homemaker was also a possibility. Such a person could encourage Mrs. Horney to more assertively undertake her homemaking and child-rearing tasks. She could also provide personal support. Parent Effectiveness Training could be used to teach the Horneys parenting skills and alternatives to harsh discipline. Finally, Mr. Horney could be encouraged to get reinvolved in a job search. An employment specialist at the agency could help him define and pursue alternative employment possibilities.

Ms. Chin discussed these alternatives with the Horneys. Together they determined which were possible and realistic. They then decided which were the most critical and should be pursued first. Mr. Horney admitted that he could use some help in finding a job, which he stated was his highest priority. He agreed to contact the agency job specialist to help him reinstitute his job search. Mrs. Horney liked the idea of having a visiting homemaker. She felt that this would help her get her work done, and it would also give her someone to talk to. Both agreed to attend a Parents Anonymous group on a trial basis. They were not interested in pursuing marriage counseling or Parent Effectiveness Training now, but would keep it in mind for the future.

Commentary

Situations involving child abuse comprise only one category among many in which social workers collect information, assess the situation, and make recommendations for intervention. These situations include unwanted pregnancy, drug and alcohol abuse, potential suicide, AIDS, poverty, mental retardation, domestic violence, racial discrimination, and grief over illness or death. For any of these situations, social workers need a base of knowledge to understand what pressures are having impacts upon their clients. They need to know what kinds of information are important and what kinds of questions to ask. Finally, workers need to assess the environmental context in which clients face their problems in order to help clients get needed services. The intent of this text is to provide the foundation for this knowledge base. (Child abuse, neglect, and sexual abuse will be discussed much more extensively in a later chapter.)

This family in Barrow, Alaska, illustrates the concept of homeostasis. Despite its members' individual preoccupations, the family stays together and functions effectively.

sional social worker is expected to behave in certain "professional" ways as defined by the professional Code of Ethics. Each of us probably fulfills numerous roles because we are involved in multiple systems. The social worker mentioned earlier may also assume the roles of spouse and parent within the family system. Additionally, that person may assume the role of executive director within the National Association of Social Workers' state chapter.

A *relationship* is "the mutual exchange, dynamic interaction, and affective, cognitive, and behavioral connection that exists" between two or more persons or systems (Barker, 1991, p. 199). For example, a social worker may have a professional relationship with a client. They communicate and interact together in order to meet the client's needs. Relationships may exist between systems of any size. A client may have a relationship with an agency; one agency may have a relationship with another agency.

Input involves the energy, information, or communication flow received from other systems. A parent may receive input from a child's grade school principal that the child is flunking physical education. A public agency may receive input from the state in the form of funding.

Output, on the other hand, is what happens to input after it has been processed by some system. For instance, take "the status of a client's problem at the time of case termination" (Chess and Norlin, 1988, p. 27). A client with an identified problem, for example, of heroin addiction may be referred to an agency. Heroin is "a potent narcotic drug synthesized from morphine," produces effects ranging from orgasmlike ecstasy to peaceful, escapist apathy, and "is highly addictive" (Barker, 1991, p. 101).

When a client receives treatment, the agency has taken its input and translated it into a process, or treatment. When the treatment process or intervention is completed, the client's progress is evaluated. Whatever progress or lack thereof that the client has made becomes one of the agency's outputs.

An issue that this text will continue to address is the importance of evaluating whether a system's (for example, an agency's) inputs are worth the outputs. In other words, is the agency using its resources efficiently and effectively? Or, can those resources be put to a better use by providing some other type of service?

Take, for example, the client with the heroin problem. The client receives six weeks of treatment, walks out of the agency, and rushes home to stick a needle in his vein for a heroin injection. To what extent was the treatment effective? And since virtually any type of treatment is expensive, was the input worth the output in this case?

If the agency typically sees little progress at the end of treatment for clients, we have to question the agency's usefulness. Should the agency's treatment process be changed to achieve better results (that is, output)? Or, should the agency be shut down totally so that resources (or input) could be better invested in some other agency or treatment system?

Feedback is a special form of input. It involves a system receiving information about its own performance. As a result of negative feedback, the system can choose to correct any deviations or mistakes and return to a more homeostatic state. For example, a supervisor may tell a social work supervisee that he or she is filling out an important agency form incorrectly. This allows the worker the opportunity to correct his or her behavior and complete the form appropriately.

Positive feedback is also valuable. This involves a system receiving information about what it is doing correctly in order to maintain itself and thrive. Getting a 97 percent on a history exam provides a sixth grader with the feedback that she has indeed mastered most of the material. An agency that receives a specific federal grant has gotten the feedback that it has developed a plan worthy of such funding.

An *interface* is "the point of contact or communication between different systems, organizations, or individuals" (Barker, 1991, p. 117). For example, one interface is the written contract established between a field instructor in an adoptions agency and a student intern placed under his or her supervision. At the beginning of the semester, they discuss plans and goals for the semester. What tasks will the student be given and what levels of performance are expected? With the help of the student's field liaison (that is, the student's university professor), a written contract is established that clarifies these expectations. Contracts generally involve written, oral, or implied agreements between persons "as to the goals, methods, timetables, and mutual obligations to be fulfilled" during some time period in their relationship (Barker, 1991, p. 50).

At his midterm evaluation, the student receives a grade of D. Although he is devastated, he still has half a semester to improve. Focusing on the interface between the field instructor and field intern (in this case, the contract they established at the beginning of the semester) provides direction concerning what to do about the problem (that the student is doing very poorly in his internship). By reviewing the terms specified in the contract, the instructor and student, with the university liaison's help, can elaborate upon problems and expectations. Where did the student go wrong? Which of the student's expectations did the field instructor fail to fulfill? They can then establish a new contract concerning the student's performance for the remainder of the semester.

It is still up to the student to "make or break" his field experience. However, the contract (or interface) provides a clearly designated means of approaching the problem. Having the field instructor and field liaison vaguely tell the student that he needs "to improve his performance" would probably accom-

plish little. Rather, identifying and using the interface in the form of the student-instructor contract provides a specific means for attacking the problem.

Interfaces are not limited to those between individual systems. Interfaces can characterize interactions among virtually any size system. For example, there is an interface between the adoptions agency providing the student placement and the university social work program that places the student intern. This interface involves the specified agreements concerning each of these two larger system's respective responsibilities and expectations.

Differentiation is a system's tendency to move from a more simplified to a more complex existence. Relationships, situations, and interactions tend to get more complex over time. For example, in the life of any particular family, each day adds new experiences. New information is gathered, and new options are explored. The family's life becomes more complex. And, as a social services agency continues over time, it may develop more detailed policies and programs.

Entropy is the tendency of a system to progress toward disorganization, depletion, and death. Nothing lasts forever. People age and eventually die. Young families get older, and children leave to start their own families. As time passes, older agencies and systems are eventually replaced by new ones.

Negative entropy is the process of a system toward growth and development. In effect, it is the opposite of entropy. Individuals develop physically, intellectually, and emotionally as they grow. Social service agencies grow and develop new programs and clientele.

Equifinality refers to the fact that there are many different means to the same end. It is important not to get locked into only one way of thinking. In any situation, there are alternatives. Some may be better than others, but nonetheless, there are alternatives. For instance, you as a social worker may get needed resources for a family from a variety of sources. These may include financial assistance, housing allowances, food stamps, grants, or private charities. You may have to choose among the alternatives available from a variety of agencies.

The Ecological Perspective: Important Concepts

Although this text primarily assumes a general systems theory approach, it also incorporates some basic concepts from the ecological perspective. There is some disagreement about the relationship between the two approaches and confusion as to what extent they are similar or different. To add to the confusion, some of the terms involved in general systems theory and the ecological perspective (for example, *input*) are components of both perspectives and have similar but slightly different meanings.

At various times, each perspective has been described as a theory, a model, or a theoretical underpinning. A theory is "a group of related hypotheses, concepts, and constructs, based on facts and observations, that attempts to explain a particular phenomenon" (Barker, 1991, p. 236). A model, on the other hand, is "a representation of reality" (Barker, 1991, p. 146). Models are guides for how to view and assess situations. Theoretical underpinnings are the theoretical foundations for any particular way of thinking.

Though systems and ecological terms may be somewhat vague and confusing, they still can help guide our way of thinking. How should we view and analyze the world around us? What aspects are important to assess when figuring out how to solve a problem? Both general systems theory and the ecological perspective provide useful means for social workers to view the world. Both focus on systems within the environment and describe how these systems interact with and affect people.

In essence, systems theory provides the foundation for the ecological perspective. We have established that general systems theory is a subset of the larger category of systems theories. The ecological model might be considered an offshoot or interpretation of general systems theory. An ecological approach provides a more specific view of the world that also fits with a social work perspective. It refers to dynamic interactions. The emphasis is on active participation. For example, people have dynamic transactions with each other and with their environments. The ecological perspective tends to place greater emphasis on individuals and individual family systems. General systems theory, on the other hand, assumes a broader perspective. It can be used to refer to the dynamics involved in a social service agency or to describe the functioning of a human family.

Either perspective can serve the purpose of conceptualizing human behavior. Each provides a framework or a way of analyzing a situation to understand more clearly why people behave the way they do. Because the ecological perspective is a subset of general systems theory, we periodically use some of the terms derived from it throughout the text. Many of these terms are especially relevant. Consider, for instance, the term *social environment* around which this text is based. The following are some of the major terms portrayed by the ecological perspective.

Social Environment

The social environment involves the conditions, circumstances, and human interactions that encompass human beings. Persons are dependent upon effective interactions with this environment in order to survive and thrive. The social environment includes the actually physical setting that the society or culture provides. This involves the type of home a person lives in, the type of work a person does, the amount of money that is available, and the laws and social rules that must be lived by. The social environment also includes all the individuals, groups, organizations, and systems with which a person comes into contact, including families, friends, work groups, organizations, and governments. Social institutions such as health care, housing, social welfare, and educational systems are yet other aspects of this social environment.

Transactions

People communicate and interact with others in their environments. These interactions or types of interactions are referred to as transactions. Transactions are active and dynamic, that is, something is communicated or exchanged. Transactions are not passive. However, they may be positive or negative. An example of a positive transaction is the revelation that the one you dearly love also loves you in return. Another positive transaction is the receipt of a paycheck after two weeks of work. An example of a negative transaction is being fired from a job that you've had for fifteen years. Another example of a negative transaction is an irritable neighbor complaining to the police about your dog barking all night long.

Energy

Energy is the natural power of active involvement between people and their environments. Energy can take the form of input or output. Input is the form of energy coming into a person's life and adding to that life. For example, an elderly person whose health is failing may need substantial physical assistance and emotional support in order to continue performing the daily tasks necessary to stay alive. Another example of input is a teacher giving a student feedback on a term paper.

Output, on the other hand, is a form of energy going out of a person's life or taking something away from it. For instance, parents may expend tremendous amounts of energy taking care of their young children. So may a person who volunteers time and effort to work on the campaign of a politician he or she supports.

Interface

The interface is similar to that in general systems theory. It is the exact point at which the interaction between an individual and the environment takes place. During an assessment of a person-in-situation, the interface must be clearly in focus in order to target the appropriate interactions for change. For example, a couple entering marriage counseling initially state that their problem concerns disagreements about how to raise their children. Upon further exploration, however, the real problem is discovered; it is their inability to communicate their feelings to each other. The actual problem, the inability to communicate, is the interface where one individual impacts the other. Each person is part of the other's social environment. If the interface is inaccurately targeted, much time and useless energy can be wasted before getting at the real problem.

The ecological perspective, however, differs from general systems theory to some extent. The former tends to emphasize interfaces concerning individuals (that is, micro systems) and small groups such as families (mezzo systems). It is more difficult to apply the ecological perspective's conception of interfaces to those involving only macro systems (communities, organizations, and other larger systems).

Adaptation

Adaptation refers to the capacity to adjust to surrounding environmental conditions. It implies change. A person must change or adapt to new conditions and circumstances in order to continue functioning effectively. As people are constantly exposed to changes and stressful life events, it is important that they be flexible and capable of adaptation. Social workers frequently help people in their process of adaptation to a new marriage partner, a new job, or a new neighborhood. Adaptation usually requires energy in the form of effort. Social workers often help direct people's energies so that they are most productive.

Not only are people affected by their environments, but environments are also affected by people in their process of adaptation. People can and do change their environments in order to adapt successfully. For instance, a person might find it hard to survive a winter in Montana in the "natural" environment without shelter. Therefore, those who live in Montana change and manipulate their environment by clearing land and by constructing heated buildings. They change their environment in order to survive in it. Therefore, adaptation is often a two-way process involving both the individual and the environment.

Coping

Coping is a form of adaptation that implies a struggle to overcome problems. Although adaptation may involve responses to new conditions that are either positive or negative, coping refers to the way people deal with the problems they encounter in life. Within their social environments people are constantly affected by the various systems with which they come into contact. These systems include families, groups, organizations, institutions, and communities. As a result of these contacts, people can experience problems with which they need to cope. For example, a person might have to cope with the sudden death of a parent, a primary family wage earner losing a job, gangs that are vandalizing the community, or vital public assistance payments that are significantly decreased.

At least five types of coping skills are important for people to develop (Barker, 1991). First, people need to solicit and obtain the types of information they need to function well. For instance, an elderly person who becomes sick needs to know how to obtain Medicare benefits. Second, people need coping skills concerning thinking about and planning for the future. For example, a person who loses a job needs to develop a plan for finding another one. Third, coping skills involve controlling emotions. For example, a minor disagreement with a spouse should not result in a major battle involving screaming, scratching, and punching. Fourth, people need coping skills to control their needs for immediate gratification. For instance, a family needs to budget its income so that there is food on the table at the end of the week, instead of spending money on a new television set. Finally, coping skills involve identifying alternative ways of approaching a problematic situation and evaluating the pros and cons of each alternative.

Social workers are frequently called upon to help clients develop coping skills. A major theme in the helping process involves working with clients to evaluate alternatives and choose the one that's best for them. Evaluating alternatives will be addressed again later in this chapter.

Interdependence

The final ecological concept is that of interdependence, which is the mutual reliance of each person upon every other person. An individual is interdependent or reliant upon other individuals and groups of individuals in the social environment. Likewise, other individuals are interdependent upon each other for input, energy, services, and consistency.

A person cannot exist without other people. The businessperson needs the farmer to produce food. He or she also needs customers to purchase goods. The farmer needs the businessperson to provide money to buy seed, tools, and other essentials. The farmer becomes the customer for the businessperson. People, especially in a highly industrialized society, are interdependent; they need each other in order to survive.

People's Involvement with Multiple Systems

The interactions between people and the various systems within their environment have tremendous impact upon human behavior. The model proposed in this text emphasizes several aspects of this interaction. General systems theory provides us with the basis for understanding our assessment model.

We have established that people are constantly and dynamically involved in interactions with their social environment. There is constant activity, communication, and change. Social work assessment tries to answer the question, "What is it in any particular

FIGURE 1.1: Human Behavior Involves Multiple Systems

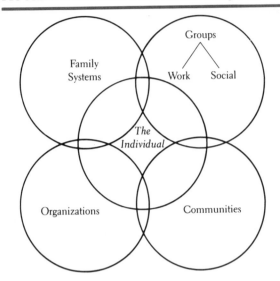

Each individual is involved in multiple systems consisting of families, groups, organizations, and communities.

situation that causes a problem to continue despite the client's expressed wish to change it?" A general systems approach provides a perspective for assessing many aspects of a situation. Clients are affected by and in constant dynamic interactions with other systems in their social environments. These include families, groups, organizations, institutions, and communities. Figure 1.1 portrays the dynamic interactions of clients with other systems in the social environment.

Micro, Mezzo, and Macro Systems

For our purposes, we will distinguish three basic types of systems throughout this text: micro, mezzo, and macro systems. Micro system refers to an individual. A system is "a combination of elements with mutual reciprocity and identifiable boundaries that form a complex or unitary whole" (Barker, 1991, p. 232). In a broad sense, this definition can apply to individual persons. Hence, a person is also a type of system (a micro system). Individual systems entail biological, psychological, and social systems. All of these systems interact to make up a person's life. Thus, for example, a micro orientation to social work practice involves "an emphasis on the individual

The micro, mezzo, and macro systems of social work: a man reading his newspaper is a micro system; a small group of children fishing is a mezzo system; and a community working to fix up low-income housing is a macro system.

client's psychosocial conflicts and on the enhancement of technical skills for use in efficient treatment of these problems" (Barker, 1991, p. 144). Micro practice, then, involves working with an individual and enhancing that person's functioning.

Mezzo system refers to any small group, including family, work groups, and other social groups. Sometimes it is difficult to clearly differentiate between a micro system (individual) and a mezzo system (small group) with which the individual is involved. This is because individuals are so integrally involved in interactions with others close to them. In many cases, we will make an arbitrary distinction between an issue concerning a micro system and one concerning a mezzo system.

Macro system refers to systems larger than small groups. A macro orientation involves "an emphasis on the sociopolitical, historical, economic, and environmental forces that influence the overall human condition, causing problems for individuals or providing opportunities for their fulfillment and equality"

(Barker, 1991, p. 136). Macro practice in social work, then, involves "bringing about improvements and changes in the general society" (Barker, 1991, p. 136).

The Social Environment

Figure 1.2 illustrates how all systems function within the social environment. We have already established that the social environment involves the conditions, circumstances, and human interactions that encompass human beings. And we have emphasized that people are dependent upon effective interactions with this environment in order to survive and thrive. Therefore, all problems should be assessed within the social environment's context. This entails focusing on micro, mezzo, and macro system interactions.

Interactions Between Micro Systems and Mezzo Systems

Individual micro systems interact with various other mezzo systems in the social environment as illus-

FIGURE 1.2: Multiple Interacting Systems in the Social Environment

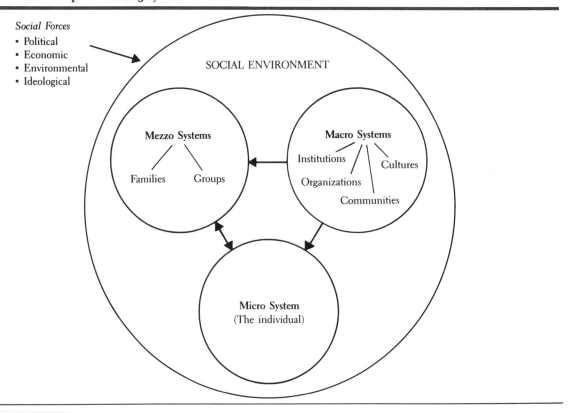

trated in Figure 1.2. These can include families and other groups, such as social and work groups. For the purposes of the diagram, only one circle is used to portray the numerous potential mezzo systems with which an individual micro system may be involved. The double pointed arrow between the circles representing micro and mezzo systems emphasizes the dynamic two-way interactions between these two types of systems.

For instance, a sixteen-year-old individual family member can affect her entire family by running away to San Francisco and roaming the streets there. The same individual may be strongly affected by her entire family group. Her family may become "fed up" with her behavior and ignore her existence, much to her surprise and dismay.

Interactions Between Micro Systems and Macro Systems

Individual micro systems are also continuously and seriously affected by the macro systems with which they interact within the social environment. Four major types of macro systems impact individual clients. The include *culture, communities, institutions,* and *organizations*. All four are intertwined.

Culture involves "the customs, habits, skills, technology, arts, values, ideology, science, and religious and political behavior" of the larger society in which individual micro systems live (Barker, 1991, p. 55). A *community* is a large "group of individuals or families that share certain values, services, institutions, interests, or geographic proximity" (Barker, 1991, p. 43). An *institution* is "a fundamental custom or behavior pattern of a culture, such as marriage, justice, welfare, and religion"; it may also be "an organization established for some public purpose and the physical facility in which its work occurs, such as a prison" (Barker, 1991, p. 116). *Organizations* are "formally structured arrangements of people, tools, and resources brought together to achieve predetermined objectives through institutionalized strategies" (Barker, 1991, p. 163).

Culture involves the life around us. It includes what goes on and how. A community is the immediate social environment in which we live, play, and work. An institution may either be one of the principles involved in the surrounding culture or an established organization. An organization is some formally structured macro system based on cultural values of what and how things should be done. Within an organization, resources are processed for some kind of outcome (for example, providing counseling to clients).

Because these terms are interconnected, they can be confusing. However, they are commonly used in the social work field, so a working understanding of the basic concepts involved is necessary. Being able to understand and assess the dynamics of human behavior provides the foundation for developing practice skills. Understanding the dynamics of human behavior is necessary to assess what needs to be done in practice situations. Assessment skills, in turn, form the basis for developing intervention skills.

We have emphasized the importance of clients' interactions with the many systems engulfing them. It is easy for practitioners, especially those who are new to the field, to focus on micro and mezzo systems. Assuming a "clinical" approach targets trying to change individuals within the context of small groups and families.

We have also emphasized that a unique and vital aspect of social work is assessing the effects of macro systems on individual client systems. Kettner, Daley and Nichols (1985) suggest that two broad theoretical perspectives most clearly underlie practice with large systems; they are organizational theory and community theory.

Organizations include virtually every structure with staff, policies, and procedures whose purpose is to continue operation in order to attain certain goals. For example, schools, public social welfare departments, and an agency operating four group homes for developmentally disabled adults are all types of organizations. Organizational theory includes several specific attempts to understand how organizations function, what improves or impairs the ability of an organization to accomplish its mission, and what motivates people to work toward organizational goals. Some approaches to organizational theory have focused on management or leadership style, while others have dealt with structural issues such as organizational hierarchy, planning, staffing patterns, budgeting, policies, and procedures.

The second theoretical framework, community

theory, has two primary components. They are the nature of communities and social work practice within communities. The task of understanding communities is easier because of the work of Roland Warren (1978), Cox, Erlich, Rothman, and Tropman (1987), and others.

Warren has conceptualized communities from multiple perspectives. For example, you may think of a community as having specific geographical boundaries like a city. Or, you can conceive of communities as groups with shared interests and beliefs. An example is the professional social work community. Cox, on the other hand, suggests that the community may be seen as a target for change, either as the problem or as the context within which change occurs. Both these perspectives have advantages. Both make it easier to assess problems, decide among several possible interventions, and evaluate possible outcomes. Both community and organizational theories will be discussed more thoroughly later on.

The Impact of Social Forces

The final aspect of Figure 1.2 to keep in mind is the impact of social forces upon the social environment. There are at least four social forces that effect changes in the social environment. They include *political, economic, environmental*, and *ideological forces.*

Political forces are the current governmental structure, laws to which people are subject, and the overall distribution of power among the populace. *Economic forces* include the resources that are available, how they are distributed, and how they are spent. *Environmental forces* concern the status of the physical environment in view of exploding populations and incessant industrialization. Finally, *ideological forces* involve the values and beliefs to which people in the social environment adhere.

The turbulent interaction of these forces and their effects on each other are striking. For example, take the national health care crisis. Political forces determine the governmental structure concerning what services must be provided to whom. The same forces govern the regulation of health care services and insurance for that health care. Economic forces involve who pays for these services. Should health services be paid for by private insurance companies with premiums paid by employers and employees? Or, should

working people pay their own premiums directly? What about the significant unemployment rate and high proportion of women and children without health insurance? Should the federal government pay for everyone's health care? If so, where will it get the money? If large amounts of money are spent on health care, which resources will be left over to care for and clean up the environment? What is more important—an expansive health care system or a livable environment? Or can we have both?

Ideologically, decisions must be made about how the political system should function, how money should be spent, and what aspects of life should receive high priority. With limited resources, should these resources be spent on cleaning up cancer-causing toxic wastes or should they be spent on heart transplants? In view of limited resources, who should receive help, an elderly man rapidly losing his mental capacities through Alzheimer's disease, a premature crack baby with a 50 percent chance of surviving with multiple health problems, or a person who has been diagnosed HIV positive who needs thousands of dollars a year for medication and treatments to survive?

The Relationships among Biological, Psychological, and Social Systems

We have established a context for assessing human behavior as one involving multiple interactions with mezzo and macro systems within the social environment. Additionally, there are biological, psychological, and social events that occur normally over an individual's life span and constantly interact with each other. For example, individuals normally master various biological, psychological, and social tasks at predictable periods in their development. We will consider these three themes (biological, psychological, and social) as separate interacting systems that have momentous impacts on the individual client system. Biological, psychological, and social systems portray critical aspects of a person's development and existence.

Figure 1.3 illustrates the dynamic interactions among the biological, psychological, and social systems within any one individual system. Double pointed arrows represent this ongoing involvement among these three systems. The individual system functions by interacting with the many other mezzo

FIGURE 1.3: The Relationships among Biological, Psychological, and Social Systems

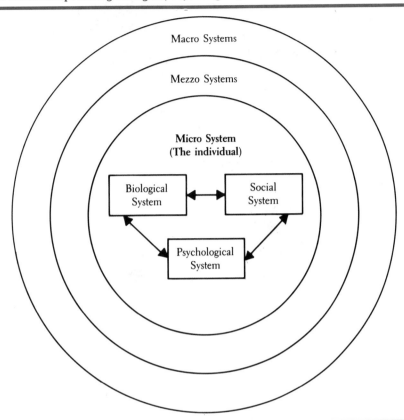

systems and macro systems within the social environment. These systems are portrayed by increasingly larger circles enveloping the circle depicting the individual, the micro system.

Two aspects of this interaction among these three systems are critical for social workers to understand. First, social workers need to know what the normal milestones are for each of these areas. Only then can they distinguish the normal from the abnormal in order to decide who is in need of intervention. Second, social workers must understand how each of these systems affects what occurs in the other systems. It's helpful to view the interactions of the systems from a chronological perspective.

Normal Developmental Milestones

Normal developmental milestones include those significant biological, psychological, emotional, intellectual, and social points of development that normally occur in a person's life span. This category focuses on the individual as a distinct entity. It provides a perspective on what can be considered normal. Topics include motor development, personality development, motivation, social development, and learning.

For example, consider a baby's normal motor development. The average baby can walk by age eighteen months (Kaluger and Kaluger, 1979, p. 116). Or, consider the normal developmental occurrences for the elderly. Older persons tend to have important changes in their sleeping patterns, such as lighter sleep and more frequent awakenings (Kimmel, 1974, p. 371).

In order to distinguish between what is normal and what is pathological, one must have a clear understanding of normal developmental milestones at any age. It should be noted that the term "normal" is used here to refer to levels of functioning that are considered appropriate for a particular age level. Social work of necessity is frequently problem oriented. Practitioners must be able to distinguish between situations that merit intervention and those that do not. Much

Learning to walk is a developmental milestone that provides a baseline for assessing the physical development of a child.

time and effort can be wasted on trying to solve "problems" that are really not problems at all. For instance, it is needless to worry about a baby who is not walking at the age of twelve months. However, it may merit investigation if that baby is still not walking at the age of twenty-four months. Likewise, consider the elderly person with sleeping problems. It may be senseless to worry about a tendency to sleep lightly when that is simply a normal sign of age. Social workers may help people adjust their expectations so that they are more reasonable. People can be helped to stop worrying about what is really the normal state of things. On the other hand, sleeping problems at the age of fifty may merit further exploration. At this earlier point in life, such problems may be caused by stress or some physiological problem.

Normal developmental milestones provide a baseline for assessing human behavior. The extent of the problem or abnormality can be assessed only to the extent that it deviates from what is normal or typical.

Bio-Psycho-Social Systems Affect Each Other

Social workers should not focus on a problem involved in only one system (that is, biological, psycho-logical, or social) and ignore how other systems are affected. Figure 1.3 connects the three systems with double pointed arrows to emphasize that they affect each other.

Consider a depressed adolescent. Although his psychological state, or depression, may be the presenting problem, problems related to other systems may also be evident. His psychological depression may cause him to withdraw from others and become isolated. Thus, his social interaction may be drastically affected. He may stop eating and/or exercising, which would have a significant impact on his biological system.

Another example involves an alcohol addicted adult. Her drinking results in her biological, psycho-logical, and social systems impacting each other. Biologically, she loses weight and has frequent physical problems such as severe hangover headaches. Her physical health affects her psychological health in that she frequently becomes disgusted with herself. Her psychological condition affects her interactions with those close to her, and they begin to avoid her. Hence, her social system is affected. Social isolation, in turn, enhances her psychological desire to drink and escape, and as a result, her physical condition continues to deteriorate.

Application of Values and Ethics to Bio-Psycho-Social System Assessments

Social workers assess problems and attempt to understand human behavior within the context of social work values and ethics. The National Association of Social Workers' (NASW) Code of Ethics (1990) focuses on six areas involving professional behavior. These include: how a worker behaves in a professional role; ethical *responsibilities to clients*; ethical *responsibilities to other social work professionals*; ethical *responsibilities to perform the job* an agency hired the worker to do; commitment to *supporting and promoting the social work profession*; and ethical *responsibility for enhancing the well-being of society at large.*

Social workers should always keep in mind their clients' rights and well-being. To the best of their ability, social workers should strive to abide by professional ethical principles, respect the rights and needs of others, and make decisions about right and wrong consistent with their professional ethics. This seems simple. You just need to think the right way and do the right thing.

But consider the following scenarios, all occurring within the context of social work assessment.

Scenario 1: You are a social worker assessing an unmarried, pregnant fifteen-year-old who has been living "on the streets." She is in her seventh month of pregnancy. She is addicted to cocaine, which she has been using throughout the pregnancy (prenatal influences will be discussed in Chapter 2). She has been informed of the potential side effects of her cocaine use upon the fetus (for example, cocaine addiction, low birth weight, lack of alertness, and other potential problems that would require more attention than that given to infants born to nonaddicted mothers). She adamantly states she will keep the baby and figure out what to to with her addiction after it's born. You have serious concerns for the infant's well-being. You personally feel that the young woman should place the baby for adoption or at least in foster care until she can solve her own problems. What is the ethical thing to do?

Scenario 2: You are a social worker assessing a client with AIDS (AIDS is covered in detail in Chapter 10). He tells you that he has had unprotected intercourse with dozens of women since he received his positive HIV diagnosis. He has shared his diagnosis with none of these women. He boldly states that he is incredibly angry that he has the disease and plans to continue having intercourse with as many women as he can. You personally feel that he is very angry and that it is not only unethical but hazardous to his sex partners for him not to tell these women about their potential exposure to the disease. Clients are supposed to be able to make choices about their own behavior. You are supposed to keep the interactions between you and your client confidential. But what about the unsuspecting victims of your client's choices? What is the ethical thing to do?

Scenario 3: You are assessing an elderly woman in her own home. Her physical and intellectual health is deteriorating. Your job as a Protective Services social worker is to make assessments and pursue interventions "on behalf of individuals—such as children, disabled people, *older people*, and mentally retarded people—who may be in danger of harm from others or who are unable to take care of their own physical needs" (Barker, 1991, p. 185). The woman lives alone in a run-down apartment in a poor section of town. She has no close family. She insists that she wants to remain in her home. Your agency supervisor has told you that elderly people deemed unable to take care of themselves must be placed in a nursing home facility. However, you also know that the only nursing home facilities available to poor elderly people in the area are run-down, understaffed, and offer a minimal quality of life. Ethically, your client has the right to make her own decisions. However, you fear that she may fall and remain helpless, turn the gas stove on and forget to light the flame, or have some other accident. What is the ethical thing to do?

Each of these situations portrays an ethical dilemma. Dilemmas involve problematic situations for which possible solutions are imperfect and unsatisfactory. In other words, your ethical guidelines conflict with each other. There is no one perfect answer that can possibly abide by all of the ethical principles in the professional code. You are "stuck" with deciding what to do. Many such dilemmas are encountered in social work practice.

Three basic suggestions guide your procedure. They are made within the context of assessing human behavior. Such assessment lays the groundwork for determining what intervention to pursue.

(continued next page)

Application of Values and Ethics to Bio-Psycho-Social System Assessments (continued)

The first suggestion is to put your theoretical and factual knowledge base about human behavior to work (This text intends to provide you with such a base.) The second is to identify your own values concerning the issues and then to discriminate between your values and professional ethics. The third suggestion is to weigh the pros and cons of each alternative available to you and your client, and then proceed with the alternative you determine is the most positive. There are no perfect answers. Following is an example of how these suggestions may be applied to Scenario 1.

In Scenario 1, the pregnant, unmarried, fifteen-year-old cocaine addict, first gather the knowledge you need. You need to know the effects of cocaine on prenatal development (described in Chapter 2), the theoretical dynamics of drug addiction (discussed in Chapter 11), and the needs of newborn infants in general (addressed in Chapters 2, 3, and 4). Such information can give you clues regarding what types of assessment information you need to know in order to plan interventions.

The second step is to recognize clearly your own personal values and biases. You should not impose your values upon your client. Strive to make decisions that coincide as much as possible with professional ethics.

Finally, identify the alternatives available to you, weigh the pros and cons of each, and make the decision you consider to be the most ethical. Knowledge of human behavior in the areas cited above can lead you to the questions you need to ask in order to make an effective, ethical decision along with your client. Questions in Scenario 1 would include:

- What are the client's drug using behaviors?
- What are the potential effects on the child?
- How motivated is the client to enter a drug treatment program?
- What resources for drug treatment and other supportive services for unmarried teen mothers are available to your client?
- If not available, can needed services be initiated and developed?
- What resources can you turn to in order to maximize the child's well-being?

You can address the dilemmas posed in scenarios 2 and 3 in a similar manner. What theoretical and factual knowledge do you have about human behavior that can be applied to your understanding of the situation? What personal values and biases do you hold concerning the client and the client's situation? What alternatives are available to you and your client? What are the pros and cons of each? What alternative is the most ethical to pursue?

A Chronological Perspective

For a coherent approach to changes that take place during a person's life span, this text will assume a chronological perspective. Each of the three systems (biological, psychological, and social) will be examined within this framework. Starting with conception and ending with death, human behavior will be explored within the context of the different phases or age periods in a person's life. These periods include infancy and childhood, adolescence and young adulthood, middle adulthood, and later adulthood.

Throughout these life periods, people tend to experience common life events. There is a greater tendency for certain types of occurrences to happen at certain times of life. For example, adolescence is a time when people establish an identity. Life is marked by striving for independence and searching for a place to fit into social peer groups. Sometimes adolescence is even more stressful. It may be marked by running away from home or by delinquency.

Marriage and having children are characteristic events of early and middle adulthood. Sometimes people face unplanned pregnancy and single parenthood during this time of life. Other people must face and deal with divorce. Life events in later adulthood include retirement and readjustments to married life when children leave home. Although many elderly people remain deeply involved in family and community life, disengagement theory predicts that others will become increasingly isolated and detached from the rest of society (Cumming and Henry, 1961). Additionally, many elderly people must cope with increasingly more serious health problems and illnesses.

These experiences or life events—identity crises, marriage and children, retirement, and detachment—all tend to happen during certain periods of life. Each of these common events will be addressed within the context of the time of life when it characteristically occurs. The variety of experiences that may be considered "typical" is great. However, there are certain life events that social workers are frequently called upon to help people cope with. We will arbitrarily select and focus on some of these experiences based on their relevance to practice.

Diversity, Oppression, and Populations-at-Risk

Social workers need to be aware of human differences and the effects they have on human behavior. Any time a person can be identified as belonging to a group that differs in some respect from the majority of others in society, that person is subject to the effects of that diversity in terms of potential discrimination. Groups meriting special attention include "minorities of color, women, and gay and lesbian persons" in addition to groups "distinguished by age, ethnicity, culture, class, religion, disablement and socioeconomic status" (Council on Social Work Education, 1991, p. 6).

Membership in groups other than the young, white, male heterosexual mainstream can place people at increased risk of discrimination and oppression. Discrimination concerns "the prejudgment and negative treatment of people based on identifiable characteristics such as race, gender, religion, or ethnicity" (Barker, 1991, p. 64). Oppression involves "placing severe restrictions on a group or institution" (p. 162). Picture a woman in an all-male business establishment. Think of a sixty-two-year-old person applying for a sales job in a department store where everyone else is under forty. Or, consider an African American person applying for membership in an all-white country club.

Membership in any group provides a certain set of environmental circumstances. A Chicano adolescent from a Mexican American inner-city neighborhood has a different social environment from that of an upper-middle-class adolescent of European descent living in the well-to-do suburbs of the same city.

Group Membership and Values

Sensitivity to group differences is critical in understanding any individual's behavior. This is important from two perspectives. First, the values or orientation of a particular group will affect how an individual chooses to or is pressured to behave. For instance, an individual with a sexual orientation for the same gender may very well choose to participate in social activities with others of the same orientation. The individual might tend to avoid bars and nightclubs aimed primarily at helping heterosexual singles meet. Instead, this person might choose to visit nightclubs and join activities or social clubs aimed at helping people with a sexual orientation toward the same gender meet each other.

The Macro System Perspective on Group Differences

There is a second important perspective concerning sensitivity to group differences. The first perspective focused on how the group member feels and chooses to act. The second perspective directs attention to how other people and groups in the social environment view the group in question. Each member of a group has a tendency to lose his or her individual identity and assume the group identity in the eyes of others in the environment. The characteristics of the group become the characteristics of the individual whether the individual actually has them or not. These are *prejudgments* and *stereotypes*. They are not based on facts about an individual but rather on predetermined notions about any person who happens to belong to a particular group.

Awareness of this second perspective is important for two reasons. The first is that professional values are one of the foundation blocks of social work. Devore and Schlesinger (1981) articulate basic social work values and emphasize the importance of adherence to them. These values include "the dignity of the individual, the right to self-determination, the need for an adequate standard of living, and satisfying, growth-enhancing relationships" (p. 128).

Stereotypes

The views of those in the surrounding social environment are important for another reason. Frequently these views, subjective opinions, and stereotypes discriminate against various groups. Pressures and limitations are often placed on members of certain groups. Alternatives are limited. Behavior is restricted. In the assessment of human behavior, it is important to know when the alternatives open to a person are limited.

For example, take a young, single, African American mother of three young children who is receiving public aid. She applies for a service job behind the counter of a local delicatessen. The deli is run by a lower-middle-class white family that holds many of the larger society's traditional values. These values include the ideas that the head of the household must be a man and that women should stay home and take care of the children. The owner of the deli, a man and head of the family, interviews the young woman and makes several assumptions.

The first assumption is that the woman has no business not being married. The second is that she should be staying at home with her children. The third assumption is that the woman, because of her color, is probably lazy and undependable anyway. He uses the excuse that she has no experience in this particular job and refuses to hire her. This young woman has run up against serious difficulties in her job search. In addition, she may have problems getting adequate day care for her young children. Taken together, all these difficulties may close to her the option of finding a job and getting off of public aid.

In assessing and understanding any person's behavior, one must be aware of limitations imposed by the environment. Otherwise, impossible alternatives might be pursued. In practice, a social worker who does not understand these things might continue to pressure the young woman in the example to go out and get a job. Since she was already trying, failing, and frustrated, this additional pressure might make her turn against the social worker and the social service system. She might just give up.

Social Work Values and Sensitivity to Diverse Populations

Sensitivity to human diversity is very important in social work practice. Therefore, this orientation is given a central role in the assessment of human behavior as presented here. Figure 1.4 portrays the two perspectives on human diversity.

The larger circle depicts the values and attitudes of the majority of people in the social environment. The

FIGURE 1.4: Value Diagram: Diverse Groups in the Social Environment

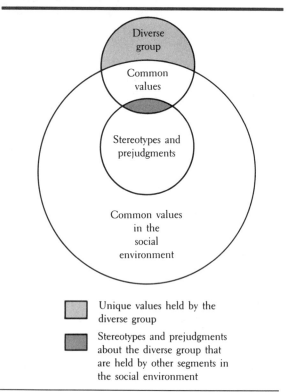

Unique values held by the diverse group

Stereotypes and prejudgments about the diverse group that are held by other segments in the social environment

smaller circle, which intersects and goes a bit beyond the edge of the larger circle, represents the values and attitudes of some group. This may be any group that is different in some way from the majority. This difference may be an ethnic diversity such as Polish or Italian American. It may be a racial diversity such as Native American or African American. It may be a diversity of sexual orientation such as being gay. A group can be distinguished from the majority in some way.

The diverse group circle extends beyond the larger circle of the entire social environment. This represents the values and attitudes held by the group that are not held by others in the environment. The small central circle represents the sum total of stereotypes and prejudgments held by people in the social environment. The fact that the diverse group circle intersects the stereotype circle reflects the prejudgments held about that particular diverse group.

The diverse group circle also intersects the other

general section of the social environment circle. The diverse group is still part of the total social environment. This intersection reflects the values and attitudes held in common with others in the social environment.

The two perspectives focused on here are reflected by the two shaded areas. The first is the perspective held by the diverse group that is different from the perspective of others in the environment. The second is where the diverse group intersects the stereotyped attitudes held in the social environment. This represents the prejudgments to which the diverse group is subjected.

The Systems Impact Model

The Systems Impact Model (SIM) proposes that social work practitioners work not only with clients to solve clients' problems but also with the many other major systems with which the client is involved. SIM proposes that a primary pursuit of social work goes far beyond counseling individual clients at the micro level or working with small groups at the mezzo level. Rather, SIM emphasizes how social workers must often work within the existing institutional and organizational structure on their clients' behalf. Often, the target must be to change or improve how services are delivered and resources distributed. Targets of change may also involve improving conditions and services within a community.

Figure 1.5 illustrates the Systems Impact Model. Circles represent the various systems involved. For instance, the three large circles above the client system depict major macro systems that strongly impact the client system. Arrows illustrate inputs or impacts. The arrows' directions indicate which system is the sender and which the receiver. Double pointed arrows indicate some degree of mutual input.

The Client System[1]

First of all, note that the client system is in the center of the model. This client system may be an indi-

1. The concept of *client system* was initiated by A. Pincus and A. Minahan in *Social Work Practice: Model and Method* (Itasca, IL: Peacock, 1973).

FIGURE 1.5: The Systems Impact Model

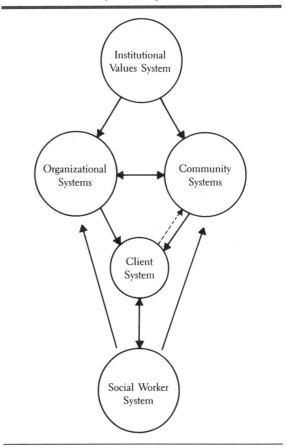

vidual, a family, or a small group struggling to cope with some serious problem. The client system may also be a community desperately battling to stay economically viable. Or, it may be an agency unable to get the resources it needs to survive and prosper.

This text focuses on individuals as they "develop over the life span and have membership in families, groups, organizations, and communities" (Council on Social Work Education, 1991). It also emphasizes their relationships and interactions with larger macro systems. Most generalist social workers will have individuals, families, and small groups as their primary client systems. For these reasons, the following discussion will refer to the individual, family, or small group as the client system. Clients will be viewed within the context of larger macro systems such as organizations and communities.

This shelter for the homeless is an example of an organization, a structure that processes and distributes resources to client systems.

The Relationship Between Organizational Macro Systems and Client Systems

Figure 1.5 shows how organizational systems can affect client systems. For our purposes, organizations will include those structures that process and distribute resources to client systems. Examples are county social service departments, residential treatment centers for behaviorally disordered teenagers, private adoption agencies, Planned Parenthood clinics, and shelters for the homeless. All use their allocated resources to provide services that meet their clients' needs. (Organizations will be discussed more thoroughly later in this chapter.)

Clients have little impact on most organizational systems, especially those providing resources to them. (They have some impact on political systems if they vote.) Clients have no formal working role within these organizations. Therefore, they have no direct means of affecting the way in which organizations function internally.

The Relationship Between the Community Macro System and the Client System

The circle to the right of the organizational systems circle in Figure 1.5 represents the community macro system. Warren (1983) describes the community as "that combination of social units and systems that performs the major social functions having locality relevance. In other words, by community we mean the organization of social activities to afford people daily local access to those broad areas of activity that are necessary in day-to-day living" (p. 28). Communities, simply put, are places where people spend their daily lives living and working.

Communities provide people with necessary input via resources, jobs, and social support systems. However, problems evident in communities can have devastating effects on community residents' ability to function in a healthy way. For instance, the increasingly poor financial condition of urban inner cities results in crime and delinquency, drug problems, environmental pollution, neglect of the elderly, child abuse, and unemployment.

Community systems have significant impacts on individuals, including your clients. Hence, Figure 1.5 shows a heavy arrow leading from the community to the client. Therefore, it's important for social workers to understand communities and how they provide the context for people's functioning. They are integral in understanding human behavior. Communities will also be discussed in greater depth later in the chapter.

Unlike the interaction depicted between the organizational system circle and the central client circle, interaction between the community and client circles is represented by two arrows. By definition, clients are units or subsystems within the larger community. As integral parts of this larger macro system, clients can develop avenues to affect their community. Many times, however, social workers can provide the needed expertise and help for clients to do so. (Social work roles concerning communities will be explored later in the chapter.) The arrow leading from the client circle to the community circle is much thinner because clients are simply subsystems of the larger macro systems. Thus, clients have less power than the much larger community system.

The Relationship Between Organizational and Community Macro Systems

In Figure 1.5, the double pointed arrow connecting the organizational system circle and the community system circle shows that these two types of macro systems affect and interact with each other. Organizational systems providing services have distinctive effects on the resources made available to community residents. Likewise, the problems and needs evident in a community influence the nature and distribution of services. For example, effective agencies do not provide services the community doesn't need.

Institutional Values Macro System

The upper circle in Figure 1.5 portrays the institutional values system. We will define this system as involving the strong, historically rooted values and beliefs governing the distribution of resources. For example, a strong institutional value is that children should not be physically damaged by adults, including their parents. Hence, we have protective service agencies and departments that exist to prevent and stop such abuse. Another example of a strong institutional value is the punishment of convicted criminals. Thus, we have a major federal and state prison system. Another example of a strongly rooted institutional value is that all citizens have the right to publicly provided education. Therefore, public schools are available to everyone in the nation. Taken collectively, these institutional values become an institutional values system.

Many institutional values are in a state of flux or confusion. This happens when large factions of peo-

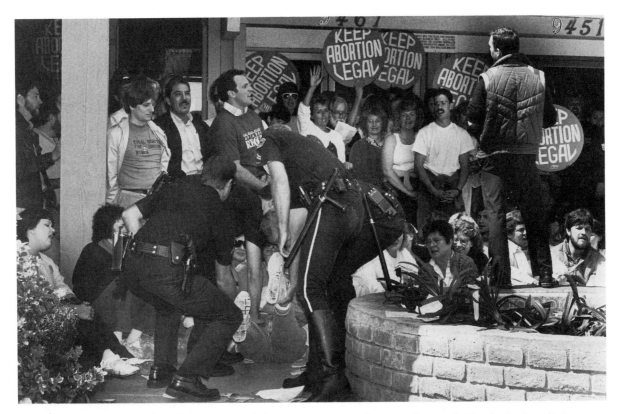

A conflict in institutional values: Police arrest anti-choice demonstrators for trespassing at a California abortion clinic.

ple in the social environment have strongly divergent opinions. For instance, many states are debating whether to institute the death penalty for those who commit murder. Most states do not have a death penalty, reflecting the institutional value that civilized nations do not kill their citizens regardless of their crimes. However, states that adopt the death penalty hold the institutionalized value that death is a fair consequence for murder.

Another example of an institutionalized value that is being debated is the controversial anti-abortion versus pro-choice issue. People have extremely strong opinions concerning abortion.

In Figure 1.5, note that the arrows connecting the institutional values systems and the organizational and community systems are directed only one way. This indicates that institutional value systems usually have tremendous impacts on organizational and community systems. However, the latter have little reciprocal impact. The services and resources provided by organizations and agencies are limited to those which institutional value systems support.

Institutional values affect the structure, function, and composition of communities. For instance, one nationally held institutional value is that all citizens have the right to a free education. However, another institutional value is that each locality should finance its public schools through local taxes. Therefore, the quality of education can vary drastically from the rich suburbs to the poor inner city.

Figure 1.5 shows no arrows leading from the organizational and community circles to the institutional values circle. This is not to imply that such values cannot be changed. Rather, this reflects that there is no clearly established means of doing so. In a practical manner, SIM emphasizes where both relationships among client, worker, and macro systems and the potential means for change can be more clearly identified.

The Effects of Institutional Values and Organizational Macro Systems on Clients

Both organizational systems and institutional values systems have impacts on clients. They dictate what resources and services clients deserve or need. If organizational systems and institutional values work

against a resource, then that resource will not be provided. For example, it is difficult, it not impossible, for single mothers receiving public assistance to find affordable and adequate day care for their children while they participate in job training programs or look for jobs. Providing these mothers with good day care is not an institutional value. This does not mean that mothers do not need this resource or that they should not have it. It simply means that this particular resource is not considered valuable enough to be offered by the institutional powers-that-be.

Client systems, on the other hand, have very little power to affect either organizational systems or the institutional values system. Hence, no arrow leads from the client system circle to the organizational systems circle or the institutional values system circle in Figure 1.5. The client may or may not understand how the systems work. Sometimes macro systems treat clients unfairly. Other times, macro systems simply deny clients the resources they need. It's during these times that your role as social worker will come into play.

Oppression and Macro Systems

Unfair and discriminatory values permeate our society. Often they infiltrate macro systems and determine how these systems treat their clients. This results in various forms of oppression. For instance, consider an armed robbery. If such an offense committed by an African American person is dealt with more severely than if it were committed by a white person, such treatment is a means of oppression. If an agency hires women at significantly less pay than it does men for doing identical work, that is a manifestation of oppression.

Various aspects of diversity and the concept of oppression will be treated more thoroughly in later chapters. The important thing to remember here is that it is critical to keep these concepts in mind whenever assessing the dynamics of human behavior.

The Social Worker System

We now come to the most critical aspect of the model, namely, how you as a social work practitioner fit in. As a worker you will probably have direct dealings with micro and mezzo systems. You may be in the position of coordinating numerous resources on behalf of your client systems. You also, however, need to be constantly aware of the impacts macro systems have on your clients.

Figure 1.5 illustrates both the social worker system's relationships with the client system and with macro systems. Client and social worker systems have reciprocal interactions, shown by the two-way arrow. They communicate and work together to solve the client's problems and meet the client's needs.

Figure 1.5 also depicts how you as the social worker may need to affect macro systems in order to get what clients need. These macro systems may either be organizations or communities. Thus, bold arrows lead from the social worker system circle to both the organization systems and the community systems circles.

The Social Worker and Organizational Systems: Promotion of Social and Economic Justice. Concerning organizational systems, two issues are relevant. First, the organizational system in need of change may be your own organization or it may be another macro system involved with the client. The methods you use to seek change probably will differ significantly in each case. Second, you probably will be working within the auspices of an organization. Therefore, you will need to be aware of its policies and restrictions. You will have to make decisions regarding the extent to which you must comply with these policies in order to perform and keep your job. You may well find yourself in the position of "bucking the system," that is, of confronting it and seeking some kind of change.

The Social Worker and Community Systems: Promotion of Social and Economic Justice. When you, as a social worker, assess a client's involvement with the community system, you may determine that there is a need for improvement or change. For instance, you may act as a catalyst for community development. This involves "efforts made by professionals and community residents to enhance the social bonds among members of the community, motivate the citizens for self-help, develop responsible local leadership, and create or revitalize local institutions" (Barker, 1991, p. 43).

The intent here is not to teach practice skills but to make you aware of the types of skills you will need in practice. The first step in the problem solving process is to teach you how to assess any client person-in-environment system. Because of macro systems' potent effects on clients, examining the macro aspects of a situation is vitally important.

The Impacts of Organizations

Organizations represent one category of macro systems that have major impacts on human behavior. We are focusing in on organizations that provide social services. Social services include "the activities of social workers and other professionals in promoting the health and well-being of people and in helping people to become more self-sufficient: preventing dependency; strengthening family relationships; and restoring individuals, families groups, or communities to successful social functioning" (Barker, 1991, p. 221). One type of social services organization frequently referred to in the social work field is the *social agency*. This is "an organization and facility that delivers social services under the auspices of a board of directors and is usually staffed by human services personnel (including professional social workers, members of other professions, subprofessional specialists)" (p. 217) and other support staff (for example, secretarial staff). The terms "social services," "human services," and sometimes "social welfare" are often used interchangeably when referring to organizations, agencies, and agency personnel.

Organizations are particularly important to you for two reasons. First, most likely you will be employed by one. Your organization's policies, goals, and restrictions will directly affect what work you can and cannot do with clients. The second reason for their significance is that often the organization and not the client may be the source of the problem. (We will discuss this later in greater depth.) Therefore, you will need to evaluate for yourself how well your own organization is functioning in order to do your work effectively.

In order to assess the effectiveness of any organization, you need to understand some basic organizational concepts. Here we will define the concept of organization, discuss a few of the primary organizational theories, and explain how organizations provide or fail to provide services and resources to clients.

What Are Organizations?

Since organizations are systems, all of the systems concepts discussed earlier apply to them. Organizations are in constant interaction with other systems in the environment. Some systems provide organizations with resources (for example, public funds, fees, or grants). Other systems are their clients who receive their services and output resources.

Organizations are defined as "social entities that are goal-directed, deliberately structured activity systems with an identifiable boundary" (Daft, 1983, p. 8). Within this definition there are four essential concepts.

First, organizations are *social entities*. They are made up of people with strengths and failings. Organizations prescribe how people should behave and what responsibilities employees are to assume in their jobs. Thus, patterns of behavior develop in organizations.

Second, organizations are *goal-directed*. They exist for some specified purpose. Social service organizations are there to provide services and resources to help people in some way. It is important to understand what an organization's goals are. It is equally important to assess whether the organization's goals are really good for clients. Finally, it is crucial to examine whether the organization is attaining its stated goals for clients.

Third, organizations are *deliberately structured activity systems*. Daft (1983, p. 8) describes what this means:

> Activity system means that organizations have a technology—they use knowledge to perform work activities. Organizational tasks are deliberately subdivided into separate departments and sets of activities. The subdivision is intended to achieve efficiencies in the work process. The deliberate structure is also characterized by a conscious attempt to coordinate and direct the separate activities.

Organizations have structures, which include policies for how the organization should be run, personnel hierarchies, and different units working in different ways to help the organization or social agency function. For instance, a family services organization might have one staff unit providing marriage and family therapy, another unit providing "family life education," and still another unit working on "community activities to enhance healthy family development" (Barker, 1991, p. 82). Each unit pursues different activities in order to achieve the agency's goal of providing family services.

The fourth major concept involves *identifiable boundaries*. A clear statement defines who is part of the organization and who is not. It should also be clearly evident how the organization is funded and what clients are provided services and resources.

Social Agencies

A social agency is "an organization and facility that delivers social services under the auspices of a board of directors and is usually staffed by human services personnel (including professional social workers, members of other professions, subprofessional specialists); clerical personnel;" and other staff necessary in the agency's performance (Barker, 1991, p. 217). A social agency is one type of social services organization.

Organizational Theories

In order to work within organizations, to evaluate them, and sometimes to change then, it is helpful to understand the major theories regarding their operation. Such a perspective is also useful in determining the kinds of organizational structures that are most effective in specific client situations.

Many organizational theories have been borrowed from the business and management fields. Businesses and social service organizations have many things in common. Both need resources (money) to operate. Both produce products via some kind of process. For example, a business might manufacture the product lawn mowers. A social services organization might produce the product improved family functioning.

Theories deal with how organizations really work, but many of them contradict each other. This is probably because there is such a vast range of organizational structures, functions, and goals. Here we will discuss four major theoretical perspectives regarding how organizations should be run. These include "classical scientific management theories," "human relations theories," "structuralist models," and "systems theories" (Sarri, 1987, pp. 30-32).

Classical Scientific Management Theories

Classical scientific management theories emphasize how a specifically designed, formal structure and consistent, rigid organizational network of employees is most important in having an organization run well and achieve its goals (Holland and Petchers, 1987; Sarri, 1987). Each employee holds a clearly defined job and is told exactly how that job should be accomplished. This school calls for minimal independent functioning on the part of employees. Supervisors closely monitor their work. Efficiency is important. How people feel about their jobs is insignificant. Nor do employees have input regarding how organizational goals can best be reached.

Traditional bureaucracies demonstrate the application of classical scientific management theories. Bureaucracies emphasize highly specialized units that perform clearly specified job tasks, minimal discretion on the part of employees (that is, ability to make independent judgments and decisions), and numerous specific rules to maintain control. The Social Security Administration, an urban county's department of social services, and the Pentagon are examples.

Human Relations Theories

Human relations theories emphasize "the role of the informal, psychosocial components of organizational functioning" (Holland and Petchers, 1987, p. 206). Satisfied, happy employees will be the most productive. Important concepts include "employee morale and productivity; . . . satisfaction, motivation, and leadership; and . . . the dynamics of small-group behavior" (Sarri, 1987, p. 31). Organizational leaders strive to enhance their workers' morale. In this system, effective leaders are important.

The immediate work group (mezzo system) is critical. Employees are encouraged to work cooperatively and participate in group decision making. Employers encourage employee input concerning organizational policies and practices.

Structuralist Models

Structuralist models emphasize "both structure and process" in viewing organization (Sarri, 1987,

p. 31). Such models focus on both the rational structure of an organization and the more irrational, imperfect behavior of the people involved in that structure. Employee satisfaction is not considered as important; however, employees' productivity is. Therefore, there is an emphasis on decision making. Decisions are made carefully and all variables are taken into consideration in order to optimize worker productivity.

Systems Theories

Systems theories involve the systems concepts we have already discussed. A systems approach "construes the organization as a social system with interrelated parts, or subsystems, functioning in interaction and equilibrium with one another. It thinks of the organization as an adaptive whole rather than as a structure that is solely rational-legal" (Holland and Petchers, 1987, p. 207). In some ways, systems theories "attempt to synthesize structuralist and human relations perspectives" (Sarri, 1987, p. 32). Systems theories generally take other theories into account to reach a more flexible, comprehensive means of viewing organizations.

Systems theories emphasize the interactions of the various subsystems involved. The importance of the environment and the impacts of other systems on the organization are also stressed. In some ways, systems theories might be considered more flexible than other theories. Irrational interactions are expected rather than ignored. Systems theories emphasize constant assessment and adjustment.

Which Organizational Theory Is Best?

No one really knows which organizational theory is best. As time passes, these theoretical perspectives rise and fall in popularity. It is beyond the scope of this text to explore organizational theory other than to provide a foundation to help you understand human behavior within the context of macro systems.

Because of its flexibility and the complexities of working with real clients, this text will view organizations primarily from a systems perspective. We've already established that general systems theory fits well with social work. However, occasionally, other theories (or ways of perceiving the world) are useful. For instance, classical scientific management theories and structuralist models provide interesting views of bureaucracy.

Here we will describe some common problems encountered by practitioners working within organizations. The concept of goal displacement and its implications for social workers will be discussed.

Viewing Organizations from a Systems Perspective

As social workers, we want to serve our clients as best we can. Because we will probably work in social service organizations, we want those organizations to be as effective as they can be. We also want other organizations with which our clients have transactions to be as effective as possible. We want to provide the best resources and services possible to help our clients. We need to maintain constant awareness of how well social service organizations are serving clients. Therefore, we continuously need to assess the effectiveness of organizations, that is, to what extent each is attaining its goals.

Social service organizations can be compared to other organizations, such as businesses, in a variety of ways. Social service organizations take input (which is, at its most primitive level, financial), process this input through service provision, and produce some output (namely, results for clients which we hope are positive). Figure 1.6 illustrates this process and compares it to that of a business organization. For the sake of example, we will compare social service organizations to a make-believe business involved in manufacturing video games that we'll call Pretendo. We will call our social services organization Financial Urban Base for Area Resources (FUBAR).

Resource Input

Figure 1.6 illustrates how both FUBAR and Pretendo take financial resources and use them to pay for raw material. Pretendo purchases materials such as metals, wires, and plastic to prepare for the production process. Pretendo gets its funds from sources such as stockholder investments and prior profits from selling Pretendo equipment.

FUBAR, on the other hand, applies its financial resources to clients. Social service organizations differ strikingly from manufacturing-business organizations in that their "raw material" is clients (Holland and Petchers, 1987). FUBAR receives its resources from public tax moneys and a variety of private sources (such as donations, fees, and grants). It then applies these financial resources to some type of helping process. The output is the help given to and progress made by clients.

Process

Both Pretendo and FUBAR process their "raw material." Pretendo sends theirs through a manufacturing production process in which materials are gradually reshaped, blended, and recombined to produce the desired product, Pretendo video game machines.

FUBAR, on the other hand, uses a completely different process on its "raw material." Instead of a manufacturing process, it provides some type of intervention. This intervention can involve counseling, financial assistance, or any other type of service provision possible in social service organizations.

FIGURE 1.6: Pretendo and FUBAR: Similar Processes

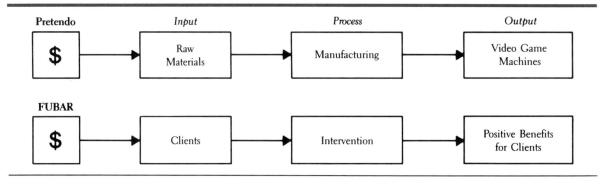

Output

Both Pretendo and FUBAR produce output (that is, some finished product) at the end of their processes. Pretendo produces new video game machines ready to be marketed. FUBAR, on the other hand, applies its process (intervention) to produce some positive effects on and for clients. Such effects may include improved family relationships, mental health, or financial status.

The Exceptional Problems of Social Service Organizations

A number of problems plague social service organizations that do not affect private businesses. Most are based on the fact that working with people is infinitely more complicated than working with material.

As populations continue to expand worldwide, resources continue to shrink. Shrinking resources means that funding and financial support become more and more difficult to obtain. It also means that competition becomes more and more intense. The result is that organizations producing higher quality products (more effectively) at lower costs requiring less input (more efficiently) will be more likely to survive than those that are less effective and efficient. Pretendo will show a profit and thrive if it produces high quality video games at competitive prices. Likewise, FUBAR will be more likely to survive and thrive if it can prove that its outcomes on clients are positive and valuable.

Before you as a practitioner can begin to assess the effectiveness of organizations for your clients and perhaps suggest changes to improve their services, you need to understand some of the problems afflicting these organizations. Organizational problems are almost never easy to address and change. You need to recognize the magnitude of the problems' causes. Organizational problems include uncertainties in the environment, vague processes, vague goals, and goal displacement.

The Shifting Environment

The environment in which social service organizations strive to exist is constantly in flux. Social forces impact other macro organizations and influence political policies, which, in turn, modify the availability of funding. Thus, Holland and Petchers (1987, p. 208) explain:

> Financial support from public and private sources must be sought, maintained, and protected while community expectations and priorities shift from one problem or need to another. Legal requirements and policies regulating operations undergo modification. Service technologies evolve in new directions, not always in consonance with consumer or public preferences.

Funding mechanisms vary widely. Social forces jar social service organizations unpredictably and severely. To survive and effectively meet their goals of helping clients, these organizations must be keenly aware of external influences and their effects. Organizations must be able to react quickly to changing needs and demands.

Vagueness of Process

Interventions performed by a variety of individual practitioners and other staff are difficult to measure and monitor. They are unlike manufacturing machines that punch out slabs of metal. Such slabs can be measured. Raw materials are predictably uniform. Effectiveness can be evaluated in terms of a machine's accuracy and efficiency (that is, how fast the machine can punch out slabs). Work routines are predictable, repetitive, and relatively easy to monitor and control.

Professional staff in social services organizations vary widely. Clients vary even more. Therefore, social service organizations have multiple, immeasurable, human factors involved in the intervention process. Because people vary drastically more than inanimate materials such as metal slabs, practitioners who work with people must have much more flexibility than metal slab punchers. Workers in organizations need to have some degree of discretion, or ability to make decisions, in working with their clients. This, in turn, makes the monitoring of the intervention process even more difficult.

Vagueness of Goals

Accountability is critically important to social work practitioners today. Accountability is "the state of being answerable to the community, to consumers of a product or service, or to supervisory groups . . . ; also, a profession's obligation to reveal clearly what its functions and methods are and to provide assurances to clients that its practitioners meet specific standards of competence" (Barker, 1991, p. 2). Individual practitioners and whole agencies are called upon to prove that their performance is productive and valuable. A way to do this is to define specific, measurable goals and monitor the extent to which they are achieved.

Superficially, this sounds simple. However, how can a practitioner prove that a client has been helped? One way is to define specific behavioral goals, a concept that will be discussed at greater length in a later chapter. This takes substantial time, effort, and expertise.

For instance, if you are teaching child management techniques to physically abusive parents, how do you know when you've been successful? When they can pass a written test quizzing them on the specific techniques? Or, when they strike their children only on the hands and rump instead of on the head? Or when they strike their children only once each day instead of a dozen times? Human behavior is difficult to define and measure.

Evaluating the outcomes of an entire organization or even of a program, including goals, effectiveness, and efficiency, is infinitely more difficult than evaluating the outcomes of micro or mezzo interventions. This is because of the increased number of variables involved. In order to evaluate program outcomes, Holland and Petchers (1987) emphasize that, first, "service content must also be made clear, with uniform definitions describing program activities." They continue, "For consequences to be attributed to an activity, it is necessary to state exactly what a client has received from a given treatment or service and to determine whether that content has remained consistent over the course of the intervention" (p. 213). This is not an easy task.

The Pros and Cons of Centralized Versus Decentralized Organizations

Organizations can be placed on a continuum to show their degree of centralization. At one end are extremely centralized organizations, run according to classical scientific management theories. Their lines of authority are clearly established, and there is a strict hierarchy of authority. The units in centralized organizations are clearly defined and cleanly separated. Workers have little discretion. Responsibilities are de-

fined and implemented from above. Feedback from below is unwanted.

An example of centralization might be a probation and parole department. Clients for any particular officer in any unit tend to have very similar characteristics. Procedures and treatment plans are relatively uniform in approach. Clients and officers must abide by clearly defined rules and regulations, and little officer discretion is possible.

On the opposite side of the centralization continuum are extremely decentralized organizations. These organizations contrast sharply with centralized organizations in terms of flexibility. Decentralized organizations provide and encourage greater worker discretion. They often have a wide variety of clients with vastly different problems, issues, and backgrounds. Workers in such organizations need discretion to make plans for viable solutions. For example, a community crisis intervention organization might be extremely decentralized. Clients coming in for help might have problems ranging from depression to illness to job loss to executive-level stress. Workers need a broad range of discretion to address a wide variety of problems.

Goal Displacement

A major problem encountered by workers in organizations involves goal displacement. Goal displacement was originally defined as "substitution of a legitimate goal with another goal which the organization was not developed to address, for which resources were not allocated, and which it is not known to serve" (Etzioni, 1964, p. 10). Holland and Petchers (1987) interpret this meaning by stating that "goal displacement often occurs when the means to a goal becomes the goal itself. In recent years, goal displacement has become a serious concern in human service organizations" (p. 208). Goal displacement occurs when an organization continues to function but no longer achieves its goals. A typical scenario in social service organizations occurs when the rules and following those rules become more important than providing services to clients.

An Example of Goal Displacement

A large county Department of Social Services (previously referred to as the "public welfare department") comes to mind. It is located in the shell of an old department store, with high ceilings and myriad small worker cubicles somewhat resembling a beehive. All outside windows have been sealed with bricks because the administration determined that the building had "heating and ventilation problems." No one really knows what that means. However, everyone in the building knows that the building's interior is isolated from the outside world.

When you enter the main door of the building, it is difficult to figure out where to go for which services even if you are a professional social worker. You probably have to stand in line for fifteen to twenty minutes simply to get the information you need to figure out where to go.

When you finally find the waiting area for the services you need, you have to stand in line again for another twenty minutes or so to get the forms you need to fill out in order to get the services. You then take the twenty pages of complicated forms to fill out and find a seat. The chairs are made of hard plastic. It then takes approximately an hour to fill out the forms. This is assuming you can read English well. You probably do not understand some of the questions, so you leave the spaces blank. You then take the forms up to the desk where they are placed in a pile. You must wait your turn in order to see an intake worker (someone who begins the process to provide services). You may wait two to three hours.

Finally, your name is called and you are instructed to go to Cubicle 57 to see Ms. Simpson. You enter the cubicle and see Ms. Simpson sitting at her desk reading your forms. You begin a discussion with her concerning the additional information she needs in order to process your application for services. It seems, she indicates, that a number of critical elements of information are missing. Look at those blanks. She then tells you that you need to get the critical information before you can continue the application process. The critical information is somewhere at home. Well, that's all right. Just go home, get it, and start this whole process over again tomorrow. At least you know where the waiting room is now.

In this example, the organization is supposed to provide services to people in need. However, the complicated process, commonly called "red tape," is more important to organization workers than whether or not clients get needed services.

People's access to resources has a major impact on the options available to them and, in effect, how they behave. Poverty and lack of resources are at the root of many of your clients' problems. Therefore, it it crucial to understand how organizations affect resource provision and clients. Such a background can enable you to identify ways to make changes in systems so that your clients are better served.

For instance, take the example concerning the county social services department above. As a worker in that agency, there are several things you might try to change. Targets of change might include working with other workers and with the administration to shorten significantly the tedious forms. You might also explore ways to get information out to community residents regarding the documentation and information they must bring when applying for services. Simple things like putting up clearly visible signs instructing people where to go when they first enter the building might be helpful. Even advocating for comfortable waiting room chairs would be useful. A wide range of social work roles to make positive change will be discussed later in this chapter and throughout the text.

General Systems Theory, Organizations, and Goal Displacement

We have established that it is helpful to view social service organizations in systems terms. Many of the concepts involved are similar to those we use to refer to business and industry. For example, in industry, resources or *input* are *processed* by the organizational system that turns out some product or *output*. Essentially the same thing happens in social service organizations. They take resources (input) and, in response to social forces and institutionalized values, apply some process (procedures for providing services) to produce output (actual service provision or some other benefits for clients).

When goal displacement occurs, however, the emphasis is often placed on the process rather than the product. People in organizational systems begin to think of the rigid process of providing services as the product. The process rather than effective provision of services then becomes the organization's product. Such goal displacement is illustrated in Figure 1.7.

FIGURE 1.7: The Process of Goal Displacement

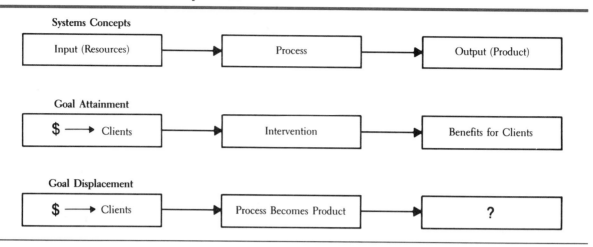

Communities and Human Behavior

We have established that organizational macro systems have major effects on clients. We have also indicated that community macro systems become extremely significant when we try to understand human behavior. Thus, the concept of community is very significant for social workers. You might ask how the word *community* can be clearly defined. Does a community include all the people living on one city block? Or is the community a group of people with common issues, problems, and concerns? For example, there is the social work community or the community of physically disabled persons. Does the word *community* connote a certain ethnic, cultural, or racial group? How large or small should a community be? Can the United States be considered a world community?

Barker (1987, p. 28) defines the community as "a group of individuals having common interests or living in the same locality." Warren (1972), who formulated perhaps the best articulated and most respected perspective on the community, defined it as "the combination of social units and social systems which perform the major social functions having locality relevance" (p. 6).

Because of the wide range of possible meanings, we will focus here on some of the major concepts inherent in both definitions of community. First, both definitions concern a group of people somehow related in terms of locality. Second, these people also

have some interests or functions in common. Third, because of their common locality, functions, or interests, people in the community interact on some level or at least have the potential to do so.

A fourth concept involved in community is important from a social work perspective. A community can be organized so that its citizens can work together and solve their mutual problems or improve their overall quality of life. Social workers can use their macro practice skills to mobilize citizens within communities in order to accomplish the goals they define for themselves.

Theoretical Perspectives on Communities

Communities vary widely. Think of a mammoth twenty-story, urban, public housing project. In contrast, consider suburban neighborhoods that require each home to be built on a minimum of four acres of land at a minimum cost of $500,000. Now contemplate neighborhoods in New York City where thousands of people work, buy groceries, eat, sleep, and play within a few city blocks of each other. Finally, consider rural farm communities where individual farmers keep cows, pigs, and chickens and harvest thousands of bushels of hay and corn.

Despite these broad contrasts, Rothman (1987) maintains that virtually any community can be examined from five major perspectives. These include "structural, social-psychological, people and territory, functional and action process, and social system" (p. 309).

Structural Perspective

Generally, structure refers to how the parts of any system are organized to become a whole. Additionally, structure shows how the components of the whole are related to each other. There are many ways of viewing a community's structure, and there are at least three subsets that demonstrate how the structural aspects of communities can be evaluated.

One way is from the *political-legal perspective*, which "refers to the official units designated as 'municipality,' 'township,' 'county,' and so forth" (Rothman, 1987, p. 309). When you think about such entities, concepts such as the public, taxes, and voting come to mind. Communities vary in their political structure.

A second subset of the structural perspective concerning communities involves their *geographical organization*. How are properties and tracts of land arranged within the community's geographical area? How are roads arranged? Is the community geographically organized like Tokyo, which developed over centuries and is composed of a maze of winding and confusing streets and alleys? Or is the community structured in terms of square blocks of land where an address such as "North 5760, West 10598" pinpoints the location exactly.

A third subset of community structure involves the *power structure*. A community can be assessed according to which of its units have the most power and influence over what happens within it. For instance, wealthier residents typically have greater power than poorer ones. It is likely, then, that those with wealth will exert greater influence over decisions made in the community than those who are poor. "Power groups" within a community involve members "who, because of their social status and positions, influence the decisions made on behalf of the community and who have greatest access to resources. Power group members usually include political leaders, financial and industrial executives, clergy," and other local leaders (Barker, 1991, p. 177).

Social-Psychological Perspective

A social-psychological perspective of a community involves how its members feel about themselves and interact with one another. One type of social-psychological approach focuses on the extent to which community members feel they have similar concerns. Do people feel that the community has a sense of identity? Do individuals feel that they are truly a part of the community? Will other community residents support them in their opinions about how the community should operate?

Another aspect of the social-psychological perspective reflects individuals' sense of well-being within the community. Do individuals feel protected and secure within the community? Or are they afraid to walk the streets? Are fellow community residents perceived as "friends" or as "foes"?

Still another social-psychological approach to communities is the "cultural-anthropological view," which emphasizes "attitudes, norms, customs, and behavior" (Rothman, 1987, p. 309). How do community members expect each other to behave? Which behaviors and attitudes are considered appropriate and which are not?

People and Territory Perspective

The people and territory perspective of communities assumes an ecological approach. We discussed some ecological concepts earlier in the chapter. This perspective views a community as a complex organism actively involved in interactions with its environment. Environmental issues such as pollution, depletion of scarce resources, and overpopulation are especially relevant.

Functional and Action Process Perspective

The function and action perspective on communities emphasizes purpose and how that purpose is achieved. Function and action are combined because they are so closely linked. A functional community is one that "includes groups of people who share some common interest or function, such as welfare, agriculture, education, [or] religion" (Ross, 1967, p. 42). Analyzing a community from a functional perspective does not necessarily involve all community members. Only those involved in the identified functions are relevant.

The action process orientation focuses on how the community has grown, acted, and matured over time. Because decisions and maneuvers change as time passes, the actions taken collectively become a process. The primary functions of the community over time directly affect the actions a community chooses to take. For instance, historically in some farming communities, almost all the community members would assist a new neighbor in building a new barn. The community's *function* focused on farming. Community *actions* were used to support that function.

Social System Perspective

The fifth and final theoretical perspective on communities involves thinking of them as social systems. This view is based on general systems theory, the major concepts of which we've already examined. This perspective emphasizes analyzing how the social subsystems within the community interact with each other. What inputs does the community have? How does the community process these inputs? Finally, what outputs does the community expend? Are enough resources entering the community to keep it healthy and thriving? Is it progressing toward disorganization and entropy? For example, are businesses moving to other more prosperous communities, leaving this community to spiral into unemployment, poverty, and despair?

Which Theoretical Perspective Is Best?

There is no answer to this question. Theoretical perspectives simply give you ways of examining things. They give you ideas about how to think and what to look for. Thinking about communities or assessing them in different ways can give social work practitioners ideas about what could be done to improve life for large groups of people in communities.

Rothman (1987) stresses that specific concepts can be helpful in determining what actually can be done to help any particular community; these concepts include "citizen participation, power structure, and social network analysis" (p. 311). These concepts can be examined and assessed from almost any of the five major theoretical perspectives on communities.

Citizen Participation. Citizen participation is the "involvement of members of the general public who are likely to be affected by a changed social policy, law, or circumstance in the process of planning and implementing that change" (Barker, 1991, p. 36). Citizen participation means that community members voluntarily contribute their efforts and participate in helping their community. Social workers who work

to improve community macro systems often employ the concept of citizen participation. Social workers can act to encourage and enable community members to improve community conditions for themselves.

Power Structure. A community's power structure is determined by "who holds the power and who calls the shots" within a community (Rothman, 1987, p. 312). Rothman also summarizes the importance of attending to and potentially using the community power structure to effect positive change:

> An understanding of the nature of power at the community level is an important consideration for community practitioners. It enables them to determine possible allies or adversaries in relation to given courses of action, and it facilitates the design of strategies stressing either consensus or conflict in regard to a given goal. It provides ongoing guidance in the general process of community appraisal.

Social Network Analysis. Social networks are "individuals or groups linked by some common bond, shared social status, similar or shared functions, or geographic or cultural connection" (Barker, 1991, p. 219). Social networks can be either formal or informal. Formal social networks are made up of various organizations and their interactions with each other. Informal social networks consist of individuals and their mutual support systems.

Formal and informal support in any community contribute strength to that community. When residents work together, it's easier to get more accomplished than when isolated individuals work alone.

One scenario involving the use of all three of these concepts (citizen participation, power structure, and social networks) comes to mind: Community members come together in citizen participation. They form a social network of support. Then they confront the primary power structure (for example, the mayor's office) and pressure this structure to make policies fairer and to distribute resources more equitably.

Social Work Practice With and Within Communities

Historically, "community organization" is the term used to refer to macro practice in social work. The methods and directions of social work practice have changed and evolved, just as the economic and social realities of the times have changed. However, reviewing the historical perspective on community practice helps us understand the significance of community assessment and work today.

Past major methods of community organization have included social action, social planning, and locality development (Rothman and Tropman, 1987). Using macro practice skills to advocate on behalf of communities of people is one logical application of social action. Frequently, social action can be used to remedy imbalances of power. For instance, African American people might be economically oppressed by white people in the same community. White residents might command the vast majority of political power positions. Whites might regulate the entrance of African Americans into other positions of power and higher paying jobs by limiting educational opportunities and employing discriminatory hiring practices. In this instance, social action might be necessary to redistribute power more equally among racial groups within the community.

The second traditional method of community organization, social planning, involves "a technical process of problem-solving with regard to substantive social problems, such as delinquency, housing, and mental health" (Rothman and Tropman, 1987, p. 6). The emphasis here is reliance on experts or consultants to work with designated community leaders to solve specific problems. People in the general community would have little, if any, participation or input into the problem solving process.

The third traditional method of community organization, locality development, emphasizes "community change . . . pursued optimally through broad participation of a wide spectrum of people at the local community level" (Rothman and Tropman, 1987, p. 4). As many people as possible within the community (ideally, everyone), in a democratic manner, define their own goals and help themselves. Locality development fits extremely well with social work values. Individual dignity and participation in addition to the right of free choice are emphasized as being vitally important.

Currently, there is considerable debate regarding which paths social work macro practice should take. National and world politics have changed since the three traditional methods of community organization were enthusiastically espoused. Resources continue to shrink and hard decisions must be made regarding

where they should be focused. Many postulate that macro practice today is substantially different than it was a few decades ago.

Macro practice, which involves effective interventions with large systems and organizations on behalf of people, is still a major thrust of generalist social work. Systems and their policies need changes and improvement. Oppressed populations need advocacy on their behalf. The focus of change must not be limited to changing the behavior of individual clients or client groups. Rather, there is a cluster of macro practice skills that social workers can use to effect change. Today most macro practice takes place within an organizational context.

The basic concept of community is no less important now than it was years ago. It remains just as critical to focus on the benefits of large groups of people, their overall well-being, their dignity, and their right of choice. The community concept provides a global perspective with which social workers can view the world, assess problems, and set goals.

Social Worker System Roles

Understanding the roles used in practice helps set the stage for skill acquisition. Roles (that is, the expected behaviors and professional functions considered important for social workers) help tie knowledge to practice. Understanding human behavior is useful in carrying out the many roles social workers have.

The following sections describe some of the roles workers use at various levels of practice. Some roles are more useful in a macro system context; others relate primarily to micro or mezzo systems. Many can be applied at all three levels of generalist practice. It should be remembered that for any particular intervention, a worker may assume a number of roles, often at the same time. Generalist practitioners need to be flexible and to be capable of working with multiple systems.

One of the most common roles for generalist practitioners is that of enabler. Roles especially useful for macro system intervention include mediator, integrator/coordinator, general manager, educator, and analyst/evaluator (Yessian and Broskowski, 1983, pp. 183–84). Still other social work roles include broker, facilitator, initiator, negotiator, and advocate. These roles are illustrated in Figure 1.8 and described briefly:

FIGURE 1.8: Social Worker System Roles in the Promotion of Social and Economic Justice

The diagrams illustrate a variety of social work roles. Most emphasize the roles' relationships to macro systems. Circles are used to represent worker, client, and macro systems. Lines and arrows depict how systems relate to each other. Macro systems are usually organizations or communities. Client systems can be individuals, families, small groups, communities, or organizations.

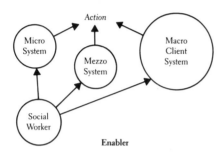

Enabler

The *enabler* role involves providing support, encouragement, and suggestions to a client system so that the client may proceed more easily and successfully in completing tasks or solving problems. The diagram above illustrates how workers can provide such support to any size system. Arrows pointing from the worker circle to the respective client system circles depict the worker's support. The desired result is that the client system will be better able to pursue some course of action.

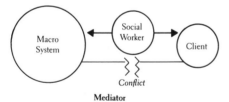

Mediator

Mediators work to help conflicting parties settle disputes and agree on compromises. A mediator maintains a neutral stance between the involved parties, taking no one's side. In the above diagram, the broken line beneath the worker circle depicts the two parties' broken lines of communication and their inability to settle differences.

Here the worker is mediating between a client system and a macro system. However, mediation can occur between virtually any size systems including that between two macro systems or two micro systems. Consider, for instance, divorce mediation where disputes are settled and agreements made between divorcing spouses.

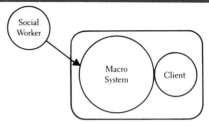

Integrator/Coordinator

The *integrator/coordinator* role concerns helping component subsystems work together to achieve goals. Although the diagram above illustrates the coordination of one macro and one client system, such coordination can occur among any number of macro, mezzo, and micro systems.

The box enclosing the macro and client systems represent the coordinated interaction between these two systems. The arrow pointing from the worker to the box depicts the worker's active involvement in coordinating all the systems involved.

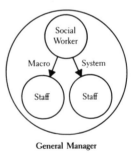

General Manager

The worker as *general manager* assumes administrative functions within an agency. Here the worker circle is pictured within the macro system. In this case the worker is employed by the macro system to supervise staff who also work for that system.

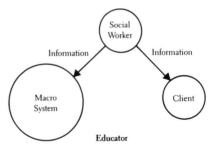

Educator

As an *educator,* a worker conveys information. The diagram above illustrates a worker teaching both a macro system and a client. The worker as educator can convey information to virtually any size system.

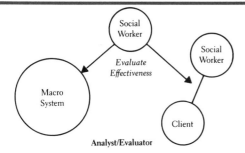

Analyst/Evaluator

Analyst/evaluator roles involve analyzing or evaluating effectiveness. In some cases, an analyst will determine the effectiveness of an entire agency or program. Recall our discussion about goal displacement which depicts one way organizations can become ineffective. The above diagram also portrays the worker evaluating an intervention with a client.

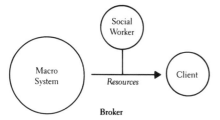

Broker

The *broker* role involves linking clients with needed resources. The line from the worker circle to the arrow portrays the worker's role. It illustrates the worker's active involvement in obtaining resources for the client. The arrow points from the macro system circle, which provides resources, to the client system circle, which receives them.

It should be emphasized that the client system could be a micro, mezzo, or macro system. Systems of all sizes need resources.

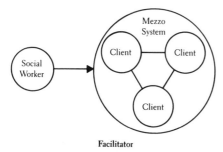

Facilitator

Facilitators lead groups. The arrow pointing from the worker circle to the mezzo system circle in the diagram depicts the worker's leadership concerning the group system. Three client system circles portray group members or subsystems within the mezzo system. Only three client

system circles are illustrated here due to lack of space. More clients could be represented depending on the size of the small group. Lines connecting the client systems represent group interaction and communication.

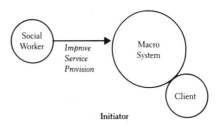

Initiator

The *initiator* role entails "starting the ball rolling," so to speak, on some new program or idea. The arrow from the worker to the macro system portrays a worker initiating a new idea regarding how the macro system could improve its service provision to clients.

Negotiator

Negotiators somewhat resemble mediators in that they function to settle disputes and/or resolve disagreements. However, unlike mediators, they clearly take the side of one of the parties involved. In the diagram, the worker is allied with the client and is proceeding to negotiate with a macro system to resolve a conflict.

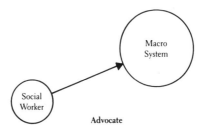

Advocate

Advocates champion the rights of others. They usually advocate with the goal of empowering their clients. The arrow in the diagram which leads from the worker to the macro system is exceptionally thick. This represents the significant amount of energy it often takes to impact larger, more powerful systems. Advocacy is an extremely significant role in generalist social work practice.

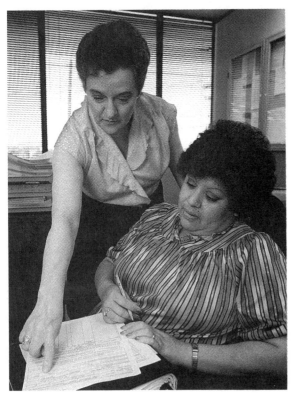

This social worker assumes the role of enabler when she helps her client apply for public assistance.

Enabler Role. In the enabler role, a worker helps a client system "become capable of coping with situational or transitional stress. Specific skills used in achieving this objective include conveying hope, reducing resistance and ambivalence, recognizing and managing feelings, identifying and supporting personal strengths and social assets, breaking down problems into parts that can be solved more readily, and maintaining a focus on goals and the means of achieving them" (Barker, 1991, p. 74). Enablers, then, are helpers. Practitioners can function in the role of enabler for micro, mezzo, or macro systems.

It should be noted that this definition of "enabler" is very different from the definition of "enabler" as used in the area of chemical dependency. There the term refers to a family member or friend who facilitates the substance abuser in continuing to use and abuse the drug of his or her choice.

Mediator Role. The mediator role involves resolving arguments or disagreements among micro, mezzo,

or macro systems in disagreement. At the macro level, mediation involves helping various factions (subsystems) within a community, or between a community system and some other system, work out their differences. At the micro and mezzo levels, mediation is becoming increasingly important in resolving divorce and child custody cases.

This role may involve improving communication among dissident individuals or groups or helping those involved come to a compromise. A mediator remains neutral; he or she does not side with either party in the dispute. Mediators make sure they understand the positions of both parties. They may help to clarify positions, recognize miscommunication about differences, and help those involved present their cases clearly.

Integrator/Coordinator Role. Integration concerns "the process of bringing together components into a unified whole" (Barker, 1991, p. 116). Coordination involves bringing components together in some kind of organized manner. A generalist social worker can function as an integrator/coordinator "in many ways, ranging from . . . advocacy and identification of coordination opportunities, to provision of technical assistance, to direct involvement in the development and implementation of service linkages" (Yessian and Broskowski, 1983, p. 184).

General Manager Role. Management in social work involves "having some level of administrative responsibility for a social agency or other unit to determine organizational goals; acquire resources and allocate them to carry out programs; coordinate activities toward the achievement of selected goals; and monitor, assess, and make necessary changes in processes and structure to improve effectiveness and efficiency" (Barker, 1991, p. 5). Management involves a number of tasks, including planning programs, getting and distributing resources, developing and establishing organizational structures and processes, evaluating programs, and implementing program changes when needed (Patti, 1983).

Educator Role. The educator role involves giving information and teaching skills to client and other systems. To be an effective educator, the worker must first be knowledgeable. Additionally, the worker must be a good communicator so that information is conveyed clearly and is readily understood by the receiver.

Analyst/Evaluator Role. Generalist social workers with a broad knowledge base of how various sized systems function can analyze or evaluate how well programs and systems work. They can evaluate the effectiveness of their own interventions.

Broker Role. A broker helps link clients (including individuals, groups, organizations, or communities) with community resources and services. A broker also helps put "various segments of the community in touch with one another to enhance their mutual interests" (Barker, 1991, p. 27). Getting resources for client systems is the key concept in the broker role.

Within the context of micro and mezzo systems, the worker can assist client systems in obtaining needed resources. This requires that the worker be familiar with community resources, have general knowledge about eligibility requirements, and be sensitive to client needs. A broker may help the client obtain emergency food or housing, legal aid, or other needed resources.

Facilitator Role. A facilitator is "one who serves as a leader for some group experience" (Barker, 1991, p. 80). The group may be a family therapy group, a task group, a sensitivity group, an educational group, a self-help group, or a group with some other focus.

The facilitator role may also apply to macro practice. In this context, a facilitator assumes "the responsibility to expedite the change effort by bringing together people and lines of communication, channeling their activities and resources, and providing them with access to expertise" (Barker, 1991, p. 80).

Initiator Role. Kettner, Daley, and Nichols (1985) define the initiator as the person or persons who call attention to an issue. The issue may be a problem existing in the community, a need, or simply a situation that can be improved. It is important to recognize that a problem does not have to exist before attention can be called to it. Often, preventing problems or enhancing existing services are good reasons for advocating change. Thus, a social worker may recognize that a policy is creating problems for particular clients and bring this to the attention of his or her supervisor. A client may identify ways that service could be improved. In each case, the person is playing the role of initiator. Usually, this role must be followed up by other kinds of work, because pointing out problems does not guarantee they'll be solved.

Negotiator Role. A negotiator represents an organization, group, or individual trying to wrestle something from other groups or systems. Somewhat like mediation, negotiation involves finding a middle ground that all sides can live with and achieving consensus whenever possible. However, unlike mediation, which is a neutral role, negotiators clearly ally themselves with one of the sides involved.

Advocate Role. Advocacy involves "the act of directly representing or defending others" and "championing the rights of individuals or communities through direct intervention or through empowerment" (Barker, 1991, p. 7). The advocate role involves stepping forward and speaking on behalf of the client system. This may be especially appropriate when a client system has little power to get what it needs. Advocacy often involves expending more effort than is absolutely necessary to accomplish the job. It also often involves taking risks, especially when advocating on a client's behalf in the face of a larger, more powerful system. This is especially so if the system is an adversary. The advocate role is one of the most important roles a generalist social worker can assume, despite its potential difficulties. It is often assumed when the client system is in the most desperate need of help. Therefore, advocacy can be extremely useful.

Problem Solving and Social Work: The Underlying Theme

Assessment involves analyzing situations in terms of interactions among client systems and other systems within the social environment. This is the initial step in helping people solve their problems and improve their lives. In practice, social workers help initiate effective change where problems are identified. Regardless of the particular role assumed, an underlying theme involves identifying alternative actions and helping client systems choose which alternative to take within the context of their social environments. The probable consequence of each alternative needs to be determined and evaluated. Finally, the most viable alternative behavior needs to be chosen regardless of the situation.

There are always reasons why people behave the way they do. The elements involved include interactions with other systems, stage of normal development, and aspects of human diversity. However, there

Case Example: Unplanned Pregnancy

Mona is a sixteen-year-old high school sophomore who just found out that she is two months pregnant. The father is Fred, a seventeen-year-old high school junior.

Mona and Fred have been going steady for two years. They think they love each other. Mona is a vivacious, outgoing cheerleader and Fred is a muscular, handsome quarterback on the school football team. They are both involved in school activities and have never thought very much about the future.

Mona hasn't told Fred about being pregnant. She's very confused about what to do. She doesn't know how he'll react. Mona hasn't told her parents either. They're very religious, and Mona is afraid that they'll be terribly disappointed in her. She doesn't know what to do.

Mona finally gets up enough courage to talk to the school worker, Ms. Peterson. Ms. Peterson is a warm, empathic individual who encourages Mona to talk about her situation. Mona shares her shock and dismay over her situation. She had simply avoided thinking about birth control or possible pregnancy. It had been easier not to worry about it and take her chances.

With Ms. Peterson's encouragement, Mona considers her alternatives. One alternative would be to have an abortion. The positive consequence of that would be a relatively fast termination of the problem and its implications. The negative consequences would include the cost, any difficulty she might encounter in setting up an appointment, and any physical discomfort the procedure would cause. The most serious negative consequence for Mona would be the guilt she says she would feel. She believes that abortion is morally wrong.

A second alternative would be to keep the baby and raise it herself. The positive consequence would be the fact that she would accept responsibility for the child she had conceived. The negative consequences would be the financial, social, and educational difficulties she would have to face in order to support and care for her child.

A third alternative would be to keep the child and marry Fred. Mona feels that this is a rather vague alternative. She doesn't know if Fred would want to get married. Although the positive consequence would be a two parent, "normal" home for the baby, Mona doesn't feel that either she or Fred is ready for the responsibilities of marriage.

A fourth alternative would be to have the baby and give it up for adoption. The positive consequences would be that her baby would live and have a home. The negative consequences would be that she would have to face the social consequences of being a pregnant high school sophomore and all of the accompanying gossip. The other major negative consequence would be the pain and regret she would experience when she gave up her baby.

Ms. Peterson should not, nor does she want to, make Mona's decision for her. It is up to Mona to weigh the positive and negative consequences of each alternative and make a decision. However, Ms. Peterson helps Mona think through her situation and her various alternatives.

Mona finally decides to have the baby and give it up for adoption. After weighing each positive and negative consequence within her own personal value system, she decides that this is the best route for her to take. She knows she will have to talk to Fred first, but feels that at least she has defined her own perspective.

---

are always other alternatives. A primary task of social work is to help people define the other alternatives available to them. Often people have tunnel vision. Because of stress or habit or lack of experience, people fail to realize that other alternatives exist. Not only do alternatives need to be defined, but they also need to be evaluated. The positive and negative consequences of each alternative need to be clearly stated and weighed. Figure 1.9 illustrates the process of evaluating alternatives. The client system might be micro, mezzo, or macro, illustrated by the three circles. A line leads from the circles to the alternative evalua-

tion process. An individual, a group, or a large organization may have to make decisions regarding how to proceed.

Much of generalist social work practice is probably done with individual clients and small groups. Thus, the case example, "Unplanned Pregnancy," shows how an individual client might be helped to identify the various alternatives available, evaluate the consequences of each, and finally select a course of action.

Within their social environments people are constantly impacted by various systems. These systems include families, groups, organizations, institutions,

FIGURE 1.9: Social Workers Help Client Systems Evaluate Alternatives

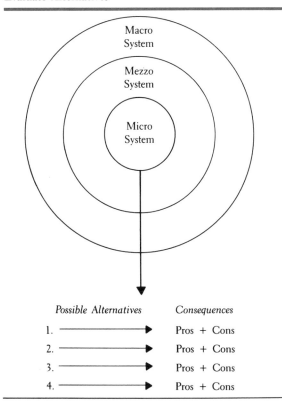

Possible Alternatives

Consequences
1. ——————▶ Pros + Cons
2. ——————▶ Pros + Cons
3. ——————▶ Pros + Cons
4. ——————▶ Pros + Cons

and communities. As a result of these impacts, people experience problems with which they need to cope. For example, a teenage daughter may run away, a primary family wage earner may lose his or her job, gangs may be vandalizing the community, or vital public assistance payments may be significantly decreased. People experiencing such impacts need to cope with them by identifying their alternatives.

The final element in our assessment of human behavior focuses on this resulting behavior and takes it one step further. There are reasons why a person opts to behave a certain way. However, there are always alternatives. A primary task of social work is to help people define the alternatives available to them. Because of stress or habit or lack of experience, people often fail to think that alternatives exist.

Summary

Foundation knowledge is essential to understanding the purpose and process of social work. This text provides knowledge necessary for the assessment of human behavior prior to acquiring practice skills. General systems concepts were explained. The multiple systems involved in human behavior were explored; the context of practice can be perceived as interacting micro, mezzo, and macro systems. Several types of interactions were discussed: interactions between micro and mezzo systems; those between micro and macro systems; the impacts of social forces; relationships among biological, psychological, and social systems that affect individuals as micro systems; and the effects on systems of diversity, oppression, and populations-at-risk.

The Systems Impact Model (SIM) was introduced. It emphasizes how organizations and communities affect client systems. Organizational and community systems were examined. Common social worker roles to enact the model were illustrated. Finally, the underlying theme of problem solving for social work practice was stressed.

PART ONE

Infancy
and
Childhood

2

Biological Systems and Their Impacts on Infancy and Childhood

Developmental Leaps

Juanita lovingly watched her one-year-old Enrico as he lay in his crib playing with his toes. Enrico was a first child, and Juanita was very proud of him. She was bothered, however, by the fact that he could not sit up by himself. Living next door was a baby about Enrico's age, whose name was Teresa. Not only could she sit up by herself, but she could stand alone and was even starting to crawl. Juanita thought that it was odd that the two children could be so different and have such different personalities. That must be the reason, she thought. Enrico was just an easy going child. Perhaps he was also a bit stubborn. Juanita decided that she wouldn't worry about it. In a few weeks Enrico would probably start to sit up.

Knowledge of normal human development is critical in order to understand and monitor the progress of children as they grow. In the example Enrico was indeed showing some developmental lags that were becoming more and more striking. He was in need of an evaluation to determine his physical and psychological status so that he might receive help.

A PERSPECTIVE

The attainment of normal developmental milestones has a direct impact on the client. Biological development affects behavior as does psychological and social development. All three systems of development operate together to affect an individual client. This chapter will explore some of the major aspects of infancy and childhood which are necessary both for providing information to clients and for making appropriate assessments of client behavior.

This chapter will:

- Describe the dynamics of human reproduction including conception, diagnosis of pregnancy, fetal development, prenatal influences and assessment, problem pregnancies, and the actual birth process.
- Explain normal developmental milestones as children progress through infancy and childhood.
- Explore abortion and infertility, two critical decision-making situations and life events which concern the decision to have children.

The Dynamics of Human Reproduction

Chuck and Christine had mixed emotions about the pregnancy. It had been an accident. They were both in their mid-thirties and already had a vivacious four-year-old daughter named Hope. Although Hope had been a joy to both of them, she had also placed serious restrictions on their personal lifestyle. They were looking forward to her beginning school. Christine had begun to work part-time and was planning on going full-time as soon as Hope turned five.

Now all that had changed. To complicate the matter, Chuck, a university professor, had just received an exciting job offer in Hong Kong—the opportunity of a lifetime. They had always dreamed of spending time overseas.

The unexpected pregnancy provided Chuck and Christine with quite a jolt. Should they terminate the pregnancy and go on with their lives in exotic Hong Kong? Should they have the baby overseas? Questions concerning foreign prenatal care, health conditions, and health facilities flooded their thoughts. Would it be safer to remain in the states as they were and turn down this golden opportunity? Christine was thirty-five. Her reproductive clock was ticking away. Soon risk factors concerning having a healthy, normal baby would begin to skyrocket. This might be their last chance to have a second child.

Chuck and Christine did some serious soul-searching and fact searching in order to arrive at their decision.

Yes, they would have the baby. Once the decision had been made, they were filled with relief and joy. They also decided to travel to Hong Kong. They would use the knowledge they had about prenatal care, birth, and infancy to maximize the chance of having a healthy, normal baby. They concluded that this baby was a blessing which would improve, not impair, the quality of their lives.

The decision to have children is a serious one. Ideally, a couple should examine all alternatives. Children can be wonderful. Family life can involve pleasurable activities, pride, and fullness to life. On the other hand, children can cause stress. They demand attention, time, and effort and can be expensive to care for.

Information about conception, pregnancy, birth, and childrearing can only help people make better, more effective decisions.

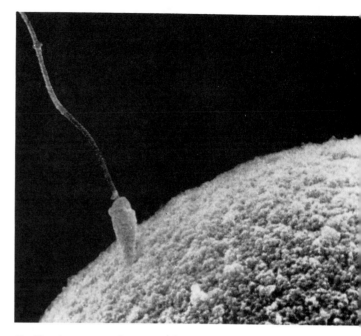

Fertilization occurs when egg and sperm combine. By the time this human sperm has reached the egg, it will have swum a distance 3,000 times its own length.

Conception

Sperm meets egg; a child is conceived. But in actuality, it is not quite that simple. Many couples who strongly desire to have children have difficulty conceiving. Many others whose last desire is to conceive do so with ease. Some amount of chance is involved. Of women having unprotected intercourse, 25 percent conceive after one month and 63 percent after three months (Shane, Schiff, and Wilson, 1976). Approximately 10 to 15 percent of couples in the United States are infertile or unable to conceive (Denney and Quadagno, 1992; Papalia and Olds, 1992). Regardless, knowledge of the process is critical for making clear and specific decisions.

Conception refers to the act of becoming pregnant. Sperm need to be deposited in the vagina near the time of ovulation. *Ovulation* involves the ovary's release of a mature egg into the body cavity near the end of one of the fallopian tubes. A woman is born with approximately 400,000 immature eggs, about half of which still remain alive at puberty. Usually the ova-

ries alternate releasing an egg on a monthly basis. Fingerlike projections called *fimbriae* at the end of the fallopian tube draw the egg into the tube by some unknown process of attraction. From there the egg is gently moved along inside the tube by tiny hairlike extensions called *cilia*. Fertilization actually occurs in the third of the fallopian tube nearest the ovary.

Conception may occur, that is, if a sperm has gotten that far. After *ejaculation*, or the discharge of semen by the penis, the sperm travels up into the uterus and through the fallopian tube to meet the egg. Sperm are equipped with a tail which can lash back and forth propelling them forward. The typical ejaculate, an amount of approximately one teaspoon full, contains about 300 million sperm. Unlike females who are born with a finite number of eggs, males continually produce new sperm. Fertilization is, therefore, quite competitive. It is also hazardous. The majority of these sperm don't get very far. Many spill out of the vagina, simply drawn by gravity. Others are killed by the acidity of the vagina. Still others swim up the wrong fallopian tube. Perhaps only as many as two hundred finally reach the egg. The journey to the egg takes approximately two hours. By the time a sperm reaches the egg, it has swum a distance 3,000 times its own length; an equivalent swim for a human being would be over three miles (Hyde, 1990).

Sperm can live up to three days. However, after about a day, they begin to lose their capacity to fertilize an egg (Guyton, 1981). Some reports of conception a full week after intercourse have been made, but this may have involved an inaccurate detection of ovulation (Masters and Johnson, 1985, p. 108). The egg, on the other hand, is capable of being fertilized for about twelve to twenty-four hours.

The actual fertilization process is thought to involve a cluster of sperm secreting an enzyme and depositing it on the egg. This enzyme apparently helps to dissolve a gelatinous layer surrounding the egg and allows for the penetration of a sperm. Some research indicates that the egg also takes an active part in the fertilization process (Schatten and Schatten, 1983, p. 32). The egg apparently selects and embraces one specific sperm with tiny projections extended from its surface. It then expels other sperm by producing a brief electrical charge on its surface. This is followed by the production of a hard coating of protein which makes it difficult for the other sperm to penetrate.

Fertilization occurs during the exact moment when the egg and sperm combine. Eggs that are not fertilized by sperm simply disintegrate. The genetic material in the egg and sperm combine to form a single cell called a *zygote*. Eggs contain an X chromosome. Sperm may contain either an X or a Y chromosome. Eggs fertilized by a sperm with an X chromosome will result in a female; those fertilized by sperm with a Y chromosome will result in a male.

The single-celled zygote begins its cell division process approximately thirty-six hours after fertilization. The cell divides to form two cells, then four, then eight, and so on. After four to seven days, the new mass of cells, first called a *morula* and now a *blastocyst*, attaches itself to the lining of the uterus. If attachment does not occur, the newly formed blastocyst is simply expelled. From the point of attachment until eight weeks of gestation, the *conceptus*, or product of conception, is called an *embryo*. From eight weeks until birth, it is referred to as a *fetus*. Gestation refers to the time passing during a pregnancy from conception to birth.

Diagnosis of Pregnancy

Pregnancy can be diagnosed by using laboratory tests, by observing the mother's physical symptoms, or by performing a physical examination. Many women first become aware of the pregnancy when they miss a menstrual period. However, women also can miss periods as a result of stress, illness, or worry about possible pregnancy. Some pregnant women will even continue to menstruate for a month or even more. Therefore, lab tests are often needed to confirm a pregnancy. These can be done at a Planned Parenthood agency, a medical clinic, or a physician's office.

Most laboratory tests fall within two categories—immunologic or biologic. Both tests depend on the detection of *HCG* (human chorionic gonadotropin) in the mother's urine. HCG is a hormone which is secreted by the placenta.

The immunologic test is fast and accurate and is currently the most common one used. A drop of the woman's urine is mixed with specific chemicals, placed on a glass slide, and observed. HCG, if present, will prevent the substance from coagulating. This means that the pregnancy test is positive. Immunologic tests are 95 to 98 percent accurate when administered two weeks after a woman misses her menstrual period.

Newer pregnancy tests are being developed. For instance, the *betasubunit HCG radioimmunoassay* is one that is 99 percent effective. It involves measuring the level of HCG in a blood sample. This test is sensitive enough to detect a pregnancy within eight days after conception. This test is becoming increasingly more available.

The biologic test also involves detection of HCG in the urine. However, here a sample of the woman's urine is injected into the bloodstream of some laboratory animal, such as a frog or rabbit. After several days the animal will ovulate if HCG was present. This ovulation indicates that the woman is pregnant.

A pelvic examination performed by a physician can also be used to diagnose pregnancy by the sixth to eighth week of gestation. Physical symptoms include a softening of the central part of the uterus just above the cervix (referred to as *Hegar's sign*), a softening of the cervix, a bluish coloration of the cervix and vagina, and a notable increase in the size of the uterus. One problem with this type of diagnosis, however, is the tremendous variability with which women experience these symptoms. The more certain method of detection of fetal heart beat, fetal movement, or identification by using X rays or sound cannot be done until at least the fourth month. By this time options such as abortion become more limited. Another problem is that several critical months have already passed when the fetus has been exceptionally vulnerable to substances such as drugs, alcohol, or tobacco. Without knowing it, irreversible damage may have already been done to the fetus.

The use of home pregnancy tests has also become very common. These are usually referred to as e.p.t.s (early pregnancy tests). These tests measure HCG levels in the urine and cost between $10 and $15. They are very convenient and can be used as early as the first day after the menstrual period was supposed to start. One such test, The Early Pregnancy Test, provides results within twenty minutes. Manufacturers claim that e.p.t.s are highly accurate, perhaps 89 to 99 percent. However, one university study found a much lower level of accuracy in which tests indicated women were not pregnant when they were (Doshi, 1987).

Despite the supposition that e.p.t.s are highly accurate, there is room for error. If instructions are not followed perfectly, results can be faulty. For instance, exposure to sunlight, accidental vibrations, using an unclean container to collect urine, or examining results too early or too late all can end in an erroneous diagnosis. False negatives (that is, showing that a woman is not pregnant when she really is) are more common than false positives (that is, showing that a woman is pregnant when she really is not). Regardless, it is suggested that a woman confirm the results either by waiting a week and administering another e.p.t. or by having a laboratory diagnosis performed. Early knowledge of pregnancy is important either to begin early health care or to make a decision about terminating a pregnancy.

Fetal Development During Pregnancy

An average human pregnancy lasts 266 days. It is most easily conceptualized in terms of trimesters, or three periods of three months each. Each trimester is characterized by certain aspects of fetal development.

The First Trimester

The first trimester is sometimes considered the most critical. Due to the embryo's rapid differentiation and development of tissue, the embryo is exceptionally vulnerable to the mother's intake of noxious substances and to aspects of the mother's health.

By the end of the first month, a primitive heart and digestive system have developed. The basic initiation of a brain and nervous system are also apparent. Small buds which eventually become arms and legs are appearing. In general, development starts with the brain and continues down throughout the body. For example, the feet are the last to develop. In the first month, the embryo bears little resemblance to a baby, as its organs have just begun to differentiate.

The embryo begins to resemble human form more closely during the second month. Internal organs become more complex. Facial features including eyes, nose, and mouth begin to become identifiable. The two-month-old embryo is approximately one inch long and weighs about two-thirds of an ounce.

The third month involves the formation of arms, hands, legs, and feet. Fingernails, hair follicles, and eyelids develop. All the basic organs have appeared, although they are still underdeveloped. By the end of the third month bones begin to replace what had been cartilage. Fetal movement is also frequently detected at this time.

During the first trimester, the mother experiences various symptoms. This is primarily due to the tremendous increase in the amount of hormones her body is producing. Symptoms frequently include tiredness, breast enlargement and tenderness, frequent urination, and food cravings. Some women experience nausea which is referred to as morning sickness.

It might be noted that these symptoms resemble those often cited by women when first taking birth control pills. This is due to the fact that the pill, by introducing hormones or artificial hormones which resemble those of pregnancy, tricks the body into thinking it is pregnant. In this way it stops the body from ovulating at all. The pill as a form of birth control is discussed more thoroughly in Chapter 6.

The Second Trimester

Fetal development continues during the second trimester. Toes and fingers separate. Skin, fingerprints, hair, and eyes develop. A fairly regular heartbeat emerges. The fetus begins to sleep and wake at regular times. Its thumb may be inserted into its mouth.

For the mother, most of the unappealing symptoms occurring during the first trimester subside. She is more likely to feel the fetus' vigorous movement. Her abdomen expands significantly. Some women suffer edema, or water retention, which results in swollen hands, face, ankles, or feet.

The Third Trimester

The third trimester involves the completed development of the fetus. Fatty tissue forms underneath the skin, thereby filling out the fetus's human form. Internal organs complete their development and become ready to function. The brain and nervous system become completely developed.

An important concept that is especially relevant during the sixth and seventh months of gestation is that of *viability*. This refers to the ability of the fetus to survive on its own if separated from its mother. It is generally accepted that at six months or twenty-four weeks, the fetus becomes viable. This issue becomes especially critical when referring to abortion. The question focuses on the ethics involved in aborting a fetus that, with external medical help, would be able to survive. This issue accents the importance of obtaining an abortion early in the pregnancy when that is the chosen course of action.

For the mother, the third trimester may be a time of some discomfort. The uterus becomes large, and the mother's abdomen becomes large and heavy. The additional weight frequently stresses muscles and skeleton, often resulting in backaches or muscle cramps. The large size of the uterus may exert pressure on other organs, causing discomfort. Energy levels during this time are low for most women (Leifer, 1980).

In the past, pregnant women were afraid of gaining too much weight. Physicians often suggested 25-pound limits. More recent recommendations, however, suggest a 26- to 35-pound gain (National Center for Health Statistics, 1986). Additionally, too little of a weight gain creates more risks than too large of a weight gain. Women who stay within the recommended weight gain limitations have significantly fewer stillbirths, low birth weight babies, and late miscarriages. Some of the added weight can be attributed to the baby itself, amniotic fluid, and the placenta. Other normal weight increases include those of the uterus, blood, and breasts as part of the body's natural adaptation to pregnancy.

Prenatal Influences

Numerous factors can influence the health and development of the fetus. Among these are the mother-to-be's nutrition, drugs and medication, alcohol consumption, age, and smoking habits.

Nutrition

A pregnant woman is indeed eating for two. Not only does the amount of food need to increase, but also the quality of food needs careful monitoring and attention. Pregnant women need approximately three hundred calories a day more than normal to provide adequate nourishment (Masters et al., 1988, p. 120). Additional vitamins and minerals are needed in order to provide adequate nutrition. Poor nutrition has been found to result in low birth weight and a high mortality rate (Holmes and Morrison, 1979). Labor also tends to be longer for women having poor diets (Newton, 1972).

Protein appears to be the most critical substance affecting intellectual development (McKay et al., 1978). One study showed that children born to women who suffered protein deficits during their pregnancies had average IQ scores 16 points less than their well-nourished peers (Winick, 1976).

Drugs and Medication

Since the effects of many drugs on the fetus are unclear, pregnant women are cautioned to be wary of drug use. Drugs may enter the bloodstream of the fetus after passing across the placenta. Drugs and medication should be taken only after consultation with a physician. The effects of such drugs usually depend on the amount taken and the gestation stage during which they were taken. This is especially true for the first trimester when the embryo is very vulnerable.

Teratogens are drugs which cause malformations in the fetus. Certain drugs can cause malformations of certain body parts or organs. The tragic example of the potential effects of drugs involves the so-called thalidomide babies of the early 1960s. Thalidomide, a type of tranquilizer, was found to produce either flipperlike appendages on newborns in place of arms or legs, or no arms or legs at all.

A variety of prescription drugs have been found to produce teratogenic effects. For instance, long-term use of antibiotics has been established as being harmful to the fetus (Hyde, 1990). One type of antibiotic, tetracycline, has been linked to stained teeth and deformed bone structures. Other antibiotics can cause deafness. Taking birth control pills during pregnancy can result in heart defects for the newborn (Heinonen et al., 1977) and a variety of other birth defects. One drug, isoretinoin or Accutane (its brand name), which is used to treat severe cases of acne, has been linked both to spontaneous abortions and to several other serious birth defects involving the brain, skull, face, thymus, and heart (Lammer et al., 1985). The Committee on Drugs of the American Academy of Pediatrics (1982) advises that women avoid taking any prescribed drugs or medication both during pregnancy and while breast-feeding unless such medication is absolutely necessary.

Even nonprescription, over-the-counter drugs— aspirin, caffeine, and insulin—should be consumed with caution (Babson et al., 1980). Ordinary aspirin, for example, when taken within the five days prior to birth, has been found to cause bleeding in both the infant and mother (Stuart et al., 1982). Such bleeding could have adverse effects in the event that the infant is born prematurely or is below normal birth weight. Caution dictates that pregnant mothers abstain from even over-the-counter drugs that contain aspirin if at all possible.

Drug addiction on the part of the mother can result in numerous problems. Such drugs may include barbiturates, heroin, and amphetamines. Potential effects include low birth weight, prematurity, convulsions, and depressed breathing (Masters et al., 1988, p. 122). Newborns of drug addicts tend to be addicted to the substance themselves; these infants actually suffer withdrawal symptoms during their first few days of life.

Papalia and Olds (1992, p. 68) describe a typical baby born to a mother using cocaine during pregnancy as "an apathetic, lethargic baby who in early childhood will have trouble loving his or her mother, making friends, and playing normally." Specific char-acteristics linked to babies whose mothers used cocaine or crack (cocaine in smokable form) during pregnancy include lack of alertness, abnormal unresponsiveness, premature birth, low birth weight, smaller head size, and urinary tract abnormalities (Chasnoff et al., 1989; Chavez et al., 1989; Hadeed and Siegel, 1989; Zuckerman et al., 1989).

Alcohol

Alcohol has been found to have serious effects on the fetus. The condition has been termed the *fetal alcohol syndrome* (FAS). Pregnant women who are heavy drinkers can cause growth deficits, impairments of the brain and nervous system, and facial aberrations (Ouellet et al., 1977; Clarren and Smith, 1978). Mental retardation is another serious effect. It has been established that about 85 percent of children affected by fetal alcohol syndrome have IQs which are approximately 70 or below (Hyde, 1986, p. 132). This sharply contrasts with the normal IQ of 90 to 110.

It has been clearly established that alcoholic mothers have the greatest likelihood of bearing babies with FAS. Evidence substantiates that women who drink six or more drinks per day cause their unborn children to be at serious risk. Even women who drink moderately may cause some adverse effects in their babies (Abel, 1980). The extent of the effects seem to be related to the amount of alcohol consumed by the mother. However, evidence is somewhat controversial regarding the effects of relatively small amounts of alcohol on the fetus. For example, Mills et al. (1984) studied almost 32,000 pregnancies and found that a minimum of one or two drinks daily significantly increased the possibility of retarded growth in the infant. However, some more recent research (Mills and Graubard, 1987) found that pregnant women who drank up to two drinks daily were no more likely to have babies suffering from FAS than pregnant women who drank nothing at all. Perhaps, some of the discrepancies in results are due to alcohol's differential effects on different people.

Smoking

Numerous studies associate smoking with "lower birth weights, shortened pregnancies, higher rates of spontaneous abortion, more frequent complications of pregnancy and labor, and higher rates of perinatal mortality (death of the fetus or newborn near the time of the birth)" (Masters et al., 1988, p. 122). The amount of smoking probably has varying effects.

One of the most striking findings is the relationship between the mothers' smoking and the significantly smaller size of their babies. Physicians at the Center for Disease Control in Atlanta have described a *fetal tobacco syndrome* which refers to the growth retardation associated with mothers who smoke at least five cigarettes each day. An additional risk of maternal smoking involves premature delivery. Shiono, Klebanoff, and Rhoads (1986) found that women who smoked a pack or more of cigarettes daily had a 60 percent greater risk of delivering their babies before thirty-three weeks of gestation.

Other research indicates that smoking during pregnancy may affect children's behavior and development even later as they continue through childhood. For instance, Stjernfeldt and associates (1986) found that children born to mothers who smoked during their pregnancy had a 50 percent greater chance of developing cancer during childhood than children of mothers who did not smoke. Dunn and colleagues (1977) found that children were twice as likely to suffer from hyperactive behavior by the time they reached age seven if their mothers had smoked heavily during pregnancy.

Age

The pregnant mother's age may affect both the mother and the child. These effects range from difficulty in labor for the mother to impacts on the child's mental and physical ability. It appears that mothers under age eighteen and over age forty are more likely to have a retarded child than women between these ages (Kaluger and Kaluger, 1984, p. 108).

Other Factors

Other factors have been found to affect prenatal and postnatal development. For example, a woman's income and social class level tend to affect prenatal development. Lower income levels and lower socioeconomic status tend to be associated with an increased number of health risks for both the prenatal child and the mother. Birth accidents also are more likely.

Illness during pregnancy may also have negative effects on the developing fetus. Take, for instance, rubella, also called German measles. Its most serious effects on the fetus occur if contracted during the first trimester of pregnancy. These include "deafness, cataracts, heart defects, mental retardation, and retarded growth" (Masters et al., 1988, p. 138). The chances of such defects decrease significantly as the pregnancy progresses to almost zero after the fourth month (Miller et al., 1982). The importance of preventive vaccinations of children should be stressed. However, no pregnant woman should ever receive a vaccination.

Transmission of Acquired Immune Deficiency Syndrome (AIDS) from mother to fetus has received major attention in recent years. Contraction of the disease may occur when the mother's blood intermingles with that of the fetus via the placenta. It is uncertain what percentage of children born to mothers with AIDS will eventually have the disease. Some research has suggested that a variety of defects may occur to the children of mothers who were infected while pregnant. Defects include small heads, various facial abnormalities such as short, flat noses and slanting eyes, and failure to grow normally (Iosub et al., 1987; Marion et al., 1986). The issue of AIDS is addressed more thoroughly in Chapter 10.

Prenatal Assessment

Tests are now available to determine if a developing fetus has any of a variety of defects. These include amniocentesis, chorionic villus sampling, ultrasound, maternal blood tests, and umbilical cord assessment.

Amniocentesis is "a means of detecting fetal abnormalities by inserting a hollow needle through the abdomen of the pregnant woman and withdrawing a sample of amniotic fluid for analysis" (Schiamberg, 1985, p. 635). The amniotic fluid contains fetal cells which can be analyzed for a variety of birth defects including Down's syndrome, muscular dystrophy, and spina bifida. The gender of the fetus can also be determined. Amniocentesis is recommended for women aged thirty-five and older and for couples who have a known history of genetic defects.

A problem with the method is that it cannot be performed until the fifteenth or sixteenth week of pregnancy, well into the second trimester of pregnancy. It takes an additional three to four weeks to obtain the results. In the event that a serious defect is discovered, the couple must face the decision of whether to abort a fetus at that stage of development or to prepare themselves to care for a potentially seriously disabled child. Another possible problem has been identified by some recent research done in Denmark, namely that there is a slightly higher risk of spontaneous abortion for women who have amniocentesis performed (Tabor et al., 1986).

Chorionic villi sampling (CVS) is "a method for diagnosing defects in the developing fetus; done by inserting a catheter through the vagina and cervix to take a small piece of tissue from the edge of the chorion, the membrane surrounding the fetus" (Masters et al., 1988, p. 681). Chorionic villi are "tiny threadlike protrusions on the chorion membrane" (Masters et al., 1988, p. 140). There are at least two major advantages of CVS. First, it can be performed by the eighth week of pregnancy. Second, results can be obtained within two days. Couples, therefore, may have a different perspective on whether to abort or keep a defective fetus at this early stage of the pregnancy. Some recent research found that the rate of spontaneous abortion is 3.8 percent when CVS is performed, a rate similar to that of women who do not have the test done (Hogge et al., 1986). Some questions have been raised, however, regarding the need for further research into other potential side effects such as damage to the chorion, infection, or damage to the fetus.

Ultrasound involves using high frequency sound waves to produce an actual picture of the fetus within the womb. A variety of abnormalities can be sighted and other information gained about the size and condition of the fetus. Many physicians use ultrasound on a regular basis to evaluate the fetal condition. However, ultrasound has been used for only a short time. Therefore, we may not yet know what long-term negative effects it may have (Kleinman et al., 1983).

Maternal blood tests can be done between the fourteenth and twentieth weeks of gestation. They detect a variety of conditions. For instance, the amount of a substance called alpha fetoprotein (AFP) can be measured. High levels of AFP can forewarn about abnormalities of the brain and spinal cord. On the other hand, low AFP levels may indicate Down's syndrome (DiMaio et al., 1987). Ultrasound, amniocentesis, or both can then be used to verify the condition.

Umbilical cord assessment entails taking small samples of fetal blood by inserting a tiny needle into the umbilical cord. The blood can be tested for a variety of conditions including "blood count, . . . liver function, . . . infection, anemia, certain metabolic disorders and immunodeficiencies, and heart failure" (Papalia and Olds, 1992, p. 55). However, certain problems may result from this procedure such as umbilical cord bleeding, premature labor, and infection (Chervenak et al., 1986; Kolata, 1988).

Problem Pregnancies

In addition to factors which can affect virtually any pregnancy, other problems including ectopic pregnancies, toxemia, Rh incompatibility, and prematurity, can develop under certain circumstances. Spontaneous abortions also happen periodically.

Ectopic Pregnancy

When a fertilized egg implants itself and begins to develop somewhere other than in the uterus, it is called an *ectopic pregnancy* or tubal pregnancy. This occurs approximately once in every one hundred pregnancies (Franklin and Zeiderman, 1973; Rubin, 1983). In most cases, the egg becomes implanted in the fallopian tube. More rarely, the egg becomes implanted outside of the uterus somewhere in the abdomen.

Ectopic pregnancies in the fallopian tubes often "spontaneously abort" and are "released into the abdominal cavity" (Hyde, 1990, p. 144). However, in some cases the fetal material continues to develop in the tube, outside the uterus, or on the ovaries, and must be surgically removed. Otherwise, the expanding fetus can cause a serious rupture of a woman's tissues, resulting in hemorrhaging and even death. In very rare instances, an ectopic pregnancy in the abdomen, if attached to the uterus, may be carried to term. There is still a high risk of hemorrhaging. Surgical removal of the fetus is necessary under these conditions.

Toxemia

Toxemia usually occurs late in pregnancy and is marked by high blood pressure, severe fluid retention resulting in swelling, and protein found in the urine.

In its most severe form, it can cause the mother to have convulsions, coma, and even death. Approximately 6 percent of all pregnancies are characterized by this condition (Masters et al., 1988, p. 138). Its cause is unknown. Toxemia is more commonly found in very young women or in women over age thirty-five. It is also more likely to occur in women of lower socioeconomic status.

Rh Incompatibility

Rh incompatibility occurs when the mother has Rh− blood and the fetus Rh+. This can only happen when the father's blood is Rh+. Since most people have Rh+ blood, the condition is fairly rare. The mother's blood forms antibodies in defense against the fetus' incompatible blood. Problems are less likely to occur in the first pregnancy than in later ones, since antibodies have not yet had the chance to form. The consequence to an affected fetus can be mental retardation, anemia, or death.

Fortunately, Rh incompatibility can be dealt with. The mother can be injected with a serum, RhoGam, which prevents the development of future Rh− sensitivity. This must be administered within seventy-two hours after the first child's birth, or even after a first abortion. In those cases where Rh sensitivity is already existent, the newborn infant or even the fetus within the uterus can be given a blood transfusion.

Prematurity

A baby is considered premature if born any time earlier than the thirty-sixth week of pregnancy. Sometimes, because the exact date of conception is difficult to determine, prematurity is gauged by birth weight. Prematurity and birth weight are thus often related. Usually an infant of 5½ pounds or less is considered to have a low birth weight. Prematurity is a condition affecting approximately 7 percent of all births in the United States (Hyde, 1990).

Premature babies, because of their lower levels of development, are much more likely to experience health problems than are full-term babies. Respiratory problems are especially common. Prematurity appears to be associated with the mother's health and nutrition, illness during pregnancy, smoking, imperfect functioning of the placenta, syphilis, and pregnancy in very young teenagers.

Spontaneous Abortion

"A spontaneous abortion or miscarriage is the termination of a pregnancy as a result of natural causes before the conceptus is capable of surviving on its own" (Denney and Quadagno, 1992, p. 163). Thirty percent of all embryos that have already fastened themselves on the uterine wall will spontaneously abort (Wilcox et al., 1988). The vast majority of miscarriages occur within the first trimester, many with the woman not even being aware of the pregnancy. Only one in four miscarriages is perceived by the pregnant woman (Beck et al., 1988). Often a miscarriage is perceived as an extremely heavy menstrual period. It appears that most miscarriages are caused by "a defective fetus, a serious maternal disease, or an abnormality of the uterus" (Denney and Quadagno, 1992, p. 164).

The Birth Process

Labor involves "rhythmic, regular contractions of the uterus that result in delivery of the child, the placenta, and membranes" (Masters et al., 1988, p. 124). Toward the end of the pregnancy, hormonal production by the placenta decreases. *Prostaglandins* are chemical substances which appear to stimulate the uterine muscles thereby causing contractions. Additionally, *oxytocin*, a substance released by the pituitary gland late in pregnancy, apparently causes the powerful uterine contractions late in the birth process which are necessary to expel or push out the fetus.

Prior to labor, several clues appear that are especially important. First, there is usually a small bloody discharge of mucus. This is actually the expulsion of the plug of mucus which remained in the cervical opening throughout the pregnancy in order to prevent germs from entering the uterus. Second, the bag of water (which acts as a cushion to protect the fetus) bursts. Although this usually happens during the end of the first stage of labor, about 10 percent of women experience this warm gush of liquid usually within twenty-four hours of the beginning of labor (Hyde, 1990).

The third major indication of beginning labor is the uterine contractions. These contractions have a clearly defined rhythm. Initially, they may be ten to twenty minutes apart and last forty to sixty seconds each. As labor progresses, these contractions increase

Pregnant women and their birth coaches practice relaxation at a Lamaze class.

in frequency, intensity, and duration as the body prepares to ease the fetus out during the birth process.

Sometimes women experience what is termed *false labor*. This condition also involves contractions called *Braxton-Hicks contractions*. However, unlike in true labor, they occur very irregularly and frequently far apart. Additionally, there is no hardening of the abdominal muscles in preparation for the birth. These contractions can be confusing and cause a mother a false alarm.

Stages of Labor

The birth process itself involves three stages. Initially during the first stage of labor, the cervix is dilated or opened in preparation for the baby to pass through it. Contractions begin between ten to twenty minutes apart in the early first stage and build to two to four minutes apart. Contractions continue to build in intensity and duration, often causing substantial pain to the mother. The water bag bursts toward the end of this stage. The first stage, the longest stage of labor, averages somewhere between twelve to fifteen hours for the first pregnancy and eight hours for later babies.

The second stage of labor marks the time when the baby is actually born. This stage begins when contractions are about two to three minutes apart and last for about sixty to seventy seconds each. The cervix is completely dilated and the baby begins to move through the vagina. The head usually emerges first. However, depending on the baby's position, some other body part may appear first. The average length of this stage is eighty minutes in first pregnancies and thirty minutes in later ones (Masters et al., 1988, p. 126).

During the second stage, the mother typically feels the urge to "bear down." This pushing, if done properly, may serve to facilitate the baby's movement out of the uterus and vagina. Each contraction also helps to move the baby farther along.

Sometimes an episiotomy is performed during this stage. An *episiotomy* involves making a small incision in the skin just behind the vagina. Its purpose is to relieve pressure on the strained tissues and help to provide a larger opening through which the baby can emerge. One reason physicians give for performing an episiotomy is that "if it is not done, the baby's head may rip" the tissue around the vagina; "a neat incision is easier to repair than a ragged tear" (Hyde, 1990, p. 133). However, many women question the necessity of having an episiotomy in view of the pain and discomfort it causes (including itching while it heals).

The baby completely emerges during this second stage. Mucus is then removed from its mouth through use of a vacuum aspiration device. Additionally, drops of silver nitrate or antibiotic ointment are placed in the infant's eyes "to prevent blindness resulting from a bacterial infection such as gonorrhea" (Kelley and Byrne, 1992, p. 89).

Finally, the umbilical cord which still attaches the baby to its mother is clamped and severed about three inches from the baby's body. As there are no nerve endings in the cord, this does not hurt. The small section of cord remaining on the infant gradually dries up and simply falls off.

The third stage of labor involves delivery of the *afterbirth*. The placenta and other fetal material making up the afterbirth detaches itself from the uterine walls and is expelled, often with the help of a few contractions. Finally, the episiotomy, if performed, is stitched up.

Birth Positions

Approximately 95 percent of babies are born with their heads emerging first. Referred to as a *vertex presentation*, this is considered the normal birth position and most often requires no assistance with in-

struments. Various birth positions are illustrated in Figure 2.1.

Another 3 percent of babies are born in a *breech presentation*. Here the buttocks and feet appear first and the head last as the baby is born. This type of birth may merit more careful attention. However, usually it can be detected ahead of time and a satisfactory delivery can be made.

A *traverse presentation* occurs in about 1 in every 200 births. Here the baby lies crossways in the uterus. During birth a hand or arm usually emerges first in the vagina. Such positions need special attention;

FIGURE 2.1: Forms of Birth Presentation

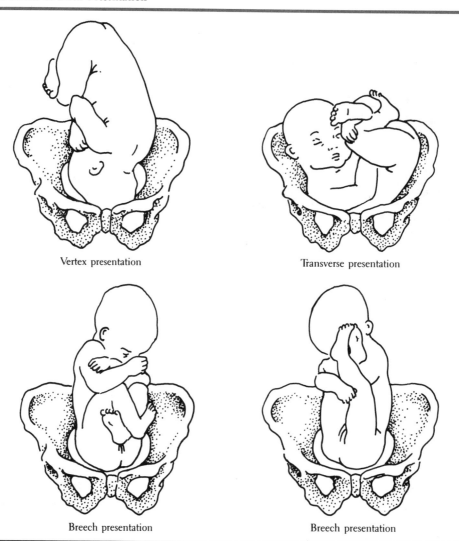

Vertex presentation

Transverse presentation

Breech presentation

Breech presentation

either the baby must be turned during labor so that a normal birth can be accomplished or a caesarean section must be performed.

A *caesarean section*, or C section, is a surgical procedure where the baby is removed by making an incision in the abdomen through the uterus. Caesarean sections account for about 25 percent of all births in the United States (Stafford, 1990). Caesarean sections are necessary when the baby is in a difficult prenatal position, when the baby's head is too large to maneuver out of the uterus and vagina, or when the labor has been extremely long and exhausting. Today it is usually safe with only minimal risks to the mother or infant. The mother's recovery, however, will be longer in order to allow for the incisions to heal.

Natural Childbirth

In natural childbirth, the emphasis is on education for the parents, especially the mother. The intent is to maximize her understanding of the process and to minimize her fear of the unknown. Natural childbirth also emphasizes relaxation techniques. Mothers are encouraged to tune in to their normal body processes and learn to consciously relax when under stress. They are taught to breathe correctly and to facilitate the birth process by bearing down in an appropriate manner. The Lamaze Method is currently popular in the United States.

Many women prefer natural childbirth because it allows them to experience and enjoy the birth to the greatest extent possible. When done correctly, pain is minimized. Anesthetics are usually avoided so that maximum feeling can be attained. It also allows the mother to remain conscious throughout the birth process. Finally, episiotomies are discouraged, which prevents the mother from suffering the subsequent discomfort resulting from incisions.

Newborn Assessment

Birth is a traumatic process, which is experienced more easily by some newborns, often referred to as *neonates*, and with more difficulty by others. Scales have been developed aimed at evaluating an infant's condition at birth. The sooner such problems can be attended to, the greater the chance of having the infant be normal and healthy. Two such scales are the Apgar and Brazelton.

In 1953 Virginia Apgar developed a scale aimed at assessing the infant's heart rate, breathing, muscle tone, reflex response, and skin color (Apgar, 1958). Each of these five variables is given a score of 0 to 2. Evaluation of these signs usually occurs twice—at one minute and at five minutes after birth. A maximum score of 10 is possible. Scores of 7 through 10 indicate a normal, healthy infant. Scores of 4 through 6 suggest that some caution be taken and that the infant be carefully observed. Scores of 4 or below warn that problems are apparent. In these cases, the infant needs immediate emergency care.

A second scale used to assess the health of a newborn infant is the Brazelton Neonatal Behavioral Assessment Scale (1973). Whereas the Apgar scale addresses the gross or basic condition of an infant immediately after birth, the Brazelton has been developed to assess the functioning of the central nervous system and behavioral responses of a newborn. This scale focuses on finer distinctions of behavior such as the infant's rooting and sucking reflexes and the ability to respond to various types of external stimuli. The scale is usually first administered two to three days after birth and then again about nine to ten days after birth. This scale has been found especially helpful for early detection of neurological problems (Als et al., 1979). There is some indication that the Brazelton scale may better predict how a baby will develop in the future than the Apgar scale (Behrman and Vaughan, 1983).

Birth Defects

Approximately 3 percent of all neonates are born with some kind of birth defect (Masters et al., 1988, p. 138). *Birth defects* refer to any kind of disfigurement or abnormality present at birth. Birth defects are much more likely to characterize fetuses that are miscarried. *Miscarriage* provides a means for the body to prevent seriously impaired or abnormal births.

No specific cause can be determined in most cases of birth defects (Wilson, 1977). However, about 20 percent can be linked to genetic factors and another 20 percent to environmental conditions such as maternal nutritional deficits, drugs, or maternal illness (Kaluger and Kaluger, 1984, p. 135). The specific types of birth defects are probably infinite; however, some tend to occur with greater frequency.

Down's syndrome is a chromosome disorder which results in various degrees of mental retardation. Accompanying physical characteristics include slanting eyes, a broad short skull, and broad hands with short fingers. The condition is also referred to as mongolism and Trisomy 21.

Chances of bearing a child with Down's syndrome increase significantly with the mother's age. For instance, at age twenty-five a mother's chance of having a baby with the syndrome is only 1 in 2,000; the chance increases with the mother's age to 1 in 40 for a woman aged forty-five or older (Papalia and Olds, 1989).

The vast majority of the research has focused on the mother's age. Hypotheses have addressed deterioration of the mother's ovum and variations in her hormonal levels. Some more recent research, however, has also found a relationship between Down's syndrome and the father's age (Abroms and Bennett, 1981). The risk rises slowly as the father ages until he turns forty-nine. An abrupt increase in risk occurs with men aged fifty-five and older.

Spina bifida is a condition in which the spinal column has not fused shut and consequently some nerves remain exposed. This birth defect occurs in approximately 1 in 500 births. Occasionally, this condition can be surgically corrected in the first months.

Low Birth Weight and Infant Mortality

Approximately 7 percent of babies born in this country (or 1 out of 14) have low birth weights (U.S. Department of Health and Human Services, 1990). That is, they are born weighing less than 5½ pounds. Low birth weight plays a major part in infant deaths. Government statistics indicate that infants born weighing 6½ pounds or less are five times more likely to die than heavier infants. Those weighing less than 3⅓ pounds at birth are ninety times more likely to die.

Infant mortality refers to the proportion of infants born in a given year that die within their first year of life. Babies are more likely to survive infancy (that is, there is a lower infant mortality rate) in twenty-one industrialized countries than in the United States, according to one survey.

Approximately 60 percent of babies born with low birth weights are premature, that is, they are born before the forty-week full-term gestation period is completed; the rest are "small-for-date babies" (Papalia and Olds, 1992, p. 90). These latter babies may or

may not be born prematurely. However, they fall in this category if they weigh less than 90 percent of what is considered normal for their gestational age. Infants born with low birth weights are likely to experience a variety of similar problems. However, premature infants with their less developed physiological systems are more likely to die than other babies with low birth weights.

Risk factors contributing to low birth weights fall into four major categories: demographic variables (for example, age, race, or education); medical factors occurring prior to the pregnancy (such as earlier miscarriages); medical factors occurring during the pregnancy (for instance, abnormally low maternal weight gain); and "prenatal behavioral and environmental factors" (such as use of alcohol or drugs) (Papalia and Olds, 1992, p. 91). It is crucial to attend to these factors and help women to have the healthiest pregnancies possible.

Social work roles to help pregnant women might include that of broker, so that women can get the resources they need. Resources include access to good nutrition and prenatal care. If such resources are unavailable, especially to poor women, social workers might need to advocate on women's behalf. Funding sources and services might need to be developed.

The consequences of low birth weight are many. They include greater vulnerability to infection (Jason, 1989), more difficulty maintaining normal body temperature due to lesser amounts of body fat, and increased respiratory distress. Long-term consequences, particularly lower IQ levels, are equally disturbing (Aylward et al., 1989; Rose et al., 1989).

Treatment for low birth weight babies includes immediate medical attention to meet their special needs and provision of educational and counseling support. Group counseling for parents and weekly home visits to teach parents how to care for their children, play with them, and provide stimulation to develop cognitive, verbal, and social skills also appear to be helpful (Infant Health and Development Program, 1990).

Other Factors at Birth Affecting the Neonate

Two other conditions that have serious effects on an infant at birth are *Phenylketonuria* (PKU) and *anoxia*.

PKU is a genetic condition whereby an infant is

unable to metabolize milk properly. It is caused by a malfunctioning of the liver so that any foods containing protein cannot be properly assimilated. Instead, substances remain and build up in the blood. These substances eventually damage the brain and result in mental retardation. Approximately 1 child in every 10,000 births is affected by this condition.

Fortunately, PKU can be detected early by a simple blood test given to the baby before leaving the hospital. On detection, a special diet can be administered which prevents the accumulation of harmful substances in the bloodstream. Mental retardation is then prevented. Eventually, some children suffering from PKU can resume a normal diet.

The other critical condition which can affect some children at birth is *anoxia*. Anoxia refers to the deprivation or absence of oxygen during birth. Oxygen deprivation can result in brain damage or even death. Anoxia can cause cerebral palsy, a condition characterized by various degrees of muscular incoordination, speech disturbances, and/or perceptual and cognitive difficulties. The Apgar rating soon after birth is helpful in identifying problems often related to anoxia.

Early Functioning of the Neonate

Most babies weigh between 5½ and 9½ pounds at birth. They tend to measure between 19 and 22 inches long (Craig and Specht, 1983, p. 42). Girls tend to weigh a bit less and are shorter than boys. Many parents may be surprised at the sight of their newborn who does not resemble the cute, pudgy, smiling, gurgling baby typically shown in television commercials. Rather, the baby is probably tiny and wrinkled with a disproportionate body and squinting eyes. Newborns need time to adjust to the shock of being born. Meanwhile, they continue to achieve various milestones in development. They gain more and more control over their muscles and are increasingly better able to think and respond.

First, newborn babies generally spend much time sleeping, although the time spent decreases as the baby grows older. Second, babies tend to respond in very generalized ways. They cannot make clear distinctions among various types of stimuli. Nor can they control their reactions in a precise manner. Any

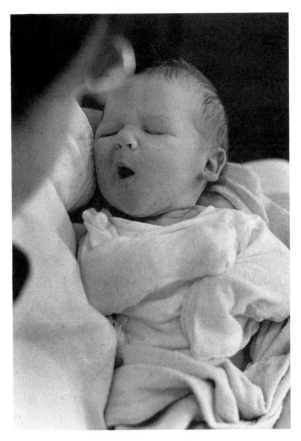

A newborn baby demonstrates the rooting reflex. A normal baby will automatically begin a sucking motion when touched on the lips or cheeks.

type of stimulation tends to produce a generalized flurry of movement throughout the entire body.

Several reflexes that characterize newborns should be present in normal neonates. First, there is the *sucking response*. This obviously facilitates babies' ability to take in food. Related to this is a second basic reflex, rooting. Normal babies will automatically move their heads and begin a sucking motion with their mouths whenever touched even lightly on the lips or cheeks beside the lips. The *rooting reflex* refers to this automatic movement toward a stimulus.

A third important reflex is *Moro's reflex*, or startle response. Whenever infants hear a sudden loud noise, they will automatically react by extending their arms and legs, spreading their fingers, and throwing their heads back. The purpose of this reflex is unknown, and it seems to disappear after a few months of life.

Three additional reflexes are the walking reflex, the grasping reflex, and the Babinski reflex. The *walking reflex* involves infants' natural tendency to lift a leg when held in an upright position with feet barely touching a surface. In a way, it resembles the beginning motions involved in walking. The *grasping reflex* refers to a newborn's tendency to grasp and hold objects such as sticks or fingers when placed in the palms of their hands. Finally, the *Babinski reflex* involves the stretching, fanning movement of the toes whenever the infant is stroked on the bottom of his or her feet.

Developmental Milestones

As the infants grow and develop, their growth follows certain patterns and principles. At each stage of their development, people are physically and mentally capable of performing certain types of tasks. Craig and Specht (1983, p. 10) define development as "the changes over time in the structure, thought, or behavior of a person as a result of both biological and environmental influences." Four major principles are involved in understanding the process of human development.

Growth as a Continuous, Orderly Process

People progress through a continuous, orderly sequence of growth and change as they pass from one age level to another. This has various implications. For one thing, growth is continuous and progressive. People are continually changing as they get older. For another thing, the process is relatively predictable and follows a distinct order. For example, an infant must learn how to stand up before learning how to run. All people tend to follow the same order in terms of their development. For instance, all babies must learn how to formulate verbal sounds before learning how to speak in complete sentences.

Several subprinciples relate to the idea that development is an orderly process (Papalia and Olds, 1992). One is that growth always follows a pattern from simpler and more basic to more involved and complex. Simple tasks must be mastered before more complicated ones can be undertaken.

Another subprinciple is that aspects of development progress from being more general to being more specific. Things become increasingly more specific and differentiated. For example, infants initially begin to distinguish between human faces and other objects such as balloons. This is a general developmental response. Later they begin to recognize not only the human face, but also the specific faces of their parents. Eventually, as they grow older they can recognize the faces of Uncle Horace, Mr. Schmidt who is the grocer, and their best friend Joey. Their recognition ability has progressed from being very basic to being very specific.

Two other subprinciples worthy of note involve cephalocaudal development and proximodistal development. *Cephalocaudal development* refers to development from the head to the toes. Infants begin to learn how to use the parts of their upper body such as the head and arms before their legs. *Proximodistal development*, on the other hand, refers to the tendency to develop aspects of the body trunk first and then later master manipulation of the body extremities (first the arms and then the hands).

Specific Characteristics of Different Age Levels

A second basic developmental principle is that each age period tends to have specific characteristics (Kaluger and Kaluger, 1984, pp. 13–14). During each stage of life, from infancy throughout adulthood, "normal" people are generally capable of performing certain tasks. Capabilities tend to be similar for all people within any particular age category. Developmental guidelines provide a very general means for determining whether an individual is progressing and developing normally.

Individual Differences

The third basic principle of development emphasizes the fact that people have individual differences (Papalia and Olds, 1981, p. 11). Although people tend to develop certain capacities in a specified order, the ages at which particular individuals master certain skills may show a wide variation. Some people may progress through certain stages faster. Others will take more time to master the same physical and mental skills. Variation may occur in the same individual from one stage to the next. The specific developmental tasks and skills which tend to characterize each particular age level may be considered an average of what is usually accomplished during that level. Any average may reflect a wide variation. People may still be very "normal" if they fall at one or the other extremes which make up the average.

The Nature-Nurture Controversy

A fourth principle involved in understanding human development is that both heredity and the surrounding environment affect development. Individual dif-

The environment in which children are raised can contribute significantly to their physical and intellectual development.

ferences, to some extent, may be influenced by environmental factors. People are endowed with some innate ability and potential. In addition, the impinging environment acts to shape, enhance, or limit that ability.

For example, take a baby who is born with the potential to grow and develop into a normal adult, both physically and intellectually. Nature provides the individual baby with some prospective potential. However, if the baby happened to be living in Ethiopia during the 1985 African famine, the environment or nature may have had drastic effects on the baby's development. Serious lack of nourishment limits the baby's eventual physical and mental potential. In severe cases, starvation results in death.

Due to the complicated composition of human beings, the exact relationship between hereditary potential and environmental effects is unclear. It is impossible to quantify how much the environment affects development compared to how much development is affected by heredity. This is often referred to as the *nature-nurture controversy*. Theorists assume stands at both extremes. Some state that nature's heredity is the most important. Others hypothesize that the environment imposes the crucial influence.

An interesting way of looking at the issue is to consider a "reaction range" for genetically inherited traits (Papalia and Olds, 1992). This involves the idea that each individual has a potential which is to some extent determined by inheritance. However, this potential is tremendously maximized or minimized by what happens to people in their own environments.

Former president Ronald Reagan maintained only a C average in college. Yet he was able to attain the most powerful position in the country. It is difficult to determine how much of his success was due to innate ability and how much to situations and opportunities he encountered in his environment.

An extensive evaluation of the very complicated nature-nurture controversy is beyond the scope of this book. Our approach is that a person develops as the result of a multitude of factors including those which are inherited and those which are environmental.

Relevance to Social Work

Knowledge of human development and developmental milestones can be directly applied to social work

Maternal Deprivation or Attentional Deprivation?

Ralph and Helen get a divorce. They have two children, Christopher, age six, and John, age ten. Helen takes custody of Christopher and Ralph of John. Helen's mother Ruth is shocked. Ruth wonders how a mother could possibly give up her own child? Ruth laments and thinks about what she did wrong to make Helen behave this way. After all, children need mothers, don't they? Or do they really?

June Cleaver, of *Leave It to Beaver,* clearly illustrated the ideal wife and mother of the 1950s. Times were relatively fruitful. People who worked hard could easily find jobs, buy homes, and upgrade their standard of living. June cooked, cleaned, and took care of her two children, Wally and the Beaver, on a full-time daily basis. Each weekday evening, Ward would come home to June whose hair would be nicely done and whose neck would be adorned by a classic string of pearls. Every day, June would be waiting for Ward at the door with a smile on her face and the daily newspaper in her hands.

As has been stated, to many this was the ideal, not necessarily the realistic, family situation of the times. Today it is clearly not the reality for most people and families. Currently both parents work outside of the home in almost 60 percent of families with children ("18 Million Moms," 1986). Almost 60 percent of women with children under the age of six (including both married and single mothers) work outside the home, and over 60 percent of all women with children under the age of eighteen do so (Matthews and Rodin, 1989).

Beginning in the Victorian era of the nineteenth century, mothers have been pressured to be the primary care givers of their children; their major tasks involved both caring for children's physical needs and conveying to them strong moral and spiritual values (Hendrick van den Berg, 1972, pp. 9–10). Prior to this children were only one part of a woman's total responsibility (Hoffnung, 1984). Women were responsible for all food and clothing preparation. They worked with men side by side to ensure the family's survival. As children and families grew, older siblings assumed child-care responsibilities for younger ones. When large extended families lived together, other family members such as grandparents helped in the overall task of maintaining the household and family.

Now you might ask, "What has all this to do with maternal deprivation?" The purpose is to set the stage for evaluating this issue. The very fact that the deprivation is labelled *maternal* and not *parental, paternal,* or *attentional* implies that when children are deprived, it's the mother's

fault. Therefore, it's important to examine how this term came about.

"Maternal deprivation" refers to the absence of opportunities for infants to interact with their mothers. Early research on maternal deprivation involved studying very young children living in institutions. These children were found to have severe cognitive and social deficits (Dennis, 1960; Dennis and Sayegh, 1965). However, it was later determined that these children were suffering from something more extensive than and different from simply the lack of a mother; they were suffering not from the *loss* of a mother's care but from a lack of care and attention (Rutter, 1972). Schiamberg (1985, p. 233) states, "It is now apparent that the institutionalized infants in many of the early studies suffered from the lack of stimulating, enriching experiences in addition to the lack of a stable, concerned care giver. When some of these infants experienced more stimulating and responsive interactions, their social and cognitive skills improved, sometimes dramatically."

The question might then be asked regarding what specific types of care infants need. What is involved in "mothering"? Lott (1987, p. 204) states that except for the physical aspect of "breast-feeding, the care and nurturance of a human being at infancy is not dependent upon the sex of the care giver." Rather, she continues, the quality of the attachment between infant and care giver depends on specific aspects in the environment and on "the previously acquired attitudes of the care giver." The five major variables include "(a) the physical presence of an infant; (b) the expectation that one will be caring for a child; (c) previously acquired nurturant responses; (d) opportunities for practice and reward; and (e) the quality of one's own remembered childhood—that is, the behavior of one's own parents."

Another related question concerns what the father's role can and should be in taking care of children. In the past, research focusing on fathers and children examined the amount of time they spent together; more current research explores how they interact when they are together (Papalia and Olds, 1989, p. 168). There is increasing evidence that positive attachment between infant and adult is related to how they spend their time together, not whether the adult is male or female (Lott, 1987, p. 205). For instance, three-month-old infants can be conditioned to increase their own vocal responses equally to the voices of both women and men (Banikiotes et al., 1972). The implication is that infants can learn to respond to fathers similarly to how they respond to their mothers.

The research concerning the similarities and differences between mothers' and fathers' reactions to their children shows some mixed results. On the one hand, for example, Berman (1980) examined the research which compared men's and women's responses to a variety of child-related stimuli including infants, young children, pictures of children and babies' cries. She found no apparent behavioral or physiological differences in their reactions. Other research has shown fathers to be responsive and nurturant toward their infants and demonstrate behavior similar to that of mothers; fathers smile at, observe, feed, and kiss their babies much like mothers do (Parke and Sawin, 1977).

On the other hand, there is some evidence that fathers and mothers do tend to treat their infants differently. For example, fathers handle their children more roughly, play more physically with them, and toss them up in the air; mothers, on the other hand, handle their children more gently and participate in more tranquil activities such as singing or reading (Lamb, 1977; Parke and Tinsley, 1981). Other research indicates that mothers tend to talk to their infants in a soft voice while fathers are more likely to physically pat their infants (Yogman, et al., 1977).

It's interesting to hypothesize how much the differences in behavior between mothers and fathers with respect to their babies are due to behaviors learned as part of their gender roles. Men are supposed to be more aggressive and physical. Women are supposed to be gentler and more verbal. Perhaps it's even more interesting to note that fathers who stay home with their babies and function as the primary caretakers assume behaviors more like mothers than do men who do not assume the major responsibility for child care (Field, 1978). The implication is that men treat children differently depending on their role and the social expectations regarding how they are supposed to act. Gender roles and sexism will be discussed in much greater depth later in Chapter 9.

The issue of maternal deprivation, or attentional deprivation, as we will refer to it here, is important because it's a matter of fairness. Most women work outside of the home. Most of these women work full-time. Additionally, women are still expected to be and indeed are the primary caretakers of children (Gilbert, 1985). There is pressure on women to be "supermoms," women who "do it all" and, even more, "do it all" well. What is the answer? Logically, if both men and women are expected to work outside of the home, then men and women should also be expected to share the work equally within the home. This is clearly not currently the case (Radloff, 1975; Englander-Golden and Barton, 1983).

The answer is *not* to say, "Oh, well, that's how it is. There's nothing we can do about it." Rather, traditional gender roles should be evaluated regarding their relevance to the here and now, not to the Cleavers or Ozzies and Harriets of the 1950s. Behaviors can be changed. People can talk about fairly sharing responsibilities and burdens. They can also talk about sharing their joys. Traditionally, men have been excluded from many of the wonders and precious moments parents can share with their children as they grow up. Lott (1987, p. 210) indicates that "men who have assumed a sizable share of responsibility for the day-to-day rearing of their children have reported an increased respect for, and appreciation of, maternal work, and that their experiences have expanded their sensitivities and capacities." Baruch and Barnett (1985) have found that fathers who are more actively engaged in child care feel greater involvement and competence in caring for their children.

Social workers need to become aware of their own opinions and biases. Only then can they avoid imposing these values on clients. Personal values concerning gender roles and how people *should be* versus how they *choose to be* are deeply rooted. It may be helpful to examine your own attitudes about the care of young children and the potential of attentional deprivation. You might consider how you would answer the following questions:

1. Do you think that mothers of young children should stay home to take care of them?
2. Should mothers and fathers share child care tasks *equally*?
3. If you marry, are married, or are living with a partner, do you share or plan to share child-care tasks equally in the event you have children?
4. Do married men and women share household tasks equally these days (for example, taking out the garbage, cleaning the bathroom, doing the laundry, washing dishes, cooking, grocery shopping, taking care of children)?
5. Do you think household tasks should be shared equally by married men and women when the women work outside of the home?
6. Do you think household tasks should be shared equally when women are homemakers who do not work outside of the home?
7. If you marry, are married, or are living with a partner, do you share or plan to share household tasks equally?

practice. Throughout the life span, assessment is a basic facet of intervention. In order to assess human needs and human behavior accurately, a knowledge of what is considered normal or appropriate is essential. Decisions must be made when intervention is necessary and when it is not. Comparing observed behavior with what is considered "normal" behavior provides a guideline for these decisions.

This book will address issues in human development throughout the life span. A basic understanding of every age level is important for generic practice. However, an understanding of the normal developmental milestones for young children is especially critical. Early assessment of potential developmental lags or problems allows for maximum alleviation or prevention of future difficulties. For example, early diagnosis of a speech problem will cue parents and teachers to provide special remedial help for a child. The child will then have a better chance to make progress and possibly even catch up with peers.

Profiles of Normal Development

The following section provides profiles of normal development for infants and young children of various ages. The intent is to provide a baseline for assessment and subsequent intervention decisions. If a child is assessed as being grossly behind in terms of achieving normal developmental milestones, then immediate intervention can be needed. If a child is assessed as being only mildly behind his or her normal developmental profile, then close observation can be appropriate. In the event that the child continues to fall further behind, help can be needed at some future time.

Gesell and colleagues (1940; 1946; 1956) initiated a number of studies concerning the development of children and their attainment of various developmental milestones. They studied hundreds of children to establish various indicators of normality such as when children typically can say their first word, run adeptly, or throw a ball overhand. Their findings reveal an organized sequence of behavior patterns through which children typically progress as they mature. Much of the information presented in "Developmental Milestones for Children from Age Four Months to Eleven Years" is taken from this research.

Significant Issues and Life Events

Two significant issues will be discussed which relate to the decision of whether or not to have children. They have been selected because of the great number of people they impact and because they often pose a serious crisis for the people involved. The issues are abortion and infertility.

The Abortion Controversy: Impacts of Social and Economic Forces

There are many unique sets of circumstances involved in any unplanned pregnancy. Individuals must evaluate for themselves the potential consequences of each alternative. Various life events such as an unplanned pregnancy impact individuals. At that juncture, the individual needs to define the available alternatives and assess the positive and negative consequences of each.

A basic decision involved in unplanned pregnancy is whether or not to have the baby. If the decision is made to have the baby, there is a subset of alternatives to evaluate from that point. One option is to marry the father, that is, of course, if the couple is not already married. A second alternative is for the mother to keep the baby and live as a single parent. Or, the mother's parents (the child's grandparents) or other relatives either could keep the baby or assist in its care. Still another option is to have the baby and place it up for adoption.

Each choice involves both positive and negative consequences. States may allow abortion as a legal alternative. Abortion is defined as "the termination of a pregnancy before the fetus can survive outside the uterus" (Masters et al., 1988, p. 679). Thus, social workers may find themselves in the position of helping their clients explore abortion as one possibility open to them.

The concept of abortion inevitably elicits strong feelings and emotions in people. These feelings can be very positive or negative. People who take stands against abortion often do so on moral and ethical grounds. A common theme is that each "unborn child" has "the right to life." On the opposite pole are those who feel strongly in favor of abortion. They feel

Developmental Milestones for Children from Age Four Months to Eleven Years

It should be emphasized that these milestones reflect only an average indication of typical accomplishments. Children need not follow this profile exactly to the letter. Normal human development provides for much individual variation. Parents do not have to be concerned if their child cannot yet stand alone at thirteen months instead of the average twelve months. However, serious lags in development or those which continue to increase in severity should be attended to. This material can act as a screening guide to determine if a child might need further, more extensive evaluation.

Each age profile is divided into five assessment categories. They include motor or physical behavior, play activities, adaptive behavior which involves taking care of self, social responses, and language development. All four topics are addressed together at each developmental age level in order to reduce confusion and to provide a more complete assessment profile.

Age Four Months

Motor: Four-month-old infants typically can balance their heads at a 90 degree angle. They can also lift their heads and chests when placed on their stomachs in a prone position. They begin to discover themselves. They frequently watch their hands, keep their fingers busy, and place objects in their mouths.

Adaptive: Infants are able to recognize their bottles. The sight of a bottle often stimulates bodily activity. Sometimes teething begins this early, although the average age is closer to six or seven months.

Social: These infants are able to recognize their mothers. Other familiar faces are also recognized. They imitate smiles and often respond to familiar people by reaching, smiling, laughing, or squirming.

Language: The four-month-old will turn his/her head when a sound is heard. Verbalizations include gurgling, babbling, and cooing.

Age Eight Months

Motor: Eight-month-old babies are able to sit alone without being supported. They usually are able to assist themselves into a standing position by pulling themselves up on a chair or crib. They can reach for an object and pick it up with all their fingers and a thumb. Crawling efforts have begun. These babies can usually begin creeping on all fours, displaying greater strength in one leg than the other.

Play: At this age, the baby is capable of banging two toys together. Many can also pass an object from one hand to the other. These babies can imitate arm movements such as splashing in a tub, shaking a rattle, or crumpling paper.

Adaptive: Babies of this age can feed themselves pieces of toast or crackers. They will be able to munch instead of being limited to sucking.

Social: Babies of this age can begin imitating facial expressions and gestures. They can play "pat-a-cake," "peek-a-boo," and wave "bye-bye."

Language: Babbling becomes frequent and complex. Most babies will be able to attempt copying the verbal sounds they hear. Many can say a few words or sounds such as "mama" or "dada." However, they don't yet understand the meaning of words.

Age One Year

Motor: By age one year, most babies can crawl well, which makes them highly mobile. Although they usually require support to walk, they can stand alone without holding on to anything. They eagerly reach out into their environments and explore things. They can open drawers, undo latches, and pull on electric cords.

Play: One-year-olds like to examine toys and objects both visually and by touching them. They typically like to handle objects by feeling them, poking them, and turning them around in their hands. Objects are frequently dropped and picked up again one time after another. Babies this age like to put objects in and out of containers. Favorite toys include large balls, bottles, bright dangling toys, clothespins, and large blocks.

Adaptive: Because of their mobility, one-year-olds need careful supervision. Because of their interest in exploration, falling down stairs, sticking forks in electric sockets, and eating dead insects are constant possibilities. Parents need to scrutinize their homes and make them as safe as possible.

Babies are able to drink from a cup. They can also

(continued next page)

Developmental Milestones for Children from Age Four Months to Eleven Years (continued)

run their spoon across their plate and place the spoon in their mouths. They can feed themselves with their fingers. They begin to cooperate while being dressed by holding still or by extending an arm or a leg to facilitate putting the clothes on. Regularity of both bowel and bladder control begins.

Social: One-year-olds are becoming more aware of the reactions of those around them. They often vary their behavior in response to these reactions. They enjoy having an audience. For example, they will tend to repeat behaviors that are laughed at. They will also seek attention by squealing or making noises.

Language: By one year, babies begin to pay careful attention to the sounds they hear. They can understand simple commands. For instance, on request they often can hand you the appropriate toy. They begin to express choices about the type of food they will accept or about whether it is time to go to bed or not. They are imitating sounds more frequently and can meaningfully use a few other words in addition to "mama" and "dada."

Age Eighteen Months

Motor: By eighteen months, a baby can walk. Although these children are beginning to run, their movements are still awkward and result in frequent falls. Walking up stairs can be accomplished by holding the baby's hand. These babies can often descend stairs by themselves but only by crawling down backwards or by sliding down by sitting first on one step and then another. They are also able to push large objects and pull toys.

Play: Babies of this age like to scribble with crayons and build with blocks. However, it is difficult for them to place even three or four blocks on top of each other. These children like to move toys and other objects from one place to another. Dolls or stuffed animals frequently are carried about as regular companions. These toys are also often shown affection such as hugging. By eighteen months, babies begin to imitate some of the simple things that adults do such as reading a book.

Adaptive: Ability to feed themselves is much improved by age eighteen months. These babies can hold their own glasses to drink from, usually using both hands. They are able to use a spoon sufficiently to feed themselves.

By eighteen months, children can cooperate in dress-

ing. They can unfasten zippers by themselves and remove their own socks or hats. Some regularity has also been established in toilet training. These babies often can indicate to their parents when they are wet and sometimes wake up at night in order to be changed.

Social: Children function at the solitary level of play. It is normal for them to be aware of other children and even enjoy having them around, however, they don't play with other children.

Language: Children's vocabularies consist of from five to twenty words. These words usually refer to people, objects, or activities with which they are familiar. They frequently chatter using meaningless sounds as if they were really talking like adults. They can understand language to some extent. For instance, children will often be able to respond to directives or questions such as "Give Mommy a kiss," or "Would you like a cookie?"

Age Two Years

Motor: By age two, children can walk and run quite well. They also can often master balancing briefly on one foot and throwing a ball in an overhand manner. They can use the stairs themselves by taking one step at a time and by placing both feet on each step. They are also capable of turning pages of a book and stringing large beads.

Play: Two-year-olds are very interested in exploring their world. They like to play with small objects such as toy animals and can stack up to six or seven blocks. They like to play with and push large objects such as wagons and walkers. They also enjoy exploring the texture and form of materials such as sand, water, and clay. Adults' daily activities such as cooking, carpentry, or cleaning are frequently imitated. Two-year-olds also enjoy looking at books and can name common pictures.

Adaptive: Two-year-olds begin to be capable of listening to and following directions. They can assist in dressing rather than merely cooperating. For example, they may at least try to button their clothes, although they are unlikely to be successful. They attempt washing their hands. A small glass can be held and used with one hand. They use spoons to feed themselves fairly well. Two-year-olds have usually attained daytime bowel and bladder control with only occasional accidents. Nighttime control is improving but still not complete.

Social: These children play alongside each other, but not with each other in a cooperative fashion. They are becoming more and more aware of the feelings and reactions of adults. They begin to seek adult approval for correct behavior. They also begin to show their emotions in the forms of affection, guilt, or pity. They tend to have mastered the concept of saying "No," and use it frequently. Perhaps this is the basis for the phrase, "the terrible twos."

Language: Two-year-olds can usually put two or three words together to express an idea. For instance, they might say, "Daddy gone," or "Want milk." Their vocabulary usually includes at least twenty-five to fifty words. Over the next few months, their acquisition of new vocabulary will be steadily increasing into the hundreds of words. They can identify common facial features such as eyes, ears, nose, etc. Simple directions and requests are usually understood. Although two-year-olds cannot yet carry on conversations with other people, they frequently talk to themselves or to their toys. It's common to hear them ask "What's this?" in their eagerness to learn the names of things. They also like to listen to simple fairy tales, especially those with which they are very familiar.

Age Three Years

Motor: At age three, children cannot only walk well, but also run at a steady gait. They can stop quickly and turn corners without falling. They can go up and down stairs using alternating feet. They can begin to ride a tricycle. Three-year-olds participate in a lot of physically active activities such as swinging, climbing, and sliding.

Play: By age three, children begin to develop their imagination. They use books creatively such as making them into fences or streets. They like to push toys such as trains or cars in make-believe activities. When given the opportunity and interesting toys and materials, they can initiate their own play activities. They also like to imitate the activities of others, especially those of adults. They can cut with a scissors and can make some controlled markings with crayons.

Adaptive: Three-year-olds can actively help in dressing. They can put on simple items of clothing such as pants or a sweater, although their clothes may turn out backwards or inside out. They begin to try buttoning and unbuttoning their own clothes. They eat well by using a spoon and have little spilling. They also begin to use a fork. They can get their own glass of water from a faucet and pour liquid from a small pitcher. They can wash their hands and face by themselves with minor help. By age three, children can use the toilet by themselves, although they frequently ask someone to go with them. They need only minor help with wiping. Accidents are rare, usually happening only occasionally at night.

Social: Three-year-olds tend to pay close attention to the adults around them and are eager to please. They attempt to follow directions and are responsive to approval or disapproval. They also can be reasoned with at this age. By age three, children begin to develop their capacity to relate to and communicate with others. They show an interest in the family and in family activities. Their play is still focused on the parallel level where their interest is concentrated primarily on their own activities. However, they are beginning to notice what other children are doing. Some cooperation is initiated in the form of taking turns or verbally settling arguments.

Language: Three-year-olds can use sentences which are longer and more complex. Plurals, personal pronouns such as "I," and prepositions such as "above" or "on" are used appropriately. Children are able to express their feelings and ideas fairly well. They are capable of relating a story. They listen fairly well and are very interested in longer, more complicated stories than they were at an earlier age. They also have mastered a substantial amount of information about themselves including their last name, gender, and a few rhymes.

Age Four Years

Motor: Four-year-olds tend to be very active physically. They enjoy running, skipping, jumping, and performing stunts. They are capable of racing up and down stairs. Their balance is very good, and they can carry a glass of liquid without spilling it.

Play: By age four, children have become increasingly more creative and imaginative. They like to construct things out of clay, sand, or blocks. They enjoy using costumes and other pretend materials. They can play cooperatively

(continued next page)

that women have "the right to choice" over their own bodies and their own lives.

The issue concerning unplanned and, in this context, unwanted pregnancy provides an excellent example of how institutional values affect the options available to clients. In June 1992, the Supreme Court ruled that states could have extensive power in restricting abortions, although they could not outlaw all abortions. If abortions are illegal or unavailable to specific groups in the population, then their choices about what to do are much more limited.

The abortion issue illustrates how clients function

Developmental Milestones for Children from Age Four Months to Eleven Years (continued)

with other children. Simple figures can be drawn, although they are frequently inaccurate and without much detail. Four-year-olds can also cut or trace along a line fairly accurately.

Adaptive: Four-year-olds tend to be very assertive. They usually can dress themselves. They've mastered the use of buttons and zippers. They can put on and lace their own shoes, although they cannot yet tie them. They can wash their hands without supervision. By age four, children demand less attention while eating with their family. They can serve themselves food and eat by themselves using both spoon and fork. They can even assist in setting the table. Four-year-olds can use the bathroom by themselves, although they still alert adults of this and sometimes need assistance in wiping. They usually can sleep through the night without having any accidents.

Social: Four-year-olds are less docile than three-year-olds. They are less likely to conform, in addition to being less responsive to the pleasure or displeasure of adults. Four-year-olds are in the process of separating from their parents and begin to prefer the company of other children over adults. They are often social and talkative. They are very interested in the world around them and frequently ask "what," "why," and "how" questions.

Language: The aggressiveness manifested by four-year-olds also appears in their language. They frequently brag and boast about themselves. Name calling is common. Their vocabulary has experienced tremendous growth, however, there is a tendency to misuse words and they have some difficulty with proper grammar. Four-year-olds talk a lot and like to carry on long conversations with others. Their speech is usually very understandable with only a few remnants of earlier, more infantile speech remaining. Their growing imagination also affects their speech. They like to tell stories and frequently mix facts with make-believe.

Age Five Years

Motor: Five-year-olds are quieter and less active than four-year-olds. Their activities tend to be more complicated and more directed toward achieving some goal. For example, they are more adept at climbing and at riding a tricycle. They can also use roller skates, jump rope, skip, and succeed at other such complex activities. Their ability to concentrate is also increased. The pictures they draw, although simple, are finally recognizable. Dominance of the left or right hand becomes well established.

Play: Games and play activities have become both more elaborate and competitive. Games include hide-and-seek, tag, and hopscotch. Team playing begins. Five-year-olds enjoy pretend games of a more elaborate nature. They like to build houses and forts with blocks and to participate in more dramatic play such as playing house or being a space invader. Singing songs, dancing, and playing records are usually very enjoyable.

Adaptive: Five-year-olds can dress and undress themselves quite well. Assistance is necessary only for adjusting more complicated fasteners and tying shoes. These children can feed themselves and attend to their own toilet needs. They can even visit around the neighborhood by themselves, needing help only in crossing streets.

Social: By age five, children have usually learned to cooperate with others in activities and enjoy group activities. They acknowledge the rights of others and are better able to respond to adult supervision. They have become aware of rules and are interested in conforming to them. Five-year-olds also tend to enjoy family activities such as outings and trips.

Language: Language continues to develop and become more complex. Vocabulary continues to increase. Sentence structure becomes more complicated and more accurate. Five-year-olds are very interested in what words mean. They like to look at books and have people read to them. They have begun learning how to count within the contexts of their mezzo and macro environments. For example, perhaps a woman's parents are unwilling to help her with a newborn. Or the child's father shuns involvement. In both these instances some of the woman's potential mezzo system options have already been eliminated.

Options are also affected by macro environments. If abortion is illegal, then social agencies are unable to provide them. Another possibility is that states can legally allow abortions only under extremely limited circumstances. For instance, they may be allowed only if the conception is the product of incest or rape,

and can recognize colors. Attempts at drawing numbers and letters are begun, although fine motor coordination is not yet well enough developed for great accuracy.

Age Six to Eight Years

Motor: Children ages six to eight years are physically independent. They can run, jump, and balance well. They continue to participate in a variety of activities to help refine their coordination and motor skills. They often enjoy unusual and challenging activities, such as walking on fences, which help to develop such skills.

Play: These children participate in much active play such as kickball. They like activities such as gymnastics and enjoy trying to perform physical stunts. They also begin to develop intense interest in simple games such as marbles or tiddlywinks and collecting items. Playing with dolls is at its height. Acting out dramatizations becomes very important, and these children love to pretend they are animals, horseback riders, or jet pilots.

Adaptive: Much more self-sufficient and independent, these children can dress themselves, go to bed alone, and get up by themselves during the night to go to the bathroom. They can begin to be trusted with an allowance. They are able to go to school or to friends' homes alone. In general, they become increasingly more interested in and understanding of various social situations.

Social: In view of their increasing social skills, they consider playing skills within their peer group increasingly important. They become more and more adept at social skills. Their lives begin to focus around the school and activities with friends. They are becoming more sensitive to reactions of those around them, especially those of their parents. There is some tendency to react negatively when subjected to pressure or criticism. For instance, they may sulk.

Language: The use of language continues to become more refined and sophisticated. Good pronunciation and

grammar are developed according to that which they've been exposed to. They are learning how to put their feelings and thoughts into words to express themselves more clearly. They begin to understand more abstract words and forms of language. For example, they may begin to understand some puns and jokes. They also begin to develop reading, writing, and numerical skills.

Ages Nine to Eleven Years

Motor: Children continue to refine and develop their coordination and motor skills. They experience a gradual, steady gain in body measurements and proportion. Manual dexterity, posture, strength, and balance improve. This period of late childhood is transitional to the major changes experienced during adolescence.

Play: This period frequently becomes the finale of the games and play of childhood. If it has not already occurred, boys and girls separate into their respective same-gender groups.

Adaptive: Children become more and more aware of themselves and the world around them. They experience a gradual change from identifying primarily with adults to formulating their own self identity. They become more independent. This is a period of both physical and mental growth. These children push themselves into experiencing new things and new activities. They learn to focus on detail and accomplish increasingly difficult intellectual and academic tasks.

Social: The focus of attention shifts from a family orientation to a peer orientation. They continue developing social competence. Friends become very important.

Language: A tremendous increase in vocabulary occurs. These children become adept at the use of words. They can answer questions with more depth of insight. They understand more abstract concepts and use words more precisely. They are also better able to understand and examine verbal and mathematical relationships.

Case Example: Single and Pregnant

Roseanne was twenty-one-years-old and two months pregnant. She was a junior at a large midwestern state university majoring in social work. Hank, the father, was a twenty-six-year-old divorcé she met in one of her classes. He already had a four-year-old son named Ronnie.

Roseanne was filled with ambivalent feelings. She had always pictured herself as being a mother someday. However, not now. She felt she loved Hank, but had many reservations about how he felt in return. She'd been seeing him once or twice a week for the past few months. Hank didn't really take her out much and she suspected that he was also dating other women. He had even asked her to babysit for Ronnie while he went out with someone else.

That was another thing—Ronnie. She felt Ronnie hated her. He would snarl whenever she came over and make nasty, cutting remarks. Maybe he was jealous that his father was giving Roseanne attention.

The pregnancy was an accident. She simply didn't think anything would happen. She knew better now that it was too late. Hank had never made any commitment to her. In some ways she felt he was a creep, but at least he was honest. The fact was that he just didn't love her.

The problem now was what she should do. A college education was important to her and to her parents. Money had always been a big issue. Her parents had helped her as much as they could, but they also had other children in college. Roseanne had worked odd, inconvenient hours at a fast-food restaurant for a while. Lately she had been working as a cook several nights a week at a diner.

What if she kept the baby? She was fairly certain Hank didn't want to marry her. Even if he did, she didn't think she'd want to be stuck with him for the rest of her life. How could she possibly manage on her own with a baby? She now shared a two-bedroom apartment with three other female students. How could she take care of a baby with no money and no place to go? She felt dropping out of school would ruin her life. The idea of "going on welfare" instead of working in welfare was terrifying. On the other hand, the idea of an abortion scared her. She had heard so many people say that it was "murder."

Roseanne made her decision, but it certainly was not an easy one. She carefully addressed and considered the religious and moral issues involved in terminating a pregnancy. She decided that she would have to face the responsibility and the guilt. In determining that having a baby at this time would be disastrous for both herself and for a new life, she decided to have an abortion.

Fourteen years passed. Roseanne is now thirty-five. She is no longer in social work although she had finished her degree. She does have a good job as a court reporter. She had always been interested in legal matters (reruns of the television show *Perry Mason* were still her favorite). This job suits her well.

She's been married to Tom for three years. Although they have their ups and downs, she is happy in her marriage. They love each other very much and enjoy their time together.

Roseanne thinks about her abortion every once in a while. Although she is using no method of birth control, she has not yet gotten pregnant. Possibly, she never will. Tom is forty-three. He had been married once before and has an adult child from that marriage. He does not feel it is a necessity for them to have children.

Roseanne is ambivalent. She is addressing the possibility of not ever having children and is looking at the consequences of that alternative. She puts it well by saying that sometimes she mourns the loss of her unborn child. Yet, in view of her present level of life's satisfaction and Tom's hesitation about having children, she feels that her life thus far has worked out for the best.

---

or if the pregnancy and birth seriously endanger the pregnant woman's life.

Even if states allow abortions, the community in which a pregnant woman lives can pose serious restrictions on her options. For instance, a community renowned for having a strong and well-organized anti-abortion movement may be supportive of actions (including legal actions) to curtail abortion services. Abortion clinics can be picketed, patients harassed, and clinic staff personally threatened. Such strong community feelings can force clinics to close.

Additionally, the abortion issue provides an excellent opportunity to distinguish between personal and professional values. Each of us probably has an opinion about abortion. Some of us most likely have very strong opinions either one way or the other. In practice, our personal opinions really don't matter. However, our professional approach does. As professionals it is our responsibility to help clients come to their own decisions. Our job is to assist clients in assessing their own feelings and values, in identifying available alternatives, and in evaluating as objectively as possible the consequences of each alternative.

In order to better understand abortion and its impacts, five aspects are discussed here. First, the current impacts of legal and political macro systems are described. Second, the abortion process itself and the types of abortion available are explained. Third, some of the psychological effects of abortion are briefly examined. Fourth, the arguments for and against abortion are compared and assessed. Fifth, a variety of social work roles with respect to the abortion issue are described.

The Impacts of Macro System Policies on Practice and Access to Services

We have established that institutional values affect laws. In many cases, laws can be considered a reflection of institutional values. Laws, in turn, regulate policy. Policy is "the explicit or implicit standing plan that an organization or government uses as a guide for action" (Barker, 1991, p. 175). Government and agency policies specify and regulate what services organizations can provide to women within communities. Subsequently, whether services are available or not controls the choices available to most pregnant women.

The abortion debate focuses on two opposing perspectives. Chilman (1987, p. 3) summarizes them as follows:

> Those who favor the legalization and ready availability of abortion are said to hold a "pro-choice" position. They believe that the human fertilized ovum is not a person, prenatally, and that the pregnant woman has a right to freedom of choice as to whether or not she will terminate an unwanted pregnancy, because a woman has a right to exercise control over her own body. Those who are against abortion are said to maintain a pro-life [or anti-choice] position. They argue that the human fertilized ovum is a human being and therefore has a right to life.

Over the past decades the political controversy over abortion has been raging. In 1973, the Supreme Court decision known as *Roe v. Wade* overruled state laws that prohibited or restricted a woman's right to obtain an abortion during the first three months of pregnancy. States still were allowed to impose restrictions in the second trimester only when such restrictions related directly to the mother's health. Finally, states could restrict abortions or even forbid them during the third trimester, excluding those necessary to preserve a woman's life and health. Women, in essence, won the right to "privacy," or, in other words, "the right to be left alone" (Hartman, 1991, p. 467). This, of course, is a pro-choice stance.

More recently, however, the Supreme Court has assumed an increasingly conservative position concerning abortion. In 1992, the Court ruled that states had the right to restrict abortions as they saw fit, except that they could not outlaw *all* abortions. Additionally, the Court has put restrictions of increasing severity into place. In *Harris v. McRae* (1980) the court confirmed that both Congress and individual states could legally refuse to pay for abortions. This significantly impacted poor women.

In *Webster v. Reproductive Health Services* (1989), the court upheld a restrictive Missouri law. This law "prohibits performing abortions in public hospitals unless the mother's life is in danger; forbids the spending of state funds for counseling women about abortion; and requires doctors to add an expensive layer of testing before performing abortions after twenty weeks if they feel it will help them determine whether a fetus would be viable outside the womb" (Wermiel and McQueen, 1989, p. 1).

Two subsequent 1990 decisions concerned Supreme Court support of state laws requiring parental notification and consent for abortion. In *Hodgson v. Minnesota*, Minnesota teenagers were required to make their intent to have an abortion known to both parents. Likewise, in *Ohio v. Akron Center for Reproductive Health*, Ohio physicians were required to notify one of the teenager's parents before performing an abortion. Under each decision, in the event a parent refuses consent, the teenager may seek alternative permission from a judge.

In 1991, the Supreme Court upheld a Pennsylvania law that required women under age eighteen to obtain parental consent for abortion or else receive a court ruling that such consent was not required. Additionally, a woman must wait twenty-four hours before she can have an abortion during which time her physician is required to inform her both of fetal development and of other options open to her. A provision that a woman must notify her husband prior to having an abortion was omitted.

In 1991, Utah passed a law which prohibits any abortion unless absolutely necessary to save a woman's life, to prevent severe damage to her health, in those instances where it can be proven that the fetus is seriously malformed, or where the pregnancy was the result of rape or incest, as long as the woman had reported the latter to the police. By the middle of 1991, "thirteen state legislatures had introduced bills intended to ban virtually all abortions" (American Association of Sex Educators, Counselors, and Therapists, May 1991, p. 1).

The abortion debate continues to seethe and storm. New decisions are being made daily at the state and national levels. However, there are a number of issues that remain in the forefront when assessing the impacts on clients' rights and on their ability to function. Several concerns have surfaced in recent years and will probably continue to characterize the abortion debate. We will discuss a number of them here including: limiting financial support; limiting access to services; consideration of the mother's condition; consideration of fetal condition; increasing violence against abortion clinics; and testing alternative methods.

Limiting Financial Support

One clear trend since 1973 has been the anti-abortion factions' pressure to limit, minimize, and eventually prohibit any public financial support for abortion. For example, federal funding could be withheld from agencies providing counseling for pregnant women and women seeking birth control methods. Congress provides funding to thousands of clinics that serve millions of low-income women through Title X of the Public Health Service Act enacted in 1970. Thus, limiting public funding would have the greatest impact upon poor women who cannot afford expensive private care.

Planned Parenthood organizations throughout the country provide an example of agencies that would be affected if public funding were to be withheld. Planned Parenthood's philosophy is that women have the right to control their own bodies. This includes having the right to accurate information about available options. Planned Parenthood espouses the concept of family planning. This refers to "making deliberate and voluntary decisions about reproduction . . . [including] the number and timing of pregnancies after considering economic circumstances, life goals, the nature of the reproductive process, and contraception methods" (Barker, 1991, p. 81). Planned Parenthood clinics do not pressure women to have abortions. Rather, abortion is presented as a viable alternative that women can choose to take.

Hartman (1991) questions the anti-choice stance. She asks why those supporting "life" and the restriction of resources for abortion do not also support "life" for the child and family before and after the birth. She states:

> The right to life, if it truly begins at conception, should not end at the moment of birth. The inconsistency of the positions of our "pro-life" federal administration has been dramatic. Although the rights of the unborn have been defended, social and health programs needed to enhance the lives of infants and children have been decimated. If we really care so much about life, about children, how can we allow one in five to live in poverty? How can we tolerate being nineteenth among the nations in infant mortality? If we believe in the fetus' right to life, why have funds been cut for prenatal care? If we want to protect children, we must make social and economic supports available to their parents. (P. 468)

Limiting Access to Services

Any court rulings that impose limitations on decision making make getting an abortion more difficult. We have discussed how escalating costs make access to abortion more difficult for poor women. Additionally, tactics such as not allowing abortions to be performed in public hospitals (to which poor women have primary access) significantly inhibits their ability to choose abortion.

Another way of limiting access is to require an arbitrary waiting period after a woman has made her decision (for example, twenty-four hours) before she can have an abortion. The decision to abort can be very painful for many reasons. Such a waiting period can result in a woman experiencing significant stress for no clearly articulated reason.

Still another way of limiting access to services is to have young women notify or get permission from their parents before having an abortion. Fear of confronting parents may cause many young women to delay making and carrying out the decision to have an abortion. One other means of limiting access to abortion involves requiring extensive testing for fetal viability. As we have discussed, viability refers to a fetus's ability to survive independently outside of the womb. Anti-choice factions have suggested that a number of complex and expensive tests be required before second trimester abortions can be performed. Cost, of course, would inhibit access. Additionally, experts report that "chances are slim that a fetus can survive outside the womb at less than twenty-four weeks.... At twenty-two weeks or less, survival is virtually unheard of." Medical experts, therefore, conclude that the only "true test of viability is time" (Rosenberg, 1989, p. 4A).

Condition of the Woman

Some people support the idea that abortion is acceptable under specific conditions. One involves the mother's health. Should an abortion be performed if carrying the fetus to term will kill the mother? Whose life is more important, that of the woman or that of the fetus?

Another aspect of the woman's condition involves her status as rape victim. Should a woman impregnated during rape or incest be forced to carry the fetus to term? Is it fair for a woman who has already been forced to undergo the horror of a sexual assault to be forced to live with the result of that assault, an unwanted child, for the rest of her life?

Fetal Condition

The condition of the fetus illustrates another circumstance in which some people consider abortion acceptable. If the fetus is severely damaged or defective, should the woman be forced to carry it to term? A subsidiary question relates to that posed by Hartman (1991) earlier. If a woman is forced to carry and bear a child, why isn't similar force or support used to provide her with resources to care for herself and the child before and after birth? To what extent should a woman being forced to bear a severely disabled child also be forced to provide the huge resources necessary for maintaining such a child?

Violence Against Clinics

Anti-choice groups have picketed and attacked abortion clinics in increasing numbers. Pickets plague patients entering clinics with provocative and abusive slurs. Clinic physicians and other staff often receive threatening phone calls and have their own homes picketed. To what extent should such harassment be legally allowed, or is it simply a manifestation of free speech? Further, should police interfere with such harassment? Should perpetrators be fined or jailed?

One incident provides an example of the raging debate involved and the subsequent dilemma about what to do (Elson, 1991). In August 1991, Operation Rescue, a forceful anti-choice organization that supports aggressive action against clinics' operation, staged blockades outside three abortion clinics in Wichita, Kansas. Operation Rescue members "physically tried to prevent employees and patients from entering the clinics, harassing them all the while with slogans like 'Abortion stops a beating heart' " (p. 22).

As the disturbance escalated, two of the clinics petitioned Federal District Judge Patrick F. Kelly to do something to stop it. The clinics based their right to operate freely on an 1871 law, sometimes referred to as the "Ku Klux Klan Act," that was intended to keep newly freed slaves from being harassed. The abortion clinics argued that patients seeking abortion were being similarly harassed, a stance that some federal courts have ruled appropriate in the past. Thousands of pickets were arrested after ignoring Kelly's court order that they stop the blockades. Pickets persisted, many returning to the blockade after being removed more than once. In desperation Judge Kelly instructed federal marshals to adopt a "jail-or-else" approach. In addition, he accepted the marshals' protection for himself after receiving a number of anonymous threats to his own safety.

The U.S. Department of Justice then interfered with Kelly's ruling by saying that federal courts had no jurisdiction over such a case. Rather, the issue should be addressed by the state courts. Shocked, Kelly responded that his "non-interference" would result in "a license for mayhem" (Elson, 1991, p. 22). He was only doing what he considered absolutely necessary to stop unruly violence.

The Bush administration vehemently denied that it was siding with the anti-abortion group. Rather, it indicated that it was focusing on some legal details.

Further, the administration indicated that the 1871 law was aimed at protecting a specific group of people being discriminated against. They argued that both men and women were involved with the abortion process and clinics, in addition to being targets of harassment. Thus, they asserted that the law did not apply because those affected were not viewed as being a specific category of citizens in need of protection from discrimination and the law.

The Supreme Court overturned the lower court's decision in January 1993 and ruled in *Bray v. Alexandria Women's Health Clinic* that women seeking abortion were not considered a protected class under the 1871 law. Therefore, abortion providers and their clients cannot legally be protected against harassment and violence exhibited by anti-choice extremists.

This incident illustrates how complicated the abortion debate has become. Pro-choice groups stress that they are functioning legally and need protection from harassment and violence. Anti-choice groups, on the other hand, pursue extreme courses of action in order to inhibit and stop abortions from being performed. So far, anti-choice groups can legally blockade clinics and harass staff and clients to make it as difficult as possible for women to obtain abortions.

Alternate Forms of Abortion

A final issue involves allowing alternate forms of abortion to be explored and tested in this country. Should women be given the choice to use newer abortion methods which may be cheaper and easier? An example of a new method is the French abortion pill RU 486. This pill, which induces a miscarriage in early pregnancy, is used in France, Britain, and China.

Other Issues

These issues and others concerning abortion will probably continue to be raised. We have just scratched the surface of the debate. Social workers need to understand the issues and the context in which they occur in order to help clients make difficult decisions. The next section will describe common abortion procedures followed by an examination of the pros and cons of abortion. Finally, various social work roles concerning the issue will be discussed.

Methods of Abortion

Several different procedures are used to perform abortions. The major factor in determining which to use is how far the pregnancy has progressed. The procedures include vacuum curettage, dilation and curettage, dilation and evacuation, induced labor, and hysterotomy, among others.

Vacuum Curettage

Vacuum curettage is by far the most common abortion technique, performed in 96 percent of all abortions (Centers for Disease Control, 1989). It is a relatively simple procedure done during the first trimester of pregnancy under local anesthetic.

The procedure involves first dilating the cervix (that is, widening the opening into the uterus). Then an instrument called a vacuum curette, which consists of a tube with a small scoop on the end, is inserted into the vagina and then through the cervix into the uterus. The scoop is used to scrape out fetal material and any material remaining is vacuumed out through the tube.

Vacuum curettage can be performed up to twenty weeks into the pregnancy, although it is usually done during the first trimester. The length of pregnancy is established by timing the beginning of the last menstrual period. The entire procedure takes about ten minutes. It can be performed on an outpatient basis in a physician's office, a clinic, or a hospital.

The vacuum curettage method is the most effective abortion method for several reasons. First of all, it is the safest for the mother. There are no additional risks posed by general anesthesia. No sutures are necessary. It is relatively fast and simple. Second, the fetal tissue is removed early in its developmental process. It is as yet nowhere near the time of viability. Third, the process is the least expensive of any of the procedures.

If this is the best type of abortion procedure, the question might be raised why it is not always used. Reasons often fall into two categories. First, the pregnant woman may not identify or acknowledge the fact that she is pregnant this early in the pregnancy. Especially if the pregnancy is unplanned and the mother is single, she may avoid thinking about the issue. She may hope that missing a menstrual period is just a fluke and that she is really not pregnant. She may also feel that by not thinking about the problem, it ceases to exist.

Some women also have difficulty deciding to have the abortion even after they realize they are pregnant. Many emotional blocks similar to those identified earlier may be operating. The decision to abort is most often a difficult one. By the time a woman verifies the fact that she is pregnant, she has only a few weeks or even days to make that decision before her pregnancy progresses into the second trimester.

Dilation and Curettage

Another abortion technique is the dilation (or dilitation) and curettage method, often referred to as the D & C. This procedure is performed during the first eight to twenty weeks of pregnancy. As with vacuum curettage, the cervical opening is dilated. A curette is used to scrape the fetal tissue and related membranes from the uterine walls. Unlike vacuum curettage, no suction is used.

Vacuum curettage is considered preferable to a D & C because the latter requires hospitalization and general anesthesia. The D & C also involves greater risks than vacuum curettage of perforation of the uterine wall, hemorrhaging, or infection. It is also more painful.

Dilation and Evacuation

Second trimester abortions are more complicated and involve greater risks. An abortion method which can be used during the fourth and fifth months of pregnancy is dilation and evacuation (D & E). This method resembles both vacuum curettage and D & C in that fetal material is initially suctioned out of the uterus and then usually scraped out with a curette. However, since this method is performed later in the pregnancy, there is a greater amount of fetal material which must be removed and the procedure is a bit more complicated.

Induced Labor

Actual labor can be induced by injecting chemicals. One such method, the saline-induced abortion, involves inserting a fine tube through the abdomen into the amniotic sac. About seven ounces of saline (salt) solution is then injected into the sac. A second method uses prostaglandins, hormonelike substances that cause uterine contractions (Hyde, 1990). A prostaglandin-induced abortion involves either injecting prostaglandins into the amniotic sac in a similar manner to that of a saline-induced abortion, slowly injecting it into a vein, or inserting a suppository containing prostaglandins into the vagina.

Either of these two methods results in the initiation of actual labor and the vaginal delivery of a dead fetus. Both of these methods have the disadvantages of taking hours of time, of causing the mother emotional and physical distress, of being more hazardous, and of being more expensive than the methods discussed so far.

Hysterotomy

A hysterotomy is similar to a caesarean section in that the fetus is surgically removed from the abdomen. It can be done throughout the second trimester. This procedure requires general anesthesia, involves greater risks than other methods, and costs more. Another major disadvantage is that the fetus is close to attaining viability. For all of these reasons, hysterotomies are rarely performed.

Other Methods

Sometimes, a stick of seaweed called laminaria is inserted into the cervix to cause dilation within about six hours. Another substance called oxytocin is occasionally used to enhance uterine contractions. Oxytocin is produced naturally by the posterior pituitary gland, but is also produced artificially.

Ovral, technically a birth control pill, is often used as a "morning-after pill" to induce abortion (Hatcher et al., 1992). Chapter 6 will discuss morning-after pills and other abortion drugs, such as RU 486, in greater detail.

The Importance of Context and Timing

Denney and Quadagno (1992, p. 250) summarize the risks associated with abortion:

> Abortion-related health risks are greatly reduced if the pregnancy is terminated as early as possible, if the patient is healthy, if the clinician is skilled and uses sterile technique, and if the woman is confident in her decision to have the abortion (Hatcher et al., 1990). . . . The most common problems include infection, retained products of conception in the uterus, continuing pregnancy, cervical or uterine trauma, and bleeding.

Long-Term Effects of Abortion

Before looking at the effects of abortion, it is interesting to identify some characteristics of the women who get them (Centers for Disease Control, 1989). About 26 percent are age nineteen or younger, about 35 percent ages twenty to twenty-four, and 39 percent are age twenty-five or over. About two-thirds of all women who get abortions are white and one-third nonwhite. About four-fifths of the women are single and one-fifth are married. Finally, over 56 percent have had no children prior to the abortion.

Positive results of abortion appear to outweigh the negative psychological effects (Osofsky et al., 1971; Osofsky and Osofsky, 1972; and Nadelson, 1978). Women report that they initially experience some anxiety and depression about the abortion experience; however, these feelings usually turn to relief after the abortion is over (Rodman et al., 1987). Less than three of every 100,000 women who have had an abortion require serious psychiatric help (Masters and Johnson, 1988).

When women are interviewed a year after their abortion, most are well adjusted (Burnell and Norfleet, 1987; Shusterman, 1979). They generally indicate that they feel neither sad nor remorseful about the abortion. Rather, they express relief and satisfaction concerning their choice. There is some evidence that psychological adjustment is enhanced when women join post-abortion support groups and are given the opportunity to communicate their feelings about their experience (Lodl et al., 1984).

Because legal abortions have been available in this country since 1973, it is difficult to get information about women who were denied access to an abortion and, hence, were forced to bear their children. However, a Czechoslovakian study examined the children of such women and compared them to a control group of children with mothers who did not seek abortions (David and Matejcek, 1981). The children were studied at age nine and between ages fourteen and sixteen. The "unwanted" children performed less well in school and had a greater tendency to leave school before finishing. Additionally, these children's teachers described them as being less gregarious and more overly and inappropriately active than control group children. Some other researchers report similar findings (David et al., 1988).

Research indicates that having an abortion has little impact on a woman's ability to have children (Hatcher et al., 1988). However, there is some indication that women who have had at least two abortions are at greater risk of miscarriage in the future (Madore et al., 1981). Whether or not to have an abortion is each individual woman's personal decision. Social workers can help women with unwanted pregnancies identify all the alternatives available to them and evaluate the pros and cons of each.

Men and Abortion

A frequently ignored psychological repercussion of abortion is the male's reaction to the whole process. Some evidence exists that, although men initially tend to deal with abortion in a calm, intellectual manner, after some time passes, these feelings change (Shostak et al., 1984). Perhaps a better way of putting it is that their true feelings may emerge. These men later begin to experience similar feelings to those that women initially experience, namely guilt, sadness, and even anger. The male's feelings toward abortion is an area which has traditionally been avoided. Perhaps it is one which also needs some attention.

Arguments For and Against Abortion

Numerous arguments have been advanced for permitting abortions:

- If abortions were prohibited, women would seek illegal abortions as they did in the past. Performed in a medical clinic or hospital, an abortion is relatively safe; but performed under unsanitary conditions, perhaps by an inexperienced or unskilled abortionist, the operation is extremely dangerous and may even imperil the life of the woman.
- If abortions were prohibited, some women would attempt to self-induce abortions. Attempts at self-induced abortions can be extremely dangerous. Women have tried such techniques as severe exercise, hot baths, pelvic and intestinal irritants, and have even attempted to lacerate the uterus with such sharp objects as hatpins, nail files, and knives.
- Recognizing abortions as being legal helps prevent the birth of unwanted babies; such babies have a higher probability of being abused or neglected.
- Permitting women to obtain an abortion allows women to have greater freedom, as they would not be forced to

Legal Abortion: Arguments For and Against

Against Legal Abortion	*For Legal Abortion*
Human life begins at conception; therefore, abortion is murder. Even scientists have not reached a consensus on any other point in fetal development which can be considered the moment the fetus becomes a person. Life is a matter of fact, not religion or values.	The belief in personhood at conception is a religious belief held by the Roman Catholic Church. Most Protestant and Jewish denominations regard the fetus as a potential human being, not a full-fledged person and have position statements in support of legal abortion. When the unborn becomes a person is a matter of religion and values, not absolute fact.
We must pass a constitutional amendment to protect unborn babies from abortion. To say the law will not be followed and should not be made is like saying people still get murdered so laws against murder should be repealed.	No law has ever stopped abortion and no law ever will. The issue is not whether abortions will be done, but whether they will be done safely, by doctors, or dangerously, by back-alley butchers or by the women themselves. History has shown that anti-abortion laws are uniquely unenforceable, as they do not prevent abortions.
Medicaid should not pay for abortion. It is wrong to try to eliminate poverty by killing the unborn children of the poor. Tax money should not be used for the controversial practice of aborting unwanted children. The decision not to have children should be made before getting pregnant.	The original intent of Medicaid was to equalize medical services between the rich and the poor and to help the poor become independent and self-sufficient. To make them ineligible for abortion defies justice, common sense, and rational policy. Women burdened by unwanted children cannot get job training or go to work and are trapped in the poverty/welfare cycle. Neither abortion nor childbirth should be forced on poor women.
If you believe abortion is morally wrong, you are obligated to work for the passage of a human life amendment to the Constitution.	Many people who are personally opposed to abortion, including most Roman Catholics, believe it is wrong to impose their religious or moral beliefs on others.
The right of the unborn to life supersedes any right of a woman to "control her own body."	In 1973, the Supreme Court affirmed that the constitutional right to privacy includes the right to terminate a pregnancy and that fetuses are not persons with constitutional rights.
The abortion mentality leads to infanticide, euthanasia, and killing of retarded and elderly persons.	In countries where abortion has been legal for years, there is no evidence that respect for life has diminished or that legal abortion leads to killing of any persons. Infanticide, however, is prevalent in countries where the overburdened poor cannot control their childbearing and was prevalent in Japan before abortion was legalized.
Abortion causes psychological damage to women.	The Institute of Medicine of the National Academy of Sciences has concluded that abortion is not associated with a detectable increase in the incidence of mental illness. The

(continued next page)

Legal Abortion: Arguments For and Against (continued)

Against Legal Abortion (cont'd.)	*For Legal Abortion (cont'd.)*
	depression and guilt feelings reported by some women are usually mild, temporary, and outweighed by feelings of relief. Such negative feelings would be substantially lessened if anti-abortion advocates were less vehement in expressing their beliefs. Women choosing abortion should be informed of the risks and benefits of the procedure and should decide for themselves what to do.
Women have abortions for their own convenience or on whim.	Right-to-life dismisses unwanted pregnancy as a mere annoyance. The urgency of women's needs to end unwanted pregnancy is measured by their willingness to risk death and mutilation, to spend huge sums of money, and to endure the indignities of illegal abortion. Women only have abortions when the alternative is unendurable. Women take both abortion and motherhood very seriously.
In a society where contraceptives are so readily available, there should be no unwanted pregnancies and therefore no need for abortion.	No birth control method is perfectly reliable, and for medical reasons many women cannot, or will not, use the most effective methods. Contraceptive information and services are not available to all women, particularly teenagers, the poor, and rural women.
Abortion is not the safe and simple procedure we have been told it is.	Before the 1973 Supreme Court rulings, illegal abortion was the leading cause of maternal death and mutilation. Having a legal abortion is medically less dangerous than childbirth.
Doctors make large profits from legal abortion.	Legal abortion is less costly and less profitable than illegal abortion was. Many legal abortions are done in nonprofit facilities. If it's proper to make money on childbirth, it is not wrong to earn money by performing legal abortions.
Parents have the right and responsibility to guide their children in important decisions. A law requiring parental notification of a daughter's abortion would strengthen the family unit.	Many teenagers voluntarily consult their parents, but some simply will not. Forcing the involvement of unsympathetic, authoritarian, or very moralistic parents in a teen's pregnancy (and sexuality) can damage the family unit beyond repair. Some family units are already under so much stress that knowledge of an unwed pregnancy could be disastrous.
Pro-abortionists are anti-family. Abortion destroys the American family.	The unwanted child of a teen-aged mother has little chance to grow up in a normal, happy American home. Instead, a new family is created: a child and her child, both destined for a life of poverty and hopelessness. Legal abortion helps women limit their families to the number of children they want and can afford and reduces the number of children born unwanted. Pro-choice is definitely pro-family.

raise a child at a time when they had other plans and commitments.

Opponents of abortion argue that the right to life is basic and should in no way be infringed. Proponents of abortion seek to counter this view by arguing that there may be a more basic right than the right to life; that is, the preservation of the quality of life. Given the overpopulation problem and given the fact that abortion appears to be a necessary population-control technique (in some countries the number of abortions is approaching the number of live births), abortion may well be a necessary measure (although less desirable than contraceptives) to preserve the quality of life.

Regardless of one's personal view, professional social workers must be aware of arguments on both sides of the issue. Many of the points and counterpoints are presented in the accompanying discussion, "Legal Abortion: Arguments For and Against."

Social Work Roles and Abortion

Social workers can assume a variety of roles when helping women with unwanted pregnancies. Among them are enabler, educator, broker, and advocate. First, as *enablers*, social workers can help women make decisions as they try to solve their problems. This involves helping clients identify alternatives and evaluate the pros and cons of each. Chilman (1987, p. 6) reflects upon how social workers can counsel women concerning abortion:

> The ultimate decision . . . should be made chiefly by the pregnant woman herself, preferably in consultation with the baby's father and family members. To make the decision that is best for the couple and their child, the pregnant woman—ideally, with the expectant father—needs to view each option in the context of the couple's present skills, resources, values, goals, emotions, important interpersonal relationships, and future plans. The counselor's role is to support and shape a realistic selection of the most feasible pregnancy resolution alternative.

A second role social workers can assume is that of *educator*. This involves providing the pregnant woman with accurate information about the abortion process, fetal development, and options available to

her. The educator role may also entail providing birth control information to avoid subsequent unwanted pregnancies.

A third social work role involves being a *broker*. Regardless of her final decision, a pregnant woman will need to associate herself with the appropriate resources. These include abortion clinics, prenatal health counseling, and adoption services. A worker can inform her of available resources, explain them, and help her obtain them.

Finally, a social worker can function as an *advocate* for a pregnant woman. A woman might want an abortion yet live in a state which severely restricts them; if she is poor, her access to an abortion is even further restricted. In such a case, a worker can advocate on this woman's behalf either to improve her access to the abortion or financial support for abortion services. Another means of advocacy would be to work to change the laws and policies themselves which inhibit the woman and others like her from getting the resources she needs.

Infertility

Ralph and Carol, both age twenty-eight, had been married for five years. Ralph was a drill press operator at a large bathroom fixture plant. Carol was a waitress at a Mexican restaurant. They both liked their jobs well enough. They were earning an adequate enough income to purchase a small three-bedroom home and to enjoy some pleasurable amenities such as going out to dinner occasionally, taking annual camping vacations, and having cable television.

However, they felt something was wrong. Although Carol had stopped taking birth control pills over three years ago, she had still not gotten pregnant. She had read in some recent issue of *Cosmopolitan* that women over age thirty-five had a much greater chance of having a child with mental retardation or birth defects. Although she still had a few years, she was concerned. She and Ralph had always wanted to have as large a family as they could afford. This meant that they had better get going.

The couple really didn't talk much about the issue. Neither one wanted to imply that something might be wrong with the other one. The idea that one or both might be infertile was not appealing. It was almost easier to ignore the issue and hope that it would

Abortion Related Ethical Dilemmas in Practice

Picture yourself as a professional social worker in practice. What happens when your own personal values seriously conflict with those expressed by your client? A basic professional value clearly specified in the National Association of Social Workers (NASW) Code of Ethics is the right of clients to make their own decisions.

By definition, an ethical dilemma involves conflicting principles. When two or more ethical principles oppose each other, it is impossible to make a "correct" decision that satisfies both or all principles involved. There is no perfect solution. For example, if a fifteen-year-old client tells you that he plans to murder his mother, you are caught in an ethical dilemma. It is impossible to maintain confidentiality with your client (another basic social work professional value) and yet do all you can to protect the mother from critical harm.

A wide range of situations involving abortion can place workers in situations involving ethical dilemmas. Loewenberg and Dolgoff (1985) have formulated a hierarchy of ethical principles to provide a guide for making difficult decisions. When two ethical principles conflict, the hierarchy suggests which principle should have priority over the other. The hierarchy can be helpful in working through difficult situations.

The hierarchy involves the following (p. 114):

Principle 1: "*Basic survival needs*" should be met first; "the means for protecting human life might include health services, food, shelter, income, and so on as appropriate in each situation."

Principle 2: After basic survival needs, "a social worker should make practice decisions that foster *a person's autonomy, independence, and freedom.*" However, it is important to keep in mind that basic survival should come first.

Principle 3: Social workers should strive to "make practice decisions that foster *equality of opportunity and equality of access for all people.*" Some groups should not be given better resources and treatment than other groups.

Principle 4: Social workers should "make practice decisions that promote *a better quality of life for all people.*" People's overall well-being is important.

Principle 5: People's *privacy and right to confidentiality* are important. However, these are less important than the well-being of all.

Principle 6: Practice decisions should allow workers to be *honest and tell the truth.* Workers should be able to provide any information which they deem necessary in any particular situation. However, the "truth" should not be told for its own sake when it violates a client's confidentiality.

Principle 7: Decisions should be made which *abide by the rules* a worker has "voluntarily accepted." For example, agency regulations should be followed, but not at the expense of clients' well-being.

Following are illustrations of ethical dilemmas concerning abortion a worker might face in practice. The first provides an example of how Loewenberg and Dolgoff's hierarchy of ethical principles might be applied. The rest furnish scenarios for you to work out yourself. Remember, there are no easy or "perfect" answers.

Illustration A

A sixteen-year-old woman becomes pregnant as a result of being raped by a middle-aged man as she walked home from school one night. Both she and her parents are horrified and plagued with worry. They come to you for help. The girl desperately wants an abortion.

Application of Ethical Principles for Illustration A

Consider Principle 1, the need to maintain basic survival needs. If you *personally* adopt an anti-abortion stance and feel that abortion is murder, what do you do? A professional social worker's personal values must be acknowledged yet put aside in professional situations. The young woman and her parents want her to have the abortion.

We then look at Principle 2, the woman's right to autonomy, independence, and freedom. She has the right to make her own decision. Your state might legally allow abortions to all women seeking them. It might restrict them to those women who have been raped or whose health would be in serious jeopardy by bringing a pregnancy to term. Or, your state might ban abortions completely.

If an abortion is legal in your state, you as a worker can help the woman get one. She has made her decision. It is her legal right. However, if your state does not allow her to have a legal abortion, you are confronted with another dilemma. Principle 3 calls for fair and equal treatment and opportunity of all people. A neighboring state, its border only twenty-five miles away, allows abortions for all women who want them. Is this fair? Is this ethical? Should you, then, help the young woman and her parents seek help in this other state which abides by contrasting rules? Or, should you work actively in your own state to advocate for change so that abortion would be a legal alternative for clients such as this?

This discussion simply raises questions and issues. Each case is unique. Circumstances and attitudes vary widely. It is a professional social worker's ethical responsibility to resolve dilemmas and help clients solve problems to the best of that worker's ability. Each client should be helped to identify alternatives, evaluate the pros and cons of each, and come to a final decision. There are no absolute answers or perfect solutions.

Consider the following cases. How would you apply the hierarchy of ethical principles for each?

Illustration B

A forty-five-year-old grandmother becomes pregnant. She already has seven children. Her personal physician refused to prescribe birth control pills for her because of her age and other health reasons. Nor did he discuss other forms of birth control with her or offer her the alternative of sterilization. Physically, it would be hazardous for her to have any more children. She comes to you, distraught and crying. She doesn't know what to do.

Illustration C

A thirty-two-year-old woman with a developmental disability becomes pregnant. She is "severely retarded" and unable to take care of herself independently. However, she has been easy prey to men as she seeks attention and has a history of numerous sexual encounters. Her genetic background indicates that she would probably have a developmentally disabled child. It is clear that she would be unable to care for any child herself.

Illustration D

A nineteen-year-old college student is six weeks pregnant. She has been going with her boyfriend for seven months.

For the past three months they have been seeing only each other, but do not consider themselves "serious" as yet. She had been using the diaphragm and contraceptive cream, but they failed to protect her. She does not want a baby right now. However, she feels terribly guilty about getting pregnant.

Illustration E

A married twenty-four-year-old woman is pregnant. She already has one child with a genetic defect. She and her husband have been through genetic evaluation and counseling at a local university. The conclusion is that since both parents have a history of significant genetic problems, the chances for a normal child are extremely unlikely. The couple was deciding upon a sterilization procedure when she became pregnant.

Illustration F

A married twenty-eight-year-old medical technician has been unaware of being pregnant until now, the seventh week of gestation. Throughout her entire pregnancy she has been exposed to dangerous X-ray radiation. The possibility that her fetus has been damaged from the radiation is very high. She and her husband want children at some time, but they dread the thought of having a baby with a serious impairment.

Illustration G

Four months ago a married man of forty-two had a vasectomy. His forty-one-year-old wife just found out she is five weeks pregnant. Some sperm apparently had still been present in his semen. The couple already have three children in their teens. They do not want any more.

Illustration H

A fourteen-year-old woman is pregnant. It just happened one night when she was out drinking. She had never considered using birth control. She's shocked that she's pregnant and is having difficulty thinking about the future.

A woman may be disappointed when she finds that she is not pregnant. Traditionally, women have placed great importance on their role of mother.

resolve itself in a pregnancy. After all, they did still have a few years.

Infertility may be defined as "the inability of a couple to achieve pregnancy, usually defined after a year or more of sexual intercourse without pregnancy" (Masters et al., 1988, p. 684). Although many people assume that they will automatically be able to conceive if they don't use birth control, this is obviously not always the case.

Infertility is considered one viable explanation after a couple has been trying to conceive, by having intercourse regularly, for one year. This one-year period is frequently considered the cue for confronting the possibility of infertility. At this point, it is usually recommended that the possibility of some physical problem in one or both members of the couple be explored. The number of infertile couples is significant. It is estimated that 10 to 15 percent of couples are unable to conceive after trying for one year (Denney and Quadagno, 1992; Papalia and Olds, 1992).

Causes of Infertility

Males are responsible for approximately 40 to 50 percent of infertility (Grunfeld, 1989). Both partners share involvement in about 15 percent of cases (Hudson et al., 1987). No specific cause for infertility can be identified in as many as 20 percent of infertile couples (Crooks and Baur, 1990).

Female Infertility

The three major causes of infertility for women (Hyde, 1990) are failure to ovulate, blockage of the fallopian tubes, and abnormally thick mucus in the cervix. Many possible causes exist for not ovulating including chronic illnesses, ovarian or hormonal abnormalities, vitamin deficiency or malnutrition, and occasionally emotional stress. Whether ovulation has occurred or not can be detected by monitoring a woman's daily morning temperature. Basal body temperature charts can be used for this purpose. A woman may experience a slight dip in body temperature on the day before ovulation. Immediately after ovulation, the body temperature rises slightly (0.2 to 0.6 degrees Fahrenheit) and maintains this higher level for ten to sixteen days. No temperature rise at all is one indication that a woman is not ovulating. Ovulation can also be determined by examining hormonal levels or scrapings of the uteral lining.

A newer and more accurate means of detecting ovulation than basal body temperature charts (March, 1985) are urine tests which can be done by individuals themselves in their own homes. These new tests, which operate on a similar principle to home pregnancy tests, monitor the levels of luteinizing hormone (LH) in the urine. Women experience a surge of LH twelve to twenty-four hours before they ovulate. Results are most accurate if the test is administered four to six days in a row. The tests, however, are expensive, ranging from $40 to $60 per one-month kit. Brand names include Ovutime, Ovustick, and First Response.

Blockage of the fallopian tubes is another major cause of infertility. Infections such as those caused by pelvic inflammatory disease can form scar tissue which blocks the tubes. Tumors or various congenital abnormalities are other possible causes. Blockage can be detected by using X rays after injecting a dye which outlines the internal structures. Potential blockage can also be explored by Rubin's test. Carbon dioxide is forced into the uterus through the cervix. Normal tubes will direct the gas into the abdomen, whereas blocked tubes will cause increased pressure in the uterus.

Abnormally thick mucus on the cervix, the third major cause of infertility in women, is sometimes referred to as "hostile mucus." In these cases, mucus acts as a barrier, preventing sperm from entering the uterus.

There are numerous other causes of female infertility. Sexually transmitted diseases (STDs) are a major cause of infertility in both women and men. One source estimates that they cause as much as 20 percent of all infertility (Office of Technological Assessment, 1988). Some women have an allergic response to sperm; in these cases antibodies are manufactured which clog the cervix and prevent sperm from entering (Witkin and David, 1988). Other women have structural abnormalities which interfere with fertilization. A woman's age may also be a contributing factor. Fertility declines after age thirty-five, with a sharper drop after age forty. There is additional evidence that weight levels 10 to 15 percent below normal (Frisch, 1988), smoking (Phipps et al., 1987), endometriosis (that is, materials from the uteral lining in the endometrium displace themselves and begin to grow in places other than the uterus), alcohol and drug abuse, and toxic substances in the environment (Office of Technological Assessment, 1988) all contribute to female infertility.

Male Infertility

Male infertility is most commonly caused by a low sperm count and decreased sperm motility (that is, the ability of sperm to swim effectively) (Crooks and Baur, 1990; Hyde, 1990). Low sperm counts can be caused by numerous conditions including varicose veins in the scrotum and testes, certain infections such as the mumps when acquired in adulthood, congenital birth defects, undescended testes, and various types of drugs including alcohol, cigarettes, narcotics, and marijuana (Masters et al., 1988, pp. 144–45). Even extremely tight underwear has been found to decrease sperm counts (Shane et al., 1976).

The relatively recent explosion of cocaine use has also been found to affect male infertility (Bracken et al., 1990). Large amounts of cocaine interfere with luteinizing hormone release which, in turn, directly affects testosterone levels. Testosterone is absolutely necessary for manufacturing sperm. Decreased testosterone levels, then, may lead to decreased sperm production. Additionally, cocaine use causes arteries to constrict. Reduced blood flow to the testes may also act to inhibit production of sperm.

Psychological Reactions to Infertility

Some people experience serious reactions to infertility. Many people "show signs of stress, anxiety, and depression while being treated for infertility" (Denney and Quadagno, 1992, p. 178). Additionally, infertility has been shown to affect a couple's sexual experiences. Sabatelli et al. (1988) found that 55 percent of infertile couples related that their sexual activity had decreased in frequency; additionally 59 percent of women and 42 percent of men indicated they did not enjoy sex as much as they had in the past.

Especially for those who really desire to have children, infertility can be associated with failure. This is compounded by the fact that even the most intimate partners often don't feel comfortable talking about their sexuality, let alone the fact that something may be wrong with it. Some men associate their potency with their ability to father children. Traditionally, women have placed great importance on their roles as wife and mother. Hopefully, with the greater flexibility of women's roles today, the technological advances aimed at improving fertility, and the new options available to infertile couples, the negative psychological reactions to infertility will be minimized.

Treatment of Infertility

Various treatments are currently available for treating infertility. For treating failure to ovulate, two kinds of drugs can be used. Clomiphene is used to stimulate the pituitary which subsequently produces the hormones necessary to induce ovulation. Pregnancies result in approximately half of all women using clomiphene. Another drug called HMG (human

A Feminist Perspective on Infertility Counseling

An infertile woman tells her story:

Oh, sure, I've had infertility counseling. I still have a bill for $2951.92 that the infertility clinic says my husband, Kenny, and I are responsible for paying. Our health maintenance plan (HMO) was supposed to pay for it, but they just stopped after paying half of the expenses. Now we're getting bills along with nasty, threatening letters from the clinic. I never did get pregnant. I guess I'm not going to have any kids. That's the bottom line.

When we first went to the clinic, they all were so optimistic and smiled all the time. Of course, we couldn't go to the first clinic we tried. They wouldn't accept HMO insurance payments; they wanted regular private insurance to pick up the tab. Anyways, the waiting room at our clinic is full of happy, smiling baby pictures. The atmosphere was all so positive. I must've asked the staff there a hundred times what their success rate was. I must've gotten the answer back a hundred times that they don't know because it's different every time. Well, of course, it's different every time. You either get pregnant or you don't. I didn't so my success rate must be zero.

So they tell you that first you have to have a laparoscopy, an endometrial biopsy, and a hysterosalpingogram. I won't bother telling you what they all are except that they're supposed to check out if I'm physically normal. They're complicated, they're time consuming, and they're expensive. That's only a few of the things you have to have done, and of course, you have to get examined every time you go in. Kenny, of course, had to have all his tests, too. He loved that. One of them involved either bringing his semen "specimen" into the clinic in a cute little jar within an hour of getting it—you know what I mean. Or else, he could do it and give it there. That was only shades of things to come.

In the end, they couldn't find anything wrong with either of us. Oh, great. We've been married for twelve years, I'm thirty-four years old, and they couldn't find anything wrong. Can you believe it? Time's gone so fast and we always thought that there'd be plenty of time for children and that it would just happen *at some point. Well, it* didn't. We knew my biological clock was ticking, so we thought we'd better be more aggressive about getting me pregnant.

So back to my story about the clinic. The first optimistic phase of treatment involves what they call an Ovustick kit. This is a slick $90 a month for the kit alone. Every month you go in on day five of your menstrual period. Okay, that's just the start. Then you have an ultrasound and they check you out to see if your follicles are developing or something like that. Then if the old follicles are okay, you go in again on day ten to have them checked again. So, then on day ten you start your Ovustick kit. You test your urine sample every day with one of the sticks that comes with the kit. When the stick "has any color change," then you're supposed to ovulate within twenty-four hours. Well, I swear in eight months, my stick never did change color right. I kept asking them "how much color change?" They kept answering "any color change" and around we'd go. Never once did I hit the old ovulation on the head, so to speak. We'd have intercourse as instructed either that night or the next morning, headache or not, and then I'd run into the clinic to see if it worked. Nope. We were always either too early for ovulation or too late. They always liked to have you pop in at the clinic around nine in the morning, too. Now I'm a homemaker who does not work outside the home. What in heaven's name would I have done if I was holding down a job?

Meanwhile, by the way, I, of course, was taking my temperature everyday and charting it because you're supposed to notice a change when you ovulate. Well, some people's temperatures may change, but mine didn't. I couldn't get that sucker to vary more than two-tenths of a degree. Tough luckski for me. That's frustration.

So they decided that doing "it," that is, having regular old intercourse by ourselves wasn't cutting it and we needed to try the next step. That's artificial insemination. This was Kenny's favorite part. Remember, I always had to figure out if it was time for the big O (that is, ovulation) first. Then for three days in a row, Kenny was supposed to have his little specimen bottle filled with semen. Kenny leaves for work every day at about 6:30 A.M. He just loved getting his specimen on demand every day for three days in a row. Of course, as I've already mentioned, he could pop into the clinic at about 9:00 A.M. when it was convenient for them and get his little specimen to give them right there. Of course, he'd have to take three half sick-days off from work every month to do it. His boss would love that. So, poor old Kenny, who reminded me frequently that he was no "spring chicken" anymore and this whole thing made him feel like a "stud bull," could never do more than two days in a row no matter how hard he tried.

I, of course, was the one who ended up taking the bottle in, getting injected with it, and lying on the table for a half hour in a humiliating wait to have it "take." That, by the way, cost $81 each time plus there was an injection fee. If you happened to ovulate, or in my case thought I might, on a weekend, my local clinic was closed. Then I had to drive way down into the city to go to another much busier clinic with a much longer waiting line.

I haven't even mentioned the hormones, worth $37, which they gave me at some point in the process to make me ovulate more regularly. All that did was make me gain 8 pounds.

And then there were the comments. I'd talk to my sister every other day or so and every other day or so like a clock, she'd ask me, "Are you pregnant yet?" What's an appropriate answer? My mother-in-law had her own approach to the matter. Her song went, "Oh, don't worry, just keep trying. You'll get pregnant yet." Please! But the best of the comments were from Kenny's brother, Steve. He thought it was cute to talk about Kenny's virility quotient as −2 on a scale from 1 to 10. Cute, very cute.

So we stopped. As they say, we had had it. If I sound like I'm angry and cynical, you bet I am. When our insurance stopped paying halfways through my treatment, the people at the clinic stopped smiling. As I popped in one day with my little bottle of Kenny's specimen, they abruptly said that they're sorry, but unless I sign this paper right this very minute which says that I will be responsible for the payments if the insurance doesn't come through, the treatment was finished right now. To say I was under duress is a vast understatement. So I signed in desperation.

How do I feel? I feel manipulated and used. There were other methods they could've used. But they wanted us to jump through the hoops first. They knew that we were an older couple. They knew that time was an issue for us. They knew that we were desperate. They could've gone to some of the other, possibly more effective methods earlier. But then it wouldn't have cost as much, would it? What about freezing some of Kenny's semen, so he wouldn't have to go through what to him was such a humiliating ordeal on a regular basis? Why couldn't they have helped us work around our established habits so that their complicated, demanding instructions would've been more "do-able" for us?

So we are kidless, and that's okay. Now I tell my sister and my mother-in-law and Kenny's brother point-blankly, "No, we're not going to have children." I am resolved and am trying to turn to other things in life.

My final thought is not earth shattering and probably not very new. Infertility counseling is only for the very, very rich.

This is the story of an infertile woman. She candidly expressed her feelings, her frustrations, and finally the resolution of her infertility crisis.

Alison Solomon (1988) suggests a feminist approach to counseling women who discover themselves to be infertile. The medical establishment tends to view infertility as a medical problem that needs to be solved, as dysfunctional equipment that needs to be fixed. Social attitudes tend to support this medical view. In many ways, Solomon continues, society views infertile women similarly to women who has been raped. First, most people in society aren't aware of the immense impact the crisis of infertility, as does rape, has upon a woman. Second, people tend to look down upon infertile women, as they do rape victims. Third, infertile women experience feelings such as shock, denial, and anger as do people confronted with any serious loss. Fourth, people in the general population tend to assign stereotypes to infertile women, as they do to rape victims. For instance, many think when a woman is infertile, she becomes "desperate," that "she loses all personal control," and that she can't possibly live a well-rounded, worthwhile life without bearing children (Pfeffer, 1985). Fifth, infertility poses a major life crisis for a woman, as does rape. People in crisis are generally more vulnerable, more suggestible, and more easily manipulated than they are during more normal times.

Solomon proposes a two-pronged approach to infertility treatment. First, women must be dealt with on a "personal level" (Solomon, 1988, p. 47). Women who are experiencing the crisis of infertility should be treated similarly to how people with other crises are treated. A woman needs to be encouraged to identify and express her feelings, even when they hurt, come to accept her situation, and eventually make decisions about how she wants to proceed. Too frequently, infertile women are told what to do by medical professionals and are led like sheep to follow extensive, expensive, complicated, time-consuming procedures which may have little chance of success. It should be acknowledged that the infertile woman is more vulnerable and more likely to respond to medical direction than when she is not experiencing a crisis. Instead of being given directions, the

(continued next page)

A Feminist Perspective on Infertility Counseling (continued)

infertile woman may need specific information about the options available to her, the risks, the amounts of effort required to pursue treatment (which is sometimes awesome), and help in evaluating which alternative is to her individual best advantage. Each woman needs to evaluate if she really wants to put forth the amount of effort needed. Infertile women need to be empowered to make their own choices.

The second level involved in the feminist treatment of infertility addresses the more general social attitudes about infertility and expectations about what infertile women should do. Infertile women are stigmatized. They are viewed by society as having something wrong with them, as being incomplete. These attitudes need to be changed. The positive qualities of any life path choice need to be emphasized. Women need to recognize their value as an individual human being, not as a failure or success because of their ability or lack of ability to bear children. People as citizens, advocates, and social workers can form pressure groups to encourage more extensive research into the causes and treatment of infertility and to alter the traditional manner in which fertility treatment is done. Women need to be and feel empowered, and to have their choices maximized.

---

menopausal gonadotropins) can also be used in a series of injections to stimulate the ovaries directly. Approximately 60 to 70 percent of all women using HMG become pregnant; 20 percent of these pregnancies are multiple (Masters et al., 1988, p. 145). However, a potential negative side effect is that either clomiphene or HMG can cause the ovaries to enlarge dramatically. Sometimes hospitalization becomes necessary as the ovaries may burst.

Microsurgery has been used to correct both blocked fallopian tubes and varicose veins in the scrotum and testes. Women having fallopian tube surgery have a 30 to 50 percent success rate (Masters et al., 1988, p. 145).

The treatment of male infertility is much less advanced. The chance of correcting problems other than varicose veins with either surgery or drugs is at present much poorer. The effects of using clomiphene, frequently positive for women, are questionable for men. Testosterone may sometimes cause a surge of sperm production after such production has been inhibited over a period of time. For specific medical disorders such as physiological defects, infections, or difficulties in hormonal production, appropriate medical procedures may be useful; unfortunately, such clearly specified causes of infertility are relatively rare.

Some research has raised questions about the actual effectiveness of infertility treatment. One study which focused on 1,145 infertile couples found that the pregnancy rate in the untreated control group was almost as good as in the treated group (Collins et al., 1983). Other research found that the pregnancy rate was 65 percent in untreated couples whose reasons for infertility were unclear (Rousseau et al., 1983). The implication of such pregnancy rates in untreated couples questions the need and effectiveness of treatment for infertility. If so many infertile couples attain pregnancy without treatment, to what extent is treatment necessary or useful? Therefore, the possible causes of infertility and the need for infertility treatment should be carefully examined for each individual couple before pursuing treatment.

Alternatives Available to the Infertile Couple

The first thing that needs to be done in the case of suspected infertility is to bring the matter out into the open. People need to talk about their ideas and feelings. Only then can the various alternatives be identified and a plan of action determined.

After at least one year of trying to conceive, both partners should probably pursue a medical evaluation to help determine if anything is physically wrong. The couple's sexual practices concerning pregnancy should also be discussed to make certain that they have accurate and specific information. Some suggestions are available for improving the chances of conception. For example, a woman can monitor her temperature to help determine when she is ovulating. After doing this for several months, an ovulation pattern may be established. Sexual intercourse right around the time of ovulation may be helpful. Additionally, ejaculations should probably not occur more than once every twenty-four to forty-eight hours in order to avoid diminishing the sperm count. The best plan is probably to have intercourse every twenty-four to forty-eight hours, or about four times, during the week of ovulation (Hyde, 1990). One other suggestion may be to have the woman assume the bottom position during intercourse, lying on her back. This helps in preventing the semen from running out of her vagina.

In those cases where treatment of infertility is impossible or unsuccessful, other alternatives, such as adoption, artificial insemination, in vitro fertilization, surrogate motherhood, and acceptance of childlessness may need to be pursued.

Adoption

Adoption is the legal, social, and psychological process which ensures a dependent child a permanent family (Friedlander, 1968). To provide a home and family to a child who has none is a viable and beneficial option.

Kadushin and Martin (1988, pp. 538–41) clearly depict the profile of children currently available for adoption in the United States. White infants are in much greater demand and lower supply than a variety of other groups of children. In summary, children who are white, younger, and without physical or mental disabilities are most readily placed (American Public Welfare Association, 1984). Therefore, it follows that children who do not fall into these categories are more readily available and easier to adopt. This is indeed the case. For instance, the percentage of African American, Hispanic, and Native American children available for adoption is significantly greater than the corresponding percentage of white children. African American families are adopting children at the same rate as white families. However, since more African American children are available for adoption, there is an "oversupply" available for adoption (Kadushin and Martin, 1988, p. 539). Additionally, it is

easier to adopt a child who is older than a child who is younger. Finally, children with disabilities represent a disproportionate number of children waiting for adoption and thus are more readily available. Mentally retarded children have the greatest difficulties finding families who want to adopt them (Cole, 1984).

Artificial Insemination

Artificial insemination refers to the process of "placing semen into the vagina or uterus by a means other than sexual intercourse" (Masters et al., 1988, p. 146). This method can be used when the woman is fertile.

Over 20,000 babies are born annually in the United States through the process of artificial insemination (CBS Reports, 1979). Human sperm can be frozen, thawed, and used to impregnate for long periods of time. (The length of time that sperm can be frozen has not been determined; it is generally acknowledged that five years would be safe with close to 100 percent assurance.)

A sperm bank collects and maintains sperm for private citizens for a fee depending on length of time. The sperm is then usually withdrawn at some later date to impregnate (with a physician's assistance) a woman.

The sperm used in artificial insemination may be the husband's (called AIH). It is possible to pool several ejaculations from a man with a low sperm count and to inject them simultaneously into the vaginal canal of his spouse, thus vastly increasing the chance of pregnancy. AIH may also be used for family planning purposes—for example, a man might deposit his sperm in the bank, then receive a vasectomy, and then later withdraw the sperm to have children. High-risk jobs might prompt a man to make a deposit in case of untimely death or sterility.

A second type of artificial insemination, called AID, involves the donor of the sperm being someone other than the husband. AID has been used for several decades to circumvent male infertility, and also used when it is known that the husband is a carrier of a genetic disease (for example, a condition such as hemophilia). In recent years an increasing number of single women are requesting the services of a sperm bank. The usual procedure involves the woman requesting the general genetic characteristics she

An Ethical Dilemma: Fertility Doctor Allegedly Uses His Own Sperm to Impregnate Unknowing Patients

In the fall of 1991, Dr. Cecil Jacobson pleaded not guilty to fifty-three felony charges for actions at his well-respected fertility clinic in Vienna, Virginia. Charges were based on two accusations. First, at least seven women accused him of using his own sperm to impregnate them without their knowledge. They stated he told them that he used a donor bank. Several patients substantiated his fatherhood after having their babies undergo genetic tests. Jacobson's rationale, according to reporters, was that by using his own sperm, he felt safe concerning HIV infection and had confidence in its effectiveness. He was quoted as saying, "I knew my semen was safe because I haven't slept with anyone but my wife in our thirty-five years of marriage" (*Milwaukee Journal*, Nov. 11, 1991). Jacobson, age fifty-five, had fathered seven children with his wife.

The second dimension of allegations involved charges that Jacobson told women they were pregnant when they really were not. He refuted this claim by saying that he had injected these women with drugs known to enhance fertility. The dosage level, which he indicated had been acceptable since the mid-1980s, was high enough to trigger positive results in pregnancy tests.

In spring 1992, Jacobson was convicted on fifty-two counts of fraud and perjury (*Wisconsin State Journal*,

March 5, 1992). He was sentenced to five years in prison with a subsequent three years of probation and was fined $116,805 (*Wisconsin State Journal*, May 9, 1992).

Jacobson has been described as "a brilliant geneticist who helped pioneer the amniocentesis procedure in the U.S." (Elmer-DeWitt, 1991). However, in 1989 he was prohibited "from practicing clinical medicine after the Virginia State Board of Medicine found that he had knowingly misled women who paid up to $5,000 for fertility treatments" (*Milwaukee Journal*, Nov. 24, 1991).

Medical advances in the fertility field have been dramatically fast moving. Numerous ethical issues are being raised and brought to the courts for settlement. At this time board certification is nonexistent and regulations concerning fertility technology are minimal.

There are many questions and, as yet, few answers. Should sperm donors be identified? Should children have access to parental health records to complete their own genetic and medical background? What rights should sperm donors have regarding the children they biologically father? In cases like Jacobson's, what reprisals or punishments should he suffer? What ethical considerations should govern artificial insemination and other reproductive technologies?

---

wants from the father, and the bank then trying to match such requests from the information known about their donors. Donors are paid for their sperm and remain anonymous. The pregnancy rate is approximately 75 percent when "fresh" sperm are used and approximately 60 percent when frozen semen is taken from a sperm bank (Masters et al., 1988, p. 146).

A third type of artificial insemination is of recent origin and has received considerable publicity. Some married couples, in which the wife is infertile, have contracted with another woman to be artificially inseminated with the husband's sperm. Under the terms of the contract this surrogate mother is paid and expected to give the infant to the married couple shortly after birth. Surrogate motherhood will be discussed more thoroughly below.

A number of ethical and legal questions have been raised about artificial insemination. Religious leaders object and claim that God did not mean for people to reproduce this way. In the case of AID, certain psychological stresses are placed on husbands and on marriages, as the procedure emphasizes the husband's infertility and involves having a baby that he has not fathered. On a broader dimension, artificial insemination raises such questions as: What are the purposes of marriage and of sex, and what will happen to male/female relationships if we do not even have to see each other to reproduce?

Some very unusual court cases suggest new laws will have to be written to resolve the questions that are arising. For instance, there is the case of Mr. and Mrs. John M. Prutting. He was medically determined to be sterile as a result of radiation received at work.

Without her husband's knowledge, she was inseminated. After the birth of the baby, he sued her for divorce on the grounds of adultery (Rifken, 1977).

In another case a wife was inseminated with the husband's consent by a donor. They later divorced. When he requested visiting privileges, she took him to court on the grounds that he was not the father and thus had no right. In New York he won, but she moved to Oklahoma, where the decision was reversed (Rifken, 1977). And finally, there was a reported case of an engaged couple who were discovered to have had the same donor through artificial insemination, and were thus half-brother and half-sister. The marriage was called off (Rifken, 1977).

There are other possible legal implications. What happens if the sperm at a bank is not paid for? Would it become the property of the bank? Could it be auctioned off? If a woman was artificially inseminated by a donor and the child was later found to have genetic defects, could the parents bring suit against the physician, the donor, or the bank? Does the child have a right to know who his or her real father is?

Sperm banks can be used in genetic engineering movements. In the spring of 1980 it was disclosed that Robert Graham had set up an exclusive sperm bank to produce exceptionally bright children. Graham stated that at least five Nobel Prize winners had donated sperm to inseminate women. Several women have already given birth through the services of this bank (*Wisconsin State Journal*, 1980, p. 7). This approach raises questions about whether reproductive technology should be used to produce superior children, and what characteristics should be defined as superior?

Surrogate Motherhood

Thousands of married couples who want children but who are unable to reproduce because the woman is infertile have turned to surrogate motherhood; a surrogate gives birth to a baby conceived by artificial insemination, using the sperm of the husband. Most frequently the surrogate is paid for her services in amounts ranging from $2,000 to $20,000, in addition to $5,000 in legal fees (Masters et al., 1988, p. 149). On birth, the surrogate mother terminates her parental rights and the child is then legally adopted by the donor of the sperm and his spouse.

Couples using the services of a surrogate mother are generally delighted with this medical technique

and believe it to be a highly desirable solution to their personal difficulty. However, other groups assert that surrogate motherhood raises a number of moral, legal, and personal issues.

A number of theologians and religious leaders firmly believe God intended conception to occur only among married couples through sexual intercourse. These religious leaders view the surrogate motherhood as ethically wrong, as the surrogate mother is not married to the donor of the sperm and because artificial insemination is viewed as "unnatural." Some religious leaders also assert that it is morally despicable for a surrogate mother to accept a fee. They maintain procreation is a blessing from God and should not be commercialized. Also criticized is the use of a human being as a commodity which can be purchased by people with enough money.

Surrogate motherhood also raises complicated legal questions which have considerable social consequences. For example, surrogate mothers usually sign a nonbinding contract stipulating the mother will give up the child for adoption at birth. What if the surrogate mother changes her mind shortly before birth and decides to keep the baby? Women who have been surrogate mothers usually report that they become emotionally attached to the child during pregnancy (Seely, 1986).

These legal questions are still being debated. In 1986, Mary Beth Whitehead of Brick Township, New Jersey, changed her mind about giving up the baby born to her as a surrogate. This was despite the fact that she had contracted with William and Elizabeth Stern to give up to them the child fathered by William Stern's sperm through artificial insemination. Upon the infant girl's birth, Whitehead found that she was too emotionally attached to the child to give her up willingly. After a controversial trial which received national attention, the courts upheld the contract and gave custody of the baby to the Sterns. This was the first judicial ruling on a disputed surrogate contract in this nation. The judge ruled the contract was valid because just as men have a constitutional right to sell their sperm, women can decide what to do with their wombs (Budiansky, 1988).

Whitehead appealed this decision to the New Jersey State Supreme Court. In 1988, this court ruled that the contract between Whitehead and Stern was invalid because it involved the sale of a mother's right to her child, which violates state laws that prohibit child selling. This decision voided the adoption of the baby by Ms. Stern; Mr. Stern was given custody and Whitehead was granted visitation rights. Whether this decision will become the legal guideline for disputed surrogate contracts will be determined by future court decisions addressing the issue.

Most surrogate mothers, to date, are married and already have children. A number of issues are apt to arise. How does the husband of a surrogate mother feel about his wife being pregnant by another man's sperm? How does such a married couple explain to their children that their half-brother or half-sister will be given up for adoption to another family? How does such a married couple explain what they are doing to relatives, neighbors, and the surrounding community? If the child is born with severe mental or physical handicaps, who will care for the child and pay for the expenses? Will it be the surrogate mother and her husband, the contracting adoptive couple, or society?

In 1983, a twenty-six-year-old surrogate mother gave birth in Michigan to a baby who was born with microcephaly, a condition in which the head is smaller than normal and mental retardation is likely. At first neither the surrogate mother nor the contracting adoptive couple wanted to care for the child. The adoptive couple refused to pay the $10,000 fee to the surrogate mother. A legal battle ensued. Blood tests were eventually taken which indicated the probable father was not the contracting adoptive father, but the husband of the surrogate mother. Following the blood tests, the surrogate mother and her husband assumed the care of the child. The question might be asked regarding what might have happened had the contracting adoptive father been proven the biological father. Would he have been forced to abide by his contract?

Many states have initiated legislation concerning surrogacy. However, the specific conditions and issues involved in regulation or prohibition are still being actively debated.

Many feminists believe that surrogate motherhood is just another means of exploiting women. Susan Ince (1989) investigated the process and procedures by which a woman became a surrogate mother. After visiting an agency as a potential surrogate, she raised many serious questions. Some involved the adequacy of the screening process. For instance, because she was "obviously bright," no intelligence testing was performed (p. 276). Additionally, she found the other medical and psychological tests extremely lacking.

Ince also raised numerous questions about the legal protections the surrogate could expect. For example, if the contracting adoptive couple decide to breach the contract, it is the surrogate, not the company, who must sue the couple for her contracted fees. Ince states, "The company holds all of the funds, makes the profit, and attempts to take a minimum of the financial/legal risks" (p. 282). One of the clauses in the contract stated that upon the physician's recommendation, the surrogate would have to undergo amniocentesis. In the event of an abnormality, the surrogate must get an abortion at the adoptive couple's request. Ince noted that the lawyer who was present while the contract was being discussed was very concerned about the abortion clause. His point was that there might be difficulties forcing the surrogate to have an abortion when the surrogate could get her full fee even if the infant was born abnormal. Nor was the surrogate protected by anonymity. The biological father would know her city of residence and would have access to a variety of personal documents including her name from the child's birth certificate, and her own medical and psychological records.

Finally, Ince noted the distant manner in which the spouse of the biological father is treated. She is referred to only rarely as "wife of the father" or "the potential stepmother," and has no clearly defined participation or place in the entire process (p. 282).

Ince (p. 281) summarizes the profits of women serving as surrogates by stating:

> It is a myth that women are easily making large sums of money as surrogates. The director of this program acknowledges that the woman who goes through a lengthy insemination process may end up being paid less than one dollar per hour for her participation. To earn this sum, she is completely "on-call" for the company. She may be required to undergo invasive diagnostic procedures, forfeit her job, and perhaps undergo minor surgery with its attendant morbidity and mortality risks. Of course, should there be a miscarriage or failure to conceive, the surrogate receives no compensation at all.

Many look upon women who serve as surrogates with disdain. They are considered to be reproductive prostitutes who sell themselves and their offspring for cash. Ince suggests that even when the surrogate's contributions to humanity and to helping others are being emphasized, the surrogate still sounds like "a happy hooker with a heart of gold" (p. 284).

A final consideration regarding surrogacy is the much overlooked well-being of the children themselves. Can or should they be considered property? Should their best interests instead of those of their procreators be taken into account? At some point in their lives, should they be told that they have a surrogate mother somewhere? How will this affect their own psychological well-being? In summary, surrogate motherhood is a very complicated issue.

In Vitro Fertilization

The common phrase for in vitro fertilization (IVF) is test-tube babies. The process involves allowing for sperm to fertilize eggs in a test tube. This obviously occurs in vitro or outside of the mother's body. The process was developed in order to help couples where the woman's fallopian tubes were so damaged that fertilization became impossible. After conception, one to three fertilized eggs are implanted in the woman's uterus where they may continue to develop as in any other normal pregnancy (Edwards and Steptoe, 1985). The procedure generally takes less than sixty seconds and rarely requires general anaesthesia.

This process is still fairly new. On July 25, 1978, the first test-tube baby was born. Louise, weighing 5 pounds, 12 ounces, was born to her parents Lesley and John Brown of Oldham, England. The world was stunned by such a feat. The physicians who developed the technique, Patrick Steptoe and Robert Edwards, had attempted the process over thirty times before, with this being the first success.

Another breakthrough in this area occurred in 1984 when an egg donated by one woman was fertilized and then implanted in another woman. Australian researchers in January 1984 reported the first successful birth resulting from a procedure in which an embryo was externally conceived, and then implanted in the uterus of a surrogate (*Wisconsin State Journal*, Feb. 4, 1984).

An unusual application of the new technology occurred in 1991 when a South Dakota woman became pregnant with her own grandchildren (Nash, 1991). Arlette Schweitzer, a forty-two-year-old librar-

ian, already had two grown children of her own, Christa, twenty-two, and Curtis, twenty-six. When Christa was fourteen, she found out she had no uterus. Even at that age, her mother indicated, Christa was devastated. In a visit to the Mayo Clinic two years later, Arlette got the idea of lending Christa her uterus. In February 1991, eggs were taken from Christa's normal ovaries, fertilized in a laboratory with her husband Kevin's sperm, and implanted in Arlette's womb. Shortly thereafter, Christa found out Arlette was pregnant with her own twin daughters.

This type of surrogate motherhood differs from the earlier type in which the surrogate mother contributes half of the genetic characteristics through the use of her egg. Here, the surrogate neither contributes her own egg nor any of the genetic characteristics of the child.

Masters et al. (1988) cite several facts about IVF. Since IVF began, over one hundred clinics have opened in the United States alone. By 1987, more than three thousand babies had been conceived in vitro. Pregnancies have a higher likelihood of involving multiple births and of requiring a caesarean section than do "normal" pregnancies. However, these latter facts may be related to the pregnant women being older mothers who have tried getting pregnant for a long time. They may also be due to the extreme importance placed on these pregnancies.

A serious criticism of IVF is its cost. Typically, a successful pregnancy may require a minimum of three or four tries. Each attempt costs almost $5,000. Most insurance companies will not cover the procedure. No public money is available for support. Thus, IVF can only be undertaken by people who can afford it. Additionally, there is no guarantee that the procedure will ever succeed. Pregnancy rates in the most successful IVF clinics in the United States range from 15 to 25 percent each time an egg is retrieved from the biological mother's uterus and fertilized (Edwards, 1984; Andrews, 1987; Seibel, 1988).

Gamete Intrafallopian Transfer (GIFT)

Gamete Intrafallopian Transfer (GIFT) differs from IVF only in where fertilization takes place. In IVF, fertilization occurs in a test tube outside of the body. In GIFT, "the egg and sperm cells are placed together in a healthy fallopian tube and fertilization takes place in the tube rather than outside the body" (Denney and Quadagno, 1992, pp. 174–75). All other aspects of the two processes are similar or identical. GIFT, of course, can only be performed in those cases where the fallopian tubes are clear and healthy. For example, it may be successfully used for women with endometriosis or where no specific cause for infertility

Embryo Case Gains International Attention

A South American-born couple, Elsa and Mario Rios, amassed a fortune (several million dollars) in real estate in Los Angeles. In 1981 they enrolled in a "test-tube baby" program at Queen Victoria Medical Center in Melbourne, Australia, after their young daughter died. Several eggs were removed from Mrs. Rios, and fertilized by her husband's sperm in a laboratory container. One of the fertilized eggs was implanted in Mrs. Rios' womb, but she had a miscarriage ten days later. The two remaining embryos were frozen so that doctors could try later at implantation.

On April 2, 1983, the couple was killed in the crash of a private plane in Chile. Since doctors have successfully thawed and implanted frozen embryos (which have resulted in births) a number of social and legal questions arise. These questions include the following:

Should the embryos be implanted in the womb of a surrogate mother in the hope that they will develop to delivery?

Are the embryos legal heirs to the Rios' multimillion dollar estate?

Does life legally begin at conception? If a surrogate mother carries the embryo to birth is she legally the mother, and is she entitled to some of the inheritance?

Do embryos conceived outside the womb have rights? If so, what rights? Should these rights be the same as those accorded humans? An Australian court ruled in 1987 that the embryos must be thawed and carried to term if a volunteer surrogate can be found—but the offspring will not be legally viewed as being entitled to inherit their biological parents' estate.

This case highlights how the rapid advance of in vitro fertilization has outstripped attitudes and laws.

SOURCES: "Embryo Case Opens New Debate," *Wisconsin State Journal*, June 19, 1984, pp. 1–2; Stephen Budiansky, "The New Rules of Reproduction," *U.S. News & World Report*, April 18, 1988, pp. 66–67.

has been identified. GIFT is not useful for women with blocked fallopian tubes, a common cause of female infertility. GIFT tends to have a lower failure rate than IVF (IVF, GIFT..., 1987) and also costs less (Seibel, 1988).

Acceptance of Childlessness

For some infertile couples, accepting childlessness may be the most viable option. Each alternative has both positive and negative consequences which need to be evaluated. The positive aspects of childlessness need to be identified and appreciated. Increasing numbers of people are choosing to remain childless for various reasons. Not having children allows the time and energy which children would otherwise demand to be devoted to other activities and accomplishments. These include work, career, and recreational activities. A couple might also have more time to spend with each other and invest in their relationship as a couple. Children are expensive and time consuming.

On the one hand, children can provide great joy and fulfillment. On the other hand, they also can cause problems, stress, and strain. Infertile couples (and also fertile couples) may benefit from evaluating both sides of the issue. There are aspects that can be identified and appreciated when pursuing either alternative.

The Effects of Macro Systems on Infertility

Unlike abortion issues, which are fairly well crystallized and articulated, the issues and institutional values concerning infertility and reproductive technologies are only now being discovered and defined. Abortion has been available for a long time. However, modern technology has only allowed for sophisticated means of artificial fertilization to be undertaken for less than two decades. Additionally, new developments are rapidly advancing.

A major issue is that most fertility enhancement techniques are expensive. They may be available, but not to poor people and the uninsured. Organizations within the community will only provide services if they are paid. Is this fair or appropriate? Should wealthy people be allowed to enjoy the luxury of such advances when infertile poor people are not? Should

Childlessness has advantages. A couple without children may have more time to share affection with each other.

such expensive advances be pursued at all in view of the world's exploding population? Vital philosophical and ethical issues are involved here. Once again, there are no easy answers.

Social Work Roles and Infertility

Social workers may assume a number of roles when helping people address infertility: enabler, mediator, educator, broker, analyst/evaluator, and advocate. Social workers can enable people in making their decisions concerning the options available to infertile people. In cases where members of a couple disagree for some reason, a social worker can assume a mediator role to help them come to some compromise or mutually satisfactory decision. The social worker as educator can inform clients about options and procedures with specific and accurate data. The broker role is used to connect clients with the specific resources and infertility procedures they need.

The role of analyst/evaluator might be used to evaluate the effectiveness of treatment generally provided by an organization. For instance, if effectiveness rates at a particular fertility clinic are 5 percent or less, a social worker might help to evaluate the reasons for this. That worker might make it known to the agency, clients, and community environment that

the clinic needs to improve its effectiveness. A related social work role is that of advocate. A worker might need to speak on behalf of clients if they are being denied services if the process for receiving infertility treatment is overly cumbersome or expensive.

Summary

Human reproduction is a complex process. Prenatal influences that affect the fetus include mother's nutrition, drugs and medication, alcohol usage, age, smoking habits, and other factors such as specific illnesses (for example, rubella or AIDS) during pregnancy. Methods of prenatal assessment include amniocentesis, chorionic villi sampling, ultrasound, maternal blood tests, and umbilical cord assessment. Four conditions which cause problem pregnancies are ectopic pregnancies, toxemia, Rh incompatibility, and prematurity. Spontaneous abortions also occur periodically. Stages in the birth process include initial contractions and dilation of the cervix, the actual birth, and afterbirth. Birth positions include the most common vertex position, breech presentations, and transverse presentations. Birth defects include Down's syndrome and spina bifida. Other factors affecting development include low birth weight, PKU, and anoxia.

"Maternal deprivation" is discussed and reframed as "attentional deprivation." There are many developmental milestones as children grow older. "Normal" motor, play, adaptive, social, and language profiles for children at various age levels are described.

Significant issues related to human reproduction are abortion and infertility. Psychological reactions to abortion and the arguments for and against abortion are explored. Professional social workers have an obligation to assist pregnant clients in evaluating the various alternatives open to them so that they can make their own decisions. Approximately 10 to 15 percent of all U.S. couples are infertile. Causes are discussed. Treatment of infertility includes drugs and microsurgery. A feminist approach to treating infertile women is proposed.

Additional alternatives to infertility include adoption, artificial insemination, surrogate parenthood, in vitro fertilization, gamete intrafallopian transfer, and acceptance of childlessness. Some ethical issues and dilemmas are addressed.

3

Psychological Systems and Their Impacts on Infancy and Childhood

Developing Cognitive Perspectives

"Hey, Barry, what did ya get on that spelling test?"

"I got an 87. What did you get?"

"Aw, I only got a 79. If I get a C in spelling, my ma will kill me."

"Yeah, Susie got a 100 again. She always ruins it for the rest of us by getting straight A's. I'm so sick of Ms. Butcherblock comparing us to her."

"Well, I hear Billy flunked again. He's never going to make it into fifth grade at this rate."

"Yeah, old Bill's an okay guy, but he sure isn't very smart."

"Only ten more minutes to recess. I'm gettin' out there first and get the best ball."

"Wanna bet? I'll race ya!"

Psychology is defined as the science of mind and behavior. Human psychological development involves personality, cognition, emotion, and self-concept. Each child develops into a unique entity with individual strengths and weaknesses. However, at the same time some principles and processes apply to the psychological development of all people. Likewise, virtually everyone is subject to similar psychological feelings and reactions which affect their behavior.

This example portrays two schoolboys discussing their current academic careers. Numerous psychological concepts and variables are impacting even this simple interaction. They are addressing their own and their peers' ability to learn and achieve. Learning is easier for some children and more difficult for others. Personality characteristics also come into play. Some children are more dominant and aggressive. Others are more passive. Some young people are more motivated to achieve and win. Others are less interested and enthusiastic. Finally, some children feel good about themselves and others have poor self-concepts.

A PERSPECTIVE

Psychological variables interact with biological and social factors to affect an individual's situation and behavior. In systems terminology we refer to each cluster of variables (that is, psychological, biological, or social) as a separate system. Each system influences the potential courses of action available to a person at any point in time. This chapter will focus on some of the psychological concepts which critically impact children as they grow up. There are four major thrusts. The first presents a perspective on how personalities develop. The second provides a basic understanding of how children think and learn. The third focuses on emotion, and the fourth on self-concept.

This chapter will:

- Summarize prominent psychological theories concerning personality development, including trait, psychodynamic, neo-Freudian psychoanalytic, behavioral, and phenomenological theories.
- Examine major theories of cognitive development, including those of Piaget and Bruner.
- Describe the concept of emotion.

- Examine the relevance of self-concept and self-esteem especially as they affect minority children.
- Explore the concepts of intelligence, intelligence testing, and learning disabilities; and examine their effects on children.

Theories of Personality

How many times have any of us heard someone make statements such as the following: "She has a great personality" or "He has a personality like a wet dish rag." *Personality* refers to the complex cluster of characteristics which distinguish a person as an individual. The term may encompass a wide array of perspectives that describe people. For instance, at one extreme a person may be described as aggressive, dominant, brilliant, and outgoing. At another extreme an individual may be characterized by terms such as slow, passive, mousy, or boring.

Because personality can include such varying dimensions of personal characteristics, explaining its development can be difficult. However, a number of theorists have proposed explanations for why individual personalities develop as they do. These explanations include trait theories, psychodynamic theory, neo-Freudian psychoanalytic developments, behavioral theories, and phenomenological theories.

Trait Theories

Trait theories distinguish between different personalities on the basis of various personality traits. For example, an individual's personality may be described by his position or scoring on an series of trait scales (Hilgard and Atkinson, 1967, p. 470). These traits may include such characteristics as intelligence and emotional sensitivity. An individual may be scaled higher or lower on each trait dimension.

Allport (1937, 1961) postulates that each person has a series of general, relatively consistent traits that tend to characterize how that person will respond in most situations. Such personality traits exist in a hierarchy of cardinal, central, and secondary traits. Allport emphasizes individuality and the importance of any particular trait to a specific individual. A *cardinal trait* is one which is so important to the individual that it might be thought to dominate. For example, Benedict Arnold's cardinal trait might be deceitfulness, while George Washington's might be honesty.

Of more frequent occurrence, according to All-port, are *central traits*. A few major traits basically characterize any individual's personality. For instance, Aunt Mabel can be generally characterized as quiet, unselfish, sensitive, and giving.

Finally, Allport hypothesizes that people also have a series of *secondary traits*. These are relatively less significant traits which characterize how an individual feels in, or responds to, a particular situation. Secondary traits do not necessarily reflect a person's general personality or manner of responding. For example, Mr. Pfeiffer's central personality traits might include being quiet, unassertive, and introverted. He lives alone, has few friends, and tends to avoid social and intimate situations. However, when his neighbor's home burns to the ground one night, he is the first to rush into the smoke and flames in order to save two small children. In this particular situation Mr. Pfeiffer is exceedingly courageous, although that trait is rarely displayed in other circumstances.

Trait theories tend to be overly simplistic. A person may respond very differently depending on the situation. Human personalities are extremely complicated, perhaps too much to ever place them into neat, distinct categories.

Psychodynamic Theory

Sigmund Freud is perhaps the best known of all personality theorists. Freud's conception of the mind was two-dimensional, as is indicated in Figure 3.1. One dimension of the mind consisted of the "conscious," the "preconscious," and the "unconscious." Freud thought that the mind was composed of thoughts (ideas), feelings, instincts, drives, conflicts, and motives. Most of these elements in the mind were thought to be located in the unconscious or preconscious. Elements in the preconscious area had a fair chance to become conscious, while elements in the unconscious were unlikely to arise to a person's conscious mind. The small conscious cap at the top of this diagram indicates how Freud theorized a person was only aware of a fraction of the total thoughts, drives, conflicts, motives, and feelings in the mind.

FIGURE 3.1: Freud's Conception of the Mind

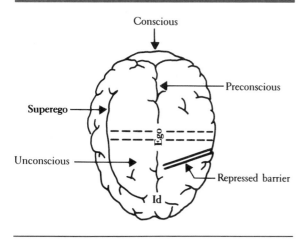

The repressed area was a barrier under which disturbing material (primarily thoughts and feelings) had been placed by the defense mechanism of repression. Repression is a process in which unacceptable desires, memories, and thoughts are excluded from consciousness by sending the material into the unconscious under the repressed barrier. Once material has been repressed, Freud thought that material has energy and acts as an unconscious irritant, producing unwanted emotions and bizarre behavior, such as anger, nightmares, hallucinations, and enuresis.

The Id, Superego, and Ego

The second dimension of the mind was composed of the id, superego, and ego. Each of these parts is interrelated and impacts the functioning of each other.

The *id* is the primitive psychic force hidden in the unconscious. It represents the basic needs and drives on which other personality factors are built. The id involves all of the basic instincts that people need to survive. These include hunger, thirst, sex, and self-preservation. The id is governed by the pleasure principle; that is, the instincts within the id seek to be expressed regardless of the consequences. Freud believed that these basic drives or instincts involved in the id provide the main energy source for personality development. When the id is deprived of one of its needs, the resulting tension motivates a person to relieve the discomfort and satisfy the need. The id's

relationship with the ego allows a person to rationally determine a means to fulfill the need.

The *ego* is the rational component of the mind. It begins to develop, through experience, shortly after birth. The ego controls a person's thinking and acts as the coordinator of personality. Operating according to the reality principle, the ego evaluates consequences and determines courses of action in a rational manner. The id indicates to a person what is needed or wanted. The ego then helps the person figure out how to get it.

The third component of this dimension of the mind is the *superego* or conscience. Normally developing between the ages of three to five, it consists of the traditional values and mores of society which are interpreted to a child by the parents. The superego's main function is to determine whether something is right or wrong. When an instinctual demand strives for expression which the superego disapproves of, the superego sends a signal of anxiety as a warning to the ego to prevent the expression of the instinct. The emotion of guilt is said to originate from the superego. Without the superego to provide a sense of right and wrong, a person would be completely selfish. That is, a person would use ego to rationally determine a means of getting what the id wanted, regardless of the consequences on other people.

An example of how the id, ego, and superego might function together is provided in the case of a nine-year-old girl looking at compact disks in her favorite store. Although the girl adores Michael Jackson, she has only $.67 to her name. Her id, functioning by the pleasure principle, urges her to get that newly released CD. Her ego reasons that she could slip the CD under her jacket and race out of the store as fast as she can manage. Her ego also encourages her to look around and see if anyone, especially those "nosey" clerks, are anywhere around. She's just about to do it when her superego propels itself into action. Clearly reminding her that stealing is wrong, it raises questions such as what would her parents think about her if she were to get caught. They would be terribly disappointed. Maybe she would even be kicked out of Girl Scouts. As a result, the girl gave the CD one last lingering look, sighed, and started on her way home. Her ego had already begun to work on how much lawn-mowing she would have to do to earn the money needed to purchase the CD honestly.

Psychosexual Development

Freud came to realize that many people had sexual conflicts and he made sexuality a focus of his theories. The term used for the energy of the id's biological instincts was *libido*. This energy was primarily conceived as being sexual energy. Freud thought sexuality included physical love, affectionate impulses, self-love, love for parents and children, and friendship associations.

Freud further conceptualized that people in their development of personality progressed through five consecutive phases. During any one of the earlier phases, conflicts or disturbances could arise which, if not resolved, could fixate that person in some ways at that particular level of development. According to Freud, the term *fixated* meant that a person's personality development was largely, though not completely, halted at the stage that was specified. In order to develop optimal mental health, an individual would either have to resolve these crises and/or use one of several defense mechanisms. A *defense mechanism* involves any unconscious attempt to adjust to conditions that are painful. These conditions may include anxiety, frustration, or guilt. Defense mechanisms are measures through which a person preserves his self-esteem and softens the blow of failure, deprivation, or guilt. Some of these mechanisms are positive and helpful. Others only help to avoid positive resolution of conflict. Definitions of common defense mechanisms postulated by Freud are given in "Definitions of Common Defense Mechanisms Postulated by Psychoanalytic Theory."

Freud's phases of psychosocial and personality development include the oral, anal, phallic, latency, and genital stages.

Oral Stage. This phase extends from birth to approximately eighteen months. It is called oral because the primary activities of a child are centered around feeding and the organs (mouth, lips, and tongue) associated with that function. Feeding is considered to be an important area of conflict, and a child's attention is focused on receiving and taking. People fixated at this stage were thought to have severe personality disorders, such as schizophrenia or psychotic depression.

Anal Stage. Between the ages of one-and-a-half and three years, a child's activities are mainly focused on giving and withholding, primarily connected with retaining and passing feces. Bowel training is an important area of conflict. People fixated at this stage have such character traits as messiness, stubbornness, rebelliousness; or they may have a reaction formation and have such opposite traits as being meticulously clean and excessively punctual.

Phallic Stage. From the third through the fifth year, the child's attention shifts to the genitals. Prominent activities are pleasurable sensations from genital stimulation, showing off one's body, and looking at the bodies of others. Also, a child's personality becomes more complex during this stage. Although self-centered, the child wants to love and be loved and seeks to be admired. Character traits which are apt to develop from fixation at this stage are pride, promiscuity, and self-hatred.

Boys and girls experience separate complexes during this stage. Boys encounter an *Oedipus complex*. This is the dilemma faced by every son at this age when he falls sexually in love with his mother. At the same time he is antagonistic toward his father, whom he views as a rival for her affections. As the intensity of both these relationships mount, the son increasingly suffers from *castration anxiety*; that is, he fears his father is going to discover his "affair" with his mother and remove his genitals. Successful resolution of the Oedipus complex occurs through defense mechanisms. A typical resolution is for the son to first repress his feelings of love for his mother and his hostile feelings toward his father. Next, the son has a reaction formation in which he stops viewing his father negatively, but now turns this around and has positive feelings toward his father. The final step is for the son to identify with his father, and thereby seek to take on the attitudes, values, and behavior patterns of his father.

Girls, on the other hand, undergo an *Electra complex* during this phallic stage. Freud believed girls fall sexually in love with their father at this age. Meanwhile, they also view their mother with antagonism. Because of these relationships, girls also suffer from castration anxiety, but the nature of this anxiety is different than for boys. Castration anxiety in a girl results from the awareness that she lacks a penis. She then concludes she was castrated in infancy and blames her mother for this. Freud went on to theorize

Definitions of Common Defense Mechanisms Postulated by Psychoanalytic Theory

Compensation: Making up for a real or fancied achievement or superiority. A common example is an effort to achieve success in one field after failure in another.

Repression: Mechanism through which unacceptable desires, feelings, memories, and thoughts are excluded from consciousness by being sent down deep into the unconscious.

Sublimation: Mechanism where consciously unacceptable instinctual demands are channeled into acceptable forms for gratification. For example, aggression can be converted into athletic activity.

Denial: Mechanism where a person escapes psychic pain associated with reality by unconsciously rejecting reality. For example, a mother may persistently deny that her child has died.

Identification: Mechanism through which a person takes on the attitudes, behavior, or personal attributes of another person whom he has idealized (parent, relative, or popular hero, etc.)

Reaction Formation: Development of socially acceptable behavior or attitudes which are the opposite of one's repressed unconscious impulses. Reaction formation is apparent in individuals who turn anal impulses into scrupulous cleanliness.

Regression: This mechanism involves a person falling back to an earlier phase of development in which he or she felt secure. Some adults when ill, for example, will act more childish and demanding with the unconscious goal of having others around them give them more care and attention.

Projection: Mechanism through which a person unconsciously attributes his own unacceptable ideas or impulses to another. For example, a person who has an urge to hurt others may turn it around and consciously feel that others are trying to hurt him.

Rationalization: Mechanism by which an individual, faced with frustrations or with criticism of his actions, finds justification for them by disguising from himself (as he hopes to disguise from others) his true motivations. Often this is accomplished by a series of excuses that are believed by the person. For example, a student who fails an exam may blame it on poor teaching, having long work hours, rather than consciously acknowledging the real reasons.

---

that because girls believe they have been castrated they come to regard themselves as inferior to boys (i.e., they have penis envy). Therefore, they perceive that their role in life is to be submissive and supportive of males. Freud did not identify the precise processes for resolution of the Electra complex in girls.

Latency Stage. This stage usually begins at the time when the Oedipus/Electra complexes are resolved and ends with puberty. The sexual instinct is relatively unaroused during this stage. The child can now be socialized and becomes involved in the educational process and in learning skills.

Genital Stage. This stage, which occurs from puberty to death, involves mature sexuality. The person reaching this stage is fully able to love and to work. Again, we see Freud's emphasis on the work ethic (i.e., the idea that hard work is a very important part of life, in addition to being necessary to attaining one's life goals), which was highly valued in Freud's time. It is interesting to observe that Freud theorized that personality development was largely completed by the end of puberty with few changes hypothesized.

Psychopathological Development

Freud theorized that disturbances can arise from several sources. One source was traumatic experiences that a person's ego is not able to directly cope with and thereby strives to resolve using such defense mechanisms as repression. Breuer and Freud (1895) provide an example of a woman named Anna O. who developed a psychosomatic paralysis of her right arm. Anna O. was sitting by her father's bedside (her father was gravely ill) when she dozed off and had a nightmare that a big black snake was attacking her father. She awoke terrified and hastily repressed her thoughts and feelings about this nightmare for fear of alarming her father. During the time she was asleep, her right arm was resting over the back of a chair and became "numb." Freud theorized that the energy connected with the repressed material then took over physiological control of her arm, and a psychological paralysis resulted.

In addition to unresolved traumatic events, Freud thought that internal unconscious processes could also cause disturbances. There was a range of possible sources. An unresolved Electra or Oedipal complex could lead to a malformed superego and thus lead a person to have a variety of sexual problems—such as frigidity, promiscuity, sexual dysfunctions, excessive sexual fantasies, and nightmares with sexual content. Unresolved internal conflicts (e.g., an unconscious liking and hatred of one's parents) may be another source that causes such behavioral problems as hostile and aggressive behavior and such emotional problems as temper tantrums. Fixations at early stages of development were another source that largely prevented development at later stages and led the person to display such undesirable personality traits as messiness or stubbornness.

As indicated earlier, the main source of anxiety was thought to be sexual frustrations. Freud thought that anxiety would arise when a sexual instinct sought expression, but the ego blocked its expression. If the instinct was not then diverted through defense mechanisms, the energy connected with sexual instincts was transformed into anxiety.

Obsessions (a recurring thought such as a song repeatedly on your mind) and compulsions (such as an urge to step on every crack of a sidewalk) were thought to be mechanisms through which a person was working off energy connected with disturbing unconscious material.

Unconscious processes were thought to be the causes for all types of mental disorders. These unconscious processes were almost always connected with traumatic experiences, particularly those in childhood.

Evaluation of Psychodynamic Theory

Freud was virtually the first to focus on the impact of the family on human development. He was also one of the earliest, most positive proponents of good mental health. However, he was a product of the past

century, and many of his ideas are subject to serious contemporary criticisms.

First, research does not support either the existence of his theoretical constructs or the effectiveness of his therapeutic method. Part of this lack may be due to the abstract nature of his concepts. It is very difficult, if not impossible, to pinpoint the location and exact nature of the superego.

The second criticism involves the lack of clarity in many of his ideas. For instance, although Freud asserts that the resolution of a boy's Oedipus complex results in the formation of the superego, he never clarifies how this occurs. The Electra complex provides another example in that the means by which girls might resolve this complex is never clearly explained.

The Electra complex leads us to a third criticism of Freud's theories. Women never really attain either an equal or a positive status within the theory. Essentially, women are left in the disadvantaged position of feeling perpetual grief at not having a penis, suffering eternal inferiority with respect to men, and being doomed to the everlasting limbo of inability to resolve their Electra complexes.

Neo-Freudian Psychoanalytic Developments

Since Freud's time, many have modified and expanded upon his theories and ideas. These theorists, often referred to as neo-Freudians, include Carl Jung, Erich Fromm, Alfred Adler, and Harry Stack Sullivan, among others. They are also referred to as ego psychologists. In general, they are more concerned with the ego and the surrounding social environment than the role of instincts, libido, and psychosexual stages, which were central to Freud's perspective.

Carl Jung, who lived from 1875 to 1961, was a Swiss psychologist originally associated with Freud. He later developed his own approach to psychology called analytic psychology. Jung thought of the mind as more than merely a summation of an individual's past experiences. He proposed the idea of the "collective unconscious," which involved an "inherited foundation of personality" (Mischel, 1976, p. 44). Each person's individual experiences somehow melded into this collective unconscious which was part of

The Relevance of Theory to Social Work

The word *theory* is defined as "a group of related hypotheses, concepts, and constructs, based on facts and observations, that attempts to explain a particular phenomenon" (Barker, 1991, p. 236). In effect, theory provides a way for people to view the world. It helps them to sort out and make sense of what they see. Likewise, it aids them in understanding how and why things are the way they are and work the way they do. Different theories provide us with different explanations.

For instance, consider the differences between general systems theory and the medical model when trying to explain the reasons for human behavior. Each theoretical approach serves as a way of examining situations in order to explain them. From the 1920s to the 1960s, social work programs used a medical model approach to human behavior. The medical model approach was developed by Sigmund Freud. This theoretical approach views clients as "patients." The task of the social worker providing services is to first diagnose the causes of a patient's problems and then provide treatment. The patient's problems are viewed as being inside the patient.

With respect to emotional and behavioral problems, the medical model conceptualizes such problems as "mental illnesses." People with such problems are then given medical labels such as *schizophrenic, psychotic, manic-depressive,* or *insane.* Adherents of the medical approach believe the disturbed person's mind is affected by some generally unknown, internal condition, thought to be due to a variety of possible causative factors inside the person. These include genetic endowment, metabolic disorders, infectious diseases, internal conflicts, unconscious uses of defense mechanisms, and traumatic early experiences that cause emotional fixations and prevent future psychological growth.

In the 1960s, social work began questioning the usefulness of the medical model. Environmental factors were shown to be at least as important in causing a client's problems as internal factors. Also, research was demonstrating that psychoanalysis was probably ineffective in treating clients' problems (Stuart, 1970). Social work shifted at least some of its emphasis to a reform approach. A reform approach seeks to change *systems* to benefit clients. The antipoverty programs, such as Headstart and the Job Corps, are examples of efforts to change systems to benefit clients.

In the past two decades social work has increasingly focused on using a general systems approach to viewing clients and the world surrounding them. This approach integrates both treatment and reform by conceptualizing and emphasizing the dysfunctional transactions between people and their physical and social environments. Human beings are viewed as being in constant interaction with other micro, mezzo, and macro systems within their social environment.

Social workers started to explore both causes and solutions in the environment encompassing any individual client instead of blaming the client. For instance, consider a person who is unemployed and poverty stricken. A social worker assuming a general systems perspective would assess the client system-in-situation. This worker would assess not only the problems and abilities of the client but would also appraise the client's interactions with the multiple systems impacting her or him. What services are available to help the person develop needed job skills? What housing is available in the meantime? What aspects of the macro systems in the environment are contributing to the high unemployment and poverty rates? What services need to be developed in order to respond to these needs?

In contrast, the medical model might orient a worker to try to cure or "fix" the individual by providing counseling to help her or him develop a better attitude toward finding a job. There would be an underlying assumption that it was the individual micro system that was somehow at fault.

Thus, theory helps us as social workers decide how to go about helping people. The medical model versus general systems theory is only one example. Throughout this text, a broad range of theories will be presented concerning various aspects of human development and behavior. Evaluation of their relevance will often be provided. You, as a future social worker, will be expected to learn how to evaluate theories for yourselves in order to apply them to your practice situations. The next section provides some suggestions for how to do this.

The Evaluation of Theory

There are many ways to evaluate theory. This is partly because theories can concern virtually anything from the best method for planting a garden to whether intelligent extraterrestrials exist. Four major approaches for evaluating theory are provided here. The approaches are applied to various theories throughout the text and are not necessarily presented in order of importance. Different theories may require different orders and emphases in terms of how they can best be evaluated.

1. Evaluate the theory's application to client situations. In what ways is the theory relevant to social work? In what ways does the theory provide a means to help us think about our clients and how to help them? For example, a theory about the mating patterns of gorillas would probably be very difficult to apply to any practice situation. However, a theory that hypothesizes how interpersonal attraction occurs between people might help you to work with an extremely shy, lonely young adult with serious interpersonal problems.

2. Evaluate the research supporting the theory. Research often involves singular, obscure, or puzzling findings. Such findings may be vague and may or may not be true. For example, the sample of people studied in a particular research project may have been extremely small. Thus, results may have been due primarily to chance. Or, the sample may not have resembled the entire population very well. Therefore, the results should be applied only to the sample studied and not to anything or anybody else. (Consider this a commercial for why you need to take a research course!) On the one hand, it's important to be cautious about assuming that any research study establishes a *fact*. On the other hand, when more and more studies continue to support each other, a fact (or, as close as we can come to a fact) may begin to develop.

A student once complained to me about her textbook. She said that the author confused her by presenting "facts"—in reality, research findings—that were contradictory. She said she hated such contradictions and wanted the author to tell her what was or was not a fact. My response to her was that I didn't think the world was like that. It cannot be so clearly divided, even though it sometimes seems that it would be more convenient that way. Facts are the closest estimation to the truth we can come to based on the limited information we have. For example, people believed that the world was flat until somebody discovered that it was round. They believed that the northern lights were reflections of sunlight off of the polar ice cap until someone discovered that they are really the effect of solar radiation on the earth's ionosphere.

Research can help to establish whether theories portray facts or not. In other words, research can help determine how accurate and useful any particular theory is. We need theories to guide our thinking and our work.

However, there are at least two problems with evaluating research in support of a theory. First, you might not have access to all, most, or any of the relevant research. There are thousands of journals where research findings (which often are interpreted as facts) can be found. Second, there may be no research specifically directed at finding the specific facts you need to help you verify a theory in your own mind.

3. Evaluate the extent to which the theory coincides with social work values and ethics. Does the theory involve an underlying assumption that "the social worker's primary responsibility is to clients" and their interests (National Association of Social Workers, NASW, Code of Ethics, II.f., 1990)? For example, take the "trickle-down theory" championed by former President Ronald Reagan and his economic policies referred to as "Reaganomics." The idea was that if the government gave major tax breaks and other advantages both to decision makers in industry and big business in addition to extremely wealthy people, then money and benefits would "trickle down" to other people in the population, including the poor. What actually happened was that the rich became richer and the poor became poorer. The number of poor people swelled and the middle class shrank. Thus, it is probably ill-advised for a social worker to employ and support the "trickle-down theory." It does not enhance social and economic justice. Rather, it encourages the oppression of the poor.

Another example of how a theory can support or contradict professional ethics involves the ethical standard that a "social worker should not practice, condone, facilitate or collaborate with any form of discrimination on the basis of race, color, sex, sexual orientation, age, religion, national origin, marital status, political belief, mental or physical handicap, or any other preference of personal characteristic, condition or status" (NASW Code of Ethics, II.F.3., 1990). Consider a theory that one group of people is by nature more intelligent than another group. This theory obviously conflicts with professional values. Therefore, it should not be used or supported by social workers.

Another example is the theory that women are too emotional, flighty, and lacking in intellectual capability to vote or hold a political office. This theory was espoused by the powerful majority of men who held public office until 1920, when women finally won the right to vote after a long, drawn-out battle for this right. This theory, too, stands in direct opposition to professional values and ethics.

(continued next page)

The Relevance of Theory to Social Work (continued)

4. Evaluate the existence and validity of other comparable theories. Are there other theories that adhere better to the first three evaluation criteria? If so, which theory or theories should be chosen to guide our assessments and practice?

The medical model and general systems theory were compared earlier. The social work profession now subscribes to general systems theory, which provides a better perspective for respecting people's dignity and rights and for targeting the macro environment in order to effect change, reduce oppression, and improve social conditions.

Sometimes two or more theories will have basic similarities. Recall the discussion concerning the differences between general systems theory and the ecological model in Chapter 1. Both approaches provide frameworks for how to analyze the world and what to emphasize. Many of the concepts they employ are similar or identical. It was concluded that the ecological model is an offshoot of general systems theory. This text assumes a general systems theory perspective, yet adopts some ecological concepts. For instance, the term *system* is used in both. Both *social environment* and *coping* are ecological terms. Thus, many times it may be determined that a combination of theories provides the best framework for viewing the world within a social work context. Each social worker needs to determine the theoretical framework or combination of frameworks best suited for his or her practice context.

At other times no theory will be perfectly applicable. Perhaps you will decide that only one or two concepts make any sense to you in terms of working with clients. The quest for the perfect theory resembles the pursuit of the perfect fact. It's very difficult to achieve perfection. Thus, when evaluating theories, be flexible. Decide which concepts in any particular theory have the most relevance to you and your work with clients.

---

all people. He theorized that this gave people a sense of their goals and directions for the future. Jung stressed that people have a religious, mystical component in their unconscious. Jung was fascinated with people's dreams and the interpretation of their meaning. He also minimized the role that sexuality plays in emotional disorders.

Erich Fromm came to the United States from Germany in 1934. Whereas Freud had a primarily biological orientation in his analysis of human behavior, Fromm had a social orientation. In other words, he hypothesized that people are best understood within a social context. He focused on how people interacted with others. Individual character traits then evolve from these social interactions with others. Fromm used psychoanalysis as a tool for understanding various social and historical processes and the behavior of political leaders.

Alfred Adler was also associated with Freud in his earlier years. After breaking with Freud in 1911 because of his basic rejection of Freud's libidinal theory, he went on to develop what he called "individual psychology" which emphasized social interaction. In summary, Adler "saw man as aiming toward his own self-created goals, rather than as a victim of his inherited drives; he viewed man's problem in his insecurity, which is apt to mislead him to emphasize his self-interest only . . . ; he believed that neuroses and psychoses are generated by an insufficient development of social feelings towards others" (Wolman, 1973, p. 10).

Harry Stack Sullivan, an American psychiatrist who lived from 1892 to 1949, made perhaps some of the most radical deviations from Freudian theory of all the neo-Freudians. He abandoned many of the basic Freudian concepts and terms. Sullivan emphasized that each individual personality developed on the basis of interpersonal relationships. He proposed that people generally have two basic needs, one for security and one for satisfaction. Whenever a conflict arose between these two needs, the result was some form of emotional disturbance. According to Wolman (1973, p. 361), "his greatest contribution was in stating that men become themselves in relationship to others, that growth, motivation, adjustment and disturbances can be understood only in their social interrelationships." He emphasized that to improve interaction, communication problems must be overcome (Newman and Newman, 1979, p. 23).

The neo-Freudians have had great impacts on the

way we think about ourselves and on the ways in which we view psychotherapy. However, Mischel (1976, p. 50) summarizes their limitations well by saying, "they have not generated specific testable hypotheses for research. Most of them are or were practicing psychotherapists and humanistic writers rather than experimental researchers and scientists. Their contribution, therefore, may prove to have more impact on the history of ideas than on the field of psychology as a formal area of science."

Behavioral Theories

Behavioral or learning theories differ from many other personality theories in one basic way. Instead of focusing on internal motivations, needs, and perceptions, they focus on specific observable behaviors.

Behavioral theories state that people learn or acquire their behaviors. This learning process follows certain basic principles. For example, behavior can be increased or strengthened by receiving positive reinforcement.

Behavioral theories encompass a vast array of different perspectives and applications. However, they all focus on behavior and how it is learned. More recently, greater attention has been given to the complex nature of social situations and how people react in them (Mischel, 1976, pp. 92–95). This involves people's perceptions about different situations and their ability to distinguish between one and another. More credit is given to people's ability to think, discriminate, and make choices. This perspective in behavioral theory is frequently called *social learning or social behavioral theory*. Behavior is seen as occurring within a social context. (Behavioral theory is discussed more extensively in Chapter 4).

Phenomenological Theories: Carl Rogers[1]

Phenomenological or self-theories of personality focus on "the person's subjective, internal experiences and personal concepts" (Mischel, 1976, p. 98). A per-

son is viewed as having various experiences and developing a personality as a result of these subjective experiences instead of one being born with a specified personality framework. It is also asserted that there are no predetermined patterns of personality development. Rather, phenomenological or self-theories recognize a wider range of options or possibilities for personality development depending on the individual's life experiences. Uniqueness of the individual personality is emphasized. Each individual has a unique configuration of personal experiences that will produce a personality unlike any others. This is a relatively positive theoretical approach in that it focuses on growth and self-actualization.

One of the most well-known self-theorists, Carl Rogers, is the founder of client-centered (more recently termed person-centered) therapy, which is based on his self-theory. One of Rogers' basic concepts in self-theory is the concept of *self*. Self is equivalent to *self-concept*. Rogers defines these terms as the "organized, consistent, conceptual gestalt composed of perceptions of the characteristics of the 'I' or 'me' and the perceptions of the relationships of the 'I' or 'me' to others and to various aspects of life, together with the values attached to these perceptions" (Rogers, 1959, p. 200). A person is the product of his or her own experience and how she or he perceives these experiences. One's self-concept is a conception of who one is. Life, therefore, provides a host of opportunities to grow and thrive.

Rogers maintains that there is a natural tendency toward self-actualization, that is, a tendency for every person to develop capacities in ways that serve to maintain or enhance the person (Rogers, 1959). People are naturally motivated toward becoming fulfilled through new experiences.

In contrast to Freud, who viewed the basic nature of humans as being "evil" (having immoral, asocial instincts), Rogers views the basic nature of humans as being inherently good. Rogers further believes that if a person remains relatively free of influence attempts from others, that person's self-actualization motive will lead to a sociable, cooperative, creative, and self-directed person.

The following are definitions of some of Rogers' other key concepts.

Ideal self: The self-concept that one would like to possess; what one would like to be.

---

1. This material on client-centered therapy is adapted from Charles Zastrow, *The Practice of Social Work*, 3rd ed., 1989, pp. 357–60. Used with permission of Wadsworth Pub. Co., Belmont, CA.

Incongruence between self and experience: A discrepancy that exists between one's self-concept and what one experiences. Example—an individual may perceive herself as outgoing, attractive, and sociable, but when together with others may generally feel ignored. When such a discrepancy exists, a person will feel tension, internal confusion, and anxiety.

Psychological maladjustment: Exists when a person denies or distorts to awareness, significant experiences. A psychologically maladjusted person is one who has an incongruence between self and experience.

Congruence, congruence of self and experience: One's concept of self is consistent with what one experiences.

Need for positive regard: Need to be valued and held in esteem by others.

Need for self-regard: Need to value oneself.

Conditions of worth: Conditions of worth result from the introjection of those values of others which are inconsistent with one's self-actualization motive. A person has conditions of worth when she feels her worth as a person is judged conditionally upon certain behaviors. Those behaviors in which she feels valued low on will be avoided. The result is that some behaviors are regarded positively which are not actually experienced as satisfying, while other behaviors are regarded negatively which are not actually experienced as unsatisfying.

The driving force in personality development is seen by client-centered theorists as the "self-actualization motive," which seeks to optimally develop a person's capacities. As an infant grows, the infant's "self-concept" begins to be formed. The development of the self-concept is highly dependent on the individual's *perceptions* of his experiences. The person's perceptions of experiences is influenced by the "need for positive regard" (to be valued by others). The need for positive regard is seen as a universal need in every person (Rogers, 1959). Out of the variety of experiences of frustration or satisfaction of the need for positive regard, the person develops a "sense of self-regard," that is, a learned sense of self that is based on the perception of the regard he has received from others.

Emotional and behavioral problems develop when the child *introjects* (takes on) those values of others which are inconsistent with his self-actualizing motive. Introjecting values inconsistent with one's self-actualizing motive results in "conditions of worth." For example, a child may introject values from his or her parents that sex is dirty or that dancing is bad.

Rogers adds that a child is apt to be influenced by others because of the need for positive regard.

When a person has conditions of worth, the result is that some behaviors are regarded positively (e.g., avoiding all sexual activity) by the person which are not internally experienced as unsatisfying. Meador and Rogers (1979, p. 144) then state:

> What happens to the actualizing tendency as conditions of worth develop in the self-regard system? The actualizing tendency remains the basic motivation for the individual. However, a conflict develops between his organismic needs and his self-regard needs, now containing conditions of worth. The individual, in effect, is faced with the choice between acting in accord with his organismic sense or censoring the organismic urging and acting in accord with the condition of worth he has learned.

Such conditions of worth lead to an "incongruence between self and experience." For example, a person may feel morally righteous and view him- or herself as being a value setter for refusing to dance or date, but yet experience that peers relate to him or her as being a prude with archaic values. When a discrepancy exists between one's self-concept and one's experiences, one will feel tension, anxiety, and internal confusion.

A person responds to this "incongruence" in a variety of ways. One way is to use various defense mechanisms. A person may *deny* that experiences are in conflict with his or her self-concept. Or the person may *distort* or *rationalize* the experiences so that they are perceived as being consistent with his or her self-concept. If a person is unable to reduce the inconsistency through such defense mechanisms, the person is forced to directly face the fact that incongruences exist between self and experiences, which will lead the person to feel unwanted emotions (such as anxiety, tension, depression, guilt, or shame).

If a person has a large or significant degree of incongruence between self and experiences which the defense mechanisms cannot cope with, "disorganization of self" generally occurs (e.g., a "psychotic" breakdown). Client-centered therapy asserts that the following three therapist attitudes are necessary and sufficient conditions to effect positive change in the client: empathy, positive regard, and genuineness or congruence. It is theorized that whenever a therapist displays these three attitudes toward a client, the actualizing potential of the client will begin to change and grow.

Empathy is the capacity of the therapist to put him- or herself in the shoes of the client so that the therapist is able to understand what the client is thinking and feeling. Empathy also involves communicating this understanding to the client.

Unconditional positive regard means that the therapist fully accepts the client and conveys a genuine caring for the client. Involved in positive regard is a nonjudgmental attitude. Also, the therapist does not express approval or disapproval, does not make interpretations, and does not probe unnecessarily. The therapist conveys that she or he fully trusts the client's resources for increased self-understanding and positive change. With this attitude the client concludes (Meador and Rogers, 1979, p. 152), "Here is someone who repeatedly tells me in one way or another that he believes in my ability to find my way in the process of growth. Perhaps I can begin to believe in myself."

Genuineness or congruence is the capacity of the therapist to "trust his own gut reactions," and then convey those feelings or reactions that the therapist believes have relevance in the relationship. This willingness of the therapist to be real, and to express what he or she is thinking and feeling, provides the client with a reality base that the client can trust. It also takes away some of the risk of sharing hidden secrets with another.

For Rogers the *nature* of the relationship between client and therapist is seen as *the* key variable in producing positive changes. Rogers (1961, p. 32) states:

> The more the therapist is perceived by the client as being genuine, as having an empathetic understanding, and an unconditional regard for him, the greater will be the degree of constructive personality change in the client.

Rogers indicates two conditions are necessary before therapy can occur. First, the client needs to be uncomfortable or anxious because of incongruences between self and experiences. (Client-centered therapy will not work well with clients who deny a problem exists, or who are unmotivated to change.) Second, a therapist must create a nonthreatening atmosphere where the client feels he or she is being fully accepted and understood, and that the therapist genuinely cares for the client.

In such a relationship, a client feels free (perhaps for the first time) to explore his or her incongruences between self and experiences. (For example, a client begins to examine the inconsistency between believing that sex is sinful while organismically her or his experiences do not agree.) The client then comes face to face with the awareness that there is this incongruence, and begins to think about what it would mean if other values were held (for example, having a value that responsible sexual experiences are desirable). During this process the client usually experiences feelings that have in the past been denied, repressed, or otherwise kept from consciousness. (Similar to Freud, Rogers believes the person in therapy should become aware of unconscious feelings and ideas, and deal with them in the conscious part of the mind.) If and when the above occurs, the concept of self becomes reorganized to include those experiences which in the past have been kept from consciousness. In addition, one's concept of self becomes increasingly congruent with one's experiences, and also more consistent with the self-actualizing processes.

The role of the therapist is best characterized as being *nondirective*. The therapist's role is to create a permissive, nonthreatening psychological atmosphere where the client feels accepted by the therapist and feels free to explore the defenses and the incongruencies between self and experiences. If growth of the individual is to occur, it is postulated that it is necessary for each person to assume responsibility for her actions, decisions, and behavior. Change that is significant and enduring, Rogers postulates, must be self-initiated. Therefore, complete responsibility for the direction of treatment sessions rests with the client. A client-centered therapist does *not* bring up subjects to discuss, give advice, make interpretations, or provide suggestions. It is postulated that a person's self-actualization motive best knows what courses of action a person should take, and therefore the focus of client-centered therapy is to help the client gain insight into values that are inconsistent with this motive, and then to allow the self-actualizing processes to make decisions and determine future directions.

Cognitive Development: Piaget

Specific theories concerning how people develop their capacities to think and understand have also been developed. Cognition involves the ability to take in information, process it, store it, and finally retrieve and use it. In other words, cognition involves the ability to learn and to think. The most noted of the cognitive theorists is probably Jean Piaget. Piaget (1952) has proposed that people go through various stages in learning how to think as they develop from infancy into adulthood. His theory, which concerns the stages through which people must progress in order to develop their cognitive or thinking ability, was derived from careful observations of his own children's growth and development.

Piaget postulates that virtually all people learn how to think in the same way. That is, as people develop they all go through various stages of how they think. In infancy and early childhood, thinking is very basic and concrete. As children grow, thinking progresses and becomes more complex and abstract. Each stage of cognitive development is characterized by certain principles or ways in which an individual thinks.

The following example does an exceptionally good job of illustrating how these changes occur. In his studies, Piaget would show children of various ages two glass containers filled with a liquid. The containers were identical in size and shape, and held an equal amount of liquid (see Figure 3.2). Children inevitably would agree that each container held the same amount of liquid. Piaget then would take the liquid from one of the containers and pour it into another taller, narrower glass container. Interestingly enough, he found that children under age six would frequently say that the taller glass held more even though the amount of liquid in each was identical. Children approximately age six or older, however, would state that despite the different shapes, both containers held the same amount of liquid. Later, it was established that the results of this experiment were the same for children of various backgrounds and nationalities.

This example might be explained by how children in different cognitive stages thought about or conceptualized the problem. Younger children tended to rely directly on their visual perceptions in order to make a decision about which glass held more or less liquid. Older children, however, were able to do more logical

FIGURE 3.2: Conservation

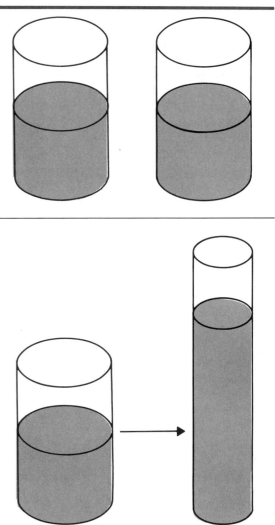

Children under age six would say that the taller glass holds more, even though the amount of liquid in each is identical.

thinking about the problem. They thought about how liquid could take various forms and how the same amount could look different depending on its container. The older children illustrated a higher, more abstract or thoughtful level of cognitive development. This particular concept involving the idea that a substance can be changed in one way (e.g., shape) while remaining the same in another (e.g., quantity) is called *conservation*.

These ways of thinking about and organizing ideas and concepts depending on one's level of cognitive development are called *schema*. A person perceives the world differently and at an increasingly more abstract level during each stage. In other words, different aspects of the environment are emphasized or even noticed depending on a person's cognitive level of development. Each stage, therefore, is characterized by its own schema.

Piaget hypothesizes that all people go through the cognitive stages in the same order. The stages are continuous rather than distinct. An individual progresses through them in a continuous manner. In other words, a child does not wake up one morning and suddenly state, "Aha, I'm now in the preoperational stage of development!" Rather, children gradually progress through each stage with smooth and continual transitions from one stage to the next. Each stage acts as a foundation or prerequisite for the next.

Thus, organization is important in understanding Piaget's theory. People go through the various stages of cognitive development in an organized, predictable manner. Three other concepts that are also important are adaptation, assimilation, and accommodation.

Adaptation refers to the capacity to adjust to surrounding environmental conditions. It involves the process of changing in order to fit in and survive in the surrounding environment. Piaget would say that adaptation is composed of the two processes, assimilation and accommodation.

Assimilation refers to the taking in of new information and the resulting integration into the schema or structure of thought. In other words, a person is exposed to a new situation, event, or piece of information. Not only is the information received and thought about at a conscious level, but it is also integrated into a way of thinking. The information is stored in a way so that it may be used later in problem-solving situations.

For example, go back to the situation where young children observe and judge the quantities of liquid in glass containers. Younger children, namely those under age six, assimilate information at a level using only their observations. Items and substances are only as they appear before their eyes. These children could not think of items as changing, as being somewhere else, or as being in a different context. They could not yet assimilate such information using higher, more

A schoolboy takes a swing at a *piñata* during a celebration of "Three Kings Day" during the Christmas season at a Boston elementary school. Piaget might call the boy's adjusting to his changed environment "adaptation."

logical levels of thought where some qualities of a substance could change while others remain the same. Children of age six or older can think about substances or items that are not immediately before their eyes. They can think about other different circumstances and situations.

Accommodation refers to the process by which children change their perceptions and actions in order to think using higher, more abstract levels of cognition. Children assimilate to take in new information and eventually accommodate it. That is, they build on the schema they already have and use new, more complex ways of thinking. Children aged six or older have accommodated the information about the liquid-filled glass containers. They have already assimilated information about shape, size, and quantity. Furthermore, they can think about changes in substance in a more abstract way. They can think of the liquid, not only as being held in a container of a specific shape and size, but also as it may be held in other containers of other shapes and sizes.

Piaget describes four major stages of cognitive development. These include the sensorimotor period, the preoperational thought period, the period of concrete operations, and the period of formal operations. Each stage will be described below. Major concepts characterizing the schema of each stage will be discussed.

The Sensorimotor Period

The sensorimotor period extends from birth to approximately two years of age. During this period, a child progresses from simple thoughtless reflex reactions to a basic understanding of the environment. Baldwin (1968) states that three major accomplishments are made during the sensorimotor period. First, children learn that they have various senses through which they can receive information. Additionally, they begin to understand that they can receive different kinds of sensory information about the same object in the environment.

For example, initially an infant may see and hear her parents squabbling over who will take the new Mercedes 500 SE with air conditioning on a 99 degree summer day and who will take the old Ford Escort with no air conditioning. Even though she will hear and see them squabbling, she will not be able to associate the two types of sensory information as referring to the same aspect of her environment, namely her parents. By the end of the sensorimotor period, she will understand that she can both hear and see her parents at the same time. She will perceive their interaction from both modes of sensory input.

A second major accomplishment during the sensorimotor period is the exhibition of *goal-directed behavior*. Instead of displaying simple responses on a random basis, the child will purposefully put together several behaviors in order to accomplish a simple goal. For example, a child will reach for a piece of a simple wooden puzzle in order to attempt placement into its appropriate slot. The child will plan to put the puzzle together. However, since a child's thinking during the sensorimotor period is still very concrete, the ability to plan very far ahead is extremely limited.

The third major accomplishment during the sensorimotor period is the understanding that objects are permanent. This is the idea that objects continue to exist even when they are out of sight and out of

hearing range. The concept of *object permanence* is the most important schema acquired during the sensorimotor period. Initially, children immediately forget about objects as soon as they no longer can perceive them. By age two, children are generally able to think about the image of something which they can't see or hear, and solve a simple problem in relationship to that image. Children begin to use *representation*, that is, the visual imagining of an image in their minds which allows them to begin solving problems.

For example, take two-year-old Ricky who is very attached to his "blanky," an ancient, ragged, yellow blanket which he loves dearly. Ricky is in the midst of playing with his action garage toy set with his "blanky" placed snuggly next to him. Ricky's mother casually walks into the room, gently picks up the "blanky," and walks down the hallway to the bedroom. Instead of forgetting about the "blanky" as soon as it's out of sight, Ricky immediately gets up and starts actively seeking out his "blanky," calling for it relentlessly. Even though he can't presently see it and he doesn't know exactly where his mother put it, Ricky is able to think of the "blanky" and begin a quest in search of it. Furthermore, he is able to run around the house and look for it in various nooks and crannies, thinking about where it might be.

The Preoperational Thought Period

Piaget's second stage of cognitive development, the preoperational thought period, extends from approximately age two to seven. Some overlap from one stage to another should be expected. A child's thinking continues to progress to a more abstract, logical level. Although children are still tied to their physical and perceptual experiences, their ability to remember things and to solve problems continues to grow.

During the preoperational stage, children progress beyond evoking simple mental images of objects. They begin to use symbolic representations for things in their environment. Children are no longer bound to actual concrete perception. They can think in terms of symbols or mental representations of objects or circumstances.

Words provide an excellent example of symbolic representation. Children may symbolize an object or situation with words and then reflect on the object or situation later by using the words. In other words, language can be used for thought even when objects and situations are not present.

Barriers to the Development of Logical Thinking

Despite children's progress toward more abstract thinking, three major obstacles to logical thinking exist during the preoperational period. These include egocentrism, centration, and irreversibility.

Egocentrism. In *egocentrism,* a child is unable to see things from anybody else's point of view. The child is aware only of him- or herself, and the needs and perspectives of others don't exist.

Piaget illustrated this concept by showing a child a doll in a three-dimensional scene. With the child remaining in the same position, the doll could be moved around the scene so that the child could observe it from different perspectives. The child would then be shown various pictures and asked what the scene would look like from the doll's perspective or point of view. Piaget found that the child would often choose the wrong picture. The child would continue to view the scene from his own perspective. It was difficult if not impossible for the child to imagine that the doll's perspective or point of view could be any different than the child's own.

Centration. *Centration* refers to a child's tendency to concentrate on only one detail of an object or situation and ignore all other aspects.

To illustrate centration, refer back to the example in which a child is asked to evaluate the amounts of liquid in two glasses. The child would observe the same amount of liquid being poured into two different shaped containers. One container was short and squat, and the other, tall and thin. When asked which container held more liquid, the child would frequently answer that the tall, thin container would. In this situation, the child was focusing on the concept of height instead of width. She was unable to focus on both height and width at the same time. Only one aspect of the situation was used to solve the problem. This is a good example of how centration inhibits more mature, logical thought.

Irreversibility. *Irreversibility* refers to a child's ability to follow and think something through in one direc-

tion without being able to imagine the relationship in reverse. For example, four-year-old Gary might be asked, "Who are your cousins?" Gary might then reply, "Sherrie, Donna, Lorrie, and Tanya." If Gary is then asked who is Sherrie's cousin, he will probably say he doesn't know. Gary is able to think through a situation in one direction, but is unable to reverse his train of thought. He knows that Sherrie is his cousin. However, he is unable to see the reverse of that relationship, namely that he is also Sherrie's cousin.

Developing Cognitive Ability

Despite barriers to the development of logical thought, several concepts illustrate ways in which children progress in their ability to think. Major changes concerning these concepts are made between the onset of the preoperational thought period and the culmination of adult logical thinking. Children gradually improve their perceptions and grasp of these concepts.

Classification. *Classification* refers to a child's ability to sort items or stimuli into various categories according to certain characteristics. The characteristics might include shape, color, texture, or size. Children gradually develop the ability to distinguish differences

Children playing with Uno cards illustrate Piaget's developmental concept of "classification."

between objects or stimuli and categorize them to reflect these differences.

For example, two-and-a-half-year-old Karen is given a bag of red, blue, and green "creepy crawlers." In this case the creepy crawlers consist of soft, plastic lizards, all of which are the same size and shape. When asked to put all the red lizards together in a heap, Karen is unable to do so. She cannot yet discriminate between the colors in order to categorize or classify the lizards according to their color. However, when Karen is given the same task at age seven, she is easily able to put the red, blue, and green lizards in their respective heaps. She has acquired the concept of classification.

Seriation. *Seriation* refers to a child's ability to arrange objects or stimuli in order according to certain characteristics. These characteristics might include size, weight, volume, or length.

For example, a child is given a number of McDonald's soda straws cut to various lengths. The child's ability to arrange such objects from shortest to longest improves as the child's cognitive ability develops (Kaluger and Kaluger, 1984, p. 242). By age four or five, a child is usually able to select both the longest and the shortest straws. However, the child still has difficulty discriminating among the middle lengths. By age five or six the child will probably be able to order the straws one by one from shortest to longest. However, this would probably be done with much concentration and some degree of difficulty. By age seven, the task of ordering the straws would probably be much easier.

The ability to apply seriation to various characteristics develops at different ages depending on the specific characteristic (Kaluger and Kaluger, 1984, p. 242). For example, children are usually unable to order a series of objects according to weight until age nine. Seriation according to volume is typically not possible until approximately age twelve.

Conservation. *Conservation* refers to a child's ability to grasp the idea that while one aspect of a substance (e.g., quantity or weight) remains the same, another aspect of that same substance (e.g., shape or position) can be changed.

For example, four-year-old Bart is given two wads of "silly putty" of exactly equal volume. One wad is then rolled into a ball and the other is patted into the shape of a pancake. When asked which wad has a greater amount of material in it, Bart is likely to say that the pancake does. Even though Bart initially saw that the two wads were exactly equal, he focused only on the one dimension of area. In terms of area alone, the pancake appeared to Bart as if it had more substance. However, by the time Bart reached age six or seven, he would probably be able to state that both wads had equal substance. He would know that matter can take different forms and still have the same amount of material.

As with seriation, children achieve the ability to understand conservation at different ages depending on the characteristic to be conserved (Papalia and Olds, 1981, pp. 263–64). For example, whereas conservation of substance is typically attained by age six or seven, the concept of conservation of weight is usually not achieved until age nine or ten. Conservation of volume is usually not mastered until age eleven or twelve.

The Period of Concrete Operations

The period of concrete operations extends from approximately age seven to eleven or twelve years. During this stage, a child develops the ability to think logically on a concrete level. In other words, a child has mastered the major impediments to logical thinking which were evident during earlier stages of cognitive development.

The child now develops the capacity to see things from other people's points of view. Understanding and empathy are substantially increased during this period.

More complex thinking is developed. Situations and events can be viewed and examined in terms of many variables. The child gradually becomes less limited by centration. A child is no longer limited to solving a problem in terms of only one variable, rather, a number of variables could be taken into account. In the glass example, the child would begin to think in terms of height, volume, substance, and shape all at the same time.

A child also develops his ability to conceptualize in terms of reversibility during this period. In other words, a child can think an issue through, and then reverse his train of thought. Relationships begin to be understood from various perspectives. Returning to an example presented earlier, Gary would now understand that not only was Sherrie his cousin, but that he was also her cousin.

The concepts of classification, seriation, and conservation would also be mastered. During the period of concrete operations a child gains much flexibility in thinking about situations and events. Events are appraised from many different points of view.

Additionally, children develop their use of symbols to represent events in the real world. Their ability to understand math and to express themselves through language greatly improves. Correspondingly, their memories become sharper.

Despite the great gains in cognitive development made during the stage of concrete operations, a child is still somewhat limited. Although events are viewed from many perspectives, these perspectives are still tied to concrete issues. Children think about things they can see, hear, smell, or touch. Their focus is on thinking about things instead of ideas. Children must enter the final stage of cognitive development, the period of formal operations, before they can fully develop their cognitive capability.

The Period of Formal Operations

The final stage of cognitive development is the period of formal operations. This period, beginning at approximately age eleven or twelve and extending to approximately age sixteen, characterizes cognitive development during adolescence. Technically, this chapter addresses childhood and not adolescence. However, for the purposes of continuity, Piaget's fourth period of cognitive development will be discussed here.

Abstract thought reaches its culmination during the period of formal operations. Children become capable of taking numerous variables into consideration and creatively formulating abstract hypotheses about how things work or about why things are the way they are. Instead of being limited to thought about how things are, children begin to think about how things could be. They begin to analyze why things aren't always as they should be.

For example, Meredy, age ten, is still limited by the more concrete type of thinking that characterizes

the period of concrete operations. She is aware that a nuclear bomb was dropped on Hiroshima near the close of World War II. When asked about why this happened, she might say that the United States had to defend its own territory and this was a means of bringing the war to an end. She can conceptualize the situation and analyze it in terms of some variables. In this case the variables might include the fact that the United States was at war and had to take actions to win that war. Her ability to think through the situation might extend no further than that. When asked the same question at age fifteen, Meredy might have quite a different answer. She might talk about what a difficult decision such a step must have been in view of the tremendous cost in human life. She might describe the incident as one of various tactical strategies which might have been taken. She also might elaborate on the political impacts caused by the event. In other words, Meredy's ability to consider numerous variables from many perspectives would improve drastically during the period of formal operations.

Three major developments characterize adolescent thought (Gallagher, 1973). First, the adolescent is able to identify numerous variables which affect a situation. An event can be viewed from many perspectives. Second, the adolescent can analyze the effects of one variable on another, that is, hypothesize about relationships and think about changing conditions. Third, an adolescent is capable of hypothetical-deductive reasoning. In other words, an adolescent can systematically and logically evaluate many possible relationships in order to arrive at a conclusion. Various possibilities can be examined. Each possibility can be scrutinized in a conditional "if-then" fashion. For instance, the adolescent might begin thinking in terms of if certain variables exist, then certain consequences will follow.

Evaluation of Piaget's Theory

Some criticisms of Piaget's theory have been expressed which both address his general approach and raise questions about specific concepts. One general criticism is that the vast majority of his suppositions are based on his observations of his own children instead of on scientific studies conducted under laboratory conditions. Questions have been raised about the manner in which he observed and interviewed his children, the language he used to obtain information from them, and personal biases which may have emerged. It is also notable that findings were primarily based on only three subjects, his own children, instead of on a variety of subjects from different backgrounds.

A second general criticism involves the fact that Piaget focuses on the "average" child. Questions can be raised regarding who the "average child" really is. Cultural, socioeconomic, and ethnic differences were not taken into account.

Consideration of "only limited aspects of human development" (Lefrancois, 1987, p. 436) poses yet a third general criticism. There is little said of personality or emotional growth except in specific instances where they relate directly to cognitive development. The effects of social interaction are virtually ignored. Piaget concentrates on how children see and think of objects instead of the people closest to them.

The idea that cognitive growth through these stages stops at adolescence is a fourth general criticism. Riegel (1973) suggests adding a fifth stage as people move into and through adulthood. In this stage, there would be "no clear plateaus—no levels of cognitive accomplishment clearly evident in the ability to solve a new class of problems." Instead, there is a renewed realization that development occurs on different levels, that it is replete with contradictions, and that different levels of behavior are entirely appropriate. As Riegel notes, a laborer might remain at the level of concrete operations, and a dancer, at a sensorimotor level (LeFrancois, 1987, p. 437).

On the other hand, some research suggests that progression to the period of formal operations does not occur for all people in all instances (Keating and Clark, 1980; Super, 1980). For example, Kohlberg and Gilligan (1971) conclude that almost half of the adults in the United States don't attain this cognitive level at all. They come to this conclusion on the basis of research which evaluates the ages at which people can perform certain formal operational level tasks. One study indicates that a substantial majority of adults do not achieve this fourth cognitive level until after age twenty-one.

Piaget (1972) has offered several possible explanations for such findings. First, an individual's social environment may influence cognitive development.

Persons from deprived environments may not be offered the same types of stimulation and support necessary to achieve such high levels of cognition. Second, individual differences might have to be taken into account. Some persons might not have the necessary ability to attain the levels of thought which characterize the formal operations period. Finally, although everyone may develop a capacity for formal operational thought, this capacity may not be versatile in its application to all problems. In other words, some individuals might be unable to use formal operations with some problems or in some situations.

Questions have also been raised regarding the meaning and appropriate age level attributed to some of Piaget's specific concepts. He appears to have erred by underestimating children's abilities concerning various conceptual achievements. Some research replicates Piaget's in terms of principle. However, by simplifying the language used to communicate with children and by using words and concepts with which they are familiar, the children's performance tends to improve. In other words, sometimes when children can relate better to the experiment, they better understand what is expected from them and thus can perform better.

For example, some recent research involves object permanence. Object permanence, as you remember, is the concept that objects continue to exist even when they're literally out of sight. According to Piaget, children don't attain this skill until nearing age two at the end of the sensorimotor period. However, Baillargeon (1987) cleverly adapted his experimental procedure to eliminate the need for infants to have a higher level of muscular coordination than is developmentally possible at their age in order to respond appropriately. He found that by four-and-a-half months, and some by age three-and-a-half months, babies indicated that they were aware of object permanence.

Piaget's examination of egocentricity has also received some criticism. Egocentrism involves the concept that a child is unable to see things from anyone else's perspective but his own.

The idea that children in this age group are so self-centered may be overly harsh. Many parents may think of the incidences where their young children appeared to show genuine empathic ability. For example, four-year-old Johnnie approaches his father after finding a robin's egg that fell from the nest. He states, "Daddy, poor birdie. She lost her baby."

Additionally, some evidence has been found to show that children are not quite as egocentric as Piaget initially proclaimed (Black, 1981; Borke, 1975; Donaldson, 1979; Hobson, 1980). A child's ability to empathize with others depends somewhat on the circumstances and the issues involved. Perhaps if a child understands a situation more clearly from a personal point of view, he is better able to see another person's perspective.

Piaget initially investigated egocentricity by having children observe three fabricated "mountains" of unequal heights placed on a table. Children were able to walk around the table and look at the mountains from various perspectives. They were then asked to sit in a chair at the table. A doll was placed in a chair on the opposite side of the table. The children were then shown a variety of photographs of the "mountains" which illustrated how they looked from a number of perspectives. Piaget asked the children to select the picture which best showed how the mountains looked from where the doll sat. Children in the preoperational stage would choose the picture which best showed the mountains from where they themselves sat, not from where the doll sat. Piaget concluded, then, that the children had not yet worked through the barrier of egocentrism since they couldn't comprehend the view of the mountains from the doll's perspective.

When a variation of the mountain task was used, the results were quite different (Hughes, 1975). Instead of "mountains," a child was seated in front of a square table with dividers on the top to divide it into four equal sectors. The researcher placed a doll in one of the sectors and a police officer figure in another sector. The child was then asked if she thought the police officer could see the doll from where he stood. The task was then complicated by placing another police officer figure somewhere on the table. The researcher then asked the child to place the doll somewhere on the table where she thought neither police officer could see her. Of thirty children aged three-and-a-half to five years, 90 percent answered or responded correctly. Most of these young children could clearly see the situation from another's perspective. These results differ significantly from Piaget's. Perhaps children had trouble understanding the con-

cept of fake "mountains" on a table, with which they were unfamiliar. On the other hand, perhaps children could better relate to and understand the concepts of police officers and dolls, both of which were familiar to them.

These and other studies point to the fact that the cognitive development of children is a very complicated process, perhaps much more so than Piaget could guess. It's interesting to note that a major thrust of these more recent studies is to emphasize what young children *can* do rather than what they *cannot* do.

Regardless of the various criticisms, Piaget must be given great credit. Decades ago, he provided us with a foundation for thinking about cognitive development and has tremendously influenced research in this area. Additionally, he set the stage for establishing appropriate expectations regarding what types of things children at various age levels can realistically accomplish.

Effects of Diversity on Cognitive Development

Some studies indicate that some children raised in minority households do not perform as well on tests designed to measure aspects of Piaget's cognitive development. For example, in Norton's study (1969) of 109 eight-year-old children, from various socioeconomic backgrounds, she discovered a strong relationship between good language models in the home and the child's ability to overcome the cognitive barrier of irreversibility. Good language referred to language with rules conducive to the development of reversible thought. For instance, children were more likely to master reversibility in thought if they had mothers who spoke in sentences and pastimes related to reading, and referred to objects by their proper names.

This was true for all subgroups except for African American children from lower socioeconomic levels. These children rated poorly on reversibility despite having "good" language models in the home. On more extensive analysis it was discovered that these homes did provide effective language models. However, the models were different from those used in white homes. The tests designed to measure reversibility apparently were not effective when applied to a different type of language model.

Norton (1983) later proposes that African American children from ghetto environments learn a language with a different "internal consistency" from that of standard English. She warns that such children may be penalized on entering school systems which don't acknowledge their different language model. Such children may not be considered as bright as others simply because they talk and structure their thinking somewhat differently. Finally, she suggests that schools need to sensitize themselves to such differences when helping children to learn and maximize their levels of cognitive development.

Cognitive Theory: Bruner

Jerome Bruner, another well-respected cognitive theorist, proposes an alternative theory of cognitive development. Bruner's theories are also based on the idea that cognition is developed through a series of stages. He maintains that basic information about any subject can be taught at almost any age level, if the material is presented in the appropriate manner (Bruner, 1972). Bruner, therefore, places great emphasis on the importance of education.

Bruner proposes three stages of development: the "enactive," the "iconic," and "symbolic representation" stages (Bruner et al., 1966). Each stage suggests that there is a preferred mode of learning at any particular time of life. Bruner maintains that infants learn best through physical and sensorimotor interaction with the environment. This is the enactive stage. The iconic stage follows for preschoolers and kindergarteners. This age group learns best through the use of mental pictures and imagery. Finally, children in middle school learn best through symbolic representation. This stage involves the use of language and more abstract thought in order to manipulate ideas.

Emotional Development

The concepts of *personality* and *cognition* are complex and abstract. No one clearly specified definition is available for either. Nor is the relationship between them explicitly defined. It is not clear exactly how thinking affects personality, or how personality affects thinking. The tremendous amount of variation from one individual to another and even one individual's varying reactions from one particular situation to another makes it even more difficult to comprehend.

Emotions are also involved in a person's development. They act to complicate the profile of an individual's personality even further. For our purposes, emotion will be defined as the complex combination of feelings and moods that involves subtle physiological reactions and is expressed by displaying characteristic patterns of behavior (Morris, 1979). For example, a four-year-old boy's goldfish might be found floating belly-up one morning when the boy gets up. On hearing the unhappy news, the boy might become upset. His heart might start beating faster, and his breathing might accelerate. Finally, he might run to his room and start to cry. In this case, the little boy experienced an emotion. His body responded as he became upset. Finally, the behavior of crying clearly displayed his emotional upset.

Infants' Emotions

Bridges (1932), a very early researcher of infants' emotions, claimed that infants initially showed only one basic emotion, namely excitement. Watson (1919), another early researcher, felt that infants were capable of three basic emotions including love, rage, and fear. Each of these emotions, according to Watson was emitted as a reflex reaction to a specific stimulus. For example, an infant would experience love if stroked softly and spoken gently to by a parent, rage if physically restrained, and fear if suddenly startled by an unexpected loud noise.

However, more recent research indicates that infants can experience a much wider range of emotion within the first few months of life. This research has focused on the interpretation of infants' facial expressions to determine the emotions they're feeling (Izard et al., 1980). Observers participating in the experiment believed that emotions including joy, interest or general excitement, sadness, fear, and to a lesser extent, disgust, surprise, and anger could be recognized.

Additional research indicates that infants become capable of experiencing specific emotions as they continue to develop (Trotter, 1983). Immediately upon birth, infants can express general interest, disgust, and distress. Other emotions including surprise, anger, and sadness occur approximately during the third to fourth month of life. Fear is displayed during months five through seven. It's interesting to note that emotions which reflect *self-awareness* tend to develop later, some not until they begin their second year. Self-awareness may be defined as "the understanding that they are separate from other people and things—which enables them to reflect on their actions and measure them against social standards" (Papalia and Olds, 1992, p. 149). Such emotions include shyness, jealousy, pride, and shame.

Crying

One means by which babies can clearly display their emotions is through crying. Wolff (1969) analyzed tape recordings of crying babies and distinguished four basic types of crying. First, there is the rhythmic hunger cry. This tends to be the most frequent cry used both when a child is hungry and also after a child has been displaying some other type of crying for a period of time. The second type of crying is the angry cry. This is a loud cry where the baby forces a large column of air through the vocal cords. Third is the cry of pain. This type of crying is characterized by an initial loud wail with no preceding sniffling or moaning. The cry may be followed by the baby holding its breath for a long period. The fourth type of crying is the cry of frustration. This begins with two or three long cries; the baby does not hold its breath when crying in this manner. Ozwald and Peltzman (1974) found that babies experiencing great strain or trouble tended to cry more loudly for longer periods of time; their crying also tended to be less steady and the babies were more apt to gag.

Mothers appear to be exceptionally responsive to the cries of their infants (Ainsworth and Bell, 1969). Mothers tend to react most quickly to cries of pain or anger, and also quite quickly when their babies cry because they're hungry (Wolff, 1969). It's interesting to note that fathers can interpret their infant's crying almost as well as mothers can (Wiesenfeld et al., 1981).

Smiling and Laughing

Babies can also express themselves emotionally through smiling and laughing. Infants smiling at their parents and their parents smiling back provides a major means for fostering the primary relationship

Fortunately for infants, most parents are exceptionally responsive to the cries of their children.

between children and parents. When a baby smiles at an adult, the adult returns the smile almost every time (Gewirtz and Gewirtz, 1968). Some infants display significantly more smiling behavior than others (Tautermannova, 1973). One might wonder what effect infrequent smiling would have on the relationship between parents and child.

Gewirtz (1965) proposed that babies progress through three phases of smiling. Reflex smiling is the first phase. Almost immediately after birth, infants can be observed smiling. At one time this was thought to be related to gas. However, research indicated that it occurs automatically as a function of central nervous system development and frequently just before a baby falls asleep (Sroufe and Waters, 1976). When an infant displays a reflex smile, only muscles in the lower part of the face, not the forehead or eyes, are involved.

The second phase involves social smiling. During this phase, infants smile in response to someone they see or hear. Their attention is being more directed toward other people. They may begin social smiling as early as their third week (Papalia and Olds, 1989, p. 156).

The final phase is the selective social phase where children smile in reaction to people they recognize. This phase begins during their second month (Papalia and Olds, 1989, p. 156). The smiling process reflects infants' gradual orientation towards other people and social relationships.

Laughing begins at about the fourth month. The older they get, the more frequently they laugh and the more things they find to laugh at. It is thought that to some extent laughter presents a means of releasing tension in situations which might otherwise be frightening or unpredictable (Sroufe and Wunsch, 1972).

Infants and Temperament

It's difficult to refer to personality with respect to infants. Personality implies a complex mixture of attitudes, expressions, and behaviors that develop over time and characterize a specific individual. Infants don't as yet have enough breadth or ability for expression to portray the complexity inherent in personality. Rather, there's a tendency for psychologists to refer to an infant's temperament instead of personality. Temperament is each individual's "characteristic style of reacting to people and situations" (Papalia and Olds, 1989, p. 157).

A classic study of infant temperament and its implications for later life was undertaken by Thomas et al. (1968, 1970), beginning in 1956. Referred to as the New York Longitudinal Study (NYLS), this research investigated eighty-five families with a total of 141 children. All families had highly educated members with professional backgrounds. The researchers identified nine components of temperament. These included: type and amount of physical activity; predictability of daily routines such as eating or sleeping; the extent to which a person approaches or withdraws from new situations; how adaptable a person is to change in the environment; the intensity of stimulation needed to elicit a response; how energetically or intensively a person responds; overall disposition ranging from "crabby" to cheerful; how readily a person can be distracted from ongoing activities; and the amount of attention a person can devote to an activity in spite of obstacles.

On the basis of these components, Thomas et al. (1968, 1970) found that children generally fall into one of three categories. *Easy* children are those whose lives have a relatively predictable, rhythmic pattern. They are generally cheerful and easy to get along with. They accept change well and are interested in

new situations. The second category of child temperament includes *difficult* children. These are children who are frequently irritable, have much irregularity in their daily pattern of activities, and have much difficulty adapting to new situations. They also tend to have intense reactions when confronted with something unfamiliar. Finally, there are the *slow-to-warm-up* children. They tend to have a generally low level of activity, a mild temperament, and moderate reactions to new situations and experiences. They tend to withdraw from the unfamiliar, at least initially, and are slow to make changes in themselves.

As with most things in life, many children do not fit neatly into one category of temperament or another. There are many children who show a combination of difficult and easy characteristics, yet still fall clearly within the realm of what is considered normal (Thomas and Chess, 1984). For instance, a child may have an extremely irregular sleeping schedule, yet reach out and adapt quickly to new, unfamiliar people. Likewise, a child may be cheerful and easygoing most of the time, but horribly stubborn and difficult to live with on some occasions such as visiting relatives. The research points to some general tendencies. However, each infant, child, and adult is a unique person.

What specifically causes the differences in temperament isn't known. It may be prenatal chemical influences or genetic inheritance. There does appear to be some biological basis. For instance, the amount of the enzyme monoamine oxidase (MAO) apparent in children is related to their levels of activity and irritability (Sostek and Wyatt, 1981). It's also been determined that the manner in which parents treat children cannot drastically or totally change the children's temperament (Thomas and Chess, 1984). Perhaps a more adequate perspective concerning temperament is that each of us is born with a general predisposition to having a certain type of temperament. Then as life proceeds, we react to various situations and make changes in how we display or manifest our temperament.

There are some findings regarding how temperament, as determined in infancy, can affect later adjustment. The study of long-term effects in the NYLS research showed that children categorized as "difficult" in infancy were more likely to have emotional or behavioral problems later which necessitated psychiatric intervention. On the other hand, the study showed that even non-difficult children (that is, children categorized as "easy" or "slow-to-warm-up") could develop problems when functioning under extremely stressful conditions.

A major variable related to overall adjustment may be the "goodness" or "poorness" of fit between the individual and the impinging social environment (Thomas and Chess, 1984). To a great extent, this is related to expectations. For instance, take parents who expect to have a dynamic, motivated child who is eager for new experiences. If they discover that what they have is a mild-mannered, hesitant, slow-to-warm-up child, they may be very disappointed. They may even place inordinate pressure on the child to be very different than the child naturally is. On the other hand, take parents who sustain a family climate where moods are intense, daily routines are irregular, and changes are assimilated slowly. A difficult child's fit in such a family may be good. The family may not view the child as difficult at all, but rather as normal.

This material on temperament can have practical applications. It's important for parents to recognize the fact that their child does have a temperament of his or her own which may be very different from their own temperaments. Then they can consciously make adjustments in their own behavior and expectations to help that child along. For instance, a slow-to-warm-up child can be given more time to adjust to new situations. And parents of a difficult child who has trouble organizing the day in a predictable manner can help by providing structure. They can help the child learn how to formulate plans and carry them out.

Handling Emotions

Emotional aspects contribute to a person's perspective of any particular situation. Psychological aspects including emotions impact an individual at any point in time. As a result of this and many other considerations, the individual will opt to behave in a certain way. Many times it is helpful for an individual to understand and be able to exert some control over his emotions. Such control may help to make more beneficial alternatives available to the individual.

Self-Concept and Self-Esteem

All individuals form impressions about who they think they are. It's almost as if each person develops a unique theory regarding who exactly she feels she is. This personal impression is referred to as the self-concept. The idea of self-concept was introduced earlier in a discussion of Carl Rogers' self-theory. A related idea is that of self-esteem. Self-esteem refers to a person's judgment of her own value. Although self-concept may include more aspects about the self than just value, many times the two terms are used interchangeably.

Self-concept is an important theme throughout mental health literature. Improving one's self-concept is often seen as a therapeutic goal for people with adjustment problems. One's self-concept is important throughout life. In order to continue working, living, striving, and positively interacting with others, one must have a positive self-concept. In other words, one must feel good enough about oneself to continue living and being productive. This is just as true for children as it is for adults.

The self-concept is an abstract idea. It is difficult to explain exactly what it involves. However, it is still an important factor in a person's ability to function. People of virtually any age need to feel good about themselves in order to be confident and enjoy life's experiences.

Theoreticians have emphasized the social significance of the self-concept and have labelled it "the meeting ground of the individual and society" (Markus and Nurius, 1984, p. 147). Middle childhood is the period when children are confronted with social expectations and demands. They become aware of the importance of the social setting and begin evaluating how they fit in.

Markus and Nurius (1984) propose that there are four developmental tasks which children must undertake for adequate development of their self-concepts. First, they must begin to empathize with others. They need to think about how other people expect them to act. They learn what various roles involve. For instance, as a student they are supposed to attend school, study, learn, and cooperate with teachers. As a friend, they're supposed to listen to their peers, talk to them, play with them, and probably be loyal to them.

Teammates of a gymnastics contest winner give her an empathic hug.

The second task children must accomplish is to learn about the complex intricacies and even inconsistencies all around them in society. These include "relationships, roles, and rules" (Papalia and Olds, 1989, p. 302). Children need to figure out that both their cousins and they have the same grandparents even though they live in different families. They also need to learn how people react differently in different social situations. For example, take Dad who comes home on a Friday night two hours after he was supposed to. Mom expected him earlier because it was their night to go out to eat. It's clear he's had more than a few beers "with the guys." Even though he and Mom usually get along well and laugh with and talk to each other, a child needs to learn that under these circumstances, Mom gets mad. When Mom is mad, she raises her voice and throws coffee cups to get her point across, and it's a good time to stay in your room.

The third task in the development of self-concept is for a child to develop certain expectations for his or her own behavior. Children must decide for them-

selves what is right and what is wrong. This is often especially difficult because children are pressured by both the standards of their peers and the standards of their parents. Often these two sets of standards are very different.

Finally, accepting responsibility for their own behavior is the fourth task involved in developing a self-concept. They must come to a resolution of what freedom of choice they have within general social expectations. They need to develop confidence in themselves so that they can choose alternatives and control their own actions. Finally, they must figure out the most effective approaches to managing their own behavior.

Another way of looking at the self-concept is to determine what characteristics a person needs to provide a sound foundation for a positive self-concept. Coopersmith (1967, 1968) interviewed eighty-five boys aged ten to twelve and their mothers in addition to administering personality and ability tests to the boys. He concluded that self-concept is founded on

The Effects of Positive and Negative Self-Concepts

Two five-year-old girls, one with a good self-concept and the other with a relatively poor self-concept illustrate the enormous effects of one's self-concept. Julie, who has a positive perception of self, is fairly confident in new situations. When she enters kindergarten, she assertively introduces herself to her peers and eagerly makes new friends. She frequently becomes a leader in their games. She often volunteers to answer her teacher's questions. Her teacher considers her happy and well adjusted.

In contrast, Mary has a relatively poor self-concept. She does not think very highly of herself or her abilities. On her first day of kindergarten, she usually stays by herself or lingers on the fringes of activities. She speaks little to others out of fear that they might criticize her. She really wants to be liked but is worried that there is nothing to like about her. Thus, it is easier for her to remain quiet and unobtrusive. For example, one day the teacher brings out pieces of colored clay for the children to play with. Being so quiet and afraid, Mary does not rush up to her teacher to get hers even though playing with clay is one of her favorite pastimes. Rather, she waits until everyone else has their clay and is returning to their seats.

By the time Mary is close to the teacher, all the clay has been handed out. Instead of clay her teacher gives her a coloring book and some crayons. Mary takes them passively and begins to color a big yellow duck. All the while she is crying silently to herself. She is very disappointed that she did not get any clay. She also is hoping no one will notice that she is different from everyone else. Mary has a poor self-concept. She is afraid of others and what they might think. She does not have much self-esteem.

four variables. The first is significance. This refers to how people feel others around them think of them and feel they are important. The second variable is competence, or their perceived ability to perform tasks which they feel are valuable. Virtue is the third variable. This involves abiding by and maintaining moral standards. The final variable is power, or the extent they feel they have power over or can influence both their own lives and the lives of others. The higher an individual scored on all of these variables, the higher was his level of self-esteem.

Furthermore, it was found that a cluster of terms tended to characterize boys with low self-esteem and those with high levels of self-esteem. Children with high self-esteem might be described as successful, active, self-confident, and optimistic. Those with low self-esteem, on the other hand, might best be described by terms such as depressed, isolated, discouraged, and fearful. In other words, children with higher levels of self-esteem exhibit traits that are valued by others and, in essence, are more competent.

A few other interesting findings involved the parents of these boys (Coopersmith, 1967, 1968). Boys with higher levels of self-esteem tended to have parents who loved and accepted them, although these parents also had higher expectations concerning school work and good behavior. These parents also tended to encourage independence in terms of expressing the boys' own thoughts. The emphasis in these homes was on rewarding good behavior rather than on using excessive punishment for behavioral control. Finally, the parents themselves tended to have higher levels of self-esteem.

Gelfand (1962) hypothesized that self-esteem is based on the number of successes and failures an individual has been exposed to during past experiences. She found that such a relationship did indeed exist. The self-esteem of people experiencing success increased while the self-esteem of those exposed to failure decreased.

This proud master builder projects a positive self-concept.

In summary, the evidence appears to bear out the importance of self-esteem as it relates to self-concept. Perhaps a high level of self-esteem provides a person not only with confidence, but also with emotional strength. Perhaps such strength is needed to reach out to others and gain social acceptance. Such strength might also contribute to an individual's ability to take risks, succeed, and achieve.

Self-Concepts of Minority Children

Conflicting evidence is found concerning the self-concepts of minority children, especially African American children. Some studies indicate that African American children tend to have poor self-concepts; others suggest that they have positive self-concepts.

Much of the evidence supporting the idea that African American children have poorer self-concepts than their white counterparts originated from the mid-thirties to the early sixties (Jenkins, 1982, p. 24). One of the methods most frequently used to measure self-concept was the evaluation of a minority child's doll preference. African American children aged three to seven years typically were shown a series of pairs of dolls, one dark skinned and one white. The children were then asked various questions designed to gain insight into their racial awareness, especially as it related to their self-concepts. The children's comments and their apparent preference for the white dolls seemed to indicate that African American children tended to have negative self-concepts as they related to race (Clark and Clark, 1952). Consequent studies with refined methodology appeared to draw similar conclusions (Jenkins, 1982, p. 24). Additionally, both African American and white children have been found to have a preference for the color white over black (Morland, 1966; McAdoo, 1977).

Other research indicates that African American children have high self-esteem (Bachman, 1970; Baughman, 1971; Taylor, 1976; McAdoo, 1985). Also the self-esteem of African American children seems to be increasing. This research interprets children's figure drawings and indicates that African American children's drawings of people are becoming much more likely to represent African American as opposed to white people (Fish and Larr, 1972; McAdoo, 1977).

Several explanations can be given for this discrepancy. Methodological problems and lack of sophistication may have been involved in some of the earlier studies finding negative self-concepts. The logic used to draw conclusions in studies finding African American children to have negative self-concepts may also be invalid. For example, perhaps a child's choice of a lighter color may have had nothing to do with the child's sense of self. Perhaps the preference only concerned a doll or a color. Children may have been trained to prefer lighter colors over darker through books and the media. For instance, the availability of real dolls having a darker skin color for children to play with is a relatively recent occurrence. Perhaps the children were not accustomed to seeing or playing with darker colored dolls. Finally, the complicated matter of self-concept and all that is involved might be much too complex to measure by using such simple techniques.

Two other aspects concerning minority children and self-concept merit attention. First, teachers and social workers who work with children need to be aware of their own ethnocentric perspectives when addressing the idea of self-concept. Children with other cultural backgrounds may manifest their self-confidence and self-concepts in different ways. Wise and Miller (1983, p. 350) provide a relevant illustration of an Ottawa Native American girl attending an urban public school "who was referred for psychological testing and counseling because her teacher felt that she had a poor self-concept and her school work was suffering because of it." On further investigation it was determined that the teacher had made the referral because of the little girl's apparent shyness and lack of eye contact. The teacher, who had had little contact with Native American children, did not know that for many Native American subcultures, looking an adult straight in the eye for any period of time implies disrespect and is inappropriate. The little girl was only displaying the good manners and behavior which she had been taught were appropriate.

The other aspect concerning minority children and self-concept which is worthy of mention involves some suggestions for reducing racial prejudice. The idea is that if prejudice is reduced, then differences in self-concept which are based on race may no longer be an issue. After testing them on groups of second- to fifth-grade children, Katz and Zalk (1978) suggest the following four techniques to combat racial prejudice. First, positive racial contacts should be increased. In the research this was done by having both African American and white children work together on teams whose task was to complete a puzzle. All of the children were then praised for their accomplishments. The intent was to reinforce and encourage both African American and white children to work together. Second, vicarious racial contact should be stressed. This means that both races should be talked about within similar positive contexts. In this research, children were told a story about an African American child who had many positive qualities. Here the intent was to help children think about a minority person in a positive light and yet in a way that children can understand. Third, the color black itself should be reinforced. During the study children were rewarded for choosing a picture of a black animal over a white one. Fourth, perceptual differentiation should be encouraged. In other words, children can be taught to differentiate people of the same race by looking at various personal characteristics. Here children were shown slides of an African American woman whose appearance was made to vary by wearing glasses or different hairdos and by changing her facial expression. Children were encouraged to discriminate between the different slides by remembering the name respectively assigned to each.

Various positive findings were gained from this research (Katz and Zalk, 1978). Groups exposed to the techniques showed less prejudice than groups who had not been exposed. A post-test one-half year later indicated that some of the gains had been maintained even over an extended period of time. One other interesting finding was that younger children were more likely to respond to the techniques and reveal less prejudice. In summary, it appears that providing some basic information about a minority group so that the unknown and strangeness is reduced can potentially have a significant effect on reducing prejudice.

Significant Issues and Life Events

Several issues and life events which can impact children have been chosen for discussion. Their selection is based on the importance of the effects they have on children and on the probability that social workers

will encounter these issues in practice. The issues include intelligence testing along with its potential problems and cultural biases, mental retardation, and learning disabilities with a focus on both types and treatment.

Intelligence and Intelligence Testing

Intelligence may be defined as the ability to understand, to learn, and to deal with new, unknown situations. Beyond this general definition, little is known about the origins of intelligence despite many attempts to refine and clarify the definition. These attempts have ranged from primitive measurement of head size, referred to as *phrenology*, to the listing of specific mental abilities supposed to be involved in intelligence. For instance, Thurstone (1938) suggested that seven independent abilities contributed to the general level of a person's intelligence. These abilities included the ability to perceive spatial relationships, perceptual speed, memory, word fluency, reasoning, numerical ability, and verbal ability. Bouchard (1968) suggested an even more complex framework for defining intelligence. Instead of a list of mental abilities, he proposed conceptualizing intelligence in terms of how people think. This involves the systematic process aspects of thinking instead of the specific mental abilities or the contents of thinking.

Cattell's Fluid and Crystallized Intelligence

Cattell (1971) identifies two different types of intelligence, fluid and crystallized. Fluid intelligence involves "the processes of perceiving relationships, forming concepts, reasoning, and abstracting" (Papalia and Olds, 1989, p. 425). This type of intelligence is innate and, therefore, theoretically not subject to change over the life span. Such native aspects of intelligence include the ability to perform abstract computations and memory capabilities. Crystallized intelligence, on the other hand, involves "a grouping of intellectual abilities that are primarily verbal and that are highly influenced by culture, experience, and education" (Lefrancois, 1990, p. 351). For instance, a person can learn a language or increase vocabulary. And a person can acquire new information and benefit from what has been learned through experience.

It would logically follow then that while fluid intel-

According to Sternberg, experimentation is "the insightful dimension of intelligence" involved in a person's actual doing of a task.

ligence would remain relatively constant throughout the lifespan, crystallized intelligence has the potential to increase. Research has established that crystallized intelligence does indeed increase as people grow older and gain experience; on the other hand, there is a tendency for fluid intelligence to show some signs of decline as people age (Horn, 1976; Horn and Donaldson, 1980). More longitudinal research is needed, however, to support these findings.

Sternberg's Triarchic Theory of Intelligence

Sternberg (1984, 1985, 1986, 1987) has proposed a triarchic theory of human intelligence which emphasizes the context in which behavior occurs. He proposes that there are three major components involved in intelligence. These components are integrally related to a person's adaptive behavior, that is, what is relevant in the individual person's environment. For example, Bill Klumpe's business was putting in septic tanks around small towns and rural farmlands in southeastern Wisconsin. Septic tanks were necessary because public sewers were unavailable throughout the area. Bill's reading skills were so poor that he had barely passed the written test to get his driver's license.

The advent of calculators was a blessing to him because he was not adept at adding and subtracting numbers when figuring out what his customers owed him. Bill, however, was the best septic tank installer people around the area had ever seen. He had learned the business as a teenager and now, in his fifties, he knew just about everything about septic tanks. He could look at a piece of schedule 40 PVC piping and know immediately if it was the right size for the proper drainage capacity. His gaskets were perfect and his pipe couplings never leaked. His "buddies" down at the bowling alley tavern sometimes would tease him, "You don't have a brain in your head, but you sure can dig!" Sternberg would say that what Bill had was intelligence. He had the capability to use his mind extremely well in those areas which were most significant to him.

Thus, Sternberg's model emphasizes the relevance of what people think about. The three specific components of intelligence are the componential, experiential, and contextual elements. The componential element involves how people think about, process, and analyze information to solve problems and evaluate their results. People who have high levels of componential intelligence also score highly on intelligence tests and are good at debate and formulating arguments.

The second component of intelligence, according to Sternberg, is the experiential element. This involves a person's actual doing of a task. It is "the *insightful* dimension of intelligence, which allows people to compare new information with what they already know or to come up with new ways of putting facts together—as Einstein did when he developed his theory of relativity" (Papalia and Olds, 1989, p. 428). Part of this has to do with being able to master some tasks or portions of tasks so that they become almost automatic. The mind then can devote greater attention to solving new parts of a problem or to working on new and better ways of accomplishing a task.

For example, Ruth, a medical transcriber at a large suburban hospital, types all the technical medical reports that physicians dictate on tape so that the information becomes part of each patient's permanent medical record. Over her many years of experience, she has identified a large body of technical medical words that are used over and over again. In order to save time and make herself more efficient, she has developed a coding system where symbols or abbreviations are used to represent long technical words and encoded these into her word processing equipment. For instance, when she types the letters *cd*, the word processor interprets the letters to mean *cethalospelvic disproportion*, which the processor automatically prints. This system allows Ruth to concentrate more closely on the new, unknown, or most difficult terminology in addition to significantly increasing her efficiency. Ruth is furious because the hospital, for some bureaucratic reason, is planning to change the word processing equipment to a system that cannot accommodate her abbreviations and symbols. However, that's another story.

Sternberg's third component of intelligence is the contextual element. This involves the practical aspect of how people actually adapt to their environment. Within an individual's personal situation, it involves what knowledge is learned and how that knowledge can best be put to use in a practical sense.

To illustrate these three components, take three undergraduate social work students, Jackie, Danielle, and Sara. Jackie had gotten almost straight A's in high school, getting B's only in physical education, art concepts, and advanced calculus. In college she was a "whiz" at taking both multiple choice and true-or-false exams. However, she did not do nearly as well on essay exams, especially when they involved applications to problem situations in practice (for example, how a social worker would intervene in a family where alcohol abuse was involved). She also had a terrible time when she entered her first social work practice course where she had to learn and apply interviewing skills in role plays. Eventually, she switched her major to sociology. She felt she could best apply her interest in working with people if she went on to graduate school in sociology and eventually did social research.

Danielle, on the other hand, did extremely well on essay exams but not as well on the objective multiple choice and true-or-false tests. She got A's in her social work practice courses which involved articulating how she would help people solve problems in the field. Her instructors praised her for her creativity and ideas. When she got into her field internship, she performed relatively well. She was able to apply her knowledge and skills to practice situations. She had some difficulty, however, working with clients who

came from socioeconomic and ethnic backgrounds radically different than hers. Her final grade in field was an A −.

Sara just barely got her college application accepted. She was in the lowest 25 percent of her high school graduating class, which meant she had to begin college on probation. She barely squeaked by each semester with the minimal cumulative gradepoint necessary. She also managed to attain the required gradepoint necessary to get into her advanced social work courses and continue on in the major. However, when she finally got into her field placement, her social work supervisor raved about what an excellent student she was. Sara was able to take on difficult cases early on in the semester and required relatively little supervision. Sara's personal manner was such that she established relationships quickly with clients. She was able to make clear applications of the practice skills she had learned in her courses. It almost seemed like working with people as a social worker came naturally to her. She seemed to have a natural sense of what to do in situations which were completely foreign to her. She received an A in field work which contrasted with her C+ cumulative grade. The agency later enthusiastically hired her.

Each of these three individuals is strong in one component in Sternberg's model of intelligence. Jackie was strong in the componential aspect of intelligence. She could conceptualize extremely well at abstract levels and clearly remember facts and details. Danielle's strength lay in the experiential component of intelligence. She was creative and insightful. She could take recommendations for what to do in a specific situation and clearly apply them. Sara excelled in the contextual aspect of intelligence. She could adapt virtually to any situation and solve problems in a very practical sense.

In real life, people can be strong in any or all of these components. They have an intellectual mixture of strengths and weaknesses.

Intelligence Testing

We have established that there is no absolute, clear, specific definition of intelligence. It is at this point that it's important to distinguish between intelligence and the intelligence quotient, commonly referred to as IQ. Many might mistakenly assume that an IQ represents the absolute quantity of intelligence that a person possesses. This is not true. An IQ really stands for how well an individual might perform on a specific intelligence test in relation to how well others perform on the same test. The IQ then involves two basic facets. One is the score that a person attains on a certain type of test. The second is the person's relative standing within the peer group.

An IQ score is the best thing available to attempt measuring whatever intelligence is. Such a statement may not inspire confidence in the value of one's IQ. However, perhaps it should elicit caution. IQ scores can be used to determine grade school placement, admission to special programs, and encouragement or lack thereof to attend college. A person who is aware of having a low IQ score may establish lower expectations. These lower expectations may act as a barrier to what actually could be achieved. She might become the victim of a self-fulfilling prophecy, that is, what she expects is what she gets.

This could have been the case, for example, for a returning student who was the mother of three children. She was also receiving social insurance benefits because of a permanent disability. Her vocational counselor had told her that her IQ was not nearly high enough for success in college. He suggested that she stay home and enjoy her moderate financial benefits. Although his statements discouraged her, she had the courage and stamina to enroll with a full course load at a well-respected state university. Her final grade report after her first semester indicated that she had achieved a perfect 4.0 average on a 4.0 scale. She immediately returned to her vocational counselor and requested financial assistance for a microcomputer to assist her in her course work. He responded by mumbling in an embarrassed manner that that might be a good idea.

Intelligence testing is done in both group and individual formats. Many school systems use group testing because it is less time-consuming and cheaper. Individual tests, however, tend to be more precise and useful in targeting specific areas of need. A commonly used group test, the Otis-Lennon Mental Ability Test, is described here. Frequently used individual tests including the Stanford-Binet Test and the Wechsler Intelligence Scale are described.

The Otis-Lennon Mental Ability Test. Children attending kindergarten through high school can be

tested by the Otis-Lennon Mental Ability Test, originally developed in 1967. It's usually administered in small groups of ten to fifteen children. It assesses children by asking them "to classify items, to show an understanding of verbal and numerical concepts, to display general information, and to follow directions" (Papalia and Olds, 1992, p. 258). Another more recent test produced by Lorne-Thorndike Tests is the Otis-Lennon School Ability Test, created in 1979.

The Stanford-Binet IQ Test. One of the most common intelligence tests is the Stanford-Binet (Terman, 1960). First used in 1905, it has continued to be tested and refined. The value of measuring intelligence is in its usefulness in predicting success in various situations. Schools frequently use the Stanford-Binet to determine program and grade placement and potential academic success.

Actually, there are over one hundred different specific kinds of tests that are part of the Stanford-Binet. They are geared to assessing a wide variety of abilities. Tests are available for adults, school-aged children, and children as young as two years old.

Scores on the Stanford-Binet can be obtained in four areas which include short-term memory, quantitative reasoning, verbal reasoning, and abstract/visual reasoning. Additionally, a composite score can be obtained which reflects the individual's IQ. The average IQ is about 100; a little more than two-thirds of all people score between 85 and 115.

Perhaps one of the most beneficial uses of IQ tests is in the targeting of potential special needs for special help. For example, the following scale has been established for describing people having normal or above intellectual ability (Morris, 1979, p. 264).

IQ	Description
Above 140	Genius
120–140	Very superior
110–120	Superior
90–110	Average, normal

Morris (1979) explains that those people who score in the 90s may be able to complete eighth grade, those scoring between 100 and 109 can finish high school, and those having an IQ of 115 or above can be expected to succeed in college. People who score within any of these ranges should be able to function well in the community if there are no additional emotional or behavioral problems.

In the past the Stanford-Binet has been criticized because of its heavy emphasis on verbal ability. Children whose verbal ability is not strong for some reason may not have had their actual intellectual ability adequately reflected. However, a new edition was published in 1985 with the intent of diminishing that bias and others.

Changes in the new edition include focusing less on verbal ability in that "there is an equal balance of verbal, nonverbal, quantitative, and memory items;" additionally, the new Stanford-Binet "assesses patterns and levels of cognitive development instead of providing the IQ as a single overall measure of intelligence" (Papalia and Olds, 1992, p. 197). The test is also designed to be more evenly responsive to a broad range of groups differing significantly in geographic location, ethnicity, and gender. Additional newly designed norms take into account socioeconomic level and the existence of handicapping conditions.

The Wechsler Tests. Several variations for the Wechsler Tests are appropriate for persons aged four to six-and-a-half, five to fifteen, and sixteen to seventy-five. In many ways the Wechsler Tests are similar to the Stanford-Binet. For instance, composite scores are available. However, an important difference is that the Wechsler provides separate sub-composite scores for both verbal and performance abilities. This makes it easier to pinpoint specific deficits and potential problems. For example, if a child performs significantly better on the performance than the verbal segments, this may provide a clue that a learning disability or some other perceptual deficit is present.

Cultural Biases and IQ Tests

It is critical to be vigilant concerning the potential for cultural biases in IQ tests. White middle- and upper-class children historically have had an unfair advantage on these tests. Biases can involve the use of words, concepts, and contexts that are more familiar to white children than minority children (Sinclair, 1983). Even the context in which children take the test can affect results. Factors within the testing context that can affect scores include the tester's attitudes, the actual words used, and how comfortable the children feel in the testing situation.

Much more attention has been paid to cultural fairness in recent years. However, since a totally "culture-free" IQ test (that is, "one with no culture-linked content" at all) is impossible to achieve, it is important to remain sensitive to fairness and strive to make tests as "culture-fair" as possible (Papalia and Olds, 1992, p. 261).

Mentally Retarded People: A Population-at-Risk

Mental retardation is "significantly subaverage general intellectual functioning existing concurrently with deficits in adaptive behavior and manifested during the developmental period" (Grossman, 1975, p. 11). Individuals are mentally retarded to one degree or another when they are unable intellectually to grasp concepts and function as well and as quickly as their peers.

There are three major parts in this definition. First, a person must score below the average in "general intellectual functioning." IQ tests can be used to make this determination. Second, a person must have "deficits in adaptive functioning." In other words, the person is unable to function well enough to be totally independent, responsible enough to take care of his or her physical needs, and/or socially responsible for his or her own behavior and interaction with others. The third important part of the definition is that retardation must manifest itself during the "developmental period," that is, between birth and age eighteen.

It's difficult to cite the exact number of retarded people. However, if scores fall in a normal distribution, it follows that two to three percent of the total population are retarded (Scheiner and McNabb, 1980). If those who function fairly well concerning their adaptive behavior are removed from this group, only one percent of the total population are retarded (Mercer, 1973). It is important to remember, however, that most of these people, approximately 75 percent, are only mildly retarded (Lefrancois, 1990, p. 357).

It appears that retarded children learn like other children learn, that is, they go through the same developmental processes; however, they learn more slowly than other children (Haywood, et al., 1982).

Multicultural IQ Test

The following questions are designed to test your multicultural IQ. Answer them to the best of your ability.

I. African American Cultural Differences Test
Define the following terms:
1. Pretend you are clean
2. Pretend you are a down person
3. Define "The Man"
4. Describe going to the crib
5. Describe yourself getting off
6. Play the dozens
7. Show your kicks
8. Feel someone's blowout
9. Pretend you are flooding
10. Define flunkying

The remaining questions are all multiple guess. Answer them to the best of your ability.

II. Chicano Cultural Differences Test
1. The treaty of Guadalupe Hildago ceded to the United States what is now known as:
   a. the state of Texas
   b. the state of New Mexico
   c. the state of California
   d. the southwestern United States
2. Cinco de Mayo is a Mexican holiday which commemorates:
   a. Mexico's independence from France
   b. the battle of Puebla
   c. the death of the Frito Bandito
   d. the decline of the Diaz regime
3. A frajo is a:
   a. short handled hoe
   b. a car
   c. a cigarette
   d. pachuco
4. A curandera is a:
   a. healer
   b. witch
   c. curious person
5. The 12th of December is:
   a. Cesar Chavez's Birthday
   b. The day of the Virgin of Guadalupe
   c. The anniversary of "pachuco" riots

6. To Chicanos their term Carnal means:
   a. brother
   b. butcher
   c. sports car
   d. enemy
7. A tio taco is a:
   a. Mexican dish
   b. individual who rejects his culture
   c. Cuban
   d. an uncle from Spain
8. The most valued institution in Chicano culture is:
   a. the educational institution
   b. the religious institution
   c. the political institution
   d. the family

III. Native American Cultural Differences Test
1. Which of the following is not an Indian invention?
   _____ Canoe
   _____ Kayak
   _____ Parka
   _____ Tomahawk
2. The Words "Kemo Sabe," popularized by the Lone Ranger's sidekick Tonto, means:
   _____ White Friend
   _____ Blue Eyes
   _____ Honky
   _____ Nothing at all
3. The phrase "The only good Indian is a dead Indian" is attributed to:
   _____ Gen. Philip Sheridan
   _____ Gen. Wm. T. Sherman
   _____ Col. Henry B. Carrington
   _____ Lt. Col. Geo. A. Custer
4. Which of the following was not a member of the League of Six Nations (Iroquois Confederacy)?
   _____ Oneida
   _____ Seneca
   _____ Kiowa
   _____ Onondaga
5. Which of the following major colleges was first instituted primarily to educate Indians?
   _____ Yale
   _____ Harvard
   _____ Dartmouth
   _____ Princeton

IV. Asian Cultural Differences Test
1. Buddha-Dharma is _____
   a. the teachings of Judo
   b. the practice of Oriental cooking
   c. the teaching of the Buddha
   d. the wife of the Buddha
2. The art of bonsai refers to _____
   a. Japanese silk screening
   b. Chinese wrestling
   c. the growing of trees to exact replicas of large trees which grow in the forest
   d. none of the above
3. The Koto is _____
   a. a Korean word for house
   b. a 13 string instrument used in Japan for many years
   c. the newest Oriental dance to hit the west coast
   d. the Vietnamese national anthem
4. This word sometimes means a japanese ghetto _____
   a. Nihon machi
   b. Sakana
   c. Kanji
   d. ghettuloheli
5. Third generation Japanese are called _____
   a. Issei
   b. Nisei
   c. Yonsei
   d. Sansei

Here are the answers to the multicultural IQ test. How well did you do? The test is designed to help you empathize with what it's like for people with different racial, cultural, or ethnic backgrounds to answer questions they don't understand. Traditional IQ tests have had cultural biases. Many minorities have tended not to do well on these tests because they don't understand what the words mean or what they mean in a certain context.

Answers to the African American Cultural Differences Test
1. Dressed real nice. Your Sunday "best."
2. A person that's cool and has his/her act together
3. Usually a white male in a position of authority, (ie, cop, boss, etc.)
4. Going home or to the apartment
5. Deeply into your music, dance or whatever turns you on (jamming)

6. Verbal word game that includes talking about someone's mother in a negative sexual way. The dozens often use phrases that rhyme.
7. Show your shoes
8. Feel someone's Afro hair style
9. Your pants legs are too short, exposing your socks
10. Working

Answers to Chicano Cultural Differences Test
1. *d.* The treaty of Guadalupe Hildago was signed by the United States and Mexico in 1848. With this treaty, Mexico accepted the Rio Grande as the Texas border and ceded the Southwest (which incorporates the present day states of Arizona, California, New Mexico, Utah, Nevada, and parts of Colorado) to the U.S. in return for $15 million.
2. *b.* This celebration is in reference to a battle in which a small Mexican army defeated a French army battalion. Cinco de Mayo celebrations are still commemorated in Mexico and all over the United States where there are a significant number of Chicanos.
3. *c.* The term frajo is a slang word for cigarette which is commonly used in the barrio.
4. *a.* The curandera is a person who is able to relieve people of their physical sickness. Many elderly Chicano people do not believe in the "doctor" as they are known in this country. They prefer to be attended by the curandera or healer.
5. *b.* Chicanos are a very religious people. The 12th of December is the day of the most patron saint of the Chicano people—the day of the Virgin of Guadalupe.
6. *a.* Carnal simply means brother. It is usually used as a greeting between males.
7. *b.* Many individuals reject their culture due to the educational system in this country. Chicanos have been taught that their culture is inferior and that the Anglo American culture is superior. Therefore, many Mexican Americans (especially second and third generations) cannot identify with their cultural heritage and the term Chicano.
8. *d.* Chicano families are traditionally very, very close. The total Chicano existence revolves around the family.

(continued next page)

Multicultural IQ Test (continued)

Answers to the Native American Cultural Differences Test

1. The tomahawk was a French invention later copied and used extensively by Indians.
2. No one knows where this phrase comes from; there are no known languages that this can be traced to—another Hollywood gimmick.
3. Gen. Sheridan's direct quote: "The only good Indians I ever saw were dead." The phrase was later simplified for laymen's use.
4. The Six Nations were composed of: Oneida, Seneca, Tuscorora, Onondaga, Cayuga, and Mohawk.
5. Dartmouth

Answers to Asian Cultural Differences Test

1. c
2. c
3. b
4. a
5. d

SOURCE: Charles A. Taylor, ed., *Handbook of Minority Student Services* (Madison, WI: Praxis Publications, 1986). Used with permission of Praxis Publications.

They probably will take longer to understand ideas and concepts. The two primary areas where mentally retarded people differ from people who have "normal" levels of intelligence are in "memory and attention span" (Lefrancois, 1987, p. 325). It's been found that they have trouble paying attention to ongoing activities and events as carefully as other people do (Mercer and Snell, 1977). They also tend to be weaker in their ability to remember things recently told to them or experienced by them (Lefrancois, 1987, p. 325). However, once they learn something, their ability to remember on a long-term basis is very similar to that of other children (Robinson and Robinson, 1976). They will also probably have difficulty grasping more abstract or complicated concepts. The degree of these difficulties, of course, will depend on the level of retardation.

Adaptive behavior refers to a person's ability to adapt or adjust to the social and physical environment. It involves an individual's ability to establish and maintain a good person-in-environment fit. Mentally retarded individuals are often capable of high levels of such behavior. They frequently can care for themselves physically and maintain good hygiene. Many can hold a job and support themselves to some extent. Mentally retarded people can often interact positively and appropriately with others. They can communicate their feelings and opinions. They can form close relationships. In summary, a person's ability to "fit in" or adapt to her surroundings is more relevant and important than absolute intellectual ability.

IQ tests are used to identify the level of mental retardation. They provide one important means of determining appropriate expectations for how well a person will be able to function both academically and independently. The respective levels of expected functioning are determined by the following scores on the Stanford-Binet:

Borderline	68–83
Mild	52–67
Moderate	36–51
Severe	20–35
Profound	Less than 20

Those people scoring within the borderline range of intelligence should be capable of independent living within the community. Although they might not be able to attain high levels of academic achievement, nonetheless they should be able to live, work, have families, and function along with everyone else in their communities. With the help of special education classes, people with IQs in the 70s are able to master academic skills including reading and arithmetic to approximately a fourth- or fifth-grade level (Morris, 1979, p. 264). Frequently they are able to "blend in," that is, to present no noticeable difference between themselves and others. Labeling such people as borderline frequently is forgotten and irrelevant when these people reach adulthood.

People who are mildly mentally retarded are often able to live independently as adults except when they are under extreme stress. During those times they may have some difficulty rationally making decisions and identifying ways to cope with the stressful circumstances. People with IQs in the 60s might be expected to reach a third-grade level of academic performance,

People with a Developmental Disability: Populations-at-Risk

Mental retardation and learning disabilities are among a number of *developmental disabilities*. These are conditions that produce "functional impairment as a result of disease, genetic disorder, or impaired growth pattern before adulthood" (Barker, 1991, p. 61). People with developmental disabilities are at risk of being oppressed, discriminated against, ignored, ridiculed, and denied equal rights.

All developmental disabilities have five aspects in common (McDonald-Wikler, 1987, p. 422). First, they all result from some specific mental and/or physical problem. Second, they appear before age twenty-two. Third, the conditions are permanent. Fourth, they result in "substantial functional limitations" that occur in at least three areas of daily life (such as the ability to communicate with others, take care of oneself on a daily basis, or live independently). Finally, developmental disabilities demonstrate the need for lifelong supplementary help and services.

Mental retardation and learning disabilities are discussed in this chapter. The remaining disabilities, which include autism, cerebral palsy, orthopedic problems, hearing problems, and epilepsy, are described here:

Autism is a condition characterized by intense inner directedness. Autistic persons pay little or no attention to what occurs in the world outside themselves. Their behavior is often bizarre. Problems include: inability to participate in normal communication with other people; indulgence in repetitive, self-stimulating movements of extremities; severe sensory distortions (such as feeling pain when being slightly touched); and lack of normal emotional reactions to others, including attachment.

Cerebral Palsy is a disability involving problems in muscular control and coordination resulting from damage to the brain's muscle control centers before or during birth. Muscle movements become very stiff and difficult, jerky, or unbalanced. Depending on the extent of damage, "lack of balance, tremors, spasms, seizures, difficulty in walking, poor speech, poor control of face muscles, problems in seeing and hearing, and mental retardation" can result (McDonald-Wikler, 1987, p. 424).

Orthopedic problems are "physical conditions that interfere with the functioning of the bones, muscles, or joints" (McDonald-Wikler, 1987, p. 424). To be classed as developmental disabilities, they must be present from birth and affect at least three areas of basic life functioning. Examples include congenital malformations of the spine, bone deformities, and missing extremities such as arms or toes.

A girl with cerebral palsy joins in the fun of a Halloween party.

Hearing problems range from mild hearing losses to total deafness. They are considered developmental disabilities because of their impact on speech development and the ability to communicate.

Epilepsy (commonly referred to as *seizure disorders*) is "a disorder characterized by recurrent, involuntary episodes of altered states of consciousness, frequently but not always accompanied by convulsive body movements" (Barker, 1991, p. 75). Symptoms range from periods of unconsciousness resembling daydreaming to violent convulsions.

Concurrent disabilities are also common. For example, a mentally retarded person can also have a hearing impairment and a malformed spine. One study indicated that about 73 percent of people with a developmental disability have one disability, 23 percent two disabilities, 4 percent three, and 1 percent four (Jacobsen and Janicki, 1984).

and those in the 50s, a second-grade level (Morris, 1979, p. 264). The term which has been used to describe people who are capable of learning some basic academic skills is educable.

Moderately retarded people have more difficulty understanding the world around them and mastering academic skills. These people are typically capable of learning the self-help skills necessary in physically caring for themselves. They can learn to communicate with others. Often they can develop enough skills to function in a home setting, a sheltered workshop, or even in an unskilled or semiskilled job. Supervision and guidance is usually needed when under mildly stressful conditions. People who are intellectually capable of learning to take care of many of their daily self-care activities, but are unable to master academic skills, at times have been described as trainable.

People with severe mental retardation may be able to learn some basic skills in caring for themselves. However, they require fairly extensive supervision. Profoundly retarded people are unable to take care of themselves. They will always require almost complete supervision and attention.

The terms used to describe people are very important. In the past negative terms such as *feeble-minded*, *moron*, *imbecile*, and *idiot* have been used to describe mentally retarded people. These terms emphasize what retarded people cannot do and have the flavor of name calling. The newer terms such as *borderline* or *mild* are more positive in that they focus less on the negative aspects of retardation. The more recently adapted term, *developmental disability*, which encompasses mental retardation, is even less negative. Placing the emphasis on the ability a person does have is much more positive than stressing retardation.

Potential Problems with IQ Scores

Two potential problems with IQ scores have already been mentioned. One is that the actual nature of intelligence is unknown. At this point in time we are talking then about a vague and subjective term. The second problem is that placing an IQ label on someone may be harmful. An individual with a low IQ may place limits on himself which may become self-fulfilling prophecies. A person labeled with a high IQ may develop an inappropriately superior attitude.

Another potential problem with IQ scores is that they do not take into account motivation or desire to work and achieve. A person with a lower IQ who works hard and is motivated to achieve may in reality attain much higher levels of achievement and success than one with a higher IQ who is not motivated to use it. Simply having the ability does not necessarily mean that it will be put to any use. Little if any information is available on the relationship between IQ and adult job performance or adult adjustment (Morris, 1979, p. 265).

IQ tests also pose a potential difficulty concerning the arbitrary manner in which people are neatly categorized purely on the basis of intelligence. Many aspects of an individual's personality, ability to interact socially, and adapt to society are not directly related to IQ. For example, can a person with a borderline IQ of 80 successfully interact with a person having a normal IQ of 100? If not, then how can a person with a normal IQ of 100 successfully interact on an equal level with a person having a superior IQ of 120? The difference for each set of individuals is 20 IQ points. Can someone with an IQ of 100 successfully interact on an equal level with a genius having a 140 IQ? What are the implications for human interaction and human rights with a 40 IQ point difference, even though both people's IQs fall at least within the normal range? How then might a person having a 60 IQ interact with one having a 100 IQ? Here is another 40 point difference.

IQ is only one facet of an individual. People have other strengths and weaknesses unrelated to IQ. Mentally retarded people are like everybody else but have less intellectual potential. They have similar feelings, joys, and needs. And they have rights.

Macro System Responses to Mental Retardation

The programs available for retarded people depend on policies that dictate where public funds should and will be spent. Once again, we see how policy (such as federal and state law) affects social work practice. Policies provide the rules for how organizations can spend money and what services they can provide Social workers must do their jobs within the context of the organizations they work for.

Services for people who are mentally retarded or have some other developmental disability are paid for primarily by federal and state programs. Ninety-five percent of the federal money designated to help developmentally disabled people is administered through various programs under the U.S. Department of Health and Human Services. The rest is administered through the Department of Education.

Here we will address two issues involved in developing programs and providing services for mentally retarded people: deinstitutionalization and community-based services. The important thing to remember throughout our discussion is that intelligence, although an important variable in terms of daily living and ability, is only one of many factors affecting people's lives. Limited intelligence may limit some of the alternatives available to an individual. For example, a person with an IQ of 70 will probably not become a brain surgeon or a nuclear physicist. However, other alternatives are available to that person to construct a rich, satisfying, and fulfilling life. A basic task of the social worker might be to help that person identify alternatives and weigh the various positive and negative consequences of each.

Deinstitutionalization. Deinstitutionalization involves "the process of releasing patients, inmates, or people who are dependent for their physical and mental care from residential-custodial facilities, presumably with the understanding that they no longer need such care or can receive it through community-based services" (Barker, 1991, p. 58). People are moved out of institutional settings and relocated in typical community settings.

Deinstitutionalization is supported by a number of rationales (Segal, 1987). First, the oppression caused by institutional living has been extensively documented. Second, costs of institutionalizing people are high and continue to grow. Third, social research and its application continue to document how total institutionalization is frequently ineffective. Fourth, institutional values have increasingly emphasized the civil rights of all citizens, including the mentally retarded; institutionalization severely inhibits civil rights. Fifth, newer policies have been and are being developed to provide aid to people in ways other than placing them in large residential facilities.

Historically, most federal money has been spent on maintaining mentally retarded people in institutional settings. Worse, most of these institutions were actually intended for housing people who were mentally

This individual with a developmental disability holds his diploma from a special high school in Mission Viejo, California.

ill (Segal, 1987). Current legislation, however, supports deinstitutionalization and the development of alternative services.

Community-Based Services. The Accreditation Council for Services for the Mentally Retarded and other Developmentally Disabled Persons supports the philosophy of enhancing "the development and well-being of individuals with developmental disabilities while maximizing their achievement of self-determination and autonomy" (McDonald-Wikler, 1987, p. 430). Thus, if part of this thrust is to move mentally retarded people out of institutions, it follows that they need to be moved *somewhere* in the community.

A subsequent question involves where in the community. Places may include housing in "smaller community-based facilities, foster homes, board and care homes, and some large group homes" (Segal, 1987, p. 379). Such settings should be structured to maximize clients' autonomy. McDonald-Wikler (1987, p. 430) summarizes what many states have done to develop family support programs. She states that numerous state legislatures

> had either passed formal family support legislation or are plotting such programs in order to secure the maintenance of the developmentally disabled person in the family home, thereby avoiding the emotional and financial cost of placing the person in an alternative living environment. Support is typically provided through cash subsidies or vouchers given directly to the family for the purchase of individually relevant support services. Services commonly include respite care, transportation, and counseling.

An important concept related to community-based services is *normalization*. This means arranging the environmental context for mentally retarded people so that it is as "normal" as possible. Mentally retarded people's lives should be as similar to those of people in the "normal," overall population as they can be.

Social Work Roles

Social workers can perform many roles when working with mentally retarded and other developmentally disabled people. Social workers can function as *enablers*, helping mentally retarded people and their families make decisions and solve problems. Social workers can be *brokers*, linking clients to the resources (for example, transportation, job placements, or group homes) which they need in order to go about their daily lives. *Educator* is another major role. Mentally retarded people may need information about employment, interpersonal relationships, and even personal hygiene, if they have not received such information previously. Social workers can also function as *coordinators* who oversee a range of supportive services mentally retarded clients need.

Social workers can also fulfill roles within the macro system context. They can assume administrative functions as *general managers* within agencies providing services to mentally retarded clients and their families. In this capacity they can *evaluate* the effectiveness of the services provided. Are clients getting what they really need? Is service provision as efficient as possible? Finally, social workers can serve as *initiators*, *negotiators*, and *advocates*. In communities and states where needed services are not readily available or nonexistent, practitioners can work with organizational, community, and government macro systems to change policies so that clients can have access to what they need.

People with Learning Disabilities: A Population-at-Risk

A learning disability is "a disorder in one or more of the basic psychological processes involved in understanding or using language . . . which may manifest itself in an imperfect ability to listen, think, speak, read, write, spell, or do mathematical calculations" (McDonald-Wikler, 1987, p. 425). A learning disability is different from either mental retardation or emotional disturbance. Rather, learning disabilities involve a breakdown in processing information. Difficulties involve either absorbing information in the first place or subsequently using this information to communicate.

At least three basic factors appear to characterize a learning disability (Morsink, 1985). First, there are distinct *discrepancies* in the child's performance. A child will perform normally or above normal in many areas but display significant deficits in other areas. A child who is mentally retarded, on the other hand, will tend to function poorly across the board.

A second characteristic of a learning disability is that the child's deficits will come together to form a convergence or *focus* in how language or math is processed. Therefore, processing problems tend to be concentrated in one of the abilities needed to develop competence in language or math. The condition then "is often manifested in disorders of listening, thinking, talking, reading, writing, spelling, or arithmetic" (Lefrancois, 1990, p. 360).

A third characteristic of a learning disability involves *nonacceptance* of other causes to explain the problem. There is no clearly identifiable reason why the deficient areas exist. For instance, the disability is not due to the fact that a child's eyes are not functioning properly or that the child is mentally retarded. In fact, learning disabled children usually have normal or higher intelligence levels and no visual or hearing problems (Feagans, 1983).

The Effects of a Learning Disability

Stevie was sixteen. He couldn't read or add numbers. As a matter of fact, he felt he couldn't do anything right. Other people seemed to think he was dumb. He even had to go to a special school. He didn't feel dumb, though. He couldn't read, but he understood things. He could even find his way all around his hometown of Milwaukee without being able to read one street sign.

His parents and his brothers and sisters had given up on trying to help him read. He knew they were tired of trying. But he never did anything right. Then they'd get mad, and he'd get mad right back. He'd go out and break some windows and shoplift. That's why he had to go to a special school. People there weren't retarded. They had what teachers and staff called "behavior problems."

One time his teachers almost taught him to write his name. He must've practiced it a thousand times. After a couple of months he almost got it right. But he just forgot it again. He liked the staff at school. Sometimes they let him do jobs like washing the chalkboards or taking messages to the cook. He liked having responsibility. Nobody ever trusted him with jobs at home.

Stevie didn't like to think about the future. The world looked pretty dim for someone who couldn't read or write.

Learning disabled students currently make up about 4 percent of all school children and 40 percent of all children placed in special education classes (Chalfant, 1989). In the past, learning disabled children were grouped under a variety of vague, negative sounding diagnoses which were not really specific. These children were said to be suffering from "hyperactivity, learning dysfunction, cerebral dysfunction, minimal brain damage, perceptual handicaps, dyslexia, or perceptual disability, or simply as being slow learners" (Lefrancois, 1990, p. 359). The term *learning disability* was initially proposed by Samuel Kirk in 1963 (Kirk, 1979). He saw it as a less negative term that characterized a grouping of more specific intellectual processing problems. The term also diminished the association of these disabilities with such negative implications as "brain damage."

Specific causes for learning disabilities have not been established (Papalia and Olds, 1992). There is some evidence that at least some learning disabilities result from brain damage or malfunction (Held, 1984). However, Lefrancois (1990, p. 361) states that "various diseases and infections, malnutrition, and other environmental or genetic factors might also be involved." The broad range of behaviors clustered under the title "learning disabilities" and their frequently vague descriptions make it difficult to pinpoint causal relationships.

It is often difficult to identify learning disabilities at first because the children in question function normally in other areas. The first clue to surface is usually a problem in academic work. Other symptoms include a lack of attentiveness in classes; thoughtless, impulsive, overly active behavior; frequent mood shifts; difficulties in remembering symbols; lack of motor coordination in writing or play activities; apparent problems in speaking or listening; and other difficulties in completing academic work (Lefrancois, 1987). These difficulties are often vague enough to raise questions about a child's emotional health, family life, motivation to achieve, or intellectual level. However, once a learning disability is suspected, a number of tests are available for assessment.

Problems in Processing

A number of possible processing problems interfere with a learning disabled individual's ability to use language. One involves the inability to grasp the individual meanings of words or how words relate to each other in terms of grammatical position. This type of disability makes it difficult for the child to understand words and their meanings.

A second processing problem related to language acquisition and usage concerns auditory processing difficulties. Some children have trouble paying attention to what is being said; the problem concerns being able to focus on the sounds most important in conveying meaning. Other children have trouble discriminating between one sound and another. For example, instead of hearing the word "bed," a child may hear the word "dead." The result is confusion for the child and difficulty in understanding and following instructions. Still other children have trouble in recalling what has been said in the correct sequence. This also makes it difficult to follow instructions correctly. They cannot understand the proper order in which they are supposed to do things. These children have special difficulties in remembering content in a series format (for example, months of the year).

A third processing problem concerning language is demonstrated by children who have trouble saying what they mean or would like to say. Sometimes this involves grammatical problems. Other children may have difficulty remembering the words they want to say. Still others have trouble telling a story so that it makes sense or describing an event or situation so that the listener can understand it.

Learning disabilities can also be involved in visual perceptual problems in which children have difficulty seeing things as they really are. Some children have problems understanding spatial relationships. They might see items or symbols reversed. They might also judge distances between one item and another inaccurately.

Other children find it difficult to complete tasks involving motor coordination. Fine motor coordination refers to the ability to control the more precise muscular movements such as those performed by the hands. Gross motor coordination, on the other hand, involves controlling larger movements of the body such as walking or running. Children with such disabilities have difficulty integrating the information they see and translating it into what they can do. Children with fine motor processing problems may have exceptionally poor handwriting or drawing skills. Those with gross motor involvement may be clumsy or inaccurate in sports activities.

Still another processing problem demonstrated in some children with learning disabilities concerns memory and recall. Such children find it difficult to remember accurately what they have seen or heard. They commonly misspell words and forget where they placed objects.

Specific Learning Disabilities

Processing problems involved in learning disabilities are difficult to deal with. We do not know enough about the nervous system to physically pinpoint where and why the nerves in the brain are not working properly. However, there are two specific conditions quite common among learning disabled people that can be identified. They are dyslexia and attention deficit hyperactivity disorder.

Dyslexia is "an impairment of reading and writing skills, often with the tendency to reverse letters or words while reading or writing them or not noticing certain letters or words" (Barker, 1991, p. 68). Of all learning abilities, dyslexia is one of the most common (McGuinness, 1986).

Attention deficit hyperactivity disorder (ADHD) "starts in infancy, childhood, or adolescence" and is "characterized by impulsive behavior, inattentiveness, and excessive motor activity and short attention span" (Barker, 1991, p. 18). This relatively new term replaces old ones used to refer to this condition such as hyperactivity or minimal brain dysfunction. Children suffering from ADHD may have difficulty focusing on tasks. The least interruption or outside stimulation in the environment may distract them. ADHD also involves excessive body movement and an inability to keep still. A child with ADHD, for example, might find it very difficult to sit at a desk for any period of time.

Effects of Learning Disabilities on Children

Learning disabilities may psychologically affect children in several ways. Eaton, Lippmann, and Riley (1980) cite several reactions which typify responses to such disabilities. They include fear of failure, withdrawal, helplessness, and low self-esteem reactions.

Learning disabled children often become experts in failure. Through no fault of their own, they are unable to learn or do things the way other children can. Some children may fail in school or in sports so frequently that they no longer will attempt new things. They begin to assume that no matter what they do, they will just fail anyway. This *fear of failure reaction* often results in almost the complete avoidance of new experiences. Since the child refuses to take any new risks, potential progress is halted.

Other children take the fear of failure reaction a step further. Not only do they avoid new experiences, but they withdraw into themselves. This is called *withdrawal reaction*. People and activities seem to have caused them only failure and humiliation in the past. The safest alternative then is to withdraw into themselves. To a limited extent, this may be a healthy means of coping. However, in extreme cases children may isolate themselves and become totally preoccupied with their own thoughts.

The *helplessness reaction* is another means of responding to a learning disability. Children may use the fact that they cannot do some things in order to get out of doing other things they are capable of doing. The vague and complicated nature of learning disabilities does not help this situation. For example, a mother may ask her daughter to do her homework. The daughter responds, "Gee, Mom, I don't know how." The daughter's learning disability involves reading. Her homework is an arithmetic assignment which she has no more difficulty completing than her peers. However, because of her learning disability, the daughter is perceived as being helpless in her mother's eyes. As a result, the mother does not make the daughter do her homework.

Another possible reaction of a learning disabled child is that of *low self-esteem*. Learning disabled children are likely to see other children do things they cannot. Perhaps others make critical comments to them. Teachers and parents may show at least some impatience and frustration at their inability to understand or perform in the areas affected by their learning disabilities. These children are likely to internalize their failures. The result may be that they feel inferior to others, and they may develop low self-esteem.

Treatment for Learning Disabilities in Educational Groups and Families

In addition to observation of performance at home and in the classroom, various tests are available to help pinpoint exactly how the disability affects the child. After diagnosis, suggestions can be made for both teachers and parents to follow in order to maximize the child's progress.

A major idea is to design an individualized special education program for the child to emphasize strengths and minimize weaknesses (Papalia and Olds, 1978, p. 298). For a child with a visual perceptual disorder, emphasis might be placed on providing material that the child can hear in order to learn it. For example, instead of reading an assignment in a textbook, a tape recording of the assignment might be made available so that the child can listen to the material. Other means of tailoring a special education program to meet a learning disabled child's needs include "breaking work down into small, manageable units" and incorporating "physical activity into the daily classroom schedule" (Papalia and Olds, 1992, p. 268).

Confronted with an unwanted task, children may exhibit the helplessness reaction.

A multisensory approach is often useful (Kaluger and Kaluger, 1984, p. 289). This involves presenting material to the child using as many senses as possible. For example, a young learning disabled boy learning how to add might be told verbally how to accomplish the task. He might be shown on the chalkboard or by using cue cards how the problem is performed. He might also be encouraged to carry out the addition task by using actual objects such as poker chips or "M & Ms." He could then manipulate the objects himself and thus use his sense of touch to enhance his learning.

A very important suggestion for treating the learning disabled child is to support and encourage development of a positive self-concept. This is important for both parents and teachers. Eaton, Lippmann, and Riley (1980, pp. 72–73) have several suggestions for enhancing self-esteem. First, the positive things that the child does should be emphasized. Problems are easy to see, but good behaviors and accomplishments often go unnoticed. Second, children should feel loved, not for their behavior, but rather for who they are. Third, confidence can be developed in children by giving them responsibility for things they are capable of accomplishing. Success at tasks helps them to develop faith in themselves. Third, comparisons to others and what they accomplish should be avoided. The learning disabled child who has probably so often failed in competition does not need to hear about how well others can do the things he can't. Rather, his own individual accomplishments should be the focus of attention. Fourth, structure in the form of clear guidelines for behavior is helpful so that the child knows what to expect. If the child knows what is acceptable and what is not, he is less likely to make mistakes. The child will also probably respond to the fact that someone cares enough to put forth the effort to provide structure.

Macro System Responses to Learning Disabilities

Major legislation has positively affected educational programming for learning disabled people in the past few decades (McDonald-Wikler, 1987). The 1975 Education for All Handicapped Children Act (P.L. 94–142) mandated that all states provide educational opportunities for all children regardless of level of ability or disability. P.L. 94–142 emphasizes the concept of *mainstreaming*. This entails "bringing people who have some exceptional characteristics into the living, working, or educational environments to which all others have access" (Barker, 1991, p. 136). Learning disabled children (in addition to mentally retarded children and children with other developmental disabilities) are thus guaranteed the right to an education. States and communities are no longer able to ignore or reject learning disabled children. Excuses such as exorbitant costs or lack of existing facilities are no longer acceptable. This illustrates how legislation forces state, community, and organizational macro systems to respond to a social need.

Social Work Roles

Social work roles with respect to learning disabled clients are similar to those used with mentally re-tarded clients. For example, social workers as brokers help link clients with resources. Practitioners as advocates work to effect positive change in macro systems that are not responsive to clients' needs.

Summary

Major theories of personality development include trait, psychodynamic, neo-Freudian psychoanalytic, behavioral, and phenomenological theories. Allport's conception of cardinal, central, and secondary traits illustrates a trait theory. Freud's psychoanalytic theory is the predominant psychodynamic theory. The neo-Freudian psychoanalytic theorists include Carl Jung, Erich Fromm, Alfred Adler, and Harry Stack Sullivan. Behavioral theory is one of the most useful theories of human behavior. The self theory of Carl Rogers is a phenomenological approach.

Two theories of cognitive development are Piaget's and Bruner's. The four periods characterizing Piaget's theory are sensorimotor, preoperational thought, concrete operations, and formal operations. Bruner's three stages are the enactive, iconic, and symbolic representation.

People begin displaying their emotions in infancy. High esteem is positively related to personality and intellectual growth. The effects of racial prejudice on the self-esteem of nonwhites are explored. Intelligence is defined, and the meaning of intelligence quotients is discussed.

Various levels of mental retardation and types of learning disabilities are described. The status of the mentally retarded and of people with learning disabilities as populations-at-risk are examined. Finally, macro system responses to mental retardation and learning disabilities in addition to appropriate social work roles are explored.

4

Social Systems and Their Impacts on Infancy and Childhood

The world beyond "me."

"My dad could punch out your dad, I bet!" Jimmy yelled at Harry, the neighborhood bully. Harry had just bopped Jimmy in the nose. Jimmy, who was small for his age, felt hurt. So he resorted to name calling as he edged further and further away from his aggressor. Since his own house was a full two blocks away, Jimmy had to do some fast thinking about how to get there without everybody thinking he was chicken. The worst thing was that Harry was also a pretty fast runner.

To Jimmy's surprise and delight, Harry was apparently losing interest in this particular quarry. Somebody called out from the next block and was trying to interest Harry, a good fullback, in a game of football.

Scowling, Harry shouted back to Jimmy, "Oh, get out of here, you punky 'fry.' Your dad sucks egg!" He then darted down the block and into the sunset.

That last remark did not make much sense, although Harry's intent was to be as nasty as possible (Harry's intellect was not his strong suit). The important thing, however, was that Harry was running in the other direction. Any of the other guys who happened to witness this incident might just think that it was Harry who was running scared. Nonetheless, Jimmy did think it best not to reply, just in case Harry decided to change his mind.

"Whew!" thought Jimmy. "That was a close one." He was usually pretty good at staying far out of Harry's way. This meeting was purely an accident. He was on his way home from a friend's house after working on a class project. That was another story. Their project involved growing bean plants under different lighting conditions. The bean plants that were supposed to be growing good beans weren't. Jimmy secretly suspected that his partner was eating the beans.

Jimmy had better things to do now at any rate. He had to finish his homework. His parents had promised to buy him a new stereo boom box if he maintained at least a B + average for the whole year. Harry would probably flunk this year anyhow. He was big, but he was also pretty stupid.

Jimmy hightailed it down the street. He imagined hearing the tones of Ear Discharge, his favorite rock group. The horrible Harry affair was soon forgotten.

A PERSPECTIVE

The attainment of primary social developmental milestones and the significant life events which tend to accompany these milestones have tremendous impacts on the developing individual and that individual's transactions with the impinging environment. Family and peer group mezzo systems are dynamically involved in children's growth, development, and behavior. Social interaction with other people in childhood provides the foundation for building an adult social personality. Children and their families do not function in a vacuum. Macro systems within the environment, including communities, government units, and agencies, can provide necessary resources to help families address issues and solve problems typically experienced with children. Impinging macro systems within the social environment can act either to help or hinder family members fulfill their potential.

This chapter will:

- Explain the concept of socialization.
- Explore the family environment, variations in family structures, the impacts of social forces on family systems, and the dynamics of family systems.
- Apply general systems theory principles to families.
- Describe the basic conepts of learning theory and how such principles as positive reinforcement, punishment, and time-out from reinforcement can be applied to effective parenting.
- Examine some common life events that affect children, including membership in sibling subsystems, gender role socialization, play with peers, television, and the school environment.
- Explore the dynamics and effects of physical abuse, neglect, and sexual abuse upon children.

Socialization

Socialization is "the process through which individuals learn proper ways (proper as defined by the society) of acting in a culture" (Zastrow and Bowker, 1984, p. 25). The process involves the acquisition of language, values, etiquette, rules, behaviors, and all the subtle, complex bits of information necessary to get along and thrive in a particular society.

Although socialization continues throughout life, most of it occurs in childhood. Children need to learn how to interact with other people. They need to learn which behaviors are considered acceptable and which are not. For example, children need to learn that they must abide by the directives of their parents, at least most of the time. They need to learn how to communicate to others what they need in terms of food and comfort. On the other hand, they also need to learn what behaviors are not considered appropriate. They need to learn that breaking windows with BB guns and spitting in the eyes of other people when they don't get their way will not be tolerated.

Since children start with knowing nothing about their society, the most awesome socialization occurs during childhood. This is when the fundamental building blocks of their consequent attitudes, beliefs, and behaviors are established.

The Family Environment

Because children's lives are centered initially within their families, the family environment becomes the primary agent of socialization. The family environment "involves the circumstances and social climate conditions within families" (Kirst-Ashman, 1983). Since each family is made up of different individuals in a different setting, each family environment is unique. The environments can differ in many ways. For example, one obvious difference lies in the socioeconomic level. Some families live in luxurious twenty-four-room estates, own a Porsche and a Mercedes in addition to the family station wagon, and can afford to have shrimp cocktail for an appetizer whenever they choose. Other families subsist in two-room shacks, struggle with time payments on their used 1988 Chevy, and have to eat macaroni made with artificial processed cheese four times a week.

This section addresses several aspects of the family environment. They include variations in family structures, positive family functioning, impacts of social forces and policies on family systems, and the application of systems theory principles to families.

Membership in Family Groups: Variations in Family Structures

Families in the United States today are no longer characterized by two first-time married parents who live blissfully together with their 2.8 children. One might wonder if the traditional "healthy" families as depicted in early television shows ever really existed as happily and contentedly as they appeared. Currently fewer than 30 percent of all families are composed of the traditional "nuclear family" (that is, one-time married parents with one or more children) (Lamanna and Riedmann, 1988).

Today's families are more likely to conform to a varied medley of configurations. We will arbitrarily define a family as "a primary group whose members assume certain obligations for each other and generally share common residences" (Barker, 1991, p. 80). Scrutinizing this definition shows how flexible the notion of family has become.

A family is a *primary group*. This entails "people who are intimate and have frequent face-to-face contact with one another, have norms [that is, expectations regarding how members in the group should behave] in common, and share mutually enduring and extensive influences" (Barker, 1991, p. 181). Thus, family members as members of a primary group have extreme influence upon each other. The second concept in the definition of family involves "obligations for each other." Obligations concern mutual commitment and responsibility for other members in the family system. The third concept in the definition entails "common residences." That is, to some extent, family members live together.

Families, then, may consist of intact two-parent families with or without children, single-parent families, reconstituted families, blended families, stepfamilies, or any other configuration that fits our definition of a family. Some of these terms are defined as follows:

A *single-parent family* is "a family unit and household comprising the children and the mother or father but not the other spouse" (Barker, 1991, p. 216). It should be noted that over 90 percent of single-parent families are headed by women.

A *reconstituted family* is "a family unit comprising a legally married husband and wife, one or both of whom have children from a previous marriage or relationship who live with them" (Barker, 1991, p. 196). Reconstituted families may also be referred to as blended families. However, a *blended family* is defined as any configuration of people, either related or unrelated, where "members reside together and assume traditional family roles" (Barker, 1991, p. 24). Such relationships may not involve biological or legal linkages. The important thing is that such groups *function* as families.

Stepfamilies are primary groups in which "members are joined as a result of second or subsequent marriages" (Barker, 1991, p. 227). Members may include stepmothers, stepfathers, and any children either may have from prior marriages. Stepfamilies may also include children born to the currently married couple. Stepfamilies have become extremely common in view of the fact that about half of all marriages end in divorce. Stepfamilies may also become very complex in cases where one or both spouses were married more than once and/or have children from a variety of relationships.

This discussion is extremely relevant to social workers (family configurations are discussed more thoroughly in Chapter 12). It is critically important that you be sensitive to and appreciative of the various configurations families may take. Open-mindedness is essential when assessing the strengths of any family group. Workers should not be limited by making assumptions about how families *should* be. Rather, practitioners should work with the family group that *is*. Carter and McGoldrick (1989, pp. 12-13) elaborate:

> It is time for professionals to give up attachments to the old ideals and to put a more positive conceptual frame around what is: two paycheck marriages; permanent "single-parent" households; unmarried couples and remarried couples; single-parent adoptions; and women of all ages alone.

Positive Family Functioning

In view of the vast range of family configurations, it is extremely difficult to define a "healthy" family. However, at least two concepts are important when assessing the effectiveness or healthiness of a family. These include how well *family functions* are undertaken and how well family members *communicate* with each other.

Family functions include "child care and child socialization, income support, [and] long-term care" in addition to other care giving functions (Barker, 1991, p. 80). Children must be nurtured and taught. All family members need adequate resources to thrive. Additionally, family members should be able to call upon each other for help when necessary (for instance, in the event of sudden disability).

Good communication is the second aspect which characterizes "healthy" families. Communication and autonomy are closely related concepts. Good communication involves clear expression of personal ideas and feelings even when they differ from those of other family members. On the other hand, good communication also involves being sensitive to the needs and feelings of other family members. Good communication promotes compromise so that the most important needs of all involved are met. In families which foster autonomy, boundaries for roles and relationships are clearly established. All family members are held responsible for their own behavior.

When faced with decisions or crises, healthy families involve all family members in developing solutions for the mutual good.

Under these conditions, family members much less frequently feel the need to tell others what to do or "push each other around." (Family communication is discussed more thoroughly in Chapter 12).

Negotiation is also clearly related to good communication and good relationships. When faced with decisions or crises, healthy families involve all family members to come to solutions for the mutual good. Conflicts are settled through rational discussion and compromise instead of open hostility and conflict. If one family member feels strongly about an issue, healthy families work to accommodate her views in a satisfactory way. As unhealthy families suffer conflict and disagreements, so do healthy families. However, a healthy family deals with conflict much more rationally and effectively.

Families can be compared and evaluated on many other dimensions and variables. The specific variables involved are not so important as the concept that children learn how to behave or are socialized according to the makeup of their individual family environments. The family environment is important in that children are taught what types of transactions are considered appropriate. They learn how to form relationships, handle power, maintain personal boundaries, communicate with others, and feel that they are an important subset of the whole family system.

Effects of Social Forces and Policies on Family Systems: Helpful or Hurtful?

We have established that families provide an immediate, intimate social environment for children as they grow and develop. However, families do not exist in a vacuum. They are in constant interaction with numerous other systems permeating the macro social environment. Families can only provide care giving and nurturance to the extent that other macro systems in the environment provide support. These macro systems, which include communities and organizations, are in turn directly impacted by the social forces surging and driving daily life.

Social forces include the political, economic, environmental, and ideological. They are abstract and difficult to define, and they are almost inseparably entangled with each other. Yet, they form the foundation resources that families need.

For example, unemployment may soar because of an economic slump. Political decisions such as increasing employer and business taxes may have sparked the slump. Ideologically, the general public may feel that in "a free country" of rugged individualists, it is each person's responsibility to find and succeed in work. The public may not support political decisions to subsidize workers by providing long-term unemployment benefits or developing programs for job retraining. At the same time, legislators concerned about the increasing unemployment rate and their reelection may hesitate to impose increasing restrictions on business and industry such as more stringent (and, subsequently, more costly) pollution control regulations. Thus, the physical environment suffers.

This example, of course, is overly simplistic. Volumes have been written on each aspect of the political, economic, environmental, and ideological aspects of the social environment. However, the point is that it is impossible to comprehend a family's situation without assessing that family within the context of the macro social environment. The resources available to a family are directly affected by the ensuing social forces. For example, economic downturns and unemployment may leave a parent jobless and poverty-stricken. That parent will then be less able to provide the food, shelter, health care, and other necessities for a family environment in which children can flourish.

Likewise, the resources available to agencies and communities for dispersal to clients depend on the legislative and organizational policies resulting from social forces. For instance, U.S. society is structured so that all citizens have the right to receive a high school education. This idea is based in ideology which, in turn, is reflected by legislative and administrative policy which regulates how that education is provided.

Public day care, on the other hand, is not provided to working parents on a universal basis. Day care involves "facilities and programs that care for children or other dependents when their parents or guardians are unavailable for their care" (Barker, 1991, p. 57). There are many historical ideological reasons for this lack. For one, traditional thought is that a woman's place is in the home and that she should be the primary caretaker of the children (Spakes, 1992). However, today almost 58 percent of women work outside of the home, most out of economic necessity (Renzetti and Curran, 1992). Over half of all mothers with children under six years old are in the work force (Kadushin and Martin, 1988). Monumental evidence suggests that although most women in heterosexual relationships work, they still continue to carry the overwhelming responsibility both for child care and other household tasks (Googins and Burden, 1987; Levant et al., 1987; Renzetti and Curran, 1992; Smith, 1984; Spakes, 1992; Thompson and Walker, 1989). Additionally, although most people marry, about one-half of all marriages end in divorce (U.S. Bureau of the Census, 1991). More than 90 percent of all single-parent families are headed by women. (Many of these issues will be discussed more thoroughly in Chapter 9.)

In summary, a number of facts point to the need for adequate day care to serve the nation's children. First, most women work outside of the home from economic necessity. Second, it remains women's additional burden to be primary homemakers. Third, many women have no mate to help in child-care responsibilities.

Yet, day-care facilities are inadequate to meet the nation's needs. Parents often struggle to find adequate, affordable, and accessible day care for their children. Many day-care centers refuse to accept small infants because of the difficulty in their care. Furthermore, it is estimated that 94 percent of all day care in the United States is provided in private homes, unregulated by public standards (Nelson, 1988). Almost one-quarter of all working parents must leave their children unsupervised by an adult on a regular basis (Hewlett, 1986; Rubin, 1987).

Why doesn't the government require that facilities be developed to meet the day-care need? There is no clear answer. Cost may be one possibility. Low priority may be another. As a student social worker, what do you think? Is the need real? How critical is it, especially for women? As you take courses in social policy and practice techniques, will you be motivated to seek out answers for how to solve this problem and others like it?

The Dynamics of Family Systems

In order to understand family functioning, it's helpful to view the family within a system's perspective. General systems theory applies to a multitude of situations, ranging from the internal mechanisms of a computer to the bureaucratic functioning of a large public welfare department to the intimate interpersonal relationships within a family. Regardless of the situation, understanding the various systems theory concepts helps to understand dynamic, active, ongoing relationships among people. Individuals are affected by others in their environment. General systems theory helps to conceptualize or formulate a mind's eye view of how a family works. Basic concepts were introduced in Chapter 1.

General systems theory also helps us understand how a family system is intimately intertwined with many other systems (Thorman, 1982, p. 174). Each member of a family is affected by what happens to any of the other members. Each member of a family and the family as a whole is also affected by the many other social and political systems in the family's environment. For instance, if Johnny flunks algebra, the family works with the school system to help him make improvements. The entire family might have to cancel their summer vacation because Johnny has to attend summer school. The school system directly impacts the family system.

A second example concerns Shirl, Johnny's mother and the family's primary breadwinner. She works as an engineering supervisor for Case International, a corporation based in Racine, Wisconsin, which makes various sized tractors. Tenneco, an immense conglomerate corporation, owns Case International. What if Tenneco decides to close down the Case International plant in Racine because of inadequate profits and decides to move the large plant to Bonetraill, North Dakota? Bonetraill is a far cry from small, but urban Racine. One possibility for the family is to move two states away to a totally different environment, as Shirl has been offered a comparable position in Bonetraill. Lennie, Johnny's father, is a journalist for the local paper. In the event of a move, he would have to find a new job if at all possible. The whole family would have to leave their neighborhood and friends. Another alternative is for mom to seek a new job in the Racine area. However, the economy there is depressed and she would have difficulty finding a position with a salary anywhere near the one she is currently earning. Thus, the family system is seriously affected by the larger Case International system, and the Case International system by the even larger Tenneco system.

Another important reason can be given for understanding general systems theory as it relates to families. Intervention in families with problems is a major concern of social work. Family therapy is "a process through which a family as a whole is enabled to change its patterns of interaction so that all members feel less pain and become more free to develop in the directions most satisfying to them" (Zastrow, 1981, p. 379). It is based on the idea that the family is a system. In finding solutions to problems within a family, the target of intervention is the family system (Minuchin, 1974, p. 14). Whether a particular problem is initially defined as an individual member's or as the entire family's, a family therapist views this problem as one involving the entire family system. Furthermore, the entire family should be the focus of treatment (Scherz, 1970, p. 222). In order to do this, the structure of the family, that is, the specific relationships between various family members in the family system, need to be closely observed (Perez, 1979, p. 19). Family interaction is discussed more thoroughly in Chapter 12.

The Family Life Cycle

One other aspect of the family needs to be examined. This book assumes a chronological framework. People functioning within their environments are not stagnant: they change. And just as people change, so do families. Families have life cycles of their own.

Several decades ago, the family life cycle and the types of experiences family members had during specified phases of the cycle were much more predictable than today. This is no longer the case. There is no "typical" cycle. We have defined the term "family" and discussed the wide range of involvements it may include. Carter and McGoldrick (1989, p. 12) recognize some of the difficulties in describing a *normal* family life cycle:

> An ever increasing percent of the population are living together without marrying (3 percent of couples at any one point in time), and a rapidly increasing number are having children without marrying. At present 6 percent or more of the population is homosexual. Present estimates are that 12 percent of young women will never marry, three times the percent for their parents' generation; 25 percent will never have children; 50 percent will end their marriages in divorce and 20 percent will have two divorces.

The traditional family life cycle was conceptualized as having six major phases (Carter and McGold-

The Application of General Systems Theory Principles to Families

Basic general systems theory concepts introduced in Chapter 1 can easily be applied to family systems. A number of these concepts will be briefly redefined and then applied to examples of family situations.

Systems

A *system* is a set of elements which form an orderly, interrelated, and functional whole. Several aspects of this definition are important. The idea that a system is a "set of elements" means that a system can be composed of any type of things as long as these things have some relationship to each other. Things may be people or they may be mathematical symbols. Regardless, the set of elements must be orderly. In other words, the elements must be arranged in some order or pattern which is not simply random. The set of elements must also be interrelated. They must have some kind of mutual relationship or connection with each other. Additionally, the set of elements must be functional. Together they must be able to perform some regular task, activity, or function and fulfill some purpose. Finally, the set of elements must form a whole.

Families are systems. Any particular family is composed of a number of individuals, the elements making up the system. Each individual has a unique relationship with the other individuals in the family. Spouses normally have a special physical and emotional relationship with each other. In a family with seven children, the two oldest sisters may have a special relationship with each other that is unlike their relationship with any of the other siblings. Regardless of what the relationships are, together the family members function as a family system. These relationships, however, are not always positive and beneficial. Sometimes, a relationship is negative and even hostile. For example, a three-year-old daughter may be fiercely jealous of and resentful toward her newborn brother.

Homeostasis

Homeostatis refers to the tendency for a system to maintain a relatively stable, constant state of equilibrium or balance. A homeostatic family system functions effectively. The family system is surviving and maintaining itself and may even be thriving. However a homeostatic family system is not necessarily a perfect family. Mother may still become terribly annoyed at father for never wanting to go out dancing.

Ten-year-old Bobby may still be maintaining a D average in English. Nonetheless, the family is able to continue its daily existence, and the family system itself is not threatened.

Homeostasis is exceptionally important in determining whether outside therapeutic intervention is necessary in a particular family situation. Absolute perfection is usually unrealistic. However, if its existence is threatened, the system may be in danger of breaking apart. In these instances, the family system no longer has homeostasis.

For instance, an eighty-nine-year-old maternal grandmother no longer can care for herself. She has been living alone since the death of her husband twenty years ago. Her eyesight is failing and her rheumatoid arthritis puts her in constant pain. She remains fairly alert, however, with only some minor forgetfulness. Mother refuses to place grandmother in a nursing home. She feels responsible for her mother as she is the only child and she would like to "pay back" all the care she received as a child.

Father, however, hates the idea of having his mother-in-law move in. Grandmother, he feels, has always tried to intervene in their marital relationship. He feels that she takes sides with his wife and constantly tells him what to do. He also feels she talks incessantly and is so hard of hearing that she listens to old Lawrence Welk reruns loud enough to deafen him even as he works down in the basement.

Father relents and grandmother moves in. Mother and father start quarreling more and more over grandmother. Soon they seem to be quarreling over everything. Mother has to quit her job because grandmother requires more care and attention than she expected. The family had just purchased a new home with high mortgage payments. Without mother's salary, money becomes scarce for food, clothing, and other necessities. Mother and father fight over the financial situation; each blames the other for buying that ridiculously expensive new home to begin with. The children's grades in school start dropping and they begin to display some behavior problems. Father threatens to leave if things don't improve. The family system's homeostasis is threatened. At this point, intervention might take the form of family counseling to help the family clearly identify their problems, voice their opinions, and come to some mutually agreed upon resolutions. Couple's counseling might be involved to improve the communication between mother and father. Social services might be needed to help the family and grandmother decide what her best care alternative might be, including consideration of placement in a nursing home. In order for the family to survive, homeostasis must be restored and maintained.

Subsystems

A *subsystem* is a secondary or subordinate system—a system within a system. The most obvious examples of this are the parental and sibling subsystems. Other more subtle subsystems may also exist depending on the boundaries established within the family system. A mother might have a daughter to whom she feels especially close. These two might form a subsystem within a family system, apart from other family members. Sometimes subsystems exist because of more negative circumstances within family systems. A subsystem might exist within a family with an alcoholic father. Here the mother and children might form a subsystem in coalition against the father.

Boundaries

Boundaries are "invisible barriers which surround individuals and subsystems, regulating the amount of contact with others" (Nichols, 1874, p. 474). In a family system, boundaries determine who are members of that particular family system and who are not. Parents and children are within the boundaries of the family system. Close friends of the family are not.

Boundaries may also delineate subsystems within a system. For instance, boundaries separate the spouse subsystem within a family from the sibling subsystem. Each subsystem has its own specified membership. Either a family member is within the boundaries of that subsystem or he is not.

Input

Input can be defined as the energy, information, or communication flow received from other systems. Families are not isolated, self-sufficient units. Each family system is constantly interacting with its environment and with other systems. For example, one type of input into a family system is the money received for the parents' work outside of the home. Another type of input involves the communication and supportive social interaction family members receive from friends, neighbors, and relatives. Schools also

A subsystem may be subtle—a mother might feel especially close to one child.

provide input in the form of education for children and progress reports concerning that education.

Output

Output can be described as energy, information, or communication emitted from a system to the environment or to other systems. Work, whether it be in a job situation, a school setting, or in the home, can be considered output. Financial output is another form. This is necessary for the purchase of food, clothing, shelter, and the other necessities of life.

An important thing to consider about output is its relationship to input. If a family system's output exceeds its input, family homeostasis may be threatened. In other words, if more energy is leaving a family system than is coming in, tensions may result and functioning may be impaired. For example, in a multiproblem family troubled

(continued next page)

rick, 1980). Each phase focused on some emotional transition in terms of intimate relationships with other people and on changes of personal status. The first stage involved an unattached young adult separating from his or her family of origin. During this phase, the young adult established a personal identity and developed new interpersonal relationships. Stage two concerned marrying and realigning life's joys and responsibilities within a couple's framework. Stage three entailed having children and meeting these

The Application of General Systems Theory Principles to Families (continued)

by poverty, illness, lack of education, isolation, loneliness, and delinquency, tremendous amounts of effort and energy may be expended simply to stay alive. At the same time, little help and support may be coming in. The result would be severely restricted family functioning and lack of homeostasis.

Feedback

Feedback is "any kind of direct information from an outside source about the effects and/or results of one's behavior" (Wolman, 1973, p. 143). Feedback can be given to an entire family system, a subsystem (such as a marital pair), or an individual within the family system.

Feedback can be information obtained from outside of the system. For example, a family therapist will provide a family having problems with information about how it is functioning. Feedback can also be given from one individual or subsystem within the family system to another. For example, the sibling subsystem might communicate to the alcoholic mother that they are suffering from the consequences of her alcoholic behavior. Finally, a system, subsystem, or individual within a system can give feedback to those outside of the family system. For instance, a family might contact their landlord and give him feedback that their kitchen sink is backing up. They might also add that he won't see another rent check until it's fixed.

Feedback can be either positive or negative. Positive feedback involves information about what a system is doing right in order to maintain itself and thrive. Positive feedback can provide specific information so that members in a family system are aware of the positive aspects of their functioning. For example, a mother works outside her home as a computer programmer. During her job performance evaluation, her supervisor may tell her that she has maintained the highest accuracy record in terms of her work in the entire department. This indicates to her that her conscientiousness in this respect is valued and should be continued.

Negative feedback can also be valuable. Negative feedback involves providing information about problems within the system. As a result of negative feedback, the system can choose to correct any deviations or mistakes and return to a more homeostatic state. For example, the mother mentioned earlier who works as a computer programmer can receive negative feedback during the same job evaluation. Her supervisor indicates that she tends to fall behind on her weekly written reports. Although she feels the reports are extraordinarily dull and tedious to complete, her supervisor's feedback gives her the information she needs to perform her job better.

A family might also receive feedback concerning its annual income tax returns. Suppose the parents failed to report some savings' interest in the hopes that no one would notice and it would save them some money. Feedback might be in the form of a terse letter informing them that they owe the Internal Revenue Service an additional amount in taxes, along with an interest penalty. This negative feedback would clearly indicate to the couple that it doesn't pay to try to cheat the government.

Perhaps the most relevant example for social workers concerning feedback is its application in a family treatment setting. When a family comes in for help about a particular problem, feedback can raise their awareness about their own functioning. It can help them correct areas where they are making mistakes. It can also encourage them to continue positive interactions. For example, if every time a husband and wife discuss housework responsibilities they yell at each other about what the other does not do, a social worker can give them feedback that their yelling is accomplishing nothing. Constructive suggestions might then be given about how the couple could better resolve their differences over who takes out the garbage, who makes the breakfast orange juice, and who separates the colors from the whites in the laundry.

Positive feedback might also be given. The husband and wife may not be aware that when asked a question about their feelings for each other or about how they like to raise children's needs. Stage four concerned dealing with adolescent children, whose needs and strivings for independence called for different types of interactions from those appropriate for very young children. Stage four also often marked a refocusing of the couple's relationship and addressing the needs of their own aging parents. Stage five involved sending children forth into their own new relationships, addressing midlife career issues, and coping with the growing disabilities of their own parents. Finally, stage six

their children, they are very supportive of each other. They immediately look to each other to check out the other's feelings. They smile at each other and encourage the other's opinions. Giving them specific positive feedback about what is occurring and describing their behaviors to them may be helpful. Such feedback may encourage them to continue these positive interactions. It may also suggest to them that they could apply similar positive means to resolving other differences.

Entropy

Entropy is the natural tendency of a system to progress toward disorganization, depletion, and in essence, death. The idea is that nothing lasts forever. People age and eventually die. Young families get older, and children leave to start their own families. Family systems are constantly in the process of change; conditions change.

Homeostasis itself is dynamic in that it involves constant change and adjustment. Families are never frozen in time. Family members are constantly changing and responding to new situations and challenges.

Negative Entropy

Negative entropy is the process of a system moving toward growth and development. In effect, it is the opposite of entropy. Goals in family treatment often involve striving to make conditions and interactions better than they were before. A relationship between quarreling spouses can improve. Physical abuse of a child can be stopped. Negative entropy must be kept in mind when helping family systems grow and develop to their full potential.

Equifinality

Equifinality refers to the fact that there are many different means to the same end. It is important not to get locked into

only one way of thinking, since in any particular situation, there are alternatives. Some may be better than others, but nonetheless, there are alternatives. It's easy to get trapped into an orientation of tunnel vision where no other options are apparent. Frequently, family systems need help in defining and evaluating the options available to them.

Take, for instance, a family where the father abruptly loses his job. Instead of wallowing in remorse, other alternatives might be pursued. The family might consider relocating geographically where a similar position might be available. The mother, who previously had not worked outside of the home, might look into the possibility of attaining a job herself, thereby helping the family's financial situation. Moving to less expensive housing might be considered. Finally, the father might look into other types of work, at least temporarily. There are always alternatives. The important thing is to recognize them and consider them.

Differentiation

Differentiation is a system's tendency to move from a more simplified to a more complex existence. In other words, relationships, situations, and interactions tend to get more complex over time instead of more simplified.

For example, two people might fall in love, marry, and begin to establish their lives together. They have three children, and each parent works full time in order to save enough for a modest home of their own. As time goes on, marital problems and disputes develop as their lives grow more complicated with children and responsibilities. Their initial simple life becomes clouded with children's illnesses, car payments, job stresses, and other mundane occurrences. General systems theory provides a framework for viewing this couple's relationship. It provides for the acknowledgment of an increasing complexity. From a helping perspective, the basic fact of the couple's affection and commitment to each other may need to be identified and emphasized.

entailed adjustments to aging and addressing the inevitability of one's own death.

Carter and McGoldrick (1989) propose an alternative to the traditional family life cycle. This new approach employs the flexibility necessary for application to a wide variety of family variations. It recognizes that the traditional phases of the cycle should not be forgotten; these phases do focus on some of life's major potential transitions. However, included in the family life cycle are a number of other major transitions which have become increasingly common and relevant. Foremost are the transitions of divorce and remarriage.

Carter and McGoldrick (1989) emphasize how "peaks of emotional tension" involved in divorce and remarriage can lead to additional transitions within the cycle (p. 21). A number of these additional transitions can induce serious stress and thus merit attention. These "peaks" most likely involve the following (Carter and McGoldrick, 1989):

1. making the determination that separation or divorce is inevitable;
2. telling family, friends, and others about the separation or divorce;
3. addressing issues such as financial distribution and child custody;
4. going through the actual process of separation;
5. participating in the legal divorce process;
6. addressing significant issues such as "money or children," especially, when the interaction involved is uncomfortable or aversive;
7. participating in subsequent events which involve the children, such as graduations, marriages, sicknesses, births, or funerals;
8. accepting critical points in the life of the ex-spouse such as remarriage, illness, or death.

Carter and McGoldrick (1989) explain that there are a number of other variables in addition to divorce and remarriage which influence and shape any particular family's individualized life cycle. One such variable is poverty. For instance, a family unable to pay the rent may suddenly become homeless. Such an incident can mark an obvious transition in a family's life. Another variable involves cultural values and variations. For example, the extent to which an unmarried teen's pregnancy is accepted or condemned by family members might vary according to ethnic or cultural expectations.

Any of these additional pressure points can add a number of "stages" to a particular family's life cycle. Why is it important to be prudently aware of such individualized transitions? Social workers are often called upon to help clients determine what alternatives are available to them at these decision-making intersections, evaluate the pros and cons of various choices, and decide which actions are best for them to take.

Within the context of the family system which progresses through its own life cycle, we will now turn our attention back to the social development of young children within this system. We will focus on how children become integrated into their family system and on how they learn to behave (or misbehave). Learning theory provides a relevant, conceptual base for understanding how socialization and learning occur. Thus, substantial emphasis will be placed on understanding the theoretical basis for learning theory and its applications to practical parenting.

Learning Theory

"Mom! I want a candy bar! You promised! I want one right now! Mom!" Four-year-old Huey screamed as loudly as he possibly could. He and his mother were standing in the checkout line at the local supermarket. An elderly woman was checking out in front of them. Two other women and a man were waiting in line behind them.

Huey's mother saw everybody looking at her and her young son. Huey simply would not stop screaming. She tried to "shush" him. She scolded him in as much of a whisper as she could muster. She threatened that he would never see the inside of a McDonald's again. Absolutely nothing would work. Huey just kept on screaming.

Finally, in total exasperation, his mother grabbed the nearest candy bar off the shelf, ripped off the wrapper, and literally stuck the thing into Huey's mouth. A peaceful silence came over the grocery store. All witnessing the event breathed a sigh of relief. Huey stood there with a happy smile on his sticky face. One might almost say he was gloating.

The family environment has already been established as a primary agent of children's socialization. It provides the critical social environment in which

A dispute at a day-care center provides a learning situation for how to get along with others.

children learn. The next logical question to address concerns how children learn. The social and emotional development of children is frequently a focus of social work intervention. Children sometimes create behavior problems. They become difficult for parents and other supervising adults to manage. When they enter school, these management problems often continue. Teachers and administration find some children difficult to control. Frequently, as children get older, problems escalate.

Children can learn how to be affectionate, considerate, fun-loving, responsible people. But they can also learn how to be selfish, spoiled, inconsiderate hellions. This latter state is not good for parents and other supervising adults. It is certainly not good for the children themselves. Children need to cooperate with others. They need to know how to get along in social settings in order to become emotionally mature, well-adjusted adults. Social learning theory concepts are useful for recognizing why anyone, child or adult, behaves the way he or she does. However, the concepts are especially helpful when addressing the issue of behavior management.

Evaluation of Theory

In order to change behavior, it first must be understood. Learning theory provides a framework for understanding how behavior develops. Learning theory has been chosen for elaboration for several reasons. First, it emphasizes the social functioning of persons within their environments (Schwartz and Goldiamond, 1975, pp. 1-2). The total person in dynamic interaction with all aspects of the environment is the focus of attention. This is in contrast to many other theoretical approaches which focus primarily on the individual's personality or isolated history.

Second, learning theory provides "a specific conception of human behavior" (National Association of Social Workers, 1977, pp. 1309-12). It emphasizes the importance of the assessment of observable behaviors (Thomas, 1970, p. 200). It also emphasizes the use of behaviorally specific terms in defining behaviors. This helps to make any particular behavior more clearly understandable.

Finally, learning theory provides a positive approach. The underlying idea is that behaviors develop through learning them, and, therefore, can be un-learned. This allows for positive behavioral changes. Instead of individuals being perceived as victims of their personal histories and personality defects, they are conceptualized as dynamic living beings capable of change.

Behavior modification is the therapeutic application of learning theory principles. Much evidence supports the effectiveness of behavioral techniques for a wide variety of human problems and learning situations (Bandura, 1969; Schutte and Hopkins, 1970; Macmillan, 1973; O'Leary and Wilson, 1975; Schwartz, 1975; Craighead et al., 1976; Fischer, 1978).

Respondent Conditioning

Respondent conditioning refers to the emission of behavior in response to a specific stimulus. It is also referred to as classical or Pavlovian conditioning. A particular stimulus elicits a particular response. The stimulus can be a word, a sight, or a sound.

For example, Martha, who has been on a strict diet for a week, stops by to visit her friend Evelyn. Evelyn is in the process of preparing a lobster dinner. She is also baking a German chocolate cake for dessert. Martha begins salivating at the thought of such appetizing food. Martha's response, salivation, occurs as a result of the stimulus, witnessing Evelyn's preparation of the wonderful, albeit fattening, food. Figure 4.1 portrays this relationship.

Much respondent behavior is unlearned; that is, a response is naturally emitted after exposure to a stimulus. This stimulus is called an unconditioned stimulus. Respondent conditioning occurs when a person learns to respond to a new stimulus which does not naturally elicit a response. This new stimulus is called a conditioned stimulus. In order to accomplish this, the new stimulus is paired with the stimulus that elicited the response naturally. The person then learns to associate the new stimulus with a particular

FIGURE 4.1: A Stimulus-Response Relationship

Lobster and German chocolate cake (*Unconditioned stimulus*) ➡ Martha's salivation (*Response*)

FIGURE 4.2: Respondent Conditioning

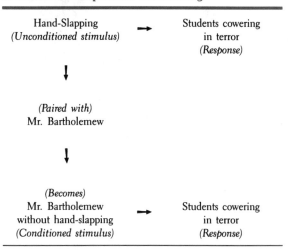

response even though it had nothing to do with that response originally.

For example, Mr. Bartholomew, a third grade teacher, slaps students on the hand when they talk out of turn. It might be noted that he slaps them very hard on the hand. As a result of this stimulus, the slapping, students fear Mr. Bartholomew. By associating Mr. Bartholomew with getting a slap on the hand, the students eventually learned to fear Mr. Bartholomew even when he wasn't slapping them. Mr. Bartholomew himself had been paired with the hand slapping until he elicited the same response that the slapping did. Figure 4-2 helps to illustrate this relationship.

Some behavioral techniques used by social workers involve the principles of respondent conditioning. Systematic desensitization is an example (Kazdin, 1989, pp. 13-14). This technique can be applied when a person is subject to extreme fear or anxiety over something, for example, snakes, enclosed places, school. Systematic desensitization usually has two major thrusts. First, the client is exposed to the thing he fears very gradually. Second, while the client is being exposed to the fearful item or event, he is also taught an incompatible response. The incompatible response must be something which cannot occur at the same time as the anxiety and fear. A good example of an incompatible response is progressive relaxation.

For example, the client learns how to control his

body and relax. At the same time the standard procedure is that he is exposed to the feared item or event in increasing amounts or degrees. A person who fears rats might first be shown a picture of a rat in the distance while, at the same time, using his newly acquired relaxation skills. Anxiety and fear cannot occur at the same time that the individual is in a relaxed state. They are incompatible responses.

The individual might then be shown an 8-by-10-inch photo of a rat. Once again, the individual would use relaxation techniques to prevent anxiety from occurring. The client would be exposed to rats in a more and more direct manner until the client could actually hold a rat in his hand. The client would gradually learn to use the incompatible relaxation technique to quell any anxiety that rats might once have elicited.

A variety of techniques based on respondent conditioning have also been used to treat enuresis, or bed-wetting, overeating, cigarette smoking, alcohol consumption, and sexual deviations (Mowrer and Mowrer, 1938; Kazdin, 1984; Kazdin, 1978). However, they are not nearly as many nor are they as common as those behavioral techniques based on operant conditioning.

Modeling

The second type of learning is called *modeling*. Modeling refers to the learning of behavior by observing another individual engaging in that behavior. In order to learn from a model, an individual does not necessarily have to participate in the behavior. An individual need only to watch how a model performs the behavior in order to learn how the behavior is accomplished. For obvious reasons, modeling is also called observational learning. A behavior can be learned simply by observing its occurrence.

Modeling is important within the context of practical parenting. Parents can model appropriate behavior for their children. This provides an effective means for children to watch and learn. For example, a father might act as a model for his son concerning how to play baseball. The father can teach his son how to throw and catch a ball by doing it himself. The child can learn by watching his father.

In social work intervention, modeling can be used

to model appropriate treatment of children so that parents may observe. For example, five-year-old Larry, who frequently has behavior problems, may pick up a pencil that the social worker accidentally dropped and return it to the social worker. The social worker may then model for the parent how the child can be positively reinforced for his good behavior. The social worker may say, "Thank you for picking up my pencil for me, Larry. That was very nice of you."

Another example of modeling within a social work practice context is role playing. For example, a social worker might ask a parent who has trouble controlling her son to role play that son and mimic his behavior. She is instructed to act the way she thinks her son would act. The social worker may then model for the parent some appropriate, effective things to say to the son when the son behaves in that way. Such modeling provides the opportunity for the parent to learn new ways of responding to her son.

Modeling can also teach children inappropriate and ineffective behavior. For example, consider a mother who strikes other family members whenever she gets the least bit irritated with them. She is likely to act as a model for that type of behavior. Her children may learn that striking others is the way to express their anger.

Some classic research studied the effects of positive and negative consequences upon modeling (Bandura, 1965). Children were shown a film of an adult hitting and kicking a large doll, obviously modeling aggressive behavior. Afterward, the children were divided into three groups. Each group then observed the model experiencing different respective consequences. One group of children viewed the model being punished for the aggressive behavior. Another group of children saw the model being rewarded for the same behavior. A third group of children saw the model being ignored. The children were then placed in situations where they themselves could display aggression. Children who saw the model receive a reward for aggressive behavior and those who saw him experience no consequences clearly displayed more aggressive behavior than those children who saw the model punished. It was ascertained that all the children had learned the aggressive behavior; when they were told they themselves would receive a reward for being aggressive, they all could indeed be aggressive. The conclusion is that modeling behavior can be

---

Consequences and Recurring Behavior

The Johnsons hired their neighbor, nine-year-old Eric, to mow their lawn once a week during the summer. Eric, not being sophisticated in the ways of money management, failed to discuss how much he would be paid per hour. Eric slaved away for four hours one Saturday afternoon when he would rather have been playing baseball.

When Eric had finished, Mr. Johnson came out, complimented Eric on what a fine job he had done, and gave him $3.50 for his trouble. Unfortunately $3.50 worked out to be $.875 per hour. Mr. Johnson thought this was more than adequate. Mr. Johnson himself had been paid only a grand total of $.50 for doing a similar job when he was a boy. Eric, however, felt this was more than chintzy on Mr. Johnson's part. He knew $3.50 would only cover a few brief video games down at Video Heaven. It would not nearly begin to finance the new baseball glove he wanted.

The consequences for Eric's lawn-mowing behavior were not positive. He did not receive his expected $12. Thus, Eric never mowed Mr. Johnson's lawn again. Instead he turned to other more generous and benevolent neighbors to upgrade his financial future. He also learned to make salary one of his first items on his business agenda. If Mr. Johnson had given him his expected rate of $3 an hour, Eric would have been a dependable and industrious worker throughout the summer. In other words, more favorable consequences for Eric would have encouraged his lawn-mowing behavior. He would have been conditioned to mow Mr. Johnson's lawn. As it turned out, Mr. Johnson was doomed to mowing his own lawn for the remainder of the summer.

---

affected both by consequences to the model and to the observer.

Other conditions can also affect the effectiveness of modeling or the degree to which modeling works. These include: "the similarity of the model to the observer; the prestige, status, and expertise of the model; and the number of models observed. As a general rule, imitation of a model by an observer is greater when the model is similar to the observer, more prestigious, and higher in status and expertise than the observer and when several models perform the same behavior" (Kazdin, 1989, p. 21).

Modeling has been used in a variety of clinical settings including the control of fear and the development of social skills. Usually, it's used in conjunction with other behavioral techniques.

Operant Conditioning

Operant conditioning is the dominant type of learning focused on in the United States (National Association of Social Workers, 1977, p. 1310). It allows for the easiest and most practical understanding of behavior. Most treatment applications are based on the principles of operant conditioning (Hosford and de Visser, 1974; Schwartz and Goldiamond, 1975; National Association of Social Workers, 1977; Kazdin, 1989).

Operant conditioning is "a type of learning in which behaviors are altered primarily by regulating the consequences which follow them" (Kazdin, 1989, p. 343). New behaviors can be shaped, weak behaviors can be strengthened, strong behaviors can be maintained, and undesirable behaviors can be weakened and eliminated. The emphasis lies on the consequences of behavior. In other words, whatever follows a particular behavior affects how frequently that behavior will occur again, as illustrated in "Consequences and Recurring Behavior."

The ABCs of Behavior

One way of conceptualizing operant behavior is to divide it into its primary parts. These include antecedents, behaviors, and consequences (Schwartz and Goldiamond, 1975, p. 17). Another way of referring to them is the ABCs of behavior.

Antecedents refer to the events occurring immediately prior to the behavior itself. These event set the stage for the behavior to occur. For instance, some individuals state that they are able to quit smoking cigarette except when they are socializing in a bar or nightclub. The bar conditions act as a stimulus or incentive for smoking behavior, whereas other environments do not. In other words, the bar setting acts as an antecedent for smoking behavior.

The behavior refers to "any observable and measurable response or act. . . . Behavior is occasionally broadly defined to include cognitions, psychophysiological reactions, and feelings, which may not be directly observable but are defined in terms that can be measured by means of various assessment strategies" (Kazdin, 1989, p. 337). The important phrase here is that behavior is "defined in terms that can be measured." Therefore, even thoughts and feelings can be addressed and changed as long as words can be found to clearly describe what they are. In order to bring about a behavior change, you must know exactly what it is that you are changing. In other words, it must be measurable. For instance, specific messages that people send to themselves can be altered as long as these messages can be clearly defined and measured. A person who frequently tells herself, "I am so fat," can have that message changed to, "I am a worthwhile person." Each time she tells herself each message, it can be noted and, therefore, the overall frequency measured.

Most behavior involved in operant conditioning is observable. Even thoughts and feelings frequently occur with accompanying behaviors. For example, Shirley is a six-year-old child who has been clinically diagnosed as depressed. Any thoughts she has about being depressed are not noticeable. However, she makes frequent statements about what a bad girl she is, how her parents don't like her, and what it would be like to die. These statements can be observed and noted. Such statements might be used as indicators for childhood depression.

Shirley's statements can also be measured; that is, the types of statements she makes and how often she makes them can be counted and evaluated. She might make a statement concerning what a bad girl she is twelve times per day, about how her parents dislike her five times per day, and about her own death sixteen times per day. When her depression begins to subside, these types of verbal statements may decrease in frequency and severity. For example, Shirley may only make derogatory remarks about herself four times per day instead of twelve. She may say her parents dislike her only once each day. Statements about death may disappear altogether.

In addition to verbal behavior, physical behavior or actions may also be observed and measured. Besides making statements which indicate she's depressed, Shirley may spend much of her time sitting in a corner, sucking her thumb, and gazing off into space. The exact amount of time she spends displaying these specific behaviors may be observed and measured. For example, Shirley initially may spend five hours each day sitting in a corner. When depression begins to wane, she may only spend one-half hour in the corner.

The final component as a basis for operant conditioning involves the consequences of the behavior. A consequence may be "either something that is presented or something that is taken away or postponed" (Schwartz and Goldiamond, 1975, p. 18). In other words, something happens as a direct result of a particular behavior. Consequences are best described in terms of reinforcement and punishment.

Reinforcement

Reinforcement refers to a procedure or consequence that increases the frequency of the behavior immediately preceding it. If the behavior is already occurring at a high frequency level, then reinforcement maintains the behavior's frequency. A behavior occurs under certain antecedent conditions. If the consequences of that behavior serve to make that behavior occur more often or be maintained at its current high rate, then those consequences are considered reinforcing. Reinforcers strengthen behavior and make them more likely to occur in the future (Patterson, 1975, p. 10).

Positive Reinforcement

Reinforcement can either be positive or negative. *Positive reinforcement* refers to positive events or consequences which follow a behavior and act to strengthen that behavior. In other words, something is presented or added to a situation and encourages a particular behavior. For example, eight-year-old Herbie receives a weekly allowance of $10 if he straightens out his room and throws all of his dirty laundry down the clothes chute. Receiving his allowance serves to strengthen or positively reinforce Herbie's cleaning behavior.

Negative Reinforcement

Negative reinforcement is the removal of a negative event or consequence which serves to increase the frequency of a particular behavior. There are two important aspects of this definition. First, something must be removed from the situation. Second, the frequency of a particular behavior is increased. In this manner positive and negative reinforcement resemble each other. Both function as reinforcement which, by definition, serves to increase or maintain the frequency of a behavior.

A good example of negative reinforcement is a seat belt buzzer in a new car. The car door is opened and a loud and annoying buzzer is activated. It will not stop until the driver's seat belt is fastened. The intent is to encourage people to buckle up. Conceptually, the buzzer functions as a negative reinforcer. The buzzer acts as reinforcement because it increases the frequency of buckling seat belts. The buzzer is also negative or aversive. It increases seat belt buckling behavior because people are motivated to stop it, not because they are motivated to hear it.

Another example of negative reinforcement is Orlando, a college sophomore trying to study in his dorm room one Thursday night. His next-door neighbor, Gavin, has decided that Thursday nights are much better for partying than for studying. Gavin, therefore, decides to invite a bunch of his friends over to participate in some illegal substance which will remain nameless. Gavin also cranks up his CD player to the highest vibration level it can tolerate.

Orlando tries to ignore this nuisance and continues trying to study until he can't stand it anymore. In a state of fury, he stomps up to the wall that he, unfortunately, shares with Gavin next door, smashes his fist on it several times, and screams, "Shut the #$@*$%& up in there!!!"

On the other side of the wall, Gavin says to his buddies, "That guy is such a dweeb. If I don't turn it down, he'll probably 'narc' on me to the hall director. Let's go somewhere else." He turns off his CD player and leaves with his friends.

Evaluating this scenario in learning theory terms leads to several conclusions. First, Orlando's screaming behavior served as negative reinforcement for Gavin's turning off his CD player and leaving the room. Orlando's screaming was aversive to Gavin. In order to terminate it, Gavin turned off his music and left. Moreover, from then on, Gavin made it a point to turn off his CD player whenever Orlando was around and leave his room when he wanted to party. Thus, Orlando's (aversive) screaming reinforced (increased the frequency of) Gavin's turning off his CD player and leaving his room when he wanted to party behaviors.

Looking at his situation from another perspective, Gavin's turning off his CD and room leaving behaviors served as positive reinforcement for Orlando's screaming behavior. Orlando was positively reinforced for screaming because he got what he wanted, namely, peace and quiet. Orlando became much more likely to scream at Gavin in the future (that is, Orlando was reinforced), because he immediately received something positive as a result of his behavior.

Although at first glance this may appear obvious and simplistic, it is easy to become confused about the type of reinforcement which is occurring. In any particular situation, both positive and negative reinforcement may be taking place at the same time. Take, for instance, the example given initially to illustrate learning theory. It involved four-year-old Huey and his mother at the supermarket. Huey yelled for a candy bar. His mother finally gave in and thrust one into his mouth. His crying immediately stopped. Both positive and negative reinforcement were occurring in this example. Mother's giving Huey the candy bar served as a positive reinforcer. Huey received something positive which he valued. At the same time he learned that he could get exactly what he wanted from his mother by screaming in the supermarket. Giving him the candy bar positively reinforced his bad behavior. That type of behavior would be, therefore, more likely to occur in the future.

At the same time negative reinforcement was occurring in this situation. Mother's giving-in behavior was encouraged or strengthened. She learned that she could stop Huey's obnoxious yelling by giving him what he wanted, namely, a candy bar. Huey's yelling, therefore, acted as negative reinforcement. It increased his mother's "giving-in" behavior by motivating her to stop or to escape from his yelling.

Punishment

Punishment and negative reinforcement are frequently confused. Perhaps this is because they both concern something negative or aversive. However, they represent two distinctly different concepts.

Punishment is the presentation of an aversive event or the removal of a positive reinforcer which results in the decrease in frequency of a particular behavior. Two aspects of this definition are important. First, the result of punishment by definition is the decrease in frequency of a behavior. This is in direct opposition to negative reinforcement, where, by definition, the frequency of a behavior is increased.

Second, punishment can be administered in two different ways. One way involves presenting a negative or aversive event immediately after a behavior occurs. Negative events may include spankings, scoldings, electric shocks, additional demands on time, or embarrassing criticisms. For example, ten-year-old Susie hadn't studied for her social studies exam. Her parents had already complained about the last report card. She just hadn't given the test much thought until Ms. McGuilicutte was handing out the test papers. Susie looked over her test paper and gasped. Nothing looked even vaguely familiar. She was sitting next to Janet, whom she considered the class genius. She figured that just a few brief glances at Janet's paper wouldn't hurt anybody. However, Susie was wrong. Ms. McGuilicutte, whose vision equalled that of a hawk's, immediately noticed Susie's wandering attention. Ms. McGuilicutte swooped down on Susie and confiscated Susie's test paper. In front of the entire class Susie was told that cheating resulted not only in an F grade, but also in two weeks worth of detentions after school. Susie was mortified. She vowed to herself that she would never cheat again.

Susie received extremely aversive consequences as the result of her cheating behavior. The consequences included not only a failing test grade and two weeks of detentions, but also devastating humiliation in front of her peers. Her cheating behavior decreased in frequency to zero.

The second way in which punishment can be administered is by withdrawing a positive reinforcer. Once again, the result must be a decrease in the frequency of a particular behavior. For example, seven-year-old Robbie thought it was funny to belch at the table during dinner. Several times his parents asked him to stop belching. Each time Robbie was quiet for about a minute and then started belching again. Finally, his mother stated loudly and firmly that such belching was considered rude behavior and that, as punishment, Robbie would not receive the banana split she had planned for his dessert. Robbie whined and pleaded, but his mother refused to give it to him. Robbie loved desserts, and banana splits were his favorite. Robbie never belched at the table again,

at least not purposefully. Removal of the positive reinforcer, namely the banana split dessert, had served as punishment. The punishment resulted in an abrupt decrease in belching behavior.

It should be emphasized that the term punishment as it is used in learning theory does not necessarily mean physical punishment. For some of us, the word may bring to mind pictures of parents putting children over their knees and spanking them. As we've indicated, punishment does not have to be physical. Verbal reprimands such as a mother saying how disappointed she is that she caught her daughter "necking" with her boyfriend in the basement family room can also serve as punishment. The reprimand functions as a punishment if her "necking" behavior decreases. Likewise, withdrawal of a valued activity such as not allowing a child to go to a popular movie can be a punishment if it acts to decrease or stop some negative behavior.

Extinction

Extinction involves "the cessation of reinforcement of a response," which results in the eventual decrease in frequency and possible eradication of that behavior (Kazdin, 1989, p. 36). Reinforcement simply stops; nothing is actively taken away. It should be noted that extinction and punishment are two separate concepts. As Kazdin notes (1989, p. 36), "In extinction, no consequence follows the response; an event is neither taken away nor presented. In punishment, some aversive event follows a response or some positive event is taken away." In everyday life, extinction usually takes the form of ignoring a behavior that was previously reinforced with attention.

An example of extinction concerns the reduction of tantrum behaviors in a twenty-one-month-old child (Williams, 1959). When put to bed, the child would scream until his parents returned to the room to comfort him. This provided positive reinforcement for the child's behavior. The parents were instructed to put the child to bed, leave the room, and ignore his screaming. The first night, the child screamed for forty-five minutes. However, the next night when the parents left the room, no screaming occurred. Eventually, withdrawing the positive reinforcer of attention resulted in the total elimination of the child's tan-

FIGURE 4.3: Positive Reinforcement, Negative Reinforcement, Punishment, and Extinction

Below the differences between positive reinforcement, negative reinforcement, punishment, and extinction are summarized. Important differences involve what happens and what results with each behavior approach.

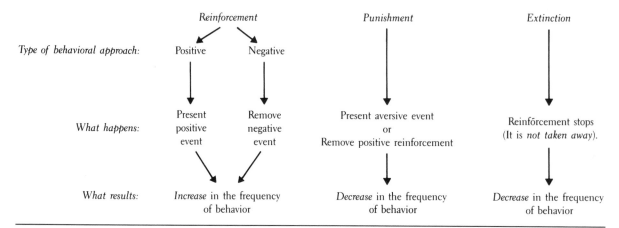

trums. Ignoring, therefore, can be used as an effective means of extinction.

This example uses attention as a positive reinforcer. However, extinction occurs with many other reinforcers in various daily situations. For example, if putting a quarter in a coffee machine results in nothing but a gush of clear, hot water without the cup, use of that coffee machine will probably be extinguished. Likewise, say you're having difficulty in your biology lab course. You don't understand what the professor is saying during lectures and you're not sure what he wants from you on exams (you've already received a D+ grade on two of them). Three times you try to see him during his office hours and every time he is not there. Eventually, you stop trying to see him, despite your frustration. Your behavior involved in seeing him to get help has been extinguished.

One other aspect of extinction is important to note. Frequently, when reinforcement initially is stopped, a brief increase in the frequency of the behavior may occur. This is referred to as an *extinction burst* (Kazdin, 1975, p. 180). This occurs despite the eventual elimination of the behavior. For example, consider again tantrums in a small child. When the reinforcement of attention is withdrawn, the child's behavior might escalate temporarily. The intensity of the undesirable behavior can seriously strain the patience and tolerance of parents (Patterson and Reid, 1970). One way of looking at this might be to see it

from the child's perspective. If the child in the past had always received positive reinforcement through attention for his behavior, it might be very confusing suddenly to receive no attention for that very same behavior. The child may try exceptionally hard to get the attention to which he was accustomed. However, eventually the child will learn that the tantrums are not reinforced and are, therefore, simply not worth the effort. Thus, the tantrum behavior is extinguished.

The relationships between extinction, punishment, positive reinforcement, and negative reinforcement are summarized in Figure 4.3.

Applications of Learning Theory to Practice

As children become socialized, they learn and assimilate various behaviors. Because learning is a complicated process, the behaviors they sometimes learn are not those that their parents would prefer. Behavior management is a major issue for many parents.

When a child behaves in a particular way, parents have various alternative ways of responding to this behavior. At any point in time there are alternative plans of action an individual can take. For each alternative there are consequences. The critical task is to evaluate each alternative and select the one with the most advantageous results. Learning theory concepts provide parents with a means of understanding the alternatives open to them and of predicting the potential consequences of each alternative. It can serve to help them gain control over their children's behavior.

An example of parental alternatives in response to behavior is provided by Danny, age four. At the dinner table with his whole family present, Danny nonchalantly and without warning says an unmentionable four-letter word. Danny's parents are shocked. At this point, they can respond in several different ways. One alternative is to ignore the fact that Danny said the word. Without being given undue attention, saying the word may be stopped. A second alternative is to tell Danny calmly that the word is not considered a very nice word. They might add that some people use it when they're angry and that other people don't really like to hear it. They might also ask him to please not use the word anymore. A third alternative is for the parents to display their horror and disbelief, scream at Danny never to say that word again, and send him up to bed without being allowed to finish his supper.

When this incident actually occurred, the parents opted to respond as described in the third alternative. Poor Danny really didn't understand what the word meant. He had just heard it on the playground that afternoon. He was amazed at the response of his parents and at the attention he received. His mother reported that for the following two years, he continued to repeat that unmentionable four-letter word virtually everywhere. He said it to the dentist, to the grocer, to the police officer, and even to his grandmother. His mother reported that after a while she would have been willing to pay Danny to stop using that word, if such a strategy would have worked.

In Danny's situation, his parents' attention became a tremendously strong positive reinforcer. Perhaps if they would have stopped and thought in terms of learning theory principles, they could have gained immediate control of the situation and never thought another thing of it.

The Use of Positive Reinforcement

Positive reinforcement is based on the very fundamental idea that behavior is governed by its consequences. If the consequences of a particular alternative behavior are positive or appealing, then the individual will tend to behave that way. In other words, the frequency of that behavior will be increased.

Positive reinforcement provides a valuable means of behavioral control. It has been established as an appropriate technique for achieving positive behavioral changes in numerous situations (Kazdin, 1975, p. 105). Rose (1973, p. 87), who expresses a strong preference for positive reinforcement over the use of aversive techniques, explains that the use of positive reinforcement helps to reduce the risk that clients begin associating the negative effects of punishment, for example, with the therapist, resulting in an aversion to therapy. Positive reinforcement also provides the advantage of teaching an individual exactly how to improve his or her behavior.

Various aspects of positive reinforcement will be discussed here. First, the types of reinforcers available will be examined. The differences between positive reinforcement and the use of rewards will be explained. Finally, suggestions for maximizing the effectiveness of positive reinforcement will be presented.

Types of Positive Reinforcers

Reinforcers can be separated into two major categories, primary and secondary. Primary reinforcers are rewarding in themselves, without any association with other reinforcers (Morris, 1979, p. 152). They include objects and activities that people naturally find valuable. Food, water, candy, and sex are examples of primary reinforcers. Individuals respond positively to them naturally without having to learn their value.

Secondary reinforcers, on the other hand, have values which are learned through association with other reinforcers (Morris, 1979, p. 152). The key idea here is that they must be learned. Alone they have no intrinsic value. Money perhaps is the most easily understood example. A one thousand dollar bill in itself is nothing but a small piece of high quality paper with printed symbols on it. However, it is associated with things of value. It can be used to purchase actual items ranging from diamonds to pistachio nuts. Money is valuable only because it is associated with other concrete primary reinforcers.

The concepts of primary and secondary reinforcers can readily be applied to treatment situations. For example, a developmentally disabled child may not initially value verbal praise. He may not yet have learned to associate verbal praise with his actual behavior. A social worker may be working with the child concerning his ability to dress himself. Initially, saying, "That's good," may mean nothing to the child. However, saying, "That's good," while at the same time giving the child a small chocolate star, may eventually give the verbal praise some meaning. The child learns to associate verbal praise with the positive value of the candy. Eventually, the praise itself becomes reinforcing to the child, even without the candy. This technique involves pairing a primary reinforcer, the chocolate star, with a secondary reinforcer, verbal praise. The secondary reinforcer becomes valuable to the child through its initial association with the candy.

Secondary Reinforcers

Four major types of secondary reinforcers will be addressed here. They include material reinforcers and nonfood consumables, activities, social reinforcers, and tokens (Fischer and Gochros, 1975; Kazdin, 1989).

Material Reinforcers and Non-Food Consumables

Material reinforcers are specific objects or substances which can be used as rewards to increase specific behaviors. Eight-year-old Herbie received an allowance for cleaning his room. Herbie's cleaning behavior was strengthened or reinforced by receiving an allowance.

Money might be considered an object or a specific, tangible thing which reinforces a behavior. Other objects which might have been used as tangible reinforcers for Herbie include records and toys. Each of these items would have acquired their value through learning. Therefore, they would be considered secondary reinforcers.

Food has already been established as a primary reinforcer along with a number of other things that are naturally reinforcing; learning is not involved. There are additionally some non-food consumables that people can learn to value. Examples include cigarettes, gum, and chewing tobacco. Although these are not naturally desired, a taste for them can be acquired. Since they are material substances, they

will be included in this category of secondary reinforcers.

Activities

Activities make up the second category of secondary reinforcers. Activities are tangible events whose value has been learned. Positively reinforcing activities for children might include watching television, playing with friends, staying up late at night, being read to, going shopping, or visiting the stock car races.

For example, twelve-year-old Gina hates doing her homework at night. However, she loves going to the movies on Saturdays. Her parents positively reinforce her for doing an hour's worth of homework five nights per week by giving her money to go to the movies on Saturday. Going to the movies is an activity that serves as positive reinforcement for Gina's doing her homework.

Premack (1965) recognized that people have hierarchies of preferred behavior. In other words, any individual when given a choice will choose one behavior over another behavior. For instance, an individual, if given a choice, might personally prefer to plant flowers in the garden over doing the laundry. The *Premack Principle* states that "of any pair of responses or activities in which an individual engages, the more frequent one will reinforce the less frequent one" (Kazdin, 1989, p. 31). Thus, more preferred activities can be used to reinforce less preferred activities. Take the person who prefers garden work over laundry. Allowing him to plant the garden after he completes the laundry will serve to reinforce the laundry-related behavior. He will be more likely to do the laundry if he knows he can plant the garden afterwards.

We've established that fun, exciting activities can serve as secondary reinforcers if they are indeed valued and enjoyed by the person involved. The Premack Principle implies that activities needn't be special or extremely valued but simply preferred in order to act as a secondary reinforcer. The garden work might not be something the same individual would choose if a weekend at Las Vegas were also given as an option. However, he still would choose the garden over the laundry. Therefore, the garden could be used as a secondary reinforcer for the laundry. Following the same line of thinking, a trip to Las Vegas could be

Activities can be effective behavioral reinforcers, particularly if they're fun and exciting. Kids who would just as soon skip cleaning their rooms in the morning might be more willing if they can play in the park in the afternoon.

used as a secondary reinforcer to working in the garden or to doing the laundry.

One of the implicit assumptions here is that each individual will have a different hierarchy of preferred activities. For example, on camping trips, Nick prefers the following specific activities in this order from most preferred to least preferred: reading *Peterson's 4-Wheel & Off-Road* magazine; cooking the food; doing the dishes; reading science fiction, especially space horror stories. Karen, on the other hand, prefers the specified camping activities in this order: reading science fiction, especially space horror stories; doing the dishes; cooking the food; reading *Peterson's 4 Wheel & Off-Road* magazine ("Winch Wisdom," the title of the leading article, doesn't excite her at all). For Karen, reading science fiction would function as a secondary reinforcer for any of the other three activities. She would be more likely to do any of them if she could read science fiction afterwards. For Nick, however, the science fiction would not serve to reinforce any of the other activities, whereas reading *Peterson's 4-Wheel & Off-Road* magazine would.

Social Reinforcers

Material and activities are not the only things that people learn to value. Various aspects of social interaction can also be considered very valuable. Social reinforcement includes words and gestures used to indicate caring and concern toward another person. This can be communicated in one of two ways, either by giving verbal or physical praise. Verbal praise involves stating words or phrases that indicate approval or appreciation of someone's specific behavior, such as "Good job," "You did that very well," or "That's terrific!"

Effective verbal praise is directed at a specific behavior or activity. The person receiving the praise should be clearly aware of what the praise concerns.

A smile is a means of social reinforcement.

For instance, eight-year-old Linda did the dishes without being asked for the two days her mother was out of town attending a professional conference. Her mother, on her return home, stated, "Thank you very much for helping out and doing the dishes. I understand you did them without even being told. I really appreciate your help." Linda's mother made it very clear to Linda exactly what she did that was appreciated. When such praise acts to strengthen Linda's dish-washing behavior in the future, it is positive reinforcement. If Linda's mother instead had stated to Linda, "You're a very good girl," it may not have been clear to Linda exactly why she was good. The positive regard communicated by such a statement, of course, is valuable in itself. However, Linda may have understood her mother to mean that she was good because she didn't cry when her mother left or because she only stayed up one-half hour past her bedtime. Linda may not have understood that her mother appreciated her washing dishes, and thus may never have done so without being told again.

The second type of social reinforcement is physical praise. Physical praise involves communicating appreciation or praise through physical gestures or body posture. This may simply involve a smile or a nod of the head. Hugging, clapping, or even winking can also indicate praise.

Consider, for example, how a smile might acquire significance. An infant may not initially value her mother's smile. However, the infant may soon learn to associate the smile with comfort, warmth, and food. Eventually, the smile itself becomes reinforcing. It is a secondary reinforcer. The infant learns to value it. The smile is valued not because it is of value itself, but because the infant has learned to associate it with things of value.

The effects of social reinforcement are illustrated by Beverly, age five. Beverly had acquired a role in the kindergarten play. Her part involved playing a duck whose job it was to waddle back and forth across the stage. Beverly was extremely nervous about her part, as she was an exceptionally shy child. She even had to get a new yellow dress and wear red rubbers to help characterize her role. She had been practicing her waddling for days before the play. Finally, the critical night arrived. It was almost time to initiate her waddle and dare to venture out on the stage. At the last minute, she almost backed down and started crying. However, she looked out into the audience and there were her parents in the second row, looking directly at her. They were both smiling proudly and nodding their heads. With such encouragement, she waddled across that stage like no one had ever waddled before. Her parents' obvious approval and encouragement had served to positively reinforce her acting and waddling behavior. After this experience, she was much more likely to volunteer and participate in activities that required performing before an audience.

Tokens

Tokens provide the fourth category of secondary reinforcers. Token reinforcers are defined as "objects that symbolize various units of value desirable to an individual that can be exchanged for something that person wants" (Fischer, 1975, p. 61). Tokens can include poker chips, slugs or artificial coins, points, checkmarks, or gold stars. In and of themselves, they mean nothing. However, they can be associated with something of value and eventually be exchanged for that item or activity.

A practical application of tokens is the use of a token economy in child management. For example, a bicycle might serve as a strong positive reinforcer for a particular child. However, it is absurd to give the child a bicycle every time the child cleans his/her room. Rather, a system can be designed where a child can earn tokens. The child can be told that if she earns a certain number of tokens, she can exchange them for a bicycle. Tokens become a secondary reinforcer. A large sum of tokens can be used to acquire a bicycle, the item of real value.

Reinforcers versus Rewards

A distinction must be made between reinforcers and rewards. A reward is not necessarily a positive reinforcer. A reward is something that is given in return for a service or a particular achievement. It may or may not increase the frequency of a particular behavior. A soldier might receive a medal of honor at the end of a war for shooting down twenty-seven enemy planes. This is a reward. This reward does not, however, increase the frequency of this individual's shooting down more planes during his civilian life.

Reinforcers, by definition, increase the frequency of a behavior. Receiving an A on an exam is a positive reinforcer for studying behavior if it serves to increase the frequency of the particular student's studying in preparation for exams. However, the student may not value the grade very much. The A may not serve to motivate him to increase or maintain studying behavior. The student becomes bored with studying and receives C and D grades on the next two exams. In this case, the grade might be considered a reward for performance on one exam. However, the grade is not a positive reinforcer because it neither maintained nor increased the frequency of his studying.

By definition, something serves as reinforcer only if it increases behavior. A positive reinforcer needs to be valued by an individual for it to be effective. Not all items, activities, and social interactions are reinforcing to all people. For example, a roller coaster ride at Disney World may be very positively reinforcing for a third grader whose dream it is to visit Disney World. However, that same ride may not be at all reinforcing or valuable to the third grader's father who tends to become ill on roller coasters.

Suggestions for Using Positive Reinforcement

Four suggestions to enhance the use of positive reinforcement involve the quality, the immediacy, and the frequency of positive reinforcement, and the use of small steps for shaping behavior.

Quality of Positive Reinforcement

In order to be considered reinforcement, an item or event must actually increase the frequency of some behavior. It's already been established that what is reinforcing for one person may not be reinforcing for another.

A more subtle issue, however, involves the varying degrees of reinforcement value within any particular reinforcer. A particular positive reinforcer might be more reinforcing in a particular form or under certain conditions. It might be more preferable in one form than in another. For example, animals can be positively reinforced for pressing a bar by giving them food. However, they will perform with a higher frequency of bar pressing behavior when they receive foods that taste sweet than when they receive foods that are sour or neutral (Hutt, 1954). Perhaps they are not so different in this respect from human beings.

A high school senior working as a part-time janitor at a small local inner tube factory provides another example. The young man, Dave, is working to save for a downpayment on his own car. The idea of owning a car is very reinforcing to him. However, the make of the car makes a difference in terms of its value to him. Because of the tremendous costs involved in purchasing a car, Dave had decided to be satisfied with almost anything that he could reasonably afford. However, when he found a 1990 red Mazda RX7 with yellow flames printed on the hood for sale down the block, his working behavior sharply increased. He asked if he could double his working hours. To Dave, the Mazda served as a much stronger positive reinforcer than an older, beat-up station wagon.

Immediacy of Positive Reinforcement

Positive reinforcement has a greater effect on behavior if it is administered immediately or shortly after the behavior occurs (Skinner, 1953). In other words, it's important that the behavior and the positive reinforcement occur very close to each other in time. Positive reinforcement loses its effect if it is delayed too long. For example, a five-year-old boy brushes his teeth without being told one morning. Praising him for this behavior immediately after he's finished or even while he's brushing will have a much greater effect on whether he brushes his teeth again this way than if he's praised when he gets into bed at night. By the time bedtime arrives, he is likely to forget that he ever brushed his teeth. It becomes much more difficult for him to associate the praise with the specific teeth-brushing behavior.

Frequency of Positive Reinforcement

Positive reinforcement which is administered consistently is the most effective (Fischer and Gochros, 1975, p. 66; Patterson, 1975, pp. 36-37). In other words, the most effective way to increase a particular behavior is to reinforce it every time it occurs. This is referred to as *continuous reinforcement*. For example, Gertie, age twelve, is supposed to do her math homework every night. If Gertie's teacher collects the assignments every morning and gives Gertie credit for doing them, Gertie is likely to complete her homework every night. However, if Gertie's teacher only collects the Thursday night homework, Gertie is less likely to do her homework every night.

An advantage of continuous reinforcement is that it is the most effective in establishing a particular behavior. However, a disadvantage is that if the positive reinforcement stops for some reason, the behavior is likely to extinguish rapidly. For example, Gertie's teacher collects her homework every morning for two months. Suddenly, her teacher decides that it's no longer necessary to collect the homework. As a result, there is a fairly strong likelihood that Gertie will stop doing her homework if she no longer gets credit for it.

An alternative to continuous reinforcement is *intermittent reinforcement*. This is where a behavior is not reinforced every time it is performed. Instead it is reinforced only occasionally. In the real world, continuous reinforcement is difficult to administer. It is difficult to be with a person every minute of the day in order to observe that person's behavior. Sometimes intermittent reinforcement is a viable alternative.

Intermittent reinforcement is not as powerful in initially establishing a behavior. It may take longer to establish the behavior. The behavior may not occur as regularly as it would under the conditions of continuous reinforcement. For example, Gertie might not do her homework every night because there would be a chance it wouldn't be collected the next day.

However, intermittent reinforcement is less subject to extinction. That is, suppose Gertie's teacher had only intermittently or occasionally collected her homework. Suddenly, the homework is no longer being collected. Gertie would be more likely to continue doing the homework after an intermittent schedule of reinforcement than after a continuous schedule. When she was accustomed to occasional or intermittent reinforcement, she would be more likely to continue doing her homework on the chance that it might be collected again. If homework collection stops abruptly after continuously being collected, Gertie would probably think that her teacher no longer liked to collect it. As a result, Gertie would probably stop doing her homework.

Each type of intermittent reinforcement dictates a different procedure for how frequently or in what order reinforcement should be administered. These various procedures are referred to as *schedules of reinforcement*.

Shaping Behavior

Sometimes the behavior that's supposed to be positively reinforced never occurs. It is impossible to reinforce a behavior that isn't there. Therefore, a technique called *shaping* can be used. Shaping refers to the reinforcement of successive approximations, that is, small steps of progress, made toward the final desired behavior.

For example, seven-year-old Ralph is terrified of the water. His mother thinks that it would be valuable for him to learn to swim. However, swimming behavior cannot be reinforced because Ralph simply refuses to enter a swimming pool. In this case, shaping might be useful. Instead of attempting to positively reinforce Ralph's dogpaddle, which isn't occurring, it might be useful to break down the specific behavior into smaller, more manageable pieces of behavior. For instance, swimming might be broken down into the following smaller segments of behavior: going to the beach and playing far away from the water, playing several feet away from the water, playing while sitting in an inch of water, wading, entering the water waist deep, moving arms around in the water, briefly dunking head beneath the water, and finally starting to practice beginning swimming strokes. At each step, Ralph could be positively reinforced with praise, attention, or toys for participating in that step. Eventually, his behavior could be shaped so that he would participate in behavior resembling swimming. Specific swimming techniques could then be initiated and reinforced.

The Use of Punishment

Punishment is frequently and often unwillingly chosen as the first alternative in controlling children's behavior. Often punishment is used in the name of discipline. Punishment involves either the application of an aversive consequence or the removal of a positive reinforcer. In either case the result is a decrease in the frequency of a behavior. Application of aversive events will be discussed first.

Potential Negative Consequences

Before using punishment as a means of behavioral management, it's important to consider the potential negative consequences involved. Five of them will be mentioned here. First, punishment tends to elicit a negative emotional response (Fischer and Gochros, 1975, p. 48). The child may come to dislike the learning situation. He or she may become despondent and uninterested in learning in general. For example, if a child is punished for spelling some words wrong in a composition, the child may no longer want to write at all. The child may also have a negative reaction toward the person administering the punishment.

For example, a young woman in junior high school was walking through the crowded halls from study hall to her next class. The gruff, varsity football coach grabbed her by the shoulder and shouted, "Act like a lady!" She had no idea what he was referring to. However, from that time on, she avoided both crowded hallways and that football coach whenever she could. She had developed an intense dislike for the man.

This example also illustrates the second possible negative side effect of punishment, namely avoidance of either the punishing person or the punitive situation (Kazdin, 1989, p. 166). In homes where physical punishment is used freely and regularly, children may try to stay away from the home as much as possible. Lying may provide another effective means of avoiding punitive situations. (Children sometimes learn to lie because parents set the price for honesty too high.)

The third possible negative effect of punishment is that it can teach children to be aggressive (Wagonseller et al., 1977, p. 6). Another way of saying this is that a punishing agent models aggressive behavior (Kazdin, 1989, p. 167). Children can learn that the way to deal with frustration or with not getting their own way is to hit or scream. This can carry over to their interactions with peers, siblings, or adults. An example is a sixteen-year-old adolescent who was diagnosed as "emotionally disturbed." When he was a small child, physical punishment was used frequently and plentifully in the home. By the time he reached age sixteen and had grown to be 6 feet, 3 inches tall, a different problem became apparent in the home. The boy began to physically assault his mother whenever they had disagreements. He had learned to be aggressive.

The fourth potential problem with using punishment, specifically physical punishment, is the possibility of physically harming the child. A parent may lose control or not be aware of his or her real strength. Without initial intent, physical damage may result.

Finally, there is a fifth reason for questioning the use of punishment. Punishment teaches people what they should not do but gives them no indication as to what they should do (Thorndike, 1932). Scolding a child for being impolite when visiting Aunt Edna gives the child no indication about how she could have treated Aunt Edna more appropriately.

In summary, all five of these considerations involve losing control of the consequences of punishment. The outcome of punishment is unpredictable and, therefore, it should be used with extreme care.

Effectiveness of Punishment

Despite these considerations, there is some evidence that punishment can be effective. Punishment has been used successfully to treat specific types of problems with specific types of children.

For instance, punishment using mild electric shock applied to the leg of a nine-month-old infant was found to stop chronic vomiting (Linscheid and Cunningham, 1977). It should be emphasized, however, that such extreme forms of punishment as electric shock might be used only very rarely when the problem is extremely serious and all other forms of treatment have failed. The infant was suffering from severe weight loss. Death was imminent. At other times electric shock has been used "to suppress such potentially harmful behaviors as self-injury, playing with dangerous equipment, and climbing dangerous places" (Kazdin, 1989, p. 147).

Some other specific types of punishment have been used to decrease specific behaviors. In one instance, mentally retarded adolescents continued to injure themselves by continuously striking themselves on the head or biting themselves. Spraying a fine mist of water into the adolescents' faces immediately after the behavior occurred was found to reduce this self-destructive behavior (Singh et al., 1986). It should be stressed that such punishments were administered only in very specific instances in which the clients were suffering from serious damage. Punishment, if used at all, is best applied in the context of a treatment program which also uses positive reinforcement (Kazdin, 1989).

Parke (1977) concludes that superficial punishment does have a place in behavior modification programs. However, he cautioned that punishment is a complex process with varied effects. Variables such as timing, intensity, consistency of the punishment, and the relationship between the punishing agent and the client, directly affect the results of punishment. He warns that decreasing behavior is not the only issue involved in view of the possible negative side effects.

The Nature of Punishment

Punishment has several characteristics. First, a decrease in the frequency of a behavior usually occurs immediately after the punishment is presented (Azrin and Holz, 1966; Kushner, 1968). If the behavior doesn't decrease almost immediately after the supposed punishment starts, there is a good possibility it never will. The implication is not to continue punishment if it doesn't work almost immediately.

For example, one-year-old Tyrone was crawling happily on his mother's kitchen floor when he accidentally discovered the electric socket. His mother, who was watching him out of the corner of her eye, ran over to him, slapped his hand, and raised her voice in a loud, "No!" He looked at her and returned his attention immediately to the socket. This occurred four times after which his mother slapped him even harder. He then started crying and she removed him to another room. In this incident, scolding and

hitting was not effective. Tyrone's mother's attention appeared to positively reinforce Tyrone's playing with the electric socket. Scolding and hitting was not effective even after several attempts. It was not likely that it would ever work. Calmly diverting Tyrone's attention might have been a more effective approach to controlling Tyrone's behavior.

Another characteristic of punishment is that its effects, although often immediate, frequently do not last very long (Kazdin, 1989, p. 171). Relatively soon after receiving punishment, a person has the tendency to revert to the old behavior. For example, a driver may receive a speeding ticket for driving 87 mph on a 55 mph expressway. He is temporarily disgusted and takes care to drive within the speed limit. However, he soon finds it too restrictive and time consuming to drive so slowly. His speeds gradually creep up to the old levels of 85 to 90 mph.

A third characteristic of punishment is that its effects are frequently limited to the conditions where the punishment occurred (Kazdin, 1989, p. 170). In other words, punishment tends to work only in the specific situation in which it occurred or only with the person who actually administered the punishment. One study found that punishment which worked to suppress autistic behavior in a treatment setting was found not to work in the home (Risley, 1968). For example, Trudy, age seven, likes to spit at people as they pass by her on the sidewalk. Her mother spanks her when she sees this behavior. Therefore, Trudy never spits in front of her mother. However, when her mother is in the house or at the grocery store, or when Trudy is at the babysitter's, she continues to spit at passers-by. The babysitter tried spanking her twice, but it didn't work. Spanking functioned as punishment for Trudy, but only when her mother was present and only when her mother administered it.

Selective Use of Punishment

Perhaps the most humane and ethical perspective to assume concerning punishment is to use it sparingly and then only in certain types of severe situations. There are at least two situations when it may be appropriate.

First, it may be used to eliminate self-destructive behavior which, in itself, is dangerous to the child's well-being (Fischer and Gochros, 1975, p. 49). This might include the self-pinching or head-banging behavior of an autistic child. It might also include immediately stopping a child from ingesting a dangerous drug.

Second, punishment might be necessary where there is no other way to make a child stop a particular inappropriate behavior so that another more appropriate behavior can be reinforced (Krumboltz and Krumboltz, 1972, p. 186). For example, three-year-old Mickey's only means of relating to other children is to walk up to them and punch them. In order to reinforce more appropriate means of relating to and playing with others, Mickey's punching behavior must be eliminated or at least suppressed. Punishment might be an effective means of accomplishing this.

Suggestions for Using Punishment

When the decision is made to use punishment, Patterson (1975) makes the following four suggestions for maximizing its effectiveness. First, intervention should occur early; that is, punishment should be administered as soon as possible after the behavior that is to be punished occurs.

For example, ten-year-old Santiago had been stealing compact disks for about six months. One afternoon he decided to shoplift a CD from K-Mart. Although he made it out to safety in the parking lot, his friend and colleague, Maynard, was not so lucky. A huge male clerk grabbed Maynard by the wrist as he was hoisting a CD under his t-shirt. Santiago, although feeling very bad that his friend got caught, also felt relieved that he did not.

Two weeks later Santiago's father received a phone call from the police. Apparently under duress and with the promise of a lesser punishment, Maynard had relented and given the police Santiago's name. Santiago's punishment was being grounded for the following month. Being grounded involved reporting in by 8:00 P.M. every night including weekends. Although Santiago was not particularly happy about his situation, he was more unhappy about being caught than about stealing a CD. He interpreted his punishment to mean, "Don't get caught." The punishment had virtually no effect on his CD-stealing behavior. He continued to steal CDs, but did so with exceptional care. In this situation, since the punishment was not administered soon after the stealing behavior occurred, it had little effect.

A second suggestion for using punishment is to administer the punishing consequences every time the behavior occurs. In Santiago's situation, he was punished only one time. Many other times his stealing behavior was strongly positively reinforced by his getting and enjoying the CDs he wanted. Receiving a punishment every time a behavior occurs helps to strengthen the idea that the consequence of that particular behavior is unappealing.

The third suggestion for using punishment is to remain calm while administering it. Excessive attention directed at a particular behavior may serve as a positive reinforcer for that behavior rather than a punishment. For example, eighteen-month-old Petey discovered a book of matches lying on the living room coffee table. He immediately sat down and started to play with them. His mother saw him, ran over to him, and spanked him. She also took away the matches. As both of Petey's parents smoked, it was fairly likely that Petey would find more matchbooks lying around the house. As a matter of fact, he found some the next day. His mother responded in a similar manner. Petey learned that he could get a lot of attention from his mother by playing with matches. As a result, he loved to find matches and play with them. Although his mother's attention was negative, it was forceful enough to serve as positive reinforcement. Petey continued to play with matches every chance he got.

The fourth suggestion concerning the use of punishment is the most important. At the same time that punishment is used, a complimentary program should be used to reinforce other more appropriate behaviors. Punishment has been found to be most effective when an individual is being reinforced for adapting more appropriate behaviors at the same time (Azrin and Holz, 1966; Kircher et al., 1971). For example, a therapeutic goal for a profoundly retarded child was to walk instead of crawl (O'Brien et al., 1974). Punishment for crawling involved restraining him from movement for five seconds. However, this did not really serve as punishment because the child's crawling behavior didn't decrease. Nor did his walking behavior increase. Eventually, a new approach was assumed. At the same time that the child was being restrained from crawling, he was also encouraged or positively reinforced for moving his body. This included being helped to walk. As a result, his walking behavior increased and his crawling behavior decreased. In this case punishment was effective when the child was reinforced for a more appropriate behavior at the same time.

It has been found that the negative side effects of punishment such as resentment toward the punitive person, aggressive behavior, and avoidance of the punitive situation are not nearly as great when reinforcement for alternative appropriate behaviors is used (Carey and Bucher, 1986).

Generally speaking the effects of punishment have seemed to be less negative when observed in real-life treatment settings than in research laboratory situations; Kazdin (1989, p. 169) suggests that this may be due to the fact that simultaneous reinforcement of positive behavior is almost always used in treatment settings, but much more rarely as an integral part of laboratory experiments.

Additional Issues

In addition to the focus on positive reinforcement and punishment, three additional issues merit attention here. They concern common elements encountered in practice. The additional issues include accidental training, the use of behaviorally specific terminology, and the importance of parental attention.

Accidental Training

Thus far, the discussion has emphasized planned behavioral change. The focus has been on gaining control of behavior. However, many times reinforcement and punishment affect behavior without conscious planning. Behavior can be increased or decreased without intention. When attempting to understand the dynamics of behavior, it's important to understand that accidental training does occur.

Negative attention is frequently an effective means of providing accidental training. Attention, even in the form of yelling, can function as positive reinforcement. Even though it is supposed to be negative, the social reinforcement value can be so strong that the behavior will be strengthened instead of weakened. For example, if mother yells at Freddie for picking her favorite peonies, then Freddie may learn that picking those peonies will make his mother yell. If Freddie continues to pick the peonies and his mother continues to yell at him for it, the yelling has served to reinforce his peonie-picking behavior.

Accidental Training

Tommy was an only child. His parents, who were in their late thirties, had tried to have children for years without success. When Tommy came along, they were overjoyed. Both parents thought almost everything Tommy did was "simply darling." One time when Tommy was three years old, he approached some dinner guests and asked for money. He had learned that money bought ice cream, and so on. Two things occurred. First, his parents thought it was cute, so they laughed. Then they appropriately told him that asking for money was not a good thing to do. But they maintained happy, smiling faces all the while. Tommy thus received massive social reinforcement in the form of praise and attention for his begging behavior. Second, Tommy did receive fifty cents, which he later spent for choco-moca-fudge ice cream. The guests were not quite as entertained by Tommy's behavior as his parents were. However, they felt he was a cute kid and gave him money to avoid embarrassment in front of his parents.

The next time Tommy's parents had guests, Tommy did the same thing. He came out for display, said hello, and then asked them if he could have some money. He received a similar reaction. As time went on, Tommy consistently continued his begging behavior in front of guests. His parents became less entertained as the years passed. They discovered that an eight-year-old Tommy coming out and asking guests for money was no longer as cute as a three-year-old doing the same thing. However, by the time Tommy was eight, they were having a terrible time trying to decrease or extinguish his begging behavior. For an extended period of time, Tommy had accidentally been trained to beg. Such extensive accidental training had become very difficult to extinguish.

Behaviorally Specific Terminology

A major advantage of conceptualizing behavior in terms of learning theory is the emphasis on specificity. A behavior must be clearly and concisely defined. A clear description of behavior allows for all involved in the behavioral management of a child to understand exactly what behavior, including problem behavior, involves.

For example, Bertha, age nine, has been described by her teachers as being too passive. It is difficult to know what is meant by "too passive." The word *passive* is relatively abstract. The image of a passive Bertha is quite vague. However, if Bertha's passivism is defined in terms of her behavior, as it would be with a learning theory conceptualization, the image of Bertha becomes more distinct. Bertha's passivism might be described behaviorally in the following way:

Bertha sits quietly by herself during classes and recesses at school. She avoids social contact with peers during recess by walking to the far side of the playground away from the other children. She does not volunteer information during class. When asked a question, she typically shrugs her shoulders as if she does not know the answer. She then avoids eye contact and looks down toward the ground. She is consistently standing last in lines for lunch, for recess, or for returning to school. When other children push her out of their way, she allows herself to be pushed without comment.

Learning theory mandates clear behavioral descriptions in order to conceptualize any particular behavior. The antecedents, the behavior itself, and the consequences of the behavior must be clearly defined in order to make changes in the behavior. The behavioral description of Bertha provides a much clearer picture than merely labeling Bertha as being too passive.

Measuring Improvement

Because of the high level of specificity necessary in order to conceptualize behavior in terms of learning theory, observation of the behavior becomes much easier. Subsequently, improvements in behavior become more clearly discernable. For example, it might be difficult to establish if Bertha is becoming less passive. However, it is much easier to determine the number of times Bertha assertively raises her hand to answer a question in class.

Behavior must be observable in order to measure if it has improved. In other words, it must be very clear when the behavior occurs and when it does not. In Bertha's situation, the frequency of hand-raising in class has been targeted as a behavior which involves passivism. If Bertha never raises her hand to answer a question in class, she will arbitrarily be considered passive. If she raises her hand frequently, on the other hand, she will not be considered passive.

For the sake of this illustration, hand-raising is used as a means to measure passivism. In an actual situation, Bertha's other behaviors could also be used to measure her degree of passivism. These might include behaviors such as the amount of time she spends talking to peers or the number of times she answers her teacher's questions. Her improvement might be measured by using a summation of a variety of measures.

The first step, then, is targeting a behavior to change. The next step is determining how severe the problem is in the first place. This must be known in order to tell when improvements have been made. In Bertha's case, the hand-raising must be counted and a baseline established. A baseline refers to the frequency with which a behavior occurs before a behavior modification program is started. After a baseline is established, it is easy to determine when a change in the frequency of the behavior has occurred. The change is reflected by the difference between how frequently that behavior occurred while the baseline was being established and how frequently the behavior occurs after the behavior modification program has begun.

For example, during the first month of school, Bertha raises her hand to answer a question zero times per school day. However, by the seventh month of school, she raises her hand to answer a question an average of six times per day. If one of the means of measuring passivism is considered to be the number of times Bertha assertively raises her hand in class, then Bertha can easily be described as less passive during the seventh month of school than during the first.

Clearly stated behaviors can be counted. Therefore, increases or decreases in behavior can be more clearly determined. Improvements in behavior can be established and documented. For example, in Bertha's case, each time she raised her hand above shoulder level after her teacher had asked the class a question could count as one hand-raising behavior.

The final point concerning behavioral specificity involves how the behaviors are counted in the first place—who keeps track of the frequency of the behavior and how this is done. Behavior checklists and charts can be developed for this purpose.

A behavior checklist simply allows for a place to make note of when a behavior occurs. For example, a two-dimensional chart might have each day of the week listed on the horizontal axis. Each day might be broken down into individual hours on the vertical axis

FIGURE 4.4: Behavior Chart: Number of Times
Bertha Raises Her Hand

	Mon.	Tues.	Wed.	Thurs.	Fri.
8:00–9:00 A.M.	0	0	0	0	0
10:00–11:00 A.M.	0	0	0	0	0
11:00 A.M.–12:00 P.M.	0	0	0	0	0
12:00–1:00 P.M.	0	0	0	0	1
1:00–2:00 P.M.	0	1	1	0	1
2:00–3:00 P.M.	0	0	1	3	3

on the left-hand side. Figure 4.4 illustrates how this might be applied to Bertha's situation.

Whenever Bertha would raise her hand in class, her teacher would make a note of it on her behavior checklist. The total number of times could be counted. It could thus be clearly established if an improvement occurred.

We have not addressed the specific types of treatment that could be used in Bertha's situation to decrease her passivism. A treatment program could be established in various ways. For example, positive reinforcement could be administered whenever she raises her hand. This could be in the form of a piece of candy, verbal praise, or a token which could be applied to something she really wanted.

The Importance of Parental Attention

One of the criticisms of the application of learning theory might be that it is a rigid and somewhat cold dissection of human behavior. Warmth, caring, and human concern are not readily evident. This certainly does not have to be the case. The importance of parents communicating with their children and genuinely showing spontaneous concern for them should not be overlooked. Learning theory provides a framework for analyzing and gaining control over behavior. Other important aspects of human relationships can occur concurrently.

For example, Gordon (1975) emphasizes the importance of active listening in his suggestions for effective parenting. He describes active listening as a process where parents can become actively receptive to what a child is saying. A parent and a child often have different ways of saying things. They each have a different perspective. Active listening encourages a parent to stop for a moment and consciously examine what the child is saying. The idea is for the parent to try to look at the issue from the child's perspective. This may not be clear from the particular words the child has spoken. The parent then is urged to reflect these feelings back to the child. The end result of a parent taking the time to understand a child should be an enhancement of the warmth and caring between them.

Charlene and her mother provide an example of active listening. Charlene, age seven, comes home after school, crying. She says to her mother, "Betty invited everybody to her birthday party but me." Instead of passing it off as a simple childhood disappointment, Charlene's mother stops for a moment and thinks about what this incident might mean to Charlene. She replies to Charlene, "You really feel left out and bad about this, don't you, honey?" Charlene comes into her mother's arms and replies, "I sure do, Mom." In this instance, her mother simply reflected to Charlene her empathy and concern. As a result, Charlene felt that her mother really understood. Warmth and feeling was apparent in their relationship.

Although this interaction is not structured within learning theory terms, it certainly illustrates the basic components of warmth and empathy necessary in the parent-child relationship. Feelings and communication are ongoing, dynamic parts of that relationship. They occur simultaneously along with the ongoing management of children's behavior.

A Specific Treatment Situation: Time-Out from Reinforcement

Extensive volumes have been written concerning the various aspects of learning theory and its applications. Specific concepts have already been discussed. The use of positive reinforcement and punishment have been emphasized. A specific treatment situation has been selected to illustrate the application of these concepts by using specific techniques. It focuses on concepts frequently used by social work practitioners. The treatment situation presented here involves the use of a time-out from reinforcement procedure.

The term *time-out* refers to time-out from reinforcement. In this procedure, previous reinforcement is withdrawn with the intended result being a decrease in the frequency of a particular behavior. It is a form of extinction. Instead of applying some aversive consequences such as a spanking after a behavior occurs, a child is simply removed from the reinforcing circumstances. If a child gets no attention or positive reinforcement for a behavior, that behavior will eventually diminish.

For example, four-year-old Vernite loves to play with her Legos. However, Vernite has difficulty sharing them with other children. When another child picks up one of the pieces, Vernite will typically run over to that child, pinch him, take the toy, and place it in a pile with the rest of her own Legos. As a result, other children don't like Vernite very much.

The goal here might be to decrease Vernite's selfish behavior. Selfish behavior is defined as the series of behaviors involved in pinching and taking toys away from other children. A time-out from reinforcement procedure can be used here in order to control Vernite's selfish behavior. Whenever Vernite pinches another child or takes a Lego away from that child, her mother immediately picks her up and puts her in a corner behind a screen for three minutes. At the end of that time, her mother picks Vernite up again and puts her back in the play situation. What happens is that the positively reinforcing situation filled with fun, Legos, and other children is removed. In actuality, of course, it is Vernite who is removed. Nevertheless the positively reinforcing conditions are taken away from or made unavailable to Vernite. Without receiving the reinforcement of having the toys for herself. Vernite's selfish behavior should eventually disappear. She should learn that such behavior is inappropriate, and, in effect, not worth its consequences. In other words, Vernite's selfish behavior should eventually be extinguished.

Improving Effectiveness

Several aspects of time-outs tend to improve their effectiveness. The following are suggestions for using time-outs:

1. A time-out should be applied immediately after the targeted behavior occurs in order for it to be effective.
2. Time-outs should be applied consistently. A time-out should occur as a consequence every time the targeted behavior occurs.

3. Time-outs should extend from ten seconds to five minutes. Such short periods of time have been shown to be effective (Bostow and Bailey, 1969). Longer periods of time do not increase the effectiveness of the time-out (White et al., 1972). The relationship between the targeted behavior and the time-out becomes too distant. An extended time-out of an hour, for instance, may also take on some of the potential negative consequences of a more severe form of punishment such as resentment toward the person administering the time-out.
4. The time-out should take place in a very boring place (Patterson, 1975, pp. 75–76). An ideal time-out should provide absolutely no positive reinforcement. This might be a chair facing a corner or another room devoid of stimulating objects and pictures. If the time-out location is exciting or stimulating, it might serve to positively reinforce a negative target behavior rather than to extinguish it.
5. The person, frequently a parent, who is administering the time-out should be careful not to give the child positive reinforcement in the form of attention while the time-out is taking place. A parent might simply state to the child, "Time-out" (Wagonseller et al., 1977, p. 5). The child should then be removed to the time-out location with as little show of emotion as possible. No debate should take place.
6. A child should be told ahead of time exactly which behaviors will result in a time-out. The length of the time-out should also be specified (Wagonseller et al., 1977, p. 5). The intent is to help the child understand exactly what he is doing wrong and what the resulting consequences will be.
7. If the child refuses to go to the time-out location, he may have to be physically taken there. This should be done with as little show of emotion as possible. The child should be gently restrained from all activity until the time-out can begin.
8. The most important thing to remember about using the time-out procedure is that positive reinforcement should be used to reinforce more appropriate replacement behaviors for the same situation. Appropriate behavior should be praised as soon as it occurs after the time-out has taken place. For example, when Vernite is returned to the play scene, she should be praised for playing with her own toys and not taking them away from other children. Her mother might simply say, "Look how well you're playing and sharing now, Vernite. Good girl."

A simple anecdote taking place in a local supermarket illustrates the ingenuity and creativity with which a time-out might be used. A mother was shopping with her two-year-old sitting in a shopping cart. Suddenly for no apparent reason the child began to scream. Much to the surprise of onlooking shoppers, the mother calmly removed her raincoat and placed it over the child's head for twenty seconds. People who are unfamiliar with the time-out technique may have thought she was trying to suffocate the child. However, she performed the procedure calmly and gently. When she removed the raincoat, there sat a peaceful and quiet child. The mother had no further problems with screaming behavior in the supermarket that day. What this mother did was to remove the child from all positive reinforcement for a brief period of time. The child learned that screaming led to no positive consequences. Thus the screaming stopped.

Related Research

When these suggestions are followed, the time-out procedure can provide an effective means of behavior change. Research has established its effectiveness in various settings. These include controlling the disruptive behavior of delinquents (Burchard and Tyler, 1965; Tyler and Brown, 1967), controlling loud classroom noise (Schmidt and Ulrich, 1969), reducing stuttering (Adams and Popelka, 1971), curbing alcohol consumption among hospitalized alcoholics (Bigelow et al., 1974), and suppressing self-stimulating and self-destructive behaviors in developmentally disabled adults (Pendergrass, 1972).

"Grounding"

One other thing should be noted regarding the use of time-outs. Frequently, parents use grounding or sending children to their rooms to curb children's behavior. Although superficially these techniques might resemble time-outs, they don't seem to be very effective (Patterson, 1975, p. 81). Perhaps too many positive reinforcers are available in a child's room. Oftentimes this form of time-out is administered long after the actual behavior occurs. The actual time of restriction is certainly longer than the recommended time period of a maximum of five minutes.

Impacts of Common Life Events on Children

Some basic aspects of family functioning have already been examined. These included a conceptualization of family systems and an examination of learning theory applied to parenting situations. Several other social aspects of childhood merit attention. Common events or situations involving the family that frequently impact the lives of children are discussed. These include membership in sibling subsystems, the effects of family size, and gender role socialization. The social aspects of play with peers, the influence of television, and the school environment are examined. The incidence and dynamics of physical abuse, neglect, and sexual abuse of children are explored. Finally, treatment of child abuse and neglect are explained.

Membership in Family Systems

We have established that the family environment is of crucial importance to a child. Even though as children grow they become more and more involved with their peers, the family itself remains the most important group to them (Furman and Buhrmester, 1985). A good family environment provides nurturance, support, guidance, and a safe, secure place to which children can turn.

An interesting series of studies evaluated how parents actually go about their business of parenting (Baumrind, 1977, 1971, 1966). Three basic styles of parenting emerged. First, *permissive* parenting encourages children to be independent and to make their own decisions. Permissive parents are very nondirective and avoid trying to control their children. The second parenting style is *authoritarian*. Parents adopting this style have definite ideas about how children should behave. These parents do not hesitate to make rules and tell their children what to do. They emphasize control and conformity. The third parenting style is *authoritative*. Parents using this style are neither permissive nor authoritarian, but somewhere in the middle. On the one hand, they provide control and consistent support. On the other hand, they involve their children in decision making and encourage the development of independence.

Which style is the most effective? The answer apparently is none (Chamberlain, 1984; Skolnik, 1978). Research indicates that it is very difficult, if not impossible, to predict how children will turn out on the basis of how they were reared. Many other variables are involved. The amount of caring parents show to their children, the surrounding physical environment, peer demands and influence, cultural values, and the unique interaction between parents and child all may affect a child's development.

A variety of other issues involving children and families will be discussed in Chapter 12. These include single-parent families, families of divorce, blended families, mothers working outside of the home, family communication, family interaction, and common problems facing families.

Membership in Sibling Subsystems

Siblings compose a child's most intimate and immediate peer group. It is logical that brothers and sisters will impact the development and behavior of a child. Siblings learn how to play with each other. They act as models for each other. They also learn how to fight with each other.

The Coming of a New Baby

Picture a three-and-a-half-year-old child waiting patiently for her mother to come home from the hospital with her new baby sister. She missed her mother terribly and can't wait to see her again. She sees her parents' car turn in the driveway. She eagerly waits for her mother to ascend the steps to their upstairs flat. Imagine her surprise when she sees her beloved mother holding a blanket that looks like it has a tiny doll in it. Her mother is smiling and cooing down at the "doll." The little girl thinks to herself, "That must be my baby sister." She feels surprise, wonderment, happiness, and worry all at once, but is unable to articulate these feelings. Her general impression of the whole new situation is, "Now what?"

The coming of a new baby changes a child's family environment. Children's reactions to the change in circumstances vary dramatically. Some may withdraw into themselves and regress to more baby-like behavior. Others may show open hostility toward the new baby and suggest giving it back. One three-year-old

This young boy is displaying ambivalence about taking care of his new sibling.

boy was found holding a safety pin near his new infant brother, contemplating poking him in the eye. That situation needed immediate attention. Other problem factors were operating within the family to elicit such extreme resentment. Still other children happily and proudly accept the family's new addition and enjoy holding and playing with him or her.

It's logical that many children find it difficult at first to share their parents with a new sibling. This is especially so when they have enjoyed a monopoly on their parents' attention. Thankfully, most of the behavior problems vanish by the time the infant is eight months old (Dunn, 1985).

Evidence does indicate that mothers' reactions to their older children do change upon the advent of a newborn in the home. For instance, mothers tend to talk to their other children less, play less with them, have more friction with them, be a bit more insensitive to their immediate needs, and speak to them in a more commanding manner (Dunn, 1985; Dunn and Kendrick, 1982). Older children tend to become perplexed if their relationship with their mother prior to the birth was not filled with friction; additionally, if the mother is extremely tired or depressed after the

Sibling interactions include learning to share.

birth, a firstborn is more likely to pull back from others and isolate her- or himself (Dunn, 1985).

Because of the complexity of the issue and the lack of clear-cut research, it is difficult to propose how to make the transition as easy as possible. It has been determined that fathers who spend more time with older children after the birth of the newborn help the children accept the situation more easily. This seems logical as fathers can help to supplement the attentional demands of older children as they lose some of their mother's attention (Lamb, 1978). Dr. Benjamin Spock (Spock, 1976; Spock and Rothenberg, 1985), the famous pediatrician who has given parents advice over the past few decades about how to raise their children, provides some logical suggestions. First, children should be told in advance about all the changes they are to experience. Changes might include sharing a bedroom or having the new baby use their old high chair.

Preparing them in this way is supposed to minimize surprises. Not knowing what's going to happen is scary for children. Second, Spock suggests continuing to talk to older children and emphasizing how much they are loved and valued. Finally, children should be encouraged to express their feelings, including the negative ones, so that parents can allay their children's fears and address problems as they occur.

Sibling Interaction

Although there is always the possibility of competition between and among siblings, there is also evidence that love and affection are likely to be present (Abramovitch et al., 1979). Sibling interaction involves a multitude of behaviors and feelings. Siblings fight together but they also are found to play with each other, work together, and show affection such as hugging each other. Older siblings are more likely to act as catalysts for both positive and negative interactions (Abramovitch et al., 1979). Younger siblings are more likely to mimic older siblings, using them as models (Dunn, 1983).

The Effects of Birth Order

The effects of birth order in relationship to siblings has received some attention in the past. About a century ago Galton (1896) noticed that a large number of British scientists happened to be firstborn children. Later studies indicated that firstborn and only children tended to have some advantages, including faster language development, higher intelligence scores, higher levels of curiosity, and a greater likelihood of going to college (Ernst and Angst, 1983; Melican and Feldt, 1980; Page and Grandon, 1979). One of the prevalent assumptions has been that firstborn and only children are similar in terms of monopolizing parental attention early in life.

The research provides mixed results regarding the effects of birth order. Falbo and Polit (1986) statistically analyzed 115 studies addressing the effects of birth order. They determined that only children, along with firstborns and children with only one sibling, surpassed children with more siblings in several areas, including intelligence, academic achievement, and social adjustment. However, Hauser and Sewell (1985) studied 9,000 children and their siblings and found that birth order had very little effect on later academic or intellectual achievement. In summary, it is difficult to predict the effects of birth order on children in any particular family system. Each family system is unique.

Furthermore, if our information on firstborn and only children depicts unclear results, that concerning middle children is even less clear. Having a "middle child" implies that a family has at least three children. But, what differences might emerge if the middle child is the second of three, the third of six, or the nineteenth of twenty? Some research indicates that family size and economic status have greater affects on child development than placement in the birth order.

The Effects of Family Size

Hauser and Sewell (1985) found that family size was inversely related to academic performance; the larger the family size, the less well children tended to do academically. Other research has indicated that children in larger families tended to score lower on intelligence tests than children in smaller families (Grotevant et al., 1977; Zajonc, 1976). One implied explanation of these results might be that the larger the family, the less time parents have to devote to each individual child's development.

However, a great deal of research targeting family size has neglected to take other critical variables such as socioeconomic status into account; for example, larger families are much more likely to be poor than smaller families (Page and Grandon, 1979). To what extent, then, are lower socioeconomic status and resource deprivation (instead of either family size or sibling order) related to children's lower degrees of intellectual and academic achievement?

Lefrancois (1990, pp. 301-2) summarizes the current situation:

> It appears clear that birth order and family size are related to intellectual development. But the relationships are not very strong and seem to be due primarily to socioeconomic factors associated with large and small families (larger families are more common among lower socioeconomic groups).

This emphasizes the significance of the macro social environment, both for entire systems and for individual family members. If a family system receives decreased and/or inadequate resources, how well can individual members of that system attain their fullest potential? To what extent does impoverishment adversely affect children's growth and achievement?

Gender Role Socialization

Although there appear to be few differences in the innate behavior of boys and girls at birth (Hyde and Rosenberg, 1980), infants are treated differently by virtue of their gender from the moment they are born. Parents are more likely to treat boys more actively and roughly than girls (Maccoby and Jacklin, 1974), who are more likely to be talked to and looked at (Lewis, 1972). Perhaps this differential treatment reinforces aggressive behavior in boys and verbal behavior in girls. In one interesting study, young mothers were divided into two groups and given the same six-month-old infant to handle and play with (Walum, 1977). For one group the infant was dressed in a ruffled pink dress and called Beth. For the other group the same infant was called Adam and dressed in blue overalls. In their interactions with "Beth" mothers were much more likely to smile at the infant, give her a doll to play with, and perceive the infant as being sweet than when the same baby was "Adam." Such differences in treatment tend to become greater and more encompassing as children grow older (Block, 1976). Even parents who state that they consciously try to avoid imposing gender stereotypes on their children still treat boys and girls differently (Scanzoni and Fox, 1980).

It is appropriate and relevant to mention here the nature-nurture argument regarding why people become the people they do. Supporters of the nature idea argue that people are innately programmed with inborn, genetic, or natural predispositions. But according to the nurture perspective, people are the product of their environment. That is, people are affected by what happens to them from the day they're born. They learn from their environment and are shaped by it. Both sides of the debate have evidence and research to support their perspective. The real answer is not clear. Probably the answer lies somewhere in the middle. People are probably born with certain potentials and predispositions that are then shaped, strengthened, or suppressed by their environments.

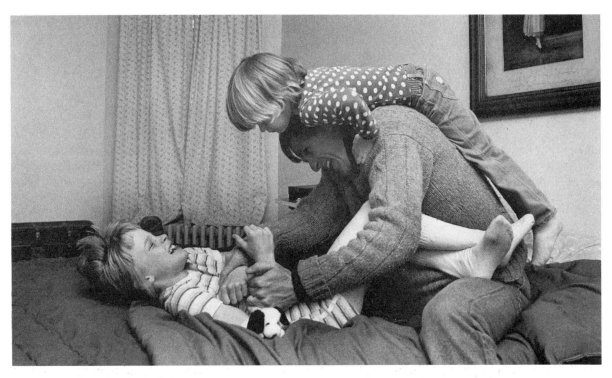

Parents are more likely to treat boys more actively and roughly than girls.

Two differences in behavior appear early in life (Hyde, 1990). Differences in aggression and in toy preference emerge as soon as children gain enough motor control to move about. Boys are more aggressive than girls and tend to choose traditionally "masculine" toys (for example, toy trucks and guns). Girls, on the other hand, are less aggressive and tend to choose traditionally "feminine toys" such as dolls. Questions can be raised regarding whether these differences are due to some innate genetic programming or to environmental influences. Boys are treated more physically than girls from the moment they're born. Aggression surely is related to physical behavior. Likewise, girls and boys are exposed to a bombardment of gender stereotypes when they observe things happening around them. For example, observations of television and of other people teach them how they are expected to behave as girls or as boys.

A relevant anecdote involves Nick, an engineer, who is married to Karen, a social work professor. When Nick's parents were cleaning out an old garage they used as a storehouse, they gathered together a box of Nick's old toys. Predictably, the toys included a steam shovel, a motorized boat, the front half of a semi truck, and some kind of a machine to move things, equipped with mini hoists and chains, and painted military green. (The interpretation of the latter item is the best the observer could do.) Karen was thankful there were no guns in the box. At any rate, there appeared to be a clear relationship between Nick's love of cogs, wheels, and machines, and the toys he was exposed to and apparently loved as a child. Karen, on the other hand, never owned a toy car or truck in her life. She never developed an affection for machinery or an intuitive sense of how to fix machines. She is also still angry that a high school counselor urged her to take typing instead of calculus (being told that girls don't really need calculus anyhow), which she obediently did and still regrets.

The point of all this is not that a causal relationship can be established between toy preference and specific, traditionally male or female abilities in adult life. In other words, we can't say that toy preference steers people into traditionally male or female roles. However, we can say that the types of experiences people have when they're young may expose them to interests and preferences they will develop later as adults. One might hypothesize that experience with toys like trucks and machines helps enhance children's ability to conceptualize spatially and thus better understand how machines work. A number of studies "support the proposition that visual-spatial skill is trainable and is related to experience" (Lott, 1987, p. 46).

Differences continue to be apparent as children reach school age. Girls tend to do better academically in school than boys do (Hyde, 1990). Several possible reasons can be given for this. First, most grade school teachers are women. Perhaps it is easier to be taught from a same-gender role model with whom one can identify more easily. Second, boys are generally rougher and more action oriented than girls. Logically this may result in more behavior management problems that might affect schoolwork. Third, boys lag behind girls in physiological development. It may be more difficult for them to master academic material at the same level as girls.

Boys are discouraged from crying. If six-year-old Susie falls, skins her knee, and comes into the house crying, her mother might respond, "You poor thing. Did you hurt yourself? It's okay now. Let me kiss it and make it better." However, if six-year-old Bill falls, skins his knee, and runs into the house, he might get a somewhat different reception. His mother might respond, "Now, now, Billy, big boys don't cry. It'll be okay. Let me put a Band-aid on it." Even very little boys are often encouraged to be strong, brave, and bereft of outward emotion. A tragic result of this is that as adults, males often maintain this facade. This sometimes creates problems in adult love and sexual relationships where men are expected to express their feelings and communicate openly (Gross, 1978).

The Social Environment: Peers, Television, and School

The family does not provide the only means of socialization for children. They are also exposed to other children as they play and to other adults, especially in the school setting. The transactions children have with their peers and with adults in school directly affect both the children's behavior and their social development. Children learn how to relate to others socially. They also learn what types of social behaviors

others expect from them. They also are influenced by the tremendous amounts of time they spend watching television. Issues to be addressed here include the social aspects of play, the influence of television, and the role of the school. The impact of each will be related to the social development of children.

The Social Aspects of Play with Peers

Luther, who is eight, screamed at the top of his lungs, "Red light, green light, hope to see the ghosts tonight!" He spun around and peered through the darkness. He was playing his favorite game, and he was "it." That meant that he counted to twenty and then had to find the others and tag them. The first one tagged had to be "it" the next time.

"Where were those other kids anyway?" he said silently to himself. Randy usually hides in the garbage can. He thinks that that makes him smell so unappealing that no one will look for him there. Siggy, on the other hand, likes to hide in the bushes by the drainage ditch. However, a lot of mosquitos were likely to consume anybody brave enough to venture over in that direction.

Horace was always an enigma. Luther never knew exactly where he was likely to hide. Once he had managed to squeeze into old Charlie's dog house. Charlie was a miniature mongrel.

On serious consideration of which route to take, Luther decided that the garbage can was his fastest and easiest bet. Just as Luther could've sworn that he heard Randy sneeze inside of the garbage can, he heard his mother's call. "Luther, you get in here this minute. I told you four times that you have to be home by 8:30 on week nights. Come in right now, do you hear!"

"Aw, rats," mumbled Luther. Just when he started to have some fun, he always had to quit and go home. Along came the other guys. See, he was right. Randy was in the garbage can and, sure enough, Siggy popped out from behind the bushes by the drainage ditch. As usual, he was scratching. Randy's mother was really going to give it to him when he got home. He did smell awfully bad. Horace appeared suddenly out of nowhere. He wasn't about to waste a good secret hiding place for nothing.

All four boys dragged themselves home. They walked as slowly as they could and procrastinated appropriately. Another hard summer's day of play was done, but they were already thinking about tomorrow.

Children's play serves several purposes. It encourages children to use their muscles and develop physically. It allows them to fantasize and think creatively. Finally, play enables children to learn how to relate to peers. Play can be seen as a means of socialization. Play provides a format for learning how to communicate, compete, and share. It functions as a major avenue of socialization.

Garvey (1977) defines play as activity that involves the following five qualities. First, play must be something that is done purely for enjoyment and not for a reward or because it is considered appropriate. Second, play has no purpose other than to be an end in itself. Play is done for the sake of playing only. Third, people who play choose to do it. No one can force a person to play. Fourth, play involves active participation in an activity. Either mentally or physically the individual must be involved. Pure observation does not qualify as play. Fifth, play acts to enhance socialization and creativity. Play provides a context in which to learn interaction, physical, and mental skills.

Play and Interaction

There are at least two basic ways of looking at how children play. These include social play and fantasy play. Social play involves the extent to which children interact with other children as they play. Fantasy play involves what children think about and how they imagine their pretend games as they play.

Social Play

Parten (1932) conceptualized a model for how children progress in their development of social play. Her research, which was done in the 1920s, focused on children aged two to five. Observations of the children in action led to the proposition that there are actually six different levels of play. Theoretically, children progress through the following levels as they get older:

1. Unoccupied behavior. Unoccupied behavior involves little or no activity. A child might be sitting or standing quietly. Frequently, the child's attention is focused on observing something going on around him.
2. Onlooker play. A child involved in onlooker play is simply observing the playing behavior of other children. The child is mentally involved in that attention is focused on what the other children are doing. However,

the child is not physically participating in the play. Onlooker play differs from solitary play in that the child's attention is definitely focused on the play of peers, instead of on simply anything that might be happening around him/her.

3. Solitary play. Solitary play involves the child playing independently. No attention is given to other children or what they might be doing.
4. Parallel play. A child involved in parallel play is still playing independently. However, the child is playing in a similar manner or with similar toys as other children in the immediate vicinity. The child is playing essentially the same way as the other children, although no interaction occurs.
5. Associative play. Here children play together in that there is some interaction. However, the interaction is not organized. For example, children may share toys or activities and talk with each other. However, their play is very individualized. Each child plays independently from the others. Attention is focused on each child's individual activities.
6. Cooperative play. Cooperative play involves organized interaction. Children play with each other in order to attain a similar goal, make something together, or dramatize a situation together. Attention is focused on the group activity. Cooperation is necessary. Children clearly feel that they are a part of the group.

Parten proposed that different age levels are characterized by different types of play. Two-year-old children tend to play by themselves. By age three years, parallel play begins to be evident. Associative play is engaged in by more and more children as they reach the age of four years. By age five years, most children participate in cooperative play.

There have been some questions raised about the total validity of Parten's conceptualization of play. Barnes (1971) studied three- and four-year-olds and found that these children did not progress nearly as rapidly as those Parten studied. What caused this difference? Barnes suggested that changes in the child's environment may account for the delay. Changes include the proliferation of extravagant, complex toys which don't require other children, the immense amount of time most children spend watching television, and the fact that families tend to be smaller so children have fewer siblings.

Fantasy and "Pretend" Games

Fantasy is an important means of self-expression for young children. It allows children to be creative, empathize with other people's feelings and perspectives, and develop problem-solving skills. Before children reach kindergarten, about 10 to 17 percent of their play involves fantasy, with the figure increasing to about one third in kindergarten (Rubin et al., 1976; Rubin et al., 1978).

Not only does fantasy play increase as children get older, but it also changes somewhat. A preschooler will fantasize by himself, whereas by kindergarten or later a child will tend to fantasize about situations involving other children. At age three, a child will sit alone at a desk and scribble with crayons, creating houses and dragons and dinosaurs. By age six, that same child will prefer to play office with other children while sitting at the same desk. It becomes much more fun to write out bills and shuffle papers and pretend to read important documents as real adults do.

Saltz et al. (1977) did some interesting research on the relationship between fantasy and the development of intelligence. Economically disadvantaged preschoolers were divided into four groups. The first group of children were read fairy tales such as "The Three Little Pigs" and "The Three Billy Goats Gruff." This group was then encouraged to actually pantomime the fairy tales. The second group of preschoolers were asked to act out a series of everyday experiences such as going to the grocery store and visiting the zoo. The third group was simply read various fairy tales. Although the children discussed the stories afterward, they did not actually act out the parts. Finally, the fourth group acted as the control group. They simply participated in supervised play activities such as cutting and pasting.

The first group of children, those who actually acted out the fairy tales, had a marked improvement in intellectual functioning as measured on a variety of tests. The group that acted out everyday experiences also showed improvement, although not as great. Both the group that was read the fairy tales and the control group showed no such increases. The conclusion was that fantasy actually helps children develop their thinking ability.

An implication is that fantasy play should be encouraged in children. It is a normal part of developing their intellectual ability. Thinking things through in fantasy apparently helps them to think in real situations.

One other aspect of fantasy which frequently concerns parents is a child's imaginary friend. Between

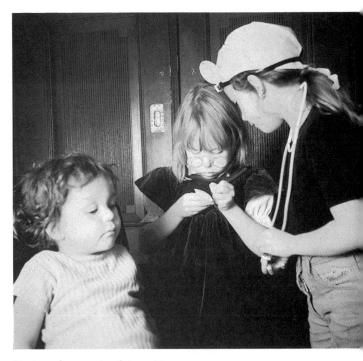

Fantasy play can simulate reality.

15 and 30 percent of all children from the ages of three to ten have an imaginary playmate (Schaefer, 1969). This friend can appear as early as age two and one-half. Frequently the friend disappears when the child begins school (Ames and Learned, 1946). This friend usually takes the form of another child or an animal. For example, one four-year-old girl had virtually no peers to play with in her rural environment comprised mostly of farmlands. For two years, she played with "Ahkey," an imaginary friend whom she explained lived out in the forest and frequently came to play with her. Manosevitz et al. (1973) found that first-born and only children were more likely to have imaginary friends. This appears to be a normal way for a child to cope with being lonely. The friend usually disappears when other children take his/her place.

It's interesting to note several parental characteristics are indeed related to children's fantasy play (Fein, 1981). Children who have active, creative fantasy play lives have parents who generally talk a lot to their children, provide their children with new and thought-provoking experiences, avoid spanking their children, and have a good marital relationship.

Parents need to be aware of the normal developmental aspects of play at different age levels. Expectations of parents and other caretakers of children need to be realistic. Children should be encouraged to play with other children in ways appropriate to their age level. Yet, children should not be pushed into activities which are beyond them. Children who are isolated in their play activities at an age when they need to be more outgoing may need encouragement in that direction. Parents and other caretakers can help children develop their play and interactional skills.

Gender Differences in Play

We have established that two gender-related differences in behavior appear early in life (Hyde, 1986, pp. 371-72). One is a difference in aggressive behavior with respect to play. Boys behave more aggressively than girls. The other early behavioral difference is in toy preference. By age three or four girls begin choosing to play with dolls and participate in sewing and housekeeping play. Boys, on the other hand, are oriented toward more masculine toys such as trucks and guns. The reasons for these differences are not clear. Perhaps children play with the toys they are given and encouraged to play with. Some research does indeed find that boys and girls tended to have different types of toys (Liss, 1981; Rheingold and Cook, 1975). Girls' rooms are filled with dolls and items devised for playing house. Boys' rooms, on the other hand, display various action-oriented toys such as cars, trucks, guns, and sports equipment.

For example, when Aunt Karen took three-year-old Andrea, her niece and the "apple of her eye," to K-Mart one day to buy her a toy, Andrea headed straight for the "girls' toys," not the "boys' toys." When Aunt Karen suggested Andrea look at some *fun* trucks and cars (Aunt Karen knew that it was good for girls to become oriented to cars and trucks, both because they'll have to use real ones someday and because such play aids in the development of spatial perception skills), Andrea screwed up her nose and said "NO! Those are boys' toys!" So much for that idea. It was interesting because in real life, Andrea's mother was the person who did most of the mechanical fixing and all of the outdoor work at their four-acre home. The impact of the media, especially television, and her observation of other people and

how they behave must have been very great. (Gender roles and gender-role stereotypes will be discussed much more thoroughly later in Chapter 9.)

Another reason for the differences in toy preference may be that children, who become conscious of gender by age two and one-half or three (Masters and Johnson, 1985, p. 272), learn early how they should be playing. They watch television and observe Mommy and Daddy; they learn that girls and boys should like to do different things.

Lott (1987, p. 41) suggests that there are at least three logical reasons why girls' behavior is less aggressive than that of boys. They all seem to relate to and reinforce each other. First, girls have less chances to "practice" aggressive behavior such as fighting, breaking, or hurting things. Second, girls' aggressive behavior is less likely to be encouraged by adults than the aggressive behavior of boys.

For instance, Aunt Karen had another opportunity to observe her three-year-old niece Andrea in the company of her male and female nursery school peers. They were on a field trip to a local pumpkin farm in the cold, November rain with the idea of picking some small pumpkins. All of the boys in Andrea's group were kicking, screaming, punching, bumping, running, and making "BRRRRRRRR" and "GRRR-RRRRR" sounds. Meanwhile, several of the mothers calmly observed, smiled, and made proud comments like, "Isn't he a *real* boy." Meanwhile all of the girls stood silently on the sidelines watching the boys have "fun." When one girl tried to get involved, her mother said, "Oh, no, Chrissy, you might get hurt. Those boys are so rough."

A third reason why girls are less aggressive, according to Lott, is that girls are less likely to "experience success" at being aggressive than are boys. Boys are encouraged by adults to be more practiced at aggression than girls. Girls, on the other hand, are reinforced for being gentler and more "ladylike."

The Peer Group and Popularity

The peer group is made up of a child's equals. It can have an increasing impact on children as they get older, more independent, and more experienced. On a positive note, the peer group provides an arena for children to learn about themselves, build their self concepts, and learn how to interact with other people. On a more negative note, the peer group can place pressure on children to do things they would never consider doing on their own.

Some children get along fabulously with peers; others are avoided, isolated, and withdrawn. What makes a child popular (for that matter, what makes an adult popular)? Researchers have studied popular and unpopular children and concluded that a series of characteristics tend to be associated with popularity.

It appears that a child's level of social skill development is clearly linked to status within the peer group (Asher and Renshaw, 1981). Popular children are friendly with others and interact eagerly (Putallaz and Gottman, 1981). Popular children tend to be bright and creative; slow learners and people who are retarded tend to be less popular (Green et al., 1980). Finally, physical attractiveness is related to popularity (Hartup, 1983; Lerner and Lerner, 1977).

On the other hand, children who are unpopular tend to be characterized by opposite traits. They are socially immature. They tend either to be too pushy and demanding, or very shy and withdrawn. They might not be the brightest children around or the most attractive. They may not have the listening skills and the ability to empathize with others that popular children seem to have. It should also be noted that such children tend to find friends with similar types of social problems (Hartup, 1989).

A common technique for examining children's interaction is referred to as *sociometry*. This involves asking children questions about their relationships and feelings toward other people. After the information is gathered, the relationships can be illustrated on a diagram called a *sociogram*. Children in a group might be asked questions such as which three peers do they like the best, which three do they like the least, who do they most admire, who would they like to sit next to, or who are they most afraid of. Each child can be represented by a circle. Arrows can then be drawn to the people they indicate in answer to each question.

Sociograms are depicted in Figure 4.5. A sociogram can be created to illustrate the results of each question asked. Our example plots out two questions. The first reflects students' feelings about who they thought was the strongest leader in the group. The second illustrates which peer they most liked in the group.

Sociogram A clearly illustrates that Toby is thought

FIGURE 4.5: Sociograms of a Special Education Class

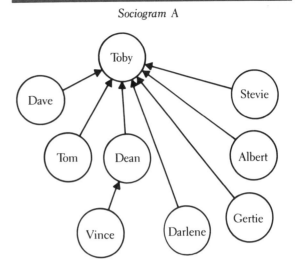

Sociogram A

Students were asked whom they felt was the strongest leader in the group. Arrows reflect their feelings. Toby clearly has that status.

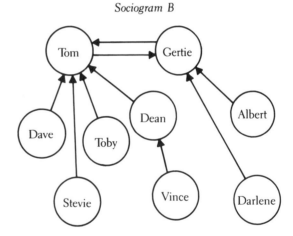

Sociogram B

Here students were asked which person they liked the most in the group. Tom and Gertie appear to be the most popular.

to be the strongest leader in the group. He is bright, energetic, and very "street smart." However, Sociogram B clearly illustrates that he is not the most popular or best liked in the group. Both Tom and Gertie shine there. They both are more mature than the other group members. They are assertive and fairly self-confident, yet don't impose their will on the others. They both are among the brightest in the group. Toby, on the other hand, is more feared than respected in the group. The others admire his apparent sophistication, yet don't trust him. He doesn't let anyone get close to him emotionally or physically. He keeps his distance.

Vince's opinions differ radically from those of other group members. Vince stays by himself most of the time. He loves to wander off whenever he can. He sees Dean as being both a strong and likeable leader. Dean is a very active, verbal person who is always in the center of activity. He has some trouble controlling his behavior and tends to provoke the other students. Perhaps Vince admires Dean's involvement.

These two sociograms are examples of how insights into a group's interaction can be obtained and visually pictured. Although they only begin to portray some of the complexities of the group's interaction, they do provide some interesting clues.

We've been speaking of children as being popular or unpopular during this discussion. It is as if on a popularity scale from 1 to 10, each child is either a very unpopular 1 or a very popular 10. In real life, of course, most people lie somewhere in between. They may have some of the characteristics of "the popular person," but not others.

It appears that social skills provide a primary basis for popularity. It follows, then, that since skills in general can be learned, social skills can be learned and popularity increased. Some research supports this (Bierman and Furman, 1984). Fifth- and sixth-graders who had difficulty relating to peers were given specific training about how to improve their interactions with other people. The training included such things as how to start and maintain conversations, empathize with the other person, appear interested, ask appropriate questions, and the like. Afterward, one group of children who received the training were asked to practice their new skills in a group of other children. Another group who received the training did not participate in the practice sessions. Still another group became the control group, that is, they were unpopular children who received no training.

Findings revealed that children who received both the social skill training and were given opportunities to practice their new skills were liked better by their peers both immediately after the practice sessions and

also six weeks later when a follow-up study was done. On the other hand, both trained children who had no opportunity to practice and untrained children were liked no better than before the research was begun.

There are two major implications here. First, children who receive training in social skill development can indeed improve their interactions with peers and, as a result, become better liked. Second, in order for the training to take effect, children must be able to practice and integrate these new skills. Additional implications for social workers who choose to work with young people are vast. Social skill training may provide one viable alternative for young people who are depressed, lacking in self-esteem, isolated, or suicidal.

The Influence of Television

Since television has become such a common aspect of a child's environment, it merits a few comments here. Preschool children spend more than a third of their time while awake watching television (Winn, 1985). Although children aged six to eleven spend a bit less time watching, the decrease is not great (Nielsen Television Index, 1984).

A major question raised about the impact of television concerns whether it teaches children to be violent and aggressive. Most of the research indicates that television does influence and increase children's violent behavior (National Institute of Mental Health (NIMH), 1982); television both provides models which show children how to be aggressive, and serves to impart the value that violence is appropriate behavior.

Aggressive children tend to watch a greater amount of television and to feel more strongly that it portrays what typically happens in real life (Eron, 1982). One study divided children aged five to nine into two groups (Liebert, 1972). One group watched three-and-one-half minutes of television which portrayed people shooting and fighting with each other. The other group observed a sports competition. Afterwards, children from both groups were placed in the position where they were told they were playing a "game" with a child whom they could not see. Of course, there was no such other child, but the participants didn't know that. Part of the game involved pushing either a "help" button or a "hurt" button. They were told that the help button would help the other child win and the hurt button would make the lever the other child held so hot that it would hurt that child. Children who had watched the violent television programming were both more likely to hurt the other child and to make the pain more severe than those children who only watched sports.

Other research establishes a relationship between the amount of violent television viewed in childhood and the amount of aggressiveness manifested by participants ten years later at age eighteen (Eron, 1982, 1980). In other words, children who watched more violent television actually displayed more violent behavior themselves when they grew up. One should caution, however, that a causal relationship cannot be established here. For example, maybe these children were more predisposed to violence to begin with.

Consider that over 98 percent of all children's cartoons portray violence; children's television programs depict six times more violence than adults' television shows (Gerbner, 1972). Cartoons about war increased from one-and-one-half hours per week in 1982 to forty-eight hours per week in 1987; it might be added that the number of war toys sold escalated 700 percent during that same period (Papalia and Olds, 1989, p. 245).

Picture such cartoons as *Teenage Mutant Ninja Turtles, Robocop, Mighty Mouse, Donald Duck Presents*, and the *Roadrunner*. How many times has the coyote been blown up with a stick of dynamite given him by the roadrunner? Or Donald Duck smashed by a baseball bat or pushed off a steep cliff? When you really think about it, the implications of this amount of violence depicted are scary.

There is another side to television, however. There's *Mr. Rogers' Neighborhood* where "it's a beautiful day in the neighborhood" every single day. There's also *Sesame Street*, which emphasizes the development of reading and arithmetic skills in addition to imparting such values as consideration for others' feelings. *Sesame Street* specifically has been found to have very positive effects on children (Lesser, 1977). Most children who watch it experience significant gains in their ability to recognize letters and geometric forms, for example.

Television affects children. The American Academy of Pediatrics (1986) suggests that parents scrutinize their children's viewing behavior by observing how their children act and by watching the programs themselves. Limits should be set regarding what is appropriate and what is not. When violence does occur, parents should talk to children about it. Parents can emphasize that violence is a bad way to solve problems and that there are many other better nonviolent ways available.

The School Environment

The school provides a major arena for socialization. Children are given information. They are taught social customs, rules, and communication skills. The family and peers help to shape a child's individual personality. The school also impacts a child's development. Schools influence children's dreams and aspirations about future careers (Walberg and Rasher, 1977). Schools help to mold the ways in which children think (Cole et al., 1971). Specific issues related to the school environment will be discussed here. They include the teacher's impact, freedom in the classroom, and the effects of social class and race.

The Teacher's Impact

Students frequently perform at the level of their teachers' expectations. Higher expectations, therefore, result in higher levels of achievement. Rosenthal and Jacobson (1968a, 1968b) studied the effects of teachers' expectations on the academic performance of students in a lower-middle-class school. Teachers were told that a specific group of students had been identified as "late bloomers." These children were discovered to be capable of achievement significantly above what they had achieved in the past. In reality, these students showed no more promise than other students. Teachers, however, had their expectations raised with this information. The results indicated that these students really did do significantly better with higher expectations. Younger students displayed the greatest improvement, which indicates that the greatest gains might be achieved if expectation levels are raised very early in children's educational careers.

Freedom in the Classroom

The classroom provides the major unit of structure in the school environment. One of the basic issues concerning the classroom is its atmosphere. The question centers on whether an open atmosphere is more productive and beneficial for learning than a traditional closed, structured setting.

A classic study concerning leadership style in the classroom was that of Lewin, Lippett, and White (1939). Ten-year-old boys participating in recreational groups were exposed to different leadership styles—authoritarian, democratic, and laissez-faire. The authoritarian leaders made all decisions and plans for the group without allowing any member input. The democratic leaders, on the other hand, structured activities so that group members had input into virtually all groups decisions. Finally, the laissez-faire or permissive group leaders allowed the group complete freedom. No direction or leader involvement was apparent.

Results indicated that the boys in the democratic group were more productive, happier, and more congenial toward each other. Boys in the authoritarian groups related poorly to each other. They tended to be either passive or aggressive, and they worked poorly together. Boys in the laissez-faire groups were disorganized and bored. Disgruntlement and disputes were frequent.

Although the Lewin, Lippett, and White study seemed to indicate that a democratic leadership style is the most effective, more recent evidence does not confirm this. Open classrooms which allow a lot of freedom and individual determination do not appear to enhance productivity (Featherstone, 1971). In other words, children in open classrooms don't seem to do any better academically than children in traditional classrooms. However, they do like both school and their teachers better than students in traditional classrooms. Children in open classrooms also generally are more likely to volunteer the expression of their ideas and feelings (Harvey et al., 1968). Additionally, the overall activity level is higher in open classrooms. In summary, although academic advances are not apparent, more subjective benefits seem to be derived from an open classroom atmosphere. Children appear to learn to think more independently. This may prove valuable in future decision-making situations, although this benefit would be difficult to measure.

The Effects of Social Class and Race

Children from families in lower socioeconomic levels generally do not do as well in school as middle-class children. One source estimates that lower-class children are one whole academic year behind their middle-class peers by the third grade, two years by sixth grade, and two-and-one-half years by ninth grade (Rioux, 1968, p. 92). Lower-class children are also much less likely to go to college than children raised in middle-class homes (DeLury, 1974).

Many reasons can be given for this discrepancy. First, the schools put forth and espouse middle-class values. Texts teach about middle-class parents raising middle-class children in middle-class neighborhoods. For children from other environments, the examples and reference points may be hard to comprehend. Second, the language used is middle-class language. Street terms are most frequently neither understood nor even tolerated by teachers. Street language which is the everyday tongue of many lower-class, urban youth is considered vulgar slang in the middle-class environment. How can children be expected to understand what is said if the language used is literally one that's foreign to them?

A third reason is that the school environments and level of teaching are often poorer for lower-class students. For example, Deutsch (1960) estimates that lower-class students actually receive one-third less actual education time than middle-class students. He continues that this is probably due to the fact that teachers in lower-class schools spend up to 80 percent of their time either disciplining or participating in mundane activities like taking attendance.

A fourth reason may be that teachers' expectation levels for their students' performance may be too low. Teachers may have white middle-class biases about the capabilities of lower-class and minority students. We've already established that teachers' expectation levels affect students' performance.

These differences become even more severe when considering ethnic and racial minority children in schools. Minorities are disproportionately clustered in the lower class. One study showed that teacher perceptions of students were directly related to the individual teacher's race and background (Gottlieb, 1966). African American teachers were both less critical and less pessimistic about their lower-class students. It was hypothesized that perhaps teachers who were raised in similar backgrounds could better identify and empathize with the difficulties that their students faced.

How might these conditions and inequities be corrected? Not only would more financial resources benefit the poorer localities and schools, but also the targeting of teacher attitudes and skills might help. Teachers need to be made aware of other perspectives. Those teaching in lower-class schools need to understand the language of their students. They need to open their minds and be more objective. Teacher training and sensitivity sessions directed toward these ends might be one way to begin.

Child Abuse and Neglect

Ralphie, age eight, came to school one day with his arm in a gigantic cast. His teacher asked him what had happened. He said he fell down the steps and broke it. He didn't seem to want to talk about it much more. When pressed about why the cast had to be so large, he replied, "Oh, that's 'cause I busted it in a couple of places." The teacher thought to herself how strange it was that he suffered such a severe injury from a simple fall. Eight-year-olds are usually so resilient.

Angel, age four, didn't want to sit down when one of her caretakers at the day-care center asked her to. It was almost as if she was in pain. The caretaker called the center's nurse so that she could examine Angel. The nurse found a doughnut-shaped burn on her buttocks. When asked how it happened, Angel said she didn't remember. The nurse thought to herself how strange this situation was.

As the Kirby Vacuum salesman left the porch of the last house he visited, he wondered to himself how people could possibly live that way. There were three filthy, unkempt small children eating Fruit Loops and glued to a blaring television set. He chastised himself for his poor judgment. That family certainly didn't look like it could afford a dust cloth, let alone a Kirby. He couldn't believe the woman's comments as he was leaving the home. There was a small puppy who leisurely urinated on the porch before his and the woman's very eyes. She looked at the salesman, making no effort to clean up the mess, and said, "Well, at least he didn't do it inside the house." She then turned around and walked back into the house.

Tony thought Alicia, one of his classmates at school, was just beautiful, albeit a little shy. They were both fourteen. He finally mustered up the courage to go over, talk to her, and ask her if she would like to go to the school dance next Friday night. She shrunk back from him as if she were terrified and said, in a whisper, that she couldn't possibly go. She added apologetically that her mother worked Friday nights and her "Daddy" always took her to the movies. That just struck Tony as being odd. However, he wasn't up to fighting with parents. Alicia was cute, but she wasn't the only girl around.

Each of the vignettes illustrate children who are being maltreated. There are a number of ways in which children can be abused or neglected. The umbrella term which may be used to include all of them is child "maltreatment" (Kadushin and Martin, 1988, p. 226). Maltreatment includes: physical abuse; being given inadequate care and nourishment; deprivation of adequate medical care; insufficient encouragement to attend school consistently; exploitation by being forced to work too hard or too long; "exposure to unwholesome or demoralizing circumstances"; sexual abuse; and emotional abuse and neglect (Kadushin and Martin, 1988, p. 226). Definitions used by legal and social service agencies vary from locality to locality and state to state. However, most definitions include the above eight aspects of how children can be maltreated.

Many entire books have been written about each form of maltreatment. It is beyond the scope of this book to address them all in great depth. Usually, however, all can be clustered under two headings, child abuse (which includes both physical and sexual abuse) and child neglect. Child maltreatment is a critical issue for social workers to understand. They need to be aware of the clues that maltreatment is occurring. They also need to understand the dynamics of how child victims and their abusers behave in order to assess the situation and make treatment plans. Here we will discuss the incidence and demographics of child maltreatment, the definitions of physical abuse, neglect, and sexual abuse, the characteristics of victims and abusers, and some basic treatment approaches.

Incidence and Demographics of Child Abuse and Neglect

The actual number of child abuse and neglect cases is difficult to determine. Specific definitions for who can and who can't be included in specific categories vary. How cases are reported and data gathered also vary dramatically. One thing, however, is certain. Chances are that any figures which are reported reflect a minimal number of actual cases. All indications are that vast numbers of cases remain unreported.

Some of the best statistics available indicate that nearly 2 million cases of child maltreatment were reported in 1985 (Kadushin and Martin, 1988, p. 244). Of these, 55.7 percent were for neglect, 33 percent for physical abuse, and 11.3 percent for sexual abuse.

Kadushin and Martin (1988) summarize the typical profile of the maltreated victim. They state, "The average age of the maltreated child is slightly over seven years of age. Younger, more vulnerable children are disporportionately underrepresented. Boys are more frequently abused than girls, but this was true only for children up to age ten or eleven. Girls are more frequently reported abused from ages eleven to seventeen" (p. 245). They continue that the increase in abuse to girls is due to the fact that sexual abuse begins to be reported at about that age level. Girls are much more likely to be reported as victims of sexual abuse than boys.

The variables described below tend to characterize maltreating families (Russell and Trainor, 1984). It should be emphasized, however, that these variables do not characterize all families in which abuse and neglect occur. Child maltreatment can happen in any family.

Families in which abuse and neglect occur tend to have low incomes and include two or three children. Families who receive public assistance, are headed by a female single parent, and are poor tend to be overrepresented among reported cases. However, it should be noted that families falling within those three categories are more likely to suffer economic and emotional stress, and to be involved with social service agencies. Such agencies are more frequent sources of abuse and neglect reports than are private agencies. It is possible that maltreatment occurring in wealthier families often remains hidden. Wealthier families have better access to private clinics, physicians, and other services. Private agencies and practitioners are much less likely to report abuse.

Although most maltreatment occurs in white families, nonwhite families are disporportionately represented. African American families were involved in 18.7 percent of the reported cases and Hispanic families in 9.8 percent. However, when maltreatment is divided into the three categories, nonwhites are no more likely than whites to abuse their children either physically or sexually. Reports of neglect, on the other hand, are much more likely to be made concerning nonwhites than whites. In view of the higher poverty levels of nonwhites and frequently lower socioeconomic status, this is not surprising. Many nonwhites may have significantly fewer resources to take care of both themselves and their children.

Women are more likely to abuse or neglect children than men. Perpetrators consist of 59.6 percent women and 40.4 percent men. However, women are much more likely to have access to children. Note the disproportionately higher number of female-headed, single-parent families. Also, in many cases, even when a male is the actual abuser, the female is still held responsible and assumed to be the primary caretaker (Martin, 1984).

Physical Child Abuse

Physical abuse can be defined very generally, although it becomes much more difficult upon examination of real-life situations. Kadushin and Martin (1988, p. 228) define physical abuse as "beating a child to the point at which the child sustains some physical damage." However, they continue that in reality there often is a very fine line between physical abuse and parental discipline. Historically, parents have had the right to bring up their children as they see fit. This has included administering punishment to curb behavior when they thought it was necessary. Take a father who beats his thirteen-year-old daughter on the buttocks with a belt because her math grade dropped over the course of a year from an A− to a C. Is that his right or is that child abuse?

As we've mentioned, there is some variation in how child abuse is defined from one place to another. Some definitions focus on whether the alleged abuser's purpose is to intentionally harm the child. Other definitions ignore the intent and instead emphasize the potential or actual harm done to the child.

Characteristics of Physically Abused Victims

Both physical indicators and behavioral indicators provide clues that a child is being physically abused.

Physical indicators can be broken down into six basic categories:

1. *Bruises.* Bruises on any infant should be suspect. Infants are not yet mobile. Therefore, it's not likely that they can bruise themselves. Bruises in unusual places or forming unusual patterns may be indicators of physical abuse. Bruises that take a recognizable shape such as a hand mark or a belt mark should be noted. Finally, bruises that display a variety of colors may portray abuse. This may be an indication that a series of bruises have been received over time. Bruises usually progress from an initial bright red to blue to blackish-purple within the first day; they become shaded with a dark green color after four to six days and finally turn pale green or yellow after five to ten days have passed (Davis, 1982).

2. *Lacerations.* Cuts, scrapes, or scratches, especially if they occur frequently or their origin is poorly explained may indicate physical abuse. Lacerations on the face and genitalia should be noted. Bite marks also may indicate abuse.

3. *Fractures.* Bone fractures and other skeletal injuries may indicate abuse. Strangely twisted fractures and multiple fractures are especially telltale signs. Infants' fractures may be the result of abuse. Additional indicators are joint dislocations and injuries where the periosteum, the thin membrane covering the bone, is detached.

4. *Burns.* Burns, especially ones that take odd forms or are in patterns, may indicate abuse. Children have been burned by cigarettes and ropes (from being tied up and confined). Burns that occur on inaccessible portions of the body such as the stomach, genitals, or soles of the feet are clues to abuse. Patterned burns may indicate that the child has been burned with some hot utensil. Sacklike burns result when a hand or foot has been submerged into a hot liquid (Davis, 1982). A donut-shaped burn will occur on the buttocks if a child has been immersed in very hot water. The central unburned area results from where the child's skin touched the bottom of the receptacle holding the water (Schmitt, 1980).

5. *Head Injuries.* Head injuries that can indicate abuse include skull fractures, loss of hair due to vigorous pulling, and subdural hematomas (that is, blood collected beneath the outer covering of the brain after strenuous shaking or hitting has occurred). Black eyes should be suspect. Retinas may detach or hemorrhage if a child is shaken vigorously.

6. *Internal Injuries.* Children have received injuries to their spleen, kidneys, and intestines due to hitting and kicking. The vena cava, the large vein by which blood is brought from the lower extremities to the heart, may be ruptured. Peritonitus, where the lining of the abdominal cavity becomes inflamed, can be another indicator of abuse.

Some of the major questions to ask yourself if you think a child may have been physically abused include the following:

- Does this child get hurt too often for someone his or her age?
- Does the child have multiple injuries?
- Do the injuries occur in patterns, assume recognizable shapes, or look like some of the injuries described earlier?
- Are the injuries such that they don't seem possible for a child at that stage of development?
- Do the explanations given for the injuries make sense?

If something doesn't seem right to you, something may be wrong. This might be called a "gut reaction." If a little voice in the back of your mind is saying, "Oh-oh, that certainly is odd," pay attention. It might be a clue to abuse.

In addition to physical indicators, behavioral indicators provide a second major dimension of clues to physical abuse. A physically abused child tends to adopt behavioral extremes. Virtually all children may display these extreme behaviors at one time or another. However, the frequency and severity of these behaviors in abused children are clearly notable. Four categories plus a variety of specific behavioral indicators have been established (U.S. Department of Health, Education and Welfare, 1979, pp. 25-27). The categories include (p. 25):

1. "Overly compliant, passive, undemanding behaviors aimed at maintaining a low profile, avoiding any possible confrontation with a parent which could lead to abuse." Abused children can be exceptionally calm and docile. They have learned this behavior in order to avoid any possible conflict with the abusive parent. If they are invisible, the parent may not be provoked. Many times abusive children will even avoid playing because it draws too much attention to themselves. Martin and Beezley (1976) call this approach "hypervigilance."

2. "Extremely aggressive, demanding and rageful behaviors, sometimes hyperactive, caused by the child's repeated frustrations at getting basic needs met." Other physically abused children assume an opposite approach to the overly passive manner identified earlier. These children are so desperately in need of attention that they will try almost anything to get it. Even if they can only

provoke negative attention from their parents, their aggressive behavior is reinforced.

3. "Role reversal behavior or extremely dependent behavior in response to parental emotional and even physical needs." Some physically abused children form behavioral patterns in reaction to their parents' own needs. For instance, parents who are seriously immature and in need of nurturance themselves may elicit overly mature, responsible, almost adultlike behavior from their children. These parents will expect their children to assume the parental role. The children will then act like little adults. On the other hand, some abusive parents will desperately need to keep their children dependent and to feel themselves in control. Children of these parents will behave in ways appropriate for children much younger. They will cling to their parents and often display babyish behavior.

4. "Lags in development." Because abused children are forced to direct their attention and energy to coping with their abusive situation, they will frequently show developmental delays. These may appear in the form of language delays, poorly developed social skills for their age level, or lags in motor development.

There are a number of specific situations where physically abused children will tend to behave differently than children who are not abused. Child behavior in the presence of strangers in one scenario. Abused children who behave aggressively will tend to be equally and overly friendly with virtually any new persons they meet. They will not discriminate in their treatment of people. They will seek attention from anyone around who might be able to give it. On the other hand, abused children who have assumed the withdrawn approach will be excessively shy and noticeably withdrawn when in the presence of strangers.

Sometimes abused children will show abnormal eating behaviors. For instance, a two-year-old may be excessively neat while eating, showing "manners" far beyond what are usually mastered by a child that age. Another example involves a child aged four. Four-year-olds generally are at a stage where they are seeking independence and like to do things their own way. If the child is exceptionally submissive and carefully eats exactly as the adult instructs, this may be a clue that abuse is taking place. Both these children may be trying very hard to obey their parents and comply with their wishes in order to avoid further abuse.

Abused children frequently don't know how to play. Perhaps they have not been allowed to express themselves through playing in their home environment. They may have made life more bearable by just sitting there and avoiding conflict instead of making themselves noticeable by playing. Some abused children are very aggressive when interacting with their peers. Their parents have modeled aggression for them at home. Therefore, this is the way they learned to interact. Additionally, aggression may provide a means for them to express the anger and resentment they are harboring inside.

Additional symptoms of abuse may include "enuresis (inability to control bladder functions), encapresis (fecal soiling), temper tantrums, and bizarre behavior" (Tower, 1989, p. 67).

Characteristics of Abusers

Perpetrators of child abuse tend to have problems in seven majors areas, the first four of which are personal and the last three environmental (U.S. Department of Health, Education and Welfare, 1979). Although no one person may have all seven problems mentioned, most abusers will be characterized by at least some of them.

First, they themselves most likely have serious needs for support and nurturance which remain unfulfilled from their own childhoods. A basic quality characterizing abusers is low self-esteem. Since they never had their own needs met, they are unable to meet the needs of their children. They often invite rejection and hostility because they have little confidence in their own abilities. They don't know how to reach out for support. On the one hand, they often feel they are undeserving. On the other hand, they still have desperate needs for human support. Many perpetrators have been abused as children themselves.

A second problem characterizing abusers involves social isolation. Their own self-confidence is low. They feel like no one will like them anyway, so they isolate themselves. They reject attention, even though they really need others for emotional support. They fear rejection so they don't even try to reach out to others. As a result, when normal everyday stresses build up, they have no one to talk to and help them cope.

Inability to take care of a child adequately because of their own emotional needs is a third problem characterizing abusive parents. We've already mentioned how abused children either display a role reversal with their abusive parents or become extremely dependent on their parents. This is the other side of that coin. Some parents look for parental support from their children. Others feel the need to control their children and keep them dependent. Sometimes the child becomes "an extension of self" (p. 29). Parents see themselves as being bad, and so their children are also bad and deserving of punishment. Children with physical or mental disabilities are at special risk because of the additional resentment they may elicit.

A related problem is the fourth characterizing abusive people. They don't know how to raise their children in a nurturant family environment. Their own family environment of origin may have been hostile and abusive. Since they don't know how to get their own needs met, they may never have observed nurturant behavior on the part of their own parents and caretakers. Their expectations for what constitutes appropriate behavior at the various developmental levels may be lacking. For instance, their demands upon the child for behavioral submission and even perfection may be very inappropriate.

Several environmental problems also tend to characterize child abusers. The fifth of their common problems involves the lack of support systems. Since these people tend to isolate themselves due to their poor self-esteem, they have no one to turn to for help in times of stress.

The sixth problem involves the marital relationship. Low self-esteem also can impact the marital subsystem. Abusers may not know how to get their needs met. They may allow their disappointments and anger to build up within them because they don't know how to express these feelings more appropriately to others. They may feel isolated and alone even within the marriage. Children may become easy targets for parents who can't communicate with each other. Children may provide a conduit for the expression of violence and anger really directed at a spouse.

The seventh problem often facing abusers is that of extreme external stress and life crises. We've noted that some child abuse is related to lower socioeconomic status and to single parenthood. Poverty causes stress, as can the lack of a partner to provide emotional support. The abuser may feel isolated and incompetent. Additional life crises like losing a job, illness, a marital dispute, or even a child's behavior problem may push people over the brink so that they cannot control themselves and cope. They may take out their stress on the easiest, most available targets, namely their children.

Helfer and associates (1976) state that abusive parents have failed to learn several basic skills in order to become good parents. In addition to not knowing how to meet their own emotional needs, they haven't learned to separate their feelings and emotions from their behavior. Therefore, if they get mad, they don't talk about it; they hit. Another unlearned skill involves the appropriate delineation of responsibility. On the one hand, there is a tendency to blame others for their mistakes. For example, it's the child's fault he got hit and broke his arm because he was naughty. On the other hand, abusers tend to accept the blame for others' behavior. For instance, it's my fault that Hubby hit the child because I didn't have his supper hot enough when he got home. Still another unlearned task involves decision making. Abusers tend to have little confidence in their own ability. Therefore, they tend to have little faith in their own judgment. They have difficulty articulating and evaluating their alternatives, with the respective pros and cons of each choice, and are indecisive. One other skill abusers often fail to master is how to delay their own gratification. The here and now becomes all-important. If a child misbehaves, a kick will take care of it immediately. If their stress level is too high, they need immediate relief. They focus on the moment and have trouble looking at what the consequences of their behavior will be in the future.

Child Neglect

Because neglect involves the absence of resources instead of the presence of something which is negative, it is difficult to define. Every social environment is different. When does a family environment cease being adequate and instead display neglect?

Wolock and Horowitz (1984, p. 15) define child neglect as "the failure of the child's parent or caretaker, who has the material resources to do so, to provide minimally adequate care in the areas of health, nutrition, shelter, education, supervision, affection or attention." Two of the most frequent aspects of neglect involve "deprivation of necessities" and "inadequate supervision" (Kadushin and Martin, 1988, p. 230).

Whereas child abuse involves harming a child through actions, child neglect concerns causing a child harm by *not* doing what's necessary. Neglect occurs when children are not given what they need to survive and thrive. This includes children's need for supervision. They need someone there to direct them, care for them, support their daily activities such as going to school, and give them emotional support.

We've already discerned that many times neglect is related to poverty. Many neglectful parents haven't the resources to take care of themselves or their children. For instance, one woman who was charged with child neglect described her living conditions to a judge at her hearing. She lived in a small, third floor flat without hot water. She said, "It is an awful place to live. The wallpaper is in strips, the floor board is cracked. The baby is always getting splinters in his hands. The bathroom is on the floor above and two other families use it. The kitchen is on the first floor. I share it with another woman. I have no place to keep food. We buy for one meal at a time" (Hancock, 1963, p. 5).

A young social worker recounts a visit to a family suspected of child neglect:

It was my first visit to the Peterson's home, or should I say second floor flat. The house was in a very poor area in the inner city of Milwaukee. I was supposed to do an initial family assessment. Both parents and three small children were there. The house was filthy even by my standards, and I have never been renowned for my domestic ability. Dirty laundry was heaped in piles on the living room floor. The walls were smeared with grease. Wads of dust rolled along the floor; if they had been at my apartment, I would've called them dinosaur dust bunnies.

The flat was small. The only furniture I could see included two double beds in the tiny living room, and a cheap, old dinette and appliances in the kitchen. The family asked me to sit at the old kitchen table. The chairs were black; I had to restrain myself from wiping one off with a Kleenex before I sat down. But I didn't want to offend my clients. I was clearly aware of my middle-class bias already. None of the children were wearing shoes, which might not be too unusual for summer. However, black dirt streaked all of the children's white arms, legs, feet, hands, and faces. Their hair was dirty and snarled.

As we talked, the parents asked me if I'd like a cup of coffee. The coffee maker in front of me was filthy as was

the cup they gave me. It matched the dirty dishes heaped high in the sink. Again, not wanting to offend my clients, I gratefully accepted the coffee. As we talked, I accepted the second cup of coffee and then a third. That was my mistake. Suddenly it occurred to me I desperately needed to use the bathroom. I wondered where it was. I asked if I could, and Mr. Peterson said, "Sure, just a minute." He stood up from the table, picked up a door which had been leaning against the wall around the corner, pointed to a literally open door out of my direct view around the refrigerator. Mortified as I was, I stepped into the bathroom. He laid the door in place (there were no hinges) and said he'd hold it until I was finished. Well, what else was there to do at that point? After I finished, I meekly said, "I'm through," at which point he picked up the door and put it back in its place leaning against the wall. We continued with the interview. One thing is for sure; my coffee drinking behavior on home visits will never be the same!

Characteristics of Neglected Children

Each of us has infinite needs. To define and categorize all that we need to maintain physical and emotional health would be an awesome task. This is why neglect is often difficult to define for any specific family situation. Nonetheless, seven general indicators of child neglect will be presented here (U.S. Department of Health, Education and Welfare, 1979). They provide at least a basis for assessment of situations in which neglect may be involved. As with the characteristics of physically abused children, it should be noted that not all of these characteristics apply to all neglected children. However, any one of them might be an indicator of neglect.

1. Abandonment. The most blatant form of neglect is abandonment. Children are deserted and left to fend for themselves either forever or for long periods of time.
2. Often or almost always left alone without adequate supervision. Examples of incidents reflective of this situation include when very young children or infants are left unattended. Another common situation is when very young children are left in the supervision of other children who themselves are too young to assume such responsibility. A third common situation occurs when unsupervised children get involved in activities in which they may harm themselves. For example, we periodically read in the newspaper how a young, unsupervised child plays with matches, starts a fire, and burns down the house or apartment building and usually dies in the fire.

3. Inadequate clothing and poor hygiene. Children may not be wearing jackets, gloves, and hats when it is cold. Their clothing might be ripped, filthy, and threadbare. Their hair might be unkempt and dirty. They themselves might be unbathed.
4. Lack of adequate medical and dental care. Illnesses are not attended to or proper dental care is not maintained.
5. Inadequate education. Frequent truancy or tardiness can be caused by neglect. Parents may fail to supervise their children and provide the minimum support needed to get them to school.
6. Inadequate nutrition. Children who frequently complain that they're hungry and searching for food may be victims of neglect. Children receiving food that provides them with inadequate nutrition may be neglected. Significant delays in development resulting from malnutrition may also be a clue to neglect.
7. Inadequate shelter. Housing with inadequate heat, ventilation, safety features, or sanitation may be involved.

Two pronounced physical conditions that can result from extreme neglect are nonorganic failure to thrive syndrome and psychosocial dwarfism (Tower, 1989). *Nonorganic failure to thrive syndrome* occurs in infancy. It is characterized by infants who are below the fifth percentile in weight, and sometimes in height (Faller, 1981). This means that 95 percent of all other infants that age weigh more. Additionally, the infant must have had normal health at one time. Lags in psychomotor development are also apparent (English, 1978).

Psychosocial dwarfism (PSD) can affect children aged eighteen months to sixteen years. In these children, "emotional deprivation promotes abnormally low growth. PSD children are also below the fifth percentile in weight and height, exhibit retarded skeletal maturation, and a variety of behavioral problems" (Tower, 1989, p. 88). Additionally, they tend to have speech difficulties and problems in their social interactions.

Characteristics of Neglectful Parents

Tower (1989, p. 91) describes a typical neglectful parent as "an isolated individual who has difficulty forming relationships or carrying on the routine tasks of everyday life. Burdened with the anger and sadness over unmet childhood needs, this parent finds it impossible to consistently recognize and meet the needs of her or his children." This description, in some ways, resembles the description of the physically abu-

sive parent. However, an abuser lashes out, whereas a neglectful parent tends to withdraw and fails to provide adequately for children.

A Macro System Response: Protective Services

An abused or neglected child is usually referred to a protective services unit which then provides assessment, treatment, and referral to other necessary services. Protective services has been defined as "a specialized casework service to neglected, abused, exploited, or rejected children. The focus of the service is preventive and nonpunitive and is geared toward rehabilitation through identification and treatment of the motivating factors which underlie" the problem (DeFrancis, 1955, p. 2).

Treatment of Physical Abuse and Neglect: Social Work Role

Treatment of physical abuse and neglect follows the same sequential steps used in other areas of social work intervention. These include intake or receipt of the initial referral, gathering of information about the case through doing a social study, assessment of the situation, case planning including goal-setting, provision of treatment, evaluation of the effects of treatment, and termination of the case (Kadushin and Martin, 1988). Assessment focuses on many of the aspects, characteristics, and dynamics of the case which we've already discussed. A number of variables have been found to affect a worker's decision that a case merits agency intervention (Kadushin and Martin, 1988; Meddin, 1985; Rosen, 1981; Craft et al., 1980; DiLeonardi, 1980). These include:

1. Clearly visible proof of abuse or environmental characteristics which obviously endanger a child;
2. The degree of the child's helplessness and vulnerability (for example, a physically disabled child or an infant are extremely vulnerable);
3. Self-destructive behavior on the part of the child;
4. A long history of severe abuse;
5. Abusers who show no or little regret for their child's abuse and have difficulty accepting responsibility;
6. Abusers who openly reject the child or blame the child for the problem.
7. Serious emotional disturbances on the part of parents;
8. Lack of cooperation on the part of the parents;
9. Families who are exposed to numerous and severe psychological and social pressures;
10. Isolation of the family and lack of social support systems.

After the family is assessed, treatment planning is undertaken. Most maltreated children remain in their own homes; only 20 percent are removed and placed elsewhere and many of those placed have been sexually abused (Kadushin and Martin, 1988, p. 268).

For both assessment and case planning, it's very important to be specific because the potential impact on the victim and family is so great. Behaviorally specific terminology, which was discussed earlier in the chapter, is very useful in accomplishing these tasks.

Treatment often progresses through phases (National Society for the Prevention of Cruelty to Children, 1976). The first three months after referral to the social service agency is a period of crisis for the family. An initial goal for the worker is to establish trust and develop a workable relationship with the family. Months four through twelve are characterized by mothers being very dependent on their workers. Much of this time is spent building parental self-esteem. During the second year, parents continue to be dependent on their worker. However, they are able to verbalize this, articulate the goals of their treatment, and acknowledge their progress. During the third year, parents become much more independent and rely very little on the worker and agency.

The primary goal of treatment is to stop the abuse. The parents' personalities don't have to be changed, but any factors that feed into the abusive situation do. Parents' own needs must be met. Tower (1989, p. 266) summarizes what parents need to learn in order to prevent future abuse. This includes:

- Recognizing what feelings or events led to the initial abuse;
- Learning to read the warning signals that immediately precede the abusive behavior;
- Learning alternative coping skills to handle anger and frustration;
- Gaining more pride in themselves as parents and in their child;
- Understanding child development so they can adapt realistic expectations of their children.

Parents need to improve their communication skills. They need to learn how to identify their feelings and express them appropriately. They need to learn how to communicate their needs to others and, in two-parent homes, to each other. They need to build their self-concepts. They also need to master effective child management techniques in order to gain control and avoid abusive situations. They need to be taught how to provide a nurturant family environment for their children and improve their parent-child relationships.

Many times outside resources are helpful. Daycare for children can provide some respite for parents and time for themselves. Homemaker service provides training for household management. It also makes an individual available to them to give support and nurturance. Parental aides can work in homes, form relationships with parents, and model both how to nurture children and effective child management techniques.

Abused children also need treatment including medical services for physical damage. Children suffering from developmental delays may need special therapy or remedial help. Exposure to appropriate adult role models through daycare is often used. Becoming involved with organizations such as Big Brothers and Big Sisters provides another means of support.

There may be a need for individual or group counseling of the child. Tower (1989) mentions three major categories of victims' needs that should be addressed. These categories relate directly to the characteristics of abused children that we've already discussed. The first need involves improving the victim's relationships with other people, including both peers and adults. Their old behavior patterns most likely involved either defensive withdrawal or inappropriate aggression. New, more effective social interaction techniques need to be established. The second need involves helping victims learn how to express their feelings. Some abused children withhold and suppress their feelings to avoid confrontations. Other abused children have never learned how to control their aggressive impulses. The third need concerns the abused child's self-concept. For the many reasons we've discussed, abused children have a poor opinion of themselves and have little confidence in their own abilities.

Much of the treatment given abusive families also applies to families tho neglect their children. One major difference is that neglectful families are more likely to be multiproblem families that suffer from economic, educational, and social deficits. The most effective approach seems to be assisting them in getting needed resources. "Situational changes rather than psychological changes" seem to be the most helpful for them (Kadushin and Martin, 1988, p. 270). Social workers can help neglectful families in the following ways: by connecting families with the resources and services they need; by helping parents learn and improve their communication skills; by providing supportive counseling when it's needed; by showing the family that someone cares about them; by supplying clear step-by-step suggestions for how to address their problems and attain their goals; and by modeling effective techniques for raising their children (Tower, 1989, p. 280).

A Macro System Response: Involvement of the Courts

Courts become involved in maltreatment cases when "parents abandon their children, severely injure or kill them, place them in imminent danger, sexually abuse them, or fail to cooperate with the protective services agency" (Tower, 1989, p. 256). This is a very difficult and scary process for both the family and victim. Juvenile court procedures vary from state to state. However, most involve three processes, namely the petition, the adjudication, and the disposition.

The *petition* involves a written complaint being submitted to the court that the alleged abuse or neglect has occurred. *Adjudication* involves a hearing where the alleged abuse or neglect is proven or discounted. Both parents and victim are represented by separate counsel. The *disposition* involves a hearing where the court determines what is to be done with the child. This is a separate hearing from the adjudication where it is determined whether the abuse or neglect actually happened. The court process is complex and often lengthy. A large number of variations including additional investigations and settlements are possible. (For additional information on court involvement, see Tower, 1989, for an excellent description of the process.) Protective service workers and other social workers are frequently called upon to provide input to aid in the court's decision. Such input often is very influential and can have direct impact on what happens to a child.

Sexual Abuse

As with physical abuse and neglect, there is a range of definitions for sexual abuse. Kadushin and Martin (1988, pp. 292-93) identify the variables involved in the breadth of the definition. They cite the definition proposed by the National Center for Child Abuse and Neglect; it reads that sexual abuse involves "contacts and interactions between a child and an adult in which the child is being used for the sexual stimulation of the perpetrator or another person." For our purposes, "children" include all who are under age eighteen; "adults" will include people who are five years older than the child who is being abused and are in a position to have power over the victim. This definition emphasizes both the fact that an adult has power over the child and that the sexual activity takes place in order to provide sexual satisfaction for the abuser. Other definitions exist which stress the amount of harm done the victim and how the victim is in the position of relying on the perpetrator for support.

Incest is a particular form of sexual abuse. As with sexual abuse, there is a variation of specific definitions. Mayer (1983, p. 4) defines incest simply and directly as "any sexual contact or interaction between family members who are not marital partners." This definition includes a wide variation of sexual behaviors which may be involved including "pornographic photography, sexual gestures, parental exposure of genitalia, fondling, petting, fellatio, cunnilingus, intercourse and any and all varieties of sexual contact" (Mayer, 1983, p. 4). Additionally, this definition allows for a variety of incestuous relationships within the family including nonbiological relatives such as stepparents, stepsiblings, mothers' boyfriends and fathers' girlfriends who live in the home, uncles, and cousins. Protective service agencies have adopted broad definitions of incest relative to assessment and provision of services (Kadushin and Martin, 1988).

As with other types of child abuse and neglect, it's difficult to determine how prevalent sexual abuse really is. Reports vary widely as to the percentage of people who have been sexually abused. For example, Russell (1983) found that one out of three women have been sexually abused, whereas Kercher and McShane (1984) found one in thirteen. Likewise, percentages of incest, when placed in a category by itself, vary widely. Professionals agree that regardless of the number reported, the actual number of sexual abuse cases is three to four times higher than those which come to the attention of authorities and social service agencies (Kadushin, 1988, p. 295).

The Dynamics of Child Sexual Abuse

A major myth involved in child sexual abuse is that children should be warned about strangers. They're told that they should not get into cars when strange men offer them lollipops and they should not talk to strange men who are hiding behind park bushes. The reality is that children are in much greater danger from people who are close to them, from people whom they trust.

Children are easy victims for sexual abuse. Because of the anxiety most people harbor about sexuality in general, children have little information about sex. They have limited life experience upon which to base judgments. Thus, they can easily be misled and tricked. They are small compared to adults and are easily intimidated. Adults, in some ways, are godlike to children. Adults tell them what to do, when to go to bed, when they can cross the street, and if they can go to McDonald's. They are oriented toward obeying adults and most likely want to please them, especially those adults who control their access to being loved, having food and shelter, and feeling safe.

Sixty percent of sexual abuse occurs within the family (Tower, 1989). This does not mean that the remaining 40 percent is perpetrated by strangers. Rather, much extrafamilial abuse is done by others who are close to the family and trusted by the child. When sexual abuse is perpetrated by someone outside the family, that person is usually called a *pedophile* (someone who prefers children for sexual gratification). Because of its prevalence, we will focus on incest in the following discussion.

Progression of the incestuous relationship is usually gradual. It may even appear innocent enough at first. For instance, the adult might appear nude or undress before a child. It then progresses to greater and greater intimacy. Carnes (1983) suggests that there are five phases of sexual abuse. First comes the *engagement* phase. Here the perpetrator will experiment with the child to see how close he can get and how the child will react. The second phase is the *sexual interaction* phase. Sexual activity in various degrees of intimacy occurs during this phase. Often the longer this phase lasts, the more intimate the abuser becomes with the victim. The third phase is one of *secrecy*. Sexual activity has already occurred so the abuser will use some tricky manipulations to hold the victim ensnared in the abuse. For instance, the

perpetrator might say, "Now don't you tell your mommy; she won't like you anymore," or, "This is our special little secret because I love you so very much," or "If you tell anybody, I'll punish you." Threats and guilt are used to maintain the secret. The fourth phase is the *disclosure*. For one reason or another, the victim reveals that abuse has occurred. It may be physically initiated if the child contracts a sexually transmitted disease or is damaged in some way. It may be the result of an accident if the sexual activity was observed or someone noted and reported the child's indicative behavior. It may be that the victim feels she must tell someone because she can't stand it anymore. The fifth and final phase is *post-disclosure*. This is a time of high anxiety for both victim and family. Feelings may include denial on the part of the perpetrator, guilt and insecurity on the part of the victim, and anger on the part of other family members.

Kadushin and Martin (1989, p. 295) describe the typical perpetrator and victim:

> The perpetrator is generally a white male in his late thirties or early forties, generally older than male physical abusers. The family is generally an intact two-parent family. The marriage has been in existence for some time. The perpetrator group is better educated, more continuously employed, and at a higher income level than in cases of physical abuse. The daughter, victim in 85 percent of the cases, is generally of early pubertal age (10.5 years average). The abuse has been continuing for one-half to three years and began when the girl was prepubescent.

Several other factors add to a child's risk of sexual abuse (Kadushin and Martin, 1988; Finkelhor and Baron, 1986). Families who are socially isolated have an increased risk. Role boundaries among family subsystems tend to be blurred. Because secrecy is a necessity for abuse to occur, there is a tendency for the family to intensify its isolation. Fathers tend to be overinvolved with their daughters who in turn are underinvolved with their mothers (Reposa and Zuelzer, 1983). Communication is usually poor between mothers and daughters. Therefore, it becomes even more difficult for daughters to turn to their mothers for help. Gradually fathers turn their affections toward their daughter.

One of the greatest risk factors for sexual abuse is

the presence of a stepfather. However, any type of parental absence during childhood increases risk. Related factors include mothers who are ill or are working outside of the home. Conflict and isolation between the parents themselves is common. When conflict is present between husband and wife, the husband may turn to his daughter to fulfill his needs. Alcoholism has been linked to increased risk as have high levels of stress experienced by the perpetrator. There is also some relationship between sexual abuse and the perpetrator having been sexually abused himself.

Interestingly enough, neither social class nor race has been found to increase risk of abuse. This differs somewhat from physical abuse and neglect, which are linked to lower socioeconomic status.

Kadushin and Martin (1988) also describe the characteristics of perpetrators and their spouses. The sexually abusive father tends to be a shy person with poor social interaction skills. He thus focuses his energies and attention on his family. As we have already noted, he also has difficulties communicating with his wife which results in marital problems. Turning to a daughter to meet his needs provides the incestuous father with additional control. The daughter is readily available because, as his child, she has little power and already feels affection toward him.

A common profile of the spouse of the perpetrator is "a diffident, depressed, unassertive, subservient woman. Dependent on her husband for support and affection, at whatever levels of adequacy, she has a lot to risk if she openly challenges him by breaking open his relationship with her daughter" (Kadushin and Martin, 1988, p. 303). Indeed, some unknown proportion of mothers do not know that the incest is occurring. The marriage is conflictual. Communication is lacking between the woman and her husband and the woman and her daughter. She may see things that are strange, but works hard to deny them. She has potentially a lot to lose if the incest is brought out into the open. She may feel resentment toward a daughter who has taken her husband and lover away from her. She may feel shame that this taboo is occurring within her very own family. She may feel guilt for being such a failure to her husband that he had to turn to another. She may desperately fear losing her husband and having her family ripped apart. It is a very difficult situation for a mother in the incest triangle. She is not the abuser. Yet there are no alternatives available to her which offer her a happy solution to the dilemma.

In some ways the mother in the incestuous triangle is also a victim (Wattenberg, 1985; McIntyre, 1981). She has been raised in a patriarchal society where she has been taught to be dependent, unassertive, and passive. She has also been taught that she is supposed to be the caretaker of the emotional well-being of her family and be deferent to her husband. She has not been given the skills needed to aggressively fight for herself and her daughter in this desperate situation.

Characteristics of Sexual Abuse Victims

Children who are sexually abused may display a variety of physical and behavioral indicators. Physical indicators may include a variety of physical problems that are sexually related such as venereal disease, problems with the throat or mouth, difficulties with urination, penile or vaginal discharge, or bruises in the genital area. Pregnancy is also an indicator.

Behavioral indicators may also be evident. Some of these resemble symptoms of physical abuse. For instance, sexually abused children may become either very withdrawn or very aggressive. They also may experience difficulties in peer interaction. Behavior related to sex which strikes you as being odd, may also be an indicator. This refers once again to your "gut reaction" that something's wrong. For example, a child may know sexual terms or display sexual gestures which strike you as being inappropriate for her age level. A child may touch herself or others inappropriately in a sexual manner. A child may express desperate fears about being touched, undressing and taking showers in gym class, or of being alone with a certain gender or with certain people.

Specific things that children say may strike you as being odd and may be indicative of sexual abuse. For instance, a child may say: "Daddy and I have a secret"; "My babysitter wears red underwear"; or "I don't like going to Aunt Shirley's house. She diddles me."

Long-Term Effects of Sexual Abuse

Victims of sexual abuse are not necessarily destined to be poorly adjusted for the rest of their lives because of the abuse (Kadushin and Martin, 1988). Vast strides have been made in treatment techniques and availability.

However, a number of variables have been found to be associated with "a worse prognosis" (Browne and Finkelhor, 1986, p. 175). It must be emphasized that there is tremendous variation in how the experience affects different individuals. No specific variables have been established that are consistently linked to long-term problems. What has been established are a number of trends.

The following variables are related to greater traumatization for the victim: longer lasting abuse; involvement in more than one incident; perpetration by fathers or stepfathers; accompaniment by the use of force; perpetration by adults who are men versus women or teenagers; and lack of support by families after disclosure and/or removal of the victim from the home. Other variables have been found to have negative or confusing effects. These include the age of the victim when the sexual abuse began, what physical forms the abuse took, how the abuse was revealed, and whether effects were more severe if the abuse was perpetrated by family members other than fathers or stepfathers than by other adults outside of the family. It remains as yet undetermined what other variables may be operating under these conditions which may influence the long-term effects.

Treatment of Sexual Abuse: Social Work Role

Because of its prevalence, we will focus on treatment of the incestuous family. Treatment usually progresses through three phases (Tower, 1989, pp. 289-90). The first is the "disclosure-panic" phase. Strong feelings characterize this period of crisis. Family members display much anger and denial. The victim is often frightened about what will happen and eager to blame herself. The second phase is the "assessment-awareness" phase. During this phase, the family acknowledges that the abuse has occurred and struggles to deal with its consequences. Family members learn about themselves and the dynamics involved in their family interaction. The social worker works to redefine and realign the boundaries of subsystems within the family. This phase tends to be characterized by conflicting feelings. On the one hand, they are angry that the abuse has occurred and eager to blame each other. On the other hand, they are struggling to realign their relationships and express the feelings of love they have for each other. The third phase is the "restructure" phase. Here the family regains emotional health. Boundaries are clearly established and family members learn how to function within them. Communication is greatly enhanced and members can use it to work out their differences. Parents take responsibility for their behavior and the victim feels much better about herself.

On the average, treatment lasts approximately nine months and has several major objectives (Kadushin and Martin, 1988). The first is to have the abuser accept responsibility for his behavior. The second is for the victim to acknowledge that the abuse was not her fault, that she can forgive other family members, and that she feels more confident in her ability to say "no" in potentially abusive situations. A third is to have the mother improve her own self-esteem, her feeling of significance and control within the family, and her ability to protect her children from abuse. A fourth objective is to develop communication among all family members, especially the marital subsystem, in order to maintain the appropriate subsystem boundaries.

Treatment themes for all family members include enhancement of self-concept and self-confidence, improved communication of feelings and ideas with each other, and definition and maintenance of appropriate boundaries between the various subsystems. Several specific goals are important for the victim to achieve (Mayer, 1983). First, she needs to learn how to identify, express, and share her feelings, even when they are negative and frightening. Second, she needs to develop her assertiveness skills. She needs to develop confidence that her own needs are important and that both her needs and the needs of others should be addressed in her relationships with others. Many times group treatment is also helpful for her to achieve these goals.

Prevention of Sexual Abuse: The Need for a Macro System Response

The ideal way of dealing with sexual abuse is to prevent it from happening at all. Information and education are the keys to prevention. Parents need both education about how to raise children and also knowledge that in the event they are in crisis there are resources available to help. Parenting education could be made a required part of all high school curricula. Special programs could be made readily available in the community to help parents with these issues.

Educating Children about Sexual Abuse

Children also need to be educated about sexual abuse. There are three basic preventative approaches. First, children should be taught that their bodies are their own and that they have private places where nobody can force them to be touched. What comes to mind are the parents who tell their four-year-old son to go up to each relative at the culmination of an extended family event and "give them a kiss." The child obviously finds this distasteful. He frowns, looks down at his shoes, and hides behind his mother. He knows that old Aunt Hilda gives really slobbery, wet ones. And, she hugs him like The Crusher in a wrestling match, too. He hates the very thought of it, even though his aunt is a kind person who loves him.

Children should have the right to say no if they don't want to have such intimacy. Parents and teachers can help children determine what are good touches and what are bad touches. They can also help children develop the confidence to say "no" to adults in uncomfortable situations involving touching them in ways they don't like.

A second preventative measure for children is to learn correct sexual terminology right from the beginning. It's easy for parents, especially if they're uncomfortable with sexual terminology themselves, to sugar-coat words and refer to "ding-dongs" and "bumps." One three-year-old girl came out into the midst of a family gathering and told her mother, "My pooderpie hurts." She had her hand placed over her clothes on her genital area. Her mother, with a look of terror, desperation, and embarrassment, jumped up and dashed off with her to the bathroom. Apparently, the little girl had to urinate and didn't identify the feeling as such. A few months later, the same three-year-old was chattering on about some topic that was desperately important to a three-year-old, pointed to her buttocks, and interjected something about her pooderpie again. My reaction was, "Yikes, the pooderpie has moved. Where will it go next?"

The point is that if this little girl would tell someone that a person touched her pooderpie, that someone might respond, "Oh, that's nice." Whomever she tells would have no idea what she was talking about. Using inaccurate, childish terminology does not equip children with the communication skills they need in the event that they encounter a sexually abusive situation. Children need to be able to specify what people

---

Suggestions for Talking to Children Victimized by Sexual Assault

- Always believe the child. It takes courage to talk about such difficult things, and it's easy to turn the child off.
- Be warm and empathic. Encourage the child to talk freely to you. Reflecting the child's feelings back is useful.
- Don't react with shock or disgust no matter what the child tells you. That only communicates to the child that he or she is the one to blame.
- Encourage the child to share all feelings with you, including the negative ones. Even getting the angry feelings out helps the child overcome the feelings of victimization. Give the child the chance to ventilate his or her feelings so he or she can deal with them.
- *Listen* to the child. Don't disagree or argue. Interrupt only when you have to in order to understand what the child is saying.
- Talk to the child in a private place. The child may feel much more comfortable if others aren't around to hear.
- Tell the child that he or she is not the only child who has had this experience. Other children have, too.
- Allow the child to express feelings of guilt. Emphasize to the child that it was *not* his or her fault. The adult abuser is the one who has a problem and needs help.
- Talk in language that the child can understand. Give accurate information when it's needed. Let the child repeat things back to you to make certain he or she understands.
- Tell the child that you are very glad he or she told you about the incident(s). Emphasize that it was the *right* thing to do.
- Ask if the child would like to ask you any questions and be sure to answer them honestly.
- Do not treat the child any differently after he or she has told you. This only communicates that you think he or she is to blame or did the wrong thing.
- If the child asks you to keep the abuse secret, answer honestly. Tell the child that you only want to help, that secrets that hurt people aren't good to keep, and that the secrets need to be brought out into the open in order to help the person who abused him or her.
- Finally, depending on your own situation, don't let the issue drop. If you are the social worker involved, pursue the problem. Otherwise, tell the parents and/or go to the appropriate authorities so that the child can get help.

are doing or have tried to do to them. Only then can their caretakers adequately protect them.

This leads us to our third preventative suggestion. Lines of communication between caretakers and children should be encouraged and kept open. Children need to be able to feel that they can share things with parents, including the things that bother them. In the event that children are placed in a potentially abusive situation, they need to be encouraged and to be able to "tell someone."

Summary

Socialization refers to the process through which individuals learn proper ways of acting in a culture. Social forces and macro systems can affect families both positively and negatively. Children are socialized by their families, peers, and schools. The family can be viewed as a system. A healthy family system strives to maintain homeostatis or equilibrium. Just as individuals go through developmental phases, so do families progress through life cycles.

Learning theory provides an exceptionally useful means of conceptualizing and understanding human behavior. The three basic types of learning are respondent conditioning, modeling, and operant conditioning. Learning theory concepts, such as positive reinforcement and punishment, can easily be applied to effective parenting. Although punishment is frequently used to attempt to control children's behavior, it should be used cautiously as it has several potential negative effects. Important issues in applying learning theory concepts include accidental training, the importance of behaviorally specific terminology for stating goals and measuring improvement, and the importance of parental attention. An effective behavioral technique is time-out from reinforcement.

Some life events and situations that influence the social development of children are the presence of siblings, social play with peers, watching television, and attending school.

Large numbers of children are physically abused, neglected, or sexually abused. There are profiles which characterize victims, perpetrators, and the family dynamics involved. Macro system responses to child abuse and neglect involve Protective Services. The social work role concerns specific techniques regarding how to treat maltreated children and their families.

5

Ethnocentrism and Racism

BACK OF THE B̶U̶S̶ BOARD ROOM

Abraham Lincoln has the reputation of being the key person in ending slavery in our country. Yet, it appears that Lincoln held racist beliefs, as indicated in the following excerpt from a speech he delivered in 1858:

> I will say, then, that I am not, nor ever have been in favor of bringing about in any way the social and political equality of the white and black races; that I am not, nor ever have been, in favor of making voters or jurors of Negroes, nor of qualifying them to hold office, nor to inter-marry with white people . . . and inasmuch as they cannot so live, while they do remain together there must be the position of superior and inferior, and I as much as any other man am in favor of having the superior position assigned to the white race.

Such a statement needs to be viewed in its historical context. Our country was more racist years ago than it is today. Lincoln, who was in the vanguard of moving for greater equality for African Americans, was also socialized by his culture to have racist attitudes.

A Perspective

Nearly every time we turn on the evening news on television we see ethnic and racial conflict—riots, beatings, murders, and civil wars. In recent years we have seen clashes resulting in bloodshed from Northern Ireland to South Africa, from Lebanon to Israel, and from the United States to South America. Practically every nation with more than one ethnic group has had to deal with ethnic conflict. The oppression and exploitation of one ethnic group by another is particularly ironic in democratic nations, as these societies claim to cherish freedom, equality, and justice. In reality, the dominant group in all societies that controls the political and economic institutions rarely agrees to share (equally) its power and wealth with other ethnic groups. Ethnocentrism and racism are factors that can adversely affect the growth and development of minority group members.

This chapter will:

- Define and describe ethnic groups, ethnocentrism, racial groups, racism, prejudice, discrimination, oppression, and institutional discrimination.
- Outline the sources of prejudice and discrimination.
- Summarize the effects and costs of discrimination and oppression and describe effects of discrimination upon human growth and development.
- Suggest strategies to combat discrimination and oppression.
- Outline some guidelines for social work practice with racial and ethnic groups.
- Forecast the pattern of race and ethnic relations in the United States in the future.

Ethnic Groups and Ethnocentrism

An ethnic group has a sense of togetherness, a conviction that its members form a special group, and a sense of common identity or peoplehood. Milton M.

Gordon (1964, pp. 27-28) defines an ethnic group as

any group which is defined or set off by race, religion, or national origin, or some combination of these categories [which] have a common social-psychological referent, in that all of them serve to create, through historical circumstances, a sense of peoplehood.

Korean musicians perform a five-drum dance during a folk and harvest festival in Queens, New York. Members of ethnic groups share a feeling of common identity and peoplehood.

Practically every ethnic group has a strong feeling of *ethnocentrism*, "the tendency to view the norms and values of one's own culture as absolute and to use them as a standard against which to judge and measure all other cultures" (*Encyclopedia of Sociology*, 1974, p. 101). Ethnocentrism leads members of ethnic groups to view their culture as the best, as being superior, as being the one that other cultures should adopt. Ethnocentrism also leads to prejudice against foreigners, who may be viewed as barbarians, uncultured people, or savages.

Feelings of ethnic superiority within a nation are usually accompanied by the belief that political and economic domination by one's own group is natural, is morally right, is in the best interest of the nation, and perhaps also is God's will. Ethnocentrism has been a factor in leading to some of the worst atrocities in history, such as the American colonists' nearly successful attempt to exterminate Native Americans and Adolf Hitler's mass executions of over 6 million European Jews, and millions more gypsies, people with disabilities, and other minority group members.

In interactions between nations, ethnocentric beliefs sometimes lead to wars and serve as justifications for foreign conquests. At practically any point in the last several centuries at least a few wars have occurred between nations in which one society has been seeking to force its culture on another or to eradicate another culture. For example, Israel has been involved in bitter struggles with Arab countries in the Middle East for more than four decades over territory ownership. Bosnians, Serbs, Croats, and others are fighting for domination in what was once Yugoslavia.

Race and Racism

Although a racial group is often also an ethnic group, the two groups are not necessarily the same. A *race* is believed to have a common set of physical characteristics. But the members of a racial group may or may not share the sense of togetherness or identity that holds an ethnic group together. A group that is both a racial group and an ethnic group is Japanese-Americans, as they are thought to have some common physical characteristics and also have a sense of peoplehood. (Coleman and Cressey, 1984, pp. 188-90). On the other hand, white Americans and white Russians are of the same race, but they hardly have a sense of togetherness. In addition, there are ethnic groups that are composed of a variety of races. For example, a religious group (such as Roman Catholic) is sometimes considered an ethnic group and is composed of members from diverse racial groups.

In contrast to ethnocentrism, racism is more likely to be based on physical differences than on cultural differences. Racism is "... a belief in racial superiority that leads to discrimination and prejudice toward those races considered inferior" (*Encyclopedia of Sociology*, 1974, p. 236). However, similar to ethnocentric ideologies, most racist ideologists assert that members of other racial groups are inferior. Some white Americans in this country have gone to extreme and morally reprehensible limits to seek to attain greater control and power over other racial groups.

Aspects of Social and Economic Forces: Prejudice, Discrimination, and Oppression

Prejudice, in regard to race and ethnic relations, is making negative prejudgments. Gordon Allport (1954, p. 7) defines *prejudice* as thinking negatively of others without sufficient justification. His definition has two elements: an unfounded judgment and a feeling tone of scorn, dislike, fear, and aversion. Prejudiced people apply racial stereotypes to all or nearly all members of a group according to preconceived notions of what they believe the group to be like and how they think the group will behave. Racial prejudice results from the belief that people who have different skin color and other physical characteristics also have innate differences in behaviors, values, intellectual functioning, and attitudes.

The word *discriminate* has two very different meanings. It may have the positive meaning to be discerning and perceptive. However, in minority group relations, it involves making categoric differentiations based on a social group ranked as inferior, rather than judging an individual on his or her own merits. Racial or ethnic discrimination involves denying to members of minority groups equal access to: opportunities, residential housing areas, membership in religious and social organizations, involvement in political activities, access to community services, and so on.

Prejudice is a combination of stereotyped beliefs and negative attitudes, so that prejudiced individuals *think about people* in a predetermined, usually negative, categorical way. *Discrimination* involves physical actions, unequal *treatment of people* because they belong to a category. Discriminatory behavior often derives from prejudiced attitudes. Robert Merton (1949), however, notes prejudice and discrimination can occur independently of each other. Merton (1949, p. 47) describes four different types of people:

1. *The unprejudiced nondiscriminator*, in both belief and practice, upholds American ideals of freedom and equality. This person is not prejudiced against other groups and, on principle, will not discriminate against them.
2. *The unprejudiced discriminator* is not personally prejudiced but may sometimes, reluctantly, discriminate against other groups because it seems socially or financially convenient to do so.
3. *The prejudiced nondiscriminator* feels hostile to other groups but recognizes that law and social pressures are opposed to overt discrimination. Reluctantly, this person does not translate prejudice into action.
4. *The prejudiced discriminator* does not believe in the values of freedom and equality and consistently discriminates against other groups in both word and deed.

An example of an unprejudiced discriminator is the unprejudiced owner of a condominium complex in an all-white middle-class suburb who refuses to sell a condominium to an African American family because of fear (founded or unfounded) that the sale would reduce the sale value of the remaining units. An example of a prejudiced nondiscriminator is a personnel director of a fire department who believes Mexican Americans are unreliable and poor fire fighters yet complies with affirmative action efforts to hire and train Mexican American fire fighters.

It is very difficult to keep personal prejudices from eventually leading to some form of discrimination.

Violence Against Minorities in the United States

Minorities have been subjected to extensive violence by whites in our society. (It has been a two-way street as a number of whites have been subjected to violence by non-whites.)

During the second half of the nineteenth century frequent massacres of Chinese mining and railroad workers occurred in the West. During one railroad strike in 1885, white workers stormed a Chinese community in Rock Springs, Wyoming, murdered sixteen persons, and burned all the homes to the ground. No one was arrested. In 1871 a white mob raided the Chinese community in Los Angeles, killing nineteen persons and hanging fifteen to serve as a warning to survivors (Pinkney, 1972, p. 73).

Pinkney (1972, p. 73) comments on the treatment of African American slaves by their white owners.

> Few adult slaves escaped some form of sadism at the hands of slaveholders. A female slaveholder was widely known to punish her slaves by beating them on the face. Another burned her slave girl on the neck with hot tongs. A drunken slaveholder dismembered his slave and threw him piece by piece into a fire. Another planter dragged his slave from bed and inflicted a thousand lashes on him.

Slaveowners often used a whip, made of cowskin or rawhide, to control their slaves. An elaborate punishment system was developed, linking the number of lashes to the seriousness of the offenses with which slaves were charged.

Shortly before the Civil War, roving bands of whites commonly descended on African American communities and terrorized and beat the inhabitants. Slaves sometimes struck back and killed their slaveowners or other whites. During Reconstruction, it has been estimated that over 5,000 African Americans were killed in the South by white vigilante groups (Pinkney, 1972, p. 79).

Following the Civil War lynching of African Americans increased and continued into the 1950s. African Americans were lynched for such minor offenses as peeping into a window, attempting to vote, using offensive remarks, seeking employment in a restaurant, getting into a dispute with a white person, and expressing sympathy for another African American who had already been lynched. Arrests for lynching African Americans were rare. Lynch mobs not only included men, but sometimes also women and children. Some lynchings were publicly announced and the public was invited to participate. The public often appeared to enjoy the activities and urged the active lynchers on to greater brutality.

Race riots between whites and African Americans have also been common since the Civil War. During the summer of 1919, for example, twenty-six major race riots occurred, the most serious of which was in Chicago. In this riot, which lasted from July 27 to August 2, 38 persons were killed, 537 were injured, and over a thousand were left homeless (Waskow, 1967).

Native Americans have been subjected to kidnapping, massacre, conquest and forced assimilation, and murder. Some tribes have been completely exterminated. The treatment of Native Americans by whites in North America stands as one of the most revolting series of acts of violence in history.

The extermination of Native Americans began with the early Christian Pilgrims. They were the first to establish a policy to massacre and exterminate Native Americans in this country. In 1636 the Massachusetts Bay Puritans sent a force to massacre the Pequot, a division of the Mohegan tribe. The dwellings were burned, and six hundred inhabitants were slaughtered (Pinkney, 1972, p. 96).

In 1642 the governor of New Netherlands began offering bounties for Native American scalps. A year later this same governor ordered the massacre of the Wappinger tribe. Pinkney (1972, p. 96) describes the massacre:

> During the massacre infants were taken from their mother's breast, cut in pieces and thrown into a fire or into the river. Some children who were still alive were also thrown into the river, and when their parents attempted to save them they drowned along with their children. When the massacre was over, the members of the murder party were congratulated by the grateful governor.

A major motive for this violence was that the European settlers were land hungry. The deliberate massacre and extermination of Native Americans continued from the 1660s throughout most of the 1800s. The whites frequently made and broke treaties with Native Americans during these years—and ended up taking most of their land and sharply reducing their population. For example, in a forced march on foot covering several states, an estimated 4,000

(continued next page)

Violence Against Minorities in the United States (continued)

Cherokees died from cold and exhaustion in 1838 (Pinkney, 1972, p. 107). During these years Native Americans were considered savage beasts. Whites felt, "The only good Indian is a dead one," and they exterminated Native Americans because it was felt they impeded economic progress.

Today, racial clashes between minority group members still occur, but on a smaller scale on the street and in some of our schools. Recent years have seen a resurgence of the Ku Klux Klan, the American Nazi Party, and other white power groups such as "skin heads" in many areas of the country. Demonstrations by these organizations have led to several bloody clashes between supporters and these opposed to these racist groups.

Throughout our country's history there have also been incidents of police brutality by white officers against mem-

bers of minority groups. For example, police brutality received national attention in 1991 when an African American motorist, Rodney King, was stopped after a lengthy car chase and beaten by four club-wielding white police officers in Los Angeles. The beatings were videotaped by a bystander. Mr. King received over fifty blows from clubs and sustained eleven fractures in his skull, a broken ankle, and a number of other injuries. In April 1992, a jury (with no African American members) found the police officers "not guilty" on charges of using excessive force. The reaction of African Americans and others in Los Angeles has been described as the worst civil unrest in over a century—nearly sixty people were killed and over $800 million in damage occurred from rioting, looting, and destruction over a period of three days.

Strong laws and firm informal social norms are necessary to break the relationships between prejudice and discrimination.

Discrimination is of two types. *De jure discrimination* is legal discrimination. The so-called Jim Crow laws in the South (enacted shortly after the Civil War ended) gave force of law to many discriminatory practices against African Americans including denial of the right to trial, prohibition against voting, and prohibition against interracial marriage. Today, in the United States, there is no de jure racial discrimination, as such laws have been declared unconstitutional.

De facto discrimination refers to discrimination that actually exists, whether legal or not. Most acts of de facto discrimination abide by powerful informal norms that are discriminatory. Marlene Cummings (1977, p. 200) gives an example of this type of discrimination and urges victims to confront assertively such discrimination:

Scene: department store. Incident: Several people are waiting their turn at a counter. The person next to be served is a black woman; however, the clerk waits on several white customers who arrived later. The black woman finally demands service, after several polite gestures to call the clerk's attention to her. The clerk pro-

ceeds to wait on her after stating, "I did not see you." The clerk is very discourteous to the black customer; and the lack of courtesy is apparent, because the black customer had the opportunity to observe treatment of the other customers. De facto discrimination is most frustrating . . . ; the customer was served. Most people would rather just forget the whole incident, but it is important to challenge the practice even though it will possibly put you through more agony. One of the best ways to deal with this type of discrimination is to report it to the manager of the business. If it is at all possible, it is important to involve the clerk in the discussion.

Oppression is the unjust or cruel exercise of authority or power. Members of minority groups in our society are frequently victimized by oppression from segments of the white power structure. Oppression and discrimination are closely related, as all acts of oppression are also acts of discrimination.

Racial and Ethnic Stereotypes

Racial and ethnic stereotypes involve attributing a fixed and usually inaccurate or unfavorable conception to a racial or ethnic group. Stereotypes are closely related to the way we think—as we seek to perceive and understand things in categories. We need categories to group things that are similar in order to study them and to communicate about them. We have stereotypes about many categories, including mothers, fathers, teenagers, communists, Republicans, school teachers, farmers, construction workers, miners, politicians, Mormons, and Italians. These stereotypes may contain some useful and accurate information about a member in any category. Yet, each member of any category will have many characteristics that are not suggested by the stereotypes and is apt to have some characteristics that run counter to some of the stereotypes.

Racial stereotypes involve differentiating people in terms of color or other physical characteristics. For example, historically there was the erroneous stereotype that Native Americans become easily intoxicated and irrational when using alcohol. This belief was then translated into laws that prohibited Native Americans from buying and consuming alcohol. A more recent stereotype is that African Americans have a natural ability to play basketball and certain other sports. While at first glance, such a stereotype appears complimentary to African Americans, it has broader, negative implications. The danger is that, if people believe the stereotype, they may also feel that other abilities and capacities (such as intelligence, morals, and work productivity) are also determined by race. In other words, believing this positive stereotype increases the probability that people will also believe negative stereotypes.

Racial and Ethnic Discrimination Is the Problem of Whites

Gunnar Myrdal (1944) pointed out that minority problems are actually majority problems. The white majority determines the place of nonwhites and other ethnic groups in our society. The status of different minority groups varies in our society because whites apply different stereotypes to various groups: for example, African Americans are viewed and treated differently from Japanese. Elmer Johnson (1973, p. 344) notes, "Minority relationships become recognized by the majority as a social problem when the members of the majority disagree as to whether the subjugation of the minority is socially desirable or in the ultimate interest of the majority." Concern about discrimina-

tion and segregation has also received increasing national attention because of a rising level of aspiration among minority groups who demand (sometimes militantly) equal opportunities and equal rights.

Our country was supposedly founded on the principle of human equality. The Declaration of Independence and the Constitution assert equality, justice, and liberty for all. Yet, in practice, our society has always discriminated against minorities.

From its earliest days, our society has singled out certain minorities to treat unequally. A *minority* can be defined as a group that has a subordinate status and is being subjected to discrimination.

The categories of people who have been singled out for unequal treatment in our society have changed somewhat over the years. In the late 1800s and early 1900s, people of Irish, Italian, and Polish descent were discriminated against, but that discrimination has been substantially reduced. In the nineteenth century, Americans of Chinese descent were severely discriminated against. However, this also has been declining for many decades.

Race Is a Social Concept

Ashley Montagu (1964) considered the concept of race to be one of the most dangerous and tragic myths in our society. Race is erroneously believed by many to be a biological classification of people. Yet, there are no clearly delineating characteristics of any race. Throughout history, the genes of different societies and racial groups have occasionally been intermingled. No racial group has any unique or distinctive genes. In addition, biological differentiations of racial groups have gradually been diluted through various sociocultural factors. These factors include changes in preferences of desirable characteristics in mates, effects of different diets on those who reproduce, and such variables as wars and diseases in selecting those who will live to reproduce (Johnson, 1973, p. 350).

In spite of definitional problems, it is necessary to use racial categories in the social sciences. Race has important (though not necessarily consistent) social meanings for people. In order to have a basis for racial classifications, a number of social scientists have used a social, rather than a biological, definition. A social definition is based on the way in which members of a society classify each other by physical characteristics. For example, a frequently used social definition of an African American in America is anyone who either displays overt African American physical characteristics or is known to have an African American ancestor (Rose, 1964).

A social definitional approach to classifying races sometimes results in different societies using different definitions of *race*; for example, in the United States, anyone who is known to have an African American ancestor is considered to be African American; in Brazil, anyone known to have a white ancestor is considered to be white (Ehrlich and Holm, 1964).

Race, according to Ashley Montagu (1964), becomes a dangerous myth when it is assumed that physical traits are linked with mental traits and cultural achievements. Every few years, it seems, some noted scientist stirs the country by making this erroneous assumption. For example, Arthur Jensen (1969) asserted that whites, on the average, are more intelligent, as IQ tests show that whites average scores of 10 to 15 points higher than African Americans. Jensen's findings have been sharply criticized by other authorities as falsely assuming that IQ is largely genetically determined (Ashley Montagu, 1975). These authorities contend that IQ is substantially influenced by environmental factors, and it is likely that the average achievement of African Americans, if given similar opportunities to realize their potentialities, would be the same as whites. Also, it has been charged that IQ tests are racially slanted. The tests ask the kinds of questions which whites are more familiar with and thereby more apt to answer correctly.

Elmer Johnson (1973, p. 50) summarizes the need for an impartial, objective view of the capacity of different racial groups to achieve.

> Race bigots contend that, the cultural achievements of different races being so obviously unlike, it follows that their genetic capacities for achievements must be just as different. Nobody can discover the cultural capacities of any population or race . . . until there is equality of opportunities to demonstrate the capacities.

Most scientists, both physical and social, now believe that, in biological inheritance, all races are alike in everything that really makes any difference (such as problem-solving capacities, altruistic tendencies, and communication capacities). With the exception of several very small, inbred, isolated, primitive tribes, all racial groups appear to show a wide distribution of every kind of ability. All important race differences that have been noted in personality, behavior, and achievement (e.g., a higher percentage of white students graduate from high school as compared to African American students) appear to be primarily due to environmental factors.

Institutional Values and Racism: Discrimination in Macro Systems

In the last three decades, institutional racism has become recognized as a major problem. Institutional racism refers to discriminatory acts and policies against a racial group that pervade the major macro systems of society, including the legal, political, economic, and educational systems. Some of these discriminatory acts and policies are illegal, while others are not.

Institutional values form the foundation for macro system policies. These policies are enacted in organizations and communities. Here we will refer to institutional racism as a prevailing orientation demonstrated in policies and procedures throughout our entire culture. It is an all-encompassing term that envelopes institutional values, communities, and organizational macro systems.

Carmichael and Hamilton (1969, p. 4) make the following distinction between individual racism and institutional racism:

> When white terrorists bomb a black church and kill five black children, that is an act of individual racism, widely deplored by most segments of society. But when in the same city . . . five hundred black babies die each year because of the lack of proper food, shelter, and medical facilities, and thousands more are destroyed and maimed physically, emotionally, and intellectually because of conditions of poverty and discrimination in the black community, that is a function of institutional racism.

Discrimination and Oppression in Organizational Macro Systems

Discrimination is built, often unwittingly, into the very structure and form of our society. It is demonstrated by how organizational macro systems treat clients. The following examples reflect how agencies can engage in institutional discrimination. A family counseling agency with branch offices assigns less-skilled counselors and provides lower-quality services in an office located in a minority neighborhood. A public welfare department encourages white applicants to request funds for special needs (e.g., clothing) or to use certain services (e.g., day care and homemaker services with the costs charged to the agency), while nonwhite clients are not informed or are less enthusiastically informed of such services. A public welfare department takes longer to process the requests of members of minority groups for funds and services. A police department discriminates against nonwhite staff in work assignments, hiring practices, promotion practices, and pay increases. A probation and parole agency tends to ignore minor violations of the rules for parole of white clients but seeks to return to prison nonwhite parolees having minor violations of parole rules. A mental health agency tends to assign psychotic labels to nonwhite clients, while assigning labels indicating a less serious disorder to white clients. White staff at a family counseling center are encouraged by their white executive board to provide intensive services to clients with whom they have a good relationship (often white clients). On the other hand, they are told to give less attention to those clients "they aren't hitting it off well with" (these clients may be disproportionately nonwhite).

Discrimination and Oppression in Community Macro Systems

Globe Magazine (1971, p. 6) carried a news story of a case example of institutional discrimination that ended in tragedy. During the evening of April 27, 1971, the mother of Claris Blake (a twelve-year-old African American girl) called police requesting help in searching for her daughter who failed to return after going to a corner grocery store. The police never made a search, and the FBI refused to enter the case. On May 7, Claris called her mother and asked if her mother loved her—then the phone clicked. On May 15, Claris's body was found; she had been shot to death. Explained one official, "Look, let's face it; the

wheel turned damned slowly in this case. It's not just the police. It's the double standard of our whole society. If a twelve-year-old girl disappears on her way to the store and she's *white*, the assumption is she's met foul play. If a little girl disappears on her way to the store and she's *black*, everyone assumes she's just run away."

Institutional racism infiltrates community life. It is a contributing factor to the following. The unemployment rate for nonwhites has consistently been over twice that for whites. The infant mortality rate for nonwhites is nearly twice as high as for whites. The life expectancy age for nonwhites is several years less than for whites. The average number of years of educational achievement for nonwhites is considerably less than for whites (Kornblum and Julian, 1989).

Other Examples of Institutional Racism in Macro Systems

Many examples of institutional racism are found in the educational macro system. Schools in white suburbs generally have better facilities and more highly trained teachers than those in minority neighborhoods. Minority families are, on the average, less able to provide the hidden costs of free education (higher property taxes, transportation, class trips, clothing, and supplies), and, therefore, their children become less involved in the educational process. Textbooks generally concentrate on achievements of white people and give scant attention to minorities. Jeannette Henry (1967, p. 22) writes about the effects of history textbooks on Native American children:

> What is the effect upon the student, when he learns from his textbooks that one race, and one alone, is the most, the best, the greatest; when he learns that Indians[1] were mere parts of the landscape and wilderness which had to be cleared out, to make way for the great "movement" of white population across the land; and when he learns that Indians were killed and forcibly

---

1. The term *Indian* was originally used by early European settlers to describe the native populations of North America. Because of its nonnative derivation and the context of cultural domination surrounding its use, many people, particularly Native Americans, object to the use of the word. The term *Native American* is now generally preferred.

removed from their ancient homelands to make way for adventurers (usually called "pioneering goldminers"), for land grabbers (usually called "settlers"), and for illegal squatters on Indian-owned land (usually called "frontiersmen")? What is the effect upon the young Indian child himself, who is also a student in the school system, when he is told that Columbus discovered America, that Coronado "brought civilization" to the Indian people, and that the Spanish missionaries provided havens of refuge for the Indians? Is it reasonable to assume that the student, of whatever race, will not discover at some time in his life that Indians discovered America thousands of years before Columbus set out upon his voyage; that Cornonado brought death and destruction to the native peoples; and that the Spanish missionaries, in all too many cases, forcibly dragged Indians to the missions?

Our criminal justice macro system also has elements of institutional racism. Our justice system is supposed to be fair and nondiscriminatory. The very name of the system, *justice*, implies fairness and quality. Yet, in practice, racism is evident. Although African Americans compose only about 12 percent of the population, they make up 47 percent of the prison population. (There is considerable debate as to what extent this is due to racism as opposed to differential crime rates by race.) The average prison sentence for murder and kidnapping is longer for African Americans than for whites. Nearly half of those sentenced to death are African American (U.S. Bureau of the Census, 1992, pp. 198-201). Police departments and district attorney's offices are more likely to enforce vigorously the kinds of laws broken by lower-income groups and minority groups than by middle- and upper-class white groups. Poor people are substantially less likely to be able to post bail. As a result, they are forced to remain in jail until their trial, which often takes months or sometimes more than a year—until their case comes up. Unable to post bail, they are more likely to be found guilty, as Paul Wice (1973, p. 23) notes:

> Numerous studies clearly show that detained defendants are far more likely to be found guilty and receive more severe sentences than those released prior to trial. Limited visiting hours, locations remote from the counsel's office, inadequate conference facilities, and censored mail all serve to impede an effective lawyer-client relationship.

Sources of Prejudice and Discrimination

No single theory provides a complete picture of why racial and ethnic discrimination occurs. By being exposed to a variety of theories, the reader should at least be better sensitized to the nature and sources of discrimination. The sources of discrimination come from inside and outside a person.

Projection

Projection is a psychological defense mechanism in which one attributes to others characteristics that one is unwilling to recognize in oneself. Many people have personal traits they dislike in themselves. They have an understandable desire to get rid of such traits, but this is not always possible. Such people may project some of these traits onto others (often to some other group in society), thus displacing the negative feelings they would otherwise direct at themselves. In the process, they then reflect and condemn those onto whom they have projected the traits.

African Americans make up 47 percent of the prison population.

For example, a minority group may serve as a projection of a prejudiced person's fears and lusts. People who view African Americans as lazy and preoccupied with sex may be projecting their own internal concerns about their industriousness and their sexual fantasies onto African Americans. While some whites view African Americans as being promiscuous, historically, it has generally been white men who forced African American women (particularly slaves) into sexual encounters. It appears many white males felt guilty about these sexual desires and adventures and dealt with their guilt by projecting their own lusts and sexual conduct onto African American males.

Frustration-Aggression

Another psychic need satisfied by discrimination is the release of tension and frustration. All of us at times become frustrated when we are unable to achieve or obtain something we desire. Sometimes we strike back at the source of frustration, but many times direct retaliation is not possible—for example, we are apt to be reluctant to tell our employers what we think of them when we feel we are being treated unfairly, as we fear repercussions.

Some frustrated people displace their anger and aggression onto a *scapegoat*. The scapegoat may not be a particular person but may be a group of people. Similar to people who take out their job frustrations at home on their spouses or family pets, some prejudiced people vent their frustrations on minority groups. (The term *scapegoat* derives from an ancient Hebrew ritual in which the goat was symbolically laden with the sins of the entire community and then chased into the wilderness. It "escaped," hence the term scapegoat. The term was gradually broadened to apply to anyone who bears the blame for others.)

Countering Insecurity and Inferiority

Still another psychic need that may be satisfied through discrimination is the desire to counter feelings of insecurity or inferiority. Some insecure people seek to feel better about themselves by putting down another group, as they thus then can tell themselves that they are better than these people.

Authoritarianism

A classic work on the causes of prejudice is *The Authoritarian Personality* by Adorno, Frenkel-Brunswik, Devinson, and Sanford (1950). Shortly after World War II, these researchers studied the psychological causes of the development of European fascism and concluded there was a distinct type of personality associated with prejudice and intolerance. The *authoritarian personality* is inflexible and rigid and has a low tolerance for uncertainty. This type of personality has a great respect for authority figures and quickly submits to their will. Such a person highly values conventional behavior and feels threatened by unconventional behavior of others. In order to reduce this threat, such a personality labels unconventional people as being immature, inferior, or degenerate and thereby avoids any need to question his or her own beliefs and values. The authoritarian personality views members of minority groups as being unconventional, degrades them, and tends to express authoritarianism through prejudice and discrimination.

History

Historical explanations can also be given for prejudice. Marden and Meyer (1962) note that the groups now viewed by white prejudiced persons as being second class are groups that have been either conquered, enslaved, or admitted into our society on a subordinate basis. For example, African Americans were imported as slaves during our colonial period and stripped of human dignity. Native Americans were conquered, and their culture was viewed as inferior. Mexican Americans were allowed to enter this country primarily to do seasonal, low-paid farm work.

Competition and Exploitation

Our society is highly competitive and materialistic. Individuals and groups are competing daily with one another to acquire more of the available goods. These attempts to secure economic goods usually result in a struggle for resources and power. In our society, whites have historically sought to exploit nonwhites.

As previously mentioned, they have either conquered, enslaved, or admitted nonwhites into our society on a subordinate basis. Once the white group achieved dominance, it then used (and still is using) its power to exploit nonwhites through cheap labor—for example, as sweatshop factory laborers, migrant farm hands, maids, janitors, and bellhops.

Members of the dominant group know they are treating the subordinate group as inferior and unequal. To justify such discrimination, they develop an ideology (set of beliefs) that their group is superior—and that it is right and proper that they have more rights, goods, and so on. Often, they assert God divinely selected their group to be dominant. Furthermore, they assign inferior traits to the subordinate group (lazy, heathen, immoral, dirty, stupid) and conclude that the minority needs and deserves less, as it is biologically inferior. Throughout history in most societies, the dominant group (which has greater power and wealth) has sought to maintain the status quo by keeping those who have the least in an inferior position.

Socialization Patterns

Prejudice is also a learned phenomenon and is transmitted from generation to generation through socialization processes. Our culture has stereotypes of what different minority group members "ought to be" and the ways minority group members "ought to behave" in relationships with members of the majority group. These stereotypes provide norms against which a child learns to judge persons, things, and ideas. Prejudice, to some extent, is developed through the same processes by which we learn to be religious and patriotic or to appreciate and to enjoy art or to develop our value system. Prejudice, at least in certain segments in our society, is thus a facet of the normative system of our culture.

Evaluation of Discrimination Theories

No one theory explains all causes of prejudices, as prejudices have many origins. Taken together, however, they identify a number of causative factors. All theories assert that the causative factors of prejudice are in the personality and experiences of the person holding the prejudice and not in the character of the group against whom the prejudice is directed.

A novel experiment documenting that prejudice does not stem from contact with the people toward whom prejudice is directed was conducted by Eugene Hartley (1946). Hartley gave his subjects a list of prejudiced responses to Jews and African Americans and to three groups that did not even exist: Wallonians, Pireneans, and Danireans. Prejudiced responses included such statements as all Wallonians living here should be expelled. The respondents were asked to state their agreement or disagreement with these prejudiced statements. The experiment showed that most of those who were prejudiced against Jews and African Americans were also prejudiced against people whom they had never met or heard about.

Impacts of Social and Economic Forces: The Effects and Costs of Discrimination and Oppression

Grace Halsell is a white woman who through chemical treatments changed the color of her skin to look like an African American for a brief period of time in order to determine what it means to live as an African American in a white world. Halsell (1969, pp. 157-58) reports on her experiences in working one day as a maid for a white woman in the South:

Long before I have one job completed, there are new orders: "Now sweep off the front porch, the side porch, the back porch, and mop the back porch." The tone is unmistakably that of the mistress-slave relationship—

I feel sorry for her. We are two women in a house all day long, and I sense that she desperately wants to talk to me, but I can never be as an equal. She looks on me as less than a wholly dignified and developed person . . .

My eight hours are up. She asks if I know where to catch the bus. No, I say, should I turn left or right "when I go out the front door?" The *front* door comes out inadvertently, because I am only trying to get an idea of directions. She hands me five dollars and ushers me to the back door, quite pointedly.

Two bus transfers and an hour later, I am back in "nigger-town." Near the Summers Hotel, young bright-eyed Negro[2] children I've come to know wave, smile, and say "hi!"

---

2. When this was written in 1969, the term *Negro* was still used widely.

I want to tell each one of them because I feel so degraded, so morally and spiritually depressed, "Don't do what I did! Don't ever sell yourself that cheap! Don't let it happen to you."

And I want to add, ". . . whatever you do, don't do what I did." The assault upon an individual's dignity and self-respect has intolerable limits, and I believe at this moment my limits have been reached.

Racial discrimination is a barrier in our competitive society to obtaining the necessary resources to lead a contented and comfortable life. Being a victim of discrimination is another obstacle which has to be overcome. Being discriminated against due to race makes it more difficult to obtain adequate housing, financial resources, a quality education, employment, adequate health care and other services, equal justice in civil and criminal cases, and so on.

Discrimination also has heavy psychological costs. All of us have to develop a sense of identity—who we are and how we fit into a complex, swiftly changing world. Ideally, it is important that we form a positive self-concept and strive to obtain worthy goals. Yet, as we have noted before, according to Cooley's (1902) "looking glass self," our idea of who we are and what we are is largely determined by the way others relate to us. When members of a minority group are treated by the majority group as if they are inferior, second-class citizens, it is substantially more difficult for such members to develop a positive identity. Thus, people who are the objects of discrimination encounter barriers to developing their full potential as human beings.

In 1965, prior to "black pride" movements, Kenneth Clark (1965) described the devastating effects of discrimination on African Americans:

Human beings who are forced to live under ghetto conditions and whose daily experience tells them that almost nowhere in society are they respected and granted the ordinary dignity and courtesy accorded to others will, as a matter of course, begin to doubt their own worth. Since every human being depends upon his cumulative experiences with others for clues as to how he should view and value himself, children who are consistently rejected understandably begin to question and doubt whether they, their family, and their group really deserve no more respect from the larger society than they receive. These doubts become the seeds of pernicious self- and group-hatred, the Negro's complex and debilitating prejudice against himself. . . . Negroes have come to believe in their own inferiority.

Young children of groups who are the victims of discrimination are likely to develop low self-esteem at an early age. Porter (1971) found that African American children who have been subjected to discrimination have a preference for white dolls and white playmates over black.

Pinderhughes (1982, p. 109) has noted that the history of slavery and oppression of African Americans, combined with racism and exclusion, have produced a "victim system."

A victim system is a circular feedback process that exhibits properties such as stability, predictability, and identity that are common to all systems. This particular system threatens self-esteem and reinforces problematic responses in communities, families and individuals. The feedback works as follows: Barriers to opportunity and education limit the chance for achievement, employment, and attainment of skills. This limitation can, in turn, lead to poverty or stress in relationships, which interferes with adequate performance of family roles. Strains in family roles cause problems in individual growth and development and limit the opportunities of families to meet their own needs or to organize to improve their communities. Communities limited in resources (jobs, education, housing, etc.) are unable to support families properly and the community all too often becomes an active disorganizing influence, a breeder of crime and other pathology, and a cause of even more powerlessness.

Discrimination also has high costs for the majority group. It impairs intergroup cooperation and communication. Discrimination also is a factor in contributing to social problems among minorities—for example, high crime rates, emotional problems, alcoholism drug abuse—all of which have cost billions of dollars in social programs. Albert Szymanski (1976) argues that discrimination is a barrier to collective action (e.g., unionization) among whites and nonwhites (particularly people in the lower income classes) and, therefore, is a factor in perpetuating low-paying jobs and poverty. Less affluent whites who could benefit from collective action are hurt.

The effects of discrimination are even reflected in life expectancy. The life expectancy of nonwhites is six years less than that of whites in the United States (U.S. Bureau of the Census, 1992, p. 76). The fact is that nonwhites tend to die earlier than whites because they receive inferior health care, food, and shelter.

Finally, discrimination in the United States undermines some of our nation's political goals. Many other nations view us as hypocritical when we advocate human rights and equality. In order to make an effective argument for human rights on a worldwide scale, we must first put our own house in order by eliminating racial and ethnic discrimination. Few Americans realize the extent to which racial discrimination damages our international reputation. Nonwhite foreign diplomats to America often complain about being victims of discrimination, as they are mistaken for being members of American minority groups. With most of the nations of the world being nonwhite, our racist practices severely damage our influence and prestige.

The Effects of Discrimination on Human Growth and Development

The effects of discrimination will be illustrated by examining the research conducted on African Americans, the largest racial minority group, composing about 12 percent of the population in the United States. We shall begin by examining some background material on the history and culture of African Americans in our society.

History and Culture of African Americans

The United States has always been a racist country. Although our country's founders talked about freedom, dignity, equality, and human rights, our economy prior to the Civil War depended heavily on slavery.

Many slaves came from cultures that had well-developed art forms, political systems, family patterns, religious beliefs, and economic systems. However, their home culture was not European, and, therefore, slave owners viewed their cultural patterns as being of no consequence and prohibited slaves from practicing and developing their art, language, religion, and family life. For want of practice, their former culture soon died in America.

The life of a slave was harsh. Slaves were viewed not as human beings but as chattel to be bought and sold. Long, hard days were spent working in the fields, with the profits of their labor going to their white owners. Whippings, mutilations, and hangings were commonly accepted white control practices. The impetus to enslave African Americans was not simply racism, as many whites believed that it was to their economic advantage to have a cheap supply of labor. Cotton growing, in particular, was thought to require a large labor force that was also cheap and docile. Marriages among slaves were not recognized by the law, and slaves were often sold with little regard to effects on marital and family ties. Throughout the slavery period and even after it, African Americans were discouraged from demonstrating intelligence, initiative, or ambition. For a period of time, it was illegal to teach African Americans to read or write.

Some authorities (Henderson and Kim, 1975, p. 180) have noted the opposition to the spread of slavery preceding the Civil War was primarily due to the Northern fears of competition from slave labor and the rapidly increasing migration of African Americans to the North and West rather than to moral concern for human rights and equality. Few whites at the time understood or believed in the principle of racial equality—not even Abraham Lincoln, who believed that African Americans were inferior to whites.

Following the Civil War, the federal government failed to develop a comprehensive program of economic and educational aid to African Americans. As a result, most African Americans returned to being economically dependent on the same planters in the South who had held them in bondage. Within a few years, laws were passed in the Southern states prohibiting interracial marriages and requiring racial segregation in schools and public places.

A rigid caste system in the South hardened into a system of oppression known as Jim Crow laws. The system prescribed how African Americans were supposed to act in the presence of whites, asserted white supremacy, embraced racial segregation, and denied political and legal rights to African Americans. African Americans who opposed Jim Crow laws were subjected to burnings, beatings, and lynchings. Jim Crow laws were used to teach African Americans to view themselves as inferior and to be servile and passive in interactions with whites.

World War II opened up new employment opportunities for African Americans. A large migration of African Americans from the South began. Greater mobility afforded by wartime conditions led to upheavals in the traditional caste system. Many African Americans served in the armed forces during this war, fought and died for their country, and yet their country maintained segregated facilities. Awareness of disparity between the ideal and reality led many people to try to improve race relations, not only for domestic peace and justice, but to answer criticism from abroad. With each gain in race relations, more African Americans were encouraged to press for their rights.

A major turning point in African American history was the U.S. Supreme Court decision in *Brown v. Board of Education* in 1954, which ruled that racial segregation in public schools was unconstitutional. Since 1954, there have been a number of organized efforts by both African Americans and certain segments of the white population to secure equal rights and opportunities for African Americans. Attempts to change deeply entrenched racist attitudes and practices have produced much turmoil: the burning of our inner cities in the late 1960s, the assassination of Martin Luther King, Jr., and clashes between African American militant groups and the police. There have also been significant advances. Wide-ranging civil rights legislation, protecting rights in areas such as housing, voting, employment, and use of public transportation and facilities, has been passed. During the riots in 1968 the National Advisory Commission on Civil Disorders (Gelman, 1988, p. 19) warned that our society was careening "Toward two societies, one black, one white—separate and unequal." David Gelman (1988, p. 19) summarizes the current atmosphere of black-white relations in our society.

America today is not the bitterly sundered dual society that the riot commission grimly foresaw. Nor is it King's promised land of racial amity. Rather, it is something uneasily between the two: a society less unequal but also less caring that it was in the '60s. . . . Blacks and whites now more often work together, lunch together, even live side by side, yet few really count each other as friends.

Four out of five African Americans now live in metropolitan areas, over half of them in our central cities (U.S. Bureau of the Census, 1992). American cities are still largely segregated, with African Americans primarily living in African American neighborhoods. In recent years, the main thrust of the civil rights movement among African Americans has been economic equality. The economic gap between African Americans and whites continues to be immense. African American families are three times as likely as white families to fall below the poverty line (U.S. Bureau of the Census, 1992). Since the early 1950s, the African American unemployment rate has been approximately twice that for whites. Unemployment is an especially severe problem for African American teenagers, whose rate of unemployment is substantially higher than for white youth and has run as high as 50 percent (U.S. Bureau of the Census, 1992).

We, as a nation, have come a long way since the U.S. Supreme Court's decision in 1954. But we still have a long way to go before we eliminate African American poverty and respond to the deep frustrations of African Americans in our ghettos. Living conditions in African American ghettos remain as bleak as they were when our inner cities erupted in the late 1960s. Dissatisfaction with living conditions in the 1960s led African Americans in many inner city areas to torch and burn down numerous buildings—these buildings were largely owned by white absentee landlords.

Two developments have characterized the socioeconomic circumstances of African Americans in the past twenty-five years, as Gelman (1988, pp. 19-20) notes:

Two striking developments mark the black situation since the '60s. One is the emergence of an authentic black middle class, better educated, better paid, better housed than any group of blacks that has gone before it. As measured sometimes by white-collar occupation— anything from bank clerk to engineer—sometimes by incomes of $20,000 a year and up, the middle class grew to near 56 percent of black wage earners by 1980.

The second development is, in a way, the reverse side of the first. As comparatively well off blacks move to better neighborhoods, they have left behind a stripped-down, socially disabled nucleus of poor people who have come to be called (somewhat pejoratively) the "underclass." With a population estimated at 2.5 million— roughly three times what it was in the '70s—this group generates a disproportionate share of the social pathology usually associated with the ghetto, including high crime rates.

The use of terms such as "underclass" may be disparaging, and may set in motion a self-fulfilling prophecy. Gans (1992, p. A56) notes:

> By the mid-1980's, the term underclass had become so popular in scholarly circles that social scientists, like journalists, began using the term to grab *their* audiences, for example, by using the term in the titles of journal articles. . . .
> Underclass is a particularly nasty label, however. Earlier terms such as pauper, vagrant, and tramp were openly pejorative, but underclass is a technical-sounding word that hides its pejorative meaning. Moreover, once people are labeled as underclass, they are often treated accordingly. Teachers decide that they cannot learn, the police and the courts think that they must be incorrigible, and welfare agencies feel justified in administering harsh policies. Such treatment sets in motion the self-fulfilling prophecy: If the poor are treated like an underclass, their ability to escape poverty is blocked further. In addition, the term is turning into a racial code word, since by now it is increasingly applied solely to blacks. The public expression of racial prejudice being no longer respectable, underclass becomes an acceptable euphemism.

The use of certain terms by social scientists, such as "underclass," may contribute to the perpetuation of a social problem.

African Americans who live in inner-city areas tend to be characterized by being chronically on welfare, teenagers dropping out of high school, families headed by single parents, and males not participating in the work force. Around 55 percent of all African American families are headed by a single female parent. The rate of pregnancy among fifteen to nineteen-year-old African American women is more than twice that of whites in that age group. African Americans account for about half of all crimes of violence (U.S. Bureau of the Census, 1992).

In a study of pregnant teenagers on Chicago's West Side, Orfield (quoted in Gelman, 1988, p. 20) indicated the data, "showed that most of these girls didn't know anyone who had a job, anyone who went to college, anyone who was married. Within their society, it looks rational to have a baby when you're a teenage girl."

Over half of all African American children are being raised in single-parent families. Morton (1983) notes, however, that many African American children living in single-parent families are living in family structures composed of some variation of the extended family. Many single-parent families move in with relatives during adversity, including economic adversity. In addition, African American families of all levels rely on relatives for their children while they work. Notes Norton (1983, p. 183):

> Many middle-class families pay an aunt or cousin or mother to come into their homes and babysit, with formal salary arrangements. Having reached financial stability themselves, they not only share that stability by providing economic opportunity for other family members but also assure that their children will receive responsible, loving and interested family-oriented child care. Other, less well off families drop their children at the home of relatives, making financial arrangements that are probably lower in cost. For others, there are no financial arrangements, but reciprocity is given in returned child care, sharing of food, clothing or shelter.

While it is a reality that many African American families are headed by single mothers, it would be a serious error to view such family structures as inherently pathological. A single parent with good parenting skills, along with a supportive extended family, can lead to healthy family functions.

Solomon (1983, p. 420) noted that

> black culture contains elements of 'mainstream' white culture, elements from traditional African culture, and elements from slavery, reconstruction and subsequent exposure to racism and discrimination.

Subcultures of African Americans have vocabularies and communication styles that differ from the dominant white culture. Young children raised in these subcultures often have difficulty understanding the English language spoken in schools. African American dialects appear to be the result of a creolized form of English that was at one time spoken on Southern plantations by slaves (Dillard, 1972). (*Creolize* refers to a language based on two or more languages that serves as the native language of its speaker.) It has been estimated that approximately 80 percent of African Americans speak a "radically nonstandard" English (Wilson, 1978). Present-day African American English is a combination of the linguistic remnants of its Southern plantation past and a reflection of the current African American sociocultural situation. As such, it is important to recognize it as a dialect in its own right and not perceive it as just a distortion of standard English. Most adult African Americans are at least bicultural, being fluent in an African American dialect and in standard English.

Religious organizations that are predominantly African American have tended to have not only a spiritual mission, but also have been highly active in social action efforts to combat racial discrimination against African Americans. Many prominent African American leaders, such as Martin Luther King, Jr., and Jesse Jackson, have been members of the clergy. African American churches have served to develop leadership skills. They have served as social welfare organizations to meet basic needs, such as clothing, food, shelter. African American churches are natural support systems for troubled black individuals and families.

Many African Americans have had the historical experience of being subjected to negative evaluations by school systems, social welfare agencies, health care institutions, and the justice system. Because of their past experiences, African Americans are likely to view such institutions with apprehension. Schools, for example, have erroneously perceived African Americans as being less capable of developing cognitive skills. Such perceptions about school failure are often a self-fulfilling prophecy. If African American children are expected to fail in school systems, teachers are likely to put forth less effort in challenging them to learn, and African American children may then put forth less effort to learn, resulting in a lower level of achievement.

African American Reactions to Discrimination

African American response to discrimination and oppression may be expressed in a variety of ways: anger, hostility, passiveness, dependency, distrust, frustration, and feelings of powerlessness.

William Grier and Price Cobb (1968, p. 204) have identified three possible defensive postures taken by African Americans in their interactions with whites:

1. Cultural paranoia that assumes that anyone white or any social institution dominated by whites will potentially act against a black's best interest.
2. Cultural depression that is a consequence of life experiences and serves to define a black as less capable, less worthy than whites.
3. Cultural antisocialism that develops from a black's experience with laws, policies, and institutional procedures, which have no respect for him or her as an individual or blacks as a group; the black, in turn, has no respect for, or obligation to conform to, these laws, policies, or procedures.

In developing their personalities, African Americans have the task of achieving a balanced response to the experience of racism and discrimination. Chestang (1972) contends that African Americans have dual personality components. One is a depreciated element that recognizes the low status that society ascribes to them and responds with feelings of hopelessness and worthlessness. The other is a transcendent element that seeks to overcome this low status and to actualize the potential for successful psychosocial functioning. If either of these two elements becomes too dominant, problems are likely to arise. For example, the overly depreciated personality conveys an image of a deserving victim, while the overly transcendent personality conveys a self-centered, conceited image.

Some of the attitudes and behaviors exhibited by African Americans who seek services from white social agencies are often labeled resistance. However, the attitudes and behaviors can better be viewed as attempts at coping with powerlessness and racism. For example, if there are delays in provision of services, African Americans may convey apathy or disparage the agency as they interpret the delay as being due to racism and then respond in ways they have learned in the past to handle discrimination.

Effects of Discrimination on Development of Self-Concept

The term *self-concept* refers to the positive and negative thoughts and feelings that one has towards one's self. It is often used interchangeably with such terms as self-image, sense of self, self-esteem, and identity. A positive self-concept is a key element in school achievement, in positive social interactions with others, and in emotional, social, and intellectual growth (Moss and Kagan, 1958).

Barnes (1972) reviewed the theoretical perspectives on self-concept. He notes that African American families have been socialized to believe they are substandard human beings and that African American children learn that their skin color and hair texture is culturally viewed as being undesirable. He concludes that such discrimination is apt to lead to: "incomplete self-image; negative self-image and preference for white; and rejection of and expressed hostility toward his own group" (p. 168). Barnes (1972, p. 169) also concludes the African American child's cognitive status, emotional well-being, and achievement orientation are apt to be adversely affected by discrimination in the following ways:

- High anxiety level.
- High level of maladjustment.
- Neuroticism and rejection of other African Americans.
- Inability to delay gratification.
- Low-level orientation toward achievement.
- Proneness toward delinquency.
- Confusion of sexual identity or sex role adoption.
- Sense of little personal control over the environment.
- Low achievement motivation.
- Unrealistically high aspirations.

Barnes' major conclusion is that the possibilities of an African American child developing a positive self-concept in this society are nil. Most authorities are not as pessimistic as Barnes.

Solomon (1983) notes that if African American adults accept society's label of inferiority, they are likely to convey such thoughts and feelings to their children. Such children are not only likely to develop a negative self-concept, but then are also likely to put less effort into developing cognitive skills, and less effort into achieving in school. Because of low self-esteem and underdeveloped cognitive skills they are less likely to develop interpersonal or technical skills, which then results in having difficulties in social interactions and to being restricted in adulthood to low-paying, low-skill jobs. The vicious circle is then completed when such difficulties confirm and reinforce feelings of inferiority and of negative value, which are then begun to be passed on to their children.

A number of studies have in recent years been conducted on the extent to which discrimination adversely affects self-concept development in African American children. Very significantly, these studies indicate that the African American child's conceptualization of self does not necessarily have to be impaired by racism. Concludes Powell (1983, p. 73):

> Afro-Americans have survived a harsh system of slavery, repression, and racism. Although there have been casualties, there have been many more survivors, achievers, and victors. The cultural heritage of coping with adversity and overcoming has been passed on from generation to generation, laced with stories of those with remarkable courage and fortitude.

Given the pervasiveness of racism and discrimination in our society, why is it that many African American children overcome this obstacle in self-concept development, and develop a fairly positive sense of self-esteem? The reason appears to involve the fact that every person is embedded simultaneously in at least two systems: one is the larger society and the other is one's immediate social and physical environment. The latter environment includes family members, other relatives, peers, friends, and neighbors. One's immediate environment appears to be the predominant system in shaping one's self-concept. It appears that the child who is loved, accepted, and supported in his immediate environment comes to love and respect himself as someone worthy of love.

African American children, as they grow older, learn of the larger society's devaluation. Practically all African American children are aware by age seven or eight of the social devaluation placed on their racial group (Baumrind, 1972). The awareness of this devaluation does not necessarily extend to the African American child's evaluation of himself as an individual. The sense of self developed in the immediate environment acts as a buffer against the potential devaluation by the larger society.

Certainly racism has the potential for adverse effects on the self-esteem development for African American children. In spite of racism in our economic, political, and social structures, African American families have not only survived but have interacted with their children in ways that foster the development of a positive identity.

Enhancing Social Justice: Strategies to Combat Discrimination and Oppression

A wide range of strategies have been developed to reduce racial and ethnic discrimination and oppression. These strategies include the following: mass media appeals, strategies to increase interaction among racial and ethnic groups, civil rights laws, activism, school busing, affirmative action programs, human relations programs, confrontation of racist and ethnic remarks and actions, confrontation of the problems in inner city ghettoes, and grass-roots organizations. Since racism is a more serious problem in our society than ethnocentrism, most of the strategies against discrimination primarily focus on curtailing racial discrimination and oppression.

Mass Media Appeals: Striving to Change Institutional Values

Newspapers, radio, and television present programs that are designed to explain the nature and harmful effects of prejudice and promote the harmony of humanity. Mass media are able to reach large numbers of people simultaneously. By expanding public awareness of the existence of discrimination and its consequences, the media may strengthen control over racial and ethnic extremists. But mass media have limitations in changing prejudiced attitudes and behaviors; they are primarily a provider of information and seldom have a lasting effect in changing deepseated prejudices through propaganda. Broadcasting such platitudes as "all people are brothers and sisters" and "prejudice is un-American" is not very effective. Highly prejudiced persons are often unaware of their own prejudices. Even if they are aware of their prejudices, they generally ignore mass media appeals as irrelevant to them or dismiss the appeals as propaganda. However, the media probably have had a significant impact in reducing discrimination through showing nonwhites and whites harmoniously working in commercials, on news teams, and on TV shows. It

The child who is loved, accepted, and supported in his immediate environment comes to view himself as someone worthy of love.

provides at least one avenue for changing institutional values rooted in racism and discrimination.

Greater Interaction Between Minority Groups and the Majority Group

Increased contact between minority groups and the majority group is not in itself sufficient to alleviate prejudice. In fact, increased contact may, in some instances, highlight the differences between groups and increase suspicions and fear. Simpson and Yinger (1965, p. 510) reviewed a number of studies and concluded that prejudice is likely to be increased when contacts are tension laden or involuntary. Prejudice is likely to subside when individuals are placed in situations where they share characteristics in nonracial and nonethnic matters; for example, as co-workers, fellow soldiers, or classmates. Equal status contacts, rather than inferior-superior status contact, are also more apt to reduce prejudices (Sullivan, 1980, p. 437).

Civil Rights Laws: Changing the Legal Macro System

In the past thirty-five years, equal rights have been legislated in areas of employment, voting, housing, public accommodation, and education. A key question is, "How effective are laws in changing prejudice?"

Proponents of civil rights legislation make certain assumptions. The first is that new laws will reduce discriminatory behavioral patterns. The laws define what was once normal behavior (discrimination) as now being deviant behavior. Through time, it is expected that attitudes will change and become more consistent with the forced nondiscriminatory behavior patterns.

A second assumption is that the laws will be used. Civil rights laws were enacted after the Civil War but were seldom enforced and gradually were eroded. It is also unfortunately true that some officials will find ways of evading the intent of the law by eliminating only the extreme, overt symbols of discrimination, without changing other practices. Thus, the enactment of a law is only the first step in the process of changing prejudiced attitudes and practices. However, as Martin Luther King, Jr., noted, "The law may not make a man love me, but it can restrain him from lynching me, and I think that's pretty important."

Activism

The strategy of activism attempts to change the structure of race relations through direct confrontations of discrimination and segregation policies. Activism has three types of politics: the politics of creative disorder, the politics of disorder, and the politics of escape (Johnson, 1973, pp. 374-79).

The *politics of creative disorder* operates on the edge of the dominant social system and includes school boycotts, rent strikes, job blockades, sit-ins, public marches, and product boycotts. This type of activism is based on the concept of nonviolent

resistance. A dramatic illustration of nonviolent resistance began on December 1, 1955, in Montgomery, Alabama, when Rosa Parks refused to give up her seat on a bus to a white person. Alabama and many other Southern states at that time had Jim Crow laws which were designed to enforce segregation. One such law required African Americans to sit in the back seats of buses. Mrs. Parks refused to get up and move to the back. She was arrested, and the famous Montgomery Bus Boycott ensued. The boycott lasted for a year and resulted in a U.S. Supreme Court ruling that declared ordinances which required segregated seating on public conveyances to be unconstitutional. The boycott had an even more important psychological impact, as it suggested that minority citizens had rights equal to those of whites and that united nonviolent resistance could overturn discriminatory laws (Cummings, 1977, pp. 197-206).

The *politics of disorder* reflects alienation from the dominant culture and disillusionment with the political system. Those being discriminated against resort to mob uprisings, riots, and other forms of violence.

In 1969, the National Commission on Causes and Prevention of Violence reported that two hundred riots had occurred in the previous five years when inner cities erupted (Sullivan et al., 1980, p. 438). In 1992, there was a devastating riot in the inner city of Los Angeles following the "not guilty" verdict by a jury (which had no African American members) to charges that four white police officers used excessive force in arresting Rodney King, an African American; the brutal arrest of Mr. King had been videotaped by a bystander. The focus of most of these riots has been minority group aggression against white-owned property.

The *politics of escape* engages in rhetoric about how minorities are being victimized. But, since the focus is not on arriving at solutions, the rhetoric is not productive, except perhaps for providing an emotional release.

The principal value of social protest seems to be the stimulation of public awareness of certain problems. The civil rights protests in the 1960s made practically all Americans aware of the discrimination to which nonwhite groups were being subjected. With this awareness, at least some of the discrimination has ceased, and race relations have improved. Continued protest beyond a certain (although indeterminate) point, however, appears to have little additional value (Sullivan et al., 1980, p. 376).

School Busing: A Community Initiative

Housing patterns in many large metropolitan centers have led to de facto segregation; that is, African Americans and certain other nonwhite groups live in one area, while whites live in another. This segregation has affected educational opportunities for nonwhites. Nonwhite areas have fewer financial resources, and, as a result, the educational quality is often substantially lower than in white areas. In the past two decades courts in a number of metropolitan areas have ordered that a certain proportion of non-whites must be bused to schools in white areas, and that a certain proportion of whites must be bused to schools in nonwhite areas. The objectives are twofold: to provide equal educational opportunities and to reduce racial prejudice through interaction.

In some areas, school busing has become accepted and appears to be meeting the stated objectives. In other areas, however, the approach is highly controversial and has exacerbated racial tensions. Busing in these areas is claimed to be highly expensive; to be destructive of the neighborhood school in which the facility serves as a recreational, social, and educational center of the community; and to result in lower-quality education. A number of parents in these areas feel so strongly about busing that they are sending their children to private schools. In addition, some have argued that busing increases white flight from neighborhoods where busing has been ordered (Sullivan et al., 1980, p. 439).

Additional concerns have been expressed about busing. Busing children a long distance is very costly and uses funds that could otherwise be used to im-

A police officer directs arriving African American high school students on the first day of Federal court ordered desegregation of previously *de facto* all-white local schools in South Boston, 1975.

prove the quality of education. Busing lessens local control and interest in schools, and it makes it less practical for parents to become involved in school affairs, as the school is less accessible.

Busing may also intensify racial tensions. For example, in Boston in 1975, a federal judge ordered school busing in order to counter housing segregation patterns. The Irish and Polish residents of South Boston (who saw themselves as oppressed ethnic minorities) violently opposed the busing, and racial tensions intensified for several years. Sociologists also voice concern that school busing in an atmosphere of hostility may reduce the quality of education and increase racial prejudices and tensions.

Two decades of school busing has failed to deliver all the benefits its boosters hoped for and its critics demanded, but it has produced clear gains for African Americans and whites. Scores of studies generally agree that white students do not suffer academically from school integration via busing, and African American students probably benefit academically, as their scores on standardized tests tend to increase after school integration (Tye, 1992, p. 9A). How much such integration increases scores on standardized tests has not as yet been determined (Tye, 1992, p. 9A).

There have been other benefits of integration via busing. African Americans who attended elementary and high schools with whites are substantially more likely to attend white-majority colleges, get jobs in desegregated workplaces that offer higher pay, and have white friends as adults (Tye, 1992, p. 9A). Also, African American students who go to integrated suburban schools rather than segregated city ones are less likely to drop out of high school, get in trouble with the police, drop out of college, bear a child before age 18, and are more likely to have white friends and live in integrated neighborhoods (Tye, 1992, p. 9A). Whites also benefit from attending school with African American students, as they learn more about diversity and tend to more thoroughly confront their racial stereotypes (Tye, 1992, p. 9A).

School busing to achieve integration was vigorously pursued by the court system and the federal Justice Department in the 1970s. In 1981, the Reagan administration stated it would be much less active in advocating that busing be used as a vehicle to achieve integration. The Bush administration continued the policies of the Reagan administration and was fairly inactive in advocating for school busing. Bill Clinton, elected president in 1992, ran on a platform that included a promise to be more active in using the powers of the federal government to promote racial integration. Whether the Clinton administration will be an advocate for school busing for integration purposes is unclear. In the past decade there has been less emphasis in many communities on using busing to achieve integration. In 1991, the U.S. Supreme Court ruled that busing to achieve integration, when ordered, is not to be considered permanent. The ruling allows communities to end court-ordered busing by convincing a judge that they have done everything reasonable to eliminate discrimination against African Americans.

Affirmative Action: A Macro System Response

Affirmative action programs require that employers demonstrate they are actively employing minority applicants. Employers can no longer defend themselves by claiming that a decision not to hire a minority group member was based on some criterion other than ethnic group membership. If the percentage of minority group members in their employ is significantly lower than the percentage in the workforce, employers must accept a goal for minority employment and set up timetables stating when these goals are likely to be met.

Affirmative action programs provide for preferential hiring and admission requirements (e.g., admission to medical schools) for minority applicants. Affirmative action programs cover all minority groups including women. These programs also require that employers make active efforts to locate and recruit qualified minority applicants and, in certain circumstances, have hard quotas under which specific numbers of minority members must be accepted to fill vacant positions (e.g., a university with a high proportion of white, male faculty may be required to fill half of its faculty vacancies with women and other minority groups). Affirmative action programs require that employers must demonstrate according to a checklist of positive measures that they are not guilty of discrimination.

A major dilemma with affirmative action programs

is that preferential hiring and quota programs involve reverse discrimination, where qualified majority-group members are sometimes arbitrarily excluded. Several successful adults have claimed reverse discrimination. The best-known case to date has been that of Alan Bakke, who was initially denied admission to the medical school at the University of California at Davis in 1973. He alleged reverse discrimination, as he had higher grades and higher scores on the Medical College Admissions Tests than several minority applicants who were admitted under the university's minorities quota policy. In 1978, his claim was upheld by the U.S. Supreme Court in a precedent-setting decision (Sindler, 1978). The court ruled that strict racial quotas were unconstitutional, but the court did not rule out that race might be used as one among many criteria in making admissions decisions. Undoubtedly more court cases will be decided before a coherent policy emerges in this area.

Henderson and Kim (1980, p. 403) summarize some of the views of whites and minority groups about affirmative action:

> The minority worker in white agencies often asks himself: "Why have I been hired?".... The worker may meet resistance from white colleagues if he or she is a product of "affirmative action," seen by some white people as simply "reverse discrimination." Whites may be quick to say that competence is what counts. Blacks perceive this as saying that they are not competent. Considering the many ways in which whites have acquired jobs, blacks wonder why competence is now suggested as the only criterion for employment. For every white professional who may dislike affirmative action to compensate for past exclusions and injustices, there is a black professional who feels that it is tragic that organizations have had to be forced to hire minorities.

Supporters of affirmative action programs also note that the majority group expressed little concern about discrimination when its members were the beneficiaries instead of the victims of discrimination. They also assert there is no other way to make up rapidly for past discrimination against minorities—many of whom may presently score slightly lower on qualification tests simply because they did not have the opportunities and the quality of training that the majority group members have had.

With affirmative action programs, some minority

Admission to educational programs and securing well-paying jobs are crucial elements in working toward integration.

group members are given preferential treatment, which results in some whites being discriminated against. But minority group members still face more employment discrimination than whites do.

Affirmative action programs raise delicate and complex questions about achieving equality through giving preferences in hiring and admissions to minorities. Yet, no other means has been found to end subtle discrimination in hiring and admissions.

Admissions to educational programs and securing well-paying jobs are crucial elements in working toward integration. The history of immigrant groups who have made it (such as the Irish, Japanese, and Italians) suggests equality will be achieved only when minority group members gain middle-and upper-class status. Once such status is achieved, the minority group members become an economic and political force to be reckoned with. The dominant groups are pressured into modifying their norms, values, and stereotypes. For this reason, a number of authorities have noted that the elimination of economic discrimination is a prerequisite for achieving equality and harmonious race relations (Featherman and Hauser, 1976, pp. 621-51). Achieving educational equality between races is also crucial, as lower educational attainments lead to less prestigious jobs, lower incomes, lower-living standards, and the perpetuation of racial inequalities from one generation to the next.

Human Relations Programs

Some school systems have human relations programs, which are designed to alleviate prejudice and discrimination. One program has been developed by the public school system in Madison, Wisconsin (Buchanan and Cummings, 1975). The goal is to help children gain a better awareness of themselves as individuals and a better understanding of, and respect for, individual differences in others.

The program has several steps, along with some suggested activities, books, and other helpful hints for parents and teachers to use with their children. Some of the key concepts are the following:

- Each person is unique, with all people having common needs.
- Each person can do some things better than other things. It is a serious mistake to use yourself as a yardstick to measure others' abilities or to use others as a yardstick to measure yours. Words such as "stupid" or "dumb" hurt deeply, especially when one is doing one's best.
- Each person has different attitudes, ideas, beliefs, and values. Although the beliefs of others may differ from one's own, they are no less important.
- Prejudice differs from a dislike. Prejudice is defined broadly as "when you are against someone you do not know because of some/one of their differences" (Buchanan and Cummings, 1975, p. 13).

The program assists children in learning personal differences and how a lack of understanding about these differences can be related to prejudice. The program explains that melanin is the pigment responsible for light and dark skin color differences. The more melanin you have, the darker you are; but

melanin, of course, in no way governs the personality or behavior of a person. Tanning occurs because the skin produces more melanin to protect it from the hot sun; yet tanning does not change the inner self, only the outside wrapping. Students are given an understanding of other individual differences such as retardation, religious differences, epilepsy, and hearing impairments so that they can be more respectful of such differences. The program also assists students in learning about and appreciating cultural and ethnic differences.

Such programs offer considerable promise of being a highly effective strategy in alleviating discrimination in the following areas: race, sex, ethnic or cultural differences, religious or political differences, physical or mental disabilities, and sexual orientation.

Confronting Racist Remarks and Actions

Racist jokes and sarcastic remarks help shape and perpetuate stereotypes and prejudices. Whites and nonwhites need to tactfully but assertively indicate they do not view such remarks as being humorous or appropriate. It is also important that people tactfully and assertively point out the inappropriateness of racist actions by others. Such confrontations make explicit that subtle racist remarks and actions are discriminatory and harmful, which has a consciousness raising effect. Gradually, it is expected that such confrontations will reduce racial prejudices and actions.

Noted author, lecturer, and abolitionist Frederick Douglass (1977, p. 201) stated:

> Power concedes nothing without a demand—it never did, and it never will. Find out just what people will submit to, and you've found out the exact amount of injustice and wrong which will be imposed upon them. This will continue until they resist, either with words, blows, or both. The limits of tyrants are prescribed by the endurance of those whom they oppress.

Confronting Community Problems: Inner-City Ghettos

It is difficult to find the right adjectives to describe the dismal living conditions in inner-city ghettos.

As the words scrawled on this wall indicate, inner-city housing projects can be like a prison.

The following apply: decaying, inhuman, dreadful, distasteful, shocking, and degrading. Ghettos are primarily inhabited by the poor, the elderly, and members of minority groups, particularly African Americans and Hispanics. Many ghettos have an ethnic concentration, such as African American, Mexican American, Cuban, or Puerto Rican.

Ghettos have high rates of crime, illiteracy, births out of marriage, single parent households, mental illness, suicide, drug and alcohol abuse, unemployment, infant mortality, rape, aggravated assault, and delinquency. High proportions of the residents are on welfare. Many city services are inferior in ghettos. Schools are inferior, streets are narrow and often filled with pot holes. Police and fire protection services are inadequate to meet the needs of the neighborhoods.

The housing is crowded, decaying, and much of it is substandard. Heat in winter is often inadequate. Many units lack adequate plumbing. Broken win-dows, peeling paint, and doors hanging off their hinges are common sights. Minority group members inhabit much of this substandard housing because most cannot afford an alternative, and because discrimination makes it difficult to relocate—even for those whose incomes would enable them to move.

One of the factors that is leading to the decline of inner cities is the sharp decline of blue-collar jobs in our society. Many blue-collar jobs are unskilled or semi-skilled jobs which require less training and education than white-collar and service jobs. The employable in inner cities have in the past largely held blue-collar jobs. For a neighborhood to resist deterioration, a minimal economic base must be maintained. As blue-collar jobs decline, and the quality of municipal services (such as transportation and public schools) deteriorate, faith in community restoration and revitalization fades.

Ghettos are a national disgrace. Our country is the

richest and most powerful in the world, yet we have been unable to improve living conditions in our inner cities.

Our country has tried a variety of approaches to improve ghetto living conditions. Programs and services provided include work training, job placement, financial assistance through public welfare, low interest mortgages to start businesses, Headstart, drug and alcohol treatment, crime prevention, housing, rehabilitation, day-care services, health care services, and public health services.

One of the most comprehensive undertakings to assist inner cities was the Model Cities Program, which was part of the War on Poverty in the 1960s. Several inner cities were targeted for this massive intervention. The program involved tearing down dilapidated housing and constructing comfortable living quarters. Salvagable buildings were renovated. In addition, these Model City projects had a variety of programs that provided job training and placement, health care services, social services, and educational opportunities. The results were more than depressing. The communities have again become slums. Living conditions are as bleak, or bleaker, than at the start of the Model City interventions (Weltner, 1977).

To date, all programs that have been tried have had, at best, only short-term success. No other conclusion can be made. Ghettos continue to have abysmal living conditions. In the 1980s and early 1990s the federal government, at least for the time being, appears to have given up trying to improve living conditions, as federal programs for inner cities have either been eliminated or sharply cut back.

Ghetto living is becoming a way of life. Poverty and dependency on welfare are becoming a life-style in ghettos, and is being passed on from one generation to another.

On January 25, 1986, CBS aired a program entitled "CBS Reports: The Vanishing Black Family." The program presented alarming information that the single parent family headed by a mother is becoming the typical family in inner cities. The program suggested that unless dramatic changes are made, by the year 2000, 70 percent of African American families will have a single female head of household. This program also indicated that many young African American mothers (and the unwed fathers) are using AFDC payments to support their families. For example, one twenty-five-year-old male who had been unemployed for the past two and one-half years was interviewed— he was proud that he had fathered six children by four different women, and took it for granted that welfare programs would pay the bills for raising his children. The program suggested that AFDC mothers in inner cities are resigned to raising their children on welfare, and that such values are being passed on from generation to generation.

Our society, for better or worse, is a materialistic one. The two main legitimate ways to get material goods are by getting a good education and by obtaining a high paying job. It appears that many ghetto residents believe that prospects are bleak for getting a good education (when only inferior schools exist in their areas) or a high paying job (when they have few marketable job skills). As a result, many turn to illegitimate ways to get material goods (shoplifting, drug trafficking, robbery, and con games). Many have also turned to immediate gratifications (including sex and drug highs). Their value system includes being dependent on the government through welfare for a substandard life-style.

One approach that has been suggested to try to combat the problems of inner cities is to use birth control technology to stabilize (and perhaps even slightly reduce) the population size in inner cities. Residents of large cities could be encouraged to have only one child. Sex education programs in schools could be expanded to teach responsible sexual behavior. Birth control information and services could be provided by the government at no cost to recipients. Increased taxes might be levied on those who had more than one or two children. Health clinics (which provide free birth control information and services) could be located in every inner-city high school. Mothers and their teenage daughters who are receiving AFDC benefits might be given higher monthly grants for voluntarily using effective birth control methods. If effective contraceptives are developed for males, teenage male children who are receiving AFDC benefits could also be given higher monthly grants for using effective contraceptives.

Such a proposal is designed to gradually reduce the number of children on AFDC, to reduce poverty being passed from one generation to another, and to seek to strengthen inner-city families. With smaller sized families on AFDC, the AFDC parents should be better able to provide higher quality care to the children they presently have.

There are a number of criticisms of this proposal. There is a strong value in our country that holds that every person has a right to be a natural parent to as many children as he or she desires. Some religions, such as the Roman Catholic church, strongly object to birth control. Encouraging AFDC recipients to use birth control is viewed by many as being "nonwhite genocide"; a higher percentage of nonwhites receive AFDC assistance, and a policy of encouraging AFDC recipients to receive birth control would thereby have the greatest impact on the birth rates of nonwhites.

Our society has tried a variety of programs in the past to combat the problems faced by inner-city residents. All past programs have largely failed to improve our inner cities. At the present time our federal government has a laissez-faire approach, and conditions are deteriorating in many of our inner cities. Will our country try an unpopular program such as using birth control technology to stabilize population size in inner cities? Or, are there other workable alternatives? One alternative is the development and support of grass-roots organizations.

Grass-Roots Organizations: Implementing Change in Community Macro Systems

The efforts of some grass-roots organizations at times have positive, long-lasting effects. Grass-roots organizations are composed of community residents who work together to improve their community. (It may be that lasting changes can be made in a neighborhood only when the residents are inspired, in some way, to improve their community.) The following description is an illustration of a successful grass-roots effort in Cochran Gardens, St. Louis, Missouri (Boyte, 1989).

Cochran Gardens, a low-income housing project, was typical of many deteriorating housing projects in large urban areas. It was characterized by rubbish, graffiti, broken windows, frequent shootings, crime, drug trafficking, and angry and fearful people.

Bertha Gilkey grew up in this housing project. If it had not been for her efforts this neighborhood would have continued to deteriorate. At a young age, Gilkey believed the neighborhood could improve if residents worked together. As a teenager she attended tenant

An ongoing rehabilitation program conducted by a resident grass-roots organization has contributed to the success of Cochran Gardens, a low-income housing project in St. Louis, Missouri.

meetings in a neighborhood church. When she was twenty years old, she was elected to chair this tenants' association. The neighborhood has since undergone gradual yet dramatically positive changes.

Gilkey and her group started with small projects. They asked tenants what they really wanted that was realistic to achieve. There was a consensus that the housing project needed a usable laundromat, because previous laundromats had all been vandalized and the only working one in the project had no locks; in fact the entry door had been stolen. Bertha and her group requested and received a door from the city housing authority. The organization then held a fund-raiser for a lock and another fundraiser for paint. After the organization painted the laundromat residents were pleased to have an attractive working laundromat, which increased their interest in joining and supporting the tenants' association. The association then organized to paint the hallways of the housing project, floor by floor. Everyone who lived on a floor was responsible for being involved in painting the hallway floor. Gilkey (quoted in Boyte, 1989, p. 3) states:

> Kids who lived on the floor that hadn't been painted would come and look at the painted hallways and then go back and hassle their parents. The elderly who couldn't paint prepared lunch so they could feel like they were a part of it too.

The organization continued to initiate and successfully complete new projects to spruce up the neighborhood. Each success inspired more and more residents to take pride in their neighborhood and to work toward making improvements. While improving the physical appearance of this housing project, Gilkey and the tenants' organization also reintroduced a conduct code for the project. A committee formulated rules of behavior and elected monitors on each floor. The rules included no loud disruptions, no throwing garbage out the windows, and no fights. Slowly residents got the message and living conditions improved, one small step at a time. The building was renamed Dr. Martin Luther King, Jr., Building. (Symbols are important in community development efforts.) The organization also held a party and a celebration for each successfully completed project.

Another focus of Gilkey's efforts was to reach out to children and adolescents. The positives were highlighted. The young people wrote papers in school on "What I Like about Living Here." In art class they built a cardboard model of the housing project that included the buildings, streets, and playground. Such efforts were designed to build the self-esteem of the young people, and to instill a sense of pride in their community.

Today, Cochran Gardens is a public housing project with flower-lined paths, trees, and grass—a beautiful and clean neighborhood filled with trusting people who have a sense of pride in their community. The high rises have been completely renovated. There is a community center, tennis courts, playgrounds, and

town house apartments to reduce density in the complex. Cochran Gardens is managed by the tenants. The association (now named Tenant Management Council) has ventured into owning and operating certain businesses: a catering service, day-care centers, health clinics, and a vocational training program.

The Cochran success has been based on the principles of self-help, empowerment, responsibility, and dignity. Gilkey (quoted in Boyte, 1989, p. 5) states:

> This goes against the grain, doesn't it? Poor people are to *be* managed. What we've done is cut through all the bullshit and said it doesn't take all that. People with degrees and credentials got us in this mess. All it takes is some basic skills. . . . If we can do it in public housing, it can happen anywhere.

Such successes suggest it is desirable for our federal, state, and city governments to seek to improve inner-city conditions by encouraging and supporting (including financially) grass-roots efforts.

Social Work Practice with Racial and Ethnic Groups

Social workers and other helping persons have many of the prejudices, stereotypes, and misperceptions of the general society. There is a danger that a social worker will use her or his own cultural, social, or economic values in assessing and providing services to clients.

The problematic nature of cross-cultural social work does not preclude its effectiveness. While many white practitioners can establish productive working relationships with minority clients, others cannot. In other instances, minority practitioners are sometimes effective and sometimes not with others of the same race or ethnic group (Mizio, 1972). This concept is illustrated by the following statement by a client who is African American and a Roman Catholic:

> In answering the question of whether a white middle-class psychiatrist can treat a black family, I cannot help but think back over my own experiences. When I first came to New York and decided to go into psychotherapy I had two main thoughts: (1) that my problems were culturally determined and (2) that they were related to

my Catholic upbringing. I had grown up in an environment in which the Catholic Church had tremendous influence. With these factors in mind, I began to think in terms of the kind of therapist I could best relate to. In addition to being warm and sensitive, he had to be black and Catholic. Needless to say, that was like looking for a needle in a haystack. But after inquiring around I was finally referred to a black Catholic psychiatrist.

Without going into too much detail, let me say that he turned out to be not so sensitive and not so warm. I terminated my treatment with him and began to see another therapist who was warm, friendly, sensitive, understanding and very much involved with me. Interestingly enough, he was neither black nor Catholic. As a result of that personal experience, I have come to believe that it is not so much a question of whether the therapist is black or white but whether he is competent, warm and understanding. Feelings, after all, are neither black nor white. (Sager, Brayboy, and Waxenberg, 1970, pp. 210-11)

In order for a worker to be effective in working with diverse racial and ethnic groups, the worker needs to learn the culture of the group or groups he is working with; be aware of his own values, prejudices, and stereotypes; and learn which intervention approaches are apt to be effective, and which are apt to be ineffective, with the group or groups he is working with.

Learning the Culture of the Group

In working with a diverse culture the following questions are crucial: How are the members likely to view someone from a different culture? What kinds of communications and actions are likely to lead to the development of a relationship? How do members view asking for help from a social agency? If the agency is viewed as being part of the dominant white society which has devalued this group in the past, how are the members likely to view the social agency? What are the values of the group? When the members of this group need help, who are they most likely to turn to—relatives, friends, neighbors, church, social agencies, school system, or local government? What are culturally acceptable ways of providing help to people in need?

Take as an example a white social worker who is serving low-income, inner-city, African American clients. Barbara Draper (1979, p. 279) briefly describes in the following extract some of the ways to learn about the culture:

> The white worker must try to enter the life span of the black client. He/she must listen to the expression of black language, its sounds and meaning. Read black literature and newspapers. Listen to black radio stations to get with the tempo and temper of blacks' feelings. Leave the office and walk around in black neighborhoods—look at the parts that are slums, but also acknowledge the blocks that are kept with pride. . . . Look at the addict and the pimp but also see those who carry themselves with dignity. Look at the hustler but also see the shopkeeper, the dentist, the doctor. Go with the black client to the hospital and the social service agency. Notice the very real differences in the way services are often given to black and white clients. . . . There is infinite variety among blacks whether in the metropolis or the small town.

As a corollary of becoming accepted by clients of diverse racial or ethnic groups, the social worker must live his or her personal life in a manner that will not offend important values and mores of those groups.

There are an *immense* number of different racial and ethnic groups in our society. It is beyond the scope of this chapter to describe the unique characteristics of these diverse groups. Instead, a few characteristics of some minority groups will be summarized to illustrate the importance of learning about the minority group of a client. When working with Native Americans it is considered rude—an attempt to intimidate, in fact—to maintain direct eye contact (Lewis and Ho, 1975).

Chicano men, as contrasted to Anglo men, have been described as exhibiting greater pride in their maleness (Schaefer, 1984, pp. 311-12). *Machismo*—a strong sense of masculine pride—is highly valued among Chicano men and is displayed by males to express dominance and superiority. *Machismo* is demonstrated differently by different people. Some may seek to be irresistible to women and to have a number of sexual partners. Some resort to weapons or fighting. Some interpret *machismo* to mean pride in one's manhood, honor, and ability to provide for one's family. Others boast of their achievements, even those that never occurred. Recent writers have noted that the feminist movement, urbanization, upward mobility, and acculturation are contributing to the decline of *machismo* (Schafer, 1984, p. 312). Chicanos also tend to be more "familistic" than Anglos. Familism is the belief that the family takes precedence over the individual. Schaefer (1984, p. 312) notes:

> Familism is generally regarded as good . . . as an extended family provides greater emotional strength at times of family crisis. The many significant aspects of familism include: (1) the importance of the *compadrazo* (godparent-godchild relationship); (2) the benefits of financial dependency on kin; and (3) the availability of relatives as a source of advice.

On the negative side, familism may discourage youth from pursuing opportunities that will take them away from the family. It should be noted that differences between Chicanos and Anglos with regard to *machismo* and familism are ones of degree, not of kind.

Delgado and Humm-Delgado (1982) suggest that natural support systems are a useful resource in providing assistance to Chicanos. These support systems include: extended family, folk healers, religious institutions, and merchant and social clubs. The extended family includes the family of origin, nuclear family members, other relatives, godparents, and those considered to be like family. Folk healers are prominent in Chicano communities. Some use treatments that blend natural healing methods with religious or spiritual beliefs. Religious institutions (especially the Roman Catholic church) provide such services as pastoral counseling, emergency money, job-locating and housing assistance, and some specialized programs, such as drug-abuse treatment and prevention. Merchant and social clubs can provide such items as native foods, herbs, referral to other resources, credit and information, prayer books, recreation, and the services of healers. The reluctance of Chicano clients to seek help from a social welfare agency can be reduced by greater use of these natural support systems. Outreach can be done through churches and community groups. If a social welfare agency gains a reputation of utilizing such natural support systems in the intervention process, Chicanos will have greater trust in the agency and be much more apt to seek help. Utilizing such natural support systems also increases the effectiveness of the intervention process.

Religious organizations that are predominantly African American usually have a social and spiritual mission. They are apt to be highly active in efforts to combat racial discrimination. Many prominent African American leaders, such as the late Martin Luther King, Jr. and Jesse Jackson, have been members of the clergy. African American churches have served to develop leadership skills. They have also served as social welfare organizations to meet such basic needs as food, clothing, and shelter. African American churches are natural support systems that workers need to utilize to serve troubled African American individuals and families.

Self-Awareness of Values, Prejudices, and Stereotypes

Since social workers live in a society in which racial and ethnic prejudices abound, they also have prejudices and stereotypes.

Think about these questions: In the past year, have you listened to some racial or ethnic jokes? Did you laugh? If you did laugh, do you think your laughter, in a minute way, was perpetuating some racial or ethnic stereotypes? Have you told in the past year some racial or ethnic jokes? If yes, was the content derogatory? By telling such jokes, are you demonstrating some of your prejudices and stereotypes? By telling such jokes, are you not, in a small way, reinforcing some of the harmful stereotypes and prejudices that exist in our society?

Racial and ethnic prejudices can be demonstrated by the following exercise:

Assume you are single; place a check mark by the following ethnic and racial groups that you would be hesitant or reluctant to marry a member of.

—— Iranian	—— Egyptian
—— Chinese	—— Irish
—— Japanese	—— Cuban
—— Samoan	—— Puerto Rican
—— Filipino	—— German
—— African American	—— Vietnamese
—— Native American	—— French
—— Italian	—— Russian
—— Mexican	

If you have checked some of these (and most people check several), analyze your thoughts as to why you would be hesitant to marry those you have checked. There is a fair chance that such an analysis will help you identify some of your prejudices.

Since practically everyone has racial and ethnic stereotypes and prejudices, a helping professional needs to be aware of them in order to remain objective in working with clients. When a helping professional is working with a client of a racial or ethnic group that he or she has negative perceptions about, the helping professional should continually be asking the following questions: Am I individualizing this person as a unique person with worth, or am I making the mistake of viewing this person in terms of my prejudices and stereotypes? Am I working up to my full capacities with this individual? Or am I seeking to cut corners by probing less deeply, by not fully informing this person of the services he or she is eligible for, or by wanting to end the interview before fully exploring all the client's problems and fully exploring all possible alternatives?

Application of Theory to Practice: Techniques of Intervention

The third area is for the social worker to learn which intervention approaches are likely to be effective, and which are likely to be ineffective with the ethnic or racial group he or she is working with. Several guidelines will be presented for illustrative purposes.

Social workers should seek to use their own patterns of communication and avoid the temptation to adopt the client's accent, vocabulary, or speech (Hull, 1985, p. 254). The worker who seeks to do this is apt to make mistakes in enunciations, and thereby come across as a phony, or may offend the client if the client interprets the worker's communication to be mimicry.

A social worker with an urban background who has a job in a small rural community needs to live his personal life in a way that is consistent with community values and standards. A worker who gains a reputation as being a violator of community norms will not be effective in a small community. Neither the power structure nor a majority of clients are likely to give such a worker credibility. A worker in a small community needs to identify community values in areas such as the following: religious beliefs and patterns of expression, dating and marriage patterns, values towards domestic and wild animals (for example, opposing deer hunting in many communities

may run counter to strong local values), drug usage, political beliefs and values, and sexual mores. Once such values are identified, the social worker needs to seek to achieve a balance between the kind of lifestyle he wants and the kind of life-style the community expects he will live.

Kadushin (1972) recommends using all of the formalities in initial meetings with adult clients of diverse racial and ethnic groups. Such usage should include the formal title (Mr., Miss, Mrs., Ms.), the client's proper full name, greeting with a handshake, and the other courtesies usually extended. In initial contacts workers should also usually show their agency identification and state reasons for the meeting.

Agencies and social workers should establish working hours that coincide with the needs of the groups being served. Doing so may mean having evening and weekend hours to avoid forcing clients, already with financial difficulties, to lose time from their job.

In the area of group services to racially diverse clients, Davis (1979) recommends that membership be selected in such a manner that no one race vastly outnumbers the others. Sometimes it is necessary to educate clients about the processes of individual or group counseling. Using words common to general conversation is much better than using technical and sophisticated jargon that clients are not likely to comprehend.

In working with adult clients who are not fluent in the English language, it is generally a mistake to use bilingual children of the clients as interpreters (Norton, 1978, p. 22). Having children as interpreters is embarrassing to the parents as it places them in a position of being partially dependent on their children and erroneously suggests the parents are deficient in learning essential communication mechanisms. In addition, children often lack an adult's knowledge, which reduces their value as interpreters. Also, in using interpreters the worker should direct his conversation to the client and not to the interpreter. To talk to the translator diverts attention from the client and places the client in the position of bystander rather than the central figure in the relationship.

Native Americans place a high value on the principle of self-determination (*Good Tracks*, 1973, p. 30). This sometimes provides a perplexing dilemma for a social worker who wonders "How can I help if I can't intervene?" Native Americans will request intervention only infrequently, and the white worker needs to have patience and wait for the request. How long this will take varies. During the waiting period the non-Native American worker should be available and may offer resistance as long as there is no hint of coercion. Once help is accepted, the worker will be tested. If the client believes the worker has been helpful, the word will spread and the worker is likely to have more requests for help. If the client concludes the worker is lacking in helpful capacities, this assessment will also spread, and the worker will have an even more difficult task in being sought out by potential clients.

In establishing rapport with African American, Hispanic, Native American, or clients of other groups who have suffered from racial oppression, a peer relationship should be sought in which there is mutual respect and mutual sharing of information. A white superiority type of relationship should be rejected totally, as it is likely to be interpreted by racially diverse clients as being offensive—which in fact it is.

Social Work Roles to Counter Discrimination

Social workers have an obligation to work vigorously to end racial discrimination as well as other forms of discrimination. The major professional social work organizations have, over the years, taken strong positions aimed at ending racial discrimination. The National Association of Social Workers, for example, has lobbied for the passage of civil rights legislation. The Code of Ethics of NASW (National Association of Social Workers, 1979) has the following explicit statement about discrimination:

> The social worker should act to prevent and eliminate discrimination against any person or group on the basis of race, color, sex, sexual orientation, age, religion, national origin, marital status, political belief, mental or physical handicap, or any other preference or personal characteristic, condition, or status.

The Council on Social Work Education (CSWE) has an accreditation requirement for baccalaureate and master's programs that content on racism must be included throughout the social work curriculum. CSWE also has an accreditation standard that prohibits racial discrimination and mandates affirmative action programs in social work educational programs.

In working to end racial discrimination as well as other forms of discrimination, there are a variety of roles that social workers can take on. They can be advocates for equal treatment for those who are being oppressed or discriminated against. They can be analysts of societal conditions that result in institutional racism and then be advocates for the development of programs to counter such racism. They can be initiators of action by seeking to inform social service systems and the political systems of social injustices and then advocating for changes in policies and programs to counter such injustices. At times, in working with oppressed groups, they can fulfill an educator role by giving information on options to counter oppression and by conveying information on how to organize and advocate for change. If several organizations are working somewhat independently to counter related forms of discrimination and oppression, social workers can serve as integrators/coordinators by seeking to have these organizations form a coalition in which they work together in some organized manner to effect change. At times, social workers may, in the role of counselor, work with oppressed individuals and small groups to problem solve personal concerns related to being victimized by oppression and discrimination. Social workers may also be brokers by linking oppressed client systems (individuals, groups, families, and organizations) with needed resources.

The Future of American Race and Ethnic Relations

The 1980s turned into a decade of struggle for minorities as they tried to hold onto past gains in the face of reactions against minority rights. Vowing to take "big government" off the back of the American people and to strengthen the economy by giving businesses the incentive to grow and produce, President Reagan and his administration largely removed the federal government from its traditional role as initiator and enforcer of programs to guarantee minority rights. President Bush and his administration continued to follow a similar strategy. The federal government under the Reagan and Bush administrations asserted that private businesses were in the best position to correct the problems of poverty and discrimination. (Since businesses generally profit from paying low wages, most businesses in the 1980s and early 1990s did not aggressively seek to improve the financial circumstances and living conditions of minorities.) Perhaps because of the federal government's shift in policies, minorities were less active in the 1980s in using the strategy of activism. In the 1980s and early 1990s, minority groups were experiencing difficulties in maintaining the gains they achieved in the 1960s and 1970s in the job market through affirmative action and equal employment opportunity programs. Bill Clinton, elected president in 1992, ran on a platform that promised a more active federal government role in promoting harmony in race and ethnic relations in this country.

It is clear that minorities (such as African Americans, Hispanics, Asian Americans, and Native Americans) will assertively, and sometimes aggressively, pursue a variety of strategies to change racist prejudices and actions. Counteractions by certain segments of the white dominant group are also likely to occur. (Even in the social sciences, every action elicits a reaction.) For example, in recent years, there have been increased memberships in organizations that advocate white supremacy, such as the Ku Klux Klan.

In 1988 a report released by the Commission on Minority Participation in Education and American Life asserted (quoted in Collison, 1988, p. 1):

America is moving backward—not forward—in its efforts to achieve the full participation of minority citizens in the life and prosperity of the nation. . . .

In education, employment, income, health, longevity, and other basic measures of individual and social well-being, gaps persist—and in some cases are widening —between members of minority groups and the majority population.

If we allow these disparities to continue, the United States inevitably will suffer a compromised quality of life and a lower standard of living.

In brief, we will find ourselves unable to fulfill the promise of the American dream.

Minorities have been given hope of achieving equality of opportunity and justice. Their hope has been kindled, and they will no longer submit to a subordinate status. Struggles to achieve racial equality will continue.

What will be the pattern of race relations in the future? Milton Gordon (1961, pp. 363-65) outlined three possible patterns of intergroup relations: Anglo-conformity, melting pot, and cultural pluralism:

Anglo-conformity assumes the desirability of maintaining modified English institutions, language, and culture as the dominant standard in American life. In practice, "assimilation" in America has always meant Anglo-conformity, and the groups that have been most readily assimilated have been those that are ethnically and culturally most similar to the Anglo-Saxon group.

The *melting pot* is, strictly speaking, a rather different concept, which views the future American society not as a modified England but rather as a totally new blend, both culturally and biologically, of all the various groups that inhabit the United States. In practice, the melting pot has been of only limited significance in the American experience.

Cultural pluralism implies a series of coexisting groups, each preserving its own tradition and culture but each loyal to an overarching American nation. Although the cultural enclaves of some immigrant groups, such as the Germans, have declined in importance in the past, many other groups, such as the Italians, have retained a strong sense of ethnic identity and have resisted both Anglo-conformity and inclusion in the melting pot.

Members of some European ethnic groups such as the British, French, and Dutch formed the dominant culture of the United States. Other European ethnic groups such as the Irish, Italians, Polish, Germans, Scandinavians, Greeks, and Hungarians are now nearly fully assimilated and integrated.

Cultural pluralism, however, appears to be the form that race and ethnic relations are presently taking. Renewed interest on the part of a number of ethnic European Americans in expressing their pride in their own customs, religions, and linguistic and cultural traditions is evident. Slogans on buttons and signs say "Kiss me, I'm Italian," "Irish Power," and "Polish and Proud." African Americans, Native Americans, Hispanics, and Asian Americans are demanding entry into mainstream America but are not demanding assimilation. They want coexistence in a pluralistic society while seeking to preserve their own traditions and cultures. They are finding a source of identity and pride in their own cultural backgrounds and histories.

Some progress has been made toward ending discrimination since the *Brown v. Board of Education* decision in 1954. Yet equal opportunity for all people in America is still only a dream.

A Dream of the End of Racism

In 1963, Martin Luther King, Jr., delivered a speech in which he stated a hope and a goal that racism will one day be ended. An excerpt from that speech follows:

> I say to you today, my friends, even though we face the difficulties of today and tomorrow, I still have a dream. It is a dream deeply rooted in the American dream. I have a dream that one day this nation will rise up, live out the true meaning of its creed: "We hold these truths to be self-evident, that all men are created equal."
>
> I have a dream that one day on the red hills of Georgia sons of former slaves and the sons of former slave-owners will be able to sit down together at the table of brotherhood. I have a dream that one day even the state of Mississippi, a state sweltering with the heat of injustice, sweltering with the heat of oppression, will be transformed into an oasis of freedom and justice.
>
> I have a dream that my four little children will one day live in a nation where they will not be judged by the color of their skin, but by the content of their character.
>
> When we allow freedom to ring—when we let it ring from every city and every hamlet, from every state and every city, we will be able to speed up that day when all of God's children, black men and white men, Jews and Gentiles, Protestants and Catholics, will be able to join hands and sing in the words of the old Negro spiritual, "Free at last, Free at last, Great God Almighty. We are free at last." (Bishop, 1971, pp. 327-28)

For most nonwhite Americans, this dream is still far from being a reality.

Summary

Our country has always been racist and ethnocentric. Discrimination and oppression continue to have tragic consequences for those who are victims. In our country's history, racial discrimination has had violent and tragic consequences for many nonwhite groups. Individuals who are targets of ethnic or racial discrimination are excluded from: certain types of employment, educational and recreational opportunities, certain residential housing areas, membership in certain residential housing areas, membership in certain social and religious organizations, certain political activities, access to some community services, and so on. Discrimination is also a serious obstacle to developing a positive self-concept, and has heavy psychological and financial costs. Internationally, racism and ethnocentrism severely damage our credibility in promoting human rights.

Theories of the sources of discrimination include: projection, frustration-aggression, countering insecurity and inferiority, the authoritarian personality, historical explanations, competition and exploitation, and socialization processes. There are numerous racial and ethnic groups in our society. These groups each have a unique culture, language, history, and special needs. This uniqueness needs to be understood and appreciated if we are to achieve progress towards ethnic and racial equality.

Strategies against discrimination include mass media appeals, increased interaction between minority groups and the majority group, civil rights legislation, protests and activism, affirmative action, school busing, human relations programs in school systems, confronting racist and ethnic remarks and actions, confronting problems in inner-city ghettos, and grassroots organizations. Three possible patterns of intergroup ethnic and race relations in the future are Anglo-conformity, melting pot, and cultural pluralism. Cultural pluralism is the form that race and ethnic relations are presently taking, and may well take in the future.

PART TWO

Adolescence
and Young
Adulthood

6

Biological Systems and Their Impacts on Adolescence and Young Adulthood

Growing Into It

Roger sat in study hall gazing out of the window. He had an intense, pained expression on his face. Roger was fifteen years old, and not one thing was going right for him. His arms were too long for the rest of his body. He felt like he couldn't walk from the desk to the door without tripping at least once. Homecoming was coming up soon, and his face had suddenly managed to look like a pepperoni pizza. Shirley, the light of his life, wouldn't even acknowledge his existence. To top it all off, even if he managed to get Shirley to go to homecoming with him, he'd still either have to scrounge up another older couple to drive or else have his father drive them to the dance. How humiliating. Roger continued to gaze out of the study hall window. The primary theme in his thoughts was, "Life is hard."

Change and adjustment characterize adolescence and young adulthood. Roger is not unique. Like other people his age, he is trying to cope with drastic physical changes, increasing sexual awareness, desires to fit in with the peer group, and the desperate need to develop a personal identity.

We have established that the attainment of developmental milestones is directly related to human behavior. We have also established that within any individual (micro system), the biological, psychological, and social systems mutually affect each other. Together, they interact and significantly impact growth, development, and ultimately well-being.

Biological development and maturation affect both how adolescents perceive themselves and how they behave. Rapid and uneven physical growth may cause awkwardness. Awkwardness may result in feeling self-conscious and consequently uncomfortable in social interactions. As we will point out, for example, some psychological behavioral differences exist between males who develop earlier and later than most others their age.

Biological development often affects the transactions between individuals and their immediate social environments. For instance, when adolescents begin to attain physical and sexual maturity, sexual relationships may begin to develop. Likewise, new and different alternatives become available to adolescents and young adults as they mature. For example, alternatives concerning sexuality may range from no sexual activity to avid and frequent sexual relations. These new alternatives merit evaluation in terms of their positive and negative consequences. Decisions need to be made about such critical issues as whether to have sexual relations or not, which if any methods of birth control to use, and whether or not to enter into marriage.

A PERSPECTIVE

Chapters 6, 7, and 8 address, respectively, the biological, psychological, and social-environmental aspects of adolescence and young adulthood. The goal is to provide a framework for better understanding this difficult, yet exciting, time of life.

This chapter will:

- Explore some of the major physical changes that occur during adolescence and puberty.
- Describe the adolescent growth spurt, the secular trend, and both primary and secondary sex characteristics.

Adolescence

Adolescence is the time of life between childhood and adulthood. The word is derived from the Latin verb *adolescere,* which means "to grow into maturity." There is no precise point in time when adolescence begins or when it ends. Adolescence should be differentiated from puberty, which is more specific. *Adolescence* might be considered a cultural concept that refers to a general time during life. *Puberty,* on the other hand, is a physical concept that refers to the specific time during which people mature sexually and become capable of reproduction.

Some societies have specific rites of passage or events to mark the transition from childhood into adulthood. For example, among the Mangaia of the South Pacific (Marshall, 1980), when a boy reached the age of twelve or thirteen years, he participated in a ceremony where a superincision was made on his penis. The cut was made along the entire length of the top of the penis. After the extremely painful ceremony was completed, the boy ran out into the ocean or a stream to ease the pain, and typically exclaimed, "Now I am really a man."

Our society has no such distinct entry point into adulthood. Although we might breathe a sigh of relief at not having such a painful custom, we're still left with the problem of the vague transitional period we call adolescence. There are no clear-cut guidelines for how adolescents are supposed to behave. On the one hand, they are children, but on the other hand, they are adults.

Some occurrences tend to contribute to becoming an adult. These include graduating from high school, getting a driver's license, graduating from college, and perhaps getting married. However, not all individuals do these things. Some young people drop out of high school, and many high school graduates don't go on to college. A substantial number of young people choose not to marry or to marry much later in life. Even people who do go through these rites do so with varying levels of maturity and ability to handle

responsibility. At any rate, becoming an adult still remains a confusing concept.

Nor do the gradual, but major, physical changes help to clarify the issue. Adolescents must strive to cope with drastic changes in size and form, in addition to waves of new hormones sweeping through their bodies. Resulting emotions are often unexpected and difficult to control. Within this perspective of change and adjustment, we will look more closely at specific physical changes and at the effects of these changes on the developing personality.

Puberty

Puberty is the period when a person becomes physically mature and able to reproduce. It is marked by the sudden enlargement of the reproductive organs and sexual genitalia and the development of secondary sex characteristics (Tanner, 1967).

Girls begin the changes of puberty somewhere between eight and thirteen years of age. Boys generally start about two years later than girls. Girls reach their full adult height by about seventeen years of age, and boys by about twenty-one years of age (Roche and Davila, 1970).

The two year age difference in beginning puberty causes more than its share of problems for adolescents. Girls tend to become interested in boys before boys begin noticing that girls are alive. One dating option for girls involves older boys of the middle or late teens. This can serve to substantially raise parental anxiety. An option for boys is to date girls who tower over them.

There is a wide age span for both boys and girls when puberty begins. Although in general there is a two-year difference between the sexes, there are also substantial individual differences that must be taken into account. In other words, one boy may begin puberty four years earlier than another.

Acting as a catalyst for all of these changes is an increase in the production of hormones. *Hormones* are chemical substances secreted by the endocrine glands. Among other things, they stimulate growth of sexual organs and characteristics. Each hormone targets a specific area or areas and stimulates growth. For example, testosterone directly affects growth of the penis, facial skin, areas in the brain, and even cartilage in the shoulder joints (Tanner, 1971). In women the uterus and vagina respond to the female hormones of estrogen and progesterone (Garrison, 1973).

There is some evidence that hormonal production during adolescence is associated with increased aggression in boys and both increased aggression and depression in girls (Brooks-Gunn, 1988). However, the relationship between hormones and emotions is not a simple one (Papalia and Olds, 1992). Social forces in adolescence are formidable. As we will see in later chapters, peer influence and approval are critically important. For instance, adolescents tend to become sexually active not only when their hormone production escalates but when their friends start to be sexually active (Brooks-Gunn, 1988). An individual's biological subsystem is intertwined with both the psychological and the social subsystems.

The Growth Spurt

The initial entrance into puberty is typically characterized by a sharp increase in height. During this spurt, boys and girls typically grow between 2 and 5 inches (Tanner, 1970). Prior to the growth spurt, boys tend to be 2 percent taller than girls. However, since girls start the spurt earlier, they tend to be taller, to weigh more, and to be stronger than boys during ages eleven to thirteen years. By the time both sexes have completed the spurt, boys once again are larger than girls by about 8 percent (Papalia and Olds, 1992).

The adolescent growth spurt affects virtually the entire body including most aspects of the skeletal and muscular structure. However, boys and girls grow differently during this period. Boys' shoulders get relatively wider, and their legs and forearms relatively longer than those of girls (Tanner, 1964). Girls, on the other hand, grow wider in the pelvic area and hips. This is to enhance childbearing capability. Girls also tend to develop a layer of fat over the abdomen, hips, and buttocks during puberty. This eventually will give a young woman a more shapely, rounded physique. However, the initial chubby appearance

can cause the adolescent a substantial amount of emotional stress. Crash and starvation diets can create a physical health hazard during this period.

Adolescents tend to have unequal and disproportionate growth. Most adolescents have some features that look obviously disproportionate. The head, hands, and feet reach adult size and form first, followed by the legs and arms. Finally, the body's trunk reaches its full size. A typical result of this unequal growth is motor awkwardness and clumsiness. Until the growth of bones and muscles stabilizes, and the brain adjusts to an essentially new body, awkward bursts of motion and misjudgments of muscular control will result.

The Secular Trend

People generally grow taller and bigger than they did a century ago. They also reach sexual maturity and their adult height faster than in the past. This tendency toward increasing size and earlier achievement of sexual maturity is referred to as the *secular trend*.

The trend apparently has occurred on a worldwide basis, especially in industralized nations such as those of western Europe and Japan (Chumlea, 1982). It has not been as evident in less developed countries (Eveleth and Tanner, 1976). This suggests that an increased standard of living along with better health care and nutrition is related to the trend (Chumlea, 1988; Lefrancois, 1990).

This secular trend seems to have reached its peak and stopped. A fourteen-year-old boy of today is approximately 5 inches taller than a boy of the same age in 1880. However, growth has seemed to stabilize for most of the American population (Schneck, 1976).

Primary and Secondary Sex Characteristics

A major manifestation of puberty is the development of both primary and secondary sex characteristics. Primary sex characteristics are those directly related to the sex organs and reproduction. The key is that they have a direct role in reproduction. For females these include development of the uterus, vagina, and ovaries. The uterus is an organ about the size of a fist and is shaped like an upside-down pear. It provides the environment where the fetus can develop. The vagina is the barrel-shaped organ into which a penis is inserted during intercourse and through which a baby passes when it is born. The ovaries are the major sex glands in a female which both manufacture sex hormones and produce eggs which are ready for fertilization.

For males primary sex characteristics include growth of the penis and development of the prostate gland and the testes. The penis is the male sexual organ through which urine passes out of the body as waste and through which semen passes during orgasm. The prostate gland, which is located below the bladder, is responsible for most of the ejaculate or whitish alkaline substance that makes up semen, which carries the sperm. The testes are the male sex glands which both manufacture sex hormones and produce sperm.

Secondary sex characteristics include those traits which distinguish the sexes from each other, but play no direct role in reproduction. These include menstruation, hair growth, development of breasts, voice changes, skin changes, and nocturnal emissions.

Proof of Puberty

The most notable indication that a female has achieved the climax of puberty is her first menstruation, also called *menarche*. Menstruation is the monthly discharge of blood and tissue debris from the uterus when fertilization has not taken place. This initially occurs when a girl's height spurt has slowed down. The average age is 12.8 to 13.2 years. Usually, the first periods do not include ovulation, or release of a ripened egg by the ovaries. Therefore, a young girl is usually unable to conceive until twelve to eighteen months after her first period (Tanner, 1978).

A wide variation in the age of occurrence for first menstruation is found from one female to another. A Peruvian girl of age five is the youngest mother ever recorded to have a healthy baby. This occurred in 1939. The baby was born by Caesarean section. At the time, physicians found that she was mature sexually, and that she apparently had begun menstruation at the age of one month. The youngest parents known are an eight-year-old mother and nine-year-old father. This Chinese couple had a son in 1910 (Hyde, 1982).

Despite the fact that menstruation represents a major change in young girls' lives, they don't appear to suffer much upset. Ruble and Brooks-Gunn (1982) studied the reactions of six hundred Canadian girls in grades five through twelve to the onset of menstruation. Most felt fairly comfortable about the occasion. They found it neither painful nor confining. Instead, they seemed to converse readily about their individual symptoms. However, girls who experience it early find it more difficult to deal with, as do girls who are not prepared for it. Young women who either had too little or the wrong information about it tended to remember their first menstruation period as a distasteful experience (Rierdan et al., 1986). The implication is that girls need adequate, accurate information about menstruation early in their lives.

It is somewhat more difficult to establish that a boy has entered the full throes of puberty. One of the more reliable signs is the presence of live sperm in the urine. Both semen which contains sperm and urine travel through the penis via a tube called the *urethra*. Sometimes sperm remain in the urethra after ejaculating and are later transported out of the penis by urine.

Hair Growth

Hair begins to grow in the pubic area during puberty. After a period of months and sometimes years, this hair changes in texture. It becomes curlier, coarser and darker. About two years after the appearance of pubic hair, axillary hair begins to grow on the armpits. However, the growth of axillary hair varies so much from one person to another that in some people axillary hair growth appears before the appearance of pubic hair (Tanner, 1970). Boys' facial hair also begins to grow on the upper lip and gradually spreads to the chin and cheeks. Chest hair appears relatively late in adolescence.

Development of Breasts

Breast development is usually one of the first signs of sexual maturity in girls. The nipples and areola, the darkened areas surrounding the nipples, enlarge. Breasts initially tend to be cone-shaped and eventually assume a more rounded appearance. Breasts usually grow to their full adult size before menarche.

Some women in our culture tend to be preoccupied with breast size and feel that breasts come in one of two sizes—too large or too small. However, all breasts are functionally equipped with fifteen to twenty clusters of mammary or milk-producing glands. Each gland has an individual opening to the nipple or tip of the breast into which the milk ducts open. The glands themselves are surrounded by various amounts of fatty and fibrous tissue. The nipples are also richly supplied with sensitive nerve endings which are important in erotic stimulation. There is some indication that smaller breasts are actually more erotically sensitive per square inch than larger ones (McCary, 1973).

Some adolescent boys also undergo temporary breast development. Although this may cause some anxiety concerning their masculinity, this enlargement is not abnormal. Hyde (1982) indicates this occurs in as many as 80 percent of all boys in puberty. The probable cause is small amounts of female sex hormones produced by the testes. The condition usually disappears within about a year.

Voice Changes

Boys undergo a noticeable lowering in the tone of their voices which usually occurs fairly late in puberty (Tanner, 1970). The process involves a significant enlargement of the larynx or Adam's apple and a doubling in the length of the vocal cords. Many times it takes two years or more for boys to gain control over their new voices (Garrison, 1968).

Girls also experience a slight voice change during adolescence, although it's not nearly as extreme as the change undergone in boys. Girls' voices achieve a less high-pitched, more mature tone due to a slight growth of the larynx.

Skin Changes

Adolescence brings about increased activity of the sebaceous glands which manufacture oils for the skin. Skin pores also become coarser and increase in size during adolescence. The result is frequently a rapid production of blackheads and pimples on the face and sometimes on the back, commonly referred to as acne. Unfortunately, a poor complexion is considered unappealing not only in our society but also in most cultures (Hyde, 1982). Acne adds to the stress of adolescence. It tends to make young people feel even more self-conscious about their bodies and physical appearance.

Nocturnal Emissions

Approximately 80 percent of all males have nocturnal emissions at one time or another (Kinsey, 1948; Ortiz, 1989). A nocturnal emission is the ejaculation or emission of semen while a person is asleep. The highest frequency of approximately once a month tends to occur during the late teens. The number then tapers off during the twenties, and finally stops after age thirty. However, occasionally men up to age eighty will have a nocturnal emission.

Noctural emissions are simply a natural means of relieving sexual tension. Often, but not always, they are accompanied by sexual dreams. It's important that adolescents understand that this is a normal occurrence and that there's nothing physically or mentally wrong with them.

Some evidence indicates that females also have orgasms during sleep. However, these apparently don't occur as frequently or as early as males's nocturnal emissions. Almost 40 percent of women experience a nocturnal orgasm by the age of forty-five (Kinsey, 1948; Ortiz, 1989). Only 8 percent reported having orgasms during sleep more frequently than five times per year. Almost all of the women who had experienced orgasms during sleep also had experienced them knowingly while awake. In other words, it seems that females must know what an orgasm is in order to identify that it has occurred during sleep.

Psychological Reactions to Physical Changes

One thing that marks adolescence is self-criticism. Physical imperfections are sought out, emphasized, and dwelled on. It may be a large lump on a nose. Or it may be an awesome derriere. Or it may even be a dreadful terror of braces locking unromantically during a good night kiss. Adolescents seek to conform to their peers. Any aspect that remains imperfect or too noticeable becomes the object of criticism. Perhaps it's partly because the age is filled with change and the mandatory adjustment to that change that adolescents strive to conform. Perhaps before an individual personality can develop and grow, a person needs some predictability and security.

A substantial amount of research focuses on adolescents' perceptions of themselves. Special areas of intense interest include body image, self-concept, weight level, weight worries, and eating disorders.

Body Image and Self-Concept

Physical appearance is very important to an adolescent. Both males and females tend to express dissatisfaction and unhappiness about their physical attributes (Bibby and Posterski, 1985; Segal, 1982). Adolescent boys would like to see themselves as tall and well-built, with broad shoulders, and oozing with athletic ability. Girls, on the other hand, would prefer to have a slender but curvaceous body, a beautiful face, an immaculate complexion, and attractive hair (Tobin-Richards, et al., 1983).

Perception of one's own body image and attractiveness is related to one's level of self-esteem (Berscheid et al., 1973). People who consider themselves attractive tend to be more self-confident and satisfied with themselves. One study found that physical appearance is the most critical factor affecting self-worth for children as young as those in grades three through eight (Harter, 1987).

A person's level of physical attractiveness in adolescence seems to have some carry-over effects in adulthood. Berscheid, Walster, and Bohrnstedt (1971) did a survey of approximately 62,000 people. Although the respondents in no way could be said to represent all segments of the total population, some interesting results were obtained. People who felt they were unattractive as adolescents were the least happy group of all the people participating in the survey. On the other hand, until they reached the age of forty-four, people who were the most attractive adolescents made up the happiest group of people in the survey. After this age, happiness seemed to level out among both groups, the more and the less beautiful.

Weight Worries

Weight is a primary concern of adolescents, particularly adolescent females. This is related to their intensified concerns about physical appearance, the effects of these concerns upon self-esteem, and the extreme cultural emphasis on thinness, especially for women.

Hendry and Gillies (1978) studied almost one thousand fifteen- and sixteen-year-old male and fe-

Adolescents seek to conform to their peers.

male adolescents. After placing them in underweight, average, or overweight categories, they compared the groups using several variables, including physical fitness, self-esteem, personality, body esteem, social class, academic attainment, extracurricular activities, and leisure companions.

Surprisingly, no major differences were found among any of the groups regarding how popular or outgoing the young people were. However, overweight adolescents were the least happy with their bodies. They were also the least physically fit.

Teachers tended to perceive the overweight girls less positively on several dimensions. They were seen as having a less attractive appearance and as being less enthusiastic than other groups. Teachers perceived underweight males and females as being more socially nervous. Additionally, underweight girls were seen as being less competitive. Male and female adolescents who were either overweight or underweight were less likely to date someone steadily than adolescents of average proportions.

Although both genders appear to express concern about "their weight, their complexion, and their facial features" (Papalia and Olds, 1992, p, 315), there are gender differences. For one, girls tend to be even more unhappy about their physical appearance than their male peers (Tobin-Richards et al., 1983). This is probably due to the extreme importance placed on females' physical appearance in this culture. Girls are more specific about what they see wrong with their bodies and appearance (Frazier and Lisonbee, 1950; Tobin-Richards et al., 1983). For example, when asked what she feels is wrong with her body, a girl might say, "My thighs are too fat and my rump sticks out too much. I'd really like to fit into a size 7 jeans, but can't get under a size 9. Can girls my age have cellulite?" Boys, on the other hand, when asked the

Masturbation

Masturbation refers to self-stimulation of the genitals that causes sexual arousal. Research indicates that most adolescents masturbate. Kinsey, Pomeroy, and Martin (1948) discovered a striking increase in the incidence of masturbation among boys aged thirteen through fifteen years. Twenty-one percent of all males studied had masturbated by age twelve. However, this percentage drastically increased to 82 percent by fifteen years of age. A substantial number of girls were also found to begin masturbating by age fifteen (Kinsey et al., 1953). However, girls generally tended to start masturbating later than boys. A higher proportion of girls when compared to boys never masturbate at all.

More recent studies support the findings that most adolescents masturbate. Sorenson (1973) surveyed the sexual attitudes of 393 adolescents. He found that 58 percent of adolescent boys and 39 percent of adolescent girls masturbated by age fifteen. By age nineteen, virtually all boys and most girls masturbate. Boys tend to masturbate to orgasm an average of two or three times per week. Girls tend to do so approximately once a month (Hass, 1979).

One interesting difference between young men and women in the incidence of masturbation is the relationship between masturbation and sexual activity with other people. Sexually active male adolescents tend to masturbate less than those who aren't having sexual intercourse. Sexually active female adolescents, on the other hand, tend to masturbate more than their virgin counterparts (Sorenson, 1973). This may have to do with differences in sex roles and sexual expectations between males and females. It may also have to do with the fact that the sex drive of women tends to develop relatively later than men's. This sex drive continues to develop well into the adult years.

It's important to address the issue of masturbation. As we've already established, it is very common among adolescents. However, it is also looked down on. The numerous slang terms used to describe it are very uncomplimentary. These include, "beat the meat," "shoot the wad," "choke the chicken," "pound pud," and "carrot cuffing." Perhaps the negative attitude traditionally convened about masturbation can best be expressed by the statements of H.R. Stout in the 1885 edition of *Our Family Physician:*

> When the evil has been pursued for several years, there will be an irritable condition of the system; sudden flushes of heat over the face; the countenance becomes pale and clammy; the eyes have a dull, sheepish look; the hair becomes dry and split at the ends; sometimes there is pain over the region of the heart; shortness of breath; palpitation of the heart (symptoms of dyspepsia show themselves); the sleep is disturbed; there is constipation; cough; irritation of the throat; finally the whole man becomes a wreck, physically, morally, and mentally.

After such a tirade it would be a wonder if a person would dare to masturbate. This presents quite a contradiction and source of confusion for adolescents. They are actually participating in the activity of masturbation. Yet, there is some tendency for it to be considered an unappealing and even disgusting behavior. Sorenson (1973) found that many adolescents felt anxiety, defensiveness, or embarrassment over their behavior. A few felt guilty about it. Hass (1979) found that most adolescents have negative feelings about masturbation.

Adolescents need to understand that masturbation is not abnormal or harmful. In a period of their lives when they are coping with many physical changes and new life situations, they do not need to be burdened with unnecessary confusion and even guilt. Masturbation is a normal means of relieving sexual tension and other stress, allowing a means of self-discovery, developing confidence in oneself, learning to control sexual needs and impulses, and fighting isolation and loneliness (Barbach, 1980; Clifford, 1978; Sorenson, 1973). Masturbation is even a prescribed means of treatment for sexual dysfunction. Women with orgasmic dysfunctions, that is, the inability to experience orgasms, are counseled to use masturbation (Kaplan, 1981). This helps them overcome anxiety and understand their sexual responses. This information can later be transferred to a partner.

same question might respond something like, "Aww, I don't know," or "I guess I'd like to be stronger."

Girls also tend to have higher frequencies of depression. This may be due to their intensified levels of self-criticism. Before puberty, boys and girls display similar levels of depression; however, by approximately age fourteen, depression rates for girls are double those of boys (Rierdan et al., 1988, 1989).

Weight, Women, and Eating Disorders

Lott (1987) addresses the general issue of women's situation within our culture. She posits that virtually all applicable research and information point to the fact that women spend much more time than men criticizing their own physical appearance and worrying about their weight. She asserts that:

> women's preoccupation with appearance is normative in our society, that it results from social pressure, from the greater punishments experienced by obese women than men, and from the strong relationship between women's judged attractiveness and thinness.... Most women regard . . . [their] weight as a crucial index of acceptability and attractiveness. (P. 266)

In view of this intense concern, women manifest the vast majority of eating disorders, most of which begin in adolescence. In general, eating disorders involve "a group of mental disturbances . . . involving maladaptive or unhealthy eating patterns" (Barker, 1991, p. 46). Due to their frequency, of special concern during adolescence are anorexia nervosa and bulimia. Anorexia nervosa is

> an eating disorder most often encountered in girls and young women whose extended refusal to eat leads to severe weight loss, malnutrition, and cessation of menstruation. The usual medical criteria for this diagnosis include the loss of one-fourth or more of one's body weight. This life-threatening condition is thought to be related to a disturbed body image and an exaggerated fear of becoming obese. (Barker, 1991, p. 9)

Ninety-five percent of those affected with anorexia nervosa are females (Koch et al., 1993). These young women become so obsessed with being thin that their need to control and limit their weight essentially takes over their lives. Estimates indicate that as

many as 1 in 100 to 1 in 800 female adolescents suffer from this condition; between 5 and 18 percent of anorexics die from it (Koch et al., 1993). In essence, these young women starve themselves to death.

Bulimia, on the other hand, is

> a pathologically excessive appetite with episodic eating binges, sometimes followed by purging through such means as self-induced vomiting, laxative abuse, and diet pills or diuretics. Bulimia usually starts as a means of dieting. Then when hunger occurs, the person eats, feels guilty, and purges, which leads to more eating, more dieting and so on. (Barker, 1991, p. 18)

Bulimia, too, involves primarily adolescents and young women. It appears to be even more common than anorexia nervosa. An accurate prevalence of bulimia is difficult to establish. Bulimics tend to guard this "secret" carefully, and they often appear "normal" in terms of weight. However, bulimia can take control of women's lives. Estimates of bulimia's incidence among adolescents and young women range from 4.5 to 18 percent (Koch and Dotson, 1989).

Eating disorders are discussed in much greater depth in Chapter 9. There the dynamics of such disorders will be explored. However, because concern about weight is so critically significant to young women and the effects of this concern so potentially lethal, it needs to be identified here. These concerns and conditions clearly illustrate the intimate interactions of the biological, psychological, and social subsystems operating developmentally within any one individual (micro system).

What do *you* think about these concerns and issues? Is it right or fair to place so much importance upon external physical appearance, especially as such emphasis concerns weight? Is it equitable that the burden of weight control rests even more heavily upon women than upon men? How have these concerns about weight and physical appearance affected you and your own aspects of biological, psychological, and social development?

Early and Late Maturation in Boys

Some adolescents mature earlier than others; some much later. Some are lucky enough to fall within the

An early maturing boy is more popular, confident, and successful in heterosexual relationships.

average range of maturation. That is, these average maturers experience their physical changes at roughly the same time that many of their peers are dealing with similar changes. Tremendous importance is placed both on physical appearance and on conformity to the peer group. Average maturers are able to conform to the group, at least in this physical respect. They have others to talk to and relate to about their physical and sexual changes.

A number of long-term studies concerning early and late maturation in boys have revealed fairly consistent results (Crockett and Petersen, 1987; Jones et al., 1950, 1957, 1965). Early maturers, those who mature earlier than most of their peers, have the advantages of increased size and athletic ability. Peers are more likely to look up to them. Lefrancois (1990) summarizes the psychological effects on early maturers: "Early maturing boys are typically better adjusted, more popular, more confident, more aggressive, and more successful in heterosexual relationships. In addition, they appear to have clear advantages with respect to self-concepts" (p. 422).

It's important not to assume that early maturers

will automatically become team quarterbacks and class presidents (or gang leaders, for that matter). Many other factors such as individual personalities and environmental influences also affect an individual's development. Papalia and Olds (1992) caution that there is some evidence that early maturers can also be "more worried about being liked, more cautious, and more bound by rules and routines" (p. 314). Early maturers may suffer more pressure from both peers and adults. Peers are more likely to look up to them for exemplary behavior and leadership. Similarly, adults are more likely to treat early maturers as if they were older than they are. Adults tend to place higher expectations upon them.

Late maturing boys, on the other hand, are perceived as being less physically attractive and not as well poised. They also appear to be more tense and are more likely to engage in immature, attention-getting behavior. Perhaps such behavior serves as their means of expressing themselves. Late maturers may be denied the respect and attention given more mature looking boys. Acting out behavior may provide late maturers a means of getting at least some attention and recognition, even though it may not be very positive.

By adulthood, the differences between early and late maturers become much less clear (Clausen, 1975; Peskin, 1973). Most, in fact, tend to disappear. There is some indication, however, that two differences tend to remain (Jones, 1957). First, early maturers continue to make better first impressions than do late maturers. Perhaps this follows from their apparent increased levels of self-confidence and social skills patterned in adolescence.

The second difference involves the increased flexibility shown by the late maturers as adults. They appear to be more tolerant of situations that are less clear or out of their control. Livson and Peskin (1980) reflect on the reasons why late maturers seem to have this particular advantage. Adolescents who mature late must learn to cope early with their disadvantaged and more stressful situation. As a result, as adults they are more flexible and are better equipped with creative problem-solving skills. They paid their dues as adolescents, but reap the rewards of their experience as adults.

Early and Late Maturation in Girls

The maturation picture for girls is more confusing and ambiguous. There is some evidence that early maturing girls, in contrast to early maturing boys, are initially disadvantaged compared to average and late maturers (Siegel, 1982). In early adolescence, early maturers tend to be less comfortable in social situations, less outgoing, and less positive about beginning menstruation (Jones, 1958; Livson and Peskin, 1980; Ruble and Brooks-Gunn, 1982). There is additional evidence that early maturers are more critical about their physical appearance and feel generally less positively about themselves (Simmons, et al., 1979). However, in later adolescence the drawbacks seem to vanish (Faust, 1960).

Early maturing girls in fifth or sixth grade may feel out of place when compared to their peers. It may be difficult for them to communicate about their new developments with other girls who have not experienced these developments and probably don't understand them. However, as early as seventh grade the picture changes. Early maturers rapidly gain prestige

as their classmates also begin to develop. These higher levels of prestige tend to be maintained throughout the rest of adolescence. There is some indication that social advantages tend to continue into adulthood (Jones and Mussen, 1958; Livson and Peskin, 1980).

It should be emphasized that the differences between early and late maturing girls, when they exist at all, are not nearly as striking as those between early and late maturing boys. Also, there is wide variation in overall adjustment from one individual to the next. Such adjustment is dependent on many factors other than physical maturation.

Young Adulthood

It is difficult to pinpoint the exact time of life we are referring to when we talk about young adulthood. The transition into adulthood is not a clearcut dividing line. People become voting adults by age eighteen. However, in most states, they are not considered adult enough to drink alcoholic beverages until twenty-one. A person cannot become a U.S. senator until age thirty or president until age thirty-five. All this presents a confusing picture of what we mean by adulthood.

Various theorists have tried to define young adulthood. Buhler (1933) clustered adolescence and young adulthood together. He felt that this period included the ages from fifteen to twenty-five. During this time, people focus on establishing their identities and on idealistically trying to make their dreams come true. Buhler continues that the next phase includes young and middle adulthood. This period lasts from approximately age twenty-three to forty-five or fifty. This group focuses on attaining realistic, concrete goals and on setting up a work and family structure for life.

Levinson and his colleagues (1974), on the other hand, break up young adulthood into smaller slices. They state that in the process of developing a life structure, people go through stable periods separated by shorter transitional periods. The stage from ages seventeen to twenty-four is characterized by leaving the family and becoming independent. This is followed by a transitional phase from ages twenty-two to twenty-eight, which involves entering the adult world. The age thirty transition focuses on making a decision about how to structure the remainder of life. A settling-down period then occurs from about ages thirty-two to forty.

For our purposes, we will arbitrarily consider young adulthood as including the ages from eighteen to thirty. This is the time following the achievement of full physical growth when people are establishing themselves in the adult world. Specific aspects of young adulthood addressed in this chapter will include physical development, health status, and the effects of lifestyle on health.

Physical Development

Young adults are in their physical prime. Maximum muscular strength is attained between the ages of twenty-five and thirty, and generally begins a gradual decline after that (Bromley, 1975). After age thirty, decreases in strength occur mostly in the leg and back muscles. Some weakening also occurs in the arm muscles.

Top performance speed in terms of how fast tasks can be accomplished is reached at about age thirty (Lehman, 1966). Young adulthood is also characterized by the highest levels of manual agility. According to Troll (1985), hand and finger dexterity decrease after the mid-thirties.

Sight, hearing, and the other senses are their keenest during young adulthood. Eyesight is the sharpest at about age twenty. A decline in visual acuity isn't significant until age forty or forty-five, when there is some tendency toward *presbyopia* (farsightedness). What happens is that there is a reduction in the elasticity of the lens in the eye. The result is that the lens can no longer change its curvature in order to focus on very near point of vision. When people of age forty or more read their newspapers by holding them three feet in front of them, they are likely to be suffering from presbyopia.

Hearing is also sharpest at age twenty. After this there is a gradual decline in auditory acuity, especially in sensitivity to higher tones. This deficiency is referred to as *presbycusis*. It results from a natural aging process where there is a slow degeneration and hardening of the auditory cells and nerves. Most of the other senses, namely touch, smell, and taste, tend to remain stable until approximately age forty-five or fifty.

Health Status

Young adulthood can be considered the healthiest time of life. Young adults are generally healthier than when they were children and they have not yet begun to suffer the illnesses and health declines which develop in middle age (Timiras, 1972). Over 90 percent of people ages seventeen to forty-four perceive of their health as being either good or excellent (U.S. Department of Health and Human Services, 1990). There is significant interest on the part of many in all socioeconomic classes in health measures. For example, running and other forms of exercising, health foods, and weight control have become very popular.

Despite the fact that young adulthood is generally a healthy time of life, health differences can be seen between men and women. For example, women tend to visit physicians more than men (Sapiro, 1990). Women also spend more time in hospitals (U.S. Bureau of the Census, 1987). However, women's more frequent visits may be attributed to health issues related to gender. These include contraception, pregnancy, or an annual pap test, instead of more general reasons of poor health. Perhaps women are also more conscientious about preventive health care in general.

Of all the acute or temporary pressing health problems occurring during young adulthood, approximately one half are caused by respiratory problems. An additional 20 percent are due to injuries. The most frequent chronic health problems occurring in young adulthood include spinal or back difficulties, hearing problems, arthritis, and hypertension. These chronic problems occur even more frequently in families of lower socioeconomic status. Young African Americans experience hypertension more frequently than their white counterparts (USDHHS, 1990). People are hospitalized most frequently during young adulthood due to childbirth, accidents, digestive tract disturbances, and genital or urinary system illnesses (USDHHS, 1985).

Young adults are most likely to die in accidents, especially those involving cars. The next important causes of death are cancer, heart disease, and suicide. When dividing people into racial and gender groups, some differences emerge. Death rates for men are twice as high as those of their female peers; additionally, women are more likely to die of cancer and men in car accidents (USDHHS, 1990).

Breast Cancer

According to the American Cancer Society, 1 in 9 women will develop breast cancer during her lifetime (*Milwaukee Journal*, Jan. 25, 1991). This has increased from 1 in 10, which was evident in 1987, and 1 in 11 in 1981 (Silverberg, 1981). Part of the increase is attributed to the fact that more and more women are getting regular mammograms (low dose X-ray photographs of the breasts). Mammograms have enabled earlier detection and better reporting of cancer. They often detect cancers too small to feel with the fingers.

Being knowledgeable about the issue of breast cancer is especially important for you in helping your female clients become aware of risks, prevention, and treatment. If you are a female, it's important for your own health. If you are a male, it's important for the women who are close to you.

Benign Lumps

Eighty percent of all breast lumps are benign. Therefore, significantly more than 1 in 9 women will develop some kind of lump in their breast during their lifetime. Benign lumps usually take one of two forms. First, there are *cysts*, which are "fluid-filled sacs"; the other common form of benign lump is an *fibroadenoma*, which is a "solid, rounded tumor" (Crooks and Baur, 1993, p. 102).

Symptoms

A number of symptoms other than identification of a tumor can indicate malignancy. Tumors can assume a number of shapes and forms. Generally, any change in the external appearance of the breasts should make one suspicious. For instance, one breast becoming significantly larger or hanging significantly lower than the other are potential warning signs. Discharges from the nipple or nipple discoloration are additional indications. Dimpling or puckering of the nipple or skin of the breast should be noted. Finally, any swelling of the upper arm or lymph nodes under the arm should be investigated.

Risk Factors

A number of risk factors are involved in getting breast cancer. Age is one. The older the person, the higher her risk. Family history is also significant. If a woman's mother and/or sisters, aunts, or grandmothers have had breast cancer, the risk is increased. Having developed breast cancer in the past automatically increases the risk factor. Women who have their first child after thirty are at slightly greater risk than women who have their first baby before age thirty. Having begun menstruation at age eleven or younger increases risk. Finally, being overweight increases the risk of breast cancer.

Treatment of Breast Cancer

In the event that a suspicious lump is detected, a number of options can be pursued. First, *needle aspiration* can be used to attempt drawing the fluid out of the lump. If fluid can be removed, the lump is likely to be a cyst. If the lump subsequently disappears, it was a cyst. There is no need for further alarm. Another means of examining a lump involves a *biopsy*. Here a small section of tissue is surgically removed and examined for cancer cells. Other less common techniques include *ultrasonagraphy*, in which sound waves are used to examine breast tissue, and *thermography*, which measures heat emitted from different parts of the breast.

Once it has been established that a lump is cancerous, there are several alternative treatments. First, there are surgeries of increasing complexity and severity. The simplest surgical procedure is a *lumpectomy*, in which only the tumor and a small portion of the surrounding tissue are removed. This allows for the least disruption of the breast's external appearance. The next alternative is a *partial mastectomy*, in which a portion of the breast containing the cancerous tumor is taken out along with some of the muscle tissue right below it and breast skin above it. The third option is a *simple mastectomy*. Here, the entire breast is removed, sometimes along with some of the lymph nodes under the arm. Although some of us find it offensive to use the term "simple" in this context ("It's simple for you to say my breast should be removed."), the term refers to the fact that the musculature in the chest will remain pretty much intact after this procedure. Removal of muscle tissue usually impairs arm movements. The fourth surgical alternative is a *modified radical mastectomy* where the breast, lymph nodes, the covering over the chest muscles, and sometimes one of the chest muscles are removed. Finally, as the name implies, the most extreme surgical procedure, a *radical mastectomy* involves removal of the breast, the skin, the chest muscles, and all lymph nodes under the arm.

(continued next page)

Breast Cancer (continued)

The surgical procedure chosen depends on a number of factors. One, of course, is how far the cancer has progressed. All cancerous cells must be removed. In the past, the most common procedure by far was the most severe, namely, the radical mastectomy. Various types of mastectomies remain the most common. More recent evidence indicates that in those cases where the malignant tumor is less than a centimeter in size, lumpectomies are just as effective as extreme procedures; in fact, both have a 90 percent effectiveness rate (*Milwaukee Journal*, June 22, 1990).

Why have radical procedures been used so commonly? One reason might be that, in the past, women did not pursue the preventative recommendations described below to the extent they do now. Another reason for the numerous mastectomies might be surgeons' lack of sensitivity to the psychological effects of mastectomies on women. Such impacts can be massive (Meyerowitz, 1980). Women generally react first to the abrupt revelation that they have cancer and second to the fact that their breast will be amputated. Breasts are given tremendous significance in this society. Additionally, external appearance and physical shape are highly acclaimed. A woman's perception of herself, of how others perceive her, and of the effects on her sexual relationships all can be severely affected.

After a mastectomy, there is the option of reconstructive surgery. This involves plastic surgery to implant an artificial breast and to make it look as natural as possible. It's estimated that over 2 million breast implants have been done so far and over 150,000 will be done each year. Breast implants are of two types: those containing silicone gel and those filled with saline water. Serious questions have been raised regarding the safety of silocone gel implants. Saline water implants have not been under such fire. The Food and Drug Administration has expressed a range of health concerns about silicone gel implants including: "infection, pain, hardening of breasts, false mammography results and silicone leaks. Questions also have been raised about potential long-term risks such as immune reactions and cancer" (*Milwaukee Journal*, April 11, 1991).

In addition to surgery, several other treatments exist for breast cancer. Radiation is used as the major means of treatment for very early cancers and to supplement surgery and prevent recurrence. *Chemotherapy* is administered when cancer has spread to the lymph nodes. Such a spread of cancer cells implies that other organs may be involved. Finally, *hormone therapy* is sometimes used to diminish the growth of breast cancer that has returned or spread to other parts of the body.

Early Detection of Breast Cancer

There are three primary recommendations for early detection of breast cancer (Crooks and Baur, 1990). The first involves seeing a health care practitioner on a regular basis, and having an annual Pap smear (examination of a small scraping of cells from the bottom of the uterus, the cervix), a pelvic examination (a check of the genital and reproductive areas for abnormalities), and breast palpation (a manual checking of the breasts).

The second recommendation for breast cancer detection is regular mammograms. The meaning of "regular" varies according to a woman's age. Every woman between ages thirty-five and forty should have a mammogram to establish a baseline. This early mammogram can be compared with later ones to identify any changes in breast tissue. Women with high risk factors such as having close female family members with breast cancer may prompt a physician to begin doing mammograms much earlier. During her forties, a woman should have one every one to two years. Finally, she should have a mammogram every year after age fifty. It should be emphasized, however, that many cancers cannot be detected by mammography. One study indicated that 22 percent of cancers established during biopsies were not detected by earlier mammographies (Edeiken, 1988).

The third recommendation for breast cancer detection is a monthly breast self-examination. If a woman checks regularly, she will be able to detect minor, subtle changes in her breasts. She can develop much greater expertise in checking herself than a physician or other health professional who checks her only once a year or less often.

It is best to do a breast self-examination seven to ten days after a menstrual period ends, because the breasts are least likely to be swollen at that time. After menopause, it is suggested that women perform examinations on the first day of each month, an easy pattern to remember. A breast self-examination can be done in three phases. First, in the shower, use the flat pads of the three middle fingers to check for lumps. Using fingertips can easily push lumps away and out of touch. Both superficial and deeper pressure should be used. Superficial pressure will detect tiny lumps that will slip away from the fingers when greater pressure is used. Deeper pressure gets at mid-level tissues. Because cancer

FIGURE 6.1: Breast Cancer Detection

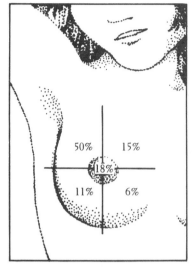

a) Where cancer tends
to develop.

b) The spiral method
of breast self-examination.

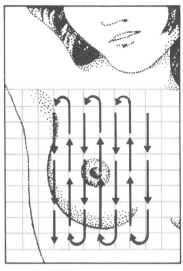

c) The grid method
of breast self-examination.

also can occur in the lymph nodes under the arm, areas near the armpit and collarbone should also be checked. About one-half of all tumors occur in this area. See figure 6.1a, which illustrates the likelihood that cancer will develop in any particular area of the breast.

Breast self-examinations should be systematic to make certain no areas of the breast are missed. Two very common methods are the *spiral method* and the *grid method*. They are illustrated, respectively, in figures 6.1b and 6.1c. Either method helps a woman make certain she has not missed some portion of the breast.

Using the spiral method, a woman should start at the top of the breast and follow the line as indicated up into the armpit, around, up to the collarbone, and then back down to the breast. At least three smaller circles should then be made around the breast ending up at the nipple. This should be done twice, once with light pressure and once with deeper pressure.

The grid method involves imagining a grid on the upper torso encompassing each breast. The woman systematically works her way from square to square exerting first light pressure and then deeper pressure to check for lumps. The second phase of the breast self-examination entails observing the breasts in a mirror. The woman should look for any changes in size or shape. She should lift her arms above her head, and then shrug her shoulders. She should bend over to see if her breasts hang evenly. Finally, she should check her nipples for any discharge. The third phase of the breast self-examination involves lying down and once again using either the spiral method or the grid method. A folded towel should be placed under the mid-back so that the breast tissue is more evenly distributed.

A Final Note

Breast cancer is a critically important issue. Some important principles for women to remember include:

1. Women should become experts on their bodies. They should perform monthly breast self-examinations. The earlier a lump is found, the smaller it will probably be, and the easier it will be to treat.
2. In the event that a lump is found, women should be knowledgeable about alternative remedies. They should consider the pros and cons of each.

Racial differences in death rates also occur. For instance, the death rate for African American young adults is more than double that of their white counterparts. The incidence of violent death in the two groups contributes to this difference. Murder is the number one cause of death for young African American men compared to the fifth cause for comparably aged white men. Furthermore, in the United States, three times as many of these killings result from guns compared to other industrialized nations (Fingerhut and Kleinman, 1990). You might ask yourself why you live in such a violent society.

The difference in the death rates of African Americans and whites reflects a significant difference in environment. Of course, there are people of virtually every ethnic and racial background who are poor. However, in the United States, if you are African American or a member of a number of other minorities, including Hispanics and Native Americans, you are more likely to be poor than if you are white. This is a complicated issue. However, much of the difference in circumstances is due to a long history of prejudice and discrimination. If you're poor, you're more likely to be living in the crowded urban center of a city than in the suburbs. If you're poor and live in the inner city where the crime rate is higher, you are more likely to be a homicide victim.

If you are poor, you are also more likely not to have employment that provides adequate health insurance. You're more likely to find yourself in a position where you can't go to a doctor when you're sick because you have no money and no insurance. Young adulthood is supposed to be the healthiest time of life and it is for most people. However, overall health status varies drastically depending on environment and living conditions. It's important for social workers to be aware of the impact that poor environments can have on people.

Poverty is often linked to minority status. Many minorities have been oppressed, that is, physically abused, burdened by the abuse of others' power, and treated unfairly. The result is the likelihood of a poor standard of living including a poor health status with more health problems. Instead of asking what people can do to get out of poor environments, social workers need to ask how these environments can be changed to improve the living conditions of the oppressed people.

Life-Style and Good Health

Good health doesn't just happen. It is related to specific practices and to a person's individual life-style. Several simple, basic habits have been found to prolong life (Belloc and Breslow, 1972). People who follow all of them tend to live longer than people who follow only some of them. As a matter of fact, a clear relationship seems to exist between the number of the suggested habits followed and the state of overall health.

These positive health habits include eating breakfast and other meals regularly. Snacking should be avoided. Moderate eating in order to maintain a normal, healthy weight is important. Smoking and heavy alcohol consumption are dangerous to health and should be avoided. Moderate exercise and adequate sleep are important and contribute to good health.

Different life-styles involve different behaviors. In other words, an individual's typical way of life will involve specific types of activities. Some of these activities have been found to have direct effects on a person's health.

For instance, excessive consumption of alcohol has very negative effects on health. Alcoholics are people who have a continual and compulsive need for alcohol. Physical dependence occurs when body tissues become dependent on the continuous presence of alcohol. Approximately three quarters of all alcoholics show some impaired liver function. Cirrhosis of the liver is eventually developed by about 8 percent of all alcoholics. The chances of developing cirrhosis are about six times greater for alcoholics than for nonalcoholics (Girdano and Dusek, 1980). Cirrhosis involves gradual deterioration of the liver tissue until it no longer can adequately perform its normal function. These functions include involvement in the process of converting food to usable energy. Other effects of alcoholism include cancer, heart problems and heart failure, a variety of gastrointestinal disorders including ulcers, damage to the nervous system, psychoses, and others (*Morbidity and Mortality Weekly Report*, 1989; National Institute on Alcohol Abuse and Alcoholism, 1981; Papalia and Olds, 1992).

Cigarette smoking is another activity that is clearly associated with health problems. Many of the deaths related to smoking are due to heart disease. Cigarette smoke contains nicotine, which acts as a stimulant. As nicotine enters the lungs, it is quickly absorbed by the small blood vessels in the lungs and immediately transported throughout the body. As a stimulant it causes both an increased heart rate and increased blood pressure. Over time the heart will be over-worked and eventually be damaged (Girdano and Dusek, 1980).

Lung cancer is another major cause of death attributed to smoking. Cigarette tars and other parti-cles in the smoke gradually accumulate in the tubes and air sacs of the lungs. This causes a gradual change in the lung tissue's normal cells. Eventually these affected cells may reproduce new cells that are different from the original ones. The new cancerous cells begin frantic reproduction of more cancerous cells which eventually kill off and take over the nor-mal cell tissue. The result is the growth of a malig-nant tumor which invades the lung and spreads to other parts of the body.

To make matters worse, it's been found that a combination of excessive alcohol consumption and tobacco usage results in an increased risk of develop-ing cancer of the mouth, larynx, and esophagus (Winder, et al., 1976; Moore, 1971, 1965). Since approximately 90 percent of all alcoholics also smoke (Dreher and Fraser, 1968), this becomes a serious health risk.

Stress is another variable related to health prob-lems. Holmes and Rahe (1976) found a strong rela-tionship between stress and illness. The more stress a person is experiencing, the greater is the chance of becoming ill. An interesting finding is that stress is caused not only by negative occurrences such as the death of a close relative, but also by new, positive occurrences. These include outstanding personal achievements and even vacations. Apparently change in general causes stress. Adjustment to new situations required expending energy. This additional energy and need for adjustment is apparently related to stress regardless of whether the adjustment is to a happy or a sad occasion.

Once again, it must be emphasized that one's capacity to establish and follow positive health habits depends on one's accessibility to resources. A poor person does not have the choices available that a middle- or upper-class person does. A poor person can't join the local Sun Valley Health Club or the Elm Grove Racquet Club in order to get adequate exercise. First, such places probably don't exist in the area. Second, there certainly is no money for such extravagances. Third, these places often have explicit and implicit requirements regarding their members' background, financial status, appearance, and social standing.

Poor people are also likely to suffer additional stress related to their lack of resources. They may be worry-ing about what to feed their kids near the end of the month when money has run out. Maybe all they have in the house is a bag of macaroni and a hunk of a generic brand of artificial process cheese. Maybe they're worried about having their phone discon-nected or their electricity turned off because they couldn't pay the bills.

Some behaviors have been found to be positively related to good health. For example, physical exercise "helps to maintain desirable body weight; build mus-cles; strengthen heart and lungs; lower blood pressure; protect against heart attacks, cancer, and osteoporosis (a thinning of the bones that tends to affect older women, causing fractures . . .); relieve anxiety and depression; and possibly lengthen life" (Papalia and Olds, 1992, p. 373).

Diet has also been found to affect health. Being overweight increases risks of heart disease, high blood pressure, and other health problems. On the other hand, choosing a well-balanced diet, limiting food intake, and avoiding foods that are infused with salt and fat can promote good health, especially in con-junction with exercise. For instance, limiting choles-terol intake decreases the risks of heart disease (Lipid Research Clinics Program, 1984a, 1984b). Choles-terol is "a soft, fat-like substance found among the fats in the bloodstream (American Heart Association, 1984, p. 1). It can collect in arteries, thereby stalling blood flow. Extreme blockages can arrest the blood flow into the heart and, ultimately, cause a heart attack. Eating foods low or lacking in cholesterol can significantly decrease these risks.

Significant Issues and Life Events

Certain significant experiences and life events tend to characterize adolescence and young adulthood. Some issues are of special concern to people in this age group. Several of these issues have been selected arbitrarily for discussion here. They were chosen on the basis of their relevance and impact on the physical well-being of young people. As adolescence is a period of sexual development, sexuality will be emphasized. The issues include sexual activity in adolescence, unplanned pregnancy, teenage fatherhood, motivation for pregnancy, sex education, sexually transmitted diseases, and contraception.

Sexual Activity in Adolescence

Two major trends have characterized adolescent sexual activity in recent years. First, there has been a dramatic increase in the proportion of teenagers who have sexual intercourse. Second, the age at which first intercourse occurs has become younger (Masters et al., 1988). Both of these trends are more true for girls than for boys.

In the 1940s, Kinsey (1948, 1953) found that about one-third of all females and almost three-quarters of all males under age twenty-five reported that they had had nonmarital intercourse. Today, by age nineteen, over half of all women and 78 percent of all men indicate that they have had sexual intercourse; 17 percent of girls and 38 percent of boys have had intercourse by age fifteen (Gordon and Gilgun, 1987).

The fact that teenagers are more likely to gain sexual experience at earlier ages than decades past does not mean, however, that they are becoming promiscuous. It does not mean that they indiscriminately have many partners during any particular period. In fact, almost 90 percent of adolescents indicate that having sexual intercourse on the first date is inappropriate; after a few dates, on the other hand, almost half feel it is appropriate (Bibby and Posterski, 1985). Most adolescents feel that sexual intercourse should occur within a relationship with someone they really care about (Christopher and Cate, 1984; Coles and Stokes, 1985).

Some petting occurs on most first dates and in almost all relationships progressing to several dates (McCabe and Collins, 1984). It appears that adolescents generally expect sexual activity to become more and more involved within the context of a "meaningful" relationship. Although young men usually want to have sexual intercourse earlier than women, women's desire soon matches men's as their relationship

Adolescents generally expect sexual activity to become more involved within the context of a "meaningful" relationship.

deepens (McCabe, 1987). However, it should not be assumed that all adolescents feel that they should or must have sexual intercourse. Some maintain that dating should involve only necking and some light petting (Lawrence et al., 1984).

Despite the fact that most adolescents have sex, they often have very mixed feelings about it (Coles and Stokes, 1985; Weis, 1985). On the one hand, they may experience excitement, intimacy, and pleasure. On the other hand, they may also feel guilt, anxiety, or fear of pregnancy and disease.

Unplanned Pregnancy in Adolescence

It is estimated that about 1 million of the 11 million sexually active adolescent females in the United States become pregnant every year. Of these pregnancies, "approximately 40 percent are aborted, 10 percent end in spontaneous abortions or stillbirths, and 50 percent result in live births (roughly one-fifth of all births annually in the United States)" (Crooks and Baur, 1990, pp. 467–68). The birth rate for single adolescent women is one of the highest in the world.

It is about seventeen times higher than Japan's and twice as high as Canada's (Jones, 1986).

The vast majority of babies born to single teens, a total of 93 percent, remain at home with their young mothers. Another 3.5 percent of the children are placed for adoption, and the other 2.5 percent, with relatives or friends (Zelnik and Kantner, 1974). This places these young women in a very different situation than that of most of their peers. Adolescence and young adulthood is the usual time of life for meeting and socializing with friends, dating, possibly selecting a mate, obtaining an education, and making a career choice. The additional responsibility of motherhood poses serious restrictions on the amount of freedom and time available to do all of these other things. Additionally, such young women are most often ill-prepared for motherhood. They are usually in the midst of establishing their own identities and learning to care for themselves.

Eighty percent of all teens who get pregnant are not married and most do not marry after becoming pregnant (Zelnik et al., 1979). Of those who do marry, the decision is often based on the fact that the young mother and father "have to" marry because of the pregnancy. Teen marriages have a very poor chance of survival. The chance of divorce is two to four times greater for teens who marry than for older people (Gordon, 1973).

Often the young mother will not have a spouse to help her in caring for and raising her new child. Furthermore, even if she does marry the father, it's likely that the marriage will be marred by turbulence and struggle, as the high divorce rate indicates.

There are a number of other strikingly negative consequences to teen pregnancy. First, such pregnancies are marked by increased physical risks, both to the child and to the mother (Felsman, 1987; Fielding, 1978; McKenry et al., 1979). Such problems include prolonged labor, anemia, toxemia, hemorrhaging, miscarriage, and, in the extreme, the pregnant teen's death. The babies have a much greater chance of either being premature or of having a lower than normal birth weight. They are twice as likely to suffer from neurological defects. The mortality rate for these babies is 200 percent higher than that of babies born to older mothers (Bright, 1987). A related finding concerning maternal and child health is that many teenage mothers are poverty stricken and re-

ceive very little prenatal health care (Brown, 1985). This contributes to the health risks of the mothers and their babies.

Other longer term research indicates that negative effects continue long after the baby's birth. Teen mothers are much less likely to finish high school than their peers who are not mothers (Furstenberg, 1976; Papalia and Olds, 1992). Furstenberg, Brooks-Gunn, and Mogan (1987) studied poor urban African American adolescent mothers. Only one-half of them had graduated from high school five years after having their babies. However, ten years later, about two-thirds of them had finished high school.

Adolescent mothers are also likely to be poor, receive public assistance, and have subsequent pregnancies (Papalia and Olds, 1992; Teti and Lamb, 1989). Later in life they are more likely than their peers without children to be unemployed or underemployed (Felsman et al., 1987; Furstenberg, 1976; Furstenberg et al., 1987). Teen mothers tend to have poorer parenting skills and are more likely to abuse their children when compared to more mature mothers (Felsman et al., 1987; Lamb et al., 1987). Thus, the added stress and responsibility of motherhood tend to take a toll on teen mothers. Raising a child demands time, energy, and attention. Time taken to care for a baby must be subtracted from the time available for school, recreational, and educational activities. There are potentially serious impacts on the mental health and daily functioning of young mothers. This is supported by the fact that pregnant teens are more likely to attempt suicide than other girls in their age group (McKenry et al., 1979).

Long term studies also reveal negative effects on the children themselves. As the children of teen mothers mature, they tend to have more emotional, intellectual, and physical problems than their counterparts born to adult mothers (Furstenberg et al., 1987; Klein and Cordell, 1987). More specifically, these children tend to perform more poorly in school and have lower IQs than other children (Baldwin and Cain, 1980; Kinard and Reinherz, 1987; Trussell, 1988). Academic difficulties do not diminish with time; children born to teen mothers tend to be low achievers even in high school (Brooks-Gunn and Furstenberg, 1986).

The consequences of teenage parenthood are emphasized here not to be cynical but to provide a

Portrait of a Single Father

Gary didn't know what to do. Linda had just ruined his day and probably his life. She had just told him that she was pregnant. How could this happen? What could he do?

Gary, a seventeen-year-old high school sophomore, had never done very well in school and had even flunked sixth grade once. Ever since then, he'd been taking "Special Ed" classes and was just barely squeaking by.

He had always considered himself a freak. He liked to do a lot of drugs, that is, whenever he had the money to get them. He also liked to listen to booming rock and was intimately familiar with radio station WROK's top ten hits. His uniform included well-patched blue jeans, construction worker boots, and 18-inch long, healthy but somewhat scraggly, greasy hair.

Beneath this exterior, Gary was an extremely sensitive, bright person. He really cared about other people, although sometimes he had trouble showing it. This thing about Linda and a baby had really shaken him up. He really loved Linda. As a matter of fact, she was the best thing that had ever happened to him. She actually cared about him. It seemed like nobody had ever done that before. Gary really didn't have much self-confidence. The fact that Linda cared simply amazed him.

Gary lived with his mother and younger sister, Hillary, age eleven. He cared about Hillary but they really didn't have much in common. There was too much of an age difference. Sometimes they stuck up for each other, though, when their mother went out with some new boyfriend and came home drunk. That happened pretty often. His mother

was really something else. She was pretty nice. It seemed like she loved him, but she had always had a horrible problem accepting responsibility. A lot of time he felt like he had to take care of her, instead of vice versa. No, she wasn't one to depend on much.

Another problem was that they were dirt poor. He could never remember having a lot of things. For years he had wanted to learn how to play the guitar. He picked one up two years ago at a sleazy neighborhood auction, but it never really sounded like much. The other problem, of course, was that he felt he had absolutely no talent. He often thought the guitar looked good, though, sitting on an old peach crate in his basement room, his place of retreat.

Sometimes Gary thought about his father out in Utah. Although he only actually saw him once in the last ten years, he talked to him sometimes on the phone on holidays. His big dream was to go out and live with his dad and his dad's new family. Gary liked nature and camping. He thought that Utah would be the perfect place to go to and get away. In his more somber moments, he realized this was only a dream. His dad was pleasant enough on the phone, but he knew he really didn't care. It was fun to think about sometimes, though. Sometimes when he got a better batch of drugs, he'd just sit in his room and think. He dreamed of all the wonderful things he'd do in Utah. That's what it was though, just a dream.

Gary dreamed a lot. He didn't have much hope for the future. He thought that was pretty hopeless. One of his teachers asked him once if he ever thought about going to

---

realistic perspective on teen pregnancy. Teenagers need to be at least intellectually aware of the impacts of motherhood. They need this information in order to make better, more realistic decisions for themselves concerning their sexual activity and their use of birth control. The other reason why it's important to focus on the consequences of teenage pregnancy concerns helping young mothers who already have their babies. Social workers need to understand the problems of teenage parenthood. This is needed to help young mothers realistically appraise their situations, make decisions about what to do for themselves, and get involved with the supportive services they need.

Teenage Fathers

The single father's paternal rights and needs merit some attention. The male teenager's role of biological father is now being distinguished from the role of the mother's potential husband.

In one survey (Robinson, 1969) of 149 single fathers, the men did not appear to shun responsibility. In fact, 61 percent indicated that they wanted to marry the child's mother. They indicated that these feelings went beyond pure moral obligation to do the right thing. In many of these cases, the mother decided against a marriage. The survey also found that

college. College, hah! How could he ever afford to go to college. He couldn't even afford a K-Mart guitar. The other problem was how poorly he always did in school. He stopped studying really years ago. Now he was so far behind he knew he'd never catch up. He didn't like to think much about the future. There was no future in it.

But now Gary's problem was Linda—Linda and the baby. It's funny how he already thought of it as a baby even though it wasn't born yet. He liked the thought of having something that was really his. He liked Linda, too, and he didn't want to lose her. She was crying when she told him she was pregnant. He bet she'd like it if they lived together, or maybe even got married. Then he could move out of his mother's apartment. He could be free and on his own. He could drop out of school. School wasn't much anyhow. Maybe he could get that second shift job slinging burgers at the local hamburger shack. That wouldn't be too bad. He could see his friends there. They could have a good time.

Yeah, that's what he'd do. He'd do a good thing for once in his life. He'd marry Linda and be a father. Maybe everything would be all right then. Maybe they'd all live happily every after.

Epilogue

Gary and Linda did get married four months later. They had a 6 pound, 8 ounce baby boy who they named Billy. The problem was that things really didn't get any better. They didn't change much at all. Gary was still poor. Now,

however, he was poor but with adult responsibilities. He still couldn't afford a guitar. He had to go to work at the hamburger shack every day at 5:00 P.M. just like he used to have to go to school every morning. There wasn't much money for him and Linda to have any fun with. As a matter of fact, there wasn't much money to do anything much at all. Their efficiency apartment was pretty cramped. Sometimes the baby's crying drove him almost crazy. He and Linda weren't doing too well either. When they weren't fighting, they weren't talking. Things hadn't changed much at all. He still didn't have much hope for the future.

Commentary

This case example isn't meant to portray the thoughts of a typical or representative unwed father. For example, Gary was very poor. In reality unwed parents originate in all socio-economic levels. However, this example is intended to illustrate the lack of experience and information adolescents often have available to them. Without information it's difficult to make insightful, well-founded decisions. A major job of a social worker is to help young people in a situation like this rationally think through the alternatives available to them. Potential services need to be talked about and plans need to be made. Young people often need both support and suggestions regarding how to proceed. They need to examine their expectations about the future and make certain that they're being realistic.

more than 60 percent of the fathers visited the babies while they were still in the hospital. These fathers also expressed strong feelings about being the child's father.

However, relatively few single fathers maintain contact with the child or the child's mother after the child reaches the age of two years (Earls and Siegel, 1980). Sawin and Parke (1976) propose that this exclusion is actually due to the larger society's prejudice against single teenage fathers. They hypothesize that our society has a very negative view of teenage males who have intercourse with and impregnate teenage females.

As with teenage mothers, teenage fathers also tend to do less well educationally (Marsiglio, 1986) and economically (Card and Wise, 1978). Because of the obligation to support their family, many opportunities apparently are denied them. They are more likely to leave school and have less education than others their age. They are also more likely to have lesser skilled, more poorly paying jobs than their peers. Finally, as we've already indicated, marital problems are more frequent and divorce is more likely. In other words, teenage fathers, like teenage mothers, have both more disadvantages and greater difficulties surviving than do their peers.

However, a teenage father has a role in relationship to his child. He not only has feelings concerning the birth and existence of the child, but he also has attachments and responsibilities. It is not helpful to be punitive about what he's done wrong. Rather, it is important to help him to express his feelings, to more clearly define his role, and to contribute where he can in taking over responsibilities for his child.

Why Do Teens Get Pregnant?

Adolescents often do not use contraception conscientiously and frequently don't use it at all (Beck and Davies, 1987; Strassberg and Mahoney, 1988). Most adolescents fail to use any kind of contraception the first few times they have sex (Crooks and Bauer, 1990). Even when sexual activity is not new to them, most adolescents fail to use a reliable birth control method consistently (Furstenberg, 1984; Zabin et al., 1984). More than a quarter of sexually active teenagers say they *never* use birth control; two-thirds of them say they don't *always* use it (Harris et al., 1986). Why don't teens use birth control?

There are a number of reasons (Harris et al., 1986). When asked, adolescents often say that they don't anticipate having sex and therefore don't get ready for it. This does not agree with their explanations for why other adolescents fail to use contraception. Reasons expressed for the peers' behavior include: not really caring about it; wanting to get pregnant; not liking to use birth control; getting more pleasure from sex without bothering with contraception; having trouble getting it; not knowing how to use it; feeling embarrassed; fearing that parents will find out; and feeling invulnerable to something like pregnancy, which only happens to other people.

One reason for not using contraception involves a type of psychological avoidance. Adolescents are most likely to use some type of contraception when they are involved in a relationship that has some consistency over time (Baker et al., 1988). Avoidance of contraception may be due to their unwillingness to admit to themselves that they're sexually active. Traditionally, the values of virginity in women and intercourse only within marriage were considered important. Some traces of these historic approaches may still subsist. Some young women may illogically feel that if they ignore the issue, it will cease to exist. If they don't think about their own sexual activity, then they don't have to worry about it. Other teenagers may simply want to get pregnant, even when marriage is not anticipated.

Still another reason for not using contraception may be unwillingness to address the issue with a partner. A young woman may feel uncomfortable talking to a partner about such intimate issues. Another fear may be giving her partner a wrong impression. If she appears to know a lot about contraception, she may fear her partner will think her too knowledgeable and experienced.

Lack of accurate information may be yet another reason for the failure to use contraception. For instance, many teens inaccurately believe that they are not old enough to conceive, that they have to have intercourse much more often than they do in order to conceive, that it is perfectly safe to have sex during certain times of the month, and that withdrawal before ejaculation is an effective birth control method (Shah et al., 1975).

Several variables are related to a teenager's likelihood or risk of getting pregnant. For instance, teenagers who are African American or Hispanic, who have parents with relatively low levels of education, and who reside with a single parent are less likely to use contraception (Ford et al., 1979; Harris et al., 1986).

Other variables putting adolescents at higher risk of pregnancy include age and the amount of time that has passed since their first sexual encounter. The younger a woman is when she has sex, the less likely she will be to use any form of birth control (Tanfer and Horn, 1985). Additionally, a young woman is more likely to get pregnant if she has just started having intercourse. Half of initial pregnancies to single adolescents occur within the first year of having sex; about 20 percent of these pregnancies happen in the first month (Zabin et al., 1979).

On a more positive note, young males apparently are taking more responsibility for contraception than they have in the past (Sorenson, 1973). About 40 percent of young women using birth control depend on their male partners to do it (Adams et al., 1989). This coincides with an increased use of condoms in response to AIDS awareness.

Sex Education

A heated controversy often develops over the issue of providing teens with information about sex. This is true even in the age of AIDS (Acquired Immunodeficiency Syndrome) (Gibbs, 1991). The fear is that giving adolescents information about sexuality will encourage them to start experimenting sexually. An underlying assumption is that adolescents won't think about sex or be interested in it unless someone around them brings up the subject.

Two fallacies can be pointed out in this approach. First, it assumes that adolescents have little or no access to sexual information other than that which adults around them choose to give. Hunt (1974) did an extensive study of sexual attitudes and behavior by surveying 982 males and 1,044 females. He found that 59 percent of the males and 46 percent of the females felt that they had obtained most of their sexual information from friends. An additional 20 percent of the males and 22 percent of the females gave reading material as their primary source of information. The fact that friends are the primary source of sex information for young people has been supported by other research (Handelsman et al., 1987; Kallen et al., 1983; Kirby et al., 1979).

Obviously, adolescents are functioning within a complex environment which exposes them to many new things and ideas. They are not locked up in a sterile cage. A tremendous emphasis is placed on sexuality and sexual behavior by the media; television, magazines, newspapers, and books are filled with sexual episodes and anecdotes. Adolescents have numerous exposures to the concept of sex.

A second fallacy is that adolescents will automatically try anything they hear about. If a parent tells a young person that some people are murderers, will the young person automatically go out and try murdering someone? Of course not. Although adults, especially parents, might wish they had such control over adolescents, they do not.

Perhaps an analogy concerning sex education could be made to the situation of buying a used Chevy van. An analogous assumption would be that it would be better to have no information about how the van works prior to buying it and hope for the best. This is ludicrous. In this situation you would want as

Parents tend to issue orders rather than discuss sexual issues with their children.

much information as possible to make the best decision about whether to buy the van or not. It would behoove you to take the van to your favorite mechanic to have it thoroughly evaluated. You would both need and want information. People, including adolescents, need as much information as possible in order to make responsible decisions about their own sexual behavior and avoid ignorant mistakes. It is illogical to deprive them of information and have them act on the basis of hearsay and chance.

The primary source of information about sex is friends, and yet friends probably don't know much more about sex than they do. Information that is available is likely to be vague and inaccurate. Just because adolescents use sexual terms does not mean they are very knowledgeable about sexuality. Often these words refer to genital or sexually related body parts. Frequently these terms are vulgar and shocking.

Another aspect of the sex education controversy is the idea that sex education should be provided by parents in the home. This is a virtuous idea. However, on closer scrutiny some problems are evident. Hass (1979, p. 166) found that approximately two-thirds of both male and female adolescents felt that they were not able to talk about sexuality with their parents. Libby and Nass (1971) examined the reactions of parents to adolescent sexual activity. They discovered a tendency for parents to issue orders rather than discuss sexual issues with their children. The following statements were typical of the type of comments made by parents: "I try to keep them from knowing too much"; "I think sex education corrupts the minds of fifteen- or sixteen-year-olds"; "My parents didn't tell me about it. I don't discuss it either"; "Kids know too much already" (p. 230). Needless to say, these statements reflect a negative attitude concerning talking about sex. An implication is that it's easier to avoid the whole issue. This approach interferes with open, honest communication about sex between parents and child.

One Cleveland study examined the attitudes of 1,400 parents toward sex education. Most parents thought it was a good idea for their children to learn about sexuality and reproduction before they became adolescents. However, only 8 percent of the fathers studied and less than 15 percent of the mothers said that they were comfortable enough or knowledgeable enough to talk about sexual intercourse with their children (Roberts and Holt, 1980).

Public opinion polls over the past fifteen years indicate that 80 to 86 percent of adults in America support the provision of sex education in schools (Gordon, 1992). Additionally, when sex education is made available, only 5 percent of parents refuse to allow their children to participate (Alan Guttmacher Institute, 1981; Kirby et al., 1979). Sex educators do not want to take the parents' place as sex educators (Dickman, 1982, p. 21). Rather, they want to ensure that children have adequate and accurate information about sex. Many times parents are uncomfortable or embarrassed talking about sex with their children. Often they feel they don't know enough of the specifics to intelligently educate a child. One student shared her eight-year-old son's reaction to her own discomfort in talking to him about sex. As she was trying to explain to him some of the basics of human reproduction, he put his hand on her arm and said, "It's okay, Mom, I get the general idea."

With the extensive publicity given to AIDS in the past few years, more schools have opted to provide sex education programs. Gordon (1992) asserts that "perhaps 10 percent of American children are exposed to anything approaching a legitimate sex education program" (p. 1). However, there is a wide range of course content which can be included in a sex education curriculum. A sex education course can focus only on physical content. Specific topics such as birth control may or may not be covered. Community, parental, and moral values may or may not be integrated into the curriculum. Masters, Johnson, and Kolodny (1988) urge that "sex education should cover the problems surrounding sexuality, but it should also discuss such aspects of sex as love, intimacy, and interpersonal responsibility" (p. 236).

There has been increasing support that sex education can both increase the amount of information teenagers have about sexuality and alter their sexual behavior (Benson et al., 1986; Marks and Cates, 1986; Kirby et al., 1979). For example, a Johns Hopkins University study of students in an inner-city senior high school found that providing an extensive sex education curriculum in addition to furnishing free contraception and birth control counseling resulted in 30 percent fewer pregnancies; additionally, girls chose to postpone having sexual relations for significantly longer periods of time (Zabin et al., 1986). Other research supports the relationship between sex education programs and decreased pregnancy rates (Zelnik and Kim, 1982). Significant decreases in the incidence of sexually transmitted diseases such as gonorrhea has also been clearly linked to the provision of good sex education programs in schools (Levine, 1970).

It is each individual's responsibility and our professional aim as social workers to assist people in making the best choices possible in their unique situations. The choice to become sexually active also has potential positive and negative consequences. Positively, one can potentially gain warmth, love, and physical enjoyment from sexual activity. Negatively, however, one can either procreate an unwanted pregnancy or contract a sexually transmitted disease.

Sex Education in the Age of AIDS

When AIDS was identified in the early 1980s, the two highest risk groups in the United States were intravenous drug users and gay or bisexual men (Strunin and Hingson, 1987). However, now the spread of infection in the general heterosexual population is growing at a faster rate than in these initial high-risk groups. AIDS transmission through heterosexual sexual activity is significant. The number of adolescent cases identified doubles every fourteen months (Gibbs, 1991). Additionally, the Centers for Disease Control (1988) report that 21 percent of all AIDS cases identified are people in the twenty- to twenty-nine-year-old age group. Because it often takes a period of up to ten years to exhibit any symptoms of AIDS, many of these young adults probably contracted the disease during their adolescent years. (Because AIDS can impact people throughout their life spans, it will be covered in greater depth in Chapter 10.)

AIDS merits intense concern when talking about sex education with adolescents and young adults. In the 1980s, it was established that adolescents generally had inadequate information about AIDS and that they did not feel they were vulnerable to contracting the disease (McGill et al., 1989; Price et al., 1985; Simkins and Kushner, 1986; Taylor-Nicholson et al., 1989). Likewise, adolescents tended not to use protection when engaging in high-risk behaviors (DiClemente et al., 1986; Strunin and Hingson, 1987).

It appears that adolescents today are better informed about the prevention and contraction of AIDS than in years past (Adame et al., 1991). In view of the extensive publicity given to AIDS, many more schools have opted to develop or intensify their sex education programs. However, serious gaps in education still exist. One study found that over half of entering freshman felt they were at less risk of contracting AIDS than other people (Adame et al., 1991). Another interesting finding is that young people who had AIDS education in high school are no more knowledgeable than those who did not (Adame, et al., 1991). There is also some indication that Hispanic students are less knowledgeable about AIDS than either African American or white students; to some extent, this might be due to a language barrier (Negy and Webber, 1991).

Fielstein, Fielstein, and Hazelwood (1992) studied 175 new college freshman. They found that most of the freshmen had gotten the bulk of their information about AIDS from the media. The students were able to answer questions about AIDS transmission and prevention correctly 90 percent of the time. However, between 12 and 20 percent of the freshmen harbored some significantly inaccurate perceptions. For example, they did not understand the high risks involved in such behaviors as anal intercourse (penetration by one person's penis of another person's anus). They also perceived certain behaviors as being high risk that really were not. For example, a number of young people thought that homosexual behavior, donating blood, and sharing drinking cups put people at high risk of contracting AIDS. Similarly, Adame, Taylor-Nicholson, Wang, and Abbas (1991) found that 17 percent of college freshmen interviewed thought that kissing was dangerous and 27 percent felt that sharing combs and toothbrushes were high-risk behaviors.

Almost all of the research discussed here examines the attitudes and knowledge base of *college students*. We do not know about the attitudes and knowledge base of adolescents who do not go to college. It might be argued that they have even less access to information about AIDS than their college-bound peers. Thus, there continues to be a great need to improve the quality of AIDS education. The U.S. Department of Health and Education (1988, pp. 17–18) makes the following recommendations for selecting material to use in educational programming about AIDS:

1. Teach about high-risk behaviors. Because of their high rates of sexual activity, adolescents should know specifically which behaviors are the most dangerous and which are the safest. They should be taught and encouraged to take responsibility for their own safety. For instance, using condoms during sexual intercourse makes transmission of contaminated body fluids less likely, although avoidance of intercourse is the safest course of all. Likewise, young people should be aware of the dangers of sharing needles when using illicit drugs.

2. Present the facts in a straightforward manner. The facts about AIDS, its transmission, and its prevention should be taught honestly and directly. This is true even when talking about explicit sexual behavior and condom use. Responsible behavior should be clearly defined in adolescents' minds. It is important that AIDS educators themselves be comfortable in talking about these potentially anxiety-producing topics.

3. Convey values about responsibility and respect for oneself and for the well-being of others. The importance of values should be emphasized throughout AIDS education. Behaviors can be discussed within the context of

evaluating alternatives. For example, adolescents can be helped to evaluate the potential positive and negative consequences of sexual behavior and drug use. They can be encouraged to establish a firm set of values regarding what they feel is right and wrong. One focus involves enhancement of their own self-esteem. They have the right to control their behavior and not be subject to the oppressive pressure of peers. They can also be helped to examine the consequences of their own behavior upon others.

4. Select appropriate materials. Depending on the age level, children and adolescents need access to different types of information. For example, in kindergarten through third grade, the "primary goal is to allay children's fears of AIDS and to establish a foundation for more detailed discussion of sexuality and health [later] at [the] sixth grade level" of AIDS education (National Coalition of Advocates for Students, NCAS, 1987). In grades four and five, the thrust should be similar to that used earlier, but with "increased emphasis on acknowledging that bodies have natural sexual feelings [and] helping children examine and affirm their own and their families' values" (NCAS, 1987). Finally, in grades six through twelve, "the primary goal should be to teach students to protect themselves and others from infection with the AIDS virus" (NCAS, 1987). It is beyond the scope of this text to detail an entire AIDS or sex education curriculum. However, there are numerous excellent curriculum development aids available.[1]

5. Promote parental involvement. AIDS education addresses a broad range of sensitive topics. Parents should be integrally involved in planning and developing the curriculum. They should be fully aware of what and how content will be presented. For instance, one means of soliciting parental involvement is to form a task force including both parents and educators. Subsequently, other parents can be invited to attend previews of the proposed educational programming prior to presenting it to students.

Sexually Transmitted Diseases (STDs)

Sexually transmitted diseases, often referred to as STDs, are infections that people can contract through sexual relations. They include some conditions which can also be transmitted in other ways not involving sexual contact. In the past STDs were referred

---

1. The San Francisco AIDS Foundation, 333 Valencia St., PO Box 6182, San Francisco, CA 94101-6182 is one source of educational materials targeting AIDS education.

---

to as veneral diseases or VD. The term STD is preferable because it doesn't sound quite as negative and demeaning as VD.

We've already established that young people are choosing to become sexually active earlier. Yet, when young they have very limited experience. It's critical that they have as much information as possible in order to make up for their lack of experience. They need to make responsible decisions both for themselves and for their partners. They need information about what common STDs are, how they are transmitted, what could be their effects, if and how they can be cured, and, perhaps most importantly, how they can be prevented. Discussion here will focus on information about some of the most common STDs. These include gonorrhea, chlamydial infections, syphilis, and genital herpes. Because of its deadliness, recent increase, easy transmission, variety of methods of transmission, and massive social, economic, and legal ramifications, AIDS will be discussed in much greater detail later in Chapter 10.

Gonorrhea

It is estimated that 1.8 to 2 million people contract gonorrhea each year (Centers for Disease Control, 1987; Hatcher, et al., 1990). Gonorrhea is easily transmitted by various sexual contacts including intercourse, oral stimulation of the genitals, and possibly even kissing (Robertson et al., 1980). A woman has a 50 percent chance of contracting gonorrhea if she has intercourse with a contagious man one time (Platt et al., 1983). A man's chance of becoming infected after having intercourse with a contagious woman is one in four or five (Hooper et al., 1978). It's also been established that the gonorrhea organism can live up to two hours on materials like wet toilet paper or on toilet seats (Gilbaugh and Fuchs, 1979).

A man's symptoms will include a yellowish, puslike discharge secreted from the opening at the tip of the penis. Urination is usually quite painful. Only about 10 percent of men have no symptoms. Symptoms may first appear as early as one day or as late as a month after contraction.

Most women, on the other hand, are asymptomatic. That is, as many as 80 percent have no noticeable symptoms (Hatcher, et al., 1990). This is because in the vast majority of cases, the infection invades the cervix. Thus, a woman is not as likely as a man either to notice the discharge or to experience pain. The bad thing about this is that without symptoms, a woman won't know she has it. If she doesn't know she has it, she won't seek treatment and, therefore, will continue to be contagious.

If unchecked, gonorrhea usually spreads from the cervix, up the uterus, and into the fallopian tubes. It then can cause pelvic inflammatory disease and possibly sterility if the fallopian tubes become blocked with scar tissue. Since men feel pain as a symptom, they are much more likely to seek treatment. Otherwise, the organisms can move into other sexually related organs, causing pain and possibly fever. Sterility is possible, although it occurs infrequently. Other possible results of gonorrhea include infection and the resulting inflammation of other organs such as the heart, brain, or joints.

Diagnosis of gonorrhea involves "identification of the bacteria in a smear from the tip of the penis, vagina, anus, or throat or by culture of the bacterium" (Denney and Quadagno, 1992, p. 529). Treatment entails administering antibiotics. People remain contagious to others until they are cured.

Chlamydial Infections

Chlamydial infections are now the most common STDs in the United States; 4.5 million new infections are diagnosed annually (Centers for Disease Control, 1987; Ferris, 1990). Chlamydia is a specific type of bacterium that invades and lives in the cells of an infected person. A number of diseases can result. Among the most common are mucopurulent cervicitis in women and nongonococcol urethritis or NGU (also referred to as nonspecific urethritis or NSU) in men.

Mucupurulent cervicitis is "an infection of the cervix which causes a discharge" (Denney and Quadagno, 1992, p. 531). If not treated, long-term effects for women may include cervical damage, pelvic inflammatory disease, infected fallopian tubes, and potentially sterility. About 40 percent of women experience no symptoms (Mundy et al., 1986). Therefore, as with gonorrhea, many women do not seek treatment. NGU is an infection of a man's urethra. It is usually, although not always caused by chlamydia. Symptoms usually include a thin, clear discharge and pain upon urination. If not treated, it can lead to infertility.

Chlamydial infections can easily be passed back and forth between sexual partners even when one has been cured. People contracting chlamydial infections are supposed to refer all previous sexual partners for treatment. It should be noted that as many as 45 percent of all people contracting gonorrhea also have a chlamydial infection (Centers for Disease Control, 1989). Diagnosis of a chlamydial infection can be done using a variety of techniques including scraping cells from the genitals and growing a culture. Treatment commonly involves the administration of antibiotics such as tetracycline or erythromycin.

Syphilis

Syphilis is contracted by 30,000 to 85,000 people each year in the United States (Centers for Disease Control, 1987; Hatcher et al., 1990). Although it is not as common as either gonorrhea or chlamydial infections, syphilis is much more deadly. Syphilis is transmitted during sexual intercourse and through blood transfusions. Also, a fetus may get it from its mother.

The symptoms progress through four phases. The first is the *primary stage*. Most notable during this phase is the appearance of a round, crater-like sore, which, despite its very unpleasant appearance, is painless. The chancre, as this lesion is called, marks the spot where the bacteria initially penetrated the body. Most frequently, syphilis enters the body through a mucous membrane, around the tip of the penis, in the vagina, or at the cervix. Syphilis can, however, also be contracted through a cut anywhere on the skin. The chancre usually appears within three to four weeks after syphilis has been contracted; however, this period may be as short as ten days or as long as three months (Hyde, 1986). Within several weeks the chancre disappears.

The *secondary stage* begins with a rash that spreads all over the body. It neither itches nor hurts. This stage begins one week to six months after the chancre disappears. By this time, the bacteria have spread throughout the body. A number of other symptoms may characterize this stage, including sore throat, hair loss, headaches, weight loss, nausea, joint pains, and fever. Most of these symptoms could also characterize a number of other illnesses. This might mask the fact that a person has syphilis. The individual might not seek treatment at all or seek treatment for some other illness.

There is another aspect of the disease that makes it difficult to pin down and diagnose. The time periods during which these generalized symptoms occur vary greatly and can be long. It's difficult to relate the symptoms of a disease like syphilis to a time perhaps six months earlier when it was contracted. These symptoms may last from two weeks to sporadic appearance for six months.

The *latent stage* begins sometimes after all secondary-stage symptoms have disappeared. No symptoms occur during this stage. The bacterial concentrate in some organ of the body like the brain, spinal cord, or bones. Fifty to 70 percent of all people who contract syphilis remain in this stage forever and live out their lives in a normal way. After about one year in this stage, they are no longer contagious. One exception is a pregnant woman, who may pass the disease on to her child.

However, the rest of the people who progress to the latent stage enter the final *late stage* of syphilis. During this phase the bacteria viciously attack the organs where they've concentrated. The heart, eyes, brain, spinal cord, digestive organs, liver, or endocrine glands may be involved. The results can include "paralysis, insanity, blindness, and death" (Masters et al., 1988, p. 564).

Blood tests are usually used to diagnose syphilis, although a number of other tests can also be used. Penicillin is the preferred treatment, although antibiotics such as tetracycline are also effective.

Genital Herpes

Genital herpes is caused by a virus and is characterized by small, painful blisters. Other symptoms may include headache, fever, muscular aches, and painful urination. Between 200,000 and 500,000 people contract genital herpes each year, adding to the 5 to 20 million people already estimated to be infected (Centers for Disease Control, 1987; Hatcher et al., 1990).

The technical name for genital herpes is *herpes simplex virus type 2* (HSV-2). Except for minor differences in its genetic code, this virus closely resembles herpes simplex virus type 1 (HSV-1), which causes fever blisters or cold sores often found in and around the mouth. Approximately 85 percent of the herpes sores found on people's genitals result form HSV-2; the remainder from HSV-1 (Gunby, 1983). Likewise,

15 percent of herpes found around the mouth is HSV-2 and the remaining 85 percent HSV-1. Either virus, if it affects the genitals, can be referred to as genital herpes. Transmission from mouth to genitals or vice versa can occur during oral-genital sex. It can also occur by touching fingers to infected areas and subsequently touching other receptive mucous membranes such as those in the genital area or in the mouth.

The first outbreak of genital herpes usually lasts an average of twelve days and frequently is the most painful and uncomfortable; this outbreak typically occurs two to twenty days after exposure to the virus (Denney and Quadagno, 1992). After the initial outbreak, recurrences vary from one individual to another. That is, outbreaks will vary greatly in frequency, duration, and severity. Some people never experience another outbreak. Others experience them regularly. One study indicated that people with herpes average four outbreaks each year (Corey and Spear, 1986). For some people, outbreaks seem to be related to high levels of stress.

One of the most serious consequences of herpes is that it may be passed on to a developing fetus through the placenta. Although this occurrence is not common, herpes can cause birth defects. Herpes also may be contracted by the newborn during delivery if contact is made with an infected cervix or vagina. Mothers who have herpes are often urged to have a cesarean section performed so that the baby avoids contagion. Another serious aspect of herpes is that it appears to be related to cancers of the vulva and cervix. Since both of these cancers are usually responsive to treatment, women with herpes are encouraged to have gynocological examinations and pap smears every six months.

Since herpes is a virus, there is no cure. Like a bad cold or flu, which are also caused by viruses, a cure has not been found. Although not a cure, the drug Acyclovir when applied to the blisters appears to ease the discomfort, especially during the first outbreak. This drug is also now available in a pill form called Zovirax. When used on a long-term basis, the drug seems to diminish the number and severity of outbreaks. However, such long-term use runs the danger of encouraging the development of new, mutated strains of the virus that would be more resistant to the drug's effects.

A woman's chances of contracting herpes if she has sexual intercourse with an infected man is 80 to 90 percent (Straus et al., 1985). A man, on the other hand, has a 50 percent chance of contracting the disease from an infected woman (Masters et al., 1988). Herpes is most contagious during an outbreak of painful blisters. The blisters should not be touched. However, there is increasing evidence that herpes can also be transmitted when no symptoms are apparent (Brock et al., 1990; Rooney et al., 1986).

Other STDs

A number of other STDs may occur. However, it is beyond the scope of this text to address them all in detail. For instance, pubic lice or "crabs" are tiny creatures who live at the base of pubic hair and feed on blood. They can cause severe itching. A prescription drug sold under the brand name Kwell kills pubic lice within twenty-four hours. Genital warts are yet another STD. The warts have a texture resembling cauliflower and are found on the genitals. They can be treated with a solution of Podophyllin mixed with alcohol, which causes the warts to fall off within several days or weeks. There appears to be a relationship between genital warts and cervical cancer.

Preventing STDs

Suggestions for preventing STDs include using condoms because they prevent contact between the penil tissues and a woman's genital tissues. Spermicides have also been found to help kill some STDs. Washing the genital areas with soap and water before sexual contact can help. Urinating both before and after intercourse can also help clear the urethra of bacteria.

These are specific behaviors that people can follow to help prevent contracting an STD. However, perhaps suggestions concerning thought and choice are the most effective. Masters et al. (1988, pp. 598–99) make six suggestions for preventing the transmission of STDs. First, each person should "be informed." Know what STDs are and how they can be contracted. Second, each individual should "be observant." This doesn't necessarily mean one should say, "Well, excuse me, dear, but may I please take a moment to examine your genitals for symptoms of STDs?" However, it does mean that being aware and

watching for symptoms may help a person avoid contracting a disease. Third, "be selective." Choose sexual partners carefully. A partner who's had several other sexual partners recently can significantly increase his or her risk of having an STD. Fourth, "be honest." That means if a person has an STD, he or she should tell a prospective partner about it. It also means that if someone is worried about a potential partner having an STD, that person should ask about it. Fifth, "be cautious." Follow the suggestions mentioned earlier, such as using condoms for protection. Sixth, if a person thinks he or she might have an STD, that person should "be promptly tested and treated."

Major Methods of Contraception

Anyone who is considering becoming sexually active and who is not intentionally trying to conceive a child needs accurate and specific information about contraceptive methods. This includes adolescents. Without adequate information, responsible decisions cannot be made. Information helps to prevent people from taking unnecessary risks. We've already established the importance of sex education. Information concerning contraception is especially important. The risk of unplanned pregnancy and the resulting impact on the lives of adolescents is too critically important to ignore.

Major methods of contraception are described in the following sections. Their levels of effectiveness are indicated, and the advantages and disadvantages of each method are explored. No one best method of birth control exists for everybody. Each individual must select a method according to how it fits with his or her individual lifestyle. Some methods are easier to use than others. Some methods require responsible adherence to a schedule. Other methods are best suited for persons who only have occasional sexual contacts.

The Pill

Birth control pills or oral contraceptives are the most effective form of contraception other than sterilization (Masters et al., 1988). Over 16 million women used some type of birth control pill in 1991, an increase from 11.8 million in 1985 (Hatcher et al., 1992).

A family planning clinician assists teenagers with a questionnaire on premarital sex. With the advent of AIDS, parents, teachers, and health administrators are recognizing the growing need for sex education in clinics and schools.

There are two major types of pill.[2] Various companies produce over twenty-five brands of these two types of pills. The most commonly used type of birth control pill combines a synthetic estrogen and a progestin (both primary female hormones). The combined pill targets a twenty-eight-day menstrual cycle and is distributed in monthly packs.

Combined pills are taken in one of two ways. The most commonly used brands of combined pills are sold in packages of twenty-one pills, which should be taken daily until they are used up. A woman then refrains from starting her next monthly pack of pills for seven days. During this time she will have her menstrual period. Other brands of combined pills come in packs of twenty-eight pills. These include placebos or ineffective sugar pills for the last seven days of the cycle. This serves to reinforce a woman's habit of taking one pill each day.

Combined pills prevent the ovaries from ovulating, or releasing a ripened egg ready for fertilization. In a sense, they trick the body into thinking that the woman is pregnant. A pregnant woman temporarily stops ovulating in order to prevent multiple pregnancies.

Combined pills are *theoretically* 99.9 percent effective, which is considered excellent (Hatcher et al., 1990). Theoretical effectiveness rates refer to the number of women out of 100 in whom pregnancy is prevented. A theoretical effectiveness rate of 100 percent means that for every 100 women, none should become pregnant.

___

2. It is beyond the scope of this text to provide all the practical, detailed information currently available about the various methods of contraception. However, many extremely useful materials are available. For instance, Elizabeth Thompson Ortiz has written *Your Complete Guide to Sexual Health* (Englewood Cliffs, NJ: Prentice Hall, 1989) for Planned Parenthood. She provides practical, straightforward information concerning a broad range of contraceptive and other health issues. Hatcher et al. provide current, detailed information in *Contraceptive Technologies* (New York: Irvington, 1990, 1992).

However, the combined pill's *actual* effectiveness rate is approximately 97 percent (Hatcher et al., 1990). Theoretical effectiveness refers to the supposed effectiveness of a means of contraception when it is used correctly. Actual effectiveness, on the other hand, refers to how effective it is in actual use. The differences between the two rates probably can be explained by human error. For example, forgetting to take a pill one day increases the chance of pregnancy. Or, with other birth control methods, failing to use them every time a person has sexual intercourse decreases the actual effectiveness rate.

The other major type of birth control pill is usually referred to as the mini-pill, which provides a lower dosage of hormones than the combined pill, and is slightly less effective. Its theoretical effectiveness rate is 99.5 percent, but its actual effectiveness rate can be as low as 90 percent (Hatcher et al., 1990). Mini-pills contain only artificial progestin, and women who take them may continue to ovulate. Rather, mini-pills cause changes in the interior uterine lining, the consistency of cervical mucus, and the functioning of the fallopian tubes so that it is more difficult for an egg to be fertilized and implanted on the uterine wall. Mini-pills can provide a good contraceptive alternative. There are indications that such pills pose fewer health risks than do combined pills (Ortiz, 1989). Both combined pills and mini-pills should be taken regularly at approximately the same time each day.

Today's birth control pills have relatively lower dosages of hormones than they did two decades ago. This is to minimize unpleasant side effects. However, the fact that they are low dosage pills makes it more important that they be taken at approximately the same time each day. Otherwise, there is a chance that their pregnancy inhibiting abilities will be decreased to the point where they will not work. With combination pills, it is important that the hormonal levels maintained by the pill do not drop to a level that makes ovulation possible. Once ovulation occurs, pregnancy is possible. With mini-pills, if the internal reproductive environment is not kept hostile enough to prevent fertilization and implantation, pregnancy may occur.

Ortiz (1989) cautions that "even the best organized woman will forget a pill once in a awhile" (p. 206). She suggests: "If you forget one pill, take two the next day. If you forget two pills in a row, catch up by taking two each for the next two days, and use a back-up method such as the condom for the rest of the cycle. If you forget three pills in a row, your protection for that cycle is probably lost, so stop taking them and wait for your period. Then start again. Use another form of birth control, such as condoms or foam, until you start the pills again. If you are on the mini-pill, keep on taking the pills but use another method of contraception as well until after your next period" (p. 206).

Advantages of taking either form of birth control pill are numerous. They are very effective. They are fairly easy to use, in that they must simply be swallowed daily. Nothing needs to be inserted into the vagina. No complicated process is involved. Nothing interferes with the spontaneity of a sexual encounter. Those who are frequently sexually active are always prepared.

Disadvantages to taking birth control pills include undesirable side effects such as nausea, headaches, constipation, water retention and the resulting swelling, minor increases in blood pressure, and irregular vaginal discharges. These side effects resemble those of the first trimester of pregnancy. This is because they are due to similar changes in hormonal levels. These symptoms usually disappear after two to three months, as they do in pregnancy. Changing brands of birth control pills sometimes helps because different brands often have minor variations in hormonal dosages. Such variations affect various women differently. Additionally, women taking the combined pill who suffer more severe side effects might consider trying the mini-pill. Negative consequences tend to be less severe with the mini-pill.

Another disadvantage to taking birth control pills is possible weight gain due to increased water retention. Some women indicate that they have an increased incidence of vaginal infections due to changes in their vaginal mucus. Additionally, since the pill is a prescription drug, cost is somewhat prohibitive.

Birth control pills should not be taken when a woman is pregnant as there are some indications that they can cause damage to a fetus. Nor should pills be taken during breastfeeding as they "cause a decrease in the amount and quality of milk produced" (Ortiz, 1989, p. 205). Birth control pills also have interactive effects with some other drugs, such as insulin, blood-thinning medications, and some tranquilizers, that can be harmful to the user. Some medications such as antibiotics and some tranquilizers can decrease the pill's effectiveness. Thus, any woman taking birth control pills should check with her physician regarding possible interactive effects with any other drugs she may be taking.

The most serious health risks in taking the pill are cardiovascular problems, such as an increased chance of blood clots in the circulatory system. The danger is that the clot can cause damage to the lungs or the brain. However, this danger must be viewed in perspective. Blood clots cause 2 or 3 deaths annually for every 100,000 women who take the pill (Rinehart and Piotrow, 1979). The death rate for pregnancy and delivery is 14 deaths per 100,000 (Hyde, 1982, p. 142). A second cardiovascular danger is the increased risk of having a heart attack. However, this is true primarily for women who smoke and for women over the age of thirty (Mann and Inman, 1975; Rosenberg et al., 1980).

Because of the associated cardiovascular problems, women over age thirty-five are discouraged from taking the pill. This is especially true for those who smoke (Planned Parenthood Association of Wisconsin, undated).

In the past, questions have been raised regarding the relationship between the pill and cancer. There is no credible evidence that the pill causes cancer (Kols et al., 1982; Rinehart and Piotrow, 1979). As a matter of fact, there is evidence that birth control pills actually protect women against some kinds of cancer, particularly ovarian cancer and cancer of the uterine lining (Centers for Disease Control, 1983). It might be noted that an earlier form of birth control pill which was referred to as the sequential pill was found to bring about uterine cancer. Of course, its use has since been prohibited.

The possible relationship between birth control pills and breast cancer has also been an issue. However, some large-scale research has shown this not to be the case (Cancer and Steroid Hormone study, 1986; Lipnick et al., 1986).

There should be a note of caution here, however. It is too early to make a definite statement that birth control pills never cause cancer under any circumstances. Some forms of cancer may take twenty, thirty, or even forty years to develop. Longer term research is necessary to counter this possibility.

Birth control pills have some positive side effects. Women who take the pill tend to have a decreased menstrual flow, have less painful cramping, and menstruate on a more regular basis (Mishell, 1982). They are only half as likely to fall prey to pelvic inflammatory disease, which can cause sterility (Kols et al., 1982; Senanayake and Kramer, 1980).

One fear about the pill has proven to be unfounded, namely, that women who take the pill will have difficulty getting pregnant later. Although it appears that women must usually wait about three months after stopping the pill in order to get pregnant, no long-term effects in fertility have been found (Maier, 1984, p. 262).

One important aspect to consider before using the pill as a means of contraception is a person's general approach to life. In other words, a person must be notably responsible and conscientious in order to take the pill regularly every day. Many people, despite their good intentions, find it difficult to follow a regimented procedure. Women who are only occasionally sexually active might also find it unappealing to take the pill every day.

The Morning-After Pill

A "morning-after pill" can be taken after a woman has had intercourse. The treatment of choice in the United States has the brand name Ovral (Hatcher et al., 1992). The procedure involves taking two Ovral pills twelve hours apart after intercourse has occurred. Then two more Ovral pills are taken twelve hours after the first dose. It is critically important that the pills be taken within seventy-two hours after intercourse. It is highly recommended that they be taken within twelve to twenty-four hours following intercourse to maximize their effectiveness. Ovral has a high success rate and few unpleasant side effects (Hatcher et al., 1992).[3]

The pills may cause some nausea the first day or so after ingestion. A woman should begin menstruating again within two to three weeks. In the event that she does not begin her period within that time or experiences any of a number of danger signs, she should see

---

3. Pregnancy will probably be prevented if an intrauterine device (IUD) is inserted in the uterus within five days after intercourse or if a woman takes a high dose of birth control pills (this procedure, however, usually has a number of negative side effects).

her physician immediately. Danger signs include severe abdominal pains, severe chest pain or cough, severe headache or dizziness, eye problems such as blurred vision, and severe leg pain in the calf or thigh (Hatcher et al., 1992).

The U.S. Food and Drug Administration has approved Ovral for birth control purposes only. It is not approved for use as a morning-after approach in preventing pregnancy.

There has been considerable debate over another French abortion drug, RU 486, which, as of this writing, cannot be distributed legally in the United States. The controversy heightened when a twenty-nine-year-old pregnant woman identifying herself only as Leona purchased the drug in England and publicly attempted to bring it into the United States for her own use (*Milwaukee Journal*, July 2, 1992). Customs agents confiscated the substance at the airport as she tried to enter the country. She later sought another method of abortion.

The Food and Drug Association (FDA) originally banned the drug in 1989 after being pressured by anti-abortion groups. However, in January 1993, the FDA removed RU 486 from the list of drugs considered illegal for "personal use." Therefore, the drug is legal in the United States if individuals import it themselves for their own use. The FDA, however, has not approved the drug for general sale and distribution.

The fact that the drug has been banned for so long and still cannot be distributed widely has curtailed research in the United States on its effectiveness. Research being done in other countries indicates it has "possible promise in treating endometriosis, glaucoma, and breast and adrenal cancer" (*Milwaukee Journal*, Oct. 8, 1992). Even if the FDA approves RU 486 for general distribution, the future of research on the drug looks bleak. Planned Parenthood Federation of America (1993, p. 2) summarizes the situation:

> In the U.S. today, most pharmaceutical firms have abandoned research and development on new contraceptives. Daunted by the time and money required to bring a drug to market (an average of seven to ten years and an estimated $70 million per drug), and concerned about product liability litigation and liability insurance costs, they have given up. The anti-abortion movement has

contributed to this climate by attempting to block sales of RU 486, calling for boycotts against any company willing to bring it to market.

In the U.S., the one remaining source for major funding of research and development of a drug like RU 486 is the federal government. Unfortunately, the federal government now spends less on contraceptive research in a single year than the Defense Department spends in 15 minutes.

Hormonal Implants and Injections

The first significantly new birth control method the Federal Drug Administration (FDA) has approved in twenty-five years is a hormonal implant called Norplant. The implant consists of six small tubes containing levonorgestrel, a synthetic female hormone, which are placed underneath the skin in the upper arm. The hormones are gradually absorbed by the body over a five-year period, after which the nonbiodegradable implants must be removed.

A major advantage of Norplant is its effectiveness. The implants appear to approach 100 percent in both theoretical and actual effectiveness rates, making it the most effective reversible contraceptive ever sold (Hatcher et al., 1992). Thus, Norplant provides an effective long-term contraceptive method which involves virtually no effort after initial insertion.

Disadvantages include a range of menstrual abnormalities. Almost "80 percent of women using Norplant experience menstrual irregularities during the first six to eight months of usage. These irregularities may include longer menstrual periods, spotting between periods and, in some cases, . . . cessation of menstruation" ("Enter Norplant," 1991, p. 1). The problems usually stop after a year of use. However, it appears that women's adjustment varies widely depending on their "individual chemistry" (pp. 1–2). Some women seem to love them. Others seem to hate them.

A number of other concerns have been expressed ("Enter Norplant," 1991). For instance, the National Women's Health Network recommends that long-term research should have been undertaken to evaluate potential negative consequences before the implants were approved. Other concerns involve the possibilities of encouraging heightened sexual activity among adolescents and forcing implants upon mothers who receive public assistance benefits to prevent them from having more children. Medicaid pays for

Norplant's insertion in all fifty states (Hatcher et al. 1992).

Hormonal Injections

Multitudes of contraceptive methods used around the world have not been approved for distribution in the United States. These include progesterone injections. The most common of such injections, Depo-Provera, is administered once every three to four months. Its actual effectiveness rate appears to approach 100 percent. However, Depo-Provera has been found to cause cancer in some animals; additionally, there are questions regarding its potential for harming a fetus when pregnancy does occur (Denney and Quadagno, 1992).

It is interesting that women in the United States have much less access to contraceptive methods than do women in other countries ("What Else Is Out There?" 1991). Norplant, for instance, was tested in forty-four countries and made available in fourteen before it was approved in the United States. There are a number of reasons for this:

> One reason for the lack of new contraceptives in the U.S. is the long and costly FDA approval process. Another reason is that the number of large companies performing contraceptive research has declined. . . . injectible contraceptives and morning-after therapy are widely used throughout the world. . . . However, political and financial barriers have kept these contraceptives from being made available in the U.S. ("What Else Is Out There?" 1991, pp. 2–3)

Other New Hormonal Approaches

Vaginal rings, which can remain in the vagina for one to six months after insertion, are being tested on an international basis (Denney and Quadagno, 1992). It is possible to take such rings out during sexual intercourse if they cause any discomfort. One vaginal ring is currently being studied which targets nursing mothers; it can be inserted as early as six weeks after a baby's delivery. Other contraceptive approaches under study include "a contraceptive vaccine, a single implant for a woman rather than the six small implants of Norplant, and an IUD [intrauterine device] containing hormones" ("What Else Is Out There?" 1991, p. 3).

The Diaphragm

The diaphragm is one of the barrier methods of birth control. This means that the device acts as a barrier to keep sperm from reaching and fertilizing the egg. The diaphragm is a circular thin piece of rubber stretched over a flexible ring of wire. It is shaped like a dome. A woman inserts it by pushing it with her fingers up into the vagina to cover the cervix.

Before insertion, approximately one teaspoonful of spermicidal cream or jelly should be placed at the bottom of the dome. Then using her finger, she would spread a small amount of cream or jelly around the rim to maximize the potential for contacting sperm. These substances kill any sperm that manage to get around the diaphragm's barrier. The diaphragm can be placed in the vagina up to six hours before intercourse. Then, it should be left in the vagina at least six to eight hours after intercourse to make certain that all of the sperm are disposed of. An additional application of spermicide must be inserted after each act of intercourse. The diaphragm should be checked for holes before each use, which can be done by holding it up to the light.

The diaphragm, when used with a spermicide, can be a very effective form of birth control. Its theoretical effectiveness rating is 94 percent. Actual effectiveness rates vary from 82 to 98 percent depending on the study referred to (Hatcher et al., 1990). Women who use it responsibly every time they have intercourse have an effectiveness rate of approximately 98 percent (Vessey et al., 1982).

Failures may be due to slippage while in use or the development of tiny holes in the diaphragm itself. Additional failures may be due to its inconvenience and difficulty in use. That is, it takes time to prepare for use and insert before every sexual encounter. Sometimes a woman may not have it with her when she needs it. At other times, she may not use it with a spermicide. This greatly decreases its effectiveness. Sometimes it might not be used because it would interfere with spontaneity.

A major advantage of the diaphragm is its safety factor. That is, it causes virtually no health problems. No chemicals are forced into the body. No device is inserted into delicate organs to cause irritation. The only potential difficulty suffered by only a small minority of people is an allergic reaction to a particular brand of spermicide.

Another advantage is its relatively reasonable cost. The diaphragm requires a visit to a physician. Different women need different sizes. After this initial evaluation, a diaphragm is prescribed. It can then be used over a long period of time, provided it is not damaged. In the case of a weight gain or loss of 10 pounds or more, a woman should be reexamined to make certain that her diaphragm still fits.

For individuals who are only occasionally sexually active, the diaphragm need only be used when needed. A person does not have to undergo the ongoing health risks involved in other contraceptive methods when contraception is not needed all of the time.

The major disadvantages of the diaphragm include its relatively complicated method of use and its potential interruption of spontaneity. A person must be willing to go through the correct procedure consistently for it to be an effective birth control method. As is indicated by the high failure rate, this is not always so easy.

The Cervical Cap

The cervical cap, made of a soft plastic or rubber, resembles the diaphragm. Smaller and deeper than a diaphragm, the cap fits snugly over the cervix and is held in place by suction. Like a diaphragm, it acts to keep sperm from entering the uterus. Its theoretical and actual effectiveness rates are similar to the diaphragm's (Hatcher et al., 1990). However, the user's "personal fertility characteristics and . . . her ability to use the method consistently and correctly" impact the cervical cap's effectiveness (Hatcher et al., 1992, p. 200). For example, a woman under age twenty-five who has intercourse more than four times a week is more likely to experience contraceptive failure than a woman who is thirty years old or older and has intercourse less than four times per week. Additionally, misuse increases the chance of pregnancy.

Cervical caps must be fitted to each individual woman's cervix. Women usually can be fitted with one of the available standard sizes. As with the diaphragm, spermicidal jelly or cream should be used, although in a somewhat lesser amount. The cap should be left in the vagina six to eight hours after intercourse. At the latest, it should be removed after seventy-two hours. Leaving the cervical cap in longer poses risks of disagreeable odor and of toxic shock syndrome (Hatcher et al., 1992).

Advantages and disadvantages related to the cervical cap are similar to those of the diaphragm. Although insertion and removal is a bit more difficult than that of the diaphragm, the cervical cap is smaller and less likely to be felt during sexual intercourse.

The Condom

A condom, also called a prophylactic or rubber, is a thin sheath made of latex rubber that fits over the penis. Some are made of the thin tissue of a lamb's intestine; these tend to be more expensive. The condom is initially rolled up into a little circular packet. This packet must be unrolled and placed on the penis. As it fits rather snugly, it acts as another of the barrier methods of birth control. After ejaculation, sperm are contained in the rubber sheath. They are never allowed to enter the vagina. Some condoms have a small bulge at the tip to allow room for semen. Otherwise some empty space must purposefully be left at the tip of the condom so that there is a place to hold the semen.

Condoms are available with a number of variations. Some are lubricated. They come with slightly different textures and a variety of colors.

The theoretical effectiveness of a condom is 98 percent (Hatcher et al., 1990). The effectiveness level rivals that of the pill when the condom is used in conjunction with a contraceptive foam.

The actual effectiveness rate of the condom is 88 percent (Hatcher et al., 1990). Once again, this decrease in actual effectiveness can be attributed to human error. The condom must be held at the base of the penis as the penis is withdrawn from the vagina. This is to make sure that none of the sperm is spilled and can enter the vagina. Condoms should not be reused.

There are many notable advantages to using the condom. First of all, it is the only nonsurgical means to giving the male some direct responsibility for contraception. Condoms are readily available at relatively low cost. They don't require a prior physical examination or a medical prescription. They are small and easy to carry along for use at any time. They cause no side effects, and serve to prevent venereal disease. Latex condoms "lubricated with the spermicide nonoxynol-9" provide the best protection against sexually transmitted diseases (Denney and Quadagno, 1992, p. 224).

Of course, their use has been given much publicity and encouragement over the past few years to help prevent the spread of AIDS (AIDS and its spread will be discussed much more thoroughly later in Chapter 10). (Condoms made from lambs intestines do not protect one from some STDs such as AIDS.) One interesting advantage for some men is that the snug fit helps to maintain an erection for a longer period of time in the cases where this is desirable.

One disadvantage of using the condom is the minor intrusion of spontaneity when placing it on the penis. It is also important that it be withdrawn shortly after ejaculation to avoid spilling semen. Some young men have indicated that they hesitate to carry condoms with them. They feel it looks to a prospective partner as if they were expecting to have intercourse. This might give a bad impression. However, the important thing is to evaluate the potential risks that are involved. The costs of an unwanted pregnancy must be weighed against risking a minor poor impression.

Female Condoms

Two new types of female condoms are currently being evaluated. Both serve to prevent semen from entering the vagina. One type is a latex G-string. A sack is located at the entrance to the vagina. During penile penetration, this sack envelopes the penis and is shoved up into the vagina along with the penis. Neither the penis nor semen can make direct contact with the woman's tissues.

The second type of female condom currently being tested is made of two rings connected by latex. One ring fits over the cervix; the latex protects the cervix from contact with either penis or semen. The other ring rests outside the vagina; here the latex forms a pouch for the penetrating penis, thus protecting the penis from vaginal contact.

The IUD (Intrauterine Device)

The IUD is a plastic device that is placed in a woman's uterus. IUDs have been made in various shapes. They need to be inserted by a physician or trained health professional. Because of potential health problems and the resultant law suits, most major manufacturers have ceased producing IUDs in this country. However, half of the women who use contraception in China use the IUD as do approximately 20 percent of Scandinavian women (Piotrow

et al., 1979). About 60 million women around the world use an IUD (Masters et al., 1988). IUDs are still approved by the Food and Drug Administration. Therefore, U.S. companies are still manufacturing them and marketing them elsewhere. As of 1992, two IUDs, Progestasert and Para Gard, were still available in the United States.

Exactly how the IUD works is a mystery. It is thought that the IUD functions as a "foreign body" or invader inside of the uterus. As a result, the woman's body responds by resisting fertilization and implantation. There is some evidence that this rejection response involves the prevention of eggs being fertilized more than the prevention of a fertilized egg being implanted on the uterine wall (Denney and Quadagno, 1992; Hatcher et al., 1990; Sivin, 1989). The Progestasert contains hormones and the Para Gard contains copper, both of which are thought to contribute to the rejection process.

The IUD is attached to a string that hangs out of the cervix. A woman must check this string regularly to be assured that the IUD is still in place. She can check the IUD by inserting her finger into the vagina and feel if the string is still there.

After initial insertion, a woman should check the string regularly. The IUD is most likely to be expelled during the first three months of use (Hyde, 1982, p. 144). During this time, the string should be checked prior to each sexual encounter. Women are also encouraged to use an additional form of birth control during this period to better insure protection against pregnancy. After three months, women should check the string at least once a month to ensure that the IUD is still in place.

The IUD is considered a very effective form of birth control. Its theoretical or potential rate of effectiveness is 98 to 99 percent, and its actual effectiveness rate 97 percent (Hatcher et al., 1990). This takes its actual or real-life failure rate into account. This is the lowest difference between theoretical and actual failure rate of any of the major methods of birth control.

The major advantage of the IUD is its ease of use. Additionally, it provides continuous protection at a high level of effectiveness.

Two serious health problems when using the IUD are possible. The first is the possibility that the device will perforate or puncture the lining of the uterus.

This occurs in approximately 1 out of every 1,000 insertions of the device (Hatcher et al., 1980). Such perforation of the uterus can cause death.

The other serious potential consequence of using the IUD is pelvic inflammatory disease (PID). PID refers to an infection located in either the uterus or the fallopian tubes. Although PID can have many causes, the IUD appears to be one of them. Apparently, some women are more prone to acquiring PID than others. It is thought that the IUD in its role as an irritant can either aggravate minor existing infections or encourage the development of new infections in some women. It appears that bacteria can travel up the protruding string to cause infections.

The long-term danger of PID is sterility. With serious and repeated infections, scar tissue eventually builds up and blocks the fallopian tubes. This prevents sperm from meeting and fertilizing the egg. Women who are prone to pelvic inflammations are discouraged from using the IUD as a means of birth control.

Other potential side effects of the IUD include increased menstrual cramping and pain in the abdomen, increased level of menstrual flow, and irregular bleeding. Between 10 and 20 percent of women using the IUD experience at least some of these symptoms. They tend to disappear after the first couple of months, however.

Cost is another factor to consider. Despite the initial cost of insertion, the extended length of use over time makes the cost relatively reasonable.

Vaginal Spermicides

Spermicides are chemical contraceptives that function in two ways. First, the chemicals act to kill sperm. Second, the substance itself acts as a barrier that inhibits sperm from entering the uterus. Spermicides are available in creams, jellies, and foams that are squeezed or thrust into a tube, which in turn is inserted into the vagina. Other spermicides include suppositories and thin, tissuelike sheets of spermicide, either of which is placed directly into the vagina. Some condoms are lubricated with a spermicide.

Advantages of spermicides include their relative ease of use, their ready availability, their low cost, their use only when needed, and their lack of health risks. There is also an increasing body of research which supports how spermicides help to prevent some

sexually transmitted diseases including gonorrhea and pelvic inflammatory disease (Cates et al., 1982; Hatcher et al., 1990; Sherris et al., 1984). Despite these advantages, the actual effectiveness rate of spermicides is only about 81 percent; their theoretical effectiveness rate is 97 percent (Hatcher et al., 1990). A woman using a spermicide for contraception has almost 1 chance in 5 of getting pregnant. However, spermicides used in conjunction with other forms of contraception can be very effective. For instance, spermicides used along with a condom approach the effectiveness of the pill, both theoretically and actually.

The Contraceptive Sponge

The contraceptive sponge is a soft, cuplike sponge device that can be inserted into the vagina and covers the cervix. It is saturated with a spermicide to provide additional protection. It was first approved by the U.S. Food and Drug Association in 1983 and is currently available without a prescription at almost any drugstore. Although in some ways it functions like a diaphragm, it does not have to be fitted by a physician. It is universally sold under the brand name Today.

The sponge's effectiveness is based on three principles. First, it acts like a barrier to prevent sperm from entering the cervix. Second, the chemical spermicide it contains acts to kill sperm. Third, its potential for absorbing sperm is also thought to be beneficial.

The sponge is used by dampening it with a little water, squeezing it gently until the spermicidal foam appears, and inserting it into the vagina. It can be inserted up to twenty-four hours prior to having intercourse and should remain in place at least six hours after. Removal involves simply pulling on the attached ribbon and guiding it out of the vagina.

The sponge appears to be more effective for women who have never borne children than for those who have. The sponge's theoretical effectiveness is 94 percent for nonmothers and 91 percent for mothers; the actual effectiveness rates are 87 and 78 percent, respectively (Hatcher et al., 1990). Thus, the sponge resembles the diaphragm and cervical cap in terms of effectiveness for women who have not borne children. There is also some evidence that the sponge is more effective for women during the second year than the first year of their using it (North and Vorhauer, 1985). Failures are due to human mistakes. Apparently, women become more responsible and adept at using the sponge with experience. Failures may be related to simply forgetting to use it or to finding it too inconvenient to insert prior to having sexual intercourse. Another problem may be removal of the sponge too soon after intercourse has occurred.

There are several apparent advantages of the contraceptive sponge. First, it is relatively inexpensive and easy to obtain. It is also easy to insert and use without any messiness. It can be inserted a relatively long time before intercourse occurs, so that it need not interfere with spontaneity. Finally, the sponge provides protection for more than one sexual encounter without having to take additional precautions such as inserting more spermicide into the vagina.

Primary disadvantages involve the fact that there still is some risk of pregnancy. This risk decreases significantly when the sponge is used concurrently with some other means of birth control such as the condom. The other potential disadvantage is a very mild irritation of the vagina or penis, which occurs in only a small percentage of users (Masters et al., 1988).

Withdrawal

Withdrawal refers to withdrawing the penis prior to ejaculating into the vagina. This is not considered a very effective means of birth control. Its actual effectiveness level is 82 percent (Hatcher et al., 1990). The problem is that a few drops of semen are expelled by a pair of glands called the Cowper's glands before the full ejaculation. Both urine and semen pass through the urethra. Urine is acidic. An acidic environment is not conducive for sperm. It is thought that these few drops of liquid are discharged prior to ejaculation in order to clear the urethra of some of its acidic quality and better prepare it for sperm. However, sometimes live sperm remain in the urethra. These can be transported out through the tip of the penis by the Cowper's glands' secretion and still impregnate a woman.

The major advantage of withdrawal is that no extraneous devices or substances are needed. A major disadvantage of withdrawal is that it is not very effective. Another critical disadvantage is that a man does not always have perfect control over his ejaculation. There is the potential for him to lose control and ejaculate directly into the woman's vagina.

The Rhythm Method

The rhythm method refers to monitoring a woman's ovulation cycle and initiating sexual relations only during the safe times of her cycle. The problem is that it is very difficult to determine and accurately chart any woman's particular cycle. The theoretical effectiveness rate ranges from 91 to 97 percent and the actual effectiveness rate ranges from 77 to 85 percent (Hatcher et al., 1990). The rhythm method is considered a poor method of birth control.

There are three types of rhythm methods. Due to their complicated procedures, we will not address them in detail here. The calendar method is the simplest of the three. It involves counting the days of the menstrual cycle and trying to determine when ovulation occurs. The idea is to have intercourse only when it is certain that the woman is not ovulating.

The second method is the basal body temperature method. A woman's body temperature undergoes minor predictable variations depending on where she is in her ovulatory cycle. Using this method involves taking her temperature every morning as soon as she wakes up. A problem with this method is that the major temperature differential occurs only after ovulation has taken place. By this time pregnancy prevention could be too late.

The third type of rhythm method is the cervical mucus method. It necessitates that a woman examine her cervical mucus throughout her menstrual cycle. The consistency, amount, and clarity of the mucus tends to change predictably depending on where she is in her ovulatory cycle.

Many women choose to use these methods in conjunction with each other. This can be considered a complicated, ineffective method of birth control. It is also difficult to maintain.

Sterilization

Sterilization is the most common form of contraception in the United States. Fifty-one percent of all married couples choose to use it (Hatcher et al., 1990). It is considered to be permanent, although it can be reversed in some cases.

Sterilization for women involves a *tubal ligation*, in which the fallopian tubes leading from the ovaries to the uterus are severed. Hence, sperm are unable to reach the egg. Sterilization for men entails a *vasectomy*; a small section of the vas deferens is removed near the place where the scrotum is attached to the body. The vas deferens is "the sperm-carrying tube that begins at the testicle and ends at the urethra" (Crooks and Baur, 1990, p. 781). Thus, sperm are not ejaculated.

Many young people ask whether sterilization interferes with sexual responsiveness. They wonder if having a vasectomy means that a man will not be able to ejaculate or have an orgasm. This, of course, is not the case. Most of the milky liquid contained in semen is produced by the seminal vesicles and the prostate gland, other organs that feed into the vas deferens later in the ejaculation process. This liquid is still ejaculated or spewed forth, but without any sperm in it. Because sperm are so tiny, the volume of semen ejaculated is virtually unaffected. Sterilization has no effect on either men's or women's ability to respond sexually or enjoy sexual activity.

Contraceptive Methods of the Future

Denney and Quadagno (1992) recognize six methods of birth control that are being investigated for future use. These include:

1. Small vaginal rings containing hormones. A ring is inserted in the upper part of the vagina and left there for three days. It is not supposed to be felt or to disrupt sexual activity. It works by changing the cervical mucus so that sperm cannot swim up through the cervix and into the uterus.
2. Immunizations and vaccines to inhibit fertilization and implantation. Vaccines for women would obstruct fertilized eggs from implanting on the uterine walls. Vaccines for men would employ hormones to inhibit sperm production.
3. Drugs to inhibit sperm production that are applied by using "nosedrops or nasal sprays" (Denney and Quadagno, 1992, p. 246).
4. Determining ovulation in women by examining breath or saliva. Some chemicals have been found to increase significantly in women's breath and saliva during ovulation. Further research needs to establish whether this is consistently the case and whether measurement of such chemicals is possible and practical.
5. Oral contraceptives for men. Some substances have been found to interfere with sperm production.

6. Drugs to prevent sperm from fertilizing eggs. The idea is to develop a drug for either men or women that would target the fertilization process and make it impossible for sperm to penetrate the egg.

Summary

Numerous physical changes mark adolescence. These include a growth spurt and the development of primary and secondary sex characteristics. Adolescents have strong psychological reactions to their physical changes. It is important for adolescents to feel they are physically attractive.

Adolescents mature at different rates. Male adolescents who mature early tend to be more self-confident and are more apt to assume leadership positions among their peers. They are more apt to be perceived as physically attractive and are treated more like adults. Differences between early and late maturing females are not nearly as striking as the differences between males.

Young adulthood, from ages eighteen through thirty, is the healthiest time of life. Some life-styles contribute to good health, while others have a negative effect on health.

Significant issues and life events that concern adolescents and young adults include: sexual activity in adolescence, unplanned pregnancy, teenage fatherhood, motivation for pregnancy, sex education, methods of contraception and sexually transmitted diseases. Of those pregnant adolescents who choose to have their babies, the vast majority keep them.

Sex education is important because it allows adolescents to make responsible decisions about their sexual behavior. This is especially true in this age of AIDS. In addition to AIDS, millions of young people contract other sexually transmitted diseases each year, including gonorrhea, chlamydial infections, syphilis, and genital herpes.

Adolescents tend not to use birth control when they first become sexually active. There is no one best method of birth control for all people. Each person should evaluate the pros and cons of each method to determine the most effective method for him or her.

7

Psychological Systems and Their Impacts on Adolescence and Young Adulthood

Identity Search

"Teen Alcoholism Shows Dramatic Increase"
"Twenty-Two-Year-Old Hangs Self in Kenosha Jail"
"$300,000 Worth of Cocaine Found In College Drug Bust"
"Teen Mother Shoots Infant Daughter, Husband, and Self"
"Four Killed by Drunk Teen Driver"

These statements might all be seen in newspaper headlines. They refer to tragedies which involve adolescents and young adults. Although the media often do address sensationalistic and tragic events, the fact that such things are occurring merits our attention. What psychological variables operate to help cause such happenings?

A PERSPECTIVE

This chapter will focus on some of the major psychological growth tasks and pitfalls confronting adolescents and young adults. Psychological systems involve such aspects of growth and development as forming an identity and developing a personal morality. An individual's psychological system interacts with biological and social systems to affect behavior.

We have already addressed some of the interactions between biological and psychological systems. For example, maturation rate and body weight (which relate to the biological system in an individual) can affect body image and self-concept (which relate to the psychological system of a person). Knowledge of psychological milestones normally negotiated during adolescence and young adulthood is important for the overall assessment of behavior and functioning. Additionally, this chapter will discuss two categories of critical life events that affect many persons in this age group: suicide and substance abuse.

This chapter will:

- Explore identity formation in adolescence by examining Erikson's eight stages of psychosocial development and Marcia's categories of identity.
- Explain and evaluate Kohlberg's theory of moral development, and present Gilligan's alternative model for women.
- Examine some critical issues and life events, including suicide and assertiveness, which have special impacts on adolescents and young adults.

Identity Formation

Personal identities crystallize during adolescence. Through experimentation and evaluation of experience and ideas, the adolescent should establish some sense of who he or she really is. In other words, people get to know themselves during adolescence.

Erik Erikson (1950) proposed a theory of psychological development comprising eight stages. A key component is the development of the ego or sense of self. This theory focuses on how personalities evolve throughout life as a result of the interaction between biologically based maturation and the demands of society. The emphasis is on the role of the social environment in personality development. The eight stages are based partly on the stages proposed by Freud and partly on Erikson's studies in a wide variety of cultures. Erikson writes that the society within which one lives makes certain psychic demands at each stage of development. Erikson calls these demands crises.

Erikson's Eight Stages of Development

Stage	Crisis	Age	Important Event
1	Basic trust versus basic mistrust	Birth to 18 months	Feeding
2	Autonomy versus shame and doubt	18 months to 3 years	Toileting
3	Initiative versus guilt	3 to 6 years	Locomoting
4	Identity versus inferiority	6 to 12 years	School
5	Identity versus role confusion	Adolescence	Peer relationship
6	Intimacy versus isolation	Young adult	Love relationship ▪
7	Generativity versus stagnation	Maturity	Parenting and creating
8	Ego integrity versus despair	Old age	Reflecting on and accepting one's life

During each psychosocial stage, the individual must seek to adjust to the stresses and conflicts involved in these crises. The search for identity is a crisis that confronts people during adolescence.

Although Erikson's psychosocial theory addresses development throughout the life span, it is included here because of the importance of identity formation during adolescence. After the entire theory is discussed, its application to adolescence will be explored in greater depth. The stages are described in "Erikson's Eight Stages of Development."

Erikson's Psychosocial Theory

Each stage of human development presents its characteristic crises. Coping well with each crisis makes an individual better prepared to cope with the next. Although specific crises are most critical during particular stages, related issues continue to arise throughout a person's life. For example, the conflict to trust versus mistrust is especially important in infancy. Yet, children and adults continue to struggle with whether or not to trust others.

Resolution of each crisis is an ideal, not necessarily a reality. The degree to which crises in earlier stages are resolved will affect a person's ability to resolve crises in later stages. If an individual doesn't learn how to trust in stage 1, that person will find it very difficult to attain intimacy in stage 6.

Stage 1: Basic Trust versus Basic Mistrust

For infants up to eighteen months of age, learning to trust others is the overriding crisis. To develop trust, one must understand that some people and some things can be depended on. Parents provide a major variable for such learning. For instance, infants who consistently receive warm, loving care and nourishment learn to trust that these things will be provided to them. Later in life, people may apply this concept of trust to friends, an intimate partner, or their government.

Stage 2: Autonomy versus Shame and Doubt

The crisis of autonomy versus shame and doubt characterizes early childhood, from eighteen months to three years. Children strive to accomplish things independently. They learn to feed themselves and to use the toilet. Accomplishing various tasks and activities provides children with feelings of self-worth and self-confidence. On the other hand, if children of this age are constantly downtrodden, restricted, or punished, shame and guilt will emerge instead. Self-doubt will replace the self-confidence that should have developed during this period.

Stage 3: Initiative versus Guilt

Preschoolers aged three to six years must face the crisis of taking their own initiative. Such children are extremely active physically. The world fascinates them and beckons them to explore it. They have active imaginations and are eager to learn. Preschoolers who are encouraged to take initiative to explore and learn are likely to assimilate this concept for use later in life. They will be more likely to feel confident in initiating relationships, pursuing career objectives, and developing recreational interests. Preschoolers who are consistently restricted, punished, or treated harshly, are more likely to experience the emotion of guilt. They want to explore and experience, but they are not allowed to. Instead of learning initiative, they are likely to feel guilty about their tremendous desires to do so many things. In reaction, they may become "passive spectators" who follow the lead of others instead of initiating their own activities and ideas (Kaluger and Kaluger, 1984, p. 233).

Stage 4: Industry versus Inferiority

School-age children six to twelve years old must address the crisis of industry versus inferiority. Children in this age group need to be productive and succeed in their activities. In addition to play, a major focus of their lives is school. Therefore, mastering academic skills and material is important. Those who do learn to be industrious by expending energy master activities. Comparison with peers becomes exceptionally important. Children who experience failure in school, or even in peer relations, may develop a sense of inferiority.

Stage 5: Identity versus Role Confusion

Adolescence is a time when young people explore who they are and establish their identity. It is the transition period from childhood to adulthood when people examine the various roles they play (for example, child, sibling, student, catholic, native American, basketball star, or whatever), and integrate these roles into a perception of self, an identity. Some people are unable to integrate their many roles and have difficulty coping with conflicting roles; they are said to suffer from *role confusion*. Such persons are confused; their identity is uncertain and unclear.

Stage 6: Intimacy versus Isolation

Young adulthood is characterized by a quest for intimacy and involves more than the establishment of a sexual relationship. Intimacy includes the ability to share with and give to another person without being afraid of sacrificing one's own identity. People who do not attain intimacy are likely to suffer isolation. These people have often been unable to resolve some of the crises of earlier psychosocial development. Various types of intimate relationships and how people experience them will be discussed in more detail in Chapter 8.

Stage 7: Generativity versus Stagnation

Mature adulthood is characterized by the crisis of generativity versus stagnation. During this time of life, people become concerned with helping, producing for, or guiding the following generation. In a way, generativity is unselfish. It involves a genuine concern for the future beyond one's own life track. Generativity does not necessarily involve procreating one's own children. Rather, it concerns a drive to be creative and productive in a way that will aid people in the future. Adults who lack generativity become self-absorbed and inward. They tend to focus primarily on their own concerns and needs rather than on those of others. The result is stagnation, that is, a fixed, discouraging lack of progress and productivity.

Stage 8: Ego Integrity versus Despair

The crisis of ego integrity versus despair characterizes old age. During this time of life, people tend to look back over their years and reflect on them. If they appreciate their life and are content with their accomplishments, they are said to have *ego integrity*, that is, the ultimate form of identity integration. Such people enjoy a sense of peace and accept the fact that life will soon be over. Others who have failed to cope successfully with past life crises and have many regrets experience despair.

Implications of Identity Formation in Adolescence

Achieving genital maturity and rapid body growth signals young people that they will soon be adults. They, therefore, begin to question their future roles as adults. The most important task of adolescence is to develop a sense of identity, a sense of "Who I Am." Making a career choice is an important part of this search for identity.

The primary danger of this period, according to Erikson, is identity confusion. This confusion can be expressed in a variety of ways. One way is to delay acting like a responsible adult. Another way is to commit oneself to poorly thought-out courses of action. Still another way is to regress into childishness to avoid assuming the responsibilities of adulthood. Erikson views the cliquishness of adolescence and its intolerance of differences as defenses against identity confusion. Falling in love is viewed as an attempt to define identity. Through self-disclosing intimate thoughts and feelings with another, the adolescent is articulating and seeking to better understand his/her identity. Through seeing the reactions of a loved one to one's intimate thoughts and feelings, the adolescent is testing out values and beliefs and is better able to clarify a sense of self.

Adolescents and young adults experiment with roles that represent the many possibilities for their future identity: students take certain courses to test out their future career interests. They also experiment with a variety of part-time jobs to test out occupational interests. They date and go steady to test out their relationships with the opposite sex. Dating also allows for different self-presentations with each new date. Adolescents and young adults may also experiment with drugs—alcohol, tobacco, marijuana, cocaine, and so on. Many are confused about their religious beliefs and seek in a variety of ways to develop a set of religious and moral beliefs that they can be comfortable with. They also tend to join, participate in, and then quit a variety of organizations. They experiment with a variety of interests and hobbies. As long as no laws are broken (and health is not seriously affected) in the process of experimenting, our culture gives teenagers and young adults the freedom to experiment in a variety of ways in order to develop a sense of identity.

Erikson (1959) uses the term *psychosocial moratorium* to describe a period of free experimentation before a final sense of identity is achieved. Generally, our society allows adolescents and young adults freedom from the daily expectations of role performance. Ideally, this moratorium allows young people the freedom to experiment with values, beliefs, and roles so that they can develop a personal conception of how they can best fit into society so as to maximize their personal strengths and gain positive recognition from the community.

The crisis of identity versus role confusion is best resolved through integrating earlier identifications, present values, and future goals into a consistent self-concept. A sense of identity is achieved only after a period of questioning, reevaluation, and experimentation. Efforts to resolve questions of identity may take the young person down paths of emotional involvement, overzealous commitment, alienation, rebellion, or playful wandering.

Many adolescents are idealistic. They see the evils and negatives in our society and in the world. They cannot understand why injustice and imperfection exists. They yearn for a much better life for themselves and for others and have little understanding of the resources and hard work it takes for advancements. They often try to change the world and their efforts are genuine. If society can channel their energies constructively, their contributions can be meaningful. Unfortunately, some become disenchanted and apathetic after being continually frustrated with obstacles.

Importance of Achieving Identity

Adolescents and young adults struggle with developing a sense of who they are, what they want out of life, and what kind of people they want to be. Arriving at answers to such questions is among the most important tasks people face in life (Glasser, 1972). Without answers, a person will not be prepared to make such major decisions as which career to select; deciding whether, when, or whom to marry; deciding where to live; and deciding what to do with leisure time. Unfortunately, many people muddle through life and never arrive at well-thought-out answers to these questions. Those who do not arrive at answers are apt to be depressed, anxious, indecisive, and unfulfilled.

The Formation of Identity

Identity development is a lifetime process. It begins during the early years and continues to change throughout one's lifetime. During the early years one's sense of identity is largely determined by the reaction of others. A long time ago, Cooley (1902) coined this labelling process as resulting in the "looking-glass self"—that is, persons develop their self-concept (who and what they are) in terms of how others relate to them. For example, if a neighborhood identifies a teenage male as being a trouble-maker or delinquent, neighbors are then apt to distrust him, accuse him of delinquent acts, and label his behavior as such. This labelling process, the youth begins to realize, also results in a type of prestige and status, at least from his peers. In the absence of objective ways to gauge whether he is in fact a delinquent, the youth will rely on the subjective evaluations of others. Thus, gradually, as the youth is identified as a delinquent he is apt to begin to perceive himself as such, and begin to enact the delinquent role.

Labels have a major impact on our lives. If a child is frequently called stupid by his or her parents, that child is apt to develop a low self-concept, anticipate failure in many areas (particularly academic) and thereby put forth little effort in school and in competitive interactions with others, and end up failing.

Since identity development is a lifetime process, positive changes are probable even for those who view themselves as failures. In identity formation, it is important to remember that what we want out of the future is more important than our past experience in determining what the future will be. The past is fixed and cannot be changed. It has brought us to where we are today. However, the present and the future can be changed. Because our past may have been painful and traumatic, it does not follow that our present and the future must be painful and traumatic. Since we are in control of our lives, we largely determine what out future will be.

Marcia's Categories of Identity

Marcia (1980) has done a substantial amount of research on the Eriksonian theory of psychosocial development. He identifies four major ways in which people cope with identity crises: (1) identity achievements, (2) foreclosure, (3) identity diffusion, and (4) moratorium. People may be classified into these categories on the basis of three primary criteria: first, whether the individual experiences a major crisis during identity development; second, whether the person expresses a commitment to some type of occupation; and, third, whether there is commitment to some set of values or beliefs.

Identity Achievement

To reach the stage of identity achievement, people undergo a period of intense decision making. After expending much effort, they develop a personalized set of values and make their career decisions. Although there are positive and negative aspects to each identity status category, the attainment of identity achievement is usually thought of as the most beneficial.

Foreclosure

People who fall into this category are the only ones who never experience an identity crisis as such. They glide into adulthood without experiencing much turbulence or anxiety. Decisions concerning both career and values are made relatively early in life. Thus, these decisions are often based on the values and ideas of their parents rather than their own. For example, a woman might become a traditional housewife and mother, not because she makes a conscious choice, but rather because she assumes it's what she is expected to do. Likewise, a man might become a Democratic millwright in a shipbuilding factory simply because his father was also a Democratic millwright and felt that it provided a good living.

It's interesting that the term *foreclosure* is used to label this category. Foreclosure involves shutting someone out from involvement, as one would foreclose a mortgage and bar a person who mortgaged his/her property from reclaiming it. To foreclose one's identity implies shutting off various other opportunities to grow and change.

Identity Diffusion

People who experience identity diffusion suffer from a serious lack of decision and direction. Although they go through an identity crisis, they never resolve it. They are not able to make clear decisions concerning either their personal ideology or their career choice. These people tend to be characterized by low self-esteem and lack of resolution. For example, such a person might be a drifter who never stays more than a few months in any one place and defies any serious commitments.

Moratorium

The moratorium category includes people who experience intense anxiety during their identity crisis, yet have not made decisions regarding either personal values or a career choice. However, moratorium people experience a more continuous, intense struggle to resolve these issues. Instead of avoiding the decision-

How to Determine Who You Are

Forming an identity essentially involves *thinking* about, and arriving at, answers to the following questions: (1) What do I want out of life? (2) What kind of person do I want to be? (3) Who am I?

The most important decisions you make in your life may well be in arriving at answers to these questions. In answering these questions, you are literally developing beliefs and attitudes about who you are and what you want out of life.

Answers to these questions are not easy to arrive at. They require considerable contemplation and trial and error. But if you are to lead a gratifying, fulfilling life, it is imperative to find answers to give direction to your life and to have a chance of living the kind of life you find meaningful. Without answers, you are apt to muddle through life by being a passive responder to situations that arise, rather than a continual achiever of your life's goals.

To determine who you are, it is very helpful to answer to the following more specific questions:

1. What do I find satisfying/meaningful/enjoyable? (Only after you identify what is meaningful and gratifying, will you be able to consciously seek involvement in activities that will make your life fulfilling, and avoid those activities that are meaningless or stifling.)
2. What is my moral code? (One possible code is to seek to fulfill your needs and to seek to do what you find enjoyable, doing so in a way that does not deprive others of the ability to fulfill their needs.)
3. What are my spiritual beliefs?
4. What are my employment goals? (Ideally, you should seek employment in which you find the work stimulating and satisfying, that you are skilled at, and that earns you enough money to support your lifestyle.)
5. What are my sexual mores? (All of us should develop a consistent code that we are comfortable with and that helps us to meet our needs without exploiting others. There is no one right code—what works for one may not work for another, due to differences in lifestyles, life goals, and personal values.)
6. Do I desire to have a committed relationship? (If yes, to what type of person and when? How consistent are your answers here with your other life goals?)
7. Do I desire to have children? (If yes, how many, when, and how consistent are your answers here with your other life goals?)
8. What area of the country/world do I desire to live in? (Variables to be considered are climate, geography, type of dwelling, rural or urban setting, closeness to relatives or friends, and characteristics of the neighborhood.)
9. What do I enjoy doing with my leisure time?
10. What kind of image do I want to project to others? (Your image will be composed of your dressing style and grooming habits, your emotions, personality, assertiveness, capacity to communicate, material possessions, moral code, physical features, and voice patterns. You need to assess your strengths and shortcomings honestly in this area, and seek to make improvements.)
11. What type of people do I enjoy being with, and why?
12. Do I desire to improve the quality of my life and that of others? (If yes, in what ways, and how do you hope to achieve these goals?)
13. What type of relationships do I desire to have with relatives, friends, neighbors, and with people I meet for the first time?
14. What are my thoughts about death and dying?
15. What do I hope to be doing five years from now, ten years, twenty years?

To have a fairly well-developed sense of identity, you need to have answers to most, but not all, of these questions. Very few persons are able to arrive at rational, consistent answers to all the questions. Having answers to most of them will provide a reference for developing your views to the yet unanswered areas.

Honest, well-thought-out answers to these questions will go a long way toward defining who you are. Again, what you want out of life, along with your motivation to achieve these goals, will primarily determine your identity. The above questions are simple to state, but arriving at answers is a complicated, ongoing process. In addition, expect some changes in your life goals as time goes on. Environmental influences change (for example, changes in working conditions). Also, as personal growth occurs, changes are apt to occur in activities that you find enjoyable and also in your beliefs, attitudes, and values. Accept such changes, and if you have a fairly good idea of who you are, you will be prepared to make changes in your life goals so that you will be able to give continued direction to your life.

(continued next page)

How to Determine Who You Are (continued)

Your life is shaped by different events that are the results of decisions you make and decisions that are made for you. Without a sense of identity, you will not know what decisions are best for you, and your life will be unfulfilled. With a sense of identity, you will be able to direct your life toward goals you select and find personally meaningful.

making issue, they address it almost constantly. They are characterized by strong, conflicting feelings about what they should believe and do. For example, a moratorium person might struggle intensively with a religious issue, such as whether or not there is a god. Moratorium people tend to have many critical, but as yet unresolved, issues.

One study of thirty-three college students (Orlofsky et al., 1973) supported the Eriksonian idea that there is a relationship between stage 5 (identity versus role confusion) and stage 6 (intimacy versus isolation). It appears that people need to confront and resolve their identity crises before they can form positive intimate relationships. Students who were found to have the best potential for developing close relationships were those falling in the identity achievement category. Shallow, stereotyped relationships tended to characterize people in both the foreclosure and identity diffusion categories. Moratorium people showed the widest variation in their ability to form relationships.

The Evaluation of Theory and Application to Client Situations

Both Erickson's and Marcia's theories provide interesting insights into people's behavior and their interaction with others. Both provide a framework for better understanding "normal" life crises and events as they occur over the life span. For example, stage 2 of Erickson's psychosocial theory focuses on age eighteen months to three years. Most of this period is frequently referred to as "the terrible twos." Understanding that children in this age group are striving to achieve some autonomy and control over their environment during this time interval helps us also understand that their behavior is full of action and exploration. Children should not be reprimanded for the types of behavior that are normal and natural during this stage of development. Such insight can better prepare social workers for helping parents develop age appropriate expectations and behavioral management techniques.

Marcia's emphasis on the acquisition of coping skills also provides insights for work with clients. Those people who are trapped in foreclosure, identity diffusion, or moratorium identity crises may benefit from help in the resolution of these crises. Social workers can give feedback in addition to helping people formulate and evaluate new alternatives. Acknowledgment of the existence of such crises and understanding their dynamics are the first steps toward resolution.

Both Marcia's and Erickson's theories emphasize the importance of identity formation. Looking at adolescence and young adulthood with some understanding of the forces at work can help social workers better understand the dynamics of human behavior within the social environment. For instance, strife between parents and children is common during adolescence. It is also understandable. Parents try to maintain some control with their leadership roles. Adolescents struggle to define themselves as individuals and become independent. Knowing that these are natural occurrences provides clues to the type of insights social workers can give to clients regarding their feelings and behaviors. The struggle for control can be identified and discussed. Parental restrictiveness and adolescent rebelliousness can be examined. New behavioral options for interaction can be explored.

We established in an earlier chapter that social workers need to evaluate theory and determine for themselves what theoretical concepts and frameworks are most suited for their own practice with clients. Questions to keep in mind while doing this include:

1. How does the theory apply to client situations?
2. What research supports the theory?
3. To what extent does the theory coincide with social work values and ethics?
4. Are other theoretical frameworks or concepts available that are more relevant to practice situations?

Value and Ethical Issues Relating to Theory on Identity Development

Questions might be raised regarding the extent to which Erickson's and Marcia's theories apply to all people. This includes various racial and ethnic groups. For instance, some cultures emphasize respect for and deference to older family members. Younger people are expected to conform until they, too, become older and "wiser." To what extent, then, is it important for each individual to struggle in order to achieve a strikingly unique and independent personality? Must this particular aspect of behavior be stressed to a great extent? Or, should the ability to assume a strong identification with the family and cultural group be given precedence?

Lesbian and Gay Adolescents

Lesbian and gay adolescents in this culture suffer even more extreme obstacles to identity development than their heterosexual peers. Perhaps their biggest obstruction is the constant oppression of homophobia. Homophobia is an extreme and irrational fear and hatred for lesbian and gay people simply because they are lesbian and gay (Chapter 13 addresses sexual orientation and homophobia in greater detail). Homophobia and the oppressive reactions of others to homosexuality isolates lesbian and gay youth. On the one hand, lesbian and gay adolescents are trying to establish individual identities, just as heterosexual adolescents are. On the other hand, lesbian and gay youth are severely discouraged from expressing and establishing their sexual identities. The question should be raised, To what extent do Erickson's and Marcia's theories concerning identity development apply to these young people? Do these theories go far enough to explain the serious crises lesbian and gay people go through?

Kaplan and Saperstein (NASW, 1985) stress the isolation young lesbian and gay people feel. If they "come out"[1] and reveal their homosexuality, they are ostracized and demeaned. On the other hand, if they cautiously hide their true feelings and identity, they

---

1. "Coming out" refers to "the process of self-identification as a lesbian woman or a gay man, followed by revelation of one's sexual orientation to others" (Barker, 1991, p. 42).

risk depression, avoidance behaviors such as drug or alcohol abuse, and rebellious acting out, such as running away or truancy.

Kaplan and Saperstein (NASW, 1985) suggest that social work practitioners be especially sensitive to the issues facing lesbian and gay adolescents. First, social workers need to evaluate their own homophobic attitudes. They should work to develop a caring, empathic, nonjudgmental perspective that can be communicated to their lesbian and gay clients. Second, social workers "need to pay attention to the 'coming out' process as it may be a cause of acting-out behavior, for example, truancy or homelessness" (p. 18). Such youth may need help in answering questions such as should they come out or not. What should they say? Whom should they tell? How will people react? Additionally, workers can help lesbian and gay youth become connected with others of their own sexual orientation. Many cities have helplines, support groups, speakers bureaus, and activities available for lesbian and gay young people. If no such resources exist in a worker's area, might it not be possible for the worker to develop them?

In summary, it appears that Erickson's and Marcia's theories have only limited relevance for lesbian and gay identity development. The theories can be applied to a certain extent; they indicate that all young people go through an identity crisis. However, they do little to focus upon the special issues of lesbian and gay young people.

It is up to you as a social worker to scrutinize theories closely and use what you can from them. However, it is just as important to recognize limitations of theories.

Moral Development

Adolescence is fraught with identity crises. Young adulthood is filled with avid quests for intimate relationships and other major commitments involving career and life goals. A parallel pursuit is the formulation of a personal set of moral values. Morality involves a set of principles regarding what is right and what is wrong. Many times these principles are not clearly defined in black or white, but involve various shades of grey. There is no one absolute answer. For example, is the death penalty right or wrong? Is it good or bad to have sexual intercourse before marriage?

A parent volunteer discusses drug problems with high school students. Such sessions reinforce Stage 4 of Kohlberg's Six Stages of Moral Development: the need to adhere to law and respect higher authority.

Moral issues range from very major to minor day-to-day decisions. Although moral development can take place throughout life, it is especially critical during adolescence and young adulthood. These are the times when people gain the right to make independent decisions and choices. Often, the values developed during this stage remain operative for life.

Kohlberg's Theory of Moral Development

Lawrence Kohlberg (1963, 1968, 1969) has proposed a series of six stages through which people progress as they develop their moral framework. These six stages are clustered within three distinct levels.

The first level, the preconventional or premoral level, is characterized by giving precedence to self-interest. People usually experience this level from ages four to ten. Moral decisions are based on external standards. Behavior is governed by whether a child will receive a reward or punishment. The first stage in this level is based on avoiding punishment. Children do what they are told to in order to avoid negative consequences. The second stage focuses on rewards instead of punishment. In other words, children do the "right" thing in order to receive a reward or compensation. Sometimes this involves an exchange of favors, a form of "I'll scratch your back if you'll scratch mine."

Level 2 of Kohlberg's theory is the conventional level, where moral thought is based on conforming to conventional roles. Frequently, this level occurs from ages ten to thirteen. There is a strong desire to please others and to receive social approval. Although moral standards have begun to be internalized, they are still based on what others dictate, rather than on what is personally decided.

Within Level 2, stage 3 focuses on gaining the approval of others. Good relationships become very important. Stage 4, "authority-maintaining morality," emphasizes the need to adhere to law. Higher authorities are generally respected. "Law and order" are considered necessary in order to maintain the social order.

Level 3, the post conventional level, concerns developing a moral conscience that goes beyond what others say. People contemplate laws and expectations and decide on their own what is right and what is wrong. They become autonomous, independent thinkers. Behavior is based on principles instead of laws. This level progresses beyond selfish concerns. The needs and well-being of others become very important in addition to one's own. At this level, true morality is achieved.

Within Level 3, stage 5 involves adhering to socially accepted laws and principles. Law is considered good for the general public welfare. However, laws are subject to interpretation and change. Stage 6 is the ultimate attainment. During this stage, one be-

Kohlberg's Six Stages of Moral Development

Level	Description
Level 1: Preconventional (Conventional Role Conformity)	Controls are external. Behavior is governed by receiving rewards or punishments.
Stage 1: Punishment and Obedience Orientation	Decisions concerning what is good or bad are made in order to avoid receiving punishment.
Stage 2: Naive Instrumental Hedonism	Rules are obeyed in order to receive rewards. Often favors are exchanged.
Level 2: Conventional (Role Conformity)	The opinions of others become important. Behavior is governed by conforming to social expectations.
Stage 3: "Good boy/girl morality"	Good behavior is considered to be what pleases others. There is a strong desire to please and gain the approval of others.
Stage 4: Authority-Maintaining Morality	The belief in law and order is strong. Behavior conforms to law and higher authority. Social order is important.
Level 3: Post Conventional (Self-Accepted Moral Principles)	Moral decisions are finally internally controlled. Morality involves higher level principles beyond law and even beyond self-interest.
Stage 5: Morality of Contract, of Individual Rights, and of Democratically Accepted Law	Laws are considered necessary. However, they are subject to rational thought and interpretation. Community welfare is important.
Stage 6: Morality of Individual Principles and Conscience	Behavior is based on internal ethical principles. Decisions are made according to what is right rather than what is written into law.

SOURCE: Adapted from Kohlberg (1968, 1981).

comes free of the thoughts and opinions expressed by others. Morality is completely internalized. Decisions are based on one's personal conscience, transcedent of meager laws and regulations. Examples of people who attain this level include Martin Luther King and Ghandhi.

Most people reach only the second level of moral functioning (Kaluger and Kaluger, 1984, p. 454). This morality is based on what others in society dictate. People respond to the pressures of the group, rather than to their own personally developed principles. Only 5 to 10 percent of all people ever reach stages 5 or 6 (Kaluger and Kaluger, 1984, p. 454).

Evaluation of Kohlberg's Theory

Many questions have been raised concerning the absolute validity and general application of Kohlberg's theory (Yussen, 1977; Rubin and Trotten, 1977; Austin et al., 1977). These include potential cultural biases inherent in the categorization, limitations imposed by children's limited vocabulary and expression of their ideas, the lack of clear-cut divisions between one category and another, and the absolute order in which the levels occur.

There have been some discrepancies in findings, especially concerning the cross-cultural application of Kohlberg's theory. Kohlberg (1970) has found support for the application of his stages to the children in numerous countries including Mexico, New Zealand, Taiwan, Thailand, Kenya, and Canada. One review of the cross-cultural research supported the idea that Kohlberg's approach can apply to other countries (Edwards, 1977). This review established that people who were older in age tended to attain higher levels of moral functioning. Despite the fact that only the first four levels tended to characterize cultures that were non-Western in orientation, this still provides some support for a general application of the theory (Snarey, 1985; Carroll and Rest, 1982). Questions must be raised, however, concerning the application of the theory's final stage to other societies. Baumrind has criticized the theory because it does not really consider the moral development possible in other cultures. He believes that it suffers from "moral absolutism."

Another major criticism involves the idea that the distinction between moral attitudes and actual behavior is not clear (Power and Reimer, 1978). Major differences can be found between what people think is right and what they actually do. Many times the most difficult moral decisions must be made in crisis situations. If you find yourself in a burning building with a crowd of other people, how much effort will you expend to save others before yourself? What is the discrepancy between what you think is right and what you would really do in such a situation?

Kohlberg (1978) has conceded that there are valid criticisms of his theory. He has given credence to the idea that people learn and respond according to their moral context. The implication is that, depending on the specific situation and culture, morality, even true morality, may be interpreted differently. He has resolved the fact that stage 6 may not generally be applied across all cultures, societies, and situations. Kohlberg has even dropped stage 6 from his evaluation in view of extensive criticism, apparent cultural bias, and the infrequency with which research subjects seem to attain it even after long periods of time (Muson, 1979, p. 57).

Moral Development and Women: Gilligan's Approach

A major criticism of Kohlberg's theory is that virtually all of the research on which it is based used only men as subjects. As a result, women have fared poorly when measured on the traditional Kohlberg tasks. They often become fixated at stage 3, unable to quite make the transition to stage 4 (Papalia and Olds, 1981, pp. 414–15). In other words, women tend to view morality in terms of personal situations instead of societal situations. Women often have trouble moving from a very personalized interpretation of morality to a focus on law and order. This bridge involves a generalization from the more personal aspects of what is right and wrong (how individual moral decisions affect one's own personal life) to morality within the larger, more impersonal society (how moral decisions, such as those instilled in law, affect virtually everyone). Kohlberg has been criticized because he has not taken into account the different orientation and life circumstances common to women.

Gilligan (1982) reasons that women's moral development is often based on their personal interest and commitment to the good of others close to them. Frequently, this involves giving up or sacrificing one's own well-being for others. Goodness and kindness are emphasized. Moral decisions often involve very specific personal situations. This contrasts with a common male focus on assertively making decisions and exercising moral judgments.

Gilligan targeted twenty-nine women who were receiving pregnancy and abortion counseling. She postulated that pregnancy and birth was an area in women's lives where they could emphasize choice. Yet, it still was an intimate area to which they could relate. Gilligan interviewed the women concerning their pregnancies. She arrived at a sequence of levels which relate specifically to women. She found that women tend to view morality "in terms of selfishness and responsibility, as an obligation to exercise care and avoid hurt. People who care for each other are the most responsible, whereas those who hurt someone else are selfish and immoral. While men think more in terms of justice and fairness, women think more about specific people" (Papalia and Olds, 1981, p. 461).

Gilligan describes the following levels and transitions of moral development for women.

Level 1: Orientation to Personal Survival

This level focuses purely on the woman's self-interest. Her needs are salient. The needs and well-being of others are not really considered. At this level, a woman focuses first on personal survival. What is practical and best for her is most important.

Transition 1: Transition from Personal Selfishness to Responsibility

This first transition involves a movement in moral thought from consideration only to self to some consideration of the others involved. During this transition, a woman comes to acknowledge the fact that she is responsible not only for herself but also for others, including the unborn. In other words, she begins to acknowledge that her choice will impact others in addition to herself.

Level 2: Goodness as Self-Sacrifice

Level 2 involves putting aside one's own needs and wishes. Rather, the well-being of other people becomes important. The "good" thing to do is to sacrifice herself so that others may benefit. A woman at this level feels dependent on what other people think. Often a conflict occurs between taking responsibility for her own actions and feeling pressure from others to make her decisions.

Transition 2: From Goodness to Reality

During this transitional period, women begin to examine their situations more objectively. They draw away from their dependence on others to tell them what they should do. Instead, they begin to take into account the well-being of everyone concerned, including themselves. Some of the concern for personal survival apparent in Level 1 returns, but in a more objective manner.

Level 3: The Morality of Nonviolent Responsibility

Level 3 involves women thinking in terms of the repercussions of their decisions and actions. At this level, a woman's thinking has progressed beyond mere concern for what others will think about what she does. Rather, it involves accepting her responsibility for making her own judgments and decisions. She places herself on an equal plane with others, weighs the various consequences of her potential actions, and accepts the fact that she will be responsible for these consequences. The important principle operating here is that of minimizing hurt, both to herself and to others.

Gilligan's sequence of moral development provides a good example of how morality can be viewed from different perspectives. It is especially beneficial in emphasizing the different strengths potentially manifested by men and women. The emphasis on feelings, such as direct concern for others, is just as important as the ability to decisively make moral judgments.

Application of Theory to Client Situations

Social work has a sound foundation of professional values expressed in the National Association of Social Workers (NASW) Code of Ethics. Ethics involve making decisions about what is right and what is wrong. Ethics provide social workers with guidelines for practice with clients.

Gilligan emphasizes the relationship between responsibility and morality. People develop morally as they gradually become more and more capable and willing to assume responsibility. Morality provides the basis for making ethical decisions. Gilligan "bases the highest stage of decision making on care for and sensitivity to the needs of others, on responsibility for others, and on nurturance" (Rhodes, 1985, p. 101). This principle is central to the NASW Code of Ethics. A theory such as Gilligan's can provide some general ethical guidelines to which we can aspire in our day-to-day practice with clients. Social workers should strive to be sensitive to the needs of their clients. They should assume responsibility for effective practice with clients. Finally, they should provide help and nurturance to meet their clients' needs.

Significant Issues and Life Events: Suicide and Assertiveness

Each phase of life tends to be characterized by issues that receive considerable attention and concern. Two issues command special attention as they relate to adolescence and youth. These are suicide and assertiveness. Although these issues continue to elicit concern with respect to any age group, they have a special critical quality for those whose lives are just beginning. Young lives terminated at such an early age represent tragic and regrettable losses of potential. Likewise, lives marked by either docile meekness and nonassertiveness on the one hand, or pushy, self-serving aggression on the other can be thwarted, damaging, or nonproductive.

Each of these issues may be viewed either from a psychological or a social perspective. They will arbitrarily be addressed in this chapter, which focuses on the psychological aspects of adolescence and young adulthood.

Suicide

Why do people decide to terminate their lives? Is it because life is unbearable, painful, hopeless, or useless? Suicide can occur during almost any time of life. However, it might be considered especially critical in adolescence and youth. This is the time of life when people could enjoy being young and fresh and looking forward to life's wide variety of exciting experiences.

Instead, many young people decide to take their own lives.

Incidence of Suicide

Suicide is one of the most critical health problems in the United States today. Consider these frightening facts. In recent years, suicide rates have increased disturbingly, especially for white males age fifteen to twenty-four. Suicide is the *second* major cause of death for this group (USDHHS, 1990). Accidents pose the most common cause of death for this group (Papalia and Olds, 1992). No one knows how many of those accidents were really suicides. Only about 15 percent of all people who kill themselves leave a note (Lefrancois, 1990). Eighty-five percent of adolescents think about suicide at some time. Fifty percent of these make some plan or seriously consider suicide as a means of solving their problems (Jensen, 1984).

Causes of Adolescent Suicide

Freese (1979) discusses five variables that seem to be related to adolescent suicide.

Feeling Helpless and Hopeless

As adolescents struggle to establish an identity and function independently of their parents, it's no wonder that many feel helpless. They must abide by the rules of their parents and schools. They suffer from peer pressure to conform to the norms of their age group. They are seeking acceptance by society and a place where they will fit in. At the same time, an adolescent must strive to develop a unique personality, a sense of self that is valuable for its own sake. At times such a struggle may indeed seem hopeless.

Loneliness

Feelings of isolation and loneliness also tend to characterize adolescents who attempt suicide. Most often, "there is little communication between these teens and their parents" (Griffeths and Pecora, 1986, p. 2). Consequently, there is a lack of emotional ties and a disengagement from one another resulting in profound feelings of isolation. Therapists frequently are told, "There's no one to talk to who understands" (p. 2).

Impulsivity

Impulsivity, or a sudden decision to act without giving much thought to the action, is yet another variable related to adolescent suicide. Confusion, isolation, and feelings of despair may contribute to an impulsive decision to end it all.

Adolescents today must face a hard transition into adulthood. Social values are shifting. Peer pressure is immense. Adolescents have not had time to gain life experience and so tend to behave impulsively. Any trivial incident may become a crisis (Harvard Medical School Mental Health Letter, Feb. 1986). For example, being "dumped" by a boyfriend or girlfriend can be devastating. Failing an exam or even doing poorer than expected can mean that life is over. Every moment of the day can feel like the end of the world if something goes wrong.

Lack of a Stable Environment

Many times, turbulence and disruption at home contribute to the profile of an adolescent suicide. Lack of a stable home environment contributes to the sense of loneliness and isolation. It also eats at the base of a person's social support.

One study that reviewed the case histories of completed adolescent suicides found that a family conflict occurred prior to the suicide in 43 percent of the cases (Litt et al., 1983). Other research involved administering a wide range of tests to adolescents who had visited a hospital emergency room (McKenry et al., 1982). The tests evaluated such things as level of depression and family dynamics. The adolescents were divided into two groups, those who came to the emergency room because of a suicide attempt and those who came for some other reason. Several characteristics became apparent in families where adolescents had attempted suicide. First, the adolescents felt they had a negative relationship with their parents. Second, adolescents in the suicide group felt their mothers were less interested in them than did adolescents in the nonsuicide group. Third, their fathers had lower self-esteem. Fourth, their mothers had been more likely to have thought about suicide before. Fifth, alcohol use was more apparent on the part of both mothers and fathers in the suicide group.

Increased External and Internal Pressures

Many teenagers today express concern over the many pressures they have to bear. To some extent, these pressures might be related to current social and economic conditions. Many families are breaking up. Pressures to succeed are great. Many young people aren't even certain they will find a job when they get out of school. Peer pressures to conform and to be accepted socially are constantly operating. Suicidal

Joany—A Victim of Suicide

Joany, age fifteen, was one of the "fries." People said that she used a lot of drugs and was wild. She did poorly in school, when she did manage to attend. Her appearance was striking. Her hair was cropped short somewhat unevenly, and was characterized by a different color of the rainbow every day, including purple, green, and hot pink. Short leather miniskirts, heavy chainlike jewelry, and dark, exaggerated makeup were also part of her style. She hung around with a group who looked and behaved much like herself. More studious, straight, upper middle-class, college-bound peers couldn't understand why she behaved that way. It was easy for them to point and snicker at her as she walked down the senior high school halls.

One day she came to school almost looking normal, noted one of her straight classmates, Karen. Karen had at times felt sorry for her in the past when people made fun of her. Today Joany was wearing an unobstrusive skirt and sweater. More noticeably, her hair was combed in an attractive manner. Today Joany finally looked like she fit in with her other classmates. Karen called out a compliment to her as she was walking down the hall, laughing with some of her other weird-looking friends. Joany turned, smiled, gave a hurried thanks, and returned to her active conversation with the others.

The next day the word spread like wildfire throughout the student population. Joany, it seemed, had hung herself in her parents' basement. The rumor was that she was terribly upset because her parents were getting a divorce. No one really knew why she had killed herself. People didn't understand the sense of hopelessness and desolation she felt. Nor did anyone know why she did not turn to friends or family or school counselors for help. There seemed to be so many unanswered questions.

All that remained of Joany several months later was an over-sized picture of her on the last page of the high school yearbook. It was labeled, "In Memoriam."

Many pressures and anxieties exert themselves on adolescents. Young people are not sure that they will find a job when they get out of school.

adolescents may simply lose any coping powers they may have had and simply give up.

There is evidence that teenagers who are either overachievers or underachievers experience greater stress and, therefore, are more likely to commit suicide (U.S. Congress, 1984). Overachievers may expect too much of themselves and respond to pressure from parents, school, and friends in an overly zealous manner. One teenager comes to mind. Terri was a popular high school cheerleader. She had been Homecoming Queen last fall. She was an A student and editor of the yearbook. When she killed herself, everyone was surprised. Most of the people around her felt that she had everything and wondered why she threw it all away. They said it was such a shame. Apparently, she had hidden her inner turmoil very well. Perhaps she was just tired of working (and playing) so hard. Or, maybe, no matter how well she seemed to others, she never measured up to her expectations when she looked at herself. At any rate, no one will ever know. We all probably know of someone like Terri.

Underachievers also may experience greater stress. There is evidence that learning disabilities are related to suicide in some cases (Kenny, 1979). Learning disabled adolescents are at a distinct disadvantage. There will always be something they can't do as well or can't do at all through no fault of their own. Yet they may be pressured to perform just like everybody else. They may break from the perceived futility of their own situations.

Suicidal Symptoms

Patterson, Dohn, Bird, and Patterson (1983) cite various risk factors that are related to a person's actual potential of carrying through with a suicide. They propose a mechanism for evaluating suicide potential which is called the "SAD PERSONS" scale. Each letter in the acronym corresponds to one of the high risk factors.

It should be emphasized that any of the many available guidelines to assess suicide potential are just that—guidelines. People who actually threaten to commit suicide should be believed. The very fact that they are talking about it means that they are thinking about actually doing it. This means that there is some chance that they may kill themselves. However, the following variables are useful as guidelines for determining risk, that is, how high the probability is that they actually will attempt and succeed at suicide.

Sex

Among adolescents, females are nine times more likely to try to kill themselves than males; however, males are seven times more likely to succeed in their attempts (Jensen, 1984, p. 12). Adolescents of either gender may have serious suicide potential. However, greater danger exists if the person threatening suicide is a male. One reason for this is that males are more likely to choose a more deadly means of committing suicide.

Age

Although a person of almost any age may attempt and succeed at suicide, the risks are greater for some age groups than for others. Statistics indicate that

Suicide Notes

The following are suicide notes written by people of various ages shortly before they successfully committed suicide.

Whomever—I wrote this sober, so it is what I planned, sober or drunk. I love you all and please don't feel guilty because it is what I planned drunk or sober. Life still happens whether it is today or tomorrow. But after twenty-three years I would think that I could have met a person that I would mean more than personal advantage. If only I meant something. People just don't seem to care. Is it that I give the impression that I don't care? I wish and want to know. I feel so unimportant to everyone. As though my presence does not mean anything to anybody. I wish so much to be something to someone. But I feel the harder I try the worse I do. Maybe I just have not run into the right person. I am still 6 feet underground. My mind just didn't want any of it obviously. Make sure _____ goes to mom. No matter what I do, in my life, I still am going to die. By someone else's hands OR MY OWN.

> (Female, age twenty-three, of a gunshot wound.)

I can't put up with this shit. I'm sorry I have to do this, but I have nothing left.
P.S. Closed casket please.
Give my guns to _____
> (Male, age twenty-five, of a gunshot wound.)

Mom and Dad
don't feel bad—I have problems—don't feel the blame for this on you_____
> (Male, age eighteen, of a gunshot wound.)

Please forgive me for leaving you. I love you very much, but could not cope with my health problems plus financial worries etc. Try to understand and pray for me.
I wish you all the best and that you will be able to find the happiness in life I could not.
> Love and Kisses

I can't take the abuse, the hurt, the rejection, the isolation, the loneliness. I can't deal with all of it. I can't try anymore. The tears are endless. I've fallen into a bottomless pit of despair. I know eternal pain and tears . . .
No one knows I'm alive or seems to care if I die. I'm a terrible, worthless person and it would be better if I'd never been born. Tabby was my only friend in the world, and now she'd dead. There's no reason for me to live anymore. . . .
Mom and Dad, I hate you!
> Love Tommy

SOURCE: These notes were recorded in "A Cry for Help: Teen Suicide," prepared and presented by Tom Skinner, Edison Junior High School, Janesville, WI. Reprinted by permission of the Rock Country Coroner's Office, Beloit, WI.

---

people who are age nineteen or younger, or age forty-five or older are in the high-risk groups (Patterson et al., 1983).

Depression

Depression contributes to a person's potential to commit suicide. *Depression* is "a psychoneurotic or psychotic disorder marked by sadness, inactivity, difficulty in thinking and concentration, a significant increase or decrease in appetite and time spent sleeping, feelings of dejection and hopelessness, and sometimes suicidal tendencies (*Webster's New Collegiate Dictionary*, 1991, p. 341). It doesn't involve simply feeling bad. Rather, it involves a collection of characteristics, feelings, and behaviors which tend to occur in conjunction with each other. People experiencing this collection are referred to as being depressed. These characteristics and feelings include a general feeling of being unhappy or blue, a low level of physical energy, problems in relating to and interacting with others, guilt feelings, feelings of being stressed and burdoned, and various physical problems such as sleep disturbances, headaches, and loss of appetite (Lewinsohn et al., 1978).

Previous Attempts

People who have tried to kill themselves before are more likely to succeed than people who are trying to commit suicide for the first time. Thirty to 40 percent of all the people who succeed in killing themselves have tried before (Harvard Mental Health Letter, March 1986).

The SAD PERSONS Scale

S (Sex)

A (Age)

D (Depression)

P (Previous Attempt)

E (Ethanol Abuse)

R (Rational Thinking Loss)

S (Social Supports Lacking)

O (Organized Plan)

N (No Spouse)

S (Sickness)

SOURCE: The SAD PERSONS scale was developed by W. M. Patterson, H. H. Dohn, J. Bird, and G. A. Patterson and is reported in the "Evaluation of Suicidal Patients: The SAD PERSONS Scale," *Psychosomatics* 24(4): 343–49. Used by permission of the Academy of Psychosomatic Medicine.

Ethanol and Other Drug Abuse

People who abuse alcohol and other drugs are much more likely to commit suicide than people who do not. Such substance abuse is involved in half of all adolescent suicide attempts (Papalia and Olds, 1992). The suicide rate among narcotics addicts is five times greater than that in the non-using population (Harvard Medical School Mental Health Letter, Feb. 1986).

Rational Thinking Loss

People who suffer from mental or emotional disorders, such as depression or psychosis, are more likely to kill themselves than those who do not. Hallucinations, delusions, extreme confusion or anxiety all contribute to an individual's risk factor. If a person is not thinking realistically and objectively, emotions and impulsivity are more likely to take over, and a person is more likely to act in a desperate manner.

Social Supports Lacking

Loneliness and isolation have already been discussed as primary elements contributing to suicide. People who feel that no one cares about them may begin to feel useless and hopeless. Suicide potential may be especially high in cases where a loved one has recently died or deserted the individual who's threatening suicide.

Organized Plan

The more specific and organized an individual's plan regarding when and how the suicide will be undertaken, the greater the risk. Additionally, the more dangerous the method, the greater the risk. A plan involving placing the loaded rifle you have hidden in the basement to your head tomorrow evening at 7:00 P.M. is more lethal than a plan of somehow getting some drugs and overdosing sometime. There are several questions that might be asked when evaluating this risk factor. How much detail is involved in the plan? Has the individual put a lot of thought into developing the specific details regarding how the suicide is to occur? Has the plan been thought over before? How dangerous is the chosen method? Is the method or weapon readily available to the individual? Has the specific time been chosen for when the suicide is to take place?

No Spouse

Single people are much more likely to commit suicide than married people. People who have never married are twice as likely; divorced and widowed people have the highest suicide rates of all (Harvard Medical School Mental Health Letter, Feb. 1986; Resnick, 1980). Generally, single people have a greater chance of being lonely and isolated.

Sickness

People who are ill are more likely to commit suicide than those who are healthy (Farberow and Litman, 1975). This is especially true for those who have long-term illnesses, which place substantial limitations on their lives. Perhaps in some of these instances, their inability to cope with the additional stress of sickness and pain eats away at their overall coping ability; they then simply give up.

Other Symptoms

Other characteristics operate as warning signals for suicide. For example, rapid changes in mood, behavior, or general attitude are other indicators that a person is in danger of committing suicide. A potentially suicidal person may be one who has suddenly become severely depressed and withdrawn. On the other hand, a person who has been depressed for a long period of time and suddenly becomes strikingly cheerful may also be in danger. Sometimes in the latter instance, the individual has already made up his/her mind to commit suicide. In those instances, the cheerfulness may stem from relief that the desperate decision has finally been made.

Suddenly giving away personal possessions that are especially important or meaningful is another warning signal of suicide potential. It is as if once the decision has been made to commit suicide, giving things away to selected others is a way of finalizing the decision. Perhaps it's a way of tying up loose ends, or of making certain that the final details are taken care of.

How to use the SAD PERSONS Scale

Patterson, Dohn, Bird, and Patterson (1983, p. 348) suggest a framework for using the SAD PERSONS scale when evaluating suicide potential. One point is assigned to each condition that applies to the suicidal person. For example, if a person is depressed, he or she would automatically receive a score of 1. Depression in addition to alcoholism would result in a score of 2, and so on. Although the SAD PERSONS scale was developed specifically to teach medical students how to evaluate suicidal potential, social workers might use it in a similar manner. It may be helpful in assessing the intensity of treatment any individual might need. The following decision-making guidelines are recommended:

Total Points	Proposed Clinical Actions
0 to 2	Send home with follow-up
3 to 4	Close follow-up; Consider hospitalization
5 to 6	Strongly consider hospitalization, depending on confidence in the follow-up arrangement
7 to 10	Hospitalize or commit

Zero to 2 points might indicate a mild potential that still merits some follow-up and attention. On the other hand, a score of 7 to 10 indicates severe suicide potential. These cases would merit immediate attention and action. Hospitalization or commitment are

among available options. Scores ranging from 3 to 6 represent a range of serious suicide potential. Although people with these scores need help and attention, the immediacy and intensity of that attention may vary. In each case, professional discretion would be involved.

It should be noted that the SAD PERSONS scale was developed to aid physicians in training. It is most likely that such physicians will not be proficient in addressing mental health problems themselves. Thus, there is an emphasis on referral to someone else and on hospitalization. Social workers, on the other hand, may often be called upon to work with suicidal people. Some guidelines are described below.

Guidelines for Helping Suicidal People

Two levels of intervention are possible for dealing with a potentially suicidal person. The first involves addressing the immediate crisis. The person threatening to commit suicide needs immediate help and support literally to keep him or her alive. The second level concerns addressing the other issues which worked to escalate his or her stress. This second level of intervention might involve longer-term treatment to address other issues of longer duration which were not necessarily directly related to the suicide crisis.

For example, take a fifteen-year-old male who is deeply troubled over the serious problems his parents are currently experiencing in their marriage. This preoccupation, in addition to his normally shy personality, has alienated him from virtually any social contacts with his peers. The result is serious consideration regarding whether it is all worth it or not. The first priority is to prevent the suicide. However, this young man also needs to address and resolve the problems which caused the stress in the first place, namely, his parents' conflicts and his lack of friends. Longer-term counseling or treatment might be necessary.

Reactions to a Suicide Threat

You might get a phone call in the middle of the night from an old friend you haven't heard from in a while who says she cannot stand living anymore. Or, a client might call you late Friday afternoon and say that he is planning to shoot himself. Kiev (1980,

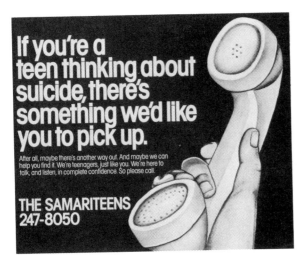

The Samariteens are teenaged volunteers from the Boston area who listen to and befriend their suicidal peers.

p. 307) makes several specific suggestions for how to treat the potentially suicidal person that include the following:

- *Remain calm.* Don't allow the emotional distress being experienced by the other person to spread and contaminate your own judgment. The individual needs help in becoming more rational and objective. The person does not need someone else who is drawn into the emotional crisis.
- *Be supportive.* It's helpful to talk about positive qualities the person has. For example, the individual might be pleasant, unselfish, hard working, conscientious, bright, attractive, and so on. People who are feeling suicidal are most likely focusing primarily on the "bad things" they perceive about themselves and their life situations. They forget their positive characteristics. One can also focus on the positive coping skills which one has used in the past.
- *Focus on the problem.* The person needs help in dealing with the immediate crisis. The top priority is to prevent the suicide from occurring. A person who is overwhelmed with problems and stress may be easily sidetracked. In these instances, you can be most helpful by remaining objective and helping the person evaluate his or her situation as objectively as possible.
- *Identify the loss.* Help the person clearly identify what is causing the excessive stress. The problem needs to be recognized before it can be examined. The individual

may be viewing an event way out of perspective. For example, a sixteen-year-old girl was crushed after her steady boyfriend of eighteen months dropped her. She felt that life was no longer worth living. In this instance, the loss of her boyfriend overshadowed all of the other things in her life—her family, her friends, her membership in the National Honor Society, and her favorite hobby of jogging. She needed help focusing on exactly what her loss had been, namely the loss of her boyfriend. To her, it felt like she had lost her whole life which was a gross distortion of reality.

- *Latch on to the will to live.* The very fact that the suicidal person came to talk to you indicates that he or she is reaching out. Especially with adolescents, there is almost always ambivalence about wanting to die. On the one hand, they want to die; but on the other hand, they want to live. It is helpful to identify and concentrate on that part of them that clutches at life.
- *Don't get into a debate.* Avoid arguing with the suicidal person about the philosophical values of life versus death. Don't use cliches like, "There's so much that life has to offer you," or, "Your life is just beginning." This type of approach only makes people feel like you're operating on a different wavelength, and really don't understand how they feel. People who threaten suicide have real suicidal feelings. They're not likely to be exaggerating them or making them up. What they need is objective, emphatic support.
- *Suggest feasible options.* Suicidal people may be in a rut of negative, depressing, suicidal thoughts. Talking with them about their other options may be very helpful. They may be blind to anything but their immediate crisis. Sometimes people in this suicidal rut have hit their lowest emotional point. Their perspective is such that they feel that life has ALWAYS been as bad as this, and that it always will be as bad as this (see Figure 6.1). In reality, the old adage, "Life has its ups and downs," is true. A suicidal person has probably been "up" before and probably will be "up" again. Many times this "sense of history" can be pointed out and used beneficially.
- *Don't give direct advice.* One of the "bottom line" dictums of social work is never, never give advice. Each individual has the right and responsibility to make his or her own decisions. A good social worker helps clients clarify their own feelings, gain an objective perspective, and make their own decisions. The client, not you, will experience the consequences of whatever decision is made.

Referrals

One of the most useful and concrete things that can be done for suicidal people is to help them get the

FIGURE 7.1: Life's Ups and Downs

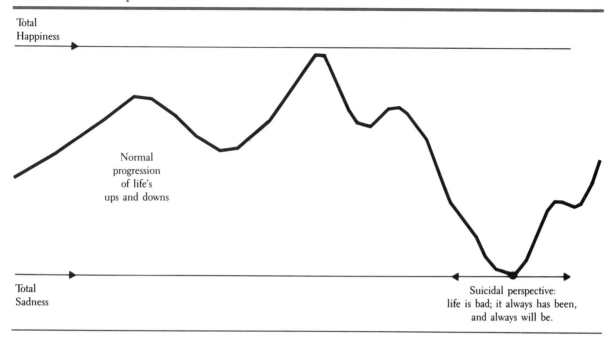

Total
Happiness

Normal
progression
of life's
ups and downs

Total
Sadness

Suicidal perspective:
life is bad; it always has been,
and always will be.

help they need. Because suicidal people tend to be isolated, this help often involves referring them to the various resources—both personal and professional—that are available. Personal sources of help may involve family or friends. There may be a minister or even a physician whom the individual trusts and could turn to. Referrals to police or hospital emergency rooms can be helpful when an emergency situation arises. Finally, professionals in mental health are available to provide long-term help to people in need.

Community Responses to Suicide: Prevention and Crisis Intervention

Community resources are critical for successful suicide prevention. You cannot refer people for help if the appropriate services don't exist. If resources are not available, you as a social worker may need to advocate to develop new programs or to expand services within your own or other agencies. There are many ways that a community system can address suicide prevention. Four will be discussed here: task forces for suicide prevention, crisis lines, peer helping

programs in schools, and training programs for community professionals.

Creation of a *suicide prevention task force* provides a potentially effective means to evaluate the need for services and decide what types of services to offer. A *task force* is "a contemporary group, usually within an organization, brought together to achieve some previously specified function or goal; an effective task force or task group knows why it is meeting, what jobs must be accomplished, who has responsibility for carrying out its decisions, and when the work is completed" (Barker, 1991, p. 235). A task force can be made up of interested individuals within an organization or a cross section of professionals and citizens within a designated community. The task force group can then make decisions regarding how the agency or community can best meet the community's need for suicide prevention services. It can answer a number of questions and decide on a plan of action. Who are the potential clients? Are there services already existing within the community that can best meet the suicide prevention need? If not, what types of programs should be initiated? What resources are available to develop such programs?

For example, the Task Force on Suicide in Canada was established in 1980. This group addressed the needs of the entire country instead of smaller community systems. Its members represented each of the twelve regions of the country. The group's purpose was to "gather and analyze the available data, to present its findings in a concise yet comprehensive report and to make recommendations where necessary and appropriate. Specific dimensions of the problem investigated include: Coroner/Medical examiners' certification procedures [to determine the cause of death]; . . . [incidence of suicide; causes of suicide]; high risk groups; primary prevention strategies; existing programs and services; the suicide prevention training of mental health professionals; and a number of insurance and legal issues" (Syer-Solursh, 1984, p. 1).

Crisis telephone lines provide one specific, useful approach to suicide prevention. Such crisis lines can be for a specific type of crisis (such as domestic violence or suicidal potential) or provide crisis intervention and referral information for virtually any type of crisis. An advantage of either type of crisis line is that people thinking about suicide can call anonymously for help at the time they need such help the most. People working on crisis lines need thorough training in suicide prevention. Additionally, such lines should have staff available at all hours of the day. Imagine the reaction of the person contemplating suicide who is told to leave her message at the sound of the beep. Finally, crisis lines should be well publicized. People will not use them if they do not know about them.

Another specific example of a community system's approach to suicide prevention is the establishment of a *peer helping program* within a school setting. One such program is "Link-Up" in Minneapolis, Minnesota (Keys, 1990). Students identified as being at risk by teachers and peers are encouraged to join. Well-adjusted students who are functioning well academically and socially are also recruited as participants. Students meet in a group for one hour weekly over the course of four or five weeks. The goal for at-risk students is to enhance self-esteem, develop more effective life coping skills, and get support from their peers. Emphasis is on developing friendships and networking with peers rather than on peer counseling. Program participants are encouraged to reach out to each other, enjoy recreational activities together,

introduce each other to other new friends, and generally improve the overall social and educational environment.

The fourth example of a community system's response to the suicide problem is the development and provision of *suicide prevention training programs for community professionals and other care givers*. Care givers include professionals such as social workers, psychologists, psychiatrists, and counselors. Care givers may also include any others that potentially suicidal people may turn to for help. These include clergy, family members, nurses, teachers, and friends. Training as many care givers as possible to deal with suicidal thoughts and threats significantly increases the chance for a potentially suicidal person to make contact with someone who can help.

Assertiveness and Assertiveness Training

Assertiveness involves behavior that is both straightforward and yet not offensive. The behavior can be either verbal or nonverbal. Assertiveness involves taking into account *both* your own rights and the rights of others. It sounds simple, but for many people appropriate assertiveness is difficult to master. For instance, take the two people sitting in front of you in a movie theater who are talking loudly. How should you react? Should you ignore them even though it's the scariest portion of the latest horror film? Should you scream "Shut up"? Or, should you tap one of them gently on the shoulder and politely ask them to please be quiet?

Your best friend asks to borrow your car. Your friend emphasizes it'll only be for one time and it's needed for *such an important reason!* You happen to know that your friend is not a very good driver, has gotten two speeding tickets in the past six months, and sometimes drives after drinking. Should you say, "No way! You know what a horrible driver you are"? Should you say, "Sure"? Should you say, "Well, okay, I guess so"? Or, should you say, "No. You know I don't let other people drive my car. Would it help if I drive you somewhere?"

Many times it's difficult to look at a situation objectively and take the feelings and needs of all concerned into account. Often, it's especially difficult for adolescents and young people who are still getting to know themselves and establishing their own identities. On the other, they want to fit in socially and respond to the feelings of others.

Assertiveness involves specific skills which can be taught. This, of course, is referred to as assertiveness training. Adolescents and young people may find assertiveness skills especially valuable as they decide how to react in new situations, especially when under social pressure. For example, they might struggle regarding how to respond in sexual situations. *What do I want to do versus what does my partner want to do?* Another example involves decisions about taking drugs. *Everyone is doing it; what should I do?* Here we will discuss in more depth the meaning of assertiveness and some concepts involved in assertiveness training.

Most people remember occasions on which they wish they could have been more assertive. Yet, at those moments they felt very uncomfortable doing so. On the other hand, many people have also experienced situations in which they "lost it," and exploded in a loud burst of anger. An example is a newly married twenty-two-year-old woman who is "at her wits' end" with her husband's best friend. He continues to make derogatory racial slurs against almost anyone who is not white, of a certain religious group, and of European heritage. The young woman, a newly graduated social worker, tries everything she can think of to turn the friend's comments off. She tries ignoring him. She tries to change the subject. Yet, she doesn't want to offend the man. After all, he is her husband's best friend. Finally, something snaps and she screams, "I can't stand it anymore. I think you're a disgusting bigot. Just shut up!" This outburst does little for their relationship.

Nonassertive, Assertive, and Aggressive Communication

On an assertiveness continuum, communication can be rated as nonassertive, assertive, or aggressive. Assertive communication involves verbal and nonverbal behavior that permits speakers to make points clearly and straightforwardly. *Assertive* speakers take into consideration both their own value system and the values of whomever is receiving their message. They consider their own points to be important; yet, they

also consider the points and reactions of the communication's receiver important.

For example, the president of the Student Social Work Club asks Maria to take notes at a meeting three meetings in a row. The club's secretary, who is supposed to take notes, is absent all three times. Maria is willing to serve, but feels it's unfair to ask her to do the work every time instead of letting others help, too. Maria assertively states to the club president, "This is the third meeting in a row that you've asked me to take notes. I'm happy to help out, but I feel that it's fair to share this task with other club members. Why don't you ask someone else to take notes this time?"

Aggressive communication involves bold and dominant verbal and nonverbal behavior in which a speaker presses his or her point of view as taking precedence above all others. Aggressive speakers consider only their views as important and devalue what the receiver has to say. Aggressive behaviors are demanding and most often annoying. Consider, for example, the man who barges in at the sales return desk in front of seventeen other people standing in line and demands *service!*

Nonassertive communication, on the other hand, is the opposite of aggressive. Speakers devalue themselves completely. They feel that the other person involved and what that person thinks is much more important than their own thoughts. For example, for lunch one day Cassie orders a hamburger well done. The waitress brings her a burger that's practically dripping in blood. Cassie, however, is afraid of what the waitress will think if she complains. Cassie doesn't want to be a "bitch." So, instead of assertively telling the waitress that the hamburger is much too rare, Cassie douses it in ketchup and forces herself to eat half of it.

There is no perfect recipe for what to say to be assertive in any particular situation. The important thing is to take into consideration both your own rights and the rights of the person you are talking to. Following are a few examples.

Situation 1: A sixteen-year-old woman is on her first date with a young man she likes. After a movie and pizza, they drive around a bit and find a secluded spot in the country where he pulls over and parks. The woman does not want to get sexually involved with the young man. She thinks this is too soon in

Before responding, these members of a high school debating club are practicing assertiveness by measuring the value of their opinions against those of the speaker.

their relationship. What will he think of her? She doesn't know him well enough yet to become intimate. What can she say?

Nonassertive Response: She says nothing and lets him make his sexual advances.

Aggressive Response: "Get your slimy hands off me, you pervert!"

Assertive Response: "I like you, Harry, but I don't think we know each other well enough yet to get involved this way. Would you please take me home now?"

Situation 2: Biff, Clay's supervisor at Stop 'n' Shop, tells Clay that he needs him to work several extra hours the upcoming weekend. Biff has often asked Clay to work extra time on weekends. However, he doesn't ask any of the other workers to do so. Clay thinks this is unfair. He needs his job, but he hates to work extra hours on weekends. What can he say?

Nonassertive Response: "Okay."

Aggressive Response: "No way, Jose! Get off my butt, Biff!"

Assertive Response: "You know I like my job here, Biff. However, I'm sorry, but I can't work extra hours next weekend. I've already made other plans."

Situation 3: Dinah Lee and Hannah, both eighteen, "hang around" with the same group of friends. However, they don't like each other very much. Dinah Lee approaches Hannah one day and says, "It's too bad you're gaining so much weight." What can Hannah say?

Nonassertive Response: "Yes, you're right. I'm trying to go on a diet."

Aggressive Response: "I'm not nearly as fat or ugly as you are, Buzzard Breath!"

Assertive Response: "No, I haven't gained any weight. I think that was a very inappropriate thing to say. It sounded as if you were just trying to hurt my feelings."

The Advantages of Assertiveness

There are many benefits to developing assertiveness skills (Lewinsohn et al., 1978; Sundel and Sundel, 1980). For one thing, you can gain more control over your interpersonal environment. Assertiveness may help you avoid uncomfortable or hostile interactions with others. You will probably feel that other people understand you better than they did before. Your self-concept can be enhanced as the result of your gain in control and interpersonal effectiveness. In the past you may have bottled up your feelings and suffered psychosomatic problems such as headaches or stomach upsets. Appropriate assertiveness helps to alleviate building up undue tension and stress and diminish such psychosomatic reactions. Finally, other people may gain respect for you, your strength, and your own demonstration of respect for others. People may even begin to use you as a role model for their own development of assertive behavior.

Assertiveness Training

Assertiveness training leads people to realize, feel, and act on the assumption that they have the right to be themselves and express their feelings freely. Assertive responses generally are not aggressive responses. The distinction between these two types of interactions is important. For example, a woman has an excessively critical father-in-law. Intentionally doing things that will bother him (bringing up topics that she knows will upset him; forgetting Father's Day and his birthday, not visiting) and getting into loud arguments with him would be considered "aggressive" behavior.

On the other hand, an effectively assertive response would be to counter criticism by saying, "Dad,

---

Each of Us Has Certain Assertive Rights

Part of becoming assertive involves believing that we are valuable and worthwhile people. It's easy to criticize ourselves for our mistakes and imperfections. And it's easy to hold our feelings in because we're afraid that we will hurt someone else's feelings or that someone will reject us. Sometimes feelings that are held in too long will burst out in an aggressive tirade. This applies to anyone, including our clients.

A basic principle in social work is that each individual is a valuable human being. Everyone, therefore, has certain basic rights.

The following are eight of your and your clients' assertive rights:

1. You have the right to express your ideas and opinions openly and honestly.
2. You have the right to be wrong. Everyone makes mistakes.
3. You have the right to direct and govern your own life. In other words, you have the right to be responsible for yourself.
4. You have the right to stand up for yourself without unwarranted anxiety and make choices that are good for you.
5. You have the right *not* to be liked by everyone (Do you like *everyone* you know?)
6. You have the right to make requests and to refuse them without feeling guilty.
7. You have the right to ask for information if you need it.
8. Finally, you have the right to decide not to exercise your assertive rights. In other words, you have the right to choose not to be assertive.

SOURCE: Most of these rights are adapted from *The New Assertive Woman* by Lynn Z. Bloom, Karen Coburn, and Joan Pearlman (New York: Dell, 1976) and *Four One-Day Workshops* by Kathyryn Apgar and Betsy Nicholson Callahan (Boston: Resource Communications Inc. and Family Service Association of Greater Boston, 1980).

---

your criticism deeply hurts me. I know you're trying to help when you give advice, but I feel that you're criticizing me. I'm an adult, and I have the right to make my own decisions and mistakes. The type of relationship that I'd like to have with you is a close adult relationship and not a father-child relationship."

As we know, social work is practical. Therefore, you can use the suggestions provided to enhance both your client's assertiveness and your own. Alberti and Emmons (1976) developed the following thirteen steps to help establish assertive behavior.

1. Examine your own actions. How do you behave in situations requiring assertiveness? Do you think you tend to be nonassertive, assertive, or aggressive in most of your communications?
2. Make a record of those situations in which you felt you could have behaved more effectively, either more assertively or less aggressively.
3. Select and focus on some specific instance when you felt you could have been more appropriately assertive. Visualize the specific details. What exactly was said? How did you feel?
4. Analyze how you reacted. Examine closely your verbal and nonverbal behavior. Alberti and Emmons (1976, pp. 31–32) cite the following seven aspects of behavior that are important to monitor. They include:
   a. "Eye contact." Did you look the person in the eye? Or, were your eyes downcast? Did you find yourself avoiding eye contact when you were uncomfortable?
   b. "Body posture." Were you standing up straight or were you slouching? Were you leaning away from the person sheepishly? Were you holding your head up straight as you looked the person in the eye?
   c. "Gestures." Were your hand gestures fitting for the situation? Did you feel at ease? Or, were you tapping your feet or cracking your knuckles? In the beginning of his term, people often criticized President George Bush for moving his arms and hands around during his public speeches. This tended to give the public the impression that he was frantic. Professional coaches helped him gain control of this behavior and present a calmer public image.
   d. "Facial expressions." Did you have a serious expression on your face? Were you smiling or giggling uncomfortably, thereby giving the impression that you were not really serious?
   e. "Voice tone, inflection, volume." Did you speak in a normal voice tone? Did you whisper timidly? Did

you raise your voice to the point of stressful screeching? Did you sound as if you were whining?

    f. "Timing." It is best to make an appropriately assertive response just after a remark is made or an incident happens. It's also important to consider whether a particular situation requires assertiveness. At times it might be best to remain silent and just "let it go." For example, it might not be wise to criticize your professor for being a "dreary bore" in a class presentation you are giving that your professor is simultaneously grading.

    g. "Content." What you say in your assertive response is obviously important. Did you choose your words carefully? Did your response have the impact you wanted it to have? Why or why not?

5. Identify a role model and examine how he or she handled a situation requiring assertiveness. What exactly happened during the incident? What words did your model use that were particularly effective? What aspects of his or her nonverbal behavior helped to get points across?

6. Identify a range of other new assertive responses that could address the original problem situation you targeted. What other words could you have used? What nonverbal behaviors might have been more effective?

7. Picture yourself in the identified problematic situation. It often helps to close your eyes and concentrate. Step by step, imagine how you could handle the situation more assertively.

8. Practice the way you have envisioned yourself being more assertive. On the one hand, you can target a real-life situation that remains unresolved. For example, perhaps, the person you live with always leaves dirty socks lying around the living room or drinks all your pop and forgets to tell you the refrigerator is bare. On the other hand, you can ask a friend, teacher, or counselor to help you role play the situation. Role playing provides effective mechanisms for practicing responses before you have to use them spontaneously in real life.

9. Once again, review your new assertive responses. Emphasize your strong points and try to remedy your flaws.

10. Continue practicing steps 7, 8, and 9 until your newly developed assertive approach feels comfortable and natural to you.

11. Try out your assertiveness in a real-life situation.

12. Continue to expand your assertive behavior repertoire until assertiveness becomes part of your personal interactive style. You can review the earlier steps and try them out with an increasingly wider range of problematic situations.

13. Give yourself a pat on the back when you succeed in becoming more assertive. It's not easy changing longstanding patterns of behavior. Focus on and revel in the good feelings you experience as a result of your successes.

Application of Assertiveness Approaches to Social Work Practice

Helping clients learn to be more assertive is appropriate in a wide range of practice situations. For example, teenagers may need to develop assertiveness skills to ward off the massive peer pressure engulfing them. This means more than "just saying no" to drugs, sex, or any other activity they may not want to participate in but feel pressured to do so. Assertiveness training involves enhancing people's self-concepts and helping people identify alternative types of responses in uncomfortable situations. Finally, assertiveness training concerns working out and practicing these alternative responses ahead of time so that they become easier and more natural.

Other examples of clients needing assertiveness training include a shy, reserved client who needs to assertively ask his landlord to do some repairs desperately needed in the client's apartment. Still another client might need help becoming more assertive in preparation for a job interview.

Workers themselves need to develop assertiveness skills in order to advocate for services on the behalf of their clients. Good communication skills and a respect for others are basic necessities for social work practice. You can lead your clients through each step in assertiveness training to become more competent and effective communicators.

Women: A Population-at-Risk

Because of traditional gender role stereotypes, women continue to manifest a number of problems related to lack of assertion. Collier (1982, p. 65) states it well:

> The culture teaches women that they are mediators and conciliators, not direct parties to conflict; they are to be gentle, nurturing, softspoken, and unaggressive. But this suppression of the ability to confront frustration, disappointment, conflicts of interest, anger, and even minor

irritation demands a high price. Most women need to learn how to improve the direct expression of their needs, wants, and feelings. This need is so widespread that it accounts for the instant popularity of what is called "assertiveness training," which gives women the tools for expressing themselves. The need of many women, however, is deeper; they need to learn that their emotions are valid, that they have a right to express them, and that other people have the obligation to respond.

For many women, assertiveness training is just a beginning.

Summary

Adolescent identity is discussed, and Erikson's eight stages of psychosexual development are described. One of these stages, the crisis of identity versus role diffusion that occurs during adolescence is discussed in some detail. Marcia's four categories of identity include identity achievement, foreclosure, identity diffusion, and moratorium. Kohlberg's theory of moral development has three levels: preconventional, conventional, and post-conventional.

Two issues that are especially significant in adolescence and young adulthood are suicide and assertiveness. Potential causes of suicide include feelings of helplessness, loneliness, impulsivity, lack of a stable environment, and increased external and internal pressures. People need to distinguish between nonassertive, aggressive, and assertive styles of interaction. Assertive rights are reviewed. Thirteen steps involved in assertiveness training are explained, and how assertiveness training may be used in social work practice is discussed.

8

Social Systems and Their Impacts on Adolescence and Young Adulthood

Defining. Refining. Combining.

Laura Sardina is nineteen years old and is wondering what the future holds for her. She lives with her parents and has a job as a hotel maid for which she receives the minimum hourly wage. She has frequent arguments with her mother, and both of her parents have encouraged her to get a better paying job so that she can become self-supporting and move out of the house. She realizes that a minimum-wage job will not enable her to live in an apartment, buy a car, buy clothes and food, and have sufficient money for entertainment.

Laura was raised in a middle-class family. Her brother is attending college to become a minister. Religion has always been an important aspect of Laura's parents' lives, but not of Laura's. She detests going to church. She would rather party. Her parents have often called her "stupid" and negatively compared her to her brother who they believe can do no wrong. This disparagement of Laura has in many ways become a self-fulfilling prophecy. She repeated a grade in elementary school, seldom studied, and often received failing grades.

In school she saw herself as a failure and hung out with other students who viewed themselves as failures. In high school, she frequently skipped school and partied. Eight weeks before graduation, she was expelled for skipping too much school. Her parents and the school system had tried numerous times to motivate Laura to apply herself in school; she even had a number of individual sessions with three different social workers and a psychiatrist.

Laura knows her parents want her to leave home. Her parents are especially irate when she leaves home for three to four days at a time and parties in an abandoned house in the inner city of Milwaukee. She has lied to her parents about her sexual activities, when the truth is she has had a variety of partners. Fortunately, she is taking birth control pills. Some of Laura's male friends are putting excessive pressure on her to become a prostitute so that there will be more money to buy drugs and party. Laura and her friends have had several encounters with the police for shoplifting, running away from home, drinking liquor under age, kicking police officers while being arrested, and high speed auto chases after radar detected they were speeding.

Laura is asking herself a number of questions. Should she prostitute herself? Or, should she stop associating with her friends and try to make peace with her parents by seeking a high school education and a better paying job? Whenever she has tried in the past to achieve the middle-class goals set by her parents she has been criticized by her parents as being a failure—she wonders what are her chances of making it this time? The one thing she has found enjoyable in life is partying with her friends, but she realizes her friends are getting her in trouble with the police. She is worried that cutting ties with her friends will result in living a life in which she will be continually rejected and put down by others. She wants a better paying job but realizes her chances are not good, especially since she hasn't completed high school. She wants a one-to-one relationship with a caring male, but because she has a low self-concept, the only thing she feels that males will find attractive about her is sexual intercourse. This has been a factor in her having multiple sex partners. She is increasingly concerned that being so sexually active is not right and may result in her acquiring a sexually transmitted disease (such as AIDS). What should she do about all of these concerns? She is deeply perplexed and confused.

A PERSPECTIVE

This chapter will focus primarily on the social changes and social problems encountered by adolescents and young adults. The social growth from puberty to roughly age thirty involves a number of passages: from being dependent on parents to becoming more independent, from adjusting to puberty to establishing a sexual identity, from beginning to date to usually marrying, from being a child with parents to parenting children, from earning money from babysitting to selecting a career and starting one's life work, from buying baseball gloves and playing ball to buying a car and traveling, from drinking pop to drinking beer and hard liquor and experimenting with drugs. The pressures and stresses of this time period have many casualties who suffer from a variety of problems.

This chapter will:

- Describe the social system changes that adolescents and young adults undergo.
- Describe the following lifestyles and family forms that young adults may enter into: marriage, cohabitation, single life, parenthood, and childless couples.
- Describe some major problems encountered by this age group: emotional and behavioral problems, crime and delinquency, delinquent gangs, and eating disorders.
- Present theoretical material on the causes and treatments of these problems.

Social System Changes in Adolescence and Young Adulthood

During adolescence and young adulthood, people move from dependence on parents to adult independence, establish peer relationships and intimate relationships, and choose a personal lifestyle involving decisions about career, marriage, and children.

Movement from Dependence to Independence

Young people often are in a conflict between wanting to be independent of their parents and yet on another level realizing their parents are providing for many of their wants and needs: food, shelter, clothes, emotional support, spending money, and so on. Many young people see their parents as having shortcomings and conclude they know more than their parents. Yet, when their automobile breaks down and they have no idea of how to fix it, mom or dad almost always knows what to do to get it fixed.

In the pursuit of independence, adolescents often rebel against their parents' attempts to guide them and reject their views as being out of date and stupid. They sometimes do things to shock them as if to say "See, I'm my own person and I'm going to live my life my way!" Interestingly, once young people become more independent in their twenties and have to pay their own bills, they tend to have a greater appreciation of their parents' knowledge. Mark Twain noted (quoted in Papalia and Olds, 1981, p. 375) "When I was fourteen my father knew nothing, but when I was twenty-one, I was amazed at how much the old man had learned in those seven years."

Children who are raised in families where the parents have helped them in the growing-up process by providing opportunities to learn self-reliance, responsibility, and self-respect tend to make a smoother transition from dependency to adulthood interdependence. Children who are raised in families where the parents are overly permissive or where the parents take little interest in their behavior tend to have greater difficulty making the transition to adulthood as they lack structure or a system of standards and values to gauge whether their behavior is suitable and their decisions are appropriate (Scheck and El-Assal, 1973). Children who have overly protective parents

By working together, a family helps children learn self-reliance, responsibility, and self-respect.

also have difficulty making this transition as they usually do not learn how to assume responsibilities or make important decisions.

Some parents are wary about their children growing up. In particular, some fathers and mothers become alarmed and uncomfortable when their "little girl" starts dating. Many parents worry their daughter may become sexually involved and pregnant, which they believe will adversely affect her and interfere with their dreams and hopes for her having the good life. When teenagers assert their right to becoming more independent, it changes the components of the family system. Any change in the components of the system will create tension within the family. This tension is expressed by teens with such statements as "You don't understand me," "Get off my back," "I know what I'm doing—don't treat me like a baby," and "Chill out."

Parents may feel hurt by what they perceive as a lack of appreciation or gratitude. Common areas of conflict between parents and adolescents according to Kaluger and Kaluger (1984, p. 370) are: performing home chores; use of time; attitude toward studies; expenditures of money; morals and manners; choice of friends; clothes selection; use of phone; dating practices; and use of car.

How should parents seek to cope with thrusts of independence from their teenagers? Kaluger and Kaluger (1984, p. 370) recommend the following:

> The most important thing for parents to keep in mind, at any time or any age of the child, is not to do or say anything that will break down or cut off the lines of communication between parent and child. All teenagers need help, even if they do not recognize this need or seem grateful for it. They must feel free to seek that help from their parents or loved ones. If teenagers cannot talk to their parents or to other acceptable adults, they have only their peers and friends to turn to. How much advice and information on serious matters can one thirteen-year-old or fifteen-year-old give to another?

Keeping the lines of communication open is admittedly easier said than done. It requires work!

The task of becoming independent involves attaining emotional, social, and economic independence. Emotional independence involves progressing from emotional dependence on parents or on others, to relative independence while still being able to maintain close emotional ties; it involves moving from a parent-child relationship to an adult-adult relationship. Emotional independence involves becoming self-reliant with the knowledge that, "I am put together well enough emotionally that I can fend for myself, but I am willing to share my feelings with others and let them become part of me." Emotional independence involves receiving and sharing and being interdependent, without being emotionally dominated or overwhelmed.

Social independence involves becoming self-directed rather than other-directed. Many adolescents are other-directed as they are so strongly motivated for social acceptance that much of what the group says is what adolescents think and do. Self-directed people factor things out of themselves and make decisions based on their personal interests. Becoming socially independent does not mean becoming selfish, as socially independent people realize their best interests are served by becoming involved in political, civic, educational, religious, social, and community affairs.

Economic independence involves earning sufficient money to meet one's financial needs. Many older teenagers and young adults do not have special skills, and, therefore, obtaining good paying jobs to meet their financial needs is very difficult. Economic independence also involves learning to limit desires and purchases to ability to pay. To become economically independent it is necessary to develop at least one marketable set of skills that one can offer an employer in exchange for a job. As Prather (1970, p. 41) notes, it is important for people to realize that the more they earn, the more they will desire:

> The number of things just outside the perimeter of my financial reach remains constant on matter how much my financial condition improves. With each increase in my income a new perimeter forms and I experience the same relative sense of lack. I believe that I would be happy if only my earnings were increased by so much that I could then have or do these few things I can't quite afford, but when my income does increase I find I am still unhappy because from my new financial position I can now see a whole new set of things I don't have.

Interaction in Peer Group Systems

Adolescents have a strong *herd* drive and desire to be accepted by their peers. Peers are an important influence on adolescents. An extensive government study involving over three thousand teenagers concluded that peers are more of a factor than parents in determining whether a youth will become involved in serious juvenile delinquency (Papalia and Olds, 1981, p. 376).

This study does not mean that peers are more of an influence than parents in all areas. Brittain (1963) conducted a study of teenage females which found that whether parents or peers have more influence depended on the particular situation. The respondents relied more on peers for deciding how to dress and on how to resolve school-centered dilemmas. The respondents relied more on parental opinions for deciding which job to take, on how to resolve complicated moral conflicts, and on other long-range issues.

The particular kind of peer group that an adoles-

cent selects depends on a variety of factors: socioeconomic status (most peer groups are class bound); values derived from parents; the neighborhood that one lives in; nature of school; special talents and abilities; and the personality of the adolescent. Once an adolescent becomes a member of a peer group, the members of that subgroup influence each other in their social activities, study habits, dress, sexual behavior, use or nonuse of drugs, vocational pursuits, and hobbies.

Not all adolescents join cliques. Some prefer to be loners. Some are already pursuing what they believe will be their life goals. Some may be busy babysitting for younger children in the family. Some prefer having only one or two close friends. Some are excluded from the cliques that exist in their areas.

Adolescents tend to identify with other teenagers, rather than with adults or younger children. Sorenson (1973) suggests this identification may be due to teens believing that most other teens share their personal values and interests, while younger and older people are seen as having more divergent interests and values. Compared to people in their forties and fifties, adolescents view themselves as being less materialistic, more idealistic, healthier sexually, and better able to understand friendships and what is important in life.

Friends and peer groups help adolescents and young adults to make the transition from parental dependence to independence. Friends give each other emotional support and also serve as important points of reference for young people to compare their beliefs, values, attitudes, and abilities. In a number of cases friendships forged during adolescence endure throughout life.

Weiss and Lowenthal (1976) conducted a study on adolescent friendships and found the following five dimensions were important in selecting and maintaining friendship relationships:

1. *Similarity*—in values, personality, attitudes, shared activities or experiences.
2. *Reciprocity*—understanding, helping, accepting each other, mutual trust, and ability to share confidences.
3. *Compatibility*—enjoyment of being together.
4. *Structure*—geographic closeness, and long duration of acquaintanceship.
5. *Role-modeling*—respect and admiration for the friend's good qualities.

Interaction in Families: Effective Communication Between Parents and Children

Thomas Gordon (1970) in Parent Effectiveness Training has identified four communication techniques that are designed to improve relationships between parents and their children.

Active Listening

This technique is recommended for use when a child indicates he or she has a problem; for example, when a sixteen-year-old daughter looks in a mirror and states "I'm fat and ugly—all of my friends have boyfriends, and not me." For such situations Gordon recommends that the parent use active listening. The steps involved in active listening are the receiver of a message tries to understand what the sender's message means or what the sender is feeling, and the receiver then puts this understanding into his or her own words and returns this understanding for the sender's verification. In using this approach, the receiver does *not* send a message of his or her own, such as asking a question, giving advice, expressing feelings, or giving an opinion. The aim is to feed back only what he or she feels the sender's message meant. An active listening response to the sixteen-year-old girl in the above example might be "You want very much to have a boyfriend and think the reason you don't is related to your physical appearance." An active listening response involves either *reflecting feelings* or *restating content.*

Dr. Gordon lists a number of advantages for using active listening. It facilitates problem solving by young people, which fosters the development of responsibility. By talking a problem through, a person is more apt to identify the root of the problem and arrive at a solution than by merely thinking about a problem. When a teenager feels his or her parents are listening, a by-product is that he or she will be more apt to listen to the parents' point of view. In addition, the relationship between parent and youth is apt to be improved because when children feel they are being heard and understood, they are apt to feel warmth toward the parent. Finally, the approach helps a teen to explore, recognize, and express his or her feelings.

Dr. Gordon mentions certain parental attitudes are required to use this technique. The parent must view the young person as being a separate person with his or her own feelings. The parent must be able to accept the youth's feelings, whatever they may be. The parent should genu-

inely want to be helpful and must want to hear what the child has to say. Additionally, the parent must have trust in his or her capacities to handle problems and feelings.

I-Messages

Many occasions arise when a young person causes a problem for the parent: for example, a daughter may turn up the stereo so high that the music is irritating, or she may stay out after curfew hours, or she may recklessly drive an auto. Confronted with such situations many parents send either a solution message (they order, direct, command, warn, threaten, preach, moralize, or advise), or a put-down message (they blame, judge, criticize, ridicule, or name-call). Solution and put-down messages can have devastating effects on a child's self-concept and are generally counterproductive in helping a child become responsible.

Solution and put-down messages are primarily *you-messages:* "you do what I say," "don't you do that," "why don't you be good," "you're lazy," "you should know better."

Dr. Gordon advocates that parents should instead send *I-messages* for those occasions when a teenager is causing a problem for the parent. For example, take a parent who is riding in a car where the son is driving and exceeding the speed limit. Instead of the parent saying "Slow down, you idiot, do you want to get us killed," Dr. Gordon urges the parent to use an I-message: "Driving this fast really frightens me."

I-messages, in essence, are nonblaming messages that communicate only how the sender of the message believes the receiver is adversely affecting the sender. I-messages do not provide a solution nor are they put-down messages. It is possible to send an I-message without using the word I, as the essence of an I-message involves sending a nonblaming message of how the parent feels the child's behavior is affecting the parent.

You-messages are generally put-down messages that either convey a message to youths that they should do something or convey to them how bad they are. In contrast, I-messages communicate to young people much more honestly the effect of the behavior on the parent. I-messages are also more effective because they help teenagers to learn to assume responsibility for their own behavior. An I-message tells teenagers that the parent is trusting them to respect the parent's needs and that the parent is trusting them to handle the situation constructively.

You-messages frequently lead to an argument between parent and youth, while I-messages are much less likely to produce an argument. I-messages lead to honesty and openness in a relationship, and generally foster intimacy. Teenagers, as well as adults, often do not know how their behavior affects others. I-messages produce startling results as parents frequently report that their teenagers express surprise upon learning how their parents really feel.

No-Lose Problem Solving

In every parent-teenager relationship there are inevitable situations where the youth continues to behave in a way that interferes with the needs of the parent. Conflict is part of life and not necessarily bad. Conflict is bound to occur because people are different and have different needs and wants, which at times do not match. What is important is not how frequently conflict arises, but how the conflicts get resolved. Generally in a conflict between parent and youth, a power struggle is created.

In many families the power struggle is resolved by one of two win-lose approaches. Most parents try to resolve the conflict by having the parent winning and the young person losing. Psychologically, parents almost always are recognized as having greater authority. The outcome of the parent winning is that it creates resentment in the teenager toward his parents, leads to low motivation for him to carry out the solution, and does not provide an opportunity for him to develop self-discipline and self-responsibility. Such teenagers are likely to react by becoming either hostile, rebellious, and aggressive, or submissive, dependent, and withdrawing.

In other families, fewer in number, the win-lose conflict is resolved by the parents giving in to their teenagers out of fear of frustrating them or fear of conflict. In such families teenagers come to believe their needs are more important than anyone else's. They generally become self-centered, selfish, demanding, impulsive, and uncontrollable. They are viewed as being spoiled by others, have difficulty in interacting with peers, and also do not have respect for property or feelings of others.

Of course, few parents use either approach exclusively. Oscillating between the two approaches is common. There is evidence that both approaches lead to the development of emotional problems in children (Gordon, 1970, p. 161).

Dr. Gordon seriously questions whether power is necessary or justified in a parent-teenager relationship. For one reason, as teenagers grow older, they become less dependent, and parents gradually lose their power. Rewards and punishments that worked in young years become less effective as youths grow older. Teenagers resent those who have power over them, and parents frequently feel guilty after using power. Dr. Gordon believes that parents continue to use power because they have had little experience in using nonpower methods of influence.

Dr. Gordon suggests a new approach, the *no-lose approach* to solving conflicts. The approach involves each parent and youth solving their conflicts by finding their own unique solutions acceptable to both.

The no-lose approach is simple to state—each person in the conflict treats the other with respect, neither person tries to win the conflict by the use of power, and a creative solution acceptable to both parties is sought. The two basic premises to no-lose problem solving are (a) that all people have the right to get their needs met and (b) that what is in conflict between the two parties involved is not their *needs* but their *solutions* to those needs.

Dr. Gordon (1970, p. 237) lists the six steps to the no-lose method as:

Step 1: Identifying and defining the needs of each person.
Step 2: Generating possible alternative solutions.
Step 3: Evaluating the alternative solutions.
Step 4: Deciding on the best acceptable solution.
Step 5: Working out ways of implementing the solution.
Step 6: Following up to evaluate how it worked.

This approach motivates youths to carry out the solution because they participated in the decision. It develops their thinking skills and a sense of responsibility. It requires less enforcement, eliminates the need for power, and improves relationships between parents. It also develops their problem-solving skills.

(continued next page)

Interaction in Families: Effective Communication Between Parents and Children (continued)

Collisions of Values

Collisions of values are common between parents and their children, particularly as the children become adolescents and young adults. Likely areas of conflict include values about sexual behavior, clothing, religion, choice of friends, education, plans for the future, use of drugs, hairstyles, and eating habits. In these areas emotions run strong and parents generally seek to influence their offspring to follow the values the parents hold as important. Teenagers, on the other hand, often think their parents' values are old fashioned and stupid and declare that they want to make their own decisions about these matters.

Dr. Gordon asserts there are three constructive ways in which parents and teenagers can seek to resolve these conflicts. (For the sake of simplicity, we will use the term *mother* in describing what should be done—a father or a teenager can also use these same techniques.)

The first way a mother can influence her offspring's values is to model the values she holds as important. If she values honesty, she should be honest. If she values responsible use of drugs, she should exhibit a responsible model. If she values openness, she should be open. She needs to ask herself if she is living according to the values she professes. If her values and behavior are incongruent in certain areas, she needs to change either her values or behavior in the direction of congruency. Congruence between behavior and values is important if she wants to be an effective model.

The second way she can influence her teenagers' values is to act as a consultant to them. There are some do's and don'ts of a good consultant. First of all, a good consultant finds out whether the other person would like her consultation. If the answer is "yes," she then makes sure she has all the available pertinent facts. She then shares these facts—once—so that the other person understands them. She then leaves the other person the responsibility for deciding whether to follow the advice, or not. A good consultant is neither uninformed nor a nag, otherwise she is not apt to be used as a consultant again.

The third way for a mother to reduce tensions over values issues is to modify her values. By examining the values held by her teenagers, she may realize their values have merit, and she may move toward their values or at least toward an understanding of why they hold them as values.

(It should be noted all of these techniques can be used to improve communication and relationships in practically all interactions, such as adult-adult, and counselor-client. The techniques are much broader in application than just parent-teenager.)

SOURCE: Adapted from Charles Zastrow, *The Practice of Social Work*, 2nd ed., (Homewood, IL: Dorsey, 1985). Used with permission of the Dorsey Press.

Intimacy versus Isolation

Erikson (1950) theorized that after young people develop a sense of identity, they next face the psychosocial crisis of intimacy versus isolation, which generally occurs in young adulthood (roughly during the twenties). Intimacy is the capacity to experience an open, tender, supportive relationship with another person, without fear of losing one's own identity in the process of growing close. In such a relationship the partners are able to understand, cognitively and emotionally, each other's points of view. An intimate relationship permits the sharing of personal feelings as well as the disclosure of ideas and plans that are not fully developed. There is respect for each other and mutual enrichment in the interactions. Each person perceives an enhancement of his or her well-being through the stimulating interactions with the other.

Intimacy involves being empathetic and being able to give and receive pleasure within the relationship. Although intimacy is often established within the context of a marital relationship, marriage itself does not produce intimacy. In some marriages there is considerable intimacy (including sharing and mutual respect). However, in empty-shell marriages and in marriages with considerable conflict, there is very little intimacy. There are additional contexts where

As these teen "Punkers" in Cologne, Germany, demonstrate, peer group members influence each other in dress, social activities, and behavior.

intimacy is apt to develop. The work setting is one of these, where close friendships are often formulated. Close friendship are also apt to develop through membership in social and religious organizations.

Traditional socialization patterns in our society create different problems for males and females in the establishment of intimacy. Boys are taught to be restrained in expressing their feelings and personal thoughts. They are also socialized to be competitive and self-reliant. They are raised to believe that they should be sexually aggressive and seek to "go as far as possible" in order to demonstrate their virility to their male friends. Males are thus unprepared for intimate heterosexual relationships—which require that they express their feelings, be supportive rather than competitive, and have a commitment to continuing the relationship rather than piling up sexual trophies.

Traditionally, women are socialized to be better prepared for the emotional demands of intimacy. They are socialized to express their feelings and personal thoughts and to be nurturant. They may, however, enter an intimate relationship with inappropriate expectations based on traditional gender-role stereotypes. For example, they may expect their partner to be stronger or more resourceful than he is. (The women's movement is changing sex role expectations and socialization practices for males and females; hopefully, the difficulties that men and women experience in forming intimate relationships will be reduced in future years).

The negative pole of the crisis of young adulthood is isolation. People who resist intimacy must continually erect barriers between themselves and others. Some people view intimacy as a blurring of the boundaries of their own identity and, therefore, are reluctant to become involved in intimate relationships. Some people are so busy seeking or maintaining their identity that they cannot share and express themselves in an intimate relationship.

Isolation may also result from situational factors. A young person may be so involved in studying to get into medical school that he or she may not have the time for an intimate relationship. Or, a teenage female may become pregnant, deliver and start raising the child, and then have few opportunities to become involved in a close relationship with an adult.

Theories about Why People Choose Each Other as Mates

The reasons that people choose each other as partners are complex and vary greatly. Certainly, such factors as religion, age, race, ethnic group, social class, and parental pressures influence the choice of mates. In addition, many theories suggest additional factors. Some of these theories are summarized here. (No theory fully identifies all of the factors involved in mate selection.)

Propinquity theory asserts that nearness or being in close proximity is a major factor in mate selection. This theory suggests we are apt to select a mate with whom we are in close association, such as at school or at work or whom we meet through neighborhood, church, or recreational activities (Rubin, 1973).

Ideal mate theory suggests we choose a mate who has the characteristics and traits we desire in a partner. This theory is symbolized by the statement, "He's everything I've ever wanted."

Congruence in values theory holds that our value system consciously and unconsciously guides us in selecting a mate who has similar values (Grush and Yehl, 1979).

Homogamy theory suggests that we select a mate who has similar racial, economic, and social characteristics.

Complementary needs theory holds that we either select a partner who has the characteristics we wish we had ourselves or someone who can help us be the kind of person we want to be.

Compatibility theory asserts we select a mate with whom we can enjoy a variety of activities. This is someone who will understand us, accept us, and with whom we feel comfortable in communicating because that person has similar feelings and a similar philosophy of life.

Isolation may also result from diverging spheres of activity and interest. Newman and Newman (1984, pp. 387–88) provide an example of how isolation may develop in a traditional marriage:

> The wife stays at home most of the day, interacting with the children and the other wives of the neighborhood. The husband is away from home all day, interacting with co-workers. When the partners have leisure time, they pursue different interests. The woman likes to play cards, and the man likes to hunt. Over the years, the partners have less and less in common. Isolation is reflected in their lack of mutual understanding and their lack of support for each other's life goals or needs.

Interaction in Family Systems: Choosing a Personal Life-Style

Most people make decisions about how they want to live their adult years during their young adult years. (As time goes on, it is important to remember that a person has a right to make changes in the following decisions). Decisions about life-styles include whether to marry or stay single; whether or not to have children; what kind of career to pursue; what area of the country to live in; whether to live in an apartment, duplex or house; and so on. In choosing a life-style, what is actually experienced by many is not a matter of ideal choice, but rather a result of opportunities. In other words, financial resources, personal deficiencies, discrimination, and so on may greatly prevent or modify free choice. In addition, unexpected life events (such as unplanned pregnancy, divorce, or death of a spouse) can greatly alter a person's life-style and family living arrangements. In regard to life-styles and family forms, we will take a brief look at the following areas: marriage, cohabitation, single life, parenthood, and childless couples.

Marriage

Throughout recorded history, regardless of the simplicity or sophistication of the society, the family has been the basic biological and social unit in which most adults and children live. In addition, all past and present societies sanction the family through the institution of marriage (Glick, 1979). Clayton (1975) suggests one of the primary reasons for instituting the custom of marriage was to enable the two partners to enjoy sexuality as fully as possible with a minimum of anxieties and hazards. The natural sex drive of men and women needs to be satisfied, yet control needs to be exercised over the spread of sexually transmitted

Romantic Love versus Rational Love

Achieving a gratifying, long-lasting love relationship is one of our paramount goals. The experience of feeling in love is exciting, adds meaning to living, and psychologically gives us a good feeling about ourselves. Unfortunately, few people are able to maintain a long-term love relationship. Instead, many people encounter problems with love relationships, including: falling in love with someone who does not love them; falling out of love with someone after an initial stage of infatuation; being highly possessive of someone they love; and having substantial conflicts with the loved one because of differing sets of expectations about the relationship. Failures in love relationships are more often the rule than the exception.

The emotion of love, in particular, is often viewed (erroneously) as being a feeling over which we have no control. A number of common expressions connote or imply that love is a feeling beyond our control, such as, "I *fell* in love," "It was love at first sight," "I just couldn't help it," and "He swept me off my feet." It is more useful to think of the emotion of love as being primarily based on our self-talk (that is, what we tell ourselves) about a person we meet.

Romantic love can be diagrammed as follows.

Event
Meeting or becoming acquainted with a person who has *some* of the overt characteristics you adore in a lover.

Self-talk
"This person is attractive, personable; has *all* of the qualities I admire in a lover/mate."

Emotion
Intense infatuation, being romantically in love; a feeling of being in ecstasy.

Romantic love is often based on self-talk that stems from intense unsatisfied desires and frustrations, rather than on reason or rational thinking. Unsatisfied desires and frustrations include extreme sexual frustration, intense loneliness, parental and personal problems, and extensive desires for security and protection.

A primary characteristic of romantic love is to idealize the person with whom we are infatuated as being a perfect lover; that is, we notice this person has some overt characteristics we desire in a lover and then conclude that this person has all the desired characteristics.

A second characteristic is that romantic love thrives on a certain amount of distance. The more forbidden the love, the stronger it becomes. The more social mores are threatened, the stronger the feeling. (For example, couples who live together and then later marry often report living together was more exciting and romantic.) The more the effort necessary to be with each other (e.g., traveling long distances), the more intense the romance. The greater the frustration (e.g., loneliness or sexual needs), the more intense the romance.

The irony of romantic love is that, if an ongoing relationship is achieved, the romance usually withers. Through sustained contact, the person in love gradually comes to realize what the idealized loved one is really like—simply another human being with certain strengths and limitations. When this occurs, the romantic love relationship either turns into a rational love relationship, or the relationship is found to have significant conflicts and dissatisfactions and ends in a broken romance. For people with intense unmet desires, the latter occurs more frequently.

Romantic love thus tends to be of temporary duration and based on make-believe. A person experiencing romantic love never loves the real person—only an idealized imaginary person.

Rational love, in contrast, can be diagrammed in the following way.

Event
While being aware and comfortable about your own needs, goals, identity, and desires, you become well acquainted with someone who fulfills, to a fair extent, the characteristics you desire in a lover/spouse.

Self-talk
"This person has many of the qualities and attributes I seek in a lover/spouse. I admire this person's strengths, and I am aware and accepting of his or her shortcomings."

Emotion
Rational love.

The following are ingredients of a rational love relationship: (a) you are clear and comfortable about your desires, identity, and goals in life; (b) you know the other person well; (c) you have accurately and objectively assessed the

(continued next page)

Romantic Love versus Rational Love (continued)

loved one's strengths and shortcomings and are generally accepting of the shortcomings; (d) your self-talk about this person is consistent with your short- and long-term goals; (e) your self-talk is realistic and rational, so that your feelings are not based on fantasy, excessive desires, or pity; (f) you and this person are able to communicate openly and honestly, so that problems can be dealt with when they arise and so that the relationship can continue to grow and develop; (g) rational love also involves giving and receiving; it involves being kind, showing affection, knowing and doing what pleases the other person, communicating openly and warmly, and so on.

Because love is based on self-talk that causes feelings, it is we who create love. *Theoretically*, it is possible to love anyone by making changes in our self-talk. On the other hand, if we are in love with someone, we can gauge the quality of the relationship by analyzing our self-talk to determine the nature of our attraction and to determine the extent to which our self-talk is rational and in our best interests.

SOURCE: Charles Zastrow, *You Are What You Think: A Guide to Self-Realization* (Chicago: Nelson-Hall, 1993).

diseases. Children that result from sexual relationships need to be raised and cared for.

Close to 92 percent of all adults will get married in our society. Over 90 percent of all married couples will have children (Papalia and Olds, 1992, pp. 409–15). In our society people marry for a variety of reasons including desire for children, economic security, social position, love, parents' wishes, escape, pregnancy, companionship, sexual attraction, common interests, and adventure (Bowman, 1970). Goldin (1977) indicates other reasons for marrying include societal expectations, and the psychological needs to feel wanted more than anyone else by someone and to be of value to another person. In our impersonal and materialistic society, marriage helps meet the need to belong as it helps in providing

emotional support and security, affection, love, and companionship.

Predictors of Marital Success

A number of studies have sought to identify factors associated with marital happiness and marital unhappiness (Kirkpatrick, 1955; Campbell, 1975; Goodrich, et al., 1973; Kornblum and Julian, 1989; Markman, 1981; Barry, 1970; Sears, 1977; Schultz, 1980; and Snyder, 1979). Some factors are associated in a predictive manner with whether the marriage will be happy or not. Other factors are related to whether an already existing marriage is happy or not. The findings in these studies are summarized in "Predictive Factors Leading to Marital Happiness/Unhappiness."

Benefits of Marriage

Marriage leads to the formation of a family, and the family unit has become recognized as the primary unit in which children are to be produced and raised. The marriage bond thus provides for an orderly replacement of the population. Children require care and protection until adulthood, and the family is the primary institution for the rearing of children. The family is also an important institution for socializing children into the culture; for example, in helping children to acquire a language, learn social values and mores, and learn how to dress and behave within the norms of society.

Marriage also provides an available and regulated outlet for sexual activity. Failure to regulate sexual behavior would result in clashes between individuals due to jealousy and exploitation. Every society has rules that regulate sexual behavior within family units; for example, incest taboos.

A marriage is also an arrangement to meet emotional needs of the partners, such as affection, emotional support, companionship, approval, encouragement, and reinforcement for accomplishments. If people do not have such affective needs met, emotional, intellectual, physical, and social growth will be stunted. (Our high divorce rate indicates this ideal of achieving an emotionally satisfying relationship is not easily obtained). Campbell, Converse, and Rodgers (1976) in a study of over two thousand adults found that married people of all ages reported higher

Predictive Factors Leading to Marital Happiness/Unhappiness

Marital Happiness	*Marital Unhappiness*
Premarital Factors	*Premarital Factors*
Parents' marriage is happy	Parents divorced
Personal happiness in childhood	Parents or parent deceased
Mild but firm discipline by parents	Incongruity of main personality traits with partner
Harmonious relationship with parents	Acquainted less than one year before marriage
Gets along well with the opposite sex	Loneliness as a major reason for marriage
Acquainted more than one year before marriage	Escape from one's own family as a major reason for marriage
Parental approval of marriage	Marriage at a young age, particularly under age twenty
Similarity of age	Predisposition to unhappiness in one or the other spouse
Satisfaction with affection of partner	Intense personal problems
Love	
Common interests	
Optimistic outlook on life	*Factors During Marriage*
Emotional stability	Husband more dominant
Sympathetic attitude	Wife more dominant
Similarity of cultural backgrounds	Jealous of spouse
Compatible religious beliefs	Feeling of superiority to spouse
Satisfying occupation and working conditions	Feeling of being more intelligent than spouse
A love relationship growing out of companionship rather than infatuation	Living with in-laws
Self-insight and self-acceptance	Whining, acting defensive, being stubborn, and withdrawing by walking away or not talking to spouse
Awareness of the needs of one's partner	
Coping ability	
Interpersonal social skills	
Positive self-identity	
Holding common values	
Factors During Marriage	
Good communicative skills	
Equalitarian relationship	
Good relationships with in-laws	
Desire for children	
Similar interests	
Responsible love, respect, and friendship	
Sexual compatibility	
Enjoying leisure-time activities together	
Companionship and an affectional relationship	
Capacity to receive as well as give	

Guidelines for Building and Maintaining a Happy Marriage

A successful and satisfying marriage requires ongoing work by each partner. Middlebrook (1974) provides the following guidelines—which are elaborated on here—on how to achieve and maintain a successful marriage.

1. Keep the lines of communication open. Learn to bite the bullet on minor or unimportant issues. Voice the concerns that are important to you, but in a way that does not attack, blame, or threaten the other person. Seek to use I-messages which were described in "Interaction in Families: Effective Communication between Parents and Children."
2. Seek to foster the happiness, personal growth, and well-being of your spouse as much as you seek to foster your own happiness and personal growth.
3. Seek to use the no-lose problem-solving technique to settle conflicts with partners (as described in "Interaction in Families: Effective Communication between Parents and Children," rather than the win-lose technique. Be tolerant and accepting of trivial shortcomings and annoyances in partner.
4. Do not try to possess, stifle, or control your partner. Also, do not seek to mold your partner into a carbon copy of your opinions, values, beliefs, or of your personal likes and dislikes.
5. Be aware that everyone has up and down mood swings. When your partner is in a down cycle, seek to be considerate and understanding.
6. When arguments occur—and they will—seek to fight fair. Limit the discussion to the issue, and keep past events and personality traits out of the fight.
7. Be affectionate, share pleasant events, be a friend, and a good listener.

feelings of satisfaction about their lives than people who are single, divorced or widowed. Two alternative factors may be operating here—either a number of people do find happiness in marriage or else happy people are more apt to be married. The happiest of all groups in the study were married people in their twenties with no children.

Marriage also correlates with good health. Married people live longer, particularly men (Papalia and Olds, 1992, p. 410). But we cannot conclude that marriage confers health. Healthy people may be more interested in getting married, may be better marriage partners, and may attract mates more easily. Or, married people may lead safer, healthier lives than single people.

Widowed and divorced men have shorter life expectancies than single men, whose life expectancy is closest to the rate of married men. Fuchs (1974) suggests that widowed and divorced men may have shorter life expectancies because they lose the desire to live.

The marriage relationship encourages personal growth; it provides a setting for the partners to share their innermost thoughts. In a marriage a lot of decisions need to be made. Should the husband and wife buy a new car or a house? Should they both pursue careers? Do they want children? How will the domestic tasks be divided? How much time will be spent with relatives? Should a vacation be taken this year; if so, where? Problems in these areas can erupt into crises that if resolved constructively can lead to personal growth. Through successful resolution, people often learn more about themselves and are better able to handle future crises. However, if the problems remain unresolved, conflict may fester with considerable discord resulting.

Cohabitation

Cohabitation is the open living together of an unmarried couple. Most such couples live together for a relatively short time (less than two years) before they either marry or separate (Papalia and Olds, 1981, p. 443). For some, cohabitation serves as a trial marriage. For others it offers a temporary or permanent alternative to marriage. And for many young people, it has become the modern equivalent of dating and going steady.

Cohabitation does not appear to have much of an effect on eventual marital adjustment or marital success. Jacques and Chason (1979) found no significant differences between those who had lived with someone premaritally and those who had not.

Why do a number of couples decide to live together without a marriage ceremony? The reasons are not fully clear. Many people want close intimate and sexual arrangements and yet are not ready for the financial and long-term commitments of a marriage. With our society being more accepting than in the past of cohabitation, some couples appear to be choosing this living arrangement. To some extent, they can have friendship, companionship, and a sexual relationship, without the long-term commitment of marriage. Living with someone helps many young adults to learn more about themselves, to better understand what is involved in an intimate relationship, and to grow as a person. Cohabitating may also help some people clarify what they want in a mate and in a marriage.

Cohabitating also has its problems, some of which are similar to those encountered by newlyweds: adjusting to an intimate relationship, working out a sexual relationship, overdependency on the partner, missing what one did when living alone, and seeing friends less. Other problems are unique to cohabitation, such as explaining the relationship to parents and relatives, discomfort about the ambiguity of the future, and a desire for a long-term commitment from their partner.

Closely related to cohabitating is a relationship in which the man and woman maintain separate addresses and domiciles, but, for several days a month, (perhaps on weekends) live together. This latter form is more of a trial honeymoon than a trial marriage. When people only live together for a few days a month, they are apt to seek to put their best foot forward.

In some recent instances courts have decided that cohabitating couples who dissolve their nonmarital living arrangements have certain legal obligations to one another. For example, some courts (under certain circumstances, such as an oral agreement between the two individuals to pool their earnings) view assets acquired during the time the couple was living together as being "marital property," which then is divided (sometimes not equally) between the two individuals after the relationship is dissolved.

Single Life

Some people choose to remain single; they like being alone and prefer not being with others much of the time. Others end up being single as they do not find a partner they want to marry or because they are in relationships where their partner chooses not to marry. Historically, there was a greater expectation that people would marry than at the present time. Now, people are freer to make decisions about whether to marry and what kind of a lifestyle to seek.

Single people have fewer emotional and financial obligations. They do not need to consider how their decisions and actions will affect a spouse and children. They are freer to take economic, physical, and social risks. They can devote more time to the pursuit of their individual interests.

Stein (1976) interviewed over sixty single men and women between the ages of twenty-two and sixty-two and found the following reported advantages to being single: satisfaction of being self-sufficient, increased career opportunities, an exciting lifestyle, mobility, sexual availability, the freedom to change, opportunities to have a variety of experiences, opportunities to play a variety of roles, and opportunities to have friendships with a variety of people. The following negative aspects of being married were reported: boredom, obstacles to self-development, feeling trapped, unhappiness, having to conform to expectations, sexual frustration, poor communication, limited mobility, restriction of new experiences, and lack of friends. (It appears the respondents in this study were biased toward the single life. Different results might have been found if the researchers had interviewed single people who wanted to be married, but who as yet had not found a marriageable partner.)

Parenthood

The birth of a baby is a major life event. Caring for a baby changes lifestyles of parents and also the marriage. For some, caring for child (who is totally dependent) is a troublesome crisis. For others, caring for a baby is viewed as a fulfillment and an enhancement of life. For many couples, parenthood has troublesome aspects, while it also enhances their lives.

What are some of the problem areas of parenthood? The birth of a baby signals to parents that they are now adults and no longer children; they now have responsibilities not only to themselves, but also in caring for someone who needs twenty-four-hour care. A baby demands a huge amount of time and atten-

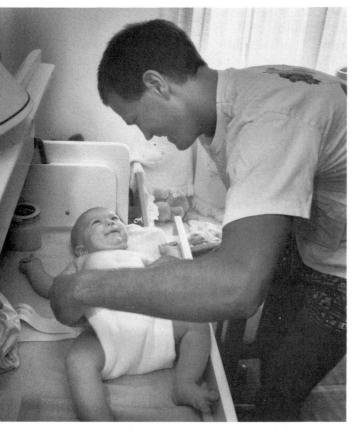

Fathers who enjoy parenting usually see it as being one of their most important life roles.

tion. Some demographic statistics should be noted. In 1991, 57 percent of women and 76 percent of men sixteen years of age and older were in the paid labor force (U.S. Bureau of the Census, 1992, p. 384). Women in the labor force are as likely to work full-time as men. More than half of women with children less than one-year-old are in the labor force (Office for Economic Cooperation and Development, 1988). Women generally assume the majority of both household and child-care responsibilities (Gilbert, 1985). Thus, they tend to have more difficulties adjusting to the parental role than their husbands do (Hobbs and Cole, 1976). Belsky, Lang, and Huston (1986) have found that the more the division of labor in a marriage changes from egalitarian to traditional, the more marital happiness declines, especially for nontraditional wives.

Thompson and Walker (1989) found about one-third of mothers view mothering as both enjoyable and meaningful, a third find it unpleasant and not meaningful, and another third report mixed experiences. Fathers tend to treasure and to be emotionally committed to their children, but they generally report less enjoyment in looking after them than mothers do.

Russell (1974) studied 271 middle- and working-class couples in which the children ranged in age from six to fifty-six weeks. The study found that the wives were bothered most by interrupted rest and sleep, fatigue, feeling edgy, and concerns about changes in their figures and about their personal appearances. Interestingly, the more highly educated a woman was, the greater her difficulty in adjusting to parenthood. Perhaps this was due to viewing parenthood as interfering with her career goals. Women who had the most positive reactions to the child's birth tended to be those who had easy pregnancies and deliveries, who were in excellent health, and who had been married a longer time.

The husbands in the Russell study tended to have different concerns than the wives, although they were also bothered by interruptions in sleep and rest. The husband's concerns included having to change lifestyle because of the baby, increased financial pressures, additional work in caring for the baby, and interference from in-laws in child rearing. Those fathers who most enjoyed the parental role were those who had prepared for parenthood by reading books and attending classes, those who had been involved in taking care of someone else's children, and those who saw being a father as being one of their most important life roles. Not surprisingly, those couples who made the most positive adjustments to parenthood were those who wanted and planned for the birth of the baby, and those who were happily married.

Why do people have children? Historically, in agricultural and preindustrial societies children were an economic asset, as their labor was important in planting and harvesting crops and in tending of domestic animals. Parents wanted large families to help out with the work. When the parents became elderly, the children tended to provide much of the care. Because children were an economic asset, values were gradually established that it was natural and desirable for married couples to want to have children. Motherhood became invested with a unique emotional aura. Some psychological theories reflected this aura by asserting that women (interestingly, not men) had a nurturing instinct that could only be fulfilled by having and caring for children. (It appears the supposed nurturing instinct was in reality a value that was learned by women through socialization practices.)

Today, children are an economic liability, rather than an economic asset. Overpopulation is increasingly being recognized as one of the world's greatest problems. In our society there is an expectation that Social Security and other government programs will primarily care for elderly parents, rather than this being a responsibility of the children. Children can have negative, as well as positive, effects on life-styles and on marital relationships. For these, and other reasons, married couples in our society over the years have gradually decided to have fewer children; now most couples usually want zero to three children. Birth control devices now make such wishes a reality.

Hoffman and Manis (1979) conducted an extensive study to identify the psychological satisfactions of having children. Love of children, fun, and stimulation headed the list.

Price-Bonham and Skeen (1979) conducted a survey of 160 African American and white husbands who were working full-time, were parents of at least two children, and were living with their spouses. According to this study, these husbands rated the best things about being a father as having someone to love and love them, the feeling that their children made them feel respectable, and that they would have someone to care for them in old age. Discipline problems and increased responsibilities were the worst things about being a father. A number of these husbands stated that fatherhood was more demanding than they had anticipated. Many said if they had a chance to do it over again, they would not have children. They felt children made their life financially harder, interfered with their previous life-styles, and interfered with what they had wanted to do in their lives. The study led the researchers to recommend extensive education for fatherhood in the elementary and secondary school curriculum.

Children have a pervasive influence on a marriage (Feldman, 1971). It is common for spouses to have disagreements about how to raise and discipline children; such dissension is perhaps to be expected as the two partners were raised somewhat differently and, therefore, have acquired different philosophies on how to raise children. Feldman (1971) found that couples who were most likely to report an increase in marital satisfaction after the birth of the first child were those who had known each other a substantial amount of time before they were married, and those who were pursuing their individual interests in the marriage. Those who were excessively dependent on each other tended to experience a decrease in marital satisfaction following the birth of a baby.

Rollins and Galligan (1978) found that a decline in marital satisfaction after the birth of a child is more common among working-class families than among middle-class families. These researchers also suggest that children are less likely to lower marital satisfaction in families where the parents desired to have children, and where the parents have outside resources for helping to care for the children. Belsky and Rovine (1988) found that in marriages that deteriorate after parenthood, one or both partners tend to have low self-esteem, and the husbands were likely to be less sensitive. The partners in deteriorating marriages were also more likely to be younger and less educated, to earn less money, and to have been married for fewer years.

Even when parenting has a negative influence on marital satisfaction, parenting often has a positive effect on the self-concepts of the parents and on their work roles (Feldman and Feldman, 1977). Thus, parenting appears to contribute to the personal development of an individual.

The Group for the Advancement of Psychiatry (1973) views parenting as a developmental process and has identified the following four stages:

1. *Anticipation:* This stage occurs during pregnancy and involves the expectant parents thinking about how they will raise their children, how their lives will change, and the meaning of parenthood. Some expectant parents have ambivalent feelings about what lies ahead. During this stage the expectant parents begin the process of viewing themselves as their children's parents, instead of being their parents' children.
2. *Honeymoon:* This stage occurs after the birth of the first child and lasts for a few months. Parents are often very happy about having and holding a baby. It is also a time of adjustment and learning, as attachments are formed

Parental Sex Preferences

In most countries boys are generally preferred to girls. Although it is the male's sperm that determines the sex of the child,* in many developing countries and countries where the status of women is low, a woman's capacity to remain married may depend on her producing sons. In some of these countries, boys are fed better, given better medical care, and receive more schooling. The death rate for female children is significantly higher than for male children, as female children are more apt to be neglected.

In this country, couples who want only one child usually desire a boy. Those who want two, generally desire one of each; and those who prefer three usually want two boys and one girl. Husbands, in particular, tend to have a strong preference for a boy. The reasons a couple desires a boy or a girl vary. Those couples desiring a boy generally prefer someone to carry on the family name and bring honor to the family; those who prefer a girl want someone who is easier to raise, is lovable, is fun to dress, and is able to help with the housework (Williamson, 1978).

---

*Sperm carrying the X chromosome will produce a female, while sperm carrying the Y chromosome will produce a male.

---

between parents and child, and family members learn new roles in relation to one another.
3. *Plateau:* This stage occurs from infancy through the teenage years. Frequent adjustments must be made by the parents, as parents need to adapt their parenting behavior to the level of the child.
4. *Disengagement:* This stage occurs at the time when the child disengages; for example, when the child marries. Because the child disengages, the parents should also change their behavior and disengage from the child. Relationships change from parent-child in nature to adult-adult.

These stages illustrate the fact that children have a great effect on parents. The Group for the Advancement of Psychiatry (1973) also notes that parents often judge their parenting on how well their children turn out. When children fulfill their expectations, the parents usually pat themselves on the back for a job well done. The danger of this approach is that if the children fall short of meeting parental expectations (which sometimes are unrealistic), the parents are apt to conclude they failed. Parents need to realize the final product is not entirely under their control as children are influenced by many other factors that are external to the family.

Childless Couples

Having children is recognized legally and religiously as being one of the central components of a marriage. In our society there still continues to be a value that something is wrong with a couple if they decide not to have children. This value, however, is no longer as strongly held as it once was. Perhaps in the future this value will cease to exist due to the overpopulation problem and the high cost of raising children; the average cost of raising a child from birth to age eighteen is estimated to be over $140,000 (Brophy, 1986, p. 59).

Married couples may decide not to have children. Some feel they do not have what it takes to be good parents. Some have heavy commitments to their careers or to their hobbies and do not want to take time away from them to raise a family. Others feel that having children would be an intrusion into their marital relationship. Still others enjoy the freedom to travel, to make spur-of-the-moment plans, and do not want their life-style changed with having children (Papalia and Olds, 1981, p. 453). Some feel choosing not to have children is desirable in order to avoid contributing to the problem of overpopulation.

Rollin (1970) found that marriages without children are happier. Campbell (1975) found that marriages are happiest before children are born and after the children leave home. Apparently, children place demands and strains on a marriage that can lead to some dissatisfaction.

Houseknecht (1979) compared fifty childless (by choice) female spouses and fifty mothers and found a very small difference in overall marital satisfaction. Childless women were slightly more satisfied. Childless couples were more likely to work together on projects to have more frequent exchanges of stimulating ideas, to discuss things more calmly, and were more likely to engage in outside interests. The childless women agreed more with their husbands on career decisions, leisure time activities, and division of household tasks. The childless women also expressed a stronger desire to continue the marriage. Additionally, they tended to be better educated, less religious, and more apt to be employed than mothers (Papalia and Olds, 1981, p. 454).

Dytrych and associates (1975) found that unwanted children are adversely affected in a variety of ways; they are more apt to be abused, have more frequent illnesses, receive poorer school grades, and have more behavior problems than children whose births are desired. Such findings suggest that if couples do not want to have children, it is probably in their best interest and that of society for them not to have children.

Social Problems

In addition to going through normal phases of social development (such as developing an identity and choosing a life-style), there are a number of situations and life crises that tend to occur. The following material will focus on certain social problems: eating disorders; emotional and behavioral problems; crime and delinquency; and delinquent gangs. The latter two can be viewed as macro system problems, as large systems are often involved in the planning and carrying out of criminal activity, and large systems are involved in investigating, prosecuting, preventing, and curbing criminal activity.

Eating Disorders

Eating disorders are occurring in epidemic proportions. While eating disorders have existed for a long period of time, the dramatic increase in the number of individuals affected is now a major concern for mental health professionals. A majority of the people who have an eating disorder are female. The first life event or social problem addressed here that can affect adolescents and young adults is an eating disorder. The three primary eating disorders are anorexia nervosa, bulimia nervosa, and compulsive overeating. All three are serious disorders that create life-threatening health problems.

Anorexia Nervosa

Anorexia nervosa means "loss of appetite due to nerves." This definition is inaccurate, as people with

The mind set leading to anorexia nervosa is reinforced by our society's valuing thinness in women.

anorexia do not actually lose their appetite until the late stages of their starvation. Until then, they do feel hungry, but they just do not eat. Anorexia nervosa is a disorder characterized by the excessive pursuit of thinness through voluntary starvation. The predominant features of this disorder include excessive thinness, and intense fear of gaining weight or becoming fat, a distorted body image in which anorexics view themselves as being overweight, and amenorrhea (cessation of menses) in females.

Anorexics refuse to accept the fact that they are too thin. They eat very little, even when experiencing intense hunger. They insist they need to lose even more weight. They erroneously believe that having an ultra-thin body is a perfect body, and that achieving such a body will bring happiness and success. As they lose more and more weight, their health deteriorates and they tend to become increasingly depressed. Symptoms of physical deterioration include reduced heart rate, lowered blood pressure, lowered body temperature, increased retention of water, fine hair growth on many parts of their body, amenorrhea in females, and a variety of metabolic changes (Koch et al., 1993). Even while their health is deteriorating, anorexics stubbornly cling to the belief that through controlling their body weight, they can get control of their lives.

On the surface someone who is prone to develop anorexia appears to be a model child. She is eager to please, is well-behaved, a good student, and someone who appears to get along well with her peers. She rarely asks for help, and she is unlikely to indicate anything is wrong. Behind this mask is an insecure, self-critical perfectionist who feels she is unworthy of any praise that she receives. She is also apt to be concerned about whether other people like her.

The development of this disorder usually proceeds according to the following pattern.

Step 1: It begins with a diet. Dieting for these individuals usually begins just before or just after a major change occurs—such as beginning of puberty, breaking up with a boyfriend, or leaving home for college.

Step 2: Dieting creates a feeling of control. At first the person feels better about herself as dieting is something she can do successfully. Soon, however, food and the fear of becoming fat become the major concerns in her life.

Step 3: Exhausting exercise is added. The anorexic exercises excessively, such as running ten miles before eating.

Step 4: Health begins to fail. Weight loss and malnutrition begin leading to mental and physical deterioration. Although the person may sense something is wrong, she refuses to conclude that she needs to start eating more. Anorexia can lead to the shrinking of any internal organ, including the brain, heart, and kidneys. As the heart muscle weakens, the chances of irregular heart rhythm and congestive heart failure increase. Other complications include muscle aches and cramps, swelling of joints, constipation, and difficulty urinating, inability to concentrate, digestive problems, and injuries to nerves and tendons. In addition, loss of fat and muscle tissue makes it difficult for the body to keep itself warm, which leads to the sensation of feeling "cold." The unusual growth of fine body hair (especially on the arms and legs) on anorexics may be the body's response to seek to make up for heat loss.

A large number of anorexics engage in excessive exercise for prolonged periods of time in an attempt to lose more weight. They prefer solitary activities (such as running and exercise machines) over team sports. At mealtimes, to avoid conflicts with others over eating so little, they are apt to lie and say that they already have eaten, or, if they are forced to be at the table with others, they may dispose of their food by slipping it into a container under the table. Because they are always hungry, anorexics are preoccupied with food, grocery shopping, nutritional information, and cooking. They may collect cookbooks and memorize calorie charts.

Anorexics, even in warm weather, tend to wear several layers of bulky clothing, or sweaters and baggy pants, to warm their cold bodies and to conceal their thinness. (Their thinness often brings questions and criticisms from relatives and friends, so wearing bulky clothing is a way to attempt to avoid being questioned.) Anorexics usually deny they need help with their eating patterns as they insist their bodies are normal and attractive.

Anorexics tend to maintain rigid control over nearly all aspects of their lives. To avoid criticism, they often withdraw from others and are introverted. They often develop compulsive rituals involving exercise, food, housekeeping, studying, and other aspects of their lives. A favorite ritual is to weigh themselves several times a day. They may cut their small morsels of food into tiny pieces and then spend extended time eating each piece. They find security in discipline and order. To achieve greater control of their lives they tend to avoid social activities, sexual relationships, parties, and friends.

Some anorexics occasionally yield to their hunger pangs and eat—and perhaps even binge. After eating and binging, they are apt to feel guilty because they failed in their efforts to always follow a restricted (and health-threatening) diet.

Anorexics tend to think in black-and-white terms. They view themselves, and others, as being right or wrong, successes or failures, beautiful or ugly, fat or thin, and so on. They do not deal well with complexity or with shades of gray. Anorexics seek to be perfectionists in all aspects of their lives: relationships, school or job responsibilities, personal appearance, and so on. An anorexic is apt to feel success in school only when she obtains straight A's; even when she does, she tends not to celebrate but begins worrying about her next exam.

Ninety-five percent of those affected with anorexia nervosa are females (Koch et al., 1993). Onset usually occurs during adolescence, although the onset can occur from prepuberty to the early thirties. Estimates of the number of teenage females affected by this disorder range from one in one hundred to one in eight hundred (Koch et al., 1993). Although this disorder is found in all ethnic and socioeconomic groups, especially vulnerable are overly perfectionistic "model" children from upper-middle and upper-class backgrounds.

To prevent death through starvation, hospitalization is frequently needed for anorexics. Studies estimate mortality rates of between 5 and 18 percent of anorexics, due to a variety of medical complications (Koch et al., 1993). These complications include: heart attack, kidney damage, liver impairment, malnutrition, and starvation. Starvation weakens the body's immune system, which leaves the anorexic vulnerable to pneumonia and to other infections. Suicide following severe depression is also a danger. The mortality rate for anorexia nervosa is thought to be higher than for any other psychiatric disorder (Koch et al., 1993).

Bulimia Nervosa

The term *bulimia* is derived from a Greek word meaning "ox-like hunger." But the binge-purge cycle that is characteristic of bulimics is triggered not by physical hunger but by emotional upset. Binge-eating is the rapid, uncontrolled consumption of large amounts of food. A binge may last from a few minutes to several hours. Purging is the process of getting rid of the food eaten during a binge. The most frequent method of purging is self-induced vomiting. Other methods of purging include strict dieting or fasting, vigorous exercise, diet pills, and abuse of diuretics and laxatives. Some bulimics chew food to enjoy the taste and then spit it out to avoid calories and weight gain.

The development of bulimia tends to proceed according to the following pattern:

Step 1: A diet is started. The person wants to lose weight and improve self-esteem. However, dieting increases hunger and leads to a craving for sweet, high-calorie food.

Step 2: Overeating begins. The overeating is often triggered by stress, such as anger, depression, loneliness, frustration, and boredom. Food helps to relieve hunger and also is a comfort for relieving emotional pain.

Step 3: Guilt develops. The person feels guilty about gaining too much weight in a society where "thin is in."

Step 4: Purging is discovered. The person discovers self-induced vomiting or other forms of purging will allow her to binge and at the same time not gain any weight.

Step 5: A binge-purge habit takes hold. Binge eating and purging become a way of daily coping with life and emotional pain. Bulimics tend to fear that others will discover their habit and view the habit as being disgusting.

Estimates of the incidence of bulimia nervosa among high school and college-age females range between 4.5 and 18 percent (Koch et al., 1993). Bulimics binge in an effort to escape painful problems in their lives. The average bulimic binge involves between 1,000 and 5,500 calories, although day-long binges of more than 50,000 calories occur in some bulimics. (The average American's food intake is about 3,000 calories a day). Bulimics tend to binge on high-calorie junk foods, such as sweets and fried foods. Because bulimics fear weight gain, they then purge themselves. Bulimics generally feel considerable shame about their binging and purging, but continue to resort to the binge-purge cycle as a way to relieve the pain of their daily problems.

Most bulimics are within a normal weight range, although some are somewhat overweight or underweight. Obesity in adolescence may be a contributing factor in the development of the disorder in some bulimics. The parents of bulimics are often overweight, and close relatives of bulimics have a higher than chance frequency of alcoholism and depression (Koch et al., 1993).

The usual age of onset for bulimia nervosa is late adolescence or early adulthood. Alcohol and other substance abuse is fairly common among bulimics. This is because the psychological dynamics that lead a person to abuse drugs are similar to the dynamics that lead a person to be bulimic. (Drug abuse may be easier to treat than bulimia, however, as a drug abuser can completely abstain from using drugs, but a bulimic needs to continue to eat (which acts as a trigger to binging) in order to survive.

Because bulimia nervosa is seldom incapacitating,

the disorder can go undetected by family and friends for years. Physical complications, however, begin to develop. Chronic vomiting can lead to gum disease and innumerable cavities, due to the hydrochloric acid content of vomit. Vomiting can also lead to severe tearing and bleeding in the esophagus. Chronic vomiting may result in a potassium deficiency, which then may lead to muscle fatigue, weakness, numbness, erratic heartbeat, kidney damage, and in severe instances, paralysis or death. Digestive problems range from stomach cramps, nausea, ulcers, colitis, and to a fatal rupturing of the stomach. Sore throats are also common. Bulimia can also lead to diabetes.

Dehydration and electrolyte imbalance can occur and in some cases cause cardiac arrhythmias and even death. Psychotropic drugs (such as tranquilizers and antidepressant drugs) may affect the body differently due to changes in body metabolism. For those bulimic individuals who are substantially below normal weight, physical complications associated with anorexia nervosa may also occur.

Both anorexia and bulimia lead to serious health problems. Stating the obvious, nutritious meals are needed for good health and survival. Anorexics risk starvation, and both bulimics and anorexics risk serious health problems. Fat synthesis and accumulation are necessary for survival. Fatty acids are a major source of energy. When fat levels are depleted, the body must draw on carbohydrates (sugar). When sugar supplies dwindle, body metabolism decreases, which often leads to drowsiness, inactivity, pessimism, depression, dizziness, and fatigue. Additional medical problems associated with eating disorders are described in Boskind-White and White (1983).

Although a few bulimics at times binge with friends, usually bulimics binge alone and secretly. Since binging leads to guilt, anxiety, and fear of weight gain, the process of purging serves as a reinforcer for binging, as purging often results in a sense of again being in control with a flat stomach. However, many bulimics feel shame and personal disgust about their binging-purging cycle.

Bulimics tend to be people-pleasers who crave affection, attention, and approval from others. Unlike anorexics, they usually have active social lives with a number of friends and acquaintances. However, they are often filled with self-doubt and insecurity. While they want close personal relationships, they also tend to fear such relationships, partly because they feel their eating disorder is more apt to be discovered if they enter into such relationships. Many bulimics are sexually promiscuous, partly because they want affection and have low self-esteem. Some bulimics may shoplift and steal food. Most bulimics feel they do not have decent control of their lives, and feel especially out of control around food. They worry that once they begin to eat, they will be unable to refrain from binging. Bulimics are more likely to ask for help than anorexics.

Compulsive Overeating

Compulsive overeating is the irresistible urge to consume excessive amounts of food for no nutritional reason. In most cases, compulsive overeating is a response to a combination of familial, psychological, cultural, and environmental factors. Compulsive overeating results in excessive accumulation of body fat. Compulsive eaters are overweight. Estimates are that one out of five Americans are overweight (Koch, et al., 1993).

Treatment is recommended for persons whose body weight is in excess of 20 percent over ideal body weight (Koch, et al., 1993). The more overweight a compulsive overeater is, the greater the health risks. Being overweight is correlated with such health problems as hypertension, hypercholesterolernia, and diabetes. People who are overweight are also prone to heart attacks and to other heart diseases.

Compulsive overeaters have many of the characteristics that are commonly found in bulimics. (A key distinguishing factor between the two disorders is that bulimics frequently engage in purging, while compulsive overeaters seldom, if ever, do.) Similar to bulimics, compulsive overeaters tend to binge in an effort to temporarily escape painful problems in their lives. Compulsive overeaters generally feel considerable shame and embarrassment about their eating patterns and being overweight. Alcohol and other substance abuse are common. Compulsive overeaters tend to be people pleasers who crave attention, approval, and affection from others. They are often filled with self-doubt and insecurity. Overeaters have a high incidence of depression and are apt to have a low self-esteem. Age of onset of the disorder is usually during adolescence.

Compulsive overeaters are apt to display one or more of the following:

1. Frequent diet plan failures. Overeaters attempt and fail at numerous diet plans. They are apt to try nearly every new "diet" fad briefly, believing that their latest effort will be the one that achieves permanent weight loss. No diet fad really works for them. Repeated diet failures result in a sense of hopelessness and self-deprecation.
2. Avoidance of health warning signs. Being excessively overweight eventually leads to health problems, such as diabetes and hypertension. Compulsive overeaters tend to ignore early warning signs of health problems, choosing instead to continue binging rather than making a commitment to developing healthier eating patterns.
3. Social isolation. Overeaters often feel shame and guilt about being overweight, and as a result they may seek to reduce interpersonal contact. For some, avoiding interactions with others becomes a dominant behavioral pattern.
4. Nutritional ignorance. Compulsive overeaters often lack adequate knowledge of basic nutrition. Many have a distorted view of what constitutes a well-balanced and healthy diet.
5. Selective eating amnesia. Compulsive overeaters are unlikely to conscientiously count their calorie intake. They are also apt to binge several times a day without keeping track of the frequency of their binging.
6. Overeating as a response to unwanted emotions. When overeaters feel such unwanted emotions as loneliness, frustration, insecurity, anger, and depression, they are apt to ease the pain of these emotions through binging. (Binging temporarily takes their mind off their concerns, so this does work—but only during the short time while they are eating.) After binging, overeaters are not only apt to feel the pain of their original unwanted emotions, which now return, but they also feel the additional unwanted emotions of shame and guilt over their excessive eating.

Interrelationships among Eating Disorders

As noted above, there are a number of differences between these three eating disorders, but there are also interrelationships. Some people have symptoms of both anorexia and bulimia, and are identified as having the disorder bulimarexia. Many of those who have bulimarexia occasionally move back and forth between being anorexic and bulimic. In addition, some overeaters occasionally have episodes of purging, and, at time, fit the criteria for being bulimic. Koch, Dotson, and Troast (1993, p. 458) indicate it is

important to conceptualize these three eating disorders as existing on a continuum, ranging from being overly thin to being excessively overweight:

> Eating disorders seem to exist on a continuum. On one end are the restricting anorexics, who achieve drastic weight loss by severely restricting food intake. In the middle are the anorexic bulimics who eat, and even binge on occasion, but who still maintain a much lower-than-normal weight by a combination of strict dieting and purging. Also included are normal-weight bulimics who binge and purge but who are not significantly underweight. These bulimics usually diet when they are not binging and may repeatedly gain and lose ten or more pounds because of their food behaviors. At the other end of the continuum, the compulsive overeater will repeatedly binge, gaining significant amounts of weight without engaging in any of the purging behaviors associated with anorexia or bulimia nervosa. Individuals may move back and forth along this continuum, alternately restricting or binging, depending on their circumstances.

Causes

Many factors contribute to the development of an eating disorder. The factors differ from one individual to another. Some bulimics and compulsive overeaters may be genetically predisposed to these disorders. Depression or alcoholism tends to be present in parents or other family members. People with an eating disorder tend to feel inadequate and worthless. Their low self-esteem combined with their quest for perfectionism leads them to be intolerant of any flaws. People with an eating disorder usually have not formed a stable sense of self. They tend to compare themselves to others, and usually conclude "I'm not good enough." A significant number of anorexics and bulimics have been victimized by molestation, rape, and incest (Rubel, 1980).

Anorexics and bulimics have some similarities (Boskind-White and White, 1984). Both are likely to have been brought up in middle-class, upwardly mobile families, where their mothers are overinvolved in their lives and their fathers are preoccupied with work outside the home. For the most part, bulimics and anorexics were good children eager to comply and eager to achieve in order to obtain the love and approval of others. Both tend to lack self-esteem, feel ineffective and have a distorted body image in which they view themselves as being fatter than others view them as being. Both have an obsessive concern with food. Their parents tended to be overprotective and did not allow them to become more independent and learn from their mistakes. Their parents still treat them as if they were young children rather than teenagers and young adults. In contrast, a smaller number of anorexics and bulimics come from nonsupportive and non-nourishing families that were demanding, critical and rejecting. Others with an eating disorder were raised by parents who combined obsessive concern with criticism and rejection, which places the children in a double bind of wanting to protest but feeling guilty because their parents are so "caring." Still others with an eating disorder were raised by parents who have good parenting skills and who love and act appropriately with their children. In such families other factors lead to the development of an eating disorder.

Bulimics are often overachievers, and in college tend to attain high academic averages. Purging for bulimics often becomes a purification rite, as it is frequently viewed as a way to overcome self-loathing. They tend to believe they are unlovable and inadequate. Through purging, they feel completely fresh and clean again. These feelings of self-worth are only temporary. They are extremely sensitive to minor insults and frustrations, which are often used as excuses to initiate another food binge.

Impacts of Social Forces

One reason for the increased incidence of anorexia and bulimia may be the increasing value that our society places on being slim and trim. Why are bulimics and anorexics primarily women? Orbach (1978) makes a strong case that there are many more pressures on women to be slender and trim than on men. Our socialization practices also overemphasize the importance of women being slender.

Eating disorders have become epidemic in the United States in the past fifteen to twenty years. Prior to that time, society allowed all people, and especially women to be rounder and heavier. Weight-gain products and breast enhancers were then popular products that were purchased by thin women who wanted to look like Marilyn Monroe. However, norms for what is attractive have changed. Koch, Dotson, and Troast (1993, p. 461) note:

The weight, bust, and hip measurements of magazine centerfolds and beauty contest winners over the past twenty-five years have progressively decreased, although the average weight for women in the general population has increased by six pounds. Today, the cultural ideal is pencil slimness, and, according to advertisements and fashion magazines, even mature women should look like adolescent boys.

Medical research and life insurance statistics indicate people are healthier, live longer, and function better when they have a degree of roundness and fatty reserves beyond that allowed by fashion. Vulnerable people who believe they will be happy and admired when they are thin can precipitate an eating disorder when their bodies rebel against an inadequate diet. Researchers believe an eating disorder may develop after prolonged dieting when people try to achieve or maintain a body size that is in direct conflict with their biology. They maintain that one's weight is genetically determined and that family history is the best indication of what a person's appropriate weight or "set point" should be. Any effort to go below the body's "set point" is resisted by an increase in appetite, a reduction in body metabolism, and lethargic behavior, all designed to increase body weight.

Treatment

Professional intervention is generally needed for people with an eating disorder as these disorders are complex and serious. Treatment for an eating disorder usually has the following three goals: (1) resolution of the psychosocial and family dynamics that led to the development of the eating disorder, (2) medical services to correct any medical problems that resulted from starving, binging and purging, or being obese, and (3) reestablishment of normal weight and healthy eating behavior.

Many anorexics and bulimics who enter treatment for eating disorders want to be treated for their unhealthy eating habits, but still want to be very thin. These two objectives are incompatible. Unless anorexics and bulimics truly comprehend that ultra-thinness is unhealthy, they will soon return to their starving or binging/purging behavior. Treatments must be comprehensive and multifaceted, as eating disorders are complex, and multidimensional problems. Each person's unique circumstances need to be carefully assessed so that the specific needs of each client can be treated.

The client may be treated on an inpatient or outpatient basis. Hospitalization of a person with an eating disorder is sometimes needed. Inpatient care should be considered for anorexics when weight loss continues or when there is an absence of weight gain after a reasonable length of time in outpatient treatment. It should be considered for bulimics who are unable to break the binge-purge cycle after a reasonable period of time in outpatient treatment. If a client with an eating disorder displays signs of suicide ideation or severe self-destructive behavior, inpatient care should be seriously considered. Hospitalization is usually necessary when physical complications require close medical supervision; for example, when an anorexic is in danger of severe heart dysfunction, or when a bulimic needs treatment for dehydration and electrolyte imbalance that is caused by excessive vomiting and abuse of diuretics and laxatives. A compulsive overeater may occasionally need to be hospitalized for such medical conditions as heart disease or problems associated with diabetes. Since hospitalization severely disrupts a person's life, it should only be used when necessary.

Individual psychotherapy is a prominent part in practically all comprehensive treatment plans with people who have an eating disorder. Goals of individual therapy include the establishment of healthy eating patterns, increased self-esteem, increased sense of power and control over one's life, resolution of negative and unwanted emotions such as guilt and depression, and resolution of internal conflicts and personal problems. Individual psychotherapy may also have the goals of increased assertiveness, reducing stress, and exploring relationship issues and career options.

Since family dynamics are usually contributing factors to the development and maintenance of an eating disorder, family therapy is also important, particularly if the affected person is living at home. Other family members are always affected, and sometimes victimized, by the turmoil experienced by the individual with the eating disorder. Family members are able through therapy to better understand the dynamics of the eating disorder, and family members can make changes that will provide increased support and guidance for the affected person. The family therapist seeks to initiate interventions to improve family functioning, which facilitates the recovery of the individual. Family sessions are also helpful to those eating disordered individuals who are struggling with issues of separation from their primary family.

Group therapy is also an important intervention. It may be provided in a variety of forms, including self-help, psycho-educational and behavioral. Through group interaction, members are able to put their problems in perspective, as they see others have problems as serious as theirs. Groups also enable members to test out more appropriate interaction patterns. Members can also share their unwanted emotions and problematic behaviors, and discover ways to think and act in more realistic ways. Groups also provide a sense of belonging and provide interpersonal support. Groups also are useful in confronting members about the health hazards of their eating patterns. Group treatment provides an arena for: diminishing feelings of isolation and secrecy, sharing successful techniques for better coping with common problems, demystifying eating disorders, expressing feelings, obtaining feedback from other members, and facilitating realistic goal setting.

Nutritional counseling is an essential component of any treatment plan. A registered dietician can provide information about proper nutrition and the body's need for nutritious food. The dietician can provide information on the physiology of dieting and weight management, and also can help the affected person to establish healthier eating patterns.

Since some persons with an eating disorder are depressed, antidepressant medication is sometimes beneficial. Such medication is prescribed by a psychiatrist or physician. Couples therapy is sometimes needed when there is significant conflict in a couple's relationship. Couples therapy assists couples in problem solving and in resolving interactional conflicts. Some elementary, secondary, and higher education school systems are now developing preventive programs which seek to inform students about the risks of eating disorders and which seek to identify and provide services for students who are beginning to develop an eating disorder.

Emotional and Behavioral Problems

Emotional problems (involving unwanted feelings) and behavioral problems (involving irresponsible actions) are two comprehensive labels covering an array of problems. Emotional difficulties include depression, feelings of inferiority or isolation, feeling guilty, shyness, having a low self-concept, having a phobia, and excessive anxiety. Behavioral difficulties include being sadistic or masochistic, being hyperactive, committing unusual or bizarre acts, being overly critical, being overly aggressive, abusing one's child or spouse, being compulsive, committing sexual deviations, showing violent displays of temper, attempting suicide, and being vindictive.

Everyone, at one time or another, will experience emotional and/or behavioral problems. Severe emotional or behavioral problems have been labeled as being mental illnesses by certain members of the helping professions. The two general approaches to viewing and diagnosing people who display severe emotional disturbances and abnormal behaviors are the medical model and the interactional model which asserts mental illness is a myth.

Medical Model

The medical model views emotional and behavioral problems as a mental illness, comparable to a physical illness. The use of mental illness labels involves applying medical labels (schizophrenia, paranoia, psychosis, insanity) to emotional problems. Adherents of the medical approach believe the disturbed person's mind is affected by some generally unknown, internal condition. That condition, they assert, might be due to genetics, metabolic disorders, infectious diseases, internal conflicts, unconscious use of defense mechanisms, and traumatic early experiences that cause emotional fixations and hamper psychological growth.

The medical model has a lengthy classification of mental disorders that are defined by the American Psychiatric Association (see "Major Mental Disorders According to the American Psychiatric Association").

In DSM-III-R (1987) numerous mental disorders are defined. A few examples of these disorders are described briefly in the following paragraphs:

Schizophrenia. This malady encompasses a large group of disorders, usually of psychotic proportion, manifested by characteristic disturbances of language and communication, thought, perception, affect, and behavior that last longer than six months.

Paranoia. Paranoia is a rare condition characterized by the gradual development of an intricate, complex, and elaborate system of thinking based on (and often proceeding

logically from) misinterpretation of an actual event. A person with paranoia often considers himself or herself endowed with unique and superior ability, or has systematized delusions of persecution.

Hypochondriasis. This is a chronic maladaptive style of relating to the environment through preoccupation with shifting somatic concerns and symptoms, a fear or conviction that one has a serious physical illness, the search for medical treatment, inability to accept reassurance, and either hostile or dependent relationships with care givers and family.

Bipolar Disorder. This is a major affective disorder with episodes of both mania and depression; formerly called manic-depressive psychosis. Bipolar disorder may be subdivided into manic, depressed, or mixed types on the basis of currently presenting symptoms.

Phobia. A phobia is characterized by an obsessive, persistent, unrealistic, intense fear of an object or situation. A few common phobias are *acrophobia* (fear of heights), *algophobia* (fear of pain), *claustrophobia* (fear of closed spaces), and *erythrophobia* (fear of blushing).

Personality Disorders. Personality disorders are deeply ingrained, inflexible, maladaptive patterns of relating, perceiving, and thinking of sufficient severity to cause either impairment in functioning or distress. Some personality disorders and their characteristics are:

Antisocial: A lack of socialization along with behavior patterns that bring a person repeatedly into conflict with society; incapacity for significant loyalty to others or to social values; callousness; irresponsibility; impulsiveness; and inability to feel guilt or learn from experience or punishment.

Borderline: Instability in a variety of areas, including interpersonal relationships, behavior, mood, and self-image.

Compulsive: Restricted ability to express warm and tender emotions; preoccupation with rules, order, organization, efficiency, and detail; excessive devotion to work and productivity to the exclusion of pleasure; indecisiveness.

Narcissistic: Grandiose sense of self-importance or uniqueness; preoccupation with fantasies of limitless success; need for constant attention and admiration; and disturbances in interpersonal relationships such as lack of empathy, exploitativeness, and relationships that vacillate between the extremes of over-idealization and devaluation.

Passive-aggressive: Aggressive behavior manifested in passive ways such as obstructionism, pouting, procrastination, intentional inefficiency, and obstinacy.

Schizoid: Manifested by shyness, oversensitivity, social withdrawal, frequent daydreaming, avoidance of

Narcissism is characterized by a grandiose sense of self-importance or uniqueness that seals the individual off from others.

close or competitive relationships, and eccentricity. Persons with this disorder often react to disturbing experiences with apparent detachment and are unable to express hostility and ordinary aggressive feelings.

The medical model approach arose in reaction to the historical notion that the emotionally disturbed were possessed by demons, were mad, and were to be blamed for their disturbances. These people were "treated" by being beaten, locked up, or killed. The medical model led to viewing the disturbed as being in need of help, stimulated research into the nature of emotional problems, and promoted the development of therapeutic approaches.

The major evidence for the validity of the medical model approach comes from studies that suggest that some mental disorders, such as schizophrenia, may be influenced by genetics (heredity). The bulk of the evidence for the significance of heredity comes from studies of twins. For instance, in a sample of over 15,000 twins, Hofer and Polin (1970) found a concordance rate (that is, if one has it, both have it) for schizophrenia of 15.5 percent for identical twins and 4.4 percent for fraternal twins. Critics of such studies argue that findings may be due to the fact that the physical similarity of identical twins leads family and friends to treat them alike. However, some research suggests a higher concordance rate among identical twins even if they were raised separately (Kety, 1976).

Interactional Model

Critics of the medical (mental illness) approach assert that such medical labels have no diagnostic or treatment value and frequently have an adverse labeling effect.

Thomas Szasz (1961a) was one of the first authorities to assert that mental illness is a myth—that it does not exist. Szasz's theory is an interactional theory, as it focuses on the processes of everyday social interaction and the effects of labeling on people. Beginning with the assumption that the term *mental illness* implies a "disease of the mind," he categorizes all of the so-called mental illnesses into three types of emotional disorders and discusses the inappropriateness of calling such human difficulties mental illnesses:

1. *Personal disabilities*, such as excessive anxiety, depression, fears, and feelings of inadequacy. Szasz says such so-called mental illnesses may appropriately be considered mental (in the sense in which thinking and feeling are considered mental activities), but he asserts they are not diseases.
2. *Antisocial acts*, such as bizarre homicides and other social deviations. Homosexuality used to be in this category, but was removed from the American Psychiatric Association's list of mental illnesses in 1974. Szasz says such antisocial acts are only social deviations and he asserts they are neither mental nor diseases.
3. *Deterioration of the brain with associated personality changes*. This category includes the disorders labeled as mental illnesses in which personality changes result following brain deterioration from such causes as arteriosclerosis, chronic alcoholism, general paresis, or serious brain damage following an accident. Common symptoms are loss of memory, listlessness, apathy, and deterioration of personal grooming habits. Szasz says these disorders can appropriately be considered diseases, but are diseases of the brain (i.e., brain deterioration which specifies the nature of the problem) rather than being diseases of the mind.

Szasz (1961b, p. 87) asserts the notion that people with emotional problems are mentally ill is as absurd as the belief that the emotionally disturbed are possessed by demons:

Major Mental Disorders According to the American Psychiatric Association

Disorders Usually First Evident in Infancy, Childhood, or Adolescence: Include, but are not limited to, mental retardation, attention deficit disorders (including hyperactivity), eating disorders (including anorexia), pervasive developmental disorders (e.g., infantile autism), and others

Organic Mental Disorders: Can be induced by substances (alcohol, drugs) or can be organic brain syndromes (delirium, dementia, and such)

Substance Use Disorders: Include abuse of alcohol, barbiturates, amphetamines, and so on

Schizophrenic Disorders: Include all forms of schizophrenia

Delusional (Paranoid) Disorders: Include all forms of paranoia and persistent irrational delusions, often with a fear of persecution

Mood Disorders: Emotional disorders such as depression or exaggerated mood swings, including manic behavior

Anxiety Disorders: Phobias, panic, extreme anxiety, and stress from traumatic experiences (for example, battle shock)

Somatoform Disorders: Psychological problems that manifest themselves as symptoms of physical disease (for example, hypochondria)

Dissociative Disorders: Problems in which part of the personality is dissociated from the rest (for example, multiple personalities and amnesia)

Sexual Disorders: Sexually related problems such as transsexualism, exhibitionism, and inhibited sexual desire

Sleep Disorders: Insominia and other problems with sleep

Disorders of Impulse Control: The inability to control certain undesirable impulses (for example, kleptomania, pyromania, and pathological gambling)

Adjustment Disorders: Difficulty in adjusting to the stress created by such common events as unemployment or divorce

Personality Disorders: Inflexible and maladaptive patterns of sufficient severity to cause either significant impairment in adaptive functioning or subjective distress.

SOURCE: DSM-III-R *(The Diagnostic and Statistical Manual of Mental Disorders)*, 3rd Ed., rev. (Washington, DC: American Psychiatric Association, 1987).

The belief in mental illness as something other than man's trouble in getting along with his fellow man, is the proper heir to the belief in demonology and witchcraft. Mental illness exists or is "real" in exactly the same sense in which witches existed or were "real."

The point that Szasz and many other writers are striving to make is that people do have emotional problems, but they do not have a mystical, mental illness. Terms that describe behavior, they believe, are very useful; for example, depression, anxiety, an obsession, a compulsion, excessive fear, hallucinations, or feelings of being a failure. Such terms describe personal problems that people have. But the medical terms, they assert (such as schizophrenia and psychosis) are not useful because there is no distinguishing symptom which would indicate whether a person has, or does not have, the illness. In addition, Offer and Sabshin (1966) point out there is considerable variation between cultures regarding what is defined as a mental illness. The usefulness of the medical model is also questioned because psychiatrists frequently disagree on the medical diagnosis to be assigned to those who are disturbed (Koll, 1969).

In a dramatic study psychologist David Rosenhan (1973) demonstrated that professional staff in mental hospitals could not distinguish insane patients from sane patients. Rosenhan and seven normal associates went to twelve mental hospitals in five different states claiming they were hearing voices; all eight were admitted to these hospitals. After admission these pseudopatients stated they stopped hearing voices and acted normally. The hospitals were unable to distinguish their sane status from the insane status of other patients. The hospitals kept these pseudopatients hospitalized for an average of 19 days, and all were then discharged with a diagnosis of "schizophrenia in remission."

The use of medical labels, it has been asserted, has severe adverse labeling effects (Scheff, 1966). The person labeled mentally ill (and frequently the therapist) believes that he or she has a disease for which unfortunately there is no known cure. The label gives the labeled person an excuse for not taking responsibility for his/her actions (for example, innocent by reason of insanity). Since there is no known cure, the disturbed frequently idle away their time waiting for someone to discover a cure, rather than assuming responsibility for their behavior, examining the reasons why there are problems, and making efforts to improve. Other undesirable consequences of being labeled mentally ill are they may lose some of their legal rights (Szasz, 1963); may be stigmatized in their social interactions as being dangerous, unpredictable, untrustworthy, or of weak character (Phillips, 1963); and may find it more difficult to secure employment or receive a promotion (Lemert, 1951).

The question of whether mental illness exists is indeed important. The assignment of mental illness labels to disturbed people has substantial implications for how the disturbed will be treated, for how others will view them, and for how they will view themselves. Cooley's "looking glass self-concept" (1902) crystalizes what is being said here. The looking glass says we develop our self-concept (our idea of who we are) in terms of how other people react to us. If someone is labeled mentally ill, other people are apt to react to him as if he were mentally ill, and that person may well define himself as being different, crazy, and begin playing that role.

Assessing and Treating Unwanted Emotions: Application of Theory to Client Situations

A variety of theoretical frameworks can be used for assessing and treating emotional problems. (A summary of these frameworks is in Zastrow, 1992.) The rational therapy approach will be described here as it is one of the more useful approaches. The primary developer of rational therapy is Albert Ellis (1962).

Many people erroneously believe that emotions are primarily determined by experiences (that is, by events that happen to us). Rational therapy has demonstrated that the primary cause of all of our emotions is what we tell ourselves about events that happen to us.

All emotions occur according to the following format:

Events
(Our experiences)

Self-talk
(Self-talk is the set of evaluating thoughts we give ourselves about facts and events that happen to us.)

Emotions
(May include remaining calm.)

This basic principle is not new. The stoic philosopher Epictetus wrote in *The Enchiridion* in the first century A.D.: "Men are disturbed not by things, but by the view which they take of them" (quoted in Ellis, 1979, p. 190). An example will illustrate this process:

Event
Jane Adams studies extensively for her first human behavior exam, takes the exam, and receives a C.

Jane's Self-Talk
"Gee, this is awful. I studied so hard for this exam, and bombed out. It sure looks like I'm going to fail this course. Human behavior is not for me. I'm simply dumber than other students. Since this is a required course in the social work major, it looks like I'll never make it as a social worker. I'm a failure. Maybe I should drop out of college right now, rather than continuing to waste my money when I'll never graduate anyway."

Jane's Emotions
Depressed, feeling of being a failure, disgusted with self.

If on the other hand, Jane tells herself the following about receiving a C, her emotions will be very different:

Event
Jane Adams studies extensively for her first human behavior exam, takes the exam, and receives a C.

Jane's Self-Talk
"Wow—I just got by on this exam. Nearly half the class got a C or lower on the exam, so it looks like I'm doing about as well as others. All I need is a grade of C in this course to pass the course and fulfill the requirement. I see where I made some mistakes that I shouldn't have made, so I think I will be able to do better on the next exam. I'll also talk with the instructor to get some ideas on how I can improve in this course. I feared I flunked this exam, and I wound up doing

better than I expected. I'm progressing satisfactorily in the social work major, and I think I can do better.

Jane's Emotions
Mildly anxious about receiving a C, relief that the exam was not flunked, optimistic about improving her grade on the next exam, and optimistic about passing the course.

The most important point about this process is that our self-talk determines how we feel, and by changing our self-talk we can change any unwanted emotion. An unwanted emotion can be defined as either an emotion we want to change or an emotion we have that others have become significantly concerned about—for example, excessive depression that has continued since a loved one died several years earlier. It is possible that an emotion that is generally viewed as being positive can be an unwanted emotion; for example, if you find you are feeling happy at a funeral, you may want to change the emotion. Also, emotions generally viewed as negative can be a wanted emotion in certain situations, for example, sadness at a funeral.

Changing Unwanted Emotions
There are only five ways to change an unwanted emotion, and only the first three of them are constructive. These three are: getting involved in meaningful activity, changing the negative and irrational thinking that underlies the unwanted emotion, and changing the distressing event.

Meaningful Activity. The first constructive way is to get involved in some meaningful or enjoyable activity. When we become involved in activity that is meaningful, it provides satisfaction and structures and fills time, thereby taking our mind off a distressing event.

Practically all of us encounter day-to-day frustrations and irritations—having a class or two that are not going too well, having a job with irritations, or having a blah social life. If we go home in the evening and continue to think about and dwell on the irritations, we will develop such unwanted emotions as depression, anger, frustration, despair, or feeling of being a failure. (Which of these emotions we will have will directly depend on what we tell ourselves.)

By having an escape list of things we enjoy doing,

Format for Rational Self-Analysis

A
(facts and events)

B
(self-talk)
1. _____
2. _____
etc.

C
(emotional consequences of B)

D(a)
(camera check of A)

D(b)
(rational self-talk challenges of B)
1. _____
2. _____
etc.

E
(emotional goals and behavioral goals for
similar future events)

---

we can nip unwanted emotions in the bud. Everyone should develop an escape list of things they enjoy doing: taking a walk, golf, going to a movie, tennis, shopping, needlework, visiting friends, routine physical activity, and so on. By getting involved in things we enjoy, we take our mind off our day-to-day concerns and irritations. The positive emotions we will instead experience will directly stem from the things we tell ourselves about the enjoyable things we are doing.

In urging people to compile and use an escape list, the authors are not suggesting that people should avoid doing something about trying to change unpleasant events. If something can be done to change an unpleasant event, all constructive efforts should be tried. However, we often do not have control over unpleasant events and cannot change them. Although we often cannot change unpleasant events, we always have the capacity to control and change what we tell ourselves about unpleasant events. It is this latter focus that is often helpful in learning to change our unwanted emotions.

Changing Self-Talk. A second approach to changing unwanted emotions is to identify and then change the negative and irrational thinking that leads to unwanted emotions. M. Maultsby (1975) developed an approach entitled Rational Self-Analysis (RSA) that is very useful for learning to challenge and change irrational thinking. An RSA has six parts as shown in "Format for Rational Self-Analysis."

The goal in doing an RSA is to change any unwanted emotion (anger, love, guilt, depression, hate, and so on). An RSA is done by recording the event and self-talk on paper. Under Part A (facts and events), simply state the facts or events that occurred. Under Part B (self-talk), write all of your thoughts about A. Number each statement in order (1, 2, 3, 4, and so on). Also write either good, bad, or neutral after each self-talk statement to show yourself how you believed each B section statement reflected on you as a person. (The RSA example which is presented in the inset "A Rational Self-Analysis of a Broken Romance" illustrates the mechanics of this, and other components, of doing an RSA).

Under Part C (emotional consequences) write simple statements describing your gut reactions/emotions stemming from your self-talk in B. Part D(a) is to be written *only* after you have written sections A, B, and C. Part D(a) is a camera check of the A section. Reread the A section and ask yourself "If I had taken a moving picture of what I wrote was happening, would the camera verify what I have written as facts?" A moving picture would probably have recorded the facts, but not personal beliefs or opinions. Personal beliefs or opinions belong in the B section. A common example of a personal opinion mistaken as a fact is: "Marty made me look like a fool when he laughed at me while I was trying to make a serious point." Under D(a) (camera check of A), correct the opinion part of this statement by only writing the factual part: "I was attempting to make a serious point when Marty began laughing at what I was saying." Then add the personal opinion part of the statement to B (that is, "Marty made me look like a fool").

Part D(b) is the section designed to challenge and change negative and irrational thinking. Take each B statement separately. Read B-1 first and ask yourself if it is inconsistent with any of the five questions for rational thinking. It will be irrational if it does one or more of the following:

1. Does not fit the facts. For example, you tell yourself no one loves you after someone has ended a romantic relationship—and you still have several close friends and relatives who love you.
2. Hampers you in protecting your life. For example, if you decide you can drive 30 miles to some place when you are intoxicated.
3. Hampers you in achieving your short- and long-term goals. For example, you want to do well in college and you have two exams tomorrow which you haven't studied for, but instead you decide to go out and party.
4. Causes significant trouble with other people. For example, you think you have a right to challenge anyone to a fight whenever you interpret a remark as being an insult.
5. Leads you to feel emotions that you do not want to feel.

If the self-talk statement is rational, merely write "that's rational." If, on the other hand, the self-talk statement meets one or more of the guidelines for irrational thinking, then think of an alternative "self-talk" to that B statement. This new self-talk statement is of crucial importance in changing your undesirable emotion, and needs to: be rational and be a self-talk statement you are willing to accept as a new opinion for yourself. After writing down this D(b-1) self-talk in the D(b) section, then consider B-2, B-3, and so on in the same way.

Under Part E write down the new emotions you want to have in similar future A situations. In writing these new emotions that you desire, keep in mind that they will follow from your self-talk statements in your D(b) section. This section may also contain a description of certain actions you intend to take to help you achieve your emotional goals when you encounter future A's.

In order to make a rational self-analysis work, you have to put effort into challenging the negative and irrational thinking with your rational debates whenever you start thinking negatively. With effort, you can learn to change any unwanted emotion. This capacity is one of the most important abilities you have. (Once you gain considerable skill in writing out

A Rational Self-Analysis of a Broken Romance

A twenty-one-year-old male college student wrote the following rational self-analysis:

A
(facts and events)

Last year I became very involved with a person named Cindy. At the beginning of our relationship I could tell she was really more infatuated with me that I was with her. Realizing this, I sat down with her and explained that she was coming on too strong for me and that I wasn't ready for a serious relationship yet. I didn't want to hurt her. So there I was, big Joe Authority. I had been in two relationships before and dated a lot, so I knew what could happen if we got involved too quickly. But in all my relationships I had never really felt badly or pondered on them (never had my heart broken). So we went out, and I gradually started to feel more attracted to her. We got along really well. We could talk very easily with one another, and we shared many things and experiences with each other. We had a small fight now and then, but everything seemed to be going all right. It was at this point I could have used some of my own medicine. I started to believe the things she said, like "I'll never leave you" and "I don't know what I'd ever do without you," thereby setting myself up for a big let down. Then it happened. When she came back to college after summer vacation, she said she didn't want to go steady anymore. Well, needless to say, I was pretty shocked at the suddenness of this. I asked her why, and she said it hurt her too much my being away from her (I live 50 miles away) and that she needed someone around all the time. After this, I told her how I felt and tried to change her mind. I even offered some alternatives, but it didn't work. I could not change her mind, so I left and pretended it didn't bother me, but it did.

Da
(camera check)

Da. This is all factual.

B
(my self-talk)

B-1. That bitch! she just wants to go out with other guys.

Db
(my rational self-talk challenges of B)

Db-1. She's not a bitch. A bitch is a mother dog. Cindy is someone I really love and care about. She might want to go out with other guys even though she said this wasn't the case, not to mention it would be the logical thing to do if she wasn't going out with me. I had also said the same thing, that I wanted to date others earlier in our relationship.

B-2. She's probably seeing another guy behind my back.

B-3. I cannot live without her.

B-4. I'll never find anyone like her again.

B-5. She just doesn't want to put the effort into it because I live so far away.

B-6. She's just a flirt! All she wants to do is hang around in bars so she can be just like her friends.

B-7. I'm never going to get involved with anyone again.

B-8. I'm just going to treat girls like s—and take advantage of them.

B-9. I'll just go out with other girls.

B-10. Maybe I'll wait and she'll call me back.

B-11. I have never felt this bad about breaking up with someone.

B-12. I will wait and call her in a few months from now and I can find out what the real reasons are and how she's doing.

B-13. I'd still like to see her, at least we could still be friends.

Db-2. I don't know this as a fact, and besides, I asked her and she said she was not.

Db-3. This is certainly not true. I lived well without her before I met her, and I can do the same in the future.

Db-4. There are over 2 million eligible women to date—surely some of those have characteristics I'll admire as much as the positives about Cindy.

(This is rational thinking on my part, and therefore does not need a rational self-talk challenge)

Db-6. I told her from the beginning I wanted her to go out with her friends. Also, I can't really say she's a tease or a flirt. Although she did mention, commenting about a friend, how nice it must be to have guys wanting to take you out all the time. I really think she began to feel this way later on.

Db-7. Not too smart, especially if I want to get married some day. Besides, I know if I meet someone I really like I would go out with her. Besides that, I know there's a risk involved.

Db-8. This is not like me. I could never do this. Besides, it's not right to take things out on other people.

(This is rational thinking. It is a positive start, probably the smartest thing I've thought so far. After all, there are plenty of fish in the sea.)

Db-10. I don't want to do this because it will give me false hopes and lead me to feel more lousy and depressed.

Db-11. True, I have never felt this bad, but it happened. Now I know what it's like and I can learn from this experience.

(This is rational thinking. I would like to know the real reason, so if I feel like calling I will. I'm very concerned about her and know there's some very emotional things bothering her about her family life and would like to make sure that these things aren't bothering her.)

(This is rational thinking. I don't want bad feelings between us, but still I shouldn't get too carried away with this, otherwise it could bring me down.)

C
(my emotions)

Angry, jealous, confused, concerned, lonely and depressed.

E
(my emotional and behavioral goals)

To realize that I'm not some victim of some sort of crime, and also realize that this is normal and things like this happen. I'm going to go out with other women, knowing that this is a risk I'm going to have to take.

an RSA, you will be able to do the process in your head without having to write it out.)

This process of challenging negative and irrational thinking *will* work in changing unwanted emotions if you put the needed effort into it. Just as dieting is guaranteed to lose weight, so is this approach guaranteed to change unwanted emotions. Both, however, require an effort and commitment to use the process in order to make it work.

Changing the Distressing Event. A third way to change unwanted emotions is to change the distressing event. Some distressing events can be changed by directly confronting the events and taking constructive action to change these events. For example, if we are let go from a job, we can seek another; when we find one we will feel better. Or, if we are receiving some failing grades, one way of constructively handling the situation is to meet individually with the instructors of these courses to obtain their suggestions on how to do better. If suggestions are received that appear practical and have merit, we will feel better.

Not all distressing events can be changed. For example, we may have a job that we need and be forced to interact with other employees who display behaviors we dislike. If we cannot change their behaviors, the only other constructive option is to bite the bullet and seek to adapt to the circumstances. However, when it is feasible and practical to change distressing events, we should seek to change these events; if we are successful we are apt to feel better because we will then give ourselves more positive self-talk about the changed events.

Destructive Ways to Change Unwanted Emotions

There are two other ways to change unwanted emotions which, unfortunately, some people turn to. One of these ways is by seeking to temporarily relieve intense unwanted emotions through the use of alcohol, other drugs, or food. Unfortunately many people seek to relieve unwanted emotions through the use of such mind-altering drugs as alcohol, cocaine, tranquilizers, and so on. When the effects of the drug wear off, a person's problems and unwanted emotions still remain, and there is a danger that through repeated use a person will become dependent on the drug. Some people overeat for the same reasons— loneliness, insecurity, boredom, and frustration. The process of eating and the feeling of having a full stomach provide temporary relief from intense unwanted emotions. Such people are apt to become overweight or bulimic—or both.

The only other way to relieve unwanted emotions is a sure-fire way—a bullet to the head (or some other form of suicide). This way is the ultimate destructive approach to changing unwanted emotions.

Assessing and Changing Deviant Behavior: Application of Theory to Practice

Our thinking is not only the primary determinant of our emotions, but also of our actions, as depicted in the following diagram:

Events

↓

Self-talk

↓

Emotions

↓

Actions

To demonstrate this principle, reflect on the last time you did something bizarre or unusual. What self-talk statements were you giving yourself (that is, what were you thinking) prior to and during the time when you did what you did?

Thinking processes primarily determine behavior. The reasons for unusual or dysfunctional behavior occurring can always be identified by determining what the perpetrator was thinking prior to and during the time when the act is being committed. Examples of cognitions that lead to dysfunctional behavior are the following:

Cognition: A seventeen-year-old sees an unlocked Camaro and thinks, "Hey, this is really a neat car to take a ride in. Let me cross the starting wires, and take it for a drive."
Behavior: Car theft

Cognition: A twenty-seven-year-old male is on his second date, is in his date's apartment, and thinks, "She is really sexy. Since I've now wined and dined her twice, it's now time for her to show her appreciation to me. She wants it as much as I do. I'll show her what a great lover I am. She may protest a little, but I'll overcome that with force. Once we get involved sexually, she'll be emotionally attracted to me."

Behavior: Date rape

Cognition: A thirty-one-year-old bartender thinks, "Cocaine gives me such a great high. Unfortunately I don't make the kind of money to buy as much as I need. I have no other choice but to buy more than I use, and then sell some of it for a profit."

Behavior: Drug trafficking

Cognition: A sixteen-year-old female who has run away from home thinks, "Now what am I going to do? Where am I going to stay? Where will I get enough money to eat? Maybe I can find some guys on the street who will give me a place to stay and some money. They'll probably want to jump on me—but that's O.K. That's better than going back home and being beaten by my father when he's drunk."

Behavior: Prostitution

Cognition: A forty-eight-year-old bookkeeper of a retail computer firm thinks, "This is an awful financial mess I'm in. I've got so many bills: mortgage payments, gambling debts, and tuition payments for two kids in college. Hopefully I can win at the next poker game. But I need a stake. The only way to get a stake is to take a couple grand from this company and pay the money back in a few weeks. With me handling the books, no one will ever miss it."

Behavior: Embezzlement

It should be noted that the cognitions underlying each dysfunctional behavior may vary considerably among perpetrators. For example, possible cognitions for shoplifting a shirt might be the following. "This shirt would look really nice for the wedding I'm going to on Saturday. Since I'm buying a number of other items from this store, they still will make a profit from me even if I take this without paying for it." Another may be: "This will be a challenge to see if I can get away with taking this shirt. I'll put it on in the fitting room and put my own shirt and coat on over it, and no one will see me walk out of the store with it. Since I've taken a number of things in the past, I'll act real casual as I walk out of the store." Or: "My son really needs a decent shirt. He doesn't have any nice ones to wear. I don't get enough money from AFDC to buy

Our Thinking Determines Our Behavior and Our Emotions

One of the authors was describing to a class the concept that our thinking primarily causes our emotions and our actions. A male student voluntarily self-disclosed the following:

What you're saying makes a lot of sense. It really applies to something that happened to me. I was living with a female student who I really cared about. I thought, though, that she was going out on me. When I confronted her about it, she always said I was paranoid and denied it.

Then one night I walked into a bar in this town and I saw her in a corner hugging and kissing some other guy. I told myself things like "She really is cheating on me. Both of them are playing me for a fool." Such thinking led me to be angry.

I also told myself "I'm going to set this straight. I'm going to get even with them. I'll break the bottoms off these two empty beer bottles and then jab each of them with the jagged edges." I proceeded to knock off the bottoms on the bar, and then started walking toward them. I got to within eight feet of them and they were still arm in arm and didn't see me. I began, though, to change my thinking. I thought that if I jabbed them, the end result would be that I would get eight to ten years in prison, and I concluded she isn't worth that. Based on this thinking I decided to drop the beer bottles, walk out, and end my relationship with her—which is what I did.

my children what they need. I know my son is embarrassed to wear the rags that he has. I'll just stick this shirt under my coat and walk out with it."

Assessing human behavior is largely a process of identifying the cognitions that underlie unwanted emotions or dysfunctional behavior. The stages of this process are as follows:

Step 1: Identify as precisely as possible the unwanted emotions and/or dysfunctional behavior that a client has.

Step 2: Identify the cognitions or thinking patterns that the client has during the time when that client is having unwanted emotions or is displaying dysfunctional behavior. There are two primary ways of identifying these cognitions. One way is to ask the client what he was thinking prior to and during the time when the client was having unwanted emotions or displaying dysfunctional behavior. If this approach does not work (perhaps because the client refuses to divulge what he was thinking), a second approach is to obtain information about the client's life circumstances at that time. Once these life circumstances are identified, the professional conducting the assessment needs to place herself mentally into the life circumstances of the perpetrator, and then reflect on the kinds of cognitions that would lead this client to have his specific unwanted emotions or dysfunctional behavior. For example, if the client is a sixteen-year-old female who has run away from home and is unemployed, it is fairly easy to identify (to some extent) the kinds of cognitions that would lead such a person to turn to prostitution.

A deduction of the principle that thinking processes determine dysfunctional behaviors and unwanted emotions is that in order to change dysfunctional behaviors or unwanted emotions it is necessary for the affected person to change his thinking patterns. These concepts are illustrated in "Our Thinking Determines Our Behaviors and Our Emotions."

Macro Systems Problems: Crime and Delinquency

A life event or social problem frequently experienced during adolescence or young adulthood is crime or delinquency. A crime is a violation of the criminal law. Practically everyone occasionally breaks the law. For example, if a person drives a car, it is likely that person has intentionally or unintentionally broken such laws as speeding, driving the wrong way on a one-way street, or making an illegal turn. Many people have also committed such offenses as jaywalking, taking something of value from work, and perhaps some liquor violations. If a criminal is defined as someone who has violated the law, then in a broad sense all of us are criminals.

The people who tend to get arrested and spend time in jail or prison are those who generally commit more serious crimes—such as armed robbery, burglary, or rape. (At times, however, some people are arrested, convicted, and treated as criminals for committing crimes that are no more serious than the bulk of the population commits). On rare occasions, a person may be arrested, charged, and convicted of a

Adolescents and young adults commit the bulk of crimes and by far are the most arrested age group in our society.

crime he or she did not commit. This has adverse effects on the person's emotional well-being, trust in the justice system, reputation, and finances.

Adolescents and young adults commit the bulk of crimes and by far are the most arrested age group in our society (Kornblum and Julian, 1989, pp. 171–73). Juveniles can be arrested for committing all of the same crimes as adults. However, they can also be arrested for violating an additional set of laws involving status offenses—that is, acts that are defined as illegal if committed by juveniles but not if committed by adults. Status offenses include running away from home, being truant from school, violating curfew, having sexual relations, being ungovernable, and being beyond the control of parents.

Juveniles when arrested are generally treated differently than adults. The juvenile court tries to act in the best interests of the child, as parents should act. Juvenile courts (in theory) have a treatment orientation. In adult criminal proceedings, the focus is on charging the defendant with a specific crime, holding a public trial to determine if the defendant is guilty as charged, and if found guilty, punishing the wrongdoer via a sentence. In contrast, the focus in juvenile courts is on the current physical, emotional, psychological and educational needs of the children as opposed to punishment for their past misdeeds. Reform or treatment of the juvenile is the goal, even though the juvenile or his family may not agree that the court's decision is in the juvenile's best interest.

Of course, not all juvenile court judges live up to these principles. In practice, some juvenile judges focus more on punishing, rather than treating, juvenile offenders. Court appearances by children can have adverse labeling effects, such as youths viewing themselves as delinquent and then continuing to break the law.

Why do people violate the law? There are many theories about crime causation. For a review of these theories, see Cole (1992, p. 53–70). Crime is a comprehensive label covering a wide range of offenses, such as drunkenness, possession of narcotics, rape, auto theft, arson, shoplifting, attempted suicide, purse snatching, incest, gambling, prostitution, fraud, false advertising, homicide, and kidnapping. Obviously, since the nature of these crimes varies widely, the motives or causes underlying each must vary widely.

The self-talk theory as described by Zastrow and Navarre (1979), in essence, asserts the reasons for any criminal act can be identified by discovering what the offender was thinking prior to and during the time when the crime was being committed. This theory is a derivation from rational therapy which was described earlier in this chapter. A case example of this theory is presented in "Self-Talk Explanation for a Presidential Assassination Attempt."

Macro System Problems: Delinquent Gangs

Juvenile gangs have existed for many decades in the United States and in other countries. In recent years in the United States there have been increases in the number of gangs, the number of youths belonging to gangs, gang youth drug involvement, and gang violence. Violent, delinquent urban gang activity has become a major social problem in the United States. The scientific knowledge base about delinquent gangs is very limited. Longres (1990, p. 320) notes:

No consensus exists for a definition of a youth gang. In addition, no agreed upon recording system exists, and no data on gang offenses are collected in systematic ways by disinterested agencies. Furthermore, attempts to eradicate gangs through social service and criminal justice programs have met with little success.

Self-Talk Explanation for a Presidential Assassination Attempt

On March 30, 1981, President Ronald Reagan was shot in Washington, DC, by a .22 caliber bullet, which pierced the left side of his chest and collapsed his left lung. Also injured was a secret service agent, a Washington policeman, and White House press secretary James Brady. Fortunately, all four men survived. Arrested for this assassination attempt was John W. Hinckley, Jr., twenty-five, the son of a multimillionaire Colorado oil executive.

Born into wealth, John Hinckley, Jr., has been described as a loner and a drifter, a misfit who craved fame. In high school, Hinckley was an average student but had few friends. He went to college for seven years, off and on, but never graduated. His father was a self-made millionaire, and his brother was vice president of his father's firm. His family members were known as strong Reagan supporters.

John Hinckley, Jr., became infatuated with actress Jodie Foster, although they had never met. In the film *Taxi Driver*, Jodie Foster played a teenage prostitute. The film was about a disturbed loser who stalks a political figure. This film appears to have influenced Hinckley's assassination attempt, as he described his self-talk in an unmailed letter to Miss Foster:

> I would abandon this idea of getting Reagan in a second if I could only win your heart and live out the rest of my life with you, whether it be in total obscurity or whatever. I will admit to you that the reason I'm going ahead with this attempt now is because I just cannot wait any longer to impress you . . .
>
> Jodie, I'm asking you to please look into your heart and at least give me the chance with this historical deed to gain your respect and love. (Lang, 1981, p. 26)

Apparently John Hinckley, Jr., shot President Reagan because he thought (erroneously) that such a shooting would impress Jodie Foster, and lead to a relationship with her.

The inadequacy of the knowledge base about delinquent gangs is a major obstacle to developing effective intervention strategies with this population. There have been numerous definitions of gangs, but no consensus exists on their distinguishing characteristics (Goldstein, 1991). The lack of consensus among investigators is indicated by the numerous and diverse categories that have been used by different investigators to classify gangs: corner group, social club, conflict group, pathological group, athletic club, industrial association, predatory organization, drug addict group, racket organization, fighting-focused group, defensive group, unconventional group, criminal organization, turf group, heavy metal group, punk rock group, satanic organization, skinhead, ethnic or racial group, motorcycle club, and scavenger group (Goldstein, 1991).

Morales's Classification

An illustration of a categorization is provided by Morales (1989, pp. 419–21), who classified youth gangs into four types: criminal, conflict, retreatist, and cult/occult.

According to Morales (1989), the primary goal of criminal gangs is material gain through criminal activities. Criminal activities include theft of property from persons or premises, extortion, fencing, and obtaining and selling illegal substances (particularly drugs). Drug trafficking of rock cocaine is presently a major source of income for criminal gangs.

Conflict gangs are turf oriented and will engage in violent conflict with individuals or rival groups that invade their neighborhood or that commit acts that they consider degrading or insulting. Respect is highly valued and defended. Hispanic gangs are heavily represented among conflict gangs. Sweeney (1980, p. 86) notes that the Code of the Barrio mandates that gang members watch out for their neighborhood and that gang members must be willing to die for their neighborhood.

Retreatist gangs focus on getting "high" or "loaded" on alcohol, cocaine, marijuana, heroin, or other drugs. Individuals tend to join this type of gang in order to secure continued access to drugs. In contrast to criminal gangs that become involved with drugs for financial profit, retreatist gangs become involved with drugs for consumption.

Some gangs become involved in "devil worship."

These groups are often referred to as occult groups. *Occult* means keeping something secret or hidden, or a belief in supernatural or mysterious powers. However, not all occult groups are involved in criminal activity or in devil worship. Unlike the gangs mentioned earlier, which are primarily composed of juveniles, the majority of occult groups are composed of adults.

Contradictions in Conceptualizing Gangs

Contradictions abound in conceptualizing delinquent gangs. Gangs are believed to be composed largely of ethnically homogeneous adolescents (African American, Hispanic, and Asian youths); yet some gangs composed of white youths exist. Most gang members are believed to be between ages twelve and eighteen, yet, recent evidence indicates some gangs include and may be controlled by adults (Klein and Maxson, 1989). Gangs are believed to be composed of males; yet, some gangs have female members, and a few gangs consist exclusively of females (Longres, 1990, p. 323). Gangs are believed to be primarily involved in drug trafficking; yet, some delinquent gangs have other illegal foci, such as burglary, robbery, larceny, or illegal drug consumption. Gang activity is thought to be primarily located in large, inner city, urban areas; yet gang activity is flourishing in many smaller cities and in some suburbs (Goldstein, 1991).

At the present time there is inadequate statistical data on the number of gangs, the number and characteristics of members, and their criminal activities. Longres (1990, p. 325) notes:

> Statistics on gangs and their criminal behavior are not obtained easily. Many cities have gang control units that collect data but do not report them in any systematic way. Even when such data are obtained, they are difficult to interpret because no uniform definition of gang offenses exists, no recording system has been in place long enough to discern trends, and arrest data from police departments may reflect bias. Additionally, no uniform definition of a gang-related offense exists across police jurisdictions even within the same state, city, or county.

Sociological Theories: Applications of Theories to Gangs

There are numerous theoretical explanations as to why youths join gangs and why gangs engage in delinquent or criminal activities. These explanations include biological, psychological, and sociological theories (see Goldstein, 1991, for a review). As yet no consensus exists as to which theories are most useful, and insufficient research has been conducted to ascertain the validity of the theories. In order to provide illustrations of existing theoretical conceptualizations, four sociological theories will be summarized: differential association theory, anomie theory, deviant subcultures theory, and control theory.

Edwin Sutherland (see Sutherland and Cressey, 1970) advanced his famous *theory of differential association* in 1939. This theory asserts that criminal behavior is the result of a learning process that primarily stems from small, intimate groups—family, neighborhood peer groups, and friends. In essence, the theory states, "A person becomes delinquent because of the excess of definitions favorable to violation of law over definitions unfavorable to violation of law" (p. 76). Whether a person decides to commit a crime is based upon the nature of present and past associations with significant others. People internalize the values of the surrounding culture. When the environment includes frequent contact with criminal elements and infrequent contact with noncriminal elements, a person is apt to engage in delinquent or criminal activity. Past and present learning experiences in intimate personal groups not only define whether a person should violate laws, but, for those deciding to commit crimes, the learning experiences also include which crimes to commit, the techniques of committing these crimes, and the attitudes and rationalizations for committing them. Thus, a youth whose most admired person is a member of a gang involved in committing burglaries or in drug trafficking will seek to emulate this model, will receive instruction in committing these crimes from gang members, and will also receive approval from the gang for successfully committing these crimes.

Robert Merton (1968) applied *anomie theory* to delinquency and crime. This approach views delinquent behavior as resulting when an individual or a gang is prevented from achieving high status goals in a society. Merton begins by noting that every society has both approved goals (for example, wealth and material possessions) and approved means for attaining these goals. When certain members of society want these goals but have insufficient access to the approved means for attaining them, a state of anomie results. (Anomie is a condition in which the acceptance of the approved standards of conduct is weakened.) Unable to achieve the goals through society's legitimately defined channels, the individuals' and gangs' respect for these channels is weakened, and they seek to achieve the desired goals through illegal means. Merton asserts that higher crime rates are apt to occur among those groups discriminated against (that is, those groups facing additional barriers to achieving the high status goals). These groups include the poor and racial minorities. Societies with high crime rates (such as the United States) differ from those with low crime rates because, according to Merton, they tell all their citizens that they can achieve, but in fact they block achievement for some of these people.

Deviant subcultures theory is another explanation for delinquent gang behavior. This theory asserts that some groups have developed their own attitudes, values, and perspectives that support criminal activity. Walter Miller (1958), for example, argues that American lower-class culture is more conducive to crime than middle-class culture. He asserts that lower-class culture is organized around six values—trouble, toughness, excitement, fate, smartness (ability to con others), and autonomy—and allegiance to these values produces delinquency. Miller concludes that the entire lower-class subculture is deviant in the sense that any male growing up in it will accept these values and almost certainly violate the law.

Albert Cohen (1955) advanced another subculture theory. He contended that gangs develop a delinquent subculture that represents solutions to the problems of young male gang members. A gang gives them a chance to belong, to amount to something, to develop their masculinity, to fight middle-class society. In particular, the delinquent subculture, according to Cohen, can effectively solve the status problems of working-class boys, especially those who are rejected by middle-class society. Cohen contends that the main problems of working-class boys revolve around status.

Control theories (Hirschi, 1969) ask the question, "Why do people *not* commit crimes?" Theories in this category assume that all people would "naturally" commit crimes and therefore must be constrained and controlled by society from breaking the law. Control theorists have identified three factors for preventing crime. One is the internal controls through the socialization process that society builds up in an individual; it is believed that developing a strong conscience and a sense of personal morality will prevent most people from breaking the law. A second factor is thought to be a strong attachment to small social groups, such as the family, which prevents individuals from breaking the law, because they fear rejection and disapproval from the people who are important to them. A third factor is that people do not break the law because they fear arrest and incarceration. Control theories assume that the basic nature of humans is asocial or evil. Such an assumption has never been proved.

Hirschi (1969) suggests that the prospects of delinquent behavior decline as the adolescent is controlled by such social bonds as affective ties to parents, involvement in school activities, success in school, high educational and occupational aspirations, and belief in the moral rightness of conventional norms. The weaker the social bonding, the greater the likelihood that an adolescent will become involved in delinquent gang activities. Social bonding is weakened by such factors as parental criminality, parental difficulties such as excessive drinking and extensive unemployment, inadequate parental supervision and monitoring, parental rewarding of deviant behavior, parental modeling of aggressive behavior, and inadequate parental warmth.

Social Work Roles and Intervention Programs

A wide variety of programs have attempted to reduce delinquent gang activities. These have included detached worker programs, in which workers join gangs and seek to transform antisocial into prosocial attitudes and behaviors; formal supervision of those gang members adjudicated delinquent through juvenile probation departments; placement of delinquent gang members in group homes, residential treatment facilities, or reform schools; drug treatment of gang members who have a chemical addiction; programs to support and strengthen families, particularly single-parent families in urban areas; and programs to prevent dropping out of school and to provide academic support.

The outcomes of such interventions have not been sufficiently researched. The factors that lead adolescents to join delinquent gangs and to then engage in delinquent activities are multifaceted and highly complex. It is clear that delinquent gang activities are on the increase in our society. The reasons for this increase are largely unknown. Also unknown are the most effective programs to reduce delinquent gang activities.

Of all the helping professions, it would appear that social work is best suited from a knowledge, values, and skills perspective to develop intervention strategies to use with gangs. Gangs as a focus for practice find the social worker intervening with individuals, groups, families and the community (that is, micro, mezzo, and macro level intervention).

Social workers intervene on a one-to-one level with a delinquent gang member in a variety of settings—as a juvenile probation officer, as a counselor at a group home or residential treatment facility, as a school social worker in a school setting, and as an alcohol and drug counselor in a chemical dependency treatment program. On a one-to-one level, social workers may assume the following roles: enabler, counselor, educator, case manager, and broker.

Social workers intervene on a mezzo level with a delinquent gang with a group approach; the worker is viewed as a "detached worker" or "gang group worker." Working with gangs requires that the social worker spend a considerable amount of time in the gang's immediate environment rather than in the agency, hence the term "detached worker" or "street worker." Fox (1985) found that most gangs are receptive to a worker engaging the gang as a group within the purposes of social work practice, and that a social worker can help urban gangs to change from being a destructive force to being a constructive contributor to the community while maintaining the gang's right to self-determination. In working with gangs, a worker can function in the roles of group facilitator, educator, enabler, and advocate in helping the gang obtain needed resources. The worker can also function as a negotiator or a mediator when there is intragang conflict or when there is a conflict between rival gangs. At a mezzo level a worker may also work with the families of gang members to assist them in being constructive forces in curbing their children's delinquent behavior.

A female inmate charged with drug violations talks with adolescent offenders. Social workers may become closely involved in programs that attempt to dissuade young people from crime.

In a very real sense, a delinquent gang is created because the needs of youths are not being met by the family, neighborhood, or traditional community institutions (such as the schools, police, and recreational and religious institutions). A social worker can function as an analyst and evaluator of community conditions that are conducive to the formation of gangs. A worker can also function as an initiator and an advocate for social policy changes. Some useful changes are a reduced access to handguns; improved educational resources; access to recreation, job training, jobs, family counseling, drug rehabilitation, and mobilization of community groups and organizations to restrain gang violence (such as neighborhood watch groups). Social policy changes are also needed at state and national levels in order to funnel more resources to urban centers. Funds are needed to improve the quality of life for city residents, including youths, so that the needs of youths are met in ways other than through gang involvement. Social workers have an obligation to advocate for such local, state, and national changes in social policy.

Summary

This chapter focuses on the social changes and social problems encountered by adolescents and young adults. Young people during this time period face the social developmental tasks of moving from parental dependence to adult interdependence, establishing peer relationships, forming intimate relationships with others, and choosing a personal lifestyle. Choosing a personal lifestyle partly involves making career decisions. Young adults may also enter into a variety of family living arrangements, including: marriage, cohabitation, single life, parenthood, and childless couples.

Social problems described in this chapter include emotional and behavioral problems, crime and delinquency, delinquent gangs, and eating disorders. There are a wide variety of emotional and behavioral problems. Two models of conceptualizing such problems were summarized: the medical model which views emotional and behavioral problems as being mental illnesses, and an interactional model which holds mental illness does not exist. Adolescents and young adults commit the bulk of crimes. Juvenile courts have more of a treatment orientation than the adult criminal justice system. Delinquent gang activity has become a major social problem in the United States; but the scientific knowledge base about delinquent gangs is very limited.

Eating disorders (anorexia nervosa, bulimia nervosa, and compulsive overeating) have recently been recognized as a serious problem. Anorexics eat very little food, bulimics binge and purge, and overeaters binge.

The chapter also summarized the rational therapy approach for assessing and treating unwanted emotions and dysfunctional behaviors. This approach asserts that thinking patterns primarily determine all emotions and behaviors, and that assessing human behavior is largely a process of identifying the cognitions that underlie unwanted emotions or dysfunctional behaviors. Furthermore, the approach asserts that in order to change dysfunctional behaviors or unwanted emotions it is necessary for the affected person to change his or her thinking patterns.

9

*Gender
Roles
and
Sexism*

"Nice briefcase! . . ."

Girls are pretty. Boys are strong.
Girls are emotional. Boys are brave.
Girls are soft. Boys are tough.
Girls are submissive. Boys are dominant.

These ideas refer to some of the traditional stereotypes about how men and women should be.

Stereotypes are "preconceived and relatively fixed ideas about an individual, group, or social status. These ideas are usually based on superficial characteristics or overgeneralizations of traits observed in some members of the group" (Barker, 1991, p. 227). The problem with such fixed images is that they allow no room for individual differences within the group. One of the major values adhered to in social work is that each individual has the right to self-determination. Clinging to stereotypes violates this basic value.

Stereotypes about men and women are especially dangerous because they affect each and every one of us. To expect all men to be successful, strong, athletic, brave leaders places an impractical burden on them. To expect all women to be sweet, submissive, pretty, and born with a natural love of scrubbing kitchen floors places tremendous pressure on them to conform.

A PERSPECTIVE

Sexism involves individual attitudes and institutional arrangements that discriminate against people, usually women and girls, because of sex role stereotyping and generalizations (Barker, 1991, p. 212). Prejudice involves negative attitudes and prejudgments about a group. Discrimination involves the actual treatment of that group's members in a negative or unfair manner. Aspects of diversity directly affect how individuals function and interact with other systems in the social environment.

The aspect of diversity addressed here is gender. Since men in our society have traditionally held the majority of positions of power, this chapter will focus on the state and status of women as victims of sexism.

This chapter will:

- Identify and discuss traditional gender role expectations and stereotypes as they affect people over the life span.
- Assess the impacts of sexism on both men and women.
- Examine some of the differences between men and women including personality, abilities, and communication styles.
- Discuss and examine the issues of comparable worth, sexual harassment, sexist language, rape and sexual assault, battered women, and special counseling needs of women.
- Present strategies for combating sexism and achieving sexual equality.

Gender Role Stereotypes

From the moment they're born, boys and girls are treated very differently. Girls are wrapped in pink blankets and parents are told that they now have "a beautiful little girl." Boys, on the other hand, are wrapped in blue blankets and parents are told that they now are the proud parents of "a bouncing baby boy." The process of gender stereotyping continues through childhood, adolescence, and adulthood.

Gender stereotyping involves expectations about how people should behave based upon their gender. Female stereotypes include being "nurturant, supportive, intuitive, emotional, . . . needful, dependent, tender, timid, fragile, . . . childlike, . . . passive, . . . obedient, . . . [and] . . . and submissive"; in stark contrast male stereotypes include being "powerful, creative, intelligent, rational, independent, self-reliant, strong, courageous, daring, responsible, . . . forceful, . . . authoritative, . . . [and] successful" (Ruth, 1990, p. 126). These stereotypes have nothing to do with an individual's personality, his or her own personal strengths and weaknesses, or likes and dislikes.

A major problem with gender-based stereotypes is that they often limit people's alternatives. Pressure is exerted from many sources on people to conform to gender-based expectations. This pressure affects the individual and affects the alternatives available to him or her.

For example, until 1920, when women finally were allowed to vote, concrete political input was not available to them. Prior to that time, the political macro system (the United States government) dictated that women could not vote. Gender-based stereotypes

about women which helped maintain that stance may have included the ideas that women were not bright enough to partake in decision making; that women belonged in the home caring for husband and children, not in the hectic world of politics; and that women were destined to be the virtuous upholders of purity and human dignity (Rothman, 1978), qualities not to be muddied in the political arena. For whatever reasons, women were simply not allowed to vote.

In order to understand and assess human behavior one must be aware of the pressures that gender-based stereotypes bring to bear on people. Social workers need to understand how human diversity affects behavior. Gender is one critical type of diversity. Gender-based differences and stereotypes will be examined within the contexts of childhood, adolescence, young adulthood, and later adulthood.

Childhood

We established in Chapter 4 that females and males are treated differently from the moment they are born. Even parents who state that they consciously try to avoid imposing gender stereotypes on their children

From birth, boys and girls are treated differently because of gender-based stereotypes. Boys, such as these in Höchst, Germany, are given toy guns, and girls are given dolls.

still treat girls and boys differently (Scanzoni and Fox, 1980). Thus, it's difficult to separate out any inborn differences from those that are learned.

We established that parents generally treat male children in a more physical manner than female children. Parents also tend to communicate to male and female children differently. For example, they tend to respond positively to boys who behave actively and to girls who talk calmly or touch gently.

Gender differences are demonstrated in how children play. Boys are more aggressive than girls. Additionally, children tend to choose gender-related toys. Boys are drawn to "masculine" toys such as guns and trucks, while girls tend to prefer "feminine" playthings like Barbies and Little Ponies.

Adolescence

Because it is a time of change, adolescence can be difficult. Bodies change drastically, sexual desires emerge, peers exert tremendous pressure to conform, personal identities are struggling to surface, and conflicts with parents are rampant. In addition to these other issues, adolescents must deal with powerful pressures to conform to gender stereotypes.

Masters, Johnson, and Kolodny (1988) indicate that there are three basic rules by which male adolescents are expected to abide. First, they must achieve success at athletics. Second, they have to become enthralled with girls and sex. Third, they don't dare show any interest in feminine things or manifest any feminine behavior. Young men who violate these rules are subject to social ostracism and ridicule. The reasons for these pressures to conform are probably twofold. The first reason is that masculinity and femininity are often seen as two opposite extremes. If a male shows any signs of leaning toward feminine behavior, he may be shifted into the feminine category. The second reason is to avoid any suspicion that he may be homosexual (see Chapter 13).

Adolescent girls, on the other hand, have problems of their own. Until adolescence, girls tend to excel over boys in academic achievement. However, as they approach adulthood, the concept of achievement conflicts with other gender role stereotypes such as dependence, submissiveness, and nurturance. It's difficult for women to achieve at higher levels than

men and be passive, dependent, and submissive at the same time. This problem is termed *femininity-achievement incompatibility* (Hormer, 1972; Hyde, 1985). For arbitrary reasons femininity and achievement traditionally have not been considered compatible in our society. A female adolescent gets messages from many sources that achieving academically will detract from her femininity (Reskin and Hartman, 1986; Sherman, 1982; Tobias and Weissbrod, 1980). Parents and teachers may encourage young women to learn domestic or secretarial skills instead of working toward a profession. Guidance counselors frequently discourage women from taking college prep courses, especially those in science and math (Marini and Brinton, 1984).

For example, one seventeen-year-old female high school senior happened to be tall, beautiful, and poised. She was also ranked sixth academically in a class of 467 students at a prestigious suburban high school. Her high school guidance counselor emphatically urged her to think about selling fashion clothing for some large department store. No mention was made of becoming an astrophysicist, a corporation attorney, or a brain surgeon. Those, of course, were so-called masculine professions. But the fact is that femininity and achievement are two unrelated concepts. One has nothing to do with the other.

There might be change for the better. Now women are entering the workforce to a much greater extent and assuming positions of power and influence. If more alternative options are available to women in the future, women will have greater freedom to choose what they would like to do with their lives.

Abolition of stereotypes would give men more options. It would give them more freedom to express feelings. The pressure for them to succeed and lead all the time would be lessened. It would also give them greater opportunities to participate in domestic and child-rearing tasks. Men often miss many of the joys of watching their children grow up simply by not being around them very much.

Young Adulthood

Women are taught that they should be fulfilled by becoming wives and mothers (Hyde, 1990). Men, on the other hand, are taught that their main source of self-satisfaction should come from their jobs (Hyde, 1986). The pressures and expectations resulting from both of these stereotypes often create serious problems for the gender involved.

A woman who devotes herself entirely to being a wife and homemaker makes herself entirely dependent on her husband. If her husband dies, becomes ill, or leaves her, such a woman is in a vulnerable position. About one out of two marriages ends in divorce (U.S. Department of Commerce, 1990). This striking rate has gradually increased. Divorce was a rare occurrence prior to World War II.

Gove (1979, pp. 39-40) identifies various other problems with which women in traditionally stereotyped roles are confronted. First, by putting all of their eggs in one basket, or directing all of their energy toward one goal, women limit their sources of gratification. Men, on the other hand, have both their work lives and their home lives from which they can derive pleasure. Second, many women find the tasks involved in childrearing and housework to be unrewarding and are disenchanted with the low status typically attributed to this work. Others find the unstructured and repetitive tasks of homemaking to be boring. Third, even when married women work outside the home, they are still expected to do most of the domestic tasks.

Men don't have the best situation in the world either. Not only is a man expected to hold a steady job outside the home, but he's also expected to be successful at it (Tavris, 1977). The man of the house is expected to be a strong leader all of the time. Not everyone is, can be, or even wants to be a leader. Such gender expectations place great burdens on men who are naturally passive, easygoing, or nonassertive. Whereas women are expected to lean all of the time, men are expected to bolster and support all of the time.

Later Adulthood

As they reach middle age some women suffer from what has been called the *empty-nest syndrome* (Bart, 1971). This involves the sense of depression and loss that can occur when children grow up and leave home. It is logical that a woman who has focused all of her efforts on her family needs to reevaluate her position when her major function, namely that of being a mother, almost disappears. Some recent research conflicts with the idea that middle-aged mothers have to suffer the empty-nest syndrome (Rubin, 1979). Interviews with women during this period revealed that they were not so much depressed as they were relieved. They indicated that for the first time in a long time, they felt free. The implication is that women at this point need to take control and pursue other interests rather than wallow in their loss. Perhaps women who have diversified their interests and talents prior to this time in their lives have an easier time with such transitions.

Another problem that plagues women as they get older is losing their physical beauty and attractiveness. Our society places a lot of emphasis on beauty. All one needs to do is watch a television commercial depicting a woman having a bad date because she didn't use the right kind of lipstick. Look at all the advertisements in the media for wrinkle removers, exercise programs, and hair tints. As women age, it becomes much more difficult to maintain a beautiful appearance. Unless women put beauty in perspective as being only one minor aspect affecting the quality of life, they have a greater potential for suffering serious problems with both adjusting to the aging process and maintaining self-esteem.

Men in middle age are affected by different gender stereotypes. Whereas a great deal of a woman's worth is traditionally based on her beauty, much of a man's worth is traditionally based on his ability to succeed (Hyde, 1986). For example, rich, successful men are frequently associated with gorgeous women. Physically attractive women do tend to marry men of higher social and economic status (Udry and Eckland, 1984; Elder, 1969).

But not all men are or can be successful. Even men who are moderately successful tend to enter a midlife crisis (Kaluger and Kaluger, 1984, pp. 538-39). This is a time when men, who were supposed to be successful in their careers, reevaluate their accomplishments and their expectations. At least half of a man's life is probably over by this time. It is a time for facing the fact that if he hasn't become president of the United States or even of the company by now, there is a good chance that he never will. At age twenty many more career options look (and indeed probably are) possible than at age fifty. By middle age, men who had worked very hard at their jobs and careers and who had espoused traditional values tend to raise serious questions about what all that hard work and commitment to values really means (Levinson, 1977). Some of the crises and difficulties middle aged men experience include addressing the emergence of some of the more feminine portions of their identities and choosing what aspects of their lives need to be changed and adjusted (Levinson et al., 1978). (For a fuller discussion of midlife crisis, see Chapter 10.)

Gender stereotypes pressure people to conform. Perhaps a more effective way of dealing with midlife crises for men is to be more flexible throughout life. If gender stereotypes begin to dissolve, maybe people will become more objective in assessing themselves from youth on. Then they may not feel pressured to be something they're not. Abolishing gender stereotypes may give people the freedom to develop more realistic expectations and to live the way they choose.

Male/Female Differences

Some differences do emerge between males and females. To what extent they are due to biological predisposition or to environmental effects is unknown. These differences are evident in personality, in abilities, and in communication styles.

Personality

Males do tend to be physically more aggressive than females (Maccoby and Jacklin, 1974, Sapiro, 1990). This difference begins to emerge with age two and continues throughout life. As with other traits, it's difficult to determine to what extent this is an innate difference and to what extent it is learned.

Some evidence shows that females tend to have less self-esteem than males (Block, 1983, 1976). This has several negative implications for females. People who are less aggressive may also be less assertive in climbing a career ladder. People who have lower self-esteem may not have the confidence it takes even to attempt to achieve and climb that ladder.

Ability Level

Although there are no differences between male and females in terms of intellectual ability or IQ, there

has been heated debate for many years regarding the differences in males' and females' verbal ability. Males have traditionally been thought to have better mathematical ability and females better verbal ability. However, recent research has raised some serious questions about the extent of these differences and even whether significant differences exist at all.

For example, Hyde and Linn (1988) found no differences in verbal ability between boys and girls. Another study used a technique call *meta-analysis* to examine one hundred research articles published between 1962 and 1988 (Hyde et al., 1990). The technique employs systematic analysis of the results of numerous studies in order to come to some general conclusions that reflect all the research involved. Findings indicated that males cannot be distinguished from females in terms of mathematical ability.

Other research complicates the issue. For example, Deaux (1984) found that girls in grades four through six perform better on both math and verbal achievement tests. However, girls later fall behind by the end of high school. Why does this happen? Does innate ability simply dry up over time for girls?

A major Baltimore study on first graders reveals that by the time children first enter school, they have begun to know that different things are generally considered important for girls and boys (Entwisle, et al., 1987). Freeman (1989, pp. 206-7) comments on their findings:

> Boys were more concerned with learning quickly; girls were more concerned with obeying rules and being honest. Being able to do arithmetic was an important aspect of the academic self-concept of boys; for girls, it was irrelevant. . . . Where did these differences come from? The study suggests that, for girls at least, they originate partly in parental expectations—and parental expectations for girls focus strongly on 'being good' rather than on academic achievement.

We confront once again the nature-nurture controversy. To what extent are such abilities innate and to what extent are they the result of the differential treatment of boys and girls? The debate continues. The important thing is not to make assumptions regarding an individual's ability on the basis of gender. The fact is that some girls score higher on mathematical achievement tests than the majority of boys; some boys score higher on verbal achievement tests than the majority of girls (Deaux, 1984).

Communication Styles

Another area where differences between males and females are evident is verbal and nonverbal communication style (Deaux, 1976; Key, 1975). Contrary to popular belief, men spend more time talking than women do. (Henley and Freeman, 1984, p. 472). Again contrary to popular belief, men also interrupt conversations more than women do (Deaux, 1976). If people are interrupted while speaking, they tend to submit to others whom they feel are superior (Eakin and Eakin, 1976). The implication is that in conversational contexts, women frequently place themselves and/or are placed in inferior positions.

Women are also more likely to give information or make self-disclosures than men are (Cozby, 1973). Self-disclosure can place a person in a vulnerable or inferior position. It involves increasing the other person's power (Henley and Freeman, 1984, p. 469). The person who receives the information can choose to criticize the discloser or give the information to other people. Research has indicated that people working in business organizations are more likely to disclose themselves to their supervisors than to those they supervise (Slobin et al., 1968).

It is interesting to note that the less people adhere rigidly to traditional gender role stereotypes, the more flexible they are in their levels of self-disclosure (Sollie and Fischer, 1985; Gerdes et al., 1981). That is, they are more likely to vary their amount of self-disclosure depending on the situation, how much others are sharing about themselves, and the topic they're discussing.

Nonverbal behavior also differs between men and women. Men more frequently touch other people, while women are most likely to be the ones who are touched (Henley, 1973a). Touching has also been found to be associated with status (Henley, 1973b). Persons of higher status are much more likely to touch persons of lower status than the other way around. The fact that women are more likely to be touched implies that somehow they are perceived to have a lower status.

Another difference in communication styles is that women often tend to be coy in their behavior. Henley and Freeman (1984, pp. 472-73) define being coy as involving gestures of submission including lowering the eyes from another's gaze, falling silent when interrupted or pointed at (or not beginning to speak at all), and cuddling to the touch. These may be considered by some to be typically "feminine" behaviors. Picture the stereotypical nineteenth-century Southern belle fluttering at every eligible man around. Being coy, along with its sexual connotations, conveys deference, dependence, and a sense of needing leadership and protection.

Although many of these differences in communication styles are subtle and minor, in combination they mean a lot. Many of women's most salient issues involve unfairness and victimization due to sexism. To begin to examine the issues and to initiate change, some of the foundations of sexism need to be understood. Changes in these behaviors, when they're all considered together, may bring about significant adjustments in gender role expectations and the distribution of power.

People

Men and women are more similar than dissimilar. The differences we refer to are differences in treatment and differences in what people have learned. Sexism needs to be addressed because it's unfair. It causes people to be treated differently because of their gender when there are no objective reasons for differential treatment.

Each individual, whether male or female, has the right to make choices. Cutting through and obliterating gender stereotypes and sexism will give people as individuals more freedom. Each individual will then have a better chance of being the way he or she naturally is comfortable being. The idea is to confront the hidden rules which pressure people to conform on the basis of gender. Women can then be assertive without being pushy. Men won't have to be strong all of the time and will be freer to express their feelings. Tasks and the burdens of leadership can then be shared or divided on the basis of mutual decision making. The best of each individual's personality traits can then blossom and be nurtured.

Table 9.1: Gender/Racial Comparison of Median Annual Income

Gender Racial Group	1988 Median Annual Income
White males	$25,180
Minority males	$17,004
White females	$16,536
Minority females	$14,248

SOURCE: Taeuber and Valdisera (1986), p. 29; U.S. Department of Commerce (1990), p. 409.

Significant Issues and Events in the Lives of Women

Women have been the victims of sexism in many striking and concrete ways. Historically, they have had fewer rights and have been financially less well off to a significant degree. They are victims of life events (rape and domestic violence) that do not touch the lives of men.

The issues addressed here were selected on the basis of prevalence, severity, and current relevance. They include comparable worth, sexual harassment, sexist language, sexual assault, battered women, and the special counseling needs of women.

Comparable Worth: Economic Inequality

It is a well-known fact that women generally earn less than men. Today, women earn about 70 percent of what men earn (Renzetti and Curran, 1992). The wage gap between women and men becomes even worse when race is taken into account. That is, minority women are significantly more disadvantaged than white women, as table 9.1 reflects.

The condition of some subgroups of minority women is worse than other subgroups (Renzetti and Curran, 1992). Figures for 1980 (the most recent year for which comparable information is obtainable) are shown in table 9.2.

A number of reasons have been given for gender-based salary differences. A major one is that women and men tend to be clustered in different kinds of occupations. Occupations more likely to be characterized by men usually pay higher salaries.

The principle of comparable worth may be defined as "calling for equal pay for males and females doing work requiring comparable skill, effort, and responsibility under similar working conditions" (Bellak, 1984, p. 75). That is, questions are being raised regarding the fact that men make substantially more money doing work requiring similar levels of preparation and skill than women do. Comparable worth refers not to jobs that are identical but to jobs that are similar. For example, a male janitor might receive a substantially higher salary than a female secretary, even though both jobs might require similar levels, not types, of training and experience. Comparable worth is a concept that needs to be introduced in the context of women's earning power, employment picture, and political status within this society.

The majority of American women work outside of the home (Fox and Hesse-Biber, 1984, p. 1). Their work is critical to their livelihood and, in many cases, to their self-concept. As we have noted, however, women tend to be clustered in occupations that historically are relatively low paying. These occupations include secretaries, childcare workers, receptionists, typists, nurses, hairdressers, and cashiers (U.S. Bureau of the Census, 1981). Men, on the other hand, tend to work in better paying occupations as physicians, managers, engineers, and construction workers. Perhaps an even more striking finding is that for most of these job categories (including those which are viewed as being feminine and those viewed as being masculine) women will earn less than men in the same job category doing the same work. A U.S.

Table 9.2: Gender Subgroup Comparison of Median Annual Income, 1980

Subgroup	Income
White	$11,189
African American	$10,381
Puerto Rican	$10,171
Native American	$10,069
Cuban	$ 9,703
Mexican American	$ 9,217

SOURCE: Renzetti and Curran (1992); Smith and Tienda (1988).

A school superintendent gives students a talk on the value of education while the teacher looks on. Although less than half of all teachers are men, 99 percent of all school superintendents are men.

Labor Department study evaluated the earnings of women and men in one hundred occupations (National Commission of Working Women, 1983). It was found that women's full-time earnings were less than men's in every single category studied. For example, the percentages of women's earnings compared to men's are reflected in the following job categories: 80 percent for computer programmers; 75 percent for lawyers; 73 percent for bookkeepers; 61 percent for office managers; 68 percent for cooks; and 80 percent for social workers. Other studies have found similar gender differences in salary for physicians, engineers, and accountants (Schreiner, 1984).

In 1986, 90 percent of all college and university presidents were men; those few who were women tended to head small, religious and women's colleges, most of which lacked in prestige when compared to those headed by men (Maeroff, 1986). A similar situation characterizes elementary and secondary schools. Women also have less direct political power in terms of the actual number of political offices they hold. In 1993, for example, 48 of 435 House of Representatives members and 6 of the 100 U.S. Senators were women. It is ironic that the 1992 election year was often referred to as "the year of the woman." Although women made some gains (for example, their numbers in the House increased from 29 to 48), their numbers in office did not approach their proportion of the total population (about 51 percent).

The statistics cited here reflect ways in which women are disadvantaged and undervalued in our society. In view of this situation, comparable worth has risen to become one of the most pressing issues confronting women today. If achieved, it would have significant impacts on women's financial status and personal power.

The Status of Comparable Worth

Bellak (1984) describes the comparable worth situation. Although many state laws refer to the concept of comparable worth either directly or indirectly, they

Table 9.3: Employment Positions Held by Women, 1991

Position	Percent Female	Average Weekly Salary
Secretary	99.1%	$343
Dental assistant	98.7	300
Receptionist	97.1	273
Child-care worker	96.1	203
Private household worker	95.6	190
Registered nurse	94.6	608
Bookkeeper	92.1	338
Bank teller	91.0	273
Textile sewing machine operator	90.1	214
Nursing aide	89.8	251
Data entry keyer	88.2	316
Librarian	85.4	489
Elementary school teacher	84.8	519
Cashier	82.2	215
Architect	14.6	695
Police officer	13.4	645
Engineer	7.3	814
Furnace operator	6.9	467
Truck driver	4.3	430
Logger	4.2	314
Material-moving equipment driver	4.1	415
Airplane pilot or navigator	3.1	898
Fire fighter	2.9	595
Aircraft engine mechanic	.7	576

SOURCE: U.S. Department of Labor (1991).

tend not to be specific about what should be done, if anything, to remedy problematic situations. The issue has been addressed primarily by government in the public sector. The private sector has yet to be targeted on a large-scale basis. Comparable worth is being used as a basis for an increasing number of pay discrimination suits. It appears that comparable worth is not clearly law at this time; it probably won't be until either Congress passes more specific laws or the courts make clear determinations about what must be done. However, several states currently have laws concerning comparable worth. Many of these laws are directed only at the state as employer; other states have laws that apply not only to themselves but to other employers. Still other states are struggling to address the issue.

Comparable worth is not a simple concept. Those on both sides of the issue have developed rationales for their perspectives. Since money lies at the base of the issue, the answer cannot be easy. To better grasp the essence of the debate, some of the arguments for and against comparable worth will be discussed.

For Comparable Worth

The core of the argument for comparable worth concerns fairness and values (Schwab, 1984, p. 90). That is, it is simply not fair that women, for whatever reasons, earn less than men for similar efforts. The Equal Pay Act passed in 1963 dictates that both men and women should be paid equally for equal work (Grune, 1984, p. 166). Comparable worth takes this basic right one step further. Women have the right to receive equal pay or to have pay equity for doing work comparable to that which men traditionally do. The intent of comparable worth is to overcome any effects of discrimination which have built up and multiplied over time.

Against Comparable Worth

Perhaps the nucleus of the arguments against comparable worth concerns both the cost it would involve (Newman and Owens, 1984, p. 146) and the infringement on the freedom of organizations and businesses to hire at the rate established by market value. Salaries of workers, primarily female, in those jobs determined as being unfairly paid would have to be raised because it probably would not be feasible to cut salaries in the "masculine" professions in order to spread the money out more evenly. Therefore, more money would have to be found or raised or taxed to increase the salaries of those in the "feminine" professions.

Opponents also charge that comparable worth threatens the freedom of organizations and businesses. The market value of workers and jobs is related to supply and demand. When there is a large supply of workers and few jobs, workers will probably be willing to accept relatively low pay levels. In other words, the demand for workers is low although the supply of workers is high. Opponents of comparable worth worry that implementing comparable worth will curb the freedom and competitiveness now available in the job market. Employers might no longer be able to adjust the salaries that they offer according to supply and demand principles. Organizations might have to offer a controlled set of salary levels based on the principles of comparable worth and not on how much an individual's job performance would be worth on the open market.

There have also been criticisms concerning the establishment and implementation of job evaluation systems. Job evaluation is not a new concept (Schwab, 1984, p. 86).

Implementing Comparable Worth

Questions have been raised regarding how comparable worth would actually work (Remick 1984). First, what factors would be chosen as the basis for job comparison? For example, what factors could be used in comparing driving a cement truck and pouring cement, with handing out paychecks at a cashier's window? Second, how would these factors be rated? How would the amount of strength needed and physical fatigue involved in working a drill press be weighed against the amount of skill necessary to type eighty words per minute? Third, how would the evaluation system be applied? Who would make decisions about how the categories were determined? Would everyone in an organization be involved including the top executives, or would just certain levels of employees be included? Fourth, how would salaries for each job classification be determined? How much salary would people in each job classification get?

First, a system of job evaluation would have to be developed. Job evaluation would involve evaluating each job in an organization on the basis of "skill requirements, effort, responsibility, and working conditions" (Schwab, 1984, p. 86). A system would have to be worked out whereby these job aspects could be analyzed, compared, and rated on a scale. The end result would be comparable job classifications with comparable salaries.

The second recommendation for implementing the doctrine of comparable worth would be to establish legislation to mandate compliance. That is, laws would have to be created to require both governmental and private business organizations to abide by comparable worth. This would require the development of job evaluation systems. It would also necessitate careful monitoring of organizations to make certain that they comply with or obey the rules.

The Future of Comparable Worth

We have just touched on a few of the basic issues involved in the comparable worth debate. Only the future can tell to what extent the doctrine will be implemented and how effective it will be. A few recent developments merit attention.

What has been referred to as the Tanner decision in *AFSCME v. the State of Washington* (Bellak, 1984, pp. 75-76) seems to have raised some eyebrows. Although the decision was later overturned by a higher court, U.S. District Court Judge Jack E. Tanner initially ruled that the state of Washington knowingly had failed to pay people in female-dominated jobs as much as people in male-dominated jobs after it had initiated, on its own accord, a job evaluation study. In other words, Washington failed to compensate people even after it knew that inequities existed. This was really a "failure to pay" suit rather than strictly a comparable worth suit. However, it still suggests the possibility that people can file suits concerning issues which involve comparable worth. The fact that the initial win was later overturned complicates the matter.

At this point, both Washington and Minnesota have laws requiring the enforcement of comparable worth principles (Renzetti and Curran, 1992). However, these apply only to jobs in the public sector.

Sexual Harassment

Sexual harassment is a serious form of sex discrimination that recently has gained public attention. It affects business, industrial, academic, and public work environments.

Sexual harassment is illegal. Title VII of the Civil Rights Act of 1964 outlaws discrimination on the basis of sex along with discrimination on the basis of race. Legal precedents have been established which include sexual harassment as a form of sex discrimination (Maypole and Skaine, 1983). Additionally, individual state laws can prohibit sexual harassment and provide legal recourse to victims.[1] Title IX of the Higher Educational Amendments of 1972 prohibits sex discrimination from taking place specifically on university campuses. Finally, individual agencies, organizations, or universities may have established policies prohibiting sexual harassment.[2]

The following section will define sexual harassment. Research concerning how frequently it occurs will be presented. The effects of harassment on victims will be addressed. Finally, some strategies for confronting sexual harassment will be proposed.

The Definition of Sexual Harassment

Sexual harassment involves unwelcome sexual advances, requests for sexual favors, and other verbal or physical conduct of a sexual nature under the following conditions: First, submission to such conduct is required as a condition of employment or education. Second, submission to such conduct is used as a basis for decisions that affect an individual's employment or academic achievement. Such conduct results in a hostile, intimidating, or anxiety-producing work or educational environment.[3]

Sexual harassment occurs when a female employee is made to tolerate the regular touching of her arms, waist, neck, and buttocks by her male supervisor in order to ensure that she gets good supervisory reviews. Sexual harassment exists when a female administrative assistant is pressured to become sexually involved with the vice president she works for if she wants to keep her job. Sexual harassment also is evident when a male college professor likes to touch young male students in suggestive ways and refers to them as "pretty boys."

Sexual harassment almost always involves elements of unequal power and coercion. Sometimes it

involves promising a victim a reward or threatening a punishment on the basis of the victim's sexual cooperation. Other times it involves becoming overly and inappropriately personal with a victim, ether by sharing intimacies or prying into the victim's personal life.

Although most victims are women, sexual harassment can be directed at either males or females. In this respect it can be considered a human rights issue. A member of either gender may be the victim of harassing, offensive behavior of a sexual nature. Homosexual people are also victims. They can be targets of inappropriate sexual advances, threats, and promises when such overtures involve someone of their same gender or the opposite gender.

Sexual harassment can also take place when verbal remarks make the work or academic atmosphere offensive or stifling. Sexual remarks which are not related to the work at hand can interfere with productivity and performance. For example, female students might be forced to endure condescending, derogatory remarks of a male instructor which focus on women's anatomy and on their inferior ability. Or female employees might force themselves to tolerate their supervisor's annoying behaviors. These might include a male's constant reference to women as "girls," his comments that "it must be that time of month" whenever a woman is moody, his remarks about how he likes "his girls" to wear short skirts, and his placing of pictures of naked women on the office bulletin board. Any of these behaviors act to disrupt a positive, productive working environment.

The Extent of Sexual Harassment

An accurate, specific profile of when, where, how, and to whom sexual harassment occurs does not exist. However, some surveys suggest that it is quite prevalent in a variety of settings. Almost 90 percent of women who voluntarily responded to the *Redbook* survey (Safran, 1976) indicated that they had been victims of sexual harassment at some time during their working careers. This survey also found that typical victims were married women in their twenties and thirties.

Research reveals that between 20 and 49 percent of faculty women and 20 to 30 percent of female stu-

---

1. For example, the state of Wisconsin's Fair Employment Act as amended in 1978 prohibits sexual harassment.

2. For example, the University of Wisconsin System Board of Regents have stated in their Resolution #2384 of May 8, 1981, that sexual harassment "is unacceptable and impermissible conduct which will not be tolerated."

3. The definition of sexual harassment is taken from Resolution #2384 of the Board of Regents of the University of Wisconsin System dated May 8, 1981. The Equal Employment Opportunity Commission has published a similar definition of sexual harassment in "Guidelines on Discrimination because of Sex, Title VII, Sec. 703," *Federal Register*, 45 (April 11, 1980).

Vignettes of Sexual Harassment

Ann's boss states that if she doesn't have sex with him, she won't make it through her six-month probationary period. She really needs the job. She doesn't know what to do.

Barbara's male supervisor likes to sneak up behind her and surprise her by putting his arms around her. This makes her feel very uncomfortable. However, he's responsible for scheduling her hours, evaluating her, and giving her raises. She is terrified of confronting him.

Harry really needs to get a good grade in his course with a female professor, Dr. Getsom, in order to keep his scholarship and stay in school. So far he has a "D+" in the course. When he goes to see Dr. Getsom, she likes to touch him a lot and acts very friendly. Last Thursday she said she would "see what could be done about helping him with his grade" if they'd start dating. He feels trapped. He doesn't know what to do.

One of the other financial assistance workers in the county social services department really annoys Buella. The man is constantly telling dirty jokes about women. Additionally, he likes to whistle at any woman under twenty-five who passes his desk.

dents have been subjected to some form of sexual harassment (Cole, 1990; Dzeich and Weiner, 1990; Project on the Status and Education of Women, 1986; Reilly et al., 1986; Sandler and Hall, 1986). Only 2 to 3 percent of female undergraduates experienced the most severe forms of *sexual* harassment such as being offered a better grade in return for sexual favors or being threatened in some way. However, a large number of women encountered less severe forms of sexual harassment such as verbal abuse or being touched inappropriately (Reilly et al., 1986; Sandler and Hall, 1986).

One of the most massive studies to date was undertaken by the U.S. Merit Systems Protection Board (MSPB 1981). A stratified random sampling procedure was used to involve over 23,000 federal employees. Of the female employees surveyed, 42 percent stated that they were victims of sexual harassment of some kind during the two-year period prior to the survey. Only 1 percent reported being victims of actual sexual assault. However, 29 percent indicated that "severe sexual harassment" had occurred to them. This included harassing telephone calls, unsolicited touching and embracing, and unwanted pressure to participate in sexual activities. An additional 12 percent experienced "less severe harassment." This included inappropriate sexual jokes and comments, leering looks, and excessive pressure to date the harasser.

Interestingly enough, women were not the only ones to consider themselves victims of sexual harassment. Fifteen percent of the men in the MSPB study felt that they also had been harassed.

Several variables made victimization more likely according to the MSPB research. Youth was one variable. A woman under age twenty was twice as likely to be sexually harassed as one between age twenty and forty. A second variable was marital status. Unlike findings in the *Redbook* survey, divorced and single women were more likely to be harassed than women who were married or widowed. Finally, education appeared to be a variable related to sexual harassment. Unlike what might be expected, sexual harassment was more likely to occur to women with higher levels of education. Perhaps this latter finding was due to the fact that more highly educated women were more aware of sexual harassment issues and also to the fact that more highly educated women assumed job positions traditionally not held by women.

Sexual harassment appears to be a serious problem. Despite the lack of a definitive profile of its occurrence, sexual harassment occurs frequently in a variety of employment and educational settings.

Effects of Sexual Harassment

Negative psychological effects of sexual harassment include humiliation and anger. One study which examined the various emotional reactions to sexual harassment indicated that over three quarters of the victims felt angry (Silverman, 1976-77). Additionally, almost half felt upset, almost one fourth felt afraid, and more than one fourth felt other negative emotions such as feelings of isolation, desertion, loneliness, and guilt.

Anita Hill versus Clarence Thomas: A Case of Sexual Harassment?

It was unimaginable that two such people would stand in total opposition before the entire nation during October, 1991. Anita Hall, a law professor at the University of Oklahoma, gave graphic, detailed, and consistent testimony that Clarence Thomas, soon to be appointed to the U.S. Supreme Court, sexually harassed her over a two-year period. The debate commenced during Senate hearings conducted to evaluate Thomas's qualifications for becoming a Supreme Court Justice. As Smolowe eloquently states:

> Viewers had to weigh the testimony of two admirable people—both of whom had escaped, through diligence and perseverance, a background of rural poverty to scale great heights, both of whom are known to be grounded in strong religious and spiritual values, both of whom have reputations for great personal integrity—and pronounce one of them a liar.

The Accusations

Hill, a thirty-five-year-old African American woman, worked for Thomas, a forty-three-year-old African American man, at the Department of Education's civil rights office and subsequently at the Equal Employment Opportunity Commission (EEOC) from 1981 to 1983. Hill alleged:

> He spoke about acts that he had seen in pornographic films involving such matters as women having sex with animals, and films showing group sex or rape scenes. . . . He talked about pornographic materials depicting individuals with large penises or large breasts involved in various sex acts. On several occasions Thomas told me graphically of his own sexual prowess. (Smolowe, 1992, p. 38)

One of the most infamous accusations involved Hill testifying to Thomas's alleged comment while reaching for a Coke, "Who has put pubic hair on my Coke?" Another involved Thomas's alleged comment referring to the large penis of an actor in a pornographic movie as "Long Dong Silver," also the character's name. Additionally, Hill said that Thomas had asked her to go out with him five to ten times, something Thomas vehemently denied. Instead, he maintained that he had always tried to be a help and support to Hill in her career. He indicated that he felt deeply betrayed by her testimony.

The core controversy throughout the Senate concerned Hill's ability to present her case in a detailed, consistent, and convincing fashion versus Thomas' ability to believably and consistently deny that what she said was true (Smolowe, 1991). Thomas had a Supreme Court Justiceship to lose.

A Question of Motive

A major question raised during the hearings involved Anita Hill's motive for her disclosures a decade after the alleged incidents occurred. In fact, she had not initially volunteered to raise these issues. Senate investigators had interviewed her as part of a routine investigation of someone being considered for the Supreme Court. Somehow, the press found out about Hill's FBI statement and brought it to the attention of the public. Hill indicated that when this occurred in early October 1991, she felt she had to step forward and tell the public her story.

The scene transmitted to the public displayed a "cool and unflappable" Hill who testified for almost eight solid hours, "her hands folded on the lap of her teal blue dress, her demeanor polite, cooperative and never defensive, she painted a vivid and sobering portrait of what it means to be victimized by sexual harassment—from the fears, embarrassments and humiliations she experienced to the repercussions it had on her work, health and career" (Smolowe, 1991, p. 37).

Thomas, on the other hand, consistently and adamantly denied each allegation. He dramatized his agony in a believable manner. He maintained again and again that he was simply a victim. He hypothesized that "Some interest groups came up with this story, and this story was developed specifically to destroy me" (Smolowe, 1992, p. 37). He emphasized that the whole ordeal targeted African American men for attack by focusing on negative stereotypes.

Why did Anita Hill step forward? Was it to enjoy the publicity? Did she enthusiastically seek an audience with the fourteen white males who would ultimately pass judgment upon her? Did she enjoy the grueling eight hours during which she had to respond to question after question, including those which were intensely personal? Was she eagerly looking forward to the condescending questions about her own statements and behavior by white males who would probably have difficulty even understanding the issues?

Or, did she feel it was in the interest of her conscience and her concern for other women in similar situations? Did she feel the need to share her deep reservations about a man who would soon assume one of the most important positions in the country, a man whose attitudes about women would soon begin to shape the policies that, in turn, molded women's lives?

Why didn't Anita Hill step forward sooner? Her critics say she probably would not have lost her job. However, they failed to differentiate between a career involving a progressive series of carefully sought career moves and a cashier job paying minimum wage at a local drug store. Typically, when women are asked why they don't report sexual harassment, they reply, "Why commit professional suicide?" (Painton, Sachs, and Reid 1991, p. 63). Women, like men, need supervisors and administrators to help them along their career paths. Would a supervisor be likely to write a woman positive letters of reference after she reported his alleged sexual harassment? Or, would he be likely to blackball her and "spread the word" that she is a troublemaker?

For example, Angela Johal accused her supervisor at Canteen Corporation in San Jose, California, of grabbing her breasts in April 1991 (Smolowe, 1992). She then was transferred to a new supervisor. However, her previous supervisor received no admonishment. The incident appeared to have been ignored. Her new boss, a friend of the old one, "accused her of incompetence.... Johal became so depressed that she sought therapy and was put on antidepressants. Finally, she went on disability leave and hired a lawyer" (Smolowe, 1992, p. 57). The attorney then filed a complaint initiating a suit.

Even when women win suits, they encounter unseen costs (Smolowe, 1992). For instance, "in 1987 Regina Rhodes filed charges against the owners of the Apollo Theater in Harlem after they refused to take seriously her complaints of unwelcome overtures from a co-worker and fired her" (Smolowe, 1992, p. 57). In 1992, she finally won $85,000. However, she could not get the money because the Apollo's owners had appealed to a higher court. She doesn't know how long it will take to get the case resolved. The case also damaged her career. She states that she had to begin another line of work. No one would hire her because in their eyes she had double-crossed a major theater.

Impacts of the Hearings

The result of the hearings, of course, is history. The senators who judged Anita Hill's testimony "merely turned their heads" (Gibbs, 1991, p. 35). They did not acknowledge her story. Clarence Thomas became a Supreme Court Justice.

What happened a year after the hearings? One report indicates that Clarence Thomas:

> ... who friends say has stopped reading newspapers, ... seldom gives speeches or appears at legal conferences, and complains that he does not feel comfortable eating out in public. He is also becoming distanced from some of his supporters in the Senate and elsewhere who have expressed disappointment that Thomas was far more conservative in his first term than they thought he would be.
>
> Eric Schnapper, an early opponent of Thomas from the NAACP Legal Defense fund, said that Thomas' conservative record on the court raises questions over his truthfulness during confirmation hearings about his judicial philosophy and therefore about his denial of Anita Hill's charges of sexual harassment. (*Milwaukee Journal*, Oct. 8, 1992)

Thomas gave little or no indication regarding the extent of his ultraconservative perspective during the Senate hearings. A group of African American democrats from Alabama indicated that Thomas had pledged to them that he would not follow Supreme Court Justice Antonin Scalia's ultraconservative outlook. However, in 1991, Thomas's decisions agreed with Scalia 89 percent of the time (*Milwaukee Journal*, Oct. 8, 1992).

Anita Hill continues as a law professor at the University of Oklahoma. During the 1992-93 academic year she took a sabbatical and traveled the national lecture circuit speaking out against sexual harassment. One newspaper cites her comments on NBC's *Today* during early October 1992 (*Milwaukee Journal*, Oct. 8, 1992): "I regret in many ways that [the situation] was manipulated or misperceived. And I have my moments when I just wish that I could go back to the way things were before. But that's not realistic. When I think of what has happened in a larger sense, beyond myself," she went on, "then I would not change anything" (p. A14).

People's opinions apparently reversed in the year following the hearings (Smolowe, 1992). A Wall Street Journal/NBC News poll found that 44 percent of registered voters

(continued next page)

Anita Hill versus Clarence Thomas: A Case of Sexual Harassment? (continued)

felt Hill was telling the truth, up from 24 percent the year before. Thomas's believers, however, dropped from 40 to 34 percent.

There were other impacts from the hearings (*Milwaukee Journal*, Oct. 8, 1992). The EEOC received 70 percent more complaints about sexual harassment during the three months immediately following the hearings than they did during the same time period the year before. Additionally, organizations supporting female candidates in preparation for the 1992 election reported a swell of campaign contributions. A number of women seeking office indicated they chose to do so because Anita Hill made them face the reality that 98 percent of the Senate was made up of men.

However, Hill's critics still remain. For instance, Wisconsin Representative Tim Pope is quoted as saying (*Milwaukee Journal*, Oct. 8, 1992), "What surprises me is how many people actually believe her. She's set up as some martyr for what she has done for women's rights when all she told was lies in the first place" (p. A14).

SOURCE: Many of the facts presented here are taken from two articles by Jill Smolowe, "He Said, She Said," *Time*, Oct. 21, 1991, and "Anita Hill's Legacy," *Time*, Oct. 19, 1992. Other facts are from "After 1 Year, Thomas-Hill Hearings Still Echo Across the Land," *Milwaukee Journal*, Oct. 8, 1992, p. A14.

Despite such negative consequences, many women feel it is hopeless to complain about sexual harassment. Only one fourth of the women in the *Redbook* (1976) survey felt that it would do any good to complain. Most women preferred to cope by assuming an air of cold indifference or by wearing extremely unrevealing, conservative clothing.

The MSPB (1981) survey revealed that only 2 percent of the women who were victimized by sexual harassment actually filed a formal complaint. Of those who did, half felt their complaints were unsuccessful.

Sexual harassment incurs financial costs as well. The MSPB study estimated that sexual harassment costs the federal government about $50 million annually. Contributing to this figure were job turnover costs such as hiring and training new employees, costs due to absenteeism and increased health problems, and reduced worker productivity due to emotional stress. The personal and emotional costs placed on the victims themselves cannot even be measured.

Sexist Language

One form of sexual harassment involves making verbal remarks that establish an offensive or stifling work or educational environment. Such language can include jokes with inappropriate sexual connotations. It can also include derogatory comments about ability based on gender. For example, a male professor might say to his students, "Girls don't usually do very well in this major. They're usually not as bright as men. They just run off and get married anyway." Such a comment is discriminatory. The professor is making an unfounded, unfair prediction. He is not attending to each student's ability to perform on an individual basis.

Many times English words themselves reflect an aura of sexism and unfairness. For instance, the word *man* seems to occur everywhere. Consider such words and phrases as *mankind, chairman, salesman, congressman,* and the *best man for the job.* Such terms often imply that women are included, but in a subsidiary way.

Another example of how sexism has infiltrated the English language is in the proper titles for men and women. On reaching adulthood, a man becomes a "Mr." for the remainder of his life. This is a polite term which makes no reference to the status of a man's personal life. A woman, however, starts as a "Miss." She becomes a "Mrs." upon marriage, which clearly establishes her marital status. At least it establishes the fact that at one time or another she has been married.

Confronting Sexual Harassment

Victims of sexual harassment have several alternative routes available to them. Each has its own potential positive and negative consequences. Alternatives include ignoring the harassing behavior, avoiding the harasser, or asking the harasser to stop (Martin, 1984). The MSPB (1981) study found that ignoring the behavior had virtually no effect. Asking the harasser to stop, however, effectively stopped the harassment in half of the cases.

Avoiding the harasser is another option. A severe shortcoming of this approach is that the victim is the one who must expend the effort. The ultimate avoidance measure is actually quitting the job or dropping the class in order to avoid contact with a sexual harasser. This is the least fair (and potentially most damaging) alternative to the victim. Further, it does nothing to re-educate the harasser, prevent harassment from recurring, or prepare the victim to deal with it in subsequent incidents.

There are, however, several other suggestions to help victims confront sexual harassment. In many cases using these strategies will stop harassment. First, a victim needs to know his or her rights. A call to the Equal Employment Opportunity Commission (EEOC), the federal agency designated to address the issue of sexual harassment, is helpful. Many women can obtain necessary information about their rights and the appropriate procedures to follow for filing a formal complaint.

Many states also have state laws which make sexual harassment illegal. Such states often have agencies or offices that victims may call for help and information. For example, the state of Wisconsin has the Wisconsin Equal Rights Division to address such issues. Additionally, organizations and agencies also have specific policies against sexual harassment. Filing a formal complaint through established procedures is often an option.

Most victims, however, choose not to pursue the formal complaint route (Martin, 1984; MSPB, 1981). Some victims fear reprisal or retaliation; others don't want to be labeled troublemakers. Still others don't choose to expend the time and effort necessary in carrying out a formal process. Most victims simply want the harassment to end so that they can work peacefully and productively.

In addition to knowing your rights, the following suggestions can be applied to most situations where sexual harassment is occurring.

1. Confront your harasser. Tell the harasser which specific behaviors are unwanted and unacceptable. If you feel you cannot handle a direct confrontation, write the harasser a letter. It is helpful to criticize the harasser's behavior rather than the harasser as a person. The intent is to stop the harassment and maintain a pleasant, productive work environment. There is also the chance that the harasser was not aware that his or her behavior was offensive. In this case, giving specific feedback is frequently effective.

2. Be assertive. When giving the harasser feedback, look him or her directly in the eye. Look like you mean what you're saying. Don't smile or giggle even though you're uncomfortable. Rather, look the harasser directly in the eye, stand up straight, adopt a serious expression, and calmly state, "Please stop touching me by putting your arms around me and rubbing my neck. I don't like it." This is a serious matter. You need to get a serious point across.

3. Document your situation (Farley, 1978). Record every incident that occurs. Note when, where, who, and what was said or done, what you were wearing, and any available witnesses. Be as accurate as possible. Documentation does not have to be elaborate or fancy. Simple handwritten notes including the facts will suffice. It is also a good idea to keep copies of your notes in another location.

4. Talk to other people about the problem. Get support from friends and colleagues. Sexual harassment often erodes self-confidence. Victims do not feel they are in control of the situation. Emotional support from others can bolster self-confidence and give victims the strength needed to confront sexual harassment. Frequently sharing these problems with others will also allow victims to discover they're not alone. Corroboration with other victims will not only provide emotional support, but it will also strengthen a formal complaint if that option needs to be taken sometime in the future.

5. Get witnesses. Look around when the sexual harassment is occurring and note who can observe it. Talk to these people and solicit their support. Try to make arrangements for others to be around you when you anticipate that sexual harassment is likely to occur.

Using Nonsexist Language

There are ways to minimize the use of sexist language. Frequently, all it takes is becoming accustomed to a different way of phrasing words and sentences. The following are some suggestions aimed at maximizing fairness and objectivity through language.

1. Replace the word *man* with other more inclusive terms such as *human* or *person*. For example, *mankind* can becomes *humankind*, *chairman* can becomes *chairperson* or *chair*, and the nature of man can become the nature of *humankind*.
2. Use the term *Ms.* instead of *Miss* and *Mrs*. Ms. and Mr. are equivalent terms. Such usage will seem natural once people becomes accustomed to using the new term.
3. Try to phrase sentences so that the masculine pronouns *he*, *him*, and *his* can be avoided. This can be done in several ways. First, pronouns can be eliminated altogether. For example,

    "The average American likes to drink *his* coffee black."

can be changed to:

    "The average American likes black coffee."

Second, phrases can frequently be rephrased into the plural:

    "Average Americans like their coffee black."

Third, masculine pronouns can be substituted with *one*, *you*, or *his or her*. For example, a statement could be phrased in the following manner:

    "The average American likes to have his or her coffee black."

4. Avoid using patronizing and derogatory stereotypes. These include phrases such as *sweet young thing, the little lady, bubble-brained blonde, hen-pecked husband, frustrated spinster, nagging mother-in-law, dirty old man*, and *dumb jock*.

Many good suggestions can be found for using nonsexist language. However, the main idea is for a person to be sensitive to what he or she is saying. Subtle implications need to be examined in order to communicate accurately and objectively. This is especially true for social workers and is pertinent to what they say and write.

SOURCE: McGraw-Hill (1974).

Rape and Sexual Assault

The most intimate violation of a person's privacy and dignity is sexual assault. Sexual assaults involve any unwanted sexual contact where verbal or physical force is used. A commonly used legal definition of rape involves a sexual assault where penile penetration of the vagina occurs without mutual consent (Masters et al., 1988).

Throughout their lives the fear of assault and rape lingers in the minds of women. It is an act of violence over which they have neither control nor protection. Several aspects of sexual assault and rape will be addressed here to give an understanding of the effects on women and how women might best cope with the fact that rape exists. They include the fre-

quency with which rapes occur, some theoretical perspectives on why rape exists in our culture, some common myths about rape, typical victim reactions to rape, and some suggestions for counseling rape victims.

Incidence of Rape

A total of 91,111 rapes were reported in 1987 (U.S. Department of Justice, 1987). Because women often do not report rape, the FBI and other experts in criminology indicate that probably ten times that many rapes actually occurred (Freeman, 1989). Formal reports indicate that a woman is raped in this country every six minutes (U.S. Department of Justice, 1987). Due to the notable underreporting of rape, the FBI conjectures that in reality a woman is raped every *two* minutes.

Women fail to report being raped for many reasons. Victims whose bodies have been brutally violated often desperately want to forget that the horror ever happened. To report it means dwelling on the details and going over the event again and again in their minds. Other victims fear retribution from the rapist. If they call public attention to him, he might do it again to punish them. No police officer will be available all of the time for protection. Other victims feel that people around them will think less of them because they've been raped. It's almost as if a part of them has been spoiled, a part that they would prefer to hide from other people. Rape is an ugly crisis which takes a great amount of courage to face.

Theoretical Views of Rape

Albin (1977) summarizes three theoretical perspectives on why rape occurs. These include theories on victim precipitation of rape, the psychopathology of rapists, and the feminist perspective. The intent is not to state which one is the best theory but to present three different ways of conceptualizing or thinking about rape.

Victim-Precipitated Rape

This perspective assumes that the victim is actually to blame for the rape—that the woman "asked for it." Perhaps she was wearing provocative clothing. A common belief is that women subconsciously desire to be raped (Strong and Reynolds, 1982, p. 507). This view focuses on how women really want to be overpowered and taken by force.

An unfortunate example of how destructive this perspective can be is provided by a young female student who came to her instructor seeking help for her friend. Her friend, age eighteen, had attended a local festival during the prior summer. The woman somehow got separated from her friends and found herself talking and flirting with two men about age twenty. As it had been a hot July day, the woman was wearing a halter top and jeans. Suddenly, before she realized what had happened, the men shoved her into the car and swept her away to a city apartment. There they raped her throughout the night.

The next morning the men put her into the car and dropped her off at the festival entrance. In terror and tears, she called her father and, sobbing, explained to him what had happened. His response to her was, "I told you not to ask for it. Why do you have to dress like that?" The woman was crushed.

This father had adopted the victim-precipitated view of rape. He immediately assumed it was his daughter's fault. Unfortunately, the young woman did not recover very well. What she had really needed from her father was support and help. What she had gotten was blame. Six months later the young woman found herself terrified of men. Her reaction was so extreme that on the following New Year's Eve at midnight, she could not bear to watch people give each other New Year's kisses. She rushed from the room crying.

The instructor listening to the story strongly suggested that the young rape victim get counseling help. She needed to work through her feelings and put the blame where it belonged, namely, on her attackers.

Many male students have also found the victim-precipitated view rather offensive. The implication is that men are rather animalistic and cannot control their own impulses. Various men have indicated that they find this you-know-how-men-are point of view as degrading as women might find the you-know-how-women-are perspective. Neither perspective takes into account individual differences or personal morals and values.

Rapist Psychopathology

A second theoretical perspective concerns rapist psychopathology. This view proposes that the rapist is emotionally disturbed or mentally unbalanced. He rapes because he is sick. This view places virtually none of the blame on society or on social attitudes.

The Feminist Perspective on Rape

The feminist perspective emphasizes that rape is the logical reaction of men who are socialized to dominate women. Rape is seen as a manifestation of men's need to aggressively maintain power over women. It has little to do with sexuality. Sexuality only provides a clearcut means for exercising power. Rape is seen as a consequence of attitudes toward women that are intimately intertwined throughout the culture. The feminist perspective sees rape as a societal problem, rather than only an individual one.

Herman (1984) elaborates on this view. She points out that both aggressors and victims are brought up to believe that sexual aggression is natural. As a result, victims often blame themselves for the assault. The rationale is that they should have expected to be raped. They should have been prepared or have done something to prevent it.

An analogous situation concerning self-blame is the example of a woman who has her purse snatched while shopping on a Saturday afternoon. If the self-blame concept were applied, it would follow that the woman would blame herself for the incident. She would chastise herself by saying it was her fault. She never should have taken her purse with her to shop in the first place. Maybe she should shop only through the home-shopping channel on cable television from now on. Of course, taking that course of action would be absurd. It was not the woman's fault. It was the purse snatcher who broke the law. He is the one who should be held responsible.

The feminist view holds that society is wrong for socializing people to assume that male sexual aggression is natural. Socializing women to consider themselves weak and nurturant also contributes to the problem. It helps to develop a victim mentality, that is, an expectation that it's natural for women to be victims. The feminist perspective emphasizes that these attitudes need to be changed. Only then can rape as a social problem disappear.

Common Myths about Rape

Various myths about rape need to be examined and corrected. Women need accurate information in order to make responsible decisions. They need to learn what types of conditions and circumstances prompt rape so that they may be avoided.

Spontaneous Rape

Most rapes are thought to occur because of spontaneous bursts of aggression and/or sexual desire. To the contrary, most rapes are planned in advance. Some research discloses that in 71 percent of all reported rapes, the rapists made arrangements in advance and in an additional 11 percent, at least some planning

was involved (Amir, 1967). In planning, they usually try to maximize their victim's vulnerability.

The Dark Alley Rape

Another myth is that rapes tend to occur in dark alleys. Although some circumstances such as hitchhiking or walking home alone in the dark tend to increase the chances of being raped, there is a good chance of being raped right in one's own home. According to Lott (1987, p. 151), "the single most common place of attack is in a woman's own residence—approximately 30 percent of all reported cases." A study of university students found that 39 percent of assaults occurred in the victim's own home, while altogether 42 percent occurred in someone's residence; another 32 percent of assaults were perpetrated outdoors, and 24 percent of those occurred in parking lots (Lott et al., 1982).

In cases occurring indoors, especially in their own homes, victims are very likely to know the rapist. This presents a problem as people tend to feel safe when they're in their own homes with a person they know (Schneider et al., 1981). However, knowledge of this fact is important if it helps people be more cautious.

One incident emphasizes the importance of caution. A twenty-year-old female student sheepishly approached her instructor and finally blurted out that she had been raped at a party the past Saturday night. Although it was not in her own home, it was in the home of a good friend of hers. Apparently, people attending the party were drinking and not concerning themselves with the noise level. The student found herself talking with a young male lawyer while sitting on the bed in one of the bedrooms. Suddenly, the lawyer closed and locked the door. He pinned her to the bed and began to rape her. She was awestruck that this could be happening. Although he was not a good friend, he was an acquaintance of hers. They shared several mutual friends. After all, he was even a lawyer. She resisted to the best of her ability. She was too ashamed to scream.

As she was talking about the incident several days later, her main concern was what her friends would think about her if they ever found out. Although she dreamed about getting revenge, she didn't want to jeopardize her reputation. As she continued to relate her story, her instructor discussed her feelings, the potential physical ramifications, and potential legal alternatives. Her instructor also helped the student gain a more objective perception of the incident. It was especially important for this victim to place the blame where it belonged, namely on the rapist. Finally, her instructor referred her to counseling to give her a chance to work out and deal with the feelings she had about having such a horrible experience.

Stranger Rape

Another myth is that only strangers are potential rapists (Koss, 1972). Between 60 and 80 percent of all rapes involve women who knew their assailant (Renzetti and Curran, 1992). This is known as acquaintance or date rape. Acquaintance rapes are particularly prevalent on college campuses. Koss, Gidycz, and Wisniewski (1987) surveyed college students over a three-year period. One in eight female students indicated that they had been sexually assaulted within the prior year. Of those whose rapes had been completed, 83 percent said they knew the rapist. About two-thirds of these women were raped while on dates.

It appears that rape by someone known to the victim causes the most severe psychological trauma (Bart, 1975). Perhaps the trauma has to do with the violation of trust. If a woman is not safe with a person she knows and trusts, who might she be safe with? This thought is frightening.

Interracial Rape

Most rapes are committed by a member of the same race as the victim (Herman, 1984, p. 27). The traditional, prejudicial perspectives that African American men rape white women and white men rape African American women are not true. The vast majority of rapes are intraracial, not interracial. The unfortunate myth of African American/white rape may be perpetuated by the inordinate amount of media attention given these incidents when they do occur ("Police Discretion . . . ," 1968, p. 318).

Additional Facts about Rape

Victim Age

Women have been raped at ages as young as six months and as old as ninety-three years (Herman, 1984, p. 28), but most rapes involve younger women. One of every three young women will be sexually

A perfectly normal-seeming and trustworthy "date" could become a rapist.

assaulted by the time they are eighteen years old (Ruth, 1990). Rush (1980) estimates that one-quarter of all rape victims are under age twelve and one-half are under age eighteen. Another source indicates that the majority of rapes happen to women age sixteen to twenty-five (Meeks and Heit, 1982, p. 447). It appears that young women in their teens and early twenties are at the greatest risk of rape, although rape may occur at virtually any age.

Profile of a Rapist

Most rapists are young; over half of all rapists are under age twenty-five (Federal Bureau of Investigation, 1981) and three-fourths are under age thirty (Masters and Johnson, 1985, p. 476). Many tend to repeat their crime (Cohen et al., 1971). Alcohol is often involved (Masters et al., 1988).

A problem with looking at a profile of convicted rapists is that it reflects only those who have been brought to court and found guilty. Only a small fraction of rapes are reported in the first place. Consequently, not all alleged rapists are convicted. Many cases are unfounded, that is, police decide not to recommend that the case be prosecuted (Bourque, 1989; Estrich, 1987; Herman, 1984). Sexual assaults are frequently treated as "private squabbles or misunderstandings rather than prosecutable crimes" (Renzetti and Curran, 1992, p. 239). Therefore, an accurate profile of all the people who commit rape might be very different from the picture of those who are convicted for the crime.

Some research has compared rapists (men who revealed that they have forced women to have sexual intercourse with them) with nonrapists. Kanin (1985) studied male college students who fell into these two categories. Men who raped reported that they applied much more pressure to women in order to have sex. For example, almost 80 percent of the rapists indicated that they had tried to get a woman drunk in order to have sex with her. This compared to 23 percent of the nonrapists. Approximately 86 percent of the rapists recounted telling a woman that they "loved" her in order to persuade her to have sex with them. This compared to 25 percent of the nonrapists. It should be noted here that although the rapists were significantly more coercive, about one-quarter of "normal" men (that is, nonrapists) studied reported using such pressuring techniques.

Rapists were more likely to have a peer group that both endorsed violent sex and pressured them to expand their sexual experience. Finally, 86 percent of the rapists reported that they thought rape was appropriate under some circumstances. This compared with 19 percent of the nonrapists. Once again, note that almost one-fifth of the nonrapists felt that rape might be appropriate under some conditions. What does this say about our society's attitudes? Other research has supported the fact that peer group acceptance of rape and hardened attitudes toward women as sexual objects tend to characterize men who rape (Crooks and Baur, 1993; Malamuth, 1986). Men who rape often have low levels of self-esteem and are socially inadequate (Crooks and Baur, 1993).

Finally, there is growing evidence that exposure to pornography that depicts violent sexual behavior with women can make men insensitive to women as human beings. These men may become less likely to view sexual assault as a criminal offense and be more likely to rape (Crooks and Baur, 1993; Donnerstein

and Linz, 1984). It should be pointed out that it appears to be the violent nature of this pornography and not the pornography itself that is related to subsequent rape (Scott and Schwalm, 1988).

One study of two thousand college men revealed that rapists may be categorized into four types (Koss et al., 1985). *Sexually assaultive* men, who comprised 4.3 percent of the sample, admitted to having forced women to have sexual intercourse with them by threatening harm or by using actual physical violence. Another 4.9 percent were *sexually abusive*. These men had sexually assaulted women by using force, but did not have sexual intercourse with them. The third group, *sexually coercive* men, tried to verbally intimidate women into sexual contact, using such ploys as threatening emotional withdrawal. Finally, 59 percent of the men were *sexually nonaggressive*. These men felt that they never had used force and that their sexual interaction had always been desired by both them and their partners. The researchers were unable to classify the remaining 9.4 percent. In summary, almost one third of these two thousand young men had used some kind of force or extreme pressure to solicit sexual cooperation from their female partners. Thus, the idea that it is appropriate to force women into sexual activity appears to be fairly common.

Date Rape

We've already established that women are in danger both of being raped by someone they know and in a place where they feel safe. We've also established that it seems many men feel that it is appropriate or expected or at least tolerable to force women to have sex with them. Dates provide the perfect opportunity. The frightening fact is that the vast majority of date rapes go unreported. For example, the Koss and associates (1985) study mentioned earlier found that many of the female victims of sexual assault did not label it as such. Somehow, because they had been "in love" with the perpetrator, rape was within the realm of acceptable behavior.

Another dynamic of date rape involves the misconception that although her words say "no, no," her eyes say "yes, yes." In other words, there is a mythical idea that women really love being raped, that they "really want it." Related to this is the idea that "she shouldn't have started it or let it go so far if she wasn't ready to go all the way." These misconceptions trap women. Women can't win under these conditions. On the one hand, there's the idea that "all she needs is a good ————," which implies that all women really want to have their animal sexual drives released by sex with a "good" man. So, the man, of course, is expected to try to release these imprisoned sexual drives. Women, in return, are expected to respond and to participate in some kind of sexual interaction with men they really care about. However, once a woman becomes involved in the developing sexual interaction, she loses her right of choice to stop. She's expected to finish what she has allowed to start.

Consider a recent article in *TV Guide*. Waggett (1989) pleads with afternoon and night-time soap operas to stop making their rapists into heroes who even marry their victims. He reports that on *"Dynasty*, Adam (Gordon Thomson) raped Kirby (Kathleen Beller) one season and proposed to her the next" (p. 11). He continues that Ross from *All My Children* "had engaged in a brief affair with his father's fiancee, Natalie. . . . When Natalie's slip of the tongue cost Ross his marriage and his position in his father's company, Ross raped her in a drunken rage. Natalie pressed charges, and Ross went to prison. . . . Ross immediately changed from criminal to hero. He broke out of jail to rescue his adopted daughter, Julie . . . from an escaped convict. He worked undercover in the prison to uncover an arsonist. On furlough for a wedding, he risked his life to save his family and friends from a bomb" (p. 11). The point is not that rapists are worthless scum. From a helping professional's perspective, they are people who have problems, cause damage, and need help. However, the trouble is that, in so many instances, the act of rape is glamorized and associated with such positive behaviors and results.

Gang Rape

One study found that 43 percent of rapes are gang rapes (performed by two or more persons) (Amir, 1971). Herman (1984, p. 25) proposes that a man participating in this behavior "is not only expressing his hostility toward women and asserting his masculinity to himself but also proving his manhood to others." These rapes tend to be characterized by violence (Medea and Thompson, 1974, p. 34) and often involve sexual humiliation (Brownmiller, 1975, p.

196). It appears that rape in these cases provides a means for these men to exercise dominance over women in a way that gains recognition and attention from others.

Victim Reactions to Rape

Burgess and Holmstrom (1974a, 1974b), studying the reactions of ninety-two rape victims, found that women can experience serious psychological effects that can persist for a half year or more following a rape. They call these emotional changes the *rape trauma syndrome*. The syndrome has two basic phases. The first is the acute phase, which involves the woman's emotional reactions immediately following the rape and up to several weeks thereafter. The victim reacts in one of two ways. She may show her emotions by crying, expressing anger, or showing fear. On the other hand, she may try to control these intense emotions and keep them from view. Emotions experienced during the acute phase range from humiliation and guilt to shock to anger and desire for revenge.

Additionally, during this phase women will often experience physical problems including difficulties related directly to the rape, such as irritation of the genitals or rectal bleeding from an anal rape. Physical problems also include stress-related discomforts such as headaches, stomach difficulties, or inability to sleep.

The two primary emotions experienced during the acute phase are fear and self-blame. Fear results from the violence of the experience. Many rape victims report that during the attack they felt their life had come to an end. They had no control over what the attacker would do to them and were terrified. Such fear can linger. Oftentimes victims fear that rape can easily happen again. The second emotion, self-blame, results from society's tendency of blaming the victim as discussed in the theory of victim-precipitated rape and the feminist perspective on rape.

The second stage of the rape trauma syndrome is the long-term reorganization and recovery phase. The emotional changes and reactions of this phase may linger on for years. Nadelson and associates (1982) found that three-fourths of rape victims felt that the rape had changed their lives in one way or another. Reported reactions included fear of being alone, depression, sleeplessness, and, most frequently, an attitude of suspicion toward other people. Other long-term changes that sometimes occur include avoiding involvement with men (Masters and Johnson, 1985, p. 474) and suffering various sexual dysfunctions such as lack of sexual desire, aversion to sexual contact, or difficulties in having orgasms (Kolodny et al., 1979).

It is very important for victims of rape to deal with even the most negative feelings and get on with their lives. In some ways rape might be compared to accepting the death of a loved one. The fact that either has occurred cannot be changed. Survivors and victims must learn to cope. Life continues.

Suggestions for Counseling Rape Victims

Three basic issues are involved in working with a victim of rape. First, she is most likely in a state of emotional upheaval. Her self-concept is probably seriously shaken. Various suggestions for helping a rape victim in such a traumatic emotional state will be provided. Second, the rape victim must decide whether to call the police and press charges. Third, the rape victim must assess her medical status following the rape, for example, injuries or potential pregnancy.

Emotional Issues

Collier (1982) suggests that counseling victims of rape involves three major stages. First, the counselor or social worker needs to provide the victim with immediate warmth and support. The victim needs to feel safe; she needs to feel free to talk. She needs to ventilate and acknowledge her feelings before she can begin to deal with them. To the extent possible, the victim should be made to feel she is now in control of her situation. She should not be pressured to talk, but rather encouraged to share her feelings.

Although it is important for the victim to talk freely, it is also important that she not be grilled with intimate, detailed questions. She will have to deal with those enough if she reports the incident to the police.

Frequently, the victim will dwell on what she could have or should have done. It is helpful to emphasize what she did right. After all, she is alive, safe, and physically not severely harmed. She managed to survive a terrifying and dangerous experience. It is also helpful to talk about how she reacted normally, as anyone else in her situation would most probably have reacted. This does not mean minimizing the incident. It does mean objectively talking about how traumatizing and potentially dangerous the incident was. One other helpful suggestion for dealing with a rape victim is to help her place the blame where it belongs, namely on the rapist. He chose to rape her. It was not her doing. Research bears out the fact that the majority of rapes have absolutely nothing to do with the behavior of the victim (Amir, 1971).

The second stage of counseling, according to Collier (1982), involves creating support from others. This support may include that of professional resources such as local rape crisis centers as well as support from people who are emotionally close to the victim. Sometimes those close to the victim need to be educated. They need to find out that what the victim needs is warmth and support, and to feel loved. Questions which emphasize her feelings of self-blame such as why she didn't fight back or why she was wearing a low-cut blouse should be completely avoided.

Collier's (1982) third stage of counseling involves rebuilding the victim's trust in herself, in the environment around her, and in her other personal relationships. Rape weakens a woman. It destroys her trust in herself and in others. This stage of counseling needs to focus on the victim's objective evaluation of herself and her situation. Her strong points need to be clarified and emphasized so that she may gain confidence in herself.

The victim also needs to look objectively at her surrounding environment. She cannot remain cooped up in her apartment for the rest of her life. It is impractical and unfair. She can take precautions against being raped, but needs to continue living a normal life.

Finally, the victim needs to assess her other personal relationships objectively. Just because she was intimately violated by one aggressor, this has nothing to do with the other people in her life. She needs to concentrate on the positive aspects of her other relationships. She must not allow the fear and terror she

Suggestions for Rape Prevention

Rape is not the victim's fault. Women do not have control over being attacked. However, there are some measures that women can take to minimize their chances of being assaulted. Most of these suggestions are simply matters of common sense. It is unfortunate that women must be extra cautious, must plan ahead, and sometimes must change patterns of behavior in minor ways. However, it is necessary.

The following suggestions are included among those made by Women Organized Against Rape (WOAR)* in order to avoid being raped.

The first suggestion is to be aware of the things around you. Notice the people and cars in your immediate surroundings. Think ahead about what areas might be especially dangerous in your usual walking routes. If you have to travel through such areas, think ahead about what you would do if you were attacked. Try to stay in well-lighted areas and walk in the middle of the sidewalk. Walking in the middle of the street when there is little traffic is also a possibility. If you can, use different routes to get where you are going, especially at night. Avoid establishing a predictable pattern for a potential assailant.

Also try to be aware of your own behavior. Notice how you're standing or walking, and how you might appear to other people. Always walk with an air of confidence and strength. Try not to appear confused, vulnerable, or preoccupied, as attackers often look for such people. Walking with others or taking public transportation are other options.

If you think someone is following you, don't be afraid to look behind you. You might want to cross the street or travel in another direction. If you continue to have the feeling that someone is following you, it's best to go to the nearest lighted store or house and call a friend or the police for help. Don't hesitate to scream for help if you feel you are in danger. Screaming such words as "fire" or "police" is usually better than screaming "help" or "rape."

Some specific suggestions can also be followed for avoiding sexual assault when you are in situations involving driving your car. First of all, try to park in well-lighted areas and have your car keys ready to use. Check the back seat before getting in. While driving, keep your car doors locked and your windows partly rolled up. If approached by someone while at a stoplight, put your hand on your horn and be ready to blow it. It's also a good idea to keep at least a quarter tank of gas in the car whenever you drive to avoid running out of gas in potentially dangerous situations.

If you should have car trouble, pull over to the side of the road and stay in the car with doors locked and windows raised. When no one is around, get out and raise the car's hood to alert others to your distress. It's best to wait until police come to assist you. In the event that a man should stop and volunteer help, roll your window down only slightly and ask that he call for police help. Although such persons offering assistance may have only the best intentions, there is no way to know for sure.

Hitch-hiking is very dangerous and should be avoided. The best way to prevent sexual assault when hitch-hiking is simply not to hitch-hike at all.

There are also ways to maintain your safety at home. Outside entrances and hallways should all be well lighted. Doors should have good dead-bolt locks instead of simple key locks which offer virtually no protection. Windows should also have locks so that potential assailants cannot enter in that manner. Women who live by themselves or with other women should use only their first initials on the mailboxes, which helps prevent potential assailants from targeting women. It's also very helpful to know your neighbors even if you live in a large, relatively impersonal apartment complex. You should know where you can go for help when you need it. Don't allow strangers in your home. If a man knocks on your door and says he's a serviceman, ask for identification and have him slide it under the door, or call his company for identification.

In the event of an attack, there are some guidelines which may help to lessen the probability of being raped (Sexual Assault Treatment Center, 1979). The first suggestion is simply to run. It's more advantageous to get angry instead of scared and to react immediately. Screaming loudly is also suggested.

Traditional weapons such as guns or knives usually do not provide an effective defense. It's too easy for the attacker to take them away and use them on the victim. Rather, carrying ordinary objects such as whistles, keys, rings, umbrellas, or hatpins is helpful. To fight back, aim for the face, including eyes, ears, nose, and mouth, which are more sensitive to pain. Pulling hair is another option and loud screams in the attacker's ear will stun him. Biting or kicking sometimes is effective. A kick aimed at his knees may be more effective in order to knock an attacker off balance, as he will be most likely to protect his genitals first.

*WOAR is located at 1233 Locust Street, Philadelphia, PA 19107; telephone (215) 985-3315.

experienced during that one unfortunate incident to color and taint other relationships. She must clearly distinguish the rape from her other relationships.

A raped woman may initially want to talk with another woman. However, it might also be important to talk to men, including those close to her. It is important for the victim to realize that not all men are rapists. Sometimes there is a male partner. His willingness to let the victim express her feelings, and in return offer support and empathy, is probably the most beneficial thing that can be done for the victim (Masters and Johnson, 1985, pp. 474-75).

Reporting to the Police

The initial reaction to being raped might be to call the police and relate the incident. However, many victims choose not to do this. Masters and Johnson (1985, p. 470) list numerous reasons why this is so. Included are fear that the rapist will try to get revenge, fear of public embarrassment and derogation, an attitude that it won't matter anyway because most rapists get off free, and fear of the legal process and questioning. It's financially expensive and emotionally draining to take a rape case to court (Herman, 1984, p. 30). In reality, even when they are persistent, women have found it difficult to have rapists prosecuted. In many cases, as we've already discussed, police determine that the case is unfounded. In cases where police do believe that a rape occurred, only half of the alleged rapists are apprehended and arrested (Herman, 1984, p. 32). Even fewer of these are actually convicted.

Some positive changes are occurring in police investigation of rape cases (Moody and Hayes, 1980) and in legal handling (Lasater, 1980). Many police departments are trying to deal with rape victims more sensitively. Some departments in larger cities have special teams trained specifically for dealing with rape victims. In many states information about the victim's past sexual history is no longer permissible for use in court. When such information is introduced, it can serve to humiliate and discredit the victim. Some states have more progressive laws. Wisconsin,[4] for example, has established four degrees of sexual assault in addition to forbidding the use of the victim's past sexual conduct in court. According to Wisconsin law

---

4. See Wisconsin State Statute 940.225.

the severity of the crime and the corresponding severity of punishment is based on the amount of force used by the rapist and on the amount of harm done to the victim. A wife if also able to prosecute her husband for sexual assault when sexual relations are forced on her.

Despite the potential difficulties in reporting a rape, the fact remains that if the victim does not report it, the rapist will not be held responsible for his actions. A rape victim needs to think through the various alternatives that are open to her and weigh their respective positive and negative consequences in order to come to this often difficult decision.

In the event that a victim decides to report, she should not take a shower. Washing will remove vital evidence. However, victims often feel defiled and dirty, and it is a logical initial reaction for them to want to cleanse themselves and try to forget that the incident ever occurred. In counseling situations, it's important to emphasize the reason for not washing immediately.

Reporting a rape should be done within forty-eight hours at the absolute longest. The sooner the rape is reported and the evidence gathered, the better the chance of being able to get a conviction.

Medical Status of the Victim

A third major issue that rape victims need to address is their medical status following the assault. At some point the victim needs to attend to the possibility of pregnancy. She should be asked about this issue at an appropriate time and in a gentle manner. She should be encouraged to seek medical help both for this possibility and for screening sexually transmitted diseases. The negative possibilities should not be emphasized. However, the victim needs to attend to these issues at some point. And the victim should, of course, be urged to seek immediate medical care for any physical injury.

Battered Women

Terms associated with wife beating include domestic violence, family violence, spouse abuse, and battered women. Strong and DeVault (1983, p. 403) describe battering as a catch-all term that includes, but is not limited to, the practices of slapping, punching, knocking down, choking, kicking, hitting with objects, threatening with weapons, stabbing, and shooting. The *battered woman syndrome* implies the systematic and repeated use of one or more of the above against a woman by her husband or lover.

Some of the myths about battered women include the following (Cultural Information Service, 1984):

- Battered women aren't really hurt that badly.
- Beatings and other abuses just happen; they aren't a regular occurrence.
- Women who stay in such homes must really enjoy the beatings they get.
- Wife-battering only occurs in lower-class families.

It is estimated that two to six million women are beaten by their male partners each year in this country; a woman is battered every eighteen seconds (Renzetti and Curran, 1992). One estimate indicates that wives will be the victim of violence in two-thirds of all American marriages (Roy, 1982). Ninety-five percent of all spouse abuse is committed by husbands (Cultural Information Service, 1984). One-third of all murdered women are killed by their husbands or lovers (McGrath, 1980). Although there has been some mention in the media of battered husbands, the overwhelming majority of domestic violence victims are women (Gelles, 1979; Renzetti and Curran, 1992). Battering women is so prevalent that women are more likely to be beaten in their own homes than police officers are likely to be assaulted on the job (U.S. House of Representatives, 1988).

Battery victims don't like being beaten. Women attend domestic violence programs for help in stopping the beatings and maintaining their marriages (Norman and Mancuso, 1980, p. 115). They do not enjoy the pain and suffering. For reasons that will be discussed later, they tolerate it.

Wife battering is not limited to poor families, minorities, people in blue-collar occupations, or families of lower socioeconomic status (Gelles, 1974). Battered wives come from virtually every socioeconomic level. It's more likely for wife battering to be reported to police, public agencies, and hospitals when it happens in lower-class families (Stark and McEvoy, 1970). Middle- and upper-class families have more resources available to them either to deal with battering in other ways or to keep it hidden from public scrutiny.

A Profile of the Victim

Walker (1979) describes the battered woman as tending to have certain characteristics. First, she has very low self-esteem. Social workers who counsel battered women indicate that psychological abuse is frequently also involved. The battering husbands tend to criticize their wives and make derogatory remarks. They also tend to emphasize how their wives couldn't possibly survive without them. Over an extended period of time, their wives start to believe them.

A second characteristic of battered women is their tendency to believe in the common myths about battering. These women are especially likely to believe that the battering is somehow their own fault. The typical battered woman believes that it is her responsibility to nurture and maintain the marriage and will often blame herself completely for a bad one (Martin, 1976, p. 81).

A third characteristic is the battered women's traditional beliefs concerning gender roles. They tend to believe in men being the dominant decision-makers and leaders of the family, and they feel women should

Women perform domestic chores in a battered women's center group house.

"My Place"

The lake. It was my spot to go and dream of my future. It was always so calm and beautiful there. From spring until fall, I sat on my pier, gazing at the sun as it set on yet another day. The setting sun did wonderful things to the calm water. It glistened and sparkled and left a trail of its beauty for my soul to behold. I always felt cleansed somehow, ending my days in this way. When it was warm, I would swim out to the raft and lie on my back, turning the clouds into imaginary shapes. There were mountains and faces, animals and forests, always changing, only to be held in a glimpse.

I was safe here, in nature's arms. She wrapped me up and held on to me. She was always there for me, she was constant in her love for me. I cherished her beauty, her wonder, her incredible power and control. Nothing could stop her, no power greater than herself. You see, that is what she gave to me, her strength. She always replenished my supply. Being a part of her, watching her change and grow, taught me that where I was then, would also change, that time never stood still.

And so I endured my situation, my adolescent years as a member of an alcoholic home. I did all the usual things a girl of fifteen liked to do. I went to school, football games, and the prom but I also did things that others did not. Daily I cooked the meals, did the dishes, the laundry for seven, the ironing. I worked part time, babysat for my brother and sister, fulfilled many different roles. I poured Mom and Dad into bed to protect my younger siblings after another night of booze. I lied, kept secrets, didn't talk, didn't tell—the family code. I enabled my parents to drink, I know that now. Then, I was only trying to keep crisis to a minimum. So, my place of solitude was the lake. I would walk down the lane to regather and regroup for tomorrow. Once I was by her side, I knew I could go on.

It was a hot summer night. The anticipation of cooling off in the lake made me hurry through my work. I quickly changed into my bathing suit, grabbed a towel and hurried down to my pier. The lake appeared to be glass, inviting me to glide across it to the raft. I dove in, swam effortlessly one hundred yards to my floating island. I lay on my back watching the sun change the horizon from hot orange to cool pink. The tension left my body like steam leaves a boiling pot, rising away to be caught and carried off by her wind.

The moon was out, illuminating my way back to the pier. I swam slowly to the shore. Climbing up the ladder, I was startled by a figure standing before me. I looked closer, relieved that it was only Mike, my next door neighbor. He was twenty-one years old. He and three of his friends had rented the cottage next door to my house. I remember being excited when they moved in. My family got to know them fairly well. My mother would sometimes invite them over for drinks—drunks. Mike was so good looking; dark black hair, black mustache, dark eyes. I was friendly to him but kept my distance. I didn't trust easily. Now, he was on my pier, invading my time and my space. I wanted him to leave. I didn't want to share her with him. He asked if I swam a lot at night. I lied. I didn't ever want him here again. Suddenly I felt exposed. He must have seen me walk past his cottage every night. He knew I was lying. I wrapped my towel around me. He stepped towards me, telling me how much he liked my family. He'd never say that if he knew the truth, I thought. I was nervous. What was he going to do? I was beautiful in my swimming suit, he said, so tall, so thin. He kissed me. I liked it. He kissed me again, drawing me in to his body. He felt warm against my wet, cool suit. He began to hold me tighter and tighter. His grip on my arms began to hurt. I struggled to free myself but his grip became stronger. My fear pulsed, raced through my young body. I began to scream. He hit my face, telling me to shut the fuck up or he would really hurt me. I began to cry and plead with him to let me go. How could this be happening to me in my place? Where was her power and control to save me? Her strength was betraying me. Was she testing my strength? Had I not been grateful to her freely giving me her wonder? Oh what had I done wrong?

His power overwhelmed me. He knocked me down on the pier. I hit my head as my body smashed against the hard wood. I was dizzy, disoriented, tied with ski rope to the pier, naked. I struggled to free my arms and legs. The rope bit into my skin. Why was he doing this to me? I screamed as loud as I could, someone please hear me. He laughed, told me to scream, no one can hear you. It was true. My house was three or four hundred yards away, through trees, on a dead-end road. No one was listening. I begged him to let me go. I wouldn't tell anyone if he stopped. I thought then that if I threaten telling my mother if he continued, he might stop. "Your mother is nothing but a fucking drunk," he laughed. I knew in my head he was correct, but in my heart, with all of my love for her, she would make this right.

He towered over me as he lowered his shorts to the pier and stepped out of them. I felt so small and frightened and powerless. I wished for a bolt of lightning to come from her dark sky and strike him dead. "You've wanted this all summer long, strutting down here every night past my window. Now you will get what you've wanted." He plunged into me like a rod is driven into wood; hammered, splitting, making its way until it is one with the board, flush and deep within. I was riveted in pain. I sobbed uncontrollably. Otherwise, there were no sounds. He said nothing as his heavy body retreated. I spit on him as he got up. He hit my face, I could feel blood dripping down my cheek and into my ear. He left me tied up, numb and broken, never to be the same. I didn't move for what seemed to be hours.

I began to try to free my arms and legs. As I wiggled, the rope cut my skin. I continued until I freed my left hand. I untied my right hand, sat up, untied my feet. I cradled myself in my arms, rocking back and forth. How could the solitude of my place betray me so? I began to look around me. My suit lay beside me, my towel behind me. The stars and the moon were not bright anymore. They had lost their luster, their sparkle, their innocence. There was no more strength here. They had been raped also. My place was gone forever.

My skin burned. I was bleeding from the openings in my body. My mind was jumbled, racing; I couldn't think. I felt dirty and used. I fell into the lake, frantically trying to scrub him off. How could I get home? I'd have to walk past his house. I was paralyzed with fear that he might come back or he would get me as I went past his cottage. The woods! I could sneak through the bushes. I dressed quickly, wrapped my towel around me. Straining to see my way in the dark, through my tears, through the thick brush, I ran barefoot colliding into branches, cutting my feet on the ground's debris. With every quick step I took, I could hear my heart pounding, louder and louder until I believed he could hear me coming. I could see the back of his cottage fifty yards to my left. I ran faster until I saw my home, the door, my Mom. I slammed the door behind me, startling my mother awake on the couch. I fell onto the couch next to her, I was home. Frantically, I cried out what he had done to me. Mom was quiet, looking away from me. Inside I was saying, "Mom didn't you hear me? Oh Mom hold me, I'm hurting Mom, help me, make it right." I desperately needed her to gather me in her arms, hold me, love me. But she was cold, silent and distant. Then, very calmly she said, "You are a big girl now, there is nothing I can do, you can handle it!" I was frozen in time, stunned by her reaction. She left me

sitting in the darkness of my living room, alone, broken and terrified. I was wrong. She wasn't going to make it right. WHY? What had I done wrong? I was raped again.

For the next two days, I lay in my bed, stayed in my room. I didn't sleep, I didn't eat, I wanted to die. I had no one. I believed I was worthless, used and dirty. If my own mother felt this way, so would everyone else. With resolve, on the third day I tried to kill myself. But of course, since you are reading this, I failed. It was my cry for help. But again, no one was listening, no one stepped forward to help a lost fifteen-year-old girl. So, it was my responsibility to pick myself up and go on. And that's what I did. I continued in my roles at home and at school, putting up a brave front. No one knew I was any different. Oh, but I knew!

Inside, the brick walls were building. They were my protection against the offenders. My pain and anger were buried in those bricks. I became isolated. I went to school, cared for and protected my sister and brother, did my work and went to bed. Life was meaningless. All the things I had held dear to me were gone. I was only going through the motions of living. I learned not to feel, not to talk, not to dream. I continued this way for the next three years. High school graduation was approaching. The only thing I knew was I was going to leave that town, that house and get out, leaving behind my nightmares. So, the very day I turned eighteen, I left, moving to Madison. I thought then that my life would fall into place. But my coping skills followed and haunted me. I had an explosive temper, overreacting to the smallest provocation. Drinking and drugs became a way of life. Flashbacks didn't occur as often when I was drinking. I was desperately trying to fill a void.

The years went by. During my early twenties, I was married and had two sons. Life felt pretty good. I was determined, almost driven to be a wonderful mother. I wanted to be everything my mother was not. I loved my sons immensely. I gave my time to them freely. I stayed home with them full time, which to this day I don't regret. But during this time I lost what little self-esteem I had left. I became frightened to even leave my home just to go to the curb to get the mail. I became even more isolated. I was self-destructing. I knew in my heart I had to deal with the past before I could have a future. I had to learn how to feel.

The past three years of my life have been painful but enlightening. I had to go back through some awful years and experiences to attach feelings to the memories. I know

(continued next page)

"My Place" (continued)

now that I was not responsible for the rape or for the reaction of my mother. I know now that I didn't entice him to rape me. I know now that it had nothing to do with sex. I know now that I can love myself, heal myself, make myself whole again. You see, one doesn't receive their strength from outside forces. One receives one's strength from deep within.

I love the lakes and the stars again. For years I let him take them away from me, too. I had been afraid when the sun set because it had been full of fear and pain. But with knowledge comes power. I have my own power, voice and control over the direction of my life now. I can't change the past. I can only acknowledge that it exists, that it happened, love myself and look forward to another day. Sharing my secret today, I am free of its power over my life. I can reach the stars!

SOURCE: Reprinted with permission from Rachel A. Kolberg. It is included here because it powerfully reflects the profoundness of trauma and the abyss of pain experienced by women who are raped. Ms. Kolberg won a Superior Writing Award for this story from the College of Letters and Sciences, the University of Wisconsin-Whitewater, in Spring, 1989.

---

be submissive and obedient. Perhaps they feel they deserve to be beaten for not adequately obeying their husbands and doing what they are told. Walker (1979, p. 51) refers to a sense of learned helplessness which may develop. She states, "Women are systematically taught that their personal worth, survival and autonomy do not depend on effective and creative responses to life situations, but rather on their physical beauty and an appeal to men. They learn that they have no control over the circumstances of their lives." The more they are battered, the more helpless they feel and the less they are able to see their way out of their plight.

The Abusive Husband

Strong and Devault (1983, pp. 405-6) propose a series of traits that tend to characterize men who batter their wives. Many of the attitudes and beliefs resemble those of their wives. For instance, they tend to have low self-esteem, to believe in the common myths about battering, and to firmly maintain traditional gender-role stereotypes. Additionally, men who batter are frequently emotionally immature and tend to use wife beating as a means of alleviating stress. Abusive men, in their personal insecurity, frequently become very jealous and possessive of their wives. Much of the research about the battered woman syndrome suggests that alcohol is frequently involved (Norman and Mancuso, 1980, p. 117).

Some evidence is found that men who batter have learned from their own parents to use aggressive behavior as a coping mechanism (Gelles, 1976; Marsden and Owens, 1975; Straus, 1974). This coincides with some of the ideas in learning theory. First, the male child can learn abusive behavior by observing the behavior modeled by his parents. For the male adult, the battering itself becomes reinforcing. It can be negatively reinforced when the wife is made to stop doing whatever it is she's not supposed to be doing. The battering can be a positive reinforcer when it provides the satisfaction of being able to exert control at least over something in life.

The fact that battering is rarely punished might also encourage it. As McGrath (1980) states, wife battering incidents "have had a police priority somewhere just above that of cats stuck in trees." Perhaps this indifference has to do with the assumption that domestic matters are no one's business but the marital partners involved. It may also stem from the traditional idea that women are something to be owned like property (Norman and Mancuso, 1980, p. 119). Therefore, the husband has the right to keep control. Also, battered women have been known to actually protect and defend their battering spouse when police enter a home and try to intervene in a violent argument. Finally, intervening is downright dangerous for

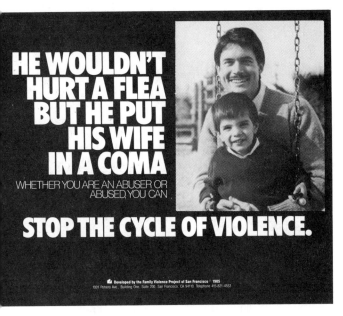

Battered wives come from every socioeconomic level. Middle- and upper-class families, however, have more resources to keep the problem hidden from public scrutiny.

the officers. Twenty-two percent of all police deaths and 40 percent of all injuries happen while they're trying to intervene in domestic violence disputes (McGrath, 1980). Despite the historic stance of police, there is some indication that police policy is changing in some locales from that of mediation to arrest. At this point, we're uncertain of how this will affect police intervention.

The Battering Cycle

Walker (1979) found that wife abuse tends to occur in three basis phases. The first phase involves building up stress and tension. The wife tries to make things okay and avoid confrontations. There may be a few minor abusive incidents. However, this phase is primarily characterized by the build-up of excessive tension.

The second phase in the battering cycle is the explosion. This is when the battering occurs. This is generally the shortest of the three phases, but it may last for up to several days.

The third phase involves making up. Since his tension has been released, the batterer now adamantly states that he is truly sorry for what he has done. He swears he will never do it again. The battered woman relents and believes him. He is forgiven and all seems well, that is, until the cycle of violence begins again.

Why Does She Stay?

One of the most frequently asked questions about domestic violence is why the battered woman remains in the home and in the relationship. Approximately 60 to 70 percent of women who seek help from shelters and even those who initiate separation through the courts eventually return to their abusive home situations (Norman and Mancuso, 1980, p. 120). There are many reasons why these women return. Reasons include lack of self-confidence, traditional beliefs, guilt, economic dependence, fear of the abuser, fear of isolation, fear for their children, and love.

Lack of Self-Confidence

Because battered women frequently have low levels of self-esteem, it takes great initiative and courage to leave even a painful situation and strike out for the unknown. The unknown is frightening. At least if the battered woman stays in the home, she knows she has a place to stay.

Adherence to Traditional Beliefs

Because battered women tend to believe in traditional gender-role stereotypes, they believe in their husbands as caretakers and providers. They dislike the alternatives of being separated or divorced. It's often difficult for them to comprehend what they would do on their own.

Guilt

As discussed, many feel that it is their own fault that they are abused. To some extent this guilt may be due to their husbands telling them that they're to blame for causing trouble. Perhaps because of their low levels of self-esteem, it's easy for them to be critical of themselves. Their beliefs in traditional gender-role stereotypes may cause them to wonder how they have failed in their submissive, nurturant role of wife.

Economic Dependence

Many battered women are not financially secure in their own right. Many do not have the skills and training necessary to obtain jobs where they could maintain their current standard of living.

Fear of the Abuser

It is logical for a battered woman to fear brutal retaliation by her husband if she leaves him. A person who has dealt with stress by physical brutality before might do so again when it is initiated by the stress of his wife leaving him. The battered woman might even fear being murdered by an abandoned husband.

Fear of Isolation

Battered women often try to keep the facts of their battery a secret. They may feel isolated from friends and family. They may indeed actually be isolated by the time their battery reaches such crisis proportions. Many times "familial ties have been strained over the years, and closeness is lacking" (Norman and Mancuso, 1980, p. 120).

Fear for Her Children

The battered woman might also fear for the safety of her children. First, she might be worried about her ability to support them financially without her husband. Second, she may firmly believe the traditional belief that children need a father. She may believe that a father who abuses his wife is better than no father at all. Third, she may even fear that she may lose the custody of her children. Her husband may threaten to take them. She may have little knowledge of the complicated legal system and may believe that he can and will do it.

Love

Battered women still love their abusive husbands. Most abused women who seek help still would prefer to remain in their marriages if the battering could be stopped (Geller, 1978). Walker (1979) cites one elderly woman's reactions to the death of her husband, who had battered her throughout their fifty-three-year marriage. The woman stated, "We did everything together. . . . I loved him; you know, even when he was brutal and mean. . . . I'm sorry he's dead, although there were days when I wished he would die. . . . He was my best friend. . . . He beat me right up to the end. . . . It was a good life and I really do miss him."

Community Responses to Battered Women: Their Alternatives

Despite the difficulties in dealing with domestic violence, there are definite intervention strategies that can be undertaken. They involve police departments, shelters, and specific counseling approaches (Hutchins and Baxter, 1980).

The Police and Battered Women

It is likely that police officers will be the first outside means of intervention involved in episodes of domestic abuse (Hutchins and Baxter, 1980, p. 201). Many police departments, despite their previously mentioned reluctance, are taking an increasingly active interest in addressing family violence (Hutchins and Baxter, 1980, p. 203). Because of the seriousness of the issue and the high potential for fatality and injury, they are acknowledging that something must be done. For example, training programs targeting domestic violence are being developed for police personnel (Bard and Zacker, 1971). One thrust of such programs is the development of specialized interpersonal skills for dealing with such situations. There is also a growing awareness that female officers may play a special beneficial role in the intervention process (Hutchins and Baxter, 1980, p. 203).

Legally, however, most states still consider battery a form of assault. Thus, it must be subject to the same requirements for prosecution as other assaults, that is, observation by a witness, filing an official complaint, and issuing a warrant for arrest (Renzetti and Curran, 1993). Some states have implemented mandatory arrest laws in which police must remove people who have been violent. Other states provide for the removal of the batterer from the home in order to avoid harm to the spouse and children. There is some evidence that such policies do help to thwart recurrent violent episodes (Dutton, 1987). However, there is also evidence that such laws frequently are not enforced (Ferraro, 1989).

Shelters for Battered Women

The most immediate need of a battered woman who seeks to flee the situation is a place to go. For this

The Burning Bed

March 9, 1977. Francine Hughes has been arrested for setting fire to her house while her ex-husband, Mickey, was sleeping. He died in the blaze. She is charged with premeditated murder. In the county jail, Fran recounts her story to Ayron Greydanus, a court-appointed attorney.

The trouble begins soon after their 1964 marriage. Out of work, living with his parents, Mickey becomes intensely possessive of Fran and jealous of her interests. One day he slaps her for "sassing him" in front of his friends. It is only the first of many incidents. The violence escalates to regular beatings in which Fran is often literally knocked across the room. The battering continues after the births of their three children.

In 1971, Fran decides she must do something about her situation. Informed by the welfare office that she will have to divorce her husband in order to qualify for financial aid, Fran leaves Mickey and moves into an apartment. However, that same year, he is seriously injured in an automobile accident. She gives in to pressure from his family to visit him in the hospital. Later, she takes a place near his mother's house, intending to stay only until he recuperates.

Although they are divorced, Mickey begins to pay regular visits to her house. When she rejects his advances, he beats her in front of the children. Terrified, Fran hides in a closet. She appeals to his parents and the police for help, but nothing changes. Mickey threatens that if she leaves him, "those kids aren't going to have a mother."

After one brutal battering, Fran runs away with the children to her mother's house. Mickey appears at the door demanding the children, and to appease him, Fran's mother sends them out to him. Convinced that he will kill her, Fran again goes to the authorities, but she cannot even

get the children back. Meanwhile, Mickey tries to persuade her that he has changed. He has quit drinking and promises he will not hurt her again.

In the courtroom, the trial of Francine Hughes is in progress. Mickey's mother testifies, and Christy Hughes, Fran's oldest daughter, describes her father's violence and threats. Then Fran is called to the stand to tell her side of the story.

Fran had been reunited with her children and had enrolled at a local community college. On the evening of March 9, she returned home late to find Mickey drunk and angry. Insisting that she quit school, he ripped up her notebooks and ordered her to burn them. After beating her nearly senseless, he demanded that they have sex.

Fran waited until he had fallen asleep. She told the children to get in the car. She poured gasoline around his bed and started the fire. As the house burst into flames, Fran and the children drove away.

In the courtroom, Fran explains her feelings that night: "I thought about all the things that had happened to me; how much he had hurt me my whole life." The jury returns the verdict for the murder charge: not guilty by reason of temporary insanity.

SOURCE: Reprinted with permission from a "Viewer's Guide" prepared by Cultural Information Service (CI-Sems, Inc.) in consultation with The National Coalition Against Domestic Violence. "The Burning Bed" was a two-hour movie presented by the NBC Television Network in October 1984. The story is a true narration of the life of Francine Hughes, a Michigan woman who took the law into her own hands after enduring twelve years of domestic abuse. The story is based on the 1980 book, *The Burning Bed*, by Faith McNulty.

---

purpose, shelters have been developed around the country. Late 1973 marked the opening of the first American shelter for battered women, Rainbow Retreat, in Phoenix, Arizona (Hutchins and Baxter, 1980, p. 206). Unfortunately these shelters are usually overcrowded. Most can take in fewer than half of the women who approach them for help (Renzetti and Curran, 1993).

All such programs provide a safe place where battered women can go to obtain temporary shelter. Hutchins and Baxter (1980) conceptualize the range

in philosophies adopted by such shelters. At one end of the continuum are the more traditionally oriented agencies. These emphasize the traditional values of keeping the family together. They orient themselves toward helping women resolve their problems with their mates, stopping the battering, and enabling these women to safely return home.

At the other end of the continuum are those shelters adopting a purely feminist perspective. For these, "wife abuse is seen as a social problem, rooted in sexism and manifested in the suffering of countless individual women. The women are regarded as victims in need of immediate protection and long-term life change. Some of the refuges with this philosophy actively encourage permanent separation of the couple" (Hutchins and Baxter, 1980, p. 207). Here the idea is that women need not be dependent on men, especially those who have been cruelly abusive to them. Rather, such abused women need to nurture confidence in themselves and to develop their own alternatives.

Many shelters, however, adopt philosophies somewhere in between the purely traditional and the purely feminist. These shelters encourage women to think through their own individual situations, evaluate their own alternatives, and make their own decisions concerning what they feel is best for them.

Counseling Strategies

The following are some basic suggestions gathered from a range of sources regarding how social workers and counselors can help battered women:

Offer Support. A battered woman has probably been weakened both physically and emotionally. She needs someone to empathize with her and express genuine concern. She needs some time to sit back, experience some relief, and think.

Review Alternatives. A battered woman may feel trapped. She may be so overwhelmed that alternatives other than surviving in her abusive situation may not even have occurred to her. Her alternatives may include returning to the marriage, getting counseling help for both herself and her husband, temporarily separating from her husband, establishing other means of financial support and independent living conditions for herself, or filing for divorce.

Furnish Information. Most victims probably don't have much information about how they can be helped. Information about available legal, medical, and social services may open up alternatives to them to better enable them to help themselves (Resnick, 1976).

Advocate. An advocate can seek out information for a victim and provide the victim with encouragement (Resnick, 1976). An advocate can also help the victim

get in touch with legal, medical, and social service resources and help the victim find her way through bureaucratic processes.

Counselor Training

Resnick (1976) has developed a training manual for counselors of battered women. She makes some excellent and specific suggestions regarding the initial interview, the range of the victim's emotional reactions, and specific counseling techniques.

The Initial Interview. A battered woman is probably very anxious during her initial meeting with a social worker or counselor. She may be worried about what to say to the counselor. The counselor should try to make the victim as comfortable as possible and emphasize that she doesn't have to talk about anything she doesn't want to.

The victim may also feel that the counselor will be judgmental and critical. Resnick emphasizes that it is important that the counselor put personal feelings aside and not pressure the battered woman into any particular course of action. This may be especially difficult when the counselor has some strong personal feelings that the victim should leave the abusive situation. A basic principle is that it is the victim's decision regarding what she will choose to do. In those cases where the victim chooses to return home, it may be useful for the counselor to help her clarify the reasons behind the decision.

Confidentiality may also be an issue for the battered woman. She may be fearful of the abuser finding out that she is seeking help and of his possible retaliation. The counselor needs to assure her that no information will be given to anyone without her consent. In the event that the victim does need a place to go, it should be made clear to her that the shelter is available.

The victim may show some embarrassment at being a "battered woman." The label may make her feel uncomfortable. The counselor should make an effort to downplay any embarrassment by emphasizing that she is a victim and that her situation has nothing to do with her character or with her intrinsic human value.

Emotional Reactions. Many battered women will display a range of emotional reactions including helplessness, fear, anger, guilt, embarrassment, and even doubts about her sanity. The counselor needs to encourage the victim to get all of these emotions out in the open. Only then will she be able to deal with them. The counselor can then help the victim to look objectively at various aspects of her situation and help get control of her own life.

Specific Counseling Techniques. Resnick emphasizes that the foundation of good counseling is good listening ability. The victim needs to know that she can talk freely to the counselor.

A battered woman is often overwhelmed and confused. One of the most helpful things a counselor can do is to help her sort through her various problems. A victim cannot do everything at once. However, she can begin getting control of her life by addressing one issue at a time and making decisions step by step.

One aspect of counseling which is very easy to forget is focusing on the victim's strengths. A battered woman will probably be suffering from low self-esteem. She probably needs help in identifying her positive characteristics.

One other important counseling technique is helping the victim establish a plan of action. She needs to clearly understand and define what she chooses to do. This choice may include formulating major goals such as divorcing her husband. It may involve setting smaller subgoals such as developing a list of existing daycare centers she can call to find out available child care options.

Special Counseling Needs of Women

In this chapter we have discussed the special life events and experiences that often confront women by virtue of their gender. The issues are intimately intertwined with characteristics and qualities of traditional gender role expectations. Women often bring to counseling situations issues related both to traditional gender roles and to the situations in which they often find themselves. It's not that men never suffer from any of these needs. Rather, it's that women are more likely to have these needs because of their gender role socialization. Collier (1982, pp. 57-68) describes five problems among others that women frequently bring to counseling situations. They include the following:

1. *Powerlessness:* Women who have been taught to be deferent and dependent often don't feel they can take control over their lives and situations. They feel no matter what they do, it won't change anything. It won't matter. Because of lack of practice in being assertive and in making decisions, they don't feel they have the potential to do so.

2. *Limited Behavioral and Emotional Options:* Because of being herded down certain gender-role related paths, women don't often see the variety of alternatives which may be open to them. For instance, it may not even occur to a divorced woman who has never worked outside of the home that she may be able to establish a career for herself. A battered woman may be so cowed by her perpetrator that she might not even think leaving him is an option. It simply might not exist in her world as she sees it. Such women may have tunnel vision where they don't know what else to do.

3. *Anger:* Women often come to counseling harboring deep feelings of anger. They may be angry at the condescending treatment they've been receiving in their outside workplaces or in their homes. They may be angry that they're trying to be super-moms, super-workers, and super-wives all at the same time, and they just can't do it. Or, they may be angry at how their perceived expectations of how they should be (that is, gentle, nurturant, passive) is conflicting with how they really want to be. Many times the anger is turned inward. Instead of targeting the real cause of the anger, the woman may become angry at herself, which results in depression.

4. *Inadequate Communication Skills:* Women who come to counseling may not have the words to say what they mean clearly and straightforwardly. Additionally, they may not feel that they have the right to say what they think. Opportunities to discriminate between nonassertion, aggression, and appropriate assertion may never have been available to them.

5. *Failure to Nurture Self:* Finally, women who have devoted themselves to nurturing and caring for others, may feel their own identities are lost. They may be searching for who they are and what they can do for themselves. They may have sacrificed so much for others that they no longer know what they, as independent individuals, need or want.

Working with Women

Social workers can help women regain their senses of having power and of being in control of their lives. Lott (1987, p. 277) asserts that the "personal traits that have clearly been shown to relate posi-

Strategies for Combating Sexism and Achieving Sexual Equality

In many ways problems discussed in this chapter are simply manifestations of the core problem of sexism. Sexism refers to prejudice, discrimination, and stereotyping based on gender. Sexism, therefore, involves misinformation and attitudes that result in behavior which discriminates against women. Some basic suggestions for combating sexism involve supplying accurate information, revising attitudes, and changing behavior:

Become conscious of the gender-role stereotypes affecting people from birth on. Don't force boys to be little men who must be actively aggressive and never dare cry when they're sad or hurting. Likewise, don't force girls to be little ladies who must wear frilly pink dresses, play with dolls, and be appropriately passive and submissive. The concept of *androgyny* may be helpful here. Androgyny refers to the capacity to have both traditionally feminine and masculine characteristics and qualities at the same time. It does not mean that men should be like women, or that women should be like men. Instead, androgyny implies that each individual, regardless of gender, be allowed to develop positive personal qualities. It means that males could be freer to express their emotional feelings and develop their communication skills. It also means that women could be freer to be assertive and have a greater share in leadership and decision making.

Throughout life place less emphasis on the need to conform with gender-based stereotypes. If less pressure was placed on men to be dominant, successful leaders, perhaps the midlife crisis would no longer exist for most men. Likewise, if less emphasis was placed on women to be beautiful, docile homemakers, perhaps they would be happier, more self-satisfied, and more comfortable in their relationships with men.

To combat the discriminatory effects of sexism on women, encourage women to develop their assertiveness skills, enhance their self-confidence, and learn to develop and appreciate analytical and spatial manipulation skills, the lack of which seems to be barring them from many of the more profitable career alternatives. Encourage both males and females to pursue whatever interest they have from early on. Females should be encouraged to develop their mathematical ability. Males should be equally encouraged to develop their domestic skills.

Encourage more freedom in adult domestic relationships. Allow individual couples to negotiate both household tasks and outside work career goals without external pressure and criticism. Encourage men and women to share in child-caring tasks. Doing so would not only allow children to know their fathers better, but also fathers to know their children. Don't criticize men who opt to stay home and manage the house and women who choose to work outside the home. Allow people the freedom to live their lives the way they want.

Confront laws and regulations that are discriminatory and restrictive on the basis of gender. Raise questions about them if you feel they're unfair. Vote for legislators and support administrators who adopt nonsexist stances. If necessary, fight for your own rights and advocate for the rights of your clients.

---

tively to measures of self-esteem or subjective well-being are the same for women as for men; and include assertiveness, independence, self-responsibility, and efficacy, characteristics typically included in the stereotype of masculinity." Thus, social workers can help women build up their self-confidence and self-esteem. Positive qualities can be identified and emphasized. Social workers can help women recognize the various alternatives available to them and evaluate the pros and cons of each. Decision-making and problem-solving skills can be taught. Success at using such skills breeds more success. Once women have learned the process of making their own decisions and solving their own problems, they can apply these skills to more decisions and more problems. This can help to build their feelings of being in control.

Social workers can teach women about assertiveness and how to develop assertiveness skills. They can provide practice situations and guide their female clients through more effective ways of handling difficult or uncomfortable situations. Assertiveness improves personal interactions, which, in turn, builds confidence.

Social workers can also encourage women to express their anger instead of holding it in. The real causes and targets of their anger can be identified. Once causes are recognized, social workers can "help the client learn to deal with anger directly through verbal and nonverbal communications styles, negotiation, confrontation, alliances and networks, compromises and resoluteness" (Collier, 1982, p. 277). Women can be helped to address the situations that cause their anger. If a woman is angry with her spouse, she can be taught how to express her feelings effectively so that whatever is happening to cause the anger can be changed.

Finally, social workers can encourage women to take care of themselves. The qualities they like about themselves can be nurtured. Women can learn that they have the right to their own time for themselves and to participate in activities they enjoy.

All of these suggestions are related to each other. Each one enhances the accomplishments of the others. Becoming more assertive enhances one's sense of control. An increased sense of control improves self-esteem. Greater self-esteem increases one's confidence in being assertive. The overall intent is to establish a confident, competent sense of self which is every person's right.

Summary

Traditional gender-role stereotypes pressure males to be strong, dominant, successful, and career-oriented, and females to be nurturant, passive, and beautiful homebodies. The socialization process and gender-role stereotyping have led to a number of problems. There is sex discrimination in employment, with men earning significantly more than women. There are double standards of conduct for males and females. There are power struggles between males and females, because men are socialized to be dominant in interactions with women, while women increasingly seek equalitarian relationships. Gender-role stereotyping is pervasive in our society and can be found in child-rearing practices, the educational system, language, the mass media, the business world, and marriage and family patterns.

Several significant issues and life events related to sexism are examined in this chapter, including: the concept of comparable worth, sexual harassment, the use of sexist language, rape and sexual assault, and battered women.

Special counseling needs of women are identified and counseling approaches suggested. Finally, general strategies for combating sexism are proposed. These strategies involve supplying accurate information, revising attitudes, and changing behavior.

PART THREE

Middle
Adulthood

10

*Biological
Systems and
Their Impacts
on Middle
Adulthood*

Crisis Time

Patrick and Laura Bailey have been married for twenty-three years and have had relatively few serious conflicts. They have one daughter who is in college. Patrick is fifty years old, and has been a bus driver for the city of Milwaukee for the past eleven years. Laura, age forty-eight, has been a carrier for Federal Express for the past thirteen years. They have a family income in excess of $45,000 a year. Their early years together were a financial struggle; the past ten years, however, have been better. Except for the monthly mortgage payment on their small house, they have no major outstanding debts to pay. They are active in church activities and enjoy taking walks, gardening, playing softball, and bowling. For the past five summers they have been spending their vacations travelling to various places in the United States in their Chevrolet Lumina van.

A PERSPECTIVE

For many people, middle adulthood has been referred to as the prime time of life (Bromley, 1974, p. 243). Patrick and Laura Bailey illustrate this. Most people at this age are in fairly good health, both physically and psychologically. They are also apt to be earning more money than at any other age and have acquired considerable wisdom through experiences in a variety of areas. However, middle adulthood also has developmental tasks and life crises. This chapter will examine human biological subsystems in middle adulthood and discuss how they impact people's lives. The chapter will:

- Describe the physical changes in middle adulthood, including those affecting physical appearance, sense organs, physical strength and reaction time, and intellectual functioning.
- Discuss the midlife crises associated with female menopause and male climacteric.
- Summarize sexual functioning in middle age.
- Describe AIDS—its causes, effects, origin, how it is contracted, and how the spread of this devastating disease can be prevented. Also discussed is AIDS discrimination, and helping persons with AIDS.

The Age Span of Middle Adulthood

Middle age has no distinct biological markers. The beginning of middle adulthood has been identified as ranging from thirty to forty by different writers. The ending of this age period has been viewed as ranging from age sixty to seventy. Somewhat arbitrarily, this text will view the age limits for the beginning and ending of middle adulthood to range from age thirty to age sixty-five. This period covers a large number of years.

Physical Changes in Middle Age

Changes in Physical Functioning

Most middle-aged people are in good health and have substantial energy. Small declines in physical functioning are barely perceptible. At age forty-eight, for example, Althea Gipson, who jogs, may notice it takes her a little longer to run the course. These decreases in physical functioning may be sufficient to make people feel they are aging.

Schanche (1973) asserts the major physical

change is a reduction in reserve capacity, which serves as a backup in times of stress and during a dysfunction of one of the body's systems. Schanche reports that the following changes occur:

- The heart of a forty-year-old pumps only 23 liters of blood per minute, compared to the 40 liters that it pumped at age twenty.
- The gastrointestinal tract secrets fewer enzymes, which increases the chances of constipation and indigestion.
- The kidneys have a reduced capacity to concentrate waste materials.
- The diaphragm weakens, which results in an increase in the size of the chest.
- In some males the prostate gland (the organ surrounding the neck of the urinary bladder) enlarges, which then can cause bladder and sexual problems.

In addition to gradual reductions in energy levels, middle-aged adults also have less capacity to do physical work. A longer time period is needed to recoup strength after extended and strenuous activity. Working full time at a job and socializing into the wee hours of the evening is harder. Recovering from colds and other common ailments generally takes longer. For those who begin an exercise program, it takes longer to get the body back into physical shape, and it takes longer to get the pain out of joints and muscles after extensive physical exercise. Welford (1977) notes that middle age adults are best at tasks that require endurance rather than rapid bursts of energy. These adults need to make adjustments in their physical activities to compensate for these changes in energy level.

Health Changes

In the early forties a general slowing down in metabolism usually begins. Individuals who reach this age either begin to gain weight or have to compensate by eating less and exercising more.

Health problems are more apt to arise. Signs of diabetes may occur; and the incidence of gall stones and kidney stones increases (Lindeman, 1975). Hypertension, heart problems, and cancer also have higher rates of occurring during the middle adult years as compared to the younger years. Back prob-

lems, asthma, arthritis, and rheumatism are also more common. But because nearly all these ailments can be treated, middle age adults need to have periodic physical examinations in order to detect and treat these illnesses in their early stages of development.

One major health problem during middle age is hypertension, or high blood pressure. The disorder predisposes people to heart attacks and to strokes. The disorder affects one out of five adults in the United States, and is more prevalent among black people and poor people (Papalia and Olds, 1989, p. 488). Fortunately the disorder is now often detected by blood pressure screening, and can generally be effectively treated with medication.

The three leading causes of death between the ages of thirty-five and fifty-four are, in order: cancer, heart disease, and accidents. Between ages fifty-five and sixty-four the leading causes are: cancer, heart disease, and strokes (Papalia and Olds, 1992, p. 434).

Changes in Physical Appearance

Gradual changes in appearance take place. Some people discover these changes when they look at themselves in a mirror and become alarmed. Gray hairs begin to appear. The hair may thin. Wrinkles gradually appear. The skin may become dry and lose some of its elasticity. There is a redistribution of fatty tissues; males, for example, are apt to develop a "tire" around their waist, and the breasts of women may decrease in size. Minor ailments develop that cause a variety of twinges.

Some studies with interesting results have been conducted on personal appearance. Bush (1976), who showed slides of both women and men to students, found that those judged to be physically attractive were also judged to be brighter, richer, and more successful in their social and career lives.

Having a physically attractive body has become a cult in our society. Americans spend thousands of hours and millions of dollars on grooming themselves, exercising, and dieting. The body beautiful cult leads those who judge themselves to be attractive to feel that they are superior to those they judge to be less attractive physically.

Berscheid and Walster (1975) found that women

who were physically attractive during college days tended during middle adulthood to be less happy, less satisfied with their lives, and less well adjusted than women who were more ordinary looking during their college years. (Men's happiness did not appear to be related to physical attractiveness.)

Why do physically attractive women have a less satisfying life as they grow older? One explanation is that physically attractive women develop their sense of self-worth in terms of their physical features. As their physical beauty begins to fade in middle adulthood, they may feel a greater sense of loss than ordinary looking women who have developed a sense of self-worth that emphasizes other features—for example, a pleasing disposition, being friendly, being a caring and honest person, and being productive and competent. Because women are more apt to be judged on their physical features in our society than men, perhaps men are less apt in middle adulthood to be adversely affected psychologically by changes in their physical appearance.

The Double Standard of Aging

Gray hairs, coarsened skin, and "crow's feet" wrinkles are considered attractive in men as they are viewed as signs of distinction, experience, and mastery. Yet, the same physical changes in women are viewed as unattractive and as indicating they are "over the hill." There is also a tendency in our society for many men to view such women as having less value as a sexual and romantic partner and even as a business associate or prospective employee (Papalia and Olds, 1989, p. 487). For example, some middle-age television anchorwomen have been discharged from their positions because normal changes in their physical features are considered "unattractive."

The double standard of aging is dramatically illustrated in a 1979 survey of employment among actresses and actors conducted by the Screen Actors Guild (Allgeier and Allgeier, 1984, p. 454). The study found that actresses aged twenty to twenty-nine slightly outnumber actors in both days worked and average income. From ages thirty to thirty-nine actors slightly outnumber actresses in both days worked and average income. As actors and actresses grow older, the gaps in days worked and average income between the sexes become more pronounced. Female members of the Guild over age forty work approximately one day for every three days worked by male members over forty. Fifty-year-old actors earn more than double the daily wage paid to actresses that age. In addition, while there are more women than men in the Guild who are in the twenty to twenty-nine age category, there are substantially more men over age forty in the Guild as compared to women.

The physical changes that generally occur with age appear to have more of an effect on a husband's sexual responsiveness to his wife than on a wife's responsiveness to her husband. In a study of 1,509 married men and women fifty-five years old or less, Margolin and White (1987, p. 25) conclude:

> Men who believe that their spouse is declining in physical attractiveness, but that they themselves are not are more likely than other men to report sexual problems in their marriage. . . . No such pattern exists for women.

These men tended to become less interested in their wives sexually, and were more apt to be unfaithful.

It is interesting to note that in a different area, career advancement, men are more apt than women to feel old before their time if they have not achieved career or financial success. Apparently more pressure is placed on men in our society to have a successful career.

Changes in Sense Organs

A gradual deterioration occurs in the sense organs during middle adulthood. Middle age adults are apt to develop problems with their vision that may force them to wear bifocals, reading glasses, or contacts lenses. As the lens of the eye becomes less elastic with age, its focus does not adjust as readily. As a result, many people develop *presbyopia*—which means they become far-sighted. They have an inability to focus sharply for near vision and thus need reading glasses. The psychological impact of being required to wear glasses may be minor or can be fairly serious if the person is fearful about growing older.

During middle age there is also a gradual hardening and deterioration of the auditory nerve cells. The most common deterioration in middle adulthood is *presbycusis*, which is a reduction in hearing acuity for high frequency tones. Timiras and Vernadakis (1972) have found that middle-aged men generally have significantly greater losses of high frequency tones than middle-aged women. Sometimes the hearing loss is enough so that a hearing aid is needed.

Engen (1977) has found that there are generally some minor changes in taste, touch, and smell as a person grows older. Most of these changes are so gradual that a person makes adjustments without recognizing that changes are occurring.

Changes in Physical Strength and Reaction Time

Physical strength and coordination are at their maximum in the twenties and then decline gradually in middle adulthood. Generally these declines are minor. Manual laborers and competitive athletes (boxers, football players, weightlifters, wrestlers, ice skaters) are most apt to be affected by these gradual declines. Some sports figures who have excelled in athletic contests and have been applauded and worshipped by fans may experience a traumatic identity crisis in middle adulthood when they no longer are as competitive. Their lifestyle and identity have been based on excelling with athletic skills, and now that those skills are fading they need to find new interests and another livelihood.

Simple reaction time reaches its optimum at around age twenty-five and is maintained until around age sixty, when the reflexes gradually slow down (Woodworth and Schlosberg, 1954). As people grow older they learn more and are generally better at a number of physical tasks in middle adulthood than they were in their twenties—such tasks include driving ability, hunting, fishing, and golf. The improvement that comes from experience outweighs minor declines in physical abilities. The same is true in other areas. Persons aged forty-five to fifty-four have been found to sort mail with the fewest mistakes (Papalia and Olds, 1981, p. 468). Skilled industrial workers are most productive in their forties and fifties, partly because they are more careful and conscientious (Belbin, 1967). Middle-aged workers are less likely to have disabling injuries on the job—which is probably due to learning to be careful and learning to use good judgment (Hunt and Hunt, 1974). An addi-

tional factor in reduced accident rates for this age group may be a reduction in the abuse of mind-altering substances among middle-aged workers.

Changes in Intellectual Functioning

Contrary to the notion that "You can't teach an old dog new tricks," mental functions are at a peak in middle age." Middle-aged adults can continue to learn new skills, new facts, and can remember those they already know well. Unfortunately, many middle age people do not fully use their intellectual capacities. Many settle in to a job and family life and are less active in using their intellectual capacities than they were in their younger years when they were attending school or when they were learning their profession or trade. Some middle-aged adults are unfortunately trapped by the erroneous belief that they can't learn anything new.

If a person is mentally active, that person will continue to learn well into later adulthood. Practically all cognitive capacities show no noticeable declines in middle adulthood. Adults who are trapped by the belief that they completed their education in their twenties are apt to show declines in their intellectual functioning in middle adulthood. There is truth in the adage "What you do not use, you will begin to lose."

In regards to specific intellectual capacities, there are variations. People in middle adulthood who use their verbal abilities regularly (either on the job or through some other mental stimulation such as reading) further develop their vocabulary and verbal abilities. There is some evidence that middle-aged adults may be slightly less adept at tests of short-term memory, but this is usually compensated by wisdom gained from a variety of past experiences (Papalia and Olds, 1981, p. 470). If middle-aged adults are mentally active, their IQ scores on tests are apt to show slight increases (Kangas and Bradway, 1971).

Creative productivity is at its optimum point in middle age. In a study of scientists, scholars and artists, Dennis (1966) found the highest rate of output was generally in the forties and that productivity remains high for many people in their sixties and seventies. Troll (1975, p. 39) suggests there are different age peaks for different types of creative production: "In general, the more unique, original and inventive the

An Identity Crisis: When the Applause Stops

Chuck Walters excelled in sports in grade school and high school. In high school he lettered in basketball, football, and baseball. In his senior year he was 6 feet 1 inch tall and weighed around 220 pounds. He was a halfback on the football team and scored ten touchdowns in eight games. He was an outfielder on the baseball team and batted .467, hitting thirteen home runs. Especially good at basketball, he was quick and averaged 23.4 points a game.

He was recruited by a number of universities for both his football and basketball skills. He chose to accept a basketball scholarship at a major midwestern university. As a bonus for accepting a scholarship, an alumnus bought him a Pontiac Firebird. He was also given a summer job by another alumnus as a construction worker, which paid well and didn't require much work. Chuck had concentrated on sports and partying in high school and college. In college he chose the easiest major (Physical Eduction) he could find and only occasionally went to class. By taking the minimum number of credits needed to maintain his basketball eligibility and by having a tutor, he managed to make his grades and play varsity basketball. He loved college. He had plenty of money, a new car, many dates, and was worshipped on campus as being a hero. He thought this was the way to live. In his junior year he averaged 16.7 points as a

guard, and in his senior year he was an all-conference selection and averaged 22.3 points a game.

He also began experimenting with cocaine. He loved being applauded and adulated. He thought the merry-go-round would keep whirling around. To his surprise, he wasn't drafted by the pros. So he went to Europe to play basketball there, hoping to excel so that some pro team would give him a try out. He played in Europe for five years and was traded several times. At age thirty he was finally cut.

This cut led to a major identity crisis. He realized the applause and adulation were now coming to a screeching halt. He drank and used cocaine to excess in order to try to numb the pain of his loss. He had failed to graduate from college, having only junior standing when his scholarship eligibility ran out. He had been carried in college by his tutor, as his reading and writing skills were at the tenth grade level. He is uncertain what his career interests are—he now fears he has no saleable skills and is worried his money may soon run out. He can no longer support his extravagant lifestyle. At the present time he is considering trying to get some fast money by smuggling cocaine into the United States. His cocaine habit is costing him $100 per day. What should he do? He doesn't know, but he's dulling the pain with cocaine.

production, the more likely it is to have been created in the twenties and thirties rather than later in life. The more a creative act depends on accumulated development, however, the more likely it is to occur in the later years of life."

Middle-aged adults tend to think in an integrative way; that is, they tend to interpret what they see, read, or hear in terms of its personal and psychological meaning. Instead of accepting, for example, what they read at face value (as younger people are apt to do) middle-aged adults filter through their own information learning and experience. This ability to interpret events in an integrative way has a number of benefits. It enables a person to better identify scams and "con games," as an integrative thinker is less naive. It enables many adults to come to terms with childhood events that once disturbed them, partly because of their earlier narrow interpretations. It en-

ables middle-aged people to create inspirational legends and myths by putting truths about the human condition into symbols that younger generations can turn to for guidelines in leading their lives. Papalia and Olds (1992, p. 438) note that people need to be capable of integrative thought before they can become spiritual and moral leaders.

Integrative thinking also enables people in their forties and fifties to be at the peak of their *practical problem solving capacities*. People in this age group are best able to arrive at quality solutions for everyday problems and crises, such as what is wrong with an automobile that fails to start, how to repair a hole in drywall in a house, and what types of injuries require medical attention.

In the past decade an increasing proportion of middle-aged adults have been returning to college. Some want an additional degree to move up a career

In the past decade, an increasing proportion of middle-aged adults have returned to college.

ladder. Some seek training that will help them to perform their present jobs better. Some are preparing to seek a new career. Some are taking courses to fill leisure time and to learn about subjects they find interesting and challenging. Some attend to expand their knowledge in special interest areas, as in photography or sculpturing. Some want to expand their interests in preparation for retirement years. Professionals in rapidly expanding fields (such as computer science, law, medicine, gerontological social work, the sciences, engineering, and teaching) need to keep up with new developments. (Social work practitioners often take workshops and continuing education courses to keep abreast of new treatment techniques, new programs, and changes in social welfare legislation.)

Stubblefield (1977, p. 351) eloquently summarizes the importance of viewing education as a lifelong process: "In our modern complex society, no one ever completes his or her education. Learning throughout the lifespan is a requirement, not an option."

Life is more meaningful if one's intellectual capacities are challenged and used. College instructors are generally delighted to have returning students in their classes, as such students have a wealth of experiences to share and are usually highly committed to learn as much as they can. Compared to younger students, they are less apt to be majoring in "having a good time."

When middle-aged adults return to college, it often takes a few weeks to get used to the routine to taking notes in classes, writing papers, and studying for exams. A few courses, such as mathematics and algebra, tend to be particularly difficult, as returning students have forgotten some of the basic concepts they learned years ago. Since people at age fifty learn at nearly the same rate and in the same way as they did at age twenty, most returning students do well in their courses.

Colleges are not the only places that offer adult education courses. Such courses are also provided by vocational and technical centers, businesses, labor unions, professional societies, community organizations, and government agencies. The concept of lifelong education has been a boon for many colleges and universities as the increase in returning students has generally offset the seats left empty by decreased enrollment of younger students.

There is generally only a small amount of deterioration in physical capacities, and almost no deterioration in potential for mental functioning in middle adulthood. Cognitive functioning may actually increase well into later adulthood (Kaluger and Kaluger, 1984, pp. 526-27). The sad fact is that many people are not sufficiently active, both mentally and physically. As a result, their actual performance, physically and mentally, falls far short of their potential performance.

Female Menopause

Menopause is the event in every woman's life when she stops menstruating and can no longer bear children. The median age when menopause occurs is forty-nine years, although the event may occur in some women as young as thirty-six, or may not occur until a woman is in her mid fifties (Olds, 1970). The time span ranging from two to five years during which a woman's body undergoes the physiological changes that bring on menopause is called the *climacteric*. There is some evidence of a hereditary pattern for the onset of menopause, as daughters generally begin and end menopause at about the same age and in the same manner as their mothers. Menopause is caused by a decrease in the production of estrogen, which leads to a cessation of ovulation.

Menopause begins with a change in a woman's menstrual pattern. This pattern varies between women. Periods may be skipped and become irregular. There may be a general slowing down of flow of blood during menstruation. There may be irregularity in the amount of blood flow and in the timing of periods. Or, there may be an abrupt cessation of menstruation. The usual pattern is skipped periods, with the periods occurring farther and farther apart.

During menopause there is a reduction of activity of the ovaries. This change of life affects other glands and may produce disturbing symptoms. Goodman, Grove, and Gilbert (1978) report that approximately 75 percent of women undergoing menopause encounter few, if any, disturbing symptoms. Kirby (1973) notes that about 25 percent of women experience serious symptoms and need medical therapy.

During menopause a number of biological changes occur. The ovaries become smaller and no longer secrete eggs regularly. The fallopian tubes (having no more eggs to transport) become shorter and smaller. The vagina loses some of its elasticity and becomes shorter. The uterus shrinks and hardens. The hormone content of urine changes (Sherman, 1971). All of these changes are biologically related to cessation of functioning of the reproductive system.

The most common symptom of menopause is the "hot flash," which affects approximately 75 percent of menopausal women (Masters, Johnson and Kolodny, 1988, p. 264). A hot flash generally occurs quite rapidly, involves a feeling of warmth over the upper part of the body (very similar to generalized blushing), and is usually accompanied by perspiring, reddening, and perhaps dizziness. Some women have hot flashes infrequently (once a week or less), while others may have them every few hours. A hot flash may last just a few seconds and be fairly mild, or it may last for fifteen minutes or more. They tend to occur more often during sleep than during waking hours. A hot flash while sleeping tends to awaken the woman, which contributes to insomnia.

Hot flashes appear to be due to a malfunction to temperature control mechanisms in the hypothalamus (Masters, Johnson and Kolodny, 1988, p. 264). Estrogen deficiency contributes to this malfunction, and therefore estrogen therapy effectively combats hot flashes. Hot flashes generally disappear spontaneously after a few years even without estrogen treatment. Deciding whether to receive estrogen treatment is largely a subjective decision for each woman.

There are other changes that may occur during menopause. Most of these changes are due to reduced estrogen. The hair on the scalp and external genitalia may become thinner. The labia may lose their firmness. The breasts may lose some of their firmness and become smaller. There is a tendency to gain weight, and the body contour may change, though some women lose weight. Itchiness, particularly after showering, may occur. Headaches may increase, and insomnia may occur. Some muscles, particularly on the upper legs and arms, may lose some of their elasticity and strength. Some masculine characteristics may appear, such as growth of hair on the upper lip and at the corners of the mouth. Many of these symptoms can be minimized by the use of estrogen replacement therapy and regular exercise. In approximately one out of four women who are postmenopausal, the decrease in estrogen leads to osteoporosis.

A variety of psychological reactions also accompany menopause, but certainly not every woman encounters psychological difficulties. If a woman is well adjusted emotionally before menopause, she is unlikely to experience psychological difficulties (Flint, 1976).

The psychological reactions that a woman has about menopause are determined by her thoughts and interpretations of this life change. If a woman sees this change as simply being one of many life changes, she is not apt to have any adverse difficulties. She may even view menopause as being a positive event, for she no longer has to bother with menstruation or worry about getting pregnant.

On the other hand, if a woman views menopause negatively, she is apt to develop such emotions as anxiety, depression, feelings of low self-worth, and lack of fulfillment. Some women believe menopause is a signal they are losing their physical attractiveness, which they further erroneously interpret as meaning an ending of their sex life. Some no longer feel needed, as their children have left the nest and they have a low paying, boring job—or no job at all. Some are widowed, separated or divorced, and regret still having to "scrimp and save to make ends meet." For many women this is a time of reexamining the past; if the past is interpreted as having been something else than what they had desired, they feel unfulfilled and cheated. Even worse, if they appraise the chances for a better life to be nil, they are apt to be depressed and have a low sense of self-worth. If they viewed their main role in life as being a mother and raising children, they now will feel a sense of rolelessness; and if their children fall far short of meeting their hopes and expectations, they are apt to view themselves as being a failure. Some women seek to relieve their problems through alcohol. Others seek out understanding lovers. Some isolate themselves, while others cry much of the time and are depressed.

There is no clear-cut way to identify the exact time when menopause ends. Most authorities agree that the climacteric can be considered as ending when there has been no menstrual period for one year. (Some women may go several months during menopause before having one of their last periods.) Physical symptoms of menopause usually end when ovulation ceases.

Some doctors urge that some type of birth control be continued for two years after the last period in order to prevent pregnancy. "Change-of-life" babies are rare because conception, although possible, is unlikely to occur. Middle-aged pregnancies do present increased health risks. The child has a higher chance of having a birth defect. For example, the rate of Down's syndrome in the children of younger mothers is 1 in 600, while the rate for older mothers rises to 1 in every 50 births (Kaluger and Kaluger, 1984, p. 533). Spontaneous abortions are more common in women who become pregnant after the age of forty years. In addition, older women are more apt to have a prolonged labor due to the loss of elasticity of the vagina and the cervix.

All in all, menopause does not appear to have serious consequences for most women. Neugarten, Wood, Kraines, and Lommis (1963) surveyed several hundred women and found that women who had been through it had a much more positive view than women who had not. As one woman noted, "I've been healthier and in much better spirits since the change of life. I've been relieved of a lot of aches and pains" (cited in Neugarten, 1968, p. 200).

Male Climacteric

In recent years there has been considerable discussion about "male menopause." (In a technical sense the term male menopause is a misnomer, as menopause means the cessation of the menses. The term *male climacteric* is more accurate.) It should be noted that men who have gone through male climacteric still retain the potential to reproduce.

Sometimes between the ages of thirty-five and sixty men reach an uncertain period in their lives that has been termed a *mid-life crisis*. It is a time of high risk for divorce, for extramarital affairs, for career changes, for accidents, and even for suicide attempts. All men experience it to some degree and emerge a bit changed, for better or for worse (Schanche, 1973). It is a time of questions: "Is what I'm doing with my life really satisfying and meaningful? Would I be better off if I had pursued a different vocation or career? Do I really want to be married to my wife?"

Male climacteric is a time when a man reevaluates his marriage and his family life (Pierce, 1976). This period of reassessment if often characterized by nervousness, decrease in sexual activity, depression, decreased memory and concentration, decreased sex-

Osteoporosis

Osteoporosis is a thinning and weakening of the bones. As a result of a drop in the blood calcium level, bones becomes thin and brittle, with a consequent reduction in bone mass. Osteoporosis is a major factor leading to broken bones in later life. Women are much more susceptible to osteoporosis, particularly women who are white, thin, and smokers, and those who do not get enough exercise or calcium. Women who have had their ovaries surgically removed in middle age are also more susceptible to osteoporosis.

One of the dangers of osteoporosis is fractures of the vertebrae, which can lead to those affected becoming stooped from the waist up, with a height loss of four inches or more (Notelovitz and Ware, 1983). Osteoporosis also often leads to hip fractures in elderly women.

Osteoporosis is preventable. The most important preventive measures include exercising, getting more calcium, and avoiding smoking. Exercise appears to stimulate new bone growth. It should become part of the daily routine early in life, and continue at moderate levels throughout life. Weight-bearing exercises (such as jogging, aerobic dancing, walking, bicycling, and jumping rope) are particularly beneficial in increasing bone density.

Most women in the United States drink too little milk and eat few foods rich in calcium. It is recommended that women should get between 1,000 and 1,500 milligrams (or more) of calcium daily, beginning in their youth (Papalia and Olds, 1989, p. 485). Dairy foods are calcium-rich. To avoid high cholesterol dairy products, low-fat milk and low-fat yogurt are recommended. Other foods rich in calcium include canned sardines and salmon (if eaten with the bones still present), oysters, and certain vegetables, such as broccoli, turnips, and mustard greens.

A somewhat controversial approach to preventing osteoporosis is the administration of estrogen to women who are at high risk for developing osteoporosis, such as those who have had their ovaries removed at a fairly young age. Estrogen is controversial because there is some evidence that it may increase the risk of cancer of the uterus (Masters, Johnson, and Kolodny, 1988, pp. 264-74).

ual interests, fatigue, sleep disturbances, irritability, loss of interest or self-confidence, indeciveness, numbness and tingling, fear of impending danger, and/or excitability. Other possible symptoms are headaches, vertigo, constipation, crying, hot flashes, chilly sensations, itching, sweating, and/or cold hands and feet (Reitz, 1977).

A man going through male climacteric usually encounters some event which forces him to examine who he is and what he wants out of life. During this crisis he looks back, as well as ahead, upon his successes and failures, his degree of dependency on others, the outcomes of his dreams, and his capabilities for what lies ahead. Depending on what he sees and how he deals with it, this experience can be either exhilarating or demoralizing. He sees the disparity between youth and age, between hope and reality (Schanche, 1973).

Male climacteric is caused by a combination of biological and psychological factors. As a male grows older, his hair thins and begins to turn gray. He develops more wrinkles and tends to develop a "tire" around his waist. His physical energy gradually decreases, and he can no longer run as fast as he once did. There are changes in his heart, his prostate, his sexual capacity, his chest size, his kidneys, his hearing, and his gastrointestinal tract.

The production of testosterone gradually decreases. Testosterone is an androgen which is the most potent naturally occurring male hormone. It stimulates the activity of male secondary sex characteristics, such as hair growth and voice depth, and helps to prevent deterioration in the sex organs in later life. The male sex glands are essential for the vitality of youth. These glands are the first glands to suffer when aging occurs. Two of the more subtle changes—as compared to hair loss, wrinkles, slowing blood circulation, more sluggish digestion—are a decline in the number of sperm in an ejaculation and a reduction of testosterone present in the plasma and urine. The testes lose their earlier vigorous functioning and produce decreasing amounts of hormones (Zaludek, 1976). Older men generally take a longer time to achieve an erection. It also takes a longer time before an erection can be regained after an orgasm.

Some men do have greater hormonal fluctuations at menopause. Kimmel (1974) summarizes studies which have found evidence of monthly cycles in some men with hormonal fluctuations in a thirty-day rhythm. The majority of men move into menopause gradually as far as biology is concerned. Dr. Herbert Kupperman has defined what he calls a true male climacteric. These males suffer from testicular dysfunctions, hot flashes, neurological symptoms, and psychosomatic symptoms (Reitz, 1977).

For this pure climacteric male the treatment of choice is hormone replacement therapy. Androgens consistently injected for four to six years can halt and actually reverse thinning of bones that weaken the body. The treatment returns the male to potent sexual functioning and helps him to control premature ejaculation or incomplete erection. The man first undergoes a battery of laboratory and clinical tests to determine his general state of health and the depth of his hormonal needs. He is checked every four to six months. If he has a testosterone deficiency, he may need treatment for the rest of life (Zaludek, 1976).

While biological changes (including the diminishing production of sex hormones) play an important part in male climacteric, perhaps even more important is the problem of being middle aged in a culture that worships youth (Reitz, 1977). Many of the problems associated with male climacteric are due to psychological factors.

There is the fear of aging, which is intensified by the awareness that mental and physical capacities are declining, including sexual capacities. Also involved is the fear of failure, either with a job or in the man's personal life. Fear of women may be a part of this. A man may think that his sexual prowess is waning, and then may fear women's greater sexual capacities. He may also have a fear of failing in his sexual activities. The man with self-doubts is especially susceptible to the fear of rejection. He is very sensitive to derogatory comments about his age, his physique, or his thinning hair. A fear of death may be apparent as he realizes he has probably lived at least half of his life. All of these fears are apt to have an adverse impact on his emotional and sexual functioning (Zaludek, 1976).

A significant part of male climacteric is due to depression, which is often brought on when a man fears aging and recognizes that his sexual powers are waning (Pierce, 1976). He also realizes that he will never achieve the successes that he envisioned for himself years earlier. His bouts with depression may

be so profound that he may contemplate suicide (Zaludek, 1976). Depression during this mid-life crisis may also be triggered by: a reevaluation of childhood dreams, conflicts in need of resolution, new erotic longings and fantasies, sadness over opportunities lost, and a new questioning of values. All of this is coupled with a search for new meaning in life. He realizes half of his life may be gone, and time becomes more precious. He worries over things undone and there does not seem to be enough time for everything. He has the feeling of missing out on a big chunk of life. The man who is engaged in activities outside his daily job is a less likely candidate for depression. It is unbalanced to be so busy with getting ahead that the pleasures of life are missed (Reitz, 1977). To recapture some of his former enthusiasm and perhaps to shake some of his unsettling doubts and fears, he may drive himself to work harder, to exercise more, or to seek younger women (Zaludek, 1976).

A man at mid-life is also apt to experience a growing dissatisfaction with his job. He feels a sense of entrapment as the pressure to pay bills forces him to continue working at a job that he finds increasingly boring and unfulfilling. Along these lines is the fact that his personal identity is deeply entwined with his work roles. His job has provided him with an opportunity to define his self with others, to enter into a stable set of relationships with colleagues and/or clients, and to explain his place in the world. Now he questions that place. Occupational aspirations may change several times during this time period. The emphasis may shift from measuring success in terms of achievement to measuring it in terms of economic security. Also at this time, movement up the occupational ladder is largely completed. If he has not achieved his work goals by age forty or fifty, he may realize he may never achieve his goals; he may even be demoted one or two steps down the occupational ladder (Wallberg, 1978).

Midlife Crisis: True or False?

The ease or panic with which a man faces his midyears will depend on how he has accepted his faults and his strengths throughout life. The man who has developed a strong affective bond with his family will fare better than the man who followed a more isolated

Some men and women experience a new sense of freedom once their children are grown.

and career-oriented course. To age gracefully is to realize that he has done the best he could with his life (Pierce, 1976).

Many physicians will prescribe antidepressant therapy and counseling, along with requesting the support and understanding of family and close friends (Zaludek, 1976). Men who undergo a midlife crisis need to realize that there is still a great deal of pleasure and satisfaction to be gotten out of life. This is not the end; there are still things left for them to do.

Women go through similar psychological worries; for example, the empty nest syndrome. Recent research indicates a declining proportion of women are affected by the empty nest syndrome as more women are emphasizing careers. Midlife is a time of reassessment for both sexes as people in this age group look over their life and see where they are and how they got there. It is a time of reprioritizing one's life. With the right attitude, this time period can become a time of reappraisal, renewed commitment, and growth.

Life is full of crises and transitions: learning to walk, entering school, starting to date, marrying, becoming a parent, and being informed that someone close has died. All of these events are apt to be both a crisis and a transition to living somewhat differently. Similarly, psychologically realizing that there is slow deterioration in one's physical capacities, and realizing that there is disparity between one's earlier dreams and present reality is apt to be a crisis for many people.

Some health evidence exists showing that midlife is a time of crisis for many people. Hypertension, peptic ulcers, and heart disease are most often diagnosed in middle-aged patients (Rosenberg and Farrell, 1976). The rate of first admissions for alcoholism treatment for middle-aged individuals is higher than for younger adults (U.S. Bureau of the Census, 1992). These statistics suggest that middle adulthood can be a period of stress and turmoil.

But midlife need not be a serious crisis. Neugarten (1970) has noted that a person who develops an inner sense of the life cycle and who is aware of expected life events is not apt to experience a midlife crisis. Such an individual is apt to encounter a variety of normal crises and stresses, but is not apt to experience an intense identity crisis (Neugarten, 1970).

Thus, it appears the midlife (compared to other age periods) is a time of transition and change. For some it is a crisis, but not for others (Hultsch and Deutsch, 1981). For some women, menopause is a precipitating factor that sets off a midlife crisis; while for other women some of the symptoms may be uncomfortable, but an identity crisis is not precipitated. For some men and women, their children leaving home precipitates an identity crisis, while other men and women delight in seeing their children grow and develop, and experience a new sense of freedom in being able to travel more and in being able to pursue more vigorously special interests and hobbies. Lowenthal and Chiriboga (1972) report that most men and women look forward to the departure of the youngest child.

In an extensive study Costa and McCrae (1980) conclude that men who undergo a midlife crisis are apt to have had adjustment problems for a long time. Kaluger and Kaluger (1984, p. 541) conclude: "Midlife crises may be the result of unadjusted adolescents and young adults who grow up to be unadjusted middle-aged adults rather than the result of a universal crisis confined to midlife."

Sexual Functioning in Middle Age

Sexual expression is an important part of life for practically all age groups. In this section we will focus on sexual functioning during middle adulthood: in marriage, in extramarital relationships, for those who are divorced or widowed, and for people who never married.

Sex in Marriage

A close relationship exists between overall marital satisfaction and sexual satisfaction, particularly for men (Maier, 1984, p. 325) These two factors probably influence each other. Marital satisfaction probably increases the pleasure derived from sexual intercourse; and a satisfying sexual relationship probably increases the satisfaction derived from a marriage. Women are much more likely to be orgasmic in very happy marriages than in less happy marriages (Masters, Johnson and Kolodny, 1985, p. 393).

Generally speaking, marriage partners report satisfaction with marital sex. Hunt (1974) found most spouses rated sexual intercourse with their partners to be "very pleasurable" or "mostly pleasurable." Interestingly, the ratings given by husbands were generally higher than those of the wives. For men, satisfaction was highest in the sixteen to twenty-five age group and decreased slightly as men grew older. For women, satisfaction was highest in the thirty-six to forty-five age group. These findings are consistent with studies which have found that a man's sex drive reaches its peak at a relatively young age, while that of a woman tends to peak in her late thirties or early forties (Maier, 1984).

The median frequencies of marital coitus by age groups as found in the Hunt (1974) study are presented in figure 10.1. Similar results were found in a more recent study by Trussel and Westoff (1980). The frequency of marital coitus is highest when the individuals are in their twenties (between two and four times a week), and then gradually declines to about once a week in couples over age forty-five. It is important to note that there is wide variability in these

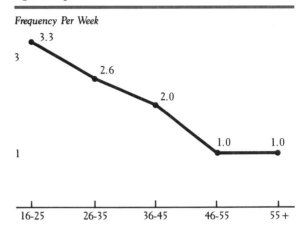

FIGURE 10.1: Median Frequency of Marital Coitus by Age Groups

Frequency Per Week

3.3 — 2.6 — 2.0 — 1.0 — 1.0

16-25   26-35   36-45   46-55   55+

(People should not seek to assess their sex life by median figures. Some couples enjoy sex more frequently, and others less frequently. The important aspect of sex is satisfaction and comfort and not frequency.)

average frequencies, and it is a serious mistake for anyone to judge themselves or to judge their marriage by the frequency of marital sex.

Westoff (1974) found that women who have a job because they wish to work report a higher frequency of marital intercourse than either wives without a paid job or wives who work out of economic necessity. Master, Johnson, and Kolodny (1985, pp. 393-94) note there is a strong correlation between the frequency of intercourse and satisfaction with marital sex for women. These researchers add that there is a strong correlation between a wife's ability to communicate her sexual desires and feelings to her husband and the quality of marital sex.

After the birth of their first child, couples report less sexual satisfaction on the average than childless couples (Maier, 1984). The presence of children in a family generally functions as an inhibition to sexual relations (James, 1974). Contrary to popular belief, the highest frequencies of sexual intercourse occur in childless couples. Many adjustments, pressures, and problems can be associated with parenthood.

For some couples the birth of the first child produces difficulties, particularly if the pregnancy was unplanned. Wives usually experience the most stress after the birth of the first child. They are apt to be concerned about their physical appearance, have increased responsibilities which lead to fatigue, and sometimes feel neglected by their husbands as the husband-wife interactions and social activities tend to decline. The arrival of more children tends to further lessen sexual satisfaction in the marriage. The frequency of sexual intercourse appears to be negatively related to the number of children in a family (Maier, 1984, p. 326). To some extent the reduction of sexual activity and sexual gratification with parenthood are offset by the increased gratifications that most parents receive from being parents—watching and helping their children grow and develop, and feeling pride in performing parental roles.

Married couples now use a greater variety of sexual techniques than couples in earlier generations. The female-on-top position is increasingly being used, as it gives the female greater control over stimulation of the clitoris than the man-on-top position. Oral sex has also become more popular. Couples today also spend a longer time making love. The amount of sex play has lengthened to an average of fifteen minutes, and the duration of actual coitus has increased from an average of two minutes in the Kinsey, Pomeroy, and Martin (1948) study to about ten minutes in the Hunt (1974) study. This change may reflect a greater awareness by married men and women that women are more likely to enjoy sex more and to be orgasmic if intercourse is unhurried.

Hunt (1974) also found that about 72 percent of young husbands masturbated and so did 68 percent of young wives. Sex therapists generally view masturbation to be a normal and useful sexual outlet.

Extramarital Sexual Relationships

About 50 percent of husbands and approximately 25 percent of wives report having experienced extramarital coitus (Nass, Libby, and Fisher, 1984; Tavris and Sadd, 1977; Hyde, 1990), even though most Americans frown on this practice. Levitt and Klassen (1973) found that 72 percent of the people they surveyed stated extramarital sex is "always wrong," while an additional 14 percent regarded it as "almost always wrong."

For males, the frequency of extramarital coitus decreases with age, while with females there is a gradual increase up to around age forty. These sex differences may reflect differences in the peaking of the sex drive. Wives with full-time jobs are more apt to have extramarital affairs than housewives (Tauris and Sadd, 1977). Wives with full-time jobs outside the home have an increased opportunity to become acquainted with a variety of men who are not known by the husband.

Spouses become involved in extramarital coitus for a variety of reasons. In some cases marital sex may not be satisfying. The spouse's partner may have a long-term illness, a sexual dysfunction, or the couple may be separated. The extramarital affair may represent an attempt to obtain what is missing in the marriage. Some seek extramarital involvements to obtain affection, to satisfy curiosity, to find excitement, or to add to their list of sexual conquests. Some become involved in extramarital affairs to get revenge for feeling wronged by their spouse. Some want to punish their spouse for not being more affectionate or appreciative. In many cases there are a combination of reasons for an extramarital affair. (Greene, Lee, and Lustig, 1974).

The Hunt (1974) survey found that extramarital sex is generally less satisfying than marital sex. In that survey more than half of the wives reported reaching orgasm "almost always" with their husbands, but only 39 percent did so in extramarital coitus. Two thirds of the husbands reported marital intercourse as "very pleasurable," but less than half the men who had had an extramarital affair rated extramarital coitus this highly. Perhaps those who become involved in extramarital affairs feel guilty that they are doing something wrong, or may fear their spouse may find out which may lead to an uproar. They may also discover that the grass on the other side of the fence is not as green as they fantasized. Some may fear acquiring a venereal disease. (This fear is intensifying as more people become aware of the perils of AIDS.) In regard to extramarital sexual relationships, Nass, Libby, and Fischer (1984, p. 207) note:

. . . physical acts are invested with symbolic meaning by the people involved. To have intercourse—still the main focus of ideas about sex—with someone outside our central relationship means quite different things to different people. To some, it's a serious infringement on a love commitment. Sex outside marriage may be viewed as a breach of a monogamous legal and/or religious contract. At the opposite extreme some people applaud any close relationship. Thy believe that it is good to express the warmth, love, or sexual desire they feel for others. In their minds such feelings may enhance life in the central relationship rather than detract from it.

Some surveys have examined why a high percentage of married couples do not have an extramarital affair. The most mentioned reason is that it would be a betrayal of trust in the love relationship. Other stated reasons are that it would damage the marital relationship, that it would hurt the spouse, and that the probable benefits of an affair are not worth the consequences (Hunt, 1974; Sprey, 1972).

In most cases extramarital affairs are carried out in secret. Sometimes the spouse later discovers the affair. Typical reactions to the affair are summarized by Maier (1984, p. 322) through his experiences as a marriage counselor:

Among the most common feelings expressed by a spouse after such a discovery are anger and a sense of being deceived and betrayed. In addition, the affair is often seen as a symbolic insult to the spouse's affection and sexual adequacy. Certain subcultures consider it appropriate to seek some type of revenge or retribution.

Generally speaking, isolated sexual experiences are less disturbing to spouses than prolonged extramarital affairs. Brief sexual encounters can sometimes be written off as temporary reactions to sexual frustration; however, longer affairs are seen as greater threats to the marital love relationship.

The discovery of an extramarital affair may lead to a divorce, but not always. Sometimes the discovery of an affair is a crisis that forces a couple to recognize that problems (sexual or nonsexual) exist in their marriage, and the couple then seek to work on these to improve the marriage. Some spouses reluctantly accept and adjust to the affair without saying much. They may be financially dependent on their partner, or they may have a low sense of self-worth and have made adjustments to being emotionally abused by their spouse in the past. Others show little reaction because they realize a divorce is expensive, socially degrading, and may result in loneliness. In such marriages the relationship may become devitalized with

The Coolidge Effect in Males Who Join Swinging Groups

Denfield and Gorden (1970) have found that some men in swinging groups report greater potency with a variety of sexual partners than with a single partner. This has been called the *Coolidge effect*, derived from the following story:

One day the President and Mrs. Coolidge were visiting a government farm. Soon after their arrival they were taken off on separate tours. When Mrs. Coolidge passed the chicken pens she paused to ask the man in charge if the rooster copulates more than once each day. "Dozens of times" was the reply. "Please tell that to the President," Mrs. Coolidge requested. When the President passed the pens and was told about the roosters, he asked, "Same hen every time?" "Oh no, Mr. President, a different one each time." The President nodded slowly, then said "Tell that to Mrs. Coolidge." (Bermant, 1976, pp. 76-77)

Some researchers on animals have reported comparable results. Maier and Maier (1970) found an average bull will couple with a cow about ten times, resting for increasing periods of time between ejaculations and finally appearing to be exhausted. However, if additional cows are then presented to the bull, he may copulate up to seventy times in a twenty-four-hour period. Part of the Coolidge effect may be due to novelty. Peters (1980) found that a sexually exhausted male rat again became sexually aroused when researchers provided a discolike atmosphere with intermittent musical tones and flashing lights. Interestingly, no evidence of a Coolidge effect has been found in human females or in female animals (Daly and Wilson, 1983). Also, the Coolidge effect does not appear to exist for some mammalian species (Dewsbury, 1981).

the partners having little emotional attachment to each other.

A few spouses react to an extramarital affair by gradually entering into a consensual extramarital relationship. In such a relationship extramarital sexual relationships are permitted and even encouraged by both partners. One type of a consensual extramarital sex arrangement is *mate swapping*. In this arrangement two or more couples get together and exchange partners, either retiring to a separate place to have sexual relations or having sex in the same room with various combinations of partners.

Sex Following Divorce

Hunt and Hunt (1977) found that a great majority of formerly married persons become sexually active within a year. When matched for age, divorced men have a slightly higher frequency of coitus than married men. Divorced men also tend to have a variety of partners (Hunt, 1974). Divorced women also generally have a fairly active sex life, although the incidence of postmarital sex tends to be lower than when they were married. They also tend to have smaller number of partners than divorced men (Hunt, 1974). Divorced women report a higher frequency of orgasm than they experienced in marital sex (Hunt, 1974). Divorced men also report sexual relationships are satisfying. These results should not be interpreted as meaning that sex following a divorce is more satisfying than marital sex. People who have a satisfying sexual relationship may be less likely to get a divorce. People who get a divorce are probably not as likely to give high ratings to their sexual relationship when they were married.

Hunt and Hunt (1977) report that divorced people are less concerned about hiding their sexual relationships from their children than were divorced people a generation ago. Divorced people apparently now have more liberal views on sexuality than was true in the past.

Sex in Widowhood

Ending a marriage by divorce can be traumatic, but a marriage ended by the death of one's spouse is usually more traumatic. In a divorce a spouse has input into the decision to part, but most widows and widowers have no input and wish their partner was still alive. They have to adjust not only to being single, but also to the death of a loved one.

Widowers are more likely than widows to establish a new sexual relationship. Around 90 percent of widowers form a new sexual relationship, while less than half of widows do (Gebhard, 1968). In middle and later adulthood there are substantially more eligible

single women than single men. There is greater cultural acceptance of older men dating younger women, than vice versa. Cultural patterns also encourage widowers to establish new sexual relationships, while widows feel pressure to be sexually loyal to their deceased spouse. Widows also tend to receive more emotional support from friends and family; and therefore, may feel less need to form a new sexual relationship.

Sex among the Never-Married

Very little research has been conducted on the sexual life-styles of never-married adults. The attitudes of singles about their status very widely. Some plan never to marry. Some want to marry, but haven't found the right partner, or have found someone they want to marry but that person refuses to marry. Some desperately seek a partner.

The life-styles of the never-married vary tremendously. Some contently become celibate. Others are highly involved in the singles scene—living in apartments for single people, going to singles bars, and joining singles clubs. Some singles have numerous sexual partners. Some singles, on the other hand, become involved in their careers or hobbies, and while they occasionally may date, they do not want the restrictions of a marriage. Some singles are content to date someone steadily for a few years, and when that relationship sours, they move on to another. Some occasionally cohabit with the opposite sex. Some become addicted to alcohol or to some other drug, and spend relatively little time in romantic relationships.

Celibacy

A small minority of people choose to abstain from sexual intercourse. Certain religious leaders (such as Buddhist monks and Roman Catholic nuns and priests) are required to remain celibate. In other cases, individuals choose to abstain for a variety of reasons. They may not want the entanglements of sexual relationships. They may have a low sex drive. They may enjoy other ways, such as masturbation, of expressing their sexuality. They may fear acquiring sexually transmitted disease or have a sexually trans-

The End of the Sexual Revolution

In the 1960s and 1970s there was a "sexual revolution," during which there was an increase in premarital and extramarital relationships, and a trend to view sex as relational or recreational rather than procreative. In the 1980s and early 1990s there has been substantial publicity about epidemics of seemingly new sexually transmitted diseases, particularly genital herpes and AIDS. The AIDS epidemic has been likened to a modern-day plague. Cures have as yet not been found for either genital herpes or AIDS. Publicity about AIDS and the realization that prevention cannot be guaranteed short of sexual abstinence or sexual monogamy with an uninfected partner have led millions of people to shift their patterns of sexual behavior, with some choosing celibacy and others becoming more selective in their choice of sexual partners (Masters, Johnson, and Kolodny, 1988, p. 23). There are also some Americans who have not changed their sexual practices at all, while others have added cautionary steps to their sexual behaviors (for example, using condoms). The late 1980s and early 1990s are a time when large numbers of people are rethinking their sexual patterns. The sexual revolution of the 1960s and 1970s is grinding to a halt.

Masters, Johnson, and Kolodny (1988) surveyed single adults about changes in their sexual practices with the advent of the AIDS peril. Although some single adults are not as yet changing their sexual behavior, Masters, Johnson and Kolodny (1988, p. 255) report the following attitudes expressed by a single adult woman as typical:

> I used to enjoy the singles bar scene as a way of connecting with men. Now I wouldn't sleep with a guy I met at a bar no matter how terrific he looked or what a great "catch" he might be. You might say I'm getting conservative in my old age, but it's really just a matter of adjusting to the harsh realities out there. Anyone who pretends that isn't so is simply a fool.

mitted disease and do not want to risk passing on the disease to someone else. They may be in a conflictive relationship with a partner and, therefore, may not desire to become sexually intimate. They may have a partner who has a low sex drive or one who is physically incapable of intercourse.

Although some people find abstinence to be very difficult, others experience it as satisfying. Coyner (1976), a feminist, suggests that periods of celibacy may be important for self-exploration and recovery from broken romances.

People Living with AIDS: A Population-at-Risk

The remainder of this chapter will focus on AIDS (Acquired Immunodeficiency Syndrome). AIDS is a devastating disease that has the potential to kill more people than any other. It is a contagious, presently incurable disease that targets the body's immune system and greatly reduces the body's capacity to defend itself against disease.

AIDS became headline news in 1985 when it was revealed that Rock Hudson (the prominent actor) had contracted AIDS—he died from the disease a few months after public release of the news. Since 1985, AIDS has continued to periodically make national headlines. The public was stunned in 1991 when NBA star Magic Johnson announced he had tested positive for HIV (the virus causing AIDS).

The following topics will be addressed here: what causes AIDS; how it is contracted; diagnosis; origin of AIDS; effects of HIV; treatment and prevention of AIDS; AIDS discrimination; social, legal, and ethical issues; and helping persons with AIDS.

What Causes AIDS?

AIDS is caused by a type of virus called HIV, an abbreviation for human immunodeficiency virus. A virus is a protein-coated package of genes that invades a healthy body cell and alters the normal genetic apparatus of the cell, causing the cell to reproduce the virus. In the process, the invaded cell is often killed. The HIV virus falls within a special category of viruses called *retroviruses*, so named because they reverse the usual order of reproduction within the cells they infect.

In recent years it has become clear that more than one virus is linked with the development of AIDS. The first virus to be identified, and the one that causes the largest number of AIDS cases, has been designated as human immunodeficiency virus type 1

Improving Love Relationships

Before presenting specific suggestions for improving love relationships, it is important to have an understanding of the various stages of a love relationship. Leslie Cameron-Bandler (1985) has developed the following framework of stages in a relationship. (As you read these stages, it may well be useful for you to identify your current stage in a love relationship.)

1. *Attraction/Infatuation:* All of us have in our heads a picture of our ideal date or mate. This picture may include a variety of characteristics about such items as: physical appearance, color of hair, color of eyes, age, height, weight, personality, hobbies, personal interests, religion, musical interests, sports, education, career interests, family background, financial security, and sexual values and interests. Such pictures vary from person to person. When we meet someone who comes close to having the characteristics we desire, we tell ourselves that this is an "ideal" potential partner. We feel strongly attracted to the person and are in a stage of infatuation. After a few dates, the infatuation may intensify. Cameron-Bandler (1985, p. 119) notes this is "a fun time, full of intensity and excitement and romance."

2. *Appreciation:* In this stage the two persons are a couple who are seriously dating, living together, or even married. They are delighted to be together. They focus on the positive qualities of each other. They appreciate each other, rather than taking one another for granted. Cameron-Bandler (1985, p. 120) notes:

> This phase can be based on a wide range of illusion or varying degrees of knowledgeable understanding of each other's wants and needs. The extent to which it is based on knowledgeable understanding is the extent to which it can be depended upon to last.

There are three basic elements for achieving and maintaining appreciation in a relationship. First, each partner has to know what he or she needs and wants in a relationship. Second, each partner must know what specifically fulfills these needs and wants. Third, each person much be able to elicit these fulfilling behaviors, lovingly, from his or her partner.

3. *Habituation:* Habituation is the stage of becoming accustomed to something. It involves being comfortable and secure with dependability and familiarity. For people who seek security, habituation is viewed as equalling safety and commitment. However, for people seeking adventure, habituation can be viewed as equalling boredom. Came-

ron-Bandler (1985, p. 121) notes, "The phase of habituation can be a very positive one, provided it cycles back to appreciation and includes an occasional trip back to attraction."

Partners in this state of a relationship are advised to engage in old and new activities that they enjoy. One suggestion is for the partners to commit two weekends each year for enhancing the relationship. The partners first agree on how much money will be spent for each weekend. Then one of the partners arranges the activities that are designed to meet his or her fantasies of how he or she wants to spend time with the partner. The next weekend the other partner similarly arranges for his or her fantasy weekend. Among other benefits, these weekends serve as a learning experience for each partner as to the other's previously unexpressed or newly formed desires.

4. *Expectation:* Cameron-Bandler (1985, p. 122) notes, "The difference between duty and pleasure often rears its ugly head in the phase of expectation. "Many of the things that one did and were appreciated by one's partner now become an expectation. For example, at first A expressed intense appreciation when B shopped for groceries and cooked on certain evenings. Now these tasks have become expected duties and B receives frowns and criticisms when they aren't done. This stage in a relationship is usually signaled by more complaints than compliments. Each partner focuses on what the other is not doing, rather than on what he or she is doing to benefit the relationship. One way of seeking to halt further deterioration in a relationship when this stage is reached is an intervention in which each partner is encouraged to once again treat the other as a lover instead of as a spouse.

5. *Disappointment/Disillusionment:* Unless the couple works on their relationship, disappointment and disillusionment soon follow expectation. In this stage the partners become increasingly disappointed because each is failing to fulfill the other's expectations. In this stage partners are apt to say their mate has started some bad habits; however, closer investigation usually shows the mate has been engaging in the undesirable behavior all along. In this stage the partners still remember the past as being wonderful and want things to be "the way they used to be." A relationship at this stage can be improved by a mutual commitment from each partner to put forth efforts to elicit those fulfilling behaviors, lovingly, from his or her partner.

6. *Threshold/Perceptual Reorientation:* The threshold is reached when one or both partners decide the relationship

is over. The partner reaching this stage has a memory change—from remembering past pleasurable experiences to remembering primarily past unpleasant memories. Such partners are no longer able to *feel* the good times, even when they think about earlier good times. Sometimes the threshold is reached by the occurrence of a minor event that, like the straw that broke the camel's back, leads a partner to conclude the relationship is over. The partner reaching this threshold has a perceptual reorientation of discounting the partner's positive qualities and instead seeks to find evidence in the partner's behaviors that warrant terminating the relationship.

7. *Verification:* In this stage the partner who has decided to end the relationship focuses on observing the other's behaviors and qualities to find evidence that warrants termination. Sometimes during this phase one or both partners experience the feeling that "I can't live with him/her and I can't live without him/her." Considerable emotional energy is generated by anyone with this feeling as such a person is under intense stress.

Usually one of the partners reaches this stage sooner than the other. One wants out, and the other seeks to maintain the relationship. The person seeking to maintain it may engage in a variety of behaviors such as seeking to please the partner in every way, attempting to make the other partner feel guilty, seeking to have a child in order to "lock" the partner into the relationship, flirting with others to make the partner jealous, and threatening suicide. Relationships at this stage are not fun. The partner who wants out has the most "power" as he or she decides whether the relationship continues or ends.

8. *Termination:* At this stage one or both partners decide to end the relationship. This stage is usually a painful experience for both. Property must be divided. Goodbyes are said—sometimes with considerable anger and animosity. If there are children involved, custody and child support arrangements need to be worked out. If the couple is married, the legal divorce process must be gone through. In addition, each person has to work on forming a new life without the former partner.

Improving an Intimate Relationship

We often tend to treat strangers with more respect than the people close to us. If a stranger does something we dislike, we usually ignore it or politely express our concerns. But if someone we love does something we dislike, we are apt to criticize and attempt to "train" the partner to meet our expectations. A major suggestion for improving intimate relationships is to seek to treat a partner with the same kind of respect given to strangers. Here are a number of additional suggestions a social worker might offer to a couple that wants to improve their relationship:

1. Analyze the relationship to determine whether your attraction is based on an unrealistic idealization or on an objective assessment of your partner's strengths and shortcomings. Is your attraction realistic and rational, or is it based on fantasy and excessive desires?

2. To maintain a high-quality relationship, *both* need to continue to work on the relationship by seeking new and exciting things to do that *both* enjoy.

3. Try to establish a comfortable, rational relationship, which is much more lasting than romantic-high relationships (see Chapter 8 for a discussion of romantic love versus rational love).

4. Often, it's minor irritants that gradually turn a relationship sour. For example, you may not like your partner leaving hair in the bathroom sink, while your partner may not like your leaving your dirty clothes on the bedroom floor. Communicate what irritates you in a nonblaming way and encourage your partner to communicate his or her concerns. Relationships work best when each partner communicates the irritants, and each partner then tries to avoid doing the things that irritate the other.

5. Try to communicate what you appreciate and enjoy about your partner. This includes aspects of your sexual relationship. For example, you may, or may not, like oral sex. Unless you communicate your preferences to your partner, she or he has no way of knowing. You can't expect your partner to be able to read your mind.

6. Do not stifle or possess your partner. If you feel your partner is too possessive of you, discuss it and work it out before such a high level of resentment builds up that you stop putting effort into making the relationship work.

7. Communicate honestly and openly in all areas so that problems can be dealt with when they arise.

8. Stop playing destructive games in a relationship (see Chapter 11). Destructive games wear a relationship thin after awhile.

9. Seek to grow as a person in the relationship. The more

(continued next page)

Improving Love Relationships (continued)

you seek to develop a positive self-identity, the better able you will be to develop a rational, comfortable, long-term relationship. There is truth in the cliché, "Before you can love someone else, you must first love yourself." Also seek to facilitate the growth of your partner in a relationship.

10. Take a positive view of events that happen to you (see Chapter 8). Both thinking positively and thinking negatively frequently become self-fulfilling prophecies. If you usually take a negative view, you will set up barriers between you and your partner because your partner will stop sharing things that she or he antici-pates will upset you. The price your partner pays for honesty will be too high, which will force your partner to either lie or withhold information from you.

11. Instead of reacting nonassertively or aggressively to things that bother you, seek to become more assertive (see Chapter 7).

12. Seek to become more attractive physically, perhaps through exercise, dieting, proper sleep, personal hy-giene, grooming, and selection of clothes. If you feel good about yourself, others are going to be more attracted to you.

13. Show affection to your partner. We all need to feel

loved. Unless you convey your affection, your partner will not know that it exists.

14. If your partner has a problem that she or he wants to share with you, use active listening to help the person talk it through (see Chapter 8).

15. If you have a concern about something your partner is doing (or failing to do), express this concern with I-messages rather than you-messages (see Chapter 8).

16. If you and your partner have a conflict, try to resolve it with the no-lose problem solving approach rather than the win-lose approach (see Chapter 8).

17. If there is a major conflict that your partner and you are unable to resolve, seek help from someone with exper-tise in this area, such as a professional counselor.

18. To receive in a relationship you must give. Relationships work only when both partners are givers *and* receivers.

19. Acknowledge your mistakes. Avoid blaming your part-ner for your errors. Also, avoid calling your partner derogatory names.

20. Develop and use humor. Look for humor in your life and develop the habit of being able to laugh at yourself.

21. Touch your partner in ways that are pleasing, and communicate to your partner how you like to be touched and held.

(HIV-1). This virus appears to be the most virulent member of the growing family of AIDS and AIDS-related viruses. HIV is a formidable enemy in that it is constantly changing, or mutating, and is present in multiple strains. To simplify our discussion of AIDS in the following pages, we refer to the infectious agent simply as HIV.

The HIV virus invades cells involved in the body's normal process of protecting itself from disease and causes these cells to produce more of the virus. Apparently HIV destroys normal white blood cells which are supposed to fight off diseases invading the body. As a result, the body is left defenseless and can fall prey to other infections. The virus devastates the body's immune or defense system so that other dis-eases occur and eventually cause death. Without a functioning immune system to combat germs, the affected person becomes vulnerable to bacteria, fungi,

malignancies, and other viruses which may cause life-threatening illnesses, such as cancer, pneumonia, and meningitis.

HIV is a tiny delicate shred of genetic material. As far as scientists know, it can live in only a very limited environment. It prefers one type of cell—the T-helper cell in human blood. Outside of blood and other bodily fluids, the virus apparently dies.

How Is AIDS Contracted?

Documented ways in which the AIDS virus can be transmitted are: by sexual intercourse with someone who has HIV, by using hypodermic needles which were also used by someone who has the virus, and by receiving contaminated blood transfusions or other products derived from contaminated blood. Babies may also contract the AIDS virus before or at birth from their infected mothers and through breast milk (San Francisco AIDS Foundation, 1987).

HIV has been isolated in semen, blood, vaginal secretions, saliva, tears, breast milk, and urine. Only blood, semen, vaginal secretions, and to a much lesser extent, breast milk have been identified as capable of transmitting the AIDS virus (Lloyd, 1990, p. 18). Many experts doubt whether there is enough of the virus present in tears and saliva to be transmitted in these fluids. Experts rule out casual kissing or swimming in pools as a means of contracting AIDS. Sneezing, coughing, crying, or handshakes also have not proven to be dangerous. Only the exchange of body fluids (for example, through anal, oral, or genital intercourse) permits infection. The virus is very fragile and cannot survive long without a suitable environment, nor is it able to penetrate the skin. In summary, evidence has not been found to show that AIDS can be spread through any type of casual contact. You cannot get AIDS from doorknobs, toilets, or telephones.

Few lesbians have contracted AIDS. Lesbians are at low risk unless they use intravenous drugs or have unsafe sexual contact with people in high risk groups. Female-to-female transmission is possible, however, through vaginal secretions or blood (San Francisco AIDS Foundation, 1987).

Women who use sperm for artificial insemination from an infected donor are also at risk of infection. Donors should be screened by licensed sperm banks as a preventative measure (San Francisco AIDS Foundation, 1987).

Pregnancy itself could jeopardize a woman's health if she is carrying the AIDS virus. Women who are concerned about AIDS and pregnancy should be referred to a physician who is knowledgeable about the disease.

Another question commonly raised is whether HIV can be transmitted by blood-sucking insects such as mosquitoes or ticks. Evidence suggests that this is not the case for a number of reasons (Zuckerman, 1986). First, children rarely are infected by HIV despite being among the people most frequently bitten by insects. Rather, the incidence of infection increases dramatically with the amount and type of sexual activity in which a person engages. Second, most infected people live in urban areas, which have

Magic Johnson, an American Hero, Joins the Battle Against the AIDS Virus

On November 18, 1991, millions of people throughout the world were stunned when Earvin "Magic" Johnson announced at a news conference that he had contracted the AIDS virus. He also announced his retirement from the Los Angeles Lakers and the National Basketball Association after twelve superb seasons. He added, "I will now become a spokesman for the HIV virus."

Thirteen years earlier, Magic Johnson made his first appearance in the public eye by leading Michigan state, as a sophomore, to the NCAA (National Collegiate Athletic Association) championship. At 6 feet 9 inches, he could play every position, including center.

In his twelve years with the Los Angeles Lakers, he led the Lakers to five world championships, and in the process acquired three Most Valuable Player awards. Magic Johnson is not only one of the most talented individuals ever to play basketball, he is also charismatic and has an appealing smile. A few days after the news conference Johnson indicated he believes he became infected with the virus from sexual intercourse with a female. He further acknowledged that over the years he has had a large number of female partners.

As of 1991, Johnson, age thirty-two, is the most recognized celebrity to acknowledge publicly that he is infected by HIV. The only person of comparable fame was the late actor Rock Hudson, who revealed in July 1985 that he had AIDS. That announcement galvanized public attention to a disease that had largely been ignored. Hudson had acquired HIV through homosexual contact. The publicity surrounding Hudson's battle with AIDS resulted in intense media attention and the infusion of hundreds of millions of dollars in government financing into AIDS research and prevention.

A few days after Johnson's news conference, he appeared on the *Arsenio Hall Show* and stated, "You don't have to feel sorry for me because if I die tomorrow, I've had the greatest life." His main message to Hall's audience and to the general public: "Practice safe sex, start using condoms and be aware. . . . Please put your thinking caps on and put your cap on down there" (gesturing below his belt).

the fewest if any insects. Third, there is a close analogy between how hepatitis B, a disease which inflames the liver, and HIV are transmitted. Laboratory evidence indicates that the hepatitis B simply disappears as the mosquito ingests it. HIV is even more difficult than hepatitis B to transmit. Therefore, it is more than likely that HIV also simply disappears upon insect ingestion. Additional factors preventing the transmission of HIV by insects include structure of the mouthparts, such as one-way valves allowing blood to flow in but not out, and infrequent feeding patterns.

If a person is exposed to the virus, the virus usually becomes inactive. Once it is in the body it apparently needs help to stay active. Such help might include a history of infections with certain other viruses, general poor health, the abuse of certain recreational drugs (such as butyl nitrite), malnutrition, and genetic predisposition. For those who do develop AIDS, the mortality rate is nearly 100 percent. In the early 1980s the AIDS virus was transmitted in some cases through blood transfusions. Since blood that is used in blood transfusions is now tested for the presence of antibodies to the AIDS virus, it is unlikely that the virus will be transmitted by transfusions. Because antibodies do not form immediately after exposure to the virus, a newly infected person may unknowingly donate blood after becoming infected but before his or her antibody test becomes positive. It is estimated that this might occur less than once in 100,000 donations (Koop, 1987, p. 22). As an added precaution, donated blood is heat treated to inactivate HIV. There is no risk of contracting the AIDS virus by being a blood donor.

Nearly everyone who is infected by HIV will eventually develop AIDS. The length of time between initial infection of HIV and the appearance of AIDS symptoms is called the incubation period for the virus. The average incubation period is estimated to be seven to eleven years (Findlay, 1991, p. 21). There is considerable variation in this incubation period, ranging from a few months (particularly for babies who are HIV positive) to twenty years or more. Drugs such as AZT (azidothymidine) and DDI (didanosine) can slow the deterioration of the immune systems in HIV-infected persons and delay the onset of full-blown AIDS, perhaps for years. Once AIDS is evident, median survival times are between nine and

thirteen months in developed countries (Lloyd, 1990, p. 25).

Another major health problem involves people who are HIV positive but have no symptoms of AIDS. Most of these individuals have not been tested for the AIDS virus and therefore are unaware they have the virus. These people can infect others, although they experience no life-threatening symptoms themselves. The following are high risk factors in contracting AIDS:

■ Having multiple sex partners without using safe sex practices (such as using condoms). The risk of infection increases according to the number of sexual partners, male or female. In considering the risks of acquiring AIDS a person should heed the assertion, "When you have sex with a new partner, you are not only going to bed with this person but also with all this person's previous sexual partners."
■ Sharing intravenous needles, as HIV may be transmitted by reusing contaminated needles and syringes.
■ Having anal intercourse with an infected person
■ Having sex with prostitutes, as prostitutes are at high risk as they have multiple sex partners and are more apt to be intravenous drug users.

Sexually active, heterosexual adolescents and young adults are increasingly becoming a high-risk group for contracting HIV. Persons in this age group tend to be sexually active with multiple sex partners, which increases the risk of contracting HIV. The risk of male-to-female transmission through sexual intercourse is higher than that of female-to-male, but the degrees of risk have not as yet been established. The risk of woman-to-woman transmission through sexual contact appears to be low, but has as yet not been determined. Although multiple exposures to HIV infection through sexual intercourse are not necessary for transmission, multiple sexual partners increase the likelihood that transmission will occur.

Lloyd (1990, p. 19) describes the ways in which sexual transmission of HIV can be prevented or reduced:

Only two methods of completely preventing sexual transmission have been identified: (1) abstaining from sex or (2) having sexual relations only with a faithful and uninfected partner. The risk of infection through sexual intercourse can be reduced by practicing what has been called "safer sex," which is using a condom for all sexual penetration (vaginal, oral, and anal) whenever there is any doubt about a sexual partner's HIV status; engaging in nonpenetrative sexual activity; limiting the number of sexual partners; and avoiding sexual contact with people such as prostitutes who have had many partners.

Although many people believe any contact with someone who is HIV positive guarantees illness and death, such fears are not justified. Body fluids (such as fresh blood, semen, urine, and vaginal secretions) infected with the virus must enter the bloodstream in order for the virus to be transmitted from one person to another. Male homosexuals account for so many AIDS cases because they are apt to engage in anal intercourse. Anal intercourse often results in a tearing of the lining of the rectum, which allows infected semen to get into the bloodstream. Sharing a needle during mainlining a drug with someone who is carrying the virus is also dangerous as there is transmission of blood. The reason sharing intravenous drug needles poses such a risk of the transmission of HIV is that a small amount of the previous user's blood is often drawn into the needle and then injected directly into the bloodstream of the next user.

At the present time, there is no evidence that the virus can be spread by "dry" mouth-to-mouth kissing. Although unproven, there is a theoretical risk of transmitting HIV through vigorous "wet" or deep tongue kissing (Lloyd, 1990). Nevertheless, the announcement that saliva can contain the virus has led the Screen Actors Guild to inform their members that they have the right to refuse to do kissing scenes if they are afraid of contracting AIDS. In studies of families of people with AIDS, there has not been a single reported case as of 1992 of the virus being passed by close family contact (eating together, hugging, sharing food, sharing towels and cups, and any other kinds of nonsexual contact).

Diagnosis

Several tests have been developed to determine if a person has been exposed to the virus. These tests do not directly detect the virus, but only the antibodies a person's immune system develops to fight the virus. Two of the most widely used tests are called the ELISA and the Western blot. ELISA stands for "Enzyme-Linked Immunosorbent Assay." ELISA can be used in two important ways. First, donated blood can be screened to prevent the AIDS virus from being transmitted by blood transfusions. Second, individuals who fear they may be carriers of the virus can be tested. A positive ELISA does not mean that a person has AIDS, but only that he or she has had contact with the virus. For a person who has been infected with HIV, it generally takes two to three months before enough antibodies are produced to be detected by the test.

ELISA is an extremely sensitive test and is therefore highly accurate in detecting the presence of antibodies. It rarely gives a negative result when antibodies are present. However, it has a much higher rate of false positive. That is, it indicates antibodies are present when in reality they are not. Therefore, it is recommended that positive results on the ELISA be confirmed by another test called the Western blot or immunoblot. This latter test is much more specific and less likely to give a false positive. Since the Western blot is expensive and difficult to administer, it can't be used for mass blood screening as can the ELISA. It must be emphasized that neither test can determine if a person already has AIDS or will actually develop it. The tests only establish the presence of antibodies which indicate exposure to the virus.

Origin of AIDS

The origin of AIDS is unknown, although there have been a variety of speculations. (We probably never will be able to identify the origin, particularly now since AIDS is in existence throughout the world.) One theory postulates that the virus first developed in Africa about two decades ago. Samples of blood taken from Ugandan children in 1973 appeared to contain antibodies for the AIDS virus or a virus very similar to it. The presence of antibodies imply that these children had been exposed to the virus. Furthermore, the sudden appearance of AIDS may have resulted from the fast paced urbanization of portions of Africa. Previously isolated enclaves harboring the disease might suddenly have been exposed to the outside world. Some authorities have found that some species of monkeys have the AIDS virus, and there is speculation that the virus may have been transmitted to humans perhaps through a monkey bite or perhaps through eating monkey meat.

Another theory is that some military research unit (sponsored by the government of some unknown country) may have developed the virus as a way to exterminate large numbers of the population of "enemy" countries. Somehow, the virus may have escaped during experimental tests.

Another recent theory links the birth of AIDS to polio vaccine (Curtis, 1992, pp. 1-2). In 1957, an experimental oral vaccine for polio was developed by Dr. Hilary Koprowski of Philadelphia's Wistar Institute. This vaccine was made from weakened polio viruses grown in a culture of monkey kidney cells. Several monkey viruses have been known to contaminate such cultures (vaccine makers now have processes to eliminate these contaminants). The people of the African nation of Zaire became the first large group to receive this experimental polio vaccine. Extrapolating from a number of coincidences—the testing of the vaccine in the very site where AIDS is thought to have originated; Koprowski's recollection that he cultured the virus in the tissue of green monkeys (a species that harbors a virus similar to HIV)—has led some authorities to speculate that the polio vaccine was contaminated with a virus that evolved into the deadly HIV. (There is no reason to worry about standard present-day polio vaccines; they are rigorously screened for contamination.)

Some feel that the advent of AIDS in the United States can be traced to a single individual (Shilts, 1987), Gaetan Dugas, a Canadian airline steward. As early as 1979, it was noted that several men began to suffer from a rare form of skin cancer named Kaposi's sarcoma, a disease that the body's immune system could normally resist easily. By 1981 it was established that AIDS had invaded the United States. Investigation of many of these men and their lives revealed that either they or someone with whom they had sexual relations had also been sexually involved with Gaetan. Allegedly, Gaetan was noted for exceptional pride in his appearance and his ability to attract many lovers. He reportedly continued to have sexual relations with men even after he understood his diagnosis and knew such behavior could be fatal to these partners. Gaetan died on March 30, 1984. This was only one month after he turned thirty-one and almost four years after he sought a doctor's help to remove an

unattractive purple spot near his ear, the beginning of his first bout with Kaposi's sarcoma.

The fact that Gaetan was a homosexual is inconsequential. It cannot be proven that he was the first person to bring AIDS to the United States. The fact that he knowingly continued to practice unsafe sex without regard for the lives of others is the significant and deadly part of the story. AIDS appears now to be spreading significantly throughout the heterosexual community. Gaetan provides an excellent lesson for all people who choose to be sexually active, namely, that it is an absolute necessity that they be concerned about the well-being of other people. The gay community merits credit for providing the first major impetus in the fight against AIDS. Many gay people banded together, brought the issue of AIDS to the attention of the general public, advocated for research, identified and lauded the use of safer sex practices, closed down facilities such as bathhouses where men met for sexual encounters, and helped people afflicted with the disease.

The Effects of HIV

Persons with the AIDS virus are now classified as being either HIV asymptomatic (without symptoms of AIDS) or HIV symptomatic (with symptoms of the syndrome). HIV invades particularly a group of white blood cells (lymphocytes) called T-helper cells or T-4 cells. These cells in turn produce cells which are critical to the body's immune response in fighting off infections. When HIV attacks T-4 helper cells, it stops them from producing immune cells which fight off disease. Instead, HIV converts T-4 cells so that they begin producing HIV. Eventually the infected person's number of healthy T-4 cells is so reduced that infections cannot be fought off.

Once a person is infected with HIV, several years are apt to go by before symptoms of AIDS appear. Initial symptoms include dry cough, abdominal discomfort, headaches, oral thrush, loss of appetite, fever, night sweats, weight loss, diarrhea, skin rashes, tiredness, swollen lymph nodes, and lack of resistance to infection. (Many other illnesses have similar symptoms, so it is irrational for persons to conclude they are developing AIDS if they have some of these symptoms.) As AIDS progresses, the immune system is less and less capable of fighting off "opportunist" diseases, making the infected person vulnerable to a variety of cancers, nervous system degeneration, and infections caused by other viruses, bacteria, parasites, and fungi. Ordinarily, opportunistic infections are not life threatening to people with healthy immune systems, but they are frequently fatal to people with AIDS, whose immunological functioning has been severely compromised.

The serious diseases that afflict persons with AIDS include Kaposi's sarcoma (an otherwise rare form of cancer that accounts for many AIDS deaths), pneumocystic carinii pneumonia (a lung disease that is also a major cause of AIDS deaths), and a variety of other generalized opportunistic infections, such as shingles (herpes zoster), encephalitis, severe fungal infections that cause a type of meningitis, yeast infections of the throat and esophagus, and infections of the lungs, intestines, and central nervous system. The incidence of tuberculosis, a disease once nearly eradicated in the United States, has escalated rapidly in recent years due largely to the epidemic of HIV infection and AIDS.

Until recently, HIV infection was diagnosed as AIDS only when the immune system became so seriously impaired that the infected individual developed one or more severe, debilitating diseases, such as Kaposi's sarcoma or pneumocystic carinii pneumonia. However, effective April 1, 1992, The Centers for Disease Control broadened its definition of AIDS: now anyone who is infected with HIV and has a helper T-cell count of 200 cells per cubic millimeter of blood or less is said to have AIDS, regardless of other symptoms that person may or may not have. (Normal helper T-cell counts in healthy people not infected with HIV range from 800 to 900 per cubic millimeter of blood).

AIDS as a syndrome is not any one specific disease. AIDS simply makes those infected by the virus increasingly more vulnerable to any disease that might come along. The disease process of AIDS involves a continuum whereby those affected become more and more vulnerable to devastating diseases.

Some recent evidence on women's manifestations of AIDS concern chronic gynecological infections and other conditions distinctively characteristic of women (*Contemporary Sexuality*, Feb. 1991, p. 4). Two-thirds of HIV infected women have been found to suffer from such maladies. One study indicated that 63 percent of HIV positive women have abnormal pap smears compared to 5 percent of women not infected. Unlike men, women rarely develop Kaposi's sarcoma, and tend to develop pneumocystis carinii pneumonia only in the very late stages of the disease.

In some patients AIDS may attack the nervous system and cause damage to the brain. The deterioration, called AIDS-dementia complex, occurs gradually over a period of time (sometimes a few years).

AIDS-dementia complex involves a significant decrease in intellectual functioning. In one study, the brains of seventy people with AIDS were examined during autopsies (Navia et al., 1986). It was found that less than 10 percent of the brains were normal. This implies that AIDS affects the brain in the majority of cases at some time during the progression of the disease.

Several specific intellectual functions are affected by AIDS (Cummings, 1986). These include inability to concentrate on the task at hand, forgetfulness, inability to think quickly and efficiently, visuospatial problems which make it difficult to get from place to place or to perform complex and simultaneous tasks, and slowed motor ability. It is interesting that language capacity and the ability to learn, difficulties which characterize people with Alzheimer's disease, do not seem to be affected.

Contrary to popular belief, people who are HIV positive can live for an indeterminately long time. Gavzer (1988, p. 5) summarizes the characteristics that long-term AIDS survivors tend to have:

- They are realistic and accept the AIDS diagnosis but do not take it as a death sentence.
- They have a fighting spirit and refuse to be "helpless-hopeless."
- They are assertive and have the ability to get out of stressful and unproductive situations.
- They are tuned in to their own psychological and physical needs, and they take care of them.
- They are able to talk openly about their illness.
- They have a sense of personal responsibility for their health, and they look at the treating physician as a collaborator.
- They are altruistically involved with other persons with AIDS.

People react idiosyncratically to learning they have HIV infection or AIDS. Certain patterns of reaction, however, have been observed. Lloyd (1990, p. 36) notes a typical reaction progresses through the following stages: shock, denial, crisis, transition, fear, depression, panic, guilt, anger, self-pity, bargaining, search for meaning, and fighting to a stage of sense of self, positive action, and acceptance. People with HIV infection or AIDS may experience losses in physical strength, health, career development, community standing, control over decision making, and the opportunity to have children, among others. Friends and family also feel loss and sometimes anger toward the person with HIV infection, which often is followed by guilt about these feelings.

Unfortunately, those who have AIDS are further victimized as they have to deal with the public hysteria and powerful prejudice against gays. Because gay men were some of the first people identified as suffering from AIDS in the United States, some people have associated having AIDS with being gay. Prejudice and discrimination make staying alive even more difficult.

Treatment and Prevention of AIDS

At this time there is no cure for AIDS. There are a multitude of hurdles to overcome in combatting the disease. AIDS is caused by a form of virus. Even with modern technology, we don't know how to cure a virus. The common cold is caused by virus; although pharmaceutical companies have spent millions of dollars on research in the hopes of finding an effective treatment, such a treatment has as yet not been found. Currently, serious research is being undertaken to understand, prevent, and fight AIDS.

Prevention can be pursued in two major ways. First, people can abstain from activities and behaviors that put them at risk for contracting the disease. Second, scientists can work on developing a vaccine to prevent contracting the disease, similar in a way to vaccines which prevent polio or measles. A vaccine might either block the virus from attacking a person's immune system or bolster the immune system so that HIV is unable to invade it.

Drugs are being studied in the hope of fighting AIDS after it has already been contracted. However, serious problems are being encountered. For one

thing, many of the drugs have serious toxic effects on the people who take them. Additionally, it is difficult and time-consuming to test drugs and get them to the point where they can be tested on humans. Animal-rights activists have protested using monkeys and orangutans for testing which inevitably results in their deaths. Testing drugs is enormously costly. Only within the past few years have substantial funds been channelled into AIDS research. In the early and middle 1980s, AIDS was frequently seen as a disease contracted only by drug abusers and homosexuals. There seemed to be an attitude that "people were getting only what they deserved." Many gay people were outraged and demanded that national attention be given to fighting a disease that was killing people, regardless of who they were. Nonetheless, the early resistance to providing money for research has set back our progress in overcoming the disease. Finally, there is the major problem that the virus mutates and changes form. This complicates finding a cure even further.

The drug called AZT (azidothymidine) has been found to delay the progress of the disease in some people (Recer, 1988). First synthesized in 1964 and initially developed as a cancer drug, AZT helps to extend life and provide hope. It does not cure AIDS and there are some serious difficulties with the drug. AZT or Retrovir (its brand name) must be taken every four hours both night and day. People often experience very uncomfortable side effects. These include nausea, headaches, anemia, lowered white blood cell counts, liver function changes, kidney effects and bone marrow damage. The longer the drug is taken, the more likely the person is to experience side effects with increasing severity. Additionally, the drug is very difficult to manufacture, involving seventeen chemical steps plus six more steps to make it marketable. The result is scarcity and high costs. Nonetheless, the existence of a drug which at least can delay the effects of such a devastating disease has provided hope and has fought the black curtain of pessimism which has shrouded AIDS.

Other drugs to combat the AIDS virus are being developed. In 1991, the Food and Drug Administration approved DDI (didanosine) for treatment of adults and children with advanced AIDS who cannot tolerate or are not helped by AZT (Scanlan, 1991).

The United States has historically been much slower than many other nations in allowing the widespread testing and use of new drugs.

In the coming years there is hope that doctors will be able to treat persons with the AIDS virus by sending bits of genetic material into the infected cells of the body, which will destroy the virus's lethal capacity to reproduce itself (Brownlee, 1992).

The best way to presently stop the spread of AIDS is through educating people to avoid exposing themselves to known risk behavior. In order to avoid getting the AIDS virus, C. Everett Koop (1987, p. 27) recommends:

> The most certain way to avoid getting the AIDS virus and to control the AIDS epidemic in the United States is for individuals to avoid promiscuous sexual practices, to maintain mutually faithful monogamous sexual relationships and to avoid injecting illicit drugs.

Impacts of Social and Economic Forces: AIDS Discrimination and Oppression

People who test positive to HIV or who have AIDS often are victimized by discrimination. Many Americans have a "them and us" mentality about those who test positive to HIV or who have AIDS. They want to have no contact with anyone who has HIV. They erroneously think casual social contact may put them at risk. As a result, those having the AIDS virus are apt to be shunned, risk losing their jobs, and often are abandoned by family, spouse, lovers, and friends. In some communities where it becomes public knowledge that a child has the AIDS virus, parents of other children have reacted by not allowing their children to attend the same school and by prohibiting their children from having any contact with the child who is HIV positive.

Patrick Haney (1988, p. 251), a person with AIDS, describes some of the negative aspects of being diagnosed as having the AIDS virus:

> Like no other illness since the advent of modern medicine, AIDS carries with it a stigma of shame and pointed finger of blame, suggesting those of us who are sick are at fault for being infected. This is a very negative impact of AIDS, yet it is also illogical. Do we blame Legionnaires for Legionnaires' disease, children for mumps, measles or chicken pox; the elderly for Alzheimer's disease or death, or epileptics for seizures? It makes no sense to blame anyone for AIDS. AIDS is caused by a virus, not by behavior or identity.

> Moreover, shame and blame can lead persons with AIDS into denial and hiding, which may cause potential avoidance of medical care, involvement in unsafe sexual activity, and a lack of support from a support system that doesn't know the person is HIV infected. This further isolates the person with AIDS and exacerbates feelings of aloneness and despair.

Professional Values and AIDS

Social work has traditionally supported and advocated for oppressed and disenfranchised groups in our country—African Americans, Hispanics, the poor, the elderly, gays and lesbians, and women. Social workers have an ethical obligation to combat the numerous injustices connected with AIDS. AIDS is not a gay disease or an intravenous drug users disease. It is a human disease.

Ethical Dilemmas: Confidentiality

The major social concerns and controversies encompassing AIDS are far too numerous for all to be addressed here. The focus will be on a select few. The intent is to provide a perspective for how massive and complicated the issues are.

A core concern and one that has many offshoots is that of confidentiality. Once a person has been positively diagnosed as having antibodies to HIV and is, therefore, contagious, who else should have access to this information? For instance, take Harvey who has just been positively diagnosed. He has been dating Chris steadily for about a year and a half. Although she is under the impression that the relationship is monogamous, Harvey has had approximately two dozen sexual encounters with other women since he and Chris first had intercourse. Harvey adamantly states that he does not want Chris to know about his other sexual experiences. Since Harvey is contagious, Chris is in a high risk group for developing AIDS. Should Chris be told about Harvey's test results?

When a Friend Has AIDS

While serious illness is a fact of everyday life, AIDS has posed new challenges for everyone involved: not only people with AIDS, but also their friends and loved ones. People who are young have become ill, and their hopes for a long life have been severely affected. Their situation is not an isolated one, but is shared by people close to them.

When someone you know becomes ill, especially with a serious illness like AIDS, you may feel helpless or useless. If this person has been a good friend you may say, "Just call if you need anything." Then out of fear or insecurity you may dread the call, if it comes. Here are some thoughts and suggestions that may help you to help someone who is very ill.

- Don't avoid your friend. Be there, it gives hope. Be the friend, the loved one you've always been, especially now when it is most important.
- Touch your friend. A simple squeeze of the hand or a hug can let him or her know that you still care. (Don't be afraid . . . you cannot contract AIDS by simply touching.)
- Call before you plan to visit. Your friend may not feel up to a visitor that day. Don't be afraid to call back and visit on another occasion. Your friend needs you, and may be lonely and afraid.
- Weep with your friend, and laugh with your friend. Don't be afraid to share these intimate experiences. They can enrich you both.
- Call and say you're bringing your friend's favorite dish. Be specific about what time you are coming. Bring the food in disposable containers, so your friend won't have to worry about washing dishes. Spend time sharing a meal.
- Take your friend for a walk or outing, but ask about and respect any limitations.
- Offer to help answer any letters or phone calls your friend is having difficulty dealing with.
- Call your friend and find out if anything is needed from the store. Ask for a shopping list and make a "special delivery."
- Help celebrate holidays—and life—with your friend by offering to decorate his or her home or hospital room.

Bring flowers or other special gifts. Include your friend in your holiday plans. A holiday doesn't have to be marked on a calendar; you can make any day a holiday.

- Check in with the people who are taking care of your friend. They may also be suffering. They may also need a break from the illness from time to time. Offer to stay with the person with AIDS in order to give the loved ones some free time. Invite them out. Offer to accompany them places. Remember, they may need someone to talk with as well.
- Your friend may be a parent. Ask about and offer to help care for any children. Offer to bring them to visit if they do not live with your friend.
- If there are young children living with your friend, offer to take them to, or pick them up from, day care or school. Ask if you can make them lunch or supper, or take them to the dentist, eye doctor, etc.
- Be creative. Bring books, magazines, taped music, a poster for a wall, home baked cookies or favorite foods to share. All of these become especially important now, and can bring warmth and joy.
- Bring along another old friend who perhaps hasn't yet been to visit.
- Don't be reluctant to ask about the illness. Your friend may need to talk about the condition. Find out by asking, "Do you feel like talking about it?"
- Like everyone else, a person with AIDS can have both good and bad days. On good days treat your friend the same as your other friends. On the bad days, however, treat your friend with extra care and compassion.
- Don't feel that you both always have to talk. It's okay to sit together silently reading, listening to music, watching television, holding hands. Much can be expressed without words.
- Can you take your friend somewhere? Transportation may be needed to a treatment, to the store or bank, to a doctor, or perhaps to a movie or community event. How about just a ride to the beach or the park?
- Appointments at Social Security or Medicaid can be exhausting and frustrating. Offer to accompany your friend and help fill out the forms. Stay with him or her until their business is finished.

- If your friend is a recovering alcoholic or drug user and is unable to get to a twelve-step program meeting, offer to call some other people in the program to arrange for them to come to his or her hospital room or home in order to have a meeting.

- If your friend is in outpatient treatment for drug addiction, he or she may need help getting to and from the treatment facility.

- Help your friend feel good about his or her looks if possible. If your friend's appearance has changed, don't ignore it. Acknowledge the fact. But be gentle.

- Include your friend in decision making. Illness can cause a loss of control over many aspects of life. Don't deny your friend a chance to make decisions, no matter how simple or silly they may seem to you.

- Tell your friend what you'd like to do to help. If your friend agrees, do this. Keep any promises you make.

- Be prepared for your friend to get angry with you for "no obvious reason," although you've been there and done everything you could. Permit this, and don't take it personally. Remember, anger and frustration are often taken out on the people most loved because it's safe and will be understood.

- What's in the news? Discuss current events. Help your friend from feeling that the world is passing him or her by. Keep your friend up to date on mutual friends and other common interests. Your friend may be tired of talking about symptoms, doctors and treatments. Take your cues from the person with AIDS.

- Offer to do household chores, perhaps taking out the laundry, washing dishes, watering plants, feeding and walking pets. This may be appreciated more than you realize. Don't take away chores that your friend can still do. He or she's already lost enough. Ask before doing anything.

- Send a card that says simply, "I care!"

- If you and your friend are religious, ask if you could pray together. Don't hesitate to share your faith with your friend. Spirituality can be very important at this time.

- Don't lecture or direct your anger at your friend if he or she seems to be handling the illness in a way that *you*

think is inappropriate. Your friend may not be where *you* expect or need him or her to be.

- Don't permit your friend to blame himself for his illness. Remind him that lifestyles don't cause disease, germs do. Help him through this one. It may be especially hard for him.

- If you and your friend are going to engage in sex, be informed about the precautions which make sex safer for both of you. Heed them! Be imaginative... touch, stroke, massage. Sex need not always be genital to be fun.

- A loving family member can be a source of strength. Remember that by being a friend or lover you are also part of the family.

- Do not confuse acceptance of the illness with defeat. This acceptance may free your friend and provide him or her with a sense of power.

- Don't allow the person with AIDS or their care-partner to become isolated. Let them know about the support groups and other concrete, practical services offered without charge by local AIDS service provider agencies, community organizations or hospitals.

- Talk with your friend about the future: tomorrow, next week, next year. It's good to look toward the future without denying the reality of today. Hope is important at this time.

- Bring a positive attitude. It's catching.

- Finally, take care of yourself! Recognize your own emotions and honor them. Share your grief, anger, feelings of hopelessness, or whatever is coming up for you, either individually with friends and loved ones or in a support group. Getting the support you need during this crisis will help you really be there for your friend.

This information is taken from the June 6, 1989, edition of a brochure written by Dixie Beckham, Diego Lopez, Luis Palacios-Jimenez, Vincent Patti, and Michael Shernoff. At the time this brochure was written, the authors all worked at Chelsea Psychotherapy Associates, a group practice of New York State Licensed social workers located at Suite 1305, 80 Eighth Avenue, NYC 10011. Copyright © 1984 Chelsea Psychotherapy Associates.

Should Harvey be forced to tell her and, if so, how can he be forced? Should Harvey's positive test results be reported to a public health agency? If results are reported, what if Shirley, an administrative assistant working for the agency who happens to know Chris and Harvey, sees the results? Should Shirley alert Chris? If Shirley tells Chris about the results, should Shirley be legally prosecuted for breaking confidentiality? Should Chris be forced to be tested so that she can take precautions from spreading the contagion? If Chris is forced, who will pay for the testing? Should she be required to pay? What about the other women with whom Harvey's had sexual contact? Should Harvey be required to tell them of his positive test results? If so, should they be required to be tested?

The dispute focuses on the individual's rights to confidentiality and privacy versus the rights of significant others to know about their vulnerability and possible condition. Few states have laws which specify when, if, and how social workers and others in the helping professions who become aware of an infected person and the potential harm to his or her intimate others should notify these other people at risk. Ryan and Rowe (1988, p. 328) suggest that "workers must continue to use their professional judgment in determining whether they should disclose this information to interested third parties by weighing failure to notify against the potential for harm." There are no easy answers.

The scenario of Harvey and Chris depicted earlier is really not so farfetched. One study by two California psychologists, Susan Cochran and Vickie Mays, resulted in some frightening conclusions (*Milwaukee Journal*, Aug. 14, 1988). The study's subjects included 422 Southern California men and women aged eighteen to twenty-five, all of whom indicated they were sexually active. Over one half of the women surveyed indicated that asking their partner questions about their past sexual encounters and about use of intravenous drugs was a major precaution they used to protect themselves from AIDS. Ironically, over one-half of the women felt that they had been lied to by men. Over one-third of the men surveyed indicated that they had indeed lied to a woman about their pasts (the researchers felt this finding was very conservative). Men indicated that typically lies would include exaggerating their positive feelings for a woman, leading a woman to believe that there were no other

existing relationships, and understating the number of past sexual contacts they really had. One other scary finding was that two-thirds of the men in higher risk categories (that is, having been sexually involved with other men or with persons who were intravenous drug users, having had a number of sexual partners, or having had a history of sexually transmitted diseases) did not use condoms. They felt it was the woman's responsibility to practice birth control.

In a University of California–San Francisco survey of people tested anonymously for infection with the AIDS virus, more than 25 percent said they did not intend to inform their sexual partners of a positive result (Goode, 1988).

Lise Van Susteren, a psychiatrist in private practice, describes her dilemma with a client who tested positive for HIV antibodies. Her client was "deeply disturbed" and yet continued to have numerous sexual partners (Van Susteren, 1989). He neither told his partners of his condition nor used any precautions such as condoms. He knew he was contagious and that the result of his behavior could be that people died. He had a stormy emotional history and had been in and out of mental hospitals. Lise Van Susteren was appalled at his behavior. She struggled with the issue of her patient's confidentiality. Finally, she had him voluntarily committed to a mental hospital and shared her concerns with the staff there. Despite knowledge of his condition, the client was discharged. Van Susteren approached many people for help including a magistrate, a judge, the U.S. District Attorney's office, and hospital staff. All was to no avail. None of them felt they could take the initiative and stop the man's destructive behavior. There were no directives for what could be done. Despite the fact that the client was hospitalized again at a later date, he was once again discharged. Van Susteren ends her story by lamenting that "no one has wanted to take a stand on this controversial issue." She raises the question, "How many people will suffer the consequences?"

Ethical Dilemmas: HIV Testing

An issue related to confidentiality is mandatory testing for antibodies to the AIDS virus. Who should be tested and what should be done with the results? At this point there are many other questions involved before these issues can be resolved. Should all health care officials be required to be tested? Should public employees? What about private industry? Should all university students be tested as a prerequisite for admission? If so, should students be required to pay for the testing as part of their tuition?

Ryan and Rowe (1988, p. 331) address the issue of HIV testing. They indicate that more and more states are requiring that people be informed of testing for communicable diseases including HIV before such testing actually occurs. They maintain that "an important precept for HIV testing is that it should be voluntary and free from coercion; in no instance should the provision of services be predicated on taking the test" (p. 331). There are many ramifications to testing. People have lost jobs, been thrown out of residences and schools, and been denied services that they desperately needed. For instance, some physicians and other health care professionals have refused to serve people with AIDS. Morticians have refused to prepare the bodies of persons with AIDS for burial. People with AIDS need to have their rights protected, including their right of free choice. Mandated testing does not guarantee protection from discrimination.

Sometimes people are tested without their knowledge. For example, one study indicates that only 10 percent of tests for HIV antibodies performed in a particular hospital during a period of more than a year were done with the patient's knowledge and consent (Henry, 1988).

An important issue is that of the distinction between "confidential" and "anonymous" testing. In confidential testing, the identity of the person being tested is recorded, although not made public. Questions have been raised with confidential testing regarding who has (or should have) access to a person's positive results—those having access may include secretaries in testing sites, the state's communicable disease center, the person's physician, and even insurance companies. With confidential testing there is a danger that those who have access to a positive test result for the tested person may then discriminate against the person. For example, an insurance company may seek to find an excuse to cancel a health or life insurance policy. Anonymous testing, on the other hand, involves no identification. An individual goes in for testing, uses a code word or number, and returns approximately two weeks later to receive testing results. Names are neither mentioned nor

recorded. A drawback of anonymous testing is that the state's communicable disease center is not informed of a positive test result for a tested individual and therefore is unable to contact and encourage past and present sexual partners of that person to be tested for HIV.

Ryan and Rowe (1988) continue that a body of law has begun to be established that extends the legal protection against discrimination (already available to those with a physical disability) to people with AIDS. However, most of these laws involve employment discrimination. Some involve housing. Fewer legal cases target the issues of "education, credit, and insurance." Therefore, people with AIDS are very often not protected from discrimination in these important parts of their lives.

Another controversial issue is that of home testing. It is possible to make testing packets available for home use. An individual could prick a finger for a blood sample, submit the sample by mail for anonymous testing, and then call the testing laboratory a week later to obtain results. Testing would be anonymous because code numbers could be used; no names would be involved. A positive thing about this is the maintenance of confidentiality. However, several problems are also involved. The accuracy of home testing has been questioned. Additionally, it is generally recommended that counseling is necessary both before and after testing because of the critical implications of the test result. Although some people maintain that counseling could be provided over the phone, this type of contact seems pretty weak in view of a positive test result and its impact on a person. People need to be prepared to receive a positive result and to know what to do and expect next. In view of a negative result, people need to examine their prior behaviors to decrease or minimize their risks.

Macro System Responses to AIDS

Health care costs involve another mammoth issue looming on the horizon. Being sick is expensive. Being very sick is very expensive. Many people who have AIDS have found their resources increasingly exhausted. People with AIDS tend to get sick very fast because of their immune system's vulnerability. If they have a job, sick days are easily used up. If they get too sick for too long, they lose their jobs. When they lose their jobs, they probably will also lose their health insurance. Any savings can be quickly used up in hospital, physician, and drug expenses. People then turn to overburdened public assistance and Medicaid systems for help.

Our health care system is not presently oriented toward treating people with conditions like AIDS. The system responds slowly and addresses itself to long-term, relatively predictable illnesses. For instance, a sixty-three-year-old man is diagnosed as having a prostate problem. (The prostate is a male organ which is the primary producer of semen; problems with the prostate gland become more and more common as men grow older.) This man experiences severe pain in the area of the prostate and goes in to see his physician. The physician diagnoses the problem as involving the prostate gland, prescribes medication to ease the pain, and refers the man to a specialist for surgery. The man contacts the specialist. The specialist replies that she would be happy to perform the surgery but is leaving for a three-week vacation in the Bahamas. She asks if the man would wait five weeks before the surgery is scheduled. In view of the facts that the man's pain has been relieved by the prescription drugs and that the prostate condition is one that is not critically dangerous, the man agrees to have the surgery five weeks later. The surgery to correct the problem is performed and the man takes the predicted six weeks for recovery. He continues to feel better and better and remains under the care of his physician. There has been plenty of time to schedule appointments, fill out insurance and hospital forms, and take care of himself.

This is anything but a typical scenario for a person with AIDS. A devastating disease like pneumocystis carinii pneumonia or Kaposi's sarcoma may strike with awesome force. The person with AIDS cannot afford five weeks or one week or even perhaps one day without immediate and sometimes extensive medical attention. There will be little or no time to fill out forms, make arrangements for complicated financing, or make any other extensive plans. Immediate action is often needed to avoid death. The health care system as it now exists finds it very difficult to respond in such an immediate fashion.

A related problem faced by people with AIDS is that often the health care system does not respond until whatever condition the person has is severe. There is an idea that care is expensive and it needn't be given until it's absolutely necessary. The problem with people who have AIDS is that diseases and conditions progress so rapidly that by the time the condition becomes severe enough, the person is on the brink of death.

Historically, a problem has been that HIV infected people could qualify for insurance, Social Security benefits, and other benefits only if they contracted any one of the increasingly growing list of specific diseases determined to characterize AIDS. In December 1992, the Bush administration issued new regulations that allow HIV positive people to receive Social Security benefits if they are unable to participate in "any substantial gainful activity"; they no longer have to wait until they contract one of the specific diseases on the AIDS list to get help (*Contemporary Sexuality*, Feb. 1992, p. 6). Qualifying for and receiving benefits has been a major problem for people with AIDS. (We will discuss the problem of macro system responsiveness in the form of health care later in this section.)

As of April 1992, people are considered to have full-blown AIDS if their normal, healthy, T-4 cell count falls below 200 per cubic milliliter; normal people have about 900 T-4 cells per cubic milliliter (Denney and Quadagno, 1992). HIV positive persons with T-4 cell counts under 200 no longer have to contract specific diseases in order to be classified as having AIDS and are often eligible for Social Security benefits.

Yet another issue concerning health care directly involves the providers of such care. A number of people in the health care professions either refuse to treat people with AIDS or treat them very differently than their other patients. For example, one medical attendant would talk to a person with AIDS only when wearing surgical clothing including gown, gloves, and mask. Under no circumstances would he touch or shake hands with a person having AIDS. How would such behavior make a person with AIDS feel? Such a person may already be feeling isolated and scourged. Such differential treatment could make anyone feel much like a leper must have felt in Biblical times.

Other health care issues involve nursing homes. Many such homes refuse to admit people with AIDS. Is this fair or right? What other alternatives are available to people with AIDS when their health is seriously fading and they need extensive care?

Solutions to the last two problems must involve educating people about AIDS and preparing them to work with people who have it. Health care professionals need to learn what is safe and what is not safe. They need to work on their own fears and personal conflicts. It is unlikely that making new laws and mandating to people how they must behave will not be enough.

In 1991, the American public was shocked when it was revealed that Florida resident Kimberly Bergalis had apparently contracted the AIDS virus from her dentist while receiving dental services. An extensive investigation led to the conclusion that four other dental patients also contracted the AIDS virus from the same dentist. Exactly how these patients became infected with the AIDS virus is unknown. Nationwide, there have been very few people who have contracted the AIDS virus from health care workers—such as dentists, physicians, or nurses. Because five patients are believed to have contracted the AIDS virus from the Florida dentist (who died from AIDS), some authorities have questioned whether this dentist intentionally engaged in dental procedures that put his patients at risk (Findlay, 1991). The risk of contracting the AIDS virus from infected health care workers is minimal. Findlay (1991, p.66) notes:

> Even if the doctor is infected, most procedures, such as a routine checkup or blood-pressure reading, put patients at no risk . . . Even in surgery, risk is minimal. Odds are between 1 in 42,000 and 1 in 417,000 of your picking up the virus from an infected surgeon who uses proper precautions, says the CDC [Centers for Disease Control]. In contrast, your chance of dying in a car accident this year is 1 in 5,300. . . . The CDC puts your chance of contracting HIV from an infected dentist at between 1 in 263,000 and 1 in 2,632,000.

The danger of patients becoming infected by health care workers has led the American Medical Association, the American Dental Association, and the Centers for Disease Control to recommend to health care workers who know they are infected to stop doing certain "at risk" procedures. The only time for concern is when a health care procedure exposes some of the patient's blood to the blood of an infected health care worker.

Actually, health care workers are at a greater risk of contracting the AIDS virus from infected patients, than vice versa. Drawing blood from an infected patient, for example, can result in an accidental needle prick to the health care worker, and perhaps transmission of the AIDS virus. Substantially more health care workers have contracted the AIDS virus from infected patients than patients have contracted the virus from health care workers (Findlay, 1991). The risk of transmission of the virus between health care workers and patients has raised a number of complex questions. When should patients be informed that one of their health care providers has the AIDS virus? Are there circumstances or medical conditions that would warrant health care workers being informed that a patient is HIV positive? Most patients and health care workers who are HIV positive are unaware they are infected. Are there circumstances or medical conditions for which HIV testing of either patients or health care workers should be mandated?

There are many other issues which have not even been mentioned here. There are opposing views regarding the conditions under which children with AIDS can go to school. Likewise, there are opposing views over whether free needles should be distributed to intravenous drug users. Will this procedure prevent them from sharing needles and thereby contracting AIDS or will it only encourage their antisocial drug abusing behavior? Another controversial issue is whether condoms should be distributed at no charge to adolescents at school. Proponents of distribution say it will help prevent the spread of AIDS, while opponents claim it promotes sexual promiscuity.

All of these matters merit serious attention and consideration. A picture of Japanese American citizens forced into concentration camps during World War II might flash before one's eyes. In those days irrational fear resulted in acts of discrimination against American citizens. Basic individual rights were violated. Those people who are unfortunate enough to contract this deadly disease deserve attention and compassion.

Social Work Roles: Helping Persons Living with AIDS

In regard to the role of social work in helping persons with AIDS, Lloyd (1990, p.13) notes:

Given the epidemiology and demography of HIV and AIDS, it is doubtful that social workers can practice anywhere without being directly or indirectly involved with people affected by HIV infection and AIDS. Therefore, all social workers should be knowledgeable about HIV transmission and prevention, capable of adapting practice methods to needs of those affected by HIV or AIDS, and committed to applying social work values to ensure that people are not discriminated against in the workplace, social service agencies, or health care facilities because of their HIV status.

Social workers have numerous roles to play in helping persons with AIDS and in preventing and/or reducing the transmission of HIV. Social workers practicing with people affected by AIDS should use the same professional skills they would use in working with any other group. Services provided by social workers include: testing and counseling people for HIV infection, educating the general public and high-risk groups to reduce risk behavior for HIV infection, assisting HIV-affected persons to remain active and productive, encouraging HIV-affected persons to reduce the risk of passing the infection on to others, and providing support and information to family and friends of persons with HIV. Services to persons with AIDS include information and education, crisis intervention, case management, facilitating support groups, facilitating therapy and bereavement groups, brokering needed services and resources, facilitating support networks, advocacy, and financial and legal assistance, linkage to Social Security entitlements, providing services to AIDS-specialized foster family homes, and finding living arrangements for homeless HIV infected babies.

Empowerment is a key concept for social workers helping persons with AIDS. Empowerment involves feeling good about ourselves and feeling that we have some control and direction over our lives. Empowerment is clearly related to hope.

Patrick Haney (1988), a person with AIDS, founded the first AIDS information and referral service in Palm Beach, Florida in 1984 and established a support network entitled Persons with AIDS Coalition. He reflected on the concept of empowerment and how vital it is for persons with AIDS. He spoke of how many physicians make two statements to people shortly after they receive their positive diagnosis. The first statement, "There's nothing we can do," and the second is, "You have x months to live" (p. 251). It would be difficult to think of something to say which would be more negative and depressing. These statements imply complete lack of control and direction over one's life and hopelessness for the future. Haney continues that "predictions about how long the person with AIDS has to live is simply a game of statistics and fortune-telling." It is true that most people with

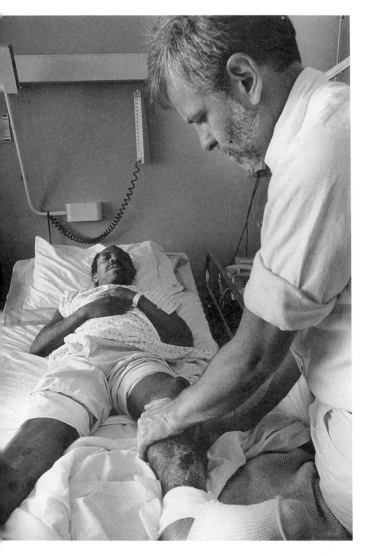

A volunteer massage therapist provides comfort and reassurance for a man with AIDS. Warm, physical contact is too often overlooked for patients in their last months of life.

AIDS die within two years of diagnosis. However, some people live significantly longer and continue to enjoy productive lives.

Dan Turner, now age forty, was first diagnosed as having AIDS in February 1982 when he discovered he had Kaposi's sarcoma (Moore, 1988). He was one of the first people in the San Francisco area to be positively diagnosed. He emphasizes living one day at a time, appreciating the positive things one can enjoy, and making positive plans for the future. After three years of counseling others, he enrolled in the Social Work program at San Francisco State University. He continues to think about things he wants to accomplish in the future. Upon completing his field placement in a mission where he counsels children, he plans to continue a career in counselling. Dan Turner provides an excellent example of someone who focuses on his personal empowerment and plans to lead a fruitful life for as long as he can.

Persons with AIDS should never be referred to as victims. Rather, they should be referred to as people *living with* AIDS, with an emphasis on living. The word *victim* implies helplessness, powerless, and lack of control. People with AIDS need to be viewed as people capable of empowerment, not as hopeless victims.

Hope should be maintained (U.S. Department of Health and Human Services, 1986). Many people with AIDS have years of living fruitful lives ahead of them. Much research and effort is being directed at combatting the disease. Some drugs (such as AZT and DDI) help to forestall the disease's progression for some people. New drugs are also being developed.

Moynihan, Christ, and Silver (1988) suggest that maintaining a meaningful quality of life is important for persons living with AIDS. Strengths should be emphasized. Part of this involves focusing on the positive instead of the negative aspects of life. Almost any situation in life can be looked at either positively or negatively. Take, for example, a couple who built a spacious new home with cathedral ceilings, which was just what they had always wanted. It had taken years of thrift and saving to build a home that was "just perfect." However, perfection was not to last. One morning they woke up and saw that there was a three foot long crack extending down from one of their beautiful "just perfect" skylights. With changes in the weather, they learned, walls typically shift in

homes with cathedral ceilings and cracks may result. Fixing the cracks wouldn't help either as it is a basic structural problem which caused the cracks. They would simply return with the passage of time. The man and the woman in the example each had a choice of how to think about the crack. The man chose to dwell on how awful the crack looked. Whenever visitors came, the first thing he did was show them the crack and complain about the construction company's incompetence. The woman, however, chose to ignore the crack and instead concentrated on all the other wonderful aspects of their brand new home—the spaciousness, the large picture windows, and how comfortable the home really was. You might guess who was the happier person of the two.

This story highlights the importance of focusing on the positive aspects of any particular situation. Something wrong can be found about virtually any situation. The winner of a $10,000 gift certificate from a major department store must pay thousands of dollars in taxes on the money before a cent can be "spent." Women who take pride in their long fingernails inevitably break one off. There is always something that one's boyfriend, girlfriend, or spouse doesn't do exactly as one wishes. Although these examples are silly when compared to the literal life or death situation encompassing AIDS, they still illustrate the point. People with AIDS need to work all the harder on identifying, concentrating on, and enjoying the day to day positive happenings in their lives.

Haney (1988) emphasizes that positives can come from any negative experience. Working through difficulties makes people stronger and wiser. He lists some of the positives which he has experienced since contracting AIDS. These include "learning to accept (his) limitations; learning to cope by getting in touch with (his) strengths, experiencing a clarity of purpose; learning to live one day at a time; learning to focus on the good in (his) life here and now; and the incredibly moving experience of having complete support from (his) family, friends, lover, people (he) hardly know(s), and sometimes even complete strangers" (p. 252).

Empowerment can come from reconnections (Haney, 1988). Having AIDS often results in people feeling isolated and disconnected from their old lives. Social workers can help people with AIDS to reconnect with other people. Support systems are essential. These can include families, friends, intimate others, or co-workers. Lines of communication need to be maintained. Of course, people with AIDS have strong feelings about their condition, but so do people close to them. Fear, guilt, anger, depression, hopelessness, feelings of abandonment, and many other emotions may be involved. Regardless of how people feel, it is crucial to bring these feelings out in the open so that significant others learn how to cope with them instead of hiding them and withdrawing from the person with AIDS.

The person living with AIDS should also be encouraged to express his or her feelings openly, even when they are negative. Suicidal thoughts and plans should be discussed openly and the potential for suicide assessed (see Chapter 7 for a more extensive discussion of how to assess and treat suicidal people). Additionally, sometimes medications to curb anxiety and depression are helpful.

Support groups provide another excellent means of enhancing empowerment. People can talk with others in similar situations. They need no longer feel so alone. They can see that there are other people who understand their concerns and feelings. Additionally, such groups provide excellent channels for gaining information on how others have worked out similar problems. A common social work role is that of facilitator of such groups. The acquisition of coping skills can help empower people with AIDS. Social workers can help to identify and emphasize coping skills used in the past.

It is important for people with AIDS to deal not only with life but also with death. Moynihan, Christ and Silver (1988) stress that people with AIDS need to learn how to cope with their fears of death (coping with death will be addressed in much greater detail later in Chapter 15). Spiritual issues may be involved. Helping people with AIDS discuss plans for what will happen after their death can be useful. In a way this may help them gain greater control. They may need to write up a will or make funeral arrangements. They may want to finish unsettled business or settle conflicts they have with others. A useful concept for working with people who are addressing death is the idea of making them the "star of their own death." In other words, instead of avoiding the issues which concern them because it makes us uncomfortable, rather emphasize that they have the right to make decisions and settle their affairs. Encourage them to

talk openly about these matters and have as much control over them as possible.

One specific aspect of AIDS which it is helpful for social workers to know about is the AIDS-dementia complex. It has already been pointed out that the symptoms of this complex, which is experienced by many people with AIDS, include forgetfulness, inability to concentrate, visuospatial problems, difficulties performing complex tasks, and slowed motor ability. Buckingham and Van Gorp (1988) present a number of implications for social work practice when dealing with AIDS-dementia. First, they suggest the use of a variety of environmental aids. Some aids, (such as reminder notes and calendars) can help to minimize the effects of forgetfulness. Living arrangements should allow easy access for people with motor impairments. Additionally, situations which would require quick thinking and decisions should be identified and avoided.

Second, structure can help people living with AIDS-dementia continue to function. A familiar environment and people available to help with daily tasks (such as giving medication and presenting meals) are important. These, too, help fight forgetfulness.

Third, the difference between initiation and motivation should be stressed. People living with AIDS-dementia often are motivated to complete a task but have trouble starting out. Once started, they can frequently carry it out themselves.

Fourth, people who help take care of those with AIDS-dementia should be well educated about what the condition involves. These helpers should know what the person is and is not capable of in order to have appropriate expectations.

Additional recommendations include having a clinical assessment for depression performed and providing psychotherapy in those cases where it would be useful. Legal contracts and estate planning should also be initiated before the dementia progresses to the point where these are no longer feasible.

Caputo (1985) suggests that the social work roles of educator, advocate, mediator, social broker, and enabler can all be applied to working with persons with AIDS. As an educator, the social worker can supply persons with AIDS and those close to them with information about the disease so that they are better prepared to cope with their situations. The

Persons Living with AIDS

The following are scenarios of people who have been diagnosed as having AIDS or as testing positive to HIV. In what ways could empowerment take place? In what ways could social workers be helpful? What laws and social policies would be helpful to them in their situations?

Mary has AIDS. She's thirty-eight years old and used to have a lucrative Milwaukee law practice. She had been dating Norm and having intercourse with him for a year and a half before he told her that he was bisexual, that he had tested positively for having AIDS antibodies, and that she had better get tested, too. She dropped him immediately. The first time she went in for a test, the results were negative. However, the physician told her to come in once again in three months just to be sure. The second time she tested positive. Her rage was almost uncontrollable. It wasn't fair! She didn't "sleep around!" She didn't use intravenous drugs! Now Mary rarely leaves her apartment. She's terrified of being vulnerable to the multitude of diseases running rampant among all of the people out there. She knows that people are much more dangerous to her than she to them. Her savings are declining. She can't afford to worry about the future.

Harry has been diagnosed positive for having AIDS antibodies in his system. Harry is only twenty-two and likes to party. He can hardly remember how many women he's had sexual intercourse with over the past two years. He's tall and handsome. Women have found him attractive as long as he can remember. He's always left the birth control responsibility to them. He thought they all must be on the pill anyway. He never thought of using a condom. He thought

AIDS was a gay disease. He found out it is not. He doesn't know if or when he'll actually come down with AIDS, but he does know he's potentially contagious. He's very scared.

Bill has AIDS. He's twenty-eight. He's been feeling very rundown for the past few months and finally went in to have the purple splotches of skin on his back checked. It is Kaposi's sarcoma. He's been together with Mike for almost three years, a relationship they've committed to as being permanent. However, before he met Mike, Bill dated a lot of men. He didn't think about such things as "safer sex" three years ago. He must've gotten AIDS from one of his many intimate partners. He wonders who. Now he's worried about Mike. They haven't been practicing "safer sex" either because they're monogamous. What if Mike has it, too? He truly loves Mike and prays that Mike is all right. Mike's going in for his test results tomorrow. Bill is very worried.

Tonya has AIDS. She's nineteen. She comes from a very poor side of town where living is tough. It seemed everybody was "into" using intravenous drugs. "Shooting up" was easy. Heroin let her escape. Needles were expensive so she shared them with her friends. Now she's very sick. She's in the hospital with some kind of strange pneumonia. This time deep down she doesn't think she'll ever make it home again.

Cheryl has AIDS. She's two months old. She got it from her mother who also has it. Cheryl's very weak now. She probably won't last very long.

advocate role allows the social worker to speak out on behalf of clients. A social worker can help clients to fight for their rights, especially in those cases where discrimination is occurring. As a mediator, the social worker may become a go-between between the person with AIDS and others with whom he's in conflict. For example, the client may have been shunned by his family or fired from his job. A social worker might help both sides better understand the concerns of the other and come to some mutually agreeable plan. The social workers as social broker can help the per-

son with AIDS come into contact with needed health, financial, and social support sources. Finally, as enabler, the social worker may help the client cope with his situation. A social worker can help the client to express his feelings, look closely at his relationships, and make plans to do the best he can with each day of his life.

The NASW *Practice Digest* (Spring, 1984) addresses the issue of helping gay people with AIDS and discusses the Gay Men's Health Crisis program in New York City, which was developed for this purpose.

It is an example of how persons with AIDS and those close to them can be helped. A wide variety of services are provided, many to social workers. After an extensive assessment interview, persons with AIDS are referred to the appropriate services. These may include legal assistance, financial aid, support groups, and recreational programming. Almost all persons with AIDS receive crisis counseling. Persons with AIDS suffer not only from the fact that they have contracted a deadly disease, but also as a result of attitudes of others who shun them, fire them, and evict them from apartments.

Summary

For many people, middle adulthood is the prime time—most middle-aged adults are in good health (both physically and psychologically) and tend to earn more money than at any other age. Middle adulthood covers a range of years; somewhat arbitrarily, the authors consider middle adulthood to range from age thirty to age sixty-five. Some decline in physical capacities occurs in middle adulthood. There is also a higher incidence of health problems than in younger years. Cognitive functioning may actually increase during middle adulthood. The sad fact is that many people fail to be sufficiently active both mentally and physically so that their actual performance *mentally* falls short of their potential performance.

Female menopause is the event in every woman's life when she stops menstruating and can no longer bear children. For a few women menopause is a serious crisis, but for many it is just another of life's developmental changes. It appears that many males reach an uncertain period in their lives which is referred to as a midlife crisis. The ease or panic with which a man faces his mid-years will depend on how he has accepted his weaknesses and strengths throughout life.

A man's sex drive reaches its peak in the early twenties, while that of a woman tends to peak in her thirties or early forties. There appears to be a close relationship between overall marital satisfaction and sexual satisfaction. Extramarital sex is usually reported as being less satisfying than marital sex.

AIDS is a contagious, presently incurable disease that destroys the body's immune system. AIDS is caused by the HIV virus. The two primary ways in which AIDS is now being spread are by sexual intercourse with someone who is HIV positive and by using hypodermic needles which were also used by someone who is HIV positive. Presently, the best way to stop the spread of AIDS is through educating people to avoid exposing themselves to known risks. People who test positive to HIV or who have AIDS often are additionally victimized by discrimination.

11

Psychological Systems and Their Impacts on Middle Adulthood

Games We Play

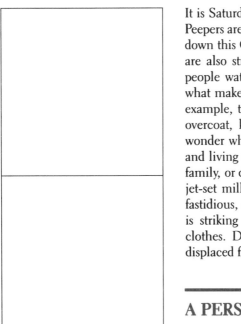

It is Saturday night on Michigan Avenue in Chicago, and Doug and Shirley Peepers are engaged in a favorite activity on a warm summer evening: strolling down this Gold Coast street and watching the thousands of other people who are also strolling and people watching. Americans have a fascination with people watching. While strolling, Doug and Shirley enjoy gossiping about what makes people tick; that is, discussing why people do what they do. For example, they look at the elderly bag lady dressed in a moth-eaten red plaid overcoat, knee-high nylon hose, and ancient, shaggy blue sneakers. They wonder what happened in her past that resulted in her now being homeless and living on the street? Is she the victim of some tragic story? Where is her family, or doesn't she have any? Likewise, Doug and Shirley look at the sleek, jet-set millionaire pulling up to the curb in his Maserati Biturbo so that a fastidious, uniformed doorman can help him out of the car. The millionaire is striking with his fashionable haircut, glowing gold jewelry, and Gucci clothes. Doug and Shirley wonder if he is a self-made computer magnate displaced from Silicon Valley, or if he's the product of generations of wealth.

A PERSPECTIVE

Figuring out the underlying reasons that cause others' actions often has substantial payoffs. If a salesperson knows what motivates people to buy a certain product, he or she can then structure the sales pitch around this focus. If a social worker knows why a father is abusing his child, the worker then knows what has to be changed to stop the abuse. If a mother knows what discipline techniques will be effective with her children, she is then better prepared to curb unwanted behavior in her children.

The primary focus of this human behavior and social environment text is to provide theoretical frameworks that will help the reader to observe and assess human behavior. The Systems Impact Model described in Chapter 1 provides a model for identifying a multitude of variables that influence human behavior.

Shirley Peepers is a computer programmer, and her husband, Doug, is a mechanical engineer. Although they have had little formal training in assessing human behavior, playing amateur psychologist is one of their favorite leisure time activities. As with anything else, assessments of human behavior are apt to be more accurate when one has greater knowledge and awareness of the significant cues to attend to. Professional social workers who will be planning interventions with people and organizations have a special need to develop their assessment skills. Middle adulthood provides as critical a stage as earlier developmental periods to examine some of the psychological dynamics of human behavior. Because there is a paucity of psychological theories specifically directed at middle adulthood, the primary focus of this chapter will be on describing contemporary theories and models for assessing human behavior throughout the life span.

This chapter will:

- Describe Erikson's (1963) and Peck's (1955) theories of psychological development during middle adulthood.
- Describe Levinson's (1978) theories of life structure, life eras, and transitions during adulthood.

Generativity versus Stagnation

Erikson's (1963) seventh life stage developmental crisis is generativity versus stagnation. Generativity involves a concern and interest in establishing and guiding the next generation. The crisis of generativity versus stagnation is perceived by a middle-aged adult to involve a commitment to improve the life conditions of future generations. The achievement of generativity involves a willingness to care about the people and the things that one has produced. It also involves a commitment to protecting and enhancing the conditions of one's society.

The achievement of generativity is important for the survival and development of any society. It involves having the adult members committing themselves to contributing their skills, resources, and creativity to improve the quality of life for the young.

The contributions may be monumental, as were Martin Luther King, Jr.'s, and Gandhi's to equality and human rights. For most people, however, the contributions are less well known—for example, the work done by volunteers for human service organizations. Adults serve on school boards, are active members of parent-teacher associations, serve on local government boards, are active in church activities, and so on. In each of these roles, adults have opportunities to positively influence the quality of life for others. To some extent it is a reciprocity situation—when these adults were younger they were recipients of such services from other adults; now they are providers of such services. In this regard, Newman and Newman (1984, p. 445) note:

> Adults serve as advisers, government leaders, religious leaders, and educators. In each of these roles, individuals have opportunities to extend the impact of their values and goals to others. Through their loving response to their children, through the care they take to perform their work at a high standard of excellence, and through their expressed respect for the diverse people they encounter, adults model a capacity for generativity that promotes optimism and perseverance among younger generations.

The opposite of generativity is stagnation. Stagnation indicates a lack of psychological movement or growth. Some adults are self-centered and seek to maximize their pleasures at the expense of others; such people are stagnated as they have difficulty in looking beyond their own needs or experiencing satisfaction in taking care of others. Having children does not necessarily guarantee generativity, as adults who are unable to cope with raising children or with maintaining a household are likely to feel a sense of stagnation. Burnout has been identified as being one of the signs of stagnation (Pines and Aronson, 1981).

Different individuals manifest stagnation in different ways. A narcissistic individual is egocentric, and generally relates to others in terms of how others can serve him. Such an individual may be fairly happy until the physical and psychological consequences of aging begin to occur. Such individuals often then experience an identity crisis when they realize their beautiful bodies and other physical attributes are waning. Many of these individuals experience a conversion to finding other meanings in living than a totally self-involved life-style. For example, they coach Little League teams or become active in church activities.

On the other hand, a depressed person is likely to perceive him- or herself as having insufficient resources to make any contribution to society. Such a person is apt to have low self-esteem, to be pessimistic about opportunities for improvement in the future and, therefore, to be unwilling to invest effort in self-improvement or in seeking to help others.

Peck's Theories of Psychological Development

Peck (1955) expanded Erikson's concepts by suggesting that there are four psychological advances critical to successful adjustment in middle adulthood:

1. Socializing versus sexualizing in human relationships. Peck suggests it is psychologically healthy for middle-age adults to redefine the men and women in their lives so that they value them as individuals, friends, and companions, rather than primarily as sex objects. (The women's movement and other groups have been advocating that all age groups should view people as being individuals worthy of respect, rather than as being sex objects.)
2. Valuing wisdom versus valuing physical powers. Peck views wisdom as the capacity to make wise choices in life. He suggests that well-adjusted middle-aged adults are aware that the wisdom they now have more than compensates for decreases in stamina, physical strength, and youthful attractiveness.
3. Cathectic flexibility versus cathectic impoverishment. Cathectic flexibility is the capacity to shift emotional investments from one activity to another, and from one person to another. Middle-aged adults are apt to experience breaking of relationships due to the deaths of friends, parents, and other relatives and the growing independence of children and their moving out of the home. Physical limitations may also necessitate a change in activities.
4. Mental flexibility versus mental rigidity. By middle age, most people have completed their formal years of education and have been sufficiently trained for their jobs or careers. They have also arrived at a set of beliefs about an afterlife, religion, politics, desirable forms of entertainment, and so on. Some middle-aged adults stop seeking new information and ideas and become set in their ways and closed to new ideas. Such people are apt to be stymied in their intellectual growth and are apt to view life as mundane, unfulfilling, and unrewarding. Others are apt to continue to seek new experiences and be challenged by additional learning opportunities. They use their prior experiences and answers they've already arrived at as provisional guides to the solution of new issues. Such people are likely to view life as being meaningful, rewarding, and challenging.

Levinson's Theories of Life Structure, Life Eras, and Transitions for Men

Levinson (1978) and his colleagues studied forty men aged thirty-five to forty-five who had the following careers and occupations: business executives, academic biologists, novelists, and hourly workers in industry. These men were interviewed and given personality tests. From this data, Levinson constructed some developmental theories of life changes in adulthood.

The concept of *life structure* is at the heart of Levinson's theory. This term is defined as "the underlying pattern or design of a person's life at a given time" (Levinson, 1986, p. 6). A person's life structure shapes and is shaped by the person's interactions with the environment. Components of the life structure include the people, institutions, things, places and causes that a person decides are most important, as well as the dreams, values, and emotions that make them so. Most people build their life structures around their work and their families. Other important aspects in one's life structure may include religion, racial identification, ethnic heritage, societal events (such as wars and economic depressions), favorite vacation spot, hobbies, and preferred types of music.

According to Levinson, life involves a number of passages: from the freedom of childhood to entering school, from school to the work world, from not dating to dating, from dating to breaking up or marrying, from marrying to divorce, and so on. Levinson sees some structure to these series of life passages. Levinson asserts that people shape their life structures during the following four overlapping eras (with each era being twenty to twenty-five years in length):

1. Preadulthood (birth to age twenty-two) is the formative time from conception to the end of adolescence.
2. Early adulthood (age seventeen to age forty-five) is the era in which people make choices that significantly influence their lives and it is the era in which people display the greatest energy and experience the most stress.
3. Middle adulthood (age forty to age sixty-five) is the era in which people tend to have reduced biological capacities but increased social responsibilities.
4. Late adulthood (age sixty and beyond) is the final phase of life.

There are transitional periods within some of these eras, and there are also transitional periods of about five years each which connect these eras. These transitional periods are graphically displayed in Figure 11.1. (All ages are approximate.)

During these transitional periods, men review the life structures they built and explore options for restructuring their lives. According to Levinson, people spend nearly half their adult lives in transition. These transitional periods are described in the following sections.

Early adult transition (ages seventeen to twenty-two). During this transition (which may take three to

FIGURE 11.1: Eras and Transitional Periods in Levinson's Theories of Adult Development (Males)

Eras	Transitions
1. Preadulthood (age 0 to 22)	Early adult transition (age 17 to 22)
2. Early adulthood (age 17 to 45)	Entry life structure for early adulthood (age 22 to 28) Age 30 transition (age 28 to 33) Culminating life structure for early adulthood (age 33 to 40) Midlife transition (age 40 to 45)
3. Middle adulthood (age 40 to 65)	Entry life structure for middle adulthood (age 45-50) Age 50 transition (age 50-55) Culminating life structure for middle adulthood (age 55 to 60) Late adult transition (age 60 to 65)
4. Late adulthood (age 60 and beyond)	

five years) men need to move from preadulthood into adulthood. A person moves out of his parents' home and becomes more financially and emotionally independent. Going to college or joining the military service serves as a transitional institutional situation between being a child in a family and reaching full adult status.

Entry life structure for early adulthood (ages twenty-two to twenty-eight). This phase has been called "Entering the Adult World." During this phase a young person becomes an adult and builds the entry life structure for early adulthood. Aspects of this phase often include: involvement with work which may lead to a career choice, intimate relationships with others which may lead to marriage and children, choosing a home, involvement with social and civic groups, and relationships with family and friends. Two important features of this phase are "dream" and "mentor." Men during this phase often have a dream of their future, which is usually viewed in terms of a career. The vision of becoming a highly successful corporate president or a famous writer spurs them on and energizes their work activities. A man's success during these apprenticeship years is strongly influenced by finding a mentor. A mentor is older (usually by about eight to fifteen years). The relationship with the mentor is a friendship with adult equality, but the mentor also performs the fatherly tasks of teaching, caring, criticizing, helping, and offering constructive suggestions in both career and personal matters.

Age thirty transition (ages twenty-eight to thirty-

three). During this phase men take another look at their lives. They may review whether the commitments made during the previous decade were premature, or they may consider making strong commitments for the first time. Some men move fairly effortlessly through this transition. Others experience crises in which they decide their present life structures are intolerable, yet they have grave difficulty in formulating better ones. Marriage conflicts may erupt during this phase, and divorce is common. Work responsibilities may shift as the man is promoted, changes jobs, or settles into his job after a period of uncertainty. Some men seek counseling to help clarify their goals.

Culminating life structure for early adulthood (ages thirty-three to forty). This phase is ushered in by a period of "settling down." The person makes a concerted effort to realize youthful dreams. The apprenticeship is over. Men during this phase make deeper commitments to family, work, and other important aspects of their lives. They set specific goals for themselves (such as a certain level of income and moving into their own house) with a set timetable. They work at formulating their niche in society, by anchoring their lives in terms of such aspects as career, family, and community involvement. They also work on advancing themselves to: build a better life, become more creative, improve their skills, and so on. In the middle to late thirties, toward the end of the settling-down period, comes a phase called "Becoming One's Own Man" (BOOM). During BOOM a man often becomes independent of his mentor and may be at odds with his wife, boss, children, friends, lover, or coworkers. During this phase a man chafes under the authority of those who have power and influence over him, and seeks to break away and speak with his own voice. However, he also fears a loss of respect from significant others during this time period.

Midlife Transition (ages forty to forty-five). This transition is focused on a person completing the work of early adulthood while learning the ropes of middle adulthood. Similar to all other transitional periods, this transition is both an ending and a beginning. During this period men (now more acutely aware of their mortality) question nearly every aspect of their lives. Most men find this is a time of moderate or severe crisis. Many men act irrationally during this period, which is related to the stresses they are experiencing. People in this stage undergo a midlife reappraisal that often involves emotional turmoil. Previous values are reviewed. Such a review is often healthy; through examining the choices that they made early

in life, they have the opportunity to focus on aspects of themselves that may have been neglected. Those who successfully negotiate this phase come to terms with the dreams of their youth and emerge with a more realistic view of themselves. Many men at this stage experience a midlife crisis that is described in Chapter 10. A man at midlife feels older than the younger generation, but is not yet ready to call himself middle-aged. A person at this age needs to integrate his need for separateness and his need for attachment to others. People at this age need to become "more compassionate, more reflective and judicious, less tyrannized by inner conflicts and external demands, and more genuinely loving of themselves and others" (Levinson, 1986, p. 5). People who fail in this task lead lives that become increasingly stagnant and trivial.

Entry life structure for middle adulthood (ages forty-five to fifty). During this transition a man in his mid-forties begins a life structure that may involve

Volunteers assemble playground equipment for an elementary school. According to Levinson, men in their late thirties and early forties are more likely to participate in community activities.

new choices: perhaps a new wife or a different way of relating to his wife, or perhaps a new career or a restructuring of his present work. The most successful people often find middle age to be the most gratifying and creative time of life as they utilize opportunities that arise to allow new facets of their personalities to flower. Those who are unsuccessful in resolving the tasks of midlife lead a constricted life or they keep busy in an organized but unfulfilling life-style.

Age fifty transition (ages fifty to fifty-five). This transition is likely to be an especially difficult time for men whose midlife transition has been relatively smooth. Most men experience a moderate crisis at this time. It is another time at which men review where they have come from, and make plans for where they are heading.

Culminating life structure for middle adulthood (ages fifty-five to sixty). This phase is generally a stable transition in which men finish the framework of their life structure for middle adulthood. During this phase those who are able to rejuvenate themselves enrich their lives. Generally, such individuals find the fifties a time period of great fulfillment.

Late adult transition (ages sixty to sixty-five). This is a major transitional turning point as it is a time for ending middle age and preparing for late adulthood.

It should be noted that Levinson primarily studied middle-aged men. As a result, he has only limited and speculative information of the transitions and adjustments that occur in late adulthood.

An important finding of Levinson is that life is a series of passages—from periods of stability to periods of instability. This cycle continues throughout life.

Application of Levinson's Theories to Women: An Evaluation

Although women were not subjects in Levinson's studies, he asserts that women go through similar kinds of age-linked changes as men. Papalia and Olds (1992, pp. 403-4) reviewed four unpublished dissertations describing studies using women subjects and Levinson's research design. The four investigators interviewed a total of thirty-nine women from twenty-eight to fifty-three years old. The women were primarily white, although eight respondents were African American. Most respondents were employed, but some were not. The studies had a mix of married and unmarried respondents, with and without children.

These studies tend, in general, to support Levinson's views that women undergo similar kinds of age-linked changes as men but identify some important differences. These differences are summarized as follows:

The Mentor: Women were substantially less likely to have a mentor. Many of the women identified role models during their twenties, but only four achieved a true mentor relationship. If these women's patterns are typical, many women may be hampered in their career pursuits for lack of a mentor.

The Love Relationship: Levinson found men want a "special woman" who helps them pursue their dreams. In the studies on women, all thirty-nine respondents sought a "special man," but these women mostly saw themselves as supporting their special man's dreams, rather than wanting a special man who would support them in achieving *their* goals.

The Dream: Most respondents had dreams (goals they wanted to achieve in life). But their dreams were more vague, more complex, more tentative and temporary, and less career oriented than those of men. Most women's dreams were split between achievement and relationships. Women were more likely to define themselves in relation to others—husbands, children, parents, or colleagues. While men tended to "find themselves" by separating from their families of origin and pursuing their own interests, women tend to develop their identity through the responsibilities and attachments of relationships.

While men dream of achievements in occupations or careers, women dream of a mix of family and career interests. Although many female respondents sought to help their "special man" achieve his goals, others began at about age thirty making greater demands on their husbands to accommodate their interests and goals in regard to career, marriage, and raising children.

Maslow's Hierarchy of Needs

Abraham Maslow (1954, 1968, 1971) viewed humans as having tremendous potential for personal development. He believed it was human nature for people to seek to know more about themselves and to strive to develop their capacities to the fullest. He viewed human nature as being basically good and saw the striving for *self-actualization* as a positive process as it leads people to identify their abilities, to strive to develop them, to feel good as they become themselves, and to be beneficial to society.

Maslow saw most people as being in a constant state of striving. Very few people fully attain a state of self-actualization. The vast majority of people are in a state of disequilibrium and are striving to satisfy their needs.

Maslow identified a hierarchy of needs which motivate human behavior. When people fulfill the most elemental needs, they strive to meet those on the next level, and so forth, until the highest order of needs is reached. In ascending order, these needs are:

1. Physiological: food, water, oxygen, rest, and so on.
2. Safety: security; stability; and freedom from fear, anxiety, threats, and chaos. A social structure of laws and limits assists in meeting these needs.
3. Belongingness and love: intimacy and affection provided by friends, family, and lover.
4. Self-esteem: self-respect, respect of others, achievement, attention, and appreciation.
5. Self-actualization: the sense that one is fulfilling one's potential and is doing what one is individually suited for and capable of. This need results in efforts to create and to learn. A fully developed, self-actualized person displays high levels of all of the following characteristics: acceptance of self, of others, and of nature; seeks justice, truth, order, unity, and beauty; has problem-solving abilities; is self-directed; has freshness of appreciation; has a richness of emotional responses; has satisfying and changing relationships with other people; is creative, and has a high sense of moral values.

Maslow's hierarchy of needs is illustrated in Figure 11.2. The needs at each level must be fairly well satisfied before the needs at the next level become important. Thus, physiological needs must be fairly well satisfied before safety needs become important, and so on. As applied to social work practice, Maslow's theory indicates social workers must first help clients meet basic needs (e.g., physiological needs). Once clients' basic needs are met, higher level needs can be dealt with.

Maslow did not offer an age-stage approach to development. Striving for self-actualization is seen as a universal process that can be observed at nearly all ages. However, it is likely that there is some progression among age groups. Infants probably have a strong

FIGURE 11.2: Maslow's Hierarchy of Needs

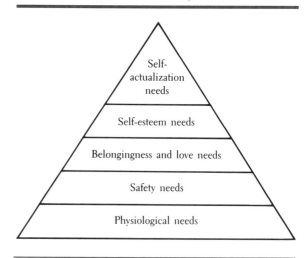

emphasis on physiological needs. As a person gradually grows older, safety needs are emphasized, and then belongingness and love needs, and so on. Since middle-aged adults have had a variety of learning experiences and tend to be at the peak of their earning potential, they tend to have a greater opportunity to focus on meeting self-actualization needs. However, such crises as unemployment, prolonged illness, and broken relationships can switch the emphasis to a lower area of need.

Game Analysis and Script Analysis

Analyzing human behavior in terms of games and scripts provides another useful theoretical framework for understanding and changing human behavior. Both game analysis and script analysis were developed by Eric Berne, who is recognized as being the founder of Transactional Analysis (TA), which is a psychotherapy approach. (See Dusay and Dusay, 1984, for a summary of TA.)

Game Analysis

A game (Berne, 1964) can be defined as a set of transactions with a gimmick (that is, a hidden scheme for attaining an end). In a game one or more participants are consciously or unconsciously striving to achieve an ulterior outcome by using a hidden scheme. For example, in the following exchange a salesperson uses a gimmick to sell the product:

> *Salesperson:* "This one is better, but you can't afford it."
> *Male Customer:* "That's the one I'll take."

The salesperson arouses the customer's pride by telling him that he is unable to afford the better, but more expensive item. Psychologically, the customer says to himself, "I'll buy the expensive item just to show that arrogant so-and-so that I'm as good as anyone."

People who are attempting to achieve a hidden outcome may or may not be aware of their intentions—or aware of the gimmick they are using. For instance, a husband who has a vague fear that his wife may desert him may not be aware he is playing a game when he says to her, "Honey, why don't you quit work and stay home to take care of the house? I can earn enough to support both of us." He may not be aware with his communication that he wants his wife to stay home so that she becomes financially dependent on him, and so that she has less opportunity to meet other men.

Although some games may lead to substantial financial loss or mental anguish for some participants, not all games are necessarily undesirable. For instance, an individual having a strong need for social approval may perform many altruistic and charitable deeds.

A game may also be repeated over and over. A few people, for instance, continually play "one-up." For some, playing a certain game may become so much a part of their personality that it can aptly be called their style of life. A male alcoholic who denies that he has a drinking problem is an example of this. (The alcoholic's payoffs for denying his drinking problem are the rewards he receives from drinking—such as feeling high and temporarily escaping facing his problems.)

The alcoholic game also illustrates another aspect of games—several people may be involved. In the alcoholic game described by Berne (1964), a nagging, masochistic wife drives her husband to drink so he will abuse her when inebriated. This wife receives two sets of payoffs. The abuse received is a form of

recognition or attention.[1] The second reward the wife receives is that the day after the drunken episode she has ammunition to belittle and berate her husband, and to get him to do things for her to atone for his behavior. The alcoholic is also apt to have companions who frequently say: "Let's go have a drink—a drink will be good for you." Their payoff is the fun and partying they have. Then there may also be a sympathetic listener to the alcoholic—perhaps a bartender who listens in order to get the alcoholic to spend his money. (Readers should note that Berne's description of the alcoholic game appears sexist as it tends to stereotype wives as being nagging and masochistic, and as receiving rewards for being victimized in a marriage in which they are being abused.)

Some people are involved in playing games that have destructive outcomes for themselves and for others. Often people are unaware that a destructive game is being played. For example, family members of an alcoholic may make elaborate efforts to keep the drinking problem hidden from others, without realizing they are continuing to make it possible for the alcoholic to drink.

Two levels of communication—social and psychological—are involved in games. The social level is the overt or manifested, and the psychological level is the covert or latent. Prochaska (1979, pp. 237-38) gives the following example of these two levels of communication in a game:

> For example, if a woman asks a man, "Why don't you come by my place to see my collection of sculpture?" and the man responds, "I'd love to. I'm really interested in art," they may be . . . communicating a message at a different level, such as . . . "Boy, I'd really like to get you alone in my apartment" and "I'd sure love to look at your curves."

For a game to progress, at least one of the participants has to pull a switch, as described in this example by Prochaska (1979, p. 238):

---

1. Transactional analysis makes an important psychological point by asserting that in the absence of receiving positive strokes, a person will seek negative strokes. Strokes are forms of human recognition. Positive strokes include greetings, smiles, approval, cheers, and applause. Negative strokes include cold looks, disapproval, criticism, and frowns.

For the payoff to occur, one of the players has to pull a switch. In this case, after fixing drinks and sitting close on the couch examining a reproduction of Rodin's The Kiss, the woman still seems to be sending a seductive communication. The man's vanity convinces him to proceed, and he puts his hand on her leg, only to be rebuffed by a slap on the face and an irate "What kind of woman do you think I am?"

The couple has just completed a heavy hand of RAPO.[2] Besides gaining mutual recognition, excitement, and some structured time together, there is also a strong emotional payoff for each. The woman is able to proudly affirm her position in life that she is OK, while feeling angry toward men for not being OK, just as her mother always said. The payoff for the man is to feel depressed and thereby reaffirm his conviction that he is not OK.

Examples of Games

Eric Berne (1964) lists a large number of psychological games in *Games People Play*. People tend to have a repertoire of favorite games they play; many people base their social relationships on finding suitable partners to play the corresponding opposite roles. The following are common games played by people.

In the game, "Why don't you? Yes, but . . . ," a person consistently asks for suggestions or advice, and then consistently rejects any that is offered. The other participants in this game assume that the principal player is attempting to solve a real problem in a concrete manner, so they offer suggestions. The principal player in this game is able to get at least two payoffs—one is attention from other people, and the other is a payoff that comes from being able to put others down by implying "That's really a dumb suggestion." The other participants may get a payoff through telling themselves "I must be a warm, caring person as this person respects and trusts me enough to share this problem with me."

In the "One-up" game, one person seeks to top whatever someone else says. If the conversation is about big fish, the one-upper always has a story about how he caught this mammoth fish. If the topic is about bad grades received, the one-upper seeks to amaze everyone with how bad his or her grades are. If jokes are being told, the one-upper begins by saying, "I've got one that'll top that. Have you heard about . . ."

"Wooden leg" is a game in which people attempt to manipulate others to not expect too much from them because of such wooden legs as having a physical handicap, being raised in a ghetto, having had a tragic romance, having emotional problems such as being depressed, and so on. Closely related, "If it weren't for . . ." is a cop-out game in which players seek to rationalize not succeeding at tasks and goals.

A person who plays "Poor me" is seeking sympathy and may at times try to get others to do things for him or her. Closely related is someone who plays "Ain't it awful" by taking a negative view of events. Such a person is usually seeking attention and sympathy. In the game "There I go again," the player seeks to excuse away his or her ineffective behavior without taking responsibility.

Some clients enjoy playing "Confession" where they seek to tell all their personal and interpersonal troubles in the hope of receiving recognition and help from others. Some unhappily married men get together and enjoy discussing "Wives are a pain" as a way of ventilating their unhappiness. Some unhappily married wives enjoy discussing "Men aren't worth it" as a way of ventilating their frustrations. Parents enjoy discussing "Look how hard I've tried" when a home situation is particularly uproarious and hostile as a way to relieve their frustrations that the goals for their family have not been achieved. Many people seek to avoid assuming responsibility for their failures and shortcomings by placing the blame on others and playing "It's all them."

Some individuals who have received few positive strokes end up seeking a lot of negative strokes, which to them is better than receiving no strokes. One game that is played to receive negative strokes is "Kick me" in which the player seeks to do things which will elicit negative reactions from others.

People who enjoy creating trouble for others are apt to play "Let's you and him/her fight," with the payoff being the spectator pleasure they receive in watching others tangle.

People who receive psychological rewards in analyzing others and in giving advice often play "Psychiatry." A person who seeks to see how many different sexual relationships he or she can have often seeks to play "Love 'em and leave 'em." Traditionally, men in our society have been socialized to play "Mr. Macho" and women "Miss America."

---

2. Eric Berne defines RAPO in its milder forms as "Kiss Off" or "indignation."

"Monday morning quarterbacks" seek to make themselves feel important by telling you what you should have done differently after things have not turned out well for you.

The number of different games that can be played is best described as infinite. Only a few of the more typical ones have been summarized here.

Application of Game Analysis to Practice

Game analysis can be defined as a treatment technique in which a counselor enables clients to gain insight into some of their interactions through the use of game concepts. The kinds of games which are the main focus of game analysis are those which lead to undesirable outcomes for clients.

The social worker's role in analyzing games is to teach clients the terminology of game analysis. This perhaps can best be accomplished on the first occasion in which a worker helps a client to gain insight into a game. The social worker needs to point out to the clients that playing games is not necessarily undesirable. This may be therapeutically valuable as some clients may feel it is wrong to play games because games have an exploitative connotation. Such a feeling may cause resistances to examining games. These resistances may be reduced by informing clients that everyone plays games, with some games having beneficial outcomes, while others have undesirable outcomes. Social workers must help clients recognize those games which are destructive for them or for other players and also enable them to gain insight into how these games are being played. Clients should be encouraged to explore new ways of responding after they are aware of how their role in a game leads to undesirable consequences. Clients need help in assigning specific names to those undesirable games they are playing. Using colloquial names for games is often acceptable and advantageous as they may be more precise and have more meaning for clients. Social workers can teach people the kind of games they need to play in order to achieve their goals. Some people have goals considered beneficial for themselves and society, but do not know what they have to do to achieve these goals. Often such people can be instructed in ways to use game concepts. For example, a person seeking a job may need to learn to play "How to get an interview," and "How to sell yourself in an interview." Or, a couple who is frequently feuding

Game concepts may be helpful in learning job interviewing skills.

may need to learn "How to fight fairly" and "How to get what you want in a relationship through giving."

There are three reasons why game analysis appears to be a useful therapeutic approach: (1) One of the important functional values of naming something (in this case a certain kind of game) is that it increases clients' capacities to identify when similar transactions are occurring in the future. Once clients recognize and have insight into a game which is causing them difficulty, they are in a better position to cease their destructive behavior and to explore alternative modes of behavior. (2) Analyzing behavior in terms of games is apt to be intriguing to clients and, therefore, may lead to greater personal involvement in therapy and increase their motivation to resolve their difficulties. (3) Game analysis provides clients with a method of analyzing certain problematic interactions. After learning how to analyze such interactions, clients should be better able to analyze other problematic games beyond those specifically discussed in counseling.

Life Scripts

Every person has life scripts (plans) that are formed during childhood and are based on early beliefs about oneself and others. These plans are developed from early interactions with parents and others and are largely determined by the pattern of strokes that are received.

Many details of a life script are supplied by parental opinions, suggestions, and encouragements: Examples include "She's such a cute girl, everyone loves her," "He's stupid and will never amount to much," "He'll be famous some day," "He's sure nutty," "All the girls will want to date him." Fairy tales, myths, TV shows, early life experiences, and children's stories are also important sources of life scripts. While parental influences and fairy tales are important contributing factors, the life script is still the creation of a young child. One's life script may be either winning or losing, success or failure, exciting or dull. Each script also includes specific roles, such as heroes and heroines, villains and victims, and so on.

Harris (1969) theorizes that each person chooses one of four general life scripts in regard to how he or she views him- or herself in comparison with others. These four scripts are (1) I'm OK—You're OK, (2) I'm OK—You're not OK, (3) I'm not OK—You're OK, and (4) I'm not OK—You're not OK.

People who decide "I'm OK—You're OK" tend to be productive, law abiding people who are successful and who have positive, meaningful relationships with others.

People who decide "I'm OK—You're not OK" predispose themselves to exploit others, cheat others, rob others, or succeed at the expense of others. This type of person may be a criminal, a ruthless business executive, or a destructive lover who loves them and leaves them.

People who decide "I'm not OK—You're OK" feel inferior in the presence of those they judge as superior. Such a life script frequently leads to withdrawal from others as a way to avoid being reminded of not being OK. Withdrawal is not the only alternative. The person can write a counterscript based on lines borrowed from early authority figures: "I can be OK if. . . ." The person is then driven to achieve the "if" contingencies. Examples of such contingencies include: making huge sums of money, being submissive, and being entertaining by making others laugh. Such a person strives to meet these contingencies in order to receive approval from others.

People who decide "I'm not OK—You're not OK" tend to be the most unhappy and disturbed. Prochaska (1979, p. 241) states:

The extreme withdrawal of schizophrenia or psychotic depression is their most common fate. They may regress to an infantile state in the primitive hope that they may once again receive the strokes of being held and fed. Without intervention from caring others, these individuals will live out a self-destructive life of institutionalization, irreversible alcoholism, senseless homicide, or suicide.

Decisions about life scripts are generally made early in childhood. James and Jongeward (1971, pp. 84-85) provide an incident in the life of a client, forty-three, that led her to conclude "I'm not OK, and men are not OK either."

My father was a brutal alcoholic. When he was drunk he would hit me and scream at me. I would try to hide. One day when he came home, the door flew open and he was drunker than usual. He picked up a butcher knife and started running through the house. I hid in a coat closet. I was almost four years old. I was so scared in the closet. It was dark and spooky, and things kept hitting me in the face. That day I decided who men were—beasts, who would only try to hurt me. I was a large child and I remember thinking, "If I were smaller, he'd love me" or "If I were prettier, he'd love me." I always thought I wasn't worth anything.

Based on this script, she married an alcoholic at age twenty-three and for the next twenty years lived her life drama of feeling worthless and living with a "beast."

Scripts (as in a play in a theater) are plans which we learn and then carry around in our heads. These scripts enable us to conceptualize where we are in our activities, and are plans for directing what we need to do to complete our activities, and to accomplish our goals. Scripts are also devices for helping us to remember what we have done in the past.

One area in which our behavior is largely guided by scripts is sexual behavior. Sexual scripts result from elaborate prior learning of an etiquette of sexual behavior. Scripts tell us who are appropriate sexual partners, what sexual activity is expected, where and when the sexual activity should occur, and what should be the sequence of the different sexual behaviors.

Scripts vary greatly from one culture to another. Powdermaker (1933, pp. 276-77) provides the following description of a script about female masturbation that is generally held by the Lesu of the South Pacific:

A woman will masturbate if she is sexually excited and there is no man to satisfy her. A couple may be having intercourse in the same house, or near enough for her to see them, and she may thus become aroused. She then sits down and bends her right leg so that her heel presses against her genitalia. Even young girls of about six years may do this quite casually as they sit on the ground. The women and men talk about it freely, and there is no shame attached to it. It is a customary position for women to take, and they learn it in childhood. They never use their hands for manipulation.

A life script and a theatrical script have many similarities. Each has a cast of characters, dialogue, themes and plots, acts and scenes, and generally both move towards a climax. Often, however, a person is unaware or only vaguely aware of the life scripts he or she is acting out. Public stages on which people act out their scripts include home, social gatherings, church, school, office, and factory. As Shakespeare wrote, "All the world's a stage."

As children grow they learn to play roles—villains, law enforcers, heroes, heroines, victims, and rescuers—and seek others to play complementary roles. Through playing roles, children integrate new themes and parts into their roles and gradually develop their life scripts. The particular scripts that are developed are substantially influenced by the reactions they receive from significant people in their lives.

Cultural Scripts and Family Scripts

Individuals follow scripts and so do families and cultures. Cultural scripts are expected patterns of behavior within a society. In regard to cultural scripts, James and Jongeward (1971, p. 70) note:

Script themes differ from one culture to another. The script can contain themes of suffering, persecution, and hardship (historically the Jews); it can contain themes of building empires and making conquests (as the Romans once did). Throughout history some nations have acted from a "top-dog" position of the conqueror; some from an "underdog" position of the conquered. In early America, where people came to escape oppression, to exploit the situation, and to explore the unknown, a basic theme was "struggling for survival." In many cases this struggle was acted out by pioneering and settling.

Women in our society have been socialized to have different life scripts than men. American women traditionally were expected to be affectionate, passive, conforming, sensitive, intuitive, dependent, and "sugar and spice and everything nice." They are supposed to be primarily concerned with domestic life, to be nurturing, to instinctively love to care for babies and young children, to be deeply concerned about their personal appearance, and to be self-sacrificing for their family. They should not appear to be ambitious, aggressive, competitive, or more intelligent than men. They are expected to be ignorant of and uninterested in sports, economics, or politics. In relationships with men they should not initiate forming the relationships. Additionally, women are expected to be tender, feminine, emotional, and appreciative. These traditional scripts for women are changing in our society; these changes are largely a result of the women's rights movement.

Males also have a number of traditional gender role expectations in our society. A male is expected to be tough, fearless, logical, self-reliant, independent, and aggressive. He should have definite opinions on the major issues of the day and is expected to make authoritative decisions at work and at home. He is expected to be strong, to never be depressed, vulnerable, or anxious. He is not supposed to be a sissy, or feminine. He is expected not to cry or openly display emotions. He is expected to be the provider and to be competent in all situations. He is supposed to be physically strong, self-reliant, athletic, to have a manly air of confidence and toughness, to be daring and aggressive, to be brave and forceful, to always be in a position to dominate any situation. He is supposed to initiate relationships with women and is expected to be dominant in relationships with them.

The women's movement is initiating changes in these gender role scripts. The ultimate result would be to take pressure off both men and women to conform to rigid gender role stereotypes. Each individual, either male or female, would then be free to develop the personality characteristics and strengths naturally fitting that person. (Gender role stereotypes are discussed in Chapter 9.)

In our society (as well as in other large and complex societies) there are a number of subcultures, and each subculture has its own scripts. Street gangs, dentists, and college students, to name only a few of the subcultures, have their own subcultural scripts. For example, common aspects of scripts for college

Families have scripts which provide directions for the behavior of each family member.

students include cramming at the last moment for exams, procrastination, partying, idealism, shortage of money, and expectation of success, happiness, and money following graduation.

Families also have scripts. These scripts provide a set of directions for family members. Examples include:

We Winships have always been pillars of the community.
We Navarres have always been rowdy.
We Hubbards have always been in trouble with the police.
We Schomakers have always been gamblers.
We Hepps have never had to ask for a handout from anyone.
We Rices have always been Democrats.

If a family member does not live up to the script expectation, he or she is often viewed as a deviant. The importance of scripts in determining human behavior is emphasized by Berne (1966, p. 310):

Nearly all human activity is programmed by an ongoing script dating from early childhood, so that the feeling of autonomy is nearly always an illusion—an illusion which is the greatest affliction of the human race because it makes awareness, honesty, creativity, and intimacy possible for only a few fortunate individuals. For the rest of humanity, other people are seen mainly as objects to be manipulated. They must be invited, persuaded, seduced, bribed or forced into playing the proper roles to reinforce the protagonist's position and fulfill his script.

There are an infinite number of script themes. A few of the more common themes are the following:

I must be loved by everyone.
I've got to be perfect.
My purpose in life is to save sinners.
People will only love me if I make them laugh.
My life will always be one big party.
I'm cut out to be a leader.
I'll never get anywhere.
I will never let anyone get the best of me.
I'm headed for fame and fortune.

James and Jongeward (1971, pp. 84-85) provide the following example of how a life script is played:

. . . a woman, who had taken the position "Men are bums," marries a sequence of bums. Part of her script is based on "Men are not OK." She fulfills her own prophecy by nagging, pushing, complaining, and generally making life miserable for her husband (who has his part to play). Eventually, she manipulates him into leaving. Then she can say, "See, I told you. Men are bums who leave you when the going gets rough."

Often people play games as part of their life scripts. A person who has a script of being a Casanova plays the game "Love 'em and leave 'em." A person who has a script of "I won't let anyone get the best of me" is apt to play "One up." A person who has a script of "I'll always find a way to seduce people into helping me" is apt to play "Poor me."

Application of Script Analysis to Practice

Script analysis can be defined as a treatment technique in which a counselor enables clients to gain insight into the scripts they are acting out through the use of script concepts. The types of scripts which are the primary focus of script analysis are those which lead to undesirable outcomes for clients or for others.

The counselor's role in analyzing scripts is to: (1) teach clients the terminology of script analysis; (2) point out to clients that everyone is playing a variety of scripts, and that scripts largely determine human behavior (they need to indicate that some scripts have beneficial outcomes, while others have undesirable outcomes); (3) help clients to recognize those scripts which have undesirable outcomes; (4) help clients to assign names to the scripts they are playing so that they can be more readily identified when they are being acted out in the future; and (5) help clients develop new, desirable scripts to act out and encourage and teach clients more effective ways of responding in the future.

Mezzo System Interactions: Nonverbal Communication

In seeking to assess human behavior, it is important to attend to nonverbal communication. Sigmund Freud (1981, p. 253) noted, "He that has eyes to see and ears to hear may convince himself that no mortal can keep a secret. If his lips are silent, he chatters with his finger tips; betrayal oozes out of him at every pore."

It is impossible not to communicate. No matter what we do, we transmit information about ourselves. Even an expressionless face communicates messages. As you are reading this, stop for a minute and analyze what nonverbal messages you would be sending if someone were observing you. Are your eyes wide open or half closed? Is your posture relaxed or tense? What are your facial expressions communicating? Are you occasionally gesturing? Do you occasionally roll your eyes? What would an observer deduce you are now feeling from these nonverbal cues?

At times nonverbal cues (such as sweating, stammering, blushing, and frowning) convey information about feelings that we desire to hide. Through developing our skills in reading nonverbal communication, we will be more aware of what others are feeling and be better able to interact effectively. Since feelings stem from thoughts, nonverbal cues such as blushing also transmit information about what people are thinking.

In literature, perhaps the greatest reader of nonverbal cues was Sherlock Holmes. In the following ex-

change Holmes (Doyle, 1974) makes certain deductions about his friend and colleague Watson:

> "How do I know that you have been getting yourself very wet lately, and that you have a most clumsy and careless servant girl?" . . . "It is simplicity itself," said he; "my eyes tell me that on the inside of your left shoe, just where the firelight strikes it, the leather is scarred by six almost parallel cuts. Obviously they have been caused by someone who has very carelessly scraped round the edges of the sole in order to remove crusted mud from it. Hence, you see, my double deduction that you had been out in vile weather, and that you had a particularly malignant boot-slitting specimen of the London slavey."

The Functions of Nonverbal Communication

Nonverbal communication interacts with verbal communication. Nonverbal communication has the following functions in relation to verbal communication:

1. Nonverbal messages may *repeat* what is said verbally. A husband may say he is really looking forward to becoming a father and repeat this happy anticipation with glowing facial expressions.
2. Nonverbal messages may *substitute* for verbal ones. If a close friend has just failed an important exam, you can get a fairly good idea what he or she is thinking and feeling by looking at the facial expressions.
3. Nonverbal messages may *accent* verbal messages. If someone you are dating says he or she is angry and upset with something you did, the depth of these feelings may be emphasized by pounding a fist and pointing an accusing finger.
4. Nonverbal messages may serve to *regulate* verbal behavior. Looking away from someone who is talking to you is a way of sending a message that you are not interested in talking.
5. Nonverbal messages may *contradict* verbal messages. An example of such a double message is someone with a red face, bulging veins, and a frown on the face, yelling, "Angry! Hell no, what makes you think I'm upset?" When nonverbal messages contradict verbal messages, the nonverbal messages are often more accurate. When receivers perceive a contradiction between nonverbal and verbal messages, they usually believe the nonverbal. (Adler and Towne, 1981, p. 257)

While nonverbal messages can be very revealing, they can also be unintentionally misleading. Think of the times when people have misinterpreted your non-verbal messages. Perhaps you tend to say little when you first wake up, and others have interpreted this as meaning that you are preoccupied with a personal concern. Perhaps you have been quiet on a date because you are tired or because you're thinking about something that has recently happened. Has your date at times misinterpreted such quietness to mean you are bored or unhappy with the relationship? When you have been thinking deeply on a subject, have you had an expression on your face that others have interpreted as being a frown? Nonverbal behavior is often difficult to interpret. A frown on the face, for example, may represent a variety of feelings: being tired or angry, or feeling rejected, confused, unhappy, irritated, disgusted, bored, or simply lost in thought. Nonverbal messages should not be interpreted as facts but as clues that need to be checked out verbally to determine what the sender is thinking and feeling.

The remainder of this section will examine some examples of how we communicate nonverbally through posture, body orientation, gestures, touching, clothes, personal space, territoriality, facial expressions, eye movements, voice, physical appearance, and the environment.

Many of these examples are taken from white middle-class American nonverbal communication. Nonverbal communication is strongly culture based. In other words, the identical nonverbal behavior may be interpreted differently depending on the cultural/ethnic/racial background of the observer. For example, a comfortable interpersonal distance may be six inches in some cultures and six feet in others. Awareness of these differences is especially critical when communicating with clients of different cultural/ethnic/racial backgrounds. Such awareness is the only thing that makes accurate understanding possible. To illustrate, direct eye contact by a social worker is usually considered desirable by white clients but is considered rude and intimidating by many Native Americans. Kissing between adult males is usually interpreted as indicating a homosexual relationship in our culture, but such kissing is a greeting custom in some European cultures. Adult males who wear skirts in our culture are viewed as weird, but kilts (knee-length pleated skirts) are commonly worn by men in Scotland and by Scottish regiments in the British armies.

Posture

In picking up nonverbal cues from posture, one needs to note the overall posture of a person and the changes in posture. We tend to take relaxed postures in nonthreatening situations and to tighten up when under stress. Some people never relax, and their rigid posture shows it.

Watching the degree of tenseness has been found to be a way of detecting status differences. In interactions between a higher status person and a lower status person, the higher status person is usually more relaxed, while the lower-status person is usually more rigid and tense (Mehrabian, 1981). For example, note the positions that are usually assumed when a faculty member and a student are conversing in the faculty member's office.

Teachers and public speakers often watch the posture of listeners to gauge how the presentation is going. If members in the audience are leaning forward in their chairs, it is a sign that the presentation is going over well. The audience slumping in their chairs is a cue that the presentation is beginning to bomb.

An indication of how posture communicates is the large number of verbal phrases which use posture as a metaphor:

> "He is able to stand on his own two feet."
> "She won't take that lying down."
> "She's got a lot of backbone."
> "Stand tall."

Body Orientation

Body orientation is the extent to which we face toward or away from someone with our head, body, and feet. Facing directly towards someone signals an interest in starting or continuing a conversation, while facing away signals a desire to end or avoid conversation. The phrase "turning your back" on someone concisely summarizes the message that is sent when you turn away from someone. Can you remember the last time someone signaled that they wanted to end a conversation with you by turning away from you?

Gestures

Most of us are aware that our facial expressions convey our feelings. When we want to hide our true feelings, we concentrate on controlling our facial expressions. We are less aware that our gestures also reveal our feelings, and, therefore, we put less effort into controlling our gestures when we want to cover up our feelings. As a result, our gestures are sometimes better indicators of how we really feel.

People who are nervous tend to fidget. They may bite their fingernails, tap their fingers, rub their eyes or other parts of their body, bend paperclips, or tap a pencil. They may cross and uncross their legs. They may rhythmically swing one leg or move one foot back and forth.

Many gestures provide cues to a person's thoughts and feelings. Clenched fists, whitened knuckles, and pointing fingers signal anger. When people want to express friendship or attraction, they tend to move closer. Hugs can represent a variety of feelings: physical attraction, good to see you, best wishes in the future, and friendship. Shaking hands is a signal of friendship and a way of saying "Hello" or "Goodbye."

Albert Scheflen (1974) notes that a person's sexual feelings can be signaled through gestures. He describes preening behavior, which is designed to send a message that the sender is attracted to the receiver. Preening behavior includes rearranging one's clothing, combing or stroking one's hair, and glancing in a mirror. Scheflen cites a number of invitational preening gestures that are specific to women: exposing or stroking a thigh, protruding the breast, placing a hand on the hip, and exhibiting a wrist or palm. Naturally these gestures do not always suggest sexual interest, as they may occur for a variety of other reasons. (It is interesting to note that comparable research has not been conducted on males. Conducting this research only on women may indicate a sexist bias.)

Gestures are also used in relation to verbal messages for a variety of purposes: repeating, substituting, accenting, contradicting, and regulating. Some people literally speak with their hands, arms, and head movements. Many people are unaware of the number of gestures they use, and then (if videotaped) are surprised to view the extent to which they communicate with gestures.

Touching

Rene Spitz (1945) has demonstrated that young children need direct physical contact, such as being cud-

---

Nonverbal Behavior among Poker Players

Oswald Jacoby has noted that poker players use nonverbal messages extensively. He has divided poker players into three classes: (1) ingenuous players, (2) tricky players, and (3) unreadable players.

Ingenuous players. These players are usually beginning players who possess few skills. When they look worried, they probably are. When they have a mediocre hand, they take a long time to bet. When they like their hand, they bet quickly. When they dislike their hand, they frown and scowl and look like bad luck has bit them. When they bluff, they look a little guilty. When they have a really good hand they immediately seek to raise the bet. This ingenuousness is seldom found in veteran players. Ingenuous players reveal their hands by their body language. Players of this type usually quit poker at an early stage because they generally lose.

Tricky players. Most poker players fall into this category. Tricky players act opposite of the way they really feel. When they have a poor hand they exude confidence, and when they have a good hand they tremble a little and look nervous as they bet. Sometimes they do a triple cross by acting the way they feel their hand is.

Unreadable players. Unreadable players have no consistency. They will randomly exude confidence or look nervous, and such nonverbal messages will give no clue to the nature of their hand. Unreadable players are excellent players.

SOURCE: Oswald Jacoby, *Oswald Jacoby on Poker* (New York: Doubleday, 1974).

---

dled, held, and soothed. Without such direct physical contact, the emotional, social, intellectual, and physical development of children will be severely stunted. Spitz observed that in the nineteenth century high proportions of children died in some orphanages and other child care institutions. The deaths were not found to be due to poor nutrition or inadequate medical care, but instead to lack of physical contact with parents or nurses. From this research came the practice of nurturing children in institutions—picking the baby up, holding her close, playing with her, and carrying her around several times a day. With this physical contact, the infant mortality rate dropped sharply in institutions.

Ashley Montagu (1971) describes findings which suggest that eczema, allergies, and certain other medical problems are in part caused by a person's lack of physical contact with a parent during infancy. Physical stimulation of children will facilitate their intellectual, social, emotional, and physical development.

Adults also need physical contact. People need to know that they are loved, recognized, and appreciated. Touching (through holding hands, hugging, pats on the back) are ways of communicating warmth and caring. Unfortunately, we have been socialized to refrain from touching, except in sexual contacts.

Our language is a mirror of our culture. Common phrases suggest that more importance is placed on the senses of sight and hearing than on touch:

"Seeing is believing."
"It's good to see you again."
"It's really good to hear from you."
"I've got my eye on you."

We have coined few phrases that include words for touch. For example, when leaving someone we say "See you again soon" rather than "Touch you again soon." If we should say the latter, it would be apt to be interpreted as having sexual connotations.

Touching someone is in fact an excellent way of conveying a variety of messages, depending on the context. A hug at a funeral will connote caring, while a hug when meeting someone connotes "It's good to see you." A hug between parent and child conveys "I love you," while a hug on a date may have sexual meanings. A number of therapists have noted that communication and human relationships would be vastly improved if people reached out and touched others more—with hugs, squeezes of the hand, kisses, and pats on the back. Touch is crucial for the survival and development of children, and touch is just as crucial for adults to assure them that they are worthwhile and loved.

Clothing

Clothes keep us warm, protect us from catching colds and other illnesses, and cover certain areas of our body so we are not arrested for indecency. But clothes have many other functions. Certain uniforms tell us what a person does and who we can receive services from: for example, uniforms of police officers, fire fighters, nurses, physicians, and waiters. The way we dress sends signals about sexuality. People intentionally and unintentionally send messages about themselves by what they wear. Clothes give messages about our occupations, personality, interests, groups we identify with, social philosophies, religious beliefs, status, values, mood, age, nationality, and personal attitudes. For example, the way an instructor dresses sends messages to the class as to the kind of atmosphere he or she is seeking to create.

There are numerous "wardrobe engineers" (tailors, manufacturers, and sellers of clothes) who assert that we can better obtain what we want by improving our selection of clothes. There is truth to the phrase "Clothes make a person."

The importance of clothes in determining judgments that people make about strangers was demonstrated in a study of Hoult (1954, pp. 324-28). Hoult began by having 254 students rate the photos of male strangers on such things as "best looking," "most likely to succeed," "most intelligent," "most like to date or double date with," and "best personality." For these photos, Hoult obtained independent ratings of clothes and the models' heads. Hoult then placed high-ranked outfits on models with low-ranked heads. Lower-ranked clothing was placed on models with higher-ranked heads. He found through a reranking that higher-ranked clothing was associated with an increase in rank, while lower-ranked clothing was associated with loss of rank.

Any given item of clothing can convey several different meanings. For example, the tie a man selects to wear may reflect sophistication or nonconformity. In addition, the way the tie is worn (loosened, tightly knotted, thrown over one's shoulder, soiled and wrinkled) may provide additional information about the wearer.

A problem often encountered by women is that they lack a socially dictated business uniform. Men wear ties and suits in bland, dark colors. Women interested in developing professional and business careers are still seeking clothing which will convey the best impression. Often they must choose between masculine-looking, unattractive, bland clothing and clothing which is more colorful and aesthetically attractive.

Clothes also affect our self-image. If we feel we are well dressed in a situation, we are apt to be more self-confident, assertive, and outgoing. If we feel we are ill dressed in a situation, we are apt to feel more reserved, less confident, and be less assertive. When we're feeling at a low tide, dressing up will make us feel better about ourselves and raise our spirits.

There is a real danger of misreading nonverbal messages. We often stereotype others on skimpy information, and frequently our interpretations are in error—which may lead to serious adverse consequences. One of the authors remembers a client he interviewed in a correctional facility who for the previous four years had lived in an elegant fashion, traveled all over Europe and North America, and stayed in the finest hotels. He financed this life-style by writing bad checks. He stated that whenever he needed money, he would carefully dress in an expensive suit and would have no trouble cashing his bogus checks.

Personal Space

We dislike uncomfortable crowding and other perceived invasions of our personal space. We can sometimes tell how people are feeling toward each other by noting the distance between them. Each of us carries around a kind of invisible bubble of personal space wherever we go. The area inside this bubble is perceived as our private territory. The only people we are comfortable in allowing to enter our private territory are those we are emotionally close to. We feel we are being invaded when strangers and people we are not emotionally close to enter our private territory.

Edward Hall (1969) has identified four distances or zones that we set in our daily interactions. We use these distances to guide us in setting the type of interactions we want to have with others. The particular zone we choose depends on the context of the conversation, how we feel toward the other person, and what our interpersonal goals are. These zones include the intimate zone, the personal zone, the social zone, and the public zone.

Intimate Zone

This zone begins with skin surface and goes out about 18 inches. We generally let only people we are emotionally very close to enter this boundary, and then mostly in private situations—comforting, conveying caring, making love, and showing love and affection. When we voluntarily let and want someone to enter this zone, it is a sign of trust. We lower our defenses. Think about the dates you have. If the person moves within this zone and sits tight against you, it is a signal that he or she is comfortable with the relationship and may want it to progress further. On the other hand, if the person seeks to maintain a safe distance of 2 or more feet, the person is still sorting out the relationship or wants a more distant relationship.

When someone moves into this intimate zone without our wanting them to, we feel invaded and threatened. Our posture becomes more upright, and our muscles tense. We may move back, and avoid eye contact, as a way of signaling we want a more distant relationship. When we are forced to get close to strangers (on crowded buses and elevators), we tend to avoid eye contact and try not to touch others, probably as a way of conveying, "I'm sorry I'm forced to invade your territory. I'll try not to bother you."

Personal Zone

This zone ranges from about 18 inches to approximately 4 feet. This is the distance at which couples

The personal zone ranges from about 18 inches to 4 feet. Couples in public usually maintain this distance.

stand in public. Interestingly, if someone of the opposite sex at a party stands this close to someone we are dating or are married to, we tend to become suspicious of that person's intentions. Also, if we see our spouse or date move this close to someone of the opposite sex at a party, we also may become suspicious and sometimes jealous.

The far range of the personal zone (from about 2½ to 4 feet) is the distance in which we convey that we are seeking to keep the other person at arm's length. It is the distance just beyond the other person's reach. Interactions at this distance may still be reasonably close, but they are much less personal than the ones that occur at a closer distance. Sometimes the communication at an arm's length distance represents a testing out by people regarding whether they want the relationship to become emotionally closer.

Social Zone

This zone ranges from about 4 feet to about 12 feet. Business communications are frequently exchanged in this zone. The closer part of this zone (from 4 to about 7 feet) is the distance at which people who work together usually converse, and it is the distance at which salespeople and customers usually interact.

Hall (1969) indicates that the 7 to 12 foot range is the distance for more impersonal and formal situations. For example, this is the distance at which our boss talks to us from behind his or her desk. If we were to pull our chair around to the boss's side of the desk in order to sit closer, a very different kind of relationship would be signaled. The way furniture is arranged and the kind of plants and wall hangings that people have in their office convey signals about their values and interests, and the type of relationship they want to have. For example, an office in which the office-holder has a desk between the customer/client/student suggests that a formal and impersonal interaction is being sought. An office in which a desk is not used as a barrier, or one that has plants, suggests that a warmer, less formal interaction is being sought.

Public Zone

This zone runs outward from 12 feet. Teachers and public speakers often use a distance of 12 to 18 feet from their audience. In the farther distances of public space (beyond 25 feet) two-way communication is very difficult. Any speaker who voluntarily chooses to have considerable distance from the audience is not interested in having a dialog.

Territoriality

Territoriality is behavior characterized by identification with an area in such a way as to indicate ownership and defense of this territory against those who may invade it (Knapp, 1978, p. 115). Many animals will strike back against much larger organisms if they feel their territory is being invaded.

Territoriality also exists in humans. There are things we feel we own that we really do not own. Students tend in each class to select a certain seat to sit in. If someone else should happen to sit in your chosen seat, do you feel your ownership rights are being violated and that you are being invaded? Clearly, the college/university owns the chairs—not you.

What we acquire as property is a strong indicator of our interests and values. The things we acquire are often topics of conversation—cars, homes, leisure-time equipment, plants, clothes. The material things we acquire also communicate messages about our status. Wealthy people acquire more property. Interestingly, we generally grant more personal space and greater privacy to people of higher status. For example, we will knock at the boss's office and wait for an invitation to walk in before entering. With people of a status similar to ours or of a lower status, we frequently walk right in.

Facial Expressions

For most people, the face and eyes are the primary sources of nonverbal communication. Facial expressions often are mirrors that reflect our thoughts and feelings. Yet, facial expressions are a complex source of information for several reasons. First, facial expressions can change rapidly. Slow motion films have found that a fleeting expression can come and go in as short a time as a fifth of a second (Adler and Towne, 1981, p. 266). In addition, researchers have found that there are at least eight distinguishable positions of the eyes and lids, at least eight positions for the eyebrows and forehead, and at least ten for the lower face (Adler and Towne, 1981, p. 266). Multiplying these different combinations together leads to several hundred different possible combinations. Therefore, compiling a directory of facial expressions and their corresponding emotions is almost impossible.

Ekman and Friesen (1975) have identified six basic emotions that facial expressions reflect—fear, surprise, anger, happiness, disgust, and sadness. These expressions appear to be recognizable in all cultures. People seeing photos of these expressions are quite accurate in identifying these emotions. Therefore, although facial expressions are complex, these six emotions can fairly accurately be identified.

A word of caution should be noted about reading facial expressions. Because people are generally aware that their facial expressions reflect what they are feeling and thinking, they may seek to mask their facial expressions for a variety of reasons. For example, a person who is angry and doesn't want others to see the anger, may seek to hide this feeling by smiling. Therefore, in reading facial expressions we should be aware that the sender may be seeking to conceal his or her real thoughts and feelings.

The eyes are also great communicators. When we want to end a conversation, or avoid a conversation, we look away from the other person's eyes. When we want to start a conversation we often seek out the other's eyes. We may wait until the receiver looks at us as a signal to begin.

The eyes also communicate dominance and submission. When a high status person and a low status person are looking at each other, the low status person tends to look away first. Downcast eyes signal submission or giving in. (Downcast eyes may also signal sadness, boredom, or fatigue.)

Good salespeople are aware that eyes are a sign of involvement. They seek to catch our eye. When they know they have caught our eye, they begin their pitch and seek to maintain eye contact. They know there are social norms in our society such as the courtesy of hearing what a person has to say once we allow the person to begin speaking. These social norms trap us into hearing the sales pitch once eye contact has been made. Good salespeople watch eyes in a store in another way. They observe what items we are most looking at, and then seek to emphasize those items in their sales pitch.

The importance of eyes in communicating is reflected in common phrases:

"He could look right through you."
"He's got shifty eyes."
"Did you see the gleam in her eye?"
"His eyes shot daggers across the room."

Eye expressions suggest a wide range of human emotions. Wide open eyes suggest wonder, terror, frankness, or naiveté. Raised upper eyelids may mean displeasure. A constant stare connotes coldness. Eyes rolled upward suggest another's behavior is unusual or weird.

When we become emotionally aroused or interested in something, the pupils of our eyes dilate. Some counselors are sufficiently skilled in reading pupil dilation that they can tell when they touch on a subject that a client is sensitive about.

E. H. Hess and J. M. Polt (1960, pp. 349-50) measured the amount of pupil dilation while showing men and women various kinds of pictures. The greater the subject's interest in the picture, the larger the eyes dilated. Women's eyes dilated an average of 20 percent when looking at pictures of nude men. Men's eyes dilated an average of 18 percent when looking at pictures of nude women. Surprisingly, the greatest increase in pupil size occurred when women looked at a picture of an infant and a mother.

Voice

The same word or phrase may have many meanings. Therefore, the way we say the word is the meaning we give to the word. For example, Knapp (1978, p. 323) shows how the meaning of the following sentence is changed by the word which is emphasized.

> *He's* giving this money to Herbie. (HE is the one giving the money; nobody else.)
> He's *giving* this money to Herbie. (He is GIVING, not lending the money.)
> He's giving *this* money to Herbie. (The money being exchanged is not from another fund or source; it is THIS money.)
> He's giving this *money* to Herbie. (MONEY is the unit of exchange, not a check or wampum.)
> He's giving this money to *Herbie*. (The recipient is HERBIE, not Eric or Bill or Rod.)

When we ask a question, we usually raise our voice at the end of the sentence. When we make a declarative statement, we usually lower our voice at the end of the sentence. Sometimes we intentionally manipulate our voice to contradict the verbal message.

In addition to emphasizing certain words in a sentence, our voice can communicate in many other ways. These ways include length of pauses, tone, pitch, speed, volume, and disfluencies (such as stammering or saying "uh," "um," and "er"). All of these factors together have been called *paralanguage.* Paralanguage deals with how something is said and not with what is said (Trager, 1958).

Using paralanguage we can communicate the exact opposite of what the verbal message is. You might practice through changing your voice how you would seek to convey literally, and then sarcastically, messages such as:

"I really like you."
"I'm having a perfectly wonderful time."
"You're really terrific."

Albert Mehrabian (1981) has found that when the paralanguage and the verbal message are contradictory, the former will carry more meaning. When there is a contradiction between words and the way something is said, subjects usually interpret the message in terms of the way it is said.

An excellent way to learn more about the way you are using paralanguage is to videotape one of your conversations or speeches, and then watch the replay. Such a process will also give you valuable feedback about your other forms of nonverbal communication.

Physical Appearance

While it is common to hear people say that only inner beauty really counts, research shows that outer beauty (physical attractiveness) plays an influential role in determining responses for a broad range of interpersonal interactions. Singer (1964) found that college professors tended to give higher grades to females who were physically attractive than to those who were less attractive. Mills and Aronson (1965) found that attractive females were more effective in modifying the attitudes of male students on national issues than were less attractive females.

Widgery and Webster (1969) found that attractive persons, regardless of sex, are rated high on credibil-

ity. If attractive people are rated high initially on credibility, it greatly increases their ultimate persuasiveness in a variety of areas—sales, public speaking, counseling, and so on.

Unattractive defendants are more likely to be judged guilty in courtrooms and more likely to receive longer sentences (Solender and Solender, 1976). The evidence is clear that *initially* we respond much more favorably to those perceived as physically attractive than those seen as less attractive. Attractiveness serves to open doors and create greater opportunities.

Physically attractive people have been found to outstrip less attractive people on a wide range of socially desirable evaluations, including personality, popularity, success, sociability, persuasiveness, sexuality, and often happiness (Knapp, 1978, p. 156). For example, attractive women are more apt to be helped and less likely to be the objects of aggressive acts (Berscheid and Walster, 1974). Less attractive people are at a disadvantage from early childhood on. Teachers, for example, interact less (and less positively) with unattractive children (Algozzine, 1976). Physical attractiveness is also a crucial factor in determining who we decide to date and who we decide to marry. In many situations practically everyone prefers the most attractive date regardless of her or his own attractiveness and regardless of being rejected by the most attractive date (Knapp, 1978, p. 159).

Unattractive men who are seen with attractive women are judged higher in a number of areas than are attractive men who are seen with attractive partners (Bar-Tal and Saxe, 1976). They are judged as making more money, as being more successful in their occupation, and as being more intelligent. Apparently, the evaluators reasoned that unattractive males must have to offset this imbalance by succeeding in other areas to be able to obtain dates with attractive women.

Being physically attractive does *not* mean that a person will be more intelligent, more successful, better adjusted, and happier than less attractive people. Attractiveness *initially* opens more opportunities to be successful, but after a door is opened, it is performance that determines outcome.

The shape of our body suggests certain stereotypes that may or may not be accurate. People who are overweight are judged to be older, more old-fashioned, less strong physically, more talkative, less good looking, more agreeable and good natured, more sympathetic, more trusting of others, more dependent on others, and more warm-hearted and sympathetic. People who are muscular are rated as being stronger, better-looking, younger, more adventurous, more self-reliant, more mature in behavior, and more masculine.

People with a thin physique are rated as younger, more suspicious of others, more tense and nervous, less masculine, more pessimistic, quieter, more stubborn, and more inclined to be difficult (Parnell, 1958). Overweight people and very thin people have been found to be discriminated against when seeking to obtain jobs, obtain life insurance, adopt children, and receive entrance into college (Knapp, 1978, p. 166). Being tall is a strong advantage in the business world for men but not for women. Shorter men are shortchanged on salaries and job opportunities (Knapp, 1978, p. 167).

We have considerable capacity to improve our physical appearance. Dieting, exercising, learning to manage stress, learning to be assertive, getting adequate sleep, improving grooming habits, and improving choice of clothes will substantially improve our physical appearance. Improving our physical appearance will open more doors and create more opportunities.

The Environment

Perhaps all of us have been in immaculate homes that have "un-living rooms" with furniture coverings, plastic lamp coverings, and spotless ashtrays that send nonverbal messages of: do not get me dirty, do not touch, do not put your feet up, and stay alert to avoid a mistake. In such homes we are not able to relax. Owners of such homes wonder why guests cannot relax and have a good time. They are unaware that the environment is communicating messages which lead guests to feel uncomfortable.

A study by Maslow and Mintz (1956) found that the attractiveness of a room shapes the kind of communication that takes place and also influences the happiness and energy of people working in it. The researchers used an unattractive room that looked like a janitor's closet and a beautiful room that was furnished with curtains, carpeting, and comfortable furniture. Subjects were required to rate a series of pictures in regard to the energy level and the feelings of well-being that the pictures conveyed. When sub-

jects were in the ugly room, they became tired and bored sooner and took longer to complete their task. They described the room as producing fatigue, headaches, monotony, and irritability. When the subjects moved to the beautiful room, they displayed a greater desire to work, they rated the pictures they were judging higher, and they communicated many more feelings of comfort, importance, and enjoyment. This experiment provides evidence supporting the common sense notion that workers do a better job and generally feel better when they are in an attractive environment.

The color of rooms apparently affects mood and productivity. Mehrabian found that children who were tested on an I.Q. test scored about 12 points higher in rooms they described as being beautiful in contrast to rooms they described as having ugly colors (Mehrabian, 1976). Blue, orange, yellow, and yellow-green were considered beautiful colors; black, brown, and white were considered ugly. The beautiful rooms appeared to stimulate alertness and creativity. Friendly words and smiles increased in the beautiful rooms, while irritability and hostility decreased. Mehrabian says the most pleasant colors are, in order, blue, green, purple, red, and yellow. The most arousing colors are, in order, red, orange, yellow, violet, blue, and green. The pastel colors of pink, baby blue, and peach are thought to have a calming effect. Some prisons and jails are now painting cells in pastel colors, hoping that it will have a calming and relaxing effect on inmates.

Businesses have found that they can control the rate of customer turnover by environmental design. Dim lighting, comfortable seats, and subdued noise levels will encourage customers to talk more and spend more time in a bar or restaurant (Sommer, 1969). If the goal is to run a high-volume business (as in a fast food place) businesses can encourage customer turnover by bright lights, uncomfortable seats, and high noise levels (for example, by having poor sound-proofing). Chairs can be constructed to be comfortable, or to be uncomfortable by putting pressure on the sitter's back. Airports seek to get travelers into the restaurants and bars where they will spend money by having comfortable chairs, tables where people can converse, and dim lighting. They discourage travelers from sitting in waiting areas by bright lighting, and by having uncomfortable chairs bolted shoulder to shoulder in rows facing outward which make conversation and relaxation next to impossible.

Casino owners in Las Vegas have built their facilities without windows or clocks so that customers will be less aware of how long they have been gambling. The aim is to keep people gambling as long as possible. Without windows, some customers are unaware that they are gambling into the next day.

The shape and design of buildings affect interaction patterns in many ways. In apartment buildings people who live near stairways and mailboxes have more contact with neighbors than those who live in less heavily traveled parts of the building. Access to neighbors increases communication. Fences, rows of trees, and long driveways increase privacy.

Wall decorations, types of furniture, and placement of furniture in offices convey messages as to whether the officeholder wants informal, relaxed communications, or wants formal, to-the-point communications. A round table, for example, suggests the officeholder is seeking to have the communication be seen as equalitarian, while a rectangular table suggests the communication should recognize status and power differentials. With a rectangular table, the high-status people generally sit at one end of the table. If the meeting is between sides of equal strength, one side tends to sit at one end, and the other at the other end, rather than intermingling the members. A classroom in which the chairs are in a circle suggests the instructor wants to create an informal, discussion atmosphere. A classroom with the chairs in rows suggests the instructor wants to create a formal, lecture-type atmosphere.

Control Theory

William Glasser (1984) has developed a control theory explanation of human behavior. A major thrust of the theory is that we have pictures in our heads of what reality is like, and pictures of how we would like the world to be. Glasser (1984, p. 32) asserts that "all our behavior is our constant attempt to reduce the difference between what we want (the pictures in our heads) and what we have (the way we see situations in the world)."

An example may illustrate the process. Keith Fitzpatrick (age thirty-seven) has been dating Sonja Noddelson (age thirty-eight) off and on for three and one-half months. Keith was divorced nineteen months ago; Sonja has never been married. Gradually Keith discovers he is becoming more and more attached to Sonja. He develops a picture of them making a commitment to each other and perhaps getting married in a year or two. This picture motivates him one night when they are having dinner to inform her that he increasingly feels attracted to her, and he asks how she views their relationship. Sonja indicates that she enjoys being with him, but also wants her independence. She adds she is occasionally dating others. Keith's reaction to the last statement is to feel "crushed" as he realizes there is a wide discrepancy between the way he wants their relationship to be and what Sonja wants out of the relationship. After several moments of small talk, Keith gradually regains his composure. He concludes that he will try a variety of strategies to entice Sonja into making a commitment to him.

In the next few weeks Keith wines and dines Sonja. He also unobtrusively observes what she likes and dislikes. He tries to present himself in the way that he thinks she likes. For example, she mentions she detests men who drink and smoke to excess. So he cuts down on his drinking when he is with her and also announces to her he has given up smoking. He discovers she likes theatrical plays, so (even though he dislikes such plays) he buys tickets and takes her to some plays and then tells her that he really loves going to them.

When Sonja mentions she has had a date with someone else, he feels hurt and jealous. In an attempt to also make her feel jealous, he then asks someone else on a date. Afterwards, he informs Sonja that the date really went well (even though it didn't).

Keith also shows his interest in her by sending her cards and flowers. Three weeks later, when he asks her to go with him to Thanksgiving dinner at his parents' house, she indicates she thinks that will give the wrong impression as she does not at this time want to make a commitment to anyone. At this point Keith feels he has put a lot into this relationship and realizes that Sonja is remaining rather uninvolved. To attempt to force her to make more of a commitment to him, he displays by his verbal and nonverbal communication that he is angry and that he thinks she has an obligation to go with him. He adds that his folks will be disappointed if she fails to attend.

Unfortunately for Keith, Sonja has learned in the past that it is a mistake to be controlled in relationships by guilt trips and obligations. She tactfully and politely informs Keith that she not only will not go with him to the Thanksgiving dinner, but that she has decided that their present noncommittal dating relationship is not working, and, therefore, she no longer will date him. Keith immediately gives up the tactics of anger and making her feel obligated to go. Instead, he pleads with her to continue dating him. However, Sonja adheres to her decision. When Keith realizes this latest strategy is not going to work, he feels he has to regain some of his honor in this lost cause. He resorts to name calling, four letter words, and pointing our her faults as he perceives them.

At this point, their relationship ends in an uproar. In this example, all of Keith's efforts to achieve the picture of an ongoing relationship with Sonja fail. After the uproar, he chooses to start dating others, hoping to find someone who comes close (as Sonja did) to having the characteristics contained in the picture in his head of his ideal mate.

How do we develop the pictures in our heads that we believe will satisfy our needs? Glasser asserts that we begin to create our picture albums at an early age (perhaps even before birth), and that we spend our whole lives enlarging these albums. Essentially what happens is that whenever what we do gets us something that satisfies a need, we store the picture of what satisfied us in our personal picture albums. Glasser (1984, p. 19) gives the following example of this process by describing how a hungry child added chocolate-chip cookies to his picture album:

> Suppose you had a grandson and your daughter left you in charge while he was taking a nap. She said she would be right back, because he would be ravenous when he awoke and she knew you had no idea what to feed an eleven-month-old child. She was right. As soon as she left, he awoke screaming his head off, obviously starved. You tried a bottle, but he rejected it—he had something more substantial in mind. But what? Being unused to a howling baby, and desperate, you tried a chocolate-chip cookie and it worked wonders. At first, he did not seem to know what it was, but he was a quick learner. He quickly polished off three cookies. She returned and almost polished you off for being so stupid as to give a baby chocolate. "Now," she said, "he will be yelling all day for those cookies." She was right. If he is like most of us, he will probably have chocolate on his mind for the rest of his life.

When this child learned how satisfying chocolate chip cookies are, he placed the picture of these cookies in his personal picture album.

Glasser notes that when he uses the term *pictures*, he means *perceptions* from the five senses of sight, hearing, touch, smell, and taste. When we get hungry, or thirsty, or have some other needs or wants, we select one or more pictures from our albums and then seek to obtain what that picture represents. For example, if we are really hungry we may select a picture of a prime rib dinner (or lobster, or two hamburgers) from our album and then seek to obtain what our picture represents.

The pictures in our albums do not have to be rational. Anorexics have a picture that they are too fat and starve themselves to come closer to their irrational picture of unhealthy thinness. Alcoholics have a picture of themselves satisfying many of their needs through alcohol. Child molesters have pictures of satisfying their sexual needs through sexual activities with young children. Rapists have pictures of satisfying their power and perhaps sexual needs through sexual assault. To change a picture, we have to replace it with another that will at least reasonably satisfy the need in question. People who are unable to replace a picture may endure a lifetime of misery. Some battered women, for example, endure brutal beatings in marriage because they do not believe they can replace their husbands in their albums.

Glasser notes that whenever there is a difference between the picture we now see and the picture we want, a *signal* is generated by this difference which starts us behaving in a way to obtain the picture we want. In order to obtain what we want, we examine our behavioral systems and select from these behaviors one or more that we judge as being the best available behaviors to reduce this difference. These behaviors not only include straightforward problem-solving efforts, but also such manipulative strategies as becoming angry, pouting, and trying to make others feel guilty. People who are acting irresponsibly or ineffectually have either failed to select responsible behaviors that they have in their behavioral repertoires or as yet have not learned responsible courses of action for the particular situation they are facing.

Glasser believes humans are driven by five basic, innate needs. As soon as one need is satisfied, another need (or perhaps more than one) pushes for satisfaction. The first basic need is *to survive and reproduce*. Included in this need are such vital functions as breathing, digesting food, sweating, regulating blood pressure, and meeting the demands of hunger, thirst, and sex.

A second need is *to belong*— to love, share, and cooperate. This need is generally met through family, friends, pets, plants, and material possessions such as a beloved car or boat.

A third need is *power*. Glasser says this need involves getting others to obey us so that we receive the esteem and recognition that accompanies power. The drive for power is sometimes in conflict with the need to belong. For example, two people in a relationship may struggle to take control of the relationship, rather than seeking an equalitarian relationship.

A fourth need is *freedom*. People want the freedom to choose how they live their lives, to express themselves, to read and write what they choose, to associate with whom they select, and to worship or not worship as they believe.

A fifth need is *fun*. Glasser believes learning is often fun, which then is a great incentive to assimilate what we want to satisfy our needs. Classes without fun (those that are grim and boring) are major failings of our educational system. Laughing helps fulfill our need for fun. Fun is such a vital part of living that most of us have trouble conceiving how life would be without it.

Glasser adds there may be other (yet unidentified) needs in addition to these basic five. He also notes that there are differences between individuals in the intensity of each of these needs. Few people, for example, have such an intense need for power as Adolf Hitler, who wanted to control the world.

Glasser asserts that any theory which contends our behavior is simply a response to outside stimuli or events is wrong. He rejects behaviorism's stimulus-response (S-R) system. He asserts that people are in control of what they do. When a person is thirsty, and then seeks water (because a glass of water is a thirst-quenching picture in his or her head) then that person's behavior is that of a well-functioning control system. An S-R theory, in contrast, would suggest a person would keep drinking water (perhaps drinking himself to death) every time he was handed a glass of water.

Intuition

The cerebrum (the area of conscious mental processes of the brain) is composed of two cerebral hemispheres. The right hemisphere has been called the right brain, and the left hemisphere has been called the left brain. Anatomically, the two hemispheres appear to be quite similar, but there is abundant evidence that their functions are by no means identical (Gleitman, 1986, pp. 39-45). Movements of the left side of the body are under the control of the right hemisphere; movements of the right side of the body are controlled by the left hemisphere.

The left hemisphere of the brain ordinarily controls language and speech functions. It appears the left hemisphere is also more centrally involved in rational thought processes, logic, deduction, and mathematical skills. In contrast, the right hemisphere may be more centrally involved in creativity, musical abilities, intuition, and feelings. (It should be noted that research on the location of different functions is somewhat speculative, and further, that there is considerable overlap in functions across the two hemispheres.)

The self-talk approach, described in Chapter 8, demonstrates that humans, by thinking rationally, can learn to better control their emotions and their actions, and obtain better control of their lives. However, Shakti Gawain (1986) theorizes that it is also important for humans to develop and use their intuition. Gawain (1986, p. 18) notes:

> A strong body/personality structure is not created by eating certain foods, doing certain exercises, or following anybody's rules or good ideas. *It is created by trusting your intuition and learning to follow its direction.*

Gawain asserts that it is important for all of us to learn to trust our intuitive knowledge. She states (1986, p. 69):

> Most of us have been taught from childhood not to trust our feelings, not to express ourselves truthfully and honestly, not to recognize that at the core of our being lies a loving, powerful, and creative nature.

Through re-educating ourselves to listen to and trust our intuition, Gawain asserts that we will gain integrity, creativity, and wholeness. Learning to trust this inner voice may feel risky and frightening at first, as we are no longer playing it safe, doing what we "should" do, pleasing others, deferring to outside authority, or following rules.

An important step toward identifying and following your intuition is simply taking time (perhaps several times a day) to relax and listen to your "gut feelings." The inner voice of intuition will present itself in a variety of ways, including images, feelings, and words. When you have an important decision to make, your true gut feelings will more easily be identified if you are very relaxed. When you are relaxed (perhaps through using meditation or some other relaxation technique) your intuition will inform you which alternative is in your personal best interest. Frequently your intuition will inform you of creative alternatives that you previously were unaware of.

Human intuition is similar (and perhaps identical) to the instinct in geese that guides them to fly south in fall and north in spring. It is similar to the instinct in dogs that makes them wary upon seeing a bear in the wild—even when they have never seen a bear before.

Your intuition can assist you in making such major decisions as whether to stay in college, choosing a career, whether to end a romantic relationship, what kind of automobile to purchase, what hobbies to pursue, and so on. Your intuition can also lead you to be a more creative, productive, contented, and fulfilled person.

Neuro-Linguistic Programming

A variety of psychological frameworks and theories to explain the dynamics of human behavior have been discussed in this chapter. Another recently developed model that helps in understanding human behavior is Neuro-Linguistic Programming.

Neuro-Linguistic Programming (NLP) was developed by John Grinder, Richard Bandler, and others (Lankton, 1980). NLP is the study of the structure of subjective experience (Lankton, 1980, p. 13). It clarifies patterns of behavior and change that have previously been only intuitively understandable. Although relatively recent in origin, it promises to have substantial applications in assessing human behavior, in developing rapport, in influencing others (in education, public speaking, and sales), and in changing behavior (therapy).

The components of the term *neuro-linguistic programming* refer to the following:

> *neuro:* nervous system through which experience is received and processed via the five senses.
> *linguistic:* language and nonverbal communication systems through which neural representations are coded, ordered, and given meaning.
> *programming:* ability to organize our communication and neurological systems to achieve specific desired outcomes.

This section will focus on summarizing concepts from NLP that are useful in assessing human behavior. For other uses of NLP, see Lankton (1980) and Laborde (1983).

Representational Systems

Everyone has, at most, five sensory systems through which they make contact with physical reality. These are the eyes (visual), ears (auditory), skin (kinesthetic), nose (smell), and tongue (taste). Before reading further, take a few minutes to identify what you remember most about the following:

> The last grocery story you were in.
> What you did on your last birthday.
> Your most enjoyable sexual experience.

For each of those events, you probably responded with remembrances involving only one or two senses. Taking the grocery store question, you may have had an *image* of fresh fruits and vegetables; or *heard* the hustle and bustle of the activity; or remember *feeling* the Charmin bathroom tissue; or remember *smelling* the pleasant aromas of fresh flowers; or remember *tasting* the free samples of freshly cooked pizza.

Anytime a person interacts with the external world, he does so through sensory representations. My sensory contact with a grocery store is apt to be quite different from yours. The same applies for everyone. Your most enjoyable sexual experience may be a visual one, while your partner's may be auditory or kinesthetic.

We operate out of our sensory representations of the world and not on reality itself. Our sensory representations provide us with a *map* of the territory. But it is important to note that the *map is not the territory*.

NLP asserts that in order to accurately assess another's actions, one needs to identify the sensory representational system being used by that person. If we are able to identify the other's representational system, and then join with that system in our interactions with that person, communication is apt to flow much more smoothly and rapport is enhanced. On the other hand, if two people are not able to join together with the same representational system, then communication is apt to be tangential, and rapport will be adversely affected. The importance of this point is immense. Successful salespersons, educators,

and therapists are those who are able to identify and join with the representational systems of the persons they are seeking to influence.

Representational System Predicates

The adverbs, adjectives, and verbs that people select while speaking reveal which sensory system they are most conscious of at that point in time. NLP calls these words "predicates."

In our culture people primarily use the visual, auditory, and kinesthetic systems. (A few cultures in other countries place greater emphasis on the senses of smell and taste.) Unless the listener is aware of what sensory representational system the speaker is using, the listener may misinterpret what the speaker

Our interactions with the world are mediated through our senses. Therefore, each person's perception of reality is unique. What are some of the sights, sounds, and smells this field study group in rural Ireland might experience?

Predicates to Identify Sensory Representational Systems

Visual	Auditory	Kinesthetic
Appear	Babble	Back away
Clear	Buzz	Break down
Colors	Drumming	Caress
Enlighten	Earshot	Catch
Farsighted	Give a hoot	Clutch
Features	Grumble	Cold
Foresee	Harmony	Dig in
Glance	Hear	Feel
Green with envy	In tune with	Firm
Hindsight	Keep your ears open	Get in touch
Image	Lend an ear	Grasp
In the clear	Listen	Handle
In the dark	Loud	Hard
Inspect	Muffled	Have a feel for
Keen	Mumble	Hold
Look	Noisy	Impressed
Observe	Pronounced	Kiss
Overview	Quiet	Lukewarm
Perspective	Resound	Nudge
Picture	Rings a bell	Poke
Red tape	Roar	Press
Resemble	Rumbling	Rack your brains
Scan	Screech	Ran up against
See	Shriek	Rubs me the wrong way
Seeing red	Silence	Run through
Show	Sound judgment	Sensuous
Tint	Sound off	Soft
Unsightly	Squawk	Stroke
Vague	Squeal	Tender
Vision	Stammer	Tickle
Watch	Thundering	Toss around
The whole picture	Whispering	Touch

is intending. For example, when Mary says "I understand you," the intended message depends on the representational system she is using:

Visual—That looks real good to me.
Auditory—I hear you clearly.
Kinesthetic—What you are saying feels right to me.

See "Predicates to Identify Sensory Representationl Systems" for further examples.

The following case example may help to illustrate the importance of sensory representational systems. A married couple sought counseling because they felt their sexual relationship was deteriorating rapidly. After rapport had been established, the counselor asked each, "What tends to turn you on sexually?" The husband mentioned it was hearing romantic things said to him, while the wife mentioned it was being softly touched in a variety of areas. Not too surprisingly, the husband was trying to excite his wife by saying romantic things (without touching her much), while the wife was seeking to excite her husband by touching him while remaining silent. A simple description of the importance of joining with the other's representational system greatly enhanced their love life with the husband spending much more time in tenderly caressing his wife, and the wife romantically talking to her husband.

In the course of growing up, people learn to favor particular representational systems for particular events. People are not totally visual or auditory or kinesthetic. The sense in use depends on the situation or context. It appears, though, that people tend to have a primary mode, in that they have a tendency to use more of one mode than the others (Laborde, 1983, p. 57).

Mismatched predicates interfere with communication and rapport, as indicated by the following example:

> *Client:* I *feel* so awful! The IRS has just audited me and I just can't *handle* it!
>
> *Counselor:* I *hear* you. It *sounds bad, but tell* me what it is that's so bad.
>
> *Client:* I just can't *lift* this *feeling*. It's so *heavy!*
>
> *Counselor:* Yes, but I don't *hear* what the problem is. *Listen* to me and *tell* me what's so bad!

In this illustration, the client is apt to end up viewing the counselor as being insensitive. An example of matched predicates in this situation is:

> *Client:* I *feel* so awful! The IRS has just audited me and I just can't *handle* it!
>
> *Counselor:* You *feel* like you're *breaking down* because of the *heaviness* of the audit.
>
> *Client:* That's exactly it. I'm *stumbling*, but yet *grasping to hold on.*
>
> *Counselor:* What do you *feel* you need to *hold on?*
>
> *Client:* *Support* and understanding from my wife, my tax accountant, and you.

In this example the counselor phrases his responses to be consistent with the client's representational system, which leads to better understanding, and increased trust and rapport.

Eye Accessing Cues

Listening to the predicates in another's speech is just one reliable way to determine which representational system is dominant at a given time. Eye accessing cues are another way (see Figure 11.3).

As always with rules there are exceptions; for example, some left handers' kinesthetic representational system is eyes down and to the left, with the eyes down and to the right being their auditory representational system. To test out this information, ask friends or acquaintances questions such as "What do you remember most about your last vacation?" and watch how the eye accessing cues are apt to be consistent with responses that are either visual, kinesthetic, or auditory.

The Four-Tuple

The four-tuple is a way of representing a person's sensory experience at a moment in time. Its general form is V, K, A, O. These capital letters are abbreviations for the major sensory channels: visual, kinesthetic, auditory, and olfactory/gustatory.

Distinguishing between experiences that are internally generated (remembering or imagining a visual image, feeling, sound, or smell), and experiences that are externally generated (sights, sensations, sounds, or smells that we receive from the external world) is useful. Therefore the superscript *e* is used to refer to external cues and *i* to internal cues. The experience of someone whose senses are fully turned outward is: V^e, K^e, A^e, O^e. Someone attending fully to an internal event, oblivious of the immediate surroundings is: V^i, K^i, A^i, O^i.

Most of us at any point in time are generally in a mixed state in which some of our senses are outwardly attending and some of our experience is remembered or imagined. Many times one or more of the sensory systems will not be in use. The following example shows how this notational system can be used. Whenever Mrs. Worth *hears* about the Christmas season, she *visualizes* being at her husband's funeral several years ago. (He was killed in an automobile accident.) She remembers how depressed she *felt* afterwards. These cues in sequence are: A^e, V^i, K^i.

The usefulness of this concept can be readily dem-

FIGURE 11.3: Eye Accessing Cues

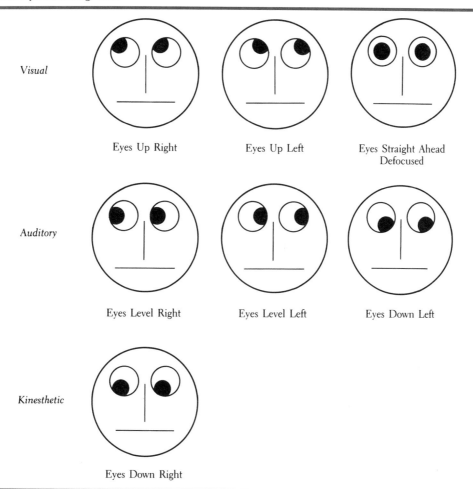

Eyes Up Right   Eyes Up Left   Eyes Straight Ahead
                                             Defocused

Eyes Level Right   Eyes Level Left   Eyes Down Left

Eyes Down Right

onstrated. Think about the last time you said something to someone and received an unusual response. Undoubtedly what happened was that your intended message led the listener to remember auditory, visual, kinesthetic, or olfactory events from the past, which then led the listener to respond primarily in terms of the internal cues. NLP makes an important point by asserting that the meaning of a communication is the response it elicits, regardless of the intent.

Chemical Substance Use and Abuse

There was going to be a big party at Evelyn's on Saturday night. Georgia, a high school junior, couldn't wait to go. Everybody was going to be there. Evelyn said she had some great hash. Georgia didn't like to smoke all that much. However, people would think that there was something wrong with her if she didn't, and that was the last thing she wanted.

Marty, age fifteen, liked to drink a couple of six packs on the weekend. After all, his father did, and Marty was almost an adult.

Virgil, age eighteen, liked to get high because then he could forget about all his problems. He wouldn't have to think about his alcoholic mother and all the problems she and his father were having. He wouldn't have to worry about all the pressures he had in school. He wouldn't even have to think about how his girlfriend recently dumped him. He just couldn't wait until the next chance he had to get high.

Drugs have become part of our daily lives. We use drugs to relax, to increase our pleasure, to feel less inhibited, to get rid of unwanted emotions, to keep awake, and to fall asleep. Practically all Americans use drugs of one kind or another. People have coffee in the morning, soda (which has caffeine) during the day, cocktails before dinner, and aspirin to relieve pain.

When the Pilgrims set sail for America, they loaded on their ships 14 tons of water—plus 10,000 gallons of wine and 42 tons of beer (Ian Robertson, 1980, p. 438). Ever since, Americans have been widely using and abusing drugs.

Pharmacologically, a *drug* is any substance that chemically alters the function or structure of a living organism. Such a definition includes food, insecticides, air pollutants, water pollutants, acids, vitamins, toxic chemicals, soaps, and soft drinks. Obviously, this definition is too broad to be useful. For our purposes, a definition based on context is more useful. In medicine, for example, a drug is any substance that is manufactured specifically to relieve pain or to treat and prevent diseases and other medical conditions.

Here drugs will be addressed within the context most useful for social workers. We will focus on drugs that can dramatically impact human behavior and have serious consequences on people's lives. A drug, then, is any habit-forming substance that directly affects the brain and the nervous system; it is a chemical substance that affects moods, perceptions, bodily functions, or consciousness and that has the potential for misuse as it may be harmful to the user.

Drug abuse is "the regular or excessive use of a drug when, as defined by a group, the consequences endanger relationships with other people, are detrimental to a person's health, or jeopardize society itself" (Zastrow, 1984, p. 114). All of the drugs mentioned earlier are types of chemicals. Another way of referring to drug abuse is *chemical substance abuse*. Drug or chemical substance intake becomes abusive when an individual's mind and/or body are affected in negative or harmful ways.

Both legal drugs such as alcohol and tobacco and prescription drugs are frequently abused. Among the most abused prescription drugs are sedatives, tran-quilizers, painkillers, and stimulants. Americans are obsessed with taking pills. Many prescribed drugs have the potential to be psychologically and physiologically addicting. Drug companies spend millions in advertising to convince customers that they are too tense, too irritable, take too long to fall asleep, that they should lose weight, and so on. These companies then assert that their medications will relieve these problems. Unfortunately, many customers accept this easy symptom-relief approach and end up dependent on pills, rather than making the necessary changes in their lives to be healthy. Such changes include exercise, stress management techniques, positive thinking, and a healthy diet.

Illegal drugs such as cocaine and heroin are also frequently abused. People use them to distort their own realities. They can be used to attain unrealistic "highs" or to escape unpleasant real life situations. However, as we will see, heavy drug use can often result in serious physical deterioration and slave-like psychological and physical dependence.

A variety of legal over-the-counter, prescription, and illegal drugs will be described. How and why people use and abuse alcohol and other drugs will be examined. The family dynamics which are often involved will be explained. Some treatment approaches for drug abusers will be identified. Finally, the relationship between knowledge about drug use and assessment in social work practice will be proposed.

Specific Drugs—What They Are and What They Do

Knowing what a specific drug is and what it does to a person is important both in treatment and in considering its use and abuse (Zastrow and Bowker, 1984, pp. 119-34). Specific drugs discussed here include depressants, stimulants, narcotics, hallucinogens, marijuana, tobacco, and anabolic steroids.

Depressant Drugs

Depressant drugs are those which slow down bodily functioning and activity. Alcohol, barbiturates, tranquilizers, Quaaludes, and PCP all fall within this category.

Alcohol. Alcohol is a colorless liquid that is in beer, wine, brandy, whiskey, vodka, rum, and other intoxicating beverages. The type of alcohol found in beverages is ethyl alcohol (it is also called grain alcohol, as most of it is made from fermenting grain).

Who Drinks? The average American over the age of fourteen consumes the equivalent of 591 cans of beer or 115 bottles of wine or 35 fifths of whiskey, gin, or vodka each year (Kornblum and Julian, 1989, p. 130). The vast majority of teenagers and adults in our society drink.

Several factors are related to whether an individual will drink, and how much a drinker will use. These variables include socioeconomic factors, gender, age, religion, urban-rural residence, and geographic region (Kornblum and Julian, 1989, pp. 133-36).

1. *Socioeconomic Factors:* College educated persons are more apt to drink than those with only high school educations. Young men at the highest socioeconomic level are more apt to drink than young men at lower socioeconomic levels. However, drinkers at the lower socioeconomic levels are more apt to drink more than those at higher socioeconomic levels.
2. *Gender:* Men are more apt to use and abuse alcohol than women. Yet, recent decades have seen a dramatic increase in alcoholism among adult women. Why? One explanation is that cultural taboos against heavy drinking among women have weakened. Another explanation is that increased drinking is related to the changing roles of women in our society.
3. *Age:* Older people are less likely to drink than younger people, even if they were drinkers in their youth. Heavy drinking is most common at ages twenty-one through thirty for men, and ages thirty-one through fifty for women.
4. *Religion:* Nonchurchgoers drink more than regular churchgoers. Heavy drinking is more common among Episcopalians and Catholics, while conservative and fundamentalist Protestants are more apt to be nondrinkers or light drinkers.
5. *Urban-Rural Residence:* Urban residents are more apt to drink than rural residents.
6. *Geographic Region:* People who live in the Northeast and along the West Coast are more apt to drink than people who live in the South and Midwest.

Recently there has been a marked decline in drinking, especially of hard liquor, in many segments of the American public (Kornblum and Julian, 1989, p. 133). For example, some business executives have switched from martini luncheons to jogging and working out. In recent years the federal government has put considerable financial pressure on states to raise the drinking age to twenty-one; if a state does not raise the age, federal highway funds are withheld. Practically all states have now raised the drinking age to twenty-one. Many secondary schools, colleges, and universities have initiated alcohol awareness programs. Many businesses and employers have developed Employee Assistance Programs which are designed to provide treatment services to alcoholics and problem drinkers. Many states have passed stricter drunk driving laws, and police departments and the courts are more vigorously enforcing such laws. Organizations, such as Mothers Against Drunk Driving and Students Against Drunk Driving, have been fairly successful in creating greater public awareness of the hazards of drinking and driving. A cultural norm is emerging in many segments that it is stylish not to have too much to drink. Despite these promising trends, rates of alcohol use and abuse in the United States remain extremely high.

What Alcohol Does. Many drinkers believe alcohol is a stimulant, as it relaxes tensions, lessens sexual and aggressive inhibitions, and seems to facilitate interpersonal relationships. However, it acts as a depressant to the central nervous system, as it reduces functional activity of this system. Its chemical composition and effects are very similar to ether (an anesthetic used in medicine to induce unconsciousness).

Alcohol slows down mental activity, reasoning ability, speech ability, and muscle reactions. It distorts perceptions, slurs speech, lessens coordination, and slows down memory functioning and respiration. In increasing quantities, it leads to stupor, sleep, coma, and finally death. A hangover (the aftereffects of too much alcohol) includes having a headache, thirst, muscle aches, stomach discomfort, and nausea. Alcohol can seriously affect how one drives an automobile. Behavior resulting from excessive alcohol intake can also negatively interfere in family, friend, and work relationships.

The effects of alcohol vary with the percentage of alcohol in the bloodstream as it passes through the brain. Generally, the effects are observable when the concentration of alcohol in the blood reaches one-tenth of a percent. Five drinks (with each drink being

Courts Are Getting Tougher on Drunk Drivers

Larry Mahoney was a thirty-four-year-old father who was described by a friend as "somebody who wouldn't hurt anybody for the world." On Sunday evening May 14, 1988, while drunk, Larry climbed into his pickup truck and drove the wrong way down a Kentucky interstate. He had 0.24 percent alcohol in his blood, more than twice Kentucky's statutory level. He slammed head-on into an old school bus carrying sixty-seven passengers, mainly teenagers, on a church outing from Radcliff, Kentucky.

Twenty-four teenagers and three adults were killed in this crash. Larry Mahoney was charged with "capital murder," which carries the death penalty.

In December 1989, Mahoney was found guilty of twenty-seven counts of second-degree manslaughter, twenty-seven counts of first-degree wanton endangerment, twelve counts of first-degree assault, fourteen counts of second-degree wanton endangerment, and one count of drunken driving. He was sentenced to sixteen years in prison. This lengthy prison sentence is one more indication that the court system is taking a tougher stand on drunk driving. Many states have enacted legislation to suspend drivers' licenses of offenders immediately and have mandated jail terms for repeat offenders. Many states now also mandate instant suspension of the driver's license for those failing, or refusing to take, a breath test.

SOURCE: "Kentucky's Textbook Case in Drunk Driving," *U.S. News & World Report*, May 30, 1988, pp. 7-8; and "Man Sentenced in Fatal Church Bus Accident." *Wisconsin State Journal*, Feb. 24, 1990, p. 3A.

one ounce of 86-proof alcohol, or twelve ounces of beer, or three ounces of wine) in two hours for a 120-pound person will result in a blood alcohol concentration of one-tenth of a percent, which is the legal criterion in most states for being intoxicated.

Alcohol also has long-term effects on a person's health. Alcoholics have a life expectancy that is ten to twelve years less than nonalcoholics (Kornblum and Julian, 1989, p. 132). There are several reasons why the life span is shorter. One is that alcohol, over an extended period of time, gradually destroys liver cells and replaces the cells with scar tissue. When the scar tissue is extensive, a medical condition occurs called *cirrhosis*. This is the sixth most frequent cause of death in the United States, numbering about 27,000 deaths per year (U.S. Bureau of the Census, 1991, p. 79). Also, although it has no nutritional value, alcohol contains a high number of calories. As a result, heavy drinkers have a reduced appetite for nutritious food and thus frequently suffer from vitamin deficiencies and are more susceptible to infectious diseases. Heavy drinking also causes kidney problems, contributes to a variety of heart ailments, is a factor in diabetes, and also appears to contribute to cancer. In addition, heavy drinking is associated with over 10,000 suicides annually (Julian and Kornblum, 1986).

However, for some as yet unknown reason, the life expectancy for light-to-moderate drinkers exceeds that for nondrinkers (Noble, 1978, p. 13). Perhaps an occasional drink helps people to relax and thereby reduces the likelihood of life-threatening psychosomatic illnesses developing.

Alcohol also can seriously affect sexual response. Even relatively low dosages of alcohol can inhibit erections (Farkas and Rosen, 1976). Research has also shown that alcohol can suppress men's ability to experience the pleasure of orgasm (Malatesta, 1979). Women are similarly affected. Sexual arousal can be suppressed (Wilson and Lawson, 1976, 1978), and orgasms become more difficult to have (Malatesta et al., 1982).

Many people are surprised at the actual effects of alcohol on sexuality. Initial psychological reactions tend to make people feel less nervous and inhibited. Hence, a person might at first feel more comfortable getting sexually involved. However, physiologically alcohol is a depressant. It acts to impede the body's ability to respond in many ways including sexually.

In alcoholics (persons who drink alcohol obsessively and compulsively), major sexual dysfunctions can occur. Five percent of all alcoholic men have primary erectile dysfunctions, that is, they are unable "to have or maintain a penile erection" (Hyde, 1986, p. 525); "an additional 40 to 50 percent have varying degrees of erectile or orgasmic dysfunction," according to Geller (1984, p. 15). Geller continues that information concerning the effects of long-term alcohol use by women is scarce by comparison. Although a high proportion of recovering alcoholics will experience some form of sexual dysfunction, the majority of alcohol related sexual problems will disappear after a few months of abstinence (Geller, 1984, pp. 19, 22).

Combining alcohol with other drugs can have disastrous, and sometimes fatal, effects. Two drugs taken together may have a *synergistic interaction*—that is, they interact to produce an effect much greater than either would cause alone. For example, sedatives such as barbiturates (often found in sleeping pills) or Quaaludes taken together with alcohol can so depress the central nervous system that a coma or even death may result.

Other drugs tend to have an antagonistic response to alcohol—one drug negates the effects of the other. Many doctors now caution patients not to drink while taking certain prescribed drugs, as the alcohol will reduce, and even totally negate, the beneficial effects of those drugs.

Whether drugs will interact synergistically or antagonistically depends on a wide range of factors: the properties of the drugs, the amounts taken, the amount of sleep of the user, the kind and amount of food that has been eaten, and the user's overall health and tolerance. The interactive effects may be minimal one day and extensive the next.

When used by pregnant women, alcohol may gravely affect the unborn child by causing mental retardation, deformities, stunting of growth, and other abnormalities. This effect has been named the *fetal alcohol syndrome.*

Withdrawal from alcohol, once the body is physically addicted, may lead to the DTs (delirium tremens) and other unpleasant reactions. The DTs include rapid heartbeat, uncontrollable trembling, severe nausea, and profuse sweating.

Barbiturates. Barbiturates, another type of depressant, are derived from barbituric acid, and depress the central nervous system. Barbiturates were first synthesized in the early 1900s, and there are now over 2,500 different barbiturates. They are commonly used to relieve insomnia and anxiety. Some are prescribed as sleeping pills, and others are used during the daytime by tense and anxious persons. They are also used to treat epilepsy, high blood pressure, and to relax patients before or after surgery. Barbiturates are illegal, unless obtained by a physician's prescription.

Taken in sufficient doses, barbiturates have effects similar to alcohol. Users experience relief from inhibitions, have a feeling of euphoria, feel "high" or in good humor, and are passively content. However, these moods can change rapidly to gloom, agitation, and aggressiveness. Physiological effects include slurred speech, disorientation, staggering, appearance of being confused, drowsiness, and reduced coordination.

Prolonged heavy use of barbiturates can cause physical dependence, with withdrawal symptoms similar to those of heroin addiction. Withdrawal is accompanied by body tremors, cramps, anxiety, fever, nausea, profuse sweating, and hallucinations. Many authorities believe barbiturate addiction is more dangerous than heroin addiction, and it is considered to be more resistant to treatment than heroin addiction. Abrupt withdrawal (*cold turkey*, the sudden and complete halting of drug use) can cause fatal convulsions. One forensic pathologist noted, "Show me someone who goes cold turkey on a bad barbiturate habit, and I'll show you a corpse" (Dunning and Chang, 1977, p. 177).

Barbiturate overdose may cause convulsions, coma, poisoning, and sometimes death. Barbiturates are particularly dangerous when taken with alcohol, as alcohol acts synergistically to magnify the potency of the barbiturates. Accidental deaths due to excessive doses are frequent. One reason for this is that the user becomes groggy, forgets how much has been taken, and takes more until an overdose level has been reached. Barbiturates are also the number one drug used for suicide. A number of famous people have fatally overdosed on barbiturates.

Barbiturates are generally taken orally, although some users also inject them intravenously. Use of barbiturates, like alcohol, may also lead to traffic fatalities.

Tranquilizers. Yet another depressant is the group of drugs classified as tranquilizers. Common brand names are Librium, Miltown, Serax, Tranxene, and Valium. Tranquilizers reduce anxiety, relax muscles, and are sedatives. Users have moderate potential of becoming physically and psychologically dependent. The drugs are usually taken orally, and the effects last four to eight hours. Side effects include slurred speech, disorientation, and behavior resembling being intoxicated. Overdoses are possible, with the effects including cold and clammy skin, shallow respiration, dilated pupils, weak and rapid pulse, coma, and possibly death. Withdrawal symptoms are similar to those from alcohol and barbiturates and include anxiety, tremors, convulsions, delirium, and possibly death.

Quaalude. *Methaqualone* (better known by its patent name *Quaalude*) has effects similar to barbiturates and alcohol, although it is chemically different. It has a reputation as a love drug, as users believe it makes them more eager for sex and enhances sexual pleasure. These effects are probably due to the fact that it lessens inhibitions (similar to alcohol and barbiturates). Quaaludes also reduce anxiety and give a feeling of euphoria.

Users can become both physically and psychologically dependent on Quaaludes. Overdose can result in convulsions, coma, delirium, and even death— most deaths occur when the drug is taken together with alcohol, which vastly magnifies the drug's effects. Withdrawal symptoms are severe and unpleasant. Abuse of the drug may also cause hangovers, fatigue, liver damage, and temporary paralysis of the limbs.

PCP. *Phencyclindine* (better known as PCP) was developed in the 1950s as an anesthetic. This medical use was soon terminated because patients displayed symptoms of severe emotional disturbance after receiving the drug. PCP is used legally today to tranquilize elephants and monkeys, as they apparently do not have the adverse side effects.

PCP is primarily used by young people who are often unaware of its hazards. It is usually smoked, often after being sprinkled on a marijuana joint. It may also be sniffed, swallowed, or injected.

PCP is a very dangerous drug. It distorts the senses, disrupts balance, and leads to an inability to think clearly. Effects produced are similar to those of hallucinogens. Larger amounts of PCP may cause a person to become paranoid, lead to aggressive behavior, and may cause the user to display temporary symptoms of severe emotional disturbance. Continued use can lead to the development of a prolonged emotional disturbance. Overdose can result in coma or even death. Research has as yet not concluded whether PCP induces physical and/or psychological dependence. The drug has a potential to be used (and abused) extensively, as it is relatively easy to prepare in a home laboratory, with the ingredients and recipes being widely available.

An additional danger of PCP is that even one-time users sometimes have flashbacks in which the hallucinations are re-experienced, even long after use has ceased. It may be that many accidents and unexplained disasters are due to people's use of PCP or other undetectable hallucinogenic substances.

Stimulants

In this section we will examine the following drugs which are classified as stimulants. Stimulants are substances which produce a temporary increase in a person's activity level or efficiency. They include caffeine, amphetamines, cocaine, crack, amyl nitrate, and butyl nitrate.

Caffeine. Caffeine is a stimulant to the central nervous system. It is present in coffee, tea, cocoa, and many soft drinks. It is also available in tablet form (for example, No-Doz). Caffeine is widely used—practically all Americans use it on a daily basis. It reduces hunger, fatigue, boredom, and improves alertness and motor activity. The drug appears addictive, as many users develop a tolerance for it. A further sign that it is addictive is that heavy users (for example, habitual coffee drinkers) will experience withdrawal symptoms of mild irritability and depression.

Excessive amounts of caffeine cause insomnia, restlessness, and gastrointestinal irritation. Excessive doses can even, surprisingly, cause death.

Because caffeine has the status of a "nondrug" in our society, users are not labeled criminals, there is no black market for it, and no subculture is formed to give support in obtaining and using the drug. Because caffeine is legal its price is low compared to other drugs. Users are not tempted to resort to crime to support their habit. Some authorities assert that our approach to caffeine should serve as a model for the way we react to other illegal drugs (such as marijuana) that they feel are no more harmful than caffeine (Timson, 1978, pp. 57-59).

Amphetamines. Another type of stimulant, *amphetamines*, are often called "uppers" because of their stimulating effect. When prescribed by a physician, they are legal. Some truck drivers have obtained prescriptions in order to stay awake and more alert while making a long haul. Dieters have received prescriptions to help them lose weight, and they often find that the pills tend to give them more self-confidence and buoyance. Others who have used amphetamines to increase alertness and performance for relatively short periods of time include college students, athletes, astronauts, and executives. Additional nicknames for this drug are speed, ups, pep pills, black beauties, and bennies.

Amphetamines are synthetic drugs. They are similar to adrenalin, a hormone from the adrenal gland that stimulates the central nervous system. The better known amphetamines include dexedrine, benzedrine, and methedrine. Physical reactions to amphetamines are extensive: consumption of fat stored in body tissues is accelerated, heartbeat is increased, respiratory processes are stimulated, appetite is reduced, and insomnia is common. Users feel euphoric, stronger, and have an increased capacity to concentrate and to express themselves verbally. Prolonged use can lead to irritability, deep anxiety, and an irrational persecution complex that can lead to sudden acts of violence.

Amphetamines are usually taken orally in tablet, powder, or capsule form. They can also be sniffed or injected. "Speeding" (injecting the drug into a vein) produces the most powerful effects and can also cause the greatest harm. An overdose may cause a coma, with possible brain damage, and, in rare cases, death. Speeders may also develop hepatitis, abscesses, convulsions, hallucinations, delusions, and severe emotional disturbances. Another danger is that, when sold on the street, the substance may contain impurities which are health hazards.

An amphetamine high is often followed by mental depression and fatigue. Continued amphetamine use leads to psychological dependence. It is unclear whether amphetamines are physically addictive, as the withdrawal symptoms are uncharacteristic of withdrawal from other drugs. Amphetamine withdrawal symptoms include sleep disturbances, apathy, decreased activity, disorientation, irritability, exhaustion, and depression. Some authorities believe such withdrawal symptoms indicate that amphetamines may be physically addicting (National Clearinghouse for Drug Abuse Information, 1974, pp. 9-10).

One of the legal uses of certain amphetamines is in the treatment of *hyperactivity* in children. Hyperactivity (also called hyperkinesis) is characterized by a short attention span, extensive motor activity, restlessness, and mood shifts. Little is known about the causes of this condition. As children become older, even without treatment, the symptoms tend to disappear. Interestingly, some amphetamines (Ritalin is a popular one) have a calming and soothing effect upon hyperactive children—the exact opposite effect occurs when Ritalin is taken by adults. It should be noted that, in the past, treating uncontrollable children with amphetamines was frequently abused. Fort and Cory (1975, p. 41) note:

> Many of the children for whom Ritalin is prescribed are not really hyperactive to begin with. They are normal children who simply refuse to submit to what their teachers and parents consider orderly school and family routines. Categorizing children who are different as hyperactive often is a seductively convenient way to blame the victims for teachers' and parents' own shortcomings. Drugging these children, however, brands them as troublemakers and helps to further institutionalize drug use.

One of the amphetamines that has had increasing illegal use in recent years is methamphetamine hydrochloride, known on the street as "meth" or "ice." In liquid form it is often referred to as "speed." Under experimental conditions, cocaine users often have difficulty distinguishing cocaine from methamphetamine hydrochloride. There is a danger this drug may be increasingly abused, as the "high" lasts longer than that from cocaine and the drug can be synthesized relatively easily in laboratories from products that are sold legally in the United States. As a "last resort," methamphetamine hydrochloride (Desoxyn) is legally used to treat obesity as one component of a weight-reduction regimen. There is, however, a serious side effect of this drug when used for weight reduction: The user's appetite returns with greater intensity after withdrawal from the drug.

Cocaine and Crack. *Cocaine* is obtained from the leaves of the South American coca plant. It is rapidly replacing other illegal drugs in popularity. Although legally classified as a narcotic, it is in fact not related to the opiates from which narcotic drugs are derived. It is a powerful stimulant and antifatigue agent.

In the United States, it is generally taken by sniffing and is then absorbed through the nasal membranes. The most common method is sniffing up through a straw or a rolled-up bank note, known as "snorting." It may also be injected intravenously, and in South America the natives chew the coca leaf. It may be added in small quantities to a cigarette and smoked. Cocaine has been used medically in the past as a local anesthetic, but other drugs have largely replaced it for this purpose.

Cocaine constricts the blood vessels and tissues, and thereby leads to increased strength and endurance. It also is thought by users to increase creative and intellectual powers. Other effects include a feeling of euphoria, excitement, restlessness, and a lessened sense of fatigue.

Larger doses, or extended use, may result in hallucinations and delusions. A peculiar effect of cocaine abuse is "formication," the illusion that ants, snakes, or bugs are crawling on or into the skin. Some abusers have such intense illusions that they literally scratch, slap, and wound themselves trying to kill these imaginary creatures.

Physical effects of cocaine include increased blood pressure and pulse rate, insomnia, and loss of appetite. Heavy users may experience weight loss or malnutrition due to appetite suppression. Physical dependence on cocaine is considered to be a low to medium risk. However, the drug appears to be psychologically habituating. Termination of use usually results in intense depression and despair, which drives the person back to taking the drug (Andrews and Solomon, 1975). Additional effects of withdrawal include apathy, long periods of sleep, extreme fatigue, irritability, and disorientation. Serious tissue damage to the nose can occur when large quantities of cocaine are "sniffed" over a prolonged period of time. Regular use may result in habitual sniffing, and sometimes leads to an anorexic condition. High doses can lead to agitation, increased body temperature, and convulsions. A few people who overdose may die if their breathing and heart functions become too depressed.

Crack, also called "rock," is obtained from cocaine by separation of the adulterants from the cocaine by mixing it with water and ammonium hydroxide. The water is then removed from the cocaine base by means of a fast drying solvent, usually ether. The resultant mixture resembles large sugar crystals, similar to rock sugar. Crack is highly addictive. Some authorities claim that one use is enough to lead to addiction. Users generally claim that after they have finished one dose, they crave another.

Crack is generally smoked, either in a specially-made glass pipe, or mixed with tobacco or marijuana in a cigarette. The effects are similar to cocaine, but the "rush" is more immediate, and the drug gives an intensified high.

An overdose is more common when crack is injected than when it is smoked. Withdrawal effects include an irresistible compulsion to have the drug, as well as apathy, long periods of sleep, irritability, extreme fatigue, depression, and disorientation.

Communal use of needles spreads AIDS. Cocaine and crack can have serious effects on the heart, straining it with high blood pressure, with interrupted heart rhythm, and with raised pulse rates. Cocaine and crack may also damage the liver. Severe convulsions can cause brain damage, emotional problems, and sometimes death. Smoking crack may also damage the lungs.

Amyl Nitrate and Butyl Nitrate. *Amyl nitrate* (poppers) is prescribed for patients who risk certain forms of heart failure. It is a volatile liquid that is sold in capsules or small bottles. When the container is opened, the chemical begins to evaporate (similar to gasoline). If the vapor is sniffed, the user's blood vessels are immediately dilated and there is an increase in heart rate. These physical changes create feelings of mental excitation (head rush) and physical excitation (body rush). The drug is supposedly only sold by prescription, but (as with many other drugs) the illicit drug market distributes it.

Butyl nitrate is legally available in some states without a prescription and has an effect similar to amyl nitrate. Trade names under which it is sold are Rush and Locker Room. Similar to amyl nitrate, butyl nitrate vapor is sniffed. It is available at some sexual aid and novelty stores.

Both of these drugs have been used as aphrodisiacs and as stimulants while dancing. The drugs have some short-term, unpleasant side effects that may include fainting, headaches, and dizziness. A few deaths have been reported due to overdoses. Both drugs are classified as stimulants.

Narcotics

The most commonly used narcotic drugs in the United States are the opiates (such as opium, heroin, and morphine). The term *narcotic* means sleep-inducing. In actuality, drugs classified as narcotics are more accurately called analgesics, or painkillers. The principal effect produced by narcotic drugs is to create feelings of euphoria.

The opiates are all derived from the opium poppy. The opium poppy grows in various parts of the world; Turkey, Southeast Asia, and Colombia have in the recent past been major sources of the opiates. The drug opium is the dried form of a milky substance that oozes from the seed pods after the petals fall from the flowers. It has been used for centuries.

Morphine is the main active ingredient of opium. It was first identified early in the 1800s, and has been used extensively as a painkiller. Heroin was first synthesized from morphine in 1874. It was once thought to be a cure for morphine addiction, but later was also found to be addictive. Heroin is a more potent drug than morphine.

Opium is usually smoked, although it can be taken orally. Morphine and heroin are either sniffed (snorted) or injected into a muscle or into a vein (called "mainlining"), which maximizes the drugs' effects.

Opiates affect the central nervous system and produce feelings of tranquility, drowsiness, or euphoria. They produce a sense of well-being that makes pain, anxiety, or depression seem unimportant. Blaze-Gosden (1987, p. 95) notes that opiates have

> been described as giving an orgasmlike rush or flash that lasts briefly but memorably. At the peak of the euphoria, the user has a feeling of exaggerated physical and mental comfort and well-being, a heightened feeling of buoyancy and bodily health, and a heightened feeling of being competent, in control, capable of any achievement, and being able to cope.

Overdoses can cause convulsions and coma, and, in rare cases, death by respiratory failure. All opiates are now recognized as highly addictive.

Heroin is the most widely abused opiate. In addition to the above-mentioned effects, heroin slows the functioning parts of the brain. The user's appetite and sex drive tend to be dulled. After an initial feeling of euphoria, the user generally becomes lethargic and stuporous. Contrary to popular belief, most heroin

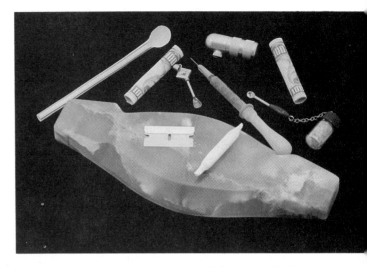

Drug use in our society ranges from social drinking to hard narcotics.

users take the drug infrequently and do not as a rule become addicted (Abadinsky, 1989, pp. 90-97), although frequent use is highly addictive.

Opiate addiction occurs when the user takes the drug regularly for a period of time. Whether addiction will occur depends on the opiate drug taken, the strength of the dosages, the regularity of use, the characteristics of the user, and the length of time taken—sometimes as short as a few weeks. Users rapidly develop a tolerance, and may eventually need a dose that is up to one hundred times stronger than a dose that would have been fatal during the initiation to the drug (Abadinsky, 1989, pp. 90-97).

The withdrawal process is very unpleasant. Symptoms include chills, cramps, sweating, nervousness, anxiety, running eyes and nose, dilated pupils, muscle aches, increased blood pressure, severe cramps, sometimes extreme nausea, and a fever. Most addicts are obsessed with securing a fix to avoid these severe withdrawal symptoms.

Addiction to opiates is extremely difficult to break, partly because intense craving for the drug may recur periodically for several months afterward. Brecher et al. (1972, p. 84) note that the opiate drug

> is one that most users continue to take even though they want to stop, decide to stop, try to stop, and actually succeed in stopping for days, weeks, months, or even

years. It is a drug for which men and women will prostitute themselves. It is a drug to which most users return after treatment. . . . It is a drug which most users continue to use despite the threat of long-term imprisonment for its use—and to which they promptly return after experiencing long-term imprisonment.

Most opiate addicts are under thirty, of low socioeconomic status, and poorly educated. A disproportionate number are African Americans. Distribution and addiction to narcotic drugs primarily occur in large urban centers.

When heroin was first discovered in the late 1880s, it was initially used as a painkiller, as a substitute for morphine, and as a drug taken by many to experience euphoria. A fair number of people became addicted, and in the early 1900s laws were passed to prohibit its sale, possession, and distribution.

Heroin abuse continues to be regarded by many Americans as our most serious drug problem. This stereotype does not appear warranted, as only a tiny fraction of the U.S. population has ever tried heroin, and the number of people addicted to heroin is minuscule compared to the number addicted to alcohol or tobacco. In addition, such drugs as alcohol and barbiturates contribute to many more deaths.

One reason heroin has the reputation it does is because users are thought to be "dope fiends" who commit many violent crimes, and who reject the values of contemporary society. Addicts, however, are unlikely to commit such violent crimes as rape or aggravated assault. They are more apt to commit crimes against property (shoplifting, burglary, pickpocketing, larceny, and robbery) in order to support their habit (Abadinsky, 1989, pp. 14-22). Prostitution for female addicts is also common. Because the severe withdrawal symptoms begin about eighteen hours after the last fix, addicts who have experienced these symptoms will do almost anything to avoid them.

Unsanitary injections of heroin may cause hepatitis and other infections. Communal use of needles can spread AIDS. Also, the high cost of maintaining a heroin habit—often over $100 daily—may create huge financial problems for the user.

Because the price of illicit narcotic drugs is so high, organized crime has made huge profits in the smuggling and distribution of these drugs. Often such drugs are diluted with dangerous impurities, which pose serious health hazards for the users. And, unfortunately, addicts are often economically forced into illegal activities to maintain their daily supply in order to avoid the withdrawal symptoms.

Hallucinogens

Hallucinogens were popular as psychedelic drugs in the late 1960s. These drugs distort the user's perceptions, creating hallucinations consisting of sensory impressions of "sights and sounds" that do not exist. The four hallucinogens most commonly used in this country are mescaline (peyote), psilocybin, psilocin, and LSD. All are taken orally—for example, in capsule form, on a sugar cube, or licked from the back of a stamp.

Peyote is derived from a cactus plant. Mescaline is the synthetic form of peyote. Psilocybin and psilocin are found in approximately ninety different species of mushrooms. They have been called "magic mushrooms." Both peyote and psilocybin have had a long history of use by certain American Indian tribes. Members of the Native American Church, a religious organization, have won the legal right to use peyote on ceremonial occasions (Robertson, 1980, p. 450).

By far the most popular hallucinogen is LSD (lysergic acid diethylamide). LSD is a synthetic material derived from a fungus (ergot) that grows on rye and other plants. It is one of the most potent drugs known; a single ounce will make up to 300,000 doses.

The effects of LSD vary a great deal depending on the expectations and psychological state of the user, and the context in which it is taken. A given person may experience differing reactions on different occasions. The effects that can be experienced include the apparent "seeing" of sounds, "hearing" of color, colors seeming unusually bright and shifting kaleidoscopically, exaggerations of color and sound, and objects appearing to expand and contract. Users become highly suggestible and easily manipulated.

Bizarre hallucinations are also common. The experience may be peaceful or may result in panic. Some users have developed severe emotional disturbances that resulted in long-term hospitalization ("Hallucinogens and Narcotics Alarm Public," 1976, pp. 44-45). Usually a "trip" will last eight to sixteen hours. Physical reactions include increased heartbeat, goose bumps, dilated pupils, hyperactivity, tremors, and increased sweating. Aftereffects include acute anxiety or depression. Flashbacks sometimes occur after the actual drug experience. Flashbacks may happen at any time and place, with no advance warning. If the user is driving a car when a flashback occurs, a life threatening condition is present for the user and for others in the vicinity.

There is no evidence of physical or psychological dependence on LSD by users. Users do develop tolerance to the drug very rapidly as the effects can only be achieved in the future by larger doses. Cessation of use, even for a few days, will restore sensitivity to the drug, enabling the user to take smaller quantities to experience the effects.

The effects and dangers of mescaline, psilocybin, and psilocin are similar to LSD. LSD is, however, the most potent of these hallucinogens.

Tobacco

The use of tobacco has now become recognized as one of the most damaging drug habits in the United States. Smoking can cause emphysema, cancer of the mouth, ulcers, and lung cancer, and it reduces life expectancy. It significantly increases the risk of strokes and heart disease, particularly in women who use birth control pills (U.S. Department of Health, Education, and Welfare, 1979). Smoking by a pregnant woman sometimes leads to miscarriages, premature births, and the child being born underweight. Yet, in spite of these widely publicized hazards, 27 percent of the adult population continues to smoke (*Hope Health Letter*, 1991, p. 6).

In 1988, the Surgeon General of the United States, C. Everett Koop, declared that tobacco is as addictive as heroin or cocaine (Rosellini, 1988, pp. 55-63). More people die from the health hazards of using tobacco than from all other illegal drugs combined. Koop noted that people addicted to tobacco are drug addicts.

Tobacco is highly habit-forming. Nicotine is the primary drug in tobacco. Nicotine has remarkable capacities, as it can act as a depressant, a stimulant, or a tranquilizer. Smokers quickly develop a tolerance for nicotine and often gradually tend to increase consumption to one or two packs or more a day.

There are special clinics and a variety of other educational and therapeutic programs to help people quit smoking. Studies show that less than 20 percent of smokers who make determined efforts to quit actu-

ally succeed (Hunt and Matarazzo, 1970, p. 76). Tobacco is indeed a very habit-forming drug. Withdrawal from use leads users to become restless, irritable, depressed, and to have an intense craving to smoke.

At the same time the Health Department is widely publicizing the hazards of drugs, the Department of Agriculture is subsidizing tobacco farmers. Educational programs urge people not to smoke, while tobacco companies are permitted to advertise that cigarette smoking is "cool" and "sexy," connoting rugged manliness in men and social sophistication in women.

Marijuana

Marijuana, "grass" or "pot," comes from the hemp plant, *cannabis sativa*. This hemp plant grows throughout the world, and its fibers are legally used to produce rope, twine, paper, and clothing.

The main use of the plant now, however, centers on its dried leaves—marijuana—and on its dried resin—hashish. Both may be taken orally, but are usually smoked. Hashish is several times more potent than marijuana.

The effects of marijuana (and hashish) vary, as with any other drug, according to the mood and personality of the user, according to circumstances, and according to the quality of the drug. The effects are rather complicated, and may induce a variety of emotions.

Many of the effects are produced because marijuana has sedative properties and creates in the user a sense of relaxed well-being, and freedom from inhibition. There may also be mild hallucinations that create a dreamy state in which the user may experience fantasies. Smokers become highly suggestible and may engage in actions (such as sexual activities) in which they would not otherwise be involved. The drug may induce feelings of joyousness, hilarity, and sociability. It may lead to talkativeness, disconnected ideas, a feeling of floating, and laughter. It may also intensify sensory stimulation, create feelings of enhanced awareness and creativity, and increase self-confidence. A person may gradually experience some of these emotions, followed by others.

The threat of physical dependence is rated low, while the threat of psychological dependence is rated as moderate. Withdrawal, however, may be very unpleasant for the user who may suffer from insomnia, hyperactivity, and loss of appetite.

The short-term physical effects of marijuana are minor: a reddening of the eyes, dryness of the throat and the mouth, and a slight rise in heart rate. There is some evidence that continued use by young teenagers will result in these users becoming apathetic, noncompetitive, and uninterested in school and other activities.

Frequent users may have impairments of short-term memory and concentration, and of judgment and coordination. They may find it difficult to read, or to understand what they read, or to follow moving objects with their eyes. Users may feel confident that their coordination, reactions, and perceptions are quite normal while they are still experiencing the effects of the drug; under these conditions such activities as driving a vehicle may have tragic consequences for them and for others.

An overdose of the active ingredients of cannabis can lead to panic, fear, confusion, suspiciousness, fatigue, and sometimes aggressive acts. One of the most frequently voiced concerns about marijuana is that it will be a "stepping-stone" to using other drugs. About 60 percent of marijuana users "progress" to using other drugs (*Hope Health Letter*, 1991, p. 7). However, other factors such as peer pressure are probably more crucial determinants of what mind-altering drugs people will "progress" to use.

The attempt to restrict the use of marijuana through legislation has been described as a "second prohibition" (Kaplan, 1970), that has had similar results as the first, as a large number of people are using the drug in disregard of the law. The unfortunate effect of laws that attempt to regulate acts (crimes as defined by law) without victims is that they criminalize the private acts of many people who are otherwise law abiding. Such laws also foster the development of organized crime and the illicit drug market.

For years, debates have raged about the hazards of long-term marijuana use. Some studies claim it may cause brain damage, chromosome damage, irritation of the bronchial tract and lungs, and a reduction in male hormone levels. These findings have not been confirmed by other studies, and the controversy rages on.

In 1982 the National Academy of Sciences completed a fifteen-month, extensive study on marijuana.

The study found no evidence that marijuana causes permanent changes in the nervous system and concluded that the drug probably does not break down human chromosomes. It also found that marijuana may be useful in treating glaucoma, asthma, certain seizure disorders and spastic conditions, and in controlling severe nausea caused by cancer chemotherapy. The study warned, however, that the drug presents a variety of short-term health risks and justifies "serious national concern." One of the reversible, short-term health effects is impairment of motor coordination, which adversely affects driving or machine-operating skills. The drug also impairs short-term memory, slows learning abilities, and may cause periods of confusion and anxiety. The study also found evidence that smoking marijuana may affect the lungs and respiratory system in much the same way that tobacco smoke does, and may be a factor in causing bronchitis and precancerous changes. Thus, the study found some evidence that marijuana may lead to certain adverse, long-term health problems. The major recommendation was that "there be a greatly intensified and more-comprehensive program of research into the effects of marijuana on the health of the American people" (U.S. Government Printing Office, 1982).

Anabolic Steroids

Anabolic steroids are synthetic male hormones. Although steroids have been banned for use by athletes in sporting competition, steroids are still being used by some athletes, body builders, and teenagers who want to look more muscular and brawny. From early childhood, many boys have been socialized to believe that the ideal man looks something like Mr. Universe. Such well-known athletes as Olympic sprinter Ben Johnson and Seattle linebacker Brian Bosworth are known to have taken the steroid shortcut to be more muscular and to increase running speed (Toufexis, 1989).

An estimated 1 million Americans, half of them adolescents, use black-market steroids (Schrof, 1992, p. 55). Many adolescents who use steroids want to be sports champions. Steroids are derivatives of the male hormone testosterone. Some young male body builders who use steroids to promote tissue growth and to endure arduous workouts routinely flood their bodies with one hundred times the testosterone they produce naturally (Schrof, 1992, p. 56). Most steroid users are middle class and white.

Steroid-enhanced physiques are a hazardous prize. Steroids can cause temporary acne and balding, upset hormonal production, and damage the heart and kidneys. Doctors suspect they may contribute to liver cancer and atherosclerosis (Toufexis, 1989). For teens, the drugs can stunt growth by accelerating bone maturation. Male steroid users have also experienced shrinking of the testicles, impotence, yellowing of the skin and eyes, and development of female-type breasts. In young boys, steroids can have the effect of painfully enlarging the sex organs. In female users, the voice deepens permanently, breasts shrink, periods become irregular, the clitoris swells in size, and hair is lost from the head but grows on the face and body.

Steroid drug users are prone to moodiness, depression, and irritability. Users are apt to experience difficulty in tolerating stress. Some males (who had been easygoing prior to steroid use) experience raging hostility after prolonged use, which is displayed in a variety of ways—ranging from being obnoxious to continually provoking physical fights. Some users become so depressed that they commit suicide.

Steroid users generally experience considerable difficulty in terminating steroids after prolonged use. One reason is that bulging biceps and ham-hock thighs soon fade when steroid use is discontinued. Concurrent with the decline in muscle mass is the psychological feeling of being less powerful and less "manly." Most users who try to quit wind up back on the drug. A self-image that relies on a steroid-enhanced physique is difficult to change.

Dependence on Alcohol and Other Drugs

Habit-forming drugs can lead to *dependence*, which is a tendency or craving for the repeated use or compulsive use (not necessarily abuse) of a chemical. This dependence may be physical, psychological, or both. When physical dependence occurs, the user will generally experience bodily withdrawal symptoms when drug use is discontinued. Withdrawal may take many forms and range in severity from slight tremblings to fatal convulsions.

When psychological dependence occurs, the user feels psychological discomfort if use is terminated.

Dependent users also tend to believe that they will use the chemical for the rest of their lives as a regular part of social/recreational activities. They also question whether the desired emotional state can be achieved without the use of the chemical, and they have a preoccupation with thinking and talking about the chemical and activities associated with using it.

Users also generally develop a *tolerance* for some drugs, which means they have to take increasing amounts over time to achieve a given level of effect. Tolerance partly depends on the type of drug, as some drugs (such as aspirin) do not create tolerance.

Drug addiction is difficult to define. In a broad sense addiction refers to an intense craving for a particular substance. The problem is this definition could be applied to an intense craving for a variety of substances—pickles, ice cream, potato chips, strawberry shortcake. To avoid this problem we will define addiction as an intense craving for a drug that develops after a period of physical dependence stemming from heavy use.

Why Do People Use and Abuse Alcohol and Other Drugs?

The effects of using drugs are numerous, ranging from feeling light-headed to death through overdosing. Drug abuse may lead to deterioration in health, relationship problems, automobile accidents, child abuse and spouse abuse, loss of job, low self-esteem, loss of social status, financial disaster, divorce, and arrests and convictions.

A distinction needs to be made between responsible drug use and drug abuse. Many drugs do have beneficial effects when used responsibly; aspirin relieves pain, alcohol helps people relax, tranquilizers reduce anxiety, antidepressant drugs reduce depression, amphetamines increase alertness, morphine is a painkiller, and marijuana is useful in treating glaucoma. Irresponsible drug use is abuse, which has already been defined.

Why do people abuse drugs? The reasons are numerous. Drug companies widely advertise the beneficial effects of their products. The media (such as television and movies) glamorize the mind-altering effects. Many popular songs highlight drinking. Taverns and cocktail lounges have become centers for socializing, and promote drinking. Through such channels, Americans have become socialized to accept drug usage as a part of daily living. Socialization patterns lead many people to use drugs, and for some the use is a stepping-stone to abuse.

Attitudes toward drug use also encourage abuse. For example, some college students believe that they should get blitzed or stoned after a tough exam. Ryne Duren (1979), former pitcher for the New York Yankees, raised the question: "I started becoming an alcoholic at age four, even though I had my first drink at age nine—how can this be?" Duren went on to explain that at a very young age he became socialized to believe a real man was "someone who could drink others under the table," and that the way to have fun was to get high on alcohol.

People abuse drugs for a variety of reasons. Some people build up a tolerance to a drug, and then increase the dosage to obtain a high. Physical and psychological dependence usually lead to abuse. People with intense unwanted emotions (such as intense loneliness, anxiety, feelings of inadequacy, guilt, depression, insecurity, and resentment) may turn to excessive use of drugs to relieve the intensity of their unwanted emotions. For many abusers their drug of choice becomes their best friend as they tend to personalize it and value it more highly than they value their friends. The drug is something that they can always count on to relieve pain or give them the kind of high they desire. Many abusers become so highly attached to their drug that they choose to continue using their drug of choice even though it leads to deterioration of health, divorce, discharges from jobs, automobile accidents, alienation from children, loss of friends, depletion of financial resources, and court appearances. Drug abusers usually feel they need their drug as a crutch to make it through the day.

Abusers develop an intimate relationship with their drug of choice. Even though this relationship is unhealthy, the drug plays a primary role in the abuser's life, dictates a certain life-style, fills a psychological need, and more often than not takes precedence over family, friends, and work. Most abusers *deny* their drug usage is creating problems for them, because they know that admitting they have a drug problem means they will have to end their relationship with their best friend, and they deeply believe they need their drug to psychologically handle their daily concerns and pressures. Drug abusers are apt to use the following defense mechanisms in order to

continue using drugs. They *rationalize* adverse consequences of drug abuse (such as loss of job) by twisting or distorting reality to explain the consequences of their behavior while under the influence. They *minimize* the adverse consequences of their drug use. They use *projection* to place the blame for their problems on others; for example, "If you had a wife like mine, you'd drink too."

About Drug Use

There are also a variety of theories as to why people use drugs. *Biological theories* assert that physiological changes produced by the drugs eventually generate an irresistible craving for the drug. Some biological theories also postulate that some people are predisposed by their genetic structure to abuse (or use to excess) certain types of drugs. For example, some authorities believe that genes play a role in predisposing some people to alcoholism. *Behavioral theories* hold that people use drugs because they find them pleasurable and continue to use them because doing so prevents withdrawal distress. *Interactionist theories* maintain that drug use is learned from interaction with others in our culture; for example, people drink alcohol because drinking is widely accepted. Interactionist theories assert that those who use such illegal drugs as marijuana or cocaine have contact with a drug subculture which encourages them to experiment with and to continue to use illegal drugs.

Interaction in Family Systems: A Theoretical Approach to Drug Abuse

Sharon Wegscheider (1981) maintains that chemical dependency is a family disease that involves and affects each family member. Although she focuses on the families of alcoholics, much of what she says is also frequently applied to the families of other types of chemical substance abusers.

She cites several rules that tend to characterize the families of drug abusers. First, the dependent person's alcohol use becomes "the most important thing in the family's life" (Wegscheider, 1981, p. 81). The abuser's top priority is getting enough alcohol, and the family's top priorities are the abuser, the abuser's behavior, and keeping the abuser away from alcohol. The goals of the abuser and of the rest of his or her family are at completely opposite poles.

A second rule in an alcoholic family is that alcohol is not the cause of the problem. Denial is paramount. A third family rule maintains that the dependent person is really not responsible for his or her behavior and that the alcohol causes the behavior. There is always someone or something else to blame. Another rule dictates that no one should rock the boat, no matter what. Family members strive to protect the family's status quo, even when the family is miserable. Yet other rules concern forbidding discussion of the family problem either within or outside of the family, and consistently avoiding stating one's true feelings.

Wegscheider maintains that these rules act to protect the dependent person from taking responsibility for his or her behavior, and that they actually serve to maintain the drinking problem. She goes on to identify several roles which are typically played by family members. In addition to the chemically dependent person, there is the chief enabler, the family hero, the scapegoat, the lost child, and the mascot.

The chief enabler's main purpose is to assume the primary responsibility for family functioning. The abuser typically continues to lose control and relinquishes responsibility. The chief enabler, on the other hand, takes more and more responsibility and begins making more and more of the family's decisions. A chief enabler is often the parent or spouse of the chemically dependent person.

Conditions in families of chemically dependent people often continue to deteriorate as the dependent persons lose control. A positive influence is needed to offset the negative. The family hero fulfills this role. The family hero often is the perfect person who does well at everything he or she tries. The hero works very hard at making the family look like it is functioning better than it is. In this way the family hero provides the family with self-worth.

Another typical role played by someone in the chemically dependent family is the scapegoat. Although the alcohol abuse is the real problem, a family rule mandates that this fact must be denied. Therefore, the blame must be placed elsewhere. Frequently, another family member is blamed for the problem. The scapegoat often behaves in negative ways (for example, gets caught for stealing, runs away, becomes extremely withdrawn) that draw attention to him or her. The scapegoat's role is to distract atten-

tion away from the dependent person and onto something else. This role helps the family avoid addressing the problem of chemical dependency.

Often there is also a lost child in the family. This is the person who seems rather uninvolved with the rest of the family, yet never causes any trouble. The lost child's purpose is to provide relief to the family from some of the pain it is suffering. At least there is someone in the family who neither requires much attention nor causes any stress. The lost child is simply just there.

Finally, chemically dependent families often have someone playing the role of mascot. The mascot is the person who probably has a good sense of humor and appears not to take anything seriously. Despite how much the mascot might be suffering inside, he or she provides a little fun for the family.

In summary, chemical dependency is a problem affecting the entire family. Each family member is suffering from the chemical dependency, yet each assumes a role in order to maintain the family's status quo and to help the family survive. Family members are driven to maintain these roles no matter what happens. The roles eventually become associated with survival.

Application of Theory to Client Situations: Treatment for the Chemically Dependent Person and His or Her Family

One of the first tasks in treatment is to allow the chemically dependent person to take responsibility for his or her own behavior. The abuser must acknowledge that he or she has a problem before beginning to solve it. Several concepts involving working with the family are critical (Wegscheider, 1981). Family members must first come to realize the extent of the problem. They need to identify the chemical abuse as their major problem. Additionally, they need to learn about and evaluate their family dynamics. They need to evaluate their own behavior and break out of the roles which were maintaining the dependent person's abuse. The chief enabler, in particular, must stop making excuses and assuming the dependent's responsibility. If the dependent is sick from a hangover and cannot make it to school or work the next day, it must be the dependent's responsibility, not a parent's or spouse's, to call in sick.

Family members eventually learn to confront the chemically dependent person and give him or her honest information about his or her behavior. For instance, they are encouraged to tell the dependent exactly how that person behaved while having a blackout. If the dependent hit another family member while drunk, this fact needs to be confronted. The confrontation should occur not in an emotional manner but rather in a factual one.

The family also needs to learn about the progression of the disease. We've already discussed some characteristics of drug dependence. Figure 11.4 portrays the typical progression of an alcoholic's feelings and behavior. At first only occasional relief drinking occurs. Drinking becomes more constant. The dependent then begins to drink in secret and to feel guilty about drinking. Memory blackouts begin to occur and gradually increase in frequency. The dependent feels worse and worse about his or her drinking behavior, but seems to have less and less control over it. Finally, the drinking begins to seriously affect work, family, and social relationships. A job may be lost or all school classes flunked. Perhaps, family members leave or throw the dependent out. The dependent's thinking becomes more and more impaired.

Eventually, the dependent person hits rock bottom. Nothing seems to be left but despair and failure, and the dependent admits complete defeat. It is at this point that the dependent person may make one of two choices. Either he or she will continue on the downward spiral to a probable death related to alcohol or may desperately struggle. Typically during this period, the dependent will make some progress only to slip back again. Vicious cycles of drinking and stopping are often apparent.

Finally, the dependent person may express an honest desire for help. A dependent person on the path to recovery will stop drinking. Meeting with other people who are also alcoholics or addicts is also very helpful. Support from others at this time in the process of recovery is especially critical.

Alcoholics Anonymous (AA) is a self-help organization that has provided the support, information, and guidance necessary for many dependent people to continue on in their recovery. The nationwide group is made up of other recovering alcoholics. The organ-

ization's success seems to rest on several principles. First, other people who really understand are available to give the recovering dependent person friendship and warmth. Each new member is given a sponsor who can be called for support at any time during the day or night. Whenever the dependent person feels depressed or tempted, there is always the sponsor to turn to.

AA provides the recovering alcoholic with a new social group and activities. The recovering alcoholic can no longer participate in the drinking activity. Old friends with well-established drinking patterns usually become difficult to associate with. Often social pressure is applied to drink again. AA provides a respite from such pressure and the opportunity to meet new people, if such an opportunity is needed.

AA also helps the recovering person to understand that alcoholism is a disease. This means that the alcoholic cannot cure him- or herself. He or she need no longer feel guilty about being an alcoholic. All that needs to be done is to stop drinking. AA also encourages introspection. Members are encouraged to look inside themselves and face whatever they see. They are urged to acknowledge the fact that they have flaws and will never be perfect. This perspective often helps people to stop fleeing from the pain of reality and hiding in alcohol or drugs. It helps them to redefine the expectations for themselves and to gain control. Within the context of this honesty, people often can also acknowledge their strengths. They can learn that they do have some control over their own behavior and that they can accomplish things for themselves and for others.

Organizations are also available to provide support for other family members and to give them information and suggestions. For example, Al-Anon is an organization for the families of alcoholics, and Al-Ateen is specifically for teenagers within these families. Likewise, self-help organizations similar to AA, such as Narcotics Anonymous, exist to help other types of chemical substance abusers.

Today a range of treatment approaches are available to chemical substance abusers. Types of facilities and treatment include inpatient and outpatient treatment programs at community mental health centers, chemical abuse rehabilitation centers and medical hospitals; halfway houses, and chemical treatment programs such as Antabuse. When Antabuse is taken, a person who then drinks an alcoholic beverage will

FIGURE 11.4: Alcohol Addiction and Recovery

To be read from left to right

occasional relief drinking

constant relief drinking begins

increase in alcohol tolerance

surreptitious drinking

onset of memory blackouts

urgency of first drink

increasing dependence on alcohol

feelings of guilt

unable to discuss problem

memory blackouts increase

decrease of ability to stop drinking when others do so

drinking bolstered with excuses

grandiose and aggressive behavior

persistent remorse

efforts to control fail repeatedly

promises and resolutions fail

tries geographical escapes

loss of other interests

family and friends avoided

work and money troubles

unreasonable resentments

neglect of food

loss of ordinary will power

tremors and early morning drinks

decrease in alcohol tolerance

physical deterioration

onset of lengthy intoxications

moral deterioration

impaired thinking

drinking with inferiors

indefinable fears

unable to initiate action

obsession with drinking

vague spiritual desires

all alibis exhausted

complete defeat admitted

crucial phase

chronic phase

enlightened and interesting way of life opens up with road ahead to higher levels than ever before

group therapy and mutual help continue

increasing tolerance

rationalizations recognized

contentment in sobriety

care of personal appearance

confidence of employers

first steps towards economic stability

increase of emotional control

appreciation of real values

facts faced with courage

re-birth of ideals

new circle of stable friends

new interests develop

family and friends appreciate efforts

adjustment to family needs

natural rest and sleep

desire to escape goes

realistic thinking

return of self-esteem

regular nourishment taken

appreciation of possibilities of new way of life

diminishing fears of the unknown future

start of group therapy

onset of new hope

physical overhaul by doctor

spiritual needs examined

right thinking begins

assisted in making personal stock taking

meets normal and happy former addicts

stops taking alcohol

learns alcoholism is an illness

told addiction can be arrested

honest desire for help

rehabilitation

obsessive drinking continues in vicious circles

SOURCE: M. M. Glatt, "Group Therapy in Alcoholism," *British Journal of Addiction* 54 (2). Used by permission of the Society for the Study of Addiction, Edinburgh, Scotland.

An AA Meeting

Alcoholics Anonymous is a remarkable human organization. Its chapters now cover every part of the United States and most of the world. There is more caring and concern among the members for one another than in most other organizations. Group members work together to save the lives of each other and to restore self-respect and sense of worth. AA has helped more people overcome their drinking problems than all other therapies and methods combined.

AA is supported entirely by voluntary donations from the members at meetings. There are no dues or fees. Each chapter is autonomous, free of any outside control by the AA headquarters in New York City or by any other body. There is no hierarchy in the chapters. The only office is that of group secretary. This person chooses a chairperson for each meeting, makes the arrangements for meetings, and sees that the building is opened, the chairs set up, and the tea and coffee put on. The group secretary holds office for only a limited time period; after a month or two the secretary's responsibilities are transferred to another member.

The only requirement for membership in AA is a desire to stop drinking. All other variables (such as economic status, social status, race, religion) do not count. Members can even attend meetings while drunk, as long as they do not disturb the meeting.

AA meetings are held in a variety of physical locations—churches, temples, private homes, business offices, schools, libraries, or banquet rooms of restaurants. The physical location is unimportant.

When a newcomer first arrives, he or she will usually find people setting up chairs, placing ashtrays, putting free literature on a table, and making coffee. Other members will be socializing in small groups. Someone is apt to introduce himself or herself and other members to the newcomer. If someone is shy about attending the first meeting alone, he or she can call AA and someone will take the person to the meeting, and introduce him or her to the other members.

When the meeting starts, everyone sits down around tables or in rows of chairs. The secretary and/or chairperson and one or more speakers sit at the head of a table or on a platform if the meeting is in a hall.

The chairperson opens with a moment of silence, which is followed by a group recitation of a prayer that is nondenominational. The chairperson then reads or gives a brief description of Alcoholics Anonymous and may read or refer to a section of the book *Alcoholics Anonymous* (a book that describes the principles of AA and also gives a number of case examples).

Then, the chairperson usually asks if anyone is attending for the first, second, or third time. The new people are asked to introduce themselves according to the following: "Hello, my name is (first name), and this is my first (second, third) meeting." Those who do not want to introduce themselves are not pressured to do so. New members are the lifeblood of AA, and the most important people at the meeting in the members' eyes. (All the longer term members remember their first meeting and how frightened and inhibited they felt.)

If the group is small, the chairperson usually then asks the longer term members to introduce themselves and say a few words. If the group is large, the chairperson asks volunteers among the longer term members to introduce themselves by saying a few words. Each member usually begins by saying, "My name is (first name); I am an alcoholic" and then discloses a few thoughts or feelings. (The members do not have to say they are alcoholic, unless they choose to do so. Each member sooner or later generally chooses to say this, to remind him- or herself that he or she is an addictive drinker who is recovering and that alcoholism is a lifelong disease, which must be battled daily.) Those who introduce themselves usually say whatever they feel will be most helpful to the newcomers. They may talk about their first meeting, or their first week without drinking, or something designed to make the newcomers more comfortable. Common advice for the newcomers is to get the phone numbers of other members after the meeting so that they can call them when they feel a strong urge to drink. AA considers such help as vital in recovering. The organization believes members can only remain sober through receiving the help of people who care about them and who understand what they are struggling with.

AA members want newcomers to call when they have the urge to drink, at any time day or night. The members sincerely believe that by helping others they are helping themselves to stay sober and grow. Members indicate that such calling is the newcomer's ace in the hole against the first drink, if everything else fails. They also inform newcomers that it is good to call others when lonely, just to chat.

In his own words, a newcomer explains how AA began to help him:

Here's what happened to me. When I finally hit bottom and called AA for help, a U.S. Air Force officer came to tell me about AA. For the first time in my life, I was talking to someone who obviously really understood my problem, as four psychiatrists had not, and he took me to my first meeting, sober but none too steady. It was amazing. I went home afterward and didn't have a drink. I went again the next night, still dry, and the miracle happened a second time. The third morning my wife went off to work, my boys to school, and I was alone. Suddenly I wanted a drink more than I had ever wanted one in my life. I tried walking for a while. No good. The feeling was getting worse. I tried reading. Couldn't concentrate. Then I became really desperate, and although I wasn't used to calling strangers for help, I called Fred, an AAer who had said that he was retired and would welcome a call at any time. We talked a bit; he could see that talking on the phone wasn't going to be enough. He said, "Look, I've got an idea. Let me make a phone call, and I'll call you back in ten minutes. Can you hold on that long?" I said I could. He called back in eight, asking me to come over to his house. We talked endlessly, went out for a sandwich together, and finally my craving for a drink went away. We went to a meeting. Next morning I was fine again, and now I had gone four days without a drink.[1]

After such discussion speakers may describe their life of drinking, how drinking almost destroyed their life, how they were introduced to AA, their struggles to remain sober one day at a time, how AA has helped them, and what their life is now like.

At the end of a meeting the chairperson may ask the newcomers if they wish to say anything. If they do not wish to say much, that is okay. No one is pressured to self-disclose what they do not want to reveal.

Meetings usually end after the chairperson makes announcements. (The collection basket for donations is also passed around. New members are not expected, and frequently not allowed, to donate any money until after the third meeting. If someone cannot afford to make a donation, none is expected.) The group then stands, usually holding hands, and repeats in unison the Lord's Prayer.

---

1. Clark Vaughan, *Addictive Drinking* (New York: Penguin, 1984), pp. 75-76.

Those who do not want to join in this prayer are not pressured to do so. After a meeting the members socialize. This is a time for newcomers to meet new friends and to get phone numbers.

AA is a cross-section of people from all walks of life. Anonymity is emphasized. It is the duty of every member to respect the anonymity of every person who attends. Concern for anonymity is a major reason for two kinds of meetings in AA, open and closed. Anyone is welcome at open meetings. Only people with drinking problems are allowed at closed meetings. Therefore, if a person feels uncomfortable going to an open meeting and has a drinking problem, then closed meetings are an alternative.

Members do not have to believe in God to get help from AA. Many members have lost, or never had, a faith in God. AA does, however, assert that faith in some Higher Power is a tremendous help in recovery because such a belief offers a source of limitless power, hope, and support whenever one feels one has come to the end of one's resources.

How does AA help? New members, after years of feelings of rejection, loneliness, misunderstanding, guilt, and embarrassment, find they are not alone. They feel understood by others who are in similar predicaments. Instead of being rejected, they are welcomed. They see that others who had serious drinking problems are now sober, apparently happy that way, and are in the process of recovering. It gives them hope that they do not need alcohol to get through the day and that they can learn to enjoy life without alcohol. They find that others sincerely care about them, want to help them, and have the knowledge to do so.

At meetings they see every sort of personal problem brought up and discussed openly, with suggestions for solutions being offered from others who have encountered similar problems. They can observe that group members bring up "unspeakable" problems without apparent embarrassment, and that others listen and treat them with respect and consideration. Such acceptance gradually leads newcomers to share their personal problems and to receive constructive suggestions for solutions. Such disclosure leads individuals to look more deeply into themselves and to ventilate deep personal feelings. With the support of other members, newcomers gradually learn how to counter strong desires to drink, through such processes as calling other members.

Newcomers learn that AA is the means of staying away from that first drink. AA also serves to reduce the stress that

(continued next page)

An AA Meeting (continued)

compels people to drink by: (a) providing a comfortable and relaxed environment and (b) having members helping each other to find ways to reduce the stresses encountered in daily living. AA meetings and members become a safe port that is always there when storms start raging. AA helps members to be programmed from negative thinking to positive thinking. The more positive a member's thinking becomes, the more stress is relieved, the better he or she begins to feel about him- or herself, the more the compulsion to drink decreases, and the more often and more effectively the person begins to take positive actions to solve his or her problems.

soon become flushed, his or her pulse will quicken, and he or she will feel nauseated, often to the point of regurgitation.

Treatment programs almost always advocate that abusers totally abstain from their drug of choice in the future, as research indicates that even one use will return the abuser to drug abuse. It should also be noted that when abusers complete a treatment program they are urged to view themselves as recovering rather than cured as they continually must work on abstaining in order to avoid the temptations of using. It is important that those receiving treatment also make lifestyle changes. The social activities of users almost always revolve around using the drug of choice; to successfully abstain, it is important that recovering abusers form new friendships and establish drug-free social activities and interests. Making such life-style changes is extremely difficult. Many recovering addicts fail in making these changes and then return to using their drug of choice.

Roles assumed by social workers in treating addicts and family members include counselor, group facilitator, broker, program initiator, and educator. The role of a social worker in confronting denial is described in "Working with Alcoholic Clients: The Problem of Denial."

Understanding and Treating Codependency

Codependent people are so trapped by a loved one's addiction that they lose their own identity in the process of obsessively managing the day-to-day trauma created by the addict. Codependency is unhealthy behavior learned amid chaos. Some codependents are as dysfunctional as the addict, if not more so. Living with addiction triggers excessive caretaking, suppression of one's needs, a feeling of low self-worth, and strained relationships. The life and identity of a codependent becomes "enmeshed" with the everyday problems of living with an addict.

Many codependents grow up in a dysfunctional family. (Some are adult children of alcoholics.) They marry or become romantically involved with someone who abuses alcohol or some other drug. To some extent, the addict fills the needs of the codependent—needs such as caretaking, loneliness, and addiction to destructive behavior, such as excessive partying and thrill seeking. Codependency can be viewed as a normal reaction to abnormal stress.

If the addict terminates the use of his or her drug of choice, the codependent's dysfunctional behaviors generally continue, unless he or she receives treatment. There are a variety of treatment approaches for codependents—individual psychotherapy, self-help groups (such as Al-Anon and Adult Children of Alcoholics), and codependency therapeutic groups. For many codependents, treatment involves recognition that they have a life and an identity separate from the addict; that the addict alone is responsible for his or her drug abuse; and that their life and the addict's will improve by terminating their caretaking and enabling behaviors. Through treatment, many codependents regain (or gain for the first time in their life) their own identity. Treatment is designed to banish the self-destructive habits that sabotage the codependent's happiness.

Roles assumed by social workers in treating codependents include: counselor, educator (through conveying information about addiction and codependency), facilitator (through leading treatment groups), broker (through linking codependents to self-help groups and to other human service resources), and program initiator (through being a catalyst in developing needed new programs to serve codependents in com-

Working with Alcoholic Clients: The Problem of Denial

Michael Jacobs (1981) has written an excellent handbook of counseling strategies for alcoholic persons. He addresses a variety of problems commonly encountered when working with alcoholic clients and suggests intervention strategies to deal with each. One specific problem, namely that of denial, and the accompanying intervention strategies will be summarized here.

Jacobs suggests:

During the early phases of treatment it can be difficult to differentiate between clients who genuinely do not believe they have a problem and those who privately fear they can no longer control their drinking. One surefire way of losing clients before the distinction can be made is to demand total abstinence. Even if clients are willing to return, they are likely to be hostile and resistant, because the counselor has unwittingly compelled them to entrench their denial more deeply. Early confrontation with deniers is most ill-advised. (P. 10)

Jacobs continues that goals of the first sessions should be very basic. For instance, the client might simply agree to return for the next session. We have already established the need to help the dependent person accept responsibility for his own behavior and its effects. When working with persons who deny they are alcoholics, any confrontation should be as "unthreatening" as possible (p. 10). For instance, the social worker might ask, "If you were to stop drinking, do you think your life would be any different? If so, in what ways?" or "Do you ever get the feeling you're having trouble controlling your drinking?"

More direct use of confrontation should only be used after a stronger relationship between worker and client has been established. It is crucial to time the confrontation well. A problem at work related to alcohol or a crisis in the marriage might provide exceptionally good possibilities for confronting the client about the effects of his drinking. For instance, the social worker might then say, "It looks like you're having a serious problem. Let's look at how it's related to drinking."

Many times it's tedious to work with a genuine denier. Jacobs warns that sometimes the client will choose to discontinue treatment when the worker places greater demands on him for self-assessment. However, "the counselor can take solace in knowing that he or she has done all that can be reasonably expected" (p. 12). The bottom line is that it is the client's choice and responsibility.

In conclusion, Jacobs notes that insight-oriented therapy, especially that which addresses reasons for drinking, is generally unsuccessful with the denial problem. On the other hand, becoming involved in a group therapy situation may encourage deniers to assess themselves and their problem, as they compare themselves to others.

---

munities where treatment programs for codependents are scarce or nonexistent).

The Relationship Between Knowledge and Assessment

Considerable attention has been given to the issue of chemical substance abuse. It was selected because it is especially critical and widespread. For social workers to be able to intervene and help facilitate another person's recovery from chemical dependency, a base of knowledge is necessary. Social workers need to know some of the dynamics involved in the behavior of chemically dependent individuals and families, and they need to understand the concept of enabling. Only then can they assess a family accurately and know at what point intervention is needed. With this base of knowledge, skills can be applied to help family members stop their enabling and their maintenance of false rules. Social work skills can also be used to encourage the family to realign responsibility. Other family members need to relinquish it to the chemically dependent person. In summary, the examination of such a major life issue should provide social workers with a starting point on which to begin problem assessment. The intent is to provide a map or guide to begin the process of intervention.

Summary

Erikson asserted that middle-aged adults face the developmental crisis of generativity versus stagnation. Peck theorized there are four psychological advances that are critical to successful adjustment in middle adulthood: (1) emphasizing socializing rather than sexualizing in human relationships; (2) valuing wisdom rather than physical powers; (3) having cathectic flexibility rather than cathectic impoverishment; and (4) having mental flexibility rather than mental rigidity. Levinson theorizes that people shape their life structures during four overlapping eras: preadulthood, early adulthood, middle adulthood, and late adulthood. There are transitional periods within some of these eras, and there are also transitional periods that connect these eras. According to Levinson, people spend nearly half their adult lives in transition.

This chapter also describes contemporary theories and models for assessing human behavior throughout the life span. Maslow's theory of hierarchy of needs has an ascending order of needs; physiological, safety, belongingness and love, self-esteem, and self-actualization. Analyzing human behavior in terms of games and life scripts provides another useful approach for understanding human behavior. In seeking to assess human behavior it is important to understand nonverbal communication.

William Glasser's control theory asserts that all human behavior is an attempt to reduce the differences between the pictures of what we want and the way we perceive situations in the world. Gawain asserts that it is important for all of us to learn to trust our intuitive knowingness. Neuro-Linguistic Programming (NLP) is the study of the structure of subjective experience, and makes explicit patterns of behavior and change that have previously been only intuitively understandable.

The chapter ends with an examination of the critical issue of chemical substance abuse. Chemical substances include alcohol, barbiturates, tranquilizers, Quaaludes and PCP, amphetamines, cocaine and crack, amyl and butyl nitrate, narcotics, hallucinogens, tobacco, marijuana, and anabolic steroids. As part of the treatment process, chemically dependent persons need to assume responsibility for their behavior.

12

Social Systems and Their Impacts on Middle Adulthood

Poverty is . . .

George Andrus is spending fifty-five hours a week getting his insurance business going and uses his leisure time working around his house. Jenny Savano recently got a divorce, is trying to raise her three children on a meager monthly AFDC grant, and is attending a vocational school to receive training as a secretary. Tom and Eleanor Townsend have their careers well established, their two children have grown and left home, and they enjoy traveling to such exotic places as the Greek Isles. Joan Sarauer spends much of her day caring for her husband who is dying of emphysema. Dorothy and Michael Powers attend church every Sunday and take leadership roles in church activities during the week.

A PERSPECTIVE

There is obviously considerable variation in the major social interests of middle-aged adults. However, there are some fairly common themes:

Settling into a career
Raising children and maintaining a household
Participating in some hobbies
Becoming grandparents
Adjusting to relationship changes with spouse and children after the children leave home
Socializing with friends

This chapter will:

- Describe three major sociological theories about human behavior: functionalism, conflict theory, and interactionism. These theories are macro system theories. (The differences between micro system theories and macro system theories will be described in the next section.)
- Present two prominent political philosophies in the Untied States: liberalism and conservatism.
- Discuss five social problems that middle-aged adults may encounter: poverty, unemployment, surviving in a bureaucracy, empty-shell marriages, and divorce. Single-parent families, blended families, and mothers working outside the home will also be discussed.
- Present material on assessing and intervening in family systems.

Macro System and Micro System Theories

Social scientists over the years have developed a variety of theories to explain the nature of society and its problems. One way of categorizing these theories is by dividing them into macro system theories and micro system theories. *Macro system theories* seek to make sense of the behavior of large groups of people and the workings of entire societies. This chapter will partly focus on describing the three most prominent macro system theories in sociology: functionalism, conflict theory, and interactionism. (These theories are applicable to all age groups, including middle-aged adults.)

Micro system theories, on the other hand, seek to make sense of the effects of group life on individuals. Prominent theories of this type include Erikson's theory, which was summarized in Chapter 7, and learning theory, summarized in Chapter 4.

Advocates of these various theories often disagree with one another. Each of these theories has certain merits and shortcomings. Some theories are more effective in analyzing a particular social problem, while other theories are more effective in analyzing other social problems. Therefore, it is helpful for assessors of human behavior to have a knowledge of all the contemporary theories in order to be able to select the theory or theories that are most effective in analyzing key dynamics of the social problem under study. Often, the greatest understanding of a social problem occurs when the insights gained from different theoretical perspectives are combined.

The Functionalist Perspective

In recent years functionalism has been one of the most influential sociological theories. The theory was originally developed by Emile Durkheim, a French sociologist, and refined by Robert K. Merton, Talcott Parsons, and many others. The theory views society as a well-organized system in which most members agree on common values and norms. Institutions, groups, and roles fit together in a unified whole. Members of society do what is necessary to maintain a stable society because they accept its regulations and rules.

Society is viewed as a system composed of interdependent and interrelated parts. Each part makes a contribution to the operation of the system, thus enabling the entire system to function. The various parts are in delicate balance, with a change in one part affecting the other parts.

A simple way to picture this approach is to use the analogy of a human body. A well-functioning person has thousands of parts with each having a specific function. The heart pumps blood, the lungs draw oxygen into the body and expel carbon dioxide, the stomach digests food for energy, the muscles move bodily parts to perform a variety of functions, and the brain coordinates the activities of the various parts. Each of these parts is interrelated in complex ways to the others and is also dependent on them. Each performs a vital function, without which the entire system might collapse, as in the case of heart failure.

Functionalism asserts that the components of a society, similar to the parts of the human body, do not always work the way they are supposed to work. Things get out of whack. When a component of a society interferes with efforts to carry out essential social tasks,

that part is said to be *dysfunctional*. Often, changes in society introduced to correct a particular imbalance may produce other imbalances, even when things are going well. For example, developing effective birth-control contraceptives (such as the pill) and making these readily available is quite effective in preventing unwanted pregnancies. However, contraceptives may also be a factor leading to increased premarital and extramarital sexual relationships—which is viewed as a problem by some groups.

According to the functionalist perspective, all social systems have a tendency toward equilibrium—maintenance of a steady state, or particular balance, in which the parts of the system remain in the same relationship to one another. The approach asserts that systems have a tendency to resist social change; change is seen as disruptive unless it occurs at a slow pace. Since society is composed of interdependent and interconnected parts, a change in one part of the system will lead to changes in at least some of the other parts. The introduction of the automobile into our society for example, led to drastic changes: the decline of traveling by horses, people being able to commute long distances to work, vacation travel to distant parts of the country, the opening of many new businesses (service stations, car dealerships, etc.), and sharp increases in air pollution and traffic fatalities.

Some of the functions and dysfunctions of a social system are *manifest*, that is, obvious to everyone. For example, a manifest function of police departments is to keep crime rates low. Other functions and dysfunctions are *latent*—hidden and unintended. Sociologists have discovered that when police departments label people they arrest with such stigmatizing labels as "criminal," "outlaw," and "delinquent," a hidden consequence is that those so labeled may actually commit more crimes over the long run than they would if they had never been arrested in the first place. Thus, police departments (in trying to curb crime) may unintentionally, at times, contribute to its increase.

According to functionalists, social problems occur when society, or some part of it, becomes disorganized. *Social disorganization* occurs when a large organization or an entire society is imperfectly organized to achieve its goals and maintain its stability. When disorganization occurs, the organization loses control over its parts.

Functionalists see thousands of potential causes of social disorganization. However, underlying all these causes is rapid social change, which disrupts the balance of society, producing social disorganization. In recent years more technological advances (such as the development of telephones, television, robots, and heart transplants) have occurred in less time than at any other time in human history. These advances have led basic institutions (such as the family and the educational system) to undergo drastic changes. Technological advances have occurred at such a pace that other parts of the culture have failed to keep pace. This *cultural lag* between technological changes and our adaptation to them is viewed as one of the major sources of social disorganization.

Examples of such social disorganization abound. The development of nuclear weapons has the potential to destroy civilization. Advances in sanitation and medical technology have sharply lengthened life expectancy but have also contributed to a worldwide population explosion. Advances in artificial insemination have led to surrogate motherhood, and our society has not as yet decided whether to encourage or discourage this type of motherhood. The development of technological advances in performing abortions has led to the capacity to terminate pregnancies quite safely on request, but it has also led to a national controversy about the desirability of legalized abortions.

Critics of functionalism assert that it is a politically conservative philosophy, as it takes for granted the idea that society as it is (the status quo) should be preserved. As a result, basic social injustices of society are ignored. Critics also argue that the approach is value laden, because one person's disorganization is another person's organization. For example, some people view divorce as being functional, because it is a legal way to terminate a relationship that is no longer working. Functionalism has also been criticized as being a philosophy that works for the benefit of the privileged social classes, while perpetuating the misery of the poor and those who are being victimized by discrimination.

The Conflict Perspective

Conflict theory views society as a struggle for power among various social groups. Conflict is thought to be inevitable and in many cases actually beneficial to society. For example, most Americans would view the struggle of the "freedom fighters" during the Revolutionary War as being highly beneficial to our society. (England, however, viewed these "fighters" as ungrateful insurgents.)

The conflict perspective rests on an important assumption: there are certain things (such as power, wealth, and prestige) that members of society value highly, and most of these valued resources are in scarce supply. Because of their scarcity, conflict theory asserts that people—either individually or in groups—struggle with one another to attain them. Society is thus viewed as an arena for the struggle over scarce resources.

Struggle and conflict may take many forms: competition, disagreements, court battles, physical fights and violence, and war. If the struggles usually involved violence, then nearly everyone would be involved in violent activities, and society would be impossible. As a result, norms have emerged that determine what types of conflict are allowable for which groups. For example, participating in a labor strike or acquiring a higher education is an approved way of competing for the limited money available in our society, while robbery is not an acceptable way.

From the conflict perspective, social change mainly involves reordering the distribution of scarce goods among groups. Unlike functionalism, which views change as potentially destructive, the conflict approach views change as potentially beneficial. Conflict can lead to improvements, advancements, the reduction of discrimination against oppressed groups, and the emergence of new groups as dominant forces in society. Without conflict, society would become stagnant.

Functionalism and conflict theory differ in another way. Functionalists assert that most people obey the law because they believe the law is fair and just, while conflict theorists assert that social order is maintained by authority backed by the use of force. They assert that the privileged classes hold power legally and use the legal system to make others obey their will. They conclude that most people obey the law because they are afraid of being arrested, imprisoned, or even killed if they do not obey.

Functionalists assert that most people in society share the same set of values and norms. In contrast, conflict theorists assert that modern societies are composed of many different groups with divergent values, attitudes, and norms—and, therefore, conflicts are bound to occur. The abortion issue illustrates such a value conflict. Prolife groups and traditional Roman Catholics believe that the human fetus at any stage after conception is a living human being and, therefore, aborting a pregnancy is a form of murder. In contrast, prochoice advocates assert that an embryo for the first few months after conception is not yet a human being because it is unable to survive outside the womb. They also assert that if the state were to forbid a woman to obtain an operation that she desires, the state would be violating her right to control her life.

Not all conflicts stem from disagreements over values. Some conflicts arise in part *because* people share the same values. In our society, for example, wealth and power are highly valued. The wealthy spend considerable effort and resources to maintain their position, while the poor and oppressed groups vehemently advocate for equal rights and a more equitable distribution of income and wealth. Labor unions and owners in many businesses are in a continual battle over wages and fringe benefits. Republicans and Democrats continually struggle with one another in the hopes of gaining increased political power.

In contrast to functionalism being criticized as too conservative, conflict theory has been criticized for being too radical. Critics say that if there were as much conflict as these theorists claim, society would have disintegrated long ago. Conflict theory has also been criticized as encouraging oppressed groups to revolt against the existing power structure, rather than seeking to work within the existing system to address their concerns.

The Interactionist Perspective

The interactionist approach focuses on individuals and the processes of everyday social interaction between them rather than on larger structures of society, such as the educational system, the economy, or religion. Interactionist theory views behavior as a product of each individual's social relationships. Dorwin Cartwright (1951, p. 383) has noted:

How aggressive or cooperative a person is, how much self-respect or self-confidence he has, how energetic and productive his work is, what he aspires to, what he believes to be true and good, whom he loves or hates, and what beliefs or prejudices he holds—all these characteristics are highly determined by the individual's group memberships. In a real sense, they are products of groups and of the relationships between people.

Interactionist theory asserts that human beings interpret or define each other's actions instead of merely reacting. This interpretation is mediated by the use of symbols (particularly the words and language that a person learns).

Interactionists study the socialization process in detail because it forms the foundation for human interaction. The approach asserts that people are the products of the culture and social relationships in which they participate. Coleman and Cressey (1984, p. 21) summarize this approach:

People develop their outlook on life from participation in the symbolic universe that is their culture. They develop their conceptions of themselves, learn to talk, and even learn how to think as they interact early in life, with family and friends. But unlike the Freudians, interactionists believe that an individual's personality continues to change throughout life in response to changing social environments.

The work of the American philosopher George Herbert Mead has been the driving force behind the interactionists' theories of social psychology. Mead noted that the ability to communicate in symbols (principally words and combinations of words) is the key feature that distinguishes humans from other animals. Individuals develop the ability to think and to use symbols in the process of socialization. Young children blindly imitate the behavior of their parents, but eventually they learn to "take the role of the other," pretending to be "Mommy" or "Daddy." And from such role taking children learn to understand the interrelationships among different roles and to see themselves as they imagine others see them. Eventually, Mead said, children begin to take the role of a *generalized other*. In doing so, they adopt a system of values and standards that reflect the expectations of people in general, not just those in the immediate present. In this way *reference groups* as well as actual *membership groups* come to determine how the individual behaves.

Cooley (1902) observed that it is impossible to make objective measures of most aspects of our self-concept—such as how brave, likeable, generous, attractive and honest we are. Instead, in order to gauge the extent to which we have these qualities, we have to rely on the subjective judgments of the people we interact with. In essence, Cooley asserted, we develop our self-concept through "the looking-glass self process," which means we learn what kind of person we are by seeing and hearing how others react to us.

Another important concept is that social reality is what a particular group agrees it is. Social reality is not a purely objective phenomenon.

Interactionist theory views human behavior as resulting from the *interaction* of a person's unique, distinctive personality and the groups he or she participates in. Groups are a factor in shaping one's personality, but the personality is also shaped by the person's unique qualities.

The reality we construct is mediated through symbols. We respond to symbolic reality, not physical reality. Sullivan and colleagues (1980, p. 27) describe the importance of symbols in shaping our reality.

> Symbols are the principal vehicles through which expectations are conveyed from one person to another. A symbol is any object, word or event that stands for, represents, or takes the place of something else. Symbols have certain characteristics. First, the meaning of symbols derives from social consensus—the group's agreement that one thing will represent something else. A flag represents love of country or patriotism; a green light means *go*, not *stop*; a frown stands for displeasure. Second, the relationship between the symbol and what it represents is arbitrary—there is no inherent connection. There is nothing about the color green that compels us to use that, rather than red, as a symbol for *go*; a flag is in reality a piece of cloth for which we could substitute anything, as long as we agreed that it stood for country. Finally, symbols need not be tied to physical reality. We can use symbols to represent things with no physical existence, such as justice, mercy, or God, or to stand for things that do not exist at all, such as unicorns.

A direct offshoot of the interactionist perspective is labeling theory. This theory holds that the labels assigned to a person have a major impact on that person's life. Labels often become self-fulfilling prophecies. If a child is continually called "stupid" by his or her parents, that child is apt to develop a low self-concept, anticipate failure in many areas (particularly academic),

and thereby put forth little effort in school and in competitive interactions with others, and end up failing. If a teenage girl gets a reputation as being promiscuous, adults and peers may label her as such, with other girls then shunning her, and teenage boys ridiculing her, and perhaps some seeking to date her for a one-night stand. If a person is labeled an ex-con for spending time in prison, that person is likely to be viewed with suspicion, have trouble finding employment, and be stigmatized as being dangerous and untrustworthy, even though the person may be honest, conscientious, and hard working. Scheff (1966) has developed a labeling theory to explain why some people develop a career of being mentally ill. He asserts the act of labeling someone mentally ill is the major determinant for their acting as if they were mentally ill. Once labeled, others interact with them as if they were mentally ill, which leads them to view themselves as being mentally ill, and they then enact this role.

The most common criticism of interactionist theory is that the theory is so abstract and vaguely worded that it is nearly impossible either to prove or to disprove it (Coleman and Cressey, 1984, p. 22).

Poverty: Impacts of Social and Economic Forces

The functionalist, conflict, and interactionist perspectives are further illustrated by discussing how each of these theories explains poverty. Poverty is a problem that is faced by a majority of social welfare recipients.

The Rich and the Poor

Poverty and wealth are closely related. Throughout most countries in the world, wealth is concentrated in a small percentage of the population. Abundance for a few is often created by depriving others.

There are two ways of measuring the extent of economic inequality. *Income* refers to the amount of money a person makes in a given period. *Wealth* is a person's total assets—real estate holdings, cash, stocks, bonds, and so forth.

The distribution of wealth and income is highly unequal in our society. Similar to most countries, the United States is characterized by *social stratification*—

that is, it has social classes, with the upper classes having by far the greatest access to the pleasures that money can buy.

Looking at wealth, the lowest fifth of American individuals owns only 0.2 percent of the wealth, while the richest fifth owns more than three-quarters of the wealth (Cooper, 1991). This means 20 percent of the population has three times as much wealth as all of the rest of the people combined! There are over 1.5 million millionaires in this country (Cooper, 1991). The richest 2 percent of our population owns 62 percent of all privately held corporate stock (Kornblum and Julian, 1989, pp. 222-24). It is estimated that approximately 35 percent of all assets in this country are owned by the "super rich" the top 0.5 percent of the population (Cooper, 1991). Almost 20 percent of all American families have a negative net worth, meaning they have more liabilities than assets. Paul Samuelson, an economist, provides a dramatic metaphor of the disparity that exists between the very rich and most people in the United States:

> If we made an income pyramid out of a child's blocks, with each layer portraying $1,000 of income, the peak would be far higher than the Eiffel Tower, but almost all of us would be within a yard of the ground.

A few comments appear in order. Given the huge wealth of the richest fifth, it is clear that a simple redistribution of some of the wealth from the top fifth to the lowest fifth could easily wipe out poverty. Of course, that is not politically acceptable to members of the top fifth who have the greatest control of the government. Also, many of these rich families are able to avoid paying income taxes by taking advantages of tax loopholes and tax shelters.

Similar disparities between the rich and the poor are found when looking at annual income instead of total wealth. The poorest fifth receives only 5 percent of the national income, while the richest fifth receives over 40 percent of the national income. This pattern has remained virtually unchanged since World War II (Cooper, 1991). In our society it is common for heads of major corporations to earn $500,000 or more per year. In addition, these highly paid executives enjoy many other tax-free benefits from their corporations: expense accounts, use of cars and private jets, paid memberships in health clubs, medical care, theater

The Ideology of Individualism

Wealth is generally inherited in this country. There are few individuals who actually move up the social status ladder. Having wealth opens up many doors (through education and contacts) for children of the wealthy to make large sums of money when they become adults. For children living in poverty, there is little chance to escape when they become older. Yet, there is the myth of individualism which is held by many. It states that the rich are personally responsible for their success, and that the poor are to blame for their failure. Joe Feagin (1975, pp. 91-92) has summarized the main points of this myth:

1. Each individual should work hard and strive to succeed in competition with others.
2. Those who work hard should be rewarded with success (seen as wealth, property, prestige, and power).
3. Because of widespread and equal opportunity, those who work hard will, in fact, be rewarded with success.
4. Economic failure is an individual's own fault and reveals lack of effort and other character defects.

The poor are blamed for their circumstances in our society. Blaming the poor has led to a stigma being attached to poverty, particularly to those who receive public assistance (welfare).

tickets, and vacations. Since 1980, the income gap between the rich and the poor in our society has widened substantially (Cooper, 1991).

In contrast millions of Americans regularly do not get enough to eat because they are poor. The brain of an infant grows to 80 percent of its adult size within the first three years of life. If supplies of protein are inadequate during this period, the brain stops growing, the damage is irreversible, and the child will be permanently retarded (Robertson, 1980, p. 31).

Coleman and Cressey (1990, p. 161) describe the effects of having, and not having, wealth:

> The poor lack the freedom and autonomy so prized in our society. They are trapped by their surroundings, living in rundown, crime-ridden neighborhoods that they cannot afford to leave. They are constantly confronted

Personal Income Disparities Are Astounding

In 1992, Ryne Sandberg was paid $7.1 million for playing second base for the Chicago Cubs, while veteran Chicago police officers made $35,814. Madonna in 1992 finalized a deal with a corporation that will pay her $60 million over seven years, while the average teacher in 1992 was paid $34,413 a year.

Robert Stempel, chairman of General Motors, was paid over $1 million in 1991, even though GM lost $8 billion. The president of the United States (considered by many people to be the most important job in the country) is paid less than $300,000 a year.

In 1991, Robert Goizueta, chief executive officer of Coca-Cola, was paid $86 million—including a deferred stock option worth $82 million—which works out to $41,346 per hour. Not bad in a country where the average hourly wage in 1991 was $10.56. When Goizueta explained his salary package to shareholders on April 15, 1992, they interrupted him with applause four times and gave him a standing ovation. The average *annual* income in the poorest 20 percent of the nations on this planet is less than $250!

SOURCE: Susan Dentzer, "The Wealth of Nations," *U.S. News & World Report*, May 4, 1992, p. 54; and Robert Rankin, "Imbalance of Payments," *Wisconsin State Journal*, May 10, 1992, pp. 1A-2A.

with things they desire but have little chance to own. On the other hand, wealth provides power, freedom, and the ability to direct one's own fate. The wealthy live where they choose and do as they please, with few economic constraints. Because the poor lack education and money for travel, their horizons seldom extend beyond the confines of their neighborhood. In contrast, the world of the wealthy offers the best education, together with the opportunity to visit places that the poor haven't even heard of.

The children of the wealthy receive the best that society has to offer, as well as the assurance that they are valuable and important individuals. Because the children of the poor lack so many of the things everyone is "supposed" to have, it is much harder for them to develop the cool confidence of the rich. In our materialistic society people are judged as much by what they have as by who they are. The poor cannot help but feel inferior and inadequate in such a context.

The Problem

In 1991, 34 million Americans, nearly 14 percent of our population, were living below the poverty line (Cooper, 1991). (The poverty line is the level of income that the federal government considers sufficient to meet basic requirements of food, shelter, and clothing.) One of the alarming elements about poverty is that the rate of poverty in recent years has been increasing. In addition, there are many people who do not fall under the government's poverty line, but still have very limited income and a living standard that is similar to those below the poverty line.

Poverty does not simply mean that poor people in the United States are living less well than people of average income. It means eating diets largely of beans,

The poverty rate in the United States is increasing. Children raised in poor families are likely to remain poor in their adult years.

Wealth Perpetuates Wealth, and Poverty Perpetuates Poverty

C. Wright Mills (1956, pp. 69-70) describes one way that wealth educates wealthy children to be financially successful.

The exclusive schools and clubs and resorts of the upper social classes are not exclusive merely because their members are snobs. Such locales and associations have a real part in building the upper-class character, and more than that, the connections to which they naturally lead help to link one higher circle with another. So the distinguished law student, after prep school and Harvard, is "clerk" to a Supreme Court judge, than a corporation lawyer, then in the diplomatic service, then in the law firm again. In each of these spheres, he meets and knows men of his own kind, and, as a kind of continuum, there are the old family friends and the schoolboy chums, the dinners at the club, and each year of his life the summer resorts. In each of these circles in which he moves, he acquires and exercises a confidence in his own ability to judge, to decide, and in this confidence he is supported by his ready access to the experience and sensibility of those who are his social peers and who act with decision in each of the important institutions and areas of public life. One does not turn one's back on a man whose presence is accepted in such circles, even under most trying circumstances. All over the top of the nation, he is "in," his appearance, a certificate of social position; his voice and manner, a badge of proper training; his associates, proof at once of their acceptance and of his stereotyped discernment.

In contrast, Ben Bagdikian (1964, p. 75) describes how living in poverty leads to despair, hopelessness and failure.

It was midafternoon but the tenement was dark. Grey plastic sheeting was tacked to the insides of the living room windows. . . . Plaster was off an expanse of ceiling and walls. . . . In one corner of the kitchen was a small refrigerator, in another a table with three legs and one chair. There was a stained stove bearing a basin full of children's clothes soaked in cold soapy water. . . . Through one kitchen door was a bathroom dominated by a toilet covered by boards; it had frozen and burst during the winter. Through another door was "the kids' room." . . . In this room slept seven children, in two beds. Neither bed had a mattress. The children slept on the springs. . . .

Outside, Sister Mary William . . . said: "You figure out what's going to happen to Harry Martin when he finds out he's never going to be a lawyer. And his brother's never going to be a doctor. And his sister's never going to be a nurse. The worst most of us have to resign ourselves to is that there's no Santa Claus. Wait until this hits those kids."

---

macaroni and cheese, or, in severe cases, even dog and cat food. It may mean not having running water, living in substandard housing, and being exposed to rats, cockroaches, and other vermin. It means not having sufficient heat in the winter and being unable to sleep because the walls are too thin to deaden the sounds from the neighbors living next door. It means being embarrassed about the few ragged clothes that one has to wear. It means great susceptibility to emotional disturbances, alcoholism, and victimization by criminals, as well as having a shorter life expectancy. It means few opportunities to advance oneself socially, economically, or educationally. It often means slum housing, unstable marriages, and little opportunity to enjoy the finer things in life—traveling, dining out, movies, plays, concerts, sports events.

The infant mortality rate of the poor is almost double the rate of the affluent (Kornblum and Julian, 1989, pp. 222-24). The poor have less access to medical services and receive lower quality care from health care professionals. The poor are exposed to higher levels of air pollution, water pollution, and unsanitary conditions. They have higher rates of malnutrition and disease. Schools in poor areas are of lower quality and have fewer resources. As a result the poor achieve less academically and are more apt to drop out of school. They are more apt to be arrested, indicted, imprisoned, and given longer sentences for the same offense. They are less likely to receive probation, parole, or suspended sentences (Kornblum and Julian, 1989, pp. 222-24).

Poverty also often leads to despair, low self-esteem,

The Hurt of Being Poor

Marcee Calvello was born and raised in New York City. Her father had trouble holding a job because he was addicted to cocaine, and her mother was an alcoholic who divorced her husband when Marcee was three years old. Marcee's mother at first sought to provide a better home for Marcee and her three brothers. She worked part time and also went on AFDC. However, her addiction to alcohol consumed most of her time and her money. Neighbors reported that the children were living in abject neglect, and Protective Services removed Marcee and her brothers to foster care. Marcee was placed in a total of seventeen foster homes. In one of the homes her foster father sexually assaulted her, and in another, a foster brother assaulted her. Being moved from foster home to foster home resulted in frequent school changes. Marcee grew distrustful of the welfare system, school teachers and administrators, males, and anyone else who sought to get close to her.

When Marcee turned eighteen, the state no longer paid for her care in foster care. She got a small efficiency apart-ment that cost her several hundred a month. Because she dropped out of school at age sixteen, she had few marketable job skills. She worked for a while at fast food restaurants. The minimum wages she received were insufficient to pay her bills. Eight months after she moved into her apartment, she was evicted. Unable to afford another place, she started living in the subway system of New York City. She soon lost her job at a fast food restaurant because of her poor hygiene and unkempt appearance.

Unable to shower and improve her appearance, Marcee has not been able to secure another job. For the past two years she has been homeless, living on the street and in the subway. She has given up hope of improving her situation. She now occasionally shares IV needles and has been sexually assaulted periodically in the subway by men. She realizes she is at high risk for acquiring the AIDS virus but no longer cares very much. Death appears, to her, to be her final escape from a life that is now filled with victimization and misery.

---

and stunting of one's physical, social, emotional, and intellectual growth. A second level of damage from poverty occurs from the *feeling* that lack of financial resources is preventing one from having equal opportunities and from the *feeling*, then, that one is a second-class citizen. Poverty hurts deeply when it leads to viewing oneself as inferior or second class.

We like to think that America is a land of equal opportunity and that there is considerable upward class mobility for those who put forth effort. The reality is the opposite of the myth. Extensive research has shown that poverty is almost escape proof. Children raised in poor families are apt themselves to live in poverty in their adult years. Most people have much the same social status as their parents had. Movement to a higher social status is an unusual happening in practically all societies—including the United States (Coleman and Cressey, 1990, p. 159).

Who Are the Poor?

An encouraging trend is that the proportion of people below the poverty line has gradually been de-creasing in the last eighty years. Prior to the twentieth century a majority of the population lived in poverty. President Franklin D. Roosevelt (1937) stated, "I see one third of a nation ill-housed, ill-clad, ill-nourished." In 1962, the President's Council on Economic Advisors estimated one-fifth of the population were in poverty (U.S. Bureau of the Census, 1982, p. 441). Now nearly 14 percent of the nation are estimated to be below the poverty line. Since 1978, the proportion of the population who are poor has increased.

Poverty is concentrated in certain population categories, including one-parent families, children, the elderly, large-size families, minorities and the homeless. Educational level, unemployment, and place of residence are also factors related to poverty.

One-Parent Families

Most one-parent families are headed by a female. Thirty-four percent of female-headed families are in poverty, compared to 8 percent of two-parent families (U.S. Bureau of the Census, 1992). Single mothers who are members of a racial minority (African American, Chicano, Native American) are particularly vul-

Most one-parent families are headed by a woman, and 34 percent of female-headed families live in poverty.

nerable to poverty as they are subjected to double discrimination in the labor market due to both race and sex. Women who work full time are paid on the average only 66 percent of what men who work full time are paid. (*Wisconsin State Journal*, Jan. 16, 1990, p. 1). Many single mothers are unable to work due to lack of transportation, to the lack or high cost of daycare services, and to having received little training for available job openings. Unable to work, they have to rely on public assistance (benefits which are often below the poverty line) in the form of Aid to Families with Dependent Children (AFDC). Of the families living in poverty, half are headed by a single mother (U.S. Bureau of the Census, 1992). The increase in one-parent families in the United States has led to an increase in the feminization of poverty. About one out of every five children in this country is now living apart from one parent, and because of increasing divorce rates, separations, and births outside of marriage, it is estimated that a majority of the children born today will spend part of their first eighteen years in a family headed by a single mother (Moynihan, 1988). Single-parent families now compose more than 20 percent of all families in the United States (Moynihan, 1988). The increase in one-parent families has led to an increase in the feminization of poverty.

Children

Approximately 40 percent of the poor are children under the age of eighteen. More than half of these children live in families where the father is absent (U.S. Bureau of the Census, 1992). Many of these children rely on AFDC payments for meeting the basic necessities.

The Elderly

Many of the elderly depend on Social Security pensions or public assistance payments (in the form of Supplementary Security Income) to meet basic neces-

The Poverty Trap

Louise Ferguson, age thirty-three, has recently become a grandmother. Her older daughter, Teresa, is a seventeen-year-old unmarried mother. Today, July 27, is a significant day in their lives, as Louise and Teresa are applying at Milwaukee's Public Welfare Office to place baby Rufus' name on America's welfare rolls. He will represent the third successive generation in the Ferguson family to receive AFDC benefits.

Louise's parents migrated from Mississippi to Milwaukee in 1959, shortly after Louise's birth. Her father got a job as a janitor for the school system, and her mother has been a part-time nurse's aid at a hospital. Louise started high school and received above average grades. She had hopes of getting a student loan to go to college. She wanted to get out of the ghetto in which she was being raised.

However, at the age of sixteen, she became pregnant. Her parents talked her out of an abortion, and she gave birth to Teresa. Two months after the birth, she signed up for AFDC, at the urging of her parents and friends. It would

only be temporary, she thought, until she could get a better handle on her life. She found going to school and caring for a baby to be too much work. So she dropped out of high school in her junior year. She no longer had the same interests as her former friends who did not have a baby to care for. At times Louise found it a joy to care for Teresa, and at other times the baby drove her up a wall. Louise went out as much as she could, when she had a little extra money and when she could find someone to babysit for her. Over the next fifteen years, Louise had four other children. Only one of the five different fathers ever married her, and that marriage only lasted two and one-half years. He left home one day, complaining about children and responsibilities. He never returned, and Louise has never heard from him again.

Louise has tried a variety of jobs while on AFDC—nurse's aid, dishwasher, waitress, and service station attendant. She discovered that costs for transportation, clothes, and babysitting left her no better off financially than if she

sities. Since the 1964 war on poverty programs were enacted, the population group that has benefited most from programs to reduce poverty has been the elderly. Programs such as Medicare, Supplemental Security Income, and increases in monthly payments under the Old Age, Survivors, Disability, and Health Insurance Program have reduced poverty among the elderly from over 25 percent in 1964 to around 12 percent at the present time (U.S. Bureau of the Census, 1992).

Large-Size Families

Large families are more apt to be poor, partly because more income is needed as family size increases. It costs an estimated $140,000 to raise a child from birth to age eighteen (Brophy, 1986).

Minorities

Contrary to popular stereotypes, most poor people (over 60 percent) are white (U.S. Bureau of the Census, 1992). But members of most minority groups are disproportionately apt to be poor. African Americans, for example, make up about 12 percent of the total population, yet they constitute over one-fourth of all

the poor. One out of every three African Americans is poor, compared to one out of ten white persons (U.S. Bureau of the Census, 1991). Approximately one-third of Native American families live below the poverty line, and about 25 percent of Mexican Americans (or Chicanos) live in poverty—particularly migrant workers in agriculture (U.S. Bureau of the Census, 1992). Racial discrimination is a major reason why most racial minorities are disproportionately poor.

The Homeless

One of the symptoms of poverty is people not having the financial resources to obtain housing. The homeless include those who have encountered economic problems such as unemployment, those in personal crisis (divorce, domestic violence, or health problems), and those who are classified as chronically mentally ill. In these categories may be found people evicted from their residences due to lack of funds, former institutionalized mentally ill patients, substance abusers, runaway youths, and the unemployed. Having hundreds of thousands of people homeless in the richest nation in the world is a national disgrace.

stayed home and received her monthly AFDC checks. Life has been hard for Louise. She feels like a second-class citizen and a charity case from being on welfare rolls. She has had to pinch pennies all her life to try to make ends meet. Countless days she has fed her children on beans and rice. She sharply regrets not being able to give her children the materials things that many other children have. While some parents are buying computers for their children, she takes her children to Goodwill's clothing store to try to find bargains on second-hand sneakers, shirts, blue jeans, and jackets.

She is living in a rundown area and is alarmed that her oldest son, Michael, is experimenting with heroin and other drugs. The school system is another concern—a high percentage of students drop out, the windows in the buildings are boarded up, vandalism is frequent, physical attacks on teachers sometimes occur, and the educational quality is known to be inferior.

When she discovered Teresa was sexually active at fifteen, she pleaded with her not to make the mistake she did. When Teresa continued to be sexually active, her mother even took her to Planned Parenthood to receive birth control pills. Louise's remaining dream is that her children will have a better life than hers. Tears often come to her eyes when she sees her children getting caught in the same poverty trap that she is in. Teresa took her pills for several months. When the supply ran out, she never got around to going back to Planned Parenthood to get her prescription refilled.

Yes, today is a significant day for Louise. Significant in the sense that it is sad, as the third generation in her family is now going on welfare. As Louise and Teresa are walking towards the welfare department, Louise is solemnly pondering why her life has turned out as it has and also wondering what it will take to give at least some of her children a chance for a better life.

The economic gap between the haves and the have-nots is greater than it has ever been since government began monitoring this factor over forty years ago.

Estimates of the number of homeless in the United States range from 300,000 to over 3 million. Accurate statistics on the number and characteristics of the homeless are largely unavailable. Many of the homeless live on the streets, in parks, in subways, or in abandoned buildings. Food is often sought from garbage cans and dumpsters.

A significant percent of the homeless are thought to suffer from serious and chronic forms of mental illness. Discharged from mental institutions without the support they need, tens of thousands of former patients live on the street in abominable conditions. Instead of providing adequate support services for discharged patients, many states have a deinstitutionalization program of simply drugging people and turning them back onto the street.

Although most of the homeless are single, a significant percentage are family groups, including mothers with young children. The effects on adults and on young children of being homeless has not been adequately studied. Undoubtedly, the adverse effects of being homeless are immense, due to long-term exposure to crime, violence, fear of being assaulted (both physically and sexually), drugs, inadequate health care, severe weather conditions, contagious diseases, inferior educational services, and food that may be spoiled.

There are a variety of reasons for the large increase in the number of homeless. Deinstitutionalization of state mental hospitals is one reason. Cutbacks in social services during the Reagan and Bush administrations is another. Urban renewal projects have demolished low-cost housing in many areas. The shift from blue-collar jobs to service and high-tech jobs in our society has reduced sharply the demand for unskilled labor. Yet another factor has been a recent trend in our society to ignore members of society who are unable to fend for themselves. Most of the homeless are homeless because they cannot afford the housing that is available. The United States does not have a commitment to a social policy of providing affordable housing to the poor.

The answers to the dismal conditions in which the homeless are living include: low-cost housing, job training and placement programs, and community services for those with emotional problems.

Education

Achieving less than a ninth-grade education is a good predictor of being poor. Completing high school, however, is not a guarantee for earning adequate wages and for avoiding poverty, as many of the poor have graduated from high school. Obtaining a college degree is an excellent predictor of avoiding poverty as only a small proportion of those with a college degree are poor (U.S. Bureau of the Census, 1992).

Employment

Being unemployed is, of course, associated with poverty. However, being employed is not a guarantee of avoiding poverty, as over 1 million heads of families work full time but earn less than the poverty level (U.S. Bureau of the Census, 1992). The general public (and many government officials) wrongly assume that obtaining jobs for unemployed adults is the key to ending poverty. However, jobs alone cannot end poverty.

Place of Residence

People who live in rural areas are more likely to be poor than people who live in urban areas. In rural areas wages are low, there is high unemployment, and work tends to be seasonal. The Ozarks, Appalachia, and the South have pockets of rural poverty with high rates of unemployment (Kornblum and Julian, 1989, pp. 234-36).

People who live in urban slums constitute the largest group in terms of numbers of people who are poor. The decaying cities of the Northeast and Midwest have particularly large urban slums. The urban poor are unable to take advantage of opportunities that are available to the affluent as they often lack job skills, transportation, a decent education, and they also may face racial or ethnic discrimination. Poverty is also extensive on Native American reservations and among seasonal migrant workers.

All these factors indicate some people are more vulnerable to poverty than others. Michael Harrington (1962, p. 21) notes that the poor made the simple mistake of

> being born to the wrong parents, in the wrong section of the country, in the wrong industry, or in the wrong racial

or ethnic group. Once that mistake has been made, they could have been paragons of will and morality, but most of them would never even have had a chance to get out of the other America.

What Causes Poverty?

There are a number of possible causes of poverty, including a high unemployment rate, poor physical health, emotional problems, drug addiction, low education level, racial and sexual discrimination, budgeting problems and mismanagement of resources, and mental retardation.

The above list is not exhaustive. However, it serves to show: (a) there are a large number of causes of poverty, (b) eliminating the causes of poverty would require a wide range of social programs, and (c) poverty interacts with almost all other social problems—such as emotional problems, alcoholism, unemployment, racial and sex discrimination, medical problems, crime, gambling, and mental retardation. The interaction between poverty and these other social problems is complicated. As indicated, these other social problems are contributing causes of poverty. Yet, for some social problems, poverty is also a contributing *cause* of those problems (such as emotional problems, alcoholism, and unemployment). And—being poor intensifies the effects (the hurt) of all social problems.

To some extent poverty is passed on from generation to generation. This cycle of poverty is diagrammed in Figure 12.1.

The Culture of Poverty: Evaluation of Theory and Its Application to Client Situations

Why is poverty passed on from one generation to another? Some authorities argue that the explanation is due to a "culture of poverty." Oscar Lewis (1966), an anthropologist, is one of the chief proponents of the cultural explanation. Lewis examined poor neighborhoods in various parts of the world and concluded the poor are poor because they have a distinct culture or life-style. The key elements of Lewis's cultural explanation are the following.

The culture of poverty arises after extended periods of economic deprivation in highly stratified capitalis-

FIGURE 12.1: A Macro System Problem: The Cycle of Poverty

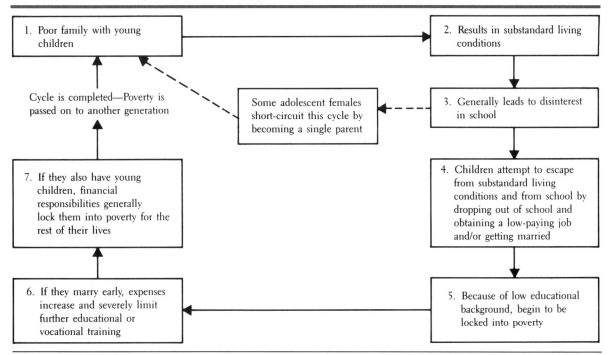

tic societies. Such economic deprivation is brought about by high rates of unemployment and low wages for those who are employed. Such economic deprivation leads to the development of attitudes and values of despair and hopelessness. Lewis (1966, p. 23) describes these attitudes and values as follows:

> The individual who grows up in this culture has a strong feeling of fatalism, helplessness, dependence and inferiority; a strong present-time orientation with relatively little disposition to defer gratification and plan for the future, and a high tolerance for psychological pathology of all kinds.

Once developed, this culture continues to exist, even though the economic factors that created it (for example, lack of employment opportunities) no longer exist. These attitudes, norms, and expectations of the poor serve to limit their opportunities and prevent their escape. A major reason they remain locked into their culture is that they are socially isolated. They have few contacts with groups outside their own culture and are hostile to the institutions (for example,

social services and education) that might be able to help them escape poverty. They reject such institutions because they perceive them as belonging to the dominant class. Furthermore, since they view their financial circumstances as private matters and hopeless and because they lack political and organizational skills, they do not take collective action to try to resolve their problems.

The culture of poverty theory is controversial and has been widely criticized. Eleanor Leacock (1971) argues that the distinctive culture of the poor is not the cause but the result of their continuing poverty. She agrees that the poor tend to emphasize instant gratification, which involves spending and enjoying one's money while it lasts. But she argues that instant gratification is a result of being poor rather than the cause, as it makes no sense to defer gratification when a person is pessimistic about the future. Deferred gratification is a rational response only when one is optimistic that postponing pleasure today by saving the money will reap greater benefits in the future. Studies (Leacock, 1971) have found that when ghetto residents are able to obtain a stable, good-paying job, they display the middle-class value of deferred gratification. Because of poverty, Leacock argues, the poor are forced to abandon middle-class attitudes and values, because such values are irrelevant to their circumstances. If they had stable, good paying jobs, they would likely take on the values of the middle class.

In an even stronger indictment, William Ryan (1976) criticizes the poverty culture theory as simply being a classic example of blaming the victim. Blaming the poor for their circumstances is a convenient excuse, according to Ryan, for avoiding developing the programs and policies thought necessary to eradicate poverty. The real culprit is the social system that allows poverty to exist. Ryan says bluntly that the poor are not poor because of their culture but because they do not have enough money.

Pro and con arguments for the culture of poverty theory continue to persist. There are many reasons, both external and internal, why a person may be poor. External reasons include high rates of unemployment, racial discrimination, automation which throws people out of work, lack of job training programs, sex discrimination, a shortage of programs to eradicate poverty, and inflation. Internal reasons include having a physical or mental impairment, being alcoholic, having obsolete job skills, becoming a parent at an early age, dropping out of school, and being uninterested in taking available jobs.

Poverty Is Functional

Obviously, poverty causes many problems, mainly to the poor themselves, but also to the affluent. However, realizing that poverty has some functions helps us to understand why some decision makers are not actively seeking to eradicate poverty.

Eleven functions provided by the poor for affluent groups are summarized by Sullivan and colleagues (1980, p. 390):

1. They are available to do the unpleasant jobs that no one else wants to do.
2. By their activities, they subsidize the more affluent (an example of such an activity is domestic service for low pay).
3. Jobs are established for those people, such as social workers, who provide services to the poor.
4. They purchase goods, such as those of poor quality, that otherwise could not be sold.

5. They serve as examples of deviance that are frowned on by the majority and that thereby support dominant norms.
6. They provide an opportunity for others to practice their "Christian duty" of helping the less fortunate.
7. They make mobility more likely for others because they are removed from the competition for a good education and good jobs.
8. They contribute to cultural activities by providing, for example, cheap labor for the construction of monuments and works of art.
9. They create cultural forms (for example, jazz and the blues) that are often adopted by the affluent.
10. They serve as symbolic opponents for some political groups and as constituents for others.
11. They often absorb the costs of change (for example, by being the victims of unemployment that results from technological advances).

Also, denigrating the poor has the psychological function for some Americans of making them feel better about themselves.

Partly because poverty is functional, our society makes only a half-hearted effort to eradicate, or at least reduce it. To eliminate it would mean a redistribution of income from the rich to the poor. Since the rich control the political power, they have generally been opposed to proposals that would eliminate poverty, such as guaranteed annual income programs. Gans (1968, pp. 133-35) emphasizes this point:

> Legislation in America tends to favor the interests of the businessman, not the consumers, even though the latter are a vast majority; of landlords, not tenants; of doctors, not patients. Only organized interest groups have the specific concerns and the time, staff, and money to bring their demands before government officials.... The poor are powerless because they are a minority of the population, are not organized politically, are often difficult to organize, and are not even a homogeneous group with similar interests that could be organized into a single pressure group.... Given the antagonism toward them on the part of many Americans, any programs that would provide them with significant gains are likely to be voted down by a majority. Legislative proposals for a massive anti-poverty effort... have always run into concerted and united opposition in Washington.

Our country has the resources to eliminate poverty—but not the will. In the present century, we have been able to find billions of dollars in resources within a

A volunteer works at a food distribution center for the poor.

few months to pay for a war, but we are not willing to allocate similar funds to improve living conditions for the homeless and millions of other people who are living in poverty in this country.

Application of Functionalism to Poverty

Functionalists view poverty as being due to dysfunctions in the economy. A wide range of dysfunctions have been identified, some of which will be mentioned here. Rapid industrialization has caused disruption in the economic system. For example, people who lack job skills are forced into menial work at low wages. Then when automation comes, they are discharged, without having work, money, or marketable job skills. Some products produced by industry also become outdated—such as steam engines, milk bottles, and horse carriages. When such products become obsolete, workers lose their jobs. In addition, work training centers and apprenticeship programs may continue to produce graduates whose skills are no longer in demand—for example, there no longer is a job market for people who are trained to repair adding machines and manual typewriters; and direct telephone

calling is sharply reducing the number of people needed as telephone operators.

Functionalists also note that the welfare system, which is intended to solve the problem of poverty, has a number of dysfunctions. Social welfare programs are sometimes established without sufficient funds to meet the needs of potential clients. Some bureaucrats are reluctant to bend the complex rules to help a deserving family that is technically ineligible for assistance. Social welfare programs at times have design dysfunctions in meeting the needs of recipients—for example, mothers of young children in some states were eligible for AFDC only when the husband was out of home—with the result that some unemployed husbands were forced to desert their family in order for the family to be fed and sheltered. (Federal legislation was enacted in 1988 to remedy this problem by requiring all states to make cash payments to two-parent unemployed AFDC families in which the breadwinner or breadwinners are actively seeking work). There are additional problems in the welfare system. Inadequate information systems fail to inform the poor about benefits to which they are entitled. Job training and educational programs sometimes train people for positions for which there are no employment openings. According to functionalists, the best way to deal with poverty is to make adjustments to correct these dysfunctions.

Many functionalists view some economic inequality (that is, poverty) as being functional. Because the poor are at the bottom of the stratification system, they receive few of the material and social rewards in the society. Functionalists view the threat of being at the bottom of the heap as an important mechanism for motivating people to perform. According to functionalists, poverty becomes a social problem when it no longer performs the function of motivating people to make productive contributions to society. Poverty is also functional as the poor do the demeaning, difficult, and low-paying jobs that are essential but that no one else wants to do.

Application of Conflict Theory to Poverty

Conflict theorists assume that, because there is such enormous wealth in modern societies, no one in such societies should go without their essential needs being met. These theorists assert that poverty exists because the power structure wants it to exist. They assert that the working poor are being exploited, since they are paid poverty level wages so that their employers can reap higher profits.

The unemployed are also seen as being the victims of the power structure. Wealthy employers oppose programs to reduce unemployment (such as educational and job training programs) because they do not want to pay the taxes to support them.

Wealthy people are apt to cling to the ideology of individualism, because they tend to view unemployment and poverty as stemming from a lack of effort rather than from social injustice or from circumstances beyond the control of the individual. As a result, the wealthy ignore the economic and political foundations of poverty, and instead get involved in charitable efforts for the poor, which leaves them feeling they have done good deeds. Conflict theorists see charity and government welfare programs as a force in perpetuating poverty and economic inequality, as such programs quell political protests and social unrest that threaten the status quo. Conflict theorists also assert that many poor people eventually come to accept the judgments passed on them by the rest of society and adjust their aspirations and their self-esteem downward.

Conflict theorists do not see poverty as either essential or functional. They see poverty as arising because some groups benefit from seeing to it that the poor have less. From the conflict perspective, poverty becomes a social problem when some group feels the existing distribution of resources is unfair and unjust and that something can and should be done about it.

Conflict theorists believe that poverty can best be dealt with by the poor becoming politically aware and organizing to reduce inequality through government action. These theorists view poor people's adjustments to poverty as being a set of chains that must be broken. Most conflict theorists believe poverty can be significantly reduced only through political action by poor people that receives at least some support from concerned members of the power structure.

Application of Interactionist Theory to Poverty

Interactionists emphasize the subjective nature of poverty. Poverty is viewed as being relative, since it de-

pends on what it is compared to. Most poor people in the United States presently have a higher standard of living than middle class people did two hundred years ago. Poor people in this country are also substantially better off than poor people in Third World countries.

The main reference for poor people in this country is their poor neighbors. A successful person in some neighborhoods is someone who knows where the next meal is coming from, and a big success may be someone who gets a job on an assembly line. People with such attitudes become trapped in their own beliefs. Another value they acquire that traps them is instant gratification, in which they are not inclined to defer immediate rewards so that long-range goals, such as a college education, can be reached.

Interactionists view poverty as a matter of shared expectations. The poor are negatively judged by influential groups. Those who are the objects of such labeling are stigmatized and may begin to behave in accordance with those expectations. Interactionists emphasize that poverty is not just a matter of economic deprivation, but involves the person's self-concept. For example, a third generation welfare recipient is apt to view him- or herself much more negatively than a person working his or her way through college, even though both have the same income.

To resolve the poverty problem, interactionists urge that the stigma and negative definitions associated with poverty be eliminated. Positive changes in the poverty problem will not occur until the poor are convinced that they no longer are doomed to live in poverty. The poverty trap can be sprung with improved public assistance programs that bring the poor up to an adequate standard of living, *combined* with programs that open up opportunities to move up the socioeconomic ladder, and programs that encourage the poor to redefine their social environment.

To resolve the poverty problem, interactionists urge that the stigma and negative definitions associated with poverty be eliminated. Positive changes in the poverty problem will not occur until the poor are convinced that they no longer are doomed to live in poverty. The poverty trap can be sprung with improved public assistance programs that bring the poor up to an adequate standard of living, *combined* with programs that open up opportunities to move up the socioeconomic ladder, and programs that encourage the poor to redefine their social environment.

Liberalism versus Conservatism: Application of Theory to Social Welfare

Two prominent political philosophies in the United States are liberalism and conservatism. The Republican party is considered to be relatively conservative and the Democratic party is considered to be relatively liberal. This discussion will focus on liberalism and conservatism in their pure forms. In reality, many people espouse a mixture of both views. For example, there are some Democrats who are primarily conservative in ideology and some Republicans who are primarily liberal in ideology.

Conservatives (derived from the verb *to conserve*) tend to resist change. They emphasize tradition and believe rapid change usually results in more negative than positive consequences. In economic matters, conservatives feel that government should not interfere with the workings of the marketplace. They encourage the government to support (for example, through tax incentives) rather than regulate business and industry in society. A free market economy is thought to be the best way to ensure prosperity and fulfillment of individual needs. Conservatives embrace the old adage that "government governs best which governs least"! They believe that most government activities constitute grave threats to individual liberty and to the smooth functioning of the free market.

Conservatives generally advocate a residual approach to social welfare programs. The residual view holds that social welfare services should be provided only when an individual's needs are not properly met through other societal institutions, primarily the family and the market economy. Social services and financial aid should not be provided until all other measures or efforts have failed and the individual's or family's resources are fully used up. In addition, this view asserts that funds and services should be provided on a short-term basis (primarily during emergencies) and should be withdrawn when the individual or the family again becomes capable of being self-sufficient.

The residual view has been characterized as "charity for unfortunates." Funds and services are not seen as a right (something that one is entitled to) but as a gift, and the receiver has certain obligations; for example, in order to receive financial aid, recipients may be required to perform certain low-grade work assignments. Associated with the residual view is the belief that the causes of social welfare clients' difficulties are rooted in their own malfunctioning—that is, clients are to blame for their predicaments because of personal inadequacies or ill-advised activities or sins. Under the residual view there is usually a stigma attached to receiving services or funds.

Conservatives believe that dependency is a result of personal failure, and they also believe it is natural for inequality to exist among humans. They assert that the family, religious organizations, and gainful employment should be the primary defense against dependency. Social welfare, they believe, should be only a temporary function that is used sparingly. Prolonged social welfare assistance, they believe, will lead recipients to become permanently dependent. Conservatives believe charity is a moral virtue and that the "fortunate" are obligated to help the "less fortunate" become productive, contributing citizens in a society. If governmental funds are provided for health and social welfare services, conservatives advocate that such funding should go to private organizations, which are thought to be more effective and efficient than public agencies in providing services. Conservatives tend to believe that the federal government is not a solution to social problems but is part of the problem. They assert that federally funded social welfare programs tend to make recipients dependent on the government rather than assisting recipients to become self-sufficient and productive.

In contrast, liberals believe change is generally good as it usually brings progress; moderate change is best. They view society as needing regulation to ensure fair competition between various interests. In particular, the market economy is viewed as needing regulation to ensure fairness. Government programs, including social welfare programs, are viewed as necessary to help meet basic human needs. Liberals advocate government action to remedy social deficiencies and to improve human welfare. Liberals feel government regulation and intervention is often necessary to safeguard human rights, to control the excesses of capitalism, and to provide equal chances for success. They emphasize egalitarianism and the rights of minorities.

Liberals generally adhere to an institutional view of social welfare. This view holds that social welfare programs are "accepted as a proper legitimate function of modern industrial society in helping individuals achieve self-fulfillment" (Wilensky and Lebeaux, 1965, p. 139). Under this view, there is no stigma attached to receiving funds or services; recipients are viewed as entitled to such help. Associated with this view is the belief that an individual's difficulties are due to causes largely beyond his or her control (for example, a person may be unemployed because of a lack of employment opportunities). With this view, when difficulties arise causes are sought in the environment (society) and efforts are focused on improving the social institutions within which the individual functions.

Liberals assert that because society has become so fragmented and complex and because traditional institutions (such as the family) have been unable to meet human needs, few individuals can now function without the help of social services (including such services as work training, job location services, child care, health care, and counseling).

Problems in the Work Setting

"What do you do for a living?" is a question that is commonly asked when two strangers meet. Work is a central focus of life, particularly for middle-aged adults who are generally at the peak of their work career in terms of earnings and prestige. Work not only enables a person to earn money to pay bills, it can also provide a sense of self-respect, provide a circle of colleagues and friends, and be a source of self-fulfillment. A challenging job can help a person to grow intellectually, psychologically, and socially. Work also largely determines a person's place in the social structure. (In the past, birth largely determined one's social position and vocational choices.) We have considerable choices in the vocations we select, and vocational choice largely determines our social status. We are largely defined by our work.

In our society we highly value the work ethic; that is, we consider work to be honorable, productive, and useful. Unemployed, able-bodied persons are often looked down on. The importance of work is shown in a study by Morse and Weiss (1955). They asked, "If by some chance you inherited enough money to live comfortably without working, do you think that you would work anyway, or not?" Eighty percent of the respondents stated they would prefer to keep on working.

Work has not always been so esteemed. The ancient Greeks, for example, viewed work as a curse imposed on humanity by the gods. Work was thought to be an unpleasant and burdensome activity that was incompatible with being a citizen. Citizens sought to have extensive leisure time so they could further develop their minds. The Greeks, therefore, used slaves and justified slavery on the basis that it freed citizens to spend their time in philosophic contemplation and cultural enrichment. Aristotle remarked, "No man can practice virtue who is living the life of a mechanic or laborer." Most Western societies until the Protestant Reformation tended to disparage work, frequently viewing it as undesirable but necessary in order to survive.

The Protestant Reformation, which began in the sixteenth century, brought about profound changes in social values concerning work. Work became highly valued for the first time. One of the Protestant reformers, Martin Luther, asserted that labor was a service to God. Since the time of Luther, work has continued to be viewed as being honorable and as having religious significance.

Another Protestant reformer, John Calvin, had even a more dramatic effect on changing the views toward work. Calvin preached that work is the will of God. Hard work, good deeds, and success at one's vocation were taken to be signs that one was destined for salvation. Calvin preached that God's will was that people should live frugally (spend very little money) and should use profits from work to invest in new ventures, which, in turn, would bring more profits for additional investments, and so on. Hard work and frugality came to have great value. Idleness or laziness came to be viewed as sinful.

One religious group that was most influenced by Calvin's teachings was the Puritans. The Puritans also developed a strong ascetic life-style, that is, the practice of denying world pleasures as a demonstration of religious discipline. Calvin's teachings were widely accepted and formed a new cultural value system which became known as the Protestant Ethic. This ethic had three core values: hard work, frugality, and asceticism.

The values of hard work and saving that were advanced by the Protestant Ethic have continued throughout history. For example, Benjamin Franklin (1980, p. 300) praised these values:

Max Weber and the Protestant Ethic

In 1904, the German sociologist Max Weber (1958) published what has become one of the most provocative theories in sociology. In *The Protestant Ethic and the Spirit of Capitalism*, Weber asserted that the Protestant Ethic encouraged, and made possible, the emergence of capitalism. Weber theorized that the ideas of puritanism (advocated by Martin Luther and John Calvin) provided the value system that led to the transformation from traditional society to the Industrial Revolution.

Weber noted that puritan Protestantism embraced the doctrine that people were divinely selected for either salvation or damnation. There was nothing people could do to alter their fate. No one knew for sure whether he or she was destined for eternal salvation or eternal damnation. However, people looked for signs from God to suggest their fate. Since they also believed that work was a form of service to God, they concluded that success at work (making profits) was a sign of God's favor. They, therefore, worked hard to accumulate as much wealth as possible.

Since the Protestant Ethic viewed luxury and self-gratification as sinful, the profits acquired were not to be spent on luxuries but reinvested in new ventures to increase income. Such new ventures included building factories and developing new machines. Thus, according to Weber, the Industrial Revolution began, and capitalism was born.

A penny saved is a penny earned.

Time is money.

After industry and frugality, nothing contributes more to the raising of a young man than punctuality.

He who sits idle . . . throws away money.

Waste neither time nor money; an hour lost is money lost.

Although we no longer value the frugal, ascetic life-style of Puritanism, we still believe strongly in the ethic of hard work. An able-bodied person, to gain approval from others, is expected to be employed (or at least to be receiving job training). People on welfare are often looked down on. There still remains a strong link between amount of income and personal worth. The more people are paid, the more highly they are regarded by others and the more highly they regard themselves.

A government report *Work in America*, (1973) found that people in low-status jobs are generally unable to form a satisfying identity from their jobs. Having an assembly line job, for example, often leads workers to view themselves as being personally insignificant. They routinely perform the same task day in and day out—such as attaching nuts to bolts. Such jobs, the report notes, lead to a worker having "an overwhelming sense of inferiority; he cannot talk proudly to his children of his job, and feels he must apologize for his status" (p. 45).

Since the status of our work has immense effects on our self-concept, having a degrading, boring, and dehumanizing job can have immense adverse effects on our psychological well-being. We judge ourselves not only by how much our job pays but also on whether the job is challenging, satisfying, and helps us grow and develop. Two of the most serious problems in the work setting are unemployment and learning to survive in a bureaucratic system.

Unemployment

The Costs of Unemployment

Unemployment can have devastating effects. Most obviously, it reduces (sometimes to poverty levels) the amount of income that a family or single person receives. Short-term unemployment, especially when a person receives unemployment compensation, may have only minor effects. But long-term unemployment may have numerous adverse effects.

Wilensky (1966, p. 129) found long-term unemployment often leads to extreme personal isolation. Work is a central part of many people's lives. When unemployment occurs, work ties are cut, and many of the unemployed see friends less, cut their participation in community life, and increasingly become isolated.

Braginsky and Braginsky (1975, p. 70) found that long-term unemployment causes attitude changes which persist even after reemployment. Being laid off (or let go) is often interpreted by the unemployed as a sign of being incompetent and worthless. Self-esteem is lowered, they are apt to experience depression, and they feel alienated from society. Many suffer deep shame and avoid their friends. They feel dehumanized and insignificant, and that they are an easily replaced statistic. They also tend to lose faith in our political and economic system, with some blaming our political system for their problems. Even when they find new jobs, they do not fully recover their self-esteem.

Brenner (1973) found a strong association between unemployment and emotional problems. During an economic recession he found that mental hospital admissions increase. The suicide rate also increases, indicating an increase in depression. Also higher during times of high unemployment are the divorce rate, the incidence of child abuse, and the number of peptic ulcers (a stress-related disease).

In many cases the long-term unemployed are forced to exhaust their savings, sell their homes, and become public assistance recipients. A few turn to crime, particularly the young. The unemployed no longer enjoy the companionship of their fellow workers. They are apt to experience feelings of embar-

rassment, anger, despair, depression, anxiety, boredom, hopelessness, and apathy. Such feelings may lead to alcoholism, drug abuse, insomnia, psychosomatic illnesses, marital unhappiness, and even violence within the family. The work ethic is still prominent in our society—when people lose their job they devalue themselves and also miss the sense of self-worth that comes from doing a job well.

Widespread unemployment can have devastating effects on society. Those still working are apt to fear they may lose their jobs. Severe unemployment leads to disenchantment with (and sometimes even rebellion against) political and social institutions. Widespread unemployment also cuts sharply government tax revenues and government services. In the late 1970s and early 1980s the auto industry in Detroit and the state of Michigan had high rates of unemployment. Revenues for the city and state were

The American Dream Becomes an Economic Nightmare Through Unemployment

Lorraine and Jim Dedrick thought they had it made. They had a five-bedroom, stone-foundation home on a lake, a landscaped yard, two well-behaved children, a car, a van, a motor-powered boat, and a sailboat. The home, the vehicles, and the boats were bought on time payments. Since both were working, they were confident they could easily make the monthly payments. Mrs. Dedrick describes what happened.

My husband worked at Dana Corporation, a car and truck-axle manufacturing plant. He was a crew supervisor and was making over $33,000 a year. I was, and still am, a legal secretary.

When the layoffs started in spring 1989, we didn't think it would touch Jim. He had six years of seniority. But by March of 1990, we knew a layoff was inevitable. Neither Dana, nor the whole American auto industry, were doing well. When the layoff came in June of 1990, we weren't surprised.

At first we weren't worried. Jim thought it would be nice to have a summer off and looked forward to doing some fishing and some fixing up around the house. Since he was thirty-nine years old and had worked steady since he was eighteen, I also thought a few months break would do him good. He was, of course, able to draw un-

employment benefits, and with my salary I was certain we could get by. Surely the auto industry would recover, and he would be called back in the fall.

In late summer, however, a rumor started and quickly spread throughout the plant that Dana was going to close its plant. In September they announced the plant was going to close.

Both of us immediately became alarmed. Jim started looking for other work in earnest. Unfortunately, there were no comparable jobs in the area—and for that matter the whole auto industry was suffering.

Jim applied at many different jobs but had no luck. I know of nothing worse than to see a once proud, secure person come home each evening with the look on his face that he had once again been rejected. Jim began developing stomach problems from the rejections, and I started having tension headaches. We used to go out a lot, laugh, and have a good time. Now, we not only cannot afford it, we no longer have an interest.

Jim grabbed at every straw. He even went to apply for jobs in Milwaukee and Chicago. In the last year he appears to have aged ten years.

In February of 1991, his unemployment benefits ended. Bill collectors began hounding us. We soon depleted all our savings. We got so many calls from bill sharply reduced, and Detroit and Michigan were forced to drastically cut services at a time when services were most needed. Such cuts further add to alienation and despair.

High unemployment also leads to high rates of underemployment. Underemployed people are working at jobs below their level of skill. A sizeable number of people who are unemployed during periods of high unemployment are forced to take whatever jobs are available. College graduates, for example, may be forced to take unskilled road construction work or become clerical workers.

Who Are the Unemployed?

In the past several years the unemployment rate nationally has ranged from 4 to 10 percent. Practically every worker risks being unemployed, and most are unemployed sometime during their working years.

There is some variation from time to time in the groups that are subjected to unemployment. In the late 1970s and early 1980s, unemployment was particularly high among steel workers and automobile workers. In the late 1970s, school teachers had high unemployment rates. In the middle 1970s, people who had Ph.D.s in the liberal arts and social sciences had high unemployment rates. In the early 1980s, the housing industry was in a slump, and there were high unemployment rates among carpenters and construction workers. In the early 1990s, there was high unemployment among automobile workers in communities where U.S. automobile corporations closed manufacturing plants.

There are groups, however, that have chronically high rates of unemployment. These groups include minorities, teenagers, women, older workers, the unskilled, and the semiskilled.

---

collectors that we took out an unlisted telephone number. Never before were we unable to pay our bills.

The months since February have been hell. Increasingly we have gotten into arguments. Whenever I bring my check home, Jim has a pained look on his face, as he feels he's not doing his share. I try to tell him that it's not his fault, but whenever we talk about it he gets hurt and angry.

At the end of February he began to advertise by word of mouth that he was an independent carpenter. He's good with his hands. Unfortunately, the few jobs he got have as yet not even paid for the extra tools he's had to buy. It has only gotten us deeper into debt.

When I drive to work, the tears often fall. It's my only time alone. Driving home I often cry as I think about our situation, and know I'll have to face Jim's sad look. We don't associate much with friends now. They either pity us or have that arrogant look that says 'I told you so' in response to our optimism when Jim was first laid off.

It just doesn't look like Jim is going to be able to get a job in this area. Next week he's going to go to Atlanta—we've heard there are a lot of job openings there.

Dennis, our twelve-year-old son, is alternately sad and angry about the possibility of leaving this area. He's got a lot of friends and loves to go boating, fishing, and sailing. Having to take our son away from something he really loves is one of the most difficult things I'll probably ever have to do.

Karen, our daughter who's fifteen, really had a bad year at school. Her grades fell, and when we asked why, she stated, 'What's the use in studying—it won't help in getting a job.' That remark hurt deeply, probably because it may have a ring of truth in it.

It looks like we're going to have to give up our dream house on this lake. [Tears came to Mrs. Dedrick as she spoke.] We've lived here for the past five years and really loved it. This is our first real home. We've added on a patio, a bedroom, and enlarged the living room. We also spent a lot of time in painting and fixing it up. It's really become a part of us. If Jim gets a job in Atlanta, we'll be forced to sell. We checked what market prices are, and there's no way we're going to get what we put into this house.

A few years ago we thought we were starting to live the American dream. This past year and a half has been hell. Here we are, broke, unhappy, and about to lose our home. At our age starting over is almost more than we can take.

High unemployment among racial minorities is partly due to discrimination that makes it more difficult to obtain employment. Unfortunately, there is truth in the saying that minorities are "last to be hired, first to be fired." Another reason for high unemployment is their lower average level of educational achievement, which leaves them unqualified for many of the available jobs. (Lower educational achievement levels and lack of marketable job skills are largely due to past discrimination.)

High unemployment among women is also partly due to discrimination. Many employers (most of them men) are still inclined to hire a man before a woman, and many jobs are still erroneously thought to be "a man's job." Women have also been socialized to seek lower paying jobs, to not be competitive with males, and to believe their place is in the home and not in the work force. (See Chapter 9 for a fuller discussion.)

There are many myths about older workers—age forty and over—that make it more difficult to obtain a new job if they become unemployed. They are thought to be less productive, more difficult to get

Unemployed men wait for work. Blue-collar workers are usually more affected by economic recessions than white-collar workers.

along with, more difficult to train, clumsier, more accident prone, less healthy, and more prone to absenteeism. Research has shown these beliefs to be erroneous. Older workers have lower turnover rates, produce at a steadier rate, make fewer mistakes, have lower absenteeism rates, have a more positive attitude toward their work, and exceed younger employees in health and low on-the-job injury rates (Butler, 1977). An additional problem for unemployed older workers is that younger workers are often available at salaries far below what the older applicants were paid at their last job.

Unemployment is high for teenagers and young people, partly because many have not received job skill training that would provide them with marketable skills.

Employers are willing to hire unskilled workers when they have simple, repetitive tasks to be performed. But unskilled workers are the first to be laid off when there is a business slump. Unskilled workers can readily be replaced if business picks up. Highly skilled workers are more difficult to replace, and employers often have much more invested in skilled workers as they have spent more time in training such workers.

Blue-collar workers are more affected by economic slumps than white-collar workers. Industries that employ large numbers of blue-collar workers (such as housing, road construction, and the auto industry) are the ones that are most quickly and deeply affected and are often forced to lay off workers. In addition, the number of blue-collar jobs in the United States is decreasing, while white-collar jobs are increasing. A major reason for this decline is automation. *Automation* is the production technique where the system of production is increasingly controlled by means of self-operating machinery. Robots are now replacing workers in many industries—particularly in doing the simple, repetitive tasks.

A major reason for the high unemployment rate in this country is that we have a structural unemployment problem, as large numbers of unemployed people are not trained for the positions that are open. In recent years a large number of blue-collar jobs have been eliminated (as in the steel industry), while at the same time a number of high skill jobs have opened in other areas (such as in the high technology field of computers). As people become trained for current positions, the employment needs of our economy will continue to shift so that there will continue to be disharmony between skills needed for vacant positions and skills of the unemployed.

Factors That Reduce Unemployment

Many factors increase the number of jobs and thereby reduce the unemployment rate. Lower interest rates encourage consumers to purchase more items through loans and by credit. Consumers buying more stimulates companies to produce more to meet the demand and thereby to hire more people. Lower interest rates also have a direct effect on businesses. Businesses often borrow money to purchase capital items (for example, additional machines to produce their goods, or buildings to expand the business) in order to increase the production. If interest rates are lower, businesses are more apt to borrow money to increase production—and when expansion in production occurs, jobs are usually created.

A war almost always reduces the unemployment rate. Some workers are drafted to fight as soldiers. Their former jobs are then available for those who are unemployed. In addition, many additional jobs are created to provide the military with the products needed to fight a war—bullets, bombs, tanks, fighter planes, food, medicine, and so on.

Businesses and governments in many other countries take a more humanistic approach to employees and to assuring that there will be jobs available for those who are unemployed. In the United States when an economic slump occurs, businesses usually lay off workers. In Japan, in contrast, businesses are much less likely to lay off workers and seek to have their employees spend their entire working lives with the same company. Governments in many other countries attempt to create jobs for those who are unemployed. Germany, for example, pays the unemployed to receive work training.

The development of new products opens up many new jobs. The invention of the automobile, airplane, television set, hair dryer, and refrigerator opened up many new jobs for not only factory workers, but also for managers and repair, sales, and insurance personnel.

In the early 1960s the economy was in a slump, with the unemployment rate fairly high. President Kennedy stimulated the economy through a tax cut for individuals and businesses. With their additional money, individuals were able to buy more. Businesses had additional money to reinvest to increase production. Kennedy's plan worked—the economy was stimulated, production increased, more jobs were created, and the unemployment rate went down. In the early 1980s we were again in an economic slump—with both a high inflation and high unemployment rate. President Reagan's plan of tax cuts to individuals and to businesses was enacted in 1981 and was again successful in stimulating the economy; individuals were able to buy more, companies expanded production, more jobs were created, and the unemployment rate went down somewhat. Another problem has developed, however. By cutting taxes, the federal deficit was sharply increased. There is a danger that the huge federal deficit may heat up the rate of inflation and result in another recession. (Inflation is a general rise in prices.)

Economics is a complicated and complex area, with the leading economists often disagreeing on the approaches that should be taken to reduce both the unemployment rate and the inflation rate. Generally, inflation and unemployment have an inverse relationship; an increase in one will usually lead to a decrease in the other. In times of high unemployment people have less money to spend. They purchase fewer goods and services, which reduces the demand for goods and services. When the demand goes down the price of the goods and services is not likely to rise and may even be depressed. Furthermore, when workers do not feel their jobs are secure due to high layoffs, they are unlikely to ask for large pay increases. When there is little pressure for price or wage increases, inflation is low.

On the other hand, when the unemployment rate is low, more people are working and are able to buy goods and services. This increased demand drives prices up. If the demand stays high, businesses produce more and make a higher profit. Labor unions want a share of this increased profit and so they ask for large wage and salary increases. The pay increases they receive are then passed on to consumers.

Surviving in Bureaucratic Systems

Material in this section will focus on how helping professionals can survive and thrive in bureaucratic systems. This material also has applications to other employees in bureaucracies, as they tend to have similar views and expectations of bureaucracies.

Knopf (1979) notes that helping professionals (including social workers) have erroneous views as to the orientation of a bureaucratic system. Helping professionals believe that the primary goal of bureaucracies should be to serve clients, while the primary goal of bureaucracies is to survive. Helping professionals believe bureaucracies should change to meet the emerging needs of clients, while bureaucracies resist change and are most efficient when no one is "rocking the boat." Helping professionals believe bureaucracies should personalize services to each client and convey that "you count as a person," while bureaucracies are in fact highly depersonalized systems in which clients (and employees) do not count as persons but are only tiny components of a large system. Figure 12.2 lists additional conflicting orientations between helping professionals and bureaucratic systems.

Any of these differences in orientation can become an arena of conflict between helping professionals and the bureaucracies in which they work.

A number of helping professionals respond to these orientation conflicts by erroneously projecting a "personality" onto the bureaucracy. The bureaucracy is viewed as being "red tape," "officialism," "uncaring," "cruel," and "the enemy." A negative personality is sometimes also projected onto officials of a bureaucracy, who may be viewed as being "paper shufflers," "rigid," "deadwood," "inefficient," and "unproductive." Knopf (1979, p. 25) states:

> The HP (helping person) . . . may deal with the impersonal nature of the system by projecting values onto it and thereby give the BS (bureaucratic system) a "personality." In this way, we fool ourselves into thinking that we can deal with it in a personal way. Unfortunately, projection is almost always negative and reflects the dark or negative aspects of ourselves. The BS then becomes a screen onto which we vent our anger, sadness, or fright, and while a lot of energy is generated, very little is accomplished. Since the BS is amoral, it is unproductive to place a personality on it.

A bureaucratic system is neither good nor bad. It has neither a personality nor a value system of its own. It is simply a structure developed to carry out

FIGURE 12.2: Orientation Conflicts Between Helping Professionals and Bureaucracies

Orientations of Helping Professionals	*Orientations of Bureaucratic Systems*
Desire a democratic system for decision making	Most decisions are made autocratically
Desire that power be distributed equally among employees (horizontal structure)	Power is distributed vertically
Desire that clients have considerable power in the system	Power is held primarily by top executives
Desire a flexible, changing system	System is rigid and stable
Desire that creativity and growth be emphasized	Emphasis is on structure and the status quo
Desire that communication be on a personalized level from person to person	Communication is from level to level
Desire shared decision making and a shared responsibility structure	A hierarchical decision-making structure and a hierarchical responsibility structure are characteristic
Desire that decisions be made by those having the most knowledge	Decisions are made in terms of the decision-making authority assigned to each position in the hierarchy
Believe feelings of clients and employees should be highly valued by the system	Procedures and processes are highly valued

various tasks. A helping person may have various emotional reactions to these conflicts in orientation with bureaucratic systems. Common reactions are anger at the system, self-blame ("It's all my fault"), sadness and depression ("Poor me," "Nobody appreciates all I've done"), and fright and paranoia ("They're out to get me," "If I mess up, I'm gone").

Knopf (1979) has identified several types of behavior patterns that helping professionals choose in dealing with bureaucracies. The *warrior* leads open campaigns to destroy and malign the system. A warrior discounts the value of the system and often enters into a win/lose conflict. The warrior generally loses and is dismissed.

The *gossip* is a covert warrior who complains to others (including clients, politicians, and the news media) how terrible the system is. A gossip frequently singles out a few officials to focus criticism upon. Bureaucratic systems often make life very difficult for the gossip by assigning distasteful tasks, refusing to promote, giving very low salary increases, and perhaps even dismissing.

The *complainer* resembles a gossip, but confines complaints to other helping persons, to inhouse staff, and to family members. A complainer wants people to agree in order to find comfort in shared misery. Complainers desire to stay with the system, and generally do.

The *dancer* is skillful at ignoring rules and procedures. Dancers are frequently lonely, often reprimanded for incorrectly filling out forms, and have low investment in the system or in helping clients.

The *defender* is scared, dislikes conflict, and therefore defends the rules, the system, and bureaucratic officials. Defenders are often supervisors, and are viewed by others as being "bureaucrats."

The *machine* is a "bureaucrat" who takes on the orientation of the bureaucracy. Often a machine has not been involved in providing direct services for years. Machines are frequently named to head study committees and policy groups and to chair boards.

The *executioner* attacks persons within an organization with enthusiasm and vigor. An executioner usually has a high energy level and is impulsive. An executioner abuses power by indiscriminately attacking and dismissing not only employees but also services and programs. Executioners have power and are angry (although the anger is disguised, denied). They have no commitment to the value orientations of the helping professionals or to the bureaucracy.

This description of bureaucratic systems highlights a number of the negatives about such systems, particularly their impersonalization. In fairness, it should be noted that an advantage of being part of a large bureaucracy is that the potential is there for changing a powerful system to the advantage of clients. In small or nonbureaucratic systems, a social worker may have lots of freedom but little opportunity or power to influence large systems or mobilize extensive resources on behalf of clients.

Survival Tips

Knopf (1979) gives a number of tips on how a helping professional can best survive in a bureaucracy, including:

1. Whenever your needs, or the needs of your clients, are not met by the bureaucracy, use the following problem-

Communication gaps between social workers and bureaucrats may be reduced when workers treat bureaucrats with as much care as they do clients.

solving approach: (a) Precisely identify your needs (or the needs of clients) that are in conflict with the bureaucracy; this step is defining the problem. (b) Generate a list of possible solutions. Be creative in generating a wide range of solutions. (c) Evaluate the merits and shortcomings of the possible solutions. (d) Select a solution. (e) Implement the solution. (f) Evaluate the solution. (The problem solving approach is described in Chapter 8.)

2. Obtain a knowledge of how your bureaucracy is structured and how it functions. Such knowledge will reduce fear of the unknown, make the system more predictable, and help in identifying rational ways to best meet your needs and those of your clients.

3. Remember that bureaucrats are people who have feelings. Communication gaps are often most effectively reduced if you treat them with as much respect and interest as you treat clients.

4. If you are at war with the bureaucracy, declare a truce. The system will find a way to dismiss you if you remain at war. With a truce, you can identify and use the strengths of the bureaucracy as an ally, rather than having the strengths being used against you as an enemy.

5. Know your work contract and job expectations. If the expectations are unclear, seek clarity.

6. Continue to develop your knowledge and awareness of specific helping skills. Take advantage of continuing

education opportunities (for example, workshops, conferences, courses). Among other advantages, your continued professional development will assist you in being able to contract from a position of competency and skill.

7. Seek to identify your professional strengths and limitations. Knowing your limitations will increase your ability to avoid undertaking responsibilities that are beyond your competencies.

8. Be aware that you can't change everything, so stop trying. In a bureaucracy, focus your change efforts on those aspects that most need change and which you also have a fair chance of changing. Stop thinking and complaining about those aspects you cannot change. It is irrational to complain about things that you cannot change or to complain about those things that you do not intend to make an effort to change.

9. Learn how to control your emotions in your interactions with the bureaucracy. Emotions that are counterproductive (such as *most* angry outbursts) particularly need to be controlled. Doing rational self-analysis on unwanted emotions (see Chapter 8) is one way of gaining control of your unwanted emotions. Learning how to respond to stress in your personal life will also prepare you to handle stress at work better.

10. Develop and use a sense of humor. Humor takes the edge off adverse conditions and reduces negative feelings.

11. Learn to accept your mistakes and perhaps even to laugh at some of them. No one is perfect.

12. Take time to enjoy and develop a support system with the people you work with.

13. Acknowledge your mistakes and give in sometimes on minor matters. You may not be right, and giving in sometimes allows other people to do the same.

14. Keep yourself physically fit and mentally alert. Learn to use approaches that will reduce stress and prevent burnout. (See Chapter 14 for a summary of stress management techniques.)

15. Leave your work at the office. If you have urgent unfinished bureaucratic business, do it before leaving work or don't leave.

16. Occasionally take your supervisor and other administrators to lunch. Socializing prevents isolation and facilitates your involvement with and understanding of the system.

17. Do not seek self-actualization or ego-satisfaction from the bureaucracy. A depersonalized system is incapable of providing this. Only you can satisfy your ego and become self-actualized.

18. Make speeches to community groups that accentuate the positives about your agency. Do not hesitate to ask after speeches that a thank-you letter be sent to your supervisor or agency director.

19. If you have a problem involving the bureaucracy, discuss it with other employees, with the focus being on problem solving rather than on complaining. Groups are much more powerful and productive than an individual working alone to make changes in a system.

20. No matter how high you rise in a hierarchy, maintain direct service contact. Direct contact keeps you abreast of changing client needs, prevents you from getting stale, and keeps you attuned to the concerns of employees in lower levels of the hierarchy.

21. Do not try to change everything in the system at once. Attacking too much will overextend you and lead to burnout. Start small and be selective and specific. Double-check your facts to make certain they accurately prove your position before confronting bureaucratic officials.

22. Identify your career goals and determine whether they can be met in this system. If the answer is no, then (a) change your goals, (b) change the bureaucracy, or (c) seek a position elsewhere in which your goals can be met.

Theory X versus Theory Y

The management styles of administrators and supervisors in organizations have considerable impact on the productivity and job satisfaction of employees. Douglas McGregor (1960) developed two theories of management styles. He theorized that management thinking and behavior are based on two different sets of assumptions, which he labeled Theory X and Theory Y.

Theory X managers view employees as being incapable of much growth. Employees are perceived as having an inherent dislike for work, and it is presumed that they will attempt to evade work whenever possible. Therefore, X-type managers believe that they must control, direct, force, or threaten employees to make them work. Employees are also viewed as having relatively little ambition, wishing to avoid responsibilities and preferring to be directed. X-type managers therefore spell out job responsibilities carefully, set work goals without employee input, use external rewards (such as money) to force employees to work, and punish employees who deviate from established rules. Because Theory X managers reduce responsibilities to a level where few mistakes can be made, work usually becomes so structured that it is monotonous and distasteful. The assumptions of Theory X are, of course, inconsistent with what behavioral scientists assert are effective principles for directing, influencing, and motivating people.

In contrast, *Theory Y managers* view employees as wanting to grow and develop by exerting physical and mental effort to accomplish work objectives to which they are committed. Y-type managers believe that the promise of internal rewards, such as self-respect and personal improvement, are stronger motivations than external rewards (money) and punishment. A Y-type manager also believes that under proper conditions, employees will not only accept responsibility but seek it. Most employees are assumed to have considerable ingenuity, creativity, and imagination for solving the organization's problems. Therefore, employees are given considerable responsibility in order to test the limits of their capabilities. Mistakes and errors are viewed as necessary phases of the learning process, and work is structured so that employees can have a sense of accomplishment and growth.

Employees who work for Y-type managers are generally more creative and productive, experience greater work satisfaction, and are more highly motivated than employees who work for X-type managers. Under both management styles, expectations often become self-fulfilling prophecies.

Family System Problems

In this section we will examine the following problems and living arrangements in families: empty-shell marriages, divorce, single-parent families, blended families, and mothers working outside of the home.

Empty-Shell Marriages

In empty-shell marriages the spouses feel no strong attachments to each other. Outside pressures keep the marriage together. Such outside pressures include: business reasons (for example, an elected official wanting to convey a stable family image); investment reasons (for example, husband and wife may have a luxurious home and other property which they do not want to lose by parting); and outward appearances (for example, a couple living in a small community may remain together to avoid the reactions of relatives and friends to a divorce). In addition, a couple may believe that ending the marriage would harm the children or may believe that getting a divorce would be morally wrong.

John F. Cuber and Peggy B. Harroff (1971) have identified three types of empty-shell marriages. In a *devitalized relationship* husband and wife lack any real interest in their spouse or their marriage. Boredom and apathy characterize this marriage. Serious arguments are rare.

In a *conflict-habituated relationship* husband and wife frequently quarrel in private. They may also quarrel in public or put up a facade of being compatible. The relationship is characterized by considerable conflict, tension, and bitterness.

In a *passive-congenial relationship* both partners are not happy, but are content with their lives and generally feel adequate. The partners may have some interests in common, but these interests are generally insignificant. The spouses contribute little to each other's real satisfactions. This type of relationship generally has little overt conflict.

The number of empty-shell marriages is unknown—it may be as high as the number of happily married couples. The atmosphere in empty-shell marriages is without much fun or laughter. Members do not share and discuss their problems or experiences with each other. Communication is kept to a minimum. There is seldom any spontaneous expression of affection or sharing of a personal experience. Children in such families are usually starved for love and reluctant to have friends over as they are embarrassed about having their friends see their parents interacting.

The couples in these marriages engage in few activities together and display no pleasure in being in one another's company. Sexual relations between the partners, as might be expected, are rare and generally unsatisfying. Visitors will note that the partners (and often the children) appear insensitive, cold, and callous to each other. Yet, closer observation will reveal that the family members are highly aware of each other's weaknesses and sensitive areas, and manage to frequently mention these areas in order to hurt one another.

William J. Goode (1976, p. 543) compares empty-shell marriages to marriages that end in divorce:

Most families that divorce pass through a state—sometimes *after* the divorce—in which husband and wife no longer feel bound to each other, cease to cooperate or share with each other, and look on one another as almost a stranger. The "empty-shell" family is in such a state. Its members no longer feel any strong commitment to many of the mutual role obligations, but for various reasons the husband and wife do not separate or divorce.

The number of empty-shell marriages ending in divorce is unknown. It is likely that a fair number eventually do. Both spouses have to put considerable effort into making a marriage work in order to prevent an empty-shell marriage from gradually developing.

Divorce

Our society places a higher value on romantic love than most other societies. In societies where marriages are arranged by parents, being in love generally has no role in mate selection. In our society, however, romantic love is a key factor in forming a marriage.

Children are socialized from an early age in this country to believe in the glories of romantic love. "Love conquers all," it is asserted. Magazines, films, TV programs, and books continually portray "happy ending" romantic adventures. All of these breathtaking romantic stories suggest that every normal person falls in love with that one special person, gets married, and lives happily ever after. This happily-ever-after ideal rarely happens.

About one out of two marriages ends in divorce (U.S. Bureau of the Census, 1991). This high rate has gradually been increasing. Prior to World War I divorce was comparatively rare.

Divorce usually leads to a number of difficulties for those involved. First, those who are divorcing face emotional concerns, such as a feeling that they have failed, concern over whether they are able to give and receive love, a sense of loneliness, concern over the stigma attached to divorce, concern about the reactions of friends and relatives, concern over whether they are doing the right thing by parting, and concern over whether they will be able to make it on their own. Many people feel trapped as they believe they cannot live with their spouse and cannot live without him or her. Dividing up the personal property is

another area that frequently leads to bitter differences of opinions. If there are children, there are concerns about how the divorce will affect them.

Other issues also need to be decided. Who will get custody of the children? Joint custody is now an alternative—with joint custody, both parents have joint responsibility for decision making involving the children and they may (or may not) share equally in the physical custody of the children. If one parent is awarded custody, controversies are apt to arise over visiting rights, and how much (if any) child support should be paid. Both spouses often face the difficulties of finding new places to live, making new friends, doing things alone in our couple-oriented society, financially trying to make it on their own, and thinking about the hassles of dating.

Studies (Papalia and Olds, 1992, p. 459) show that going through a divorce is very difficult. People are less likely to perform their jobs well and more likely to be fired during this period. Divorced people have a shorter life expectancy. Suicide rates are higher for divorced men.

Divorce per se is no longer automatically assumed to be a social problem. In some marriages where there is considerable tension, bitterness, and dissatisfaction, divorce is sometimes a solution. It may be a concrete step that some people take to end the unhappiness and to begin leading a more productive and gratifying life. It is also increasingly being recognized that a divorce may be better for the children, as they no longer may be subjected to the tension and unhappiness in a marriage that has gone sour.

Mary Jo Bane (1976, pp. 31-33) has noted that the rising divorce rate may not be as serious a threat to the institutions of marriage and family as some believe:

> It is distressing in and of itself . . . only if staying together at all costs is considered an indicator of healthy marriages or healthy societies. . . . Some things are fairly clear. The majority of marriages do not end in divorce. The vast majority of divorced people remarry. Only a tiny proportion of people marry more than twice. We are thus a long way from a society in which marriage is rejected or replaced by a series of short-term liaisons. . . . Society may be changing its attitudes toward the permanence of marriage and its notions of the roles of husbands and wives. It may simply be recognizing that there is no particular benefit to requiring permanence in unhappy marriages.

The rising rate of divorce does not necessarily mean that more marriages are failing. It may simply mean that in marriages which have gone sour, more people are dissolving the marriage than continuing to live unhappily.

Reasons for Divorce

The reason people decide to divorce may have nothing to do with specific "bad" qualities that either or both members of the couple have. Rather, Little (1982) suggests that the main reason people divorce is disappointment with each other. In other words, partners simply do not measure up to their spouse's expectations. Over time such disappointment and disillusionment lead to the decision to divorce.

It is interesting to note that the same individual might be considered horrendous by one spouse but wonderful by the next, depending on the expectations of each spouse. Take Nick, for instance. His first wife Judy found him to be cold, noncommunicative, and unaffectionate. She lamented that he refused to sit with her on the couch, hold hands, and watch television as they relaxed in the evening. She once indicated that the purchase of a single person reclining chair caused the demise of their marriage because they could no longer sit together. After the divorce, however, his second wife Karen felt that Nick was very, very affectionate, even though he demonstrated the same or at least very similar behavior toward her. She loved having her independence in the evenings and having television sets in separate rooms. To Karen, with her love of horror movies and Nick's love of *Wall Street Week in Review*, living in this more independent manner was much more appealing.

There are many sources of marital breakdown, including alcoholism, economic strife caused by unemployment or other financial problems, incompatibility of interests, infidelity, jealousy, verbal or physical abuse of spouse, and interference in the marriage by relatives and friends.

As noted earlier, many people marry because they believe they are romantically in love. If this romantic love does not grow into rational love (see Chapter 8 for a description of rational love), the marriage is apt to fail. Unfortunately, young people are socialized in our society to believe that marriage will bring them continual romance, resolve all their problems, be sexually exciting, thrilling, full of adventure and excitement, and will always be as wonderful as the courtship. (Most young people only need to look at their parent's marriage to realize such romantic ideals are seldom attained.) Unfortunately, living with someone in a marriage involves carrying out the garbage, washing dishes and clothes, being weary from work, putting up with the partner's distasteful habits, changing diapers, dealing with conflicts over such things as how to spend a vacation, and differences in sexual interests. Making a marriage work requires that each spouse put considerable effort into making it successful.

Another factor that is contributing to an increasing divorce rate is the unwillingness of some men to accept the changing status of women. Many men still prefer a traditional marriage where the husband is dominant, and the wife plays a supportive (subordinate role) as child-rearer, housekeeper, and emotional supporter to her husband. Many women no longer accept such a status and demand an equalitarian marriage in which making major decisions, doing the domestic tasks, raising the children, and bringing home paychecks are shared responsibilities.

Over half of the adult women in the United States are now in the labor force (U.S. Census Bureau, 1992). This increase in the percent of working women means women are no longer as dependent financially on their husbands. Women who are financially able to support themselves are more likely to seek a divorce if their marriage goes sour.

Another factor contributing to the increasing divorce rate is the growth of individualism. Individualism involves the belief that people should seek to actualize themselves, to be happy, to develop their interests and capacities to the fullest, to seek to fulfill their own needs and desires. With individualism the interests of the individual take precedence over the interests of the family. People in our society have increasingly come to accept individualism as a way of life. In contrast, people in more traditional societies and in extended families are socialized to put the interests of the group first, with their own individual interests being viewed as less important. In extended families people view themselves as members of a group first and as individuals second. With America's growing belief in individualism, people who conclude that they are unhappily married are much more apt to dissolve the marriage and seek a new life.

Another reason for the rise in the divorce rate is the growing acceptance of divorce in our society. With less of a stigma attached to a divorce, more people who are unhappily married are now ending the marriage.

An additional factor in the increasing divorce rate is that modern families no longer have as many functions as in traditional families. Education, food production, entertainment, and other functions once centered in the family are now largely provided by outside agencies. Kenneth Keniston (1977, p. 21) notes:

> In earlier times, the collapse of a marriage was far more likely to deprive both spouses of a great deal more than the pleasure of each other's company. Since family members performed so many functions for one another, divorce in the past meant a farmer without a wife to churn the cream into butter or care for him when he was sick, and a mother without a husband to plow the fields and bring her the food to feed their children. Today, when emotional satisfaction is the bond that holds marriages together, the waning of love or the emergence of real incompatibilities and conflict between husband and wife leave fewer reasons for a marriage to continue. Schools and doctors and counselors and social workers provide their supports whether the family is intact or not. One loses less by divorce today than in earlier times, because marriage provides fewer kinds of sustenance and satisfaction.

Consequences of Divorce

Both members of the couple, even the person who initiated the divorce, experience grief at the loss (Janzen and Harris, 1986, p. 258). Typical patterns of behavior must be changed. Even the loss of negative behavior patterns causes stress, because new ways of interacting must be established. The unknown is scary to many people. There is a tendency to feel that the old ways, even when they were bad, at least were predictable. There's safety in predictability. This makes any kind of change more difficult.

Feelings are often strong and varied after a divorce. People may feel anger and anxiety (Janzen and Harris, 1986, p. 259). Things didn't work out as they had planned. It's easy to think of how unfair it all is and to blame the other partner for the failure. People may also feel self-blame and guilt.

A major result of divorce for women is a serious decline in their standard of living. Weitzman (1985) studied divorce and its aftermath for people in California over a ten-year period. She concluded that divorced women and their children experience an immediate 73 percent drop in their standard of living in contrast to the 42 percent increase divorced men enjoy. She contends that such discrepancies are often due to the way property is legally divided. For instance, the man frequently gets half of all property. The half allotted to the woman must be shared with her children. If a home is involved, it must be sold and the mortgage paid off. Since divorce most frequently results in a severe drop in income for a divorced woman, she and her children must often move to much less expensive housing.

Weitzman continues that usually divided assets do not include occupational assets such as years of experience in full-time employment, health insurance, and future earning power potential. In families in which the man had been the primary breadwinner, women are at a serious disadvantage after divorce. Even women who work outside of the home during the marriage are likely to have been in professions earning less money than professions traditionally occupied by men. Also, they are more likely to have lost career time due to pregnancy and child-care leaves and are more likely to have worked part-time.

For older women who have not worked outside of the home, the results are even more serious. They have had no opportunity to acquire skills and experience which are traditionally valued in the workplace. Nor have they been able to acquire access to benefits such as retirement and health insurance which men traditionally have had. Because of their age, they find it difficult to get jobs which can support them.

In 90 percent of divorce cases, mothers are awarded custody of the children (Papalia and Olds, 1992, p. 459). Fathers are usually court ordered to pay child support. But the amounts awarded are generally insufficient to meet the financial needs of the children. In addition, many divorced fathers fail to pay the full amount of child-support payments, and some do not make any court-ordered child-support payments. As a result, the income for the divorced mother and her children often plunges below the poverty level. In many cases taxpayers wind up supporting the mother and her children through the welfare system.

Facts about Divorce

Age of spouses: Divorce is most likely to occur when the partners are in their twenties.

Length of engagement: Divorce rates are higher for those having a brief engagement.

Age at marriage: People who marry at a very young age (particularly teenagers) are more apt to divorce.

Length of marriage: Most divorces occur within two years after marriage. There is also an increase in divorce shortly after the children are grown—this may be partly because some couples wait until the children are ready to leave the nest before dissolving an unhappy marriage.

Social class: Divorce occurs more frequently at the lower socioeconomic levels.

Education: Divorce rates are higher for those with fewer years of schooling. Interestingly, divorce occurs more frequently when the wife's educational level is higher than the husband's.

Residence: Divorce rates are higher in urban areas than in rural areas.

Second marriages: The more often individuals have divorced, the more likely they are to divorce again.

Religion: The more religious individuals are, the less apt they are to become divorced. Divorce rates are higher for Protestants than for Catholics or Jews. Divorce rates are also higher for interfaith marriages than for single faith marriages.

SOURCES: William J. Goode, "Family Disorganization," in R. K. Merton and R. Nisbet, eds., *Contemporary Social Problems*, 4th ed. (New York: Harcourt Brace Jovanovich, 1976), pp. 511-56; Goode, *After Divorce* (New York: Free Press, 1956); Paul C. Glick, *American Families* (New York: Wiley 1957); J. Richard Udry, *The Social Context of Marriage*, 2d ed. (Philadelphia: Lippincott, 1971); William Kornblum and Joseph Julian, *Social Problems*, 6th ed. (Englewood Cliffs, NJ: Prentice-Hall, 1989), pp. 358-63.

Children of Divorce

Annually, over 1 million children under the age of eighteen experience a divorce in their family (U.S. Bureau of the Census, 1992). Many unknowns must be confronted by children involved in a divorce. For instance, there will often be a change of home environment, frequently to a home that is not as nice or expensive as the old one. Another issue children must cope with is custody. Legal custody refers to the fact that one or both parents (the latter in the case of joint custody) maintain all rights and responsibilities for the child.

Kaluger and Kaluger (1984, p. 298) note that society places two conflicting demands on parents who are contemplating a divorce:

One is that the couple's first concern should be with their parental roles and that they should try to put aside their marital problems, which imply that marriage roles are secondary to parental roles. Yet, in a society that places great emphasis on personal ego-need satisfaction in marriage, the placing of marriage in a secondary position may be difficult for the married person to accept.

A basic question parents contemplating divorce ask themselves is: Which would be better for the children: that we remain unhappily married or we end the marriage and thereby end the conflict and tension? A key to answering this question depends on what life will be like after the divorce.

Within five years after a divorce, three quarters of all divorced people are remarried (Kaluger and Kaluger, 1984, p. 298). Therefore, most children of divorce eventually return to living in a family having an adult male and female.

In most cases the mother receives custody of the children, and most divorced women conquer the difficult process of taking over the role of the father. Kaluger and Kaluger (1984, p. 298) note:

Divorced mothers, as well as all other parents without partners, feel that not having to share daily parental decisions with a partner who might not agree with his/her strategy is an advantage. They feel that the parental partner can be a great asset if the two parents agree, but if this is not usually true, one parent can probably do a better job alone.

The breakup of a marriage is traumatic not only for the parents but also for the children. Children appear to react more severely to a divorce than they do to the death of a parent, as suggested by the fact that children of divorce are more likely to get into trouble with the law than those in which a parent has died (Rutter, 1979). This delinquent behavior appears to be more of a reaction to the discontent in the home that caused the divorce, rather than a reaction to the separation and divorce itself as children from intact homes where there is considerable conflict also are more likely to commit delinquent acts (Rutter, 1979).

When parents end a marriage, the children are apt to be fearful of the future, to feel guilty for their own (usually fantasized) role in causing the breakup, to be angry at both parents, and to feel rejected by the parent who moves out. They may become irritable, accident-prone, depressed, bitter, hostile, disruptive, and even suicidal. They may suffer from skin disorders, inability to concentrate, fatigue, loss of appetite, and insomnia. They may also show less interest in their school work and their social lives (Sugar, 1970; McDermott, 1970).

Hetherington, Cox, and Cox (1975) studied forty-eight divorced families for two years after the breakup to assess the effects of divorce on children. They found that immediately after a breakup there is considerable disruption and disorganization in family life. The parents have a variety of stresses to deal with—including economic pressures (partly the result of now maintaining two households), restrictions on recreational and social activities (more so for the mother, especially if she is unemployed), and the needs for affectionate and intimate heterosexual relationships. A number of changes also occur in parent-child interactions. Divorced parents make fewer demands on the children, are less consistent in discipline, communicate less well with them, and have less control over them. These differences are greatest during the first year after the breakup. By the end of the second, a reequilibration appears to take place, particularly between mothers and children. In this study the mothers primarily received custody, and the fathers gradually became less available to their children. The study concluded that the first two years after a breakup are stressful for everyone in the family.

A child's reaction to a divorce is affected by a variety of factors, including the age and sex of the child, the length of time of severe discord in the marriage, and the length of time between the first separation and the formal divorce (Sugar, 1970). A key factor in how traumatic the divorce will be for the child is how well the parents deal with the child's concerns, fears, questions, and anxieties. It is much more traumatic when parents do not explain that the breakup is not the child's fault and if the divorce and custody arrangements are hotly contested. Another factor that increases the trauma is when one or both of the parents seek to turn the child against the other parent. Transferring anger and bitterness about the breakup to the child also increases the child's trauma.

Papalia and Olds (1989, p. 321) cite the many feelings children of divorce may experience which include "pain, confusion, anger, hate, bitter disappointment, a sense of failure, and self-doubt." One longitudinal study focused on 60 California families while they were undergoing divorces (Wallerstein, 1983; Wallerstein and Kelly, 1980). Children in the families ranged in age from three to eighteen years when the parents separated. It was found that children need to work through six major issues in order to maintain positive emotional adjustment. First, children need to accept the fact that their parents' marriage is over. They need to understand that their parents will no longer be together and that their access to one or both parents will be changed. Second, children need to withdraw from any conflicts their parents might be having and get on with their own lives and activities. Third, children need to cope with their loss. This might include their loss of contact with a parent, home situation, family rules or family routines. Fourth, children need to acknowledge and cope with their strong feelings of anger and self-blame. It's very easy for children to place blame either on their parents or on themselves. They need to forgive all involved, stop dwelling on what went wrong, and attend to the present and future. Fifth, children need to understand that the situation is a permanent one. They need to relinquish any dreams they might have that their parents will get together someday. Sixth, children need to maintain a realism about their own relationships with other people. They need to understand and accept that just because their parents' relationship failed, it does not mean their own close relationships with other people will fail.

Although the period during and immediately following the divorce is traumatic for both parents and children, the negative effects appear to lessen after two years (Hetherington et al., 1975). The worst disturbance seems to occur during the first year after the divorce. It seems that the single-parent family is able to regain its homeostasis after making adjustments to the new financial and social situation. Fathers also tend to become less and less available to their children. Perhaps children learn to accept their mother as the primary, single family leader. They have to (and do) adjust to the fact that a father is not always available.

A critical variable affecting children's adjustment to a divorce is the way the parents handle both the divorce and their children's feelings. For example, children react more negatively if the divorce proceedings are drawn out and bitter (Sugar, 1970). Children also suffer when parents use them as a buffer between each other and a means of transmitting hostility as

The Effects of a Divorce on Children Depend on What Happens after the Divorce

The Haag Family

Mary Beth and Doug Haag obtained a divorce after nine years of marriage. They had two children, John (eight years old) and David (four years old). The divorce process was filled with a fair amount of emotional trauma, as both partners were uncertain whether to end the marriage. But both partners were honest in answering their children's questions about the divorce and made crystal clear to them that they were in no way at fault for the marriage ending. Mary Beth and Doug decided to each take custody of a child, partly because John wanted to live with Doug. Doug took custody of John, and Mary Beth took custody of David. The reasons for separating the children were carefully explained to them. The children frequently visited each other on weekends, holidays, and during the summer. Telephone calls between the children were frequent and encouraged.

Mary Beth and Doug respected each other after the divorce and no longer fought. Doug was an accountant, and Mary Beth, an elementary school teacher—both earned enough so that neither was in serious financial difficulty. Doug was married a year and a half later to a woman who understood the harmonious relationship that had developed between Doug and Mary Beth after the divorce.

Mary Beth occasionally dates, but largely concentrates her free time on attending college to obtain her masters degree and on spending time with David. The home environment is now much better for all the Haags than it was in the final years of a marriage that was filled with bitterness and hostility.

The Denny Family

Robert and Corine Denny divorced after thirteen years of marriage. Robert, a dentist, asked for the divorce because he was involved with one of his dental assistants. Corine was furious when she found out. Since she had stayed home to raise the children for the last twelve years, she got the larger part of the divorce settlement. She received the house, the year-old Buick, custody of the three children, and $1,200 per month in child support. The reasons for the divorce were never fully explained to the children, because the parents wanted to hide the fact that Robert had been dating someone else for two years prior to the divorce. As a result, the children assumed they were responsible for causing the tension and arguments prior to the divorce and felt guilty because they thought they were responsible for their parents' separating.

Corine became depressed after the divorce and sought to drown her misery in vodka. She also began going out with a woman friend who was also divorced. Frequently she brought men home to stay overnight. Her standard of living dropped sharply. She refused to look for a job or seek job training and sought to live off of the child support payments. When the children visited their father (which was infrequent as Corine tended to sabotage such visits), Robert sought to dazzle his children with how well his life was now going. Both Robert and Corine sought to use the children as pawns to get back at each other. Corine viewed Robert as someone who had destroyed her comfortable life. Robert viewed Corine as a lush who was being irresponsible and who was spending his hard earned money on partying.

The children suffered greatly. Their grades dropped sharply in school. They were embarrassed to have friends over as their house was a mess, and they never knew when their mother would be intoxicated. The oldest daughter, Jill (twelve years old), began skipping school and is now sexually active without using birth control. Bob, ten years old, was recently caught for shoplifting and is on informal supervision at the juvenile probation department. Dennis, eight years old, has withdrawn. He spends most of his free time watching rock videos on TV. In school he makes practically no effort, has few friends, and is receiving Ds and Fs in all his classes.

this only fosters children's confusion and resentment. The best thing parents can do is be open with the children about the fact that the marriage has failed. Children should not be made to feel that it was their fault. Parents should clearly take responsibility for their decision to part. Finally, parents should continue to be supportive of their children and understand that the children are suffering pain and loss, too. Children need to be heard; they need to be able to express their anger, unhappiness, and shock. Only then can all family members begin to accept the new situation and start moving forward.

Papalia and Olds (1981, p. 328) summarize some things that parents can do to reduce the trauma:

> One of the most important tasks of parents facing divorce is the need to reassure their children that they are not responsible for the break. Parents also can help their children by reestablishing regular routines, by finding adults who can fill the gap left by the missing parent, and by not forcing the children to take sides. The emotional aspects of divorce, rather than the legal considerations, are hardest on children. . . . The initial break is always painful, but many children thrive in an atmosphere that brings hope for a better life after the end of a troubled marriage.

Social Work Roles: Marriage Counseling

The primary social service for people who are considering a divorce or who have an empty-shell marriage is marriage counseling. (Those who do obtain a divorce may also need counseling to work out adjustment problems—such as adjusting to single life. Generally such counseling is one-on-one, but at times may include the ex-spouse and the children, depending on the nature of the problem.)

Marriage counseling is provided by a variety of professionals, including: social workers, psychologists, guidance counselors, psychiatrists, and members of the clergy. Marriage counseling is provided (to a greater or lesser extent) by most direct social service agencies.

Marriage counselors generally use a problem-solving approach in which: (a) problems are identified, (b) alternative solutions are generated, (c) the merits and shortcomings of the alternatives are examined, (d) the clients select one or more alternatives to implement, and (e) the extent to which the problems are being resolved by the alternatives are later as-

Early in the morning, a divorced working woman checks her schedule while her teenage daughter makes a sandwich for lunch.

sessed. Since the spouses "own" their problems, they are the primary problem solvers.

A wide range of problems may be encountered by married couples. A partial list of such problems includes sexual problems, financial problems, communication problems, problems with relatives, interest conflicts, infidelity, conflicts on how to discipline and raise children, and drug abuse problems. Marriage counselors seek to have spouses precisely identify their problems and then use the problem-solving format to resolve the issues. At times, some couples may rationally decide a divorce is in their best interests.

Marriage counselors try to see both spouses together during sessions. Practically all marital conflicts involve both partners and, therefore, are best resolved when both partners work together on resolving the conflicts. (If the spouses are seen separately, each spouse is apt to become suspicious of what the other is telling the counselor.) By seeing both together, the counselor can facilitate communication between the partners and have the partners work together on resolving their concerns. (When spouses are seen individually, they are also more apt to compose exaggerated stories of the extent to which their mate is contributing to the disharmony.) Seeing both partners together allows each partner the opportunity to refute what the other is saying. Only in rare cases is it desirable to hold an individual session with a spouse. For example, if one of the partners wants to work on unwanted emotions dealing with an incestual relationship in the past, meeting individually with that spouse might be desirable. When an individual session is held, the other spouse should be informed of why the session is being held and of what will be discussed. If the other spouse is not informed, there is a danger that he or she will suspect that negative information is being related, which will increase distrust of both the spouse and the counselor.

If some of the areas of conflict involve other family members (such as the children), it may be desirable to include these other family members in some of the sessions. For example, if a father is irritated because his fourteen-year-old daughter is often disrespectful to him, the daughter may be invited to the next session to work on this subproblem.

The self-help organization of Parents Without Partners serves divorced people, unwed mothers or fathers, and stepparents. It is partially a social organization but also an organization to help members with adjustment problems of raising a family alone. Social workers may function as brokers in linking divorcing parents to this organization.

A recent development in social services is divorce mediation, which helps spouses who have decided to obtain a divorce to resolve such issues as dividing the personal property, resolving custody and child support issues, and working out possible alimony arrangements. Some social workers are now receiving specialized training to provide divorce mediation services.

Single-Parent Families

More than 20 percent of all children in the United States are raised in homes with only one parent present. Several reasons account for this. They include divorce, desertion, death of a spouse, and births outside of marriage. More than 90 percent of these families are headed by women. The rate of female-headed homes in African American families is more than twice that in white families and is over 50 percent (Papalia and Olds, 1992, p. 293). These rates have significantly increased over the past two decades. The traditional family configuration (two parents, one a mother who remains in the home to provide full-time child care) is becoming less and less common.

Papalia and Olds (1981, p. 326) summarize some of the problems children face in growing up in one-parent families:

> Children growing up in one-parent homes undoubtedly have more problems and more adjustments to make than children growing up in homes where there are two adults to share the responsibilities for child rearing, to provide a higher income, to more closely approximate cultural expectations of the "ideal family," and to offer a counterpoint of sex-role models and an interplay of personalities. But the two-parent home is not always ideal, and the one-parent home is not necessarily pathological.

Just what effect does being raised in single-parent homes have on children? Obviously, a single parent must fulfill all of the responsibilities of running a home instead of being able to share them with a partner. A single parent wrestles with responsibilities and tasks equal to two full-time jobs in the traditional two-parent family. The question concerning the effects on children is a difficult one to answer. Little research has been done on motherless families. Many questions have been raised about the validity and reliability of the available research on fatherless families.

Some of the data has focused on psychological and cognitive deficits in children produced by lack of an available father figure. Radin (1981) has reviewed the literature regarding the impacts of fathers' presence and absence on children. He found generally that boys were more significantly affected by father absence than girls. Boys are more likely than girls to assume their father's values, gestures, and roles. Such imitation especially occurs when fathers are accepting, positive, and nurturant toward their sons. Girls, on the other hand, react to their fathers in a more complicated manner. They respond best to fathers who encourage development of their intellectual potential and their ability to make independent decisions. Fathers who are obstinate, intolerant, and authoritarian have a negative effect on the intellectual development of both boys and girls. Finally, boys who lose their fathers before age five (Shinn, 1978) and girls before age nine (Radin, 1981) don't perform as well in math as children with both parental figures present.

Some research indicates that children in single-parent families are more likely to experience school difficulties. Zakariya (1982) studied 18,000 students in both elementary and high schools in fourteen states. Children from single-parent homes tended to have lower grades, more absences, more negative feelings about themselves, and more disciplinary actions brought against them than children from two-parent families. However, the results were complicated by the fact that the one-parent families were more likely than two-parent families to live in low-income housing and also to have undergone a move while school was in session. Additionally, some follow-up research found that both family income and gender had a greater impact on children's achievement than one- or two-parent home status.

It must be taken into consideration that this research was done during a time when a father's absence was considered an anomaly. Female-headed, single-parent families are much more common today. Possible negative influences upon children such as feeling different from other children or being stigmatized for their family situations may no longer have as much adverse impact. Some of the negative effects may, therefore, be neutralized.

In contrast to research that has found negative effects of single-parent families, other research portrays a more positive picture. For instance, Rutter (1983) found that children grew up to be better adjusted in single-parent families where they had a positive relationship with their parent than in two-parent families which were ridden with fighting and strife. Likewise, Hetherington (1980) found that a parent who is unapproachable, belligerent, and rejecting can cause more harm to a child than a parent who is not there at all. Another interesting finding is that there is no difference in the likelihood of emotional disturbances between children brought up in the homes of unmarried mothers and those in homes where two parents are present (Klein, 1973). In summary, it appears that how the available parent feels toward and treats the child is more important than simply having two bodies present within the home.

Poverty affects single-parent families significantly more than two-parent families. Differences in the average income levels of single-parent, female-headed families and two-parent families are striking and deplorable. Thirty-four percent of female-headed families are in poverty compared to 8 percent for two-parent families (U.S. Bureau of the Census, 1992.) The situation is worse for African American and Hispanic women and their families than for white women. In 1991, 67 percent of African American female-headed families, and 70 percent of Hispanic female-headed families, were living in poverty.

White mothers who live in poverty most likely have been married. Their current single status results from divorce, separation, or death of a spouse. African American mothers in poverty, however, are more likely to have borne their children without having been married. Children born to unmarried women accounted for 19 percent of all white births and 64 percent of all African American births in 1989 (U.S. Bureau of the Census, 1992, p. 69).

These figures are presented to make a critical point. We have a serious problem for a large proportion of women and children in this country, and the problem is increasing in size and proportion. At the same time federal, state, and local programs that help these people are proportionately decreasing or simply being cut back. The National Advisory Council on Economic Opportunity (1981) indicated that poverty for women and children results from two basic conditions. First, women as opposed to men continue to assume the major responsibility for raising their children. Second, jobs that women can and do get generally pay significantly less than jobs for men. Additionally, women's jobs frequently provide little opportunity for advancement. The issue of women's wages was addressed in Chapter 9.

Blended Families

One out of two marriages now ends in divorce (U.S. Bureau of the Census, 1992). A number of divorcees have had children while married. Most people who obtain a divorce remarry in a few years. Some people are marrying for the first time, but have parented a child while single. A variety of blended families are now being formed in our society. In blended families one or both spouses have biologically parented one or more children with someone else prior to the current marriage. In many blended families the newly married couple gives birth to additional children. In some blended families the children are biologically a combination of "his, hers, and theirs."

Many terms are used for two families that are joined together by the marriage of one parent to another. They include stepfamilies, blended families, reconstituted families, and nontraditional families. Regardless of which term is used, blended families involve complex situations. Conditions depend on variables like the number of children each member of the couple brings into the marriage and the existing relationships already established among members in the previously separate families.

In blended families a number of adjustments have to be made. The husband or wife (or both) have to adjust to raising children that are biologically parented by someone else. The children in blended families have to form relationships with other children in their family who are biologically half-brothers and half-sisters. The children in such families also often have to adjust to a prior divorce that has occurred. Many of the children in blended families have to form relationships with a biological parent who is absent from the home and with a new stepparent. A newly married husband or wife who marries someone else who has been divorced and brings children into the marriage often has to form a relationship with the ex-spouse, as the ex-spouse is apt to have visitation rights and have an impact on the family. If ex-spouses are still feuding, they are apt to use the children as "pawns" to create problems, which then generate extensive strife and turmoil in families.

Blended families are increasing in number and proportion in our society. The family dynamics and relationships are much more complex than in the traditional nuclear family. Blended families are, in short, burdened by much more baggage than are two adults who are childless and marrying for the first time. Blended families must deal with stress that arises from the losses (as a result of divorce or death) experienced by both adults and children, which can make them afraid to love and to trust. Previously

established bonds between children and their biological parents may interfere with the formation of ties to the stepparent. If children go back and forth between two households, conflicts between stepchildren and stepparents may be intensified.

Some difficulties in adjustment can be anticipated (Janzen and Harris, 1986, p. 273). They include jealousies arising between new siblings. Jealousies may focus on sharing parental attention with the new spouse and with new siblings. Another issue for children is the adjustment to a new parent who may have new ideas, values, rules, and expectations. Yet another adjustment involves sharing space and properties when children aren't used to sharing with these new people or to sharing at all. Finally, if one member of the couple comes into the marriage with no child-rearing experience, an adjustment is apt to be necessary by all family members to allow time for the new parent to learn and adapt.

People come into a blended family with ideas and issues based on past experiences. Old relationships and ways of doing things still have their impacts. In discussing blended families, Stuart and Jacobsen (1985) suggest that marrying a new partner involves marrying a whole new family. A blended family differs somewhat from a traditional family in that more people are involved; for example, ex-spouses, ex-in-laws, as well as an assortment of cousins, uncles, and aunts. The married couple can have both positive and negative interactions with this large supporting cast. If a prior marriage has ended bitterly, the unresolved emotions that remain (such as anger and insecurity) will affect the present relationship.

The area of greatest stress for most stepparents is that of child rearing. A stepchild, used to being raised in a somewhat different way, may balk at having to conform to a new set of rules. The stepchild may also have difficulty accepting the stepparent as one who has the right to parent him or her. Such a difficulty is more likely to arise if the stepchild feels sad because the missing parent is not present. If the husband and wife disagree about how to raise children, the chances of conflict are substantially increased. Stepparents and stepchildren also face the problem of adjusting to the habits and personalities of each other. Kompara (1980) recommends that stepparents should not rush into establishing a relationship with stepchildren; a gradual effort at establishing a relationship is more likely to result in a trusting and positive relationship. Kompara (1980) also notes that becoming a stepparent is usually more difficult for a woman because children tend to be emotionally closer to their biological mother and have spent more time with her than with the father.

Three myths about blended families can also be addressed (Janzen and Harris, 1986, pp. 275-76). First, there is the myth of the "wicked stepmother." This involves the idea that the stepmother is not really concerned about what is best for the children, but rather is more concerned about her own well-being. The scene from the cartoon feature "Cinderella" might be brought to mind. Here, the "wicked stepmother" cruelly keeps Cinderella from going to the ball in the hope that her own biological daughters will have a better chance at nabbing the handsome prince. In reality, stepmothers have been found to establish very positive and caring relationships with their stepchildren, provided that the stepmothers have a strong self-concept and the support of their husband (Shulman, 1972).

A second myth about blended families is that "step is less" (Wald, 1981). In other words, this myth asserts that stepchildren will never hold the same place in the hearts of parents that biological children do. This myth does not take into account the fact that people can learn to love each other and are motivated to bind members of their new family together.

The third myth about blended families is that the moment they become joined as one family, they will have "instant love" for each other (Wald, 1981). Relationships take time to develop and grow. The idea of instantly having strong love bonds for each other does not make sense. People involved in any relationship need time to get to know each other, test each other out, and grow to feel comfortable with each other.

Stinnet and Walters (1977) reviewed the research literature on stepparenthood and concluded: (1) integration tends to be easier in families that have been split by divorce than by death, perhaps because the children realize the first marriage is not working out, (2) stepparents and stepchildren come to the blended family with unrealistic expectations that love and togetherness will rapidly occur, (3) children tend to see a stepparent of the opposite sex as playing favorites with their own children, (4) most children continue to miss and admire the absent biological parent, (5)

male children tend to more readily accept a stepparent, particularly if the new parent is also a male, and (6) adolescents have greater difficulty accepting a stepparent than young children or adult children.

There are at least four tasks which stepfamilies need to pursue in order to achieve integration (Visher, 1982; Visher and Visher, 1983). The first task involves acknowledging that losses from old relationships do exist. In addition to the bad times suffered in these prior relationships, there are also memories of the good times. Recalling how good things used to be may elicit feelings of sadness that these times are gone and anger that they can be no more. As Janzen and Harris (1986, p. 284) put it, "In this case, help is usually needed to assist stepfamily members in sorting out feelings, identifying sources of sadness and anger, and looking at the new family as an opportunity to develop and share meaningful relationships, without being disloyal to friends and relatives or desecrating pleasant memories from previous experiences."

A second task for stepfamilies is the creation of new customs and traditions. New ways of doing things need to be established to replace the old ways used in the old family structures. New traditions involve a combination of values and activities enjoyed by all new blended family members. For instance, one side of a newly blended family celebrates at home on New Year's Eve and the other side celebrates the New Year on New Year's Day. A completely new tradition might be established where the family spends the New Year holiday at a resort and celebrates both on New Year's Eve and New Year's Day.

The third task for blended families involves establishing new alliances within the family. Alliances may involve not only the spouses' relationship with each other, but also relationships among siblings and between parents and children. Spending time on activities together is one of several ways of working on alliances.

The fourth task for blended families is integration. Parents have the responsibility of providing organization for the family. Children need to have their limits defined and consistently upheld. One of the difficulties is that children are faced with a new stepparent attempting to gain control, when they have not as yet enjoyed many supportive and positive experiences with their new stepparent. It is important, therefore, for this new stepparent to provide nurturance and

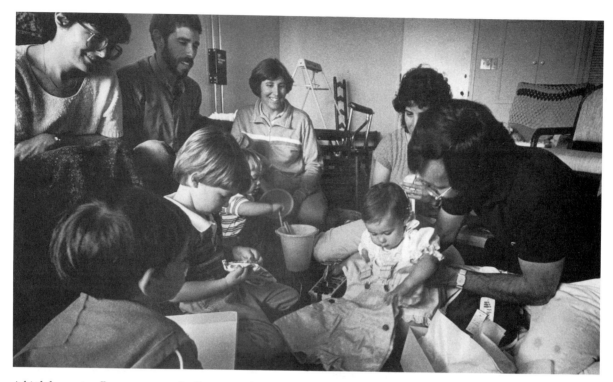

A birthday party offers an opportunity for a new adult member of a blended family to work on alliances.

positive feedback to stepchildren in addition to making rules and maintaining control.

Berman (1981) and Visher and Visher (1983) give the following suggestions to parents in blended families to increase the chances of positive relationships developing between adults and children:

a. Maintain a courteous relationship with the former spouse or spouses. Children adjust best after a divorce when there are harmonious relationships between former spouses. Problems are intensified when former spouses continue to insult each other and when the children are used as weapons for angry former spouses to hurt each other.

b. Understand the emotions of their children. Although the newly wed adults in a recently formed blended family may be fairly euphoric about their relationship, these adults need to be perceptive and responsive to the fears, concerns, and resentments of their children.

c. Allow time for loving relationships to develop between stepparents and stepchildren. Stepparents need to be aware that their stepchildren will probably have emotional ties to their absent biological parent, and that the stepchildren may resent the breakup of the marriage

between their biological parents. Some of the children may even feel they are responsible for their biological parents separating. Some may try to make life difficult for the stepparent so that he or she will leave, with the hope that the biological parents will then reunite. Stepparents need to be perceptive and understanding of such feelings, and patiently take time in allowing their stepchildren to work out their concerns and to allow them to take time in bonding.

d. New rituals, traditions, and ways of doing things that seem right and enjoyable for all members of the blended family need to be developed. Sometimes it is helpful to move to a new house or a new apartment that does not hold memories of a past life. Leisure time should be given structure so that the children spend time alone with the biological parent of the family, some time alone with the stepparent, some time with both of these parents together, some time perhaps with the absent parent or parents, and some time for the new spouses to be alone. New rituals need to be developed for holidays, birthdays, and other special days.

e. Seek social support. Parents in blended families should seek to share their concerns, feelings, frustrations, experiences, coping strategies, and triumphs with other stepparents and stepchildren. Such sharing allows parents in blended families to view their own situations more realistically and to learn from the experiences of others.

Mothers Working Outside of the Home

A major break with tradition has occurred with the surge of married women entering the workforce over the past several decades. In 1948, only 11 percent of all married women with children under age six were in the labor force. In 1989 this figure jumped to 60 percent (U.S. Bureau of the Census, 1992, p. 388). When we look at the percentage of women working outside of the home with children under eighteen, the figure jumps once again to 67 percent. Single mothers are also likely to enter the labor force. Over 53 percent of single mothers with children work outside of the home. Most working mothers work full time.

Many questions have been raised concerning the effects on the social and emotional development of children. The traditional view stressed the importance of a stable, supportive, caretaker being available consistently to meet the needs of children. In other words, it was important for a mother to remain in the home and coordinate the family's care and activities. Research indicates that women need not have to remain home in order to maintain a well-adjusted family.

Reviews of the research on working mothers and their children conclude that "if the mother is satisfied with her job and the provision for child care is reasonably good and suitable, there is no adverse effect on the child's development" (Kadushin and Martin, 1988, p. 178). The evidence is clearest for children in the three to five year age group.

Some questions have been raised concerning the effects on children under age three when mothers work outside of the home. These questions tend to revolve around the issue of maternal deprivation (that is, that infants are emotionally deprived if they do not have enough contact with their mother). Concerns were initially raised after some very early research indicated that institutionalized infants suffered negative effects. This research related these negative effects to the fact that the mother was absent. However, could these effects have been due to the fact that the infants received inadequate care and very little

attention from anyone? It may not necessarily be that they specifically missed their mother.

There is no simple answer to the question about the effects upon children of their mothers working. Children need consistent nurturance, guidance, and care. Home conditions vary widely. Not all biological mothers provide adequate care and attention to their young children. The conditions under which a mother works vary tremendously. Some mothers love their jobs; other mothers hate having to work. The level of the mother's overall satisfaction with life must affect the child.

Indications are that good daycare, that is, daycare which provides the child with consistent attention and care, does not harm a child. Much of the research on the effects on children of mothers working was performed in good facilities with high quality care. Many parents find it very difficult to get good daycare. This is due to many reasons including cost, location, hours available, type of care, and age restrictions on children. Substantial concerns exist when the single mother works outside the home (or when both parents work outside the home) and the children receive poor child care or no care.

The fact is that most mothers work outside of the home. Some work by choice; many work because they need the income to live. It seems that the ideal solution is to make enough good alternative care available so that mothers can work with the knowledge that their children are well cared for.

One other related issue concerns the role of the father in caring for children in those cases where a father is present in the home. Can't the father be a primary participant in child care? It's interesting that the term maternal deprivation is commonly used while the parallel term paternal deprivation is not. In reality, mothers, whether they work outside of the home or not, maintain the primary responsibility for child care (Gilbert, 1985). In a decade-long study of dual-career families, fathers made virtually no contributions to child care other than to provide family income in 40 percent of the families. An additional 30 percent of the fathers would put forth some effort in caring for children but would do absolutely no housework. Only 30 percent of the fathers studied shared child-care responsibilities and household tasks equally with mothers.

Child rearing is most often seen as the mother's

responsibility (Kellerman and Katz, 1978). However, perhaps this idea was more credible when few women worked outside of the home. Perhaps changing attitudes to encourage shared parenting would be in the best interest of families.

Assessing and Intervening in Family Systems

Families are characterized by multiple ongoing interactions. When social workers intervene with families there is much to observe and understand. The dimensions of family interaction that will be discussed here include communication, family norms, and problems commonly faced by families. In addition, two prominent family assessment instruments will be described: the eco-map and the genogram.

Verbal and Nonverbal Communication

Communication involves transmitting information from one person to another. To do this a common system of symbols, signs, or behavior is used. Verbal communication involves the use of words and will be addressed first.

The first phase of verbal communication involves the translation of thoughts into words. The information sender must know the correct words and how to put them together. Only then will the information have the chance of being effectively received. The sender may be vague or inaccurate with the message, and interruptions and distractions may detract from the communication process.

The information receiver, then, must be receptive to the information. That is, she or he must be paying attention both to the sender and to the words that the sender is saying. The receiver must understand what the specific words mean. Inaccuracies or problems at any point in this process can stop the information from getting across to the receiver. At any point distortions may interfere.

Verbal communication patterns inside the family include who talks a lot and who talks only rarely. They involve who talks to whom and who defers to whom. They also reflect the subtle and not so subtle qualities involved in family members' relationships.

The sender also transmits nonverbal messages along with the verbal messages. These include facial expressions, body posture, emotions displayed, and many other subtle aspects of communication. Somewhere between verbal and nonverbal aspects of communication are voice inflection, intonation, and loudness. All this gives the receiver additional information about the intent and specific meaning of the message that's being sent. Sometimes the receiver will attribute more value to the nonverbal aspects of the message than the verbal.

For example, a seventeen-year-old son asks his father, "Dad, can I have the car next Saturday night?" Dad, who's in the middle of writing up his tax returns, which are due in two days, replies, "No, Harry." Harry interprets this to mean that his father is an authoritarian tyrant who does not trust him with the family car. Harry stomps off in a huff. However, what Dad really meant was that he and Mom need the car this Saturday because they're taking their best friends, the Jamesons, out for their twentieth wedding anniversary. Dad was also thinking that perhaps the Jamesons wouldn't mind driving. Or maybe he and Harry could work something out to share the car. At any rate, Dad really meant that he was much too involved with the tax forms to talk about it and would rather do it during dinner.

This is a good example of ineffective communication. The information was vague and incomplete, and neither person clarified his thoughts or gave feedback to the other. There are endless variations to the types of ineffective communication that can take place in families. At any rate, it's up to the social worker to help clarify, untangle, and reconstruct communication patterns.

One especially important aspect of assessing messages is whether they are congruent or incongruent. Satir states that communication is incongruent when two or more messages contradict each other's meaning (Satir, 1967, p. 82). In other words, the messages are confusing. Contradictory messages within families disturb effective family functioning.

Nonverbal messages can sometimes contradict verbal messages. These double messages can also occur in families. For example, a recently widowed woman says, "I'm sorry Frank passed away," with a big grin on her face. The information expressed by the words indicates that she is sad. However, her accompanying physical expressions show that she is happy. Her words are considered socially appropriate for the situation. However, in this particular case, she is relieved to get rid of "the old buzzard" and happy to be the beneficiary of a large life insurance policy.

The double message reflected by the widow's verbal and nonverbal behavior provides a relatively simple, clear-cut illustration of potential problem communication within families. However, congruence is certainly not the only important aspect of nonverbal communication. All of the principles of nonverbal communication can be applied to communication within families.

Family Norms

Family norms are the rules that specify what is considered proper behavior within the family group. Many times the most powerful rules are those that are not clearly and verbally stated. Rather, these are implicit rules or repeated family transactions which all family members understand but never discuss. It's important for families to establish norms which allow both the entire family and each individual member to function effectively and productively.

Every family differs in its individual set of norms or rules. For example, Family A has a relatively conservative set of norms governing communication and interpersonal behavior. Although the norms allow frequent pleasant talk among family members, it is always on a superficial level. The snowy winter weather or the status of the new variety of squash grown in the garden is fair game for conversation. However, nothing more personal is ever mentioned. Taboo subjects include anything to do with feelings, interpersonal relationships, or opinions about careers or jobs. On one occasion, for example, a friend asked the family matriarch what her son and daughter-in-law would name their soon-to-be-born first baby. With a shocked expression on her face, she replied, "Oh, my heavens, I haven't asked. I don't want to interfere."

Family B, on the other hand, has a vastly different set of norms governing communication and behavior. Virtually everything is discussed and debated, not only among the nuclear family members but among several generations. Personal methods of birth control, stances on abortion, opinions on capital punish-

ment, and politics number among the emotionally heated issues discussed. Family members frequently talk about their personal relationships, including who is the favorite grandchild and who tends to fight all the time with rich old Aunt Harriet. The family is so open that price tags are left on Christmas gifts.

The rules of behavior that govern Family B are very different from those of Family A. Yet, in each family, all the members consider their family's behavior to be normal and are comfortable with these rules. Members of each family may find it inconceivable that families could be any other way.

In families with problems, however, most frequently the family rules do not allow the family or the individual members to function effectively and productively. Ineffective norms need to be identified and changed. Positive, beneficial norms need to be developed and fostered.

The following is an example of a family in which there was an implicit, invalid, and ineffective norm functioning. The norm was that no one in the family would smoke cigarettes. A husband, wife, four children, and two sets of grandparents composed this family. Although never discussed, the understanding was that no one had ever or would ever smoke. One day the husband found several cigarette butts in the ashtray of the car typically used by his wife. He thought this odd but said nothing. Over the next six months, he frequently found cigarette butts in the same ashtray. Because no one in the family smoked, he deduced that these butts must belong to someone else. He assumed that his wife was having an affair with another man, which devastated him. However, he said nothing about it and suffered in silence. His relationship with his wife began to deteriorate. He became sullen, and spats and conflicts became more frequent. Finally, in a heated conflict, he spit out his thoughts and feelings about the cigarette butts and her affair. His wife expressed shocked disbelief. The reality was that it was she who smoked the cigarettes, but only when no one else was around. Her major time to be alone was when she was driving to and from work. She took advantage of this time to smoke, but occasionally forgot to empty the ashtray. She told him the entire story, and he was tremendously relieved. Their relationship improved and prospered.

This example illustrates how an inappropriate norm almost ruined a family relationship. Such a simple thing as the wife being a "closet smoker" had the potential for destroying a marital relationship. In this instance, a simple correction in communication solved the problem. The interesting thing is that eventually the entire family learned of this incident. The wife still smokes but still insists on doing it privately. The family now functions effectively with an amended family rule that accepts smoking.

Social workers need to identify and understand family norms so that inappropriate, ineffective norms can be changed. At any point, a social worker can point out such an ineffective norm to family members, help them clarify alternative solutions and changes, and help them assess which is the best solution for them.

Family System Assessment: The Eco-Map

The eco-map is a paper-and-pencil assessment tool used by practitioners to assess specific troubles and plan interventions for clients. The eco-map is a drawing of the client/family in its social environment. An eco-map is usually jointly drawn by the social worker and the client. It helps both the worker and the client achieve a holistic or ecological view of the client's family life and the nature of the family's relationships with groups, associations, organizations, other families, and individuals. It has been used in a variety of situations, including marriage and family counseling, and in adoption and foster care home studies. The eco-map has also been used to supplement traditional social histories and case records. The eco-map is a shorthand method for recording basic social information. The technique helps users (clients and practitioners) gain insight into clients' problems and better sort out how to make constructive changes. The technique provides a "snapshot view" of important interactions at a particular point in time. The primary developer of the technique is Ann Hartman (1978).

A typical eco-map consists of a family diagram surrounded by a set of circles and lines used to describe the family within an environmental context. The eco-map user can create her or his own abbreviations and symbols. (See Figure 12.3.)

To draw an eco-map, a circle (representing the client's family) is placed in the center of a large, blank sheet of paper (see Figure 12.4). The composition of

FIGURE 12.3: Commonly Used Symbols in an Eco-Map

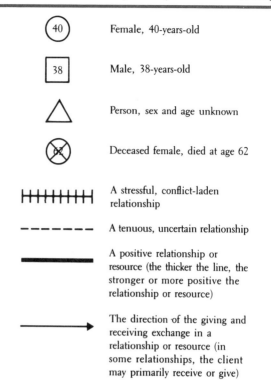

the family is indicated within the family circle. A number of other circles are drawn in the area surrounding the family circle. These represent the other systems (that is, the groups, other families, individuals, and organizations) with which the family ordinarily interacts.

Different kinds of lines are drawn to describe the nature of the relationships that the members of the client family have with the other systems. The directional flow of energy (indicating giving and/or receiving of resources and communication between the client family members and the significant systems) is expressed by the use of arrows. A case example of the use of an eco-map follows.

Barb and Mike Haynes are referred to the Adult Services Unit of Greene County Human Services Department by Dean Medical Clinic. Dean Medical Clinic has been treating Mike's mother, Ruth Haynes, for Alzheimer's disease since she was diagnosed with this disorder four years ago. For the past three years she has been living with Barb and Mike

FIGURE 12:4: Setting Up an Eco-Map

An eco-map is an assessment tool for depicting the relationships and interactions between a client family and its social environment. The largest circle in the center depicts the client family. The surrounding circles represent the significant groups, organizations, other families, and individuals that make up the family's social environment.

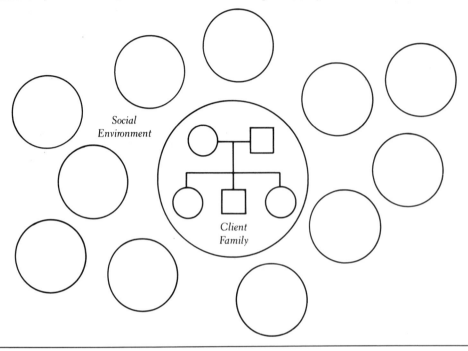

Haynes. She now requires round-the-clock care, as during the evening hours she has trouble sleeping, wanders around the house, and starts screaming when she becomes lost (in the house) and confused. Dean Medical Clinic refers Barb and Mike Haynes to the Adult Services Unit to explore alternative care-giving arrangements.

Barb and Mike Haynes meet with Maria Garcia, Adult Services Worker. Mr. and Mrs. Haynes indicate that they feel a moral obligation to continue caring for Ruth in their home, as Ruth spent most of her adult years caring for Mike and his brother and sister when they were children. However, Barb and Mike also indicate that their emotional and time resources have been stretched to the limit. They have a two-year-old child, Erin, at home. This is a second marriage for both Barb and Mike, and they are paying for Mike's son, Brian, to attend the state university. With such expenses, both believe they need to continue to work because of their financial obligations.

Mike's oldest sister, Mary Kruger, is a single parent who has two children in high school. Mary Kruger has a visual disability but is able to be the primary care giver for Ruth and Erin during the daylight hours when Mike and Barb are working outside the home. Recently, Mary informed Mike and Barb that caring for Ruth is becoming too difficult for her and that some kind of alternative care is needed. Ms. Garcia suggests adult day care for Ruth may be a useful resource during the daytime.

Tears come to the eyes of both Mike and Barb at this point. They indicate they too are emotionally and physically exhausted with working full time, caring for a two-year-old, and taking turns staying awake for four-hour shifts each night to provide care for Ruth. Mike adds that it is emotionally devastating to see your mother slowly deteriorate in front of your eyes. He indicates he is in a double bind; he feels an obligation to care for his mother but doing so is causing major disruptions in his family life. The stress has resulted in marital discord with Barb, and he adds that both he and Barb have increasingly become "short" in temper and patience with Erin.

At this point, Ms. Garcia suggests it may be helpful to graphically diagram their present dilemma. Together, the Hayneses and Ms. Garcia draw the eco-map shown in Figure 12.5. While drawing the map, Mike inquires whether Ruth's medical condition might soon stabilize. Ms. Garcia indicates that temporarily Ruth may occasionally appear to stabilize but that the long-term prognosis is gradual deterioration in mental functioning and in physical capabili-

FIGURE 12.5: Sample Eco-Map: Barb and Mike Haynes

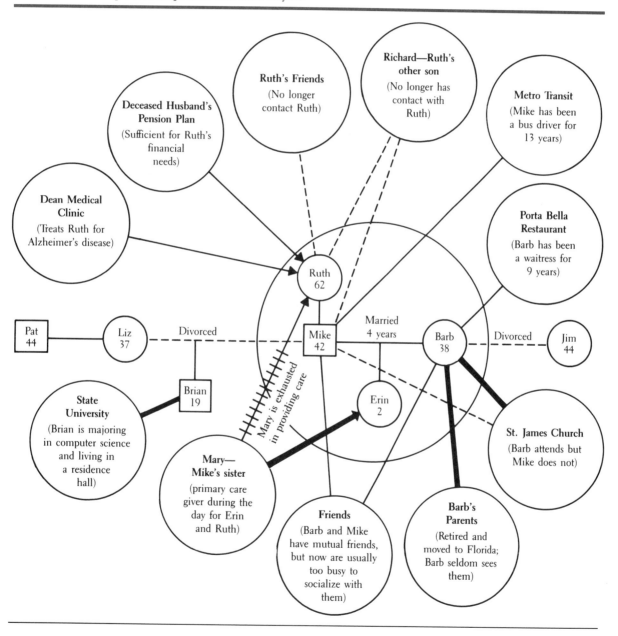

ties. The eco-map helps Mike and Barb see that even though they are working full time during the day and spending the remainder of their waking hours caring for Erin and Ruth, they are becoming too emotionally and physically exhausted to continue doing all of this. During their past three years of trying, they have also ceased socializing with friends. Now they seldom have any time to spend even with Brian. Feeling helpless and hopeless, they inquire if some other care arrangement is available besides a nursing home. They indicate that Ruth has stated on numerous occasions, "I'd rather die now than be placed in a nursing home." Ms. Garcia states that there are some high quality adult group homes in the area. The Hayneses are given the addresses.

After visiting a few of the care facilities, Barb and Mike ask Ruth to stay for a few days at one they particularly like. At first Ruth is opposed to going for a "visit." But after being there a few days, she adjusts fairly well, and soon concludes (erroneously, but no one objects) that it is a home she bought and that the staff are her "domestic employees." Ruth's adjustment eases the guilt that Barb and Mike feel in placing Ruth in a care facility and results in substantial improvements in their marital relationship and in their interactions with Erin, Brian, and their friends.

A major value of an eco-map is that it facilitates both the worker and the client viewing the client's family from a systems and an ecological perspective. Sometimes, as happened in the Hayneses case example, the drawing of the eco-map helps clients and practitioners gain greater insight into the social dynamics of a problematic situation.

Family System Assessment: The Genogram

The genogram is a graphic way of investigating the origins of a client's problem by diagramming the family over at least three generations. The client and the worker usually jointly construct the family genogram. The genogram is essentially a family tree. Murray Bowen is the primary developer of this technique (Kerr and Bowen, 1988). The genogram is a useful tool for the worker and family members to examine problematic emotional and behavioral patterns in an intergenerational context. Emotional and behavioral patterns in families tend to repeat themselves; what happens in one generation will often

FIGURE 12.6: Commonly Used Genogram Symbols

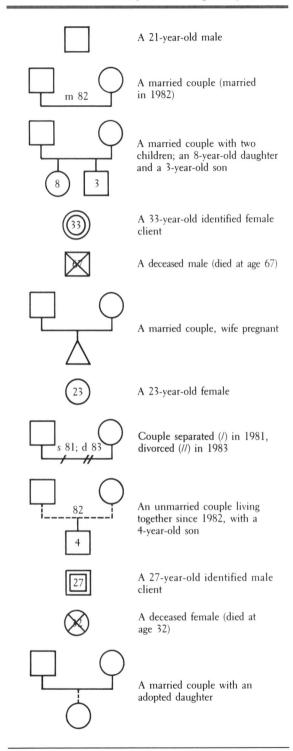

A 21-year-old male

A married couple (married in 1982)   m 82

A married couple with two children; an 8-year-old daughter and a 3-year-old son   8   3

A 33-year-old identified female client   33

A deceased male (died at age 67)

A married couple, wife pregnant

A 23-year-old female   23

Couple separated (/) in 1981, divorced (//) in 1983   s 81; d 83

An unmarried couple living together since 1982, with a 4-year-old son   82   4

A 27-year-old identified male client   27

A deceased female (died at age 32)

A married couple with an adopted daughter

occur in the next. Genograms facilitate family members in identifying and understanding family relationship patterns.

Figure 12.6 shows some of the commonly used symbols. Together, the symbols provide a visual picture of a family tree including the family members; their names, ages, and gender; marital status; sibling positions, and so on, for at least three generations. When relevant, additional items of information may be included, such as: emotional difficulties, behavioral problems, religious affiliation, ethnic origins, geographic locations, occupations, socioeconomic status, and significant life events. The use of the genogram is illustrated in the following case example.

Chris Witt makes an appointment with Kyle Nolan, a social worker in private practice. Chris is distraught. He indicates his wife, Karen, and two children are currently at Sister House, a shelter for battered women. Chris states he and his wife had a "scuffle" two days ago, and she bruised her face. Yesterday, when he was at work, she left home with the children and went to Sister House. He adds that she has contacted an attorney and is now seeking a divorce.

Mr. Nolan inquires as to the specifics of the "scuffle." Chris says he came home after having a few beers. His dinner was cold, and he "got on" Karen for not cleaning up the house. He adds that Karen then started mouthing off, and he slapped her to shut her up. Mr. Nolan then inquires whether such incidents had occurred in the past. Chris indicates "a few times" and then adds that getting physical with Karen is the only way for him to "keep her in line." He says he works all day long in his small business as a concrete contractor while his wife sits home all day long watching soap operas. He feels she is not doing her "fair share" as, he states, the house usually looks like a "disaster."

Mr. Nolan asks Chris if he feels getting physical with his wife is justifiable. He responds, "Sure," and adds that his dad frequently told him "spare the rod, and spoil both the wife and the kids." Mr. Nolan asks Chris if his dad was at times abusive to him when he was a child. Chris indicates that he was and adds that to this day he detests his dad for being abusive to him and to his mother.

Mr. Nolan then suggests that together they draw a "family tree," focusing on three areas: episodes of heavy drinking, episodes of physical abuse, and traditional versus modern gender stereotypes. Mr. Nolan explains that a traditional gender stereotype includes the husband being the primary decision maker, the wife being submissive to him, and the wife being primarily responsible for domestic tasks. The modern gender stereotype involves an equalitarian relationship between husband and wife. After an initial reluctance (Chris expresses confusion as to how such a "tree" would help get his wife back), Chris agrees. The resulting genogram is presented in Figure 12.7.

The genogram helps Mr. Witt to see that he and his wife are products of family systems that have strikingly different values and customs. In his family, the males tend to drink heavily, have a traditional view of marriage, and tend to use physical force in interactions with their spouses. Chris adds that his father also physically abused his brother and sister when they were young. Upon questioning, Chris mentions that he has, at times, struck his own children. Mr. Nolan asks Chris how he feels about repeating the same patterns of abuse with his wife and children that he despises his father for using in the past. Tears come to his eyes, and he says one word, "Guilty."

Mr. Nolan and Chris discuss courses of action that Chris might take to change his family interactions and how he might best approach his wife in requesting that she and the children return. Chris agrees to attend AA (Alcoholics Anonymous) meetings and a therapy group for batterers. After a month of attending these weekly meetings, Chris contacts his wife and asks her to return. Karen agrees to return *if* Chris stops drinking (as most of the abuse occurred when he was intoxicated) and *if* he agrees to continue to attend group therapy and AA meetings. Chris readily agrees. Karen's parents, who have never liked Chris, express their disapproval of her returning.

For the first few months, Chris Witt is on his best behavior, and there is considerable harmony in the Witt family. Then one day Chris has to fire one of his employees. Feeling bad, he stops afterward at a tavern and drinks until he is intoxicated. When he finally arrives home, he starts to verbally and physically abuse Karen and the children. This is the final straw for Karen. She takes the children to her parents' house, where they stay for several days until they are able to find and move into an apartment. She also

FIGURE 12.7: Sample Genogram: The Chris and Karen Witt Family

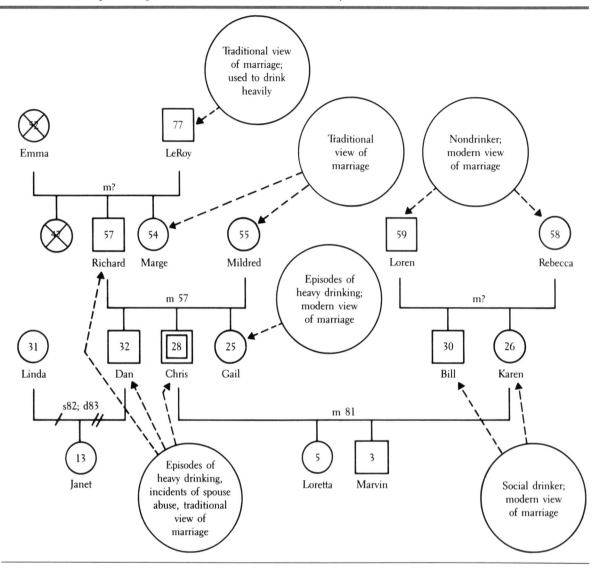

files for divorce and follows through in obtaining one.

In many ways this case is not a "success" case (in reality, many cases are not). The genogram, however, is useful in helping Mr. Witt realize that he has acquired, and is now acting out, certain dysfunctional family patterns. Unfortunately, he is not yet fully ready to make lasting changes. Perhaps sometime in the future he will be more committed to make changes. At the present time, he has returned to drinking heavily.

The eco-map and the genogram have a number of similarities. With both techniques, users gain insight into family dynamics. Some of the symbols used in the two approaches are identical. There are also differences. The eco-map focuses attention on a family's interactions with groups, resources, organizations, associations, other families, and other individuals. The genogram focuses attention on intergenerational family patterns, particularly those that are problematic or dysfunctional.

Family Problems and Social Work Roles

Thorman (1982) points out that although each family is unique, conflicts and problems within families tend to be clustered in four major categories. First, there are marital problems between the husband and wife. Second, there are difficulties existing between parents and children. Third are the personal problems of individual family members. Finally, there are stresses imposed on the family by the external environment.

Family problems do not necessarily fall neatly into one or another of these categories. Frequently, families experience more than one category of problems. Nor are these problem categories mutually exclusive. Many times one problem will be closely related to another. Consider, for instance, the wife and mother of a family who is a department store manager and the primary breadwinner for her family. The store at which she has been working for the past eleven years suddenly goes bankrupt and out of business. Despite massive efforts, she is unable to find another job with similar responsibilities and salary. This can be considered a family problem caused by stresses in the environment. However, this is also a personal problem for the wife and mother. Her sense of self-worth is seriously diminished by her job loss and inability to find another position. As a result, she becomes cranky, short-tempered, and difficult to live with. The environmental stress she is experiencing causes her to have difficulties relating to both children and spouse. The entire family system becomes disturbed.

A family therapy perspective sees any problem within the family as a family group problem, not as a problem on the part of any one individual member (Okun and Rappaport, 1980, p. 37). Social workers, therefore, need to assess the many dimensions of the problem and the impacts on all family members.

Marital problems between the husband and wife present the first category of problems typically experienced by families. Although problems between spouses impact all family members, intervention may target a subsystem of the family, in this case the marital subsystem. In other words, a social worker may work with only these two instead of the entire family to solve a specific problem. When the marital pair gets along better, the entire family will be positively affected.

The Family Service Association of America (Beck, 1973) conducted a national survey of troubled couples to determine the major causes of conflict in marital relationships. Communication surfaced as the primary complaint. Other major sources of conflict included disagreements over children, sexual problems, conflicts over recreational time and money, and unfaithfulness. This study provides some clues concerning the areas practitioners need to address when assessing a marital couple's relationship within the family.

For instance, Bill and Linda, both in their mid-thirties, had a communication problem. They had been married one year. The marriage occurred after a lengthy dating period filled with strife. A primary source of stress was Linda's desire for a permanent commitment of marriage and Bill's unwillingness to make such a commitment. In view of Linda's threats to leave him, Bill finally decided to get married.

Before the marriage another source of difficulty was the amount of time that Bill and Linda spent together. They each owned their own condominiums and lived separately. Bill was involved in a physical fitness program, working out at a health club four nights a week, including Fridays. Bill also had numerous close friends at the club with whom he enjoyed spending his time. Linda was infuriated that Bill restricted the time he spent with her to only some of the days when he didn't work out at the club. Her major concern, however, remained Bill's inability to make a commitment. Linda felt that things would change once they got married.

After marriage, things did not change very much. Although Linda and Bill now lived together, he still worked out at the club with his friends four nights a week, and Linda was still infuriated. In a discussion the two expressed their feelings. Linda said, "I hate all the time Bill spends at the club. I resent having him designate the time he thinks he can spend with me. I feel like he's putting my time into little boxes."

Bill responded, "My physical health is very important to me. I love to work out at the club. What should I do—stay home every night and become a couch potato watching television?"

One way of assessing this couple's communication is evaluating the intent, or what the speaker wants to have communicated to the receiver; and the actual impact of the communication, or what the listener actually hears (Gottman et al., 1976, pp. 1-2). Many times the intent and impact of communication are different. One therapeutic goal is to improve the accuracy and quality of communication, that is, the extent to which the intent of the speaker and the impact upon the listener resemble each other.

Although other difficulties existed in the relationship that are too lengthy to describe here, we will address some of the issues involved in this simple communication. After further meetings and discussion, the following scenario developed. Linda verbally states that she is intensely unhappy that Bill goes to the health club. The impact on Bill is that he feels Linda is trying to tell him what to do. He loves Linda but is wary of losing his independence and what he sees as his identity. When Linda places demands on him, he becomes even more protective of his time.

Linda's intent in her communication is very different than her impact; she feels Bill thinks the club and his friends are more important than she is. This is related to her basic lack of self-esteem and self-confidence.

Bill's response to Linda's statement also has serious discrepancies between its intent and impact. Bill states that he loves to work out. The impact on Linda (that is, what she is hearing Bill say) is that he likes the club and his friends more than he likes her. Bill's actual intent is to tell Linda his physical health and appearance are important to him. He also wants to communicate that his sense of independence is also important to him. He loves her and wants to be committed to her. Yet, this long-term fear of commitment is related to his actual fear that he will lose his identity in someone else's. He's afraid of losing his right to make choices and decisions. He fears being told what to do.

Eventually, Bill and Linda used a problem-solving approach to resolve this issue. Through counseling, the accuracy of their communication gradually improved. Each learned how to communicate personal needs. Instead of their old stand-off, they began to identify and evaluate alternatives. Their final solution involved several facets. Fist, Bill would continue to go to the club to work out three nights each week. Fridays, however, would be spent with Linda; it became clear that she was particularly annoyed at not being able to go out with Bill on Friday nights. Linda, who also was an avid believer in physical fitness, would occasionally go with Bill to the health club to work out. This gave her a sense of freedom to join him when she chose to. The important thing was that she no longer felt restricted. In reality, she rarely went with him to the club. Linda also chose to take some postgraduate courses in her field on those evenings when Bill visited the club. She enjoyed such activities, and they enhanced her sense of professional competence. The personal issues of Bill's need to feel free and Linda's lack of self-esteem demanded ongoing efforts by both spouses. Enhanced communication skills helped them communicate their ongoing needs.

Richard B. Stuart developed a "Couple's Pre-Counseling Inventory" which is used to assess a couple's problems (1983). Each member of the couple is asked to fill out the questionnaire separately. Later, answers can be shared during counseling and misconceptions each has about how the other person feels can be clarified. Areas which are evaluated include the following: "happiness with the relationship"; "caring behaviors" liked and perceptions of caring behaviors liked by the partner; "communication"; how conflict is managed; how moods and other as-

Marital problems between husband and wife make up the first category of family problems. For example, a woman may want to be more than a servant to her husband and his friends.

pects of personal life are managed; "sexual interaction"; how children are managed; willingness to make changes; "marital history"; and specific goals each person wants to pursue.

Such an instrument provides an excellent mechanism for assessment because misconceptions between partners can be clearly pinpointed. For instance, under the topic of "Sexual Interaction," members of the couple are asked to respond to a variety of statements and indicate their levels of satisfaction with the issue involved. The range is from 5, which means "very satisfied," to 1, which means "very dissatisfied." One statement concerns "the length of our foreplay." If one partner is very satisfied and the other very dissatisfied, this is clearly an area which needs to be addressed.

The second major type of family problem involves relationships between parents and children, including parents' difficulties controlling their children and, especially as children reach adolescence, communication problems.

There are many perspectives on child management and parent/child communication techniques. Two major approaches are application of learning theory and Parent Effectiveness Training (PET) developed by Thomas Gordon (1970).

Practitioners can help parents improve their control of children by assessing the individual family situations and teaching parents some basic behavior modification techniques. Behavior modification involves the application of learning theory principles to real-life situations. (The application of learning theory principles to positive parenting is discussed in Chapter 4.)

Personal problems of individual family members make up the third category of problems typically addressed by families.

Sometimes a family will come to a practitioner for help and identify one family member as being "the problem." However, a basic principle of family therapy is that the entire family "owns" the problem (Thorman, 1982, p. 87). Sometimes one family member becomes the scapegoat for a malfunction of the entire family system. The social worker is responsible for helping the family define the problem as a family problem rather than blaming an individual. Treatment goals will most likely involve restructuring various family relationships.

For example, a family of five came in for treatment. The family consisted of a forty-eight-year-old husband and father, a forty-five-year-old wife and mother, and three children: Bob, age nineteen, Ralph, sixteen, and Rosie, twelve. The family lived in a rural Wisconsin town of eight thousand people. The father was a successful businessman involved in local politics. The mother was a homemaker who did not work outside of the home. Bob was a freshman at the University of Wisconsin–Madison. The identified client was Ralph. For the past year, Ralph had been stealing neighbors' cars and running down mailboxes. To say the least, this behavior annoyed the townspeople. The family came to counseling as a last resort.

After several sessions of family members pointing blaming fingers at Ralph, Rosie quietly commented to her parents, "Well, you never say anything about his problem" and proceeded to point at Bob. Suddenly, as if a floodgate had been opened, the entire family situation came pouring out. Rosie was referring to her parents' difficulties in accepting Bob's recent announcement that he was gay. Bob was going through a difficult period as he was "coming out" —making life-style decisions and relating to old friends and family members. His father was terrified that the local townspeople, who were severely homophobic (see Chapter 13), would find out. He feared he would lose his social status and that his political career would be damaged. Bob's mother turned out to be an alcoholic, a secret the family kept well guarded. The parents had not had a sexual relationship for ten years and slept in separate bedrooms. The father was a harsh, stern man who felt it necessary to maintain what he considered absolute control over family members, including his wife. Highly critical of his family, he never risked sharing his own feelings. Finally, Rosie was having serious problems both with her grades and attendance in school. She was also sexually active with a variety of young men. Both she and her parents lived in constant fear that she would become pregnant.

As it turned out, Ralph was one of the better adjusted individuals in the family. He attended school regularly, had a B average, and was active in sports before being suspended for his delinquent behavior. This family provides a good illustration of a family-owned problem. The entire family system was showing disturbances. Ralph was the scapegoat, the identified client, largely because his behavior was more public. All Ralph was doing was calling attention to the family's deeper problems.

The fourth category of problems frequently found in families is problems caused by factors outside the family. These problems can include inadequate income, unemployment, poor housing, inadequate access to means of transportation and places for recreation, and lack of job opportunities (Beck, 1973, p. 91). Included in the multitude of other potential problems are poor health, inadequate schools, and dangerous neighborhoods.

To begin addressing these problems, social workers need effective brokering skills. That is, they need to know what services are available, and how to make a connection between families in need and these services.

Many times appropriate services will be unavailable or nonexistent. Social workers will need to advocate, support, or even help to develop appropriate resources for their clients (Thorman, 1982, pp. 95-99). Services that do not exist, for example, will need development. Unresponsive agency administrations will need to be confronted. Legal assistance may be needed. There are no easy solutions to solving such nationwide problems as poverty or poor health care. This is an ongoing process, and political involvement may be necessary. Such environmental stresses pose serious problems for families, and social work practitioners cannot ignore them.

Summary

Three theories about human behavior are summarized—functionalism, conflict theory, and interactionism. Functionalism views society and other social systems as composed of interdependent and interrelated parts. In contrast to functionalism, conflict theory is more radical, and views society as being a struggle for scarce resources among individuals and social groups. Interactionist theory views human behavior as resulting from the interaction of a person's unique, distinctive personality and the groups she or he participates in.

Also described are two prominent political theories in the United States: conservatism and liberalism. Conservatives generally advocate a residual approach to social welfare programs, while liberals usually emphasize an institutional approach to social welfare programs.

Much of the chapter focuses on describing the following social problems that middle-aged adults (and other age groups) may encounter—poverty, unemployment, empty-shell marriages, and divorce. Those most vulnerable to being poor include one-parent families, children, the elderly, large size families, minorities, the homeless, those without a high school education, and those living in urban slums. Surviving in a bureaucracy and unemployment are two of the major problems in the work setting.

Three types of empty-shell marriages are: devitalized relationships, conflict-habituated relationships, and passive-congenial relationships. Now, about one out of two marriages end in divorce. Although a divorce is traumatic for everyone in the family, it appears children grow up better adjusted when raised in a single-parent family in which they have a good relationship with that parent, than when they are raised in a two-parent family which is filled with discontent and tension.

Becoming more common in our society are single-parent families, blended families, and mothers working outside of the home. Poverty affects single-parent families significantly more than two-parent families. The formation of a blended family requires substantial adjustments by a number of people, including: the spouses, the children, the former spouses, and close relatives and friends. Because an increasing number of mothers are working outside of the home, our society needs to expand its effort to make good child-care arrangements available to the children in these families.

Problems faced by families tend to be clustered in the following four categories: marital problems between the husband and the wife; conflicts between the parents and the children; personal problems of individual family members; and stresses imposed on the family by the external environment. Two-family system assessment techniques are the eco-map and the genogram.

Re-Viewing Relationships

13

Sexual Orientation

John had been attending the state university for over a year now. He didn't have a chance to visit his parents in their small midwest town very often. When he did get home, his visits were usually limited to holidays. Thanksgiving of his sophomore year had finally rolled around, and he found himself hopping on the Greyhound bus headed for Slab City, Wisconsin, his home.

This trip home was a problem for him. No matter how often or how deeply he mulled it over in his mind, he couldn't find an answer. He had something to tell his parents that he didn't think they would like very much. Over the past year John had come to realize something about himself. He had come out; he was gay.

As he watched the countryside roll by from his bus seat he thought. He thought about his childhood, about his high school friends, and even about the girl he had gone steady with for two and one-half years during high school. What would they think if they found out?

He had never really been interested in girls. Sure, he pretended to be. Once a guy got labeled a "fag," he might as well run off to a monastery. He had always been pretty bright. He had learned really fast how men were supposed to act. As all-conference fullback on the high school football team, he became quite adept at telling the appropriate locker room dirty jokes and at exaggerating the last weekend's conquests with women. He often wondered why he had to pretend so hard. The others seemed to really get into it. They seemed genuinely enthralled with the ideas of big breasted women and sex. He never dared mention the fact that he'd rather spend time with Dan or Chuck. He certainly never came close to mentioning any of his secret fantasies.

He even asked Millie to go steady with him. She was a nice girl, in addition to being cute and extremely popular. With her he didn't feel the pressure of constantly having to push for sex. Typically, every Saturday night they'd go to a movie or basketball game or something like that. Then afterwards they'd "neck" in the driveway for just a bit. That couldn't last too long anyway because Millie's parents were pretty strict and imposed a midnight curfew. She was in by midnight or else. He always had to put a little bit of move on her and try to get to second base. At that point she always stopped him, told him she loved him, and firmly stated she was waiting for marriage. What a relief.

At college things were different. He had chosen the state university for a variety of reasons. He found that a person could do a lot of hiding among 40,000 other students. He also found that there were other men who felt just like he did. There was an exceptionally active gay rights group that sponsored a spectrum of social and recreational activities for gay men. Through one of these activities, he had met Hank. Lately they had been spending a lot of time together. He had never felt so comfortable in a relationship before. He found he could talk to Hank about his most intimate thoughts. He also discovered how much he enjoyed expressing his affection for Hank both verbally and physically.

John was jolted from his reverie as the bus pulled up to the local bus stop. He could see his parents waiting to pick him up. There was his father with a big smile on his face, waving at the son he was so proud of. John smiled, waved back, and thought. "Oh, boy. Well, here goes." He stepped off the bus.

Although most people have a sexual orientation toward the opposite gender, many do not. Many are attracted to members of the same gender and some to both genders.

For whatever reasons, the idea of homosexuality, which involves having a sexual orientation for members of the same gender, frequently elicits a strong negative emotional response. As future professional social workers, you need to identify and address this negative response. The National Association of Social Workers' (NASW) Code of Ethics specifics that "the social worker should make every effort to foster maximum self-determination on the part of clients" (NASW, 1979). Additionally, it specifies that a "social worker should not practice, condone, facilitate or collaborate with any form of discrimination on the basis of race, color, sex, *sexual orientation*, age, religion, national origin, marital status, political belief, mental or physical handicap, or any other preference or personal characteristic, condition or status." Clearly, determination of one's sexual orientation is a person's right.

A PERSPECTIVE

This chapter will provide information about various aspects of homosexuality. The intent is to encourage readers to examine their own feelings and reactions. Understanding the effects of diverse sexual orientations upon human behavior is necessary for objective, professional social work practice. Assessing one's own values towards people's diverse sexual orientations is a major step in developing professional social work values.

This chapter will:

- Define and explain the meanings of homosexuality and bisexuality and discuss the terms used to refer to lesbian and gay people.
- Report estimates of how many people are lesbian and gay, and discuss some of the theories attempting to explain why people have diverse sexual orientations.
- Address the issue of discrimination against lesbian and gay people and discuss the concept of homophobia.
- Review some of the myths and stereotypes about gay and lesbian people.
- Describe the lesbian and gay life-styles including lesbian and gay relationships, sexual interaction, lesbian and gay pride, sense of community, and meeting places.
- Identify some of the life situations and crises affecting lesbian and gay people, such as legal issues, violence against them, coming out, aging, and AIDS.

Homosexuality and Bisexuality

A man is committed to prison and has sexual relations with other men. Is he a homosexual? A very shy, lonely woman who has never dated any men is approached by a lesbian friend. The lonely woman decides to have an affair with her friend. Is she a homosexual? Two fourteen-year-old male adolescents experiment with each other by hand-stimulating each other to orgasm. Are they homosexuals? While having sexual intercourse with his wife, a man frequently fantasizes about having sexual relations with other men. He has never had any actual sexual contact with a man in his adult life. Is he a homosexual?

The answers to these questions are not so easy. Placing people in definite, distinct categories is difficult. It is not always easy to draw a clear distinction between a heterosexual and a homosexual person. It may make us feel more secure and in control to cordon off the world into neat and predictable little

Many theories have been advanced to explain the cause of homosexuality, but no one really knows why some people are homosexual and others are not.

boxes of black or white. However, in reality the world is an endless series of shades of gray. People frequently like to polarize others as being either heterosexual or homosexual. Perhaps such labeling makes situations appear to be predictable. If a person is labeled a heterosexual, then many assume that they know a lot of things about that person. For example, if a person is labeled a heterosexual female, then she is probably unassertive, sweet, demure, and emotional. She will date men and probably marry to become a mother and homemaker. If a person is a homosexual male, then he will probably have his hair permed, frequently flick his wrists, and become a hairdresser. In reality things are not so predictable and clear.

The problem with these neat categories is that they foster stereotypes. A stereotype is a fixed mental image of a group that is frequently applied to all its mem-bers. Often the characteristics involved in the mental picture are unflattering. Stereotypes refuse to take into account individual differences. They negate the value and integrity of the individual.

What Does Being a Homosexual Mean?

For the purposes of this chapter, the terms *homosexual*, *lesbian*, and *gay* will be defined in the following arbitrary manner. A homosexual, lesbian, or gay person is a person who is oriented toward having sexual relations with persons of the same gender.

There are two aspects of this definition that merit attention. First of all, above anything else, a homosexual is a person. In the eyes of some heterosexuals the sexuality of a lesbian or gay person often takes precedence over all other aspects of his or her personality. The person becomes lost or invisible. Figure 13.1 depicts this relationship. Most people have homophobia, which involves a fear of lesbian and gay people. This fear warps their perception of homosexuals. The homosexuality becomes prominent at the expense of all other aspects of the lesbian or gay person's personality. A more realistic view is one in which the viewer perceives homosexuality in context. The fact that a person is lesbian or gay is only one slice in a person's personality pie. A realistic perspective allows the many various aspects of the personality to be acknowledged and appreciated.

The second part of the definition states that a homosexual is someone who is oriented towards having sexual relations with people of her or his same gender. In other words, a gay male is attracted to and would choose to have sexual relations with another male over having them with a female. Likewise, a lesbian or female homosexual would opt to have sexual relations with another female instead of with a male. This part of the definition excludes people who under certain circumstances engage in homosexual activities. For instance, prisoners and other institutionalized persons might establish homosexual relationships with others simply because persons of the opposite gender are unavailable. These people will typically return to heterosexuality when the opportunity arises.

The word *homosexual* is derived from the Greek root *homo*, meaning "same." The word *homosexual*

FIGURE 13.1: The Personality Pie

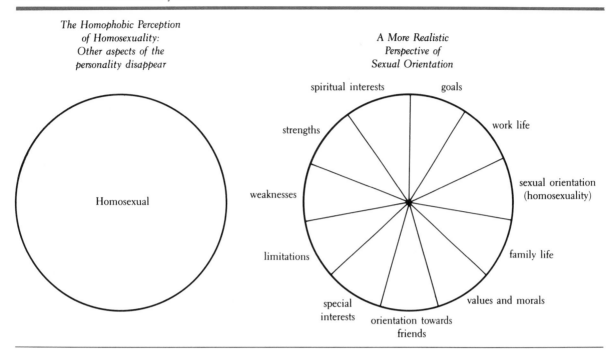

The Homophobic Perception of Homosexuality: Other aspects of the personality disappear

Homosexual

A More Realistic Perspective of Sexual Orientation

spiritual interests
goals
strengths
work life
weaknesses
sexual orientation (homosexuality)
limitations
family life
special interests
values and morals
orientation towards friends

itself, however, was not used until the late 1800s (Karlen, 1971).

Terms used to refer to lesbian and gay people can be confusing. Both women and men with same-gender orientations have been labeled homosexuals. Gay men prefer the term *gay* instead of *homosexual* because it has neither the direct sexual connotations nor the demeaning implications frequently associated with the word *homosexual*.

The word *lesbian* refers to female homosexuals. About the year 600 B.C., a woman named Sappho lived on the Greek island of Lesbos in the Aegean Sea (from which the term *lesbian* is derived). Although Sappho was married, she remains famous for the love poems she wrote to other women.

Many people who are not lesbian or gay use the term *gay* to refer both to lesbians and gay men. However, many lesbians have expressed concern that men are given precedence over women when this term is used by itself to refer to both genders. Therefore, throughout this chapter we will differentiate between the terms *lesbian* and *gay*, giving them equal status. Although we have established specific definitions of *lesbian*, *gay*, and *homosexual*, many who use these terms do not have a clear picture of what they actually mean. All three words may refer to a person with slight, moderate, or substantial interest in or sexual experience with persons of the same gender.

Definition of Bisexual

A bisexual person is sexually attracted to members of either gender. A bisexual usually, although not always, has had sexual interactions with persons of both genders (Masters et al., 1982, p. 316).

We have already initiated the idea that homosexuality is not such a clear-cut concept. Bisexuality is even less clearly defined. In the first major study of sexuality in our era, Kinsey (1948) found that it was very difficult to categorize people in terms of being homosexual, bisexual, or heterosexual. He found many people who considered themselves as being heterosexual had had homosexual experiences at some time during their lives. For example, 37 percent of the men in his sample of 5,300 had had at least one sexual experience with another male to the point of orgasm after reaching age sixteen. In his study of

5,940 women, Kinsey (1953) found that between 8 and 20 percent had had some type of homosexual contact between ages twenty and thirty-five. A significantly smaller percentage of each group had exclusively homosexual experiences throughout their lifetimes.

Because he found it so difficult to categorize people into distinct categories, namely those of homosexual and heterosexual, he developed a six-point scale which placed people on a continuum concerning their sexual experiences (see figure 13.2). A rating of 0 on the scale meant that the individual was exclusively heterosexual; the person had never had any type of homosexual experience. On the other hand, a score of 6 on the scale indicated exclusive homosexuality; this individual had never experienced any form of heterosexual behavior. Those persons scoring 3

would have equal homosexual and heterosexual interest and experience.

More recent researchers have discovered similar difficulties in clearly categorizing people in terms of their sexual orientation. Storms (1980) suggests that the Kinsey scale still failed to provide an accurate description. He developed a two-dimensional scheme to reflect sexual orientation (figure 13.2). The two dimensions involved reflect homoeroticism (sexual interest in and/or experience with those of the same gender) and heteroeroticism (sexual interest in and/or experience with those of the opposite gender).

Additionally, sexual interest in general is portrayed. Those individuals who express high interest in both sexes are placed in the upper right-hand corner. They are considered bisexuals. Those persons who have a very low sexual interest in either gender are

FIGURE 13.2: Conceptualizations of Homosexuality and Heterosexuality

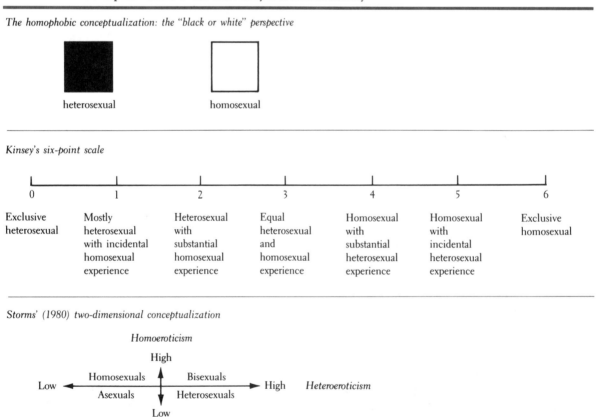

SOURCE: A.C. Kinsey, W. B. Pomeroy, and C. E. Martin (eds.), *Sexual Behavior in the Human Male.* Adapted by permission of the Kinsey Institute for Research in Sex, Gender & Reproduction, Inc., Bloomington, IN.; Adapted from M.D. Storms, "Theories of Sexual Orientation," *Journal of Personality and Social Psychology* 38(1980):783-92.

placed in the lower left-hand corner. They are considered asexuals. Persons with primary sexual interest in the same gender, the homosexuals, are placed in the upper left-hand corner. Similarly people with primary sexual interest in the opposite gender, the heterosexuals, are placed in the lower right-hand corner.

Numbers of Lesbian and Gay People

It's difficult if not impossible to state exactly how many people are lesbian or gay. However, it may be useful to consider the numbers of people who have adopted a primarily lesbian or gay orientation over an extended period of time.

Many authorities feel that the Kinsey studies (1953, 1948) still provide the most valid indicators of the proportion of lesbian and gay people. Kinsey found that, although over one-third of American men had homosexual experiences leading to orgasm during their adolescent or adult lives, only 10 percent of men were exclusively homosexual for a three-year period between ages sixteen and fifty-five. Only about 4 percent were gay throughout their lives.

Supposedly, two to three times as many men as women have a homosexual orientation. Although Kinsey found that 19 percent of American women had homosexual experiences by the age of forty, only 2 to 3 percent of these remained lesbian throughout their lives.

A problem with determining absolute numbers or percentages of lesbian and gay people is that many people have a range of homosexual and heterosexual experiences. For instance, some estimate that 2 percent of all men are exclusively gay and 1 percent of all women are exclusively lesbian throughout their lives; however, 23 percent of all men and 14 percent of all women have had both homosexual and heterosexual experiences (Crooks and Baur, 1993; Hunt, 1974). Others identify 10 to 20 percent of the population as being lesbian or gay in terms of identity regardless of their heterosexual experience. Many lesbian and gay organizations use 10 percent of the entire population as a rule of thumb. One lesbian and gay organization is called "The Ten Percent Society." Some have criticized that sexism has invaded the realm of research focusing on lesbian and gay life-styles. The conjecture is that lesbians have often been ignored. There-

fore, their actual numbers should be much higher than what has been reported.

Why Are Some People Lesbian or Gay?

Although various theories have been proposed to explain why people are gay or lesbian, none has been proven. (A similar question could be asked, "Why are people straight, that is, heterosexual?") No one can give a definitive answer concerning why some people are homosexual and others heterosexual. Some of the primary hypotheses will be reviewed here. They fall under the umbrellas of biological and psychosocial theories. Evaluation of theory, interactionist theory, ethical issues related to theory, and other recent research will also be discussed.

Biological Theories

The biological theories attempting to explain homosexuality can be clustered under two headings, genetic and hormonal. They are based on the idea that homosexuality is caused by physiological factors over which individuals have no control.

Genetic Factors

The genetic explanation for homosexuality supports the idea that people's sexuality is programmed through their genes. Kallman (1952) was a major proponent of this idea. He studied sets of identical and fraternal twins, examining the incidence of homosexuality among them. He found virtually 100 percent concordance of homosexuality among the identical twins. In other words, in all cases of the identical twins, when one was a homosexual, so was the other. He found only 14 percent concordance among the fraternal twins. From this he concluded that homosexuality was genetically caused.

However, there are numerous criticisms of this study. For example, all sets of twins were raised in the same home environment. Thus, environmental factors may have been responsible to an undeterminable extent. Another question concerned the fact that the scientific method virtually never reveals perfect, 100 percent results. This fact alone raises serious concerns about the study. Finally, subsequent research has failed to corroborate the findings (Heston and Sheilds, 1968; Zuger, 1976).

More recently, Bailey and Pillard compared groups of identical twins, fraternal twins, and brothers who were adopted (1991). Identical twins develop from the splitting of a single fertilized egg. They are therefore genetically identical. Fraternal twins, on the other hand, develop concurrently from two separate eggs that were fertilized from two separate sperm. They are only as genetically similar as any brothers might be. Brothers who are adopted, unless they are family members, have no genetic commonality. The researchers found that when one brother was gay, 52 percent of their identical twins were also gay. In only 22 percent of fraternal twins and 11 percent of adoptive brothers were both brothers gay. The researchers concluded that this provides evidence for a genetic link. They indicated that the degree of genetic contribution to homosexuality could vary from 30 to 70 percent. However, as in the earlier study mentioned, it's impossible to winnow out possible environmental elements that might also be related to homosexuality.

LeVay (1991) studied the brains of forty-one cadavers: nineteen of gay men, sixteen of supposedly heterosexual men, and six of supposedly heterosexual women. He found that the anterior hypothalamus (a marble-sized cluster of cells that regulates sexual activity in addition to appetite and body temperature) in gay men was only half the size as that in heterosexual men. He cautioned that this was by no means absolute proof of a genetic link with homosexuality but provided an interesting avenue for further research.

Most experts today feel that adopting a genetic theory to explain homosexuality is naive. Human development is too complex and is affected by numerous physical and social variables.

Hormonal Theories

Hormonal theories of homosexuality suggest that hormonal type and level cause homosexuality. One subset of hormonal theories concerns differences in hormonal levels during adulthood. Tourney (1980) examined studies completed since 1969 which were oriented toward this issue. Earlier studies were not included because of their methodological problems. He found that results were extremely contradictory. Some studies indicate that gay men had lower levels of testosterone than heterosexual men (Loraine et al.,

1970; Starka et al., 1975). Other studies found just the opposite, namely that testosterone levels were higher in gay men (Doerr et al., 1973). Yet other studies found no differences at all.

Some of the conflicting data may be due to methodological complications in the research. For example, one study done by Kolodny and associates (1971) found testosterone levels to be lower in gay men than in heterosexual men. However, on closer scrutiny it was found that some of the subjects in the study had also been smoking marijuana. Marijuana has been suspected of affecting testosterone levels. Therefore, it may have been the marijuana which caused lower testosterone levels, not the lower testosterone levels which caused homosexuality.

Another subset of the hormonal theories indicates that abnormal hormonal levels during the prenatal period may result in homosexuality (Dorner, 1976). Ehrhardt (1985), for example, studied thirty women whose mothers had been administered a synthetic hormone, DES or diethylstilbestrol during their pregnancies. These women were found to manifest a higher than average level of lesbian and bisexual activity than women whose mothers had not taken DES during pregnancy. However, these findings cannot be taken to be indicative of a clear cause-effect relationship. Three-quarters of the women, clearly the large majority, were heterosexual despite the DES. Another problem with this research is that results from a sample with possible biological abnormalities due to the DES cannot be generalized to the "normal" population.

There has been a recent surge of interest in hormonal theories of homosexuality. This probably coincides with the development of increasingly more sensitive and accurate technology for hormonal measurements. Many experts feel that there is a greater likelihood that hormones influence the predisposition of sexual orientation to one gender or the other prenatally rather than postnatally (Byer et al., 1988, p. 349; Masters et al., 1988, p. 418). However, once again, one must be cautioned not to adopt a clear cause-effect relationship. Hormonal levels vary from one individual to another, and, indeed, within the same individual over time. Human hormones are not yet clearly understood. Whatever causes homosexuality and heterosexuality is likely to be a much more complex process.

Psychosocial Theories

Behavioral theories emphasize that homosexual behavior is learned just as any other type of behavior is learned. Early in life homosexual behavior might be positively reinforced by pleasurable experiences and thereby strengthened. Or, such behavior may be punished by negative, punitive experiences and, as a result, be weakened.

For instance, a child who has several positive sexual contacts with members of the same gender might be positively reinforced or encouraged to seek out more such contacts. In a similar manner, a child who has a negative experience with a member of the same gender might be discouraged from having any more such encounters.

Feldman and MacCulloch (1971) take this idea a step further. They suggest that an adult may change his or her sexual orientation later in life through a series of such positive and negative experiences. In other words, even adults can learn to become lesbian or gay according to behavioral theory. The fact that some female victims of sexual assault become lesbians after the very negative experience of being raped lends some support to this idea (Grundlach, 1977).

Still others hypothesize that homosexuality results from certain patterns of family relationships. Freud (1905) maintained that people were born essentially bisexual. They became either homosexual or heterosexual as a result of early life experiences, especially those involving their parents. Bieber (1962) proposed that gay men tend to have dominant mothers and passive, withdrawn fathers. He suggested that homosexuality resulted from fears of heterosexual interaction caused by these problems in early family relationships. Wolff (1971) proposed that lesbians are more likely to have rejecting or indifferent mothers and distant or absent fathers. She suggested that when girls from such families grew up, they sought from other women the love they never received from their own mothers. Later research, however, has failed to support these theories.

The Evaluation of Theory: What Is the Answer?

The answer to why people are gay is multifaceted. Genetic rationales have major shortcomings. For example, we discussed the research finding concerning identical twins; when one brother was gay, 52 percent of their identical twins were gay. However, why were half of the respective twins heterosexual? If, as some researchers postulate, genetic rationales explain some component or percentage of why people are gay, then what explains the remaining components or percentages? If people are gay or lesbian because of some hormonal impact (perhaps prenatally), why aren't all people lesbian or gay who experienced similar hormonal impacts?

At least two major shortcomings can be cited with respect to psychosocial theories of homosexuality that emphasize the learning process. First, there is a tremendous amount of negative feedback about homosexuality. Children learn early on that being called a "fag" is not a compliment. The question might be raised regarding how homosexual behavior would be reinforced and increase in frequency in view of such punitive circumstances.

Second, learning theory implies that a person must first have a homosexual experience. Then, if the experience was positively reinforcing or personally rewarding, the person would seek out more such experiences. However, might it not be the case that individuals who have homosexual desires seek out sexual experiences with the same gender in the first place? In other words, might not the desire for sexual contact with the same gender be there even before any actions ever occur?

Finally, theories like Freud's that emphasize the effects of family variables on developing homosexuality have received little or no support. If family dynamics did have such impacts, why would similar family variables sometimes result in homosexual children and other times in heterosexual children? No consistency has been established.

Interactionist Theory

Michael Storms (1981) has proposed a theory that focuses on the interaction of biological predisposition and the effects of the environment. He poses that the development of a homosexual orientation is related to the rate at which people mature during preadolescence. Children tend to play and interact with people of the same gender during preadolescence. This same-sex interaction reaches its peak at about age twelve, after which heterosexual interactions begin to develop. Heterosexual dating may start around age fifteen. Storms suggests that the sex drive for some people emerges earlier than for others. If children who mature earlier are still in same-sex groupings, they may have positive sexual experiences with persons of the same gender during this time. They may develop a pattern whereby they remain oriented toward the same gender. They never become interested sexually in the opposite gender. This is where the environment plays a part. If these children happen to have positive sexual same-sex experiences, they may continue with that same sexual orientation. If early maturers do not have these experiences, they continue later to develop a heterosexual orientation as they begin interacting with people of the opposite gender.

There is some support for this theory (Van Wyck and Geist, 1984). For example, lesbians' sexuality emerges earlier than heterosexual women's as gauged by age of first masturbation, first sexual fantasies, and first indication of sexual arousal (Saghir and Robins, 1973). Much more exploration is needed before this can be accepted as an explanation for homosexuality.

Many experts agree that homosexuality probably results from some mixture of both biological and psychosocial variables. As yet we don't know what that mixture is (Crooks and Baur, 1993; Gooren, Fliers, and Courtney, 1990).

Ethical Issues Related to Theory

Some lesbian and gay people have expressed ethical concerns regarding proving any theory about homosexuality involving a biological component. On the one hand, many express relief at the thought that others might consider their homosexuality not to be their "own fault." If there's a medical basis, the general public might become more accepting of lesbians and gay men. Gelman and colleagues (1992) found that people were generally more accepting of lesbian and gay people if they felt such people were "born that way" instead of *choosing* or *learning* to lead that life-style.

On the other hand, if specific genetic or hormonal "ingredients" are found for homosexuality, lesbian and gay people might be considered defective by society at large. Taking this one step further, society at large might decide to make biological "corrections" prenatally. Might this mean changing what a person was meant to be into something else? Might potential parents be more likely to abort a fetus determined to be lesbian or gay if they learn about the homosexuality early in the gestational process? There are no easy answers to these questions in our technological age.

Other Research on the Origins of Homosexuality

Bell, Weinberg, and Hammersmith (1981) undertook a massive investigation through the Alfred C. Kinsey Institute for Sex Research concerning the causes of homosexuality. They studied 979 lesbians and gay men, and compared them to 477 heterosexual women and men. Study participants were asked extensive questions about many aspects of their lives. A statistical method called *path analysis* allowed the researchers to explore possible causal relationships between variables, such as parental characteristics and family relationships, and the development of sexual orientation.

Unfortunately, despite the fact that the research is some of the most extensive and methodologically sound available, none of the aforementioned theories to explain homosexuality were supported. If anything several of the variables proposed by these other theories were found **not** to be related to homosexuality. For instance, they found that there was no relationship between being gay and having been seduced by a person of the same gender when young. The researchers found no ultimate answers, but they did identify some interesting aspects about being lesbian or gay. Three findings are of special significance.

First, sexual orientation appears to emerge by the time both males and females reach adolescence. This is the case even when people have little or no sexual experience. Second, lesbian and gay people have a similar amount of heterosexual experience during childhood and adolescence when compared to heterosexual people. There was one basic difference, however. Despite the fact that lesbian and gay people participate in heterosexual activity, they do not enjoy it very much.

The third major finding of the study involves the

concept of gender nonconformity during childhood and the development of homosexuality. Gender nonconformity refers to a child's preference for play and activities which our society generally assumes appropriate for children of the opposite gender. For example, little girls usually choose to play with Barbie dolls and play dishes, while little boys generally prefer "GI Joes" and toy bulldozers. A little girl who only plays with tanks and footballs or a little boy who only plays with Barbie dolls would provide examples of gender nonconformity. Gender nonconformity was a much stronger causal factor for gay men than for lesbians. Other factors such as family relationships have a stronger causal relationship with lesbianism.

This research indicates that sexual orientation develops very early in life. It also suggests that whether a person is gay or lesbian or heterosexual is not a matter of choice. Just as a heterosexual person might be sexually attracted to another heterosexual person, so is a lesbian or gay person sexually attracted to another of the same gender. It appears that it would be just as impossible for a lesbian or gay person to turn heterosexual as it would be for a heterosexual person to begin choosing sexual partners of the same gender.

The fact that many lesbian and gay people externally assume heterosexual roles for appearance's sake is also logical. Numerous homophobic stigmas are placed on gay or lesbian people. They are often subjected to serious discrimination. People can choose to behave in a certain way. However, people cannot choose whom they will be sexually attracted to. In evaluating the consequences of the various alternatives open to them, some lesbian and gay people may decide that it is too difficult to survive openly as a gay/lesbian person (e.g., hold a job, relate to family members, participate in community activities). A lesbian or gay person with a heterosexual facade is burdened with pretending to be someone she or he is not. Such pretense can violate individual dignity and freedom.

Discrimination: The Impacts of Homophobia

"Did you ever hear the one about the dyke who . . ."
"Harry sure has a 'swishy' way about him. You'd never catch me in the locker room alone with that guy."
"They're nothing but a bunch of lousy faggots."

Our common language is filled with derogatory terms referring to lesbian and gay people. Just as other diverse groups are subject to arbitrary stereotypes and to discrimination, so are gay and lesbian people. Because of negative attitudes and the resulting discriminatory behavior, alternatives for lesbian and gay people are often different and limited. There are often other negative consequences. Other nonsexually related aspects of their lives are affected because of their sexual orientation.

For example, a male third grade teacher may live in deathly fear that the parents of his students will discover he's living with another man. He loves his job which he's had for nine years. If parents put pressure on the school administration about his homosexuality, he may get fired. He may never get another teaching job again.

Another example is provided by a female college student who expends massive amounts of energy to disguise the fact that she's a lesbian. She attends a state university in a small, midwest, rural town. She is terribly lonely. She keeps hoping that that special someone will walk into her life. However, she doesn't dare let her friends know she's lesbian or she really will be isolated. There wouldn't be anyone to talk to or to go to have dinner with. They would just never understand. People have committed suicide for less.

Lesbian and gay people are frequently the victims of homophobia. Homophobia is the irrational "hostility and fear that many people have towards homosexuality" (Masters et al., 1988, p. 422). It is not clear how homophobia originated. Maier (1984, p. 371) postulates that it may be people's attempts to deny homosexual feelings in themselves. Perhaps the more strongly homophobic people are, the more they are working to deny such feelings in themselves. Regardless of the cause, the manifestations and symptoms of homophobia are all around us. In the past homosexuality was considered an illness. Not until 1974 did the American Psychiatric Association remove it from the list of mental illnesses.

Whitham and Mathy (1986, p. 180) potently describe the extent of homophobia:

Not only are homosexuals criminalized, victimized, and labeled pathological, they are also regarded by some religious groups as sinners deserving to be put to death, a view reminiscent of the Inquisition. There are very few, if any, groups in American society which evoke more hostility than homosexuals.

Today there are many indications of the general public's homophobia. Only 45 percent of all people feel that a homosexual relationship between consenting adults should be legalized ("Public Perceptions of Gays," 1982). Another survey found that almost three quarters of the persons questioned felt that homosexual relations were always wrong; 59 percent felt that gay men should not be allowed to teach in colleges (Davis and Smith, 1984).

The Roman Catholic church has decried homosexual behavior as sinful. In many Protestant churches (although not all denominations) gay/lesbian people are not allowed to join the clergy. Lesbian and gay people have been denied or lost jobs and housing purely on the basis of their sexual orientation. Violence against lesbian and gay people has risen dramatically in the past few years (this topic will be addressed more thoroughly later in this chapter).

A potentially serious negative effect would be to internalize such negative attitudes. In other words, a gay/lesbian person might think, "If being homosexual is bad, and I am homosexual, then that means that I am bad, too." Weinberg and Williams (1974) have found that only slightly more than one-tenth of all lesbian and gay people feel that homosexuality is an illness. However, 80 percent of lesbians and 77 percent of gay men expressed having fears of others finding out about their sexual orientation (Jay and Young, 1979). The implication is that they fear negative consequences such as job loss, exclusion from various opportunities, and social isolation might occur.

The Lesbian and Gay Life-Styles

What is it like to be lesbian or gay? How would life be different or similar if you awoke tomorrow morning and discovered that you were homosexual? What would happen to your relationships with family, friends, and colleagues?

No one typical type of life-style is practiced by all lesbians and gay people. Lesbians and gay men have lives which are just as varied as those of heterosexuals. Being a gay man in Dickeyville, Wisconsin, is different from being a gay man in a San Francisco suburb.

Being a white lesbian mother receiving public assistance in Utah is different from being an African American upper-class lesbian mother in New York City. However, some common patterns emerge in the lives of lesbian and gay people. Several issues reflected by these patterns are addressed here. They include lesbian and gay relationships, sexual interaction, gay/lesbian pride and a sense of community, and meeting places.

Lesbian and Gay Relationships

Individual relationships vary among lesbian and gay people just as they do among heterosexuals. However, there is evidence that gay men have a greater number of partners than heterosexual men (Weinberg and Williams, 1974). It should be noted that many gay men have decreased the number of sexual relationships they have or turned to monogamy due to fears of contracting AIDS (Stulberg and Smith, 1988).

The social and legal obstacles that prevent lesbian and gay people from establishing long-term relationships may be one of the reasons for this. For example, opportunities for marriage aren't available to lesbian and gay people. Gay and lesbian marriages are illegal in every state (Crooks and Baur, 1993). Even if they are very much in love with each other and want to spend their lives together, social obstacles might exist such as pressure from family and heterosexual friends to form heterosexual relationships, marry, and have children.

Lesbians tend to have substantially fewer partners than gay men do (Schafer, 1977). Likewise, a much higher proportion are involved in monogamous relationships (Thoresen, 1984). Perhaps this is related to the fact that women in general traditionally have had fewer partners and less sexual experience than men.

Bell and Weinberg (1978) conducted a massive survey of lesbian and gay people in the San Francisco area. They recruited 4,639 volunteer respondents through various means including notices in local newspapers, personal contacts, and notices at organizations and establishments oriented toward lesbian and gay people. Respondents were given lengthy interviews concerning aspects of lesbian and gay life. Additionally, the researchers made direct observations of gay and lesbian behavior in various settings where gay and lesbian people congregated.

Stereotypes about Gay and Lesbian People

Not only are lesbian and gay people the victims of homophobia, but they are also the target of derogatory, inaccurate stereotypes. Some of the more common ones include the ideas that gay and lesbian people look "swishy" or "butchy" respectively, that they like to assume either a male or female role, that they are potential child molesters and that they all have AIDS. (Hyde, 1990). All of these stereotypes are false.

The Queen and the Butch

A prevalent stereotype about gay and lesbian people is that gay men typically look extremely feminine and that lesbians, on the other hand, appear very masculine. Terms used to refer to effeminate gay males include *swish*, *nellie*, and *queen*. Terms used to refer to masculine-looking lesbians include *dyke* and *butch* (Sagarin, 1970). In truth these stereotypes are not very accurate.

For example, male university athletes might be considered the epitome of masculinity in terms of traditional masculine stereotypes. Garner and Smith (1977) found that approximately 40 percent of such male athletes had participated in sexual relations to orgasm with another man in the two years preceding the study.

Only about 15 percent of gay men could readily be identified as gay by how they looked, acted, and dressed, according to Kinsey. More recently Voeller (1980) corroborated this statistic concerning male homosexuals. With the breakdown of some of the traditional gender roles, identifying homosexuals by appearance may be even less possible. Women normally wear slacks. Men normally can wear makeup and jewelry. They can even have their hair permed.

Much of the stereotypes about how gay and lesbian people look is the result of confusion between two central concepts: gender identity and choice of sexual partner (Hyde, 1982, p. 363). Gender identity refers to a "person's private, internal sense of maleness or femaleness—which is expressed in personality and behavior—and the integration of this sense with the rest of the personality and with the gender roles prescribed by society" (p. 62). In other words, gender identify refers to a person's self-concept of being either a male or a female. Choice of sexual partner, on the other hand, refers to "sexual attraction to members of the same gender, member of the other gender, or both" (p. 62). Here the emphasis is placed on sexual attraction.

These concepts should not be confused. For example,

whether a man prefers to have sexual relations with another man has nothing to do with his own feeling that he is also a man. Most gay men think of themselves as being men (Storms, 1980). They neither think of themselves as being women, nor do they want to become women. Therefore, a gay man can logically look and act like any other man, yet still be attracted to men.

Likewise, gender identity and choice of sexual partner should not be confused with respect to women. A woman may feel like a woman and think of herself as a woman, yet still be attracted to women (Wolff, 1971). The two concepts are separate and distinct.

Playing Male and Female Roles

Another common stereotype about gay and lesbian people is that in any particular pair, one will choose a "masculine" dominant role and the other a "feminine" submissive role. As with any heterosexual couple, this is rarely the case. Any individual, either homosexual or heterosexual, may play a more dominant or more submissive role depending on the particular mood, activity, or interaction involved. People are rarely totally submissive or totally dominant.

Gay and lesbian people do not assume "male" and "female" roles on a regular basis (Peplau, 1981; Jay and Young, 1979). Even while engaged in sexual activity, few lesbian and gay people limit themselves to only one role (Hooker, 1965). Most gay and lesbian people practice a variety of sexual activities and exchange roles.

The Myth of Child Molesting

One other derogatory stereotype targeting gay and lesbian people is that they are inclined to molest children. This stereotype is especially deleterious for homosexual teachers in that it can cause them to lose their jobs.

In reality, 80 percent of all child molesting is performed by heterosexual men whose victims are young girls. Heterosexual teachers are proportionately more likely to molest children than are homosexual teachers (Newton, 1978).

The "If They're Gay, They Must Have AIDS" Stereotype

AIDS has commanded media attention over the past few years. This concentration has focused on such issues as

(continued next page)

Stereotypes about Gay and Lesbian People (continued)

what the disease involves and what portions of the population are involved. Since gay men were among the first groups hit by the epidemic, the public has some tendency to identify them with the virus. In reality, the spread of AIDS is growing much faster in the heterosexual population (Centers for Disease Control, 1992). This is especially true for women as they are much more likely to contract the disease through heterosexual sex than are men (Ellerbrock, et al., 1991). If anything, gay men have been extremely active in AIDS prevention, education, and advocacy for research and resources. They have striven to saturate gay communities with information about safer sex and to provide mutual support. AIDS is virtually unknown among lesbians, except those who are IV drug users, a high risk group (Hyde, 1990).

AIDS is not a "gay disease." Its transmission has nothing to do with being gay. Sexual and other behaviors (such as sharing IV drug needles) can put anyone at greater risk. Both heterosexual and gay and lesbian people need to be aware of and avoid high risk behaviors.

A major criticism of the study is in its sampling methodology. First, all respondents were volunteers. The lack of a random sample representing the entire lesbian and gay population raises questions whether findings can be applied to all lesbian and gay people. Second, all respondents came from one limited geographical area. This raises doubts whether results accurately reflect the behavior and attitudes of lesbian and gay people who live elsewhere. Nonetheless, there were many interesting findings including some on lesbian and gay relationships. Bell and Weinberg found that relationships between lesbian and gay people tend to fall within five major categories: close couples, open couples, functionals, dysfunctionals, and asexuals.

Close-Couple Relationships

Bell and Weinberg resisted the temptation of labeling lesbian and gay people in close-couple relationships as being happily married. However, these relationships resembled marriage in terms of closeness. Ten percent of the males and 28 percent of the females lived in such relationships. These relationships were characterized by monogamy, closeness, and much mutual time spent together. These couples appeared to be happy and very satisfied with this life-style. An interviewer described one of the close couples in the following manner:

> She and her roommate were obviously very much in love. Like most people who have a good, stable, five-year relationship, they seemed comfortable together, sort of part of one another, able to joke, obviously fulfilled in their relationship. They work together, have the same times off from work, do most of their leisure activities together. She is helping her roommate to learn to paint, while her roommate is teaching her about photography. They sent me home with a plateful of cookies, a good symbolic gesture of the kind of welcome and warmth I felt in their home. (1978, p. 220)

Open-Couple Relationships

As with close couple relationships, people falling in this category lived with one special partner. However, the relationship was sexually open in that each partner could also seek out other sexual partners. Eighteen percent of the gay men and 17 percent of the lesbians had this type of relationship.

These relationships tended not to be as happy as the close couple ones. Partners tended to look for satisfaction outside of the relationship. More difficulties concerning sexual activity, communication, and jealousy were apparent than in close couple relationships. The following is an interviewer's description of a person involved in an open-couple relationship:

> He tries to give the appearance of happiness with his roommate but cruises continually, feels grave guilt about this, and says that it contributes to his domestic travail. He stopped me from introducing myself to his roommate, as if I were a pickup he wanted to keep secret. (Bell and Weinberg, 1978, p. 222)

A gay man who was kind enough to read this chapter over and give some feedback commented that in many gay relationships only one of the partners desires to seek out others. It brought to mind so many heterosexual relationships where one of the partners was more committed and more "in love" than the other.

Functionals

People falling in the functional category tended to orient the rest of their lives around their sexual interests. Bell and Weinberg compared them to heterosexual swinging singles. They participated in more sexual activity with a greater number of partners than did people in any of the other categories. Fifteen percent of the males and 10 percent of the females were included here. They seemed to be energetic, involved people who were generally happy with their lives. An interviewer characterizes one respondent using the following remarks:

> He was a very energetic and open kid, looking much younger than twenty-seven. He seemed to be feeling very happy, likes his job in the Merchant Marine, and enjoys being back for just short stays. Although this militates against long-term relationships, he really enjoys his feelings of independence. (Bell and Weinberg, 1978, p. 224)

Dysfunctionals

Twelve percent of the males and 5 percent of the females fell within the dysfunctional category. Although sexually active, this group was characterized by relatively unhappy, troubled people. They tended to complain about sexual difficulties and suffer psychological problems. There was also a tendency to regret the fact that they were gay or lesbian. One interviewer described a dysfunctional male as follows:

> He lives in an ugly, bleak two-bedroom apartment, where he seems to devote most of his time to watching TV. He has no close friends, and those he has he seldom sees. All relationships seem casual and unimportant to him. (Bell and Weinberg, 1978, p. 226)

Asexuals

People in the asexual category tended to be little interested in sex, have few sexual experiences, and generally spend their time alone. They also tended to report having sexual problems. Sixteen percent of the males and 15 percent of the females were classified as asexuals. Bell and Weinberg attributed their solitary apathy more to psychological problems unrelated to sexuality than to the fact that they were gay or lesbian. An interviewer described a lesbian asexual in the following account:

> She was a bit cool and businesslike. Her difficulties with interpersonal relations were hinted at when she said she tends to be suspicious of people who are "too nice." When the interview was over she was pleasant, but it felt superficial. (1978, p. 227)

Sexual Interaction

Many people find it hard to imagine what lesbian and gay people do sexually. After all, they don't have the "necessary" ingredients of both penis and vagina. The fact is that lesbian and gay people engage in the same types of activities that heterosexuals also enjoy.

Gay people in a close-coupled relationship do not differ greatly from their heterosexual counterparts. Boyce Hinman and Larry Beaty, who share a home, two cars, and a joint checking account, describe themselves as "an average, middle-aged suburban couple."

These include hugging, kissing, touching, fondling of the genitals, and oral sex.

The physiological responses of gay and lesbian people are exactly the same as those of heterosexuals (Masters and Johnsons, 1979). They become aroused or excited, enter a plateau stage of high arousal, have an orgasm, and go through a period of resolution during which the body returns to its normal, unaroused state. The process is the same for all people, male or female, gay or heterosexual.

One difference between gay and lesbian people and straight people is that gay and lesbian people tend to be more open to new techniques, take more time, and pay more attention to the ways in which they interact sexually (Masters et al., 1988, pp. 423-27). this may be partly due to the fact that there are fewer conventions or traditional rules about how sexual relations should be accomplished. For example, heterosexual men tend to quickly reach for their partner's breasts and then move on directly to stimulating her genitals; lesbians, on the other hand, will tend to spend much more time kissing, holding, and caressing each other before any genital touching occurs (Masters and Johnson, 1979).

It's interesting that a major thrust of much sex therapy for heterosexual couples is to slow down and enjoy the many various aspects of sexual interaction and to avoid being so goal oriented (Annon, 1976). Perhaps many heterosexual couples could learn a thing or two from lesbian and gay couples.

The frequency of homosexual activity (Bell and Weinberg, 1978) appears to resemble the frequency of heterosexual activity. American couples in their twenties tend to have sexual intercourse two to three times per week. This figure tends to drop to approximately once a week after people reach age forty-five (Hyde, 1986, p. 321). Lesbian and gay people participate in many of the same sexual activities as heterosexuals. As with heterosexuals, sexual preferences and techniques vary from individual to individual. However, some practices are more frequently used than others. The most common technique used by lesbians is manual stimulation of the genitals (Saghir and Robins, 1973; Bell and Weinberg, 1978). In order to reach orgasm, lesbians tend to prefer *cunnilingus*, a term for oral stimulation of the female genitals (Bell and Weinberg, 1978; Califia, 1979).

Fellatio, which refers to mouth stimulation of the male genitals, seems to be the most common sexual technique used by gay males (Saghir and Robins, 1973; Bell and Weinberg, 1978). *Anal intercourse*, which involves insertion of the penis into the rectum, also seems to be frequently used by many gay men (Saghir and Robins, 1973). However, this practice is not universal. Twenty-two percent of the white gay males in Bell and Weinberg's studies (1978) had not participated in anal intercourse within the past year. Some gay men are altering their sexual behavior by using condoms to avoid contact with semen (Gochros, 1992). AIDS is spread through bodily fluids, especially blood and semen.

Gay and Lesbian Pride and a Sense of Community

Gay and lesbian people and heterosexual people alike need places to socialize, to feel free, to be themselves, and to feel that they belong. Gay and lesbian pride and the sense of community are important concepts. One young gay man summarized these concepts well by joyously stating:

> As someone who has recently "come out," I have acquired a sense of pride in my homosexuality; a part of me I have run and hidden from for twenty of my twenty-five years. I owe much gratitude to many people in the gay community who have given me the courage to stand up for who I am. I am proud to call these people my gay brothers, the first real friends I have ever had. I'm not ashamed—I'm proud to be gay. My sense of gay pride has made me realize that I'm as good as any other person on this earth and deserving of the same basic human dignity and respect all human beings are entitled to. ("What Does Gay/Lesbian Pride Mean to You?"1985)

Heterosexual innuendos, expectations, values, and ideas saturate our society. One gay man said he always felt he had to be watchful and cautious in heterosexual groups. He carefully censored what he said to protect himself from vicious homophobic attacks on himself and his life-style.

Within the lesbian and gay communities, lesbians and gay men can be themselves. They can let down their protective facades. They can be with other people who understand what it's like to be gay in a heterosexually oriented world. This is not to say that many lesbians and gay men have not openly and proudly proclaimed their sexual orientation. This is so despite the fact that it means they expose themselves to homophobic criticism, prejudice and discrimination. In a way, by doing this, they are advocating for individual freedom and the end of discrimination.

In this homophobic world, there are a multitude of lesbian and gay activities and organizations. These range far beyond crisis lines and support groups. There are sports teams and organizations, choral groups, churches, bookstores, newspapers, magazines, advocacy groups, and computer dating services all oriented toward lesbians and gay men. The sense of community has developed and grown far beyond that of the gay bar.

Meeting Places

As we've discussed, there are many types of organizations and activities available for lesbian and gay people within the gay/lesbian community. One is the lesbian or gay bar. Because of its function as one of the most common meeting places where lesbian and gay people can talk and socialize, we will discuss it briefly here. It should be emphasized, however, that it provides only one of the many places where lesbian and gay people can come together. One gay man expressed offense at the idea that a gay bar is the only place where a gay person can have fun. He emphasized that not all gay people, like heterosexual people, like to go to bars and drink.

Historically, gay bars have been described as a sanctuary from the rest of the heterosexual world (Cory and LeRoy, 1963), a hub of communications for finding out about what's happening in the gay community (Hooker, 1967), and a major place for gay people to meet friends (Cory, 1951). They have provided a place for gay people to socialize, relax, and dance without stigma. Bell and Weinberg (1978) found that almost half of the white gay males and almost two-thirds of the African American gay males had patronized the bars at least once a week for the past year. For some people, the gay bar is the center of their social life (Warren 1974).

Most bars for gay and lesbian people orient themselves either to men or women (Rosen, 1974), al-though there are exceptions. Gay men tend to go to the bars in order to meet new sexual partners; lesbians, on the other hand, are more likely to go simply as a place to socialize with people they know (Maier, 1984, p. 364).

Significant Issues and Life Events

As members of a diverse group, lesbian and gay people are victims of stereotypes and homophobia. Discrimination may frequently limit the alternatives available to them. Social workers and other human service professionals need to be aware of the special issues and life events confronting lesbian and gay people. In order to help clients define and evaluate the alternatives available to them, social workers must understand the effects of certain life events. Significant issues and life events examined here include gay/lesbian people and the law, violence against gay/lesbian people, coming out, gay/lesbian parents, aging, and AIDS. Additionally, social work with gay and lesbian people is addressed.

The Impacts of Social and Economic Forces: Legal Issues

For hundreds of years, laws have existed to suppress homosexuality. Although some progress has apparently been made by and on behalf of lesbian and gay people in the last decade (Slovenko, 1980), homosexual acts are still illegal in many states (Maier, 1984, p. 376). Part of the reason for such antihomosexual bias lies in the homophobic fear that homosexuality will spread and prosper if legalized. Some people have expressed the fear that flagrant homosexuality would subvert the morality of society.

The Great Britain Committee on Homosexual Offenses and Prostitution (1963) came up with some findings quite to the contrary. The committee concluded that outlawing homosexuality had no effect on the incidence of homosexual behavior. They stated that it was beyond the realm of the law to regulate private morality. They recommended that adults be allowed to participate privately in homosexual behavior if they chose to do so. As an aside, the United States seems to have more laws on the subject of sexuality in general than all of the European countries put together (Slovenko, 1964, p. 9).

The laws in this country have developed over the past two centuries to "support and protect heterosexuality and nuclear family relationships"; the result is that many of the legal rights of lesbians and gay men have been ignored (Schwaber, 1985, p. 92). Six issues will be addressed concerning where lesbian and gay people are treated differently than heterosexual people under the law. The issues include employment, the military, personal relationships and finances, child custody and visitation, and criminal (sodomy) law.

Employment

Not until 1975 did the U.S. Civil Service Commission change its policy forbidding hiring of gay and lesbian people for government positions (Byer et al., 1988, p. 366). Most federal government agencies cannot discriminate against lesbian and gay people purely on the basis of their sexual orientation.

Other than for federal government jobs, there are no federal statutes that prohibit employers from discriminating against lesbians and gays. They are not considered to be one of the groups such as racial minorities included under the equal protection clause of the U.S. Constitution. Some states, cities, and counties have implemented legislation which protects the rights of lesbian and gay people in various categories. However, where these laws have been established and how they are enforced vary drastically.

In the many localities where statutory protection is absent, private employers can do what they want. Some large corporations, such as McDonald's, IBM, NBC, Exxon, and AT&T, have adopted internal nondiscrimination policies ("How Gay Is Gay?" 1979). However, the vast majority of private employers do not operate under these guidelines. Many employers, therefore, may not hire people just because they are lesbian or gay; likewise, they can fire people simply because they are lesbian or gay.

The Military

Lesbian and gay people are prohibited from joining the CIA, the FBI, or even the armed forces (McCrary and Gutierrez, 1979/80). Leonard Matlovich perhaps provides one of the most publicized examples of discrimination against gay/lesbian people

by the military. As the son of an Air Force sergeant, Matlovich was raised on air force bases. On high school graduation, he immediately joined the Air Force. He received numerous decorations for his service, which included fighting in Vietnam. He was also labeled superior in his evaluations.

Years later, at age thirty, Matlovich acknowledged that he was gay and became involved in gay activities. When he related this to his superiors, he was discharged with a general discharge, a type of discharge considered less than honorable. He eventually took his case to court. He "later collected $160,000 in back pay when the air force could not rebut his claim to an exemption from the no-gays policy." In late 1992, the U.S. Supreme Court "upheld a lower court ruling that demanded the services provide a 'rational basis' for the ban on gays" (*Newsweek*, 1993, p. 54).

President Bill Clinton has stated that he plans to revoke the fifty-year-old ban on homosexuals in the military. The implementation of this ban has been stressed since 1982; about fifteen hundred lesbian and gay people have been discharged from the military each year over the past decade (Smolowe, 1993).

The debate continues. In January 1993, President Clinton issued a "memorandum of instruction," considered less coercive than an "executive order," "to stop questioning recruits about their sexual orientation, stop investigations into soldiers' sexual orientations and end the practice of discharging soldiers who admitted they were gay" (*Newsweek*, 1993, p. 55). However, a new twist involves distinguishing between sexual *orientation* and sexual *conduct*. The military's Uniform Code of Military Justice makes oral and anal sex a criminal felony (although these regulations are enforced sporadically and unevenly for both straight and gay or lesbian people). In effect, a ban on gay or lesbian sexual behaviors would force gay and lesbian people to "keep their sex lives absolutely private—which isn't always easy in barracks" (*Newsweek*, 1993, p. 55).

One newspaper article reflects on the perspective of many military leaders (*Milwaukee Journal*, Nov. 11, 1992, pp. A1, A3):

> Such a change would be one of the most far-reaching social changes imposed on the armed services since Harry Truman ordered blacks integrated into the military in 1948. . . . Little was being done to prepare the nation's

1.8 million troops for such a major change. The subject is so sensitive "no one wants to deal with it," said one officer, speaking on condition of anonymity. . . . About 14,000 troops have been kicked out of the service during the last 10 years because they were homosexual . . . Both four-star generals [the chairman of the Joint Chiefs of Staff and the chief of staff of the Army] contend the issue affects the readiness of the troops for battle, their morale and their rights to privacy.

Even if the ban is totally lifted, an extensive homophobic reaction on the part of much of the military might be expected. Many lesbian and gay people are "anxious, fearing that a darker, more troublesome time looms as the tradition-bound military braces for one of its greatest cultural changes" (*Milwaukee Journal*, Nov. 16, 1992).

Personal Relationships and Finances

In no state in the nation can lesbian and gay people legally marry. Heterosexual unions are characterized by, hopefully, much celebration and legal support. Families and friends hold wedding showers, give gifts, and make the wedding itself a major social event. Lesbian and gay people, however, do not have this legal alternative. With few exceptions in some municipalities and companies, "partners" cannot be included in health insurance policies nor can partners file joint tax returns.

If a lesbian or gay person becomes critically ill and needs hospitalization, his or her partner may be denied visiting privileges. A gay or lesbian lover and partner has no legal rights because he or she does not fall under the legal definition of family under these circumstances. Lesbian and gay people are encouraged, therefore, to draw up a legal document involving the medical power of attorney; these may address "visitation rights, the right to be consulted and to give or withhold consent about medical decisions, and in case of death, the right to personal effects and the right to dispose of the body" (Schwaber, 1985, p. 92).

Wills and the exercising of their instructions are another source of difficulty for many lesbian and gay people. Lesbian or gay partners have no rights to any inheritance if there is no will. All inheritance will be given to legal family members. Therefore, lesbian and gay people are strongly encouraged to have a will made. Wills may clearly specify what possessions will go to which people.

Even with a will, however, relatives may still challenge it under the concept of "undue influence" (Peters, 1982, p. 24). Lesbian and gay people are, therefore, encouraged to update the contents of the will from time to time. Each time they should ascertain that the will accurately reflects their current assets and is well documented.

Child Custody and Visitation Rights

One source reports that gay or lesbian parents have only half as good a chance as heterosexual parents in winning a court battle for custody of their children (Moses and Hawkins, 1982, p. 202). Lesbian mothers are much more likely to be involved in decisions concerning custody than are gay fathers, who must even fight for the right to see their children (Hitchens, 1979/1980).

Cases have been cited where even when a lesbian mother receives custody of her child, she must abide by personal restrictions imposed by the courts. One example is a San Francisco mother who was awarded custody of her three children (Lewis, 1980). The court mandated that as a condition for custody the mother see her female lover only at specified times: when her children were at school or when they visited their father. The question must be raised whether such conditions would have been imposed had her lover been a male.

Judges presiding over custody disputes can make arbitrary judgments concerning what is in the child's best interests (Moses and Hawkins, 1980, pp, 201-2). Some judges may have homophobic ideas. Such ideas have the potential of influencing their decisions.

Moses and Hawkins (1982, pp. 199-201) cite several myths about lesbian and gay parenthood which might influence people against lesbian and gay parents. First, there is the misconception that gay/lesbian parents will influence their children to become gay or lesbian. Second, there is the idea that children will be damaged by growing up in lesbian or gay homes. Third, some people may mistakenly believe that gay and lesbian people's parenting skills are inadequate. Finally, there is the myth that gay and lesbian people are child molesters. Moses and Hawkins conclude that no evidence exists in support of any of these claims. If anything, there is supportive evidence that lesbian and gay people are as good as heterosexuals as parents. Children raised in lesbian and gay homes are

Marchers in a "Gay Pride" rally in Irvine, California, carry a banner that is considered legally obscene. Here, police officers confront the marchers with obscenity codes.

just as well adjusted as children raised in heterosexual homes.

Lesbian and gay people are slowly making progress in attaining more positive custody decisions (Green, 1978; Hitchens, 1979/1980). Several suggestions can be made to human service professionals to help lesbian and gay people fight and win these battles (Moses and Hawkins, 1982, pp 204-5). First of all, the parent must realize that although progress has been made, the odds for gaining custody are still not very good. The parent needs to realize that such cases usually take considerable time and energy. Court cases also frequently cause burdensome stress for both parent and children, and are expensive. Teaching the client such skills as assertiveness, stress management, and problem solving are frequently useful. Another suggestion is to make certain to get a highly competent attorney. Referring the lesbian or gay parent to support groups is also helpful. Finally, educating the parent by providing reading material is often beneficial.

Criminal Law

In many states homosexual activities, both public and private, are specifically illegal. There is significant variation regarding both possible penalties (although some include jail terms) and the extent to which these laws are enforced. In many places an intimate sexual relationship between two consenting adults is technically illegal and can be prosecuted.

The Future of Gay and Lesbian Rights

Although it is a fact that lesbian and gay people are not treated equally under the law, the great progress that has been made should be emphasized. Some states and localities are adopting equal housing and employment legislation for lesbian and gay people. Homosexuality is no longer considered a psychiatric illness. Most of the federal government agencies can no longer discriminate against gay/lesbian people. Lesbian and gay people, through their advocacy and hard work, have achieved a great deal.

Their struggle for equality is sometimes characterized by the phrase, "Remember Stonewall!" Stonewall was a gay bar in New York City's Greenwich Village. On June 28, 1969, police stormed and raided the bar, an incident not unusual in those times. However, how the gay people at the bar responded was indeed unusual. They fought back. The struggle continued in the street for hours (Hunt, 1974).

People involved in gay/lesbian liberation and gay and lesbian rights organizations have provided much impetus to progress made in gay and lesbian legal rights. Such groups exist in many communities, especially in urban settings. Group meetings often provide opportunities to discuss issues, plan political interventions, and get help and support concerning personal difficulties such as employment discrimination. Additionally, they provide a means of becoming acquainted with other lesbian and gay people and with the gay and lesbian community in general.

Social workers need to attend to gay and lesbian rights issues. Not only is an objective, open-minded attitude and belief in individual self-determination necessary, but an advocacy stance is also critical. Unfair, discriminatory rules in public and private agencies can be confronted. Attention can be called to any discrimination that does occur. Political candidates who encourage gay and lesbian rights can be supported. Finally, others including friends, family, and professional colleagues can be educated about gay and lesbian rights and encouraged to support them.

Community Responses: Violence Against Lesbian and Gay People

A Phoenix gay bar explodes when it is attacked with a firebomb.

Two lesbians are thrown out of their apartment after their landlady spied at them through their own apartment window and discovered their sexual orientation. Later, when the two women tried to address the issue through court action, they were assaulted by the landlady's son along with a number of his friends. The group beat up and attacked one of the women with a knife, resulting in serious injuries.

A station wagon filled with five men passes by three gay teenagers. At first the men in the wagon only scream out verbal assaults to the three. However, as the situation intensifies, one of the men in the car hauls out a golf club and hits a gay man in the head, fracturing the gay man's skull.

These and similar incidents are more and more frequently being reported in daily newspapers. David Wertheimer (1988), Executive Director of the New York City Gay and Lesbian Anti-Violence Project, reports the significant increase of violent attacks on lesbians and gay men during the 1980s. He cites one study which reports that 22 percent of all gay men surveyed had been "punched, hit, kicked, or beaten simply because they were perceived to be gay"; he continues that over one-third of the lesbians surveyed said that they had either been "sexually harassed or assaulted based on the assumption they were lesbians" (p. 52). He indicated that his own Anti-Violence Project had observed an 83 percent increase in such victimization within one year.

Wertheimer cites seven types of victimization. These include: verbal harassment, which occurs most frequently; threatening behavior such as being followed by harassers or being warned that attacks are forthcoming; physical attacks by groups of men which can result in emotional and physical injury; assaults associated with AIDS and the resentment towards gay and lesbian people related to it; sexual assaults of women and men; assaults and discrimination by po-

lice; and even murder. Homophobia seems to form the foundation for these attacks.

What can be done to curb and halt such victimization of lesbians and gay men? Wertheimer proposes four potential solutions. First, gay and lesbian civil rights legislation must be passed. Discrimination on the basis of sexual orientation must be clearly illegal. People must get the message that such behavior will not be tolerated. Victims need to feel safe in reporting abusive incidents.

Wertheimer's second suggestion involves the passage of laws which specifically address crimes committed because of hatred and prejudice toward specific groups. Such legislation would protect not only lesbian and gay people but others subjected to prejudice because of their gender, race, ethnic status, religion, or beliefs.

The third proposal involves educating the police and people working in the criminal justice system about homophobia, gay and lesbian victimization, and the needs and rights of gay people. Education could include training employees to have greater empathy for lesbian and gay people, and be more sensitive to their situations. This would encourage lesbian and gay victims to report crimes instead of fearing harassment and retribution from authorities.

Finally, Wertheimer's fourth suggestion to combat gay and lesbian victimization is to establish crisis centers for victims. Such resources would resemble the centers which have already been developed to help heterosexual victims of sexual assault and domestic violence.

Coming Out

"Coming out of the closet" or "coming out" refers to the process of a person acknowledging publicly that she or he is lesbian or gay. It is frequently a long and difficult process in view of the homophobia and stereotypes enveloping us.

Lesbian and gay people usually become aware of the fact that they are different from most others in terms of sexual orientation before the age of twenty (Moses and Hawkins, 1982). The process of coming out itself frequently takes one to two years (Jay and Young, 1979). It should be noted, however, that there is great variation regarding how any specific individual comes out. In other words, for some people it might take much longer and they might come out much later in life. For many people, especially adolescents who do not have much independence and are subject to severe peer pressure, the coming out period may be very difficult.

One way to describe coming out is to identify the four stages involved (Boston Women's Health Book Collective, 1984). The stages include: (1) coming out to oneself; (2) getting to know other people within the gay and lesbian community; (3) sharing with family and friends that one is lesbian or gay; and (4) coming out of the closet, that is, openly and publicly acknowledging one's sexual orientation.

Moses and Hawkins (1982) describe the first stage of the process, namely coming out to oneself, and elaborate on its implications. It involves thinking about oneself as a person who is lesbian or gay instead of as one who is heterosexual. The term used for this is *signification*. They suggest that there is often a period of identity shifting, during which individuals experiment with the label. They may begin conceptualizing themselves as lesbian or gay and begin thinking about what such a label will mean concerning their own life-style.

Part of the signification process involves accepting a label about which society has had so many negative things to say. Some people feel much better about themselves after applying a label of being lesbian or gay. It seems such a label helps in the process of establishing a self-identity. It also seems to give people permission to think and feel honestly about themselves. They then feel they can pursue new thoughts and experiences they feared and avoided before.

Moses and Hawkins (1982) suggest some excellent intervention strategies for human service professionals when helping lesbian and gay clients during their coming out period. To begin with, it is important to provide the client with information about what being lesbian or gay is really like. Chances are that the client thinks in terms of some of the same stereotypes and has some of the same homophobic responses that many others in society do. A gay man who is coming out may need to be educated concerning the difference between gender identity and choice of sexual partner. He would also need to understand that he was not suffering from an illness.

The issue of self-concept may need to be addressed in counseling. Many times it is initially difficult for lesbian and gay people to distinguish between society's somewhat negative view of gay and lesbian people and their own views of themselves. They need to understand that they will not suddenly become different people with odd habits. Rather, they can be made to see that there are different options available to them which may provide them with greater freedom to be themselves.

Another suggestion is the realistic identification and evaluation of the alternatives open to a lesbian or gay person. Signification may have advantages and disadvantages. Advantages might include the decreased fear and anxiety which result from pretending to be someone you're not. Another advantage might be the blossoming of new possibilities for social activities and support systems with other lesbian and gay people. Referrals to local organizations would be helpful here.

Disadvantages also need to be confronted and evaluated. These might include the discrimination in employment and social settings sometimes suffered by lesbian and gay people. Another disadvantage might be the potential loss of some friends and family members. Any anxiety about potential risks in telling people needs to be explored.

The second phase of the coming out process involves actually meeting and getting to know other lesbian and gay people. According to Lewis (1984, p. 467), this involves searching for "community—a place to belong." The best way to curb fears and rid oneself of stereotypes is to meet other lesbian and gay people and find out that all of the horrible things one has heard simply are not true. It's important to establish a social support system made up of people who understand what it is like to come out and who are easy to talk to about it.

The third phase of coming out involves telling friends and family. Most people come out to friends first, as it seems to be more difficult to tell family members (Boston Women's Health Book Collective, 1984). However, it's also difficult *not* to tell family members.

Moses and Hawkins (1982) make specific suggestions for coming out to friends and family. First, the potential consequences need to be realistically examined. They emphasize that it may not be necessary to tell all close friends, relatives, and colleagues when the consequences for the lesbian or gay person are likely to be negative.

For example, take a young man, a junior in college, who has recently come out. His relationship with his father has always been marginal in that they have never communicated well and do not feel very close to each other. However, they do attend family functions together and participate in the family system with other family members. The father has often made derogatory statements about gay people for as long as the son can remember. In this case, it may serve no purpose to come out to the father, since the relationship will probably not be improved. On the other hand, coming out may cause the son much painful criticism and potential ostracism from the family unit.

The fourth phase of coming out involves publicly acknowledging that one is lesbian or gay. As with friends and family, it's important to evaluate the potential positive and negative consequences of each alternative. That is, one must carefully consider if letting it be known that one is lesbian or gay will be to one's advantage or disadvantage in any particular setting.

Many people choose not to come out of the closet. We've already discussed the criticism, rejection, and discrimination lesbian and gay people experience. Perhaps, each individual needs to consider what's best personally. Those on one side of the issue emphasize that discrimination victimizes people unfairly and that each individual must decide for her or himself what is best. Moses and Hawkins (1982) reflect that many might consider this a conservative approach. Those on one side of the issue proclaim that one cannot be free to be oneself without honesty and openness to everyone.

A reality-oriented approach involves looking at all available alternatives. The positive and negative consequences for each alternative must be evaluated. The idea is to assist clients in making decisions which are in their best interests.

Lesbian and Gay Parents

Many lesbian and gay people have children. Bell and Weinberg (1978) found that about one-fourth of all their respondents had been married at one time. Of these, over a third of the lesbians had been married

compared to less than a fifth of gay men. More than half of all the lesbian and gay people who had been married also had children. Additionally, many lesbian and gay people who never marry are also likely to have children.

Even when a lesbian or gay parent gains custody of a child (as you remember, custody problems were discussed earlier under legal issues), there still may be some problems to overcome. For instance, lesbians with children place great importance on passing as heterosexuals (Pagelow, 1980, pp. 200-203). Losing a job or an apartment might have much greater impact on lesbians with children than lesbians who aren't parents. Much more may be at stake when the wel-

In one study, more than half of the lesbian and gay people who had been married had children. Many lesbian and gay people who never marry also have children. Here, two fathers share Gay Freedom Day with their adopted son.

Cheryl's Exploration of Her Self-Identity and Sexual Orientation

Cheryl, age nineteen, worked as a sales clerk at Shopko, the local discount store. Although she still lived with her parents primarily for financial reasons, she was starting to make her own decisions. She debated moving into an apartment with several female friends, and whether she should attend the local technical school or college part-time. These were not the issues she addressed, however, as she came in for counseling.

Cheryl hesitantly explained that she was very anxious about the sexual feelings she was having lately. Although she was steadily dating her high school sweetheart, he did not interest her sexually. She was thinking more and more about her sexual attraction toward other women. She had had these feelings for as long as she could remember. Lately she was becoming obsessed about them. She was very worried that she might be a lesbian.

On further discussion, she expressed fears about what being a lesbian would be like. She was concerned about starting to look too masculine and about becoming sex-starved for other women. Cheryl's counselor provided some information about what being lesbian or gay is really like. They discussed and discarded some of Cheryl's negative stereotypes. The counselor referred Cheryl to some written material on lesbianism and to some local organizations so Cheryl could get more information.

As counseling progressed, Cheryl began to nurture her weakened self-image. Her years of anxiety and her efforts to hide her feelings had taken an emotional toll. Her counselor helped her to work through her confusion about all the negative things she'd heard about gays and her perception of herself. Cheryl began to look at herself more realistically. She began to focus on her personal strengths. These in-cluded her good sense of humor, her pleasant disposition, and her desire to become more independent and establish a career for herself. She found that these attributes and her personal identity had nothing to do with the negative stereotypes she had previously heard about homosexuality.

Finally, her counselor helped her to define and evaluate the various alternatives open to her. For the first time, she explored the possibility of breaking up with her stable, although somewhat boring, boyfriend. She considered the possibility of pursuing a sexual relationship with one of the women she had recently met at a gay and lesbian rights organization meeting. She was already beginning to develop friendships with other women she'd met in a lesbian support group.

After several months of counseling, Cheryl had made several decisions. She had gone through the signification process. She had moved out of her parents' home and into an apartment with several of her female friends, none of whom were lesbians. After much fear and trepidation, she had come out to them. To her relief, they indicated that although they were surprised, it made no difference concerning their friendship. She had broken off with her boyfriend and had started a sexual relationship with another woman. Not only did she have no regrets about her new romantic situation, but she felt extreme relief, satisfaction, and a new sense of freedom.

Cheryl still had not decided whether to come out to her parents. She was still working on that. Nor had she yet decided what career route would be best for her. However, her new sense of self-identity provided her with new confidence and strength. The future looked hopeful and exciting instead of dull and restrictive.

---

fare, support, and living conditions of children must also be taken into consideration. Another typical worry of lesbian and gay parents is that their children's friends might discover that they are homosexual (Lewis, 1979, pp. 121-23).

Several suggestions can be made to social workers and other human service professionals in their efforts to help lesbian and gay people cope with parenthood (Moses and Hawkins, 1982, pp. 205-9). First, social workers can help the lesbian or gay parent identify and emphasize the joys of parenthood. It might be all too easy to get lost in the additional problems of being lesbian or gay and miss all of the normal pleasures of raising children.

Second, social workers can help lesbian and gay parents address the issue of coming out to children. Berzon (1978) recommends that lesbian and gay parents do this as soon as possible. This might avoid family stresses and problems in communication which could result from hiding such an important aspect about the parent. It might make daily living much more comfortable when the lesbian or gay parent can openly interact with and express affection toward a partner, without excluding the children.

Finally, sharing the truth with children might prevent them from finding out about it from someone else which, in turn, might cause them surprise and shock. Children might wonder why their parent hadn't told them. This secrecy might convey a very negative perspective about being lesbian or gay.

Third, sometimes a lesbian or gay parent will find a partner and decide to live with him or her. Social workers can help that parent address many of the same issues that need to be dealt with when a new heterosexual partner joins a household. Issues about child management need to be discussed. Expectations regarding how money will be shared or spent, how daily routines will be organized, and how the adults will act in front of the children need to be clarified openly.

Fourth, these parents may worry about the prejudice and discrimination their children might experience because of their parent's sexual orientation. Wolf (1979) suggests teaching children situational ethics. The idea here is for lesbian and gay parents to be open about their sexual orientation. Children then can learn about being lesbian or gay in a positive sense. However, at the same time, a lesbian or gay parent can teach a child that it is more appropriate to refer to and talk about sexual orientation under some conditions than under others. For example, it is perfectly appropriate to be open about mother's female lover at home with the family. However, more discretion might have to be used when the child is giving a report before her class at school.

That children learn when certain behavior is appropriate or inappropriate is a normal part of growing up. One means of teaching the concept of appropriateness is to teach about individual differences (Moses and Hawkins, 1982, p. 209). Children understand that each person is different. Every individual has his or her own ideas and beliefs. Everyone lives life a bit differently. Differences in sexual orientation are simply another type of human difference. As some people might have different ideas about sexual orientation, they might be prejudiced about it. Therefore, it is not always wise to raise the issue.

As Lesbians and Gay Men Age

The negative stereotypes of elderly homosexual people involve a man who "becomes effeminate, an 'old queen,' while a woman becomes a heartless, cruel, and 'masculine' witch" (Berger, 1985, p. 53). The stereotype continues that because elderly lesbians and gay men lose their youthful appearance, they are rejected by other lesbian and gay people in addition to homophobic heterosexuals. They become lonely, isolated, saddened human beings.

Contrary to this stereotype, the research indicates that what happens is just the opposite. There are two major summary statements about older lesbian and gay people. First, most are relatively well-adjusted, have many gay and lesbian friends and a few heterosexual ones, have some ties with the gay and lesbian community and its support network, and have an age-appropriate sexual and emotional relationship with a long-time partner (Bell and Weinberg, 1978; Minnigerode and Adelman, 1978; Kelly, 1977). The second major summary statement is that both the adjustment levels and the psychosocial needs of older lesbian and gay people are more similar to those of heterosexuals than dissimilar. As gay and lesbian people age, they are exposed to most of the same conditions and have most of the same needs as elderly heterosexuals (Berger, 1985).

If anything, lesbian and gay people may adjust better to aging than heterosexual people based on two principles. These are "mastery of independence" and "mastery of stigma" (Berger, 1985; Moses and Hawkins, 1982; Francher and Henkin, 1973). The concept of "mastery of independence" refers to how being independent is nothing new to lesbian and gay people. Heterosexuals tend to be more involved with their traditional family systems and often have difficulties coping with the death of a spouse and other peers. In a sense heterosexual people have been sheltered during their lives. Lesbian and gay people, however, have had to fend for themselves and experience a lifetime of independence. Since their life-style did not fit with the traditional heterosexual one, they always had to reach out to others and forge new paths and relationships. Coping with the "aloneness" of old age theoretically might not be such a shock to lesbian and gay people as it is to heterosexuals.

The second concept which poses an advantage to older gay men and lesbians involves "mastery of stigma." This means that lesbian and gay people are probably better at coping with the stigma of old age because they've been coping with stigma and rejection all their lives. Coping with one stigma, namely homosexuality, helps prepare them to cope with another, namely aging.

Berger (1985, p. 56) indicates that elderly homosexual people and heterosexual people have two major concerns, "good health and good finances"; he continues that in addition lesbian and gay people have three more problems specifically related to being lesbian or gay which are "institutional problems, legal problems, and emotional needs." Institutional problems many times involve being placed in a nursing home or having to be hospitalized. A person's lover and closest friends may neither be allowed input into whether and where the person is placed, nor even allowed admission to see the person. As was discussed under legal issues, the traditionally defined family can often take over and deny the lesbian or gay person's intimate other access to her or him.

We have also already established that the legal system frequently ignores gay and lesbian people and gay and lesbian relationships. If a will is not clearly written, well established, updated, and well documented, a lesbian or gay partner may lose much of what he's worked together for with a deceased partner. The biological, legal "family" may claim all.

The emotional needs of elderly gay and lesbian people are much like the emotional needs of elderly heterosexuals. They need social contacts, human warmth, and self respect. However, lesbian and gay people have the additional pressure of battling homophobia and the heterosexual bias that the world should be a heterosexual world. For instance, take a social worker who can't understand why a client would want to take a leave from work and apply for public assistance in order to care for a very close "friend." There is the constant battle lesbians and gays must wage either to explain or defend themselves and their behavior.

Berger (1985) makes several suggestions to social workers for their interventions with lesbian and gay clients. First, social workers need to know something about what homosexuality is like and also about the local gay and lesbian communities. Second, social workers must confront their own biases and ideas about homosexuality and sexuality of the elderly. Third, social workers can both work to develop new services for older lesbian and gay people and also help them receive better service from existing traditional agencies.

Gay and Lesbian People and AIDS

AIDS has been discussed in depth earlier in Chapter 10. Although initially many people labelled it a gay disease, it is now spreading among heterosexuals at a greater rate than among gay people. Therefore, in Chapter 10 AIDS was discussed as a condition that could affect anyone, heterosexual or gay or lesbian. Since gay men were among the first to contract the disease in this country, a few comments will be made here about its impact upon them.[1]

Before the existence of AIDS was acknowledged in the United States, many people had already been exposed to and contracted it. Most of the people first exposed here were gay men. As a result, many gay people have seen dozens of their friends die from it. The emotional impact on the gay community has been awesome.

Little attention was initially given to AIDS. Many saw it as something that happened to homosexuals, drug addicts, and other "bad" people. Homophobic responses by heterosexual people and the idea that AIDS is a punishment for bad behavior may have been a contributing factor to the relative inaction on the part of the government. Meanwhile, many gay men along with their friends, families, and lovers, were suffering desperately from the disease.

Gay people can be thanked for much of the publicity about AIDS, the new resources directed to research for a cure, and the strong emphasis on prevention. Gay people were infuriated that the crisis was ignored by the government. The implication was that those contracting the disease weren't that important anyway and that they deserved it. As a result, people in the gay and lesbian community banded together, wrote letters to legislators, marched, advocated for people with the disease, and demanded that it be given some attention. They helped provide the impetus for addressing AIDS as early as it was.

Gay people also took major steps to initiate a massive campaign aimed at prevention. They circulated information and provided people with information in any way they could think of. For instance, brochures emphasizing the need for safer sex practices were even distributed at gay bars. Gay people abruptly slowed

---

1. AIDS is virtually unknown among lesbians (except those who are IV drug users, a separate high risk group).

the spread of the disease within their own communities.

Any social worker who works with a gay or lesbian client needs to be aware of the ramifications and emotional impacts AIDS has had. Those close to the client have likely dealt with many of the as yet unanswered economic and social issues involved with AIDS. These include not only serious illness, but poverty when their resources have been depleted, social isolation, insurance and public assistance problems, and problems getting medication. Such sensitivity to these issues can only help social workers better serve their clients' needs.

Social Work with Lesbian and Gay People: Promoting Optimal Well-Being

Social work has at least two important thrusts concerning working with lesbian and gay people. One involves the individual practitioner's attitudes and skills. The other concerns agencies' provision of services to gay and lesbian people.

Counseling

Josephine Stewart, who chaired the NASW National Committee on Lesbian and Gay Issues, has made several suggestions for social work practitioners working with lesbian and gay clients (NASW *Practice Digest*, 1984, pp. 28-30). For one thing, it is very important to confront one's own homophobia and become comfortable with one's own feelings. One of the worst things a practitioner can do is negatively label a lesbian or gay client and criticize that client for her or his sexual orientation. This contradicts the basic social work value of the client's right to self-determination. A negatively biased practitioner can work against a client's development and maintenance of a positive self-image. Alternatives involving a lesbian or gay life-style and resources available in the gay and lesbian communities might be ignored or even rejected.

Another suggestion for working with lesbian and gay people is to become familiar both with the lesbian and gay life-styles and with the lesbian and gay communities (Moses and Hawkins, 1982, p. 77; NASW *Practice Digest*, 1984, p. 30). This knowledge is necessary in order to help clients identify and evaluate the various alternatives available to them. It's also helpful to know people within the gay or lesbian community who can update a practitioner on new events and resources.

Agency Provision of Services

The other issue concerning social work with lesbian and gay people involves agencies' provision of services. Many services are needed by lesbian and gay people which address specific aspects of lesbian and gay life. These might include lesbian support groups, groups for gay men who are in the process of coming out, legal advice for lesbian or gay parents seeking child custody, or couple counseling for lesbian or gay partners. On the one hand, such services can be provided by agencies focusing on and serving only lesbian and gay people. On the other hand, such services can be mainstreamed into traditional agencies. Either way has advantages.

Segregated services rapidly destroy preconceptions about lesbian and gay inferiority. Having their own services implies that lesbian and gay people are important and numerous enough to merit services equivalent to others. Segregated services also provide greater exposure for the gay or lesbian community.

There are several advantages of mainstreaming services into already existing social service agencies (NASW *Practice Digest*, 1984, pp. 5-7). First, a large traditional agency can provide a wider variety of services and serve more specific individual needs. For example, a lesbian mother might have access to agency-provided parent effectiveness training. She might have easy access to this service, even though it has nothing to do with her sexual orientation.

Second, lesbian and gay people do not have to be segregated from the rest of society. They can go to a social service agency just as heterosexual people can. No stigma need be involved.

Third, mainstreaming provides the opportunity for heterosexual practitioners to interact with other practitioners who are familiar with the issues of gay or lesbian life and serve a gay or lesbian clientele. This provides an excellent opportunity for practitioners to learn from each other. Stereotypes can be addressed and homophobic responses confronted.

Regardless of where services are provided for lesbian and gay people, the fact is that they are needed. Social workers need to learn about lesbian and gay life. They need to confront their own feelings and apply social work values to lesbian and gay clients. They need to learn about resources available for lesbian and gay people and make appropriate referrals. They also need to educate others about the special issues confronting lesbian and gay people in order to fight homophobia. Finally, many times social workers need to act as advocates for the rights of lesbian and gay people. Sexual orientation needs to be addressed as simply another aspect of human diversity. Sexual orientation should be respected instead of denied. Political candidates in favor of gay and lesbian rights need to be supported. Agencies that discriminate against lesbian and gay people need to be confronted, educated, and pressured to provide needed services in a fair and unbiased manner.

Summary

A homosexual, lesbian, or gay person is someone who is oriented toward having sexual relations with persons of the same gender. A bisexual is a person who is sexually attracted to members of either gender. Because of the large numbers of people who have homosexual experiences at some time during their lives, most people do not fall within the distinct categories of gay or lesbian or heterosexual. Although various theories attempt to explain why people become lesbian or gay, no definite causes have been established. Recent research has found that most lesbian and gay people establish their sexual orientation by adolescence. A strong implication of the research is that people cannot choose whether to be gay or lesbian or heterosexual.

Lesbian and gay people are frequently the victims of homophobia, the irrational hostility and fear that many people have towards homosexuality. There are a number of inaccurate stereotypes that exist in our culture, such as the false notion that lesbian and gay people are apt to molest children—the truth is that most child molesting is done by heterosexuals. There is no one type of life-style adopted by all lesbian and gay people, just as there is so single life-style for all heterosexuals.

Two important concepts for many gay men and lesbians are "gay and lesbian pride" and "a sense of community." Several significant issues and life events tend to characterize the lives of lesbian and gay people. Some laws permit discrimination against gay people. Homophobia has produced increasing violence against gay men and lesbians in recent years. "Coming out," or acknowledging that one is lesbian or gay, sometimes is difficult in view of the homophobic fears and negative stereotypes about homosexuality. Many lesbian and gay people are parents and must address coming out to their children. Lesbian and gay people face many but not all of the same issues as heterosexuals during the aging process.

Although the gay and lesbian communities have made tremendous strides in curbing the spread of AIDS, the emotional and economic impacts upon many gay people have been devastating. To work with lesbian and gay people, social workers need to confront their own homophobia and to familiarize themselves with the lesbian and gay communities.

PART FOUR

Later
Adulthood

14

*Biological
Systems and
Their Impacts
on Later
Adulthood*

Wrinkle, wrinkle, little star...

LeRoy was a muscular outgoing teenager. He was physically bigger than most of his classmates and starred in basketball, baseball, and football in high school. In football he was selected an all-state linebacker in his senior year. At age sixteen, he began drinking at least a six pack of beer each day, and at seventeen he began smoking. Since he was an athlete, he had to smoke and drink on the sly. Since LeRoy was good at conning others, he found it fairly easy to smoke, drink, party, and still play sports. That left little time for studying, but LeRoy was not interested in that anyway. He had other priorities.

LeRoy received a football scholarship and went on to college. He did well in football and majored in partying. His grades suffered, and when his college eligibility for football was used up he dropped out of college. Shortly after dropping out, he married Rachel Rudow, a college sophomore. She soon became pregnant and dropped out of college. LeRoy was devastated after leaving college. He had been a jock for ten years, the envy of his classmates. Now he couldn't get a job with status. After a variety of odd jobs, he obtained work as a road-construction worker. He liked working outdoors and also the macho-type guys with whom he worked, smoked, drank, and partied.

LeRoy and Rachel had three children, but he was not a good husband. He was seldom home, and when he was, he was often drunk. After a stormy seven years of marriage (including numerous incidents of physical and verbal abuse) Rachel moved out and got a divorce. She and the children moved to Florida with her parents so that LeRoy could not continue to harass her and the children. LeRoy's drinking and smoking increased. He was smoking over two packs a day, and sometimes drank a quart of whiskey also.

A few years later he fathered an out-of-marriage child for whom he was required to pay child support. At age thirty-nine he married Jane, who was only twenty. They had two children and stayed married for six years. Jane eventually left because she became fed up with being assaulted when LeRoy was drunk. LeRoy now had a total of six children to help support and seldom saw any of them. LeRoy continued to drink and also ate to excess. His weight went up to 285 pounds, and by age forty-eight he was no longer able to keep up with the other road construction workers. He was discharged by the construction company.

The next several years saw LeRoy taking odd jobs as a carpenter. He didn't earn much, and he spent most of what he earned on alcohol. He was periodically embarrassed by being hauled into court for failure to pay child support. He was also dismayed because he no longer had friends who wanted to get drunk with him. When LeRoy was sixty-one, the doctor discovered he had cirrhosis of the liver and informed him he wouldn't live much longer if he continued to drink. Since LeRoy's whole life centered around drinking, he chose to continue to drink. LeRoy also noticed that he had less energy and frequently had trouble breathing. The doctor indicated that he probably had damaged his lungs by smoking and now had a form of emphysema. The doctor lectured LeRoy on the need to stop smoking, but LeRoy didn't heed that advice either. His health continued to deteriorate, and he lost 57 pounds. At age sixty-four, while drunk, he fell over backwards and fractured his skull. He was hospitalized for three and one-half months. The injury permanently damaged his ability to walk and talk. He now is confined to a low-quality nursing home. He is no longer allowed to smoke or drink. He is frequently angry, impatient, and frustrated. He no longer has any friends. The staff detests working with him; his grooming habits are atrocious, and he frequently yells obscenities. LeRoy frequently expresses a wish to die to escape his misery.

ElRoy's early years were in sharp contrast to his brother LeRoy. ElRoy had a lean, almost puny muscular structure and did not excel at sports. LeRoy was his parents' favorite and also dazzled the young females in school and in the neighborhood. ElRoy had practically no dates in high school and was viewed as a prude. He did well in math and the natural sciences. He spent much of his time studying and reading a variety of books and liked taking radios and electrical appliances apart. At first, he got into trouble because he was not skilled enough to put them back together. However, he soon became known in the neighborhood as someone who could fix radios and electrical appliances.

He went on to college and studied electrical engineering. He had no social life but graduated with good grades in his major. He went on to graduate school and obtained a masters degree in electrical engineering. On graduation he was hired as an engineer by Motorola in Chicago. He did well there and in four years was named manager of unit. Three years later he was lured to RCA with an attractive salary offer. The group of engineers he worked with at RCA made some significant advances in television technology.

At RCA ElRoy began dating a secretary, Elvira McCann, and they were married when he was thirty-six. Life became much smoother for ElRoy after that. He was paid well and enjoyed annual vacations with Elvira to such places as Hawaii, Paris, and the Bahamas. ElRoy and Elvira wanted to have children, but could not. When ElRoy was in his early forties, they adopted two children, both from Korea. They bought a house in the suburbs and a sailboat. ElRoy and Elvira occasionally had some marital disagreements but generally got along well. In their middle adult years, one of their adopted sons, Kim, was tragically killed by an intoxicated automobile driver. That death was a shock and very difficult for the whole family to come to terms with. But the intense grieving gradually lessened, and after a few years ElRoy and Elvira put their lives back together.

Now, at age sixty-seven, ElRoy is still working for RCA and loving it. In a few years he plans to retire and move to the Hawaiian island of Maui. ElRoy and Elvira have already purchased a condominium there. Their surviving son, Dae, has already graduated from college and is working for a life insurance company. ElRoy is looking forward to retiring so he can move to Maui, and get more involved in his hobbies of photography and making model railroad displays. His health is good, and he has a positive outlook on life. He occasionally thinks about his brother and sends him a card at Christmas and at his birthday. Since ElRoy never had much in common with LeRoy, he seldom visits him.

A PERSPECTIVE

At age seventy-three, Ronald Reagan won reelection as president of the United States. At eighty, George Burns received his first academy award for his role in *The Sunshine Boys*. At eighty-one, Benjamin Franklin mediated the compromise that led to the adoption of the U.S. Constitution. Konrad

Adenauer was chancellor of Germany at age eighty-eight. At eighty-nine, Arthur Rubinstein gave a critically acclaimed recital in Carnegie Hall, and at the same age, Albert Schweitzer was directing a hospital in Africa. Pablo Picasso, at ninety, was producing engravings and drawings. At ninety-four, Bertrand Russell headed international peace drives. Grandma Moses began painting at age seventy-eight and was still painting at age one hundred (*U.S. News & World Report*, Sept. 1, 1980, pp. 52-53). These internationally noted individuals document that age need not be a barrier to making major contributions in life. Unfortunately the discrimination against the elderly in our society prevents many of them from having a meaningful and productive life.

This chapter will:

- Define later adulthood.
- Describe the physiological and mental changes that occur in later adulthood.
- Present contemporary theories on the causes of the aging process.
- Describe common diseases and major causes of death among the elderly.
- Present material on stress management and on other ways to maintain good physical and mental health throughout life.

What Is Later Adulthood?

Later adulthood is the last major segment of the life span. Sixty-five has usually been cited as the dividing line between middle age and old age (Hareven, 1976). There is nothing magical or particularly scientific about age sixty-five. Wrinkles do not suddenly appear on the sixty-fifth birthday, nor does hair suddenly turn gray or fall out. In 1883, Germany set age sixty-five as the criterion of aging for the world's first modern social security system (Sullivan et al., 1980, pp. 335-70). When our Social Security Act was passed in 1935, the United States followed the German model by selecting sixty-five as the age of eligibility for retirement benefits.

The elderly are an extremely diverse group, spanning an age range of over thirty years. Biologically, psychologically, and sociologically there are a number of differences between Sylvia Swanson, age sixty-five, and her mother, Maureen Methuselah, age eighty-six. Sylvia owns and operates a boutique, making frequent buying trips to Paris, Mexico City, and San Francisco, while Maureen has been a resident of a nursing home since the death of her husband thirteen years ago.

Gerontologists have attempted to deal with these age-related differences among the elderly by dividing later adulthood into two groups: *young-old* ages sixty-five to seventy-four years, and *old-old*, ages seventy-five and above (Hall, 1980).

Our society tends to define old age mainly in terms of chronological age. In primitive societies, old age is generally determined by physical and mental conditions rather than by chronological age. Such a defini-

Senescence may involve reduced agility and increased unsteadiness of the hands.

tion is more accurate than ours. Everyone is not in the same mental and physical condition at age sixty-five. Aging is an individual process that occurs at different rates in different people, and sociopsychological factors may retard or accelerate the physiological changes.

Senescence

The process of aging is called *senescence*. Senescence is the normal process of bodily change that accompanies aging. Senescence affects different persons at different rates and in various parts of the body. Some parts of the body resist aging more than others. In this section we will look at how the aging process in later adulthood affects appearance, senses, teeth, voice, skin, psychomotor skills, intellectual functioning, skeleton and joints, homeostasis, muscular structure, nervous system, digestive system, respiration, heart, and sexuality.

Appearance

Changes in physical appearance include increased wrinkles, reduced agility and speed of motion, stooping shoulders, increased unsteadiness of the hands and legs, increased difficulty in moving, thinning of hair, and the appearance of varicose veins. Wrinkling of the skin is caused by the partial loss of elastic tissue and of the fatty layer of the skin (Rossman, 1977).

Senses

The acuity of the senses generally deteriorates in later years. The sense of touch declines with age because there is drying, wrinkling, and toughening of the skin. The skin also has increased sensitivity to changes in temperature. Since the automatic regulation of bodily functions responds at a slower rate, elderly persons often "feel the cold more." Exposure to cold and to poor living conditions may cause abnormally low body temperature, which is a serious problem for some elderly. They cannot cope as well as younger people with heat either, and therefore cannot work as effectively in moderately high temperatures as younger people can.

The sense of hearing gradually deteriorates. The ability to hear very high tones is generally affected first. As time goes on, the level of auditory acuity becomes progressively lower. Many of the elderly find

it difficult to follow a conversation when there is a competing noise, as from a radio, television, or other people talking (Kalish, 1975). Impairment in hearing is five times as common in persons aged sixty-five to seventy-nine as it is in individuals between the ages of forty-five and sixty-four years. Men are more apt to experience hearing impairments than women (Kaluger and Kaluger, 1984, p. 582). People who have a hearing impairment are apt to feel lonely and isolated as they cannot as readily join into conversations. Sometimes such an impairment and the feelings of isolation facilitate the development of personality quirks that result in their being more difficult to get along with, which further increases their loneliness. (We see once again how the physical and social environment can affect emotional development.)

Vision also declines. Most people over age sixty need glasses or contact lenses to see well. The decline in vision is usually caused by deterioration of the lens, cornea, retina, iris and optic nerve (Botwinick, 1970). The power of the eye to adjust to different levels of light and darkness is reduced, and color perception is also reduced. The elderly are likely to have 20/70 vision or less, are not as able to perceive depth, and cannot see as well in the dark, a problem that keeps many of them from driving at night. (Corso, 1971). Half of the legally blind persons in the United States are over sixty-five (Papalia and Olds, 1992, p. 479).

In many of the elderly, the eyes eventually appear sunken due to a gradual loss of orbital fat. The blink reflex is slower, and the eyelids hang loosely because of reduced muscle tone.

Cataracts are a common concern of the elderly. A cataract is a clouding of the lens of the eye or of its capsule that obstructs the passage of light. The consequences of a cataract for visual functioning depend on its location. The most common form of a cataract involves hardening of cell tissues in the lens. Cataracts prevent light from passing through and thus cause blurred vision and blindness. In severe cases double vision may result. Cataracts generally can be surgically removed and a substitute lens implanted. About 16 percent of the elderly develop cataracts (Papalia and Olds, 1992, p. 479). Fortunately, with the development of corrective lenses and new surgical techniques for removing cataracts, many vision losses are at least partially restored.

A frequent cause of blindness among the elderly is

glaucoma, which occurs when fluid pressure in the eye builds up. This pressure, if untreated, damages the eye internally. If this disease (which seldom has early symptoms) is detected through routine vision checkups, it can be treated and controlled with eye drops, medication, surgery, or laser treatments.

The senses of taste and smell have reduced functional capability during advancing years. Much of this reduced sensitivity appears to be related to illness and poor health rather than to a deterioration of sense organs due to age (Rovee et al., 1975). Taste is very often based on what people can smell. More than four out of five persons over eighty years of age have major impairments in smell, and more than half have practically no sense of smell at all (Papalia and Olds, 1992, p. 480). Because food loses its taste to those who have serious impairments in smell and taste, those affected eat less and are often undernourished.

The vestibular senses, which function to maintain posture and balance, also lose some of their efficiency. As a result, the elderly are more prone to fall than younger adults. The elderly are also more apt to suffer from dizziness, which increases the likelihood they will fall.

Teeth

As people grow older, the gums gradually recede, and the teeth increasingly take on a yellowish color. Periodontal disease becomes an increasing problem. Many of the elderly eventually lose many of their teeth; the problem is more severe for people from low income levels (Papalia and Olds, 1992, p. 483). Having to have the teeth replaced with dentures takes several weeks to get adjusted to, and the person will not be able to eat or sleep as well during this adjustment period. Poor teeth or the use of dentures may also be traumatic as it drives home the fact that the person is aging physically. A person's disposition can be adversely affected. On the other hand, dentures for some people improve their appearance and may lead to an improved self-concept. Many of the facial evidences of later adulthood may be prevented by proper dental care throughout life or by using dentures. Dental health is due to a combination of innate tooth structure and lifelong eating and dental health habits.

Voice

Gradually the voice becomes higher pitched, and in later adulthood it may become less powerful and restricted in range. Public speaking and singing abilities generally deteriorate earlier than normal speaking skills. All of these changes are partly due to the hardening and decreasing elasticity of the laryngeal cartilages. Speech often becomes slower and pauses become longer and more frequent. If there are pathological changes in the brain, slurring may occur.

Skin

The skin in many of the elderly becomes somewhat splotchy, paler in color, and loses some of its elasticity. Some of the subcutaneous muscle and fat disappear, resulting in the skin hanging in folds and wrinkles.

Psychomotor Skills

The elderly can do most of the same things that younger people can do, but they do them more slowly. A key factor in the high accident rates of the elderly is a slowdown in the processing of information by the central nervous system (Papalia and Olds, 1992, p. 484). It takes the elderly longer to move in order to assess their environment, longer to make a decision after assessment, and then longer to implement the right action. This slowness in processing information shows up in many aspects of the elderly's lives. Their rate of learning new material is slowed, and the rate at which they retrieve information from memory is reduced.

Have you ever been irritated when an elderly person was driving a car slowly in front of you? Perhaps you even blasted your car horn to attempt to hurry that person along. We need to remember the elderly are probably functioning at the fastest pace that is safe for them.

The slower processing times and reaction times have practical implications for drivers. The elderly have higher accident rates than middle-age adults. Their rates are similar to those for teenagers (Papalia and Olds, 1992, p. 481). However, the reasons for these relatively high accident rates differ (Kaluger and Kaluger, 1984). Teenagers frequently have accidents because they tend to be more reckless and often take risks. The elderly, on the other hand, tend to have accidents because of being slower in getting out of the way of potential problems and because of less efficient sensorimotor coordination. The elderly have as great a need to drive as others. Being able to drive often makes the difference between actively participating in society or facing a life of enforced isolation. Papalia and Olds (1992, p. 481) suggest what needs to be done:

> For the protection of themselves and others, older drivers' vision, coordination, and reaction time need to be retested regularly. Older drivers can compensate for any loss of ability by driving more slowly and for shorter distances, by choosing easier routes, and by driving only in daylight. In many communities, defensive driving courses are given for senior citizens to help them continue to drive as long as possible.

Physical exercise and mental activity appear to reduce losses in psychomotor skills, such as in the areas of speed, strength, and stamina. Regular exercise also helps to maintain the circulatory and respiratory systems and helps people be more resistant to physical ailments that might be fatal, such as heart attacks (Bromley, 1974).

Intellectual Functioning

The notion that there is a general intellectual decline in old age is largely incorrect. (Balter and Schaie, 1974, p. 35). Most intellectual abilities hold up well with age. The elderly do tend to achieve somewhat lower scores in IQ tests than younger people, and the scores of the elderly gradually decline as the years pass (Papalia and Olds, 1981, p. 518). In explaining such differences Papalia and Olds (pp. 518-20) note that a distinction needs to be made between *performance* and *competence*. It could well be that while the elderly show a decline in performance on IQ tests, their actual intellectual competence may not be declining. Their lower performance on IQ tests could be due to a variety of factors. With diminished capacities to see and hear they have more difficulty perceiving instructions and executing tasks. Due to reduced powers of coordination and agility, they may perform less well. They may be more fatigued when older, and fatigue has been found to suppress intellectual performance (Furry and Baltes, 1973). Speed is a component of many IQ tests, and the elderly have a decline in speed because it takes them longer to perceive, longer to assess, and longer to respond (Birren, 1974). In addition, when elderly people know they are being timed, their anxiety in-

Being able to drive one's own car often makes the difference between actively participating in society or facing a life of enforced isolation.

creases as they are aware that it takes them longer to do things than it used to; such increased anxiety may actually lower performance (Papalia and Olds, 1981, p. 521).

IQ tests primarily have test items that are designed to test intelligence in younger people; as a result, some of the items may be less familiar to older people, which lowers their scores. The elderly are consistently more cautious than the young, which may hinder their performance on IQ tests, which generally emphasize risk taking and speed (Botwinick, 1966). The elderly are more apt to have self-defeating attitudes about their abilities to solve problems; such attitudes may become self-fulfilling prophecies on IQ tests as they are inhibited from doing as well as they could.

The reduced performance by the elderly on IQ tests may be partly due to a lessening of continued intellectual activity in later adulthood. It appears that reduced use of one's intellectual capacities results in a reduction of intellectual ability. Such a proposition underscores the need for the elderly to remain intellectually active.

Riegel and Riegel (1972) have found that there is a *terminal drop* in intelligence; that is, there is a sudden drop in intellectual performance a few weeks or a few months before death. Terminal drop is not limited to the elderly; it is found in younger people who have a terminal illness.

It is at this time not possible to draw definite conclusions as to whether intellectual functioning actually declines in later adulthood. IQ scores do go down, but that does not mean intellectual competence declines, for the reasons cited. Continued intellectual activity serves to maintain intellectual capacities.

Skeleton and Joints

The maximum height of a person is reached by the late teens or early twenties. In future years there is little or no change in the length of the individual bones. In elderly persons there may be a small reduction in overall height which is due to a progressive decline in the discs between the spinal vertebrae (Garn, 1975). The bones of the body also become less dense and more brittle due to changes in chemical composition. Such changes increase the risk of breakage. Joint movements also become stiffer and more restricted, and the incidence of disease (such as arthritis) affecting the joints increases with age. The elderly need to stay physically active to exercise their joints, as the joints will increase in stiffness if there is little activity.

Homeostasis

Frolkis (1977) has found that homeostasis becomes less efficient in later adulthood. The stabilizing mechanisms become sluggish, and the physiological adaptability of the person is reduced. The heart and breathing rates take longer to return to normal. Wounds take longer to heal. The thyroid gland shrinks, resulting in a lower rate of basal metabolism. The pancreas loses part of its capacity to produce enzymes that are used in protein and sugar metabolism.

Muscular Structure

After around age thirty, there is a gradual reduction in the power and speed of muscular contractions and the capacity for sustained muscular effort decreases. After the age of around fifty, the number of active muscle fibers gradually decreases, resulting in the older person's muscles being reduced in size. The hand grip strength of a seventy-five-year-old man is

Values and Aging: The Myth of Senility

Senility can be defined as an irreversible mental and physical deterioration associated with later adulthood. Many people erroneously believe that every elderly person will eventually become senile. This is simply not accurate. Although the physical condition of the elderly deteriorates somewhat, the elderly can be physically active until near death. Furthermore, the vast majority of the elderly show no signs of mental deterioration for as long as they live (Heinig, 1978).

Regarding the term *senility* Butler (1975, p. 232) notes: "[Senility] is not a medical diagnosis, but a wastebasket term for a range of symptoms that, minimally, includes some memory impairment or forgetfulness, difficulty in attention and concentration, decline in general intellectual grasp and ability, and reduction in emotional responsiveness to others."

Those elderly persons who do appear disoriented and confused are apt to be suffering from one or more of over a hundred illnesses, many of which are treatable (Henig, 1978). Infections, undiagnosed hardening of the blood vessels in the brain, Alzheimer's disease, anemia, brain tumors, and thyroid disorders are only a few of the medical conditions that can cause a person to have senilelike symptoms.

only about 55 percent that of a thirty-year-old man (Kaluger and Kaluger, 1984, p. 586). The ligaments tend to harden and contract, and sometimes result in a hunched-over body position. The reflexes respond more slowly, and incontinence (loss of bowel or bladder control) sometimes occurs. Involuntary smooth muscles that are part of the autonomic system show much less deterioration than other muscle groups.

Nervous System

Although there is little functional change in the nerves with increasing age, some of the nerve tissue is gradually replaced by fibrous cells. Reflex and reaction times of an older person become slower. The total number of brain cells may decrease, but the brain continues to function normally unless its blood supply is blocked. The brain weight of an average seventy-five-year-old man is only 56 percent of the brain weight of a thirty-year-old man (Kaluger and Kaluger, 1984, p. 586). People with certain medical conditions (such as cerebral arteriosclerosis) will have progressive deterioration of brain tissue. If such deterioration takes place, the person is apt to have a loss of recent and/or past memories, to become apathetic, to be less coordinated in body movements, to give less attention to grooming habits, and may have some personality changes (such as being more irritable, confused, and frustrated). In many of the elderly the cortical area of the brain that is responsible for organizing the perceptual processes gradually shows degenerative changes.

Digestive System

With increased age there is a reduction in the amount of enzyme action, gastric juices, and saliva, which upsets the digestion process (Rockstein, 1975). Complaints about digestive disorders are among the most common complaints of the elderly. Since the digestive system is highly sensitive to stress, to emotional disturbances, and to anxieties that accompany old age, many of the digestive disorders may be due to these factors rather than to age per se. The regularity of bowel movements also is more of a problem in later adulthood, resulting in diarrhea or constipation.

Respiration

The lungs decrease in size, resulting in a decrease of oxygen utilization. Some air sac membranes are replaced by fibrous tissue, which obstructs the normal exchange of gases within the lungs. The maximum breathing capacity and maximum oxygen intake in a seventy-five-year-old are about 40 percent of a thirty-year-old (Kaluger and Kaluger, 1984, p. 586). Moderate exercise throughout life is important for keeping oxygen intake and blood flow at their highest levels, thereby slowing down the aging process.

Heart

The heart and the blood vessels are the bodily parts in which aging produces the most destructive changes. The heart and arteries are the weakest link in the chain of life, as most of the other organs would probably last for 150 years if they received an adequate blood supply (Harris, 1975). The heart is affected by aging in a variety of ways. The heart shrinks in size, and the percentage of fat in the heart increases. The heart muscles tend to become stringy and dried out. Deposits of a brown pigment in the cells of the heart partly restrict the passage of blood and interfere with the absorption of oxygen through the heart walls. The elasticity in the valves of the heart is reduced, and deposits of cholesterol and calcium in heart valves also decrease valve efficiency.

The heart of an older person pumps only 70 percent as much blood as that of a younger person (Harris, 1975). The rhythm of the heart becomes slower and more irregular. Deposits of fat begin to accumulate around the heart and interfere with its functioning. Blood pressure also rises. These changes are not necessarily dangerous, provided the heart is properly treated. A nutritious diet, moderate exercise, adequate sleep, and a positive mental attitude will help keep the heart functioning properly.

In later life the coronary artery has a tendency to harden and become narrow, which may lead to a partial blockage. The coronary artery is the site of many heart attacks that are brought on by increased emotional stress or physical effort. Hardening of the coronary artery may also increase blood pressure and may reduce the flow of blood to many parts of the body. Poor circulation of blood may cause a variety of problems. For example, poor circulation to the brain may lead to brain deterioration and to personality changes. Poor circulation to the kidneys may result in kidney problems and even kidney failure.

Reserve Capacity

Under ordinary circumstances, people do not use their body systems and organs to their limits. This backup capacity (which allows organs and body systems to respond at greater levels during times of stress) has been called reserve capacity. Younger adults have reserve capacities that put forth four to ten times as much effort as usual (Papalia and Olds, 1992, p. 481). Reserve capacity helps to preserve homeostasis.

As people age, their reserve capacities decrease. As a result, the elderly cannot respond to stressful demands as rapidly as younger adults. An elderly person who used to be able to mow the lawn and then go water-skiing may now exhaust the capacity of the heart by mowing the lawn. Young people usually recover fairly rapidly from the flu or pneumonia, while the elderly may succumb to these illnesses.

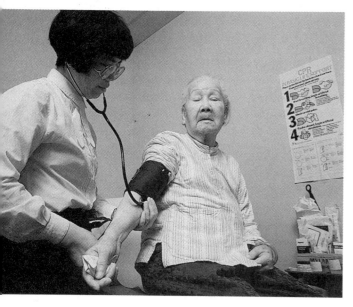

Heart and circulatory problems are a major concern of the elderly.

Because the elderly no longer have fast reflexes, vigorous heart action, and quick-responding muscles, they are at a great risk of being victims of certain accidents; for example, traffic accidents while crossing the street. As the reserve capacity continues to diminish, those affected become less able to care for themselves and more dependent on others.

Sexuality: Conceptualizing Sexual Response

Masters and Johnson (1966) identified four stages of sexual response in females and males: excitement, plateau, orgasm, and resolution. There are many similarities in the physical responses of men and women. These include the two major body changes that result from individual stimulation—myotonia, or muscle tension, and vasocongestion, or blood engorgement.

In *excitement*, blood flows into the erectile tissue of the penis (vasocongestion), resulting in erection. The scrotum (the sac surrounding the testicles) becomes thicker, more wrinkled, and the testicles move up closer to the body.

Plateau response is characterized by the continuation of erection, although it often waxes and wanes during sex play with a partner. The testicles become fully elevated, rotate toward the front, and become blood engorged causing expansion in their size. The Cowper's gland secretes a small amount of clear fluid that comes out the tip of the penis. The purpose of this fluid is generally thought to be to cleanse the urethra of urine, thereby neutralizing the chemical environment for the passage of sperm.

The *orgasm* stage in men consists of two phases. The first is ejaculatory inevitability, a short period during which stimulation sufficient to trigger orgasm has occurred and the resulting ejaculation becomes inevitable. The second phase, ejaculation, results from rhythmic contractions (myotonia) forcing sperm and semen through the urethra. Simultaneous with this is the very pleasant physical sensation of orgasm.

The final stage, *resolution*, represents a return to the unstimulated state. In resolution, the penis loses its erection and the testicles lose their engorgement and elevation.

In women, the *excitement* stage of sexual response ushers in many changes. The process of vaginal lubrication begins. This response is analogous to the male erection; it is caused by sexual stimulation and is, physiologically, a blood engorgement response. The uterus and cervix begin to move up and away from the vagina. The clitoris and labia minora (inner lips) enlarge and the labia majora (outer lips) spread. Breast size increases slightly and the nipples become erect.

In *plateau*, the uterus continues in its movement up and back, the vagina lengthens and balloons at the rear, and the outer third of the vagina contracts, causing a gripping effect. The clitoris retracts under its hood, making it seem to disappear.

At *orgasm*, the uterus and vagina become involved in wavelike muscular contractions. This response, as well as the subjective pleasure of orgasm, are very similar to the experience of the male.

In *resolution*, the cervix and uterus drop to their normal positions and the outer third of the vagina returns to normal, followed by the inner two-thirds. The clitoris and the breasts also return to normal.

There are many involuntary *extragenital* physical responses in men and women. These include muscle tension responses such as facial grimace, spastic contractions of the hands and feet, and pelvic thrusting. Extragenital blood engorgement responses include sex flush, blood pressure and heartrate increases, and perspiration on soles of feet and palms of hands.

FIGURE 14.1: Effects of Aging on Sexual Response in Men

Bodily processes slow down *but they do not stop.* A natural slowing down *does not* mean a loss of interest. *Regularity* of sexual release is most important to maintain sexual response capability in later years.

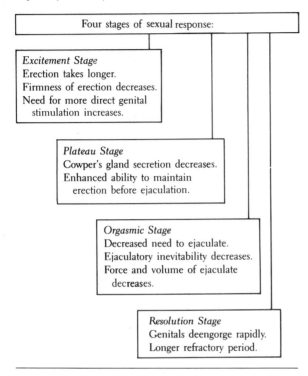

The effects of aging on sexual response are summarized in Figures 14.1 and 14.2.

Values and Sexuality

A common misconception is that older people lose their sexual drive. It is true that both sexual interest and sexual activity gradually decline among the elderly (Hyde, 1990, p. 338). However, an extensive study (Brecher, 1984) on sexual patterns among the elderly indicates that many elderly continue to engage in sexual activity. Sixty-five percent of married women and fifty-nine percent of married men over seventy years old reported in the study that they continue to have sex with their spouse. In addition, 33 percent of women and 43 percent of men over seventy years old reported they still masturbate.

The most noted studies of sexual behavior among the elderly were conducted by Kinsey, Pomeroy, Mar-tin, and Gebhard (1948, 1953), Masters and Johnson (1966, 1968, 1970), and Pfeiffer (1974). All found that the elderly who are in fairly good health are physiologically able to be sexually active into their seventies and beyond. As far as sexuality is concerned, in older years there is truth to the saying "If you don't use it, you'll lose it." The studies found that those who were most active sexually during youth and middle age usually maintained their sexual vigor and interest longer into old age. The study by Pfeiffer (1974) was particularly interesting; 15 percent of the elderly reported a rising rate of sexual activity as they grew older. (The nature of sexual activity in this study included both activity with a partner and self-stimulation.)

If sexual behavior does decline in later years, it probably is due to social rather than physical reasons. Masters and Johnson (1966) found the most important deterrents to sexual activity when one is older are

FIGURE 14.2: Effects of Aging on Sexual Response in Women

Bodily processes slow down *but they do not stop.* A natural slowing down *does not* mean a loss of interest. *Regularity* of sexual release is most important to maintain sexual response capability in later years.

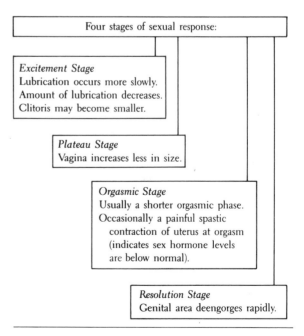

the lack of a partner; boredom with one's partner; overindulgence in drinking or eating; poor physical or mental health; fear of poor performance; negative attitudes toward menopause; and negative attitudes toward sex, such as the erroneous belief that sex is inappropriate for the elderly. Other factors deter sexual activity. One is the lack of privacy in many living arrangements, such as in nursing homes. Butler and Lewis (1977) note that the fear of death due to a stroke or heart attack deters some of the elderly from sexual activity. A variety of feelings—guilt, anxiety, depression, or hostility—also deter sexual activity. Because of some of these reasons there is usually more interest in sex than there is sexual activity. (This is true, however, for practically all age groups).

Attitudes of younger adults as to what is appropriate sexual behavior for the elderly commonly create problems. Many younger people express beliefs that it is inappropriate for an unmarried elderly person to become romantically involved with someone. A widower or widow at times faces strong opposition to remarrying from other family members. Negative views are often strongest when an elderly person becomes involved with someone younger who will become an heir if the older person dies.

Fortunately, attitudes toward sexuality in old age are changing. Taber (1975, pp. 356-57) notes:

> With the changing attitudes of younger people to alternatives to the traditional family, some older people are finding informal arrangements for living together attractive. The couple who do not have a marriage ceremony can share all the companionship and sexual satisfactions without upsetting inheritance rights and retirement benefits. When they become aware of it, their children may accept such a pattern because they find it preferable to remarriage. We have no idea of the numbers that are involved, but the old as well as the young have new options as societal norms change. The popularity of living together without marriage will probably increase.

The elderly, like other age groups, have a right to sexual expression as long as they do not hurt anyone. Think how angry you feel if someone tries to control your sexual activity. Few efforts are made to control the sexual expressions of middle-age people. It seems absurd for society to put restrictions on people as they move from middle adulthood to later adulthood. Being touched and receiving affection is something

Physical affection promotes self-worth and personal satisfaction for people of all ages.

that everyone needs at all ages to promote feelings of self-worth and personal satisfaction.

Many of the current living arrangements for the elderly (group homes, nursing homes, and foster homes) have overlooked the need for privacy. Many nursing homes, for example, place two women or two men in a small room. Butler and Lewis (1976) suggest that future care facilities for the elderly be designed to provide privacy.

What Causes Aging?

Everyone who lives to later adulthood will experience some of the physiological changes that are described in the preceding material. But what causes these changes? No one knows all of the reasons. A number of theories have been developed which involve biological, sociological, environmental, and psychological factors. Most of the theories involve biological factors.

Genetic Theories

These theories hypothesize that aging occurs due to damage or change in the genetic information involved in the formation of cellular proteins. Such changes cause cells to die, which results in aging. The following theories have been classified as genetic theories.

Cellular genetic theory of DNA damage asserts that damages or changes to DNA molecules alter the genetic information and result in the cell being unable to manufacture essential enzymes. (DNA molecules in each cell contain the genetic information of each person. Amazingly, each cell of the body is literally a blueprint of the composition of a person.) Without essential enzymes, it is theorized that aging occurs as cells gradually die.

The running-out-of-program theory asserts there is a set amount of basic genetic material (DNA molecules) in each cell. As the cells age, the DNA is used up and the cells die. Hayflick's research (1974) supports this theory as his findings showed human cells will divide only a limited number of times, usually about fifty.

The somatic mutation by radiation theory postulates that aging occurs due to abnormal chromosomes developing after exposure to radiation. Recent research suggests radiation is not the major factor causing the aging process (Shock, 1977).

The error theory of aging is due to an accumulation of errors involved in transmission of information from the DNA molecule to the final protein product. Such accumulation of errors results in "error catastrophe," which eventually leads to the death of cells.

Nongenetic Cellular Theories

This category of theories postulates that changes take place in cellular proteins after they have been formed. Such changes cause some cells to die, which results in aging. The following theories have been classified as nongenetic cellular theories.

Deprivation theory assumes that aging is caused by vascular changes which deprive cells of essential nutrients and oxygen.

Accumulation theory asserts that aging results from the accumulation of harmful substances in the cells of an organism. When the accumulation builds up, the cells eventually begin to die. The specific substances involved have not as yet been identified.

Wear and tear theory asserts that cells begin to die after long use and exposure to stressful elements during the process of living.

Free radical theory hypothesizes there are chemicals, called free radicals, that contain oxygen in a highly activated state that react with other molecules in their vicinity. Such reactions are postulated to damage and kill some cells.

Cross-linkage theory asserts that cross-linkages or bonds develop between molecules or between components of the same molecules. These bonds supposedly change the chemical and physical properties, which cause some cells to function improperly and gradually die.

Physiological Theories

These theories explain aging as due to either the breakdown of an organ system or to an impairment in physiological control mechanisms. The following theories have been classified as physiological theories.

Single organ system theory asserts that aging is due to an essential system breaking down. The precise system that is thought to control aging has not been identified, but various systems have been suggested. Those suggested include the thyroid gland, which is involved with metabolism, sex glands which regulate hormone secretions, the cardiovascular system which controls oxygen and blood flow, and the pituitary gland which regulates secretions from other glands.

Endocrine control system theory postulates that hormones control the aging process. There is evidence that hormones are involved in puberty and menopause. There is also evidence that the functions of the endocrine system decline with age.

Stress theory asserts aging is due to the accumulation of the effects of the stresses of living. Each stress encountered is thought to leave a small residual of accumulants and impairments, which results in bodily systems then aging. This theory is consistent with cliches about how stressful events will turn a person's hair gray or cause the hair to fall out.

Immunological theory assumes that individuals have an immune system which protects the body from invading bacteria, micro-organisms, and atypical mutant cells that may form. As a person grows older, it is hypothesized that fewer antibodies are produced, which decreases the protection ability of the immune system. Gradually, invading micro-organisms begin to engulf and digest body cells, which results in aging.

Control mechanisms theory of the central nervous system asserts that mechanisms in the central nervous system are responsible for aging. A variety of mechanisms may be involved. For example, the mechanisms that control the autonomic nervous system may function less effectively, which causes the autonomic nervous system to gradually degenerate. Or control mechanisms may cause the endocrine system to function less effectively, which results in a gradual reduction in the functions of practically every system in the body.

Evaluation of Theories of Aging

Everyone grows old, so the conclusion is obvious that nature has a built-in mechanism that promotes aging. We still do not know what this mechanism is. As yet, sufficient evidence has not been presented to prove which (if any) theory is valid.

Factors That Influence the Aging Process

Aging is a complex process. There seem to be many variables that accelerate and decelerate the process. A person who has a serious, long-term illness, or a severe impairment, will often age much faster and earlier than someone who is healthy (Makinodan, 1974). The precise reasons why such conditions accelerate the aging process are not known. More rapid aging in such individuals may be due to decreased exercise, or to unknown biochemical changes, or to greater stress.

Bierman and Hazzard (1973) have found that a large number of "biological insults" hastens the aging process. Such insults include accidents, broken bones, severe burns, severe psychological stress, and severe alcohol or drug abuse. Poor eating habits also accelerate aging (Kent, 1980).

Environmental factors influence the aging process. Being physically and mentally active tends to slow down the aging process. Inactivity speeds it up. A positive outlook (positive thinking) tends to slow down the aging process. Insecurity, lack of someone to talk to, negative thinking, and being in a strange environment tend to accelerate the aging process (Rosenmayr, 1980). Prolonged excessive heat or cold will also speed up the aging process (Shock, 1977).

Genetic inheritance also plays a role. People whose parents lived a long time have a longer life expectancy than people whose parents lived a shorter period of time (with the assumption that they died from natural causes). Our bodies apparently have a genetic time clock. Some individuals have a longer time than others. Within a family group, the rate of aging shows a high positive correlation for the different family members. It seems that some kind of a timing device causes tissues and organ systems to break down at specific times (Shock, 1977). This timing device can be accelerated or decelerated by a variety of factors.

Diseases and Causes of Death of the Elderly

Most older persons have at least one chronic condition and many have multiple conditions. The most frequently occurring chronic conditions are: arthritis, hypertension, hearing impairments, heart disease, orthopedic impairments, sinusitis, cataracts, diabetes, visual impairments, and tinnitus (American Association of Retired Persons, 1990). Older persons see their doctor more frequently, spend a higher proportion of their income on prescribed drugs, and, once in the hospital, they stay longer. As might be expected, the health status of the old-old (seventy-five and over) is worse than the young-old.

The medical expenses of an elderly person average four times more than those of a young adult (American Association of Retired Persons, 1990). One of the reasons medical costs are high is because the elderly suffer much more from long-term illnesses—such as cancer, heart problems, diabetes, and glaucoma.

The physical process of aging is a factor in the elderly having a higher rate of health problems. However, research in recent years has demonstrated that personal and social stresses also play major roles in causing diseases. The elderly face a wide range of stressful situations: death of family members and friends, retirement, loneliness, changes in living arrangements, reduced income, loss of social status, and a decline in physical capacities and physical energy. Medical conditions also may result from inadequate exercise, substandard diets, cigarette smoking, and excessive drinking of alcoholic beverages.

A special problem for the elderly is that when they

become ill, their new illness is often imposed on an assortment of preexisting chronic illnesses and on organ systems which no longer are functioning very well (because their reserve capacities are diminished). The health of elderly patients is thus more fragile, and even a relatively minor illness such as a flu can lead to major consequences, and even death (Papalia and Olds, 1992, p. 483).

The most common conditions that limit the activities of the elderly are high blood pressure, heart conditions, rheumatism, arthritis, orthopedic impairments, and emotional disorders. Some of these disorders, such as heart problems, high blood pressure, and arthritis, begin to appear among people in their thirties.

The discussion of these health problems needs to be put in context. The elderly have higher rates of illnesses than younger people, but it needs to be emphasized that a majority of the elderly are reasonably healthy. People over sixty-five do have a health advantage over younger persons in a few areas as they have fewer flu infections, colds, and acute digestive problems. The reasons are unclear. They may be more immune to common germs, or they may go out less and, therefore, be less exposed to germs.

Life Expectancy

The average life expectancy in ancient Rome and during the Middle Ages was between twenty and thirty years. Some people lived to be seventy or eighty, but infant mortality was very high, and famine, diseases, and conflicts took the lives of many more. The life expectancy for Americans has gradually been increasing due to better sanitation, nutrition, and disease control. In the middle of the nineteenth century Americans lived an average of forty years. At the turn of the twentieth century, the average was 49 years. The average life expectancy in 1990 was seventy-five years (United States Bureau of the Census, 1992). These gains have resulted from improvements in infant survival, medical care, diets, and sanitation. Particularly significant in leading to these gains has been immunization against many diseases that used to kill (such as whooping cough, polio, and diphtheria) and the development of antibodies to reduce the severity of such illnesses as strep throat, bronchitis, and pneumonia.

Leading Causes of Death among the Elderly

Cause of death	Of those who died, proportion who died of this cause
1. Diseases of heart	39.3%
2. Malignant neoplasms (Cancer)	21.9
3. Cerebrovascular diseases	8.2
4. Chronic obstructive pulmonary diseases (lung diseases)	4.6
5. Pneumonia and influenza	4.4
6. Diabetes mellitus	2.3
7. Accidents and adverse effects	1.8
8. Chronic liver disease, cirrhosis	.7
9. Suicide	.4
10. Homicide and legal intervention	.1
11. All other causes	16.3
Total	100%

SOURCE: U.S. Bureau of the Census, *Statistical Abstract of the United States, 1992* (Washington, D.C.: U.S. Government Printing Office, 1992), p.85.

Rowland (1977) sought to identify life events that predict death in the elderly. In a review of the literature, only two items were found to have predictive significance: death of a spouse and environmental relocation (primarily a move to nursing home). A partial explanation for both of these life events is that those who lose their spouse or are moved to a nursing home may no longer have the will to live, which hastens their death. For those being moved to a nursing home, an additional partial explanation for a higher death rate is that such individuals may be in poorer health and therefore more apt to die.

How Long Will You Live?

Figure 14.3 is a rough guide for calculating your personal longevity. The basic life expectancy for males is age seventy-two years and for females it is seventy-

Alzheimer's Disease

Tony Wiggleworth is sixty-eight years old. Two years ago his memory began to falter. As the months went by, he even forgot what his wedding day to Rose was like. His grandchildren's visits slipped from his memory in two or three days.

The most familiar surroundings have also become strange to him. Even his friends' homes seem like places he has never been before. When he walks down the streets in his neighborhood, he frequently becomes lost.

He is now quite confused. He has difficulty speaking and can no longer do such elementary tasks as balance his checkbook. At times, Rose, who is taking care of him, is uncertain whether he knows who she is. All of this is very baffling for Tony. Until he retired three years ago, he had been an accountant and excelled at remembering facts and details.

Tony has Alzheimer's disease. The disease now affects about 6 to 10 percent of all people over sixty-five and 20 to 50 percent of all people over eight-five (Papalia and Olds, 1992, p. 484). These statistics indicate the disease affects the old-old to a greater extent.

Alzheimer's disease is a degenerative brain disorder that gradually causes deterioration in intelligence, memory, awareness, and ability to control bodily functions. In its final stages, Alzheimer's leads to progressive paralysis and breathing difficulties. The breathing problems often result in pneumonia, the most frequent cause of death for Alzheimer's victims. Other symptoms of Alzheimer's include irritability, restlessness, agitation, and impairments of judgment. Although most of those affected are over sixty-five, the disease occasionally strikes people in middle age.

Over a period lasting from as few as five years to as many as twenty, the disease destroys brain cells. The changes in behavior displayed by those afflicted have some variation. Brownlee (1991, p. 40) notes:

One sufferer refuses to bathe or change clothes, another eats fried eggs without utensils, a third walks naked down the street, a fourth has the family's beloved cats put to sleep, while yet another mistakes paint for juice and drinks it. The outlandish acts committed by Alzheimer's patients take as many forms as there are people who suffer the disease. Yet, in every case, the bizarre behavior serves as a sign that the sufferer is regressing towards unawareness, a second childishness.

The cause of Alzheimer's disease continues to be a mystery. Various theories of causality have blamed viral infections, biochemical deficiencies, genetic tendencies, defects of the immune system, and even aluminum poisoning. Genetic tendencies appear to be a contributing factor as relatives of Alzheimer's patients have an increased risk of having the disease in the future (Papalia and Olds, 1992, pp. 484-85).

An examination of the brains of victims has found a distinctive tangle of protein filaments in the cortex, the part of the brain responsible for intellectual functions. This research shows that there are biochemical causes for the disease and leads to the conclusion that aging does not automatically include senility. The exact causes of Alzheimer's are as yet unknown, but it is definitely a disease.

Diagnosing the disease is difficult because the disorder has symptoms that are nearly identical to other forms of dementia. The only sure diagnosis at the present time is observation of tissue deep within the brain, which can be done only by autopsy after death. Doctors usually diagnose the disease in a living person by ruling out other conditions that could account for the symptoms (Heston and White, 1983).

The most prominent early symptom of the disease is

---

nine years. Write down your basic life expectancy. If you are in your fifties or sixties, you should add ten years to the basic figure because you have already proven yourself to be quite durable. If you are over age sixty and active, add another two years.

Significant sex differences are found in life expectancies. In 1990, females in the United States had a life expectancy at birth of seventy-nine years while males had a life expectancy of only seventy-two years

(United States Bureau of the Census, 1992, p. 76). In 1989 there was a ratio of 145 women for every 100 men. The sex ration increases with age—ranging from 120 for the sixty-five to sixty-nine age group to a high of 256 for persons eighty-five and older (American Association of Retired Persons, 1990).

In later life there appear to be both environmental and biological reasons for the higher mortality rates among men. Environmental factors are demonstrated memory loss, particularly for recent events. Other early symptoms (which are often overlooked) are reduced ability to play a game of cards, reduced performance at sports, and sudden outbreaks of extravagance. More symptoms then develop—irritability, agitation, confusion, restlessness, and impairments of concentration, speech, and orientation. As the disease progresses, the symptoms become more disabling. The care giver or care givers eventually have to provide twenty-four-hour care—which is a tremendous burden for care givers. As the disease progresses in its final stages, a nursing home placement is often necessary. Near the end, the patient usually cannot recognize family members, cannot understand or use language, and cannot eat without help.

Brownlee (1991, p. 48) briefly describes the mental and physical trauma that care givers and family members of those afflicted experience:

> They live in a private hell, one that cannot be discussed with neighbors and friends in too much detail because the details are so devastating. They grieve even as their loved ones plunge them into a maelstrom of unreality, where mothers streak through the living room wearing nothing but a shower cap and garter belt and grandfathers try to punch their baby granddaughters.

In addition, the patient's inability to reciprocate expressions of caring and affection robs relationships of intimacy.

Scientists are now investigating a number of hypotheses as to what causes Alzheimer's. One intriguing finding is that victims of Down's syndrome (a severe form of mental retardation due to a chromosome defect) who survive into their thirties frequently develop symptoms indistinguishable from Alzheimer's. Such a similarity may provide a clue as to the causes of Alzheimer's. A recent clue is the discovery of fragments of amyloid in brains of persons who died from the disorder. Amyloid is a very tough protein that in normal amounts is necessary for cell growth throughout the body. Some researchers hypothesize that abnormal patches of this protein in the brain set up a chain reaction that progressively destroys brain cells. This amyloid protein is an abnormal product formed from a larger compound called amyloid precursor protein, or APP. In August 1992, a research team at SIBIA Inc. (located in San Diego) reported initial success in developing a test that shows promise in being able to detect Alzheimer's disease in its early stages (Maugh, 1992, p. 1A). The test detects abnormalities in APP, which appears to be associated with the accumulation of the amyloid protein in the brain. Further research is needed to test the validity of this SIBIA test. If Alzheimer's disease can be detected in its early stages, people will be better able to plan for their future care and make arrangements for their families while they still retain control of their mental faculties. Furthermore, if in fact Alzheimer's disease results from an accumulation of the amyloid protein, and if the early accumulation of this protein can be detected, then it is likely that drugs can be developed to treat the disorder by blocking the formation of amyloid in the brain (Sisodia, et al., 1990). There is high hope that the causes of Alzheimer's can be found soon and treatment developed.

At the present time there is no cure for the disease. Patients with Alzheimer's disease receive some relief from drugs that reduce depression and agitation and help them sleep. Exercise, physical therapy, proper nourishment, and proper fluid intake are also beneficial. Memory aids assist somewhat in everyday functioning. Especially helpful to patients and their families are emotional and social support provided by groups and professional counseling.

by the fact that men are more likely to die from suicide, accidents, and homicide (U.S. Bureau of the Census, 1992, p. 81). Men are also more likely to die from lung cancer, heart disease, emphysema, and asthma, all of which have been linked to such environmental causes as smoking and alcohol abuse (U.S. Bureau of the Census, 1992, p. 81). A partial explanation for sex differences in mortality rates is that sex role stereotypes allow women to be much more expressive of their feelings than men. It may be that suppression of feelings leads to anger, frustration and other unwanted emotions being bottled up inside, which increases stress, results in an increased number of stress-related disorders in men, and then shortens their life span.

Biological factors are probably also involved in leading to higher mortality rates among men. The higher mortality rate among males in the fetal stage and in infancy supports the notion of an inborn difference in resistance.

The fact that there are many more women over age sixty-five than men means that women are much more apt to be widows than men are apt to be widowers. Since there is a social custom in our society for males to marry someone younger, husbands are even more likely to die before their wives. Women are thus much more likely than men to spend their later years alone.

FIGURE 14.3: Basic Life Expectancy

Decide how each item below applies to you and add or subtract the appropriate number of years from your basic life expectancy.

1. *Family history*
   Add 5 years if two or more of your grandparents lived to 80 or beyond. _____
   Subtract 4 years if any parent, grandparent, sister, or brother died of heart attack or stroke before 50. Subtract 2 years if anyone died from these diseases before 60. _____
   Subtract 3 years for each case of diabetes, thyroid disorders, breast cancer, cancer of the digestive system, asthma, or chronic bronchitis among parents or grandparents. _____

2. *Marital status*
   If you are married, add 4 years. _____
   If you are over 25 and not married, subtract 1 year for every unwedded decade. _____

3. *Economic status*
   Subtract 2 years if your family income is over $40,000 per year. _____
   Subtract 3 years if you have been poor for greater part of life. _____

4. *Physique*
   Subtract 1 year for every 10 pounds you are overweight. _____
   For each inch your girth measurement exceeds your chest measurement deduct 2 years. _____
   Add 3 years if you are over 40 and not overweight. _____

5. *Exercise*
   Regular and moderate (jogging 3 times a week), add 3 years. _____
   Regular and vigorous (long-distance running three times a week), add 5 years. _____
   Subtract 3 years if your job is sedentary. _____
   Add 3 years if it is active. _____

6. *Alcohol*
   Add 2 years if you are a light drinker (1-3 drinks a day). _____
   Subtract 5 to 10 years if you are a heavy drinker (more than 4 drinks per day). _____
   Subtract 1 year if you are a teetotaler. _____

7. *Smoking*
   Two or more packs of cigarettes per day, subtract 8 years. _____
   One to two packs per day, subtract 4 years. _____
   Less than one pack, subtract 2 years. _____
   Subtract 2 years if you regularly smoke a pipe or cigars. _____

8. *Disposition*
   Add 2 years if you are a reasoned, practical person. _____
   Subtract 2 years if you are aggressive, intense, and competitive. _____
   Add 1-5 years if you are basically happy and content with life. _____
   Subtract 1-5 years if you are often unhappy, worried, and often feel guilty. _____

9. *Education*
   Less than high school, subtract 2 years _____
   Four years of school beyond high school, add 1 year. _____
   Five or more years beyond high school, add 3 years. _____

10. *Environment*
   If you have lived most of your life in a rural environment, add 4 years. _____
   Subtract 2 years if you have lived most of your life in an urban environment. _____

11. *Sleep*
   More than 9 hours a day, subtract 5 years. _____

12. *Temperature*
   Add 2 years if your home's thermostat is set at no more than 68°F. _____

13. *Health Care*
   Regular medical checkups and regular dental care, add 3 years. _____
   Frequently ill, subtract 2 years. _____

SOURCE: Richard Schulz, *The Psychology of Death, Dying and Bereavement*, (New York: McGraw-Hill, 1978). Table 5.1, pp. 97–98. Reprinted by permission of McGraw-Hill Book Co., Inc.

Wellness: The Impact of Different Systems on Health

The preceding material echoes over and over a central theme. Elderly people are apt to experience little physical or mental deterioration (until near death) if they have a nutritious diet, are successful in managing stress, and stay mentally and physically active. A real key to good mental and physical health in later years is having a life-style throughout life that incorporates health maintenance principles. Health is one of our most important resources.

Traditionally, the health profession in this country has focused on treatment of diseases rather than on prevention. The Chinese approach to medicine has focused on helping patients maintain good health. The holistic concept of treating the whole person is gaining ground in America. There is now greater emphasis on prevention, wellness, and treating a patient psychologically and socially as well as physically.

Physical Exercise

For people who have had poor health maintenance habits, it is nearly never too late to start. For example, Arehart-Triechel (1977) reported on a study in which a group of seventy-year-old inactive men participated in a daily exercise program; at the end of a year they had regained the physical fitness levels normally associated with forty-year-olds. There is also evidence that continued exercise as people grow older reduces the degree of physical and mental slowness that occurs in many of the elderly. Before middle-aged and older adults embark on an exercise program (if they have been relatively inactive for a number of years), they should have a physical examination by their physician to identify heart conditions and other medical problems that may be unduly aggravated by exercise. DeVries (1975) suggests poorly conditioned elderly should begin an exercise program of such activities as brief walks, and perhaps later incorporate a jog-walk routine under proper medical supervision. Swimming in moderation is also suggested.

Mental Activity

Just as physical exercise maintains the level of physiological functioning, mental exercise maintains

---

Health and Longevity

In a study of 6,928 adults, Nedra Belloc and Lester Breslow found that the following seven health practices are positively related to good health and longevity:

- Eating breakfast
- Exercising regularly
- Staying within 10 percent of your proper weight
- Not smoking cigarettes
- Not drinking to excess
- Not eating between meals
- Sleeping seven to eight hours a night

At age forty-five, a person who follows these practices has a life expectancy that is eleven years longer than a person who follows fewer than four. A seventy-year-old who practices all seven is apt to be as healthy as a forty-year-old who follows only one or two.

SOURCE: A. F. Ehrbar, "A Radical Prescription for Medical Care," *Fortune*, Feb. 1977, p. 169.

---

good cognitive functioning. Denney (1982) concludes there are some age-related declines in cognitive functioning, but if a person is mentally active the declines begin to appear at a later age and to be less severe. The specific declines in intellectual functioning have been described earlier in this chapter.

Our society needs to put more emphasis on assuring that the elderly are exposed to intellectual stimulation. Some nursing homes and retirement communities now have daily programs that provide such stimulation; national issues or local issues are discussed and guest speakers on a variety of subjects are sometimes brought in.

One innovative program is Elderhostel which offers low-cost, summer college courses designed for the elderly. The elderly sign up for one-, two-, or three-week sessions to study a variety of topics at a relaxed pace. Some public universities also have provisions for the elderly to attend regular classes with either reduced or no tuition. The elderly have generally responded well to adult educational courses. Some want to update earlier studies, and others want to pursue educational programs to enrich their lives.

Some want to acquire basic learning skills, and some want to attain a high school or college diploma.

Traveling is yet another way for the elderly to stay mentally active. Some organizations, such as the American Association of Retired Persons (AARP), offer travel tours within the United States and to other parts of the world.

Most authorities on aging now believe that intellectual decline in later adulthood is largely a myth. It thus appears that our society is largely wasting a precious resource—an elderly population with extensive experience, training, and intelligence. Our society needs to develop more educational programs to help the elderly maintain their intellectual functioning, and find additional ways to allow the elderly to be productive, contributing members to society.

Sleep Patterns

Many of the elderly have one or more sleep disturbances, such as insomnia, difficulty in falling asleep, restless sleep, falling asleep when company is present, frequent awakening during the night, and feeling exhausted or tired after a night of fitful sleep.

What is a healthy sleep pattern for the elderly? The stereotype that the elderly need more sleep appears to be erroneous. It appears the elderly in fairly good health require no more sleep than those in middle adulthood (Kaluger and Kaluger, 1984, p. 591).

Sleep disturbances that the elderly experience tend to be a result of anxiety, depression, worry, or illness. Restless sleep is common for those who are inactive, those who catnap too much, and those who have physical discomforts (such as arthritic pains).

Some normal changes occur in sleep patterns for the elderly. Deep sleep virtually disappears (Kales, 1975). The elderly generally take a longer time to fall asleep and have more frequent awakenings. More importantly, the elderly distribute their sleep somewhat differently. They generally have several catnaps of fifteen to sixty minutes during the day. Pfeiffer (1974) indicates such catnaps are normal, and caution should be used in attempting to use sleep medication to keep an elderly person asleep for eight hours throughout the night as they need less sleep when they have catnaps. People develop their sleep patterns according to their physical needs and according to the responsibilities and activities they have.

Nutrition and Diet

The majority of the elderly have inadequate diets (Kaluger and Kaluger, 1984, p. 590). Because of the relationship between diet and cardiac problems, physicians recommend that the elderly have low-fat, high-protein diets.

The elderly are the most undernourished group in our society (Papalia and Olds, 1992, pp. 482-83). A number of reasons can be given for chronic malnutrition of the elderly: lack of money, transportation problems, lack of incentives to prepare a nutritious meal when one is living alone, inadequate cooking and storage facilities, poor teeth and lack of good dentures, and lack of knowledge about proper nutrition.

Some of the elderly have a tendency to overeat. One way for people to occupy their free time is to eat, and most of the elderly have a lot of free time. The caloric requirements decrease somewhat in the later years, and the excess calories that are consumed turn into fat, which increases the risks of heart disease and other medical conditions.

To improve the nutritional needs of the elderly, some programs have been developed. Many communities, with the assistance of federal funds, now provide meals for the elderly at group eating sites. These meals are generally provided four or five times a week and usually are luncheon meals. These programs improve the nutrition of elderly persons and offer opportunities for socialization. Meals on Wheels is a service which delivers hot and cold meals directly to house-bound recipients (many of whom are elderly) who are incapable of obtaining or preparing their own meals, but who can feed themselves.

Stress and Stress Management

Learning how to manage stress is important for the physical and emotional health of all age groups. Because of its importance, we will look at stress and at techniques to manage stress in considerable detail.

Stress is a contributing factor in a wide variety of emotional and behavioral difficulties, including anxiety, child abuse, spouse abuse, temper tantrums, feelings of inadequacy, physical assaults, explosive expressions of anger, feelings of hostility, impatience, stuttering, suicide attempts, and depression (Greenberg, 1980, pp. 39-49).

Stress is a contributing factor in most physical illnesses (Pelletier, 1977). These illnesses include hypertension, heart attacks, migraine headaches, tension headaches, colitis, ulcers, diarrhea, constipation, arrhythmia, angina, diabetes, hay fever, backaches, arthritis, cancer, colds, flu, insomnia, hyperthyroidism, dermatitis, emphysema, Raynaud's disease, alcoholism, bronchitis, infections, allergies, and enuresis. Stress-related disorders have now been recognized as being our number-one health problem (Greenberg, 1980).

Becoming skillful in learning how to relax is important in treating and facilitating the recovery from both emotional and physical disorders. The therapeutic value of learning how to manage stress has been dramatically demonstrated by Simonton and Simonton (1978) who have had considerable success in treating terminal cancer patients by instructing them on how to manage and reduce stress.

The increased recognition of stress management in treating physical and emotional disorders is gradually altering the traditional physician-patient relationship. Instead of being passive participants in the treatment process, patients are increasingly being taught (by social workers and other health professionals) how to prevent illness and how to speed up the recovery from illness by learning stress management strategies (Brown, 1977).

People who are successful in managing stress have a life expectancy which is several years longer than those who continually are at high stress levels (Pelletier, 1977). Effective stress management is a major factor in enabling people to live fulfilling, healthy, satisfying and productive lives (Tubesing, 1981).

Conceptualizing Stress

Stress can be defined as the physiological and emotional reactions to stressors. A stressor is a demand, situation, or circumstance which disrupts a person's equilibrium (internal balance) and initiates the stress response. There are an infinite variety of possible stressors: loss of a job, loud noise, toxic substances, retirement, arguments, death of a spouse, moving to a nursing home, heat, cold, serious illness, lack of purpose in life, and so on. Every second we are alive our bodies are responding to stressors that call for adaptation or adjustment. Our bodily reactions are continually striving for homeostasis, or balance.

Gardening provides this elderly woman with exercise that helps keep her physically fit so that she is better able to handle stress successfully. The fruits of her work reinforce her positive feelings about herself.

Selye (1956), one of the foremost authorities on stress, found that the body reacts to all stressors in the same way regardless of the source of stress. This means that the body reacts to positive stressors (for example, a romantic kiss) in the same way it reacts to negative stressors (for example, an electric shock). Selye found that the body has a three-stage reaction to stress: (a) the alarm phase, (b) the resistance phase, and (c) the exhaustion phase. Selye called this three-phase response the General Adaptation Syndrome (GAS).

In the alarm phase the body recognizes the stressor and responds by preparing for fight or flight. The body's reactions are numerous and complex and will only be briefly summarized here. The body sends messages from the hypothalamus (a section of the brain) to the pituitary gland to release its hormones.

Conceptualizing Stressors, Stress, and Stress-Related Illnesses

Stressors
{
Events or experiences: (for example, being forced to retire from a job held for twenty-seven years)

↓

Certain kind of thinking: (for example, "What will I do now with all of my time? My work has been my life. Life is over for me now. All I have left to do is die. My income now will be sharply reduced—how will I pay my bills? The company has no right to force me to retire! This is unfair.")
}

↓

Stress
{
Emotional reactions: Fear, anxiety, worry, alarm, depression, anger

↓

Physiological reactions: The alarm stage of the General Adaptation Syndrome occurs, and the body prepares for fight or flight. Adrenalin and other hormones increase heartbeat and rate of breathing, increase perspiration, raise blood sugar levels, dilate the pupils, and slow digestion. The process results in greater muscular strength, a huge burst of energy, and better vision and hearing.

↓

Stress-related disorder: If the body remains at a high level of stress for a prolonged period, a stress-related disorder will develop.
}

These hormones trigger the adrenal glands to release adrenaline. The release of adrenaline and other hormones results in the following:

- Increased breathing and heartbeat rates.
- A rise in blood pressure.
- Increased coagulation of blood, which minimizes potential loss of blood in case of physical injury.
- Diversion of blood from the skin to the brain, the heart, and contracting muscles.
- A rise in serum cholesterol and blood fat.
- Decreased mobility of the gastrointestinal tract.
- Dilation of the pupils.

These changes result in a huge burst of energy, better vision and hearing, and increased muscular strength—all changes which increase our capacities to fight or to flee. (A major problem of the fight-or-flight reaction for us is that we often cannot deal with a threat by fighting or by fleeing. In our complex civilized society fighting or fleeing generally runs counter to sophisticated codes of acceptable behavior. The fight-or-flight response was once functional for primitive humans, but now seldom is.)

In the resistance phase (the second phase) bodily processes seek to return to homeostasis. The body seeks during this phase to repair any damage caused by the stressors and may adapt to such stressors as hard physical labor and intense heat. In handling most stressors the body generally only goes through the two phases of alarm and repair. During a lifetime a person goes through these two phases hundreds of thousands of times.

The third phase of exhaustion only occurs when the body remains in a state of high stress for an extended period of time. If the body remains at a high level of stress, it is unable to repair damage that has occurred. If exhaustion continues, a person is apt to develop a stress-related illness.

There are two components of a stressor—experiences or events that are encountered and our thoughts and perceptions about these events (Tubesing, 1981). (See "Conceptualizing Stressors, Stress, and Stress-Related Illnesses.")

Stress is heavily dependent on what a person thinks about events. The following example shows how a person's thinking about a positive event can be a source of negative stress.

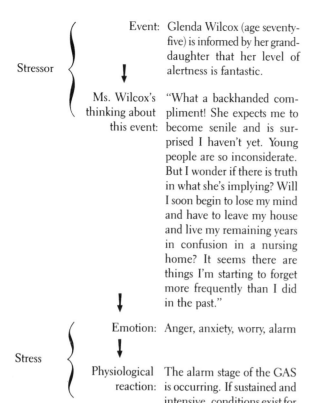

Stressor {

Event: Glenda Wilcox (age seventy-five) is informed by her granddaughter that her level of alertness is fantastic.

Ms. Wilcox's thinking about this event: "What a backhanded compliment! She expects me to become senile and is surprised I haven't yet. Young people are so inconsiderate. But I wonder if there is truth in what she's implying? Will I soon begin to lose my mind and have to leave my house and live my remaining years in confusion in a nursing home? It seems there are things I'm starting to forget more frequently than I did in the past."

Stress {

Emotion: Anger, anxiety, worry, alarm

Physiological reaction: The alarm stage of the GAS is occurring. If sustained and intensive, conditions exist for a stress-related illness to develop.

Not all stress is bad. Life without stress would be boring. Selye (1972, p. 83) indicates stress is often "the spice of life," and that it is impossible to be alive without experiencing stress. Dreaming even produces some stress. Stress at times is often beneficial to us. It stimulates and prepares us to perform a wide variety of tasks. Students, for example, often find they need to feel a moderate level of stress before they can study for an exam—too little stress results in their being unable to concentrate and may even result in their falling asleep, while too high a level of stress results in too much anxiety and interferes with their concentration. High levels of the alarm phase of the GAS are very desirable during emergencies where physical strength is needed—such as in lifting a heavy object which has fallen on someone.

The kind of stress that is harmful has been called *distress* by Selye (1974). Long-term distress occurs when we think negatively about events that have happened to us. When unpleasant events occur, we

always have a choice to react negatively or positively. If we continue to think negatively about the situation, our thinking keeps our body under a high level of stress—which can then lead to a stress-related illness. On the other hand, if we think positively about the situation, our thinking enables the body to relax and repair any damage that was done. In addition, when we are relaxed, our natural immune system is much more effective in combating potential illnesses. (When we are in the alarm phase the functioning of our immune system is sharply reduced, as our bodily resources are primarily focused on facilitating the fight or flight response.)

There are a number of signals, presented in Figure 14.4, that we can use to measure level of stress. Most of us use these signals to judge whether our friends are under too much stress. For our emotional and physical health, we need to give more attention to monitoring these signals in ourselves.

Approaches to Stress Management: Application of Theory

Of the five major categories of approaches to stress management, only three are constructive. The three constructive approaches are (1) changing the distressing event; (2) changing one's thinking about the distressing event; and (3) taking one's mind off the distressing event, usually by thinking about something else.

There are also two destructive ways that some people use to relieve stress. One is resorting to alcohol, other drugs, or food. Perhaps the major reason for abusing alcohol and other drugs is to seek relief from stress and unwanted emotions. Drugs will provide temporary relief, but the next day a person's problems still remain, and there is a serious danger that drug abuse may become a destructive habit. Compulsive overeating is also an unhealthy way of temporarily relieving stress; the activity of overeating is resorted to by some people who experience such unwanted emotions as loneliness, boredom, and insecurity.

The second destructive way of escaping stress is suicide. Most of our attention will focus on constructive ways to relieving stress.

Changing a Distressing Event. When distressing events occur it is desirable to confront them directly to try to improve the situation. If someone is grieving

FIGURE 14.4: Stress Signals

A number of signals can be used to measure whether we are at a good level of stress, or whether we are at too high a level of stress. You have to use your own judgment based on these signals to determine whether your stress level is too high.

Good Level	*Too High*
1. *Behaviors*	High-pitched nervous laughter
Creative, make good decisions	Lack of creativity
Friendly	Poor work quality
Generally successful	Overdrink or overeat
Able to listen to others	Smoke to excess
Productive—get a lot done	Stutter
Appreciate others, sensitive to others, and	Inability to concentrate
recognize contributions of others	Easily startled by small sounds
Smile, laugh, joke	Impatient
	Easily irritated
	Unpleasant to be around
	Put others down
	Engage in wasted activity and motion
2. *Feelings*	Resentful, bitter, dissatisfied, angry
Feeling of confidence	Timid, tense, anxious, fearful
Calm, relaxed	Paranoid
Feelings of pleasure and enjoyment	Weary, depressed, fed up
Feelings of excitement and exhilaration	Feelings of inadequacy or failure
	Confused, swamped, overwhelmed
	Feelings of powerlessness or helplessness
3. *Body Signals*	Loss of appetite, diarrhea, or vomiting
Restful	Accident prone
Absence of aches and pains	Frequent need to urinate
Coordinated body reactions	Trembling, nervous tics
Unaware of body, which is functioning	Feelings of dizziness or weakness
smoothly	Frequent colds and flus
Good health, absence of stress related illnesses	High blood pressure
	Tight or tense muscles
	Asthma or breathing irregularities
	Skin irritations, itches, and rashes
	Sleep problems
	Upset stomach and ulcers
	Various aches and pains—muscle aches, back-aches, neck aches, and headaches

from the death of someone close, discussing the grief with others and perhaps seeking professional counseling can be helpful. If an elderly person is concerned about what to do with his time after retiring, the person needs to work on finding meaningful and enjoyable activities to become involved in. If a person is concerned about a deterioration in health, it is desirable to see a physician and receive medical treatment. Many distressing events can be improved by confronting them head on, and taking constructive action to change them.

Changing One's Thinking about a Distressing Event. Some events cannot be changed. For example, Carlton Komarek does not want to retire from a meat packing plant when he reaches seventy in May, but the company has a rigid rule and will not make exceptions. Since Carlton cannot change the situation, the only constructive alternative is to accept it and find meaningful activities after he retires. It is counterproductive to nag, complain, or get upset about something that cannot be changed. Acceptance of the situation will also improve Carlton's disposition.

One of the structured techniques for changing one's thinking about a distressing event is to challenge and change the negative and irrational thinking through a Rational Self-Analysis, as described in Chapter 8.

Positive Thinking. When anticipated and unanticipated events occur, we have a choice to either take a positive view or a negative view. If we take a negative view we are apt to experience more stress, and also apt to alienate friends and acquaintances. Here is a summary of some of W. Clement Stone's (1966, pp. 9-10) basic tenets of positive thinking:

- Give a smile to everyone you meet (smile with your eyes) —and you'll smile and receive smiles. . . .
- Give honor, credit and applause (the victor's wreath)— you will be honorable and receive credit and applause. . . .
- Give time for a worthy cause (with eagerness)—you will be worthy and richly rewarded. . . .
- Give hope (the magic ingredient for success)—you will have hope and be made hopeful. . . .
- Give cheer (the verbal sunshine)—you'll be cheerful and cheered. . . .
- Give good thoughts (nature's character builder)—you will be good and the world will have good thoughts for you. . . .

Some books on positive thinking have become best sellers (Schuller, 1973; Ringer, 1977).

Akin to positive thinking is having a philosophy of life that allows us to take crises in stride, to travel through life at a relaxed pace, to look at the scenery with enjoyment, to approach work in a relaxed fashion so as to permit greater creativity, to enjoy and use leisure time to develop more fully as a person, and to find enjoyment in each day.

Talking to Others. Every person needs someone to share good times with and to talk with about personal difficulties. Sharing concerns with someone helps to vent emotions. Talking a concern through often helps in two ways to reduce stress. It may lead to a new perspective on how to resolve the distressing event, or it may help by changing one's thinking about the distressing event to a more positive and rational attitude. The listener may be a neighbor,

friend, member of the clergy, or professional counselor.

Closely related to discussing the distressing event with someone is having a social support group. Support groups allow people to share their lives, to have fun with others, to let their hair down, and to be a resource for help when emergencies and crises arise. Possible support groups include friends in a retirement community, one's family, one's coworkers, a church group, a community group, and so on.

Taking One's Mind Off the Distressing Event, Usually by Thinking about Something Else. This category is the third constructive approach to reducing stress. There are a variety of ways to stop thinking about a distressing event.

Relaxation Approaches. Deep breathing relaxation, imagery relaxation, progressive muscle relaxation, meditation, and biofeedback are effective techniques in reducing stress and inducing the relaxation response (becoming relaxed). For each of these techniques the relaxation response is facilitated by sitting in a comfortable position, in a quiet place, with closed eyes (Zastrow, 1989).

Deep breathing relaxation helps you to stop thinking about day-to-day concerns and concentrate your thinking on your breathing processes. For five to ten minutes, slowly and gradually inhale deeply and exhale, while telling yourself something like "I am relaxing, breathing smoother. This is soothing, and I'm feeling calmer, renewed and refreshed." Continued practice of this technique will enable a person to become more relaxed whenever in a tense situation— such as prior to giving a speech.

Imagery relaxation involves switching your thinking from your daily concerns to focusing your thinking (for ten to fifteen minutes) on your ideal relaxation place. It might be lying on a beach by a scenic lake in the warm sun. It might be relaxing in warm water while reading a magazine. Savor all the pleasantness, the peacefulness—focus on everything that you find calming, soothing, relaxing. Sense your whole body becoming refreshed, revived, and rejuvenated.

Progressive muscle relaxation is based on the principle that a person cannot be anxious if the muscles are relaxed (Jacobson, 1938). The approach is learned by having a person tighten and then relax a set of muscles. When relaxing the muscles, the person is advised to concentrate on the relaxed feeling while noting that the muscles are becoming less tense. Watson and Tharp (1973, pp. 182-83) give a brief description of the initial steps in this procedure:

> Make a fist with your dominant hand (usually right). Make a fist and tense the muscles of your (right) hand and forearm; tense it until it trembles. Feel the muscles pull across your fingers and the lower part of your forearm. . . . Hold this position for five to seven seconds, then . . . relax. . . . Just let your hand go. Pay attention to the muscles of your (right) hand and forearm as they relax. Note how those muscles feel as relaxation flows through (twenty to thirty seconds).

The procedure of tensing and then relaxing is continued three or four times until the hand and forearm are relaxed. Next, other muscle groups are tensed and relaxed in the same manner, one group at a time. These groups might include: left hand and forearm, right biceps, left biceps, forehead muscles, upper lip and cheek muscles, jaw muscles, chin and throat muscles, chest muscles, abdominal muscles, back muscles between shoulder blades, right and left upper leg muscles, right and left calf muscles, and toes and arches of the feet. With practice, capacity to relax simply by visualizing the muscles is developed.

A variety of meditative approaches are being used today. (Deep breathing relaxation and imagery relaxation are two forms of meditation.) Benson (1975) has identified four basic components common to meditative approaches that induce the relaxation response: (1) being in a quiet environment free from external distractions; (2) being in a comfortable position; (3) having an object to dwell on, such as a word, sound, chant, phrase, or imagery of a painting. Since any neutral word or phrase will work, Benson suggests repeating silently to yourself the word *one*; and (4) having a passive attitude in which you stop thinking about day-to-day concerns. This last component, Benson asserts, is the key element in inducing the relaxation response.

Biofeedback equipment provides mechanical feedback to a person about her or his level of stress. Such equipment is able to inform people about levels of stress that they are usually unaware of until a markedly high level is reached. For example, a person's hand temperature may vary 10 to 12 degrees in an hour's time, with an increase in temperature indicating an increase in becoming calm and relaxed. With biofeedback equipment, the levels of functioning of numerous physiological processes can be measured. The processes that can be measured include blood pressure, hand temperature, muscle tension, heart beat rate, and brain waves. With biofeedback training a person is first instructed in recognizing high levels of anxiety or tenseness. Then the person is instructed on how to reduce such high levels by either closing the eyes and adopting a passive letting-go attitude or by thinking about something pleasant or calming. Often, relaxation approaches are combined with biofeedback to elicit the relaxation response. Biofeedback equipment provides immediate feedback to a person about the kind of thinking that is effective in reducing stress (Brown, 1977).

Exercise. Since the alarm phase of the General Adaptation Syndrome automatically prepares us for large muscle activity, it makes sense to exercise. Through exercising, we use up fuel in the blood, reduce blood pressure and heart rate, and reverse the other physiological changes set off during the alarm stage of the General Adaptation Syndrome. Exercising helps keep us physically fit so we have more physical strength to handle stressful crises. Exercising also reduces stress and relieves tension, partly by switching our thinking from our daily concerns to the exercise we are involved in. For these reasons one needs to have an exercise program. A key to making ourselves exercise daily is selecting a program we enjoy. A wide variety of exercises are available including walking, jogging, isometric exercises, jumping rope, swimming and so on.

Pleasurable Goodies. Pleasurable goodies relieve stress, change our pace of living, are enjoyable, make us feel good, and are, in reality, personal therapies. What is a goody (pleasurable experience) to one person may not be to another. Common goodies are: being hugged, listening to music, going shopping, taking a bath, going to a movie, having a glass of wine, taking part in family and religious get-togethers, taking a vacation, singing, and so on. Such goodies add spice to life and remind us we have worth.

Personal pleasures can also be used as payoffs to ourselves for jobs well done. Most of us would not seek to short-change others for doing well; we ought not to short-change ourselves. Such rewards make us feel good and are a motivator to move on to new challenges.

An exercise class at a senior center offers participants a means to reduce stress and to improve muscle tone.

Having enjoyable activities beyond work and family responsibilities also are pleasurable goodies which relieve stress. Research (Schafer, 1978) has found that stress reduces stress; that is, an appropriate level of stressful activities in one area helps reduce excessive stress in others. Getting involved in enjoyable outside activities switches our negative thinking from our daily concerns to positive thoughts about the enjoyable activities. Therefore, it is stress reducing to become involved in activities we enjoy. Such activities may include golf, tennis, swimming, scuba diving, taking flying lessons, traveling, and so on.

Application of Theory to Client Situations

Social workers are one of the helping professionals along with psychologists, psychiatrists, and guidance counselors, who are involved in developing and providing stress management programs. Social workers have a variety of roles in stress management. They can serve as educators in providing stress management educational programs to individuals and groups. Some physicians now refer patients experiencing high levels of stress or those who have stress-related illnesses such as heart disease to such programs. Social workers can incorporate relaxation training and biofeedback training in their counseling sessions with clients, particularly those experiencing high levels of stress; if highly stressed clients learn to relax, they are often more effective in solving their difficulties. Social workers can serve as brokers in referring highly stressed individuals to stress management programs, and they can serve as group facilitators in leading therapeutic groups that emphasize stress management. Social workers can also serve as initiators and consultants in developing stress management programs in schools, businesses, and industries, and in medical settings.

Summary

Later adulthood begins around age sixty-five. This age group is an extremely diverse one, spanning an age range of over thirty years. Later adulthood is an age of recompense as it is a time when people reap the consequences of the kind of life they have lived. The process of aging affects different persons at different rates. Nature appears to have a built-in mechanism that promotes aging, but it is not known what this mechanism is.

There are a variety of factors that accelerate the aging process: poor diet, overwork, alcohol or drug abuse, prolonged illnesses, severe disabilities, prolonged stresses, negative thinking, exposure to prolonged heat or cold, and serious emotional problems. Factors that slow down the aging process include a proper diet, skill in relaxing and managing stress, being physically and mentally active, a positive outlook on life, and learning how to control unwanted emotions.

The elderly are much more susceptible to physical illnesses than younger people; yet, a majority of the elderly are reasonably healthy. The two leading causes of death are diseases of the heart and cancer. Alzheimer's disease, a malady that affects many older adults, was described. The chapter ends with a discussion of the effects of stress and descriptions of stress management techniques.

15

Psychological Systems and Their Impacts on Later Adulthood

Just Browsing

Mrs. Sandra Lombardino is sixty-nine years old. Except for being overweight and having arthritis, she is in fairly good health. She is personable, well-groomed, kind, and articulate. She retired two years ago from her job as an elementary schoolteacher; she was well liked by students and fellow staff in her thirty-three years of teaching. She raised four children, all of whom have started careers and families of their own.

Mrs. Lombardino would like to use her retirement years to travel and do volunteer work. She has worked hard for many years and has looked forward to enjoying her retirement.

She is increasingly frustrated because her husband's demands and offensive behavior are destroying her retirement dreams. Her husband, Benedito, has a number of health care needs. Benedito used to be a carpenter and at one time was a good athlete. But he has been a heavy drinker for over forty years. When drunk he has been physically and verbally abusive to his wife and to his children. His children left home to escape from him as soon as they were financially able to do so. The children love their mother but despise their father.

In many ways Sandra Lombardino has been a martyr. She took a marriage vow to live together for better or worse until death. She has fulfilled that vow, in spite of the urging of her friends and relatives to seek a divorce. Several years ago Benedito was discovered to have cirrhosis of the liver and had to stop working. He now receives a monthly disability check. Despite his illness, Benedito has continued to drink heavily and has developed high blood pressure and diabetes. He is grossly overweight and is often incontinent. The drinking and illnesses have caused brain deterioration and he now has difficulty walking, talking, and grooming himself, and he frequently hallucinates. His offensive behavior has resulted in a loss of friends. Benedito has been pressured into attending a number of alcoholism treatment programs, including Alcoholics Anonymous, but he has always returned to drinking.

Sandra Lombardino is in a quandary about what she should do. She is angry that she now has to spend most of her waking hours caring for someone who is obnoxious and verbally abusive to her. She resents not being able to travel and not being able to leave home in order to do volunteer work. Sometimes she wishes her husband would die, so that she could get on with her life. At other times she feels guilty about wishing her husband would die.

She has contemplated getting a divorce, but such a process would mean her husband would get half of the property that she has worked so many years to acquire. She also has considered placing Benedito in a nursing home, but she feels an obligation to care for him and realizes that the expenses of a nursing home would deplete her life savings. Mrs. Lombardino feels that the cruelest injustice would be for her to die before her husband, so that she would be robbed of her chances to achieve her retirement dreams.

A PERSPECTIVE

People need to make a number of psychological adjustments at all ages for their lives to be meaningful and fulfilling. Later adulthood is no exception.

This chapter will:

Developmental Tasks of Later Adulthood

Most of the developmental tasks that the elderly encounter are psychological in nature. We will look at a number of these tasks, using a couple, Douglas and Norma Polser, as an example.

1. *Retirement and lower income.* In 1980 Douglas Polzer retired from being a road construction foreman in Dubuque, Iowa. Two years earlier his wife, Norma, had retired from the post office. Retirement brought a number of changes to their lives. For several months after retiring Douglas had difficulty in finding things to do with his time. His work had been the center of his life. He seldom saw his former coworkers, and he had practically no hobbies or interests. When he was working, he always had many stories to tell about unusual situations that happened. He no longer had much to talk about. Another problem for the Polzers was that they now had a lower standard of living. Their main sources of income were social security benefits and Norma's federal pension.

2. *Living with one's spouse in retirement.* Prior to retiring Norma and Douglas did not see each other very much. Both worked during the week, and Norma worked on Saturday. Each tended to socialize with his or her coworkers. Norma and Douglas tended to annoy each other if they were together a lot.

   After Douglas retired, both were generally home. Since Norma had always done most of the domestic tasks, she kept busy. Finding things to do was not very difficult for her.

   For the first few months after Douglas retired he followed Norma around the house telling her how she should do her work. That didn't go over very well. They got on each other's nerves and had a number of arguments. As time passed, Douglas became more interested in fishing, taking walks, and getting together with his retired friends. Gradually, with Douglas being gone more, the arguments faded.

3. *Affiliating with individuals of one's own age group or with associations for the elderly.* The Polzers joined the Senior Citizens Leisure Club in Dubuque. Norma participated more frequently than Douglas. The club had a variety of activities: luncheons; speakers, bus tours, painting and craft sessions, bowling, and golf. The club also had a small library.

4. *Maintaining interest in friends and family ties.* Norma and Douglas formed a number of new friendships with members they met in the club. Through conversing with such friends, Norma and Douglas were able to gain new perspectives on the adjustments they had to make.

   Most of the Polzers' friends prior to retiring were coworkers. After retirement, they gradually saw less and less of these friends, since their interests were growing in different directions. These former friends still talked a great deal about what was happening at work, and both Norma and Douglas now thought such conversations were boring.

   The Polzers usually got together on Sunday with their son, Kirk, and his family who lived in Dubuque. Their daughter, Devi, had left home at age seventeen to marry. After three children, she obtained a divorce and was on AFDC for four years until she remarried. She is now living in California and has had two more children. The Polzers seldom see her, but their relationship with her has improved since her adolescent years. Doug and Norma wish they could see Devi and her children more.

5. *Continuing social and civic responsibilities.* Douglas has continued to be a volunteer night watchman for the county fair that is held for four days during the summer. Since they retired, Doug and Norma have been more active in attending their church and participating in church activities; Doug has become an elder for the church and Norma has become more active in the ladies aid society.

6. *Coping with illness and loss of spouse and/or friends.* After four years of retirement, life was going fairly smoothly for the Polzers. Then in 1984 Doug had a stroke which left him partly paralyzed. Doug and Norma's lives changed radically. Douglas almost never went outside the house. He became irritable, incontinent, and needed constant attention. Visiting nurse services provided some help, and so did the Polzers' son and daughter-in-law. But the major burden was Norma's. She was forced to drastically reduce her church and club activities. For the next two years she spent most of her time caring for Douglas. He never said

"thank you," and he verbally abused her. At times Norma wished he would die. Then in 1986 he did.

Norma's world again changed. For the first time in many years she was living alone. Douglas' death was very hard for her. She felt guilty since she had wished Douglas would die and believed that this may have magically contributed to his death. Initially, she was lonely. But, as the months began to pass, she gradually started putting her life back together. She became active again in the church and in the senior leisure club. Sharing her grief with other club members helped. As the years passed more of her friends died, and Norma found herself attending more funerals.

7. *Finding satisfactory living arrangements at the different stages of later adulthood.* After Douglas died, Norma was depressed and had less energy. Kirk helped, but he had his own family, career, and home to care for. Norma realized she was slowing down physically. After two years, Kirk began to encourage her to sell the house and move into an apartment complex that was especially built for the elderly. Norma resisted for over a year. Then, in 1989 Norma slipped on a stairway and broke her leg. She had to crawl to the telephone. Kirk came and took her to the emergency room where her leg was put in a cast. When she got out of the hospital, Kirk took her to his home. Norma's house was put up for sale.

Having to leave her house was almost as great a loss as when Douglas died. She spent two months with Kirk's family, but she did not get along with Kirk's wife. Each had different ways of doing things and different ideas on how children should be raised. When relationships became severely strained, Norma moved to an apartment for the elderly. The move meant that many cherished possessions had to be discarded. Norma began to realize that if her mental or physical condition deteriorated further, her next move would be to a nursing home; at times she thought she would rather die than enter a nursing home. The move also meant Norma had to establish new relationships. Fortunately, the move went smoother than even Norma hoped and she was warmly welcomed by the staff and the other residents.

8. *Adjusting to changing physical strength and health and overcoming bodily preoccupation.* For many years Norma had struggled to get used to gray hairs, wrinkles, and all the other physical changes of aging. Her arthritis often caused swelling and pain in her joints, and she no longer had as much energy and stamina as in the past.

9. *Reappraising personal values, self-concept, and personal worth in light of new life events.* A major adapta-

tion task of the elderly, according to Butler and Lewis (1977), is to conduct an evaluative life review. During this review they reflect on their failures and accomplishments, their disappointments and satisfactions and hopefully come to a reasonably positive view of their life's worth. Failure to arrive at a positive view can result in overt psychopathology.

After Norma became settled in her apartment, she again had a lot of free time. She was now seventy-six years old, and her health was declining. She spent a lot of time thinking about the past. She had enjoyed the early years of retirement, but she acknowledged that the five years since Douglas' first stroke had been rocky.

10. *Accepting the prospect of death.* It is now 1992 and Norma has been living in her apartment for three years. Her arthritis is worse, and she has cataracts. But her last three years have been fairly uneventful. Kirk and his family visit almost every Sunday, and she has made a number of friends at her apartment complex. She has attended a number of funerals, and still occasionally mourns the death of Douglas, especially on holidays and on their wedding anniversary. Norma feels her life has been fairly full and meaningful. These assessments have also led her to think about her eventual death. She worries about the pain she may experience and is fearful about slowly deteriorating. To avoid being kept alive after her mental capacities have deteriorated, she has signed a "living will" which declares that if she becomes unconscious for a prolonged period of time she does not want heroic measures to be used to keep her alive. She is fully aware and accepting of the fact that she will die in the not-too-distant future. Since her life has been full and positive, she is prepared for death. Her religion asserts there is a life after death; she is uncertain whether an afterlife exists, but if it does she is hoping to be reunited with Douglas, and to see many of her friends who have died.

Theoretical Concepts about Developmental Tasks in Later Adulthood

In this section we will examine the following theoretical concepts: integrity versus despair, shifting from work-role preoccupation to self-differentiation, shifting from body preoccupation to body transcendence, shifting to self-transcendence, life review, self-esteem, and low status and ageism.

Integrity versus Despair

The final stage of life according to Erickson (1963) involves the psychological crisis of *integrity versus despair*. The attainment of integrity comes only after considerable reflection about the meaning of one's life. Integrity refers to an ability to accept the facts of one's life and to face death without great fear. The elderly who have achieved a sense of integrity view their past in an existential light. They have a feeling of having achieved a respected position during their lifetime and have an inner sense of completion. They accept all of the events that have happened to them, without trying to deny some unpleasant facts or to overemphasize others. Integrity is an integration of one's sense of past history with one's present circumstances, and a feeling of being content with the outcome. In order to experience integrity, the elderly must incorporate a lifelong sequence of failures, conflicts, and disappointments into their self-image. This process is made more difficult by the fact that the role of the elderly is devalued in our society. There are a

lot of negative attitudes being expressed in our society that (often erroneously) suggest the elderly are incompetent, dependent, and old-fashioned. The death of close friends and relatives and the gradual deterioration of physical health make it additionally difficult for the elderly to achieve integrity.

The opposite pole of integrity is despair. Despair is characterized by a feeling of regret about one's past and includes a continuous nagging desire to have done things differently. Despair makes an attitude of calm acceptance of death impossible, as those who despair view their life as being incomplete and unfulfilled. They either seek death as a way of ending a miserable existence, or they desperately fear death because it makes any hope of compensating for past failures impossible. Some of the elderly who despair commit suicide (see Figure 15.1).

Buhler (1968) conducted a study of the extent to which the elderly achieve integrity. The study found that integrity and despair were largely ideal concepts. Most of the people she studied showed neither of the extremes of integrity or despair. Instead, most of the

FIGURE 15.1: Men, Particularly Elderly Men, Are More Apt to Commit Suicide Than Are Women

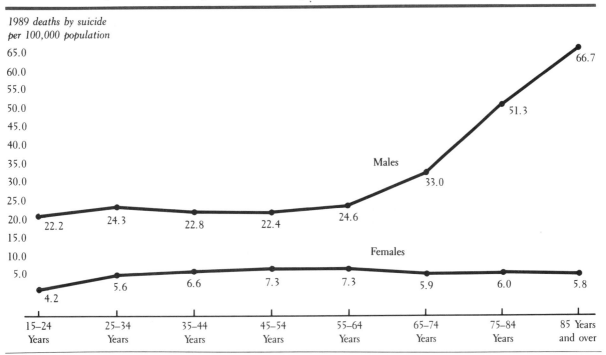

SOURCE: U.S. Bureau of the Census, *Statistical Abstract of the United States* 1991, (Washington, D.C.: U.S. Government Printing Office, 1992), p. 85.

elderly exhibited a combination of partial fulfillment of a life well lived and of goals met, tempered by many disappointments and culminating in a state of resignation. Buhler's study suggests that while Erickson's concepts of integrity versus despair may have conceptual value in describing the polar extremes of adjusting to later adulthood most of the elderly make an adjustment that falls somewhere between these polar extremes.

Three Key Psychological Adjustments

Peck (1968) suggests that there are three primary psychological adjustments that must be made in order to make later adulthood meaningful and gratifying. The first adjustment is shifting from work-role preoccupation to self-differentiation. Since retirement is a crucial shift in one's life, a new role must be acquired. The elderly person has to adjust to the fact that she or he will no longer go to work and needs to find a new identity and new interests. People who are in the process of making this adjustment must spend time assessing their personal worth. (A woman whose major work has been being a wife and a mother faces this adjustment when her children leave home or her husband dies.) A crucial question to resolve at this point is: "Am I a worthwhile person only insofar as I can do a full-time job or can I be worthwhile in other different ways . . . (Peck, 1968, p. 90)?" In making this adjustment, people need to recognize that they are richer and more diverse than the sum of their tasks at work.

A second adjustment is shifting from body preoccupation to body transcendence. Health problems increase for the elderly and energy levels decrease. One's physical appearance also shows signs of aging such as graying and thinning of hair and increasing wrinkles. Many older people, as a result, become preoccupied with their state of health and their appearance. Others, however, transcend these concerns and are able to enjoy life in spite of declining health. Those who make this transcendence have generally learned to define comfort and happiness in terms of satisfying social relationships or creative mental activities.

The third adjustment is shifting to self-transcendence. The inevitability of death must be dealt with. Although death is a depressing prospect, Peck (1968) indicates a positive acceptance can be achieved by shifting one's concerns from "poor me" to "what can I do to make life more meaningful, secure, or happier for those who will survive me?"

Life Review

Most older persons conduct an evaluative life review in which they assess their past life and consider the future in terms of the inevitability of death. Frenkel-Brunswik (1970) refers to this life review as "drawing up the balance sheet of life." The two key elements in this review are concluding that the past was meaningful and learning to accept the inevitability of death. Those who psychologically achieve this are apt to be content and comfortable with their later years; those who conclude that life has been empty and who do not as yet accept death are apt to despair.

Self-Esteem

Self-esteem (the way people regard themselves) is a key factor in overall happiness and adjustment to life. According to Cooley's (1902) "looking glass self-concept," people develop their sense of who they are in terms of the ways that others relate to them. If elderly people are treated by others as if they are old-fashioned, senile, dependent, and incompetent, they are apt to view themselves in the same way. With losses of friends and relatives through death, with the loss of the work role, and with a decline in physical appearance and in physical abilities, the elderly are vulnerable to a lowering of self-esteem.

In order for the elderly to feel good about themselves, they need feedback from others that they are worthwhile, competent, and respected. Like people in all other age groups, the elderly thrive by demonstrating their competence. People tend to feel competent when they exert control over their own lives. The more options they have, the more in control they are, and the higher their self-esteem will be. Schwartz (1975) has noted that privacy is a factor in furthering competence and self-esteem. People who have a private place to go can decide when they want to be with other people and when they want to be alone. In a nursing home those who have a private room can retreat to it whenever they find something distasteful, or too noisy, or whenever they want to rest. A private room gives them a way to control their environment.

Low Status and Ageism

The elderly suffer psychologically because our society has been generally unsuccessful in finding something important or satisfying for them to do. Roscow (cited in McTavish, 1971, p. 90) has noted: "It should be clear that the crucial people in the aging problem are not the old, but the younger age groups, for it is the rest of us who determine the status and position of the older person in the social order." The young and the middle aged not only determine the future for the elderly, they also determine their own future as they will someday be elderly.

In most primitive and earlier societies, the elderly were respected and viewed as useful to their people to a much greater degree than is the case in our society. Industrialization and the growth of modern society have robbed the elderly of their high status in our society. Prior to industrialization, older people were the primary owners of property. Land was the most important source of power; and therefore, the elderly controlled much of the economic and political power. Now, people earn their living in the job market, and the vast majority of the elderly own little land and are viewed as having no salable labor. In earlier societies the elderly were also valued because of the knowledge they possessed. Their experiences enabled them to supervise planting and harvesting and to pass on knowledge about hunting, housing, and crafts. The elderly also played key roles in preserving and transmitting the culture. But the rapid advances of science and technology have tended to limit the value of the technological knowledge of the elderly, and books and other memory-storing devices have made the elderly less valuable as storehouses of culture and records.

Papalia and Olds (1981, p. 536) summarize our society's treatment of the elderly:

> Our society does not allow many of our elderly to experience their last years positively. We don't respect old people for their wisdom and experience, but instead dismiss their ideas as outdated and irrelevant. We don't allow them to use their abilities productively, but force them into retirement when they are still eager and able to work. We don't sustain them financially, but allow them to waste away in a state of poverty that crushes the spirit.

The low status of the elderly is closely associated with ageism. The term *ageism* refers to having negative images of and attitudes toward people simply because they are old. Today, the reaction to the elderly by many people is a negative one. Ageism is similar to sexism or racism as it involves discrimination and prejudice against all members of a particular social category.

The negative stereotypes about the elderly appear to be ingrained in our society. Third graders have been found to have generally negative stereotypes of the elderly—as being mean or as being lonely, bored and inactive (Hickey et al., 1968). Many children's books do not have elderly characters, and those that do usually portray the elderly unfavorably (Flaste, 1977).

The prejudice against the elderly is shown in everyday language by the use of such terms as "old biddy," and "old fogey."

Ageism is an additional burden that the elderly encounter. Some of the elderly, particularly among the young-old, are able to refute ageism stereotypes by being productive and physically and mentally active. Unfortunately for others, ageism stereotypes become self-fulfilling prophecies. The elderly are treated as if they are incompetent, dependent, and senile; such treatment lowers their self-esteem, and some end up playing the roles suggested by the stereotypes. Ageism adversely impacts on the elderly and restricts the roles and alternatives available to them.

Theories of Successful Aging

Three theories about how to age successfully are activity theory, disengagement theory, and social reconstruction syndrome theory.

Activity Theory

This theory asserts that the more physically and mentally active people are, the more successfully they will age. Components of this theory were discussed at length in Chapter 14. One component of the theory asserts that the sexual response can be maintained in later adulthood by being sexually active. There is considerable evidence that being physically and mentally active will help to maintain the physiological, psychological, and intellectual functions of the elderly.

A volunteer teaches an English-as-a-second-language class. The more physically and mentally active the elderly are, the more successfully they will age.

Disengagement Theory

Cumming and Henry (1961) coined the term *disengagement* to refer to a process whereby people respond to aging by gradually withdrawing from the various roles and social relationships they occupied in middle age. Such disengagement is claimed to be functional for the elderly as they are thought to gradually lose the energy and vitality to sustain all the roles and social relationships held in younger years.

Societal Disengagement Theory

Disengagement theory refers not only to the elderly withdrawing from society but also to society withdrawing from the elderly, or *societal disengagement* (Atchley, 1983, p. 97). It is claimed it is functional for our society (which values competition, efficiency, and individual achievement) to disengage from the elderly, who have the least physical stamina and the highest death rate. Societal disengagement occurs in a variety of ways: employers may seek to force the elderly to retire, the elderly may not be sought out for leadership positions in organizations, their children may involve them less in making family decisions, and

the government may be less responsive in meeting their needs as compared to people who are younger. Societal disengagement is often unintended and unrecognized by employers, younger relatives, and other younger members of society. Disengagement theory also asserts that the elderly welcome this withdrawal and contribute to it.

Evaluation of Disengagement Theory

Disengagement theory has generated considerable research over the years. There is controversy regarding whether disengagement is functional for the elderly and for our society. Research has found some people do voluntarily disengage as they grow older. However, critics assert that disengagement is related less to old age itself than to the factors associated with aging, such as retirement, poor health, death of spouse and of close friends, and impoverishment. For example, when people are forced to retire they tend to disengage from coworker friendships, union activities, professional friendships, and reading in their field. Once retired, they also have less money to spend on entertainment, so disengagement from some activities is forced.

Disengagement is neither universal nor inevitable. Contrary to the theory's predictions, most older persons maintain extensive associations with friends, and active involvement in voluntary organizations (such as church groups and fraternal organizations). Also, some of the elderly, after retiring, develop new interests, expand their circle of friends, join clubs, and do volunteer work. Others rebel against society's stereotypes and refuse to be treated as if they had little to offer to society. Many of these people are marshaling political resources to force society to adapt to their needs and skills.

Disengagement theory at times advocates the exact opposite of activity theory. Activity theory asserts it is beneficial for the elderly to be physically and mentally active, while disengagement theory asserts it is beneficial to withdraw from a variety of activities (many of which provide physical and mental stimulation).

Ethical Issues

A severe criticism of disengagement theory is that the theory may be used to justify society's failure to help the elderly maintain meaningful roles. It may also be used to justify ageism. Disengagement theory may, at best, be merely a description of the age/youth relationships (and reactions to them) which we should combat as we try to combat ageism.

Social Reconstruction Syndrome Theory

This theory was developed from the *social breakdown syndrome* that was conceptualized by Zusman (1966). Zusman indicated social breakdown occurs for the elderly because of the effects of labeling. Society has unrealistic standards or expectations that all adults should work and be productive; other people label the elderly as incompetent or lacking in some ways; the elderly accept the label and view themselves in terms of the label; they then learn behavior consistent with the label and downplay their previous skills. As a result, they become more dependent and incompetent, and feel inadequate.

Kuypers and Bengston (1973) assert that this negative interaction between the elderly's environment and self-concept explains many of the problems of aging in our society. To break the vicious cycle of this labeling process, they recommend the *social reconstruction syndrome*, which has three major recommendations. First, our society should liberate the elderly from unrealistic standards and expectations. The belief that self-worth depends on a person's productivity has adverse consequences for those who are retired. Kuypers and Bengston (1973) recommend that society be reeducated to change these unrealistic standards. Fischer (1977, p. 33) specifies the direction such reeducation should take:

> The values of our society rest upon a work ethic—an ethic of doing—that gives highest value to people in the prime of their productive years. We should encourage a plurality of ethics in its place—not merely an ethic of doing, but also an ethic of feeling, an ethic of sharing, an ethic of knowing, an ethic of enduring, and even an ethic of surviving.

The second recommendation of Kuypers and Bengston (1973) is to provide the elderly with the social services they need. Such services include transportation, medical care, housing, help with housekeeping, and programs that provide physical and mental activity.

The third recommendation is to find creative ways to give the elderly more control over their lives. Bengsten (1973, p. 49) for example, recommends that at nursing homes the decision-making bodies should be "exclusively comprised of the elderly themselves. While the nursing and social service staff, for example, might be younger people, they are servants of the elderly board of directors, the elderly committee structure and the elderly administrators."

The Impact of Life Events on the Elderly

We will look at a number of life events that impact on life in later adulthood. The events we will examine are marriage, death of spouse, widowhood, never having been married, remarriage, family relationships, and grandparenthood. These events directly affect the behavior of the elderly and often limit the alternatives available to them.

Marriage

Because people are living longer, many marriages are lasting longer as well. Today, fiftieth wedding anniver-

Cultural Differences in Successful Aging

Leaf (1973) studied three societies where the elderly live much longer (some over one hundred years) and remain more vigorous than in most other places around the world. These societies were located in Abkhazia, in the southern part of Asia; the principality of Hunza in Pakistani-controlled Kashmir; and an Andean village in Ecuador.

Leaf (1973) studied the question of why the elderly in these three societies are vigorous, healthy, and live long lives. He found that several aspects of their lives, involving psychological and physical factors, were very different from the life-styles in our society. The social status of the elderly in these societies is high. They live with members of their family who respect them and who appreciate the useful contributions they make to the family and to the community. In Hunza, twenty elderly men compose a council of elders who meet daily to resolve disputes.

There is no forced retirement, and the elderly work as long as they are able. On a daily basis they perform such tasks as doing laundry, feeding poultry, planting and harvesting crops, tending animals, and caring for small children. They have a different outlook toward life and old age. They expect to be healthy and to live a long time and consider the normal life span to be about one hundred rather than seventy. They view people as being young for a long time, and believe that youth extends to about eighty years of age.

In all three communities the people eat less than we do. The average American adult consumes about 3,300 calories a day, while people in these three societies consume a low-calorie diet throughout life, usually less than 2,000 calories a day. They eat very few fats of animal origin and few dairy products. Such dietary habits may delay the development of *atherosclerosis* (fatty deposits in the arteries). The elderly Abkhazians drink some vodka and some homemade wine regularly. Almost none of the people studied are obese.

People in all three societies have a high level of physical activity. They walk up and down mountainous terrain and are involved in such physical activities as hunting, farming, and sheepherding, which maintains cardiovascular fitness and good muscle tone.

Genetic factors may also be involved in their longevity. People in these societies (just as people who live a long time in our society) generally have parents who lived to advanced ages. It could well be that people who live to advanced ages do not have genes that carry predispositions to disabling or fatal diseases.

The elderly in these societies also have an active interest in the opposite sex. They continue to have sexual intercourse with their partners well into their later years.

It is impossible to tell with exactness which (if any) of the above factors are responsible for people in these societies being in good health and living to advanced ages. The study, however, does suggest a number of factors that *may* make later adulthood a good age. Having a life of quality in later adulthood, as Abkhazians, Hunzans, and the Andean people appear to have, is much more important than living to an advanced age.

---

saries are much more common than they were in the past. But divorces are more common too.

Couples who are still married in their later years are less likely than younger couples to see their marriages as full of problems (Papalia and Olds, 1992, p. 513). There could be a variety of reasons. They may well have worked out their major conflicts. Since divorce is now quite accessible, those marriages that survive many years may be the happier and more conflict-free ones. Or, the difference may be one of development; as people learn to better cope with crises and conflicts.

The level of happiness and satisfaction in the marriages of elderly people appears to be higher than that of younger couples. Stennett, Carter, and Montgomery (1972) studied 408 married elderly men and women. Nearly 95 percent rated their marriages as very happy or happy. More than half stated that the happiest time of married life was the present and that their marriages had become better over the years.

The researchers also examined what makes a marriage happy. The respondents continued to be romantics as they stated being in love was a key factor in achieving a successful marriage. Also important were respect for each other and the sharing of common interests. The most rewarding aspects were companionship and being able to express their true feelings to each other. Most reported their marriages were now

Fiftieth wedding anniversaries are more common now than in the past.

trouble free. Those who did have conflicts stated the sources were differences in interests, in values, and in philosophies of life.

Gilford (1986) found that people over age seventy consider themselves less happily married than those age sixty-three to sixty-nine; perhaps decline in physical health aggravates the strains on marriage. Gilford also found that elderly women tend to be less satisfied with marriage than are elderly men, partly because women generally expect more warmth and intimacy from marriage than men do.

Married elderly people are happier than the unmarried and particularly happier than the widowed and the divorced (Lee, 1978). Lee (1978) also found that the extent to which elderly people, particularly women, are satisfied with their marriage influences their overall sense of well-being. Health and satisfaction with one's standard of living were also found to positively correlate with an overall sense of well-being. Chronic illness has a negative impact on the morale of couples, even when only one member is ill. The healthy partner may become depressed, angry, or frustrated with the responsibilities of taking care of the ill spouse and having to do most of the tasks to maintain the household. Ill health of one spouse may also reduce the opportunities for enjoyable activities, may drain financial resources, and may reduce sexual involvement. Other crises and life events (such as retirement) can also generate considerable marital turmoil and conflict.

Ill health can also lead to role changes in the lives of elderly couples. The spouse who develops a serious life-threatening illness is usually the husband—as women tend to be younger than their spouses and to live longer. If one spouse develops an illness (such as Alzheimer's disease) where there is progressive deterioration of mental and physical capacities, the other spouse has to take on increasing decision-making and care-giving responsibilities. Gilford (1986) found that spouses (especially wives) who must care for mates with disabilities may experience anger, isolation, and frustration. They are also more apt to develop a chronic illness themselves.

Clark and Anderson (1967) found that happily married elderly couples had fewer rigidly defined sex roles than unhappily married elderly couples. Happily married elderly couples were found to be more flexible about who does what in the marriage and tended to ignore sex-role expectations as far as carrying out household and domestic responsibilities.

Death of Spouse

The death of a spouse is traumatic at any age. It is more apt to occur in later adulthood as death rates are considerably higher in this age group. The surviving spouse faces a variety of emotional and practical problems. The survivor has lost a lover, a companion, a good friend, and a confidant. The more intertwined their life had become, the deeper the loss is apt to be felt. In most marriages, household maintenance responsibilities are divided. The survivor now finds he or she has a lot more tasks to do, some of which were never learned.

The survivor's social life changes also. At first, relatives, friends, and neighbors usually rally to give the survivor sympathy and emotional support. But gradually they return to their own lives, leaving the widower or widow to form a new life. Friends and relatives are apt to grow tired of listening to the survivor talk about his or her loss and grief and withdraw emotional and practical help. The survivor may have to make such decisions as moving to a smaller place that is easier to maintain and going to social events alone. Some survivors withdraw because they feel like a "fifth wheel," especially with other couples.

Widowhood

Forty-two percent of women over sixty-five have husbands, while 77 percent of elderly men have wives (American Association of Retired Persons, 1990). This difference is largely due to the tendency of men to marry younger women and the fact that women have a longer life expectancy. The effects of widowhood are poignantly summarized by a seventy-five-year-old widow, "As long as you have your husband, you're not old. But once you lose him, old age sets in fast" (quoted in Papalia and Olds, 1992, p. 514).

Lopata (1973) surveyed the experiences, attitudes,

People who adjust best to widowhood are those who keep busy.

and life-styles of 301 widows who were fifty years of age and over. The respondents stated that loneliness was the worst problem of widowhood. They missed their husband's companionship and love. Widowhood affects different people in diverse ways. Interestingly, women who had serious marital conflicts had more trouble adjusting to the death of their husband. Perhaps they felt guilty for things they did or said, or felt guilty for things failed to say or do. The study also found the more a woman has been dependent on her husband for her identity, the more deeply she feels his absence. This finding suggests that women should develop a strong sense of their own identity and assume a large role in family decision-making activities, including the financial areas in order to prepare themselves for the probability of eventual widowhood.

A majority of the respondents felt their life had changed significantly in one or more ways as a result of widowhood; most of these respondents stated the change was positive. Even many of the women who had been happily married came to consider themselves more competent and independent following the death of their spouse. Women who reported that there were no significant changes after the death of their spouse tended to be more socially isolated and to have less education than women who reported changes.

Widowed people of both sexes have higher rates of depression and mental illness than married people (Papalia and Olds, 1992, p. 515). Men are more likely to die within six months of a wife's death, and women are more apt to develop a chronic illness after a husband's death (Papalia and Olds, 1992, p. 515).

People who adjust best to widowhood are those who keep busy, perhaps by taking on new paid or volunteer work or by becoming more deeply involved in other activities (such as seeing friends often or taking part in community programs). Participating in support groups for widowed people is also beneficial (Papalia and Olds, 1992, p. 516).

Never Married

Gubrium (1975) surveyed twenty-two people who had never been married and who ranged in age between sixty and ninety-four years. They expressed fewer feelings of loneliness than those who had once been married. Perhaps they had made an adjustment to being single a long time ago (or even preferred to be single) and therefore were not as bothered by being alone as those who were once married. These single people also seemed to be more independent, had fewer social relationships, were generally satisfied with their lives, and seemed to be less concerned about their age than most elderly persons. Gubrium (1975) suggests they may have a unique social personality in which they generally prefer to be by themselves.

Remarriage

Our society has generally opposed the elderly dating and remarrying. We think of younger people hugging and kissing each other, but such behavior by an elderly couple is often met with stares and crude remarks. Children of the elderly are sometimes opposed to their mother or father remarrying. (They may be concerned about inheritance, or they may believe starting a new relationship is being unfaithful to or dishonoring the parent who has died.) Yet, remarriage in later adulthood is increasing (Papalia and Olds, 1992, p. 517).

Vinick (1978) interviewed twenty-four elderly couples who had remarried after both partners were over sixty years of age. Most of the respondents had been widowed rather than divorced. Most had either known each other during their previous marriages or were introduced to each other by a friend or relative. The male usually took the initiative in beginning the relationship. More than half married within the year in which they began dating.

The couples primarily remarried for companionship. The female respondents also tended to mention emotional feelings toward the man they married and noted certain positive personal qualities. Most of these couples were supported in their decision to marry by their adult children. Some reported receiving negative feedback from a few friends, partly because the friends felt either envious or abandoned.

Almost all these spouses reported being very happily married. A typical response was, "We're like a couple of kids. We fool around—have fun. We go to dances and socialize a lot with our families. We enjoy life together. When you're with someone, you're happy" (Vinick, 1978, p. 362). These spouses tended to have a "live and let live" attitude toward each other and to have less conflict.

For a variety of reasons our society should change its negative attitude about remarriage in later adulthood. Married elderly people are happier than those who are widowed or divorced. They have companionship, can share interests, provide emotional support, and can assist each other in household maintenance tasks. It is also cost effective for society to support the single elderly in remarrying as they are then less likely to need financial assistance and social services and are less likely to be placed in nursing homes (Papalia and Olds, 1992, p. 517).

About love and remarriage in later adulthood, Henri Rousseau, age sixty-five, noted:

> One can still be in love at any age without being ridiculous. It's not the same sort of love that young people go in for, but must one resign oneself to living alone just because one's old? It's dreadful going back to lonely lodgings. It's at my age that one most needs one's heart warmed up again. . . . It's not right to laugh at old people who get married again; you need the company of someone you love. (Quoted in Papalia and Olds, 1981, p. 548)

Family System Relationships

There is a popular belief that the elderly disengage somewhat from their adult children and their grandchildren. There is also a belief that there is a generation gap (conflict in values) between the elderly and younger family members. These beliefs suggest that the elderly may have strained and somewhat unfavorable family relationships.

A study by Seelbach and Hansen (1980), however, suggests that most elderly persons' family relationships are generally quite positive. These researchers asked 367 elderly people how satisfied they were with various aspects of family relations. (About 40 percent of the respondents were institutionalized, primarily in nursing homes.) Eighty-eight percent of the respondents stated they were perfectly satisfied with the treatment they received from their families. Those who were over age eighty were more satisfied than the "young-old" (age sixty-five to eighty in this study). Eighty-seven percent said they were receiving as much love and affection from their families as they ever had. Fewer than one in three wished their families would pay more attention to them. Such positive replies were surprising; most of the institutionalized elderly did not appear estranged from their families, even though their families were involved in placing them in a nursing home. The results suggest family relationships with the elderly are substantially better than suggested by popular beliefs.

In most instances, the elderly and their adult children do not live together for a variety of reasons. Many younger people live in small quarters that make it inconvenient to house another person. The elderly are reluctant to move in as they may fear they will have little privacy. They may fear that there will be somebody else's rules to follow and that they may not have visitors when they wish. They may resent having to account to their children for how they spend their time. They may fear their children may put pressure on them to make life-style changes, such as giving up smoking, changing their eating habits, and reducing the intake of alcoholic beverages. They may also fear inconveniencing or becoming a burden to their children's families. And, many simply do not want to leave their own home (castle) where they feel comfortable and have pleasant memories.

Although most of the elderly do not live with their children, they tend to live close to them and to see them frequently. A study reported by Rabushk and Jacobs (1980) found that eight out of ten elderly persons had seen at least one of their children during the past week.

Most of the elderly do not want to live with their children. Of the few who do, most are female and widowed (Papalia and Olds, 1992, p. 521). Lopata (1973) in a survey of widows who did not live with their children found that these respondents felt it would be difficult to live with their married children's families. They felt they would have trouble remaining silent about mistakes they saw their children making in such areas as handling finances, raising children, and getting along in their marriages. They felt the advice they would be compelled to give would be unwelcome.

Our society has the exact opposite views about the contributions of the elderly as held by most primitive societies. In primitive societies the advice and knowledge of the elderly are actively sought, and the elderly usually live with their children and receive needed care. In our society the role of adult children in caring for their aged parents is confused. Middle-aged adults tend to feel that their first priorities are to meet their needs and the needs of their children. The fact that many adults would rather see their parents cared for in a nursing home than living with them suggests adults do not feel as great an obligation to their parents as do members of primitive societies. The question of whether to place one's partly incapacitated elderly parent in a nursing home or to provide care in one's own home is a question that many middle-aged adults struggle with.

Most adult children help their parents in many ways. Hill (1985) found that grandparents receive substantial help from both their children and their adult grandchildren in such areas as household tasks, emotional support, and assistance during periods of illness. The grandparents in this study were more apt to receive help than to give it.

Help often goes in both directions. Grandparents may care for young grandchildren when both parents work or when the parents go out for an evening. Grandparents and parents may jointly work together helping each other around their homes. Grandparents may open their home to a son or daughter who is divorced or separated or who is temporarily unemployed. Grandparents may also help financially during emergencies, such as paying for treatment for alcohol or other drug abuse. Grandparents may also help by being good listeners to their adult children and by providing suggestions to help resolve the problems they face.

Abused Parents: A Population-at-Risk

An increasing number of incidents of elderly parents being abused by their children are being reported to adult protective service units in social service agencies. Although the public is virtually unaware of parent abuse, an estimated 4 percent (over 1 million) of the nation's elderly are victims of parent abuse (Jones and Eimers, 1988, p. 27). One example follows:

In Chicago, a nineteen-year-old woman confessed to torturing her eighty-one-year-old father and chaining him to a toilet for seven days. She also hit him with a hammer when he was asleep: "I worked him over real good with it. Then after I made him weak enough, I chained his legs together. After that, I left him and rested. I watched TV for a while." (Koch and Koch, 1980, p. 14)

Koch and Koch (1980, p. 14) report that the following four types of parent abuse are the most prevalent, as reported to adult protective services.

- Physical abuse (three-fourths of the cases) including direct beating and withholding of personal care, food, medicine, and necessary supervision.
- Psychological abuse (almost half of the cases) involving verbal assaults and threats provoking fear.
- Material abuse or theft of money or personal property.
- Violation of rights (nearly all of the cases), such as forcing a parent out of his or her dwelling, usually into a nursing home.

Adult children may abuse their parents for a variety of reasons. They may be responding to the stress of their own personal problems or to the stress of the time, energy, and finances needed to care for another person. They may be paying back their parent for having been abusive to them when they were younger. They may be upset with their elderly parent's emotional reactions, physical impairments, life-style, or personal habits such as excessive drinking. They may be intentionally abusing the parent to force him or her to move out of their home. When the elderly person is living with the abuser, finding alternative living arrangements is often necessary.

Every state is mandated by the federal government to provide adult protective services similar to those provided for children. This program serves adults—primarily the elderly and adults with physical or mental disabilities—who are being neglected or abused. (This program is described in more detail in Chapter 16.)

Grandparenthood

Neugarten and Weinstein (1964) identified five major styles of grandparenting in our society. The *fun seeker* is a playmate to the grandchildren in a mutual relationship that both enjoy. The *distant figure* has periodic contact with the grandchildren, generally on birthdays and holidays, but is quite uninvolved with their lives. The *surrogate parent* assumes considerable caretaking responsibilities, usually because the grand-

In a study of grandparents, about half were found to be fun seekers.

children's parents are working, or because the mother is single and working. The *formal figure* leaves all child-rearing responsibilities to the parents and limits his or her involvement with the grandchildren to providing special treats and occasional babysitting. The *reservoir of family wisdom* takes on an authoritarian role and dispenses special resources and skills.

In a study of 70 sets of grandparents Neugarten and Weinstein (1964) found that half the grandparents were either distant figures or fun seekers. Grandparents are not necessarily elderly adults; some are as young as thirty-five to forty years. In Neugarten and Weinstein's (1964) study those grandparents over age sixty-five were more apt to be formal figures. Perhaps as people become older they may be less interested in playing with young children and also less interested in assuming parenting responsibilities.

Kahana and Kahana (1970) asked children who ranged in age from four to twelve a variety of questions about relationships with their grandparents. These children generally felt closest to the maternal grandparents, with the favorite grandparent usually being the mother's mother. The youngest children preferred the formal figures who gave them treats, food, love and presents. The eight- and nine-year-olds preferred the fun seekers, and the oldest children preferred the formal figures. Kahana and Kahana (1970, p. 99) conclude, "It is possible that different styles of grandparenthood fit in best with the child's needs at different stages in his development." Kahana and Coe (1969) found that grandparents feel increasingly distant from their grandchildren as the children become older.

Troll (1983) has found that the tacit "norm of noninterference" by grandparents tends to evaporate in times of trouble for their adult children and their grandchildren. Grandparents tend to perform the role of family "watchdogs," according to Troll. They stay on the fringes of the lives of their children and grandchildren, with varying degrees of involvement. During times of crisis (such as serious illness, money problems, or divorce) they tend to become much more involved by stepping in and playing more active roles. During good times they are less involved, but they are still watching.

Some gender differences have been found to exist in grandparenting. Cherlin and Furstenberg (1986) found that grandmothers tend to have closer and warmer relationships with their grandchildren and are more apt to serve as surrogate parents than are grandfathers. The same study also found that the mother's parents are likely to be closer to the grandchildren than the father's parents and are more apt to become involved during a crisis. Thomas (1986) found that grandmothers tend to be more satisfied than are grandfathers with grandparenting.

Because the elderly are living longer, four and even five generational families are becoming more common. Future research will need to focus on the relationships that develop. An exploratory study by Doka and Mertz (1988) indicates that great-grandparents view great-grandchildren as a source of diversion and as evidence of their own longevity and their family renewal and continued survival.

Guidelines for Positive Psychological Preparation for Later Adulthood

Growing old is a lifelong process. Becoming sixty-five does not destroy the continuity of what a person has been, is now, and will be. Recognition of this fact should lessen the fear of growing old. For those who are financially secure and in good health, and who have prepared thoughtfully, later adulthood can be a period of, if not luxury, then at least reasonable pleasure and comfort.

Some may be able to start small home businesses based on their hobbies or become involved in meaningful activities with churches and other organizations. Others may relax while fishing and/or slowly traveling around the country. Still others may continue such interests as gardening, woodworking, reading, needlework, painting, weaving, and photography.

Our lives largely depend on our goals and our efforts to achieve these goals. How we live prior to retiring will largely determine whether later adulthood will be a nightmare or gratifying and fulfilling. The importance of being physically and mentally active throughout life was discussed at length in Chapter 14.

1. *Close personal relationships.* Close relationships with others is important throughout life. The elderly who have close friends are more satisfied with life (Lemon, Bengston, and Peterson, 1972). Practically everyone needs a confidant, a person to confide one's private thoughts and feelings. The elderly who have a confidant are better able to handle the trials and tribulations of aging (Lowenthal and Haven, 1968). Through sharing their deepest concerns with a confidant, people are able to ventilate their feelings and also talk through their problems so that they are often better able to arrive at some strategies for handling such problems.

   Lowenthal and Haven (1968) found in a study of the elderly that those who are married are more likely than the widowed to have confidants; and that the widowed are more likely to have confidants than those who have never married. For those who are married, the spouse is apt to be the confidant, especially for the men. The wives sometimes had other confidants, such as a child, a relative, or a friend. Vinick (1978) also found that elderly women are more apt than elderly men to have close friendships with children, other relatives, and with other people.

2. *Finances.* In a study of elderly adults Markides and Martin (1979) found that health and income are the two factors most closely related to life satisfaction in later adulthood. When people feel good and have money, they can be more active. These researchers found those who are active—who go out to eat, go to meetings or museums, go to church, go on picnics or travel—are

happier than those who tend to stay at home. Saving money for later years is important and so is learning to manage or budget money wisely.

3. *Interests and hobbies.* Psychologically, people who are traumatized most by retirement are those whose self-image and life interests center around their work. People who have meaningful hobbies and interests look forward to retirement in order to have sufficient time for their hobbies and interests.

4. *Self-identity.* People who are comfortable and realistic about who they are and what they want out of life are better prepared to deal with stresses and crises that arise.

5. *Looking toward the future.* A person who dwells in the past or rests on past achievements is apt to find the older years depressing. On the other hand, a person who looks to the future generally has interests that are alive and growing and is thereby able to find new challenges and new satisfactions in later years. Looking toward the future involves planning for retirement, including deciding where you would like to live, in what type of housing and community, and what you look forward to doing with your free time.

6. *Coping with crises.* If a person learns to cope effectively with crises in younger years, these coping skills will remain when a person is older. Effective coping is learning to approach problems realistically and constructively.

Grief Management and Death Education

The remainder of this chapter will present material on reactions to death in our society, models of the grieving process, guidelines for coping with grief, social work roles in grief management, guidelines on relating to a dying person and to survivors, and suggestions for becoming comfortable with your own eventual death.

Death in Our Society: The Impact of Social Forces

People in primitive societies handle death better than we do. They are more apt to view death as a natural occurrence, partly because they have a shorter life expectancy. They also frequently see friends and relatives die. Because they view death as a natural occurrence, they are better prepared to handle the death of loved ones.

In our society we tend to shy away from thinking about death. The terminally ill generally die in institutions (hospitals and nursing homes) away from our homes. Therefore, we are seldom exposed to people dying. Many people in our society seek to avoid thinking about death. They avoid going to funerals and avoid conversations about death. Many people live as if they believe they will live indefinitely.

We need to become comfortable with the idea of our own eventual death. If we do that, we will be better prepared for the deaths of close friends and relatives. We will also then be better prepared to relate to the terminally ill and to help survivors who have experienced the death of a close friend or relative.

Funerals are needed for survivors. Funerals help initiate the grieving process so people can work through their grief. (If a close survivor delays in going through the grieving process, the eventual grief may be intensified.) Funerals also serve a function of demonstrating that the person is dead. If survivors do not see the dead body some may mystically believe that the person is still alive. For example, John F. Kennedy was assassinated in the early 1960s and had a closed casket funeral. Because the body was not shown, rumors abounded for many years that he was still alive.

The sudden death of a young person is more difficult to cope with for three reasons. First, we do not have time to prepare for the death. Second, we feel the loss as being more severe because we feel the person is missing out on many of the good things in life. Third, we do not have the opportunity to obtain "closure" to the relationship; we may feel we did not have the opportunity to tell the person how we felt about him or her, or we may feel we did not get the opportunity to resolve interpersonal conflicts. (Because the grieving process is intensified when closure does not occur, it is advisable to actively work toward closure in the relationships we have with others.)

Children should not be sheltered from death. They should be taken to funerals of relatives and friends and their questions answered honestly. It is a mistake to say, "Grandmother has gone on a trip and won't be back." The child will wonder if others who are close will also go on a trip and won't be back; or, the child may be puzzled about why grandmother won't return from the trip. It is much better to explain to children that death is a natural process. It is desirable to state that death is unlikely to occur until a person is elderly, but that there are exceptions—such as an automobile accident. Parents who take their children to funerals almost always find the children handle the funeral better than expected. Funerals help children learn that death is a natural process.

It is generally a mistake for survivors to seek to appear strong and emotionally calm following the death of a close friend or relative. Usually such survivors want to avoid dealing with their loss, and there is a danger that when they start grieving they will experience intense grief—partly because they will feel guilty about denying that they are hurting, and partly because they will feel guilty because they deemphasized (by hiding their pain and feelings) the importance of the person who died.

Many health professionals (such as medical doctors) find death difficult to handle. Health professionals are committed to healing. When someone is found to have a terminal illness, health professionals are apt to experience a sense of failure. In some cases they experience guilt because they cannot do more, or because they might have made a mistake that contributed to a terminal illness. Therefore, do not be too surprised if you find that some health professionals do not know what to say or do when confronted by terminal illness.

The Grieving Process

Nearly all of us are currently grieving about some loss that we have had. It might be the end of a romantic relationship, or moving away from friends and parents, or the death of a pet, or failing to get a grade we wanted, or the death of someone.

It is a mistake to believe that grieving over a loss should end in a set amount of time. The normal grieving process is often the life span of the griever. When we first become aware of a loss of very high value, we are apt to grieve intensively—by crying or by being depressed. Gradually we will have hours, then days, then weeks, then months where we will not think about the loss and will not grieve. However, there will always be something that reminds us of the loss (such as anniversaries), and we will again grieve. The intense grieving periods will, however, gradually become shorter in duration, occur less frequently, and gradually decrease in intensity.

Two models of the grieving process will be pre-

sented: the Kübler-Ross (1969) model and the Westberg (1962) model.

The Kübler-Ross Model

Stage One: Denial. During this stage we tell ourselves "No, this can't be. There must be a mistake. This just isn't happening." Denial is often functional as it helps cushion the impact of the loss.

Stage Two: Rage and Anger. During this stage we tell ourselves "Why me? This just isn't fair!" For example, terminally ill patients resent the fact that they will soon die while other people remain healthy and alive. During this stage God is sometimes a target of the anger. The terminally ill, for example, blame God as unfairly imposing a death sentence.

Stage Three: Bargaining. During this stage people with a loss attempt to strike bargains to regain all or part of the loss. For example, the terminally ill may bargain with God for more time. They promise to do something worthwhile or to be good in exchange for another month or year of life. Kübler-Ross indicates that even agnostics and atheists sometimes attempt to bargain with God during this stage.

Stage Four: Depression. During this stage those having a loss tell themselves, "The loss is true, and it's really sad. This is awful."

Stage Five: Acceptance. During this stage the person fully acknowledges the loss. The terminally ill tell themselves, "I will soon pass on, and it's all right." Those who are not terminally ill accept the loss and begin working on alternatives to cope with the loss and to minimize the loss.

The Westberg Model

Shock and Denial. Many people when informed of a tragic loss are so numb and in such a state of shock that they are practically devoid of feelings. It could well be that when emotional pain is unusually intense that the response system in a person experiences "overload" and temporarily "shuts down" so that the person hardly feels anything, and the person then acts as if nothing has happened. Such denial is a way of avoiding the impact of a tragic loss.

Emotions Erupt. As the realization of the loss becomes evident, the person expresses the pain by crying, screaming, or sighing.

Anger. At some point a person usually experiences anger. The anger may be directed at God for causing the loss. The anger may be partly due to the unfairness of the loss. If the loss involves the death of a loved one, there is often anger at the dead person for "desertion."

Illness. Since grief is stress producing, stress-related illnesses are apt to develop, such as colds, flu, an ulcer,

FIGURE 15.2: Westberg Model of the Grieving Process

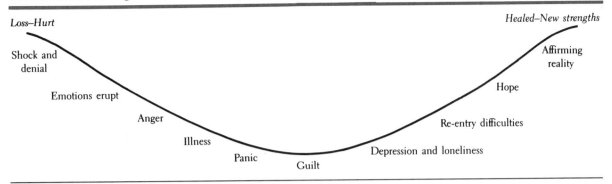

tension headaches, diarrhea, rashes, insomnia, and so on.

Panic. Because the grieving person realizes he or she does not feel like the "old self," the person may panic and worry about going insane. Nightmares, unwanted emotions that appear uncontrollable, physical reactions, and difficulties in concentrating on day-to-day responsibilities contribute to the panic.

Guilt. The grieving person may blame him- or herself for having done something that contributed to the loss or feel guilty for not doing something that might have prevented the loss.

Depression and Loneliness. At times the grieving person is apt to feel very sad about the loss and also has feelings of isolation and loneliness. The grieving person may withdraw from others, who are viewed as not being supportive or understanding.

Reentry Difficulties. At this point the grieving person makes efforts to put his or her life back together. Reentry problems are apt to arise: the person may resist letting go of attachments to the past, and loyalties to memories may hamper pursuing new interests and activities.

Hope. Gradually hope of putting one's life back together returns and begins to grow.

Affirming Reality. The grieving person puts his or her life back together again, and the old feeling of having control of one's life returns. The reconstructed life is not the same as the old, and memories of the loss remain. However, the reconstructed life is satisfactory. The grieving person resolves that life will go on.

Evaluation of Models of the Grieving Process

Kübler-Ross and Westberg note that some people remain grieving and never do reach the final stage (the acceptance stage in the Kübler-Ross model and the affirming reality stage in the Westberg model). Kübler-Ross and Westberg also caution it is a mistake to rigidly believe everyone will progress through these

stages as diagrammed. There is often considerable movement back and forth in these stages. For example, in the Kübler-Ross model a person may go from denial to depression, to anger and rage, back to denial, then to bargaining, then to depression, back to anger and rage, and so on.

How to Cope with Grief

The following suggestions are given to help those who are grieving.

- Crying is an acceptable and valuable expression of grief. Cry as you feel the need. Crying releases tension that is part of grieving.
- Talking about your loss, and about your plans, is very constructive. Sharing your grief with friends, family, the clergy, a hospice volunteer, or a professional counselor is advisable. You may seek to become involved with a group of others having similar experiences. Talking about your grief eases loneliness, allows you to ventilate your feelings. Talking with close friends gives you a sense of security and brings you closer to others you love. Talking with others who have similar losses helps put your problems into perspective. You will see you are not the only one with problems, and you will feel good about yourself when you assist others in handling their losses.
- Death often causes us to examine and question our faith or philosophy of life. Do not become concerned if you begin questioning your beliefs. Talk about them. For many, a religious faith provides help in accepting the loss.
- Writing out a rational self-analysis on your grief will help you to identify irrational thinking that is contributing to your grief (see Chapter 8). Once your irrational thinking is identified, you can relieve much of your grief through rational challenges to your irrational thinking.
- Try not to dwell on how unhappy you feel. Become

involved and active in life around you. Do not waste your time and energy on self-pity.

- Seek to accept the inevitability of death, yours and others'.
- If the loss is the death of a loved one, holidays and the anniversaries of your loved one's birth and death can be stressful. Seek to spend these days with family and friends who will give you support.
- You may feel that you have nothing to live for and may even think about suicide. Understand that many people who encounter severe losses feel this way. Seek to find assurance in the fact that a sense of purpose and meaning will return.
- Intense grief is very stressful. Stress is a factor that leads to a variety of illnesses, such as headaches, colitis, ulcers, colds, and flu. If you become ill, seek a physician's help, and tell the physician you believe your illness may be related to grief you are experiencing.
- Intense grief may also lead to sleeplessness, sexual difficulties, loss of appetite, or overeating. If a loved one has died, do not be surprised if you dream the person is still alive. You may find you have little energy and cannot concentrate. All of these reactions are "normal." Do not become worried that you are going crazy or losing your mind. Seek to take a positive view. Eat a balanced diet, get ample rest, and exercise moderately. Every person's grief is individual—if you are experiencing unusual physical reactions (such as nightmares) try not to become overly alarmed.
- Medication should be taken sparingly and only under the supervision of a physician. Avoid trying to relieve your grief with alcohol or other drugs. Many drugs are addictive and may stop or delay the necessary grieving process.
- Recognize that guilt, real or imagined, is a normal part of grief. Survivors often feel guilty about things they said or did, or feel guilty about things they think they should have said or done. If you are experiencing intense guilt, it is helpful to share it with friends or with a professional counselor. It might also be helpful to write a rational self-analysis of the guilt. Learn to forgive yourself. All humans make mistakes. If you didn't make mistakes you wouldn't be human.
- You may find that friends and relatives appear to be shunning you. If this is happening they probably are uncomfortable around you as they do not know what to say or do. Take the initiative and talk with them about your loss. Inform them about ways in which you would like them to be supportive of you.
- If possible, put off making major decisions (changing jobs, moving) until you become more emotionally relaxed. When you're highly emotional, you're more apt to make undesirable decisions.

When a person's spouse dies, he or she is apt to feel sad, lonely, and isolated. Gradually, the grieving person reaches out to others.

Application of Grief Management Theory to Client Situations

Most people are grieving about one or more losses—the end of a romantic relationship, the death of a pet, or the death of a loved one. Social workers may take on a variety of roles in the areas of grief management and death education: They can be initiators of and then educators in educational programs in schools, churches, and elsewhere for the general public. They can be counselors in a variety of settings (including hospices, nursing homes, and hospitals) in which they work on a one-to-one basis with the terminally ill and with survivors. They can be group facilitators and lead grief management groups (including bereavement groups for survivors of the death of a loved one) in settings such as hospitals, hospices, mental health clinics, and schools. They may also serve as brokers in linking individuals who are grieving or who have unrealistic views about death and dying with appropriate community resources.

In order for social workers to be effective in these roles they need to become comfortable with their own eventual death. They also need to develop skills for relating to the terminally ill and to survivors. The following summarizes some guidelines in these areas. The material is useful not only for social workers but also for anyone (including yourself) who must have contact with a dying person or with survivors.

How to Relate to a Dying Person

First, you need to accept the idea of your own eventual death and view death as a normal process. If you cannot accept your own death, you will probably be uncomfortable talking to someone who is terminally ill and will not be able to discuss the concerns that the dying person has in an understanding and positive way.

Second, convey verbally and with body language that you are willing to talk about any concerns that the other person has. Touching or hugging the dying person is very helpful. Remember the person has a right not to talk about concerns if he or she chooses. What you want to convey is that you are emotionally ready and supportive, that you care, and that you are available.

Third, answer questions as honestly as you can. If you do not know an answer, seek out a person who will accurately provide the requested information. Evasion or ambiguity in response to a dying person's questions only increases his or her concerns. If there is a chance for recovery, this should be mentioned. Even a small margin of hope can be a comfort. The chances for recovery, however, should not be exaggerated.

Fourth, a dying person should be allowed to accept the reality of the situation at his or her own pace. Relevant information should not be volunteered nor should it be withheld. People who have a terminal illness have a right to have access to all the relevant information. A useful question that may assist a dying person is, "Do you want to talk about it?"

Fifth, if people around the dying person are able to accept the death, the dying person is helped to accept the death. Therefore, it is therapeutic to help close family members and friends of the dying person to accept the death. Remember, they may have a number of concerns that they want to share, and they may need help to do this.

Sixth, if you do have trouble about certain subjects involving death, inform the dying person of your limitations. This takes the guesswork out of the relationship.

Seventh, the religious or philosophical viewpoint of the dying person should be respected. Your own personal views should not be pressed.

How to Relate to Survivors

These suggestions are similar to the suggestions on relating to a dying person. It is very helpful to become accepting of your own death. If you are comfortable about your own death, you will be better able to calmly listen to the concerns being expressed by survivors.

It is helpful to initiate the first encounter with a survivor by saying something like "I'm sorry," and then touching or hugging the person. Then convey that if he or she wants to talk or needs help, you're available. Take your lead from what the survivor expresses. You should seek to convey that you care, that you share his or her loss, and that you're available if he or she wants to talk.

It is helpful to use active listening with both survivors and persons who are terminally ill. In using active listening, the receiver of a message feeds back only what he or she feels was the intent of the sender's message. In using this approach, the receiver does *not* send a message of his or her own—such as a question, giving advice, personal feelings, or an opinion (Gordon, 1970).

It is frequently helpful to share with a survivor pleasant and positive memories you have about the person who has died. This conveys that you sincerely care about and miss the deceased person and also that the deceased person's life had positive meaning. Relating your memories will often focus the survivor's thoughts on pleasant and positive memories of his or her own.

Continue to visit the survivors if they show interest in such visits. It is also helpful to express your caring and support through a card, a little gift, or a favorite casserole. If a survivor is unable to resume the normal functions of living, or remains deeply depressed, it is advisable to suggest seeking professional help. Joining a survivor's self-help group is another possible suggestion.

The religious or philosophical viewpoint of survivors should be respected. You should not seek to press your views on the survivors.

Questions about Grief, Death, and Dying

Arriving at answers to these questions is one way to work toward becoming more comfortable with your own eventual death.

1. Which of the following describe your present conception of death:
   a. Cessation of all mental and physical activity
   b. Death as sleep
   c. Heaven-and-hell concept
   d. A pleasant after-life
   e. Death as being mysterious and unknown
   f. The end of all life for you
   g. A transition to a new beginning
   h. A joining of the spirit with an unknown cosmic force
   i. Termination of this physical life with survival of the spirit
   j. Something other than this list
2. Which of the following aspects of your own death do you find distasteful:
   a. What might happen to your body after death
   b. What might happen to you if there is a life after death
   c. Concerns about what might happen to your dependents
   d. The grief that it would cause to your friends and relatives
   e. The pain you may experience as you die
   f. The deterioration of your body before you die
   g. All your plans and projects coming to an end
   h. Something other than this list

3. If you could choose, what age would you like to be when you die?
4. When you think of your own eventual death, how do you feel?
   a. Depressed
   b. Fearful
   c. Discouraged
   d. Purposeless
   e. Angry
   f. Pleasure in being alive
   g. Resolved as you realize death is a natural process of living
   h. Other (specify)
5. For what or for whom would you be willing to sacrifice your life?
   a. An idea or moral principle
   b. A loved one
   c. In combat
   d. An emergency where another life could be saved
   e. Not for any reason
6. If you could choose, how would you prefer to die?
   a. A sudden violent death
   b. A sudden but nonviolent death
   c. A quiet and dignified death
   d. Death in the line of duty
   e. Suicide

How to Become Comfortable with Your Own Eventual Death

Perhaps the main reason people are uncomfortable about death is that in our culture we are socialized to avoid seeing death as a natural process. We would be more comfortable with our own death if we would more openly talk about it and actively seek answers to questions and concerns that we have. Comfort with our own death helps us to relate to and understand those who are dying in a more supportive manner. If you are uncomfortable about death, including your own eventual death, there are a number of sugges-tions for things you can do to become more comfort-able.

Identify what your concerns are and then seek answers to these concerns. A number of excellent books provide information on a wide range of subjects involving death and dying. Many colleges, universi-ties, and organizations provide workshops and courses on death and dying. If you have intense fears related to death and dying, you may consider talking to au-thorities in the field, such as professional counselors, or to clergy with experience and training in grief counseling.

Taboos against talking about death and dying need

---

    f. Homicide victim

    g. Death after you have achieved your life goals

    h. Other (specify)

7. If it were possible, would you want to know the exact date on which you would die?

8. Would you want to know if you had a terminal illness?

9. If you had six more months to live, how would you want to spend this time?

    a. By satisfying hedonistic desires such as sex

    b. By withdrawing

    c. By contemplating or praying

    d. By seeking to prepare loved ones for your death

    e. By completing projects and tying up loose ends

    f. By considering suicide

    g. Other (specify)

10. Have you seriously contemplated suicide? What are your moral views of suicide? Are there circumstances under which you would take your life?

11. If you had a serious illness and the quality of your life had substantially deteriorated, what measures do you believe should be taken to keep you alive?

    a. All possible heroic medical efforts

    b. Medical efforts being discontinued when there is practically no hope of returning to a life with quality

    c. Other (specify)

12. If you are married, would you prefer to outlive your spouse? Why?

13. How important do you believe funerals and grief rituals are for survivors?

14. If it were up to you, how would you like to have your body disposed of after you die?

    a. Cremation

    b. Burial

    c. Donation of parts of your body for organ transplants

    d. Donation of your body to medical school or to science

    e. Other (specify)

15. What kind of funeral would you prefer?

    a. A church service

    b. As large as possible

    c. Small with only close friends and relatives present

    d. A lavish funeral

    e. A simple funeral

    f. Whatever your survivors want

    g. Other (specify)

16. Have you made a will? Why or why not?

17. Were you able to arrive at answers to most of these questions? Were you uncomfortable in answering these questions? If you were uncomfortable, what were you feeling, and what made you uncomfortable? For the questions you do not have answers to, how might you arrive at answers?

to be broken in our society. You may find that tactfully initiating discussions about death and dying with friends and relatives will be helpful to you, and to people close to you.

It is probably accurate that we will never become fully accepting of our own death, but we can learn a lot more about the subject and obtain answers to many of the questions and concerns we have. In talking about death it is advisable to avoid using euphemisms such as "passed on," "gone to heaven," and "taken by the Lord." It is much better to be accurate and say the person has died. Using euphemisms gives an unrealistic impression of death and is part of the avoidance approach to facing death. Fortunately, an open communications approach about death is emerging in our society.

Additional ways to become more informed about death and dying are attending funerals, watching

Life after Life

Raymond Moody (1975) interviewed a number of people who had near-death experiences. These people had been pronounced clinically dead, but then shortly afterward were revived. Moody provides the following composite summary of typical experiences that are being reported. (It is important to bear in mind that the following narrative is not a representation of any one person's experience, rather it is a composite of the common elements found in many accounts.)

A man is dying and, as he reaches the point of greatest physical stress, he hears himself pronounced dead by his doctor. He begins to hear an uncomfortable noise, a loud ringing or buzzing, and at the same time feels himself moving very rapidly through a long dark tunnel. After this, he suddenly finds himself outside of his own physical body, but still in the immediate physical environment, and he sees his own body from a distance, as though he is a spectator. He watches the resuscitation attempt from this unusual vantage point and is in a state of emotional upheaval.

After a while, he collects himself and becomes more accustomed to his odd condition. He notices that he still has a "body," but one of a very different nature and with very different powers from the physical body he has left behind. Soon other things begin to happen. Others come to meet and to help him. He glimpses the spirits of relatives and friends who have already died, and a loving, warm spirit of a kind he has never encountered before—being of light—appears before him. This being asks him a question, nonverbally, to make him evaluate his life and helps him along by showing him a panoramic, instantaneous playback of the major events of his life. At some point he finds himself approaching some sort of barrier or border, apparently representing the limit between earthly life and the next life. Yet, he finds that he must go back to the earth, that the time for his death has not yet come. At this point he resists, for by now he is taken up with his experiences in the afterlife and does not want to return. He is overwhelmed by his intense feelings of joy, love, and peace. Despite his attitude, though, he somehow reunites with his physical body and lives.

Later he tries to tell others, but he has trouble doing so. In the first place, he can find no human words adequate to describe these unearthly episodes. He also finds that others scoff, so he stops telling other people. Still, the experience affects his life profoundly, especially his views about death and its relationship to life.

No one is sure why such experiences are being reported. A variety of explanations have been suggested (Siegel, 1981). One is that it suggests there may be a pleasant afterlife. This explanation gives comfort to those who dislike seeing death as an absolute end. Another explanation, however, is that these near-death experiences are nothing more than hallucinations triggered by chemicals released by the brain or induced by lack of oxygen to the brain. Scientists involved with near-death research acknowledge that so far there is no conclusive evidence that these near-death experiences prove there is life after death.

SOURCE: Raymond A. Moody, Jr., *Life after Life* (New York: Bantam Books, 1975), pp. 21–23. Reprinted by permission of the copyright owner, Mockingbird Books, St. Simons Island, GA.

quality films and TV programs that cover aspects of dying, providing support to friends or relatives who are terminally ill, being supportive to survivors, talking to people who do grief counseling to learn about their approach, keeping a journal of your thoughts and concerns related to death and dying, and planning the details of your funeral. The questions in "Questions about Grief, Death, and Dying" will help you to assess your attitudes toward these realities.

Mwalimu Imara (1975) views dying as having a potential for being the final stage of growth. Learning to accept death is similar to learning to accept other losses such as the breakup of a romantic relationship or leaving a job we cherished. If we learn to accept and grow from the losses we encounter, such experiences will help us in facing the deaths of loved ones and our own eventual death.

Having a well-developed sense of identity (that is, who we are and what we want out of life) is an important step in learning to become comfortable with our own eventual death. If we have a well-developed blueprint of what will give meaning and direction to our lives, we are emotionally better prepared to accept the fact that we will eventually die.

Summary

A number of psychological developmental adjustments must be made by the elderly, such as adjusting to retirement and lower income and to changing physical strength and health. Theoretical concepts about developmental tasks in later adulthood include: integrity versus despair; shifting from work-role preoccupation to self-differentiation; shifting from body preoccupation to body transcendence; shifting from self-preoccupation to self-transcendence; conducting a life review; the importance of self-esteem; and the negative effects of low status and ageism.

Three theories of successful aging are the activity theory, the disengagement theory, and the social reconstruction syndrome theory. Suggestions for positive psychological preparation by younger adults for later adulthood include: forming close personal relationships, preparing financially, having interests and hobbies, forming a positive self-identity, looking toward the future, learning to cope with crises, and learning to cope with death. The chapter ends with guidelines on grief management and death education, relating to a dying person, relating to survivors, and becoming more comfortable with the idea of one's own eventual death.

16

Social Systems and Their Impacts on Later Adulthood

When does the "loving" stop?

On July 14, 1985, David Pearsall had his seventieth birthday, and it was a day to remember. It was not only his birthday but also his last day of work at the company he worked for, Quality Printers. That evening, the owners of Quality Printers gave a retirement party for Dave. He received a gold watch, and the owners and many of his fellow printers gave testimonial speeches about how much Dave had contributed to the morale and productivity of the company. Dave was deeply honored, and tears occasionally came to his eyes.

Dave felt strange waking up the next morning. He was used to getting up early to go to work. Work had become the center of his life. He even socialized with his fellow printers. This morning he had nothing planned and nothing to do. He lay in bed thinking about what the future would hold for him. Dave had generally muddled through life. His father had helped him obtain a position as a printer, and Dave seldom gave much attention to planning for the future. For example, while he thought it would be nice to retire, he had given little consideration to it.

Dave got up, looked in a mirror, and noticed his thinning, gray hair, the wrinkles on his face and hands, and the tire around his waist. In concluding that the best part of his life had passed by, he anxiously wondered what the future would hold for him, and he contemplated what he should do with all of his time—he had no idea.

For the next few weeks, he followed his wife, Jeanette, around the house. David began giving Jeanette suggestions on how she could be more efficient and productive around the house. After a few weeks of such advice, Jeanette angrily told David to "get off her back." He visited the print shop where he used to work but soon realized everyone was too busy to spend time talking with him. He also stopped socializing with these printers, since they tended to talk about work. He felt useless. As the months went by, he spent most of his time sitting at home and watching TV. Occasionally, he went to a neighborhood bar, where he drank to excess.

David and his wife never gave much attention to long-range financial planning. They both had worked for many years and tended to spend their paychecks shortly after they received them. When they bought their house five years ago, they gave little thought to how they would make their mortgage payments after retiring. David had hoped the Social Security system would take care of his bills.

David and Jeanette were in for a shock when they retired. The monthly Social Security checks were much less than they had anticipated. They stopped going out to eat, to movies, and to ballgames. A few months after David retired, they realized they no longer could make the mortgage payments. They put the house up for sale and sold it four-and-a-half months later, at a price lower than what the house was worth. Both were sad about leaving their home, but financially they had no other choice. They moved into a two bedroom apartment. Both became even more inactive, as they no longer had yard work and now had fewer home maintenance tasks. One neighbor frequently played a stereo late into the night, and the Pearsalls had trouble sleeping.

In February 1987, Jeanette had a major heart attack. She was in the hospital for nearly two weeks and was then placed in a nursing home. David became deeply depressed and missed the companionship of his wife. He wished she could come home, but her medical needs wouldn't allow that, so he visited her every day. Since David had never learned to cook much, and because he was depressed, his diet consisted mainly of cheese sandwiches and TV dinners. In November 1987, Jeanette died of another heart attack.

David became even more distressed and depressed. He no longer shaved or bathed. He no longer cleaned his apartment, and neighbors began to complain about the odors. David gave up the will to live. He seldom heard from his son, Donald, who was living in a distant city. David sought to drown his unhappiness in whiskey. One night, in January 1989, he passed out in his apartment with a lighted cigarette in his hand, which set his couch on fire. David died of smoke inhalation.

David's later years raise some questions for our society. Have we abandoned the elderly to a meaningless existence? Is it a mistake for the elderly to count on the Social Security system to meet their financial needs when they retire? How can our society provide a more meaningful role for the elderly?

A PERSPECTIVE

This chapter will focus on the social problems encountered by the elderly. The plight of the elderly has now become recognized as a major problem in the United States. The elderly face a number of personal problems: high rates of physical illness and emotional difficulties, poverty, malnutrition, lack of access to transportation, low status, lack of a meaningful role in our society, and inadequate housing. To a large extent, the elderly are a recently discovered minority group. Similar to other minority groups, the elderly are victims of job discrimination and are subjected to prejudice that is based on erroneous stereotypes.

This chapter will:

- Summarize the specific problems faced by the elderly and the causes of these problems.
- Describe the current services to meet these problems and identify gaps in these services.
- Discuss the emergence of the elderly as a significant political force in our society.
- Present a proposal to provide the elderly with a meaningful, productive, social role in our society.

The Elderly: A Population-at-Risk

Human societies have different customs for dealing with the incapacitated elderly. Some societies abandoned their enfeebled old. The Crow, Creek, and Hopi tribes, for example, built special huts away from the tribe where the old were left to die. The Eskimos left the incapacitated elderly in snowbanks or they went off in a kayak. The Siriono of the Bolivian forest simply left them behind when they moved on in search of food (Moss and Moss, 1975, p. 18). Even today, the Ik of Uganda leave the elderly and disabled to starve to death (Kornblum and Julian, 1989, pp. 320-324). Generally, the primary reason such societies have been forced to abandon the elderly is scarce resources.

Although we might consider such customs to be barbaric and shocking, have we not also abandoned the elderly? We force them to retire when many are still productive. All too often, when a person is forced to retire, his or her status, power, and self-esteem are lost. Also, in a physical sense, we seldom have a place for large numbers of older people. Community facilities—parks, subways, libraries—are oriented to serving children and young people. Most housing is designed and priced for the young couple with one or two children and an annual income of over $25,000. If the elderly are not able to care for themselves (and if their families are unable or unwilling to care for them), we store them away from society in nursing homes. Our abandonment of the elderly is further indicated by our taking little action to relieve the financial problems of the elderly—nearly a quarter of the elderly have incomes close to or below the poverty line (U.S. Bureau of the Census, 1992). (In one sense, our abandonment of the elderly is more barbaric than that of tribal societies who are forced by survival pressures to abandon the elderly.) Our treatment of the elderly has only recently come to be viewed as a major social problem.

The elderly are subjected to various forms of discrimination—for example, job discrimination. Older workers are erroneously believed to be less productive. Unemployed workers in their fifties and sixties have greater difficulty finding new jobs and remain unemployed much longer than younger unemployed workers. The elderly are given no meaningful role in our society. Our society is youth-oriented and deplores growing old. Our society glorifies physical attractiveness and, thereby, shortchanges the elderly. The elderly are viewed as out of touch with what's happening, and their knowledge is seldom valued or sought. Intellectual ability is sometimes thought to decline with age, even though research shows intellectual capacity, barring organic problems, remains essentially unchanged until very late in life (Papalia and Olds, 1992, pp. 486-91).

The elderly are erroneously thought to be senile, resistant to change, inflexible, incompetent workers, and a burden on the young. Given opportunities, elderly individuals usually prove such prejudicial concepts to be wrong. They generally react to prejudice against them in the same way that racial and ethnic minorities react—by displaying self-hatred and by being self-conscious, sensitive, and defensive about their social and cultural status (Barron, 1971). As we have mentioned previously, individuals who frequently receive negative responses from others eventually tend to come to view themselves negatively.

Problems Faced by the Elderly

The social problems of the elderly are considered to be problems for two reasons. Some of the problems are conditions that the elderly encounter, such as poverty, malnutrition, poor health, and lack of transportation. Other problems are difficulties incurred by society in caring for the elderly, such as increased taxes for medical care. A point to remember is that, unlike other minorities, the problems of the elderly are problems that we all encounter eventually (assuming we do not die prematurely). By the time most of today's college students reach middle age (presumably their peak earning years), a larger proportion of the adult population will be retired, because the elderly have the highest rate of population growth in our society. Those who are retired depend heavily on Social Security, Medicare, and other government programs to assist in meeting their financial and medical needs. If we do not face and solve the problems of the elderly now, we will be in dire straits in the future.

Emphasis on Youth: The Impacts of Social and Economic Forces

Our society fears aging more than most other societies do. Our emphasis on youth is illustrated by our dread of getting gray hair and wrinkles or becoming bald and by our being pleased when someone guesses our age to be younger than it actually is.

Our society places a high value on youthful energy and action. We like to think we are doers. But why is there such an emphasis on youth in our society? Industrialization resulted in a demand for laborers who are energetic, agile, and strong. Rapid advances in technology and science have made obsolete past knowledge and certain specialized work skills. Pioneer living and the gradual expansion of our nation to the west required brute strength, energy, and stamina. Competition has always been emphasized and has been reinforced by a social interpretation of Darwin's theory of evolution, which highlighted survival of the fittest, though Darwin meant those that "fit" their environment, not those that were young and healthy. The cultural tradition of overvaluing youth in our society has resulted in a devaluation of the elderly.

The Increasing Elderly Population

There are now about ten times as many people age sixty-five and older than there were at the turn of the century. Table 16.1 shows that the percentage of older people has steadily been increasing.

Several reasons can be given for the phenomenal growth of the older population. The improved care of expectant mothers and newborn infants has reduced the infant mortality rate. New drugs, better sanitation, and other medical advances have increased the life expectancy of Americans from forty-nine years in 1900 to seventy-five years in 1990 (U.S. Bureau of Census, 1992).

Another reason for the increasing proportion of the elderly is that the birthrate is declining—fewer babies are being born, while more adults are reaching later adulthood. After World War II, a baby boom lasted from 1947 to 1960. Children born during these years flooded schools in the 1950s and 1960s. Then they moved into the labor market. At the turn of the century, this generation will reach retirement. After 1960, there was a baby bust, a sharp decline in birthrates. The average number of children per woman went down from a high of 3.8 in 1957 to a low of 1.7 in 1976 (U.S. Bureau of the Census, 1992).

The increased life expectancy along with the baby boom followed by the baby bust will significantly increase the median age of Americans in future years. The median age is increasing dramatically. The long-term implications are that the United States will undergo a number of cultural, social, and economic changes.

The Fastest Growing Age Group Is the Old-Old

As our society is having more success in treating and preventing heart disease, cancer, strokes, and other killers, more and more elderly are living into their eighties and beyond. People age seventy-five and over constitute the fastest growing age group in the United States.

Table 16.1: Composition of U.S. Population Age Sixty-Five and Older

			Year		
	1900	1950	1970	1980	1990
Number of older persons (in millions)	3	12	20	25	31
Percent of total population	4	8	9.5	11	12

SOURCE: U.S. Bureau of the Census, *Statistical Abstract of the United States*, 1992, (Washington, DC: U.S. Government Printing Office, 1992), p. 14.

In 1960, only 5.6 million Americans were age seventy-five or older. In 1990, there were 13.1 million Americans age seventy-five years or older—an increase of 235 percent, while the overall population increased only 140 percent (U.S. Bureau of the Census, 1992, p. 14).

Those who are seventy-five and over will create a number of problems and difficult decisions for our society. Otten (1984, p. 1) notes:

> It is these "oldest old"—often mentally or physically impaired, alone, depressed—who pose the major problems for the coming decades. It is they who will strain their families with demands for personal care and financial support. It is they who will need more of such community help as Meals on Wheels, homemaker services, special housing. It is they who will require the extra hospital and nursing-home beds that will further burden federal and state budgets.
>
> And it is they whose mounting needs and numbers already spark talk of some sort of rationing of health care. "Can we afford the very old?" is becoming a favorite conference topic for doctors, bioethicists and other specialists.

Many of the old-old suffer from a multiplicity of chronic illnesses. Common medical problems of the old-old include arthritis, heart conditions, hypertension, osteoporosis (brittleness of the bones), Alzheimer's disease, incontinency, hearing and vision problems, and depression.

The older an elderly person becomes, the higher the probability that the person will become a resident of a nursing home. Although only about 5 percent of the elderly are currently in a nursing home, nearly one out of three of those age eighty-five and over are placed in a nursing home at some point (Bould, Sanborn, and Reif, 1989, p. 13). The cost to society for such care is high—over $22,000 a year per person to provide nursing home care (Bould, et al., 1989). Despite the widespread image of families dumping aged parents into nursing homes, most frail elderly are still outside institutional walls, being cared for by a spouse, a child, or a relative. Some middle-aged people are now simultaneously encountering demands to put children through college and to support an aging parent in a nursing home.

The number of years spent in retirement is considerable. To maintain the same standard of living after retiring requires immense assets. Rising health care costs and superlongevity have ignited controversy over whether to ration health care to the very old. For example, should people over age seventy-five be prohibited from receiving liver transplants or kidney dialysis? Discussion of euthanasia (the practice of killing individuals who are hopelessly sick or injured) has also been increasing. In 1984 Governor Richard Lamm of Colorado created a controversy when he asserted the terminally ill have a duty to die. Dr. Eisdor Fer (quoted in Otten, 1984, p. 10) stated:

> The problem is age-old and across cultures. Whenever society has had marginal economic resources, the oldest went first, and the old people bought that approach. The old Eskimo wasn't put on the ice floe; he just left of his own accord and never came back.

Early Retirement: The Impacts of Social and Economic Forces

The maintenance of a higher rate of employment in our society is a major goal. One instrument that our society used in the past to keep the work force reduced to a level in line with demand was mandatory retirement at a certain age, such as sixty-five or seventy. In 1986, Congress (recognizing that mandatory retirement was overtly discriminatory against the elderly) outlawed most mandatory retirement policies. In many occupations, the supply of labor is exceeding the demand. An often-used remedy for the oversupply of available employees is the encouragement of ever earlier retirement. Forced retirements often create

financial and psychological burdens that retirees usually face without much assistance or preparation.

Many workers who retire early supplement their pension by obtaining another job, usually of a lower status. Nearly 90 percent of Americans sixty-five and older are retired, even though many are intellectually and physically capable of working (American Association of Retired persons, 1990).

Our Social Security program supports early retirement at the age of sixty-two. Pension plans of some companies and craft unions make it financially attractive to retire as early as fifty-five. Perhaps the extreme case is the armed forces, which permit retirement on full benefits after twenty years of service or as early as age thirty-eight.

While early retirement has some advantages to society, such as reducing the labor supply and allowing younger employees to advance faster, there are also some disadvantages. For society, the total bill for retirement pensions is already huge and still growing. For the retiree, it means facing a new life and status without much preparation or assistance. While our society has developed educational and other institutions to prepare the young for the work world, it has developed few comparable institutions to prepare the elderly for retirement.

In our society, we still view people's worth partly in terms of their work. People often develop their self-image in terms of their occupation. Because the later years generally provide no exciting new roles to replace the occupational roles lost on retirement, retirees cannot proudly say, "I am a . . ." Instead, they must say, "I *was* a . . ." The more a person's life revolves around work, the more difficult retirement is apt to be.

Retirement often removes people from the mainstream of life. It diminishes their social contacts and their status and places them in a *roleless role*. People who were once valued as salespeople, teachers, accountants, barbers, or secretaries are now considered noncontributors in a roleless role on the fringe of society.

There are several myths about the older worker that have been widely believed by employers and the general public. Older workers are thought to be less healthy, clumsier, more prone to absenteeism, more accident-prone, more forgetful, and slower in task performance (Atchley, 1988). Research has shown

Retirees who have enjoyed affluence, travel, and education are more likely to enjoy retirement.

these beliefs to be erroneous. Older workers have lower turnover rates, produce at a steadier rate, make fewer mistakes, have lower absenteeism rates, have a more positive attitude toward their work, and exceed younger employees in health and low on-the-job injury rates. However, when older workers do become ill, they usually take a somewhat longer time to recover (Atchley, 1988).

A key question regarding early retirement is the age at which people want to retire. Gerontologists have studied this question. Younger workers generally state they prefer to retire before age sixty-five. Older workers indicate they desire to retire later than the conventional age of sixty-five (Ekerdt et al., 1980). The explanation for this difference appears to be partly economic. Since Social Security benefits and pension plans are usually insufficient to provide the same standard of living as when a person was working, the elderly see an economic need to continue working beyond age sixty-five. An additional explanation is sociopsychological. With retirement often being a roleless role in our society, older workers may gradually identify more and more with their work and prefer it over retirement.

Adjustment to retirement varies for different people. One study found that at least one-third of retired people have adjustment problems (Atchley, 1978). The two most common problems were adjusting to a reduced income and missing their former jobs. Those who had the most difficulty in adjusting tended to be rigid or overly identified with their work by viewing their job as their primary source of satisfaction and self-image. Those who were happiest were able to replace job prestige and financial status with values stressing self-development, personal relationships, and leisure activities.

The golden age of leisure following retirement appears to be largely a myth. Lawton (1978) found that life in retirement is apt to be sedentary, with TV-viewing and sleep outranking such traditional leisure time activities as gardening, sports, clubs, and other pastimes. Julian and Kornblum (1986, pp. 313–14) attribute such leisure activities to the past experiences of today's elderly:

This elderly age cohort was born in an era when the average work week was fifty hours long. Their own working lives began in the period of the forty-eight-hour work week, when vacations were rare and holidays were few. Homemakers cared for larger houses and larger families, and they had few labor-saving devices or products. These people had little opportunity to develop an understanding or appreciation of leisure. Moreover, many elderly people are poorly educated—a factor that makes them less likely to enjoy reading or activities that focus on new knowledge or self-improvement. The gross reduction in income, fear of crime, lack of transportation, and reduced mobility also contribute to the sedentary life of the old.

Future generations of retirees will probably be different. Those who have enjoyed affluence, travel and education are more likely to enjoy retirement. This trend is already surfacing in the form of retirement communities that offer golf, swimming, and recreational centers.

Financial Problems of the Elderly

Many of the elderly live in poverty. A fair number lack adequate food, essential clothes and drugs, and perhaps a telephone in the house to make emergency calls. One-fifth of the elderly have incomes close to or below the poverty line (American Association of Retired Persons, 1990). Only a small minority of the elderly have substantial savings or investments.

Gordon and Walter Moss (1975, pp. 17–18) describe the plight of someone who is old and poor:

An old woman turned quickly away from the dismal scene outside her Florida hotel room window. Listlessly, she mixed her own breakfast: a cup of Sanka and a small glass of Tang. After finishing her breakfast, she looked at her wardrobe. It contained a few unwanted dresses given to her by a relative and one she had bought herself seven years ago. After choosing one, she made her bed and dusted her dresser, two small tables, and their lamps. She then turned on a small fan in anticipation of a hot, muggy day, wound her clock, straightened her small pile of old books, blew dust from the artificial flowers in a cheap vase, and sat down in her only chair to watch television. Finally, it was noon, time for her to go down to the church for a hot lunch. In the afternoon, she would watch television soap operas or perhaps spend an hour or two visiting with the many other widows in the hotel.

All the while, uncertainty gnawed at her. Already, she was paying over half of her small retirement and welfare income for rent; and if the rent went up any-

more, she would be unable to stay. The hot lunch, sponsored by the federal government, cost her only 50 cents and helped a little. Nevertheless, due especially to medical bills, she frequently ran out of money before the end of the month.

Her ulcer was her biggest worry. A few weeks earlier, it had started to bleed, and she had passed out. She had lain helpless for some time before finally managing to crawl to the phone. The desk clerk and some friends had then helped her get to the hospital. She had been more fortunate than some others in the hotel. Their lives had ended in their rooms, because they had been too weak from malnutrition to crawl for help.

The financial problems of the elderly are compounded by additional factors. One factor is the high cost of health care, as previously discussed. A second factor is inflation. Inflation is especially devastating to those on fixed incomes. Most private pension benefits to do not increase in size after a worker retires. For example, if living costs rise annually at 7 percent, after twenty years a person on a fixed pension would be able to buy only one-fourth as many goods and services as he or she could at retirement (*U.S. News & World Report*, Feb. 26, 1979, p. 57). Fortunately, in 1974, Congress enacted an automatic escalator clause in Social Security benefits, providing a 3 percent increase in payments when the Consumer Price Index increased a like amount. However, Social Security benefits were never intended to make a person financially independent—it is nearly impossible to live comfortably on monthly Social Security checks.

The most important source of income for the elderly is Social Security benefits, primarily the Old-Age Survivors, Disability, and Health Insurance Program (OASDHI). This program is described later in this chapter. In 1988, the major source of income for older couples and individuals was Social Security (39 percent) followed by asset income (25 percent), earnings (17 percent), public and private pensions (17 percent), and all other sources 2 percent (American Association of Retired Persons, 1990).

The importance of financial security for the elderly is emphasized by Sullivan and associates (1980, pp. 357-58):

Financial security affects one's entire life-style. It determines one's diet, ability to seek good health care, to visit relatives and friends, to maintain a suitable wardrobe, and to find or maintain adequate housing. One's financial resources, or lack of them, play a great part in finding recreation (going to movies, plays, playing bridge or bingo, etc.) and maintaining morale, feelings of independence, and a sense of self-esteem. In other words, if an older person has the financial resources to remain socially independent (having her own household and access to transportation and medical services), to continue contact with friends and relatives, and to maintain her preferred forms of recreation, she is going to feel a great deal better about herself and others than if she is deprived of her former style of life.

The Social Security System

The Social Security system was not designed to be the main source of income for the elderly. It was originally intended as a form of insurance that would *supplement* other assets when retirement, disability, or death of a wage-earning spouse occurred. Yet, many of the elderly do not have investments, pensions, or savings to support them in retirement, and therefore Social Security has become the major source of income for the elderly.

The Social Security system was instituted in the United States in 1935. Money is paid into the system from Social Security taxes on employers and employees. In 1935, life expectancy was only somewhat over sixty years of age. Life expectancy, however, has increased to 76 in 1990 (U.S. Bureau of the Census, 1991). Social Security taxes have sharply increased in recent years, but the old-old are the fastest growing age group and the proportion of the elderly is increasing in our society. One projection has the fund being depleted in 2048 (Saltzman and Wiener, 1988, p. 67).

The *dependency ratio* is the ratio between the number of working people and the number of nonworking people in the population. As the proportion of elderly people increases, the nonworkers will represent a greater and greater burden on the workers. Authorities predict that by the year 2020 the dependency ratio will decline from the current level of about three workers for every nonworking person to a ratio of about two to one (Kornblum and Julian, 1989, pp. 320-44).

Some problems now exist with the system. First,

Maximum Social Security Tax Paid by Employees Has Risen Dramatically

Year	Maximum Tax
1971	$ 405.60
1976	895.05
1981	1,975.05
1986	3,003.00
1987	3,131.70
1988	3,379.50
1989	3,604.80
1990	3,924.45
1991	5,123.30
1992	5,326.00
1993	5,528.70

The maximum Social Security Tax—also called FICA (Federal Insurance Contributions Act)—is calculated by a "tax rate," which has gradually been increasing over the years and by "maximum taxable earnings," which has also increased over time. In 1993, the tax rate was 7.65% on the first $57,000 of an employee's pay, plus 1.45 percent of pay between $57,600 and $135,000.

SOURCE: Social Security Administration, Department of Health and Human Services.

---

the benefits are too small to provide the major source of income for the elderly. Even with payments from Social Security included, an estimated 80 percent of retirees are now living on less than half of their preretirement annual income. And the monthly payments from Social Security are generally below the poverty line (Kornblum and Julian, 1989, pp. 320-44). Second, it is unlikely that the monthly benefits will be raised much. Our society faces some hard choices about keeping the Social Security system solvent in future years. Benefits might be lowered, but this would further impoverish the recipients. Social Security taxes might be raised, but there is little public support for this. Social Security taxes are already increasing dramatically.

The future of the Social Security system is unclear. The system is likely to continue to exist, but reduced

Ethical Issue: Should Assisted Suicide Be Legalized?

The technology of life-support equipment can keep people alive almost indefinitely. Courts and state legislatures are presently working through the legal complexities governing death and euthanasia. The technology of respirators, artificial nutrition, intravenous hydration, and so-called miracle drugs not only sustain life but also trap many of the terminally ill into surviving in a degrading mental and physical condition. Such technology has raised a variety of ethical questions. Do people who are terminally ill and in severe pain have a right to die by refusing treatment? Increasingly, through "living wills," patients are able to express their wishes and refuse treatment. However, does someone in a long-term coma who has not signed a "living will" have a right to die? How should our society decide when to continue and when to stop life-support efforts?

Should assisted death, or assisted suicide, be legalized? As of 1992, only The Netherlands permitted physicians to give qualifying terminally ill patients a lethal dose of drugs. There is considerable controversy about assisted suicide in the United States. Hemlock Society founder Derek Humphry has written a do-it-yourself suicide manual that has become a best seller. (The Hemlock Society promotes active voluntary euthanasia.) Michigan Dr. Jack Kevorkian has made national news by building a machine to help terminally ill people end their lives and by assisting several of them to do so.

Those in favor of assisted suicide argue that unnecessary, long-term suffering is without merit and should not have to be endured. They argue that people have a right to a death with dignity, which involves a death without excessive emotional and physical pain and without excessive mental, physical, and spiritual degradation. They argue that assisted suicide affirms the principle of autonomy—upholding the individual's right to make decisions about his or her dying process. Allowing the option of suicide for the terminally ill is said to be the ultimate right of self-determination.

Those opposed to assisted suicide assert that suicide is unethical and is a mortal sin for which the deceased cannot receive forgiveness. They assert that modern health care can provide almost everyone a peaceful, pain-free, comfortable, and dignified end to life. They argue that most terminally ill persons consider suicide not because they fear death but because they fear dying—pain, abandonment, and loss of control—all of which the hospice is designed to alleviate. They assert that the horror stories of intense suffering are most often the tragic results of medical mismanagement. The opposition also claims that assisted suicide legislation could easily result in the philosophy that the terminally ill

---

benefits are possible. Young people are well-advised to plan for retirement through savings and investments that are independent of the Social Security system and will supplement Social Security payments.

Death

Preoccupation with dying, particularly with the circumstances surrounding it, is an ongoing concern of the elderly. For one reason, they see their friends and relatives dying. For another, they realize they've lived more years than they have left.

The elderly person's concern about dying is most often focused on the disability, the pain, and long periods of suffering that may precede death (Moss and Moss, 1975, p. 72). People generally would like a death with dignity. They would prefer to die in their own homes, with little suffering, with mental faculties intact, and with families and friends nearby. The elderly are also concerned about the costs of their final illness, the difficulties they may cause others by the manner of their death, and whether their resources will permit a dignified funeral.

In modern America most people die in nursing homes or hospitals surrounded by medical staff (Kornblum and Julian, 1989, p. 340). Such deaths often occur without dignity. Fortunately, the hospice movement has been developing in recent years to attempt to foster death with dignity. A hospice is a program that is designed to allow the terminally ill to die with dignity—to live their final weeks in the way they want to. Hospices have their origin among European religious groups in the Middle Ages who welcomed travelers who were sick, tired, or hungry (Sullivan et al., 1980, p. 363).

have a *duty* to die, in order to avoid being a financial and emotional burden to their families and to society. At their most extreme, the opposition equate assisted suicide with homicide.

Some authorities have sought to make a distinction between active euthanasia (assisted suicide) and passive euthanasia (treatment being withheld or withdrawn). In many states it is legal for physicians and courts to choose to honor a patient's wishes to not receive life-sustaining treatment.

A recent case of passive euthanasia involved Nancy Cruzan. On January 11, 1983, when the Missouri woman was twenty-five, her car overturned. Her brain lost oxygen for fourteen minutes following the accident, and for the next several years she was in a "persistent vegetative state," with no hope of recovery. A month after the accident, her parents, Joyce and Joe Cruzan, gave permission for a feeding tube to be inserted. In the months that followed, however, the parents gradually became convinced there was no point in keeping Nancy alive indefinitely in such a hopeless condition.

In 1986 they were shocked when a Missouri state judge informed them that they could be charged with murder for removing the feeding tube. The Cruzans appealed the decision all the way to the U.S. Supreme Court, requesting the Court to overturn a Missouri law that specifically prohibits withdrawal of food and water from hopelessly ill patients. In July 1990, the Supreme Court refused the Cruzans' request that their daughter's tube be removed, but said states could sanction the removal if there was "clear and convincing evidence" that the patient would have wished it. Cruzan's family subsequently found other witnesses to testify that Nancy would not have wanted to be kept alive in such a state.

A Missouri judge decided that the testimony met the Supreme Court's test. The tube was disconnected in December 1990, and Nancy Cruzan died several days later on December 26.

At the present time, 10,000 Americans are in similar vegetative conditions, unable to communicate. Many of these individuals have virtually no chance to recover. Right-to-die questions will undoubtedly continue to be raised in many of these cases.

Do you believe that the terminally ill have a right to die by refusing treatment? Do you believe assisted suicide should be legalized? If a terminally ill close relative of yours who was in intense pain asked you to assist her or him in acquiring a lethal dose of drugs, how would you respond? Would you be willing to help? Or would you refuse?

Hospices serve patients in a variety of settings—in hospitals, in nursing homes, and in the dying person's home. Medical services and social services are provided in hospices, and extensive efforts are made to allow the terminally ill to spend their remaining days as they choose. Hospices sometimes have educational and entertainment programs, and visitors are welcome. Pain relievers are extensively used, so that the patient is able to live out his or her final days in relative comfort.

Hospices view the *disease*, not the patient, as terminal. Their emphasis is on helping people use the time that is left, rather than trying to keep people alive as long as possible. Many hospice programs are set up to assist people in living their remaining days at home. In addition to medical and visiting nurse services, hospices have volunteers to help the patient and family members with such services as counseling, transportation, filling out insurance forms and other paperwork, and respite care (that is, staying with the patient to provide temporary relief for family members).

Emotional Problems

The older person is often a lonely person. Most people seventy years or older are widowed, divorced, or single. When someone has been married for many years and the spouse dies, a deep sense of loneliness usually occurs that seems unbearable. The years ahead often seem full of nothing but emptiness. It is not surprising, then, that depression is the most common emotional problem of the elderly. Symptoms of depression include feelings of uselessness, being a burden, being unneeded, loneliness, and hopelessness. Somatic symptoms of depression include loss of weight and appetite, fatigue, insomnia, and constipation. (It is often difficult to determine whether such somatic symptoms are due to depression or to an organic disorder.)

Depression can alter the personality of an elderly person. Depressed people may become apathetic, withdrawn, and show a slowdown in behavioral actions. Levy, Derogatis, Gallagher, and Gatz (1980) have found that an elderly person's reluctance to respond to questions is apt to be due to depression rather than to the contrariness of old age.

Those who have unresolved emotional problems in earlier life will generally continue to have them when older. Often, these problems will be intensified by the added stresses of aging.

There appear to be two major barriers to good mental health in the later years: failure to bounce back from psychosocial losses (such as the death of a loved one) and failure to have meaningful life goals (Skidmore and Thackeray, 1976, p. 226). Later adulthood is a time when there are drastic changes thrust on the elderly that may create emotional problems: loss of a spouse, loss of friends and relatives through death or moving, poorer health, loss of accustomed income, and changing relationships with one's children and grandchildren.

Unfortunately, there is an erroneous assumption that *senility* and *mental illness* are inevitable and untreatable. On the contrary, the elderly respond well to both individual and group counseling (Atchley 1988, pp. 108-10). In addition, even many ninety-year-olds show no sign of senility. Senility is by no means an inevitable part of growing old.

Where the Elderly Live

We have heard so much about nursing homes in recent years that few people realize that 95 percent of the elderly do not live in nursing homes or any other kind of institution (American Association of Retired Persons, 1990). Over 70 percent of all elderly males are married and live with their wives (American Association of Retired Persons, 1990). Because females tend to outlive their spouses, over 40 percent of women over age sixty-five live alone (American Association of Retired Persons, 1990). Nearly 80 percent of older married couples maintain their own house-holds—in apartments, mobile homes, condominiums, or their own houses (American Association of Retired Persons, 1990). In addition, nearly half of the single elderly (widows, widowers, divorced, never married) live in their own homes (American Association of Retired Persons, 1990). When the elderly do not maintain their own households, they most often live in the homes of relatives, primarily children.

The elderly who live in rural areas generally have a higher status than those living in urban areas. People living on farms can retire gradually. People whose income is in land, rather than a job, can retain importance and esteem to an advanced age.

However, almost three-fourths of our population live in urban areas, and the elderly often live in poor-quality housing. At least 30 percent of the elderly live in substandard, deteriorating, or dilapidated housing (Atchley, 1988). Many of the elderly in urban areas are trapped in decaying, low-value houses needing considerable maintenance and often surrounded by racial and ethnic groups different from their own. Many of the urban elderly live in the urban inner cities in hotels or apartments with inadequate living conditions. Their neighborhoods may be decaying and crime ridden, where they are easy prey for thieves and muggers.

Fortunately, many mobile home parks, retirement villages, and apartment complexes geared to the needs of the elderly are being built throughout the country. Many such communities for the elderly provide a social center, security protection, sometimes a daily hot meal, and perhaps help with maintenance.

Transportation

Many of the elderly do not drive. Some cannot afford the cost of a car, while others have physical limitations that prevent them from driving and maintaining a car. The lack of convenient inexpensive transportation is a problem faced by most elderly.

Crime Victimization

Having reduced energy, strength, and agility, the elderly are easily victimized by crime, particularly robbery, aggravated assault, burglary, larceny, vandalism, and fraud. Many of the elderly live in constant fear of being victimized, although actual victimization rates

Many of the urban elderly live in poverty and substandard conditions. They may depend on the community for needed supplies and special services.

for the elderly are lower than rates for younger people.[1] Some are extremely hesitant to leave their homes for fear they will be mugged or from fear their homes will be burglarized while they are away. When the elderly are victims of crimes of physical assault, they are more likely than younger people to sustain serious injury and to recover more slowly.

Malnutrition

The elderly are the most uniformly undernourished segment of our population (Atchley, 1988). Chronic malnutrition of the elderly exists because of transportation difficulties in getting to grocery stores; lack of knowledge about proper nutrition; lack of money to purchase a well-balanced diet; poor teeth and lack of

good dentures, which greatly limits the diet; lack of incentives to prepare an appetizing meal when one is living alone; and inadequate cooking and storage facilities.

Health Problems and Cost of Care

As noted earlier, the proportion of the elderly in our society is increasing dramatically, and the old-old (age seventy-five and over) is the most rapidly growing age group in our society. Today, there is a crisis in health care for the elderly. There are a variety of reasons for this crisis.

As described in Chapter 14, the elderly are much more apt to have long-term illnesses. In the 1960s the Medicare and Medicaid programs were created to pay for much of their medical costs. Due to the high costs of these programs, the Reagan-Bush administrations in the 1980s said we could no longer pay the full costs of that care, and as a result there have been cuts in eligibility for payment and limits set for what the government will pay for a variety of medical procedures.

---

1. The actual victimization rates for the elderly may be considerably higher than official crime statistics indicate, because many of the elderly feel uneasy about becoming involved with the legal and criminal justice systems. Therefore, they may not report some crimes which they are victims of. Some of the elderly are afraid of retaliation from the offenders if they report the crimes and some of the elderly dislike the legal processes they will have to go through if they press charges.

Physicians are primarily trained in treating the young, and generally less interested in serving the elderly. As a result, when the elderly become ill, they often do not receive quality medical care. For example, Hugh Downs in an ABC news report described the case of an eighty-two-year-old woman who was shuffled from one hospital to another over a three month period of time, and finally dumped in a county hospital—where she eventually died of a single grossly neglected bedsore. Hugh Downs (1985, p. 11) notes:

> The revolution of longer life has produced a new complex of critical medical needs, needs this nation does not yet seem prepared to meet. For example, there seems little prospect that there will be anything like the numbers of geriatricians needed to care for the elderly. It's a field still avoided by young doctors. Because of the complicated problems of the aging, there is a need for more health evaluation services and more psychiatric and rehabilitation assistance. Even for the limited efforts we now make, funding has always been meager.
>
> The new era of the longevity revolution is already bringing with it multiplying health problems to which our society remains largely blind . . . and within this nation's vast medical complex, many old who could be helped are left adrift, trapped, their needs unrecognized.

Medical conditions of the elderly are often misdiagnosed, as physicians receive little specialized training in the unique medical conditions of the elderly. Many of the elderly who are seriously ill do not get medical attention. One of the reasons physicians are uninterested in treating the elderly is the problem of reimbursement. The Medicare program sets reimbursement limits on a variety of procedures that are provided to the elderly. As a result, most physicians prefer to work with younger patients where the fee-for-service system is much more profitable.

There have also been restrictions put on hospital payments under Medicare. In the past, the payment system covered whatever the expenses came to. To curtail rampant costs, the federal government in the 1980s set flat payments for each category of illness, which are called "Diagnostic Related Groups" or DRGs. With this system, instead of reimbursing hospitals for the actual cost of treating Medicare patients, the government now pays a set fee for each medical condition. For the medical community it's a simple message: if a hospital spends less on a patient than the fixed amount, it makes money. If it spends more, it must absorb the loss. A perverse, unintended consequence of DRGs is that many seriously ill elderly patients are being discharged prematurely (Downs, 1985). With the DRG system, hospitals that have a social conscience and continue to treat the elderly beyond the length of time allowed by the DRG regulations must cover the expenses themselves, and thereby face bankruptcy.

In addition, the elderly who live in the community often have transportation difficulties in getting medical care. And those living in nursing homes sometimes receive inadequate care as some health professionals assume such patients no longer have much time to live, and therefore the professionals are less interested in providing high quality medical care. Medical care for the elderly is becoming a national embarrassment (Downs, 1985).

Current Services: Macro System Responses

Present services and programs for the elderly are primarily maintenance in nature, as they are mainly designed to meet basic physical needs. Nonetheless, there are a number of programs, often federally funded, to provide services needed by the elderly. Before we briefly review many of these programs, we will look at the Older Americans Act of 1965, which set objectives for programs that serve the elderly.

Older Americans Act of 1965

The Older Americans Act of 1965 created an operating agency (Administration on Aging) within the Department of Health, Education, and Welfare (as of 1980, the Department of Health and Human Services). This law and its amendments are the basis for financial aid by the federal government to assist states and local communities to meet the needs of the elderly. The objectives of the act are to secure for the elderly:

- An adequate income.
- Best possible physical and mental health.
- Suitable housing.
- Restorative services for those who require institutionalized care.

- Opportunity for employment.
- Retirement in health, honor, and dignity.
- Pursuit of meaningful activity.
- Efficient community services.
- Immediate benefit from research knowledge to sustain and improve health and happiness.
- Freedom, independence, and the free exercise of individual initiative in planning and managing their own lives. (U.S. Department of Health, Education, and Welfare, 1970)

Although these objectives are commendable, in reality they have not been realized for many of the elderly. However, some progress has been made. Many states have offices on aging, and some municipalities and counties have established community councils on aging. A number of universities have established centers for gerontology, which focus on research of the elderly and training of students for working with the elderly in such disciplines as nursing, psychology, medicine, sociology, social work, and architecture. (Gerontology is the scientific study of the aging process from physiological, pathological, psychological, sociological, and economic points of view.) Government research grants are being given to encourage the study of the elderly and their problems. Publishers are now producing books and pamphlets to inform the public about the elderly, and a few high schools are beginning to offer courses to help teenagers understand the elderly and their circumstances.

A number of programs, often federally funded and administered at state or local levels, provide funds and services needed by the elderly. A number of these programs are briefly described in the following material.

Old Age, Survivors, Disability, and Health Insurance (OASDHI)

The OASDHI social insurance program[2] was created by the 1935 Social Security Act. OASDHI is usually referred to as Social Security by the general public. It is an income insurance program designed to partially replace income lost when a worker retires or becomes disabled. Cash benefits are also paid to survivors of insured workers.

Payments to beneficiaries are based on previous earnings. Rich as well as poor are eligible if insured. Benefits are provided to fully insured workers at age sixty-five or older (age sixty-two if somewhat smaller benefits are taken). Dependent husbands and wives over sixty-two and dependent children under eighteen (no age limit on disabled children who become disabled before eighteen) are also covered under the benefits.

Participation in this insurance program is compulsory for most employees, including the self-employed. The program is generally financed by a payroll tax (FICA—Federal Insurance Contributions Act) assessed equally to employer and employee. The rate has gone up gradually. Eligibility for benefits is based on the number of years in which Social Security taxes have been paid and the amount earned while working.

Supplemental Security Income (SSI)

Under the SSI program, the federal government makes monthly payments to people in financial need who are sixty-five years of age or older or to persons of any age who are legally blind or disabled. In order to qualify for payments, applicants must have no (or very little) regular cash income, own little property, and have little cash or few assets (such as jewelry, stocks, bonds, or other valuables) that could be turned into cash.

The SSI program became effective January 1, 1974. The word *supplemental* in the term "supplemental security income" is used because, in most cases, payments supplement whatever income may be available to the claimant. Since OASDHI monthly payments are often low, SSI sometimes supplements even that income source.

SSI provides a guaranteed minimum income (an income floor) for the elderly, the legally blind, and the disabled. Administration of SSI has been assigned to the Social Security Administration. Financing of the program is through federal tax dollars, primarily income taxes.

---

2. Social insurance programs are financed by a tax on employees, or on employers, or on both. In contrast, public assistance benefits are paid from general government revenues (such as revenues through income taxes). In our society, receiving social insurance benefits is generally considered a right, while receiving public assistance is usually considered charity and is stigmatized.

Medicare

In 1965, Congress enacted the Medicare program (Title XVIII of the Social Security Act). Medicare helps the elderly pay the high cost of health care. It has two parts: hospital insurance (Part A) and supplementary medical insurance (Part B). Everyone sixty-five or older who is entitled to monthly benefits under the Old Age, Survivors, and Disability Insurance program gets Part A automatically, without paying a monthly premium. Nearly everyone in the United States sixty-five or older is eligible for Part B; Part B is voluntary, and beneficiaries are charged a monthly premium. Disabled people under age sixty-five who have been getting Social Security benefits for twenty-four consecutive months or more are also eligible for both Part A and Part B, effective on the twenty-fifth month of disability.

Part A

Hospital insurance helps pay for time-limited care in hospitals and skilled nursing facilities and for home health visits (such as visiting nurses). Covered services in a hospital or skilled nursing facility include the cost of room and meals in a semiprivate room, regular nursing services, and cost of drugs, supplies, and appliances.

Part B

Supplementary medical insurance helps pay for physicians' services, outpatient hospital services in an emergency room, outpatient physical and speech therapy, and a number of other medical and health services prescribed by a doctor, such as diagnostic services, X-ray or other radiation treatments, and some ambulance services.

Medicaid

This program was established in 1965 by Title XIX of the Social Security Act. Medicaid primarily provides medical care for recipients of public assistance. It enables states to pay hospitals, nursing homes, medical societies, and insurance agencies for services provided to recipients of public assistance. Many of these recipients are indigent elderly, some of whom are in nursing homes. The federal government shares the expenses with the states on a 55-45 basis to recipients of public assistance, primarily those covered by Aid to Families with Dependent Children (AFDC) and by Supplemental Security Income. Medical expenses that are covered under Medicaid include diagnosis and therapy performed by surgeons, physicians, and dentists; nursing services in the home or elsewhere; and medical supplies, drugs, and laboratory fees.

Medicaid benefits vary from state to state. The original legislation encouraged states to include coverage of all self-supporting persons whose marginal income made them unable to pay for medical care. However, this inclusion is not mandatory, and the definition of medical indigence has generally been defined by states to provide insurance coverage primarily to recipients of public assistance.

Food Stamps

The food stamp program is designed to combat hunger. Food stamps are available to public assistance recipients and to other low-income families. These stamps are then used to purchase groceries.

Adult Protective Services

One of the services that is offered in practically all communities, usually by public welfare departments, is adult protective services. Although offered widely, the public is largely unaware of it. One in every twenty elderly people probably needs some form of protective services, and this proportion is expected to increase as the proportion of people over age seventy-five increases (Atchley, 1988, p. 176). Protective services are for adults who are being neglected or abused or for adults whose physical or mental capacities have substantially deteriorated. The aim of adult protective services is to help the elderly and adults with disabilities meet their needs in their own home if possible. Alternative placements include foster care, group home care, and elderly housing units (such as apartments for the elderly). Services provided include homemaker services, counseling, rehabilitation, medical services, visiting nursing services, Meals on Wheels, and transportation.

In New York City, a volunteer from the Federation of Protestant Welfare Agencies shops for an elderly woman who is recovering from a fall. Adult protective services, while offered in almost all communities, are often a well-kept secret.

Additional Programs

Additional programs for the elderly include the following:

- Meals on Wheels provides hot and cold meals to housebound recipients who are incapable of obtaining or preparing their own meals, but who can feed themselves.
- Senior-citizen centers, golden age clubs, and similar groups provide leisure time and recreational activities for the elderly.
- Special bus rates reduce bus transportation costs for the elderly.
- Property tax relief is available to the elderly in many states.
- Housing projects for the elderly are built by local sponsors with financing assistance by the Department of Housing and Urban Development.
- Reduced rates at movie theaters and other places of entertainment are often offered voluntarily by individual owners.
- Home health services provide visiting nurse services, physical therapy, drugs, laboratory services, and sickroom equipment.
- Nutrition programs provide meals for the elderly at group eating sites. (These meals are generally provided four or five times a week and usually are luncheon meals.)
- Homemaker services provide household tasks that the elderly are no longer able to do for themselves.
- Day care centers for the elderly provide activities that are determined by the needs of the group.
- Telephone reassurance is provided by volunteers, often older persons, who telephone elderly people who live alone. (Such calls are a meaningful form of social contact for both parties and also ascertain whether any accidents or other serious problems have arisen which require emergency attention.)
- Nursing homes provide residential care and skilled nursing care when independence is no longer practical for the elderly who cannot take care of themselves or for the elderly whose families can no longer take care of them.
- Nursing Home Ombudsman Program investigates and acts on concerns expressed by residents in nursing homes.

Nursing Homes

Nursing homes were created as an alternative to expensive hospital care and are substantially supported by the federal government through Medicaid and Medicare. More than 1.5 million older people now live in extended-care facilities, making nursing homes a billion-dollar industry. There are more patient beds in nursing homes than in hospitals (Bould, Sanborn and Reif, 1989).

Nursing homes are classified according to the kind of care they provide. At one end of the scale, there are residential homes that provide primarily room and board, with some nonmedical care (such as help in dressing). At the other end of the scale are nursing-care centers that provide skilled nursing and medical attention twenty-four hours a day. The more skilled and extensive the medical care given, the more expensive the home. The costs per resident average more than $2,000 a month (Bould, Sanborn, and Reif, 1989). Although only about 5 percent of the

Adult Protective Services

Dodge County Public Welfare Department received a complaint from a neighbor of Jack and Rosella McArron that the McArrons were living in health-threatening conditions and that Mr. McArron was frequently abusing his wife.

Vincent Rudd, adult protective service worker, investigated the complaint. When he arrived at the door, Jack McArron appeared in shabby, filthy clothes with a can of beer in his hand and refused entry to Mr. Rudd. Mr. Rudd heard someone moaning in the background, so he went to the nearest service station where he called the police department. Together, Mr. Rudd and a police officer returned to the McArrons. The officer informed Mr. McArron that a protective service complaint had been made, and that an investigation must be made. Mr. McArron grudgingly let the officer and Mr. Rudd in.

The inside of the house had the appearance of having been hit by a cyclone. Newspapers and dirty clothes were heaped together in piles on the floor. The dining room table was covered by dust, cigarette butts, beer cans, whiskey bottles, and dirty dishes. The plumbing was not working. Cockroaches were seen. The house had a wood burning stove that was covered with dirt and a burnt crust. At the very least the place appeared to be a fire trap. There was a stench that was largely due to urine.

Mr. McArron appeared to be intoxicated. Mrs. McArron was found moaning in the bedroom. Mr. McArron stated that she had arthritis and had slipped on the stairway. He further stated that her demands and her behavior were driving him to drink. Her hair was greasy and appeared not to have been washed for months. She was wearing a torn nightgown that smelled of urine. She was very thin, wrinkled, and had a variety of cuts and bruises. Her mutterings were difficult to understand, but she seemed to be saying that her husband had been battering her for months.

She was taken to a hospital where she spent two-and-one-half weeks. (She was found to be sixty-six years old, and her husband, sixty-nine.) At first she wouldn't eat, so she was fed intravenously. After several days she became more alert. Daily baths improved her appearance. It became clear that she had frequently been abused by her husband for more than a decade. She was also found to have severe arthritis and diabetes. In the hospital she stated she did not want to return to live with her husband because of the beatings. She was placed in a foster home.

The neighbors of the McArrons were interviewed; it was found that Jack McArron had had a drinking problem for years and that the neighbors seldom saw him sober. The neighbors were afraid of what he might do when intoxicated. He frequently beat his wife and was loud and obnoxious, and the neighbors were fearful he might kill someone while driving under the influence. Mr. McArron was taken to a thirty-day drug treatment center. Records showed he had been admitted to this center on seven previous occasions. This time a physician found evidence that Mr. McArron was suffering from brain deterioration due to chronic alcoholism. He seemed to be paranoid as he talked about his neighbors being gangsters. He stated that they were stealing his possessions. As the days went by, he started blaming the police and protective services for kidnapping his wife and talked about getting her back. He stated, "I'm goin' lookin' for her with my shotgun, and I'll blast anyone who gets in my way." With his increasing paranoid statements, the staff was reluctant to let Mr. McArron return to his home as it was felt that if he became intoxicated he could be dangerous. His mental capacities were deteriorating, and he was found to have a severe case of cirrhosis of the liver. As a result, procedures were followed to have a court declare him incompetent, to appoint a younger cousin as guardian, and to place Mr. McArron in a nursing home.

After Mrs. McArron was placed in a foster home for several weeks, she said that she wanted to return to live with her husband. She was informed that her husband was in a nursing home. She visited him on several occasions and became increasingly depressed about his deteriorating condition. She began talking about wanting to die. About a year and a half later, she did die of a massive heart attack. Her husband's condition in the nursing home has continued to deteriorate.

Vincent Rudd often thought about this case. It seemed that the intervention that resulted in Jack and Rosella being separated from each other was in some way a factor in facilitating both their mental and emotional deterioration. Breaking a husband-wife bond has unexpected adverse consequences. But what were the alternatives? They seemed to be killing each other by living together. Mr. Rudd realized intervention in social work is a matter of judgment, and all anyone can do is give it their best shot.

elderly live permanently in nursing homes, many spend some time convalescing in them.

One scandal after another characterizes care in nursing homes. A number of years ago in Houston, an elderly woman was so neglected in a nursing home that her death was not discovered until rigor mortis had set in. Another woman in the same home was hospitalized from rat bites (Trafford, 1978). It has been charged that some doctors are giving needless repeated injections to nursing home patients in order to make high profits (Butler, 1975). In 1980, a nursing home in Madison, Wisconsin, strapped a thirty-seven-year-old stroke patient to her wheelchair for over forty minutes at a time when the patient had no bladder or bowel control. She was not assisted to the toilet despite her repeated cries for help (Paley, 1980).

Robert Butler (1975) visited a number of nursing homes and found patients lying in their own feces or urine. He also found that the food was so unappetizing that residents at times refused to eat it, that many homes had serious safety hazards, and that boredom and apathy were common among staff as well as residents.

A federal report by the Health Care Financing Administration in 1988 found that 43 percent of the nation's nursing homes fail to meet food sanitation standards and nearly a third have problems administering drugs and providing personal hygiene for residents (Wineke, 1988). In 1987, investigators for the U.S. Senate Special Committee on Aging found that conditions in one out of ten nursing homes were "shockingly, dangerously bad." The study found neglect, medical maltreatment, and in a few isolated cases even beatings and rape. The study found that in California between 1985 and 1986, seventy-nine patients died as a direct result of neglect (Robinson, 1987, p. 13).

Donald Robinson (1988, pp. 13-14) conducted a nationwide investigation of nursing homes in 1988 and concluded:

> I learned that the majority of nursing homes are safe, well-run institutions that take good care of the sick people entrusted to them. Some are superb.

Robinson (1988) also noted a number of horrors and abuses in some of the homes. The abuses included giving new and unapproved drugs to patients without their consent, giving patients heavy doses of tranquilizers to keep them docile, kickbacks given to nursing home administrators from druggists, stealing funds from patients, submitting phony cost reports to Medicare, sexual abuse by staff of some patients, and charging patients thousands of dollars to gain admission to a home.

At the present time, people of all ages tend to be prejudiced against nursing homes, even those that are well run. Frank Moss (1977, p. 9) describes the elderly person's view of nursing homes: "The average senior citizen looks at a nursing home as a human junkyard, as a prison—a kind of purgatory, halfway between society and the cemetery—or as the first step of an inevitable slide into oblivion." There is some truth to the notion that most nursing homes are places where the elderly wait to die.

The cost of care for impoverished nursing home residents is largely paid by the Medicaid program. Since the federal government has set limits on what will be reimbursed under Medicaid, other problems may arise. There may be an effort to keep salary and wage levels as low as possible and the number of staff to a minimum. A nursing home may postpone repairs and improvements. Food is apt to be inexpensive such as macaroni and cheese, which is high in fats and carbohydrates. Congress has mandated that every nursing home patient on Medicaid is entitled to a monthly personal spending allowance. The homes have control over these funds, and some homes keep this money (Moss, 1977, p. 9).

Gordon Moss and Walter Moss (1975, p. 65) present additional complaints:

> The quality of care from both particular staff members and from the institution as a whole is another major source of problems and complaints. There may be much delay or no response to calls for help. Patients may be left sitting for a long time on bedpans. The staff may harass patients they dislike or consider to be insufficiently docile by doing these things or by withholding services, isolating them in separate rooms in little-used parts of the building, or forcing them to remain bedridden.

Complaints about the physical facilities of nursing homes include not enough floor space or too many

Community Options Program: Providing Alternatives to Nursing Home Placement

Community Options Program (COP) is an innovative Wisconsin program that provides alternatives to nursing home placement. COP is funded by the state and the federal government and is administered by county social services departments.

To qualify for the program a person must have a long-term or irreversible illness or disability and be a potential or current resident of a nursing home or a facility for the developmentally disabled. The person must also have income and assets that are below the poverty line. If these eligibility guidelines are met, a social worker and a nurse assess applicants for their social and physical abilities and disabilities to determine the types of services needed. If an alternative to nursing home placement is available, is financially feasible, and, most important, is preferred by an applicant, a plan for services is drawn up, and a start date for in-home or in-community services is determined.

A wide variety of services may be provided that are designed to be alternatives to placement in nursing homes. Typical services that are provided include homemaker services, visiting nurse services, home-delivered meals, adult foster care, group home care, and case management. COP is a coordinated program that makes use of a number of resources from a variety of agencies. Wisconsin is finding that the program is not only cost effective in comparison to nursing home care but also preferred over nursing home care by service recipients. (A number of other states are now offering COP or similar programs.)

people in a room. The call light by the bed may be difficult to reach, or the toilets and showers may not be conveniently located. And the building may be in a state of decay.

Frank Moss (1977, p. 9) along with a number of other authorities is critical of our society's response to the problems of the elderly:

> The phenomenon of large numbers of ill elderly is a comparatively recent problem in the United States, as is our "solution"—nursing homes. The solution reflects today's society: the sick and the aged are an embarrass-

ment; they remind us of our own mortality and therefore should be removed from view.

While the quality of nursing home care ranges from excellent to awful, nursing homes are needed, particularly for those requiring round-the-clock health care for an extended time. If nursing homes were abolished, other institutions such as hospitals would have to serve the elderly. Life in nursing homes need not be bad. Where homes are properly administered, residents can expand their life experiences.

Social Work with the Elderly

Social work education is taking a leading role in identifying the problems of the aged and is developing gerontological specializations within the curricula. Although in the past, social workers have not been a significant part of the staff of most agencies serving the elderly, this is changing. Some states, for example, are now requiring that each nursing home employ a social worker.

Social work has a number of skills to help meet the special needs and concerns of the aged. Social workers are needed as brokers to link the elderly with available services. In any community there are a wide range of services available, but few people are knowledgeable about the array of services and about various eligibility requirements. The social worker's knowledge of community resources prepares him or her for this broker role. The elderly are in special need of this "broker" service as some have difficulty with transportation and communication, and others may be reluctant to request the assistance to which they are entitled.

Counseling is another function social workers can provide to the elderly or to the families of the elderly. Areas involved include counseling on emotional problems, employment, finding new "meaning" in living, coping with health problems, death and dying, and whether to enter a nursing home.

Outreach is another role for social workers, including identifying and offering services to those who need financial assistance, better housing, health care services, recreational and leisure-time services, transportation, companionship, consumer protection services, sex education, and hot-meal programs. Communities are now finding it is more cost efficient—and better for most of the elderly—to provide services to the elderly in their homes than to use the alternative of a nursing home. Social workers are increasingly becoming involved in providing and co-ordinating services to the elderly in their homes (a case management role).

Other roles are opening up for social workers in the field of aging: consultants, community planners, researchers, and administrators of services. The role of advocate is also crucial. Because the elderly in our society have long been subjected to prejudice and discrimination, social workers have an obligation to help them (and society) identify specific instances of ageism and then serve as advocates in eradicating such prejudice and discrimination.

Because the elderly population is the most rapidly growing age group in our society, it is anticipated that services to the elderly will expand in the next few decades. This expansion will generate a number of ad-ditional employment opportunities for social workers.

The Elderly Are Emerging as a Powerful Political Force

Most programs for the elderly are designed to main-tain them at their current level of functioning rather than having the higher goal of enhancing their social, physical, and psychological well-being. In spite of all the maintenance programs available for the elderly, key problems remain to be solved. A high proportion of the elderly do not have meaningful lives, respected status, or adequate income, transportation, living ar-rangements, diet, or health care. The elderly are victims of ageism—prejudice and discrimination against the elderly. How can we defend urging people to retire when they are still productive? How can we defend the living conditions within some of our nursing homes? How can we defend our restrictive attitudes toward sexuality among the elderly? How can we defend providing services to the elderly that are limited to maintenance and subsistence? Gordon and Walter Moss (1977, p. 79) comment, "Just as we are learning that black can be beautiful, so we must learn that gray can be beautiful, too. In so learning, we may brighten the prospects of our old age."

In the past, prejudice has been most effectively combated when those being discriminated against

An elderly Hispanic man campaigns for senior citizens' rights at a rally in Sacramento, California. Older adults in America are politically organized and influential.

join together for political action. Therefore, it seems apparent that if major changes in the elderly's role in our society are to take place, they will have to be made through political action.

The elderly are, in fact, becoming increasingly involved in political activism and, in some cases, even radical militancy. A prominent organization is the American Association of Retired Persons. This group is lobbying for the interests of the elderly at local, state, and federal levels of government.

An action-oriented group that has caught the pub-lic's attention is the Gray Panthers. This organization argues that a fundamental flaw in our society is the emphasis on materialism and on the consumption of goods and services, rather than on improving the quality of life for all citizens (including the elderly).

The Gray Panthers seek to end ageism and to advance the goals of human freedom, human dignity, and self-development. This organization uses social action techniques, including getting the elderly to vote as a bloc for their concerns. Founder of the group Maggie Kuhn (quoted in Butler, 1975, p. 341) stated, "We are not mellow, sweet old people. We have got to effect change, and we have nothing to lose."

Another reason the elderly are becoming a powerful political group is that they tend to be more likely to vote than the young (Atchley, 1988). And the elderly will be more politically active in the future because the composition of the elderly population is changing. The educational level of this population has been steadily increasing. Between 1970 and 1988, their median level of education increased from 8.7 years to 12.1 years, and the percentage who had completed high school rose from 28 percent to 54 percent. About 11 percent in 1988 had four or more years of college (American Association of Retired Persons, 1990). The coming generation of elderly will be better-educated, better-informed, and more politically conscious.

Significant steps toward securing a better life for the elderly have been made in the last twenty-five years: increased Social Security payments, enactment of the Medicare and Medicaid programs, the emergence of hospices, and the expansion of a variety of other programs for the elderly. With the elderly becoming a powerful political bloc, we are apt to see a number of changes in future years to improve the status of the elderly in our society.

Changing a Macro System: Finding a Social Role for the Elderly

As we have discussed, the elderly face a variety of problems. Following retirement, their income drops, often to below poverty levels. Health care expenses rise considerably, as the elderly are more susceptible to chronic illness. With reduced income, their living standard drops dramatically. With less money, the elderly often reduce their physical and mental activities, which accelerates the aging process. The life expectancy of the elderly is increasing, with the old-old being the fastest-growing age group in our society. Many of the elderly depend on the Social Security

system for a large amount of their income; yet the monthly payments are inadequate, and with the increasing number of recipients, the payouts may become smaller. Young people today cannot count on the Social Security system being their primary source of income when they grow old and retire. The elderly have a roleless role in our society and are the victims of ageism. How can these problems be combated?

In a nutshell, it would seem essential to find a meaningful productive role for the elderly. At present, early retirement programs and the stereotypic expectations of the elderly often result in the elderly being unproductive, inactive, dependent, and unfulfilled. To develop a meaningful role for the elderly in our society, it appears that the productive elderly should be encouraged to continue to work and the expectations of the elderly should be changed.

The elderly who want to work and are still performing well should be encouraged to continue working past age sixty-five or seventy. Also, it is suggested here that if an elderly person wants to work half time or part time, this should be encouraged. For example, two elderly persons working half time could fill a full-time position. New roles might also be created for the elderly to be consultants after they retire in the areas where they possess special knowledge and expertise. For those that do retire, there should be educational and training programs to help them develop their interests and hobbies (such as photography) into new sources of income.

Working longer in our society would have a number of payoffs for the elderly and for society. The elderly would continue to be productive, contributing citizens. They would have a meaningful role. They would continue to be physically and mentally active. They would have higher self-esteem. They would begin to break down the stereotypes of the elderly being unproductive and a financial burden on society. They would be paying into the Social Security system rather than drawing from it. What is being proposed here is a system for the elderly to have a productive role, either as paid workers or as volunteers.

In our materialistic society perhaps the only way for the elderly to have a meaningful role is to be productive. The elderly face the choice (as do younger people) between having adequate financial resources through productive work or inadequate financial resources as a result of not working.

Objections to such a system may be raised by those who maintain that some of the elderly are no longer productive. This may be true, but some younger people are also unproductive. What is needed to make the proposed system work is jobs having realistic, objective, and behaviorally measurable levels of performance. Those at any age who do not meet the performance levels should be informed about the deficiencies and would be given training to meet the deficiencies. If the performance levels still were not met, discharge processes should be used as a last resort. (For example, if a tenured faculty member was deficient in levels of performance—as measured by student-course evaluations, peer faculty evaluations of teaching, record of public service, record of service to the department and to the campus, and record of publications—that faculty member should be informed of the deficiencies. Training and other resources to meet the deficiencies should be offered. If the performance levels then do not improve to acceptable standards, dismissal proceedings would be initiated. Some colleges and universities are now moving in this direction.)

In the productivity system that is being suggested, the elderly would have an important part to play. They would be expected to continue to be productive within their capacities. By being productive, they would serve as examples to counter the current negative stereotypes of the elderly.

Another objection we have heard to this new system is that the elderly have worked most of their lives and deserve to retire and live in leisure with a comfortable standard of living. It would be nice if the elderly really had this option. However, that is not realistic. Most of the elderly do not have the financial resources after retiring to maintain a high standard of living. When most of the elderly retire, their income and their standard of living are sharply reduced. The choice in our society is really between working and thereby maintaining a comfortable standard of living or retiring and having a lower standard of living.

We are already seeing the elderly heading in a more productive direction. A number of organizations have been formed to promote the productivity of the elderly. Three examples are Retired Senior Volunteer Program, Service Corps of Retired Executives, and Foster Grandparent Program.

The *Retired Senior Volunteer Program (RSVP)* of-fers people over age sixty the opportunity of doing volunteer service to meet community needs. RSVP agencies place volunteers in hospitals, schools, libraries, day care centers, courts, nursing homes, and a variety of other places.

The *Service Corps of Retired Executives* (SCORE) offers retired businessmen and businesswomen an opportunity to help owners of small businesses and managers of community organizations who are having management problems. Volunteers receive no pay but are reimbursed for out-of-pocket expenses.

The *Foster Grandparent Program* employs low-income older people to provide personal care to children who live in institutions. Such children include those with a developmental disability and those who have emotional or behavioral difficulties. Foster grandparents are given special assignments in child care, speech therapy, physical therapy, or as teacher's aides. This program has been shown to be of considerable benefit to both the children and to the foster grandparents (Atchley, 1988, pp. 215-16). The children served become more outgoing and have improved relationships with peers and staff. They have increased self-confidence, improved language skills, and decreased fear and insecurity. The foster grandparents have an additional (small) source of income, increased feelings of vigor and youthfulness, an increased sense of personal worth, a feeling of being productive, and a renewed sense of personal growth and development. For society, foster grandparents provide a vast pool of relatively inexpensive labor that can be used to do needed work in the community.

The success of these programs illustrates that the elderly can be productive in both paid and volunteer positions. Atchley (1988, p. 216) makes the following recommendations for using elderly volunteers:

First, agencies must be flexible in matching the volunteer's background to assigned tasks. If the agency takes a broad perspective, useful work can be found for almost anyone. Second, *volunteers must be trained.* All too often agency personnel place unprepared volunteers in an unfamiliar setting. Then the volunteer's difficulty confirms the myth that you cannot expect good work from volunteers. Third, a variety of placement options should be offered to the volunteer. Some volunteers prefer to do familiar things; others want to do *anything but familiar* things. Fourth, training of volunteers should not make them feel that they are being tested.

This point is particularly sensitive among working-class volunteers. Fifth, volunteers should get personal attention from the placement agency. There should be people (perhaps volunteers) who follow up on absences and who are willing to listen to the compliments, complaints, or experiences of the volunteers. Public recognition from the community is an important reward for voluntary service. Finally, transportation to and from the placement should be provided.

Summary

People sixty-five and older now comprise over one-tenth of our population and are the fastest growing age group in our society. The elderly tend to encounter a number of problems in our society: low status, lack of a meaningful role, an emphasis on youth, health problems, inadequate income, inadequate housing, transportation problems, malnutrition, crime victimization, emotional problems (particularly depression), and concern with circumstances surrounding dying. A majority of the elderly depend on the Social Security system as their major source of income. Yet, monthly payments are inadequate.

In many ways, the elderly are victims of ageism. But increasingly, the elderly are becoming politically active and organized to work toward improving their status.

In order to provide the elderly with a productive, meaningful role in our society it is proposed here that they should be encouraged to work (either in paid work or as volunteers) as long as they are productive and have an interest in working to maintain their standard of living. Helping the elderly to stay productive in their lives is predicted to have a number of personal payoffs for them and to be highly beneficial to society.

Bibliography

Note: National Association of Social Workers has been abbreviated to NASW.

Abadinsky, H. *Drug Abuse: An Introduction*. Chicago: Nelson-Hall, 1989.

Abel, E.I. "Fetal Alcohol Syndrome." *Psychological Bulletin* 87 (1980):29–50.

Abramovitch, R., C. Corter and B. Lando. "Sibling Interaction in the Home." *Child Development* 50(1979):997–1003.

Abroms, K., and J. Bennett. *Paternal Contributions to Down's Syndrome Dispel Maternal Myths*. ERIC, 1981.

Adame, D.D., M.E. Taylor-Nicholson, M. Wang, and M.A. Abbas. "Southern College Freshmen Students: A Survey of Knowledge, Attitudes, and Beliefs about AIDS." *Journal of Sex Education and Therapy* 17(3)(Fall 1991):196–206.

Adams, G., S. Adams-Taylor, and K. Pittman. "Adolescent Pregnancy and Parenthood: A Review of the Problem, Solutions, and Resources." *Family Relations* 38(1989):223–29.

Adams, M. "The Single Woman in Today's Society: A Reappraisal." *American Journal of Orthopsychiatry* 41(5)(1971):776–86.

Adams, M.R., and G. Popelka. "The Influence of Time-Out on Stutterers and Their Dysfluency." *Behavior Therapy* 2(1971):334–39.

Adler, R. B., and N. Towne. *Looking Out/Looking In*. 3d ed. New York: Holt, Rinehart & Winston, 1981.

Adorno, T.W., E. Frenkel-Brunswik, D.J. Devinson, and R.N. Sanford. *The Authoritarian Personality*. New York: Harper & Row, 1950.

"Affirmative Action on Employment: Top College Officials Are Still Predominantly White Males." *Project on the Status and Education of Women* 19. Washington, DC: Association of American Colleges, 1978.

"After One Year, Thomas-Hill Hearings Still Echo Across the Land." *Milwaukee Journal*, Oct. 8, 1992, p. A14.

"AIDS Update: Myths and Realities." *Playboy Magazine*, June 1986, pp. 52–53 and 179.

Aiken, L.R. *The Psychology of Later Life*. Philadelphia, PA: W.B. Saunders, 1978.

Ainsworth, M.D.S., and S.M. Bell. "Some Contemporary Patterns of Mother-Infant Interaction in the Feeding Situation." In A. Ambrose (ed.), *Stimulation in Early Infancy*. New York: Academic Press, 1969.

Alan Guttmacher Institute. *Safe and Legal: 10 Years' Experience with Legal Abortion in New York State*. New York: Alan Guttmacher Institute, 1980.

Alberti, R.E. and M.L. Emmons. *Assert Yourself—It's Your Perfect Right: A Guide to Assertive Behavior*. Obispo, CA: Impact, 1976.(a)

———. *Stand Up, Speak Out, Talk Back!* New York: Pocket Books, 1976.(b).

Albin, R. S. "Psychological Studies of Rape." *Signs* 3(1977):423–35.

Algozzine, R. "What Teachers Perceive—Children Receive." *Communication Quarterly* 24(1976):41–47.

Allgeier, A.R., and E.R. Allgeier. *Sexual Interactions*. Lexington, MA: D.C. Heath, 1988.

Allgeier, E., and A. Allgeier. *Sexual Interactions*. Lexington, MA: D.C. Heath, 1984.

Allport, G.W. *Personality*. New York: Holt, 1937.

———.*The Nature of Prejudice.* Reading, MA: Addison-Wesley, 1954.

———. *Pattern and Growth in Personality.* New York: Holt, Rinehart and Winston, 1961.

Alm, R., and R.J. Morse. "Growing Furor over Pay of Top Executives." *U.S. News and World Report*, May 21, 1984, pp. 79–81.

Als, H., E. Tronick, B.M. Lester, and T.B. Brazelton. "Specific Neonatal Measures: The Brazelton Neonate Behavioral Assessment Scale." In J.D. Osofsky (ed.), *Handbook of Infant Development.* New York: Wiley, 1979.

Altus, W.D. "Birth Order Intelligence and Adjustment." *Psychological Reports* 5(1959):502.

Amelar, R.D. *Infertility in Men.* Philadelphia, PA: Davis, 1966.

American Academy of Pediatrics. *How to Be Your Child's TV Guide: Guidelines for Constructive Viewing.* Elk Grove Village, IL: AAP, 1986.

American Academy of Pediatrics Committee on Adolescence. "Pregnancy and Abortion Counseling." *Pediatrics* 63(6)(1979): 920–21.

American Academy of Pediatrics Committee on Drugs. "Psychotropic Drugs in Pregnancy and Lactation." *Pediatrics* 69(2)(1982):241–43.

American Association of Retired Persons. "A Profile of Older Americans." Washington, DC AARP, 1988.

———. "A Profile of Older Americans." Washington, D.C.: AARP, 1990.

American Association of Sex Educators, Counselors, and Therapists. "Abortion Bans Considered in 13 States." *Contemporary Sexuality* 25(5)(1991):1–2.

American Cancer Society. *1976 Cancer Facts & Figures.* New York: ACS, 1975.

American Heart Association. *Cholesterol and Your Heart.* Dallas, TX: AHA, 1984.

American Psychiatric Association. *DSM-111-R Diagnostic and Statistical Manual of Mental Disorders.* 3 ed. rev. Washington, DC: APA, 1987.

American Public Welfare Association. *Indicator Survey 1982.* Washington, DC: U.S. Department of Health and Human Services, 1984.

Ames, L.B., and J. Learned. "Imaginary Companions and Related Phenomena." *Journal of Genetic Psychology* 69(1946): 147–67.

Amir, M. "Forcible Rape." *Federal Probation* 31(1)(1967):51.

Anastasi, A. *Psychological Testing.* New York: Macmillan, 1968.

Anderson, B., and E. Palmore. "Longitudinal Evaluation of Ocular Function." In E. Palmore (ed.), *Normal Aging.* Durham, NC: Duke University Press, 1974.

Anderson, B.E., and J.R. Dumpson, (eds.). *The State of Black America.* New York: National Urban League, 1978.

Andrews, G., and Solomon, D., eds. *The Coca Leaf and Cocaine Papers.* New York: Harcourt Brace Jovanovich, 1975.

Andrews, L. *New Conceptions.* New York: Ballantine, 1987.

Annon, J.S. *The Behavioral Treatment of Sexual Problems: Brief Therapy.* New York: Harper & Row, 1976.

"Anti-Smoking Sentiments Increasing." *Hope Health Letter* 14(4)(April 1991).

Apgar, K., and B.C. Callahan. *Four One-Day-Workshops.* Boston, MA: Resource Communications, 1980.

Apgar, V. "The Apgar Scoring Chart." *Journal of the American Medical Association* 32(1958):168.

———. "Perinatal Problems and the Central Nervous System." In U.S. Department of HEW, *The Child with Central Nervous System Deficit.* Washington, DC: U.S. Government Printing Office, 1967.

"Apparent per Capita Ethanol Consumption—United States." *Morbidity and Mortality Weekly Report* 38(46)(1989):800–803.

Arehart-Triechel, "It's Never Too Late to Start Living Longer." *New York Magazine*, April 11, 1977, p. 38.

Aristotle. *Politics.* Book 3, Section V (Jowlett translation).

Asher, S.R., and P. Renshaw. "Children Without Friends: Social Knowledge and Social Skill Training." In S.R. Asher and J.M. Gottman (eds.), *The Development of Children's Friendships.* New York: Cambridge University Press, 1981.

Ashley Montagu. *Man's Most Dangerous Myth: The Fallacy of Race.* 4th ed. Cleveland. OH: World, 1964.

———. *Touching: The Human Significance of the Skin.* New York: Harper & Row, 1971.

———. ed. *Race and I.Q.* London, UK: Oxford University Press, 1975.

Atchley, R.C. *The Social Forces in Later Life: An Introduction to Social Gerontology.* 2d ed. Belmont, CA: Wadsworth, 1977.

———. "Aging as a Social Problem: An Overview." In M.M. Seltzer, S.L. Corbett, and R.C. Atchley (eds.) *Social Problems of the Aging.* Belmont, CA: Wadsworth, 1978.

———. *Aging: Continuity and Change.* Belmont, CA: Wadsworth, 1983.

———. *Social Forces and Aging.* 5th ed. Belmont, CA: Wadsworth, 1988.

Austin, V., D. Rulle, and T. Trabasso. "Recall and Order Effects as Factors in Children's Moral Judgments." *Child Development* 48(1977):470–74.

Aylward, G.P., et al. "Outcome Studies of Low birth Weight Infants Published in the Last Decade: A Metaanalysis." *Journal of Pediatrics* 115(1989):515–20.

Ayres, A.J. *Sensory Integration and the Child.* Los Angeles, CA: Western Psychological Services, 1983.

Azrin, N.H., and W.C. Holz. "Punishment." In W.K. Honig (ed.), *Operant Behavior: Areas of Research and Application.* New York: Appleton-Century-Crofts, 1966.

Babson, S.G., M.I. Pernoll, G.I. Brenda, and K. Simpson. *Diagnosis and Management of the Fetus and Neonate at Risk: A Guide for Team Care.* 4th ed. St. Louis, MO: Mosby, 1980.

Bachman, J.G. *Youth in Transition.* Vol. 2, *The Impact of Family Background and Intelligence on Tenth-Grade Boys.* Ann Arbor, MI: Institute for Social Research, University of Michigan, 1970.

Baer, B.L. "Developing a New Curriculum for Social Work Education." In F. Clark and M. Arkava (eds.), *The Pursuit of Competence in Social Work.* San Francisco, CA: Jossey-Bass, 1979.

Baer, B.L., and Federico, R.C. *Educating the Baccalaureate Social Worker.* Cambridge, MA: Ballinger, 1978.

Bagdikian, B.H. *In the Midst of Plenty: The Poor in America.* Boston: Beacon Press, 1964.

Bailey, J.M., and R. Pillard. "A Genetic Study of Male Sexual Orientation." *Archives of General Psychiatry* 48(1991):1089–96.

Baillargeon, R. "Object Permanence in 3½- 4½-Month-Old Infants." *Developmental Psychology* 23(5)(1987):655–64.

Baker, S., S. Thalberg, and D. Morrison. "Parents' Behavioral Norms as Predictors of Adolescent Sexual Activity and Contraceptive Use." *Adolescence* 28(1988): 278–81.

Baldwin, A. *Theories of Child Development.* New York: Wiley, 1968.

Baldwin, W., and V.S. Cain. "The Children of Teenage Parents." *Family Planning Perspectives* 12(1980):34.

Baltes, P. and K. Schaie. "Aging and IQ: The Myth of the Twilight Years." *Psychology Today* 7(10)(1974):35–38.

Bandura, A. "Influence of Models' Reinforcement Contingencies in the Acquisition of Imitative Responses." *Journal of Personality and Social Psychology* 1(1965):589–95.

———. *Principles of Behavior Modification.* New York: Holt, 1969.

Bane, M.J. "Marital Disruption and the Lives of Children." *Journal of Social Issues* 32(1976):103–17.(a)

———. *Here to Stay: American Families in the Twentieth Century.* New York: Basic Books, 1976.(b)

Banikiotes, F.G., et al. "Male and Female Auditory Reinforcement of Infant Vocalizations." *Developmental Psychology* 6(1972):476–81.

Barbach, L.G. *Women Discover Orgasm.* New York: Free Press, 1980.

Bard, M., and J. Zacker. "The Prevention of Family Violence: Dilemmas in Community Intervention." *Journal of Marriage and the Family* 33(1971):677–82.

Barker, R.L. *The Social Work Dictionary.* Silver Spring MD: National Association of Social Workers, 1991.

Barnes, E.J. "The Black Community as the Science of Positive Self-Concept for Black Children: A Theoretical Perspective." In R. Jones (ed.), *Black Psychology.* New York: Harper & Row, 1972.

Barnes, K.E. "Preschool Play Norms: A Replication." *Developmental Psychology* 5(1)(1971):99–103.

Barron, M. L. "The Aged as a Quasi-Minority Group." In Edward Sagarin (ed.), *The Other Minorities.* Lexington, MA: Ginn, 1971.

Barry, J.R. and C.R. Wingrove, eds. *Let's Learn about Aging.* New York: Wiley, 1977.

Barry, W.A. "Marriage Research and Conflict: An Integrative Review." *Psychological Bulletin* 73(1970):41–45.

Bart, P. "Rape Doesn't End with a Kiss." *Viva* 11(9)(June 1975): 39–41, 100–101.

Bart, P.B. "Depression in Middle-Aged Women." In V.G. Gornick and B.K. Moran (eds.), *Women in a Sexist Society.* New York: Basic Books, 1971.

Bar-Tal, D., and L. Saxe. "Perceptions of Similarity and Dissimilarity of Physically Attractive Couples and Individuals." *Journal of Personality and Social Psychology* 33(1976): 772–81.

Bartlett, H.M. *The Common Base of Social Work Practice.* New York: National Association of Social Workers, 1970.

Baruch, G.K., and R.C. Barnett. "Consequences of Fathers' Participation in Family Work: Parents' Role Strain and Well-Being." Wellesley College, Center for Research on Women, Wellesley, MA, 1985.

Basow, S.A. *Gender Stereotypes: Traditions and Alternatives.* Pacific Grove, CA: Brooks/Cole, 1986.

Baughman, E.E. *Black Americans: A Psychological Analysis.* New York: Academic Press, 1971.

Baumrind, D. "Effects of Authoritative Parental Control on Child Behavior." *Child Development* 37(1966):887–907.

———. "Current Patterns of Parental Authority." *Developmental Psychology Monographs* 4(1971):1.

———. "An Exploratory Study of Socialization Effects on Black Children: Some Black-White Comparisons." *Child Development* 43(1972):261–67.

———. "Some Thoughts about Child Rearing." In S. Cohen and T.J. Comiskey (eds.), *Child Development: Contemporary Perspectives.* Itasca, IL: Peacock, 1977.

———. "A Dialectical Materialist's Perspective on Knowing Social Reality." *New Directions for Child Development* 2(1978).

Beavers, W.R. *Psychotherapy and Growth.* New York: Brunner/Mazel, 1977.

Becher, E.M. Marijuana: The Health Questions." *Consumer Reports*, March 1975, pp. 143–49.

Beck, A.T. *Depression.* New York: Harper & Row, 1967.

Beck, D. *Progress on Family Problems.* New York: Family Service Associations of America, 1973.

Beck, J., and D. Davies. "Teen Contraception: A Review of Perspectives on Compliance." *Archives of Sexual Behavior* 16(1987):337–68.

Beck, M., et al. "Miscarriages." *Newsweek*, Aug. 15, 1988, pp. 46–49.

Bechham, D., D. Lopez, L. Palacios-Jimenez, V. Patti, and M. Shernoff. *When a Friend has AIDS.* New York: Chelsea Psychotherapy Associates, 1984.

Behrman, R.E., and V.C. Vaughan, eds. *Nelson Textbook of Pediatrics.* 12th ed. Philadelphia, PA: Saunders, 1983.

Belbin, R.M. "Middle Age: What Happens to Ability?" In R. Owen (ed.), *Middle Age.* London: BBC, 1967.

Bell, A.P., and M.S. Weinberg. *Homosexualities: A Study of Diversity among Men and Women.* New York: Simon & Schuster, 1978.

Bell, A.P., M.S. Weinberg, S. Martin, and S.K. Hammersmith. *Sexual Preference.* Bloomington: Indiana University Press, 1981.

Bell, R.T. "Friendships of Women and Men." *Psychology of Women Quarterly* 5(1981):402–17.

Bellak, A.O. "Comparable Worth: A Practitioner's View." In *Comparable Worth: Issue for the 80's.* vol.1. Washington, DC: U.S. Commission on Civil Rights, 1984.

Belloc, N.B., and L. Breslow. "Relationship of Physical Health Status and Health Practices." *Preventive Medicine* 1(3)(1972): 409–21.

Belmont, L., and A.F. Marolla. "Birth Order, Family Size, and Intelligence." *Science* 182(1973):1096–1101.

Belsky, J., M. Lang, and T.L. Huston. "Sex Typing and Division of Labor as Determinants of Marital Change across the Transition to Parenthood." *Journal of Personality and Social Psychology* 50(1986):517–522.

Belsky, J., and M.J. Rovine. "Nonmaternal Care in the First Year of Life and the Security of Infant-Parent Attachment." *Child Development* 59(1988):157–67.

Bengston, V. *The Social Psychology of Aging.* Indianapolis, IN: Bobbs-Merrill, 1973.

Benson, H. *The Relaxation Response.* New York: Avon, 1975.

Benson, M.D., et al. "Sex Education in the Inner City." *Journal of the Medical Association* 255(1986):43–47.

Berger, R.M. "Rewriting a Bad Script: Older Lesbians and Gays." In H. Hidalgo et al. (eds.), *Lesbian and Gay Issues: A Resource Manual for Social Workers.* Silver Spring, MD: National Association of Social Workers, 1985.

Berman, C. *Making It as a Stepparent: New Roles/New Rules.* New York: Bantam, 1981.

Berman, P.W. "Are Women More Responsive Than Men to the Young? A Review of Developmental and Situational Variables." *Psychological Bulletin* 88(1980):668–95.

Bermant, G., and J.M. Davidson. *Biological Bases of Sexual Behavior.* New York: Harper & Row, 1975.

Bermant, G. "Sexual Behavior: Hard Times with the Coolidge Effect." In M.H. Siegel and H.P. Ziegler (eds.), *Psychological Research: The Inside Story.* New York: Harper & Row, 1976.

Berne, Eric. *Games People Play.* New York: Grove Press, 1964.

———. *Principles of Group Treatment.* New York: Oxford University Press, 1966.

Berscheid, E., and E.H. Walster. "Physical Attractiveness." In L. Berkowitz (ed.), *Advances in Experimental Social Psychology*, vol. 7. New York: Academic Press, 1974.

Berscheid, E., E.H. Walster, and G. Bohrnstedt. "The Happy American Body: A Survey Report." *Psychology Today* 7(6)(1973):119–31.

Berzon, B. "Sharing Your Lesbian Identity with Your Children." In G. Vida (ed.), *Our Right to Love: A Lesbian Resource Book.* Englewood Cliffs, NJ: Prentice-Hall, 1978.

Bibby, R.W., and D.C. Posterski. *The Emerging Generation: An Inside Look at Canada's Teenagers.* Toronto: Irwin, 1985.

Bieber, I., et al. *Homosexuality: A Psychoanalytic Study of Male Homosexuals.* New York: Basic Books, 1962.

Bierman, E., and W. Hazzard. "Biology of Aging." In D. Smith and E. Bierman (eds.), *The Biologic Ages of Man.* Philadelphia, PA: Saunders, 1973.

Bierman, K.L., and W. Furman. "The Effects of Social Skills Training and Peer Involvement on the Social Adjustment of Preadolescents." *Child Development* 55(1984):151–62.

Bigelow, G., I. Liebson, and R. Griffiths. "Alcoholic Drinking: Suppression by a Brief Time-out Procedure." *Behavior Research and Therapy* 12(1974):107–15.

Biller, H.B. "Father Absence and the Personality Development of the Male Child." *Developmental Psychology* 2(1970):181–201.

———. "Fatherhood: Implications for Child and Adult Development." In *Handbook of Developmental Psychology.* Englewood Cliffs, NJ: Prentice-Hall, 1982.

Birren, J.E. "Psychological Aspects of Aging and Intellectual Functioning." *Gerontologist* 8(1)(1968), part 2.

———. "Translations in Gerontology—From Lab to Life: Psychophysiology and Speed of Response." *American Psychologist* 29(11)(1974):808–15.

Birren, J.E., A.M. Woods, and M.V. Williams. "Behavioral Slowing with Age: Causes, Organization, and Consequences." In L.W. Poon (ed.), *Aging in the 1980s.* Washington, DC: American Psychological Association, 1980.

Bishop, J. *The Days of Martin Luther King, Jr.* New York: Putnam, 1971.

Black, J.K. "Are Young Children Really Egocentric?" *Young Children* 36(1981):51–55.

Blau, F.D., and A. Winkler. "Women in the Labor Force: An Overview." In J. Freedman (ed.), *Women: A Feminist Perspective,* 4th ed. Mountain View, CA: Mayfield, 1989.

Blaze-Gosden, T. *Drug Abuse.* Birmingham, G.B.: David & Charles, 1987.

Bliss, T. "Drugs—Use, Abuse and Treatment." In *Introduction to Social Welfare Institutions.* Homewood, IL: Dorsey, 1978.

Block, J.H. "Issues, Problems and Pitfalls in Assessing Sex Differences." *Merrill-Palmer Quarterly* 22(1976):283–308.

———. "Differential Premises Arising from Differential Socialization of the Sexes: Some Conjectures." *Child Development* 54(1983): 1335–54.

Bloom, L.Z., K. Coburn, and J. Pearlman. *The New Assertive Woman.* New York: Dell, 1976.

Blum, R.H. et al. *Society and Drugs and Cultural Observations.* San Francisco, CA: Jossey-Bass, 1969.

Blum, S. "The Children Who Starve Themselves." *New York Times Magazine,* Nov. 10, 1974.

Boehm, D. "The Cervical Cap: Effectiveness as a Contraceptive." *Journal of Nurse-Midwifery* 28(1)(1983):3–6.

Borke, H. "Piaget's Mountains Revisited: Changes in the Egocentric Landscape." *Developmental Psychology* 11(1975):240–43.

Boskin-White, M. and W.C. White. *Bulimarexia.* New York: Norton, 1983.

Boston Women's Health Book Collective. *The New Our Bodies, Ourselves* New York: Simon & Schuster, 1984.

Bostow, D.E., and J.B. Bailey. "Modification of Severe Disruptive and Aggressive Behavior Using Brief Time-Out and Reinforcement Procedures." *Journal of Applied Behavior Analysis* 2(1969):31–37.

Botwinick, J. "Cautiousness in Advanced Age." *Journal of Gerontology* 21(1966):347–53.

———. "Geropsychology." *Annual Review of Psychology* 21(1970):239–72.

———. "Intellectual Abilities." In J.E. Birren and K.W. Schaie (eds.), *Handbook of the Psychology of Aging.* New York: Van Nostrand Reinhold, 1977.

Bouchard, T.J., Jr. "Current Conceptions of Intelligence and Their Implications for Assessment." In P. McReynolds (ed.), *Advances in Psychological Assessment,* vol. 1. Palo Alto, CA: Science and Behavior Books, 1968.

Bould, S., B. Sanborn, and L. Reif. *Eighty-Five Plus.* Belmont, CA: Wadsworth, 1989.

Bourque, L.B. *Defining Rape.* Durham, NC: Duke University Press, 1989.

Bowerman, D.E., and D.P. Irish. "Some Relationships of Stepchildren to Their Parents." *Marriage and Family Living* 24(1962):113–21.

Bowman, H.A. *Marriage for Moderns.* 6th ed. New York: McGraw-Hill, 1970.

Boyte, H.C. "People Power Transforms a St. Louis Housing Project." *Occasional Papers.* Chicago: Community Renewable Society, 1989.

Bracken, M., et al. "Association of Cocaine Use with Sperm Concentration, Motility and Morphology." *Fertility and Sterilization* 53(1990):315–22.

Braginsky, D.D., and B.M. Braginsky. "Surplus People: Their Lost Faith in Self and System." *Psychology Today,* Aug. 1975, p. 70.

Brazelton, H.M. "Neonatal Behavioral Assessment Scale." In *Clinics in Developmental Medicine,* no. 50. Philadelphia, PA: Lippincott, 1973.

Brecher, E.M. *Love, Sex, and Aging.* Mount Vernon, NY: Consumers Union, 1984.

Brecher, E.M. "Marijuana: The Health Questions." *Consumer Reports,* March 1975, pp. 143–49.

Brecher, E.M., et al. *Licit and Illicit Drugs: The Consumers Union Report on Narcotics, Stimulants, Depressants, Inhalants, Hallucinogens and Marijuana—Including Coffee, Nicotine, and Alcohol.* Boston: Little, Brown, 1972.

Breland, H. "Birth Order, Family Configuration and Verbal Achievement." *Child Development* 45(1974):1011–19.

Brenner, H. *Mental Illness and the Economy.* Cambridge, MA: Harvard University Press, 1973.

Breuer, J., and S. Freud. *Studies in Hysteria.* London: Hogarth Press, 1895.

Bridges, K.M.B. "Emotional Development in Early Infancy." *Child Development* 3(1932):324–41.

Bright, P. "Adolescent Pregnancy and Loss." *Maternal-Child Nursing Journal* 16(1987):1–12.

Brittain, C. "Adolescent Choices and Parent-Peer Cross-Pressures." *American Sociological Review* 28(1963):385–91.

Brock, C., et al. "Frequency of Asymptomatic Shedding of Herpes Simplex Virus in Women with Genital Herpes." *Journal of the American Medical Association* 263(1990):418–22.

Bromley, D.B. *The Psychology of Human Aging.* 2d ed. Middlesex: Penguin, 1974.

Bronfenbrenner, U. "The Changing American Family." In E.M. Hetherington and R.D. Parke (eds.), *Contemporary Readings in Child Psychology.* New York: McGraw-Hill, 1977.

Brooks-Gunn, J. "Pubertal Processes and the Early Adolescent Transition." In W. Dumon (ed.), *Child Development Today and Tomorrow*. San Francisco, CA: Jossey-Bass, 1988.

Brooks-Gunn, J., and F.F. Furstenberg. "The Children of Adolescent Mothers: Physical, Academic, and Psychological Outcomes." *Developmental Review* 6(1986):224–51.

Brophy, B. "Children under Stress." *U.S. News & World Report*, Oct. 27, 1986, p. 59.

Brown, B. *Stress and the Art of Biofeedback*. New York: Harper & Row, 1977.

Brown, B.S. "The Decriminalization of Marijuana." In *Hearings of the House Select Committee on Narcotic Abuse*, March 14, 1977, First session, 95th Congress.

Brown, S.S. "Can Low Birth Weight Be Prevented?" *Family Planning Perspectives* 17(3)(1985):112–118.

Browne, A., and D. Finkelhor. "Initial Long-Term Effects: A Review of the Research." In D. Finkelhor, S. Araji, A. Browne, S.D. Peters, and G.E. Wyatt (eds.), *A Sourcebook on Child Sexual Abuse*. Beverly Hills, CA: Sage, 1986.

Brownlee, S. "Alzheimer's: Is There Hope?" *U.S. News & World Report*, Aug. 12, 1991, pp.40–49.

———. "Plotting a Fresh Attack in the War on AIDS." *U.S. News & World Report*, Jan. 6, 1992, p. 62.

Brownmiller, S. *Against Our Will: Men, Women, and Rape*. New York: Bantam Books, 1975.

Bruch, H. *Eating Disorders*. New York: Basic Books, 1973.

———. *The Golden Cage: The Enigma of Anorexia Nervosa*. Cambridge, MA: Harvard University Press, 1978.

Bruner, J.S., R.R. Oliver, and P.M. Greenfield. *Studies in Cognitive Growth*. New York: Wiley, 1966.

Buchanan, R.L., and M.A. Cummings. *Individual Differences: An Experience in Human Relations for Children*. Madison, WI: Madison Public Schools, 1975.

Buckingham, S.L., and W.G. Van Gorp. "AIDS-Dementia Complex: Implications for Practice." *Social Casework* 29(6)(June 1988):371–75.

Budiansky, S. "The New Rules of Reproduction." *U.S. News & World Report*, April 18, 1988, pp. 66–69.

Buhler, C. *Der Menschliche, Lebenslauf al Pschologishes Problem*. Leipzig: Verlag von S. Herzel, 1933.

———. "The Course of Human Life as a Psychological Problem." *Human Development* 11(1968):184–200.

Burchard, J.D., and V.O. Tyler. "The Modification of Delinquent Behavior Through Operant Conditioning." *Behaviour Research and Therapy* 2(1965):245–50.

Burgess, A.W., and L.L. Holmstrom. "Rape Trauma Syndrome." *American Journal of Psychiatry* 131(1974):981–86.(a)

———. *Rape: Victims of Crisis*. (Bowie, MD: Robert J. Brady, 1974.(b)

Burnell, G.M., and M.A. Norfleet. "Women's Self-Reported Responses to Abortion." *Journal of Psychology* 121(1987):71–76.

Bush, S. "Beauty Makes the Beast Look Better." *Psychology Today*, Oct. 1976, pp. 15–16.

Butler, R.N. "Myths and Realities of Aging." Address at the Governor's Conference on Aging, Columbia, MD, May 28, 1970.

———. *Why Survive? Being Old in America*. New York: Harper & Row, 1975.

Butler, R.N. and M. Lewis. *Sex after Sixty: A Guide for Men and Women for Their Later Years*. New York: Harper & Row, 1976.

———. *Aging and Mental Health: Positive Psychosocial Approaches*, 2d ed. St. Louis, MO: Mosby, 1977.

"By Any Other Name: Early Signs of AIDS in Women Go Unrecognized." *Contemporary Sexuality* 1(2)(Feb. 1991):4.

Byer, C.O., et al. *Dimensions of Human Sexuality*, 2nd ed. Dubuque, IA: W.C. Brown, 1988.

Bylinski, G. "What Science Can Do about Hereditary Disease." *Fortune*, Sept. 1974, pp. 148–60.

Califia, P. "Lesbian Sexuality." *Journal of Homosexuality* 4(3) (1979):255–66.

Cameron-Bandler, L. *Solutions*. San Rafael, CA: Future Pace, 1985.

Campbell, A. "The American Way of Mating: Marriage Si; Children Only Maybe." *Psychology Today*, Aug. 1975, pp. 37–43.

Campbell, A., P.E. Converse, and W.L. Rodgers. *The Quality of American Life: Perceptions, Evaluations, and Satisfactions*. New York: Russell-Sage, 1976.

Cancer and Steroid Hormone Study, Centers for Disease Control and National Institute of Child Health and Human Development. "Oral Contraceptive Use and the Risk of Breast Cancer." *New England Journal of Medicine* 315(1986):405–11.

"Cancer Society Says More Women in U.S. Will Develop Breast Cancer." *Milwaukee Journal*, Jan. 25, 1991.

Caputo, L. "Dual Diagnosis: AIDS and Addiction." *Social Work* 30(4)(1985):361–64.

Card, J.J., and L.L. Wise. "Teenage Mothers and Teenage Fathers: The Impact of Early Childbearing on the Parents' Personal and Professional Lives." *Family Planning Perspectives* 10(1978): 199–205.

Carey, R.G., and B.B. Bucher. "Positive Practice Overcorrection: Effects of Reinforcing Correct Performance." *Behavior Modification* 10(1986):73–92.

Carmichael, S., and C.V. Hamilton. *Black Power: The Politics of Liberation in America*. New York: Vintage Books, 1967.

Carnes, P. *Out of the Shadows: Understanding Sexual Addiction*. Minneapolis, MN: Comp Care, 1983.

Carroll, J.L., and J.R. Rest. "Moral Development." In B.B. Wolman (ed.), *Handbook of Developmental Psychology*. Englewood Cliffs, NJ: Prentice-Hall, 1982.

Carter, E.A., and M. McGoldrick. *The Family Life Cycle: A Framework for Family Therapy*. New York: Gardner Press, 1980.

———. "Overview: The Changing Family Life Cycle—A Framework for Family Therapy." In B. Carter and M. McGoldrick (eds.), *The Changing Family Life Cycle: A Framework for Family Therapy*, 2nd ed. Boston: Allyn and Bacon, 1989.

Cartwright, D. "Achieving Change in People: Some Applications of Group Dynamics Theory." *Human Relations* 4(1951): 381–92.

Cates, W., Jr., and S.L. Schulz. "Epidemiology of HIV in Women." *Contemporary OB/GYN* 32(1988):94–105.

Cates, W.J., et al. "Sex and Spermicides: Preventing Unintended Pregnancy and Infection." *Journal of the American Medical Association* 248(1982):1636–37.

Cattell, R.B. *Abilities: Their Structure, Growth, and Action*. Boston: Houghton Mifflin, 1971.

CBS Reports. "The Baby Makers." Oct. 1979.

Centers for Disease Control. "Oral Contraceptive Use and the Risk of Ovarian Cancer." *Journal of the American Medical Association* 249(1983):1596–99.

———. *Publications*. Atlanta: Public Information Office, 1987.

———. *AIDS Weekly Surveillance Report*. Sept. 26, 1988.

———. *Abortion Surveillance, United States, 1984-1985*. *Morbidity and Mortality Weekly Report* 38(1989):11–45.(a)

———. "Sexually Transmitted Diseases: Treatment Guidelines." *Morbidity and Mortality Weekly Report* 38(1989):1–36.(b)

———. "The HIV/AIDS Epidemic: The First 10 Years." *Morbidity and Mortality Weekly Report* 40(1991):357–58.

———. "The Second 100,000 Cases of Acquired Immunodeficiency Syndrome—United States." *Morbidity and Mortality Weekly Report* 41(1992):28–29.

Chalfant, J.C. "Learning Disabilities Policy Issues and Promising Approaches." *American Psychologist* 44(1989):392–398.

Chamberlain, R.W. "How Well Do Early Child-Rearing Styles and Child Behavioral Patterns Predict Later Home and School Functioning?" In S.A. Mednick et al., (eds.), *Handbook of Longitudinal Research*. Vol. 1, *Birth and Childhood Cohorts*. New York: Holt, Rinehart and Winston, 1984.

Chappell, D., "Forcible Rape: A Comparative Study of Offenses Known to the Police in. Boston and Los Angeles." In J.M. Henslin (ed.), *Studies in the Sociology of Sex*. New York: Appleton-Century-Crofts, 1971.

Chasnoff, I.J., et al. "Temporal Patterns of Cocaine Use in Pregnancy: Perinatal Outcomes." *Journal of the American Medical Association* 261(12)(1989):1741–44.

Chavez, G.F., J. Mulinare, and J.F. Cordero. "Maternal Cocaine Use During Early Pregnancy as a Risk Factor for Congenital Urogenital Anomalies." *Journal of the American Medical Association* 26(2)(1989):795–98.

Cherlin, A., and F.F. Furstenberg. "Grandparents and Family Crisis." *Generations* 10(4)(1986):26–28.

Cherry, R. *Discrimination: Its Economic Impact on Blacks, Women, and Jews*. Lexington, MA: Lexington Books, 1989.

Chervenak, F.A., G. Isaacson, and M.J. Mahoney. "Advances in the Diagnosis of Fetal Defects." *New England Journal of Medicine* 315(5)(1986):305–7.

Chess, W.A., and J.M. Norlin. *Human Behavior and the Social Environment*. Boston: Allyn and Bacon, 1988.

Chestang, L. "Character Development in a Hostile Environment." Occasional Paper No. 3. Chicago: School of Social Science Administration, University of Chicago, 1972.

"Child-Support Payments Lax." *Providence Evening Bulletin*, March 14, 1985.

Child Welfare League of America. *Standards for Foster Family Care*. New York: CWLA, 1959.

Chilman, C.S. "Abortion." In *Encyclopedia of Social Work*, vol. 1. New York: NASW, 1987.

Christopher, F., and R. Cate. "Factors Involved in Premarital Decision Making." *Journal of Sex Research* 20(1984):363–76.

Christopher, R. "Mother's Little Helper." *Maclean's Magazine*, March 10, 1980, p. 10.

Chumlea, W.C. "Physical Growth in Adolescence." In B.B. Wolman (ed.), *Handbook of Developmental Psychology*. Englewood Cliffs, NJ: Prentice-Hall, 1982.

Clark, K.B., and M.P. Clark. "Racial Identification and Preferences in Negro Children." In G.E. Swanson, T.M. Newcomb, and E.L. Hartley (eds.), *Readings in Social Psychology*, rev. ed. New York: Holt, Rinehart and Winston, 1952.

Clark, M., and B. Anderson. *Culture and Aging*. Springfield, IL: Charles C. Thomas, 1967.

Clarren, K.S., and D.W. Smith. "The Fetal Alcohol Syndrome." *New England Journal of Medicine* 298(1978):1063–67.

Clausen, J.A. "The Social Meaning of Differential Physical and Sexual Maturation." In S.E. Ragastin and G.H. Elder (eds.), *Adolescence in the Life Cycle: Psychological Change and Social Context*. New York: Wiley, 1975.

Clayton, R.R. *The Family, Marriage and Social Change*. Lexington, MA: D.C. Heath, 1975.

Clifford, E. "Body Satisfaction in Adolescents." *Perceptual and Motor Skills* 33(1971):119–25.

Clifford, R.E. "Subjective Sexual Experience in College Women." *Archives of Sexual Behavior* 7(1978):183–97.

Cohen, A. *Delinquent Boys: The Culture of the Gang*. New York: Free Press, 1955.

Cohen, F. "Psychological Characteristics of the Second Child as Compared with the First." *Indian Journal of Psychology* 26(1951):79–84.

Cohen, M.L., R. Garofalo, R. Boucher, and T. Seghorn. "The Psychology of Rapists." *Seminars in Psychiatry* 3(1971):307–27.

Cole, E.K., ed. *Sexual Harassment on Campus: A Legal Compendium*. Washington, DC: National Association of College and University Attorneys, 1990.

Cole, E.S. "Societal Influences on Adoption Practice." In P. Sachdev, (ed.), *Adoption: Current Issues and Trends*. Toronto, Canada: Butterworths, 1984.

Cole, G.F. *The American System of Criminal Justice*. 6th ed. Pacific Grove, CA: Brooks/Cole, 1992.

Cole, M., J. Gay, J. Glick, and D. Sharp. *The Cultural Context of Learning and Thinking*. New York: Basic Books, 1971.

Coleman, J.W., and D.R. Cressey. *Social Problems*. New York: Harper & Row, 1980.

———. *Social Problems*. 2nd ed. New York: Harper & Row, 1984.

———. *Social Problems*. 4th ed. New York: Harper & Row, 1990.

Coles, R. *Children of Crisis*. Boston: Atlantic/Little, Brown, 1967.

———. Testimony before the Select Committee on Nutrition and Human Needs of the U.S. Senate, Feb. 1969.

Coles, R., and G. Stokes. *Sex and the American Teenager*. New York: Harper & Row, 1985.

Collier, H.V. *Counseling Women*. New York: Free Press, 1982.

Collins, J.A., et al. "Treatment-independent Pregnancy among Infertile Couples." *New England Journal of Medicine* 309 (1983):1201–6.

Collison, M. "Neglect of Minorities Seen Jeopardizing Future Prosperity." *Chronicle of Higher Education* 34(37)(May 15, 1988):1.

Commission on Marihuana and Drug Abuse. *Marihuana: A Signal of Misunderstanding*. Washington, DC: U.S. Government Printing Office, 1972.

———. *Drug Use in America: Problem in Perspective*. Washington, DC: U.S. Government Printing Office, 1973.

Conger, J.J. "Adolescence: A Time for Becoming." In M.E. Lamb (ed.), *Social and Personality Development*. New York: Holt, 1978.

Consumers Union. *Licit and Illicit Drugs*, E.M. Brecher (ed.). Boston: Little, Brown, 1972.

Contemporary Sexuality. "Enter Norplant." (Jan. 1991, pp. 1–2.(a)

———. "What Else Is Out There?" Jan. 1991, pp.2–3.

———. "By Any Other Name: Early Signs of AIDS in Women Go Unrecognized." Feb. 1991, p.4. no 2:4.

———. "Sexuality and the Law: New Rules Speed Benefits to People with AIDS." Feb. 1992, p. 6.

Cooley, C.H. *Human Nature and the Social Order* New York: Scribner, 1902.

Cooper, M. "The Rich in America." *U.S. News & World Report*, Nov. 18, 1991, pp.34–40.

Coopersmith, S. *The Antecedents of Self-Esteem*. San Francisco, CA: Freeman, 1967.

———. "Studies in Self-Esteem." *Scientific American* 218(2)(1968): 96–106.

Cordes, C. "The Rise of One-Parent Black Families." *APA Monitor*, Aug. 1984, pp. 16–18.

Corey, L., and P.G. Spear. "Infections with Herpes Simplex Virus— Part Two." *New England Journal of Medicine* 314 (1986):749–57.

Corso, J.F. "Sensory Processes and Age Effects in Normal Adults." *Journal of Gerontology* 26(1)(1971):90–105.

Cory, D.W. *The Homosexual in America: A Subjective Approach.* New York: Greenberg, 1951.

Cory, D.W., and J.P. LeRoy. "Homosexual Marriage." *Sexology* 29(10)(1963):660–62.

Costa, P.T., Jr., and R.R. McCrae. "Still Stable after All These Years: Personality as a Key to Some Issues in Aging." In P.B. Baltes and O.G. Grin, Jr. (eds.), *Life-Span Development and Behavior,* vol. 3. New York: Academic Press, 1980.

Costin, L.B. *Child Welfare: Policies and Practice.* New York: McGraw-Hill, 1979.

Cottingham, P. "Black Income and Metropolitan Residential Dispersion." *Urban Affairs Quarterly* 10(March 1975):273–96.

Council on Social Work Education. *Curriculum Policy for the Masters Degree and Baccalaureate Degree Programs in Social Work Education.* New York: CSWE, 1983.

———. *Handbook of Accreditation Standards and Procedures.* Rev. ed. New York: CSWE, 1984.

———. "Curriculum Policy Statement for Baccalaureate Degree Programs in Social Work Education." Draft. Alexandria, VA: CSWE, 1991.

Council on Social Work Education Commission on Accreditation. *Handbook of Accreditation Standards and Procedures.* Washington, DC: CSWE, 1988.

Cox, F.M. "Alternative Conceptions of Community: Implications for Community Organization Practice." In F.M. Cox, et al. (eds.), *Strategies of Community Organization,* 4th ed. Itasca, IL: Peacock, 1987.

Cox, F.M., J.L. Erlich, J. Rothman, and J.E. Tropman, eds. *Strategies of Community Organization: A Book of Readings.* 4th ed. Itasca, IL: Peacock, 1987.

Coyner, S. "Women's Liberation and Sexual Liberation." In S. Gordon and R.W. Libby (eds.), *Sexuality Today and Tomorrow.* North Scituate, MA: Duxbury Press, 1976.

Cozby, P.C. "Self-Disclosure: A Literature Review." *Psychological Bulletin* 79(1973):73–91.

Craft, J.L., et al. "Factors Influencing Legal Disposition in Child Abuse Cases." *Journal of Social Service Research* 4(1)(Fall 1980):31–45.

Craib, R. "Sex and Women at UC [University of California] Berkeley—Two Surveys." *San Francisco Chronicle,* July 22, 1977.

Craig, G.J., and R. Specht. *Human Development.* Englewood Cliffs, NJ: Prentice-Hall, 1983.

Craighead, W.E., M.L. Mahoney, and A.R. Kazdin. *Behavior Modification: Principles, Issues, and Applications.* Boston: Houghton-Mifflin, 1976.

Crisp, A.H. *Let Me Be.* New York: Grune & Stratton, 1980.

Crockett, L.J., and A.C. Petersen. "Pubertal Status and Psychosocial Development: Findings from the Early Adolescence Study." In R.M. Lerner and T.T. Foch (eds.), *Biological-Psychosocial Interactions in Early Adolescence: A Life-Span Perspective.* Hillsdale, NJ: Erlbaum, 1987.

Crooks, R., and K. Baur. *Our Sexuality.* 4th ed. Redwood City, CA: Benjamin/Cummings, 1990.

———. *Our Sexuality.* 5th ed. Redwood City, CA: Benjamin/Cummings, 1993.

Cuber, J.F., and P.B. Harroff. "Five Types of Marriage." In A.S. Skolnick and J.H. Skolnick (eds.), *Family in Transition.* Boston: Little, Brown, 1971.

Cultural Information Service. "The Burning Bed: Viewer's Guide." New York: CIStems, 1984.

Cumming, E., and W.E. Henry. *Growing Old: The Process of Disengagement.* New York: Basic Books, 1961.

Cummings, J.L. "Subcortical Dementia: Neuropsychology, Neuro-

psychiatry and Pathophysiology." *British Journal of Psychiatry* 149(1986):682–97.

Cummings, M. "How to Handle Incidents of Racial Discrimination." In C. Zastrow and D.H. Chang (eds.), *The Personal Problem Solver.* Englewood Cliffs, NJ: Prentice-Hall, 1977.

Curtis, T. "Defeating One Disease May Have Spread Another." *The Milwaukee Journal,* Section D, March 16, 1992, pp. 1–2.

Daft, R.L. *Organization Theory and Design.* New York: West, 1983.

Daley, M., and M. Wilson. *Sex, Evolution, and Behavior.* 2nd ed. Boston: Willard Grant, 1983.

Davenport, R. *Making Time, Making Money.* New York: St. Martin's Press, 1982.

David, H.P., et al., eds. *Born Unwanted: Developmental Effects of Denied Abortion.* New York: Springer, 1988.

David, H.P., and Z. Matejcek "Children Born to Women Denied Abortion: An Update." *Family Planning Perspectives* 13(1981): 32-34.

Davis, J. *Help Me, I'm Hurt.* Dubuque, IA: Kendall/Hunt, 1982.

Davis, J., and T. Smith. *General Social Surveys 1972-1984: Cumulative Data.* New Haven, CT: Yale University, Roper Center for Public Opinion Research, 1984.

Davis, L.E. "Racial Composition of Groups." *Social Work* 24(May 1979):208–13.

Deaux, K. *The Behavior of Women and Men.* Belmont, CA: Brooks/Cole, 1976.

———. "From Individual Differences to Social Categories." *American Psychologist* 39(1984):105–16.

DeFrances, V. *The Fundamentals of Child Protection.* Denver, CO: American Humane Assoc. 1955.

Delgado, M., and D. Humm-Delgado. "Natural Support Systems: Source of Strength in Hispanic Communities." *Social Work* 27(1)(Jan. 1982):83–89.

DeLury, G.E. *World Almanac.* Garden City, NY: Doubleday, 1974.

Denfield, D., and M. Gordon. "The Sociology of Mate Swapping: Or the Family That Swings Together Clings Together." *Journal of Sex Research* 6(1970):85–100.

Denney, N.W. "Aging and Cognitive Changes." In B.B. Wolman (ed.), *Handbook of Developmental Psychology.* Englewood Cliffs, NJ: Prentice-Hall, 1982.

Denney, N.W., and D. Quadagno. *Human Sexuality.* 2nd ed. Chicago: Mosby, 1992.

Dennis, W. "Causes of Retardation among Institutional Children: Iran." *Journal of Genetic Psychology* 96(1960):47–59.

———. "Creative Production Between the Ages of 20 and 80." *Journal of Gerontology* 21(1966):8.

Dennis, W., and Y. Sayegh. "The Effect of Supplementary Experiences upon the Behavioral Development of Infants in Institutions." *Child Development* 36(1965):81–90.

Dentzer, S. "The Wealth of Nations." *U.S. News & World Report,* May 4, 1992, pp. 54.

Deutsch, M. "Minority Group and Class Status as Related to Social and Personality Factors in Scholastic Achievement." *Monographs of the Society for Applied Anthropology* 2(1960).

Devore, W., and E.G. Schlesinger. *Ethnic-Sensitive Social Work Practice.* St. Louis, MO: Mosby, 1981.

DeVries, H.A. "Physiology of Exercise and Aging." In D.S. Woodruff and J.E. Birren (eds.), *Aging: Scientific Perspectives and Social Issues.* New York: Van Nostrand, 1975.

Dewsburg, D. "Effects of Novelty on Copulatory Behavior: The Coolidge Effect and Related Phenomena." *Psychological Bulletin* 89(1981):464–82.

Dickman, I.R. *Winning the Battle for Sex Education.* New York: SIECUS, 1982.

DiClemente, R.J., B.A. Zorn, and L. Temoshok. "Adolescents and AIDS: A Survey of Knowledge, Attitudes, and Beliefs About AIDS in San Francisco." *American Journal of Public Health* 78(1986):1443–45.

DiLeonardi, J.W. "Decision-Making in Protective Services." *Child Welfare* 59(6)(June 1980):356–64.

Dillard, J.L. *Black English: Its History and Usage in the United States.* New York: Random House, 1972.

DiMaio, M.S., et al. "Screening for Fetal Down's Syndrome in Pregnancy by Measuring Maternal Serum Alpha-Fetoprotein Levels." *New England Journal of Medicine* 317(1987):342–46.

Division of Health Examination Statistics, National Center for Health Statistics. *Data from the Health and Nutrition Examination Survey, 1971–1974.* Washington, DC: U.S. Government Printing Office, 1975.

Dodge, K.A. "Behavioral Antecedents of Peer Social Status." *Child Development* 54(1983):1386–99.

Doerr, P., et al. "Plasma Testosterone, Estradiol, and Semen Analysis in Male Homosexuals." *Archives of General Psychiatry* 29(1973):829–33.

Doka, K.J., and M.E. Mertz. "The Meaning and Significance of Great-Grandparenthood." *Gerontologist* 28(2)(1988):192–97.

Donaldson, M. "The Mismatch Between School and Children's Minds." *Human Nature* 2(1979):158–62.

Donnerstein, E., and D. Linz. "Sexual Violence in the Media: A Warning." *Psychology Today,* Jan. 1984:14–15.

Dorner, G. *Hormones and Brain Differentiation.* Amsterdam: Elsevier, 1976.

Doshi, M. "Accuracy of Consumer Performed In-Home Tests for Early Pregnancy Detection." *American Journal of Public Health* 76(1987):512–14.

Downs, H. "Growing Old in America." ABC News Program Transcript. New York: Journal Graphics Inc., 1985.

Doyle, A.C. "A Scandal in Bohemia." In *The Adventures of Sherlock Holmes.* London: John Murray, 1974.

Draper, B.J. "Black Language as an Adaptive Response to a Hostile Environment." In C.B. Germain (ed.), *Social Work Practices: People and Environments.* New York: Columbia University Press, 1979.

Dreher, K.F., and J.G. Fraser. "Smoking Habits of Alcoholic Outpatients." *International Journal of Addictions* 3(1968):65–80.

Dreyer, P.H. "Sexuality during Adolescence." In B.B. Wolman (ed.), *Handbook of Developmental Psychology.* Englewood Cliffs, NJ: Prentice-Hall, 1982.

Drill, V.A. "Oral Contraceptives: Relation to Mammary Cancer, Benign Breast Lesions and Cervical Cancer." *Annual Review of Pharmacology* 15(1975):367–85.

Duberman, L. *The Reconstituted Family: A Study of Remarried Couples and Their Children.* Chicago: Nelson-Hall, 1975.

Duffy, M. "Calling the Doctor: Women Complain about Illnesses More Often Than Men." *New York Daily News,* Feb. 8, 1979.

Dunn, H.G., et al. "Maternal Cigarette Smoking during Pregnancy and the Child's Subsequent Development. II: Neurological and Intellectual Maturation to the Age of 6 ½ years." *Canadian Journal of Public Health* 68(1977):43–50.

Dunn, J., and C. Kendrick. *Siblings: Love, Envy and Understanding.* Cambridge, MA: Harvard University Press, 1982.

Dunn, J. "Sibling Relationships in Early Childhood." *Child Development* 54(1983):787–811.

———. *Sisters and Brothers.* Cambridge, MA: Harvard University Press, 1985.

Dunning, W.W., and D.H. Chang. "Drug Facts and Effects." In C. Zastrow and D.H. Chang (eds.) *The Personal Problem Solver.* Englewood Cliffs, NJ: Spectrum, 1977.

Duren, R. Presentation on drug abuse at University of Wisconsin—Whitewater, Oct. 18, 1985.

Dusay, J.M., and K.M. Dusay. "Transactional Analysis." In Raymond J. Corsini (ed.), *Current Psychotherapies,* 3rd ed. Itasca, IL: Peacock, 1984.

Dutton, D.G. "The Criminal Justice Response to Wife Assault." *Law and Human Behavior* 11(1987):189–206.

Dytrych, Z., Z. Matejcek, V. Schuller, H.P. David, and H.L. Friedman. "Children Born to Women Denied Abortion." *Family Planning Perspectives* 7(1975):165–71.

Dzeich, B.W., and L. Weiner. *The Lecherous Professor: Sexual Harassment on Campus.* Boston: Beacon Press, 1990.

Eakins, B., and G. Eakins. "Verbal Turn-Taking and Exchanges in Faculty Dialogue." In B.L. Dubois and I. Crouch (eds.), *Papers in Southwest English IV: Proceedings in the Conference on the Sociology of the Languages of American Women.* San Antonio, TX: Trinity University Press, 1976.

Earls, F., and B. Siegel. "Precocious Fathers." *American Journal of Orthopsychiatry* 50(1980):469–80.

Eaton, J.T., D.B. Lippmann, and D.P. Riley. *Growing with Your Learning-Disabled Child.* Boston: Resource Communications, 1980.

Edeiken, S. "Mammography and Palpable Cancer of the Breast." *Cancer* 61(1988):263–65.

Edwards, C.P. "The Comparative Study of the Development of Moral Judgment and Reasoning." In R.L. Monroe and B.B. Whiting (eds.), *Handbook of Cross-Cultural Human Development.* New York: Garland, 1977.

Edwards, R. "The Current Situation of In Vitro Fertilization." *International Planned Parenthood Federation Medical Bulletin* 18(5)(1984):1–2.

Edwards, R., and P. Steptoe. "Current Status of In Vitro Fertilization and Implantation of Human Embryos." *Human Reproduction* 1(1)(1985):6–10.

Ehrbar, A.F. "A Radical Prescription for Medical Care." *Fortune,* Feb. 1977, p. 169.

Ehrhardt, A. "Sexual Orientation after Prenatal Exposure to Exogenous Estrogen." *Archives of Sexual Behavior* 14(1)(1985): 57–75.

Ehrlich, P., and R. Holm. "A Biological View of Race." In Ashley Montague (ed.), *The Concept of Race.* New York: Free Press, 1964.

"18 Million Moms Doing Double-Duty." *Providence Evening Bulletin,* Feb. 11, 1986.

Einstein, E. "Stepfamily Lives." *Human Behavior,* April 1979, pp. 63–68.

Ekerdt, D.J., R. Bosse, and J.M. Mogey. "Concurrent Change in Planned and Preferred Age for Retirement." *Journal of Gerontology* 35(1980);232–40.

Ekman, P., and W.V. Friesen. *Unmaking the Face.* Englewood Cliffs, NJ: Prentice-Hall, 1975.

Elder, G. "Appearance and Education in Marriage Mobility." *American Sociological Review* 34(1969):519–33.

Elias, J., and P. Gebhard. "Sexuality and Sexual Learning in Childhood." *Phi Delta Kappan* 50(1969):401–5.

Elkins, D. "Some Factors Related to the Choice Status of Ninety Eighth Grade Children in a School Society." *Genetic Psychology Monographs* 58(1958):207–72.

Ellerbrock, T. et al. "Epidemiology of Women with AIDS in the United States, 1981 through 1990." *Journal of the American Medical Association* 265(1991):2971–75.

Ellis, A. *Reason and Emotion in Psychotherapy.* New York: Lyle Stuart, 1962.

———. "Rational-Emotive Therapy." In R. Corsini (ed.), *Current Psychotherapies.* Itasca, IL: Peacock, 1975.

———. "Rational-Emotive Therapy." In Raymond Corsini (ed.), *Current Psychotherapies,* 2nd ed. Itasca, IL: Peacock, 1979.

Elmer-DeWitt, P. "The Cruelest Kind of Fraud." *Time,* Dec 2, 1991, p. 27.

Elson, J. "The Feds vs. a Federal Judge." *Time,* Aug. 19, 1991, p. 22.

Emlen, A.C. "Slogans, Slots, and Slander: The Myth of Day Care Need." *American Journal of Orthopsychiatry* 43(1)(Jan. 1973):23–36.

Encyclopedia of Social Work. Silver Spring, MD: NASW, 1987.

Encyclopedia of Sociology. Guilford, CN: Duskin, 1974.

Engen, T. "Taste and Smell." In J.E. Berrin and K.W. Schale (ed.), *Handbook of the Psychology of Aging.* New York: Van Nostrand Reinhold, 1977.

England, P. "Explanations of Job Segregation and the Sex Gap in Pay." In *Comparable Worth: Issue for the 80's.* Vol. 1. Washington, DC: U.S. Commission on Civil Rights, 1984.

Englander-Golden, P., and G. Barton. "Sex Differences in Absence from Work: A Reinterpretation." *Psychology of Women Quarterly* 8(1983):185–88.

English, P.C. "Failure to Thrive Without Organic Reason." *Pediatric Annals* 7(1978):774–80.

"Enter Norplant." *Contemporary Sexuality* vol. 25(1)(Jan. 1991):1–2.

Entwisle, D.R., K.L. Alexander, A.M. Pallas, and D. Cardigan. "The Emergent Academic Self-Image of First Graders: Its Response to Social Structure." *Child Development* 58(1987): 200–209.

Erikson, E.H. *Childhood and Society.* New York: Norton, 1950.

———. "The Problem of Ego Identity." *Psychological Issues* 1(1959): 101–64.

———. *Childhood and Society,* 2nd ed. New York: Norton, 1963.

Ernst, C., and J. Angst. *Birth Order: Its Influence on Personality.* New York: Springer-Verlag, 1983.

Eron, L.D. "Prescription for Reduction of Aggression." *American Psychologist* 35(3)(1980):244–52.

———. "Parent-Child Interaction, Television Violence, and Aggression in Children." *American Psychologist* 37(2)(1982):197–211.

Espenshade, T.J. "The Economic Consequences of Divorce." *Journal of Marriage and the Family* 41(1979):615–25.

Estes, E.H. "Health Experience in the Elderly." In E. Busse and E. Pfeiffer (eds.), *Behavior and Adaptation in Late Life.* Boston: Little, Brown, 1969.

Estrich, S. *Real Rape.* Boston: Harvard University Press, 1987.

Etzioni, A. *Modern Organizations.* Englewood Cliffs, NJ: Prentice-Hall, 1964.

Evans, R.B. "Sixteen Personality Factor Questionnaire Scores of Homosexual Men." *Journal of Consulting and Clinical Psychology* 34(1970):212–15.

Eveleth, P.B., and J.M. Tanner. *Worldwide Variation in Human Growth.* Cambridge, U.K.: Cambridge University Press, 1976.

Everywoman's Center. *Results of Sexual Violence Survey.* Amherst: University of Massachusetts, 1980.

"Fact Sheet: RU486." New York: Planned Parenthood Federation of America, Inc., 1993.

Fagot, B.I., R. Hagan, M.D. Leinbach, and S. Kronsberg. "Differential Reactions to Assertive and Communicative Acts of Toddler Boys and Girls." *Child Development* 56(1985): 1499–1505.

Falbo, T., and D.F. Polit. "Quantitative Review of the Only Child Literature: Research Evidence and Theory Development." *Psychological Bulletin* 100(2)(1986):176–89.

Faller, K.C., et al. "Types of Child Abuse and Neglect." In K. Faller (ed.), *Social Work with Abused and Neglected Children.* New York: Free Press, 1981.

"Families with Children Falling Further Behind." *Providence Evening Bulletin,* Dec. 26, 1985, p. A.1.

Farberow, N.I., and R.E. Litman. "Suicide Prevention." In H.L.P. Resnick and H.L. Ruben (eds.), *Emergency Psychiatric Care.* Bowie, MD: Charles Press, 1975.

Farkas, G.M., and R.C. Rosen. "Effect of Alcohol on Elicited Male Sexual Response." *Journal of Studies on Alcohol* 37(1976):265–72.

Farley, L. *Sexual Shakedown: The Sexual Harassment of Women on the Job.* New York: Warner, 1978.

Faust, M.S. "Developmental Maturity as a Determinant in Prestige of Adolescent Girls." *Child Development* 31(1960):173–84.

Feagans, L. "A Current View of Learning Disabilities." *Journal of Pediatrics* 102(4)(1983):487–93.

Feagin, J.R. *Subordinating the Poor: Welfare and American Beliefs* Englewood Cliffs, NJ: Prentice-Hall, 1975.

Featherman, D.L., and R.M. Hauser. "Changes in the Socioeconomic Stratification of the Races, 1962-73." *American Journal of Sociology* 81(Nov. 1976):621–51.

Featherstone, J. "Open Schools—the British and U.S." *New Republic,* Sept. 11, 1971, pp. 20–25.

Federal Bureau of Investigation. *Uniform Crime Reports for the United States: 1981.* Washington, DC: U.S. Government Printing Office, 1982.

———. *Uniform Crime Reports for the United States: 1985.* Washington, DC: U.S. Government Printing Office, 1986.

Federico, R. *The Social Welfare Institution.* Lexington, MA: D.C. Heath, 1973.

Fein, G. "Pretend Play in Childhood: An Integrative Review." *Child Development* 52(1981):1095–1118.

Feldman, H. "The Effects of Children on the Family." In A. Michel (ed.), *Family Issues of Employed Women in Europe and America.* Leiden, The Netherlands: E.F. Brill, 1971.

Feldman, H., and M. Feldman. "Effect of Parenthood at Three Points in Marriage." Unpublished manuscript, 1976–77.

Feldman, M.P., and M.J. MacCulloch. *Homosexual Behavior: Therapy and Assessment.* Oxford: Pergamon Press, 1971.

Felsman, D., G. Brannigan, and P. Yellin. "Control Theory in Dealing with Adolescent Sexuality and Pregnancy." *Journal of Sex Education and Therapy* 13(1987):15–16.

Ferguson, E. *Social Work: An Introduction.* 3rd ed. Philadelphia, PA: J. Lippincott, 1975.

Ferraro, K.J. "Policing Woman Battering." *Social Problems* 36(1989):61–74.

Ferris, D. "Diagnosing Chlamydia in Minutes in Your Office." *Medical Aspects of Human Sexuality* 24(1990):41–43.

"Fertility Doctor Defends Motives." *Milwaukee Journal,* Nov. 24, 1992, p. A7.

Field, T.M. "Interaction Behaviors of Primary Versus Secondary Caretaker Fathers." *Developmental Psychology* 14(1978):183–84.

Fielding, J. "Adolescent Pregnancy Revisited." *New England Journal of Medicine* 299(1978):893–96.

Fielstein, E.M., L.L. Fielstein, and M.G. Hazlewood. "AIDS Knowledge among College Freshmen Students: Need for Education?" *Journal of Sex Education & Therapy* 18(1)(Spring 1992):45–54.

Findlay, S. "If Your Doctor Has AIDS." *U.S. News & World Report,* Feb. 18, 1991, p. 66. (a)

———. "AIDS: The Second Decade." *U.S. News & World Report*, June 17, 1991, pp. 20–22.(b)

Fingerhut L.A., and J.C. Kleinman. "International and Interstate Comparisons of Homicide among Young Males." *Journal of the American Medical Association* 263(4)(1990):3292–95.

Finkelhor, D. *A Sourcebook on Child Sexual Abuse.* Beverly Hills, CA: Sage, 1986.

Finkelhor, D., and L. Baron. "High-Risk Children." In D. Finkelhor, *A Sourcebook on Child Sexual Abuse.* Beverly Hills, CA: Sage, 1986.

Finn, P., and P.A. O'Gorman. *Teaching about Alcohol.* Boston: Allyn & Bacon, 1981.

Fischer, D.H. "Putting Our Heads to the 'Problem' of Old Age." *New York Times*, May 10, 1977, p. 33.

Fischer, J. *Effective Casework Practice: An Eclectic Approach.* New York: McGraw-Hill, 1978.

Fischer, J., and H.L. Gochros. *Planned Behavior Change: Behavior Modification in Social Work.* New York: Free Press, 1975.

Fish, J.E., and C.J. Larr. "A Decade of Change in Drawings by Black Children." *American Journal of Psychiatry* 129(1972): 421–26.

Flaste, R. "In Youngsters' Books, The Stereotype of Old Age." *New York Times*, Jan. 7, 1977, p. A12.

Flint, J. "Oversupply of Young Workers Expected to Tighten Jobs Race." *New York Times*, June 25, 1978, pp. 1, 34.

Flint, M. "Cross-Cultural Factors That Affect Age of Menopause." In P.A. Van Keep, R.B. Greenblatt, and M. Albeaux-Fernet (eds.), *Consensus on Menopause.* Baltimore, MD: University Park Press, 1976.

Flynn, M. "Poverty and Income Security." In D. Brieland, L. Costin, and C. Atherton (eds.), *Contemporary Social Work.* New York: McGraw-Hill, 1975.

———. "Aging." In D. Brieland, L. Costin, and C. Atherton (eds.), *Contemporary Social Work*, 2nd ed. New York: McGraw-Hill, 1980.

Ford, J., M. Zelnik, and J. Kantner. "Differences in Contraceptive Use and Socioeconomic Groups of Teenagers in the United States." Paper presented at the meeting of the American Public Health Association, New York, Nov. 1979.

Forssman, H., and I. Thuwe. "One Hundred and Twenty Children Born after Application for Therapeutic Abortion Refused." *Acta Psychiatrica Scandinavica* 42(1966):71–85.

Fort, J., and C.T. Cory. *American Drug Store.* Boston: Little, Brown, 1975.

Fosburgh, L. "The Make-Believe World of Teenage Maternity." *New York Times Magazine*, Aug. 7, 1977, p. 7.

Fox, J.R. "Mission Impossible? Social Work Practice with Black Urban Youth Gangs." *Social Work* 30(Jan.-Feb. 1985):25–29.

Fox, M.F., and S. Hesse-Biber. *Women at Work.* Palo Alto, CA: Mayfield, 1984.

Franklin, E.W., and A.M. Zeiderman. "Tubal Ectopic Pregnancy Etiology and Obstetric and Gynaecologic Sequelae." *American Journal of Obstetrics and Gynecology* 117(1973):220–25.

Frazier, A., and L.K. Lisonbee. "Adolescent Concerns with Physique." *School Review* 58(1950):397–405.

Freeman, J. *Women: A Feminist Perspective.* Palo Alto, CA: Mayfield, 1984.

———. *Women: A Feminist Perspective.* Mountain View, CA: Mayfield, 1989.

Freese, A.S. "Adolescent Suicide: Mental Health Challenge." New York: Public Affairs Pamphlets, 1979.

"French Abortion Drug Termed a Safe 'Morning After' Pill." *Milwaukee Journal*, Oct. 8, 1992.

Frenkel-Brunswick, E. "Adjustments and Reorientation in the Course of the Life-Span." In R.G. Kuhlen and G.G. Thomson (eds.), *Psychological Studies of Human Development*, 3rd ed. New York: Appleton-Century-Crofts, 1970.

"Freshmen Survey Shows Middle-of-Road Trend." *Willimantic Chronicle*, June 18, 1986, p. 2.

Freud, S. "Three Essays on the theory of Sexuality." In *Standard Edition*, Vol. VII. London, UK: Hogarth Press, 1905.

Friedlander, W.A. *Introduction to Social Welfare.* Englewood Cliffs, NJ: Prentice-Hall, 1968.

Friedlander, W.A. and Apte, R.Z. *Introduction to Social Welfare*, 5th ed. Englewood Cliffs, NJ: Prentice-Hall, 1980.

Frieze, I.H., J.E. Parsons, P.B. Johnson, D.N. Ruble, and G.L. Zellman. *Women and Sex Roles: A Social Psychological Perspective.* New York: Norton, 1978.

Frisch, R. "Fatness and Fertility." *Scientific American*, March 1988, pp. 88–95.

Frolkis, V.V. "Aging of the Autonomic Nervous System." In J.E. Birren and K.W. Schaie (eds.), *Handbook of the Psychology of Aging.* New York: Van Nostrand Reinhold, 1977.

Fuchs, V.R. *Who Shall Live? Health, Economics and Social Choice.* New York: Basic Books, 1974.

Furman, W., and D. Burhmester. "Children's Perceptions of the Personal Relationships in Their Social Networks." *Developmental Psychology* 21(6)(1985):1016–24.

Furry, C.A., and P.B. Baltes. "The Effect of Age Differences on the Assessment of Intelligence in Children, Adults, and the Elderly." *Journal of Gerontology* 28(1)(1973):73–80.

Furstenberg, F.F. "The Social Consequences of Teenage Parenthood." *Family Planning Perspectives* 8(4)(July-Aug. 1976):148–64.

Furstenberg, F.F., J. Brooks-Gunn, and S.P. Morgan. "Adolescent Mothers and Their Children in Later Life." *Family Planning Perspectives* 22(2)(1987):239–49.

Furstenberg, F.F., Jr., and G.B. Spanier. *Recycling the Family: Remarriage after Divorce.* Beverly Hills, CA: Sage, 1984.

Gallagher, J.M. "Cognitive Development and Learning in the Adolescent." In J.F. Adams (ed.), *Understanding Adolescence*, 2nd ed. Boston: Allyn & Bacon, 1973.

Galton, F. *Hereditary Genius: An Enquiry into Its Laws and Consequences* London, UK: Macmillan, 1896.

Gans, H.J. *More Equality.* New York: Pantheon, 1968.

———. "Fighting the Biases Embedded in Social Concepts of the Poor." *Chronicle of Higher Education*, Jan. 8, 1992, p. A56.

Gardner, R. *Understanding Children.* New York: Aronson, 1973.

Garn, S.M. "Bone Loss and Aging." In R. Goldman and M. Rockstein (eds.), *The Physiology and Pathology of Human Aging.* New York: Academic Press, 1975.

Garner, B., and R.W. Smith. "Are There Really Any Gay Male Athletes? An Empirical Survey." *Journal of Sex Research* 13(1977):22-34.

Garrison, K.C. "Physiological Changes in Adolescence." In J.F. Adams (ed.), *Understanding Adolescence: Current Developments in Adolescent Psychology.* Boston: Allyn & Bacon, 1968.

———. "Psychological Development." In J.F. Adams (ed.), *Understanding Adolescence*, 2nd ed. Boston: Allyn & Bacon, 1973.

Garvey, C. *Play.* Cambridge, MA: Harvard University Press, 1977.

Gavzer, B. "Why Do Some People Survive AIDS?" *Parade Magazine*, Sept. 18, 1988, pp. 4–6.

Gawain, S. *Living in the Light.* San Rafael, CA: Whatever Pub., 1986.

"Gays Face New Fears If Ban Ends." *Milwaukee Journal*, Nov. 16, 1992.

"Gays and the Military." *Newsweek*, Feb. 1, 1993, pp. 52–55.

Gebhard, P.H. "Postmarital Coitus among Widows and Divorcees." In P. Bohannan (ed.), *Divorce and After*. Garden City, NY: Doubleday, 1968.

Gelfand, D.M. "The Influence of Self-Esteem on Rate of Verbal Conditioning and Social Matching Behavior." *Journal of Abnormal and Social Psychology* 65(1962):259–65.

Geller, A. *Alcohol and Sexual Performance*. Minneapolis, MN: Johnson Institute, 1984.

Geller, H., and G. Steele. *Probability Tables of Death in the Next Ten Years from Specific Causes*. Indianapolis, IN: Methodist Hospital of Indiana, 1977.

Geller, J. "Reaching the Battered Husband." *Social Work with Groups* 1(1978):27–37.

Gelles, R.J. *The Violent Home: The Study of Physical Aggression Between Husbands and Wives*. Beverly Hills, CA: Sage, 1974.

———. "Abused Wives: Why Do They Stay?" *Journal of Marriage and the Family* 38(1976):659–68.

———. "The Myth of Battered Husbands." *Ms.*, Oct. 1979.

Gelman, D. "Black and White in America." *Newsweek*, March 7, 1988, pp. 19–21.

Gelman, D., D. Foote, T. Barrett, and M. Talbot. "Born or Bred?" *Newsweek*, Feb. 24, 1992, pp. 46–53.

Gerbner, G. "Violence in Television Drama: Trends and Symbolic Functions." In G.A. Comstock and E.A. Rubenstein (eds.), *Television and Social Behavior*, Vol. 1. Washington, DC: U.S. Government Printing Office, 1972.

Gerdes, E.P., et al. "The Effects of Sex and Sex-Role Concept on Self-Disclosure." *Sex Roles* 7(1981):789–98.

Germain, C.B. "An Ecological Perspective in Casework Practice." *Social Casework* 54(June 1973):323–30.

———. *Social Work Practice: People and Environments*. New York: Columbia University Press, 1979.

Germain, C.B., and A. Gitterman. *The Life Model of Social Work Practice*. New York: Columbia University Press, 1980.

Gessell, A. *The First Five Years of Life: The Preschool Years*. New York: Harper & Row, 1940.

Gessell, A., and F.L. Ilg. *The Child from Five to Ten*. New York: Harper & Row, 1946.

Gessell, A., F.L. Ilg, and L.B. Ames. *Youth: The Years from Ten to Sixteen*. New York: Harper & Row, 1956.

Gewirtz, H.B., and J.L. Gewirtz. "Caretaking Settings, Background Events, and Behavior Differences in Four Israeli Childrearing Environments: Some Preliminary Trends." In B.M. Foss (ed.), *Determinants of Infant Behavior*, Vol. 4. London, UK: Methuen, 1968.

Gewirtz, J.L. "The Course of Infant Smiling in Four Child-Rearing Environments in Israel." In B.M. Foss (ed.), *Determinants of Infant Behavior*, Vol. 3. London, UK: Methuen, 1965.

Gibbs, N. "Teens: The Rising Risk of AIDS." *Time*, Sept. 2, 1991, pp. 60–61.(b)

———. "Into the Arena There Came Two Gladiators, Fourteen Senators and an Audience of Millions. But Could Anyone Declare Victory When the Spectacle Was So Repellent?" *Time*, Oct. 21, 1991, p. 35.(a)

Gil, D.G. *Violence Against Children*. Cambridge, MA: Harvard University Press, 1973.

Gilbaugh, J.H., Jr., and P.C. Fuchs. "The Gonococcus and the Toilet Seat." *New England Journal of Medicine* 301(1979):91–93.

Gilbert, L.A. *Men in Dual-Career Families: Current Realities and Future Prospects*. Hillsdale, NJ: Erlbaum, 1985.

Gilford, R. "Marriages in Later Life." *Generations* 10(4)(1986):16–20.

Gilligan, C. "In a Different Voice: Women's Conceptions of Self and Morality." *Harvard Educational Review* 47(4)(1977):481–517.

———. *In a Different Voice: Psychological Theory and Women's Development*. Cambridge, MA: Harvard University Press, 1982.

Girdano, D.A., and D. Dusek. *Drug Education: Content and Methods*. Reading, MA: Addison-Wesley, 1980.

Glass, D., J. Neulinger, O. Brim. "Birth Order, Verbal Intelligence and Educational Aspirations." *Child Development* 45(3)(1974):807–11.

Glasser, W. *Schools Without Failure*. New York: Harper & Row, 1969.

———. *The Identity Society*. New York: Harper & Row, 1972.

———. *Control Theory*. New York: Harper & Row, 1984.

Gleitman, H. *Psychology*. 2nd ed. New York: Norton, 1986.

Glick, P.C. "The Future of the American Family." *Current Population Reports*, Special Studies Series P-23, No. 78. Washington, DC: U.S. Government Printing Office, 1979.

Gochros, H. "The Sexuality of Gay Men with HIV Infection." *Social Work* 37(1992):105–9.

Goldin, R. "Therapy as Education." Ph.D Diss. Boston University, 1977.

Goldmeier, J. "From Divorce to Family Reconstitution: A Clinical View." In C. Janzen and O. Harris (eds.), *Family Treatment In Social Work Practice*. Itasca, IL: Peacock, 1980.

Goldstein, A.P. *Delinquent Gangs: A Psychological Perspective*. Champaign, IL: Research Press, 1991.

Goldstein, J., A. Freud, and A.J. Solnit. *Beyond the Best Interest of the Child*. New York: Free Press, 1973.

Goode, E.E. "I Love You, But Can I Ask a Question?" *U.S. News & World Report*, Feb 22, 1988, p. 85.

Goode, W.J. "Family Disorganization." In R.K. Merton and R. Nisbet (eds.), *Contemporary Social Problems*, 4th ed. New York: Harcourt, Brace, Jovanovich, 1976.

Goodman, M.J., J.S. Grove, and F. Gilbert, Jr. "Age at Menopause in Relation to Reproductive History of Japanese, Caucasian, Chinese and Hawaiian Women Living in Hawaii." *Journal of Gerontology* 33(1978):688–94.

Goodrich, W., R.G. Ryder and H.L. Rausch. "Patterns of Newlyweds." In M.E. Losswell and T.E. Losswell (eds.), *Love, Marriage and Family: A Developmental Approach*. Glenview, IL: Scott, Foresman, 1973.

Good Tracks, Jimm G. "Native American Noninterference." *Social Work* 18(Nov. 1973):30–34.

Googins, B., and D. Burden. "Vulnerability of Working Parents: Balancing Work and Home Roles." *Social Work* 2(1987):295–300.

Gooren, L., E. Fliers, and K. Courtney. "Biological Determinants of Sexual Orientation." *Annual Review of Sex Research* 1(1990):175–96.

Gordon, M. "Assimilation in America: Theory and Reality." *Daedalus* 90(Spring 1961):363–65.

———. *Assimilation in American Life: The Role of Race, Religion, and National Origins*. New York: Oxford University Press, 1964.

Gordon, S. *The Sexual Adolescent*. North Scituate, MA: Duxbury Press, 1973.

———. "Can Sex Education Work?" *Contemporary Sexuality* 26(1)(1992): 1–2.

Gordon, S., and J.F. Gilgun. "Adolescent Sexuality." In V.B. Van Hasselt and M. Hersen (eds.), *Handbook of Adolescent Sexuality*. New York: Pergamon Press, 1987.

Gordon, T. *Parent Effectiveness Training*. New York: Wyden, 1970.

———. *Parent Effectiveness Training*. New York: New American Library, 1975.

Gottlieb, D. "Teaching and Students: The Views of Negro and White Teachers." *Sociology of Education* 37(1966):345–53.

Gottman, J., C. Notarius, J. Gonso, and H. Markman. *A Couple's Guide to Communication*. Champaign, IL: Research Press, 1976.

Gove, W.R. "Sex Differences in the Epidemiology of Mental Disorder: Evidence and Explanations." In E.S. Gomberg and V. Franks (eds.), *Gender and Disordered Behavior*. New York: Brunner-Mazel, 1979.

Grady, W.P. "Remarriages of Women 15-44 Years of Age Whose First Marriages Ended in Divorce: United States 1976." *Advancedata* 58(1980):1–12.

Great Britain Committee on Homosexual Offenses and Prostitution. *The Wolfenden Report*. New York: Stein & Day, 1963.

Green, K.D., R. Forehand, S.J. Beck, and B. Vosk. "An Assessment of the Relationship among Measures of Children's Social Competence and Children's Academic Achievement." *Child Development* 51(4)(Dec. 1980):1149–56.

Green, R. "Homosexuality as a Mental Illness." *International Journal of Psychiatry* 10(1972):77–98.

———. *Sexual Identity Conflict in Children and Adults*. New York: Basic Books, 1974.

———. "Should Homosexuals Adopt Children?" In J.P. Brady and H.K. Brodie (eds.), *Controversy in Psychiatry*. Philadelphia, PA: Saunders, 1978.

Greenberg, H.M. *Coping with Job Stress*. Englewood Cliffs, NJ: Prentice-Hall, 1980.

Greene, B. "Speck Admits Killing of 7 of 8 Chicago Nurses." *Wisconsin State Journal*, March 8, 1978, pp. 1–2.

Greene, B.L., R.R. Lee, and N. Lustig. "Conscious and Unconscious Factors in Marital Infidelity." *Medical Aspects of Human Sexuality* 8(1974):87–105.

Grier, W.H., and P.M. Cobb. *Black Rage*. New York: Basic Books, 1968.

Griffeths, K., and P.J. Pecora. *Utah Child Welfare Training Project Research Capsule No. 10, Teenage Suicide*. Salt Lake City, UT: University of Utah, 1986.

Grimes D. "Reversible Contraception for the 1980's." *Journal of the American Medical Association* 255(1986):69–75.

Gross, A.E. "The Male Role and Heterosexual Behavior." *Journal of Social Issues* 34(1)(1978):87–107.

Grossman, H.J., ed. *Manual on Terminology and Classification in Mental Retardation*. Rev. ed. Washington, DC: AAMD, 1975.

Grotevant, M.D., S. Scarr, and R.A. Weinberg. *Intellectual Development in Family Constellations with Adopted and Natural Children: A Test of the Zajonc and Markus Model*. Paper presented at a meeting of the Society for Research in Child Development, New Orleans, LA, 1977.

Group for the Advancement of Psychiatry. *The Joys and Sorrows of Parenthood*. New York: Scribner's, 1973.

Grundlach, R. "Sexual Molestation and Rape Reported by Homosexual and Heterosexual Women." *Journal of Homosexuality* 2(1977):367–84.

Grune, J.A. "Pay Equity Is a Necessary Remedy for Wage Discrimination." In *Comparable Worth: Issue for the 80's*. Vol. 1. Washington, DC: U.S. Government Printing House, 1984.

Grunfeld, L. "Workup for Male Fertility." *Journal of Reproductive Medicine* 43(1989):143–149.

Grush, J.E., and J.G. Yehl. "Marital Roles, Sex Differences and Interpersonal Attraction." *Journal of Personality and Social Psychology* 37(1979):116–23.

Gubrium, F.F. "Being Single in Old Age." *International Journal of Aging and Human Development* 6(1)(1975):29–41.

Guilford, J.P. "Factorial Angles to Psychology." *Psychological Review* 68(1961):1–20.

Gunby, P. "Genital Herpes Research." *Journal of the American Medical Association* 250(1983):2417–27.

Guttentag, M., and H. Bray. "Teachers as Mediators of Sex Role Standards." In A. Sargend (ed.), *Beyond Sex Roles*. St. Paul, MN: West, 1977.

Guyton, A.C. *Textbook of Medical Psychology*. 6th ed. Philadelphia, PA: Saunders, 1981.

Hadeed, A.J., and S.R. Siegel. "Maternal Cocaine Use During Pregnancy: Effect on the Newborn Infant." *Pediatrics* 84(2)(1989):205–10.

Haith, M.M., and J.J. Campos. "Human Infancy." *Annual Review of Psychology* 28(1977):251–93.

Hall, E.T. *The Hidden Dimension*. Garden City, NY: Doubleday, 1969.

Hall, E. "Acting One's Age: New Rules for Old." *Psychology Today* 13(11)(1980):66–80.

Hall, R.V., S. Axelrod, M. Foundopoulos, J. Shellman, R.A. Campbell, and S.S. Cranston. "The Effective Use of Punishment to Modify Behavior in the Classroom." *Educational Technology* 11(1971):24–26.

Hallberg, E.C. *The Gray Itch: The Male Menopause Syndrome*. New York: Stein and Day, 1978.

"Hallucinogens and Narcotics Alarm Public: Chemistry and Engineering News 48(1976):44–45.

Halsell, G. *Soul Sister*. New York: Fawcett Crest, 1969.

Hancock, C. *Children and Neglect—Hazardous Home Conditions*. Washington, DC: U.S. Government Printing Office, 1963.

Handelsman, C.D., R.J. Cabral, and G.E. Weisfeld. "Sources of Information and Adolescent Sexual Knowledge and Behavior." *Journal of Adolescent Research* 2(1987):455–63.

Haney, P. "Comments on Currents: Providing Empowerment to Persons with AIDS." *Social Work* 33(3)(May-June 1988): 251–53.

Hareven, T.K. "The Last Stage: Historical Adulthood and Old Age." *Daedalus* 105(4)(1976):13–27.

Harrington, M. *The Other America*. New York: Macmillan, 1962.

Harris, L. et al. *American Teens Speak: Sex, Myths, TV and Birth Control: The Planned Parenthood Poll*. New York: Planned Parenthood Federation of America, 1986.

Harris, R. "Cardiac Changes with Age." In R. Goldman and M. Rockstein (eds.), *The Physiology and Pathology of Human Aging* New York: Academic Press, 1975.

Harris, T. *I'm OK—You're OK*. New York: Harper & Row, 1969.

Harry, J. "Some Problems of Gay/Lesbian Families." In C.S. Chilman, et al. (eds.), *Variant Family Norms*. Beverly Hills, CA: Sage, 1988.

Harter, S. "The Determinants and Mediational Role of Global Self-Worth in Children." In N. Eisenberg (ed.), *Contemporary Topics in Developmental Psychology*. New York: Wiley, 1987.

Hartley, E. *Problems in Prejudice*. New York: King's Crown Press, 1946.

Hartley, R.E. "Sex-Role Pressures in the Socialization of the Male Child. *Psychological Reports* 5(1959):457–68.

Hartman, A. "Diagrammatic Assessment of Family Relationships." *Social Casework* 59(Oct. 1978):465–76.

———. "Toward Redefinition and Contextualization of the Abortion Issue." *Social Work* 36(6)(Nov. 1991):466–67.

Hartup, W.W. "Peer Relations." In T.D. Spencer and N. Kass (eds.), *Perspectives in Child Psychology: Research and Review*. New York: McGraw-Hill, 1970.

———. "Peer Relations." In P.H. Mussen (ed.), *Handbook of Child Psychology*, 4th ed. Vol. 4. *Socialization, Personality, and Social Development*, E.M. Hetherington (series ed.). New York: Wiley, 1983.

———. "Social Relationships and Their Developmental Significance." *American Psychologist* 44(2)(1989):120–26.

Harvard Medical School. "Suicide—Parts I and II." *Mental Health Letter* 2(2,3)(Feb. and March 1986).

Harvey, O.J., M. Prather, B.J. White, and J.K. Hoffmeister. "Teacher's Beliefs, Classroom Atmosphere, and Student Behavior." *American Educational Research Journal* 5(1968):151–66.

Hass, A. *Teenage Sexuality.* New York: Macmillan, 1979.

Hatcher, R.A. et al. *Contraceptive Technology, 1976–1977.* 8th ed. New York: Irvington, 1976.

———. *Contraceptive Technology, 1980–1981.* 10th ed. New York: Irvington, 1980.

———. *Contraceptive Technology, 1988–1989.* 14th ed. New York: Irvington, 1988.

———. *Contraceptive Technology* 15th ed. New York: Irvington 1990.

———. *Contraceptive Technology.* 16th ed. New York: Irvington, 1992.

Hauser, R.M., and W.H. Sewell. "Birth Order and Educational Attainment in Full Sibships." *American Journal of Educational Research* 22(1985):1–23.

Hayflick, L. "The Strategy of Senescence." *Gerontologist* 14(3) (1974):37–45.

Hayghe, H. "Rise in Mothers' Labor Force Activity Includes Those with Infants." *Monthly Labor Review,* Feb. 1986, pp. 43–45.

Haywood, H.C., et al. "Mental Retardation," In M.R. Rosenzweig and L.W. Porter (eds.), *Annual Review of Psychology,* vol. 33. Palo Alto, CA: Annual Reviews, 1982.

Hearn, G. *The General Systems Approach: Contributions Toward an Holistic Conception of Social Work.* New York: Council on Social Work Education, 1969.

Hedgpeth, J.M. "Empowerment Discrimination Law and the Rights of Gay Persons." *Journal of Homosexuality* 5(1,2)(1978/1980):67–78.

Heinonen, O.P., et al. "Cardiovascular Birth Defects and Antenatal Exposure to Female Sex Hormones." *New England Journal of Medicine* 296(1977):67–70.

Held, D.F. *The Intuitive Approach to Reading and Learning Disabilities: A Practical Alternative.* Springfield, IL: Charles C. Thomas, 1984.

Helfer, R., et al. "Arresting or Freezing the Developmental Process." In R. Helfer and C.H. Kempe (eds.), *Child Abuse and Neglect: The Family and the Community.* Cambridge, MA: Ballinger, 1976.

Hellman, L.M., and J.A. Pritchard, *Williams Obstetrics.* 14th ed New York: Appleton-Century-Crofts, 1971.

Henderson, C.H., and B. Kim. "Racism." In D. Brieland, L. Costin, and C. Atherton (eds.), *Contemporary Social Work,* 2nd ed. New York: McGraw-Hill, 1980.

Hendrick van den Berg, J. *Dubious Maternal Affection* (Pittsburgh, PA: Duquesne University Press, 1972.

Hendry, L., and P. Gillies. "Body Type, Body Esteem, School and Leisure: A Study of Overweight, Average, and Underweight Adolescents." *Journal of Youth and Adolescence* 7(2)(1978):181–96.

Henig, R.M. "Exposing the Myth of Senility." *New York Times Magazine,* Dec. 3, 1978, p. 158.

Henley, N.M. "The Politics of Touch." In P. Brown (ed.), *Radical Psychology.* New York: Harper & Row, 1973.(a)

———. "Status and Sex: Some Touching Observations." *Bulletin of the Psychonomic Society* 2(1973):91–93.(b)

Henley, N.M., and J. Freeman. "The Sexual Politics of Interpersonal Behavior." In J. Freeman (ed.), *Women: A Feminist Perspective.* Palo Alto, CA: Mayfield, 1984.

Henry, J. *Indian Historian* 1(Dec. 1967).

Henry, K., M. Maki, and K. Crossley. "Analysis of the Use of HIV Antibody Testing in a Minnesota Hospital." *Journal of the American Medical Association* 259(Jan. 1988):229–32.

Herman, D. "The Rape Culture." In Jo Freeman (ed.), *Women: A Feminist Perspective.* Palo Alto, CA: Mayfield, 1984.

Hess, E.H. "Imprinting." *Science* 130(1959):133–41.

Hess, E.H., and J.M. Polt. "Pupil Size as Related to Interest Value of Visual Stimuli." *Science* 132(1960):349–50.

Heston, L. and J. Shields. "Homosexuality in Twins." *Archives of General Psychiatry* 18(1968):149–60.

Heston, L.L., and J.A. White. *Dementia.* New York: Freeman, 1983.

Hetherington, E.M. "Children and Divorce." In R. Henderson (ed.), *Parent-Child Interaction: Theory, Research, and Prospect.* New York: Academic Press, 1980.

Hetherington, E.M., M. Cox and R. Cox. "Beyond Father Absence! Conceptualization of Effects of Divorce." Paper presented at the annual meeting of the Society for Research in Child Development, Denver, CO, 1975.

———. "Beyond Father Absence: Conceptualization of Effects of Divorce." In E.M. Hetherington and R.D. Parke (eds.), *Contemporary Readings in Child Psychology.* New York: McGraw-Hill, 1977.

Hetherington, E.M., and Parke, R. *Child Psychology: A Contemporary Viewpoint.* New York: McGraw-Hill, 1979.

Hewlett, S.A. *A Lesser Life.* New York: Morrow, 1986.

Hickey, T., L. Hickey, and R. Kalish. "Children's Perceptions of the Elderly." *Journal of Genetic Psychology* 112(1968):227–35.

Hilgard, E.R., and R.C. Atkinson. *Introduction to Psychology.* 4th ed. New York: Harcourt, Brace & World, 1967.

Hill, R. "Decision Making and the Family Life Cycle." In E. Shanas and G. Streib (eds.), *Social Structure and the Family: Generational Relations.* Englewood Cliffs, NJ: Prentice-Hall, 1965.

Hirschi, T. *Causes of Delinquency.* Berkeley: University of California Press, 1969.

Hitchens, D. "Social Attitudes, Legal Standards and Personal Trauma in Child Custody Cases." *Journal of Homosexuality* 5(1,2)(1979/1980):89–96.

Hobbs, D., and S. Cole "Transition to Parenthood: A Decade Replication." *Journal of Marriage and the Family* 38(1976): 723-31.

Hobson, R.P. "The Question of Egocentrism: The Young Child's Competence in the Coordination of Perspective." *Journal of Child Psychology and Psychiatry* 21(1980):325–31.

Hodges, A., and B. Balow. "Learning Disability in Relation to Family Constellation." *Journal of Educational Research* 55(1961):4–42.

Hofer, A., and W. Polin. "Schizophrenia in the NAS-NRC Panel of 15,909 Twin Pairs." *Archives of General Psychiatry* 23(1970):469–77.

Hoffman, L.W., and J. Manis. "The Value of Children in the United States: A New Approach to the Study of Fertility." *Journal of Marriage and the Family* 41(1979):583–96.

Hoffnung, M. "Motherhood: Contemporary Conflict for Women." In J. Freeman (ed.), *Women: A Feminist Perspective.* Palo Alto, CA: Mayfield, 1984.

Hogge, W., S. Schonberg, and M. Golbus. "Chorionic Villus Sampling: Experience of the First 1,000 Cases." *American Journal of Obstetrics and Gynecology* 154(1986):1249–52.

Holland, T.P., and M.K. Petchers. "Organizations: Context for Social Service Delivery." *Encyclopedia of Social Work.* Silver Spring, MD: NASW, 1987.

Holmes, D.L., and F.J. Morrison. *The Child: An Introduction to Developmental Psychology.* Monterey, CA: Brooks/Cole, 1979.

Holmes, T.H., and M. Masuda. "Psychosomatic Syndrome." *Psychology Today* 106(1972):71–72.

Holmes, T.H., and R.H. Rahe. "The Social Readjustment Rating Scale." *Journal of Psychosomatic Research* 11(1976):213.

Hooker, E. "The Adjustment of the Male Overt Homosexual." *Journal of Projective Techniques* 21(1957):18–31.

———. "An Empirical Study of Some Relations Between Sexual Patterns and Gender Identity in Male Homosexuals." In J. Money (ed.), *Sex Research: New Developments.* New York: Holt, 1965.

———. "The Homosexual Community." In J.H. Gagnon and W. Simon (eds.), *Sexual Deviance.* New York: Harper & Row, 1967.

Hooper, R.R., et al. "Cohort Study of Venereal Disease. Part I, The Risks of Gonorrhea Transmission from Infected Women to Men." *American Journal of Epidemiology* 108(1978):136–44.

Hope Health Letter. "Anti-Smoking Sentiments Increasing." April 1991.

Hormer, M.S. "Toward an Understanding of Achievement Related Conflicts in Women." *Journal of Social Issues* 28(2)(1972):157–75.

Horn, J.L. "Human Abilities: A Review of Research and Theory in the Early 1970's." In M.R. Rosenzweig and L.W. Porter (eds.), *Annual Review of Psychology.* Palo Alto, CA: Annual Reviews, 1976.

Horn, J.L., and G. Donaldson. "Cognitive Development in Adulthood." In O.G. Brim, Jr., and J. Kagan (eds.), *Constancy and Change in Human Development.* Cambridge, MA: Harvard University Press, 1980.

Hosford, R.E., and Louis de Visser. *Behavioral Approaches to Counseling: An Introduction.* Falls Church, VA: APGA Press, 1974.

Hoult, R. "Experimental Measurement of Clothing as a Factor in Some Social Ratings of Selected American Men." *American Sociological Review* 19(1954):324–28.

Houseknecht, S.K. "Childlessness and Marital Adjustment." *Journal of Marriage and the Family* 41(1979):259–66.

Howell, M.C. "Effects of Maternal Employment on the Child." *Pediatrics* 52(3)(1973):327–43.

"How Gay Is Gay?" *Time,* April 1979, pp. 72–73.

Howie, L.H., and T.F. Drury. "Vital and Health Statistics." series 10, no. 126. National Center for Health Statistics, no. (PHS) 78-1554. Washington, DC: U.S. Government Printing Office, 1978.

Hsu, L., A Crisp, and B. Harding. "Outcome of Anorexia Nervosa." *Lancet,* Jan. 13, 1976, pp. 61–65.

Hudson, B., R. Pepperell, and C. Wood. "The Problem of Infertility." In R. Pepperell, B. Hudson, and C. Wood (eds.), *The Infertile Couple.* Edinburgh, Scotland: Churchill Livingstone, 1987.

Hughes, M. *Egocentrism in Preschool Children.* Ph.D. Diss. Edinburgh University, Edinburgh, 1975.

Hull, G.H., Jr. "Urban Problems." In C. Zastrow and L. Bowker (eds.), *Social Problems.* Chicago: Nelson-Hall, 1984.

———. "Social Work Practice with Diverse Groups." In C. Zastrow (ed.), *The Practice of Social Work,* 2nd ed. Homewood, IL: Dorsey, 1985.

Hultsch, D.F., and F. Deutsch. *Adult Development and Aging: A Life Span Perspective.* New York: McGraw-Hill, 1981.

Hunt, B., and M. Hunt. *Prime Time.* New York: Stein and Day, 1974.

Hunt, L.G., and N.E. Zinberg. *Heroin Use: A New Look.* Washington, DC: Drug Abuse Council, 1976.

Hunt, M. *Sexual Behavior in the 1970s.* Chicago: Playboy Press, 1974.

Hunt, M., and B. Hunt. *The Divorce Experience.* New York: Signet, 1977.

Hunt, W.A., and J.D. Matarazzo. "Habit Mechanisms in Smoking." In W.A. Hunt (ed.), *Learning Mechanisms of Smoking.* Chicago: Aldine, 1970.

Hutchins, T., and V. Baxter. "Battered Women." In N. Gottlieb (ed.), *Alternative Social Services for Women.* New York: Columbia University Press, 1980.

Hutt, P.J. "Rate of Bar Pressing as a Function of Quality and Quantity of Food Reward." *Journal of Comparative and Physiological Psychology* 47(1954):235–39.

Hyde, J.S. *Understanding Human Sexuality.* New York: McGraw-Hill, 1982.

———. *Half the Human Experience: The Psychology of Women.* 3rd ed. Lexington, MA: D.C. Heath, 1985.

———. *Understanding Human Sexuality,* 3rd ed. New York: McGraw-Hill, 1986.

———. *Understanding Human Sexuality,* 4th ed. New York: McGraw-Hill, 1990.

Hyde, J.S., E. Fennema, and S.J. Lamon. "Gender Differences in Mathematic Performances: A Meta-Analysis." *Psychological Bulletin* 106(1990):139–55.

Hyde, J.S., and M.C. Linn. "Gender Differences in Verbal Ability: A Meta-Analysis." *Psychological Bulletin* 104(1988):53–69.

Hyde, J.S., and B.G. Rosenberg. *Half the Human Experience: The Psychology of Women.* 2nd ed. Lexington, MA: Heath, 1980.

"If You are Attacked." "Milwaukee, WI: Sexual Assault Treatment Center of Greater Milwaukee, 1979.

Imara, M. "Dying as the Last Stage of Growth." In E. Kubler-Ross, *Death: The Final Stage of Growth.* Englewood Cliffs, NJ: Prentice-Hall, 1975.

Ince, S. "Surrogate Motherhood Represents Reproductive Prostitution." In R.T. Francoeur (ed.), *Taking Sides: Clashing Views on Controversial Issues in Human Sexuality,* 2nd ed. Guilford, CN: Dushkin, 1989.

Infant Health and Development Program. "Enhancing the Outcomes of Low-Birth-Weight, Premature Infants." *Journal of the American Medical Association* 263(22)(1990):3035–42.

Iosub, S., et al. "More on Human Immune Deficiency Virus Embryopathy." *Pediatrics* 80(1987):512–16.

"IVF, GIFT, and Intraperitoneal and Intrauterine Insemination for Human Infertility." *Research on Reproduction* 19(1)(1987):1.

Izard, C.E., R.R. Huebner, D. Resser, G.C. McGinness, and L.M. Dougherty. "The Young Infant's Ability to Produce Discrete Emotional Expressions." *Developmental Psychology* 16(2)(1980):132–40.

Jacobs, H.C. "National Caucus on the Black Aged: A Progress Report." *Aging and Human Development* 3(1971):226–31.

Jacobs, J., and J. Teicher. "Broken Homes and Social Isolation in Attempted Suicide of Adolescents." *International Journal of Social Psychology* 13(1967):139–49.

Jacobs, M.R. *Problems Presented by Alcoholic Clients.* Toronto, Canada: Addiction Research Foundation, 1981.

Jacobsen, J.W., and M.P. Janicki. "Observed Prevalence of Multiple Developmental Disabilities." *Mental Retardation* 21(3)(1984):87–94.

Jacobson, E. *Progressive Relaxation.* 2nd ed. Chicago: University of Chicago Press, 1938.

Jacobson, S.B. "The Challenge of Aging for Marriage Partners." In W.C. Bier (ed.), *Aging: Its Challenge to the Individual and to Society.* New York: Fordham University Press, 1974.

Jacoby, O. *Oswald Jacoby on Poker.* New York: Doubleday, 1974.

Jacques, J.M., and K.J. Chason. "Cohabitation: Its Impact on Marital Success." *Family Coordinator* 28(1979):35–39.

James, M. and D. Jongeward. *Born to Win: Transactional Analysis with Gestalt Experiments.* Reading, MA: Addison-Wesley, 1971.

James, W.H. "Marital Coital Rates, Spouses' Ages, Family Size and Social Class." *Journal of Sex Research* 10(1974): 205–18.

Janzen, C., and O. Harris. *Family Treatment in Social Work Practice.* 2nd ed. Itasca, IL: Peacock, 1986.

Jason, J.M. "Infectious Disease-Related Deaths of Low Birth Weight Infants, United States, 1968 to 1982." *Pediatrics* 84(2)(1989):296–303.

Jay, K., and A. Young. *The Gay Report.* New York: Summit Books, 1979.

Jenkins, A.H. *The Psychology of the Afro-American: A Humanistic Approach.* New York: Pergamon Press, 1982.

Jenkins, J.L., M.K. Salus, and G.L. Schultze. *Child Protective Services: A Guide for Workers.* Washington, DC: U.S. Department of Health, Education and Welfare, 1979.

Jensen, A. "How Much Can We Boost I.Q. and Scholastic Achievement?" *Harvard Educational Review* 39(1969):1–123.

Jensen, M.L. "Adolescent Suicide: A Tragedy of Our Times." *FL Educator,* Summer 1984, pp. 12–16.

Jersild, A.T. *The Psychology of Adolescence.* 2nd ed. New York: Macmillan, 1965.

Johnson, C., et al. "Incidence and Correlates of Bulimic Behavior in a Female High School Population." *Journal of Youth and Adolescence* 13(1984):15–22.

Johnson, E.H. *Social Problems of Urban Man.* Homewood, IL: Dorsey, 1973.

Johnson, L.C. *Social Work Practice: A Generalist Approach.* Boston, MA: Allyn & Bacon, 1983.

Johnston, L.D., J.G. Bachman, and P.M. O'Malley. *1979 Highlights: Drugs and the Nation's High School Students: Five Year National Trends.* Rockville, MD: National Institute on Drug Abuse, 1979.

Jones, E.F. *Teenage Pregnancy in Industrialized Countries.* New Haven, CT: Yale University Press, 1986.

Jones, E.F., J.D Forrest, N. Goldman, S.K. Henshaw, R. Lincoln, J.I. Rosoff, C.F. Westoff, W. Wulf, and D. Wulf. "Teenage Pregnancy in Developed Countries: Determinants and Policy Implications." *Family Planning Perspectives.* 17(1985):53–63.

Jones, M.C. "The Later Careers of Boys Who Were Early or Late Maturing." *Child Development* 28(1957):113–28.

———. "A Study of Socialization Patterns at the High School Level." *Journal of Genetic Psychology* 92(1958):87–111.

———. "Psychological Correlates of Somatic Development." *Child Development* 36(1965):899–911.

Jones, M.C., and N. Bayley. "Physical Maturing among Boys as Related to Behavior." *Journal of Educational Psychology* 41(1950):129–48.

Jones, M.C., and P.H. Mussen. "Self Conceptions, Motivations, and Interpersonal Attitudes of Early and Late Maturing Girls." *Child Development* 29(1958):491–501.

Jones. R.Y., and L. Eimers. *Elder Abuse Task Force Final Report* Elkhorn, WI: Walworth County Department of Aging, 1988.

Julian, J., and W. Kornblum. *Social Problems.* 3rd ed. Englewood Cliffs, NJ: Prentice-Hall, 1980.

———. *Social Problems.* 5th ed. Englewood Cliffs, NJ: Prentice-Hall, 1986.

"Justice Kennedy Blocks Teen's Abortion." *Milwaukee Journal,* May 17, 1989, p. 52.

Kadushin, A. *The Social Work Interview.* New York: Columbia University Press, 1972.

———. *Child Welfare Services.* New York: Macmillan, 1980.

Kadushin, A., and J.A. Martin. *Child Welfare Services.* 4th ed. New York: Macmillan, 1988.

Kahana, B., and E. Kahana. "Grandparents from the Perspective of the Developing Grandchild." *Developmental Psychology* 3(1)(1970):98–105.

Kahana, E., and R.M. Coe. "Perceptions of Grandparenthood by Community and Institutional Aged." *Proceedings of the Seventy-Seventh Annual Convention of the American Psychological Assocation* (1969), pp. 735–36.

Kakvan, M., and S.D. Greenberg. "Cigarette Smoking and Cancer of the Lung: A Review." *Rhode Island Medical Journal* 60(12)(1977): 588–91, 606.

Kales, J.D. "Aging and Sleep." In R. Goldman and M. Rockstein (eds.), *The Psychology and Pathology of Human Aging.* New York: Academic Press, 1975.

Kalish, R.A. *Late Adulthood: Perspectives on Human Development.* Monterey, CA: Brooks/Cole, 1975.

Kallen, D.J., J.J. Stephenson, and A. Doughty. "The Need to Know: Recalled Adolescent Sources of Sexual and Contraceptive Information and Sexual Behavior." *Journal of Sex Research* 19(1983):137–59.

Kallman, F.J. "Comparative Twin Study on the Genetic Aspects of Male Homosexuality." *Journal of Nervous and Mental Disease* 115(1952):283–98.

Kaluger, G., and M.F. Kaluger. *Human Development: The Span of Life.* St. Louis, MO: Mosby, 1979.

———. *Human Development: The Span of Life.* 3rd ed. St. Louis, MO: Times Mirror/Mosby, 1984.

Kaluger, G., and C.J. Kolson. *Reading and Learning Disabilities.* 2nd ed. Columbus, OH: Merrill, 1978.

Kangas, J., and K. Bradway. "Intelligence at Middle Age: A Thirty-Eight-Year Follow-Up." *Developmental Psychology* 5(1971):333–37.

Kanin, E. "Date Rapists: Differential Sexual Socialization and Relative Deprivation." *Archives of Sexual Behavior* 14(1985): 219–31.

Kaplan, H.S. *The New Sex Therapy.* New York: Brunner/Mazel, 1981.

Kaplan, J. *Marijuana: A New Prohibition.* New York: World, 1970.

Kaplan, S., and S. Saperstein. "Lesbian and Gay Adolescents." In H. Hidalgo, T.L. Peterson, and N.J. Woodman (eds.), *Lesbian and Gay Issues: A Resource Manual for Social Workers.* Silver Spring, MD: NASW, 1985.

Karlen, A. *Sexuality and Homosexuality: A New View.* New York: Norton, 1971.

Katchadourian, H.A. *Fundamentals of Human Sexuality.* Chicago: Holt, Rinehart and Winston, 1989.

Katz, P., and S. Zalk. "Modification of Children's Racial Attitudes." *Developmental Psychology* 14(5)(1978):447–61.

Kavale, K., and S. Forness. *The Science of Learning Disabilities.* San Diego, CA: College-Hill Press, 1985.

Kazdin, A.E. *History of Behavior Modification: Experimental Foundations of Contemporary Research.* Baltimore, MD: University Park Press, 1978.

———. *Behavior Modification in Applied Settings.* 3rd ed. Homewood, IL: Dorsey, 1984.

————. *Behavior Modification in Applied Settings.* 4th ed. Pacific Grove, CA: Brooks/Cole, 1989.

Keating, N.C., and L.V. Clark. "Development of Phsyical and Social Reasoning in Adolescents." *Developmental Psychology* 16(1980):23–30.

Keller, Mark, and C. Gurioli. *Statistics on Consumption of Alcohol and on Alcohol.* New Brunswick, NJ: Rutgers Center of Alcohol Studies, 1976.

Kellerman, J., and E. Katz. "Attitudes Toward the Division of Child-Rearing Responsibility." *Sex Roles* 4(1978):505–12.

Kelley, K., and D. Byrne. *Exploring Human Sexuality.* Englewood Cliffs, NJ: Prentice-Hall, 1992.

Kelly, G.F., *Sexuality Today: The Human Perspective.* 2nd ed. Guilford, CT: Dushkin, 1990.

Kelly, J. "The Aging Male Homosexual: Myth and Reality." *Gerontologist* 17(4)(1977):328–32.

Keniston, K. *All Our Children: The American Family under Pressure.* New York: Harcourt Brace Jovanovich, 1977.

Kenny, T.J. "Visual-Motor Problems of Adolescents Who Attempt Suicide." *Perceptual and Motor Skills* 48(April 1979):599–602.

Kent, S. *The Life-Extension Revolution.* New York: Morrow, 1980).

Kercher, G.A., and M. McShane. "The Prevalence of Child Sexual Abuse Victimization in an Adult Sample of Texas Residents." *Child Abuse and Neglect* 8(1984):495–501.

Kerr, M.E., and M. Bowen. *Family Evaluation: An Approach Based on Bowen Theory.* New York: Norton, 1988.

Kettner, P., J. Daley, and A. Nichols. *Initiating Change in Organizations and Communities.* Monterey, CA: Brooks/Cole, 1985.

Kety, S.S. "The Biological Roots of Schizophrenia." *Harvard Magazine* 78(1976):20–26.

Key, M.R. *Male/Female Language.* Metuchen, NJ: Scarecrow Press, 1975.

Keys, D.L. "Link-Up: A Program for Youth at Risk," "Working Together," "What's Next?" and "Who Needs You." Pamphlets distributed at presentation on "Male Adolescents: Development, Suicide, and Gay Issues," Regional Council on Social Work Education Conference, Starved Rock, IL, April 20, 1990.

Kiev, A. "The Courage to Live." *Cosmopolitan,* Sept. 1980, pp. 301-8.

Kimmel, D.C. *Adulthood and Aging.* New York: Wiley, 1974.

Kinard, E., and H. Reinherz. "School Aptitude and Achievement in Children of Adolescent Mothers." *Journal of Youth and Adolescence* 16(1987):69–78.

Kinsey, A.C., W.B. Pomeroy, and C.R. Martin. *Sexual Behavior in the Human Male.* Philadelphia, PA: Saunders, 1948.

Kinsey, A.C., W.B. Pomeroy, and C.R. Martin, and P.H. Gebhard. *Sexual Behavior in the Human Female.* Philadelphia, PA: Saunders, 1953.

Kirby, D. *Sexuality Education: An Evaluation of Programs and Their Effects.* Santa Cruz, CA: Network Pub, 1984.

Kirby, D., et al. *An Analysis of U.S. Sex Education Programs and Evaluation Methods.* Atlanta, GA: U.S. Department of Health, Education and Welfare, 1979.

Kirby, I.J. "Hormone Replacement Therapy for Postmenopausal Symptoms." *Lancet* 2(1973):103.

Kircher, A.S., J.J. Pear, and G.L. Martin. "Shock as Punishment in a Picture-Naming Task with Retarded Children." *Journal of Applied Behavior Analysis* 4(1971):227–33.

Kirk, S. *Educating Exceptional Children.* 3rd ed. Boston: Houghton Mifflin, 1979.

Kirkpatrick, C. *The Family as Process and Institution.* New York: Ronald Press, 1975.

Kirst-Ashman, K.K. "Exploration of the Family Environment and Problems of Uncontrollable Adolescents." Ph.D. Diss., University of Illinois at Urbana-Champaign, 1983.

Klein, C. *The Single Parent Experience.* New York: Walker, 1973.

Klein, H., and A. Cordell. "The Adolescent as Mother: Early Risk Identification." *Journal of Youth and Adolescence* 16 (1987):47–58.

Klein, M.W., and C.L. Maxson. "Street Gang Violence." In M. Wolfgang and N. Weiner (eds.), *Violent Crimes, Violent Criminals.* Newbury Park, CA: Sage, 1989.

Kleinman, C. "Gender Gap Grows in Educational Executive Posts." *Providence Evening Bulletin,* July 26, 1983.

Kleinman, J.C., et al. *Variations in Use of Obstetric Technology.* DHHS pub. no. PHS 84-1232. Washington, DC: U.S. Government Printing Office, 1983.

Knapp, M.L. *Nonverbal Communication in Human Interaction.* 2nd ed New York: Holt, Rinehart and Winston, 1978.

Knopf, R. *Surviving the BS (Bureaucratic System.* Wilmington, NC: Mandala Press, 1979.

Koch, H.L. "Attitudes of Children Toward Their Peers as Related to Certain Characteristics of Their Siblings." *Psychological Monographs* 70(426)(1956):1–41.(a)

————. "Sibling Influence on Children's Speech." *Journal of Speech Disabilities* 21(1956):322–28.(b)

————. "Sissiness and Tomboyishness in Relation to Sibling Characteristics." *Journal of Genetic Psychology* 88(1956):231–44.(c)

————. "Some Emotional Attitudes of the Young Child in Relation to Characteristics of His Siblings." *Child Development* 27(1956):393–426.(d)

————. "The Relation of Certain Formal Attributes of Siblings to Attitudes Held Toward Each Other and Toward Their Parents." *Monographs of the Society for Research in Child Development* 25(1960):1–134.

Koch, J.P. "The Prentif Contraceptive Cervical Cap: A Contemporary Study of Its Safety and Effectiveness." *Contraception* 25(1982):135.

Koch, L., and J. Koch. "Parent Abuse—A New Plague." *Parade Magazine,* Jan. 27, 1980, p. 14.

Koch, M.O., V. Dotson, and T.P. Troast. "Treating Eating Disorders." In C. Zastrow, *Social Work with Groups.* 3rd ed. Chicago: Nelson-Hall, 1993.

Koeppel, B. "The Big Social Security Ripoff." *Progressive* 39(7)(1975):13–18.

Kohlberg, L. "The Development of Children's Orientations Toward a Moral Order. I, Sequence in the Development of Moral Thought." *Vita Humana* 6(1963):11–35.

————. "The Child as a Moral Philosopher." *Psychology Today* 2(4)(1968):25–30.

————. *Stages in the Development of Moral Thought and Action.* New York: Holt, Rinehart and Winston, 1969.

————. "The Child as Moral Philosopher." In P. Cramer (ed.), *Readings in Developmental Psychology Today.* Del Mar, CA: CRM, 1970.

————. "Revisions in the Theory and Practice of Moral Development." *New Directions for Child Development* 2(1978).

————. *The Philosophy of Moral Development.* New York: Harper & Row, 1981.

Kohlberg, L., and C. Gilligan. "The Adolescent as a Philosopher: The Discovery of the Self in a Postconventional World." *Daedalus,* Fall 1971, pp. 1051–86.

Kolata, G. "Fetuses Treated Through Umbilical Cords." *New York Times,* March 29, 1988, p. C3.

Koll, L.C., V. Bernard, and B.P. Dohrenwend. "The Problem of Validity in Field Studies of Psychological Disorder." In Bruce

P. Dohrenwend and B. Snell Dohrenwend (eds.), *Urban Challenges to Psychiatry*. New York: Wiley, 1969.

Kolodny, R.C., W.H. Masters, J. Hendryx, and G. Toro. "Plasma Testosterone and Semen Analysis in Male Homosexuals." *New England Journal of Medicine* 285(1971):1170–74.

Kolodny, R.C., W.H. Masters, and V.E. Johnson. *Textbook of Sexual Medicine*. Boston: Little, Brown, 1979.

Kols, A., et al. "Oral Contraceptives in the 1980s." *Population Reports*, Series A, No. 6 (May-June 1982).

Kompara, D. "Difficulties in the Socialization on Process of Step Parenting." *Family Relations* 29(1980):69–73.

Konig, K. *Brothers and Sisters: A Study in Child Psychology*. New York: St. George Books, 1963.

Koop, C.E. *Surgeon General's Report on Acquired Immune Deficiency Syndrome*. Washington, DC: U.S. Department of Health and Human Services, 1987.

Kornblum, W., and J. Julian. *Social Problems*. 6th ed. Englewood Cliffs, NJ: Prentice-Hall, 1989.

Koss, M.P. "The Underdetection of Rape: Methodological Choices Influence Incidence Estimates." *Journal of Social Issues* 48(1992):61–75.

Koss, M.P., C. Gidycz, and N. Wisniewski. "The Scope of Rape: Incidence and Prevalance of Sexual Aggression in a Sample of Higher Education Students." *Journal of Consulting and Clinical Psychology* 55(1987):162–170.

Koss, M.P., K.E. Leonard, D.A. Beezley, and C.J. Oros. "Nonstranger Sexual Aggression: A Discriminant Analysis of the Psychological Characteristics of Undetected Offenders." *Sex Roles* 12(1985):981–92.

Kramer, R.M., and H. Specht, eds. *Readings in Community Organization Practice*. 3rd ed. Englewood Cliffs, NJ: Prentice-Hall, 1983.

Krasner, L. "Behavior Therapy." *Annual Review of Psychology* 27(1971):483–532.

Krumboltz, J.D., and H.B. Krumboltz. *Changing Children's Behavior*. Englewood Cliffs, NJ: Prentice-Hall, 1972.

Kübler-Ross, E. *On Death and Dying*. New York: MacMillan, 1969.

Kushner, M. "Faradic Aversive Controls in Clinical Practice." In C. Neuringer and J.L. Michael (eds.), *Behavior Modification in Clinical Psychology*. New York: Appleton-Century-Crofts, 1970.

Kuypers, J., and V. Benston. "Competence and Social Breakdown: A Social-Psychological View of Aging." *Human Development* 16(2)(1973):37–49.

Laborde, G.Z. *Influencing with Integrity*. Palo Alta, CA: Syntony, 1983.

Lakein, A. *How to Get Control of Your Time and Your Life*. New York: Signet, 1973.

Lamanna, M.A., and A. Riedmann. *Marriages and Families: Making Choices and Facing Change*. 3rd ed. Belmont, CA: Wadsworth, 1988.

Lamb, M.E. "Father-Infant and Mother-Infant Interaction in the First Year of Life." *Child Development* 48(1977):167–81.

———. "Influence of the Child on Marital Quality and Family Interactions during the Prenatal, Perinatal, and Infancy Periods." In R. Lerner and G. Spanier (eds.), *Child Influences on Marital and Family Interaction: A Life-Span Perspective*. New York: Academic, 1978.

Lamb, M., K. Hopps, and A. Elster. "Strange Situation Behavior of Infants with Adolescent Mothers." *Infant Behavior and Development* 10(1987):39–48.

Lammer, E. et al. "Retinoic Acid Embryopathy." *New England Journal of Medicine* 313(1985):837–41.

Lang, J.S. "John Hinkley—A Misfit Who Craved Fame." *U.S. News & World Report*, April 13, 1981, p. 26.

Lankton, S. *Practical Magic: A Translation of Basic Neuro-Linguistic Programming into Clinical Psychotheray*. Cupertino, CA: Meta Publications, 1980.

Lasater, M. "Sexual Assault: The Legal Framework." In C. Warner (ed.), *Rape and Sexual Assault*. Germantown, MD: Aspen Systems Corp., 1980.

Lawrence, L., L. Rubinson, and T. O'Rourke. "Sexual Attitudes and Behaviors: Trends for a Ten Year Period." 1972-1982." *Journal of Sex Education and Therapy* 10(1)(Fall/Winter 1984):22–30.

Lawton, M.P. "Leisure Activities for the Aged." *Annals of the American Academy of Political and Social Science* 438(1978): 71–79.

Leacock, E. *The Culture of Poverty: A Critique*. New York: Simon & Schuster, 1971.

Leaf, A. "Everyday Is a Gift When You Are Over 100." *National Geographic* 143(1)(1973):93–118.

Lebovitz, P.S. "Feminine Behavior in Boys: Aspects of Its Outcome." *American Journal of Psychiatry* 128(1972):1283–89.

Ledger, M. "Aging." *Pennsylvania Gazette*, June 1978, pp. 18–23.

Lee, G. "Marriage and Morale in Later Life." *Journal of Marriage and the Family* 40(1)(1978):131–39.

Lee, J. "Homosexuality: Tolerance vs. Approval." *Time*, Jan. 8, 1979, pp. 48–51.

Lefrancois, G.R. *The Lifespan*. 2nd ed. Belmont, CA: Wadsworth, 1987.

———. *The Lifespan*. 3rd ed. Belmont, CA: Wadworth, 1990.

Lehman, H.C. "The Most Creative Years of Engineers and Other Technologists." *Journal of Genetic Psychology* 108(1966):263–77.

Leiber, C.S. "Alcoholic Fatty Liver: Its Pathogenesis and Precursor Role for Hepatitis and Cirrhosis." *Panminerva Medica* 18(9–10)(1976):346–58.

Leifer, M. *Psychological Effects of Motherhood: A Study of First Pregnancy*. New York: Praeger, 1980.

Lembert, E.M. *Social Pathology*. New York: McGraw-Hill, 1951.

Lembo, J. *Help Yourself*. Niles, IL: Argus, 1974.

Lemon, B., V. Bengston, and J. Peterson. "An Exploration of the Activity Theory of Aging: Activity Types and Life Satisfaction among In-movers to a Retirement Community." *Journal of Gerontology* 24(4)(1972):511–23.

Lennard, H.L., and Associates. *Mystification and Drug Misuse*. San Francisco: Jossey-Bass, 1971.

Lerner, R., and J. Lerner. "Effects of Age, Sex, and Physical Attractiveness on Child-Peer Relations, Academic Performance and Elementary School Adjustment." *Development Psychology* 13(6)(1977):585–90.

Lesser, H. *Television and the Preschool Child: A Psychological Theory of Instruction and Curriculum Development*. New York: Academic Press, 1977.

Levant, R.F., S.C. Slattery, and J.E. Loiselle. "Father's Involvement in Housework and Child Care with School-Aged Daughters." *Family Relations* 36(1987):152–57.

LeVay, S. "A Difference in Hypothalamic Structure Between Heterosexual and Homosexual Men." *Science* 253(1991):1034–37.

Levine, M.I. "Sex Education in the Public Elementary and High School Curriculum." In D.L. Taylor (ed.), *Human Sexual Development*. Philadelphia, PA: Davis, 1970.

Levinson, D. "A Conception of Adult Development." *American Psychologist* 41(1)(1986):3–13.

Levinson, D.J. "The Midlife Transition: A Period in Adult Psychosocial Transition." *Psychiatry* 40(1977):99–112.

Levinson, D.J., C.N. Darrow, E.B. Klein, M.H. Levinson, and

B. McKee. "The Psychosocial Development of Men in Early Adulthood and the Mid-Life Transition." In D.F. Ricks, A. Thomas, and M. Roff (eds.), *Life History Research in Psychopathology*. Minneapolis: University of Minnesota Press, 1974.

———. *The Seasons of a Man's Life*. New York: Knopf, 1978.

Levitt, E.E., and A.D. Klassen, Jr. *Public Attitudes Toward Sexual Behaviors: The Latest Investigation of the Institute for Sex Research*. Bloomington: Indiana University Press, 1973.

Levy, S.M., L.R. Derogatis, D. Gallagher, and M. Gatz. "Intervention with Older Adults and the Evaluation of Outcome." In L.W. Poon (ed.), *Aging in the 1980s*. Washington, DC: American Psychological Association, 1980.

Lewin K., R. Lippett, and R.K. White. "Patterns of Aggressive Behavior in Experimentally Created 'Social Climates.'" *Journal of Social Psychology* 10(1939):271–99.

Lewinsohn, P.M., R.F. Munoz, M.A. Youngren, and M.Z. Antonette. *Control Your Depression*. Englewood Cliffs, NJ: Prentice-Hall, 1978.

Lewis, K. "Children of Lesbians: Their Point of View." *Social Work* 25(3)(1980):203.

Lewis, L.A. "The Coming-Out Process for Lesbians: Integrating a Stable Identity." *Social Work* 29(5)(1984):464–68.

Lewis, M. "State as an Infant—Interaction: An Analysis of Mother-Infant Interaction as a Function of Sex." *Merrill-Palmer Quarterly* 18(1972):95–121.

Lewis, O. "The Culture of Poverty." *Scientific American* 215(Oct. 1966):19–25.

Lewis, R.G., and Man Keung Ho. "Social Work with Native Americans." *Social Work* 20(Sept. 1975):378–82.

Lewis, S. *Sunday's Women: A Report of Lesbian Life Today*. Boston: Beacon Press, 1979.

Libby, R.W., and G.D. Nass. "Parental Views on Teenage Sexual Behavior." *Journal of Sex Research* 7(1971):226–36.

Lichtenwalner, J.S., and J.W. Maxwell. "The Relationship of Birth Order and Socioeconomic Status to the Creativity of Preschool Children." *Child Development* 40(1969):1241–46.

"Like Much about AIDS, Origin Is Uncertain." *Milwaukee Journal*, Aug. 18, 1985, p. 7.

Liebert, R.M. "Television and Social Learning: Some Relationships Between Viewing Violence and Behaving Aggressively." In J.P. Murray, E.A. Rubinstein, and G.A. Comstock (eds.), *Television and Social Behavior*, vol. 2. Washington, DC: U.S. Government Printing Office, 1972.

Liebow, E. *Tally's Corner: A Study of Negro Street-Corner Men*. Boston: Little, Brown, 1967.

Lincoln, A. Speech made in Charleston, IL 1858. Reported in R. Hofstader, *The American Political Tradition*. New York: Knopf, 1948.

Lindeman, R.D. "Changes in Penal Function." In R. Goldman and M. Rockstein (eds.), *The Physiology and Pathology of Human Aging*. New York: Academic Press, 1975.

Lindgren, J.R., and N. Taub. *The Law of Sex Discrimination*. New York: West, 1988.

Linscheid, T.R., and C.E. Cunningham. "A Controlled Demonstration of the Effectiveness of Electric Shock in the Elimination of Chronic Infant Rumination." *Journal of Applied Behavior Analysis* 10(1977):500.

Lipid Research Clinics Program. "The Lipid Research Clinic Coronary Primary Prevention Trial Results. 1, Reduction in the Incidence of Coronary Heart Disease." *Journal of the American Medical Association* 251(1984):351–64.(a)

———. "The Lipid Research Clinic Coronary Primary Prevention Trial Results: II The Relationship of Reduction in Incidence of Coronary Heart Disease to Cholesterol Lowering." *Journal*

of the American Medical Association 251(1984):365–374.(b)

Lipnick, R.J., et al. "Oral Contraceptives and Breast Cancer." *Journal of the American Medical Association* 255(1986):58–61.

Liss, M.B. "Pattern of Toy Play: An Analysis of Sex Differences." *Sex Roles* 7(1981):1143–50.

Litt, I.F., et al. "Emergency Room Evaluation of the Adolescent Who Attempts Suicide: Compliance with Follow-up." *Journal of Adolescent Health Care* 4(June 1983): 106–8.

Little, M. *Family Breakup* San Francisco, CA: Jossey-Bass, 1982.

Livson, N., and H. Peskin. "Perspectives on Adolescence from Longitudinal Research." In A.J. Adelsen (ed.), *Handbook of Adolescent Psychology*. New York: Wiley, 1980.

Lloyd, G.A. "AIDS and HIV: The Syndrome and the Virus." *Encyclopedia of Social Work: 1990 Supplement*. (Silver Spring, MD: National Association of Social Workers, 1990.

Loden, M. "Disillusion at the Corporate Top: A Machismo That Drives Women Out." *New York Times*, Feb. 9, 1986, p. F2.

Lodl, K., A. McGettigan, and J. Bucy. "Women's Responses to Abortion: Implications for Post-Abortion Support Groups." *Journal of Social Work and Human Sexuality* 3(1985): 119–32.

Loewenberg, F.M. *Fundamentals of Social Intervention* (New York: Columbia Press, 1977).

Loewenberg, F.M., and R. Dolgoff. *Ethical Decisions for Social Work Practice*. 2nd ed. Itasca, IL: Peacock, 1985.

Longres, J.F. "Youth Gangs." In *Encyclopedia of Social Work: 1990 Supplement*. Silver Spring, MD: National Association of Social Workers, 1990.

Lopata, H. "Living Through Widowhood." *Psychology Today* 7(2)(1973):87–98.

Loraine, J.A., et al. "Endocrine Function in Male and Female Homosexuals." *British Medical Journal* 4(1970):406–8.

Lott, B. *Women's Lives: Themes and Variations in Gender Learning*. Belmont, CA: Brooks/Cole, 1987.

Lott, B., M.E. Reilly, and D.R. Howard. "Sexual Assault and Harassment: A Campus Community Case Study." *Signs* 8(1982):296–319.

Lovass, O.I., and J.Q. Simmons. "Manipulatoin of Self-Destruction in Three Retarded Children." *Journal of Applied Behavior Analysis* 2(1969):143–57.

Lowenthal, M.F., and C. Haven. "Interaction and Adaptation: Intimacy as a Critical Variable." In B. Neugarten (ed.), *Middle Age and Aging* Chicago: University of Chicago Press, 1968.

Lowenthal, M.F., and D. Chiroboga. "Transition to the Empty Nest: Crisis, Change, or Relief?" *Archives of General Psychiatry* 26(1972):8–14.

Luech, M., A. Orr, and M. O'Connell. "Trends in Child Care Arrangements of Working Mothers." *Current Population Reports*, Series P-23, no. 117 (1982), p. 14.

Maas, H.S. *Five Fields of Social Work Practice*. New York: National Association of Social Workers, 1966.

Maccoby, E.E., and C.N. Jacklin. *The Psychology of Sex Differences*. Stanford, CA: Stanford University Press, 1974.

MacDonald, K., and R.D. Parke. "Parent-Child Physical Play: The Effects of Sex and Age on Children and Parents." *Sex Roles* 5(1986):367–378.

MacKinnon, C.A. *Sexual Harassment of Working Women: A Case of Sex Discrimination*. New Haven, CN: Yale University Press, 1979.

Macmillan, D.L. *Behavior Modification and Education*. New York: Macmillan, 1973.

Madigan, F.C., and R.B. Vance. "Differential Sex Mortality: A Research Design." *Social Forces* 35(1957):193–99.

Madore, C., et al. "A Study on the Effects of Induced Abortion on Subsequent Pregnancy Outcome." *American Journal of Obstetrics and Gynecology* 139(1981):516–21.

Maeroff, G.I. "Making Room at the Top for Women." *New York Times* 1986, p. E9.

Maier, R.A. *Human Sexuality in Perspective.* Chicago: Nelson-Hall, 1984.

Maier, R.A., and B.M. Maier. *Comparative Animal Behavior.* Belmont, CA: Brooks/Cole, 1970.

Makinodan, T. "Cellular Basis of Immunosenescence." In *Molecular and Cellular Mechanisms of Aging.* Vol. 27 Paris: INSERM, Coll. Inst. Nat. Sante Rec. Med., 1974.

Malamuth, N. "Rape Proclivity among Males." *Journal of Social Issues* 37(4)(1981):138–57.

———. "Predictors of Naturalistic Sexual Aggression." *Journal of Personality and Social Psychology* 50(1986):953–62.

Malatesta, V.J. "Alcohol Effects on the Argasmic-Ejaculatory Response in Human Males." *Journal of Sex Research* 15(1979): 101-7.

Malatesta, V.J., R.H. Pollack, T.D. Crotty, and L.J. Pecock. "Acute Alcohol Intoxication and Female Orgasmic Response." *Journal of Sex Research* 18(1982):1–17.

Malveaux, J. "Current Economic Trends and Black Feminist Consciousness." *Black Scholar* 16(2)(1985):26–31.

"Man!" *New York Times,* Oct. 20, 1974.

Manley, M. "How to Cope with a Sense of Failure." In C. Zastrow and D. Chang (eds.), *The Personal Problem Solver.* Englewood Cliffs, NJ: Prentice-Hall, 1977.

Mann, J. "Poverty Trap: No Way Out?" *U.S. News & World Report,* Aug. 16, 1982, pp. 31–36.

Mann, J.I., and W.H. Inman. "Oral Contraceptives and Death from Myocardial Infarction." *British Medical Journal* 2(1975): 245–48.

Manosevitz, M., N.M. Prentice, and F. Wilson. "Individual and Family Correlates of Imaginary Companions in Preschool Children." *Developmental Psychology* 8(1)(1973):72–79.

March, C. "Update: Home Tests for Ovulation and Pregnancy." *Endocrine and Fertility Forum* 8(4)(1985):2–6.

Marcia, J. "Identity in Adolescence." In J. Adelson (ed.), *Handbook of Adolescent Psychology.* New York: Wiley, 1980.

Marden, C.F., and G. Meyer. *Minorities in American Society.* New York: American Book Co., 1962.

Margolin, L, and L. White. "The Continuing Role of Physical Attractiveness in Marriage." *Journal of Marriage and the Family* 49(1)(1987):21–27.

Marieskind, H.I. *Women in the Health System.* St. Louis, MO: Mosby, 1980.

Marini, M.M., and M. Brinton. "Sex Typing in Occupational Socialization." In B.F. Reskin (ed.), *Sex Segregation in the Workplace: Trends, Explanations, Remedies.* Washington, DC: National Academy Press, 1984.

Marion, R.W., et al. "Human T-Cell Lymphotropic Virus Type III (HTLV-III) Embryopathy." *American Journal of Diseases of Children* 140(1986):638–40.

Markides, K., and H. Martin. "A Casual Model of Life Satisfaction among the Elderly." *Journal of Gerontology* 34(1)(1979): 86–93.

Markman, H.J. "Prediction of Marital Distress: A 5-Year Follow-Up." *Journal of Consulting and Clinical Psychology* 49(1981):760–62.

Marks, J.S., and W. Cates. "Sex Education: How Should It Be Offered?" *Journal of the American Medical Association* 255(1986):85–86.

Markus, H., and P.S. Nurius. "Self-Understanding and Self-Regulation in Middle Childhood." In W.A. Collins (ed.), *Development During Middle Childhood: The Years from Six to Twelve.* Washington, DC: National Academy, 1984.

Marsden, D., and D. Owens. "The Jekyll and Hyde Marriage." *New Society* 32(1975):334.

Marshall, D.S. "Too Much in Mangaia." In C. Gordon and G. Johnson (eds.), *Readings in Human Sexuality: Contemporary Perspectives,* 2nd ed. New York: Harper & Row, 1980.

Marsiglio, W. "Teenage Fatherhood: High School Accreditation and Educational Attainment." In A.B. Elster and M.E. Lamb (eds.), *Adolescent Fatherhood.* Hillside, NJ: Erlbaum, 1986.

Martin, D. *Battered Wives.* San Francisco, CA: Glide Pubns, 1976.

Martin, H.P.I., and P. Beezley. "Personality of Abused Children." In H.P. Martin (ed.), *The Abused Child.* Cambridge, MA: Ballinger, 1976.

Martin, J. "Neglected Fathers: Limitations in Diagnostic and Treatment Resources for Violent Men." *Child Abuse and Neglect* 8(1984):387–92.

Martin, S.E. "Sexual Harassment: The Link Between Gender Stratification, Sexuality, and Women's Economic Status." In Jo Freeman (ed.), *Women: A Feminist Perspective.* Palo Alto, CA: Mayfield, 1984.

Marx, K. *Selected Writings in Sociology and Social Philosophy,* T.B. Bottomore, trans. New York: McGraw-Hill, 1964.

Mashek, J.W. "Massive Shift to Right: Story of '80 Elections." *U.S. News & World Report,* Nov. 17, 1980, p. 29.

Maslow, A.H. *Motivation and Personality.* New York: Harper & Row, 1954.

———. *Toward a Psychology of Being.* 2nd ed. Princeton, NJ: Van Nostrand, 1968.

———. *The Farther Reaches of Human Nature.* New York: Viking, 1971.

Maslow, A.H., and N.L. Mintz. "Effects of Esthetic Surroundings." *Journal of Psychology* 41(1956):247–54.

"Mastectomy Not So Necessary, Panel Says." *Milwaukee Journal,* June 22, 1990.

Masters, W.H., and V.E. Johnson. *Human Sexual Response.* Boston: Little, Brown, 1966.

———. "Human Sexual Response: The Aging Female and the Aging Male." In B.L. Neugarten (ed.), *Middle Age and Aging: A Reader in Social Psychology.* Chicago: University of Chicago Press, 1968.

———. *Human Sexual Inadequacy.* Boston: Little, Brown, 1970.

Masters, W.H., V.E. Johnson, and R.C. Kolodny. *Human Sexuality.* Boston: Little, Brown, 1979.

———. *Human Sexuality.* 2nd ed. Boston: Little, Brown, 1982.

———. *Human Sexuality.* 3rd ed. Boston: Little, Brown, 1985.

———. *Human Sexuality.* 4th ed. Glenview, IL: Scott, Foresman, 1988.

Matthews, K.A., and J. Rodin. "Women's Changing Work Roles: Impact on Health, Family, and Public Policy." *American Psychologist* 44(11)(1989):1388–93.

Maugh, T.H. "New Test Seems to Detect Early Alzheimer's." *Capital Times,* Aug. 22, 1992, p. 1A.

Maultsby, M.C., Jr. *Help Yourself to Happiness.* Boston: Herman, 1975.

Mayer, A. *Incest: A Treatment Manual for Therapy with Victims, Spouses and Offenders.* Holmes Beach, FL: Learning Pubns, 1983.

Maypole, D.E., and R. Skaine. "Sexual Harassment in the Workplace." *Social Work* 28(5)(Sept./Oct. 1983):385–90.

McAdoo, H.P. "The Development of Self-Concept and Race Attitudes in Black Children: A Longitudinal Study." In W.E. Cross, Jr. (ed.), *Proceedings: The Third Annual Conference on*

Empirical Research in Black Psychology. Washington, DC: U.S. Department of Health, Education, and Welfare, National Institute of Education, 1977.

———. "Racial Attitude and Self-Concept of Young Black Children Over Time." In H.P. McAdoo and J.O. McAdoo (eds.), *Black Children: Social, Educational, and Parental Environments*. Newbury Park, CA: Sage, 1985.

McArthur, C. "Personalities of First and Second Children." *Psychiatry* 19(1956):47–54.

McCabe, M.P. "Desired and Experienced Levels of Premarital Affection and Sexual Intercourse During Dating." *Journal of Sex Research* 23(1)(Feb. 1987):23–33.

McCabe, P.M., and J.K. Collins. "Measurement of Depth of Desired and Experienced Sexual Involvement at Different Stages of Dating." *Journal of Sex Research* 20(1984):377–90.

McCary, J.L. *Human Sexuality*. Princeton, NJ: Van Nostrand, 1973.

McCrary, J., and L. Gutierrez. "The Homosexual Person in the Military and in National Security Employment." *Journal of Homosexuality* 5(1,2)(1979/80):115–46.

McDermott, J.F. "Divorce and Its Psychiatric Sequelae in Children." *Archives of General Psychiatry* 23(5)(1970):421–27.

McDonald, K. "Rapid-Growth Genes Could Yield 'Super Livestock.'" *Chronicle of Higher Education*, Feb. 8, 1984.

McDonald-Wikler, L. "Disabilities: Developmental." In *Encyclopedia of Social Work*. Vol. 1. Silver Spring, MD: National Assocation of Social Workers, 1987.

McGill, L., P.B. Smith, and T.C. Johnson. "AIDS: Knowledge, Attitudes, and Risk Characteristics of Teens." *Journal of Sex Education and Therapy* 15(1989):31–35.

McGrath, C. "The Crisis of Domestic Order." *Socialist Review*, Jan./Feb. 1980, pp. 11–30.

McGregor, D. *The Human Side of Enterprise*. New York: McGraw-Hill, 1960.

McGuinness, D. "Facing the 'Learning Disabilities' Crisis." *Education Week* 22 (Feb. 5, 1986): 28.

McIntyre, J. "Victim Response to Rape: Alternative Outcomes." Final Report to the National Institute of Mental Health, ROIMH 29043, Rockville, MD, 1980.

McIntyre, K. "Role of Mothers in Father-Daughter Incest: A Feminist Analysis." *Social Work* 267(1981):26–62, 462–67.

McKay, J., L. Sinisterra, A. McKay, H. Gomez, and P. Lloreda. "Improving Cognitive Ability in Chronically Deprived Children." *Science* 200(1978):270–78.

McKenry, P.C., L.H. Walters, and C. Johnson. "Adolescent Pregnancy: A Review of the Literature." *Family Coordinator* 23 (1)(1979):17–28.

McKenry, P.C., et al. "Adolescent Suicide: A Comparison of Attempters and Nonattempters in an Emergency Room Population." *Clinical Pediatrics* 21(May 1982):266–70.

McQuade, W., and A. Aikman. *Stress*. New York: Bantam, 1974.

McTavish, D.G. "Perceptions of Old People: A Review of Research Methodologies and Findings." *Gerontologist* 11(1971): 90–101.

McWhirter, J.J. *The Learning Disabled Child: A School and Family Concern*. Champaign, IL: Research Press, 1977.

Meador, B.D., and C. Rogers. "Person-Centered Therapy." In R.J. Corsini (ed.), *Current Psychotherapies*, 2nd ed. Itasca, IL: Peacock, 1979.

Meddin, B.J. "The Assessment of Risk in Child Abuse and Neglect Investigations." *Child Abuse and Neglect* 9(1985):57–62.

Medea, A., and K. Thompson. *Against Rape*. New York: Farrar, Strauss and Giroux, 1974.

Meeks, L.B., and P. Heit. *Human Sexuality: Making Responsible Decisions*. Chicago: Saunders, 1982.

Mehrabian, A. *Public Places and Private Spaces*. New York: Basic Books, 1976.

———. *Silent Messages*. 2nd ed. Belmont, CA: Wadsworth, 1981.

Meisels, A., R. Begin, and V. Schneider. "Dysplasias of Uterine Cervix. Epedimiological Aspects: Role of Age at First Coitus and Use of Oral Contraceptives." *Cancer* 40(6)(1977): 3076–81.

Melican, G.J., and L.S. Feldt. "An Empirical Study of the Zojonc-Markus Hypothesis for Achievement Test Score Declines." *American Educational Research Journal* 17(1980):5–19.

"Men Often Lie About Sex Lives, AIDS Exposure, Survey Finds." *Milwaukee Journal*, Aug. 14, 1988.

Mercer, C.D., and M.E. Snell. *Learning Theory Research in Mental Retardation: Implications for Teaching*. Columbus, OH: Merrill, 1977.

Mercer, J.R. *Labeling the Mentally Retarded*. Berkeley: University of California Press, 1973.

———. "A Policy Statement: On Assessment Procedures and the Rights of Children." *Harvard Educational Review* 44(Feb. 1974):17–34.

———. *System of Multicultural Pluralistic Assessment Technical Manual*. New York: Psychological Corp., 1979.

Mercer, J.R., and J.F. Lewis. *System of Multicultural Pluralistic Assessment Manual*. New York: Psychological Corp., 1979.

Merton, R.K. "Discrimination and the American Creed." In R.M. MacIver (ed.), *Discrimination and National Welfare*. New York: Harper, 1949.

———. *Social Theory and Social Structure*. New York: Free Press, 1968.

Meyerowitz, B.E. "Psychosocial Correlates of Breast Cancer and Its Treatments." *Psychological Bulletin* 87(1980):108–31.

Middlebrook, P.N. *Social Psychology and Modern Life*. New York: Knopf, 1974.

Miles, C.P. "Conditions Predisposing to Suicide: A Review." *Journal of Nervous and Mental Disease* 164(1977):231–46.

"Military Uncooperative on Gay Rights." *Milwaukee Journal*, Nov. 11, 1992.

Miller, E., J.E. Cradock-Watson, and T.M. Pollock. "Consequences of Confirmed Maternal Rubella at Successive Stages of Pregnancy." *Lancet*, Oct. 9, 1982, pp. 781–84.

Miller, W.B. "Lower Class Culture as a Generating Milieu of Gang Delinquency." *Journal of Social Issues* 14(3)(1958):5–19.

Mills, C.W. *The Power Elite*. New York: Oxford University Press, 1956.

Mills, J., and E. Aronson. "Opinion Change as a Function of the Communicator's Attractiveness and Desire to Influence." *Journal of Personality and Social Psychology* 1(1965):73–77.

Mills, J.L., and B.I. Graubard. "Is Moderate Drinking During Pregnancy Associated with an Increased Risk for Malformation?" *Pediatrics* 80(3)(1987):309–14.

Mills, J.L., et al. "Maternal Alcohol Consumption and Birth Weight: How Much Drinking Is Safe During Pregnancy?" *Journal of the American Medical Association* 252 (1984):1875–79.

Milton, G.A. *Five Studies of the Relation Between Sex Role Identification and Achievement in Problem Solving*. Technical Report No. 3, Dept. of Industrial Administration, Dept. of Psychology, Yale University, Dec. 1958.

Milwaukee Journal. "Like Much about AIDS, Origin Is Uncertain." Aug. 18, 1985, p. 7.

———. "Researcher Far from AIDS Cure." Aug. 21, 1985, p. 8.

———. "Men Often Lie about Sex Lives, AIDS Exposure, Survey Finds." Aug. 14, 1988.

———. "Justice Kennedy Blocks Teen's Abortion." May 17, 1989, p. 5a.

————. "Mastectomy Not So Necessary, Panel Says." June 22, 1990.

————. "Cancer Society Says More Women in U.S. Will Develop Breast Cancer." Jan. 25, 1991.

————. "Silicone Breast Makers Given Ultimatium." April 11, 1991.

————. "RU-486 Abortion Pills Confiscated by U.S. Agents." July 2, 1992.

————. "After One Year, Thomas-Hill Hearings Still Echo Across the Land." Oct. 8, 1992, p. A14.

————. "French Abortion Drug Termed a Safe 'Morning After' Pill." Oct. 8, 1992.

————. "Military Uncooperative on Gay Rights." Nov. 11, 1992.

————. "Gays Face New Fears if Ban Ends." Nov. 16, 1992.

————. "Fertility Doctor Defends Motives." Nov. 24, 1992, p. A7.

Minahan, N. "Relationships among Self-Perceived Physical Attractiveness, Body Shape, and Personality of Teen-Age Girls." *Dissertation Abstracts International* 32(1971):1249–50.

Minnigerode, F.A., and M.R. Adelman. "Elderly Homosexual Men and Women: Report on a Pilot Study." *Family Coordinator* 27(4)(1978):451–56.

Minuchin, S. *Families and Family Therapy*. Cambridge, MA: Harvard University Press, 1974.

Mischel, W. *Introduction to Personality*. 2nd ed. New York: Holt, Rinehart, and Winston, 1976.

Mishell, D.R., Jr. "Non-Contraceptive Health Benefits of Oral Steroidal Contraceptives." *American Journal of Obstetrics and Gynecology* 142(1982):809–16.

Mizio, E. "White Worker-Minority Client." *Social Work* 17(May 1972):82–86.

Moody, J., and V. Hayes. "Responsible Reporting: The Initial Step. In C. Warner (ed.), *Rape and Sexual Assault*. Germantown, MD: Aspen Systems, 1980.

Moore, C. "Cigarette Smoking and Cancer of the Mouth, Pharynx, and Larynx." *Journal of the American Medical Association* 191(1965):104–10.

Moore, J.W. *Mexican Americans*, 2nd ed. Englewood Cliffs, NJ: Prentice-Hall, 1976.

Moore, S. "AIDS Field Beckons Social Work Students." *NASW NEWS*, Oct. 1988, pp. 4–5.

Moore, W., Jr. *The Vertical Ghetto*. New York: Random House, 1969.

Moos, R.H., and B. Humphrey. *Family, Work, and Group Environment Scales Manual*. Palo Alto, CA: Consulting Psychologists Press, 1974.

Morales, A. "Urban Gang Violence." In A. Morales and B.W. Sheafor, *Social Work, A Profession of Many Faces*, 5th ed. Boston: Allyn & Bacon, 1989.

Morin, S.F. "Heterosexual Bias in Psychological Research on Lesbianism and Male Holosexuality." *American Psychologist* 32(1977):629–37.

Morland, J. "A Comparison of Race Awareness in Northern and Southern Children." *American Journal of Orthopsychiatry* 36(1966):22–31.

Morris, C.G. *Psychology: An Introduction*. Englewood Cliffs, NJ: Prentice-Hall, 1979.

Morse, N.C., and R.S. Weiss. "The Function and Meaning of Work." *American Sociological Review*, April 1955, pp. 191–98.

Morsink, C.V. "Learning Disabilities." In W.H. Berdine and A.E. Blackhurst (eds.), *An Introduction to Special Education*, 2nd ed. Boston: Little, Brown, 1985.

Morton, H.C. "A Look at Factors Affecting the Quality of Working Life." *Monthly Labor Review*, Oct. 1977, p. 64.

Moses, A.E., and R.O. Hawkins. *Counseling Lesbian Women and Gay Men: A Life-Issues Approach*. St. Louis, MO: Mosby, 1982.

Moss, F. "It's Hell to Be Old in the U.S.A." *Parade Magazine*, July 17, 1977, p. 9.

Moss, G., and W. Moss. *Growing Old*. New York: Pocket Books, 1975.

Moss, H.A., and J. Kagan. "Maternal Influences and Early IQ Scores." *Psychological Reports* 4(1958):655–61.

Motherner, I. "Teenage Mothers USA." *RF Illustrated* (Rockefeller Foundation), May 1977.

Mowrer, O.H., and W.M. Mowrer. "Enuresis: A Method for Its Study and Treatment." *American Journal of Orthopsychiatry* 8(1938):436–59.

Moynihan, D.P. "Our Poorest Citizens—Children." *Focus* 11(1) (Spring, 1988);5–6.

Moynihan, R., G. Christ, and L.G. Silver. "AIDS and Terminal Illness." *Social Casework* 69(6)(June 1988):380–87.

Mundy, P., B. Thomas, and D. Taylor-Robinson. "The Microtrak Test for Rapid Detection of Chlamydia in Diagnosing and Managing Women with Abdominal Pain." *Genitourinary Medicine* 62(1986):15–19.

Mushkin, S. "Politics and Economics of Government Response to Drug Abuse." *Annals of the American Academy of Political and Social Science* 417(Jan. 1975):30.

Muson, H. "Moral Thinking: Can It Be Taught?" *Psychology Today* 12(9)(1979): 48–58, 67-68, 92.

Mussen, P.H., and M.C. Jones. "Self Conceptions, Motivations, and Interpersonal Attitudes of Late and Early Maturing Boys." *Child Development* 28(1957):243–56.

Muuss, R.E. "Adolescent Development and the Secular Trend." *Adolescence* 5(1970):267–84.(a)

————. "Puberty Rites in Primitive and Modern Societies." *Adolescence* 5(1970):109–28. (b)

Myers, U.S. "Illegitimacy and Services to Single Parents." In C. Zastrow (ed.), *Introduction to Social Welfare Institutions*, 2nd ed. Homewood, IL: Dorsey, 1982.

Myrdal, G. *An American Dilemma*. New York: Harper & Row, 1944.

Nadelson, C. "Relation of Vaginal Lubrication to Sexual Desires." *Medical Aspects of Human Sexuality* 12(9)(1978):98.

Nadelson, C., et al. "A Follow-Up Study of Rape Victims." *American Journal of Psychiatry* 39(1982):1266–70.

Nass, G., R. Libby, and M. Fisher. *Sexual Choices*. 2nd ed. Monterey, CA: Wadsworth, 1984.

Nass, J.M. "All in the Family: How Does That Gutsy South Dakota Grandma Feel about Being Pregnant with Her Daughter's Twins." *Time*, Aug. 19, 1991, p. 58.

National Academy of Sciences. *Marijuana and Health*. Washington, DC: U.S. Government Printing Office, 1982.

National Advisory Council on Economic Opportunity. *The American Promise: Equal Justice and Economic Opportunity. Final Report*. Washington, DC: U.S. Government Printing Office, 1981.

National Association of Social Workers. *Encyclopedia of Social Work*. New York: NASW, 1977.(a)

————. "Social Casework and Social Group Work: The Behavioral Approach." In *Encyclopedia of Social Work*. New York: NASW, 1977. (b)

————. "The NASW Code of Ethics." Silver Spring, MD: NASW, 1979.

————. *Practice Digest*. New York: NASW, 1984.

————. *Encyclopedia of Social Work*. Silver Spring, MD: NASW, 1987.

————. "Code of Ethics of the National Association of Social Workers." Silver Spring, MD: NASW, 1990.

National Center for Health Statistics. "Final Mortality Statistics, 1977." *Monthly Vital Statistics Report* 27 (Supp.)(Feb. 5, 1979):1–27.

———. *Maternal Weight Gain and the Outcome of Pregnancy, United States, 1980. Vital Statistics.* DHHS Publication No. 86–1922. Washington, DC: U.S. Government Printing Office, 1986.

National Center for Social Statistics. *Children Served by Public Welfare Agencies and Voluntary Child Welfare Agencies and Institutions, March, 1972.* Washington, DC: U.S. Government Printing Office, 1974.

National Clearinghouse for Drug Abuse Information. *Amphetamine.* Report Series 28, no. 1. Rockville, MD: Alcohol, Drug Abuse, and Mental Health Administration, 1974.

National Coalition of Advocates for Students. *Criteria for Evaluating an AIDS Curriculum.* Boston: NCAS, 1987.

National Commission of Working Women. *Women's Work: Undervalued, Underpaid.* Washington, DC: Center for Women and Work, 1983.

National Committee for the Day Care of Children. *Newsletter* 4(5)(Spring 1965).

National Council on Aging. *Fact Book on Aging: A Profile of America's Older Population.* Washington, DC: NCOA, 1978.

National Institute on Alcohol Abuse and Alcoholism (NIAAA). *Media Alert: FAS Awareness Campaign: My Baby. . . Strong and Healthy.* Rockville, MD: National Clearinghouse for Alcohol Information, 1986.

National Institute of Mental Health (NIMH). *Television and Behavior: Ten Years of Scientific Progress and Implications for the Eighties.* Vol. 1, *Summary Report* DHHS publication no. ADM 82-1195. Washington, DC: U.S. Government Printing Office, 1982.

National Institute on Drug Abuse. *Sedative-Hypnotic Drugs: Risks and Benefits.* Washington, DC: U.S. Government Printing Office, 1977.

———. *Student Drug Use in America: 1975–1981.* Washington, DC: U.S. Government Printing Office, 1982.

———. "Cocaine Use Remains Steady, Other Drug Use Declines among High School Seniors." *NIDA Notes* 2(2)1987):1.

National Society for the Prevention of Cruelty to Children. *At Risk.* Boston: Routledge and Kegan Paul, 1976.

Navia, B.A., B.D. Jordan, and R.W. Price. "The AIDS Dementia Complex. I, Clinical Features." *Annals of Neurology* 19(June 1986):517–24.

Negy, C., and A.W. Webber. "Knowledge and Fear of AIDS: A Comparison Study Between White, Black, and Hispanic College Students." *Journal of Sex Education and Therapy* 17(1)(1991):42–45.

Neiding, P.H., and D.H. Friedman. *Spouse Abuse: A Treatment Program for Couples.* Champaign, IL: Research Press, 1984.

Nelson, C. "Victims of Rape: Who Are They?" In C. Warner (ed.), *Rape and Sexual Assault.* Germantown, MD: Aspen Systems, 1980.

Nelson, M. "Providing Family Day Care: An Analysis of Home-Based Work." *Social Problems* 35(1988):78–94.

Neugarten, B. "Dynamics of Transition of Middle Age to Old Age: Adaptation and the Life Cycle." *Journal of Geriatric Psychiatry* 4(1970):71–87.

Neugarten, B., and K. Weinstein. "The Changing American Grandparent." *Journal of Marriage and the Family* 26(1964): 199–205.

Neugarten, B., V. Wood, R. Kraines, and B. Lommis. "Women's Attitudes Toward the Menopause." *Vita Humana* 6(1963):140–51.

New York Times. "Women and Power—A Status Report." May 1, 1977, sec. 3, pp. 1, 4.

Newhouse M.L., et al. "A Case Control Study of Carcinoma of the Ovary." *British Journal of Preventive and Social Medicine* 31(3)(Sept. 1979):148–53.

Newman, B.M., and P.R. Newman. *An Introduction to the Psychology of Adolescence.* Homewood, IL: Dorsey, 1979.

———. *Development Through Life: A Psychosocial Approach.* Homewood, IL: Dorsey, 1984.

Newman, G., and C.R. Nichols. "Sexual Activities and Attitudes in Older Persons." In E.B. Palmore (ed.), *Normal Aging.* Durham, NC: Duke University Press, 1970.

Newman, L.E. "Treatment for the Parents of Feminine Boys." *American Journal of Psychiatry* 133(1976):683–87.

Newman, W., and C. Owens. "Race-and-Sex-Based Wage Discrimination Is Illegal." In *Comparable Worth: Issue for the 80's.* Vol. 1. Washington, DC: U.S. Commission on Civil Rights, 1984.

Newton, D.E. "Homosexual Behavior and Child Molestation: A Review of the Evidence." *Adolescence* 13(1978):29–43.

Newton, E. *Mothercamp: Female Impersonators in America.* Englewood Cliffs, NJ: Prentice-Hall, 1972.

Nichols, M. *Family Therapy: Concepts and Methods.* New York: Gardner Press, 1984.

Nieburg, P., et al. "The Fetal Tobacco Syndrome." *Journal of the American Medical Association* 253(1985):2998–99.

Nielsen Television Index. *Report on Television Usage.* Hackensack, NJ: A.C. Nielsen Co., 1984.

Noble, E.P. *Alcohol and Health: Third Special Report to the United States Congress.* Rockville, MD: U.S. Public Health Service, 1978.

Norman, E., and A. Mancuso. *Women's Issues and Social Work Practice.* Itasca, IL: Peacock, 1980.

North, B.B., and B.W. Vorhauer. "Use of the Today Contraceptive Sponge in the United States." *International Journal of Fertility* 30(1985):81–84.

Norton, D.G. "Environment and Cognitive Development: A Comparative Study of Socioeconomic Status and Race." Ph.D. diss., Graduate School of Social Work and Social Research, Bryn Mawr College, 1969.

———. "Incorporating Content on Minority Groups into Social Work Practice Courses." In *The Dual Perspective.* New York: Council on Social Work Education, 1978.

———. "Black Family Life Patterns, the Development of Self and Cognitive Development of Black Children." In G.J. Powell (ed.), *The Psychosocial Development of Minority Group Children.* New York: Brunner/Mazel, 1983.

Notelovitz, M., and M. Ware. *Stand Tall: The Informed Woman's Guide to Preventing Osteoporosis.* Gainesville, FL: Triad, 1983.

Novak, E.R., G.S. Jones, and H.W. Jones. *Novak's Textbook of Gynecology.* 9th ed. Baltimore, MD; Williams and Wilkins, 1975.

Nyberg, K.L., and J.S. Alston. "Analysis of Public Attitudes Toward Homosexual Behavior." *Journal of Homosexuality* 2(1976/77):99–107.

Nye, F.I. "Child Adjustment in Broken and Unhappy Unbroken Homes." *Marriage and Family Living* 19(1957):356–61.

O'Brien, F., N.H. Azrin, and C. Bugle. "Training Profoundly Retarded Children to Stop Crawling." *Journal of Applied Behavior Analysis* 5(1974):131–37.

Offer, D., and M. Sabshin. *Normality: Theoretical and Clinical Concepts in Mental Health.* New York: Basic Books, 1966.

Office for Economic Cooperation and Development. *Labor Force Statistics.* Paris; OECD, 1988.

Office of Technological Assessment, U.S. Congress. *Infertility and Social Choices.* Washington, DC: U.S. Government Printing Office, 1988.

Offir, C.W. *Human Sexuality.* New York: Harcourt Brace Jovanovich, 1982.

Ogburn, W.F., and F.M. Nimkoff. *Technology and the Changing Family.* New York: Houghton Mifflin, 1955.

Okun, B.F., and L.J. Rappaport. *Working with Families: An Introduction to Family Therapy.* North Scituate, MA: Duxbury, 1980.

Olds, S.W. "Menopause: Something to Look Forward To?" *Today's Health,* May 1970, p. 48.

O'Leary K.D., and G.T. Wilson. *Behavior Therapy: Application and Outcome.* Englewood Cliffs, NJ: Prentice-Hall, 1975.

O'Leary, K.D., R.N. Kent, and J. Kanowitz. "Shaping Data Collection Congruent with Experimental Hypotheses." *Journal of Applied Behavior Analysis* 8(1975):43–51.

O'Neill, G., and N. O'Neill. *Open Marriage.* New York: Evans, 1971.

Orbach, S. *Fat Is a Feminist Issue.* New York: Paddington Press, 1978.

Orlofsky, J., J. Marcia, and I. Lesser. "Ego Identity Status and the Intimacy Versus Isolation Crisis of Young Adulthood." *Journal of Personality and Social Psychology* 27(2)(1973):211–19.

Ortiz, E.T. *Your Complete Guide to Sexual Health.* Englewood Cliffs, NJ: Prentice-Hall, 1989.

Osofsky, J.D., et al. "Psychologic Effects of Legal Abortion." *Clinical Obstetrics and Gynecology* 14(1)(1971):215–34.

Osofsky, J.D., and H.J. Osofsky. "The Psychological Reactions of Patients to Legalized Abortions." *American Journal of Orthopsychiatry* 42(1972):48–60.

Otten, A.S. "Ever More Americans Live into 80s and 90s, Causing Big Problems." *Wall Street Journal,* July 30, 1984, pp. 1, 10.

Otto, W. "Family Position and Success in Reading." *Reading Teacher,* Nov. 1965.

Ouellette, E., et al. "Adverse Effects on Offspring of Maternal Alcohol Abuse During Pregnancy." *New England Journal of Medicine* 297(1977):528–30.

Ozwald, P.F., and P. Peltzman. "The Cry of the Human Infant." *Scientific American* 230(3)(1974):84–90.

Padilla, E.R., and G.E. Wyatt. "The Effects of Intelligence and Achievement Testing on Minority Group Children." In G.J. Powell (ed.), *The Psychosocial Development of Minority Group Children.* New York: Brunner/Mazel, 1983, pp. 417–37.

Page, E.B., and G.M. Grandon. "Family Configuration and Mental Ability: Two Theories Contrasted with U.S. Data." *American Educational Research Journal* 16(1979): 257–72.

Page, E.W., C.A. Villee, and D.B. Villee. *Human Reproduction: Essentials of Reproductive and Perinatal Medicine.* Philadelphia, PA: Saunders, 1989.

Pagelow, M. "Heterosexual and Lesbian Single Mothers: A Comparison of Problems, Coping and Solutions." *Journal of Homosexuality* 5(3)(1980):189–204.

Painton, P., A. Sachs, and J.L. Reid. "Nation." *Time,* Oct. 21, 1991, pp. 63–64.

Palen, J.J. *Social Problems.* New York: McGraw-Hill, 1979.

Paley, D. "Nursing Home Is Cited Again." *Wisconsin State Journal,* May 23, 1980, sec. 4, p.1.

———. "Cocaine Becoming 'Acceptable.'" *Wisconsin State Journal,* Dec. 13, 1982, sec. 1, p. 1.

Papalia, D.E., and S. Wendkos Olds. *Human Development.* 2nd ed. New York: McGraw-Hill, 1981.

———. *Human Development.* 4th ed. New York: McGraw-Hill, 1989.

———. *Human Development.* 5th ed. New York: McGraw-Hill, 1992.

Parke, R.D., and D.B. Sawin. "Fathering: It's a Major Role." *Psychology Today,* Nov. 1977.

Parke, R.D., and B.R. Tinsley. "The Father's Role in Infancy: Determinants of Involvement in Caregiving and Play." In M.E. Lamb (ed.), *The Role of the Father in Child Development,* 2nd ed. New York: Wiley, 1981.

Parke, R.S. "Some Effects of Punishment on Children's Behavior—Revisited." In E.M. Hetherington and R.D. Parke (eds.), *Child Psychology: A Contemporary Viewpoint.* New York: McGraw-Hill, 1977.

Parnell, R.W. *Behavior and Physique: An Introduction to Practical and Applied Somatometry.* London, UK: Edward Arnold, 1958.

Parten, M. "Social Participation among Preschool Children." *Journal of Abnormal and Social Psychology* 27(1932): 243–69.

Patel, N.S. "Attempted and Completed Suicide." *Medical Science Law* 14(1974):273–79.

Patterson, G.R. *Families: Applications of Social Learning to Family Life.* Champaign, IL: Research Press, 1975.

Patterson, G.R., and J.B. Reid. "Reciprocity and Coercion: Two Facets of Social Systems." In C. Neuringer and J.L. Michael (eds.), *Behavior Modification in Clinical Psychology.* New York: Appleton-Century-Crofts, 1970.

Patterson, W.M., H.H. Dohn, J. Bird, and G.A. Patterson. "Evaluation of Suicidal Patients; The SAD PERSONS Scale." *Psychosomatics* 24(4)(April 1983):343–49.

Patti, R. *Social Welfare Administration.* Englewood Cliffs, NJ: Prentice-Hall, 1983.

Pauker, J.D. "Fathers of Children Conceived Out of Wedlock: Pregnancy, High School, Psychological Test Results." *Developmental Psychology* 4(2)(1971):215–18.

Pear, R. "Poverty Data and Families." *New York Times,* Aug. 29, 1985, p. A17.

Peck, R.C. "Psychological Development in the Second Half of Life." In B.L. Neugarten (ed.), *Middle Age and Aging.* Chicago: University of Chicago Press, 1968.

Pelletier, K.R. *Mind as Healer, Mind as Slayer.* New York: Dell, 1977.

Pendergrass, V.E. "Timeout from Positive Reinforcement Following Persistent High-Rate Behavior in Retardates." *Journal of Applied Behavior Analysis* 5(1972):85–91.

Peplau, L.A. "What Homosexuals Want in Relationships." *Psychology Today* 15(3)(March 1981):28–38.

Pepper, C. "Will There Be a Brighter Tomorrow for the Nation's Elderly?" *USA Today* 108(2420)(1980):14–16.

Perez, J.F. *Family Counseling: Theory and Practice.* New York: Van Nostrand, 1979.

Perloff, W.H. "Hormones and Homosexuality." In J. Marmor (ed.), *Sexual Inversion: The Multiple Roots of Homosexuality.* New York: Basic Books, 1965.

Peskin, H. "Influence of the Developmental Schedule of Puberty on Learning and Ego Functioning." *Journal of Youth and Adolescence* 2(1973):273–90.

Peters, H. "The Legal Rights of Gays." In A.E. Moses and R.O. Hawkins (eds.), *Counseling Lesbian Women and Gay Men: A Life Issues Approach.* St. Louis, MO: Mosby, 1982.

Peters, R. *Mammalian Communication: A Behavioral Analysis of Meaning.* Monterey, CA: Brooks/Cole, 1980.

Pfeffer, N. "Not So New Technologies." *Trouble and Strife* 5(1985):46–50.

Pfeiffer, E. *Successful Aging.* Durham, NC: Duke University Center for the Study of Aging and Human Development, 1974.

Phillips, D.L. "Rejection: A Possible Consequence of Seeking

Help for Mental Disorder." *American Sociological Review* 28 (1963)963–73.

Phillis, D.E., and P.J. Stein. "Sink or Swing? The Lifestyles of Single Adults." In E.R. Allgeier and N.B. McCormick (eds.), *Changing Boundaries: Gender Roles and Sexual Behavior.* Palo Alto, CA: Mayfield, 1983.

Phipps, W., D. Cramer, I. Schiff, S. Belisle, R. Stillman, B. Albrect, M. Gibson, M. Berger, and E. Wilson. "The Association Between Smoking and Female Infertility as Influenced by Cause of Infertility." *Fertility and Sterility* 48(1987):377–82.

Piaget, J. *The Origins of Intelligence in Children.* New York: International Universities Press, 1952.

———. "Intellectual Development from Adolescence to Adulthood." *Human Development* 15(1972):1–12.

Pierce, P. "Male Change of Life." *Ebony* 30(1976):122–28.

Pillard, R.C., J. Poumadere, and R.A. Carretta. "A Family Study of Sexual Orientation." *Archives of Sexual Behavior* 11(1982): 511–20.

Pillard, R.C., nd J.D. Weinrich. "Evidence of Familial Nature of Homosexuality." *Archives of General Psychiatry* 43(1986): 808–12.

Pincus, A., and A. Minahan. *Social Work Practice: Model and Method.* Itasca, IL: Peacock, 1973.

Pinderhughes, E. "Afro-American Families and the Victim System." In M. McGoldrick, J.K. Pearce, and J. Giordana (eds.), *Ethnicity and Family Therapy.* New York: Guilford, 1982.

Pines, A., and E. Aronson. *Burnout: From Tedium to Personal Growth.* New York: Free Press, 1981.

Pines, M. "Invisible Playmates." *Psychology Today,* Sept. 1978, pp. 38–42, 106.

Pinkney, A. *The American Way of Violence.* New York: Random House, 1972.

Piotrow, P.T., W. Rinehart, and J.C. Schmidt. "IUDs: An Update on Safety Effectiveness and Research." *Population Reports,* series B, No. 3(May, 1979).

Planned Parenthood Association of Wisconsin. "Facts about Oral Contraception." Undated handout.

Plateris, A.A. *Increases in Divorces: United States—1967.* Washington, DC: U.S. Government Printing Office, 1967.

Platt, R., P.A. Rice, and W.M. McCormack. "Risk of Acquiring Gonorrhea and Prevalence of Abnormal Adnexal Findings Among Women Recently Exposed to Gonorrhea." *Journal of the American Medical Association* 250(1983):3205–9.

Polansky, N.A., et al. *Child Neglect: Understanding and Reaching the Parent.* New York: Child Welfare League of America, 1972.

"Police Discretion and the Judgment That a Crime Has Been Committed—Rape in Philadelphia." Comment. *University of Pennsylvania Law Review* 117(1968):2.

"Poll: Women Belong in the Workplace." *Providence Evening Bulletin,* June 17, 1986, pp. A1–2.

Porter, J. *Black Child, White Child: The Development of Racial Attitudes.* Cambridge, MA: Harvard University Press, 1971.

"Poverty in the United States: Where Do We Stand Now?" *Focus* 7(Winter 1984):1.

Powdermaker, H. *Life in Lesu.* New York: Norton, 1933. Pp. 276–77.

Powell, G.J., ed. *The Psychosocial Development of Minority Group Children.* New York: Brunner/Mazel, 1983.

Power, C., and J. Reimer. "Moral Atmosphere: An Educational Bridge Between Moral Judgment and Action." *New Directions in Child Development* 2(1978).

Prather, H. *Notes to Myself.* Moab, UT: Real People Press, 1970.

Premack, D. "Reinforcement Theory." In D. Levine (ed.), *Nebraska Symposium on Motivation.* Lincoln: University of Nebraska Press, 1965.

Price, J.H., D. Desmond, and G. Kukulka. "High School Students' Perceptions and Misperceptions of AIDS." *Journal of School Health* 55(1985):107–9.

Price-Bonham, S., and P. Skeen. "A Comparison of Black and White Fathers with Implications for Parent Education." *Family Coordinator* 28(1979):53–59.

Pritchard, J.A., P.C. MacDonald, and N.F. Grant. *Williams Obstetrics.* 17th ed. Norwalk, CT: Appleton-Century-Crofts, 1985.

Prochaska, J.O. *Systems of Psychotherapy.* Homewood, IL: Dorsey, 1979.

Project on the Status and Education of Women. "Supreme Court Rules on Sexual Harassment." *On Campus with Women* 16(2)(1986):5.

"Public Perceptions of Gays: Few Changes in Past Few Years." *Sexuality Today,* Dec. 6, 1982, p. 1.

Putallaz, M., and J.M. Gottman. "An Interactional Model of Children's Entry into Peer Groups." *Child Development* 52(1981):986–94.

Rabushk, A., and B. Jacobs. "Are Old Folks Really Poor? Herewith a Look at Some Common Views." *New York Times,* Feb. 15, 1980, p. A29.

Rachal, J.V., et al. *A National Study of Adolescent Drinking Behavior, Attitudes, and Correlates.* Research Triangle Park, NC: Research Triangle Institute, 1975.

Radin, N. "The Role of the Father in Cognitive Academic, and Intellectual Development." In M.E. Lamb (ed.), *The Role of the Father in Child Development.* New York: Wiley, 1981.

Radloff, L.S. "Sex Differences in Depression: The Effects of Occupation and Marital Status." *Sex Roles* 2(1975):249–65.

Raeburn, P. "Alzheimer's Disease of the Aged." *Wisconsin State Journal,* March 5, 1984, sec. 2, p. 1.

Ramsay, O.A., and E.H. Hess. "A Laboratory Approach to the Study of Imprinting." *Wilson Bulletin* 66(1954):196–206.

Rankin, R. "Imbalance of Payments." *Wisconsin State Journal.* May 10, 1992, pp. A1–2.

Recer, P. "One Year Later: AZT Prolongs Life—and Hope—for AIDS Patients." *Milwaukee Journal,* March 27, 1988, p. 46.

Reese, H.W. "Relationships Between Self-Acceptance and Sociometric Choices." *Journal of Abnormal and Social Psychology* 62(1961):472–74.

Reevy, W.R. "Child Sexuality." In A. Ellis and A. Abarbanel (eds.), *Encyclopedia of Sexual Behavior.* New York: Hawthorn, 1967.

Reilly, M.E., B. Lott, and S.M. Gallogly. "Sexual Harassment of University Students." *Sex Roles* 15(1986):333–58.

Reilly, P. *Genetics, Law and Social Policy.* Cambridge, MA: Harvard University Press, 1977.

Reitz, R. *Menopause: A Positive Approach.* Radnor, PA: Chitton Book Co., 1977.

Remick, H. "Dilemmas of Implementation: The Case of Nursing." In Helen Remick (ed.), *Comparable Worth and Wage Discrimination.* Philadelphia, PA: Temple University Press, 1984.

Renzetti, C.M., and D.J. Curran. *Women, Men, and Society.* Needham Heights, MA: Allyn and Bacon, 1992.

Reposa, R., and M.B. Zuelzer. "Family Therapy with Incest." *International Journal of Family Therapy* 5(2)(Summer 1983): 111–25.

"Researcher Far from AIDS Cure." *Milwaukee Journal,* Aug. 21, 1985, p. 8.

Reskin, B.A., and H.I. Hartman, eds. *Women's Work, Men's Work: Sex Segregation on the Job.* Washington, DC: National Academy Press, 1986.

Resnick, H.L.P. "Suicide." In H.I. Kaplan, A.M. Freedman, and

B.J. Sadock (eds.), *Comprehensive Textbook of Psychiatry*, 3rd ed. Baltimore, MD: Williams and Wilkins, 1980.

Resnick, M. *Wife Beating Counselor Training Manual No. 1.* Ann Arbor, MI: 1977 AA NOW/WIFE Assault, 1976.

Rest, J.R. "The Hierarchical Nature of Moral Judgment: The Study of Patterns of Comprehension and Preference with Moral Stages." *Journal of Personality* 41(1)(1974):92–93.

Rheingold, H.L., and K.V. Cook. "The Contents of Boys' and Girls' Rooms as an Index of Parents' Behavior." *Child Development* 46(1975):459–63.

Rhodes, M.L. "Gilligan's Theory of Moral Development as Applied to Social Work Practice." *Social Work* 30(1985):101–5.

Rice, F.P. *The Adolescent: Development Relationships and Culture.* 2nd ed. Boston: Allyn & Bacon, 1978.

Richmond, M. *Social Diagnosis.* New York: Free Press, 1917.

Riegel, K.F. "Language and Cognition: Some Life-Span Developmental Issues." *Gerontologist* 13(1973):478–82.

Riegel, K.F., and R.M. Riegel. "Development, Drop, and Death." *Developmental Psychology* 6(2)(1972):306–19.

Rierdan, J., E. Koff, and J. Flaherty. "Conceptions and Misconceptions of Menstruation." *Women and Health* 10(4)(1986): 33–45.

Rierdan, J., E. Koff, and M.L. Stubbs. "Gender, Depression, and Body Image in Early Adolescents." *Journal of Early Adolescence* 8(2)(1988):109–17.

————. "A Longitudinal Analysis of Body Image as a Predictor of the Onset and Persistence of Adolescent Girls' Depression." *Journal of Early Adolescence* 9(4)(1989):454–66.

Rifken, L. *Who Should Play God?* New York: Dell, 1977.

Rinehart, W., and P.T. Piotrow. "OCs: Update on Usage, Safety, and Side Effects." *Population Reports*, Series A, No. 5(Jan. 1979).

Ringer, R. *Looking Out for #1.* New York: Fawcett Crest, 1977.

Rioux, J.W. "The Disadvantaged Child in School." In J. Helmuth (ed.), *The Disadvantaged Child.* New York: Brunner/Mazel, 1968.

Risley, T.R. "The Effects and Side Effects of Punishing the Autistic Behavior of a Deviant Child." *Journal of Applied Behavior Analysis* 1(1968):21–34.

Risman, B.J., and P. Schwartz. *Gender in Intimate Relationships.* Belmont, CA: Wadsworth, 1989.

Road Traffic Board of South Australia. *The Points Demerit Scheme as an Indication of Declining Skill with Age.* Adelaide, 1972.

Roberts, E.J. and S.A. Holt. "Parent-Child Communication about Sexuality." *SIECUS Report* 8(4)(March 1980):1–2,10.

Robertson, D.H., A. McMillan, and H. Young. *Clinical Practice in Sexually Transmissible Diseases.* Kent, UK: Pitman Medical, 1980.

Robertson, I. *Social Problems.* 2nd ed. New York: Random House, 1980.

Robinson, D. "Our Suprising Moral Unwed Fathers." *Ladies Home Journal*, Aug. 1969, pp. 49–50.

Robinson, D. "The Crisis in Our Nursing Homes." *Parade Magazine*, Aug. 16, 1988, pp. 13–14.

Robinson, N.M., and H.B. Robinson. *The Mentally Retarded Child: A Psychological Approach.* 2nd ed. New York: McGraw-Hill, 1976.

Roche, A.F., and G.H. Davila. "Late Adolescent Growth in Stature." *Pediatrics* 50(6)(1972):874–80.

Rockstein, M. "The Biology of Aging in Humans: An Overview." In R. Goldman and M. Rockstein (eds.), *The Physiology and Pathology of Human Aging.* New York: Academic Press, 1975.

Rodman, H., G. Sarvis, and J. Bonar. *The Abortion Question.* New York: Columbia University Press, 1987.

Rogers, C. "The Process Equation of Psychotherapy." *American Journal of Psychotherapy* 15(Jan.1961):27–45.

Rogers, C.R. "A Theory of Therapy, Personality and Interpersonal Relationships, as Developed in the Client-Centered Framework." In S. Koch (ed.), *Psychology: A Study of a Science.* Vol. 3. New York: McGraw-Hill, 1959.

Rohn, R., R. Sarles, T. Kenny, B. Reymonds, and F. Heald. "Adolescents Who Attempt Suicide." *Journal of Pediatrics* 90(4)(1977):636–38.

Rollin, B. "Motherhood: Who Needs It?" *Look*, Sept. 22, 1970, pp. 15–17.

Rollins, B., and R. Galligan. "The Developing Child and Marital Satisfaction of Parents." In R. Lerner and G. Spanier (eds.), *Child Influences on Marital and Family Interaction: A Life-Span Perspective.* New York: Academic Press, 1978.

Romero, E.R., and V. Bernal del Rio. "Mental Health Needs and Puerto Rican Children." In G.J. Powell (ed.), *The Psychosocial Development of Minority Group Children.* New York: Brunner/ Mazel, 1983.

Rooney, J.F., et al. "Acquisition of Genital Herpes from an Asymptomatic Sexual Partner." *New England Journal of Medicine* 314(1986):1561–64.

Roosevelt, F.D. Second Inaugural Address. Jan. 20, 1937.

Rorvik, D.M. "Making Men and Women Without Men and Women." *Esquire*, April, 1969, pp. 110–15.

Rose, A. *The Negro in America.* New York: Harper & Row, 1964.

Rose, S.A., J.F. Feldman, C.M. McCarton, and J. Wolfson. "Infant Visual Attention: Relation to Birth Status and Developmental Outcome During the First 5 years." *Developmental Psychology* 25(4)(1989):560–76.

Rose, S.R. *Treating Children in Groups.* San Francisco, CA: Jossey-Bass, 1973.

Rosellini, L. "Rebel with a Cause: Koop." *U.S. News & World Report*, May 30, 1988. pp. 55–63.

Rosen, D.H. *Lesbianism: A Study of Female Homosexuality.* Springfield, IL: Charles C. Thomas, 1974.

Rosen, H. "How Workers Use Cues to Determine Child Abuse." *Social Work Research and Abstracts* 17(1981):27–33.

Rosen, J., and A. Wiens. "Changes in Medical Problems and Use of Medical Services Following Psychological Intervention." *American Psychologist* 34(1979):420–31.

Rosenberg, L., et al. "Oral Contraceptive Use in Relation to Nonfatal Myocardial Infarction." *American Journal of Epidemiology* 111(1980):59–66.

Rosenberg, N.D. "Only True Test for Fetal Viability Is Time, Expert Says." *Milwaukee Journal*, July 5, 1989, p. 4A.

Rosenberg, S.D., and M.P. Farrell. "Identity and Crisis in Middle-Aged Men." *International Journal of Aging and Human Development* 7(1976):153–70.

Rosenhan, D.L. "On Being Sane in Insane Places." *Science* 179(1973): 250–57.

Rosenmayr, L. "Achievements, Doubts and Prospects of the Sociology of Aging." *Human Development* 23(1980):46–62.

Rosenthal, R., and L. Jacobson. *Pygmalion in the Classroom.* New York: Holt, Rinehart and Winston, 1968.(a)

————. "Teacher Expectations for the Disadvantaged." *Scientific American* 218(1968):19–23.(b)

Ross, M.G. *Community Organization: Theory, Principles, and Practice.* 2nd ed. New York: Harper & Row, 1967.

Rossman, J. "Anatomic and Body Composition Changes with Aging." In C.E. Finch and L. Hayflicks (eds.), *Handbook of the Biology of Aging.* New York: Van Nostrand Reinhold, 1977.

Rothman, J. "Community Theory and Research." In *Encyclopedia of Social Work*, vol. 1. Silver Spring, MD: NASW, 1987.

Rothman, J., and J. Tropman. "Models of Community Organization and Macro Practice Perspectives: Their Mixing and Phasing." In F.M. Cox, J.L. Erlich, J. Rothman, and J.E. Tropman (eds.), *Strategies of Community Organization*. Itasca, IL: Peacock, 1987.

Rothman, S.M. *Woman's Proper Place*. New York: Basic Books, 1978.

Rousseau, S., et al. "The Expectancy of Pregnancy for 'Normal' Infertile Couples." *Fertility and Sterility* 40(1983):768–72.

Rovee, C.K., R.Y. Cohen, and W. Shlapack. "Life Span Stability in Olfactory Sensitivity." *Developmental Psychology* 11(1975): 311–18.

Rowland, K. "Environmental Events Predicting Death for the Elderly." *Psychological Bulletin* 84(1977):349–72.

Roy, M., ed. *The Abusive Partner: An Analysis of Domestic Battering*. New York: Van Nostrand Reinhold, 1982.

Rubel, J. "Information Pamphlet." Eugene, OR: Anorexia Nervosa and Related Eating Disorders, Inc., 1980.

Rubin, G.L. "Ectopic Pregnancy in the United States: 1970 Through 1978." *Journal of the American Medical Association* 249(1983):1725–29.

Rubin, J.Z., F.J. Provenzano, and Z. Luria. "The Eye of the Beholder: Parents' Views on Sex of Newborns." In J.H. Williams (ed.), *Psychology of Women: Selected Reading*. New York: Norton, 1985.

Rubin, K. "Nonsocial Play in Preschoolers: Necessary Evil?" *Child Development* 53(1982):651–657.

Rubin, K. "Whose Job Is Child Care?" *Ms.*, March 1987 pp. 32–44.

Rubin, K., T. Maioni, and M. Hornung. "Free Play Behaviors in Middle-Class and Lower-Class Preschoolers: Parten and Piaget Revisited." *Child Development* 47(1976):414–19.

Rubin, K., and K. Trotten. "Kohlberg's Moral Judgment Scale: Some Methodological Considerations." *Developmental Psychology* 13(5)(1977):535–36.

Rubin, K., K. Watson, and T. Jambor. "Free-Play Behaviors in Pre-School and Kindergarten Children." *Child Development* 49(1978):534–36.

Rubin, L.B. *Women of a Certain Age: The Midlife Search for Self*. New York: Harper & Row, 1979.

Rubin, Z. *Liking and Loving*. New York: Holt, Rinehart and Winston, 1973.

Ruble, D.N., and J. Brooks-Gunn. "The Experience of Menarche." *Child Development* 53(1982):1557–66.

Rudel, R.G., with J.M. Holmes and J.R. Pardes. *Assessment of Developmental Learning Disorders: A Neuropsychological Approach*. New York: Basic Books, 1988.

"RU-486 Abortion Pills Confiscated by U.S. Agents." *Milwaukee Journal*, July 2, 1992.

Rush, F. *The Best Kept Secret*. Englewood Cliffs, NJ: Prentice-Hall, 1980.

Russell, A. "The Incidence and Prevalence of Intrafamilial Abuse of Female Children." *Child Abuse and Neglect* 7(2)(1983): 133–46.

Russell, A.B., and C.M. Trainor. *Trends in Child Abuse and Neglect: A National Perspective*. Denver, CO: American Humane Assoc., Children's Division, 1984.

Russell, C. "Transition to Parenthood: Problems and Gratifications." *Journal of Marriage and the Family* 36(1974):294–302.

Russell, M.A.H. "Cigarette Smoking: Natural History of a Dependence Disorder." *British Journal of Medical Psychology* 44(March 1971).

Ruth, S. *Issues in Feminism*. Mountain View, CA: Mayfield, 1990.

Rutter, M. *Maternal Deprivation: Reassessed*. Middlesex, UK: Penguin, 1972.

———. "Separation Experiences: A New Look at an Old Topic." *Pediatrics* 95(1)(1979):147–54.

———. "Stress, Coping, and Development: Some Issues and Some Questions." In N. Garmezy and M. Rutter (eds.), *Stress, Coping, and Development in Children*. New York: McGraw-Hill, 1982.

Ryan, C.C., and M.J. Rowe. "AIDS: Legal and Ethical Issues." *Social Casework* 39(6)(June 1988):324–33.

Ryan, W. *Blaming the Victim*. Rev. ed. New York: Vintage, 1976.

Sabatelli, R., R. Meth, and S. Gavazzi. "Factors Mediating the Adjustment to Involuntary Childness." *Family Relations* 37 (1988).

Safran, C. "What Men Do to Women on the Job: A Shocking Look at Sexual Harassment." *Redbook*, Nov. 1976.

Sagarin, E. "Language of the Homosexual Subculture." *Medical Aspects of Human Sexuality* 4(1970).

Sager, C.J., T.L. Brayboy, and B.R. Waxenberg. *Black Ghetto Family in Therapy: A Laboratory Experience*. New York: Grove Press, 1970.

Saghir, M.T., and E. Robins. *Male and Female Homosexuality*. Baltimore, MD: Williams and Wilkins, 1973.

Saltz, E., D. Dixon, and J. Johnson. "Training Disadvantaged Preschoolers on Various Fantasy Activities: Effects on Cognitive Functioning and Impulse Control." *Child Development* 48(1977):367–80.

Saltzman, A., and L. Wiener. "A Boomers' Plan." *U.S. News & World Report*, Aug. 15, 1988, pp. 64–67.

Samuelson, P. Quoted in P. Blumberg, *Inequality in an Age of Decline*. New York: Oxford University Press, 1980.

Sandler, B.R., and R.M. Hall. "The Campus Climate Revisited: Chilly for Women Faculty, Administrators, and Graduate Students." Washington, DC: Project on the Status and Education of Women, 1986.

San Francisco AIDS Foundation. *Women and AIDS*. 3rd ed. San Francisco, CA: AIDS Foundation, 1987.

Sapiro, V. *Women in American Society*. 2nd ed. Mountain View, CA: Mayfield, 1990.

Sarri, R.C. "Adolescent Status Offenders—A National Problem." In A. Kadushin (ed.), *Child Welfare Strategy in the Coming Years*. Washington, DC: U.S. Department of Health, Education and Welfare, 1978.

———. "Administration in Social Welfare." In *Encyclopedia of Social Work*, vol. 1, Silver Spring, MD: NASW, 1987.

Satir, V. *Conjoint Family Therapy*. Palo Alto, CA: Science and Behavior Books, 1967.

———. *People Making*. Palo Alto, CA: Science and Behavior Books, 1972.

Sattem, L., J. Savells, and E. Murray. "Sex-Role Stereotypes and Commitment of Rape." *Sex Roles* 11(1984):849–60.

Sawin, D.B., and R.D. Parke. "Adolescent Fathers: Some Implications from Recent Research on Parental Roles." *Educational Horizons* 55(1976):38–43.

Scales, P. "Males and Morals: Teenage Contraceptive Behavior Amid the Double Standard." *Family Coordinator* 26(1971): 211–22.

Scanlan, C. "New AIDS Drug Wins OK by FDA." *Wisconsin State Journal* Oct. 10, 1991, p. 3A.

Scanlon, J. *Young Adulthood*. New York: Academy for Educational Development, 1979.

Scanzoni, J., and G.L. Fox. "Sex Roles, Family and Society: The Seventies and Beyond." *Journal of Marriage and the Family* 42(1980):743–58.

Schachter, S. "Birth Order, Eminence and Higher Education." *American Sociological Review* 28(1963):764–67.

Schack, S., and R.S. Frank. "Police Service Delivery to the Elderly." *Annals of the American Academy of Political and Social Science* 438(July 1978):83.

Schaefer, C.E. "Imaginary Companions and Creative Adolescents." *Developmental Psychology* 1(1969):747–49.

Schaefer, R.T. *Racial and Ethnic Groups*. 2nd ed. Boston: Little, Brown, 1984.

Schafer, S. "Sociosexual Behavior in Male and Female Homosexuals: A Study in Sex Differences." *Archives of Sexual Behavior* 6(1977):355–64.

Schafer, W. *Stress, Distress and Growth*. David, CA: International Dialogue Press, 1978.

Schanche, D. "What Really Happens Emotionally and Physically When a Man Reaches 40?" *Today's Health*, March 1973, pp. 40–43, 60.

Schatten, G., and H. Schatten. "The Energetic Egg." *Sciences* 23(5)(1983):28–34.

Scheck, D.C., R. Emerick, and M.M. El-Assal. "Adolescents' Perceptions of Parent-Child Relations and the Development of Internal-External Control Operation." *Journal of Marriage and the Family* 35(1973):643–54.

Scheff, T. *Being Mentally Ill*. Hawthorne, NY: Aldine, 1966.

Scheflen, A. *How Behavior Means*. Garden City, NY: Anchor, 1974.

Scheiner, A.P., and N.A. McNabb. "The Child with Mental Retardation." In A.P. Scheiner and I.F. Abroms (eds.), *The Practical Management of the Developmentally Disabled Child*. St. Louis, MO: Mosby, 1980.

Scherz, F.H. "Theory and Practice of Family Therapy." In R.W. Roberts and R.H. Nee (eds.), *Theories of Social Casework*. Chicago: University of Chicago Press, 1970.

Schiamberg, L.B. *Human Development*. New York: Macmillan, 1985.

Schlesinger, B. "One-Parent Families in Great Britain." *Family Coordinator* 26(1977):139–41.

Schmidt, G.W., and R. Ulrich. "Effects of Group Contingent Events upon Classroom Noise." *Journal of Applied Behavior Analysis* 2(1969):171–79.

Schmitt, B. "The Child with Non-Accidental Trauma." In C.H. Kempe (ed.), *The Battered Child*. Chicago: University of Chicago Press, 1980, pp. 128–46.

Schneck, H.M., Jr. "Trend in Growth of Children and Lags." *New York Times*, June 10, 1976, p. 13.

Schneider, J., et al. "Some Factors for Analysis in Sexual Assault." *Social Science and Medicine* 15A(1)(Jan. 1981):55–61.

Schreiner, T. "A Revolution That Has Just Begun." *USA Today*, May 29, 1984, p. 40.

Schrof, J. "Pumped Up." *U.S. News & World Report*, June 1, 1992, pp. 55–63.

Schuller, R. *Move Ahead with Possibility Thinking*. Moonachie, NJ: Pyramid, 1973.

Schultz, T. "Does Marriage Give Today's Women What They Want?" *Ladies Home Journal*, June 1980, pp. 89–91, 146–55.

Schulz, D.A. *Human Sexuality*. Englewood Cliffs, NJ: Prentice-Hall, 1988.

Schutte, R.C., and B.L. Hopkins. "The Effects of Teacher Attention on Following Instructions in a Kindergarten Class." *Journal of Applied Behavior Analysis* 3(1970):117–22.

Schwab, D.P. "Using Job Evaluation to Obtain Pay Equity." In *Comparable Worth: Issue for the 80's*. Vol. 1. Washington, DC: U.S. Commission on Civil Rights, 1984.

Schwaber, F.H. "Some Legal Issues Related to Outside Institutions." In H. Hidalgo, T. Peterson, and N.J. Woodman. (eds.), *Lesbian and Gay Issues: A Resource Manual for Social Workers*. Silver Spring, MD: NASW, 1985.

Schwartz, A., and I. Goldiamond. *Social Casework: A Behavioral Approach*. New York: Columbia University Press, 1975.

Schwartz, G.D. "Biofeedback, Self Regulation, and the Patterning of Physiological Processes." *American Scientist* 63(1975):314–24.

Scott, J., and L. Schwalm. "Rape Rates and the Circulation of Adult Magazines." *Journal of Sex Research* 24(1988):241–50.

Scully, D., and J. Marolla. *Convicted Rapists: Attitudes Toward Women and Rape*. Paper presented at the meeting of the First International Interdisciplinary Congress on Women, Haifa, Israel, Dec. 1981.

Sears, R.R. "Ordinal Position in the Family as a Psychological Variable." *American Sociological Review* 15(1950):397–401.

———. "Sources of Life Satisfaction of the Terman Gifted Men." *American Psychologist* 32(1977):119–28.

"Secretive Gay Subculture at the United States Military Academy." *Sexuality Today*, Nov. 3, 1986, p. 4.

Sedney, M. "Development of Androgyny: Parental Influences." *Psychological Women's Quarterly* 11(1987):311–26.

Seelbach, W.C., and C.J. Hansen. "Satisfaction with Family Relationships among the Elderly." *Family Relations* 29(1)(1980):91–96.

Seely, R. "Love for Baby Changed Surrogate's Views." *Wisconsin State Journal*, Dec. 20, 1986, sec. 3, p. 2.

Segal, S.P. "Deinstitutionalization." In A. Minahan (ed.), *Encyclopedia of Social Work*, vol. 1. Silver Spring, MD: NASW, 1987.

Seibel, M. "A New Era in Reproductive Technology." *New England Journal of Medicine* 317(1988):828–34.

Selkin, J. "Rape." *Psychology Today* 8(8)(1975):70.

Selye, H. *The Stress of Life*. New York: McGraw-Hill, 1956.

———. *Stress Without Distress*. New York: Signet, 1974.

Senanayake, P., and D.G. Kramer. "Contraception and the Etiology of PID: New Perspectives." Paper presented at the International Symposium of Pelvic Inflammatory Disease, Atlanta, GA, April 1980.

Settlage, D.S.E., et al. "Sexual Experience of Younger Teenage Girls Seeking Contraceptive Assistance for the First Time." *Family Planning Perspectives* 5(July/Aug. 1973):223–26.

"Sexuality and the Law: New Rules Speed Benefits to People with AIDS." *Contemporary Sexuality* 26(2)(Feb. 1992):6.

Shah, F., M. Zelnik, and J. Kantner. "Unprotected Intercourse among Unwed Teenagers." *Family Planning Perspectives* 7(1)(1975):39–44.

Shah, F., and M. Zelnik. "Sexuality in Adolescence." In B.B. Wolman and J. Money (eds.), *Handbook of Human Sexuality*. Englewood Cliffs, NJ: Prentice-Hall, 1980.

Shakin, M., D. Shakin, and S.H. Sternglanz. "Infant Clothing: Sex Labeling for Strangers." *Sex Roles* 12(1985):955–64.

Shane, J.M., I. Schiff, and E.A. Wilson. "The Infertile Couple: Evaluation and Treatment." *Clinical Symposia* 28(5)(1976).

Sheets, K.R. "A Bumper Crop in Troubles." *U.S. News & World Report*, Aug. 18, 1986, pp. 14–15.

Sheldon, W.H., with S.S. Stevens. *The Varieties of Temperament: A Psychology of Constitutional Differences*. New York: Harper & Row, 1942.

Shepard, L.A., M.L. Smith, and C.P. Vojir. "Characteristics of Pupils Identified as Learning Disabled." *American Educational Research Journal* 20(1983):309–31.

Sherman, J.A. *On the Psychology of Women: A Survey of Empirical Studies*. Springfield, IL: Charles C. Thomas, 1971.

———. "Girls Talk about Mathematics and Their Future: A Partial Replication." *Psychology of Women Quarterly* 7(1982):338–42.

Sherris, J.D., S.H. Moore, and G. Fox. "New Developments in Vaginal Contraception." *Population Reports*, Series H, No. 7. (Jan./Feb. 1984).

Shilts, R. "The Eight-Year Odyssey of AIDS: Book Traces Initial Cases to Patient Zero, a Canadian Airline Steward with Many Lovers." *Milwaukee Journal*, Nov. 8, 1987, pp. 1–2, 6-7J.(a)

———. "AIDS Link: Carrier Refused to Stop Sex." *Milwaukee Journal*, Nov. 15, 1987. pp. 1–2J.(b)

———. "What's Fair in Love and War." *Newsweek*, Feb. 1, 1993, pp. 58–59.

Shinn, M. "Father Absence and Children's Cognitive Development." *Psychological Bulletin* 85(1978):295–324.

Shiono, P.H. M.A. Klebanoff, and G.G. Rhoads. "Smoking and Drinking During Pregnancy." *Journal of the American Medical Association* 255(1986):82–84.

Shock, N.W. "Biological Theories of Aging." In J.E. Birren and K.W. Schaie (eds.), *Handbook of the Psychology of Aging.* New York: Van Nostrand Reinhold, 1977.

Shostak, A., G. McLouth, and L. Seng. *Men and Abortions: Lessons, Losses, and Love.* New York: Praeger, 1984.

Shulman, G.L. "Myths That Intrude on the Adaptation of the Step Family." *Social Casework* 53(3)(1972):131–39.

———. *Identifying, Measuring, and Teaching Helping Skills.* New York: Council on Social Work Education, 1981.

Shusterman, L.R. "Predicting the Psychological Consequences of Abortion." *Social Science and Medicine* 13(1979):683–89.

Siegel, O. "Personality Development in Adolescence." In B.B. Wolman, et al. (eds.), *Handbook of Developmental Psychology.* Englewood Cliffs, NJ: Prentice-Hall, 1982.

Siegel, R.K. "Accounting for 'Afterlife' Experiences." *Psychology Today*, Jan. 1981, pp. 66–69.

"Silicone Breast Makers Given Ultimatum." *Milwaukee Journal*, April 11, 1991.

Silverberg, E. "Cancer Statistics, 1981." *Ca-A Cancer Journal for Clinicians* 31(1)(1981):13–28.

Silverman, D. "Sexual Harassment: Working Women's Dilemma." *Quest: A Feminist Quarterly*, Winter 1976-77, p. 3.

Silvers, A.R. *Abortion: Clinics Bracing for Federal Gag Rule. Milwaukee Journal*, (Nov. 24, 1991).

Simkins, L., and A. Kushner. "Attitudes Toward AIDS, Herpes II, and Toxic Shock Syndrome: Two Years Later." *Psychological Reports* 59(1986):883–91.

Simmons, R.G., D.A. Blyth, E.F. Van Cleave, and D.M. Bush. "Entry into Early Adolescence: The Impact of School Structure Puberty, and Early Dating on Self-Esteem." *American Sociological Review* 44(6)(1979):948–67.

Simonton, O.C., and S. Matthews-Simonton. *Getting Well Again.* Los Angeles: J.P. Tarcher, 1978.

Simpson, G.E., and J.M. Yinger. *Racial and Cultural Minorities.* 3rd ed. New York: Harper & Row, 1965.

Sinclair, E. "Important Issues in the Language Development of the Black Child." In G.J. Powell (ed.), *The Psychosocial Development of Minority Group Children.* New York: Brunner/Mazel, 1983.

Sindler, A.P. *Bakke, DeFunis and Minority Admissions: The Quest for Equal Opportunity.* New York: Longmans, Green, 1978.

Singer, J.E. "The Use of Manipulative Strategies: Machiavellianism and Attractiveness." *Sociometry* 27(1964)128–51.

Singh, N.N., J.E. Watson, and A.S.W. Winton. "Treating Self-Injury: Water Mist Spray Versus Facial Screening or Forced Arm Exercise." *Journal of Applied Behavior Analysis* 19 (1986):403–10.

"Single Parents Head One-Fourth of Households with Children." *Providence Journal Bulletin*, May 15, 1985.

Siporin, M. *Introduction to Social Work Practice.* New York: Macmillan, 1975.

Sisodia, S.S., E.H. Koo, K. Beyreuther, A. Unterbeck and D.L. Price. "Evidence That B-amyloid protein in Alzheimer's Disease Is Not Derived by Normal Processing." *Science* 248(April 27, 1990):492–95.

Siven, I. "IUDs are Contraceptives, Not Abortifacients: A Comment on Research and Belief." *Studies in Family Planning* 20(1989):355–59.

Skidmore, R.A., and M. Thackeray. *Introduction to Social Work.* 2nd ed. Englewood Cliffs, NJ: Prentice-Hall, 1976.

Skinner, B.F. *Science and Human Behavior.* New York: Free Press, 1953.

Skolnik, A. "The Myth of the Vulnerable Child." *Psychology Today*, Feb. 1978, pp. 56–60, 65.

Slobin, D.I., S.H. Miller, and L.W. Porter. "Forms of Address and Social Relations in a Business Organization." *Journal of Personality and Social Psychology* 8(1968):289–93.

Slovenko, R. *Sexual Behavior and the Law.* Springfield, IL: Charles C. Thomas, 1965.

———. "Homosexuality and the Law: From Condemnation to Celebration." In J. Marmor (ed.), *Homosexual Behavior.* New York: Basic Books, 1980.

Smart, R.G., and N.L. Blair. "Drug Use and Drug Problems among Teenagers in a Household Sample." *Drug and Alcohol Dependence* 5(1980):171–79.

Smith, J. "The Paradox of Women's Poverty: Wage-Earning Women and Economic Transition." *Signs: Journal of Women in Culture and Society* 10(1984):416–36.

Smith, S.A., and M. Tienda. "The Doubly Disadvantaged: Women of Color in the U.S. Labor Force." In A.H. Stromberg and S. Harkess (eds.), *Women Working.* Mountain View, CA: Mayfield, 1988.

Smolowe, J. "He Said, She Said." *Time*, Oct. 21, 1991, pp. 36–40.

———. "Anita Hill's Legacy." *Time*, Oct. 19, 1992, pp. 56–57.

———. "Sex, Lies, and the Military." *Time*, Feb. 8, 1993, pp. 29–30.

Snarey, J.R. "Cross-Cultural Universality of Social-Moral Development: A Critical Review of Kohlbergian Research." *Psychological Bulletin* 97(1985):202–32.

Snyder, D. "Multidimensional Assessment of Marital Satisfaction." *Journal of Marriage and the Family* 41(1979):813–23.

Soldo, B.J. *America's Elderly in the 1980s.* Washington, DC: Population Reference Bureau, 1980.

Solender, E.K., and E. Solender. "Minimizing the Effect of the Unattractive Client on the Jury: A Study of the Interaction of Physical Appearance with Assertions and Self-Experience References." *Human Rights* 5(1976):201–14.

Sollie, D.L., and J.L. Fischer. "Sex-Role Orientation, Intimacy of Topic, and Target Person Differences in Self-Disclosure among Women." *Sex Roles* 12(1985):917–29.

Solomon, A. "Integrating Infertility Crisis Counseling into Feminist Practice." *Reproductive and Genetic Engineering* 1(1988): 41–49.

Solomon, B.B. "Social Work with Afro-Americans." In A. Morales and B.W. Sheafor (eds.), *Social Work: A Profession of Many Faces,* 3rd ed. Boston: Allyn & Bacon, 1983.

Sommer, R. *Personal Space: The Behavioral Basis of Design.* Englewood Cliffs, NJ: Prentice-Hall, 1969.

Sorenson, R.C. *Adolescent Sexuality in Contemporary America.* New York: World, 1973.

Sostek, A.J., and R.J. Wyatt. "The Chemistry of Crankiness." *Psychology Today* 15(10)(1981):120.

Spakes, P. "National Family Policy: Sweden Versus the United States." *Affilia: Journal of Women and Social Work* 7(2)(Summer 1992):44–60.

Speroff, L., R.H. Glass, and N.G. Kase. *Clinical Gynecologic Endocrinology and Infertility.* Baltimore, MD: Williams and Wilkins, 1973.

Spitz, R. "Hospitalization: Genesis of Psychiatric Conditions in Early Childhood." *Psychoanalytic Study of the Child* 1(1945):53.

Spock, B. *Baby and Child Care.* New York: Pocket Books, 1976.

Spock, B., and M.B. Rothenberg. *Baby and Child Care.* New York: Pocket Books, 1985.

Sprey, J. "Extramarital Relationships." *Sexual Behavior* 2(1972):34–40.

Sroufe, L.A., and E. Waters. "The Ontogenesis of Smiling and Laughter: A Perspective on the Organization of Development in Infancy." *Psychological Review* 83(1976):173–89.

Sroufe, L.A., and J. Wunsch. "The Development of Laughter in the First Year of Life." *Child Development* 43(1972): 1326–44.

Stack, C. *All Our Kin: Strategies for Survival in a Black Community.* New York: Harper & Row, 1974.

Stafford, R.S. Alternative Strategies for Rising Cesarean Section Rates." *Journal of the American Medical Association* 263(1990): 683–87.

Stallard, K., B. Ehrenreich, and H. Sklar. *Poverty in the American Dream: Women and Children First.* Boston: South End Press, 1983.

Stark, R., and J. McEvoy. "Middle Class Violence." *Psychology Today,* April 1970, pp. 54-56, 110–12.

Starka, L., et al. "Plasma Testosterone in Male Transsexuals and Homosexuals." *Journal of Sex Research* 11(1975):134–38.

Stein, P.J. "Being Single: Bucking the Cultural Imperative." Paper presented at the annual meeting of the American Sociological Association, Sept. 3, 1976.

Steinberg, R.J. "Identifying Wage Discrimination and Implementing Pay Equity Adjustments." In *Comparable Worth: Issue for the 80's.* Vol. 1. Washington, DC: U.S. Commission on Civil Rights, 1984.

Stennett, N., L. Carter, and J. Montgomery. "Older Persons' Perceptions of Their Marriages." *Journal of Marriage and the Family* 34(1972):655–70.

Sternberg, R.J. "A Contextualist View of the Nature of Intelligence." *International Journal of Psychology* 19(1984):307–34.

———. *Beyond IQ: A Triarchic Theory of Human Intelligence.* New York: Cambridge University Press, 1985.

———. *Intelligence Applied: Understanding and Increasing Your Intellectual Skills.* New York: Harcourt Brace Jovanovich, 1986.

———. "The Uses and Misuses of Intelligence Testing: Misunderstanding Meaning, Users Over-Rely on Scores." *Educational Week* 22(Sept. 23, 1987):28.

Stinnet, N., and J. Walters. *Relationships in Marriage and Family.* New York: Macmillan, 1977.

Stjernfeldt, M., et al. "Maternal Smoking During Pregnancy and Risk of Childhood Cancer." *Lancet,* June 14, 1986, pp. 1350–52.

Stockard, J., and M.M. Johnson. *Sex Roles.* Englewood Cliffs, NJ: Prentice-Hall, 1980.

Stoltz, H.R., and L.M. Stoltz. "Adolescent Problems Related to Somatic Variation." In N.B. Henry (ed.), *Adolescence: 43rd Yearbook of the National Committee for the Study of Education*

Chicago: Department of Education, University of Chicago, 1944.

Stone, W.C. "Be Generous." In O. Mandino (ed.), *A Treasury of Success Unlimited.* New York: Hawthorn Books, 1966.

Storms, M.D. "Theories of Sexual Orientation." *Journal of Personality and Social Psychology* 38(1980):783–92.

———. "A Theory of Erotic Orientation Development." *Psychological Review* 88(1981):340–53.

Stout, H.R. *Our Family Physician.* Peoria, IL: Henderson and Smith, 1885.

Strassberg, D., and J. Mahoney. "Correlates of Contraceptive Behavior of Adolescents/Young Adults." *Journal of Sex Research* 25(1988):531–36.

Straus, M.A. "Leveling, Civility and Violence in the Family." *Journal of Marriage and the Family* 36(1974):13–29.

———. "Wife Beating! How Common and Why?" *Victimology* 2(3-4)(Fall–Winter 1977):443–58.

———. *Behind Closed Doors: Violence in the American Family.* New York: Doubleday, 1980.

Straus, M., R. Gelles, and S. Steinmetz. *Behind Closed Doors: A Survey of Family Violence in America.* Garden City, NJ: Doubleday, 1977.

Straus, S.E., et al. "Herpes Simplex Virus Infections: Biology, Treatment and Prevention." *Annals of Internal Medicine* 103(1985): 404–19.

Strong, B., and C. DeVault. *The Marriage and Family Experience.* 2nd ed. New York: West, 1983.

Strong, B., and R. Reynolds. *Understanding Our Sexuality.* New York: West, 1982.

Strunin L., and R. Hingson. "Acquired Immunodeficiency Syndrome and Adolescents: Knowledge, Beliefs, Attitudes, and Behaviors." *Pediatrics* 79(1987):825–28.

Stuart, M.J., et al. "Effects of Acetylsalicylic-Acid Ingestion on Maternal and Neonatal Hemostasis." *New England Journal of Medicine* 307(1982):90.

Stuart, R.B. *Trick or Treatment.* Champaign, IL: Research Press, 1970.

———. *Couple's Pre-Counseling Inventory.* Champaign, IL: Research Press, 1983.

Stuart, R.B., and B. Jacobson. *Second Marriage.* New York: Norton, 1985.

Stubblefield, H. "Contributions of Continuing Education." *Vocational Guidance Quarterly* 25(1977):351–55.

Stulberg, I., and M. Smith. "Psychosocial Impact of the AIDS Epidemic on the Lives of Gay Men." *Social Work* 33(1988): 277-81.

Sugar, M. "Children of Divorce." *Pediatrics* 46(4)(1970): 588–95.

Sullivan, T.J., K. Thompson, R. Wright, G. Gross and D. Spady. *Social Problems.* New York: Wiley, 1980.

Sundel, S.S., and M. Sundel. *Be Assertive: A Practical Guide for Human Service Workers.* Beverly Hills, Ca: Sage, 1980.

Super, C.M. "Cognitive Development: Looking Across at Growing Up." In C.M. Super and S. Harkness (eds.), *New Directions for Child Development.* No. 8, *Anthropological Perspectives on Child Development.* San Francisco, CA: Jossey-Bass, 1980.

Sutherland, E.H., and D.R. Cressey. *Criminology.* 8th ed. Philadelphia, PA: Lippincott, 1970.

Sutton-Smith, B., and B.G. Rosenberg. *The Sibling.* New York: Holt, Rinehart and Winston, 1970.

Sweeney, T.A. *Streets of Anger: Streets of Hope.* Glendale, CA: Great Western, 1980.

Syer-Solursh, D. "News and Reviews: Task Force on Suicide." *Current Awareness Bulletin,* 1 (1)(Oct., Nov., Dec. 1984).

(Calgary, Alberta, Canada, Suicide Information and Education Centre.)

Szasz, T.S. The Myth of Mental Illness. New York: Hoeber-Harper, 1961.(a)

———. "The Myth of Mental Illness." In J.R. Braun (ed.), *Clinical Psychology in Transition.* Cleveland, OH: Howard Allen, 1961. (b)

———. *Law, Liberty and Psychiatry.* New York: Macmillan, 1963.

Szymanski, A. "Racial Discrimination and White Gain." *American Sociological Review* 41(June 1976):403–14.

Taber, M. "The Aged." In D. Brieland, L.B. Costin, and C.R. Atherton (eds.), *Contemporary Social Work.* New York: McGraw-Hill, 1975.

Tabor, A., et al. "Randomized Controlled Trial of Genetic Amniocentesis in 4606 Low-Risk Women." *Lancet,* June 7, 1986, pp. 1287–93.

Taeuber, C.M., and V. Valdisera. "Women in the American Economy." *Current Population Reports,* series P-23, no. 146. Washington, DC: U.S. Government Printing Office, 1986.

Tanfer, K., and M.C. Horn. "Contraceptive Use, Pregnancy, and Fertility Patterns among Single American Women in Their 20's." *Family Planning Perspectives* 17(1(1985):10–19.

Tanner, J.M. "The Adolescent Growth-Spurt and Developmental Age." In G.A. Harrison, J.S. Werner, J.M. Tannert, and N.A. Barnicot (eds.), *Human Balance: An Introduction to Human Evolution, Variation, and Growth.* Oxford, UK: Clarendon Press, 1964.

———. "Puberty." In A. McLaren (ed.), *Advances in Reproductive Physiology,* vol. 11. New York: Academic Press, 1967.

———. "Earlier Maturation in Man." *Scientific American* 218 (1968):21–27.

———. "Physical Growth." In P.H. Mussen (ed.), *Carmichael's Manual of Child Psychology,* vol. 1, 3rd ed. New York: Wiley, 1970.

———. "Sequence, Tempo, and Individual Variation in the Growth and Development of Boys and Girls Aged Twelve to Sixteen." *Daedelus* 100(1971):907–30.

———. *Fetus into Man: Physical Growth from Conception to Maturity.* Cambridge, MA: Harvard, 1978.

Tate, B.G., and G.S. Baroff. "Adversive Control of Self Injurious Behavior in a Psychotic Boy." *Behavior Research and Therapy* 4(1966):281–87.

Tautermannova, M. "Smiling in Infants." *Child Development* 44(1973):701–4.

Tavris, C. "Masculinity." *Psychology Today,* Aug. 1977, p. 34.

Tavris, C., and S. Sadd. *The Redbook Report on Female Sexuality.* New York: Delacorte, 1977.

Taylor, C.A., ed. *Handbook of Minority Student Services.* Madison, WI: Praxis, 1986.

Taylor, H. *Making Time Work for You.* New York: Dell, 181.

Taylor, R.L. "Psychosocial Development among Black Children and Youth: A Reexamination." *American Journal of Orthopsychiatry* 46(1976):4–19.

Taylor-Nicholson, M.E., M.Q. Wang, and D.D. Adame. "Impacts of AIDS Education on Adolescent Knowledge, Attitudes, and Perceived Susceptibility." *Health Values* 13(1989):3–7.

Teenage Pregnancy: The Problem That Hasn't Gone Away. New York: Alan Guttmacher Institute, 1981.

Terman, L.M. *Standford-Binet Intelligence Scale, Manual for the Third Revision Form L-M by L.M. Terman and M.A Merrill.* Boston, MA: Houghton Mifflin, 1960.

Teti, D., and M. Lamb. "Socioeconomic and Marital Outcomes of Adolescent Marriage, Adolescent Childbirth, and Their Co-Occurrence." *Journal of Marriage and the Family* 51 (1989):203–12.

Thomas, A., and S. Chess. "Genesis and Evaluation of Behavioral Disorders: From Infancy to Early Adult Life." *American Journal of Orthopsychiatry* 14(1)(1984):1–9.

Thomas, A., S. Chess, H.G. Birch. *Temperament and Behavior Disorders in Children.* New York: New York University Press, 1968.

———. "The Origin of Personality." *Scientific American* 223(1970):102–9.

Thomas, E.J. "Behavioral Modification and Casework." In R.W. Roberts and R.H. Nee (eds.), *Theories of Social Casework.* Chicago: University of Chicago Press, 1970.

Thomas, J.L. "Gender Differences in Satisfaction with Grandparenting." *Psychology and Aging* 1(3)(1986):215–19.

Thompson, L., and A.J. Walker. "Women and Men in Marriage, Work, and Parenthood." *Journal of Marriage and the Family* 51(1989):845–72.

Thoreson, J. "Lesbians and Gay Men: Complements and Contrasts." Paper presented at the Society for the Scientific Study of Sex Conference, Philadelphia, PA: April 7, 1984.

Thorman, G. *Helping Troubled Families: A Social Work Perspective.* New York: Aldine, 1982.

Thorndike, E.L., *The Fundamentals of Learning.* New York: Teachers College, 1932.

Thurstone, L.L. "Primary Mental Abilities." *Psychometric Monographs* 1, 1938.

Timiras, P.S. *Developmental Physiology and Aging.* New York: Macmillan, 1972.

Timiras, P.S. and A. Vernadakis. "Structural, Biochemical, and Functional Aging of the Nervous System." In P.S. Timiras (ed.), *Developmental Physiology and Aging.* New York: Macmillan, 1972.

Timson, J. "Is Coffee Safe to Drink?" *Human Nature,* Dec. 1978, pp. 57–59.

Tobias, S. "Mathematics and Sex." In *Overcoming Math Anxiety.* New York: Norton, 1978.

Tobias, S., and C. Weissbrod. "Anxieties and Mathematics: An Update." *Harvard Educational Review* (1980):50, 63–70.

Tobin-Richards, M.H., A.M. Boxer, and A.C. Petersen. "The Psychological Significance of Pubertal Change: Sex Differences in Perceptions of Self During Early Adolescence." In J. Brooks-Gunn and A.C. Petersen (eds.), *Girls at Puberty: Biological, Social, and Psychological Perspectives.* New York: Plenum, 1983.

Toffler, A. *Future Shock.* New York: Bantam Books, 1970.

Tomeh, A.K. "Birth Order and Friendship Associations." *Journal of Marriage and the Family* 32(1970):361–62.

Toufexis, A. "Shortcut to the Rambo Look." *Time,* Jan. 30, 1989, p. 78.

Tourney, G. "Hormones and Homosexuality." In J. Marmor (ed.), *Homosexual Behavior.* New York: Basic Books, 1980.

Tower, C.C. *Understanding Child Abuse and Neglect.* Needham Heights, MA: Allyn & Bacon, 1989.

Townsend, C. *Old Age: The Last Segregation.* New York: Grossman, 1971.

Trafford, A. "The Tragedy of Care for America's Elderly." *U.S. News & World Report,* April 24, 978, p. 56.

Trager, G.L. "Paralanguage: A First Approximation." *Studies in Linguistics* 13(1958):1–12.

Troll, L.E. *Early and Middle Adulthood.* Belmont, CA: Wadsworth, 1975.

————. "Grandparents: The Family Watchdogs." In T.H. Brubacker (ed.), *Family Relationships in Later Life*. Beverly Hills, CA: Sage, 1983.

————. *Early and Middle Adulthood*. 2nd ed. Pacific Grove, CA: Brooks/Cole, 1985.

Trotter, R.J. "Baby Face." *Psychology Today*, Aug. 1983, pp. 14–20.

Trussell, J. "Teenage Pregnancy in the United States." *Family Planning Perspectives* 20(1988):262–73.

Trussell, J., and C.F. Westoff. "Contraceptive Practice and Trends in Coital Frequency." *Family Planning Perspectives* 12(5) (1980):246-49.

Tubesing, D.A. *Kicking Your Stress Habits*. Duluth, MN: Whole Person Associates, 1981.

Tuddenham, R.D. "Studies in Reputation. 3. Correlates of Popularity among Elementary School Children." *Journal of Educational Psychology* 42(1951):257–76.

Turnbull, C.M. *The Mountain People*. New York: Simon and Schuster, 1972.

Tye, L. "Study: U.S. Retreats on Integration." *Wisconsin State Journal*, Jan. 12, 1992, pp. 1A and 8A–9A.

Tyler, V.O., and G.D. Brown. "The Use of Swift, Brief Isolation as a Group Control Device for Institutionalized Delinquents." *Behavior Research and Therapy* 5(1967):1–9.

U.S. Bureau of the Census. "Money Income in 1976 of Families and Persons in the United States." *Current Population Reports*, Series P-60, No. 114. Washington, DC: U.S. Government Printing Office, 1978.

————. *Current Population Reports*, Series P-20, No. 349 (Dec.). Washington, DC: U.S. Government Printing Office, 1980.

————. *Statistical Abstract of the United States, 1979*. Washington, DC: U.S. Government Printing Office, 1981.

————. "Money Income and Poverty Status of Families and Persons in the United States: 1981. *Current Population Report*, Series, P-60, No. 134 (July). Washington, DC: U.S. Government Printing Office, 1982.

————. *Statistical Abstract of the United States: 1982-83*. Washington, DC: U.S. Government Printing Office, 1982.

————. *Statistical Abstract of the United States: 1984*. Washington, DC: U.S. Government Printing Office, 1984.

————. *Statistical Abstract of the United States: 1986*. Washington, DC: U.S. Government Printing Office, 1986.

————. *Current Population Reports*, P-60, no. 157, (July), Table 12, Washington, DC: U.S. Government Printing Office, 1987.(a)

————. *Statistical Abstract of the United States: 1987*. Washington, DC: U.S. Government Printing Office, 1987.(b)

————. *Statistical Abstract of the United States: 1988*. Washington, DC: U.S. Government Printing Office, 1988.

————. *Household Wealth and Ownership. 1988*.Washington, DC: U.S. Government Printing Office, 1990. (a)

————. *Statistical Abstract of the United States, 1990*. Washington, DC: U.S. Government Printing Office, 1990. (b)

————. *Statistical Abstract of the United States: 1992*. Washington, DC: U.S. Government Printing Office, 1992.

U.S. Bureau of Labor Statistics. *U.S. Working Women: A Databook*. Bulletin no. 1977. Washington, DC: U.S. Government Printing Office, 1977.

————. *Labor Force Statistics Derived from the Current Population Survey: A Databook*. Vol. 1. Washington, DC: U.S. Government Printing Office, 1982.

————. *1991 Employment and Earnings*. Washington, DC: U.S. Government Printing Office, 1991.

U.S. Congress, Senate Committee on Judiciary, Subcommittee on Juvenile Justice. *Hearings on Teenage Suicide*. Testimony by M. Herbert on teenage suicide in a public school system, Oct. 1984.

U.S. Dept. of Health, Education and Welfare. *Older Americans Act of 1965, as Amended, Text and History*. Washington, DC: U.S. Government Printing Office, 1970.

————. *Health, United States 1975*. DHEW Pub. No. (HRA) 76-1232. Rockville, MD: National Center for Health Statistics, 1976.

————. Office of the Assistant Secretary for Planning and Evaluation. *The Appropriateness of the Federal Interagency Day Care Requirements (FIDCR)*. Vol. 1 *An Overview of the Study and Findings*. Discussion draft, Feb. 17, 1978.

————. *Resource Materials: A Curriculum on CAN DHEW*. Pub. no. (OHDS) 79-30221. Washington, DC: U.S. Government Printing Office, 1979.(a)

————. *Smoking and Health*. Washington, DC: U.S. Government Printing Office, 1979.(b)

————. *Surgeon-General's Report on Smoking and Health*. Washington, DC: U.S. Government Printing Office, 1979.(c)

————. "AIDS and the Education of Our Children." Washington, DC: U.S. Government Printing Office, 1988.

U.S. Dept. of Health and Human Services, Public Health Service, Alcohol, Drug Abuse, and Mental Health Administration. *Coping with AIDS*. DHHS Pub. No. (ADM) 85–1432. Washington, DC: U.S. Government Printing Office, 1986.

————. *Health, United States 1985*. DHHS Pub. No. PHS 86-1232. Washington, DC: U.S. Government Printing Office, 1985.

————. *Health, United States 1989*. DHHS Pub. No. PHS 90-1232. Washington, DC: U.S. Government Printing Office, 1990.

U.S. Dept. of Justice, Federal Bureau of Investigation. *Crime in the United States, Uniform Crime Reports 1987*. Washington, DC: U.S. Government Printing Office, 1987.

U.S. Dept. of Labor, Employment Standards Administration, Women's Bureau. *20 Facts on Women Workers*. Washington, DC., 1975.

U.S. House of Representatives. *Women, Violence, and the Law*. Washington, DC: U.S. Government Printing Office, 1988.

U.S. Merit Systems Protection Board (MSPB). *Sexual Harassment in the Federal Workplace: Is It a Problem?* Washington, DC: U.S. Government Printing Office, 1981.

U.S. News & World Report. "A Rush of Test-Tube Babies." Aug. 7, 1978, p. 22.

————. "Battered Families: A Growing Nightmare." Jan. 15, 1979, pp. 60–62.

————. "Working Women." Jan. 15, 1979, p. 64.

————. "Will Inflation Tarnish Your Golden Years?" Feb. 26, 1979, p. 57.

————. "Where Jobs Will Be in the 1980s." Oct. 15, 1979, p. 76.

————. "Age Need Not Be a Barrier to Making Major Contributions." Sept. 1, 1980, pp. 52–53.

————. "To Raise a Child Today." Jan. 5, 1981, p. 77.

————. "The Desperate World of America's Underclass." March 26, 1984, pp. 54–56.

————. "Anacostia, an Orphan at Steps of Nation's Capital." Dec. 10, 1984, pp. 74–75.

————. "RX for AIDS: A Grim Race Against the Clock." Sept. 30, 1985, pp. 48–49.

————. "Threat of AIDS Widening to the General Public." Sept. 30, 1985, p. 49.

Ubel, E. "A World Without Disease." *Parade Magazine*, Jan. 27, 1985, pp. 11–13.

Udry, J.R., and B.K. Eckland. "Benefits of Being Attractive: Differential Payoffs for Men and Women." *Psychological Reports* 54(1984):47–56.

Utian, W.H., et al. "Successful Pregnancy after In Vitro Fertilization and Embryo Transfer from an Infertile Woman to a Surrogate." *New England Journal of Medicine* 313(1985):1351–52.

Van Susteren, L. "AIDS Victim Vows Vengeance Putting Therapist in Quandary." *Milwaukee Journal*, March 12, 1989, pp. 1, 20J.

Van Wyck, P.H., and C.S. Geist. "Psychosocial Development of Heterosexual, Bisexual, and Homosexual Behavior." *Archives of Sexual Behavior* 13(6)(1984):505–44.

Vener, A.M., and C.S. Stewart. "Adolescent Sexual Behavior in Middle America Revisited: 1970-1973." *Journal of Marriage and the Family* 36(Nov. 1974):728–34.

Verbrugge, L.M. "Marital Status and Health." *Journal of Marriage and the Family* 41(2)(1979):267–85.

Vessey, M., et al. "Efficacy of Different Contraceptive Methods." *Lancet* 1 (8276)(1982):841–42.

Vinick, B. "Remarriage in Old Age." *Family Coordinator* 27(4)(1978):359–63.

Visher, E.B. "Step Families and Stepparenting." In F. Walsh (ed.), *Normal Family Processes*. New York: Guilford Press, 1982.

Visher, E., and J. Visher. "Stepparenting: Blending Families." In H.I. McCubbin and C.R. Figley (eds.), *Stress and the Family*. Vol. 1, *Coping with Normative Transitions*. New York: Brunner/Mazel, 1983.

Voeller, B. "Society and the Gay Movement." In J. Marmor (ed.), *Homosexual Behavior* New York: Basic Books, 1980.

Waggett, G.J. "Let's Stop Turning Rapists into Heroes." *TV Guide*, May 27-June 2, 1989, pp. 10–11.

Wagonseller, B.R., M. Burnette, B. Salzberg, and J. Burnett. *Behavior Management Techniques: Discipline*. Champaign, IL: Research Press, 1977.

Walberg, H.J., and S.P. Rasher. "The Ways Schooling Makes a Difference." *Phi Delta Kappa* 58(1977):703–7.

Wald, E. *The Remarried Family*. New York: Family Service Assoc. of America, 1981.

Walker, L.E. *The Battered Woman*. New York: Harper & Row, 1979.

Walker, W.J. "Changing United States Life-Style and Declining Vascular Mortality: Cause or Coincidence?" *New England Journal of Medicine* 297(3)(1977):163–65.

Wall Street Journal. "Gains Against AIDS Have Come Rapidly But a Cure Is Distant." Aug. 5, 1985, pp. 1, 12.

Wallerstein, J.S. "Children of Divorce: The Psychological Tasks of the Child." *American Journal of Orthopsychiatry* 53(2)(1983):230-43.

Wallerstein, J.S., and J.B. Kelly. *Surviving the Break-Up: How Children Actually Cope with Divorce*. New York: Basic Books, 1980.

Walum, L.R. *The Dynamics of Sex and Gender: A Sociological Perspective*. Chicago: Rand McNally, 1977.

Warren, C.A.B. *Identity and Community in the Gay World*. New York: Wiley, 1974.

Warren, C.L., and R. St. Pierre. "Sources and Accuracy of College Students' Sex Knowledge." *Journal of School Health* 43(1973):588–90.

Warren, R. *The Community in America*. Chicago: Rand McNally, 1972.

———. *The Community in America*. Chicago: Rand McNally, 1978.

———. "A Community Model" In R.M. Kramer and H. Specht (eds.), *Readings in Community Organization Practice*, 3rd ed. Englewood Cliffs, NJ: Prentice-Hall, 1983.

Waskow, A.I. *From Race Riot to Sit-In*. Garden City, NY: Doubleday, 1967.

Watson, D.L., and R.G. Tharp. *Self-Directed Behavior*. Monterey, CA: Brooks/Cole, 1973.

Watson, J.B. *Psychology from the Standpoint of a Behaviorist*. Philadelphia, PA: Lippincott, 1919.

Wattenberg, E. "In a Different Light—A Feminist Perspective on the Role of Mothers in Father-Daughter Incest." *Child Welfare* 64(4)(May-June 1985):203–11.

Weatherly, D. "Self-Perceived Rate of Physical Maturation and Personality in Late Adolescence." *Child Development* 35 (1964):1197–1210.

Weber, M. *The Protestant Ethic and the Spirit of Capitalism*. New York: Scribner's, 1958.

Wegman, M.E. "Annual Summary of Vital Statistics—1985." *Pediatrics* 78(6)(1986):983–94.

Wegscheider, S. *Another Chance: Hope and Health for the Alcoholic Family*. Palo Alto, CA: Science and Behavior Books, 1981.

Weinberg, S., and C. Williams. *Male Homosexuals: Their Problems and Adaptations*. New York: Oxford University Press, 1974.

Weiss, D. "The Experience of Pain During Women's First Sexual Intercourse: Cultural Mythology about Female Sexual Initiation." *Archives of Sexual Behavior* 14(1985):421–28.

Weiss, L., and M. Lowenthal. "Life-Course Perspectives on Friendship." In M. Lowenthal, M. Thurner and D. Chiriboga (eds.), *Four Stages of Life*. San Francisco, CA: Jossey-Bass, 1975.

Weitzman, L.J. "Sex-Role Socialization." In J. Freeman (ed.), *Women: A Feminist Perspective*. Palo Alto, CA: Mayfield, 1975.

———. *Sex Role Socialization*. Palo Alto, CA: Mayfield, 1979.

———. *The Divorce Revolution*. New York: Free Press, 1985.

Welford, A.T. "Motor Performance." In J.E. Birren and K.W. Schaie (eds.), *Handbook of the Psychology of Aging*. New York: Van Nostrand Reinhold, 1977.

Weltner, C. "The Model Cities Program: A Sobering Scorecard." *Policy Review*, Fall 1977, pp. 73–87.

Wermiel, S., and M. McQueen. "Turning Point? Historic Court Ruling Will Widen Disparity in Access to Abortion." *Wall Street Journal*, July 5, 1989, p. 1.

Wertheimer, D.M. "Victims of Violence: A Rising Tide of Anti-Gay Sentiment." *USA Today Magazine*, Jan. 1988, pp. 52–54.

Westberg, G. *Good Grief*. Philadelphia, PA: Fortress Press, 1962.

Westoff, C.F. "Coital Frequency and Contraception." *Family Planning Perspectives* 6(3)(1974):136–41.

"What Does Gay/Lesbian Pride Mean to You? *Gaylife* 10(52)(June 27, 1985):2.

"What Else Is Out There?" *Contemporary Sexuality* 25(1)(Jan. 1991), 2–3.

White, B.L. *The First Three Years of Life*. Englewood Cliffs, NJ: Prentice-Hall, 1975.

White, G.D., G. Neilsen, and S.M. Johnson. "Timeout Duration and the Suppression of Deviant Behavior in Children." *Journal of Applied Behavior Analysis* 5(1972):111–20.

Whiteman, D. "America's Hidden Poor." *U.S. News & World Report*, Jan. 11, 1988, pp. 18–24.

Whitham, F.L., and R.M. Mathy. *Male Homosexuality in Four Societies*. New York: Praeger, 1986.

Wice, P.B. *Bail and Its Reform: A National Survey.* Washington, DC: U.S. Government Printing Office, 1972.

Widgery, R.N., and B. Webster. "The Effects of Physical Attractiveness upon Perceived Initial Credibility." *Michigan Speech Journal* 4(1969):9–15.

Wiesenfeld, A.P., C.Z. Malatesta, and L. DeLoache. "Differential Parental Response to Familiar and Unfamiliar Infant Distress Signals." *Infant Behavior and Development* 4(1981):281–95.

Wilcox, A., C. Weinberg, J. O'Connor, D. Baird, J. Schlatterer, R. Canfield, G. Armstrong, and B. Nisula. "Incidence of Early Loss of Pregnancy." *New England Journal of Medicine* (1988):189–94.

Wilensky, H.L. "Work as a Social Problem." In H. Becker (ed.), *Social Problems.* New York: Wiley, 1966.

Wilensky, H., and C. Lebeaux. *Industrial Society and Social Welfare.* New York: Free Press, 1965.

Williams, C.D. "The Elimination of Tantrum Behavior by Extinction Procedures." *Journal of Abnormal and Social Psychology* 59(1959):269.

Williamson, N. "Boys or Girls? Parents' Preference and Sex Control." *Population Bulletin.* Washington, DC: Population Reference Bureau, 1978.

Wilson, A.N. *The Developmental Psychology of the Black Child.* New York: African Research, 1978.

Wilson, G.T., and D.M. Lawson. "Effects of Alcohol on Sexual Arousal in Women." *Journal of Abnormal Psychology* 85 (1976):489–97.

———. "Effects of Alcohol on Sexual Arousal in Male Alcoholics." *Journal of Abnormal Psychology* 87(1978):609–16.

Wilson, J.G. "Embryotoxicity of Drugs in Man." In Wilson and Fraser (eds.), *General Principles and Etiology Handbook Teratology* vol. 1. New York: Plenum Press, 1977.

Wineke, W. "Report: Nursing Homes Fail U.S. Test." *Wisconsin State Journal,* Dec. 2, 1988, p. 1B.

Winick, M. *Malnutrition and Brain Development.* New York: Oxford University Press, 1976.

Winn, M. *The Plug-In Drug.* Rev. ed. New York: Viking, 1985.

Wisconsin State Journal. "Medicaid Kickbacks Called 'Way of Life.'" July 17, 1977, Sec. 1, p. 11.

———. "Exclusive Sperm Bank Rekindles Controversy." March 1, 1980, Sec. 1.

———. "Abortion Foes Gain Victory." July 1, 1980, Sec. 1, p. 1.

———. "Healthy Baby Is Born from Donated Embryo." Feb. 4, 1984, Sec. 1, p. 2.(a)

———. "Embryo Case Opens New Debate." June 19, 1984, pp. 1–2.(b)

———. "Study Cites Hunger in U.S." Feb. 27, 1985. Sec. 1, p. 8.

———. "Iacocca Earns $17.9 Million in '87." April 20, 1988, p. 6B.

———. "Incomes, Poverty Increase." Sept. 1, 1988, p. 3A.

———. "Men Still Earn More." Jan. 16, 1990, p. 1C.

———. "Infertility Doctor Convicted: Jacobson Guilty on 52 Counts of Fraud, Perjury." March 5, 1992, p. 4A.(a)

——— "Infertility Doctor Gets 5-Year Term." May 9, 1992, p. 3A.(b)

Wise, F., and N.B. Miller. "The Mental Health of the American Indian Child." In G.W. Powell (ed.), *The Psychosocial Development of Minority Group Children.* New York: Brunner/Mazel, 1983.

Witkin, S., and S. David. "Effect of Sperm Antibodies on Pregnancy Outcome in a Subfertile Population." *American Journal of Obstetrics and Gynecology* 158(1988):59.

Wolf, D. *The Lesbian Community.* Berkeley: University of California Press, 1979.

Wolf, M.M., T. Risley, J. Johnson, F. Harris, and E. Allen.

"Application of Operant Conditioning Procedures to the Behavior Problems of an Autistic Child: Follow-Up and Extension." *Behavior Research and Therapy* 5(1967):103–11.

Wolfbein, S. *Work in American Society.* Glenview, IL: Scott, Foresman, 1971.

Wolff, C. *Love Between Women.* New York: Harper & Row, 1971.

Wolff, P.H. "The Natural History of Crying and Other Vocalizations in Early Infancy." In B.M. Foss (ed.), *Determinants of Infant Behavior,* vol. 4. London, UK: Methuen, 1969.

Wolman, B.B. *Dictionary of Behavioral Science.* New York: Van Nostrand Reinhold, 1973.

Wolock, I., and B. Horowitz. "Child Maltreatment as a Social Problem: The Neglect of Neglect." *American Journal of Orthopsychiatry* 54(4)(Oct. 1984):530–43.

Wolpe, J. *The Practice of Behavior Therapy.* Elmsford, NY: Pergamon Press, 1974.

"Women and Power—A Status Report." *New York Times,* May 1, 1977, sec. 3, pp. 1,4.

Women Organized Against Rape (W.O.A.R.). "Data." Philadelphia, PA, 1975, p. 1. Mimeo.

Women's AIDS Network. "Lesbians and AIDS: What's the Connection?" San Francisco, CA, 1986.

Wood, P.L. "The Victim in a Forcible Rape Case: A Feminist View." *American Criminal Law Review* 7(2)(1973):348.

Wooden, L. *Weeping in the Playtime of Others.* New York: McGraw-Hill, 1976.

Woodruff, D.S. "Arousal, Sleep and Aging." In J.E. Birren and K.W. Schaie (eds.), *Handbook of the Psychology of Aging.* New York: Van Nostrand Reinhold, 1985.

Woodworth, R., and H. Schlosberg. *Experimental Psychology.* New York: Holt, 1954.

Work in America: Report of a Special Task Force to the Secretary of Health, Education, and Welfare. Cambridge, MA: M.I.T. Press, 1973.

Wynder, E.L., L.S. Covey, K. Mabuchi, and D. Mushinski. "Environmental Factors in Cancer of the Larynx: A Second Look." *Cancer* 35(1976):1591–1601.

Yancy, W.S., P.R. Nader, and K. Burnham. "Drug Use and Attitudes of High School Students." *Pediatrics* 50(5)(1972):739–45.

Yessian, M.R., and A. Broskowski. "Generalists in Human-Service Systems: Their Problems and Prospects." In R.M. Kramer and H. Specht (eds.), *Readings in Community Organization Practice,* 3rd ed. Englewood Cliffs, NJ: Prentice-Hall, 1983.

Yogman, M.J., S. Dixon, E. Tronick, H. Als, and T.B. Brazelton. "The Goals and Structure of Face-to-Face Interaction Between Infants and Their Fathers." Paper presented at the meeting of the Society for Research in Child Development, New Orleans, LA, 1977.

Yussen, S. "Characteristics of Moral Dilemmas Written by Adolescents." *Developmental Psychology* 13(2)(1977):162–63.

Zabin, L.S., J.F. Kantner, and M. Zelnik. "The Risk of Adolescent Pregnancy in the First Months of Intercourse." *Family Planning Perspectives* 11(4)(1979):215–22.

Zabin, L., M.B. Hirsch, B.A. Smith, and J.B. Hardy. "A School-, Hospital-, and University-Based Adolescent Pregnancy Prevention Program." *Journal of Reproductive Medicine* 29(1984):421–26.

———. "Adolescent Sexual Attitudes and Behavior: Are They Consistent?" *Family Planning Perspectives* 15(16)(1984):185.

———. "Evaluation of a Pregnancy Prevention Program for Urban Teenagers." *Family Planning Perspectives* 18(3)(May/June, 1986):119–26.

Zajonc, R.B. "Family Configuration and Intelligence." *Science* 192(1976):227–36.

Zakariya, S.B. "Another Look at the Children of Divorce: Summary Report of the Study of School Needs of One-Parent Children." *Principle*, Sept. 1982, pp. 34–37.

Zaludek, G.M. "How to Cope with Male Menopause." *Science Digest*, 1976, pp. 74–79.

Zastrow, C. *Talk to Yourself: Using the Power of Self-Talk.* Englewood Cliffs, NJ: Prentice-Hall, 1979.

———. *The Practice of Social Work.* Homewood, IL: Dorsey, 1981.

———. *Introduction to Social Welfare Institutions: Social Problems, Services, and Current Issues.* Homewood, IL: Dorsey, 1982.

———. *The Practice of Social Work.* 2nd ed. Homewood, IL: Dorsey, 1985.

———. *The Practice of Social Work.* 3rd ed. Homewood, IL: Dorsey, 1989.(a)

———. *Social Work with Groups.* Chicago: Nelson-Hall, 1989.(b)

———. *The Practice of Social Work.* 4th ed. Belmont, CA: Brooks/Cole, 1992.

———. *You Are What You Think: A Guide to Self-Realization.* Chicago: Nelson-Hall, 1993.

Zastrow, C., and L. Bowker. *Social Problems.* Chicago: Nelson-Hall, 1984.

Zastrow, C., and D. Chang. *The Personal Problem Solver.* Englewood Cliffs, NJ: Simon & Schuster, 1977.

Zastrow, C., and R. Navarre. "Self-Talk: A New Criminological Theory." *International Journal of Comparative and Applied Criminal Justice*, Fall 1979, pp. 167–76.

Zelnick, M., and J.F. Kantner. "The Resolution of Teenage First Pregnancies." *Family Planning Perspectives* 6(Spring 1974):74–80.

———. "Sexual and Contraceptive Experiences of Young Unmarried Women in the United States, 1976 and 1971. *Family Planning Perspectives* 9 (2)(1977):55–71.

———. "Sexual Activity, Contraceptive Use, and Pregnancy Among Metropolitan-Area Teenagers: 1971-1979." *Family Planning Perspectives* 12(1980):230–37.

Zelnik, M., J.F. Kantner, and K. Ford. *Sex and Pregnancy in Adolescence.* Beverly Hills, CA: Sage, 1981.

Zelnik, M., and Y.J. Kim. "Sex Education and Its Association with Teenage Sexual Activity, Pregnancy and Contraceptive Use." *Family Planning Perspectives* 14(3)(1982).

Zelnik, M., Y.J. Kim, and J.F. Kantner. "Probabilities of Intercourse and Conception among U.S. Teenage Women, 1971 and 1976." *Family Planning Perspectives* 11(3)(1979):177–83.

Zelnik, M., and F.K. Shah. "First Intercourse among Young Americans." *Family Planning Perspectives* 15(2)(1983):64–70.

Zodhiates, K., R. Feinbloom, and S. Sagov. "Contraceptive Use of Cervical Caps." Letter. *New England Journal of Medicine* 304(15)(1981):915.

Zuckerman, A. "AIDS and Insects." *British Medical Journal* 292(April 26, 1986).

Zuckerman, B., et al. "Effects of Maternal Marijuana and Cocaine Use on Fetal Growth." *New England Journal of Medicine* 320(12)(1989):762–768.

Zuger, B. "Monozygotic Twins Discordant for Homosexuality: A Report of a Pair and Significance of the Phenomenon." *Comprehensive Psychiatry* 17(1976):661–69.

Zusman, J. "Some Explanations of the Changing Appearance of Psychotic Patients: Antecedents of the Social Breakdown Syndrome Concept." *Millbank Memorial Fund Quarterly* 64(1) (1966):20.

Zylman, R. "Age Is More Important Than Alcohol in the Collision Involvement of Young and Old Drivers." *Journal of Traffic Safety Education* 20(1)(1972):7–8, 34.

Name Index

and low birth rate, 62
of the poor, 487
Inferiority, and prejudice, 213
Infertility, 83, 856
alternatives available in, 90–96
causes of, 86–87
counseling on, 88–90
definition, 86
ethical dilemmas, 92
and macro systems, 96–97
psychological reactions to, 87
and social work roles, 97
treatment of, 87, 90
Initiator role, 41, 43
with mentally retarded, 138
Inner-city ghettos, 226–29
Input, 151
definition, 10
Insecurity, countering, 213
Insightful dimension of intelligence, 128
Institution, 17
Institutional racism, 210–12
Institutional values, 27–28
and clients, 28
and racism, 210–12
Insulin, and fetal development, 55
Integrator/coordinator role, 40, 42
Integrity, v. despair, 595–96
Intellectual functioning
in elderly, 569
in middle age, 393–96
Intelligence, 127–31
crystallized, 128
fluid, 127–28
triarchic theory of, 128–29
Intelligence testing, 129–30
and cultural biases, 131, 132–34
Otis-Lennon Mental Ability test, 130
potential problems, 136
and race, 210
Stanford-Binet IQ test, 130–31
Wechsler tests, 131
Interactionist theory, 483–84
criticism of, 484
and drug use, 470
and emotional and behavioral problems,
333–35
and homosexuality, 541–42
and poverty, 496
Interdependence, in ecological perspective,
14
Interface, 11
in ecological perspective, 13
Intermittent reinforcement, 168
Internal injuries, in child abuse, 191
Interracial rape, 369
Intimacy, v. isolation, 314–16
Intimate zone, 445
Intuition, 452–53
In vitro fertilization, 95
Irreversibility, 115
Isolation
fear of, 380
and intimacy, 314–16

Isoretinoin, and fetal development, 55
IUD (intrauterine device), 274–75

Jim Crow laws, 208
Joint custody, 508

Kaposi's sarcoma, 413, 420
Kübler-Ross model of grief, 608, 609
Ku Klux Klan Act, 77
Kwell, 267

Labeling theory, 484
Labor, 58–59
induced, 79
stages of, 59–60
Lacerations, in child abuse, 191
Lamaze method, 61
Laminaria, 79
Language. *See also* Communication
nonsexist, 366
sexist, 364
Late adult transition, 433
Latency stage of development, 104
Later adulthood, 599–606, 620–30. *See
also* Agency
appearance, 567
crime victimization, 628–29
and death, 626
and death education, 607–15
definition, 566–67
demographics, 621
developmental tasks, 593–97
and digestive system, 571
diseases and causes of death, 576–80
family relationships, 603–4
financial problems, 624–25
gender role stereotypes, 353–54
grandparenthood, 605–6
grief management, 607–15
health problems, 629–30
heart, 571
homeostasis, 570
and intellectual functioning, 569
macro system responses to, 630–36
and malnutrition, 629
and muscular structure, 570
nervous system, 570–71
never married, 602–3
as political force, 637–38
as population-at-risk, 619–20
poverty, 489–90
psychological preparation for, 606–7
psychomotor skills, 568–69
remarriage, 603
reserve capacity, 571–72
residences, 628
respiration, 571
senescence, 567–74
senses, 567–68
sexuality, 572–73
skeleton and joints, 570
skin, 568
social security system, 625–26
social roles, 638–39

social work, 636–37
teeth, 568
transportation, 628
unemployment, 502
values and sexuality, 573–74
voice, 568
widowhood, 602
Laughter, 121–22
Learning disabilities
causes of, 139
characteristics of, 138–39
definition, 138
effects of, 139, 140
macro system responses to, 142
problems in processing, 139–40
specific, 140
treatment for, 141–42
Learning theory, 154–55, 531
ABCs of behavior, 158–59
accidental training in, 172
behaviorally specific terminology in,
172–73
evaluation of, 155–56
extinction in, 161–62
and homosexuality, 541
measuring improvement in, 173–74
modeling in, 157–58
negative reinforcement, 159–60
operant conditioning, 158
and parental attention, 174
positive reinforcement, 159, 163–64,
167–68
punishment, 160, 169–70, 171–72
respondent conditioning, 156–57
and rewards, 167
secondary reinforcers, 164–67
and social work practice, 162–72
Lesbians. *See* Homosexuality
Let's you and him/her fight game, 436
Liberalism, v. conservatism, 497–98
Libido, 103
Librium, 461
Lice, pubic, 267
Life expectancy, 215–16, 577–80
Life review, in later adulthood, 596
Life scripts, 437–41
Life structure, Levinson's theories on,
430–33
Life-style
choosing, 316
and good health, 254–55
Listening, active, 312
Locality development, 39
Logical thinking, development of, 115
Longevity and health, 581
Looking glass self, 283, 284
Lorne-Thorndike tests, 130
Love
and abusive relationships, 380
improving relationships, 406
romantic v. rational, 316
Love 'em and leave 'em, 436
Low birth weight, and infant mortality, 62
LSD (lysergic acid diethylamide), 466–67

Photo Credits

p. 4. Tony Stone Images © Robert E. Daemmrich

p. 10. MGA/Photri © Ellis Herwig

p. 15. (*Top Left*) Tony Stone Images © Lawrence Migdale, (*Top Right*) MGA/Photri © Lee Balterman, (*Bottom*) Tony Stone Images © Robert E. Daemmrich

p. 20. MGA/Photri © Spencer Grant

p. 26. Tony Stone Images © George Mars Cassidy

p. 27. MGA/Photri © Spencer Grant

p. 42. Tony Stone Images © Robert E. Daemmrich

p. 51. Photo Researchers © D.W. Fawcett

p. 59. MGA/Photri © Spencer Grant

p. 63. MGA/Photri © Spencer Grant

p. 65. MGA/Photri © Spencer Grant

p. 86. MGA/Photri © Brent Jones

p. 97. MGA/Photri © Ellis Herwig

p. 113. MGA/Photri © Spencer Grant

p. 115. MGA/Photri © Ellis Herwig

p. 121. Stock Boston © David Austen

p. 124. MGA/Photri © Spencer Grant

p. 125. MGA/Photri © Tom McCarthy

p. 128. Tony Stone Images © Lawrence Migdale

p. 135. MGA/Photri © Spencer Grant

p. 137. MGA/Photri © Spencer Grant

p. 141. Photri

p. 147. MGA/Photri © Frank Siteman

p. 151. Tony Stone Images © Lawrence Migdale

p. 155. Photri © David Phillips

p. 165. National Educational Association

p. 166. MGA/Photri © Frank Siteman

p. 177. MGA/Photri © Doug Wilson

p. 178. MGA/Photri © Spencer Grant

p. 180. MGA/Photri © Frank Siteman

p. 183. MGA/Photri

p. 205. NYT Pictures Ruby Washington

p. 212. Tony Stone Images © Marc PoKempner

p. 221. MGA/Photri © Lee Balterman

p. 223. MGA/Photri © Ellis Herwig

p. 225. MGA/Photri © Ellis Herwig

p. 227. Tony Stone Images © Marc PoKempner

p. 229. St. Louis Post-Dispatch

p. 245. MGA/Photri © Ellis Herwig

p. 248. MGA/Photri © Spencer Grant

p. 256. Tony Stone Images © Lawrence Migdale

p. 261. MGA/Photri © Spencer Grant

p. 268. Photo Researchers © Blair Seitz

p. 288. MGA/Photri © Spencer Grant

p. 294. MGA/Photri © Frank Siteman

p. 298. Courtesy of The Samaritans Boston, Massachusetts

p. 302. MGA/Photri © Ellis Herwig

p. 310. Stock Boston © Gale Zucker

p. 315. MGA/Photri © Spencer Grant

p. 322. MGA/Photri © Spencer Grant

p. 325. MGA/Photri © Wally Hampton

p. 333. MGA/Photri © Timothy Wilson

p. 342. Tony Stone Images © Walter Geiersperger

p. 347. Tony Stone Images © Robert E. Daemmrich

p. 351. (*Left*) MGA/Photri © David Seman, (*Right*) MGA/Photri © Diane Schmidt

p. 357. MGA/Photri © Spencer Grant

p. 369. MGA/Photri © Spencer Grant

p. 375. Tony Stone Images © Robert E. Daemmrich

p. 379. Family Violence Prevention Fund

p. 395. MGA/Photri © Ellis Herwig

p. 400. MGA/Photri © Lee Balterman

p. 422. © Sibylla Herbrich

p. 432. The Image Works © Dan Chidester

p. 437. MGA/Photri © D. Seman

p. 440. MGA/Photri © Frank Siteman

p. 445. MGA/Photri © Ellis Herwig

p. 454. Stock Boston © Jim Harrison

p. 465. Photri

p. 486. MGA/Photri © Lee Balterman

p. 489. Tony Stone Images © Carol Lee

p. 495. Tony Stone Images © Don Smetzer

p. 502. Tony Stone Images © Robert E. Daemmrich

p. 505. MGA/Photri © D. Seman

p. 514. MGA/Photri © Ellis Herwig

p. 519. MGA/Photri © Ellis Herwig

p. 531. MGA/Photri © Frank Siteman

p. 536. © Robert Pruzan

p. 547. San Francisco Examiner Elizabeth Mangelsdorf

p. 552. MGA/Photri © Spencer Grant

p. 555. San Francisco Examiner Nicole Bengiveno

p. 567. MGA/Photri © David Phillips

p. 569. MGA/Photri © Frank Siteman

p. 572. Tony Stone Images © Lawrence Migdale

p. 574. MGA/Photri © Frank Siteman

p. 583. © Fran Buss

p. 589. Tony Stone Images © Billy E. Barnes

p. 598. Tony Stone Images © Lawrence Migdale

p. 601. MGA/Photri © T. Firak

p. 602. Photri © Nina Tisara

p. 605. © TBR Photos

p. 610. (*Top*) MGA/Photri © David Phillips, (*Bottom*) MGA/Photri © Frank Siteman

p. 623. MGA/Photri © Frank Siteman

p. 629. Tony Stone Images © Lawrence Migdale

p. 633. Photo Researchers © Guy Gillette

p. 637. Stock Boston © Elizabeth Crews